REFERENCE DO NOT
TAKE FROM THIS ROOM

REFERENCE DO NOT
TAKE FROM THIS ROOM

THE ENCYCLOPEDIA OF

American
Facts and Dates

THE ENCYCLOPEDIA OF

American

Facts and Dates

EDITED BY

GORTON CARRUTH AND ASSOCIATES

REFERENCE DO NOT

Sixth Edition TAKE FROM THIS ROOM

With a Supplement of the 70s

THOMAS Y. CROWELL COMPANY, NEW YORK

Established 1834

GEORGE M. SMITH LIBRARY
CENTRAL METHODIST COLLEGE
FAYETTE, MISSOURI 65248

Copyright © 1972 by Thomas Y. Crowell Company, Inc.
Previous copyrights © 1956, 1959, 1962, 1966, 1970
by Thomas Y. Crowell Company, Inc.

All rights reserved. Except for use in a review, the reproduction or utilization
of this work in any form or by any electronic, mechanical, or other means,
now known or hereafter invented, including xerography, photocopying,
and recording, and in any information storage and retrieval system is forbidden
without the written permission of the publisher. Published simultaneously in
Canada by Fitzhenry & Whiteside Limited, Toronto.

Manufactured in the United States of America

L.C. Card 72-78262

ISBN 0-690-26302-3

3 4 5 6 7 8 9 10

To the user of

THE ENCYCLOPEDIA OF
AMERICAN FACTS AND DATES:

The three chief purposes of *The Encyclopedia of American Facts and Dates* are to present in one volume a vast number of the most interesting events from America's past, to arrange these events both in chronological order and at the same time in concurrent order, and finally to provide a complete, cross-referenced index for instant and easy consulting.

It is chronological. Decade by decade, year by year, you can follow *down* the page the facts, dates, and events of American life, from the earliest times to the present—*in chronological order.*

It is divided into the four fields of interest, in four parallel columns. Side by side you can follow *across* the page the facts, dates, and events of American life, in the four departments of knowledge—*in parallel arrangement.*

Every pair of facing pages is divided into four vertical columns. **Continuations of the columns are on the following pair of facing pages.** The subjects listed at the top of the columns are representative topics only. Actually you will find in the four columns entries on the following:

1.	2.	3.	4.
POLITICS AND GOVERNMENT	BOOKS	SCIENCE	SPORTS
WAR	PAINTING	INDUSTRY	FASHIONS
DISASTERS	DRAMA	ECONOMICS	POPULAR ENTERTAINMENT
VITAL STATISTICS	ARCHITECTURE	EDUCATION	
	SCULPTURE	RELIGION	FOLKLORE
		PHILOSOPHY	SOCIETY
SUFFRAGE	PERIODICALS		
TREATIES	CENSORSHIP	SCIENTIFIC ASSOCIATIONS	GAMES
IMMIGRATION	MUSIC AND ENTERTAINMENT		DRESS
FOREIGN AFFAIRS		SCHOLARSHIP	HOLIDAYS
DOMESTIC AFFAIRS	POETRY	MEDICINE	DANCING
WESTWARD EXPANSION	BALLET	BUSINESS	MOVIES
	POPULAR SONGS	FINANCE	EXPOSITIONS
STATEHOOD	JAZZ	AGRICULTURE	SAYINGS
EXPLORATION AND DISCOVERY	FURNITURE	TECHNOLOGY	MANNERS
	MONUMENTS	INVENTORS	FOODS
INDIAN AFFAIRS	THOUGHT AND COMMENT	COLLEGES AND UNIVERSITIES	FEMINISM
SLAVERY			TEMPERANCE
TRADE AGREEMENTS		COMMUNICATIONS	
TARIFFS		HIGHWAYS AND ROADS	
BATTLES		TRANSPORTATION	
		LABOR	

At the end of the book you will find a *thorough rapid-reference index* that covers all items and refers back—not to pages—but to the appropriate year and column.

In *The Encyclopedia of American Facts and Dates* you will find many of the milestones of American history. You are given such important dates as those of the *Mayflower* landing, the battle of Lexington, the invention of the automobile, the publication of *Uncle Tom's Cabin,* the launching of the first atomic-powered submarine. In themselves these are important events about which everyone knows a little. But all of us could learn even more about them, and therefore enriching surrounding information has been included with each item. *The Encyclopedia of American Facts and Dates* is also filled with more humble information: the favorite drink of colonial Americans, beginnings of opera and the theater, development of the typewriter, founding of the first baseball club, and a host of out-of-the-way, hard-to-find events that make a book like this a constant reading companion.

You may observe that many "obvious" dates are missing. The dates of many treaties, laws, births, deaths, and other material readily available in standard reference books have been rejected. Also—and this an editor always regrets—some material was omitted to keep this volume compact and within bounds.

The Encyclopedia of American Facts and Dates was developed from countless source books, reference books, and other printed material. When sources disagree about dates and about exactly what happened, the most recent version was usually followed. It is impossible to acknowledge all the standard multi-volume reference books and specific source books used; but particular acknowledgment should be made to those single-volume American date and reference books that have proved especially valuable: *The Reader's Encyclopedia* edited by William Rose Benét (Thomas Y. Crowell Company); *Documents of American History* by Henry Steele Commager (Appleton-Century-Crofts, Inc.); *The Columbia Encyclopedia* (Columbia University Press); *Information Please Almanac* (The Macmillan Company); *Famous First Facts* by Joseph Nathan Kane (H. W. Wilson Company); *A Short Chronology of American History, 1492–1950* by Irving S. and Nell M. Kull (Rutgers University Press); *The Encyclopedia of Sports* by Frank G. Menke (A. S. Barnes and Company); *The Encyclopedia of American History* edited by Richard B. Morris (Harper & Brothers); *The World Almanac* (New York World-Telegram and The Sun).

Thanks should also go to the staff, and especially to Mr. John Ott and to Mr. Hugh Weideman for their invaluable advice and encouragement.

THE ENCYCLOPEDIA OF

American
Facts and Dates

NOTE TO THE SIXTH EDITION

The Sixth Edition of *The Encyclopedia of American Facts and Dates* contains entries for events through 1971. The latest material is presented in the first installment of a "Supplement of the 70s," which begins on p. 891. The index to the supplement begins on p. 916.

Gorton Carruth

POLITICS AND GOVERNMENT; WAR; DISASTERS; VITAL STATISTICS.	BOOKS; PAINTING; DRAMA; ARCHITECTURE; SCULPTURE.

FROM THE BEGINNINGS TO 1599

986 1st reports of America. Herjulfson, Norse navigator, sailing from Iceland, was caught in storm and driven southward where he glimpsed new land. It could only have been coast of America.

1000 Leif Ericson settled in Vinland. This colony was probably somewhere along New England coast.

1513 Apr. 2 Juan Ponce de León discovered Florida, claiming it for King of Spain.

1536 May 3 Hernando Cortes reached Santa Cruz, Calif., with expedition he led from Mexico.

1539 May 30 Fernando de Soto landed in Florida and consolidated Spain's dominion over peninsula.

1540 Garcia Lopez de Cardenas, leader of scouting party for Coronado's expedition to New Mexico, discovered the **Grand Canyon** of Colorado.

1541 May 8 1st Europeans reached Mississippi R., members of de Soto expedition. De Soto died following year and was buried in river.

1542 Juan Rodriguez Cabrillo, sent on exploratory voyage by Spanish administrators in Mexico, landed near Ballast Point, San Diego, Calif., thus becoming **1st white man to set foot on Pacific coast** of what is now the U.S. He continued his explorations and discovered Santa Catalina Island, San Pedro Bay, the Santa Barbara Channel, and other west coast landmarks.

1562 Feb. 18 1st French colonizers of New World sailed for Florida under leadership of Huguenot Jean Ribaut. Landed 1st on St. John's R. near St. Augustine, May 1, but soon settled on Parris Island in Port Royal Sound near what is now town of Beaufort, S.C. After Ribaut returned to France, starving colonists revolted and attempted to sail to Europe. In 1564 colony was replenished by ex-

1507 Apr. 25 "America" 1st used for New World in Martin Waldseemüller's short geography book *Cosmographiae Introductio.* Wrote Waldseemüller, "But now that these parts have been more extensively examined, and another fourth part has been discovered by Americus Vespucius . . . I do not see why anyone should by right object to name it America . . . after its discoverer, Americus, a man of sagacious mind, since both Europe and Asia took their names from women." Geographer mistakenly accredited discovery of New World to Amerigo Vespucci.

c1564 1st professional painter of New World, Frenchman Jacques le Moyne de Morgues, associated with René de Laudonnière expedition of Huguenots which tried to colonize Florida. After destruction of this colony, Le Moyne escaped to France. His drawings were later engraved and used by De Bry in 1591 in second of his *Voyages.*

1588 1st eye-witness survey and written report in English of what today is part of America is **Thomas Hariot's** *A Briefe and True Report of the New Found Land of Virginia.* One of men in Roanoke Island group sponsored by Sir Walter Raleigh, Hariot returned to England to defend New World project against those who were disillusioned by 1st venture. His book set pattern for "promotion" type literature that followed throughout course of 17th century. America is pictured as abundant paradise, wherein little work will yield enormous produce.

1588 A Brief and True Report of the new found Land of Virginia by Thomas Hariot published.

1589 *The Principall Navigations, Voiages and Discoveries of the English Nation, made by Sea or Over Land to the most remote and farthest distant quarters of the earth at any time within the com-*

FROM THE BEGINNINGS TO 1599

1112 1st Bishop of America appointed. He was Eric Gnupsson, named by Pope Paschal II. His see included Greenland and Vinland (America).

1497 June 24 John Cabot discovered **Newfoundland,** which he called Prima Vista. In 1583 Humphrey Gilbert took official possession of Newfoundland in the name of the English throne. England was slow to develop her advantages in the fishing industry of the island. Richard Hakluyt reported that, in 1577, there were 150 French fishing craft, 100 Spanish, 50 Portuguese and 15 English engaged in fishing there. In the next century English fishing became dominant. The significance of Newfoundland in the history of the New World was in affording a place for an international exchange of material from countries which were elsewhere committed to ceaseless competition.

1540 Priests accompanying De Soto expedition baptized Indian guide, Peter, in waters of Acmulgee R., near present-day Macon, Ga. The **1st recorded baptism** in U.S.

1563 Spring **1st ship** built in North America to cross Atlantic Ocean. It was constructed by French Huguenots who had settled on Parris Island, S.C., but who had decided to return to France since their group was destitute. They built a pinnace, using bedding and shirts for sails. They actually arrived within sight of French shoreline, half starved, where they were rescued by English sailors.

1565 1st introduction of European livestock such as black cattle, horses, sheep, and swine into America by Spanish in Florida.

1565 Sept. 8 Parish of St. Augustine, Fla., **1st Catholic parish in present-day U.S.,** founded by Fr. Don Martin Francisco

1007 Snorro, **1st white child born in North America,** son of Thorfinn and Gudrid Karlsefni, members of Leif Ericson's Viking expedition to Vinland. Later Snorro became an important member of the Norse community in Iceland.

1540 Horse 1st introduced on large scale into what is now U.S. by Francisco Coronado, Spanish explorer, who traveled through Kansas with 260 horses, most escaping to Midwest, Mexico, and Canada. These animals eventually mingled with large French Norman horses brought to Canada by French settlers, producing wide variety of wild horses found in North America.

1550–1600 Explorations of the Spaniards in the New World brought benefits which were incidental to the main objects of the conquest and yet shaped the habits of 2 continents as much as the discovery of gold and the contests of arms. **Potatoes** were 1st brought back to Spain from Peru. In their missions in Peru the Jesuits extracted **quinine** from the bark of a cinchona tree. **Cocoa, tomatoes,** and the **cassava root,** which yields **tapioca,** were originally South American products. The conquistadores smoked **tobacco,** as they saw the Indians doing, though it was 1st used medicinally as a headache remedy. In return, the pioneers introduced livestock and plants which transformed the life of the American continents. **Pigs, cattle, poultry, rabbits, sugar-cane, wheat, oats, barley,** and **rye** were all brought over from Europe. The **horse,** let loose, found a natural home on the plains. In the course of a century the prehistoric culture of a primitive people was contacting civilization on every frontier and the amalgamation of the Old and New Worlds was fairly begun.

1564 Earliest pictures of hunting in what is now U.S. were Jacques le Moyne's

pedition under command of René de Laudonnière, whom Ribaut reinforced the next year in a second expedition.

1565 Sept. 8 Spanish forces under Don Pedro Menéndez de Aviles founded **1st permanent white colony** in U.S. at St. Augustine, Fla. Ménendez secured Spanish Catholic dominion over the territory by destroying the French Huguenot colony at Parris Island, and later he was appointed by Charles V of Spain to resist all French occupation of Florida. He captured Fort Caroline and set out to look for a water route through the peninsula.

1587 May **Roanoke Island colony,** sponsored by Sir Walter Raleigh, established by John White. Colony quickly ran into difficulties, and in the Fall White returned to England for help. Rescue expedition arrived in 1591, with additional settlers, including women and children, found no people or houses, but only a high palisade, on site.

passe of these 1500 yeares, the *magnum opus* of **Richard Hakluyt,** published. Hakluyt spent years collecting accounts of famous voyages. Between 1598 and 1600 the original edition of *The Principal Navigations* was enlarged and republished in 3 outsized folio volumes which were brought up to date with reports of the recent adventures of Drake, Frobisher, Gilbert, John and Richard Hawkins, Raleigh, and other major Elizabethan voyagers. A classic of the literature of discovery, it climaxes a century of interest in the discovery of the New World.

1598 Apr. 30 **1st theatrical performance** given in North America acted on Rio Grande near present-day El Paso. Play was a Spanish *comedia* dealing with expedition of soldiers. On July 10 same group produced *Moros y los Cristianos,* anonymous play.

1600–1609

1602 May 15 Capt. Bartholomew Gosnold, **1st Englishman to land in New England,** anchored at what is now New Bedford, Mass. On Mar. 26 he had sailed from Falmouth, Eng., in the *Concord,* touched at the Maine coast, and explored the New England coastline. He named Cape Cod, Martha's Vineyard, and other landmarks.

1604 Sieur de Monts planted earlist **Northern French** colony at Neutral Island in St. Croix R., Me. His patent had been granted by the French king.

1607 Conspiracy against the Council of Jamestown uncovered in Virginia; **probably 1st act of rebellion** in the American colonies. George Kendall, leader, was shot for mutiny.

1607 May 13 Jamestown, Va., **1st permanent English colony in North America,** founded by more than 100 colonists on left bank of "River of Powhatan" (James R.). Dispatched by London Com-

1606 Nov. 14 **One of earliest theatrical performances,** French masque *Le Théâtre de Neptune en la Nouvelle-France,* took place in Port Royal, Acadia.

1608 1st "American" book, written by **John Smith,** *A True Relation of Such Occurrences and Accidents of Noate as Hath Hapned in Virginia Since the First Planting of that Collony,* printed in London, strangely omitted famous tale of Pocahontas. It was not until 1624, with the publication of his *Generalli Historie (The General History of Virginia, New England and the Summer Isles),* that Smith included a reference to the famous romance.

1609 Oldest surviving non-Indian building in U.S., **Governor's Palace** at Santa Fe, built by Don Pedro de Peralta.

4

SCIENCE; INDUSTRY; ECONOMICS; EDUCATION; RELIGION; PHILOSOPHY.

SPORTS; FASHIONS; POPULAR ENTERTAINMENT; FOLKLORE; SOCIETY.

Lopez de Mendozo Grajales, chaplain of conquering Spanish forces.

1566 1st Jesuit mission in America founded in Florida.

1579 1st religious service in English, and hence **1st Protestant service** in New World, held in California. Participants were members of crew of Admiral Francis Drake's expedition, which having sailed around South America put into a bay at 38th parallel where, according to ship's log, "the admiral ordered divine service to be performed at his tent."

1587 Manteo, a friendly Indian, baptized in Church of England by members of Sir Walter Raleigh's expedition to Roanoke. Later named by Raleigh Lord of Roanoke, Manteo was **1st Indian converted to Protestant Christianity.**

account of Laudonnière expedition. Some drawings showed Indians stalking deer under a deerskin, Indians capturing alligators by ramming long poles down their throats, Indians fishing from pirogues (tree trunk hollowed to make crude boat).

1585 1st eye-witness picture of American Indians at play, a drawing by John White, shows Indians participating in lacrosse, archery, foot racing, and pitching balls at target on top of high tree.

1587 Aug. 18 Virginia Dare, **1st English child born** in North America. Her parents were Ananias and Ellinor Dare, members of Sir Walter Raleigh's colony at Roanoke Island, N.C. Ellinor Dare was daughter of Gov. John White, who led 150 householders to establish a colony on the Chesapeake. Landed at Hatteras on July 22. Gov. White returned to England on Aug. 27; sometime thereafter the colony disappeared.

1600–1609

1606 London Company and **Plymouth Company,** organized for colonization, were granted charters by English Crown. They divided territory of Virginia at 41° north latitude.

1607 Glassmaking practiced in 1st English colony at Jamestown with techniques that varied little from those of ancient civilizations. In 1608 **1st glass beads** were made for trade with Indians.

1608 1st cargo shipped from America to foreign country, consisting of pitch, tar, soap, ashes, and glass, dispatched from Jamestown to colony's sponsors in England. There is evidence that sassafras was shipped from Cape Cod previously, but Jamestown cargo was 1st instance of American manufactures being exported.

1608 John Robinson, English Nonconformist, led his congregation from Scrooby, England, to Amsterdam. Robinson was head of a Separatist or Independ-

1600 About 1 million **Indians** lived in North America when European exploration began. Since pattern of settlement differed from Spanish penetration of Middle and South America, change in customs of inhabitants was, at first, comparatively slow. But, in retrospect, 1st decade of 17th century was twilight of aboriginal Indian life. Pioneer groups of white colonists were small. They entered regions with sparser populations and more fluid cultures than larger and stabler Indian communities of Central America, Andes and Caribbean islands. Contact was sometimes mutually beneficial for both races, but there was no fusion of cultures as in South America.

1607 In 1st English settlement in America of some 105 men, 35 were considered **"gentlemen."** Second expedition contained 33 "gentlemen" out of 120.

1608 John Smith had two Indians teach him how to raise **Indian corn.** Faced with

5

pany, the colonists had sailed aboard the *Sarah Constant, Goodspeed,* and *Discovery.*

1607 Sept. 10 **John Ratcliffe** replaced deposed Edward M. Wingfield as president of Virginia colony. Wingfield was the 1st president of the colony.

1607 Dec. **John Smith** captured by Indians with 2 companions while in search of provisions. His companions were killed; but he was spared, Smith reported, by the intercession of Pocahontas, Chief Powhatan's daughter.

1608 Capt. **John Smith** chosen president of Jamestown.

It combined Spanish and Pueblo features in archetypical southwestern colonial style.

1609 *Virginia Richly Valued,* the last work of **Richard Hakluyt,** published. It is based upon a Portuguese work, *Relacam,* which was written by a voyager who claimed to have been with de Soto on the expedition through Florida, Georgia, Alabama, Arkansas, and Louisiana. 1 of 3 extant histories of this voyage, *Virginia Richly Valued* has been attributed to the original authorship of de Soto.

1610–1619

Estimated European **population** in colonies—210.

1612 **Beginnings of New York city.** Dutch sent 2 ships, *Tiger* and *Fortune,* to trade with Indians on Hudson R. Huts were built on Manhattan Island (approximately where 45 Broadway now stands) to house trade goods. One year later, permanent trading post was established. The next year fort was erected on tip of island.

1613 Small **French settlement,** established at Somes Sound, near Mount Desert on Maine coast, forced out by English settlers from Jamestown led by Samuel Argall.

1614 **1st important Dutch settlement** in New World, preceding New Amsterdam, was stockaded post at Albany, established by Dutch fur traders. Fort Orange, near Albany, established 1624 by Walloons. Region later dominated by patroonship of Rensselaerswyck.

1617 Dec. 23 **1st penal colony** established in America by royal proclamation providing for exile of habitual criminals to colony of Virginia.

1610 First-hand account of New World settlement by **William Strachey,** *A True Reportory of the Wrack and Redemption of Sir Thomas Gates, Knight, upon and from the Islands of the Bermudas, his coming to Virginia and the Estate of that Colony then and after the Government of the Lord La Ware,* has been offered as one of books which might have suggested *The Tempest* to Shakespeare.

1612 Detailed study of early Virginia provided in *A Map of Virginia* by **John Smith.** Book, describing country, commodities, people, government, and religion was published in Oxford, Eng.

1613 Famous early book *Purchas His Pilgrimes,* by **Samuel Purchas,** published in England, took a skeptical view of New World settlements. Typical remarks are "For what haue they to oppose our Elephants, Rhinocerotes, Camels, Horses, Kine, &c. Neither are the naturall fruits of America comparable to those of our World. Whence are their Spices, and best Fruits, but from hence, by transportation or transplantation? As for Arts, States, Literature, Diuine and Humane, multitudes of

ent community which denied the authority of any established church. When the accession of James I to the throne of England disappointed the hopes of the Puritans that there would be a larger measure of tolerance towards their beliefs, Robinson and his followers joined the wave of exiles who fled abroad to escape further persecution. The following year, Robinson moved with his parishioners to Leiden. This group became the nucleus of the colonists who sailed for America on the *Mayflower* and founded Plymouth. Robinson, his hopes of following his flock across the Atlantic never materializing, died in 1625.

starvation, colonists accepted this new grain, although opposition to it existed everywhere. In French Louisiana the women, accustomed to fancier European fare, staged "petticoat rebellion" against daily consumption of corn. The governor reported that the women ". . . inveigh bitterly against His Grace, the Bishop of Quebec, who, they say has enticed them away from home under the pretext of sending them to enjoy the milk and honey of the land of promise."

1609 Anne Burrows and John Laydon married in Virginia; probably the **1st marriage** performed in the American colonies.

1610–1619

1610 Lawrence Bohune, **1st doctor in the English colonies,** arrived in Virginia. In 1620 he was appointed Surgeon General of the London Company in Virginia.

1611 The Rev. Alexander Whitaker, a volunteer from the Puritan community at Cambridge, Eng., arrived at Jamestown to establish the **1st Presbyterian congregation in Virginia.** He is best known as the clergyman who instructed Pocahontas in Christianity and baptized her.

1612 John Rolfe, who had 1st come to Virginia in 1609, planted **1st successful tobacco crop** in the colony after several experiments with native tobacco plants. As a result, tobacco became staple crop for the Virginia colony. Rolfe later (1614) won additional renown by marrying Pocahontas.

1613 **Pocahontas** became 1st Indian convert to Christianity in Virginia. Taken hostage to compel release of colonists held by her father's tribe, she came into contact with the Rev. Alexander Whitaker, was converted, baptized, and given Christian name of Rebecca. She later married young planter named John Rolfe. On trip to England, her old friend, Capt. John Smith, introduced her to royal court.

1611 May **1st recorded game** played by white men in America was game of bowls in streets of Jamestown, Va.

1613 Dec. 25 Contemporary account of **Christmas** in Virginia tells us that "the extreame winde, rayne, froste and snow caused us to keepe Christmas among the savages where we were never more merry, nor fed on more plenty of good Oysters, Fish, Flesh, Wilde fowl and good bread, nor never had better fires in England."

1617 Better-class **women** started to arrive in Virginia. Unlike Puritans in North, Virginia settlers came over "not as men, but more as soldiers sent out to occupy an enemy's country." Arrival of women insured growth and development of permanent communities.

1618 **Governor Argall** of Virginia decreed that all who failed to attend church service would be imprisoned in guardhouse, "lying neck and heels in the Corps of Gard ye night following and be a slave ye week following." Sunday dancing, fiddling,

POLITICS AND GOVERNMENT; WAR; DISASTERS; VITAL STATISTICS.	BOOKS; PAINTING; DRAMA; ARCHITECTURE; SCULPTURE.

1619 July 30 **1st legislative assembly** in America, House of Burgesses, convened at Old Church, Jamestown, Va. All legislation needed approval of London Company.

1619 Aug. **1st slaves** arrived in Virginia when a Dutch ship carried 20 Negroes to Jamestown for sale.

Cities, Lawes, and other Excellencies, our World enjoyeth still the priuiledge of the First-borne. America is a younger brother, and hath in these things almost no inheritance at all, till it bought somewhat hereof of the Spaniards, with the price of her Freedome."

1620–1629

Estimated colonial **population**—2499.

1620 Miles Standish appointed **1st military officer** in colonies when he was named to organize defenses of the New Plymouth Colony.

1620 June 29 Early colonial **trade agreement** concluded between Crown and Virginia Company provided that tobacco would not be grown in England in return for 1 shilling per lb. duty on that produced in Virginia.

1620 Nov. 11 **Mayflower Compact,** 1st basis of government for New England colony, drafted and signed by 41 adult males in Provincetown Harbor.

1620 Dec. 21 **Pilgrims reached Plymouth, Mass.,** aboard *Mayflower* after 63-day voyage. Company consisted of 41 men and their families.

1621 **Peace treaty and defensive alliance** between Wampanoags and Pilgrims concluded at Strawberry Hill, Plymouth, Mass. Arranged by Squanto, an English-speaking Indian, it was one of earliest recorded treaties between whites and Indians in North America.

1622 Mar. 22 **1st Indian massacre,** led by Powhatan's brother, almost wiped out settlements outside Jamestown, which was itself heavily fortified.

1622 Aug. 10 Province of **Maine** granted to John Mason and F. Gorges. It

1620 Henry Ainsworth's **Psalm Book,** published in Amsterdam in 1612, brought to America by Plymouth Pilgrims, perhaps 1st music book in this country. It brought together tunes from earlier English, French, and Swiss psalters, and was best music of its kind at time.

1620 **1st public library** in British colonies established at projected college in Heunco, Virginia. Library flourished through bequests of books from English estates.

1621 Jan. 29 Rose, beautiful wife of Miles Standish, died and set stage for one of oldest and most loved traditions in America. Captain Standish thought he might win hand of **Priscilla Mullins,** and sent **John Alden** as messenger to discover whether he could court her. When Alden spoke to girl of Captain's suit, she raised her eyes and said; "Prithee, John, why do you not speak for yourself?" John eventually did and married her before long.

1622 1st detailed and accurate account of **landing of Pilgrims** at Plymouth published in journal of William Bradford and Edward Winslow. Journal has long been known as *Mourt's Relation.*

SCIENCE; INDUSTRY; ECONOMICS; EDUCATION; RELIGION; PHILOSOPHY.	SPORTS; FASHIONS; POPULAR ENTERTAINMENT; FOLKLORE; SOCIETY.

1614 **1st large-scale fishing expedition** in America, led by Capt. John Smith, sailed from Virginia in search of gold, copper, whales, and, finally, fish off coast of Maine. He caught 60,000 in one month.

1616 **Smallpox epidemic** among Indians relieved pressure on New England colonies; tribes from Penobscot R. to Narragansett Bay virtually destroyed.

1619 **1st shipment** of Virginia grown tobacco, weighing 10 tons, sent to England.

card playing, hunting, and fishing were forbidden.

1619 Enactment of **blue laws** in Virginia, requiring men to dress according to their rank. Excess in dress was also discouraged by taxing one's wardrobe.

1620–1629

1620 **Congregational Church** founded in Plymouth, Mass., by 102 Pilgrim Separatists under William Brewster, William Bradford, and Edward Winslow, all of whom comprised part of Scrooby-Leiden Congregation in Holland. Ralph Smith, 1st pastor, arrived later.

1620 Virginia colonists plan **1st American iron works** at Falling Creek, 66 miles north of Jamestown. Before work could begin in 1622, settlement of 348 was massacred by Indians. Only one boy escaped.

1620 Dec. 21 Dr. Samuel Fuller, **1st physician for New England colony,** arrived on *Mayflower;* as both doctor and administrator, he was one of the prominent members of the Pilgrim band.

1621 **1st windmill** in America set up by Gov. Yeardley in Virginia. Millers generally kept ⅙th of meal they ground.

1623 To encourage raising of **silk** in America, the Virginia Legislature compelled all settlers to grow mulberry trees.

1620 **Promotion scheme** launched by London Company to exploit New World included the shipping of many English virgins to colony and selling them to colonists for 100 to 200 lbs. of tobacco each.

1621 Dec. **Earliest American harvest festival** celebrated by Pilgrims at Plymouth, Mass.

1621 Dec. 25 Governor Bradford of Plymouth colony shocked to find some newcomers to settlement **playing games** in street on Christmas Day. Governor stopped games, which included "pitching the barr" and "stoole-ball," by confiscating necessary equipment.

1623 After 3 very lean years Plymouth colonists were ordered by Governor Bradford to **raise their own plot of corn.** Besides planting of corn, colonists were taught by Indians how to grind and cook it. Many Indian names relating to corn have thus passed into English: hominy, pone, suppawn, samp, succotash.

1623 Women and children arriving in New England this year to join their Pilgrim husbands and fathers were feasted with "a lobster or a piece of fish without bread or anything else but a cup of spring water." **Lobsters** and **fish** kept early settlers alive in uncultivated wilderness. Many lobsters weighed 25 pounds and were so abundant that smallest child could catch them.

9

POLITICS AND GOVERNMENT; WAR; DISASTERS; VITAL STATISTICS.	BOOKS; PAINTING; DRAMA; ARCHITECTURE; SCULPTURE.

included the land between Merrimac and Kennebec Rs.

1623 **1st colonists** sent by Dutch West India Company settled along Hudson R.

1624 May **New York** founded as New Netherland when Cornelis J. Mey arrived with 30 families. Mey was **1st governor of New Netherland.**

1624 Dec. 21 Charter granted by the South company of Sweden, organized as the "Australian Company," for settlement of **1st Swedish colony** in America. Colony was not established until 1638.

1626 Sale of **"Manhattes" Island** by Indians for legendary sum of 60 guilders, roughly equivalent to $24. Purchase made by Peter Minuit, 1st Director General of New Netherland, who arrived in New Amsterdam on May 4.

1628 **Thomas Morton of Ma-re Mount** deported to England by Plymouth colony. He shortly returned and was deported again in 1630. He and his companions at Merry Mount, his estate, were accused of dissolute and lawless behavior.

1629 June 7 **Patroon system** established by Charter of Freedoms and Exemptions to Patroons adopted by Dutch West India Company. Nearly all land along Hudson R. was distributed among a few patroons.

1629 June 27 1st settlers of **Massachusetts Bay Colony** entered Salem Harbor. Led by John Winthrop, they were 900 strong, and arrived in 5 ships.

1622 Summer **1st substantial building** in New England, fort of hewn oak timbers, built by Plymouth settlers.

1624 **John Smith's** *General History of Virginia, the Summer Isles, and New England* represents accumulated accounts of his various observations in New World. Besides helping to found Virginia, he had mapped coastal area of New England around Cape Cod in 1614. This exciting report provides first complete account of Smith's rescue by Pocahontas. In part this was "promotional" literature designed to encourage immigration.

1625 The Rev. William Morrell's **Nova Anglia,** Latin poem with English paraphrase, provides early picture of New England. Following is sample stanza referring to new colony:

Westward a thousand leagues, a spacious land
Is made, unknown to them that it command
Of fruitful mould, and no less fruitful main,
Inrich with springs and prey, highland and plain . . .

1626 1st translation of Ovid's **Metamorphoses** by an American, George Sandys of Jamestown, Va., published in London. Translation praised by Dryden and Pope.

1630–1639

Estimated colonial **population**—5700.

1630 **Rensselaerswyck,** only successful Dutch patroonship, founded by Kiliaen Van Rensselaer, a director of Dutch West India Company. Extended 24 miles on both sides of Hudson R. Inhabitants numbered several thousand tenants. Never seen by Van Rensselaer, who managed whole enterprise from his home in Old Amsterdam.

1630 1st account of Puritan settlement in New England, *History of Plymouth Plantation,* by **William Bradford,** 2nd governor of Plymouth colony, begun; took more than 20 years to complete and was 1st published in full in 1856. Devout, sincere, and learned, Bradford wrote feelingly of *Mayflower* crossing and of pioneer life of early settlers. His authenticity earned him title "Father of American History."

10

| SCIENCE; INDUSTRY; ECONOMICS; EDUCATION; RELIGION; PHILOSOPHY. | SPORTS; FASHIONS; POPULAR ENTERTAINMENT; FOLKLORE; SOCIETY. |

1623 Sept. 10 **1st cargo** shipped from Plymouth consisted of lumber and furs. It was dispatched to England aboard the *Anne,* a vessel of 140 tons, with William Pierce in command.

1624 **1st appointed minister** for Pilgrim colony arrived at Plymouth. John Lyford was sent by London merchants who sponsored Plymouth colony. Because Lyford was unordained, he was unable to administer sacraments. Charges of Anglican bias and conspiring to establish rival colony were leveled at Lyford by Pilgrims. Lyford was tried, convicted, and expelled from colony.

1624 Mar. Edward Winslow, later governor of Plymouth colony, imported 3 heifers and a bull from Devon, Eng. They were **1st cattle brought to New England.**

1628 1st service in newly established **Dutch Reform Church** at New Amsterdam performed by Rev. Jonas Michaelius.

1629 Ralph Smith arrived in Plymouth colony as **1st ordained minister** of colony.

1629 July 10 **1st non-Separatist Congregational Church** in America established in Salem, Mass. Church founded by Francis Higginson and Samuel Skelton, 2 newly arrived ministers from England.

1623 **Social stratification** in Virginia reflected in law excepting "persons of quality" from penal whipping because they were not considered "fit to undergo corporal punishment."

1624 **Mandatory church attendance** on Sunday required by early Virginia law. Penalty for absence was 1 lb. of tobacco. Law also stipulated that each plantation should have house or room for worship.

1625 **1st child** born in New Amsterdam to family of Jan Joris Rapaelje, marking beginning of family life in Dutch settlement.

1627 **1500 children kidnaped** in Europe arrived in Virginia. Many became great successes. A 6-year-old, kidnaped by sailor and sold in America, married his master's daughter, inherited his fortune, and bought sailor (then a prisoner).

1628 May 1 Celebration of **May Day** at Ma-re [Merry] Mount was colorfully although bitterly described by Gov. Bradford: "They allso set up a May-Pole, drinking and dancing aboute it many days together, inviting the Indean women, for their consorts, dancing and frisking together, (like so many faries, or furies rather) and worse practices. As they had anew revived and celebrated the feasts of the Roman Goddes Flora, or the beastly practieses of the Madd Bacchinalians."

1630–1639

1630 **Oldest timepiece in New England,** William Bowyer's sundial, which he made for Gov. Endicott of New England Company. It is now in Essex Institute in Salem, Mass.

1630 Summer **1st church founded** in Boston. It had been formed under a covenant adopted by John Winthrop, Thomas Dudley, Isaac Johnson, and the

1631 Feb. 22 Fast day appointed as **1st public thanksgiving** in Massachusetts Bay Colony, though many private celebrations had been recorded before this.

1632 Gov. John Winthrop of Massachusetts Bay Colony received information that Dixy Bull and 15 other Englishmen had turned **pirates** and raided Bristol, Me.; they later joined the French forces. Bull

11

1630, Sept. 17 **Boston** founded by John Winthrop. It was an extension of the colony at Salem, which was under the governorship of John Endicott.

1630 Sept. 7 Tri-mountain settlement named **Boston**. Its Indian name was Shamut, meaning living fountain.

1630 Sept. 30 John Billington, **1st criminal executed** in American colonies, was hanged for murder. A member of the original Pilgrim band, he had waylaid and shot an opponent in a quarrel.

1631 Feb. **1st great fire** occurred in Boston.

1631 May 18 **Restrictive suffrage act** passed by Massachusetts General Court limited privileges of citizenship to church members.

1632 June 20 Charter for settlement of **Maryland** granted to Cecilius, 2nd Lord Baltimore. He was given title Baron of Baltimore; at Baltimore he started Roman Catholic colony.

1634 **1st official highway regulations,** issued by General Court of Massachusetts. These regulations governed planning and construction of roadways.

1635 Aug. 17 Arrival in Boston of **Richard Mather,** founder of "Mather Dynasty," series of New England ministers who ruled Puritan community with strong, often arbitrary, hand.

1636 **1st pensions** in America awarded to wounded soldiers by Plymouth Pilgrims.

1636 June **Roger Williams** founded Rhode Island when he established Providence with small group of colonists from Massachusetts Bay. It was first English colony in America to grant complete religious tolerance.

1637 May 26 **1st large-scale battle** between colonists and Indians took place when Captains John Mason and John Underhill led colonial forces in attack on Pequot Indians who had been harassing

1630 May 29 Chronicle of events from 1630 to 1649, *Journal* or *History of New England* begun by **John Winthrop,** 1st governor of Massachusetts Bay Colony. The journal was germ for many of Longfellow's *New England Tragedies.* It was published in a 2-volume edition in 1790. When an additional manuscript was found some time later, the whole work finally appeared as *The History of New England,* published 1825–26. It thus continued to grow with the development of literature in New England and remains an unparalleled primary source for the history of the period which it covers. Winthrop touched upon some aspect of all of the major concerns of life. His work is a vast compendium of what the early colonists actually felt and thought and traces out the evolution of their ideas and ideals as they were hammered out in the crucible of action and experience.

1634 **1st Roman Catholic Church** built by English colonists raised at St. Mary's City, Md. Excavations have revealed its foundation, but nothing else is known of its appearance.

1636 **Oldest extant house** of English-speaking colonies, Adam Thoroughgood House, built near Norfolk, Va. It is the archetype of the small, southern Colonial, brick farmhouse of 17th C.

1637 Fairbanks house, **oldest frame house** still standing in U.S., built at Dedham, Mass.

1637 Book reflecting gayer side of New England life is *New English Canaan* by **Thomas Morton.** Morton founded colony at Ma-re Mount, where Maypole dances and other debauched customs stirred wrath of Puritan leaders. Morton was the square peg in the round hole of New England Puritanism. He spent his life hopping back and forth across the Atlantic, spending enough time in various colonies for the local authorities to become outraged enough at his activities to ship him back to England and prison. Before he

SCIENCE; INDUSTRY; ECONOMICS; EDUCATION; RELIGION; PHILOSOPHY.

SPORTS; FASHIONS; POPULAR ENTERTAINMENT; FOLKLORE; SOCIETY.

pastor, John Wilson, in Charlestown before these men and their followers crossed river and founded their own settlement. It was a non-Separatist Congregational church.

1630 Nov. 9 **1st ferry route** established by Massachusetts Court of Assistants in Boston. Every approved ferry operator between Boston and Charleston on Charles R. could charge 1 penny for each passenger and same amount for each 100 lb. of cargo.

1631 **Compulsory religious education** in Virginia enforced by requiring each churchwarden to take monthly oath that he was not delinquent in catechizing the young. Ministers were ordered to "examine, catechise, and instruct the youth and ignorant persons" of parish "in the ten commandments, the articles of the beliefe and in the Lord's prayer."

1631 Feb. 5 **Roger Williams,** great early American dissenter and founder of American Baptist Church, arrived at Boston from England.

1631 Nov. 3 **The Rev. John Eliot,** 1st important Protestant minister in America devoted to religious conversion of Indians, arrived at Boston from England.

1633 Adam Roelantsen, **1st schoolmaster in America,** arrived at Nieuw Amsterdam (New York). Shortly afterward he established 1st school in American colonies as adjunct of Dutch Reformed Church, known today as the Collegiate Church of New York city.

1633 **1st secondary school** in America, Boston Latin School, founded with classical curriculum derived from English schools. By 1720, 5 public schools were maintained in Boston, and were so well regarded that they enrolled students from as far away as West Indies. Boston Latin, oldest public school, is still in existence.

was probably the 1st pirate to appear on the New England coast.

1633 **Price fixing** introduced in town of Salem. Maximum price of meal at an inn was 6 pence. At Ship Tavern, famous hostelry in New England, board, lodging and wine at dinner (beer on occasion) cost 3 shillings a day. Strong intoxicating liquors were forbidden, as well as games, dancing, and singing.

1634 **Sumptuary law** passed by Massachusetts General Court prohibiting purchase of woolen, linen, or silk clothes with silver, gold, silk, or thread lace on them. Slashed clothing was limited to a slash in each sleeve and in back.

1634 Mar. 4 **1st tavern** opened in Boston by Samuel Cole. Tavern was most important social institution in colonies.

1634 Mar. 25 **Maryland Day,** state holiday, commemorates landing of 1st colonists on St. Clement's Island.

1637 Governor Kieft estimated that more than one quarter of buildings in New Amsterdam were **"grog-shops** or houses where nothing is to be got but tobacco and beer."

1637 **Taunton,** Mass., founded by "ancient maid" of 48. What signalizes this event is that unmarried women in early America had an extremely difficult time making a life for themselves. Marriages were generally prompt; after 25 unmarried women had to bear brunt of ridicule, and often law.

1638 **Anne Walker** forcibly excluded from Boston church for "intemperate drinking from one inn to another and for light and wanton behaviour." Public houses caused much disturbance.

13

settlers. Pequot forts were burned and 500 Indian men, women, and children died by fire. Pequots were a small but aggressive band of Mohegans centered along the Thames River out of New London. They were willing to trade with the Dutch and English for a time, but, in 1633, suddenly turned on the English traders and killed those in their territory. The next year they began a war with the Narragansetts and the Dutch were soon involved. Finally, when John Oldham, a New England trader, was massacred, Gov. John Endicott raised and led a war party into Connecticut. Pequots resumed attacks the following spring and New England colonists prepared large scale offensive.

1637 July 13 **Pequot war** ended when Captains Stoughton and Mason virtually wiped out remaining tribesmen near Fairfield, Conn.

1638 Mar. **1st Swedish settlers** in America landed at Fort Christiana, Del., after crossing in Dutch ships under Peter Minuit. They established **1st Lutheran congregation** in America led by Rev. Reorus Rorkillus. Later (1643) Swedish colonists from Delaware, under John Printz, settled at Upland, now Chester, Pennsylvania. They introduced the log cabin, originally a Finnish design, and the steam bath.

1638 Mar. 13 Ancient and Honorable Artillery Company chartered at Boston, Mass., one of the **1st military units** founded in the colonies.

1639 Jan. 14 The "Fundamental Orders composed by Roger Ludlow, which were in effect the **1st constitution** in the colonies written to create a government, were adopted by representatives from Hartford, Windsor, and Wethersfield in Connecticut. The resulting instrument was the 1st constitution for Connecticut and remained in force with some changes until 1818.

published his book he was engaged by English as an informer against the Massachusetts colony. It was partly revenge for the treatment which he had received there and partly a justification of his own activities. Hawthorne wrote about Morton in "The Maypole of Merry-Mount."

1638 Building of **Old College** begun at Harvard, most ambitious building of its time in U.S. Housed entire student body, library, lecture halls, etc.

1638 **American (originally Finnish) log cabin** introduced to New World by Swedish settlers of Delaware. Unlike other colonists they brought over their own timber.

1638 *An Almanak for the Year of Our Lord, 1639, Calculated for New England* published by William Pierce. It was the **1st almanac** in the English colonies. Pierce, a shipmaster, published his almanac as a broadside to attract new settlers for the colonies and new passengers for his ship.

1638 **1st printing press** in colonies established at Cambridge, Mass., and operated by Stephen Day (Daye). Day was succeeded by Samuel Green.

1639 **1st document** in English printed in America is famous broadsheet "Oath of a Free-Man." It was printed in Massachusetts by Stephen Day from case of type brought from England. "Oath" reads in part: "I doe solemnly bind myself in the sight of God, that when I shal be called to give my voyce touching any such matter of this State, in which Freemen are to deal, I will give my vote and suffrage as I shall judge in mine own conscience may best conduce and tend to the publike weal of the body, without respect of persons, or favour of any man."

1639 Hezekiah Usher, who became **1st American bookseller and publisher,** settled in Cambridge, Mass. He later (1657) imported presses and type from England to print Eliot's *Indian Bible.*

SCIENCE; INDUSTRY; ECONOMICS; EDUCATION; RELIGION; PHILOSOPHY.

SPORTS; FASHIONS; POPULAR ENTERTAINMENT; FOLKLORE; SOCIETY.

1634 Israel Stoughton granted permission by General Court at Boston to build mill and bridge on Naponsett R. at Dorchester, Mass. It may have been **1st bridge** built in English colonies.

1634 Mar. 25 **Catholic Church** gained permanent foothold in America when *Dove* and the *Ark* arrived in Maryland with colonists carefully selected by Cecilius Calvert, 2nd Lord Baltimore.

1636 **1st church** in Hartford, Conn., founded by religious refugees from England and Massachusetts. Led by the Rev. Thomas Hooker, the group proclaimed their independence of all authority except that of God.

1636 Oct. 28 **Harvard College** founded by an act of General Court of Massachusetts which allowed £400 for establishment of a school. Entrance requirements were: "When any scholar is able to understand Tully or such like classical author extempore, and make and speak true Latin in verse and prose . . . and decline perfectly the paradigms of nouns and verbs in the Greek tongue, let him then and not before, be capable of admission into the college." The Rev. **Henry Dunster** was its 1st president.

1637 Nov. 7 **Anne Hutchinson,** charged with having preached the Antinomian heresy, was condemned by ecclesiastical synod at Newtown, Mass. Banished, she fled to Rhode Island.

1638 **1st Baptist church** in America established at Providence by Roger Williams, who became its 1st pastor but remained in church for only few months.

1639 May 20 Council of Dorchester, Mass., established **1st school** maintained by community taxes. However, only certain property owners were taxed; no general tax rates were established.

1639 June 6 Bay Colony governors granted Edward Rauson 500 acres at

1638 **Dutch justice** was prompt and harsh during early days of Manhattan. Guysbert Van Regerslard was sentenced to throw himself from sail-yard of a yacht three times and receive three lashes from each sailor, for "drawing his knife upon a person."

1638 Arrival in New Amsterdam of **Dr. Hans Kiersted,** whose Kiersted Ointment is still used after 300 years, its formula closely guarded family secret.

1639 New England laws governing **clothing of men** reflect gay attire of day: men censured for wearing "immoderate great breeches," broad shoulder-bands, capes, and double ruffles; silk roses were worn as adornment on shoes.

1639 Shopkeeper Capt. Keayne accused of **unfair trade** for taking more than sixpence in the shilling profit. After being convicted and fined by court, he was severely censured by church authorities, some of whom were for having him excommunicated.

1639 **Margaret Brent** appeared before Maryland Assembly and requested right to vote, an unprecedented, in fact unheard-of, gesture for a woman of this time.

1639 Woman of Plymouth convicted of **adultery** was sentenced to "be whipt at a cart tayle," and to "weare a badge upon her left sleeue during her aboad" in community. If found in public without badge, she was to be "burned in the face with a hott iron." Generally letters AD made up badge.

1639 Sept. 4 General Court of Massachusetts enacted law against **drinking toasts.** "The common custom of drinking to one another is a mere useless ceremony, and draweth on the abominable practice of drinking healths." Impossibility of sup-

15

1639 **1st American post office** authorized in the Massachusetts Bay Colony. Richard Fairbanks, 1st postmaster, handled the mail in his home in Boston. He received 1 penny for each letter.

1639 **Governor's Castle** built in St. Mary, the 1st permanent settlement in Maryland. It covered 2,934 sq. ft. and was largest building erected in English colonies. It was blown up in 1694 when gunpowder stored in its cellar exploded.

1640–1649

Estimated colonial **population**—27,947.

1640 **Great Migration** into Massachusetts occurred between 1630 and 1640 with 16,000 arrivals, of whom only about 4,000 were church members.

1640 **Boston Common** reserved for use of municipality in maintaining some natural retreat for city dwellers.

1641 Dec. **General Court of Massachusetts** framed legal code entitled, "Body of Liberties," which contained strong hints of growing spirit of colonial independence. Five years later, in 1646, court had occasion to reply to criticism of its provisions: "Our allegiance binds us not to the laws of England any longer than while we live in England."

1643 **Cosmopolitan nature** of New York city's population had early beginning. Although administered by Dutch until 1674, there were over 20 different nationalities and sects on Manhattan Island in 1643, speaking 18 different languages.

1643 Development of coastal towns of **Boston, Salem, Dorchester,** and **Charleston** in Massachusetts Bay colony dwarfed Plymouth settlement. Estimated 20,000 inhabitants in London Company's Bay colony.

1643 Mar. **Roger Williams** embarked from his colony of Providence to return to England to obtain formal charter. In this way Rhode Island secured legal position from which to fight against pressure of hostile New England Confederacy.

1640 **High-backed settle** appeared in American households. Designed to rest in fireplaces, it was fitted with high back and arms to ward off drafts, with seats extremely narrow and left unupholstered.

1640 *The Whole Booke of Psalmes Faithfully Translated into English Metre* published in Cambridge, Mass. More commonly called *Bay Psalm Book,* it was **1st book printed** in America, contained new versions of all Psalms; early editions had no music, but explicit instructions on which tunes should be used for each Psalm. Both translations and tunes were crude, jog-trot ballads, easier to sing but much less interesting than older versions in Ainsworth's or Sternhold and Hopkins' Psalters.

1641 Calvinistic theology appeared in its most attractive form in **Thomas Shepard**'s *The Sincere Convert.* Popularity of book attested by fact that it went through 20 editions.

1641 **1st inn,** City Tavern, built in New Amsterdam. Four-story, stone house was excellent example of Dutch colonial style. It later (1654) became municipal *Stadthuys* or Town-House.

1642 **1st great Virginia mansion** built by Gov. William Berkeley about 3 miles north of Jamestown. Called "Greenspring," it was L-shaped, brick main wing nearly 100 feet long.

1643 **1st American word book,** *A Key into the Language of America, or an help*

SCIENCE; INDUSTRY; ECONOMICS; EDUCATION; RELIGION; PHILOSOPHY.	SPORTS; FASHIONS; POPULAR ENTERTAINMENT; FOLKLORE; SOCIETY.

Pecoit, Mass., to found **gunpowder mill,** probably the 1st in America.

pressing this age-old custom forced repeal of law in 1645.

1640–1649

1640 Aug. 6. Newport, R.I., 1st American community to allot large tract of **public land for school** as permanent endowment. Income from this land was to be used to educate poorer children of community.

1641 Oct. Samuel Winslow of Massachusetts granted issued **1st patent** in colonies for a process of manufacturing salt, the term of the patent to extend 10 years.

1642 **1st Dutch Reformed Church** in America begun in Manhattan by group called First Dutch Church of St. Nicholas. Church was built within a fort for protection against Indian attacks. Church was rudimentary wooden structure.

1642 **Joseph Jencks,** skilled English ironmaker, induced to come to America to help develop iron and brass works at Lynn, Mass. Became **1st American inventor,** obtaining Massachusetts patent for scythe-grinding machine in 1645.

1643 Small woolen and fulling mill, probably **1st American textile factory,** established at Rowley, Mass.

1644 **1st ship** built in Boston and named *Trial.* This marks beginning of great shipbuilding industry of New England.

1644 **1st successful iron works and manufacturing establishment** in U.S. founded on Saugus R., near Lynn, Mass. Founders, under leadership of John Winthrop, were called The Company of Undertakers for the Iron Works.

1646 1st law in Virginia providing for **education of poor** directed justices of peace to bind out children of poor parents as

c1640 Mistress Margaret Brent, colonial attorney for Cecilius Calvert, Lord Proprietor of Maryland, became **1st lady barrister** in America.

1643 **1st "cook's shop,"** or restaurant, opened in Boston after Goody Armitage, William Hudson Jr., and "William Knops wife" received licenses. They were permitted to keep "the ordinary, but not to draw wine."

1644 **1st Thanksgiving Day** celebrated in N.Y. commemorated safe return of Dutch soldiers from battle with Connecticut Indians near Stamford.

1645 June Early mention of **maypole** in New Netherland appeared in sentencing of one William Garritse, who, because he sang libelous song, was tied to maypole.

1646 General Court of Massachusetts enacted a law making it lawful to **smoke tobacco** only when on journey 5 miles away from any town. Unlike earlier laws governing smoking, this one was not based on moral objections, but on danger of fire.

1647 Connecticut enacted strange **blue law** forbidding "social" smoking. Tobacco could be used once a day, at meals or elsewhere, "and then not in company with any other." Tobacco could only be used in one's own house. Behind this law lay belief that smoking in group paved way to dissipation.

1647 Sir William Berkeley, Governor of Virginia, attempted **1st rice-planting** in American colonies. His crop did not succeed.

1647 **1st commercially successful American wines** produced by Captain Brocas.

17

POLITICS AND GOVERNMENT; WAR; DISASTERS; VITAL STATISTICS.

BOOKS; PAINTING; DRAMA; ARCHITECTURE; SCULPTURE.

1643 May 19 New England Confederation formed on May 19 uniting New Haven, Massachusetts Bay, Plymouth, and Connecticut in league for their common defense. John Winthrop of Massachusetts was 1st president.

to the language of the natives of that part of America called New England, by Roger Williams, founder of Providence, R.I., was published in London; Williams compiled his dictionary aboard ship during a journey to Southampton, England.

1644 Mar. 18 Jamestown, Va., threatened by an **Indian uprising** spearheaded by Opechancanough. Suppressed by colonists; resulting treaty forced Indians to cede additional territory and effected a peace that lasted until 1675.

1643 Oldest tide mill, gristmill operated by movement of tides, built at Hingham, Mass. One of earliest examples of industrial architecture in U.S.

1646 1st American battle cruiser commissioned by united colonies of New Haven and Hartford for patrolling Long Island Sound against incursions by Dutch.

1644 Probably 1st great democratic note struck in colonies is Roger Williams' *The Bloudy Tenent of Persecution for Cause of Conscience,* which asserted that basis of power lies in people and "that such Governments as are by them erected and established, have no more power, nor for no longer time, than the civill power or people consenting and agreeing shall betrust them with." Being regarded dangerous book was burned by public hangman in London. Fortunately Williams did not sign his own name to it.

1647 May 29–31 Rhode Island General Assembly convened at Portsmouth, drawing from 4 towns (Providence, Portsmouth, Newport, and Warwick). This body drafted remarkably liberal constitution which, among other things, called for separation between church and state.

1648 Oct. 18 Massachusetts Bay Colony authorized **1st labor organization** in U.S. "The shoomakers of Boston" were permitted to meet whenever they wanted to choose officers and clerks.

c1645 One of **earliest American books for children** published in England, entitled *Spiritual Milk for Boston babes in either England. Drawn out of the breasts of both Testaments for their souls nourishment.* It was written by John Cotton.

1649 Jan. 30 Colony of Virginia declared **allegiance to house of Stuart** after execution of Charles I, and offered haven to any threatened Cavaliers. Virginia was under the London Company until 1624. Then the Company was suspended and the colony reverted back to the crown. In 1642 a loyalist governor, Sir William Berkeley, was appointed, and he disputed Parliamentry claims to Virginia during the Commonwealth (1649–1660). Until 1652 Vir-

1647 One of most amusing works of 17th century and at same time one of most severe in its attack on toleration is **Nathaniel Ward's** *The Simple Cobler of Aggawam in America.* Professing to be reflections of a shoemaker, book attacks women's fashions, long hair on men, etc.

1647 Earliest painting of New York, by unknown artist, also provides **1st rep-**

18

apprentices in industrial or agricultural trades. No specific provision made for book learning although many justices made such a stipulation in their apprentice contracts.

1646 Sept. 1 **Cambridge Synod** of Congregational Churches convened by General Court of Massachusetts to draw up *Cambridge Platform,* constitution of Congregational churches in Massachusetts, Plymouth, New Haven, and Connecticut. Form of church in Massachusetts agreed upon was partly congregational and partly Presbyterian.

1646 Oct. 28 **1st Protestant service** for Indians in America held by the Rev. John Eliot at Nonantum, Mass.

1646 Nov. 4 Massachusetts enacted **severe heresy law** making death punishment for any person who persisted in denying that Holy Scriptures were word of God, "or not to be attended to by illuminated Christians."

1647 **1st important public education law** in U.S. passed in Massachusetts, providing that every community of 50 homeowners maintain free elementary education and that communities of more than 100 households provide secondary school education as well.

1647 Nov. 11 **1st American compulsory school law** passed by Massachusetts. It provided for appointment of teacher in every community of more than 50 families and for the establishment of a grammar school in every community of more than 100 families.

1648 **Earliest recorded orphans' court** in America held in Virginia. It delegated administration of orphans' estates to guardians and heard complaints against such guardians.

1649 Apr. 21 **Toleration Act** pushed through Maryland Assembly by Lord Baltimore, Roman Catholic Proprietor of Maryland. Though colony was haven for Roman Catholics, Lord Baltimore had from beginning encouraged Protestant im-

1647 Mrs. Clark given license to open tavern in Salem, Mass., on condition that she "provide a fitt man y^t is godlie to manage ye business." **Tavern and Innkeeping** provided means of livelihood to many widows of colonial times.

1647 Law in Rhode Island declared **marriages by agreement** illegal. Cases in colonies of self-betrothal were frequent, especially among Quakers. In one case, after living with her "husband" for 20 years, a New England woman petitioned for separation and her property. Court stigmatized her as fornicator, fined both 20 pounds and ordered them "not to lead soe scandalose life."

1647 Jan. Margaret Brent initiated **woman suffrage movement** after she had demanded right to vote in Maryland Assembly. Though outspoken and vociferous, she was refused.

1647 May 26 Massachusetts law forbade any **Jesuit** or **Roman Catholic priest** entering territory under Puritan jurisdiction. Any person suspected, who could not clear himself, was to be banished; for second offense death was penalty.

1648 Margaret Jones of Charlestown, Mass. was **1st witch executed in America.** Gov. Winthrop wrote "that she was found to have such a malignant touch, as many persons, (men, women and children), whom she stroked or touched with any affection or displeasure, etc., were taken with deafness . . . or other violent pains or sickness. . . . Her behaviour at the trial was very intemperate, lying notoriously, and railing upon the jury and witnesses, etc., and in the like distemper she died," etc.

1648 Foundations of **volunteer firefighting system** laid when Gov. Peter Stuyvesant of New York appointed 4 fire wardens who were to inspect wooden chimneys of New Amsterdam and collect 4 guilders for each chimney that was not thoroughly swept. Money collected was used to buy hooks and ladders and leathern

| POLITICS AND GOVERNMENT; WAR; DISASTERS; VITAL STATISTICS. | BOOKS; PAINTING; DRAMA; ARCHITECTURE; SCULPTURE. |

ginia stood with the Stuarts. The English Revolution brought another reversal, but the restoration of Charles II returned the colony to Berkeley and the former allegiance was reasserted.

resentation of striped flag; 4 stripes symbolized confederacy of 4 states, Plymouth, New Haven, Connecticut, and Massachusetts.

1650–1659

Estimated colonial **population**—51,700.

c1650 Establishment of **Maryland plantation** called "Aha, the Cow Pasture." Other house and plantation names in 17th-Century Maryland: Hard Bargain, Bachelor's Hope, Thrumcapped, Want Water, Dear Bought, Peddy Coat's Wish, Parrott's Cage.

1652 Dutch government agreed to exportation of **Negro slaves** to New Netherland. In colony strict laws prevented mistreatment of slaves. Whipping forbidden unless owner received permission from authorities.

1652 Apr. Peter Stuyvesant forced to grant New Amsterdam autonomous **city government.**

1652 May 31 Despite her appeal to Parliament, Massachusetts General Court ruled that **Maine** was part of Bay colony. Maine was unable to resist, and so was annexed.

1652 June 10 **1st mint** in America established in defiance of English colonial law in Boston with John Hull as 1st mintmaster. It issued famous Pine Tree Shilling designed by silversmith John Hull.

1653 Virginia settlers began to migrate through Nansemond Valley into what is now **North Carolina.** They settled north of Albemarle Sound between Chowan R. and sea. Move endorsed by Virginia Assembly, who wanted buffer settlement as protection for their southern frontier.

c1650 **1st known American cabinetmaker** with example of his work still extant, Nicholas Disbrowe, flourished in this period in Connecticut Valley—frontier of the day—site of growing furniture manufacturing.

c1650 American ingenuity shown in design of **settle table,** a dining table which could easily be changed into settle by removal of two wooden pins. See 1640. In 1844 J. W. Mason Company of New York was established to make and sell these tables. They were in great demand.

1650 New England's **1st poet,** Anne Bradstreet, wife of Massachusetts' Gov. Simon Bradstreet, published her 1st volume of verse, *The Tenth Muse,* in London. *Several Poems* was published in Boston in 1678.

1653 Beauty of **Dutch gardens** in New Amsterdam reported by early traveler, who cited "white and red roses, stock roses, cornelian roses, eglantine, jenoffelins, gillyflowers, different varieties of fine tulips, crown-imperials, white lilies, anemones, bare-dames, violets, marigolds, summersots, clove trees."

1653 Probably **1st book printed in an Indian language** in New England was *Catechism in the Indian Language* by John Eliot. Missionary to Indians, Eliot later translated Bible into Algonquian language.

1654 Dynamic account of early Puritan settlement given by **Edward Johnson** in *The Wonder-Working Providence of*

SCIENCE; INDUSTRY; ECONOMICS; EDUCATION; RELIGION; PHILOSOPHY.

SPORTS; FASHIONS; POPULAR ENTERTAINMENT; FOLKLORE; SOCIETY.

migration. As Protestant groups became more numerous, religious disturbances became more frequent and more bitter. Rise of Cromwell in England in 1642 intensified anti-Catholic feeling among Puritans in Maryland and other colonies. Increased pressure from England for subjugation of Catholicism in colonies led Baltimore to sponsor Act of Toleration as means of averting serious test of force.

buckets for fire-fighting organization called "The Prowlers," group of 8 men who patrolled streets 9 P.M. until dawn.

1649–1660 Rigid Puritan enforcement of laws relating to **sexual conduct** reflected in 122 indictments for sexual offenses in sparsely settled Essex County between 1649 and 1660.

1650–1659

1651 Famous case of **persecution of Baptists** in Massachusetts involved two Baptist ministers, John Clarke and Obediah Holmes, who were arrested during service in private home. Clarke released against his wishes by a friend's payment of his fine but Holmes whipped in streets of Boston.

1654 **Production of wool** important New England industry, partly because many early settlers had been in wool business in England.

1654 Boston selectmen commission Joseph Jencks, ironmaker of Lynn, Mass., to construct **1st American fire engine.** A machine set on wheels, it spurted water from cistern filled by bucket-passers.

1654 General Court of Massachusetts licensed Richard Thurley to build and maintain toll bridge over Newbury R. at Rowley. Court fixed toll at 2d for horses, cows, and oxen; ½d for hogs, sheep, and goats. Humans passed free. Thurley's bridge was probably **1st toll bridge** in the U.S.

1654 July 8 **1st Jew** to settle in North America, Jacob Barsimson, arrived on Manhattan Island, first of 24 Jewish emigrants to Manhattan that year.

1654 Sept. **1st Jewish immigrants** arrived in New Amsterdam, a group of 3 fleeing from Spanish Inquisition in Brazil. Others followed. Their right to stay was upheld by Dutch West India Company against wishes of Gov. Peter Stuyvesant. They founded congregation of Shearith Israel with Saul Brown as **1st rabbi.**

1650 Notices appeared describing **fox hunting** on shores of Chesapeake Bay.

1651 Relaxation of some of Puritan asceticism reflected in sale of **toys and dolls** in stores in Boston and Salem.

1652 Vogue of form of **miniature golf** began in New Netherland. Small ball was putted around green by means of crooked club.

1653 Interesting example of **New England snobbery** seen in arrest of 2 women in Newbury for adorning themselves with silk hoods and scarves and their release when they presented proof that their husbands each had net worth of £200.

1656 **Captain Kemble** of Boston made to sit 2 hours in stocks for "his lewd and unseemly behavior" in kissing his wife "publicquely" on Sunday. He had just returned from 3-year voyage.

1656 To insure that **Sunday** would be day of rest, burgomasters of New Netherland passed law forbidding drinking, sowing, mowing, building, sawing, smithing, bleaching, hunting, fishing, dancing, cardplaying, tick-tacking, bowling, jaunting in boat or carriage, etc.

1656 Law governing **baking of bread** passed in New Amsterdam. Bakers had to bake coarse and white bread twice a week, both for Christians and Indians. Price of coarse loaf of 8 lb. regulated at 14 stuyvers.

1657 **1st reference to golf** in America was complaint issued by sheriff of Fort

21

POLITICS AND GOVERNMENT; WAR; DISASTERS; VITAL STATISTICS.	BOOKS; PAINTING; DRAMA; ARCHITECTURE; SCULPTURE.

1655 After years of pressure, stubborn old **Peter Stuyvesant** broke Johan Printz's rule in Delaware and Dutch took over. Swedes and Finns living along Delaware R. gladly became English citizens when William Penn founded Pennsylvania in 1683.

1655 Mar. 25 End of **Civil War** in Maryland between Catholics and Puritans. War sparked by repeal of Toleration Act (1654), a move that denied Catholics protection under law, and won by Puritans. In ensuing seesaw struggle for control, Calverts lost proprietary control of Maryland, then regained it once more (Nov. 30, 1657).

1656 July 17 1st structure on what is now **Syracuse** built by Jesuit priests from Canada.

1656 Sept. 22 General Provincial Court in session at Patuxent, Md., empaneled **1st all-woman jury in Colonies** to hear evidence against Judith Catchpole. Defendant, accused of murdering her child, claimed she had never even been pregnant. After hearing her evidence, jury acquitted her.

1658 Aug. 12 **1st police force,** or *ratelwacht,* formed in New Amsterdam, consisting of 10 watchmen, paid 24 stuyvers (about 50¢) a night, money collected from inhabitants each month. Guard caught sleeping on duty was fined 10 stuyvers; he was enjoined not to swear, fight, or drink.

Zion's Saviour in New England, published anonymously in England. Book purports to show how emigration from England and settlement of New World were parts of God's plan for his oppressed people.

1654 Early Dutch **glassmaker** of New Amsterdam allotted ground upon which to set up his works. Jan Smedes' firm prospered to extent that Glass-makers Street was renamed Smee Street (later Smith and now William Street).

1657 **Old North Church** constructed in Portsmouth, N.H. 1st church edifice erected in colony, serving its congregation until 1708. Church was located on site offering maximum protection from Indian attacks.

1659 Puritan notion of interrelationship of God and state outlined in *The Christian Commonwealth* by **John Eliot.** Supremacy of clergy in 17th century was based on belief that "there is undoubtedly a form of Civil Government, instituted by God himself in the holy Scriptures."

1659 Probably 1st description of **Copernican astronomy** in colonies appeared in an *Almanack* issued at Cambridge. "A breif Explication and proof of the Philolaick Systeme," by Sechariah Brigden. Young Harvard graduates used often to edit these New England almanacs, which consequently included verse of their editors and featured most recent popular scientific information.

1660-1669

Estimated colonial **population**—84,800.

1660 Dec. 1 **Navigation Act,** written to govern colonial trade, stated that all goods carried to and from England must be transported by British ships manned chiefly by British sailors. It further provided that certain articles, which included sugar, to-

1662 Masterpiece of **Michael Wigglesworth** and most phenomenal work of Puritan poetry is *Day of Doom; or, A poetical description of the great and last Judgement.* A fire-and-brimstone tract, book scourges nonbelievers. 1800 copies sold 1st year; every 35th person in New England

SCIENCE; INDUSTRY; ECONOMICS; EDUCATION; RELIGION; PHILOSOPHY.

SPORTS; FASHIONS; POPULAR ENTERTAINMENT; FOLKLORE; SOCIETY.

1655 **Illiteracy of women** was about 50%, as shown by an examination of legal documents which required signature of women in Massachusetts. More than half were obliged to sign with a cross. In New Netherland it was 60% and in Virginia 75%.

1656 **Galileo's** conception of universe with sun, rather than earth, as its center formally accepted by Harvard College only 23 years after Galileo had been forced by Inquisition to repudiate it.

1656 July **1st Quakers** to land in America were Mary Fisher and Ann Austin, who had only recently secured some influential converts to Quakerism in Barbados. Arriving in Boston, they were imprisoned for five weeks and deported by Massachusetts authorities.

1656 Oct. 14 **1st punitive legislation against Quakers** in Massachusetts decreed that 40-shilling fines be levied against any one sheltering Quakers and prescribed various physical mutilations for Quakers who returned to colony after having been banished.

1657 June 1 **1st Quakers** arrived in Manhattan, 5 in number, only to be imprisoned for 8 days before being allowed to leave for Rhode Island.

1659 **1st classical elementary school** in New York established.

1659 Oct. 27 **1st Quakers** hanged on Boston Common for violating laws of 1656 against returning to Massachusetts when once banished were William Robinson and Marmaduke Stevenson.

Orange, N.Y. (Albany) against 3 men for playing kolven on Sunday. Kolven believed to be early form of golf.

1657 **Horse racing** within city limits of New Amsterdam forbidden by governor.

1658 Colonial writer noted **fortunes of women:** "They no sooner arrive than they are besieged with offers of matrimony, husbands being ready soon for those whom nature had apparently marked out and predestined for lives of single blessedness." Servants, innocent country girls kidnaped in England, coming penniless to America, married well and attained distinction.

1658 **1st New York hospital** set up by Dr. Varravanger, surgeon of Dutch West India Company. It consisted of a clean house with plenty of firewood and a fire, and was supervised by a matron. This was possibly **1st hospital in U.S.**

1659 Jan. Severity of **colonial punishments** seen in ordinance passed in New Amsterdam: "No person shall strip the fences of posts or rails under penalty for the first offence of being whipped and branded, and for the second, of punishment with the cord until death ensues."

1659 Sept. 30 **1st mention of tennis** in U.S. appeared in proclamation issued by Peter Stuyvesant forbidding tennis playing, among other things, on a certain day.

1660–1669

1661 **American Quakers held 1st yearly meeting** in Rhode Island.

1660 John Eliot founded **1st Indian church** in New England at Natick, Mass., on the Charles R. He had established Natick as a native village for "praying Indians" in 1657.

c1660 Much rejoicing and riotous activity among Dutch on **Pinkster Day** (Dutch name for Pentecost, hence Whitsunday). Celebration was at its greatest among Negro slaves of Albany. Native Congo dances staged, accompanied by tom-tom rhythms and strange African airs.

bacco, cotton, wool, ginger, and dyestuffs were to be exported to England only.

1662 May 3 **Legal charter for Connecticut** secured through efforts of Gov. John Winthrop, Jr.

1663 June 23 **New Jersey** granted to James, Duke of York, by Charles II.

1664 Maryland enacted statute providing for lifelong servitude for **Negro slaves.** Law was designed to prevent slaves who had become converted to Christianity from claiming freedom on basis of British court decisions which had held that infidel slaves must be freed once they had been baptized as Christians and had taken legal residence in the country. Similar acts passed in Virginia, North Carolina, New York, South Carolina, and New Jersey. No such action taken in Georgia, Pennsylvania, and Delaware.

1664 **New Netherland** surrendered to British, and New Amsterdam and Fort Orange became New York and Albany, but retained their Dutch characteristics for many years. Thus, Dutch power that had opened Hudson R., challenged English in Connecticut, and supplanted Swedes in Delaware was broken.

1664 Sept. 8 Fort and town of **New Amsterdam** surrendered by Peter Stuyvesant to Col. Richard Nicolls. Nicolls and his fleet of 4 ships were in pay of Duke of York, brother of Charles II.

1665 Jan. 5 **New Haven annexed** by Connecticut. New Haven colonists had choice of becoming part of Connecticut to north, or absorption into territory under jurisdiction of Duke of York.

1665 Feb. 28 **Duke's Laws** sponsored by English proprietor of New York, Duke

purchased one, a success never equaled in America. Book has been repeatedly reprinted in America and at least once in England.

1662 Strict **censorship** of printed material in Puritan New England revealed in appointment of two licensers to prevent escape of certain books which might tend "to open the door of heresy."

1664 **Richard Jackson House** constructed in Portsmouth, N.H. Built in traditional English style of time, dwelling reputed to be oldest building in state. Richard Jackson was a shipbuilder.

1664 Will of Mr. Nathaniell Rogers, of Rowley, Mass., specified **"treble vial"** valued at 10 shillings; this was the 1st known mention of musical instrument in America.

1664 **1st best selling book of sermons** in America, *A Call to the Unconverted* by Richard Baxter. Baxter was famous British Puritan preacher and author.

1664 Contemporary observers note new emergence of **Renaissance style** in Dutch colonial houses at New Amsterdam. Dutch influence continued to prevail after colony became New York.

1665 Very widely read book in Colonial America, *The Practice of Piety* by Englishman, **Lewis Bayly,** Bishop of Bangor. Book of prayer, meditation, and especially exhortations, written with Calvinistic fire.

1665 Aug. 27 **1st play performed in North American colonies,** *Ye Bare and Ye Cubb* by Philip Alexander Bruce, at Accomac, Va. 3 local residents were fined for acting in this play. Most colonies had laws forbidding public performances. What is strange is that this incident occurred in Virginia where no such legislation existed.

1669 **1st extensive account of history of New England** published at Boston, Mass. It was *New England's Memoriall,*

SCIENCE; INDUSTRY; ECONOMICS; EDUCATION; RELIGION; PHILOSOPHY.

1660 May Celebration of **Christmas** forbidden by law of Massachusetts, with fine of 5 shillings levied on violators.

1661 **1st Bible printed in America,** translated by John Eliot into Algonquian language, financed by Corporation for Propagating the Gospel in New England. Of this remarkable work, Cotton Mather wrote: "Behold, ye Americans, the greatest honor that ever you were partakers of! This is the only Bible that ever was printed in all America from the very foundation of the world."

1661 Pressures for **cultivation of silk** in Virginia increased with coronation of Charles II in robe woven of Virginia silk.

1661 Mar. 14 **Last Quaker executed** in Boston, William Leddra, for his return from banishment.

1661 Sept. **Persecution of Quakers** in Massachusetts halted by Gov. Endicott on orders from Charles II, personal friend of William Penn.

1662 Jan. **1st lime produced in America** by Mr. Hacklett of Providence.

1662 Mar. Adoption of **Half-Way Covenant** by a General Synod of Massachusetts churches led to schism in New England Congregationalism. Covenant permitted parents who had been baptized in church, but who no longer professed their faith, to have their children baptized. *Half-Way Covenant* was symptomatic of decline of power of New England founders and emergence of more liberal second generation.

1666 **First Presbyterian Church** in Elizabeth, N.J., 1st English-speaking church in state, began construction.

1666 **1st Church** built in Breuckelen (Brooklyn), heavy, square building, situ-

SPORTS; FASHIONS; POPULAR ENTERTAINMENT; FOLKLORE; SOCIETY.

1660 **1st divorce case** in Delaware involved Finnish couple. "The wife receives daily a severe drubbing and is expelled from the house like a dog." Husband was adulterer, and divorce was granted. New England at this time showed most liberality in granting divorces. New York and rest of Middle Atlantic colonies made divorce almost impossible outside of proved or confessed adultery.

1660 **Connecticut law** ordered all married men to live with their wives; a man who was separated from his wife for more than 3 years was ordered out of colony.

1660 **Sumptuary law** passed in Virginia forbade settlers importing "silke stuffe in garments or in peeces except for whoods and scarfs, nor silver or gold lace, nor bone lace of silk or threads, nor ribbands wrought with gold or silver in them."
But with Restoration in England **periwigs** came into fashion on both sides of Atlantic. Authorities in New England made repeated efforts to prevent their use.

1662 Virginia edict decreed that any parents who failed to have their **children baptized** were to be fined 2000 lb. of tobacco.

1662 Virginia General Assembly proclaimed Jan. 30, anniversary of **beheading of Charles I,** day of fasting in colony. Charles II had issued similar edict in England upon his restoration in 1660.

1665 Nov. 5 **Guy Fawkes Day** celebrated in New York. A law ordered all ministers to preach sermon on this date in memory of discovery of Guy Fawkes plot to blow up English House of Lords in 1605.

1663 Instance of **wife-trading** occurred in New York. Laurens Duyts sentenced by Dutch court to be flogged and have his right ear cut off for selling his wife.

1664 **Marriage** by justice of peace instead of clergyman made lawful in New York by Duke's Laws, actually a continua-

of York, provided for official recognition of all Protestant sects within colony. Specific mention granted to Dutch Reformed Church, only church recognized by name. This unusual toleration of Dutch Church by English authorities contrasted sharply with restrictive policies of Dutch West India Company before its loss of colony to British in 1664. Up to 1664, Dutch Reformed Church was only legal religion in colony. Yet, despite this restriction, a great many unauthorized religious groups established footholds in Dutch colony. This religious diversity inherited by British proprietor in 1664 made policy of toleration a practical necessity.

1667 Virginia legislature decreed that individuals born in **slavery** did not end their servitude once they had been baptized in Christian faith. Preamble to law expressed hope that slave owners would, by passage of this law, become more diligent in converting their slaves to Christianity.

1667 July 21 **Second Anglo-Dutch War ended** by Peace of Breda which conceded all New Netherland to England.

or a Brief Relation of the Most Memorable and Remarkable Passages of the Providence of God, Manifested to the Planters of New England in America; With Special Reference to the First Colony Therefore, Called New Plymouth, by Nathaniel Morton.

1666 Rollicking book recounting life in early Maryland is **George Alsop's** *A Character of the Province of Maryland.* Full of raw humor, often coarse and obscene, book abounds in phrases like the following: "Herds of deer are as numerous in this province of Maryland as cuckolds can be in London, only their horns are not so well dressed and tipped with silver."

1669 Classic document in annals of early American life is *New England's Memoriall* by **Nathaniel Morton,** secretary of Plymouth colony. Describing work, author writes that it is "a brief relation of the most memorable and remarkable passages of the providence of God manifested to the planters of New England, with special reference to the first colony thereof called New Plymouth."

1669 Christian view of suffering and comfort derived from it presented in a long poem by **Michael Wigglesworth,** *Meat out of the Eater; or, Meditations concerning the necessity, end, and usefulness of afflictions unto God's children, all tending to prepare them for and comfort them under the Cross.*

1670–1679

Estimated colonial **population**—114,500.

1670 Apr. **Charleston, S.C. founded.** English colonists under Joseph West settled at Port Royal Sound, then moved northward to Ashley R. at Albemarle Sound for fear of Spaniards. There they established Charles Town, later known as Old Charles Town. In 1680, this settlement was moved once again to juncture of Ashley and Cooper, present site of city.

1670 Early painting attributed to **John Foster** is Yale University's portrait of *John Davenport.* A Harvard graduate who devoted his spare time to woodcuts, Foster painted his portrait in stiff, flat manner, making him one of earliest primitives.

1670 **1st account in print** of New York city is *A Brief Description of New York* by Daniel Denton. Designed to encourage immigrants to this growing community, book sings of "the woods and fields so

SCIENCE; INDUSTRY; ECONOMICS; EDUCATION; RELIGION; PHILOSOPHY.

SPORTS; FASHIONS; POPULAR ENTERTAINMENT; FOLKLORE; SOCIETY.

ated on what is now Fulton Street. It continued to be used until 1810.

1668 May 27 **1st Baptists** sentenced to exile from Massachusetts, Thomas Gold, William Turner, and John Farnum.

1669 **1st Sunday school** of record established at Plymouth, Mass.

1669 **Fundamental Constitutions** drawn up by John Locke as expression of ecclesiastical objectives of proprietors of Carolinas. Stressing religious toleration, *Fundamental Constitutions* provided that "Noe person whatever shall disturb, molest or persecute another for his speculative opinions in Religion or his way of Worship." Although official recognition and support could be granted only to Church of England under provisions of the *Constitutions,* it was further specified that any 7 adherents of same religious faith could establish a church under any name they desired, with proviso that such church must accept existence of God and declare that parishioners of church intended to worship Him. Although *Fundamental Constitutions* never became operative as laws in colonies, they exercised profound influence on colonial religion, particularly in Carolinas.

tion of Dutch law of 1590. Since this date law has not been altered.

1664 **America's 1st organized sport,** horse racing, began when New York's 1st governor, Richard Nicolls, established Newmarket Course at Hempstead Plains, Long Island, instituted rules of racing, offered prizes to winners. His purpose was to improve breed of horses in U.S.

1666 South Carolina publicized in England this **inducement to women:** "If any maid or single woman have a desire to go over, they will think themselves in the golden age, when men paid a dowry for their wives; for if they be but civil, and under fifty years of age, some honest man or other, will purchase them for their wives."

1666 Arrival in America of **Captain and Mrs. Neale** (she former Anna Gill), who were progenitors of many of Maryland's famous names. Fleeing England after execution of Charles I, he bought tract of land in Maryland with Spanish coins called "cob dollars," hence name of his settlement, Cob Neck.

1668 **America's 1st sports trophy,** silver porringer, hand-wrought by Pieter van Inburg, presented to winner of horse race at Newmarket, Long Island race course.

1669 **Horse racing** firmly established in New York when Gov. Lovelace personally arranged race for silver crown at Newmarket Course at Hempstead Plains.

1670–1679

1670 Aug. 22 John Eliot and John Cotton of Massachusetts colony founded **Indian church** on Martha's Vineyard. Hiacoomes and Tackanash, two educated Indians, were appointed pastor and teacher. Hiacoomes continued in his office for many years as a well-liked and faithful minister.

1671 Stephen Mumford established **1st Seventh Day Baptist Church** at Newport,

1670–1690 Growth of **Southern aristocracy** seen early in Virginia, where practically every official position in Henrico County was filled by a Randolph.

1670 Following **game** available to hunters on Long Island, N.Y., very popular hunting area: "Deer, Bear, Wolves, Foxes, Racoon, Otters, Musquashes, and Skunks; Wild Fowl . . . Turkies, Heath Hen, Quailes, Partridges, Pigeon, Cranes,

27

POLITICS AND GOVERNMENT; WAR; DISASTERS; VITAL STATISTICS.

BOOKS; PAINTING; DRAMA; ARCHITECTURE; SCULPTURE.

1670 **Virginia slavery act** decreed that slaves who had become Christians before their importation were not liable to life-long servitude. This law reflected moral concern felt in America over enslavement of Christians.

1670 Virginia legislature enacted law **prohibiting importation of convicts** as indentured servants. This act sustained for a time in English Parliament but finally repealed in 1717 by act authorizing transportation of convicts to America.

1671 **1st of great Hudson Valley manors** established by English colony of New York at Fordham. Others followed: Fox Hall (Kingston), 1672; Rensselaerswyck, 1685; Livingston (160,000 acres), 1686; Pelham, 1687; Philipsborough, 1693; Morrisania, 1697; Cortlandt, 1697; and Scarsdale, 1701.

1671 Maryland act extended scope of **slavery law** passed in 1664 by declaring that conversion or baptism of slaves before or after their importation did not entitle them to freedom. Act was passed to quell fears of slave owners who hesitated to import slaves for fear of losing their investment through prior or subsequent conversion and, also, to encourage slave owners to convert their slaves to Christianity.

1672 May 15 Massachusetts General Court enacted **1st copyright law** in American colonies, issuing copyright to John Usher, bookseller, to publish a new edition of "The General Laws and Liberties of the Massachusetts Colony." Protection was for 7 years. Penalty for infringement was fine three times the manufacturing cost.

1673 **Josiah Winslow** of Plymouth elected Governor of Massachusetts, the 1st native-born person to hold that office. His term extended until his death in 1680. Winslow also succeeded Myles Standish as commander-in-chief of Plymouth military defense.

1673 Aug. 8 Dutch demand **surrender of New York** while anchored near Sandy Hook with 23 ships and 1600 men. They

curiously bedecked with roses" and "divers sorts of singing birds, whose chirping notes salute the ear of travellers."

1670 **1st portrait engraving** in colonial America is woodcut of Richard Mather, theological writer of Massachusetts.

1670 Early example of colonial portraiture is *Margaret Gibbs* by **"Freake Painter"** of Boston. Adorned in lacery, the young lady attests to side of Puritan life which is hardly religious. Though most painters of period are unknown, the fact that Boston could claim from 5 to 10 around this time reveals lively interest in portraiture.

1670 Earliest portion of **House of Seven Gables** built in Salem, Mass.; it was later much enlarged and remodeled.

1672 Oct. 2 **Castillo de San Marcos,** fort at St. Augustine, Fla., and one of most impressive structures of Spanish colonial style, begun. Completed 1756. 9 previous forts of wood and earth construction had been built and demolished on site.

1674 Early colonial naturalist employing real scientific discipline was **John Josselyn.** In his *Account of Two Voyages to New England* he reports geological and botanical observations.

1674 **Samuel Sewall** began his famous diary, which covers years 1674–1729. Like Pepys, he loved to record commonplace, daily events of his time. As a judge at witchcraft trials, he lived to recant his views.

1676 Early American satire is ballad *A Looking-Glass for the Times; or, The former spirit of New England revived in this generation* by **Peter Folger,** grandfather of Ben Franklin. In strong, manly doggerel, he lashed into Christians of New England for their behavior toward Quakers, Baptists, etc.

1677 Historical book popular enough during 17th century to be termed classic is

SCIENCE; INDUSTRY; ECONOMICS; EDUCATION; RELIGION; PHILOSOPHY.	SPORTS; FASHIONS; POPULAR ENTERTAINMENT; FOLKLORE; SOCIETY.

R.I. An English Sabbatarian Baptist, Mumford argued that the Sabbath should be observed on the last day of the week; in 1947 his group had grown to 6,462 members.

1674 Dec. 4 **1st dwelling** in what is now Chicago built by Father Marquette as a mission.

1675 Charter issued by Duke of York for a fishing corporation in New York; it may have been **1st business corporation** in America. It was a joint-stock company with capital shares valued at £10, but the other aspects of the incorporation are not clear today.

1675 May 3 Massachusetts law enacted requiring **locking of church doors** during service. Law result of too many people leaving before long sermon was completed.

1675–1676 Pressures on **Indian population** of New England resulted in King Philip's War. Tribes most affected by early colonial expansion were: (1) Wampanoags, originally from Atlantic coast, now forced back to east of Narragansett Bay; (2) Narragansetts, whose territory between Bay and Thames R. was menaced by land company which claimed it held mortgage to areas; (3) Mohegans, between Connecticut and Thames Rs.; (4) Podunks, directly to north; and (5) Nipmucks, who ranged over northern parts of Thames and Pawtucket Rs. Coalition of these tribes, known as Five Nations, was headed by Philip, chief of Wampanoags.

1676 Massachusetts **regulated price** of shoes: "Five pence half penny a size for all pleyne and wooden heel'd shoes, and above

Geese of several sorts, Brants, Ducks, Widges, Teal, and divers others."

1670 License given by Boston authorities to woman to sell coffee and chocolate. This was beginning of **coffee house** in America.

1672 New York employed Indians to carry winter **mail** from city to Albany because of extreme hardships involved. As late as 1730 notice posted that "whoever inclines to perform the foot-post to Albany this winter may make application to the Post-Master."

1673 Early **horse racing** in Virginia was strictly for aristocrats. James Bullock, York county tailor, ran his mare against Mathew Slader for 2000 lb. of tobacco. When he tried to collect, the court fined him 100 lb. of tobacco, declaring: "Racing to be a sport for gentlemen only."

1673 Appearance of **fencing school** in Boston indicated greater emphasis on recreation in Puritan life.

1673 Jan 1 **1st regular mounted mail service** inaugurated between New York and Boston. Postman rode without changing horse from New York to Hartford, through woods, over streams, keeping a lookout for runaway servants and soldiers.

1674 Plymouth Colony court ruled that "whatsoever person ran a race with any horse in any street or common road should forfeit 5 shillings or sit in the stocks for one hour." There was no prohibition of **horse racing** away from public thoroughfares.

1675 **New York city,** which had always had mixed population, began to take on really cosmopolitan air. Combination of religious toleration and commercial activity encouraged influx of Englishmen, Jews, African Negroes, Indians, Madagascan pirates, and French Huguenots.

1675 Massachusetts General Court enacted laws which upbraided **current fashions.** Indian attacks blamed on sins of people, among which was "the manifest pride openly appearing amongst us in that long hair, like women's hair, is

29

held possession of colony until Feb. 9, 1674, when British regained control.

1675 June 24 **King Philip's War** began with massacre of colonists at Swansee, Plymouth, by band of Indians.

1675 Aug. 2 **Indians attacked and destroyed** Brookfield, Mass. They were later forced to retreat under assault led by Maj. Willard.

1675 Sept. 1 **Deerfield**, Mass., set aflame by attacking Indians.

1676 Feb. 10 Indians, under **King Philip**, attacked Lancaster, Mass. Settlement destroyed by fire after all men killed and women and children taken prisoners.

1676 Aug. 12 **King Philip's War** ended when he was surprised and shot by an Indian in service of Capt. Church.

1676 Sept. 19 Nathaniel Bacon defeated Gov. Berkeley's troops and burned Jamestown in uprising called **Bacon's Rebellion.** Berkeley, royal governor of Virginia, repeatedly refused to organize necessary defensive measures to oppose marauding Indians.

1677 Aug. **1st large group of Quakers** from England to emigrate to America settled in West Jersey, founding city of Burlington.

1679 **Worst fire** in 17th-century U.S. destroyed 150 houses in Boston. Thereafter frame houses abandoned by city ordinance, and all houses were of "stone or bricke, & covered with slate or tyle."

William Hubbard's *Narrative of the Troubles with the Indians in New England;* it reflects hostility to red men, who are "treacherous villains," "children of the Devil," "the dross of mankind," "dregs and lees of the earth."

1677 Probably finest poem written in America during this era is *Elegy on the Reverend Thomas Shepard* by **Urian Oakes,** whom Increase Mather considered "one of the greatest lights that ever shone in this part of the world, or that is ever like to arise in this horizon."

1678 1st book of poems by a woman to be published in the colonies, *Several Poems Compiled with Great Variety of Wit and Learning* by **Anne Bradstreet.** This was 2nd revised and enlarged edition of her 1st publication. Coming from a cultivated background in England, and thrust into wilderness of New World, she reveals on one hand her leaning toward poets such as Sidney, Spenser, and Herbert; on other, she records the feelings of sensitive woman in contact with rude nature.

1679 Colonial best seller, *A Guide to Heaven* by **Samuel Hardy,** published in Boston. A book of Puritan rules and practices of piety, it is less fiery than Bishop Bayly's *The Practice of Piety.*

1680–1689

Estimated colonial **population**—155,600.

1680 Sept. **New Hampshire** separated from Massachusetts by royal commission.

1680 **John Banister,** famous early American botanist, made international contribution to study of natural history by presenting 52 different species of American

SCIENCE; INDUSTRY; ECONOMICS; EDUCATION; RELIGION; PHILOSOPHY.	SPORTS; FASHIONS; POPULAR ENTERTAINMENT; FOLKLORE; SOCIETY.

seven pence half penny a size for well wrought 'French falls.' " Shoes with wooden heels worn throughout 17th century.

1676 Order in Salem, Mass., regulating **church attendance** required "all ye boyes of ye towne are appointed to sitt upon ye three paire of stairs in ye meeting-house, and Wm. Lord is appointed to look after ye boys upon ye pulpitt stairs." Little girls, on the contrary, sat with their mothers. Men and women generally sat on different sides of hall.

1676 **Episcopal Church** in Jamestown, Va., 1st Protestant church in America, destroyed by Nathaniel Bacon who, in rebelling against rule of Gov. Berkeley, set fire to Jamestown, burning entire community to the ground. Ruins of church tower still standing on site of community.

1677 **1st charter guaranteeing separation** of church and state in American colonies framed by William Penn at Quaker colony of West Jersey.

1677 Puritan **hostility to Quaker methods** of conversion reflected in Samuel Sewall's account in his diary of unruly gestures and appearance of Quaker woman bursting in on Congregational meeting.

1678 **1st vessel** to penetrate Lake Ontario, the *Griffin,* carried French expedition led by Sieur de la Salle from Fort Frontenac (later Kingston) to present site of Fort Niagara.

worn by some men, either their own or others' hair made into periwigs."

1676 **Caste law** passed in Connecticut providing that any one adorned with silk ribbons, gold or silver lace, or any other luxurious fabric or metal was to be assessed for taxable property of £150 with significant exception of "such whose quality and estate have been above the ordinary degree though now decayed."

1675 38 women brought before Connecticut magistrate for wearing **clothes** that did not agree with their estate. One young girl accused of "wearing silk in a flaunting manner, in an offensive way and garb not only before but when she stood presented." This year 30 young men arrested for wearing silk and sporting long hair.

1678 Dutch inhabitants of New York were great consumers of **tobacco.** An English chaplain reported that "the Dutch are obstinate and incessant smokers, whose diet . . . being sallets and brawn and very often picked buttermilk, require the use of that herb to keep their phlegm from coagulating and curdling."

1679 James Willet, husband of daughter of Lieutenant Peter Hunt, sued latter for failing to pay him £100 offered as his wife's **dowry.** Marriage was thoroughly permeated by economics among fashionable Puritans. Often fathers haggled and bargained over their daughters' dowries.

1679 Sept. **1st methodical plan for street naming** appeared in an order of Town Meeting of Newport "to consider of making foure equall divisions of this Towne . . . (which) will be useful about ye naming of ye highways." Boston itself had no plan until later. It designated streets as "the street leading to the Neck" or "John Thwings land to the lane by Houghton's house."

1680–1689

1680 Major scientific achievement of colonial America, calculation of orbit of a comet of 1680 by **Thomas Brattle,** early Boston mathematician.

c1680 **Long straight coat** introduced into New England. Manufactured without collar, coat was worn with neck cloth which was fastened under hair in back by

1681 Mar. 10 **William Penn** received charter from Charles II that made him sole proprietor of territory which became Pennsylvania.

1682 Virginia legislature repealed **slavery law** of 1670 which had exempted from lifelong servitude all slaves who had been converted to Christianity before their importation. Repeal of 1670 statute was dictated by the sharp decline in slave importation after its passage.

1682 A site for city of **Philadelphia** was laid out by Thomas Holme, 1 of 4 commissioners sent to Pennsylvania by William Penn to prepare settlers for the new government.

1682 May 5 William Penn's **"Frame of Government"** put into effect. An unusually liberal document, it provided for a Governor, a council, and an assembly to be elected by freeholders. Council had legislative, judicial, and administrative powers. At first, Assembly could not initiate legislation, but this was altered in 1696.

1682 Aug. 24 **Delaware awarded to William Penn** by Duke of York, who had no legal title to land. This made Penn's control over Delaware tenuous, particularly since it conflicted with other claims. Issue finally resolved by Charter of 1701 which gave Delaware autonomy.

1683 Oct. 6 **1st German settlers** in America, Mennonites from Krefeld, Germany, arrived at Philadelphia. They settled Germantown, near Philadelphia, at the bidding of William Penn. Their leader, Francis Daniel Pastorius, was considered by many the most learned man in America at the time.

1684 June 21 **Massachusetts Bay Colony charter annulled** by Court of Chancery. Edmund Randolph, collector and surveyor of customs, had sent series of derogatory reports back to England, and followed these with personal prosecution of colony before court.

1685 Feb. 18 **1st European settlers in Texas** were French who were organized by La Salle.

insects to Petiver, distinguished English naturalist.

1680 **1st "hipped" or "Italian" roof** in U.S. built on Talbot County Court House, Md. Style later became popular in Georgian architecture of Revolutionary era.

c1680 Appearance of **banister-back side chair:** simple chair deriving its name from series of banisters, generally vase-shaped, which are set between upper and lower rails of back.

1681 Early account of Keystone State is provided in **William Penn's** *Some Account of the Province of Pensilvania.* Like numerous other accounts this was meant as "promotion" literature, designed to induce emigration from England by indicating ways by which living could be earned in New World.

1681 One of biggest **best sellers** in America (relative to population), **John Bunyan's** *The Pilgrim's Progress,* published only three years after its 1st English publication. Library of Congress records more than 120 American editions, a far from complete list. Some editions sold for only 10 or 20¢.

1681 **Old Ship Meeting House** erected at Hingham, Mass., by Puritans who never referred to house of worship as "church." This meeting house has been in continuous service since its completion and is last remaining example, architecturally, of foursquare meeting house, a native American contribution to art and design of church construction. The meeting house was intentionally denied cross or spire, and in their place functional tower held bell and supported practical weathervane.

1682 **Printing** in Virginia suppressed by Governor Berkeley, who had indicated his intentions a few years earlier by remarking: "But, I thank God, there are no free schools nor printing, and I hope we shall not have these three hundred years."

1682 Famous account of life among American Indians, **Mary Rowlandson's** *The Sovereignty & Goodness of God, To-*

SCIENCE; INDUSTRY; ECONOMICS; EDUCATION; RELIGION; PHILOSOPHY.

SPORTS; FASHIONS; POPULAR ENTERTAINMENT; FOLKLORE; SOCIETY.

1681 Mar. 4 **Pennsylvania** granted to William Penn in payment of debt of £16,000 due him from crown. Penn's *Frame of Government,* issued in April, 1682, expressed his conception of religious liberty in new colony.

1682 Aug. 13 **1st Welsh settlers** in America established community near Philadelphia.

1684 **1st excise tax** on liquor in America levied in Pennsylvania for governor's expenses. Governor, then William Penn, refunded revenues. Later regretting his action, Penn unable to secure consent of his legislature for reimposition of tax.

1684 Oct. 3 **Massachusetts charter revoked** by Charles II on ground that foundation of charter, religious freedom, had been violated by colony's refusal to tolerate Church of England. Charles II had dispatched royal commission to colony in 1664 with instructions to obtain relaxation of religious restrictions which effectively barred Church of England from religious life of Massachusetts. Commission's failure to secure any degree of toleration for Anglican Church and subsequent failures of King to persuade Congregationalist leaders to satisfy his ecclesiastical wishes led Charles to begin court proceedings to revoke colony's charter.

1685 **1st printing press** outside New England assembled by William Bradford in Philadelphia.

1685 Huguenot minister haled before New England court for **performing marriages** in Boston. Growing tendency to make marriage ecclesiastical function was strongly suppressed; marriage was regarded as civil contract and courts were determined to enforce this.

1686 May 15 The Reverend Robert Ratcliffe arrived in Boston with orders from Charles II to found **Anglican church** in Massachusetts. Ratcliffe's visit represented culmination of campaign by

silver buckle. Later coat appeared in flowered brocade with very large cuffs.

1681 Appearance of **1st dancing master** in Boston provoked outburst of authorities. He was cited as "a person of very insolent & ill fame that Raues & scoffes at Religion." He was driven out shortly. Dancing was constant source of complaint among ministers. Shortly after ousting of 1st French master, Increase Mather thundered forth his condemnation in tract, *An Arrow against Profane and Promiscuous Dancing, Drawn out of the Quiver of the Scriptures.*

1682 John Skene, **1st Freemason to settle in America,** arrived in Burlington, N.J. He belonged to the Lodge in Aberdeen, Scotland, and came to colonies through arrangements made by Earl of Perth, chief proprietor of New Jersey and an outstanding Freemason.

1682 **1st girl married** in Pennsylvania was Priscilla Allen, who had met her husband, Thomas Smith, only once before on Isle of Wight.

1685 Governor's Council of Pennsylvania ordered **caves** used for dwellings evacuated and filled in. Early settlers in Pennsylvania, New York, and Massachusetts lacked sawmills, even saws, and facilities for cutting and using stone. Many, poor and rich, lived in caves dug into sides of hills.

1685 Revocation of **Edict of Nantes** in France sent host of Huguenot families to New World. Predominantly cultured tradespeople, they settled in Massachusetts, New York, Rhode Island, Virginia, and South Carolina, and immediately took active part in colonial social and political life. Faneuil, De Lancey, Boudinot, Bowdoin, Bernon were prominent names before 1700.

1687 June 28 William Phipps, **1st knighted native American** dubbed by James II in ceremonies at Windsor Castle. He was honored by the King for having found a treasure ship off the coast of

1685 May 15 Chief Justice Nicolas More of Pennsylvania was brought to trial on 10 counts in **1st impeachment proceedings** in America. He was expelled from office on June 2 for having wielded "an unlimited and arbitrary power," but was later reappointed to high office by Penn.

1686 **Charter Oak** incident occurred. It began when Sir Edmund Andros assumed control of all New England colonies except Rhode Island and Connecticut. Preparing for eventuality of war against French, he proposed to set up Dominion of New England including New York, New Jersey, and Pennsylvania. His first step was to incorporate Rhode Island and Connecticut into the New England Confederation, and accordingly, he demanded their charters. But the Connecticut charter was never delivered. At meeting between governor and Connecticut officials, candles were suddenly blown out and the charter stolen from room. It was hidden in an oak tree by Capt. Joseph Wadsworth.

1689 **"Glorious Revolution"** in New England succeeded in ousting unpopular Gov. Andros. On Apr. 18, an armed uprising in Boston forced Andros to surrender. Manifesto, written principally by Cotton Mather, listed grievances of colonists and justified rebellion. Andros was returned to England to stand trial for misconduct.

1689 Aug. 1 **Protestant revolution in Maryland** ended by peace treaty. Rebellion had begun when rumors convinced many that colony was about to be taken over by Catholics. A Protestant Association was quickly formed by John Coode, who led them to St. Mary's to demand capitulation and resignation of Lord Baltimore's representative. On Aug. 22, the Association asked crown to assume control of colony. This was done in 1691.

gether With the Faithfulness of His Promises Displayed; Being a Narrative of the Captivity and Restoration of Mrs. Mary Rowlandson. It reflected hostile attitude of colonists to Indian. Book went through more than 30 editions.

1682 Most complete and authentic of extant 17th-century Virginia churches, **Newport Parish Church,** built at Smithfield, Isle of Wight County. Also called "Old Brick Church." In all details, remarkable example of Tudor Gothic (late Medieval) architecture transferred to America.

1683 **Parson Capen** house, typical 2-room Colonial structure, built at Topsfield, Mass. Very careful restoration in 1913 makes it best image extant of 17th-century New England style.

c1685 Appearance of **Pennsylvania Walnut Stretcher Table.** Ranging in size from 30 in. in length to 8 ft., table has sturdy legs framed by skirt on top containing drawers. At bottom legs are braced by stretcher all around.

1687 *The Excellent Privilege of Liberty and Property,* &c., by **William Penn,** published in Philadelphia; it contained text of Magna Charta and other English statutes on freedom and property.

1688 **Francis Bacon's** famous *Essays* rank among most widely read books in colonial times, popular in England for nearly a century before 1st publication in New World. These *Essays* stand with John Bunyan's *The Pilgrim's Progress* as 2 widely read Colonial books which are today considered classics.

1690–1699

Estimated colonial **population**—213,500.

1690 Committee of General Court of Massachusetts recommended that Court

1690 **Important theological treatise** published. It was Francis Daniel Pastorius' *Vier Kleine Doch Ungemeine und Sehr*

Charles II to establish Church of England on hostile soil of Congregationalism. Charles II had initiated his campaign as far back as 1664 and had been confronted with unusual situation of demanding toleration in a British colony for Church of England.

1687 Mar. 22 Governor Edmund Andros, royal governor of Massachusetts, an adherent of Anglican Church, inspected 3 Puritan meeting houses in Boston to determine best site for an Anglican service. South Meeting House was selected and 1st Anglican service in Boston was held there on Good Friday. A subsequent Anglican service was held on Easter Sunday from 11 A.M. to 2 P.M. to great inconvenience of Congregationalist parish who waited outside for termination of Anglican service. More satisfactory terms were later arranged for joint use of South Meeting House by Anglican and Congregationalist parishes until Anglicans were able to move into their projected church, King's Chapel, which was built the next year.

1689 Assault on economic oligarchy in New York led by Jacob Leisler, disgruntled German merchant, who seized power and held it until 1691 when he was captured and executed by colonial authorities.

1689 1st public school in America with such practical subjects as science and inventions, William Penn Charter School, founded in Philadelphia with tuition charged only to those students who could afford it.

Hispaniola. Later he returned to Massachusetts and became Governor of the colony.

1688 According to Cotton Mather supernatural happenings this year made it a veritable portentous annus mirabilis: In the summer a cabbage root was seen in Boston, out of which sprang three wonderful branches, "one of them exactly resembling a Cutlace, another of them, as exactly resembling a Rapier, and a third, extreamly like to a Club used by the Indians in their Barbarous Executions." In the winter "Red Snow" covered the ground. But extraordinary signs were not reserved only for this year. For example, on Oct. 1, 1689, a flaming sword blazed in the sky and threw thousands who observed it into deathly fear.

1689 June 30 Typical appeal for garrison aid sent to governor and council of Massachusetts Bay by frontier settlement of Wells asking for "twenty eight good brisk men that may be serviceable as a guard to us whilest we get in our harvest of hay & corn." Many of these early frontier settlements were not covered by regular string of garrison forts set up for their protection, and found it hard to do their work while fighting off drunken Indians and white renegades.

1689 Summer Legend of the naming of Nix Mate's Island in Massachusetts Bay originated this year. Captain Nix anchored his boat off the nameless island one night. Screams were heard by inhabitants of Boston, investigators found captain murdered. Mate was accused, tried, and sentenced to hang. As a final statement he said that island would wash away as proof of his innocence. By beginning of 19th century a good portion of Nix Mate's Island had disappeared.

1690–1699

1690 1st paper mill in America set up by German settlers of Pennsylvania. Paper was handmade from linen rags pounded

1690 John Locke's Thoughts on Education, published in England, had tremendous influence on rearing of children in

35

| POLITICS AND GOVERNMENT; WAR; DISASTERS; VITAL STATISTICS. | BOOKS; PAINTING; DRAMA; ARCHITECTURE; SCULPTURE. |

decide exactly where **frontier** was and maintain garrison with 40 soldiers at each frontier town. 200 years later there was no frontier line in U.S., and westward expansion, "the most important single process in American history," was over. By this time word "frontier" had special American meaning, rather edge of a settlement than a political boundary.

1690 Feb. 3 **1st paper money** issued. It was used by Massachusetts to pay soldiers who had served in war with Quebec.

1690 Feb. 8 Schenectady, N.Y., attacked and burned by **French and Indians** from Montreal.

1691 "Liberty of conscience to all Christians, except Papists," provided in **charter** which united colonies of Plymouth and Massachusetts Bay.

1691 **Jacob Leisler,** who had taken governorship of New York in 1698, hanged for high treason. Eventually he was cleared of charge.

1691 Albemarle renamed **North Carolina** and put under governorship of Deputy answerable to Crown.

1692 Connecticut sent troop of soldiers to protect Massachusetts **frontier towns** along Connecticut R., taking long step toward breaking down provincial antagonism. Frontier settlements were also learning to unite against their common enemies and hardships.

1692 **1st act of establishment** passed in Maryland Assembly provided for official recognition of Church of England in this royal colony. Act was rejected by Board of Trade and Plantations in London. It represented will of Protestant majority in Assembly, but aroused strong opposition of Roman Catholic and Quaker groups in Maryland sympathetic to Toleration Act of 1649.

1692 Apr. Patent issued to Englishman Thomas Neale to found **post office** in English colonies; 1st took effect in Virginia. Andrew Hamilton, Neale's colonial dep-

Nützliche Tractätlein, printed in Germantown, Pa.

1690 Famous **"Wayside Inn"** of Longfellow's *Tales* built in Sudbury, Mass. It was called Red Horse Tavern, and was characterized by raftered ceiling and bar in form of cage. Burned in 1955, it will be restored.

c1690 Innovation in all-purpose chest was addition of short legs, thus creating **"highboy,"** a piece of furniture that became very popular.

1690 **1st appearance** of *New England Primer,* standard colonial elementary textbook. It combined teaching of alphabet and Puritan theology in moral couplets, as "In Adam's fall—We sinned all."

1690 Sept. 25 **1st newspaper in colonies** appeared in Boston. It was Benjamin Harris' *Publick Occurrences.* It expired 4 days later because Harris had presumed to publish without official permission.

1693 Earliest known example of **"jerkin-head"** roof in U.S., Thomas Sessions house, built at Yorktown, Va. Also called "clipped gable" or "a roof hipped above the wind-beams." It was gable with top corner flattened to form additional, triangular, downswept surface.

1694 **Quaker Meeting House** in Flushing, N.Y., built on simple rectangular form with hipped roof. Oldest religious building on Long Island, has been in continuous use ever since it was built.

1695 Cornerstone laid for first building at **William and Mary College,** based on plans said to have been drawn in London by Christopher Wren. Completed 1702. Excellent example of early Georgian style in its purest, Virginian form.

1696 Richard Lyon's *Advice to a Young Gentleman Leaving the University* probably **1st book** printed in New York. Previous to this only laws of state had been set in type in New York.

SCIENCE; INDUSTRY; ECONOMICS; EDUCATION; RELIGION; PHILOSOPHY.

SPORTS; FASHIONS; POPULAR ENTERTAINMENT; FOLKLORE; SOCIETY.

into pulp. **1st American watermark** was word "company" formed in paper made by William Rittenhouse.

1690 American **whaling industry** 1st began large-scale operations out of Nantucket.

1692 Reversing long-established policy, Massachusetts Assembly gave clergymen authorization to **perform marriages.** Connecticut followed in 1694.

1692 Increase Mather, 6th president of Harvard College, received Doctor of Divinity degree from Harvard under new charter just granted by William and Mary; it was the **1st divinity degree** conferred in the American colonies.

1692 Mar. **Salem witch hunt** unleashed when some children, called upon to explain their odd behavior, claimed that three old women had bewitched them. Women were tried, convicted, and condemned on testimony of children. Although Governor Phipps halted trials in Oct., 1692, by Jan., 1693, 20 condemned witches had been executed and two had died in prison.

1692 Oct. Reaction against Salem witch trials reflected in **Cotton Mather's** *Wonders of the Invisible World,* a mystic defense of witchcraft.

1693 **Last execution for witchcraft** in Massachusetts. No trials for witchcraft took place in the 18th century. Between 1692 and 1693 mania at Salem had caused 19 to be hanged and 1 pressed to death.

1693 Feb. 8 Charter signed to found **William and Mary College.** Grant given to James Blair to "furnish Virginia with a seminary of ministers, to educate the youth in piety, letters and good manners and to propagate Christianity among the Indians."

1694 **1st brick meeting house** in Boston constructed, replacing old wooden house on Brattle St.

1695 **Epidemic** in South destroys 100,-000 head of cattle. These quickly replaced by rapidly growing flock. By 1703 colonial

colonies. His suggestion that children have their feet toughened by constant immersion in cold water and by having them wear thin-soled shoes was followed religiously. Many children spent half their time with damp feet. Locke's suggestions on sleep and the use of milk had more lasting results.

1690 Legendary hero of "Old Yarmouth," Mass., **Captain Paddock,** came to Nantucket to instruct people "in the art of killing whales." His greatest adventure was against monster Crook-Jaw, into whose mouth he wandered to pay visit to Devil and sorceress.

1691 Dutch custom of **aanspreecker,** funeral inviter, given official status by making inviter a public officer in New York. Death was marked by tolling of bells and solemn march of *aanspreecker* from house of deceased to relatives and friends, whom he informed of death and whom he invited to funeral. Etiquette forbade attendance at a funeral unless invited.

1691 **Ducking stool,** form of punishment for scolds, ordered built on wharf in front of City Hall, New York. Although this form of punishment not used frequently in New York, it was common in South.

1693 **Huguenots** of South Carolina, considered foreigners, were threatened with loss of their estates upon death. Discrimination against French was marked throughout century in South Carolina, probably through envy of their refinement, education, and superior economic abilities.

1693 Earliest description of **buffalo or bison hunting** in America appeared in French traveler Fr. Louis Hennepin's account of Louisiana. Coming upon large group of buffalo, Indians would surround them with a circle of grass fire, leaving a few openings where they waited to ambush escaping animals.

1693 **Manorial privileges** in Hudson Valley continued with award of Philipsborough to Frederick Philipse.

uty, later did much to organize widespread postal service.

1696 Board of Trade for the Plantations named by William III. Its 15 members were given jurisdiction over: (1) trade and fisheries, (2) care of poor, (3) all plantation affairs, (4) appointment of colonial officials, and (5) colonial legislation which it had power to review. Board's decisions were referred to Privy Council.

1697 Epidemic of **smallpox** ravaged Charlestown, S.C. After running its course for over a year it diminished, only to be followed in Aug., 1699, by yellow fever, killing off 150 in 6 days. Infections were generally brought from West Indies.

1697 Fire wardens for each ward, probably **1st paid firemen in U.S.,** appointed by New York city. Chiefly they were provided to enforce fire laws. Homeowners were liable to fines of 3 guilders for dangerous chimneys, 25 guilders for fires caused by negligence.

1697 Sept. 30 Treaty of Ryswick ended **King William's War.** From standpoint of American colonies war was completely pointless. Both French and English forces won a number of engagements and managed to occupy a certain amount of each other's territory. However, treaty restored all possessions to *status quo* before hostilities.

1697 New York printed its **1st almanac,** a field of enterprise which had been monopolized by New England. Rhode Island published its 1st in 1728; Virginia in 1731. In 1733, most famous of all, *Poor Richard's Almanack,* was published.

1698 Old Swedes Church erected in Wilmington, Del., by Swedish Lutherans, said to be oldest Protestant church in continuous use in America. It is now Protestant Episcopal.

1698 1st book containing sheet music published in America, *Psalms, Hymns, and Spiritual Songs,* it being 9th edition of *The Bay Psalm Book.* It had 12 tunes.

1699 Best seller, *God's Protecting Providence* by Quaker **Jonathan Dickinson,** told story of group of castaways in Florida, who, naked and starving, made their way to St. Augustine, being continually captured by, but escaping from, ferocious Indians. This was one of best adventure stories of colonial days. It went through many editions in both this country and Europe, where it was translated into Dutch and German.

1st known sliding-sash windows in the Virginia colony ordered from England for Capitol in Williamsburg. All windows previously had been leaded casements, usually very small, of medieval type.

1700–1704

c1700 **Population** of colonies was sparsely scattered over large area: Below Delaware R. isolated farm was usual settlement, save for Charleston, which had about 250 families. Philadelphia had approximately 700 houses; New York about 5000 inhabitants, Newport less than 2000, and Boston, the largest city, had about 7000. There were approximately 275,000 inhabitants in colonies.

1701 Vestry Act, providing for establishment of Church of England in North

c1700 1st appearance of American **slatback chair** simultaneously in New England, Pennsylvania, and New York. In 19th century Shakers produced quantities of this type, which were very popular for general home use. Early type used rope seat. Not to be confused with **splat-back chair,** which shows influence of Dutch craftsmanship and design and was also product of this period.

1700 Perhaps 1st American strongly to denounce enslavement of Negro in

government ordered hunters to kill cattle that were unmarked and found straying. In Virginia they were hunted like game.

1696 **Slave trading** in New England begun on large scale with termination of monopoly of Royal African Trade Company.

1696 Yearly meeting of American Quakers admonished all members against importing Negroes for **slavery,** with expulsion from membership as penalty for violators.

1697 Official repentance for **Salem witch trials** highlighted by day of praying for forgiveness by Massachusetts Court. Samuel Sewall, one of Salem judges, publicly confessed his feeling of guilt from his pew in South Church.

1697 Oct. Severe enactment against **blasphemers** and **atheists** passed in Massachusetts. Any denying divine nature of Bible could be imprisoned 6 months, confined to pillory, whipped, have his tongue bored through with a hot iron, or be forced to sit on gallows with rope around his neck.

1698 May 29 **Trinity Church** of Wilmington, Del., begun at ultimate cost to its parishioners of £800, a considerable sum for that time. Completed church of granite measured 60 ft. in length, 30 ft. in width, and 20 ft. in height.

1695 New York established overseers to administer **relief to poor.** They estimated amount to be handed out as well as poor tax. Paupers clothed by city had to sew badge on their garments "with this Mark N.Y. in blew or Red Cloath."

1695 **Street cleaning** introduced in New York. A Mr. Vanderspiegle took job for £30 a year. By 1710 city was employing public cartmen who removed trash placed before houses.

1695 **Early colonial prices** illustrated by ninepence paid for a quarter of venison. Indians would exchange stag for jackknife. In Georgia, less heavily populated, a deer cost only sixpence as late as 1735.

1699 Spring **Captain Kidd,** the notorious pirate, paid a visit to an old friend in Narrangansett and left some treasure. Thus began myth of Captain Kidd's buried treasure, which has sent thousands digging up beaches for trinkets and pieces of eight. Legend says that Kidd murdered a helper and buried him with treasure chest as means of warding off searchers.

1699 June Judge Samuel Sewall of Boston suppresses a **card game** only to find a few days later pack of cards strewn over his lawn as if to mock his efforts. Gambling was rampant in all colonies despite numerous laws against it. Even lotteries came under ban in New England by order promulgated in 1719.

1700–1704

1700 June 17 Massachusetts enactment allowed 3 months for any **Roman Catholic priest** in colony to leave. If he remained, he was to be considered an ". . . incendiary and disturber of the public peace and safety and an enemy to the true Christian religion." If found guilty, he could be imprisoned for life or executed.

1701 June **Society for the Propagation of the Gospel in Foreign Parts** chartered by William III to assist Anglican churches

1701 Boston Town Meeting authorized **street naming.** Only Newport and Philadelphia had by now officially assigned street names. At end of 7 years 109 names were submitted for ratification.

1701 **Status of American colonial women** indicated by fact that 6 sat on jury in Albany, engaged for special duty.

1702 To combat **delinquency** in Massachusetts Cotton Mather formed "Society for the Suppression of Disorders," a sort of vigilante committee to keep a wary eye

Carolina, passed by Anglican majority in Assembly over violent opposition of dissenting groups, especially Quakers and Presbyterians. Because of this spirited opposition and dangerous social possibilities it represented, proprietors of colony disallowed act. This action reflected religious diversity in North Carolina even from beginning.

1701 Passing of piracy from colonial trade signalized by capture of notorious buccaneer, Capt. **William Kidd,** wealthy New York landowner who had served as privateer for British crown against French. Kidd was tried and hanged in London on May 23, bequeathing many legends of buried treasure.

1701 July 24 New settlement in Michigan established at **Detroit** by Antoine de la Mothe Cadillac. Territory of Michigan was early known to trappers, priests, and traders from French Canada. The Jesuits, led by Isaac Jogues, founded a mission at Sault Ste. Marie in 1641. There, in 1668, Pere Marquette established the 1st permanent settlement in Michigan. When the crown lost interest in the outposts in the West, Cadillac went to France with a proposal that would save the fur trade from the English. He was granted the land by the narrows of the river connecting Lake Huron with Lake Erie where he set up a large colony which he called Fort Pontchartrain. The name Detroit comes from the French word for the narrows (*de troit*) where the fort was located.

1702 Act of establishment passed by Maryland Assembly became law after two previous acts in 1692 and 1696 were rejected by Board of Trade and Plantations in England. Act provided for official recognition of Church of England, and secured final passage largely owing to the influence of Dr. Thomas Bray, Bishop of London's Commissary, who arrived in Maryland in 1700 to push enactment and then returned to England to argue for final approval before the Board. Taxes for support of ministers were levied on all free males over 16, all male servants over 16, and

colonies was **Samuel Sewall,** whose *Selling of Joseph* provided antislavery arguments for more than century. Typical of his time, Sewall relied mainly on Biblical citations.

1700 1st pipe organs arrived in America. They were imported by Episcopal Church, Port Royal, Pa., and Gloria Dei (Swedish Lutheran) Church, Philadelphia, Pa.

1700 Popular book of the colonial period, *A Token for Children* by **James Janeway.** Subtitle: *Being an exact Account of the Conversion, Holy and Exemplary Lives, and Joyful Deaths of Several Young Children.*

1702 Compendium of early New England was magnum opus of **Cotton Mather,** *Magnalia Christi Americana; or the Ecclesiastical History of New England.* Mather wanted to bring back people to early spirit of Puritanism at a time when feeling against clergy ran high because of witch burnings.

1702 1st mention of **stove** in American house occurred in diary of Judge Samuel Sewall of Boston under date of Jan. 16. What kind of stove he meant is not known. Heat for warmth and cooking was still provided by fireplaces, and stoves did not become common for another 60 years.

1703 1st **professional acting,** in Charleston, S.C. But no important theater developed in colonies until at least a generation later because of official belief that theater bred immorality and disorder.

1704 Earliest known example of **"Dutch gambrel" roof** in U.S. built on Ackerman house in Hackensack, N.J. Became common throughout New York and northern New Jersey in 18th century.

1704 Apr. 24 1st successful newspaper in colonies, *Boston News-Letter,* appeared for first time as a weekly. John Campbell was publisher and paper lasted until Revolution. Other notable early newspapers were *American Weekly Mercury* of Philadelphia (1719), *New-England Courant* of

EDUCATION; RELIGION; PHILOSOPHY.
SCIENCE; INDUSTRY; ECONOMICS;

SPORTS; FASHIONS; POPULAR EN-
TERTAINMENT; FOLKLORE; SOCIETY.

in America. Between 1702 and 1783, the society maintained 54 missionaries in South Carolina, 33 in North Carolina, 84 in New England, 47 in Pennsylvania, 58 in New York, 44 in New Jersey, 13 in Georgia, 5 in Maryland, 2 in Virginia. Total number of missionaries maintained in America during that period was 309 (missionaries sometimes shifted territories); total number of central missions maintained by society was 202. Society spent £227,454 for its activities during this period. Although its extensive efforts gained many converts to Church of England, society was unable to make Anglicanism dominant religion in America. Separatist groups in America, Presbyterians, Congregationalists, Quakers, Baptists, and Roman Catholic minority held most of ground they had gained before Revolution. During Revolution, British ties of Anglicanism strengthened position of separatist groups. In addition, Anglicans in South, particularly in Virginia, resisted close ties to English bishops. Thus leadership of Revolutionary forces was shared by Southern Anglicans, like Washington and Lee, and Northern Congregationalists, like Samuel Adams. At same time many Anglicans supported Loyalist cause.

1701 Oct. 16 **Yale** founded as "Collegiate School" in Killingworth, Conn., by Congregationalists dissatisfied with growing liberalism at Harvard. Named after Elihu Yale, son of one of founders of New Haven, who had gained great riches in India as governor for East India Company. Moved to New Haven, Conn., in 1745 where it became Yale College. Became university in 1887. 1st degrees awarded in 1716.

1703 Mar. 28 **St. Anne's Protestant Episcopal Church** in Burlington, N.J.,

and ear open for swearing, blaspheming, and patronage of bawdy houses. By 1713 Mather had collected list of young men who frequented disreputable establishments and presented it to committee, who in turn warned each of young men.

1703 Fall The Rev. Solomon Stoddard urged the Massachusetts Bay **frontier town** of Northampton to use dogs "to hunt Indians as they do bears." Indians were too fast on their feet for frontiersmen and "act like wolves and are to be dealt with as wolves."

1704 New York **women's fashions** described by a contemporary traveler and diarist: "The English go very fasheonable in their dress. The Dutch, especially the middling sort, differ from our women, in their habitt go loose, were French muches wch are like a Capp and a head band in one, leaving their ears bare, which are sett out wth Jewells of a large size and many in number. And their fingers hoop't with Rings, some with large stones in them of many Coullers as were their pendants in their ears, which You should see very old women wear as well as Young."

1704 Francis Thrasher of Boston at his own expense laid **1st underground sewer** in Boston, and paved way for municipal regulations governing disposal of refuse and garbage. By 1710 Selectmen of Boston were giving licenses to private citizens for digging up streets for sewer construction.

1704 A number of pleasure sleighs traveled 3 or 4 miles out of New York city to place called **The Bowery** where there were many houses of entertainment, according to a famous traveler, Madame Sarah Kemble Knight.

| POLITICS AND GOVERNMENT; WAR; DISASTERS; VITAL STATISTICS. | BOOKS; PAINTING; DRAMA; ARCHITECTURE; SCULPTURE. |

all male and female slaves over 16. Appointment of ministers was prerogative of royal governor of colony. Most spirited opposition to act of establishment came from Quaker and Catholic settlers.

1704 Feb. 29 French soldiers and their Indian allies surprised **Deerfield,** a western outpost of Massachusetts, massacred 50 men, women, and children, and carried off over 100 more after burning town to ground.

Boston (1721), New York *Gazette* (1725), Maryland *Gazette* (1727), Pennsylvania *Gazette* (1730), Virginia *Gazette* (1736).

1704 Oct. Classic travel book, *Private Journal* of **Sarah Kemble Knight,** which began on this date and extended to March, 1705. A schoolmistress (young Franklin attended her school in Boston) she took trip alone to New York and reported incidents, characters, and mores of Yankee inhabitants. It was not published until 1825.

1705–1709

1705 2nd Vestry Act, providing for establishment of Church of England in North Carolina, passed by Anglican majority in Assembly after first such act had been disallowed by colonial proprietors in 1701. 2nd act, like first, caused violent controversy between Anglican interests and dissenting groups, mainly Quakers and Presbyterians. Violent civil disturbances stymied enforcement of act and matter was soon dropped.

1705 Virginia **slavery act** decreed that all imported servants were to remain in life-long servitude. Excepted were those who had been Christians in their native country or who had been free in a Christian country. This law limited slavery to Negroes and confined almost all imported Negroes to slavery. An interesting exception was inserted for "Turks and Moors in amity with her majesty."

1706 Important American customhouse built at Yorktown, Va. Yorktown had been appointed port of entry for New York, Philadelphia, and other northern cities, though many merchants disregarded law. Was site of Virginia's "tea party" in 1774, when Richard Ambler, collector of revenue, led boarding party to the *Virginia* and tossed tea cargo overboard; customhouse was restored in 1928.

1706 Jan. 17 Birth of **Benjamin Franklin** in Boston. A nonconformist, his father, Josiah, fled England in 1682 and settled down in New England, rearing 17 children.

1705 Early history of Virginia published, the *History of Virginia* by **Robert Beverley,** which was popular in England and France. A man of wealth, sprung from ancient English family, Beverley, often motivated by what he felt was English misconception of colony, painted robust picture of plantation life.

1706 Work begun on **Governor's Palace** at Williamsburg, Va., finest residence of time in colonies. Not formally completed until 1720. Occupied by royal governors until Revolution, thereafter by state governors, Patrick Henry and Thomas Jefferson, until capital was moved to Richmond in 1780.

1706 Phenomenally popular Latin grammar, **Ezekiel Cheever's** *Accidence, A Short Introduction to the Latin Tongue,* book that was to be printed in 20 editions, 20th appearing in 1785. **1st Latin grammar** published in America.

1706 Weakening of Puritan influence in America reflected in **Cotton Mather's** *The Good Old Way,* in which he complained that people had lost their reverence for clergy and did not support them as generously as before.

1707 A colonial best seller was *The Redeemed Captive* by **John Williams,** an account of author's Indian captivity. Being carried off by heathen Indians was substance of much of popular colonial literature.

SCIENCE; INDUSTRY; ECONOMICS; EDUCATION; RELIGION; PHILOSOPHY.	SPORTS; FASHIONS; POPULAR EN- TERTAINMENT; FOLKLORE; SOCIETY.

begun. 1st service held on Aug. 22, 1703, before church had been completed. Church still stands in good condition as one of most distinguished historical edifices in New Jersey.

1704 Sept. 28 Statute passed in Maryland gave ministers right to force a **separation** between a man and woman if minister disapproved of her. If the man did not obey, he was haled into court and, if convicted, could be fined, or whipped until blood began to flow.

1705–1709

1706 **1st Anglican parish** in Connecticut established in Stratford largely through efforts of Colonel Caleb Heathcote, wealthy landowner in Westchester county and active churchman.

1706 Boston surgeon, Zabdiel Boylston, sprang into prominence by performing perhaps **1st lithotomy** in New England. Following this, he performed many successful operations; in 1718 he removed cancerous breast from woman.

1706 Mar. **1st Presbytery** in America organized at Philadelphia largely through efforts of Rev. Francis Makemie, Irish Presbyterian minister, who settled in Maryland in 1683. Makemie is considered father of Presbyterianism in America.

1707 1st meeting of **Baptist Association** in America convened at Philadelphia with 5 churches represented.

1707 **Francis Makemie** tried and acquitted by New York court. This signals the end of prosecution of Protestant dissenters in New York.

1708 **Saybrook Platform,** adopted by Connecticut Congregational churches, brought them closer to Presbyterian system of church organization and further away from democratic notions of Massachusetts Congregationalism.

1709 **1st mining company charter** in America granted by Connecticut General Assembly to a copper mine at Simsbury, Conn. Mine produced 15–20% ore which was exported to England. During Revolu-

1705 **Intermarriage** between white person and Negro declared illegal in Massachusetts; minister performing such a marriage was fined £50. This prohibition remained in force until 1843, when law was repealed.

1705 Robert Beverley's *History of Virginia* gave details of various methods of **hunting in the South:** horses were taught to walk quietly at their master's side when stalking game to keep him out of sight; rabbits were hunted with fast mongrel dogs, which caught them or forced them into a hollow tree; raccoons and opossums, hunted on foot with small dogs by light of moon, were treed, and agile lads climbed trees after them and shook them down; wolves were trapped; turkeys shot or trapped.

1705 Thomas Odell of Boston arrested for counterfeiting newly issued £4 note of Massachusetts. He was sentenced to pay fine of £300 and spend a year in prison. **Counterfeiting** was relatively new to colonies, since paper money had only just been printed around turn of century. Punishments were generally severer than that administered to Odell.

1706 **Closed season** on deer established on Long Island where continual hunting had almost eliminated this popular game.

43

POLITICS AND GOVERNMENT; WAR; DISASTERS; VITAL STATISTICS.

BOOKS; PAINTING; DRAMA; ARCHITECTURE; SCULPTURE.

1708 Aug. 30 **Haverhill,** Mass., attacked and razed by French and Indians.

1709 Sept. 3 1st major influx of **Swiss and German immigrants** to the Carolinas, encouraged by grant of 13,500 acres by the proprietors to two sponsors representing German refugees from Palatinate and Swiss emigrants from Berne.

1708 Popular, extravagant satire by writer who called himself **"Ebenezer Cook,** Gentleman" was *The Sot-Weed Factor; or, A Voyage to Maryland,—a satire in which is described the laws, government, courts, and constitution of the country, and also the buildings, feasts, frolics, entertainments, and drunken humors of the inhabitants in that part of America.*

1710–1714

Estimated colonial **population**—357,500.

1710 **Great German migration** to America begun. New Berne on the Neuse R., at the mouth of the Trent R., in North Carolina settled by company, under the leadership of Baron Christopher de Graffenried, of German and Bernese Swiss in search of religious freedom. Gov. Robert Hunter, commissioned in England in 1709 governor of New York and the Jerseys, arrived in the colonies this year with 3,000 Palatines who had taken refuge in England and who were being sent to produce naval stores in the Hudson Valley. Commercially unsuccessful they migrated under Conrad Weiser in 1713 to Schoharie Valley, N.Y., then to the Mohawk Valley, N.Y., and eventually, in some instances, to Bucks County in 1723 and Berks County in 1728–29, both in Pennsylvania.

1711 Sept. 22 **Tuscarora Indian War** begun with massacre of settlers on Chowan and Roanoke R., N.C. New Bern was abandoned. White encroachment, which included the enslaving of Indian children, led to war.

1712 Jan. 28 Carolina militia, aided by friendly Indians, killed 300 **Tuscarora Indians** on the Neuse R.

1712 May 9 **Territory of Carolinas** provided with 2 governors, one for the North and one for the South. Though theoretically a single province, the settlements were far apart, and so each section had its governor. From 1691 to 1712 a single governor usually resided in Charleston.

1713 Mar. 23 End of **Tuscarora War** with capture of Indian stronghold, Fort

1710 *The Husband-Man's Guide, in Four Parts—Part first, containing many excellent rules for setting and planting. Part second, choice physical receipts for divers dangerous distempers in men, women, and children. Part third, the experienced farrier. Part fourth, containing rare receipts,* by **Eleazar Phillips** published in Boston, Mass. It became one of most popular books for farmers in American colonies.

1710–1717 **John Wise,** pastor of Ipswich, led liberal Congregationalists against centralizing forces of Massachusetts with two famous pamphlets: *The Churches Quarrel Espoused* (1710) and *Vindication of the Government of New England Churches* (1717).

1711 **Bookselling** now flourishing trade; in Boston alone about 30 shops were doing profitable business. Early booksellers, as well as printers, did not limit themselves to books. Items like tobacco, patent medicines, playing cards, etc., could be purchased in their shops.

1711 **1st cruciform church** in U.S. begun in Bruton Parish, Williamsburg; architect unknown. Though cruciform plan was usually a feature of Gothic architecture, church was in all other details characteristic of early Georgian.

1713 **King's Chapel,** Anglican church in Boston, acquired organ in bequest from Thomas Brattle. Few organs to be found in colonial churches, since Puritan practice prohibited instrumental music in religious services and most congregations of

SCIENCE; INDUSTRY; ECONOMICS; EDUCATION; RELIGION; PHILOSOPHY.	SPORTS; FASHIONS; POPULAR EN-TERTAINMENT; FOLKLORE; SOCIETY.

tionary War, diggings were used as a prison for Tories.

1709 Quakers of Philadelphia, Pa., formed **1st private home for mental illness** in U.S. In 1751 it became a part of Pennsylvania Hospital.

1708 **Closed season,** April 1–July 31, established on turkeys, heath hens, partridges, and quail in Kings, Queens, and Suffolk counties in New York.

1710–1714

1710 Spreading **ferry service** in Massachusetts controlled by legislative act regulating rates throughout colony at 1 shilling for each single passenger and 2 shillings for more than one, with each passenger paying equal fractional share of the 2 shillings.

1710 **Trinity School** established in New York city under auspices of Society for the Propagation of the Gospel. Founding of Trinity School represented victory of private and parochial school adherents over supporters of free public schools.

1711 Widely read defense of **deism,** *Characteristics,* by Lord Shaftesbury, postulated an innate moral sense in human beings that does not require religious incentives to reveal itself. Many of Shaftesbury's admirers in colonies seized upon this idea as the basis of deistic thought. *Characteristics of Men, Manners, Opinions, Times,* published in 3 volumes, was as enthusiastically received in France and Germany. The ethical ideas of Shaftesbury, which exalted the social sense at the expense of the ego, refuted the assumptions of Hobbes and Locke. They influenced much of the literature of the century: Alexander Pope, Hume, Adam Smith, Leibnitz, Voltaire, Diderot, Lessing and Herder are all indebted to the speculations of Shaftesbury.

1712 Christopher Hussey, Nantucket whaleman, took **1st sperm whale** captured by American. Event radically changed character of Nantucket whaling business. Whalers previously had plied close to

c1710 In contrast to sober dress of Quakers, **colonial fashions** were often extravagant. High heels, stiff stays, and large curled wigs worn by both men and women. Men's coat skirts stiffened with buckram, and sleeve cuffs often reached elbows. Invention of hoop in England in 1711 governed styles in America for many years. Originally these hoops were flat, projecting only at sides. Over them were worn layers of skirts, and sacque, or overdress, was hung on top. Women's hairdress was characterized by "tower" or "commode." From top of this tower "lappets," or lace pendants, hung down alongside face.

1712 **1st fines for speeding** levied against reckless carters in Philadelphia.

1713 Children's winter **sleighing and coasting** suppressed by New York edict which ordered constable "to take any slee or slees from all and every such boys and girls rydeing or offering to ryde down any hill within ye sd city and breake any slee or slees in pieces."

1714 **Tea** introduced to colonies. Favorite nonalcoholic drink of colonists, however, was chocolate. Coffee was also drunk infrequently. But favorite beverage was still rum in New England and beer in middle colonies. Of wines Madeira took 1st place, followed by canary, claret, Burgundy, port, brandy, and champagne. Use of tea, cocoa and coffee was a direct result of the new era of European expansion. Cocoa, with sugar and vanilla added, was introduced as a European beverage by Cortes in 1520, after cacao beans were dis-

Nohucke, S.C. Indians fled northward and were admitted into League of the Iroquois as a 6th nation.

1713 Mar. 31 **Treaty of Utrecht** ended Queen Anne's War, which had begun on May 4, 1702, when the Grand Alliance (England, League of Augsburg, Denmark, Portugal, and the Netherlands) declared war on France in order to prevent union of French and Spanish on the death of Charles II of Spain. Worst colonial disaster of war was the Deerfield massacre by French and Indians. By Treaty France ceded Hudson Bay territory, Newfoundland, and Nova Scotia to Great Britain. She agreed to British protectorate over Iroquois Indians. France kept Cape Breton Island and the islands of the St. Lawrence.

other denominations could not afford to import instruments from England.

1714 **1st play** to be printed in colonies was *Androboros*, published by governor of New York, Robert Hunter. Play was political satire. Hunter was military and political head of New York and New Jersey. In his play he lampooned the senate and the lieutenant-governor. It is doubtful that the farce was ever on the boards, though it is reputed to have made people laugh. The Huntington Library in California preserves a copy of *Androborus*, the 1st play known to have been composed in America.

1715–1719

1715 **3rd Vestry Act** passed by Anglican majority in North Carolina Assembly providing for official recognition and support of Church of England accepted by colonial proprietors, who had disallowed previous acts in 1701 and 1705. Passage of act due largely to efforts of Society for the Propagation of the Gospel, a missionary organization supported by Church of England. Ministers were to be supported by head tax not to exceed 5 shillings per person, to be assessed on both freemen and slaves over 16 years of age.

1718 **New Orleans** founded by French settlers from Canada and France. Canadians generally brought wives and family with them. French officers, however, usually younger sons of nobility, refused to marry lower than their rank, occasioning plea of one of early governors to France: "Send me wives for my Canadians; they are running in the woods after Indian girls."

1715 1st American instruction manual for singing, Rev. **John Tufts'** *Introduction to the Singing of Psalm-Tunes*. There is no known copy of this book in existence.

1716 **1st theater in colonies** built in Williamsburg, Va., by William Levingston.

1719 Juvenile best seller, *Divine and Moral Songs for the Use of Children* by **Isaac Watts**, over 240 editions being published in England and America. Was popular for at least 150 years.

1719 Founding of nationalistic newspaper, the *Boston Gazette*, by William Brooker. In 1741 it was combined with *New England Weekly Journal* and launched attacks on Stamp tax.

1719 Probable date of the 1st publication of gay and nonsensical **Mother Goose's Melodies for Children.** Printed by Thomas Fleet in Boston, an enterprise of some daring in those times of Puritan severity.

1719 Earliest residental building remaining in Manhattan, **Fraunces Tavern,** built at Pearl and Broad Streets, New York. Became tavern in 1762, famous for Long Room where Washington delivered his Farewell Address to his officers, 1783.

shore, seeking right whales; thereafter they hunted in deep waters on longer voyages. In 1715 Nantucket, Mass., had a fishery of 6 sloops engaged in sperm whaling.

1713 **1st American schooner-type** of sailing craft built by Capt. Andrew Robinson in Gloucester, Mass.

1714 **Iron furnaces** established along Rapidan R., Va., by Gov. Spotswood. He imported German settlers for labor.

1714 Famous Puritan theologian, Cotton Mather, accepted **Copernican** theory of universe as against Ptolemaic. His sermon of acceptance was unfavorably received by eminent Puritan moralist, Judge Samuel Sewall, who considered subject too controversial.

covered by the Spanish in Mexico. Coffee came to Europe by way of Turkey and was introduced in England in 1652 by a trader named Edward. 1st English reference to tea was in a letter, dated 1615, kept by the East India Company, and the forerunner of the teashop appeared in 1657. The colonists were not far behind the Europeans in adopting these fashionable light drinks.

1714 May 12 **1st record** of wild animal on exhibition in America made in Samuel Sewall's diary of this date when he reported sale of "a large Dromedary seven foot high, and 12 foot long, taken from the Turks at the Siege of Vienna." There is some doubt whether the dromedary, a one-humped Arabian camel, actually appeared in America.

1715–1719

1716 Probably **1st lighthouse** in colonies put up by Massachusetts on Little Brewster Island to guard Boston Harbor.

1716 June 6 **1st Negro slaves** in French Louisiana delivered by two slave ships of Company of the West.

1717 Important advance in American trade made with admission of colonial merchants into lucrative **rum trade** of French West Indies. The treaty of Utrecht (1713), which ended Queen Anne's War, ceded Newfoundland, Acadia, and Hudson Bay to Great Britain, and yielded additional trading concessions with the Spanish colonies. In America a marine and fishing boom began. After 1717 American ships were allowed in the French West Indies. French molasses was cheap and the rum distilleries of New England were more efficient than those of the West Indies. New England rum quickly became a cheap and celebrated staple of colonial trade.

1717 **1st professorship** in philosophy and mathematics in America assumed by the Rev. Hugh Jones at William and Mary.

1718 Proclamation offering substantial rewards for apprehending or killing pirates published by Alexander Spotswood, governor of Virginia. Aimed chiefly at **Captain Teach** or "Blackbeard," who had hideout in North Carolina, it brought results. Governor's men captured Blackbeard's ship and brought back his head on a pole.

1719 Beginning of **potato** cultivation in colonies with settlement of Londonderry, N.H., by Scotch-Irish immigrants.

1719 Perhaps **1st street light** in U.S., single lantern, presented to town of Boston by Eliakim Hutchinson. Selectmen ordered that it be "well fixed with Lights on all dark or Stormy Nights."

1719 Mar. New Jersey enacted its most important **statute regarding marriage.** It provided that no person under 21 years of age could be married without consent of parent or guardian. It was the result of many instances of young people being enticed into clandestine marriages. Under present law a woman may marry at 18 without consent.

1720–1724

1720 **City populations** were: Boston, 12,000; Philadelphia, 10,000; New York, 7000; Charleston, 3500; and Newport, 3800. All urban dwellers at this time comprised only 8% of total population. Estimated **colonial population—474,388.**

c1720 Period of **French expansion and entrenchment** in the Mississippi Valley. Fort erected in 1720 and 1726 at mouths of the Kaskaskia and Illinois Rs. Peace made with Indians in South; Fort Toulouse erected among Creeks on Alabama R. In North powerful Fort Louisbourg on Cape Breton Island, constructed 1720, guarded entrance to St. Lawrence R. Further south French established fortifications at Crown Point on Lake Champlain in 1731. Protecting northern approach to Mississippi Valley Fort Miami was constructed in 1704, Fort Ouiataon on the Wabash R. about 1719, and Fort Vincennes on lower Wabash R. about 1724.

1721 Mar. **1st German immigrants** to French Louisiana arrived, group of 200 settling near New Orleans.

1722 **League of 6 Nations,** an Iroquois confederation which included the Tuscarora tribe, concluded in Albany treaty with Gov. Spotswood of Virginia. Indians agreed not to cross Potomac R. or Blue Ridge Mountains. Iroquois League always remained friendly with the English and hostile to the French since the latter had often aided Indian tribes against which the warlike Iroquois had fought. Thus League of 6 Nations was an effective and very necessary guard for the English colonies' western borders during this period of French expansion in the Mississippi R.

1720 The Rev. **Thomas Symmes** of Bradford, Mass., published his essay, "The Reasonableness of Regular Singing, or Singing by Note." In it he says that "singing by note" was studied at Harvard from founding of college (1636), proving Puritans were not averse to secular music.

1721 Early painting that points to expressionism of 20th century is portrait of **Ann Pollard** by unknown artist. Subject, innkeeper of more than 100 years, claimed she was 1st to leave boat when immigrants landed in New England.

1721 **1st American book** with barred music notes, *The Grounds and Rules of Musick Explained, or, an Introduction to the Art of Singing by Note,* by the Rev. Thomas Walter, of Roxbury, Mass.

1721 **Flavius Josephus'** *Antiquities of the Jews* was favorite reading for Colonial settlers.

1721 **1st recorded public art commission** given to Gustavius Hesselius by the Vestry of St. Barnabas' Church, Prince George's county, Md., for a painted altar piece depicting "The Last Supper."

1722 Early account of western lands is given in **Daniel Coxe's** *Description of La Louisiana; as also of the Great and Famous River, Meschacebe or Mississippi, the Five Navigable Lakes of Fresh Water etc. . . .*

1722 **The Alamo,** famous Texan fort constructed at about this time as a Franciscan mission.

1723 **1st extended catalogue** of a library printed in colonies was *Catalogus Librorum Bibliothecae Collegii* put out by Harvard College.

1723 Perhaps 1st house in U.S. to have **running water** was John Headly's in New-

SCIENCE; INDUSTRY; ECONOMICS; EDUCATION; RELIGION; PHILOSOPHY.

SPORTS; FASHIONS; POPULAR ENTERTAINMENT; FOLKLORE; SOCIETY.

1720–1724

1721 Violent controversy engendered in America by Cotton Mather's suggested introduction of **smallpox inoculations** during epidemic of dread disease. Although conflict followed traditional lines of science against religion, Mather, theologian, found himself arrayed against such secular figures of science as Benjamin Franklin.

1721 Among earliest institutions of higher learning in Middle West was **Jesuit college** at Kaskaskia (in what is now Illinois) with especially distinguished library containing many volumes of 18th-century French philosophers.

1721 May 25 **1st marine and fire insurance company** in America opened on High Street, Philadelphia, Pa., by John Copson.

1721 June 26 **1st smallpox inoculations** in America given by Zabdiel Boylston in Boston, Mass. He inoculated his son, Thomas, and 2 negro slaves on the recommendation of Cotton Mather. Mather's slave, Onesimus, had previously told his master of similar inoculations administered by African tribesmen, and Mather urged Boylston to try the practice. Angry mobs stoned both the Mather and Boylston homes when they learned of the experiment.

1722 Jan. 24 Edward Wigglesworth named 1st Thomas Hollis Professor of Divinity at Harvard College. This was probably the **1st professorship of divinity** in the colonies.

1722 Oct. 23 Timothy Cutler, Daniel Brown, and Samuel Johnson sailed for England to be ordained as Anglican ministers. The 3 men, leading Congregational ministers in Connecticut, had been affiliated with Yale College. Their decision was most significant triumph of **Anglicanism** in New England up to that time.

1723 William and Mary College, Williamsburg, Va., built Brafferton hall to house **1st permanent school for Indians** in the colonies. School was maintained by

c1720 Striking interior feature of new Georgian homes of wealthy Americans was **servant's staircase,** said to have been introduced so that servants could carry full commodes from upper chambers without passing family or guests.

1720 **Governor's Palace** in Williamsburg, now completed, became center of fashion and social life in Virginia.

1720 Mar. William Smith of Charlestown, Mass., and Hannah Travis, better known as Dancing Hannah, convicted of **theft** by Philadelphia court and sentenced to death. Growth of crime was marked after 1700, an expected development with phenomenal increase in wealth and with instability resulting from frequent colonial wars. Death penalty for theft was almost universal.

1721 French government sent to Louisiana **25 prostitutes,** collected from a house of correction, to help relieve extreme shortage of women and to provide some means of getting Canadian settlers away from their Indian mistresses.

1721 May After succession of **blue laws** limiting traveling on Sunday, Connecticut passed law providing that no person could go from his or her house unless to attend worship or on some indispensable task.

1722 Apr. 30 The *New England Courant* reported that a public house in Charlestown, Mass., had set up tables for customers who wished "to Recreate themselves with a Game of **Billiards."**

1723 Philadelphians petitioned Colonial Assembly to do something "concerning the **Intermarriages** of Negroes and Whites." In Charleston, S.C., were references to young men and their "black Loves"; in

| POLITICS AND GOVERNMENT; WAR; DISASTERS; VITAL STATISTICS. | BOOKS; PAINTING; DRAMA; ARCHITECTURE; SCULPTURE. |

1722 June 4 250 **German immigrants** landed at Mobile.

1723 Discontented with manner in which his brother treated him, **Benjamin Franklin** left Boston and settled in Philadelphia, where he became famous.

1724 **Dummer's, or Lovewell's, War** (1722–25) culminated in the killing by English settlers of **Father Râle,** a French Jesuit missionary who was accused of fomenting trouble among the Abenaki Indians in northern Maine. As a result of Jesuit missionary activities the Abnakis remained friendly with the French, and for protection the English built series of border forts in northern New England. These forts contained French expansion of this period.

port, which was equipped in this year with pipe "underground from the Spring."

1723 Apr. Cornerstone of **Christ Church,** called "Old North Church," laid in Boston. Designed by William Price, who had studied Christopher Wren's London churches. It is earliest Georgian church in New England, and the oldest church in Boston. Built after the London fire of 1666, when the designs of Wren, who did much of the restoration of the city, were widely admired and imitated, the Old North Church was in the wave of Georgian style which swept across England and America. From the steeple of the church were hung the lanterns which signaled to Paul Revere whether the British were coming to Concord by land or by sea.

1725–1729

1725 Number of Negro **slaves** in North American colonies reached 75,000.

1725–1729 Albany merchants tried and sentenced for trading **blackmarket furs.** English colonists were forbidden by law to traffic in furs which had been trapped by Indians living in French territory. Similar ban restricted commerce between the French colonists and the Indians living in English territory. By 1725, a 2-way illegal trade was flourishing. Law began to be enforced and several English traders were prosecuted and punished.

1725 Feb. 20 In fight between Indians and party of whites led by Capt. Lovewell at Wakefield, N.H., 10 Indian scalps were taken; this was **1st known instance of scalping by white men.** Bounty of £100 per scalp was paid to victors in Boston.

1726 Poorer classes in Philadelphia riot in heart of town, tearing down pillory and stocks and setting them on fire. The governor declares it **riot** and puts it down accordingly. Similar outbursts crop-

1725 1st appearance of *cabriole,* curved design for table and chair legs, replacing stiff lines of previous models. At same time **Queen Anne style** furniture attained its vogue in America, 5 years after its greatest popularity passed in England and some 11 years after death of Queen Anne. This period also saw 1st appearance of **American Windsor chair** in Philadelphia. These chairs were generally painted green, brown, or red, rarely white.

1725 **1st newspaper** in New York, the *Gazette,* founded by William Bradford. Lasted until 1745.

1725 Extremely popular almanac which Franklin may have used as prototype in preparing his own was the *Astronomical Diary and Almanack* by **Nathaniel Ames,** a Massachusetts physician. Typical entries:

"Dec 7–10 'Ladies, take heed,
Lay down your fans,
And handle well
Your warming pans.'

SCIENCE; INDUSTRY; ECONOMICS; EDUCATION; RELIGION; PHILOSOPHY.	SPORTS; FASHIONS; POPULAR ENTERTAINMENT; FOLKLORE; SOCIETY.

funds left for the purpose by Robert Boyle, English scientist.

1723 Connecticut trading company became **1st recorded commercial corporation** in America. Up to this time, land companies, universities, and philanthropic enterprises were only forms of corporate enterprise. Colonial restrictions on distribution of currency and restrictions from England on local trade and industry served to inhibit formation of corporations in modern sense.

1723 German Baptists, often called Dunkards, gathered at home of one Becker in Germantown, Pa., to form **1st Dunkard Church** in America. 6 new converts were baptized in Wissahickon Creek the same day.

1724 **1st horticulturist** in America was Paul Dudley, who launched the science with his study of fruit trees in New England.

1735 sea captain and young Southerner fought a duel over "the Favours of a certain sable Beauty."

1723 **Police force** in Boston consisted of 12 men. Their beats were designated by Selectmen, who further instructed them "to walke Silently and Slowly, now and then to Stand Still and Listen in order to make discovery. And no smoking to be on their walking the rounds."

1723 Aug. 1–8 *American Weekly Mercury* reported exhibition in Philadelphia of "curious and exact Modell of the Czar of Muscovia's Country seat, near Moscow." This was probably **1st exhibition** ever advertised in colonial newspaper, and it was apparently very successful.

1725–1729

1725 **1st separate church** of Colored Baptists established in Williamsburg, Va.

1725 **U.S. Reformed Church** established by John Philip Boehm at Falkner Swamp, Pa.

1726 **1st college** established in Middle Colonies was Log College in Bucks County, Pa.

1727 Portrait of Cotton Mather engraved by **Peter Pelham.** Pelham, an English immigrant, introduced mezzotint portraiture to colonial engraving. His rare plates are now collectors' items.

1727 **Jonathan Edwards,** leading religious figure of 18th century in America, succeeded his grandfather in pulpit of Northampton church, most prominent church in New England outside Boston.

1727 Early benevolent association in America, **the Junto,** established by Benjamin Franklin, pledged its members to oppose slavery and other forms of inhumanity to men. In this, as in much else, Franklin manifested tendencies of "Age of Enlightenment."

1728 Boston began to enclose its **Common** in order to preserve grass from carts and horses. Soon it became custom after tea for gentlemen and ladies to stroll about green before going to their homes.

1728 *New England Weekly* estimated that **living expenses** of middle-class tradesman, having no more than 8 in family, were about £265. 18. 9. per year. Most families employed a maid-of-all-work at cost of £10 a year.

POLITICS AND GOVERNMENT; WAR; DISASTERS; VITAL STATISTICS.

BOOKS; PAINTING; DRAMA; ARCHITECTURE; SCULPTURE.

ped up in city: in 1729 crowds broke into mayor's gardens and destroyed his plants; in 1738 riot ensued when administration limited fishing on Schuylkill.

1729 Chaussegros de Léry sent by French to **fortify the Ohio R.** down to the Great Miami. Alarmed by incidents with English colonists who were crossing the Alleghenies and invading the territory under their control, the French took steps to prevent the westward expansion of their rivals. 8 years before, the enterprises of the English colonists had inspired the Lords of Trade to petition the King to "fortify the passes of the back of Virginia" and to cripple French activity on the Great Lakes in order to "interrupt the French communications from Quebec to the River Mississippi." Justification for this move was that the charters of the seaboard colonies had always claimed the west as an extension of their own holdings. The King, however, failed to take the offensive and positive measures were left to the initiative of the French.

1729 **Royal control** reestablished in South Carolina. Colonists of South Carolina, chafing under proprietary rule, rebelled and petitioned for a royal government. Their grievances were of long standing. They resented the failure of the proprietors to give them adequate protection against the Yamassee Indians, who had been goaded by the Spanish to wage war against them through the entire period 1715–1728. In 1719, when the proprietors vetoed the more liberal election laws of the assembly, the colonists revolted and appointed a governor who would be responsible only to the king. The proprietors were finally forced to relinquish their rights and Parliament instituted a royal government for the colony.

1729 June English Crown purchased **Carolinas** for £17,500 from proprietors. It was divided into 2 royal provinces, North and South Carolina, in 1730. Boundary was not finally settled until 1815.

"Dec 15–18 'This cold, uncomfortable weather
Makes Jack and Gill lie close together.'"

1725 **Union Oyster House,** famed Boston restaurant, built as private residence. Became public eating place in 1826.

1726 **Largest book,** folio, printed in America up to this time, *Compleat Body of Divinity* by the Rev. Samuel Willard, president of Harvard University.

1728 Important poetical work from Maryland was *The Mouse-Trap, or the Battle of the Cambrians and the Mice,* a translation by **Richard Lewis** of Edward Holdsworth's Latin poem *Muscipula,* a lampoon on the Welsh. It was printed on William Parks' Annapolis press.

1729 **Old South Meeting House** built in Boston by Joshua Blanchard, master mason who later built Faneuil Hall. Has been museum since 1876.

1729 **1st serial** in American newspaper, Daniel Defoe's *Religious Courtship,* appeared in *Pennsylvania Gazette.*

1729 Oct. **Pennsylvania Gazette** bought by Benjamin Franklin. Under title *Universal Instructor in All Arts and Sciences and Pennsylvania Gazette* it had been begun by Samuel Keimer in 1728. At this time it had a subscription list of 90. Franklin made it become in time leading newspaper between New York and Charleston. He managed the *Gazette* until 1766, and it was continued until 1815 by David Hall, Franklin's partner from 1748, and by Hall's descendants. The claim of the popular magazine *The Saturday Evening Post* (failed 1969) that it was a continuation of the *Gazette* is a myth, based on the fact that the *Post* was first issued from a shop that had printed the *Gazette.* The *Post* was founded in 1821, 6 years after the *Gazette* expired, by men who had had no connection with the *Gazette.*

SCIENCE; INDUSTRY; ECONOMICS; EDUCATION; RELIGION; PHILOSOPHY.

SPORTS; FASHIONS; POPULAR ENTERTAINMENT; FOLKLORE; SOCIETY.

1728 **Benjamin Franklin** demonstrated his belief in reason as basis of religious faith with writing of his prayer manual entitled "Articles of Belief and Acts of Religion." Franklin subordinated formal religious doctrines to common-sense logic.

1728 Jews of New York city build **1st American synagogue** in Mill Street. Building rented in 1628 had been in previous use for public worship. Congregation later added 1st school for Jewish children.

1728 One of **1st church organs** in America installed in Christ Church in Philadelphia.

1728 Social distinctions seen in Louisiana with arrival of **"casket girls,"** so-called because they received dress in casket as gift for their immigration. Since these girls were not inmates of penal institutions, as were many of their predecessors, it became and has remained a genealogical honor to be descended from "casket girl."

1729 **1st arithmetic textbook** by an American published in Boston, Mass. It was entitled *Arithmetick Vulgar and Decimal: with the Application Thereof to a Variety of Cases in Trade and Commerce,* and was written by Isaac Greenwood.

1729 **3rd Anglican parish** in Boston established in **Trinity Church.** New parish reflected rapid expansion of Anglicanism in New England.

1729 **Presbyterian churches** adopted as their doctrinal standard Westminster Confession of Faith and Catechisms.

1729 Mar. 15 Ceremony of the Profession of Sister St. Stanislaus Hachard occurred at Ursuline Convent in New Orleans, La. She was the **1st Catholic nun professed in U.S.**

1728 **Importation of rum** in colonies for this year amounted to 2,124,500 gals., or £25,000 of liquor. Drinking was extremely heavy. Printed doggerel lists one reason why people don't drink:

There's but one Reason I can Think,
Why People ever cease to drink,
Sobriety the Cause is not,
Nor Fear of being deam'd a Sot,
But if Liquor can't be got.

1728 May *New York Gazette* reported imminent arrival of **lion** at Jamaica fair. Awaited lion had begun its American tour in Boston and, caged on ox-cart, had proceeded to Philadelphia, New London, and Albany. This is 1st record of lion on exhibition in America.

1729 Rhode Island **discrimination** forced ship captains to post £50 for each immigrant coming from any place other than England, Ireland, Jersey, and Guernsey.

1729 Mar. 1 **St. David's Day,** in honor of patron saint of Wales, formally celebrated by Welsh inhabitants of Philadelphia who formed Society of Ancient Britons at gathering in Queen's Head Tavern. From there, members of the Society marched through streets, wearing leeks in their hats, to Christ Church where the Rev. Dr. Weyman delivered sermon in Cymric, after which celebrants repaired to tavern once more for further ceremonies.

1729 Apr. 23 1st celebration of **St. George's Day** in America held in Tun Tavern by St. George's Society of Philadelphia, a group of Philadelphians of English extraction.

53

1730–1734

Estimated colonial population—654,950.

1730 New England was **most populated area** of colonial America with 275,000 white people. By 1760 this rose to 425,000, and at close of Revolution to 800,000.

1730 **Baltimore, Md.,** settled. 2 previous efforts had been made to found a city named after the Lords Baltimore, but the site of the 1st is in question and only house and ruins remain of the 2nd. Baltimore was important as a seaport for the rich grain and tobacco lands which lie around the head of the Chesapeake Bay. Land for Baltimore bought by legislature in 1729.

1732 Jan. **Concession in Louisiana** surrendered to French crown by Western Company of John Law. Antoine Crozat, a French trader, held the concession from 1712 and made the grant to John Law, Scottish financier and speculator, in 1717. The Western Company (variously called the Company of the West, *Compagnie D'Occident* and the Mississippi Company) was pledged to develop Louisiana and given exclusive right to trade on the Mississippi R. Law, celebrated in fiction as well as in history, sponsored the scheme which is remembered as the Mississippi Bubble. The Duke of Orleans, regent of France, encouraged Law to start a bank which, in the name of the Western Company, floated paper money in excess of security. The collapse of this speculation ruined Law. He returned to Europe where he died in 1725.

1732 Feb. 22 **George Washington** born at Bridges Creek, Va.

1732 June 9 Royal charter granted to James Edward Oglethorpe for formation of the colony of **Georgia.** It was formed both as a defense for South Carolina against the Spanish in Florida and the French in Louisiana and as a refuge for persecuted Protestant sects and the poor but worthy classes in England.

1730 1st book of **Pennsylvania German hymns,** *Göttliche Liebes und Lobes Gethöne,* printed by Benjamin Franklin in Philadelphia for Conrad Beissel. Beissel was first composer of music in the colonies whose works were published.

1730 Probably **1st algebra book** printed in America was *Arithmetica ot Cyffer-Konst Volgens de Munten Maten en Gewigten, te Niew-York, gebruykelyk als mede een kort ontwerp van de Algebra,* by Peter Venema. It was published by J. Peter Zenger of New York city.

1730 **Old State House** in Philadelphia, known as Independence Hall, designed by Andrew Hamilton. Not completed until 1753; rebuilt in 1828. Excellent example of Georgian public architectural style.

1730 Extremely popular piece of humorous verse which caught fancy of English public when printed in *Gentleman's Magazine* is "Father Abbey's Will" by **John Seccomb,** New England minister. Father Abbey, dying, bequeaths in part the following to his widow:

> A greasy hat,
> My old ram cat,
> A yard and half of linen,
> A woolen fleece
> A pot of grease,
> In order for your spinning.

1732 **1st guide book** in America, *Vade Mecum for America: or, A Companion for Traders and Travellers* by Daniel Henchman and T. Hancock, printed. It provided information on all roads and taverns from Maine to Virginia, and also included directory of streets of Boston.

1732 Opening of the **2nd theater building** in the colonies, the New Theater, Nassau Street, New York city. On Dec. 6 it staged *The Recruiting Officer* by George Farquhar. It also produced this season *The Beaux' Stratagem* by George Farquhar; *The Busy-body* by Susannah Centlivre; and *Cato* by Joseph Addison.

1730–1734

1730 **1st stoneware furnace,** or kiln, established in New York. City became center of pottery manufacture, evidenced by designation "Potter's Hill" on early map of city.

1730 "Stampt Paper in Rolls for to **paper Rooms"** sold to wealthy merchants of colonies.

1730 Hadley's Mariner's Quadrant invented by Thomas Godfrey. It was **1st practical navigating quadrant.**

1731 Founding of Library Company of Philadelphia by Franklin represents **1st circulating library** in New World. Extent to which libraries were to grow and flourish in U.S. indicated by fact that there are at present about 6000 public libraries in U.S. with annual circulation of more than 2 volumes per capita.

1731 **1st efficient fire engine** in America, invented in England, arrived in Philadelphia and became part of Union Fire Company of Philadelphia, headed by Benjamin Franklin.

1732 Early indication of **Quaker humanitarianism** in America was founding of public almshouse in Philadelphia supported by public funds.

1732 **1st stage coach line** established between Burlington and Amboy, N.J. Connections could be made from Amboy to New York city and from Burlington to Philadelphia by boat.

1732 Feb. 26 **Only Catholic church** built and maintained in colonies until Revolutionary War held its 1st mass in Philadelphia.

c1733 Finest pottery work in America came from **Pennsylvania Dutch kilns.** Earliest specimen dates from this period—a barber basin inscribed "Putz und Balwir mich heibsh und fein das ich gefal der liebste mein (Clean and shave me nicely and fine so that I'll please my loved one)." Later Pennsylvania slip- and sgraffito-

c1730 Great craze for **white stockings** for men and women set in, replacing varicolored hose of 17th century. These were made of thread, silk, cotton, or worsted and were supported by means of ornate garters. Often name of gentleman or lady was woven into garter with a "posy." White hose worn until end of century.

1730 **Newport** began to attract rich by its healthful climate, ideal as watering place. Visitors came from as far south as West Indies and Carolinas. Boating in Bay, tea and dancing parties, good food and society, helped make this city mecca of sophisticated. It was also famous for its historical past which, in the old stone mill in Touro Park, is said to extend as far back as the Norsemen. In 1730 Newport saw the beginnings of the Philosophical Society (which became the Redwood Library 20 years later). Within a few years it was to become hub of the "triangular trade," whereby rum from Newport was traded for slaves in Africa and the slaves were exchanged for the sugar and molasses of the Barbadoes.

1730 Mr. Smith of Maryland, unhappy with chase of gray fox, imported a number of **English red foxes** and set them loose along banks of Chesapeake.

1730 Daniel Coxe became **1st appointed Grand Master of Masons** in America when he was designated "Provincial Grand Master of the Provinces of New York, New Jersey, and Pennsylvania."

1732 "A piece of land at the lower end of Broadway fronting to the fort" leased to three well-known New Yorkers, John Chambers, Peter Bayard, and Peter Jay, "to make a **Bowling Green** thereof."

1732 **1st fishing club** and **oldest sporting organization** of any kind in North America formed as Schuylkill Fishing Company in Philadelphia. It is now known as Fish House Club, its membership limited to 30, **its** function limited to annual

55

1733 **Epidemic of influenza** 1st serious outbreak in North America, swept New York city and Philadelphia.

1733 Feb. 12 **Savannah,** 1st settlement in Georgia, founded by Oglethorpe. Georgia was the last of the 13 colonies to be founded.

1733 May 17 **Molasses Act** passed, which placed high duties on rum and molasses imported from French and Spanish West Indies. Admission of American merchants into the rum trade of the French West Indies (1713) caused a boom in sugar on those islands. Planters on the English islands lost out as New England ships put into French and Dutch ports to load up with cheap sugar. They petitioned Parliament and forced passage of the Molasses Act, which levied prohibitive duties on sugar and molasses brought to the colonies from other than British possessions.

1733 July **40 Jews,** admitted to Georgia colony by its proprietors, settled in Savannah.

1734 Oct. **Peter Zenger,** publisher of *Weekly Journal* in New York, arrested for libel. Acquitted after defense by Andrew Hamilton which was later often cited in cases involving freedom of press. Sons of Liberty, an organization founded to aid Zenger's defense, later became Tammany Society of New York.

1732 **Adams mansion,** Quincy, Mass., residence of famous Adams family throughout 18th and 19th centuries, built in Georgian style. Was several times enlarged, and shows successive changes in architectural style.

1732 May *Philadelphische Zeitung,* **1st foreign-language newspaper in U.S.,** founded by Benjamin Franklin in Philadelphia, Pa.

1732 Dec. 19 Publication of **Franklin's** *Poor Richard's Almanack* began. In continuous publication for 25 years, *Almanack* sold on average more than 10,000 copies yearly and thus one of most popular writings of colonial America.

1733 **Charles Theodore Pachelbel,** noted organist from South Germany and son of famous Johann Pachelbel, precursor of Bach, arrived in America and took up his appointment as organist at Trinity Church, Newport, R.I. He died four years later at Charleston, S.C.

1733 Nov. 5 **Peter Zenger** founded *New York Weekly Journal,* newspaper which supported the popular cause in New York. Lasted until 1751.

1734 Aug. Benjamin Franklin advertised for sale his *Mason Book,* a reprint of Anderson's *Constitutions of the Free-Masons.* It was the **1st book** about Freemasonry published in the colonies.

1735–1739

1735 **1st European settlers in Indiana,** some 8 French families, founded Vincennes.

1735 Oct. 30 **John Adams,** 2nd president of U.S., born in Braintree, Mass.

1736 Famous remark by Col. Byrd II of Virginia to effect that "the Saints of

1735 Portrait of Indian chief *Lapowinsa* painted by Swedish-American painter **Gustavus Hesselius.** Born in 1682, he emigrated to Delaware in 1712, later joining Moravians in Philadelphia. This portrait of a puzzled Indian was commissioned by Penn family.

1735 Feb. 8 **1st opera** produced in colonies performed at the Courtroom, Charleston, S.C. It was *Flora; or, The Hob in the Well* by Colley Cibber.

1735 Feb. 12 3rd theater in colonies opened with *The Recruiting Officer* by

SCIENCE; INDUSTRY; ECONOMICS; EDUCATION; RELIGION; PHILOSOPHY.

SPORTS; FASHIONS; POPULAR EN-TERTAINMENT; FOLKLORE; SOCIETY.

ware characterized by little verses like the following:

In the dish on the table
Merry he who yet is single
Sad is he who is engaged.

If loving were unhealthy
Surely the doctor would avoid it
And if it would hurt the wives
Surely they would not allow it.

1734 **Jonathan Edwards** led and preached "The Great Awakening" in New England, religious revival that emphasized man's sinful nature and torments of his eternal damnation. In his parish in Northampton, Mass., Edwards lived a life of spartan dedication. His fame spread to Boston, bringing invitations to preach and print his sermons. The influence of his example was strong, especially among young people. In December 1734 there began a series of conversions, emotional in nature and increasing in frequency, which was felt throughout the county. From 1740–45 the movement was at fever pitch. It was condemned as a disruptive influence by the more conservative congregations and by the faculties at Yale and Harvard, but began a religious mode which proved congenial to many later Americans and did add to social cohesiveness in a time of great uncertainty.

meetings at the Andalusia, Pa., headquarters.

1733 Gentry of New York began to form **social clubs,** one of earliest being Political Club, which met this year at Todd's Tavern. It was followed by Hum Drum Club, Hungarian Club, and New Club, Lodge, or Society of Free Masons (1738).

1734 **Benjamin Franklin** contributed famous epigram on marriage to his *Poor Richard's Almanack* when he observed that "where there's marriage without love, there will be love without marriage."

1734 **1st jockey club** in world formed as South Carolina Jockey Club. Disbanded in 1900.

1734 Mar. Commercial notice in Boston said that shipment of **Nassau silk** "of the Colour provided for the royal wedding" had been shipped from England "early, that . . . Ladys may have them as soon as some of ours." Boston provided good market for merchants of London; latest fashions were in great demand by wealthy.

1735–1739

1735 **1st Moravian community** in America established at Savannah, Ga., under leadership of Rev. Augustus Gottlieb Spangenberg. A single Moravian evangelist had been in Pennsylvania the year before, however.

1735 **Early fire insurance company,** probably 1st in American colonies, established at Charleston, S.C. Called The Friendly Society for the Mutual Insurance of Houses Against Fire, it was ruined in the great fire of Nov. 18, 1740, which consumed half of Charleston.

1735 **Public balls** came into vogue in colonial New York. In 1736 birthday of Prince of Wales celebrated by magnificent ball at Black Horse Tavern.

c1735 Increase of wealth in colonies caused change in **status of women.** More women left their husbands when they found living together incompatible; newspapers recounted items of runaway wives and elopements.

1735 Jan. John van Zandt, Dutch burgher of New York, horsewhipped his Negro **slave** to death for having been

New England" imported so many **Negroes** into Virginia that "the Colony will some time or other be Confirmed by the name of New Guinea." Remark reflected resentment in South of moral preachments of Puritans regarding slavery.

1737 **Thomas Penn** angered Delaware Indians by hiring expert walkers to pace off land deeded to William Penn by tribe, which was to include all land a man could walk across in a day and a half. Penn's experts walked 66½ miles.

1739 **3 Negro uprisings** broke out in South Carolina this year. Source of the incidents has been attributed to the preaching of the Spanish missionaries who allegedly created in the Negroes a false expectation of deliverance. On Sept. 9 a band of Negroes from Charleston set out for St. Augustine and freedom, slaying all whites whom they met on the way. They were themselves surrounded and massacred. 21 whites and 44 Negroes perished. At Stone River a slave named Cato led another insurrection. 3d was in St. John's Parish in Berkeley County.

1739 Oct. 19 **War of Jenkins' Ear** begun with England declaring war on Spain over mistreatment of English seamen and border difficulties in Florida. Conflict soon merged with War of Austrian Succession, 1740–48. Robert Jenkins, an English merchant seaman, had reported in the House of Commons that his ear had been cut off in 1731 by Spaniards who had told him to take it to the English king. The Spaniards had punished him as a suspected smuggler. This abrupt justice was being meted out by a special Spanish fleet fitted to intercept English ships engaged in slave traffic with the Spanish colonies, although the English South Sea Company had been admitted to the trade by the provisions of the Treaty of Utrecht. Public reaction to the indignity

George Farquhar. It was the new **Dock Street Theater,** Charleston, S.C. On Feb. 23 it staged *The Orphan* by Thomas Otway. Performances were given until May 1737. Boxes were 30 shillings; pit 20 shillings; gallery 15 shillings.

1736 Aug. 6 Early **literary newspaper** *Virginia Gazette,* begun by William Parks at Williamsburg.

c1737 **Oldest extant house** in U.S. Midwest built by unknown French colonist at Cahokia, Ill. Later became Cahokia County Courthouse. Of *poteaux-sur-sole* construction, i.e., upright posts driven into earth and chinked with clay, with double-pitched, hipped roof, and surrounding *galerie.*

1737 **John Wesley,** English Methodist visiting America, published at "Charles-Town," S.C., *A Collection of Psalms and Hymns.* Wesley had been greatly influenced by hymns of German Moravians, and some of his collection were translations from their *Gesangbuch.*

1739 Famous glass designer and manufacturer **Caspar Wistar** set up glass works at Allowaystown, New Jersey. His enterprise responsible for most distinctive type of early American glass, "South Jersey": wide, bulbous forms, often with superimposed winding thicknesses on bottom.

1739 1st American edition of Dr. **Isaac Watts's** *Hymns and Spiritual Songs* published. Many of Dr. Watts's hymns had been known in America long before this; they were probably most influential factor in development of American music during 1st half of 18th century.

1739 Fine sketch of history of Rhode Island, *An Historical Discourse* by **John Callender,** minister of Baptist Church in Newport. Book traces course of events—intolerance, bigotry—of Massachusetts col-

1735 Growth of **trade** in Massachusetts reflected in joint possession by Boston and Salem of some 25,000 tons of shipping.

1735 1st published account of **lead poisoning** as a result of drinking rum distilled with lead pipes written by Thomas Cadwallader.

1735 Gov. Oglethorpe of Georgia colony, visiting England, met **John Wesley** and his brother Charles, students at Oxford. Wesleys belonged to Oxford group known variously as "Holy Club," "Bible Moths," and "Methodists." Oglethorpe invited them to come to Georgia, and they accepted. They arrived Feb. 5, 1736.

1735 Dec. 10 **John Wesley** sailed to Georgia at invitation of Oglethorpe. When he came to America the career of Wesley had not yet reached the spectacular stage of his later achievement as a public preacher. 6 years before the name of Methodists had been applied to his group of religious ascetics, but Methodism was still in the future. His stay in America is notable for his romance with Sophia Hopkey, who wooed him but did not win. When Sophia married another, Wesley barred her from his congregation and decided to leave the colony because her new husband retaliated with the threat of a lawsuit.

1736 Significant contribution to American and world medicine made by Dr. William Douglass of Boston who published 1st adequate clinical diagnosis of **scarlet fever.**

1737 **1st copper coinage** minted in colonies produced by John Higley at his furnace on Hopmeadow Brook, Simsbury, Conn. Known to numismatists today as "Higley pennies," the coins were stamped "I am good copper" and "Value me as you will."

1738 **Isaac Greenwood,** one of earliest teachers of natural science in America, ended his career in Harvard. He was succeeded by John Winthrop.

1739 1st American experimenter in **physiological botany** was the Rev. Jared

picked up at night by watch. Coroner's jury judged that "Correction given by the Master was not the Cause of his Death, but that it was by the Visitation of God." Relations between whites and Negroes were often tense in New York because slave population was about ⅙ of population of entire colony. Negroes were lynched and burned for theft, rape, etc.

1736 **60 maidens** from Bahamas arrived at Charleston and immediately advertised in local press for husbands, a commodity of which there was plenty in old South.

1737 Mar. 9 Mob of **reformers** smashed bawdy house in Boston "for harbouring lewd and dissoulte Persons." Prostitutes ranged waterfront of Boston. One girl, who entertained "Lawyers, Officers, Journeymen, Gentlemen, Merchants, Apprentices" had to be cautioned not to display her behavior "at the Window on the Lord's Day" for fear of minister.

1737 Mar. 17 1st celebration of **St. Patrick's Day** outside confines of Church held in Boston by Charitable Irish Society founded in that year. Friendly Sons of St. Patrick began St. Patrick's Day celebrations in Philadelphia in 1780. Friendly Sons of St. Patrick in New York city followed suit in 1784. An oddity of New York society was its joint sponsorship by Irish Roman Catholics and Presbyterians with 1st president of organization being a Presbyterian.

1738 Masonic warrant for **1st military Masonic lodge** issued by Grand Lodge of Massachusetts to Abraham Savage. Similar authority granted to Richard Gridley in 1756 for military expedition against Crown Point, N.Y.

1738 More than 1000 pairs of gloves given away at funeral of wife of Gov. Belcher of Massachusetts. **Funeral gifts** were customary in colonies. Generally rings given at this time were called mourning-rings. A minister or doctor accumulated thousands of these in course of a lifetime.

POLITICS AND GOVERNMENT; WAR; DISASTERS; VITAL STATISTICS.

BOOKS; PAINTING; DRAMA; ARCHITECTURE; SCULPTURE.

committed against Jenkins was so great that Walpole declared war against Spain Oct. 23, 1739. Oglethorpe called on the colonists of Georgia and South Carolina, who had their own grievances against the Spaniards in Florida, to join the war. Spanish retaliated by attempting to invade those colonies from the sea.

ony that led to emigration to and formation of Rhode Island.

1739 Book reflecting best the spiritual revivalism of 18th century is *Personal Narrative* of **Jonathan Edwards.** Edwards describes in glowing terms mystic conversion which led him to change his whole life: his sense of sin, his complete acceptance of God.

1740–1744

Estimated colonial **population**—889,000.

1740 Beginning of **War of Austrian Succession.** France, allied with Prussia, invaded southern Germany after death of Charles VI on Oct. 20. France also allied itself with Spain, at war with England, and so declared war herself on England Mar. 15, 1744. In America war was known as **King George's War.**

1740 Powerful **political attack** upon Gen. James Oglethorpe and his administration of new colony of Georgia was *A True and Historical Narrative of the Colony of Georgia* by three inhabitants who fled to Charleston, Patrick Tailfer, Hugh Anderson, and David Douglass. "Thus, while the nation at home was amused with the fame of the happiness and flourishing of the colony, . . . the poor miserable settlers and inhabitants were exposed to as arbitrary a government as Turkey or Muscovy ever felt."

1740 Jan. Oglethorpe invaded Florida in **War of Jenkins' Ear.** He was protected on the west from the French by friendly Indians. He captured Forts San Francisco de Pupo and Picolata on the San Juan R. From May to July he besieged Saint Augustine, but broke off attack when rear was threatened.

1741 **1st symphony orchestra** in America organized by Moravian settlers in Bethlehem, Pa. By 1748 had 14 pieces: 2 1st violins, 2 2nd violins, 2 violas, 1 cello, 1 double bass, 2 flutes, 2 trumpets, 2 French horns.

1741 Feb. 13 **1st magazine published** in America, **Andrew Bradford's** *American Magazine, or A Monthly View of the Political State of the British Colonies.* 3 days later came **Benjamin Franklin's** *General Magazine, and Historical Chronicle, For all the British Plantations in America.* Both magazines dated January, 1741, in Philadelphia. Bradford's magazine lasted only 3 months, Franklin's 6.

1741 Aug. **Organ for Trinity Church,** New York city, completed by Philadelphian Johann Gottlob Klemm. Klemm, 1st organ-builder in America, took more than 2 years to construct the organ, which was probably 1st built in this country.

1742 Best-known work reflecting revivalism in colonial times is **Jonathan Edwards'** *Some Thoughts concerning the Present Revival of Religion in New England.*

1742 Master carpenters of Philadelphia formed Carpenters' Company to establish an **architectural library** and teach themselves elements of design and craftsmanship. They built **Carpenters' Hall** in

SCIENCE; INDUSTRY; ECONOMICS; EDUCATION; RELIGION; PHILOSOPHY.	SPORTS; FASHIONS; POPULAR ENTERTAINMENT; FOLKLORE; SOCIETY.

Eliot who worked on fructification of maize before 1739.

1739 Caspar Wistar builds factory on tracts of wooded land in New Jersey ideal for the production of **window and bottle glass.** July 30, 1740, the factory went into operation staffed with Belgian glass blowers specially drafted in Europe, becoming one of 1st successful co-ops in America.

1739 Aug. **George Whitefield,** celebrated English preacher, arrived at Lewes, Del., to begin evangelistic tour that was to spur great Methodist revival in America.

1738 One of **1st umbrellas** in America owned by Edward Shippen. There was much religious opposition to use of umbrellas, particularly among Quakers.

1739 Some relaxation of stringent codes of behavior in New England seen in permission granted to Charles Bradstreet to teach **French dancing,** "so long as he keeps good order."

1739 **Benjamin Franklin** coined famous epigram on self-adulation in *Poor Richard's Almanack:* "He that falls in love with himself will have no rivals."

1740–1744

1740 **1st brewery in Georgia** erected by Governor Oglethorpe, supplying ample quantities of beer for all troops.

1741 Growth of **fishing industry** in New England reflected in existence of some 1000 fishing ships.

1741 Famous sermon delivered by Jonathan Edwards at Endfield, Mass., began "the **Great Awakening**" in New England. Entitled, "Sinners in the Hands of an Angry God," Edwards' sermon proclaimed man's "abominable" sinfulness in eyes of God.

1742 An antagonistic note leveled against revivalist movements launched by Edwards struck by Charles Chauncey in his *Enthusiasms Described and Cautioned Against.* Leaning toward Unitarianism, Chauncey's more cultivated sensibilities reacted against personalistic effusions of those caught in "**Great Awakening.**"

1742 Arrival of distinguished French Jesuit scholar, **Father Meurin,** in region that is now Illinois led to impressive scholarship in Indian dialects and writing of dictionary of these dialects.

1742 So-called "**Franklin stove,**" a variation of an open firebox German design, invented by Benjamin Franklin.

1743 **1st scientific association,** American Philosophical Society, established in Philadelphia, Pa. 1st president was Thomas

1740 **Mineral springs** in mountains of Virginia found to have medicinal qualities, inducing many plantation owners to travel with their families to bathe and vacation. Washington in 1769 spent a season there with his wife and step-daughter.

1740 Mar. 25 Construction began on Bethesda Orphanage, Savannah, Ga., the **oldest existing orphanage** in America. Orphanage was an indirect result of the invitation to preach in Georgia which was extended to John Wesley by Oglethorpe. Wesley was accompanied on the mission by George Whitefield. Whitefield stayed 3 months in the colony before returning to England to take orders. He had conceived the idea of a Georgian orphanage and, to raise the funds, began the practice of public speaking which was the characteristic of early Methodism and one of the major religious innovations of the century. 2 years later he went back to Georgia. Orphanage dates from this period. In 1769, the year of his last visit to America, Whitefield arranged for the conversion of the orphanage into Bethesda College.

1741 Winter Famous "**Negro Conspiracy**" occurred in New York city. 11 Negroes burned at stake, 18 more hanged along with 4 white men in New York when series of incendiary fires occurred throughout city. Public suspicion fell upon Negro slaves for no other reason than that they were present in area.

| POLITICS AND GOVERNMENT; WAR; DISASTERS; VITAL STATISTICS. | BOOKS; PAINTING; DRAMA; ARCHITECTURE; SCULPTURE. |

1741 **German Moravians** moved from Georgia, where their colony had been unsuccessful, to Pennsylvania where they joined others of their Church in the establishment of Bethlehem on the Lehigh R. Count Zinzendorf, their leader, arrived from Europe this year, bringing with him a band of new immigrants. Zinzendorf returned to Europe in 1741.

1742 Battle of Bloody Swamp, a Spanish counterattack in the **War of Jenkins' Ear,** fought on St. Simon's Island. Spanish were severely defeated.

1743 **Benjamin Franklin** retired from his business ventures in printing, publishing, and bookselling at age of thirty-seven. After this, he was free to pursue his scientific interests and to meet his forthcoming political responsibilities.

1743 Apr. 13 **Thomas Jefferson,** 3rd president of U.S., born in Shadwell, Va.

1744 Territory in **Ohio Valley** north of Ohio R. ceded by Iroquois League to England in a treaty signed at Lancaster, Pa.

1770, which became meeting place of First Continental Congress.

1742 Sept. 24 **Faneuil Hall** in Boston opened to public. A Georgian structure, designed by painter John Smibert, it was later (1805) enlarged according to plans by Charles Bulfinch, which retained original Georgian style. Famous weathervane on cupola is giant grasshopper of beaten copper.

1743 Sept. **1st important American magazine,** *American Magazine and Historical Chronicle,* in Boston. Edited by Jeremy Gridley, who devoted it largely to politics, it lasted more than 3 years.

1744 Appearance of a little book, **A Collection of Poems by Several Hands,** hailed as proof of poetic excellence in colonies. Actually various poets merely echo, rather weakly, lines of Pope.

1744 1st publication in America of best seller *Pamela* by **Samuel Richardson.** Richardson's *Clarissa, Sir Charles Grandison, Pamela* 1st of "sentimental novels," which flourished in America c1750 to c1850.

1744 Moravians at Bethlehem, Pa., most musical of dissenting sects in America, established **"Collegium Musicum"** for performance of chamber music and symphonies by Haydn, Mozart, Bach, Stamitz, and other European composers. 1st such organization in U.S.

1745–1749

1745 June 16 **Fort Louisbourg,** powerful French stronghold on Cape Breton Island, captured by New Englanders under William Pepperell and English fleet under Sir Peter Warren. This was part of **King George's War,** which was not prosecuted vigorously in America. Beginning this year Maine fortifications were raided by French and Indians. On Nov. 28–29 of this year Saratoga, N.Y., was burned by French and Indians after the English had succeeded in getting the Iroquois League on the warpath.

1745 1st appearance in American periodicals of writings of **Montesquieu.** These excerpts culled from *Persian Letters.* Later selections appeared in Boston *Gazette* were drawn from his *Spirit of the Laws,* which had profound effect on final form of U.S. Constitution.

1745 Summer 8-bell **carillon** placed in Christ Church belfry, Boston, Mass. Paid for by public subscription in Boston and London, the carillon was the 1st in America. Bells were cast in Gloucester, England.

SCIENCE; INDUSTRY; ECONOMICS; EDUCATION; RELIGION; PHILOSOPHY.

SPORTS; FASHIONS; POPULAR ENTERTAINMENT; FOLKLORE; SOCIETY.

Hopkinson; Benjamin Franklin served as group's 1st secretary. Purpose of the society was "for the promotion of useful knowledge among the British planters in America." 26 years later the society was combined with the American Society, an earlier group originated by Franklin. In the same year, it began its 1st series of publications, *Transactions.* The Royal Society of London, then almost a century old, was the inspiration of the American Philosophical Society. The society is restricted to members who are preeminent in the various fields of science, philosophy and literature. It has collected an invaluable library of documentation of the American past.

1743 Significant publisher in early American religious development was **Christopher Saur,** who began publishing Bibles in German language.

1743 John Woolman began preaching evils of **slavery** to Quaker meetings throughout colonies.

1744 **1st brewery in Baltimore** established on southwest corner of Baltimore and Hanover Streets by Leonard and Daniel Barnetz of York, Penn.

1741 Legend of **Tom Cook,** the Leveler, may be said to commence this year. The young lad was sick unto death and his mother prayed, "Only spare his life, and I care not what he becomes." He became a semi-legendary evil-doer, a sort of Robin Hood, whose name came up in scores of New England villages. Legend has it that he sold his soul to the Devil, but managed to rob even Satan of his due.

1741 Child of 4 or 5 in Philadelphia died after consuming great quantity of rum. **Drunkenness** was most prevalent vice of colonial settlers. Each colony had stringent laws meant to suppress excess drinking. Boston even went so far as to post names of drunkards; contemporary quatrain sounds this note:

This town would quickly be reclaimed,
　If drams no more had vent,
And all the sorts that could be named
　To *Strombolo* were sent.

1742 **Horse race** held on Trinity Church Farms, west of present-day City Hall Park in New York city.

1743 **Benjamin Franklin** coined biting proverb in *Poor Richard's Almanack:* "Experience keeps a dear school, yet Fools will learn in no other."

1745–1749

1745 Growth of **literacy** in early America spurred by founding of 22 newspapers between 1713 and 1745.

1745-1763 **Early Texas history** compiled by Franciscan fathers who wrote books on techniques of missionaries and on language and character of Texas Indians.

1746 1st university lectures on **electricity** in America given by John Winthrop IV at Harvard.

1745 Earliest use of term **coffee house** to designate a certain type of inn appeared in notice of opening of Widow Roberts' Coffee House in Philadelphia. Meant for entertainment of gentlemen, inn provided all newspapers and magazines from home and abroad. Tea, coffee, or chocolate and "constant Attendance" of hostess included.

c1745 **Whist** became very popular in colonies, being brought over from England where it had been the rage among men and women. Game afforded opportunity

POLITICS AND GOVERNMENT; WAR;

DISASTERS; VITAL STATISTICS.

BOOKS; PAINTING; DRAMA;

ARCHITECTURE; SCULPTURE.

1747 Some of the **1st flags** created in American colonies were those designed by Benjamin Franklin to be employed by military units opposing attacks by French.

1748 Drapers Meadows founded on Virginia's frontier. It was 1st English settlement west of Allegheny Divide.

1748 Oct. 18 Treaty of Aix-la-Chapelle ended **King George's War** (War of Austrian Succession). In the colonies situation returned to its pre-war status, with Fort Louisbourg being returned to France.

1749 Year of **great drought** in New England. Great shortage of hay forces imports from Pennsylvania and England.

1749 May 19 **Ohio Company** chartered by George II. Organized by Virginians and Englishmen it had grant of 500,-000 acres on upper Ohio R. During this year Sieur de Bienville led **French expedition** to Ohio Valley to establish French claim. He deposited inscribed lead plates at mouth of each important river.

1749, Oct. 26 Negro slavery extended to Georgia with official permission granted by proprietors. Importation of rum was also permitted. Action repeals act of 1735, which prohibited both rum and slavery. The timidity of Parliament about the presence of slaves in the colonies, who might have allied themselves with the Spanish in time of crisis, thus ended. It had already been repudiated by the colonists, especially in Georgia, where the necessity for field and house hands had encouraged the settlers to flaunt the prohibition. In England, too, shippers and traders were besieging Parliament to lift the ban. Finally, in 1749, the trustees of Georgia requested a change in policy. Parliament yielded. The legal introduction and extension of slavery into the colonies in this year mark the beginning of the plantation system in the South.

1745 Sept. 4 At **Moravian concert** in Bethlehem, Pa., hymn "In Dulce Jubilo" sung in 13 languages simultaneously: Bohemian, Dutch, English, French, German, Greek, Irish, Latin, Mohawk, Mohican, Swedish, Welsh, and Wendish. A Dane, a Pole, and a Hungarian were also present but did not join in.

1747 Most popular poem in 18th century, **Alexander Pope's** *Essay on Man.* 1st published in England in 1733, it was reprinted all over American colonies. It sold 50,000 copies in Little Blue Books edition of 1920.

1747 Long poem of nearly 700 lines in pastoral vein, *Philosophic Solitude; or, The Choice of a Rural Life* written by young **William Livingston** of New York who, despite his predilection for sequestered life, was destined to be one of illustrious statesmen of Revolution.

c1748 Style of American painting of this period excellently revealed in **Robert Feke's** *Unknown Lady,* hanging at present in Brooklyn Museum. Patterns are sharply cut into bell-shaped skirts and funnel-shaped torsos, pointing to Cubism of later date. Of artist little is known. A contemporary noted in his diary that Feke had "phiz of an artist."

1748 One of earliest attempts in America to adapt **scientific data and method** to agriculture demonstrated in *An Essay on Field Husbandry* by Jared Eliot, New England preacher, physician, and farmer.

1749 King's Chapel, 1st building in Boston to be built from Quincy granite, erected from designs by Peter Harrison of Newport. 1st King's Chapel had been erected in 1688.

1749 Aug. 22 Early troupe of **English actors,** Murray and Kean's, performed Addison's *Cato* in a Philadelphia warehouse. Protests by city council forced them to leave for New York.

1746 Oct. 22 **Princeton College** founded by an evangelical faction of Presbyterian church. In years that followed, Princeton Seminary became a stronghold of conservative doctrine in bitter conflicts within Presbyterian church.

1747 Jonathan Mayhew, 1st New England minister openly to challenge traditional **doctrine of the Trinity,** assumed pulpit at West Church in Boston.

1747 **New York Bar Association,** 1st legal society in America, organized by lawyers of New York city to defend themselves against attacks by Lieut. Governor Colden. Group spearheaded resistance to Stamp Act.

1747 May **Princeton College** began its 1st classes. Named originally College of New Jersey, in Elizabethtown, N.J., it was moved to Newark, N.J., in 1747 and to Princeton, N.J., in 1756. It became Princeton University in 1896. 1st degrees awarded in 1748.

1749 Size of **Boston's** role as a colonial seaport reflected in fact that no fewer than 489 ships used harbor as home port during year.

1749 Nov. 13 Inspired by a pamphlet on education written by Benjamin Franklin, 24 citizens of Philadelphia, Pa., joined to found an Academy with Franklin as 1st president of the trustees. In 1753 the proprietors of Pennsylvania gave $15,000 to the academy, and in 1755 it became the College, Academy, and Charitable School of Philadelphia, from which grew the **University of Pennsylvania.**

for men to keep company with women. Ladies often played for money as evidenced from accounts of Jefferson and Washington concerning their wives' expenses.

1746 **1st boarding school for girls** founded in Bethlehem by Moravian settlers. It was called Seminary for Young Ladies. It exists today under name of Moravian Seminary and College for Women.

1747 **Benjamin Franklin** coined oft-quoted proverb of prudence in *Poor Richard's Almanack:* "A Slip of the Foot you may soon recover, But a Slip of the Tongue you may never get over."

1749 Horse presses for making **cider** and abundance of apple orchards in New York noted by eminent Swedish naturalist visiting colonies. Consumption of cider rivaled consumption of beer. In winter it was used extensively; in summer it was mixed with water, sweetened, and spiced with nutmeg.

1749 Philadelphia **social life** enhanced by establishment of **Dancing Assembly.** Positions in dance determined by lot, and a gentleman and his partner were engaged for entire evening. Day following dance a gentleman usually had tea with his partner in order to develop his acquaintanceship.

1749 **Eating habits** of Dutch in New York carefully recorded by Swedish traveler: "Their Breakfast is tea, commonly without milk. . . . They never put sugar into the cup but put a small bit of it into their mouths while they drink. Along with tea they eat bread and butter with slices of hung beef. . . . They breakfast generally about seven. Their dinner is buttermilk and bread. . . . They sometimes make use of buttermilk instead of fresh milk to boil a thin kind of porridge with, which tastes very sour but not disagreeable in hot weather. To each dinner they have a great salad prepared with abundance of vinegar and little or no oil [probably

POLITICS AND GOVERNMENT; WAR; DISASTERS; VITAL STATISTICS.	BOOKS; PAINTING; DRAMA; ARCHITECTURE; SCULPTURE.

1750–1754

Estimated colonial **population**—1,207,-000.

1750 Ohio Company obtained large tract of land on upper Ohio R. and sent **Christopher Gist** out to explore the territory. Gist was a neighbor of Daniel Boone's and, by this commission, actually beat Boone for the record of being the 1st white man to survey in northeastern Kentucky. Gist read the lands of the Ohio R. like the palm of his hand. To this day the charts which he made of the region and his observations of the customs of the natives are esteemed as "models in mathematical exactness and precision in drawing."

1751 Mar. 16 **James Madison,** 4th president of U.S., born in Port Conway, Va.

1753 *Argo,* a schooner commanded by Capt. Charles Swaine, set out from Philadelphia, Pa., to search for **Northwest Passage.** Expedition had been fitted out chiefly through exertions of Benjamin Franklin; explored Hudson's Straits and returned the same year.

1753 Oct. 31 **George Washington** sent by Gov. Dinwiddie of Virginia to demand French withdrawal from Ohio territory. Dinwiddie was impressed by Washington's achievement as both a surveyor and fieldsman, and picked him for the commission although he was then only 21. As Adjutant General of the Northern Division Wash-

1750 Probably **1st use of imitation materials** in an American building, Redwood Library of Newport, R.I. A temple-form structure in late Georgian manner, its siding was of pine planks worked to imitate stone.

1750 **Parlange,** one of finest plantation houses of bayou country in Louisiana and classic example of French colonial style, built at New Roads, Pointe Coupée Parish, La., by Marquis Vincent de Ternant, whose descendants still own it.

1750 Mar. 5 **1st regular company** of comedians, Murray and Kean's, after being badly received in Philadelphia, arrived in New York and opened with *Richard III.*

1751 **Peter Pelham,** early engraver and stepfather of Copley, died. During his life he engraved many portraits of New England ministers, that of Cotton Mather being one of his best known.

1751 Significant economic theory propounded by **Benjamin Franklin** in his *Observations Concerning the Increase of Mankind,* which held that wages of workers in America must be high because of abundance of free land. This year also saw publication in London of Franklin's famous *Experiments and Observations in Electricity, Made at Philadelphia in America.* Among his friends abroad were Priestley, Hume, Burke, Adam Smith, Lafayette, Turgot, D'Alembert.

1751 **John Smibert,** earliest American artist of real merit, died. Born in 1684, he studied in England and Italy. Coming to America with Bishop Berkeley, he finally settled in Boston where he achieved fame and wealth as portrait painter. Most

"koolslaa"—modern coleslaw]. Their supper is generally bread and butter, or milk and bread."

1750-1754

1750 **1st essay on human dissection** authored by Drs. John Bard and Peter Middleton of New York city. Dissection was performed on body of Hermannus Carrol, an executed murderer.

1750 Jonathan Edwards compelled to resign from his pulpit at Northampton, Mass., by action of liberal members of his congregation who opposed his emphasis on sinful nature of man. Departure of Edwards marked end in New England of **"The Great Awakening,"** which his sermons had sparked.

1750 Invention of **flatboat** by Jacob Yoder of Pennsylvania. It was boon to colonial inland navigation.

1750 Probably **1st free manual training classes** in America established by the Rev. Thomas Bacon in Maryland. Enrollment was open to all without distinction of sex or racial origin.

1752 Jan. 31 Ceremony for the Profession of Sister St. Martha Turpin held at Ursuline Convent, New Orleans, La. She was the **1st American-born nun** in the Catholic Church.

1752 June **Benjamin Franklin** conducted experiment with kite and key to prove lightning a manifestation of electricity. Kite with projecting wire was flown during thunderstorm and spark was conducted to key by means of sleazy twine. Experiment was made in pasture near what is now corner of Fourth and Vine Sts., Philadelphia, Pa.

1753 **Benjamin Franklin** received Copley Medal of the Royal Society of London in recognition of his research in electricity. Franklin's reputation as a scientist had grown very rapidly in Europe after the publication there of his works on electricity, and the award to him had been voted unanimously by the Royal Society.

1750 Big **horse race** on the Newmarket Course on Hempstead Plains, Long Island, brought heavy business to Brooklyn ferry, which carried over 70 chairs and chaises and over 1000 horses in one day.

1750 Colonel Tasker of Belair, Md., imported **Selima,** daughter of Godolphin Arabian (one of original thoroughbred horses), who became dam of several good American racers.

1751 **1st sugar cane** grown in America introduced into Louisiana by Catholic missionaries from San Domingo. It was used to make taffia, a kind of rum.

1752 Col. Tasker's **Selima** defeated Col. Bird's *Tryall* in challenge horse race in Maryland. Colonel Tasker was so successful with offspring of *Selima* that Maryland-bred horses were barred from Virginia Jockey Club purses for several years. The colonel then sent his horses to Virginia to foal and soon was winning again.

1752 Biblical sentence, "Proclaim liberty throughout all the land unto all the inhabitants thereof," chosen by Pennsylvania Provincial Assembly as the inscription for famous **Liberty Bell.** Bell was cast in England and delivered to colony this year. While being tested in Philadelphia, it suffered its 1st crack.

1752 May 11 "Hand-in-hand," nickname of the Philadelphia Contributorship for the Insurance of Homes, dates from the adoption of the famous and suggestive seal by the 1st meeting of the board of the company. The 12 directors of the board of this early **fire insurance company** in America had been chosen Apr. 13, but it was not until the following month that they met.

1753 May 10 Beauty of **Carolinian women** led Society for the Regulation of Manners to decree that after this day "no Lady do presume to walk the Streets in a

ington set out from Williamsburg, Va., Oct. 1, 1753. With Christopher Gist as his guide he took heed of the French fortifications and estimated how they could be balanced out by similar English ones. During the expedition he kept a journal which Dinwiddie later got hold of and had printed. It was an indictment of the French intentions for the territory and attributed to a French officer the indiscreet admission that ". . . it was their absolute Design to take possession of the Ohio, and by G– they would do it."

1754 May 28 Washington's skirmish with French troops led by de Jumonville was 1st action of **French and Indian War.** French defeated, and Washington built Fort Necessity.

1754 June 19 Benjamin Franklin introduced **Albany Plan of Union.** In Albany, N.Y., representatives of New York, Pennsylvania, Maryland, and the New England states met with leaders of the Six Iroquois nations to draw up plan of defense against encroaching French. Plan called for union under a president appointed by crown. A council of delegates elected by assemblies of colonies would have legislative power subject to approval by crown and president. Plan was rejected.

1754 July 3 Washington yielded **Fort Necessity** when attacked by large French contingent from Fort Duquesne. This defeat left French in possession of Ohio Valley.

famous work is *Family of Bishop Berkeley,* now in Dining Hall of Yale University.

1752 Arrival of acting troupe from England, Lewis Hallam's **"American Company,"** marked a turning point in American theater history. Group set up repertory theater that lasted until Revolutionary War. Playing in Williamsburg, New York, Philadelphia, etc., company familiarized colonists with works of best British playwrights. It provided the best acting in America so far, and was far superior to Murray and Kean's company.

1752 **Georg Muller House** built at Milbach, Pa. Best surviving example of Pennsylvania Dutch architecture, based on designs common in Rhine Valley.

1753 Early tract, in form of a romance, which outlined plans for an ideal college in America, was *A General Idea of the College of Miriana* by **William Smith.** Brought to attention of Franklin, book influenced him in forwarding his plans for a college in Philadelphia.

1754 1st publication in England of **Thomas Chippendale's** *The Gentleman and Cabinetmaker's Director* helped shape American styles in furniture. Stressed elaborate rococo designs with formal adaptations of French, Gothic, and Oriental designs.

1754 Benjamin Franklin published cartoon, believed to have been **1st American cartoon,** in his *Pennsylvania Gazette.* Cartoon showed snake cut into 8 parts, the head representing New England and the other seven parts representing the remaining colonies; underneath was printed the caption, "Join or Die." Cartoon was provoked by rumors of an impending war with the French.

SCIENCE; INDUSTRY; ECONOMICS; EDUCATION; RELIGION; PHILOSOPHY.

SPORTS; FASHIONS; POPULAR ENTERTAINMENT; FOLKLORE; SOCIETY.

1753 **Practice of medicine** regulated in New York city for 1st time. An ordinance required that "all the physicians and surgeons and apothecaries in the province are to be licensed . . ." Law was not strictly enforced until 1760 when New York General Assembly provided a system of examination and licensing for those who intended to practice medicine or surgery within the province. Illegal practice was punished by a fine of £5.

1753 **1st steam engine** in colonies brought to North Arlington, N.J., by John Schuyler to pump water from his copper mine. Machine came from England and was assembled in this country by Joshua Hornblower.

1754 **1st clock made entirely in America** constructed by Benjamin Banneker, a 30-year-old Negro who had never seen a clock before. It continued to run accurately, striking all hours regularly, for 20 years.

1754 Strongest voice against slavery in early America was that of **John Woolman,** Quaker, whose *Some Considerations on the Keeping of Negroes* was expression of relentless campaign of exhorting Quaker slave owners to give up their slaves.

1754 Oct. 31 **Columbia University** chartered as King's College in New York city. Sponsored by Episcopalian groups, King's College was incorporated as dominant institution in state supported University of the State of New York in act passed in 1784. Bitter conflict between advocates of free public education and backers of King's College led to separation of college, now Columbia College, from University of the State of New York by act of legislature in 1787. University of the State of New York, a university in name only, then concerned itself with primary and secondary school education while Columbia College remained only higher institution of learning in state. Columbia College became a university in 1912. First degrees were awarded in 1758.

Mask, unless either the Sun or Wind is in her Face; such as are very ugly or have sore Eyes always excepted."

1754 Harvard forbade students to wear **"banyan"**—nightgown made of silk and damask that was worn as dressing gown. That these garments were very fashionable is evidenced by number of paintings in which subject is wearing one.

1754 Curious **Valentine customs** recorded by a girl: "Last Friday was St. Valentine's Day, and the night before I got five bay leaves and pinned four on the corners of my pillow and the fifth to the middle; and then if I dreamt of my sweetheart, Betty said we should be married before the year was out. But to make it more sure I boiled an egg hard and took out the yolk and filled it with salt; and when I went to bed ate it shell and all, without speaking or drinking after it. We also wrote our lovers' names on bits of paper, and rolled them up in clay and put them into water; and the first that rose up was to be our Valentine. Would you think it? Mr. Blossom was my man. I lay abed and shut my eyes all the morning, till he came to our house, for I would not have seen another man before him for all the world." It was about this time, in the middle of the century, that the history of American valentines begins. The verses or messages of these originals were often as homely as the one received by this young girl. A certain simplicity clung to the style of the sketches, too, though they often displayed a compensatory taste and not a little art. Valentine Writers were imported from England from 1723 on, and many senders were willing merely to copy their verses from these professional models.

POLITICS AND GOVERNMENT; WAR;
DISASTERS; VITAL STATISTICS.

BOOKS; PAINTING; DRAMA;
ARCHITECTURE; SCULPTURE.

1755–1759

1755 July 9 **Gen. Braddock** mortally wounded when he and his troop of 1373 men fell in French and Indian ambush. Braddock had just crossed Monongahela R. on his way to attack Fort Duquesne. Washington assumed command of retreating army.

1755 Nov. 27 1st land in America purchased for **Jewish settlement.** Joseph Salvador bought 100,000 acres near Fort Ninety-Six, S.C.

1755, Nov. 30 **1st refugees** from French and Indian War, some 900 Acadian French, deported by English authorities from Nova Scotia, arrived in Maryland. Longfellow's poem, "Evangeline," is set against this background of exile.

1756 May 17 **England** and **France** formally declared war upon each other after almost 2 years of fighting.

1756 Aug. 14 French, under Gen. Montcalm, captured **Fort Oswego, N.Y.** Montcalm then rendered fort useless for military purposes and returned to Montreal.

1757 Jan. 11 **Alexander Hamilton** born at Charles Town, on Island of Nevis in West Indies. Anniversary of his birth is observed in nation's capital by Secretary of the Treasury, who places a wreath at base of Hamilton's statue.

1757 Aug. 9 **Fort William Henry** capitulated to French commanded by Montcalm. Many British in garrison were killed by Indian allies of French next day.

1758 April 28 **James Monroe,** 5th president, born in Monroe's Creek, Va.

1758 July 8 British and colonial troops beaten back at **Ticonderoga,** N.Y., by French under Gen. Montcalm. Nearly 2,000 of attacking force of 17,000 were killed or wounded.

1758 July 26 French at **Louisburg** surrendered to British under Adm. Bosca-

1755 According to legend, Dr. Richard Shuckburg, British army surgeon, wrote words of **"Yankee Doodle"** as satire on ragged American troops. More probably song was of folk origin among British soldiers. Adopted as favorite marching tune by American troops, "Yankee Doodle" quickly lost satirical aspect and was played at British surrender at Yorktown.

1755 Prophetic reference to destiny of **George Washington** made in sermon preached in Virginia by popular minister, Samuel Davis. At about time of General Braddock's defeat, he said: "I may point out to the public that heroic youth, Colonel Washington, whom I cannot but hope Providence has hitherto preserved in so signal a manner, for some important service to his country."

1756 **Oldest continuing newspaper in** America, *New Hampshire Gazette,* began publication in Portsmouth under editorship of Daniel Fowles.

1757 **Mount Vernon,** a one-and-a-half-story cottage acquired by George Washington, remodeled 1st time; remodeled and enlarged at least 3 times in next 30 years, probably in accordance with Washington's own designs. Result not as good as other Virginia mansions, but interesting, aside from historical associations, for its record of architectural growth.

1757 Oct. Most admired of early literary magazines was **The American Magazine,** which ran to Oct., 1758. Conducted "by a society of gentlemen," this Philadelphia publication printed choice articles on philosophy and science, as well as sprinkling of belles-lettres.

1758 **Mount Airy,** one of best houses of late Georgian period in Virginia, built near Richmond. Designed by John Ariss, most important architect in Virginia at time, it is more massive and more highly decorated than earlier Georgian homes.

SCIENCE; INDUSTRY; ECONOMICS; EDUCATION; RELIGION; PHILOSOPHY.

SPORTS; FASHIONS; POPULAR ENTERTAINMENT; FOLKLORE; SOCIETY.

1755–1759

1755 June 16 1st nonsectarian college in America, University of Pennsylvania, 1st chartered as College, Academy, and Charitable School in Philadelphia through efforts of Benjamin Franklin. 1st degrees were awarded in 1757.

1755 June 28 1st English-made vessel on Lake Ontario, schooner with 40-ft. keel, equipped with 14 oars and 12 swivels, launched from its berth.

1756 Rise of **rationalistic thinking** in American religion reflected in republication of *The Humble Inquiry into the Scripture Account of Jesus Christ* by Thomas Emlyn, first self-styled Unitarian minister in Great Britain.

1756 Through stage from Philadelphia to New York city organized by 4 waggoners. They used a "Jersey Wagon" without springs and traveled in relays. Journey by stage and boat could be made in 1 long day, but 3 days was usual.

1758 Two Penny Act passed by Virginia Assembly. Clergy and some public officials were, by the provisions of act, to receive regular salaries rather than proportionate shares of tobacco crop. Due to small size of tobacco crop, this act, in effect, cut into real income of designated parties by keeping them from selling tobacco on a demand market. It was, consequently, extremely unpopular. One affected clergyman was Rev. James Maury, with whom Thomas Jefferson, then 14, began that year to study. Maury had set up log cabin on his place where he added to his income by teaching school. Jefferson boarded with the family, was one in class of 5, paid tuition of £20 per year.

1758 School for **Negroes** established in Philadelphia under the auspices of the "Associates of Dr. Bray." Organization, founded by the Rev. Thomas Bray of Maryland in 1723, was Anglican missionary group closely linked to Society for Propagation of the Gospel in Foreign Parts.

1755 Jacob Bailey, Kingston, N.H., schoolteacher, recorded **scenes of rural frolic** in poem:

The chairs in wild disorder flew quite around the room.
Some threatened with firebrands, some brandished a broom,
While others, resolved to increase the uproar,
Lay tussling the girls in wide heaps on the floor.

1756 July 26 "Bosom Bottles" advertised in *Boston Evening Post*. They were small, beribboned glasses worn on stiff dresses of the period, filled with water, and containing flowers which served much the same function as corsages do today.

1757 Lewis Morris' famous horse, **American Childers,** won race around Beaver Pond in Jamaica, Long Island.

1757 1st street-lights appeared in Philadelphia on a small scale. Whale-oil lamps, specially designed by Benjamin Franklin, were installed on a few streets.

1758 Benjamin Franklin circulated famous parable on thrift in *Poor Richard's Almanack* which went:

A little neglect may breed mischief:
For the want of a nail the shoe was lost,
For the want of a shoe the horse was lost,
For the want of a horse the rider was lost,
For the want of a rider the battle was lost,
For the want of a battle the kingdom was lost—
And all for the want of a horseshoe nail.

This year he also composed: "Early to bed and early to rise, Makes a man, healthy, wealthy and wise."

1758 July Famous legend of **"Windham Frogs"** began in Eastern, Conn. In-

71

wen and Gen. Amherst after 48-day siege. Almost 6000 prisoners taken.

1758 Aug. 27 British, under Col. John Bradstreet, captured **Fort Frontenac.**

1758 Nov. 25 British forces drove French from **Fort Duquesne,** which they renamed Pittsburgh.

1759 July 26 French abandoned **Ticonderoga** as Gen. Amherst threatened siege. French commander Bourlamaque withdrew to Crown Point, N.Y.

1759 Sept. 18 French defeated at battle of **Quebec** in which both Gen. Wolfe and Gen. Montcalm were killed.

1759 Probably **1st secular song** by a native American composer, Francis Hopkinson's *My Days Have Been So Wonderous Free.* Poem is Thomas Parnell's. It was not published until 20th century.

1759 May 31 Religious, especially Baptist, opposition to theater seen in Pennsylvania law forbidding **performance of plays** under penalty of £500.

1759 Dec. 13 **1st music store,** that of Michael Hillegas, in Philadelphia.

1760–1764

Estimated colonial **population**—1,610,000.

1760 Aug. 8 **Fort Loudoun,** Tenn., capitulated to Cherokees. Capt. Demere surrendered under condition that permitted his men to retreat unimpeded. Next day garrison was massacred by Indians while retreating to Fort Prince George.

1760 Sept. 8 French surrendered at **Montreal** to Gen. Amherst. After defeat of this last French stronghold Canada was split into 3 parts: Quebec, Montreal, and Three Rivers.

1760 Nov. 29 **Detroit** was surrendered to Maj. Robert Rogers by French Commander Belêtre.

1760 Dec. Governors of frontier colonies were instructed to deny **land grants** which encroached on Indian territories.

1761 Feb. 24 Strong colonial opposition to English rule inaugurated by **James Otis** in his controversial political speech against writs of assistance before Supreme Court of Massachusetts. Later (1764) he published his famous pamphlet, *The Rights of the British Colonies Asserted and Proved,* in which he stated that power ultimately derives from the people.

1763 Beginnings of a **free Negro tradition** in New England reflected in presence

c1760 Painstaking care in realistic portraits by **John Copley** revealed in his study of *Colonel Epes Sargent* and his *Mrs. Thomas Boylston.* Colonial sitters posed for hours on end for many days. In contrast Sir Joshua Reynolds wrote of his craft in England: "A portrait requires in general three sittings, about an hour and a half each, but if the sitter chooses it the face could be begun and finished the same day. When the face is finished the rest is done without troubling the sitter."

1761 *Urania,* collection of psalms set to music by James Lyon, published at Philadelphia. It was **1st music book** by native American. Lyon achieved considerable popularity with his songs and other compositions, although his duties as Presbyterian minister required him to spend most of his life in Nova Scotia and Maine.

1761 Benjamin Franklin, accomplished performer on guitar and harp, invented **"Glassychord,"** later called "Armonica." It was based on musical glasses which had been introduced in Europe 20 years before. Instead of filling glasses with water, Franklin made them of different sizes and balanced them on spindles which were rotated by foot action, like a spinning wheel. Thus performer could reach wide range of notes and play more rapid passages. In-

SCIENCE; INDUSTRY; ECONOMICS; EDUCATION; RELIGION; PHILOSOPHY.

SPORTS; FASHIONS; POPULAR ENTERTAINMENT; FOLKLORE; SOCIETY.

1758 Aug. **1st Indian reservation** in North America established by New Jersey colonial assembly. Reservation founded on 3,000 acre tract called Edge Pillock in Burlington County, at site of present village of Indian Mills. About 100 Indians, chiefly Unamis, settled on the reservation and attempted to set up a self-sustaining community.

1759 Thomas and Richard Penn of Philadelphia, Pa., established Presbyterian Ministers Fund, **1st recorded life insurance company** in U.S.

habitants were awakened by tremendous roaring and clashing, which drove them in nightdress from their houses where they stood until dawn waiting for final day of judgment. In morning they discovered that two armies of bullfrogs had fought for possession of a pond. Each side had invoked a leader, Col. Dyer and Col. Elderkin respectively, 2 well-known lawyers. Inhabitants swore they heard these names amid roaring and hubbub.

1760–1764

c1760 Benjamin Franklin devised **1st bifocal lenses.** 20 years later Franklin wrote to a friend, explaining that he had become tired of carrying 2 pairs of spectacles and had ordered a pair made with 2 kinds of lenses cut in the same circle of glass.

c1760 Great American contribution to transportation was **Conestoga wagon,** which 1st came into considerable use about this time. Developed in Pennsylvania where roads were somewhat better than in other colonies, wagon had these advantages: broad wheel tires, curved bottom to prevent shifting of freight, strong hemp cover stretched over 6 or 8 curved bows. They could carry 4 to 6 tons of freight.

1761 John Winthrop led expedition to Newfoundland to observe **transit of Venus** across the sun. Harvard College sponsored the expedition for the specific purpose of gathering data on the parallax of the sun. The years of the transits were 1761 and 1769. Winthrop composed 2 poems which commemorate the occasion and published them in *Pietas et Gratulatio.*

1761 One of **earliest known American cookbooks** is *The Complete Housewife; or, Accomplished Gentlewoman's Companion; Being a Collection of Several Hundred of*

1760 Mar. 25 **Thomas Jefferson a** boarding student at William and Mary College in Williamsburg, Va. Students petitioned faculty for a change in menus provided by housekeeper, Isabella Cocke. They seem not to have minded particularly being served leftovers ("scraps"), so long as everyone got the same kind of hash and the same dishes appeared on every table. They requested both salt and fresh meat for dinner and desserts, either pies or puddings, 3 times a week including Sundays.

1761 June 10 Moral preoccupation of times seen in title of play presented at Newport, R.I., by Douglass Company: *Moral Dialogues in 5 parts, Depicting the Evil Effects of Jealousy and other Bad Passions, and Proving that Happiness can only Spring from the Pursuit of Virtue.* **Othello** was play. Advertisement for performance read: ". . . Commencement at 7, conclusion at half past 10, in order that every spectator may go home at a sober hour and reflect upon what he has seen before he retires to rest." This description failed to disarm Puritan critics of theater. After few performances in Newport and Providence, Rhode Island Assembly enacted legislation barring theatrical performances in colony with penalty of £100 for each actor.

of 5214 Negroes in Massachusetts' population of 235,810. Most of them worked at menial jobs in shipyards and homes.

1763 Extreme presentation of Tory point of view were sermons of **Jonathan Boucher** between 1763 and 1775, published in 1797 under title, *A View of the Causes and Consequences of the American Revolution.* Believing in divine authority of government, he found it necessary to preach at times with a pair of loaded pistols before him.

1763 Feb. 10 **French and Indian War** came to end with signing of Treaty of Paris by England, France, and Spain. France ceded her Canadian claims to England, as well as Louisiana east of Mississippi R., excluding New Orleans, and Spain gave up Florida for return of Cuba and Philippines.

1763 June 4 Deadly game of lacrosse played by two enormous teams of Indians outside **Fort Michilimackinak** at what is now Mackinaw City, Mich. When English garrison troops manning fort had gathered to watch game, Indians seized concealed weapons and attacked, slaughtering all occupants and burning fort to ground.

strument achieved considerable popularity, and "Armonica" concerts were given in London and Paris as well as in U.S.

1762 **1st music society** in America, St. Cecilia Society, founded in Charleston, S.C. In Europe, Charleston was considered chief cultural center of pre-Revolutionary colonies, and many artists, actors, and musicians chose to settle in Charleston when they emigrated.

1763 Moravians of Pennsylvania published collection of **hymns** translated into language of the Delaware Indians.

1764 Significant development in harmonic quality of **psalmody** in American religious services effected by publication of Josiah Flagg's *A Collection of the Best Psalm Tunes.*

1764 One of papers to stay longest in existence, **Connecticut Courant,** began publication in Hartford as weekly. It continued as daily until 1940.

1765–1769

1765 **Establishment Act** passed by Anglican majority in North Carolina Assembly supplemented Vestry Act of 1715 by fixing salary of ministers at a little over £133 per annum, and placing control of ministerial appointments in hands of governor. This law was 1st of its nature in North Carolina to receive approval of British authorities. Power of appointment granted to governor antagonized local parishes, causing resistance to ministers appointed by governor and general diminution in prestige of Church of England in North Carolina.

1765 Terms **"Sons of Liberty,"** 1st used in English Parliament by Colonel Isaac Barre, one of few English opponents of Stamp Act. Later that year, clubs formed

1765 Death of **Joseph Badger,** 1st American painter to utilize realism in his portrayals of colonial figures. As Revolution approached, tendency to imitate English nobility in painting diminished in favor of simple, native representation.

1765 William Paterson, Princeton College student, founded Well Meaning Society, later called **Cliosophic Society.** This is thought to have been 1st college arts and letters society in U.S.

1765 Portrait of *John Hancock* by **Copley** reveals simple, unsophisticated style of native talent. Although Copley departed from his style upon settling in London, his impact upon young American artists was great. Their unpretentious portraits formed a characteristic school. This year he also

the most Approved Receipts in Cookery, Pastry, etc., by (Mrs.) E. Smith. It was published in New York city.

1763 **1st steamboat** built by Henry Williams, who tried his invention, inspired by James Watt of England, on the Conestoga Creek, Lancaster, Pa. Although tests were a failure, they helped encourage Fulton and his experiments.

1763 Tendency away from strict Calvinistic approach to God seen in 2 published sermons of **Jonathan Mayhew**, *On the Nature, Extent, and Perfection of the Divine Goodness.* Mayhew turned away from conception of God wielding arbitrary power and characterized by spirit of anger.

1763 Significant social change in colonial America caused by British expulsion of **French Jesuit missionaries** from trans-Appalachian area, thus depriving French settlers of effective leadership.

1764 **Spinning and carding machinery** invented by James Davenport of Pennsylvania. On Feb. 14 patent was granted and Davenport founded the Globe Mills in Philadelphia. In 1796 installed plant in Kensington, Pa.

1762 May 3 Commentary on **colonial theater** made by notice in playbill of Douglass Company: "A Pistole reward will be given to whoever can discover the person who was so very rude as to throw eggs from the gallery upon the stage last Monday, by which the cloaths of some ladies and gentlemen were spoiled and the performance in some measure interrupted. . . ."

1763 Oct. **Vermont** christened this month. Standing on a high tor, the Rev. Dr. Peters pronounces: "We have here met on the rock Etam, standing on Mount Pisgah . . . to dedicate and consecrate this extensive wilderness to *God manifested in human flesh,* and to give it a new name, worthy of the Athenians and ancient Spartans; which new name is Verd-mont, in token that her mountains and hills shall be ever green, and shall never die."

1764 **1st minister of Dutch Reformed Church to preach in English,** the Rev. Doctor Laidlie, arrived in Manhattan in 1764 and soon tried to have dancing banned in gay Dutch colony. He was unsuccessful; Dutch continued most of their festivals and frequent supper dances.

1765–1769

1765 **1st chocolate** manufactured in North America produced at Dorchester Lower Mills on Neponset R., Mass., by John Harmon. In 1780 plant came into possession of Dr. James Baker, who had sponsored Harmon, and from Baker's business evolved the world famous Walter Baker & Co., Ltd., chocolate manufacturers.

1765 **Latin schools** maintained in at least 48 of 140 Massachusetts communities with a population in excess of 100 families.

1765 May 3 Drs. John Morgan and William Shippen, Jr., organized medical department in College of Philadelphia as **1st medical school** in Colonies. Later be-

1765 **Colonial curriculum** for wealthy young Southerners described by William Kean, director of Queen Anne County School in Virginia. He instructed "in Latin, Greek, Hebrew, the Grecian and Roman Histories and Antiquities . . . reading, writing, arithmetic-vulgar, decimal, and duodecimal-geometry, planometry, trigonometry, surveying, gauging, Italian bookkeeping, navigation and the proportions of the horizontal dials."

1765 Outside New England most **marriages** of genteel folk performed with marriage license by special permission of a magistrate, instead of posting of banns as was customary still in New England.

1765 **Education for women** in colonial America rooted in practical, as illustrated

POLITICS AND GOVERNMENT; WAR; DISASTERS; VITAL STATISTICS.

BOOKS; PAINTING; DRAMA; ARCHITECTURE; SCULPTURE.

in Boston and elsewhere in colonies called "The Sons of Liberty" and in some localities "Liberty Boys."

1765 Mar. 22 **Stamp Act** passed requiring purchase of revenue stamps to be affixed to newspapers, pamphlets, almanacs, legal documents, playing cards, and dice. British hoped to raise £60,000 with this tax.

1765 May 29 **Patrick Henry** attacked Stamp Act in Virginia House of Burgesses, declaring that only colonial legislatures could impose tax on colonies. Shouts of treason interrupted Henry's speech, to which he made his famous reply: "If this be treason, make the most of it."

1765 Oct. 7 **Stamp Act Congress** met at City Hall, New York city, in answer to circular letter from Massachusetts House of Representatives; 28 delegates from 9 colonies attended to organize united resistance to Stamp Act. Resolutions adopted by this congress ultimately led to repeal of act.

1765 Oct. 19 **Stamp Act Congress** adopted 13 resolutions protesting against taxes imposed by act, and resolved not to import any goods which required payment of duty. This led to Petition of London Merchants in 1766 urging repeal of act and stressing injury to English trade caused by colonial policy of nonimportation.

1765 Nov. 1 Rising protest over Stamp Tax coincides with preparations for **Guy Fawkes Day** in New York. Colonists executed and buried "Liberty" and then proceeded to break windows, burn an effigy of governor, mock at soldiers, and loot homes of officials. Riot was gradually quelled by fearful citizens.

1767 Mar. 15 **Andrew Jackson,** 7th president, born at Cureton's Pond, N.C.

1767 June 29 **Townshend Revenue Act** passed by Parliament. It required that colonists pay import duty on tea, glass, painter's colors, oil, lead, and paper. The £40,000 that act was expected to yield was to pay salaries of royal governors and judges in colonies. In Feb., 1768, the

completed his *Portrait of Lady Wentworth.* 1768 saw his portrait of *John Amory* finished.

1766 **St. Paul's Chapel,** oldest church surviving in Manhattan, built as subsidiary to Trinity Church.

1766 1st play to be written upon an American subject was *Ponteach, or the Savages of America* by Maj. **Robert Rogers.** It concerned itself with relations of Indians and white men. It was printed in London.

1766 Oct. **1st permanent commercial theater** in America built by Douglass Company on South Street, Philadelphia, and was called Southwark Theater. Building was demolished in 1921.

1767 *Plain Tunes,* a collection of compositions by **Andrew Law,** published. Son of the governor of Connecticut, Law cultivated music assiduously and was "better music booster" of his day. He introduced system of musical notation which used no staff lines and employed notes of different shapes to signify pitch.

1767 Probably **1st libretto published** in America was *The Disappointment: or The Force of Credulity*, a light opera by Andrew Barton. It was printed in New York city.

1767 Apr. 24 One of earliest American dramatists, **Thomas Godfrey,** had his play *The Prince of Parthia* performed at the Southwark Theater in Philadelphia. This was probably the **1st American play professionally performed.**

1768 Commemorative bowl molded in silver by **Paul Revere** presented to 92 legislators in Massachusetts House of Representatives who resisted royal authority in protesting to King George III about restrictive trade measures.

1768 July 18 Probably **1st American patriotic song,** *The Liberty Song,* appeared in *Boston Gazette.* It had just been published in Boston, and was on sale at London Book Store.

1769 **Whitehall,** impressive late Georgian mansion, built in Anne Arundel

came at the University of Pennsylvania School of Medicine.

1766 **Stage coach** which ran between New York and Philadelphia advertised itself as a "flying-machine, a good stage-wagon set on springs." Trips lasted 2 days in good weather.

1766 **1st Methodist society** in America formed in New York city by Philip Embury, preacher from Ireland. At this time Methodism was a movement within the Church of England.

1766 Nov. 10 **Rutgers University** 1st chartered as Queen's College in New Brunswick, N.J. Established under Dutch Reformed auspices, Queen's College renamed Rutgers College in 1825 and Rutgers University in 1924. 1st degrees awarded in 1774.

1767 **1st planetarium** in America built by David Rittenhouse of Philadelphia. Rittenhouse, noted clock maker, plotted orbits of Venus and Mercury in 1769.

1768 A Dr. Otto of Bethlehem, Pa., presented to the American Philosophical Association the **1st cottonseed oil** made in America. He submitted samples and said he had obtained 9 pints of oil from a bushel and a half of seed.

1768 **1st botany professor** in U.S. was Adam Kuhn, who gave his 1st course at College of Philadelphia in 1768.

1768 Apr. 5 John Cruger elected 1st president of the **New York Chamber of Commerce** at founding meeting held in New York city. Organization was probably 1st of its kind in U.S.

1768 Oct. 30 **1st Methodist Church** in America dedicated. It was the Wesley Chapel on John St. in New York city. Church was rebuilt in 1817 and again in 1840.

1769 Famous American **glassmaking plant** opened at Manheim, Penn., by Henry William Stiegel, whose name became identified with a type of American glassware that reflected a German tradition.

by advertisement of Philadelphia teacher, who promised to teach young ladies to spell and point with propriety. He advised them not to be discouraged in their pursuit of knowledge by their age or fear of obtaining a husband, since he had given "the finishing stroke" to several New York ladies who married shortly afterwards.

1765–1775 **Horse racing** in Maryland entered its greatest period of fashion and popularity under Gov. Robert Eden. Course at Annapolis was one of best in U.S.

1766 Gloucester Fox Hunting Club, the **1st regularly organized fox-hunting group** in U.S., founded in Philadelphia. Most of its hunting was done across Delaware R. in Gloucester co., N.J.

1766 Some **games popular** in New York indicated by James Rivington's advertisement that he imported battledores, shuttlecocks, cricket balls, pellets, racquets for tennis and fives, and backgammon tables.

1767 Dec. 21 One of earliest **"tall tales"**—a type which was to flood literary scene in 19th century—appeared in *Boston Evening-Post*. It tells how Josiah Prescott of Deerfield, while hunting, spied a moose 100 yards away and shot it dead. Immediately 2 more appeared and his aim was perfect; then another suffered same fate at end of his gun. "One of the old ones was ten feet high and ten feet long; the other eight feet high and ten feet long. . . . After this extraordinary exploit was over, he was joined by a partner, who being at a little distance, heard the guns, came up to his assistance; and in going home he got help to dress the Mooses: A wild Cat they also killed on their return. This is a fact."

1768 According to New England legend **army of caterpillars** invaded both sides of Connecticut R. this year—3 mi. in front and 2 in depth—and in spite of efforts of 1000 frantic men, devoured everything for space of 100 miles. Then they marched into river and drowned, poison-

House of Representatives of Massachusetts sent letter to other colonial legislatures calling upon them to join with her in common action against duties. British ordered letter repudiated and threatened to dissolve any assembly in sympathy with Massachusetts. In Virginia, burgesses responded with declaration that they had exclusive right of taxing and, while protesting loyalty to king, entered into agreement not to import goods on which Parliament raised revenues and, after certain date, to stop buying long list of embargoed items.

1767 July 11 **John Quincy Adams,** 6th president, born in Braintree, Mass.

1768 June 14 Old South Church in Boston became scene of **largest mass meeting** ever held in New England. Meeting forwarded petition to governor demanding that British vessel which was hindering navigation in harbor be removed.

County, Md. It was equipped with only known interior water closet in colonial U.S.

1769 1st known American sculptor, Mrs. **Patricia Lovell Wright** of Bordentown, N.J., left America for London. Earlier she did bust of *Thomas Penn* in Independence Hall, Philadelphia.

1769 **1st of California missions,** San Diego de Alcala, established by Fr. Junipero Serra, Franciscan friar. Within 15 years he established 8 others along Camino Real (King's Highway), northernmost at San Francisco Bay. These were 1st permanent settlements in California.

1769 Sept. 18 Possibly **1st spinet** made in America, by John Harris of Boston. Some have said that Gustavus Hesselius had made spinets as early as 1743 in Philadelphia.

1770–1774

Estimated colonial **population**—2,205,000.

1770 Mar. 5   7 colonists killed by British soldiers, who were stoned by mob of men and boys. This incident became known as **Boston Massacre.**

1770 Apr. 12   **Townshend Acts** repealed through efforts of Lord Frederick North. Realizing that colonies were being pushed too far, Parliament was persuaded to withdraw all Townshend duties except that on tea. Colonists responded by lifting their embargo on goods shipped from England, thus improving relations between the two countries. Tax on tea, however, still remained as did colonists' embargo on it.

1772 **Watauga Association,** formed to govern area outside normal jurisdiction of any colony, became 1st independent local government in North America. Land was originally ceded by Six Nations to English in what is now Tennessee. Not knowing what else to do with it, British turned area over to an elected committee of 5, who

1770 *The New England Psalm Singer, or American Chorister,* containing psalms, anthems, and canons by **William Billings** of Boston, published. Billings, most popular composer among native-born Americans of 2nd half of 18th century, published several later collections, including: *The Singing Master's Assistant* (1778); *Music in Miniature* (1779); and *The Suffolk Harmony* (1786). Among his most famous hymn tunes were "Majesty," "Chester," and "The Bird," still sung in 1950 by rural congregations.

1770 1st house at **Monticello** built by Thomas Jefferson from his own designs. Shows his great interest in pure classicism, in the temple forms of Greek and Roman architecture, especially as evidenced by large porticoes. Later Monticello was completely rebuilt and enlarged upon these principles, as it is seen today. Plans for Monticello absorbed Jefferson's attention from early manhood. Foundations were dug in 1769, the year of his 1st election to House of Burgesses. It proved a project

SCIENCE; INDUSTRY; ECONOMICS; EDUCATION; RELIGION; PHILOSOPHY.

SPORTS; FASHIONS; POPULAR ENTERTAINMENT; FOLKLORE; SOCIETY.

1769 Steady hold of **religious tradition** in America's scientific community reflected in conclusion accepted at Harvard that reptiles in America were descendants of Noah's creatures.

1769 Strong ties between American Lutherans and their German brethren in Europe established with arrival in Pennsylvania of **J. H. C. Helmuth,** distinguished theologian.

1769 **Anthracite coal** 1st used in forge in Wilkes-Barre, Pa. It had been discovered as early as 1762 by Connecticut pioneers in Pennsylvania. It was little used until beginning of 19th century.

ing waters. Only arrival of millions of pigeons, which could be killed by a stick, saved Vermont from starvation.

1769 June 7 **Daniel Boone** caught his 1st glimpse of Kentucky after long trek by way of Cumberland Gap, early gateway to West. Date is now celebrated by Kentucky State Historical Society as Boone Day.

1769 Nov. 30 Following advertisement appeared in Pennsylvania *Gazette* of Philadelphia: "The Orchestra, on Opera Nights, will be assisted by some musical Persons, who as they have no View but to contribute to the Entertainment of the Public, certainly claim a Protection from any Manner of Insult." Reference is to widespread 18th-century custom of filling out inadequately staffed professional **orchestras** of time with "gentlemen amateurs," wealthy performers who donated their services out of love for music.

1770–1774

1770 **1st American chemistry textbook,** *A Syllabus of a Course of Lectures on Chemistry* by Benjamin Rush, published in Philadelphia, Pa. Rush, who taught at the College of Philadelphia, held **1st chemistry professorship** in America.

1770 **College of Charleston** established. Charter granted in 1785 and classes began in 1790. In 1837 it became 1st municipal college in U.S.

1770 Earliest production of **porcelain** in America successfully effected by Bonnin and Morris of Philadelphia.

1772 **1st foundry for casting type** in America completed; but it failed to make colonial papers self-sufficient without imports from England, with consequence that Revolutionary War, with its isolation of colonies from English production, seriously disrupted journalism in America.

1773 **1st commercial roster** put out by Robert Aitken of Philadelphia, Pa. It was entitled *Aitken's General Register and the*

c1770 Reappearance of **"tower"** (see 1710) as popular form of hairdress among rich colonial women, this time in highly exaggerated form: After being frizzled, hair was piled up high over pads until there was a mountain of curls. It was then greased with pomatum, powdered, and finally decked with all kinds of paraphernalia—beads, jewels, ribbons, lace, feathers, and flowers. From tower thick false curls dangled alongside cheeks. Sometimes an ostrich feather a yard high flew above tower. Hair-dressing took hours and hairdresser was in great demand.

1771 **Umbrella** as protection against sun was introduced in Philadelphia amidst storm of ridicule. Newspapers considered it effeminate. Doctors, however, recommended it as means of keeping off vertigo, epilepsy, sore eyes, fevers, etc.

1771 Mar. 15 Unusual **marriage** recorded in *Virginia Gazette:* "Yesterday was married, in Henrico, Mr. William Carter, aged 23, to Mrs. Sarah Ellyson, Relict of Mr. Gerard Ellyson, deceased, aged 85,

POLITICS AND GOVERNMENT; WAR;
DISASTERS; VITAL STATISTICS.

BOOKS; PAINTING; DRAMA;
ARCHITECTURE; SCULPTURE.

ruled according to the Articles of Watauga Association.

1773 Feb. 9 William Henry Harrison, 9th president, born at Berkeley, Va.

1773 Apr. 27 Tea Act passed by Parliament. This sparked chain of events that led directly to conflict ahead. Act was designed to save East India Co. from bankruptcy by remitting all British duties on tea while retaining tax on tea exported to America. This allowed company to cut back its price and undersell colonial competition. Resulting monopoly all but destroyed American merchants.

1773 Dec. 16 Group of men, dressed as Indians, boarded English ships in Boston Harbor and destroyed their cargo of tea valued at £18,000. This incident became famous as **"Boston Tea Party."**

1774 Mar. 31 1st of **Intolerable Acts** passed. They were reprisals by British as punishment to Massachusetts for "Boston Tea Party." 1st closed port of Boston until payment was made for tea destroyed by "Party." Other 3 acts were: (1) **Massachusetts Government Act,** which forbade public meetings unless sanctioned by governor; (2) **Administration of Justice Act,** under which any British officials accused of capital offenses were to be transferred from Massachusetts to England or another colony for trial; and (3) **The Quartering Act** which forced residents of Massachusetts to house and feed British troops.

1774 May 17 1st call for **intercolonial congress** issued by Rhode Island. Appeal was echoed almost immediately by Philadelphia and New York, and resulted in 1st Continental Congress.

1774 June 2 Old **Quartering Act** extended. It required that colonial homes be made available to soldiers wherever existing quarters were inadequate.

1774 June 22 Quebec Act passed, which extended boundaries of Quebec to northwest Ohio.

1774 Sept. 5 1st **Continental Congress** met in Philadelphia with all of 13 colonies

which occupied him the rest of his life. The work was difficult. There were woods to be cleared, land to be leveled, water to be carried. A year later "southeast pavilion" was finished. Jefferson lived there until after his marriage.

1771 Benjamin Franklin began writing his famous *Autobiography,* which he took up again in 1784, 1788–89. Work carries story of his life up to 1759 and was originally designed to inform his son, William, then governor of N.J., of his background. Contains wealth of remarks on religion, literary life, utilitarian philosophy, besides colorful account of Franklin in Philadelphia, Boston, London.

1772 1st life-size portrait of George Washington painted by Charles Willson Peale, versatile colonial from Maryland. He could make clocks, harnesses; stuff birds; extract and repair teeth, etc. Washington is shown at age of 40 as colonel, in same uniform he had worn during French and Indian War.

1773 Eminent cabinet maker of colonial period, **Thomas Burling,** began his career as craftsman in New York city.

1774 Tory viewpoint expressed in anonymous play attributed to Southerner, *A Dialogue Between a Southern Delegate and His Spouse on His Return from the Grand Continental Congress.* Dialogue is sharp satire on workings of Congress. Other Tory dramas were *The Americans Roused* (1775) by Jonathan Sewall, anonymous *Battle of Brooklyn* (1776), *The Blockheads* (1782).

1774 American reception of **Goethe's** *Werther,* written this year, was phenomenal. Wertherism spread wildly through colonies, occasioning countless warnings against its effects in periodicals and books. In one novel of time hero dies, holding *Werther* in his hands.

1774 Jan. 1st American magazine to use illustrations often, *Royal American Magazine.* Paul Revere contributed series of engravings attacking British oppression of colonies.

| SCIENCE; INDUSTRY; ECONOMICS; EDUCATION; RELIGION; PHILOSOPHY. | SPORTS; FASHIONS; POPULAR ENTERTAINMENT; FOLKLORE; SOCIETY. |

Gentleman's and Tradesman's Complete Annual Account Book, and Calendar, for the Pocket or Desk, for the year of our Lord, 1773.

1773 **Oliver Evans'** 1st successful experiments in steam propulsion begun. Inventor of cylinder flue boiler for high-pressure steam engines, Evans demonstrated **1st practical steamboat** on Schuylkill R. off Philadelphia in 1804.

1773 John Winthrop, astronomer and mathematician, received **1st honorary LL.D. granted by Harvard College.**

1773 **Mental hospital,** oldest institution of its kind in U.S., opened at Williamsburg, Va. Originally called Public Hospital for Persons of Insane and Disordered Minds, it later became Eastern Lunatic Asylum and is called now the Eastern State Hospital.

1773 Last year in which **Harvard students** were listed in catalogue according to their social position.

1773 Jan. 12 **1st museum** established in American colonies, at Charleston, S.C. In 1915 it was incorporated as Charleston Museum.

1773 Feb. 27 **Christ Church** in Alexandria, Va., completed after 6 years of extravagant construction at total cost of $4070. George Washington purchased a pew for himself and his family at cost of about $100. He also donated handsome brass chandelier to church.

1773 July 14 **1st annual conference of American Methodists** convened at St. George's Church, Philadelphia, Pa.

1774 Aug. 6 Ann Lee, known as "Mother Ann," arrived in America from England with small band of followers. She was leader of schismatic group of **"Shakers,"** whose official designation was United Society of Believers in Christ's Second Coming. After brief imprisonment for treason during Revolution, she established her

a sprightly old Tit, with three Thousand Pounds Fortune." Publication of property "value" of bride was common throughout colonies. As for marrying late, many widows survived 3 and 4 husbands.

1772 Nearly 100 **private carriages** in Philadelphia, indicating it as center of high society.

1773 Virginia diarist sadly noted arrival of batch of **women's stays** (corsets): "[They] are produced upwards so high that we can have scarce any view at all of the Ladies' Snowy Bosoms; and on the contrary, they are extended downwards so low that whenever Ladies who wear them, either young or old, have occasion to walk, the motion necessary for Walking, must, I think, cause a disagreeable Friction of some part of the body against the lower edge of the Stays which is hard and unyielding." Stays were worn by old and young. Little girls of 10 were forced to girdle their bodies.

1773 1st large-scale **street lighting** began in Boston, under direction of John Hancock. 310 street lamps installed; kept lighted in evenings from Oct. 1 to May 1.

1773 Mar. Rioting and wild festivities that marked **New Year's Day** in New York somewhat curbed by Legislature, which outlawed firing of guns and explosives. New Year's Day had been most important holiday in colony during Dutch rule when it was traditional day of visiting and exchanging of gifts. English took over Dutch customs completely, adding turkey shoot to day's festivities.

1774 **Ban** on horse racing, cockfighting, gambling, and theatrical exhibitions recommended by Continental Congress mainly as austerity measure. But attitude against these diversions persisted well after end of War.

1774 **Bull baiting** scheduled for every Thursday afternoon at 3 P.M. on Tower Hill in New York, according to early advertisement.

but Georgia represented. Peyton Randolph was elected president and Charles Thompson, secretary.

1774 Oct. 14 Declaration of Rights, consisting of 10 resolutions on the rights of the colonists, including rights to "life, liberty, and property," adopted by 1st Continental Congress at Philadelphia, Pa.

1774 Nov. 17 Philadelphia Troop of Light Horse, one of earliest revolutionary military groups established in colonies, founded by 26 patriots of Philadelphia after meeting of First General Continental Congress. Troop later became The First Troop Philadelphia City Cavalry, under which name it still exists.

1774 Dec. 14 1st military encounter of Revolution occurred. It was *not* the battle of Lexington. On the report (news was carried by Paul Revere) that the British intended to station a garrison at Portsmouth, N.H., Maj. John Sullivan led a band of militia to Fort William and Mary, broke into its arsenal, and carried off a store of arms and ammunition. Neither side suffered casualties.

1774 Mar. 10 1st documentary reference to appearance of **"Stars and Stripes"** was in *Boston Journal* of Isaiah Thomas. Insert reads: "The American ensign now sparkles a star which shall shortly flame wide from the skies." Actually stripes had been used earlier in colonial flags.

1774 June. John Copley, 1st great American painter, left successful practice in Boston and sailed to England. Enjoyed tremendous success in London, doing some of his finest work there: *The Death of Lord Chatham* (c1780), *Siege of Gibraltar* (1790), portraits of royal family, and famous *Family Picture* of his wife and children.

1774 Oct. 20 Theater during Revolution at standstill due to order of Continental Congress that colonies "discountenance and discourage all horse racing and all kinds of gaming, cock fighting, exhibitions of shows, plays, and other expensive diversions and entertainments." Hallam company, popular performers, emigrated to West Indies for duration of war.

1775–1779

1775 Jan. 11 1st Jew to hold elective post in New World was Francis Salvador. A plantation owner from the Ninety-Sixth District, he served in South Carolina Provincial Congress. On July 31, 1776, he was killed in a skirmish, thus being 1st Jew to die for American independence.

1775 Mar. 23 Standing before 2nd Virginia convention held in Richmond, **Patrick Henry** delivered his immortal speech against arbitrary rule of England, closing with memorable words, "Give me liberty or give me death."

1775 Apr. 14 The Society for the Relief of Free Negroes Unlawfully Held in Bondage, the **1st abolition society,** organized at Philadelphia, Pa., by Benjamin Franklin and Benjamin Rush.

1775 Apr. 19 Battle of Lexington in Massachusetts. During these 1st shots of

c1775 Influence of Copley and his bent toward **realism in portraiture** is seen in portrait of *Roger Sherman,* by Ralph Earl (1755–1801). Subject, self-made man who had risen from simple shoemaker to leader in Revolution, depicted sitting in hard wooden chair, stiff and ungainly. He is epitome of Puritan vigor and intransigence.

1775 2 cantos of **John Trumbull's** satire on American Tories in Revolution, *M'Fingal,* appeared. He labored 7 more years on poem and published it complete in 1782. Very derivative and extremely popular, work resembled *Hudibras* and Churchill's *The Ghost.*

1775 **1st note of romanticism** is said to have been struck by Copley in his painting *Brook Watson and the Shark,* depicting naked boy attacked by shark while his

SCIENCE; INDUSTRY; ECONOMICS; EDUCATION; RELIGION; PHILOSOPHY.

headquarters at New Lebanon, N.Y., and preached so forcefully that at time of her death in 1784 there were Shaker communities throughout northern states. The religion of the Shakers had, from the beginning, centered about a public confession of sins and preparations for the second coming of Christ. Ann Lee continued to profess these tenets, but added her own strictures against marriage and sex and, finally, against war, bearing arms, and oath-taking. Both in England and America she was discouraged by the authorities and the hagiography which was composed by her disciples after her death made much of these persecutions and tribulations as it does of the miraculous manner of her deliverance from her tormentors. In her lifetime Ann claimed that she had received many visions which prompted her along the way which she was to take. It was such a vision that, in 1774, told her that she should go to America.

SPORTS; FASHIONS; POPULAR ENTERTAINMENT; FOLKLORE; SOCIETY.

1774 **1st hunting scene** engraved and published in colonies appeared at head of "The Hill Tops, A New Hunting Song," in *Royal American Magazine* in Boston. Scene pictured death of stag.

1774 May Society in Virginia strictly followed British customs to point where opening of Assembly at Williamsburg marked by publication of **code of etiquette** by court herald. This code regulated society of community.

1774 "Marcolini period" of celebrated **porcelain** factory in Dresden, Germany, begins. Count Marcolini assumed management of Dresden plant. He gave his name to the porcelain products of next two generations. These pieces were in the mainstream of neo-classic style of era, began to appear in American trade after the Revolution, exerted strong influence on products of domestic potters. Finest American porcelain continued to be imports from centers in Germany, England and Holland.

1775–1779

1775 Feb. 22 **1st joint stock manufacturing company** in America established to promote production and distribution of textile products as "American Manufactory of Woolens, Linens, and Cottons." Shares sold on subscription basis at £10 apiece.

1775 Mar. 10 Widely used path of early pioneers blazed by **Daniel Boone** when he set out from Fort Wautaga on trek to mouth of Kentucky River at Otter Creek, where he established fort and terminal station called Boonesborough.

1775 July 25 Dr. Benjamin Church became **1st surgeon general of the Continental Army.** On Oct. 4, 1775, with Gen. Washington presiding, Church was court-martialed for having held "criminal correspondence with the enemy." He was sentenced to life imprisonment, but because of

1775 Appeal by Continental Congress for 13,000 **winter coats** for Continental Army answered by thousands of housewives throughout colonies. Workmanship was generally of such high order that many troops chose to accept coats rather than their bounty. Names of these troops and makers of their coats are still listed in many New England communities on what is called a "Coat Roll."

1775 Town of Forks of Tar River, N.C., became 1st American community to take name of **Washington** in honor of commander of Continental Army.

1775 Cherokee Indians in Florida played **lacrosse** with deerskin ball stuffed hard with deer's hair and bats 2 feet long with deerskin thongs, according to description by James Adair. Game usually played for very high stakes between two large

POLITICS AND GOVERNMENT; WAR; DISASTERS; VITAL STATISTICS.

BOOKS; PAINTING; DRAMA; ARCHITECTURE; SCULPTURE.

the Revolutionary War 8 of 60 Minutemen were killed and 10 wounded.

1775 May 10 **Ticonderoga, N.Y.,** taken by American forces under command of Col. Ethan Allen.

1775 May 10 **2nd Continental Congress** convened in Philadelphia.

1775 May 16 Provincial Congress of Massachusetts drafted a constitution, **1st constitution in U.S. to be tested by a popular vote.** It was rejected. Acceptable constitution was finally ratified on June 7, 1778.

1775 May 20 **Mecklenburg Declaration of Independence,** containing 5 resolutions of independence from England, said to have been approved by citizens of Charlotte, N.C., at a midnight meeting. No contemporary document has been found, and the reliability of the available drafts is considered questionable.

1775 May 25 **British reinforcements** arrived at Boston with Gens. Howe, Burgoyne, and Clinton in command.

1775 June 15 **George Washington** selected supreme commander of the Continental Army. He declined to accept pay for services, but after 8 years of war, submitted records of his expenses totalling £24,700.

1775 June 16 Col. Richard Gridley, 1st chief engineer of the Continental Army. He was appointed by the Continental Congress. He designed defense works at **Bunker Hill.**

1775 June 17 Battle of **Bunker Hill** (Massachusetts) fought. Though American forces ultimately had to evacuate their position, they demonstrated courageous tenacity while defending it.

1775 June 22 2nd Continental Congress resolved to issue **paper currency** of a "sum not exceeding 2,000,000 Spanish milled dollars." It was decided that the represented colonies (Georgia was absent) should pledge themselves to redeem the bills.

companions in skiff try to save him. Unlike other 18th century masters, Copley did not try to point moral or load painting with intellectual content.

1775 Popular play during Revolution was *The Group* by Mrs. **Mercy Warren;** it concerned early Puritan leaders. Previously Mrs. Warren, a Whig, used her pen to satirize Tory cause: *The Adulateurs* dealt with Boston Massacre; *Upper Servia* satirized contemporary figures like Adamses and Hancock.

1775 **1st pianoforte** made in America, by John Behrent in Philadelphia.

1776 **Satire of political conditions** that brought about Revolution was chronicle play *The Fall of British Tyranny, or American Liberty Triumphant . . .* by John Leacock of Philadelphia. Scenes of play shift from Lexington to Parliament to Virginia, etc.

1776 Remarkable best seller, *Common Sense* by **Thomas Paine,** sold 100,000 copies in less than 3 months. No other book in U.S. has had such a quick or large sale relative to the population. It urged dissolution of union with Great Britain.

1776 Mission of **San Juan Capistrano** established in California. 1st chapel of mission, completed following year, still stands and is California's oldest building.

1776 Jan. 8 During a production of Burgoyne's *Blockade* a sergeant of British army jumped on stage and announced: "The Yankees are attacking our work on **Bunker's Hill.**"

1776 July 6 **Declaration of Independence** 1st published in *Pennsylvania Evening Post* under title, *A Declaration by the Representatives of the United States of America, in General Congress assembled. Post* was sold for "only 2 coppers" and was published every Tuesday, Thursday, and Saturday evening. A 4-page paper, it devoted its entire front page and 1st column of 2nd page to Declaration.

1777 Best-selling book of poetry *Night Thoughts* by the Rev. **Edward Young,**

SCIENCE; INDUSTRY; ECONOMICS; EDUCATION; RELIGION; PHILOSOPHY.

SPORTS; FASHIONS; POPULAR ENTERTAINMENT; FOLKLORE; SOCIETY.

ill-health he was permitted to live in Massachusetts providing he did not leave colony. It is said that he later sailed for London, but the ship was apparently lost at sea, and Church was never heard from again.

1775 Aug. 1st article expounding **women's rights** in America written by Thomas Paine in *Pennsylvania Magazine*, which he edited.

1776 **1st American war submarine,** the *Turtle,* constructed by David Bushnell. It carried a crew of 1.

1776 July 3 Wartime incentive to building of **warships** on Lake Champlain provided by Congress in measure authorizing Marine Committee to hire skilled shipworkers from seaports on Atlantic at wage of $37\frac{2}{3}$ a month and ½ pint of rum a day.

1776 July 13 Opposition to all **titles** in America spearheaded by *Pennsylvania Evening Post.*

1776 Dec. 5 **Phi Beta Kappa** founded at William & Mary College as a social fraternity of 5 students. It was 1st social fraternity at an American college. In 1831 Phi Beta Kappa became an honorary fraternity for students who had achieved academic distinction.

1777 **Jeremiah Wilkinson** of Cumberland, R.I., invented a process for cutting nails from cold iron which made him famous.

1777 "Manufacturing Society of Williamsburg" in Virginia advertised for Negro boys and girls to serve as **weaver apprentices.** Boys to be aged 15 to 20 and girls 12 to 15. All such apprentices, however, were retained as slaves.

1778 **Pharmacopoeia Simpliciorum & Efficaciorum,** by William Brown, chief physician of government hospitals, published in Philadelphia, Pa. It is thought to have been 1st pharmacopoeia published in U.S.

groups equal in number, and ball kept in air for long periods of time, Indians evidently being very good at game.

1775 June 17 **Memorable phrase,** "Don't fire until you see the whites of their eyes," pronounced by Colonel Prescott to his band of 1500 colonials as they watched British Redcoats ascend Bunker Hill. Twice repulsed, British were finally able to dislodge "rebels."

1775 Sept. One of **1st unofficial American flags** raised over Fort Johnson on James Island in harbor of Charleston, S.C. Sept. 15, 3 companies of Americans led by Lt. Col. Isaac Motte took possession of fort from British and ran down Union Jack. It was replaced by ensign designed by Col. Moultrie: a dark blue ground with white crescent in upper left corner and word "Liberty" in white letters across flag.

1775 Dec. 3 Raising of the **1st official American flag** took place aboard *Alfred,* flagship of Commodore Esek Hopkins. Because Navy governed by Congress it was called Congress Colors, and was later variously known as Grand Union Flag and First Navy Ensign. Standard, bearing 13 red and white stripes and crosses of St. George and St. Andrew, remained colonial flag until superseded by Stars and Stripes on June 14, 1777.

1776 **1st cocktail** said to have been made by Betsy Flanagan, barmaid at Halls Corners, Elmsford, N.Y. Back of bar decorated with tail feathers. When a drunk called for a glass of "those cocktails," she made him a mixed drink and put a feather in it.

1776 Nov. 16 **1st salute** to a U.S. flag (Grand Union Ensign) was volley of 11 guns fired by Fort of Orange on St. Eustatius, Dutch West Indies. Salute was in response to like volley fired from *Andrea Doria* commanded by Capt. Isaiah Robinson.

1777 June 14 Continental Congress passed resolution providing for adoption of flag for 13 United States consisting of 13 stripes, 7 red and 6 white, and 13 white

1775 July 3 Gen. **George Washington** assumed command of troops at Cambridge, Mass., that were laying siege to Boston.

1775 July 26 **Postal system** established by the 2nd Continental Congress. Benjamin Franklin chosen postmaster general.

1775 Sept. 25 Col. **Ethan Allen** captured while attacking Montreal. He was taken to England and held prisoner till end of war.

1775 Oct. 13 Congress authorized the commission of a "swift sailing vessel to carry 10 carriage guns and an appropriate no. of swivels" thus creating **1st U.S. naval ship. Continental Navy** was established on Dec. 22.

1775 Nov. 10 **U.S. Marine Corps** organized by authority of 1st Continental Congress as a component of the navy. It was separately organized July 11, 1789.

1775 Nov. 29 Continental Congress resolved that a committee of 5 be appointed to correspond with "our friends" in England, Ireland, and France. "**Committee of Secret Correspondence**" was formed; members were Thomas Johnson, Benjamin Harrison, Benjamin Franklin, John Jay, and John Dickinson.

1775 Nov. 29 American cruiser *Lee* captured British brig *Nancy*, which was laden with guns and ammunition destined for Quebec. *Nancy* was later named *Congress*, and was instrumental in forcing **evacuation of Boston.**

1775 Dec. Esek Hopkins appointed **1st commander in chief of the Continental Navy.** His rank was to correspond with Gen. Washington's. His 1st fleet consisted of the *Alfred, Columbus, Andrea Doria,* and the *Cabot.* On Jan. 2, 1777, he was formally dismissed because he failed to observe orders from the Continental Congress.

1776 **Great fire** destroyed most of old city in New York, including much of best Dutch colonial building in U.S.

1776 Thomas Jefferson advanced plan for African resettlement of **Negro slaves.**

LL.D. Also great success in England and Europe. Popular well into 19th century.

1777 **John Milton's** *Paradise Lost* was American best seller, but popular in England long before 1777. From 1760 to 1775 *Paradise Lost* was 1 of 5 most frequent importations by American booksellers.

1777 English **Bible** 1st published in America. It consisted only of New Testament. **1st complete Bible** in English published in America came out in 1782.

1777 Late but good example of Dutch colonial building, **Lefferts' Homestead,** constructed in Brooklyn, N.Y. Thin colonnettes and sunburst design of entrance were peculiarities of New York 18th-century architecture. It is still standing and open to public.

1777 1st American publication of *The Seasons* by **James Thomson.** In spite of much moral and religious discussion, these poems still often vivid. Very popular last half of 18th century.

1778 Earliest known **mural painting** in America produced in private home. Itinerant painters traveled in groups, causing stir whenever they arrived in village to do wall. Scenes like Vesuvius erupting and marines were popular. Often painters carried stereotyped stencils of weeping willows and simple linear motifs in their kits.

1779 Rollicking satire of Boston group who avoided support of Revolution for fear of loss of social status was *The Motley Assembly,* a farce attributed to Mrs. **Mercy Warren.** Some characters in play were Esq. Runt, "a short fat old fellow: fond of gallanting the ladies"; Mrs. Flourish, Mrs. Taxall, Mrs. Bubble—all women who preferred British scarlet to Yankee blue.

1779 Jan. 9 Opening night of season at **John Street Theatre** in British-occupied New York saw following notice in advertisement: Parts will be played "by young ladies and grown gentle-women who never appeared on any stage before."

SCIENCE; INDUSTRY; ECONOMICS; EDUCATION; RELIGION; PHILOSOPHY.

SPORTS; FASHIONS; POPULAR ENTERTAINMENT; FOLKLORE; SOCIETY.

1778 Proposal for federal subsidy of **steamboat building** in America made by Thomas Paine, who recommended design of Jonathan Hulls. Hulls patented ship that would surmount both "wind and tide" in England in 1736.

1779 Under direction of Thomas Jefferson, **William and Mary College** became a university by discontinuing grammar and divinity schools and creating schools of medicine, law, and modern languages. Elective system was adopted at same time.

1779 Broad democratic program of **education** in Virginia proposed by Thomas Jefferson, providing for universal elementary education in schools supported by local districts, with boys of proved ability being provided with further education in academies and colleges, scholarships going to those gifted students who could not afford expenses of higher education.

1779 **1st Universalist congregation** in America established at Gloucester, Mass., by John Murray, English minister, who wished to formulate more humane and rational form of Christianity. His views anticipated by Charles Chauncy, liberal minister from Boston, who declared that God in his infinite goodness must have decided on universal salvation. These views were strong reaction against pessimistic accents of Calvinism.

1779 Jan. Gloucester First Church formed by 61 citizens of Gloucester, Mass. This constituted the formal establishment of the **Universalist Church** in America. John Murray, who had been preaching Universalist doctrine for nearly a decade, was 1st minister. Murray was a Calvinist Universalist who emigrated from London in 1770. The Universalist Church is, as a religious body, centered chiefly in North America, in the U.S., and Canada. It was founded by Murray as a rejection of the doctrine of eternal damnation. In the next decades after Murray's death, Universalism grew nearer to Unitarianism and, under the influence of Hosea Ballou, rejected the Calvinist strain in Murray's teaching.

stars in a field of blue "representing the new constellation." This date has since been observed as **Flag Day,** although resolution did not go into effect until Sept. 3, 1777.

1778 Feb. 14 **1st salute** to "Stars and Stripes" fired by French ship **Admiral La-Motte Picquet** in answer to John Paul Jones's 13-gun salute from *Ranger.* French volley was, in effect, acknowledgment of American independence.

1779 Very popular diversion of lower and middle classes around Charlottesville, Va., was **sprint races,** quarter-mile races between two horses of very great speed. This was also called "quarter-racing," according to officer under General Burgoyne, Thomas Anbury, who distinguished between these sprints and the two-, three-, and four-mile races held every spring and fall in big towns of Richmond and Williamsburg. The latter races compared favorably to big purse races held in England.

1779 Sept. 23 Heroic phrase, **"I have not yet begun to fight,"** sounded by John Paul Jones in reply to British commander's "Have you struck?" The scene was the engagement between the *Bonhomme Richard,* under Jones' command, and *HMS Serapis,* under Capt. Richard Pearson, With 14 ships Jones sailed to the British Isles in August with the intention of laying seige to Leith. On Sept. 23 he fell afoul of a fleet of 41 British Baltic traders, in convoy with the *Serapis.* 3 of Jones' ships challenged the British. For more than 3 hours the *Bonhomme Richard* engaged the *Serapis* directly. Jones brought them deck to deck and they fired point blank at one another. Both ships were aflame when the *Serapis* which topped her by an extra deck, struck her own colors in admission that the British commander had himself ceased to fight.

(Column 1 continued)

Similar ideas were widely held in South at this time.

1776 Jan. 1 **Norfolk,** Va., burned by British after defeat of royalist contingent.

1776 Jan. 10 1st demand for complete independence for American colonies appeared in pamphlet *Common Sense* by **Thomas Paine,** greatly influential in swinging tide in favor of clean break with mother country.

1776 Mar. Charleston, S.C., set up an **independent government** under a temporary local constitution which was to be in effect until an agreement with England could be reached. John Rutledge was chosen president. Said to be the 1st independent government within the recognized borders of the colonies. It was this government which successfully defended Charleston against the British army and fleet on June 28, 1776, thus freeing the South from attack for nearly 3 years.

1776 March 17 **Gen. Howe** evacuated Boston Harbor after Washington had seized Dorchester Heights, 2 weeks previously. Howe sailed for Halifax, N.S., to await reinforcements.

1776 Apr. 12 North Carolina Provincial Congress instructed its delegates to the Continental Congress to vote for independence. She was the **1st colony to propose independence formally.**

1776 June Most famous political document in America, **The Declaration of Independence,** drafted by Thomas Jefferson.

1776 June 27 Massed spectators watched hanging of Thomas Hickey near Bowery Lane, New York. Condemned as a traitor, Hickey was **1st American soldier executed by order of military court.** He had conspired to deliver Gen. Washington to British.

1776 July 2 New Jersey 1st colony to grant **woman suffrage.** This statute remained in force until 1807, when it was reversed.

(Continued in next column)

(Column 1 continued)

1776 July 5 President of the Congress, John Hancock, and Secretary of the Congress, Charles Thompson, signed draft copies of the **Declaration of Independence.** These copies were to be sent to the several state assemblies.

1776 July 8 John Nixon gave the first public reading of **Declaration of Independence** to an assembly of Philadelphians. He had been chosen for this distinction by the sheriff of Philadelphia.

1776 Aug. 2 Though the **Declaration of Independence** had been adopted July 4, it was not signed by members of Congress until this day. Names of the signers were withheld from public for more than 6 months because, if independence were not achieved, their treasonable act might result in their deaths.

1776 Aug. 27 Battle of **Long Island** (N.Y.), in which American forces commanded by Putnam and Sullivan defeated by British under Howe and Clinton. On Aug. 30 Americans evacuated Long Island.

1776 Sept. **Benjamin Franklin** chosen by Congress to represent the U.S. in negotiations with France for a treaty of commerce.

1776 Sept. 9 Continental Congress resolved that the words **"United States"** were to replace the words "United Colonies."

1776 Sept. 15 American forces withdrawn from **New York** and city occupied by British under Howe.

1776 Sept. 22 Capt. **Nathan Hale** of Connecticut executed by British in New York. Before he was hanged he made his famous statement: "I only regret that I have but one life to lose for my country."

1776 Nov. 16 British under Howe captured **Fort Washington,** New York city, taking about 2000 prisoners.

1776 Dec. 19 1st number of series of pamphlets, *The Crisis,* by **Thomas Paine,** written to bolster morale of Continental Army; immortalized by famous 1st sen-

(Continued in next column)

88

(Column 1 continued)

tence, "These are the times that try men's souls."

1776 Dec. 26 Washington captured nearly 1000 mercenary Hessian troops in famous early morning raid on **Trenton,** N.J.

1777 Jan. 3 Battle of **Princeton,** N.J., fought and won by Americans. Washington attacked in early morning again as he had at Trenton in previous week.

1777 June 28 Americans repulsed at battle of **Monmouth,** N.J. Many soldiers overcome by heat.

1777 July **1st state to abolish slavery and adopt universal male suffrage** without regard to property was Vermont, which drafted its constitution this month. It was followed to a lesser degree by other New England states, which with Vermont were destined to become strongholds of abolitionism in the 1850's. Vermont had declared itself an independent state Jan. 16, 1777.

1777 July 6 **Fort Ticonderoga,** N.Y., abandoned by Americans under St. Clair to superior British force commanded by Burgoyne. St. Clair, with approximately 3000 troops, joined Schuyler at Fort Edward, N.Y.

1777 Aug. 16 Americans under Stark defeated British at **Bennington,** Vt., killing about 200 and taking 600 prisoners. British detachment commanded by Col. Baum sent by Burgoyne in search of provisions.

1777 Sept. 11 Washington defeated at **Brandywine,** Pa., by Howe. Gen. Lafayette wounded in this battle.

1777 Sept. 14 Burgoyne crossed Hudson over **bridge of boats,** and encamped at Saratoga, N.Y.

1777 Sept. 19 1st engagement of Gates and Burgoyne fought at **Bemis Heights,** N.Y. British gained some ground and lost 500 men. Almost 300 Americans were killed.

1777 Sept. 27 British, under Cornwallis, took possession of **Philadelphia.**

(Continued in next column)

(Column 1 continued)

1777 Oct. 4 Washington's attack upon **Germantown,** Pa., repulsed by Howe. Americans lost about 600 men in this battle.

1777 Oct. 7 1500 British troops routed in 2nd battle of **Bemis Heights,** N.Y. British Gen. Fraser killed and Arnold wounded while attempting to force an entrance into Hessian camp.

1777 Oct. 9 Burgoyne retreated to **Saratoga.**

1777 Oct. 17 Burgoyne capitulated to Gates at **Saratoga,** N.Y., surrendering 5642 British and German troops.

1777 Nov. **1st secular community** in California, San José, established on Guadalupe R. Called a *pueblo.* Contained 66 inhabitants whose dissolute life scandalized *padres* at nearby Mission Santa Clara. Priests built road lined by shady willows (forerunner of modern Alameda) to encourage church attendance, but colonists stayed away.

1777 Nov. 15 **Articles of Confederation** adopted by Continental Congress at York, Pa. They were ratified in 1781.

1777 Dec. David Bushnell, who had invented a man-propelled submarine, launched a **mine attack** against British ships. The mines were kegs of gunpowder which would explode on contact. This was perhaps 1st marine mine field ever laid, and the feat inspired the ballad, "The Battle of the Kegs," written by Francis Hopkinson.

1777 Dec. 17 Washington retired with his troops to **Valley Forge,** Pa., for winter.

1778 Feb. 6 **Treaty with France** signed. It was in part a commercial treaty and in part a political and military alliance. France recognized U.S. independence, which was for the U.S. the object of the alliance. Said to be the 1st and only treaty of alliance made by U.S. until the North Atlantic Treaty Organization, April 4, 1949.

(Continued in column 1, next page)

(Column 1 continued)

1778 May 4   Continental Congress ratified **Treaty of Alliance** with France. Never before or after did U.S. make treaty of alliance until North Atlantic Treaty Organization, which went into effect Aug. 24, 1949.

1778 June   Directed by Aaron Burr, **Secret Service** organized as "Headquarters Secret Service," 1st such in U.S.

1778 June 18   Fearing blockade by French ships, British evacuated **Philadelphia.**

1778 July   Conrad Alexandre Gerard,

(Continued in next column)

(Column 1 continued)

appointed Ambassador to U.S. by Louis XVI, arrived in this country; he was **1st foreign diplomatic representative accredited to U.S.**

1778 July 3–4   Inhabitants of Wyoming Valley, Pa., **massacred** by 1600 Indians and Tories led by Cols. Butler and Brant. Some 200 scalped and many others burned alive when fort at Kingston set aflame.

1778 Aug. 30   American forces evacuated **Rhode Island.**

1778 Dec. 29   British troops led by Col. Campbell, took **Savannah**, Ga.

(Continued in next column)

POLITICS AND GOVERNMENT; WAR; DISASTERS; VITAL STATISTICS.

BOOKS; PAINTING; DRAMA; ARCHITECTURE; SCULPTURE.

1780–1784

1780   **Estimated colonial population—** 2,781,000.

1780 Mar. 1   Pennsylvania became **1st state to abolish slavery** (Vermont not yet admitted to Union). Law provided that no child born after date of its passage should be slave.

1780 Aug. 16   Gen. Gates defeated at Camden, S.C., by Gen. Cornwallis. Baron **De Kalb,** Prussian officer who joined American forces, mortally wounded during battle.

1780 Oct. 2   Maj. **John André,** British officer, hanged as spy at Tappan, N.Y. He was apprehended by 3 militiamen after he left West Point, which Benedict Arnold, its commander, had agreed to surrender to British.

1780 Oct. 7   British and Tories defeated at **King's Mountain,** S.C., by Americans under Cols. Campbell, Shelby, and Cleveland. British commander, Maj. Ferguson, and 150 others killed and nearly 800 prisoners taken.

1781 Jan. 17   British under Col. Tarleton suffered heavy losses at **Cowpens,** S.C. American force of about 800 men led by Gen. Morgan.

c1780   Furniture maker **Jonathan Gostelowe** of Philadelphia began to make his reputation for original American design. In 1788 he was elected chairman of Gentlemen Cabinet and Chair Makers.

1780 May 4   **American Academy of Arts and Sciences** chartered at Boston, Mass., with James Bowdoin, later governor of Massachusetts, as 1st president. In his lifetime Bowdoin was a correspondent of Franklin's and shared the same sensitivity to the expanding world of the natural sciences. He balanced his active concern for political affairs with the honors, from home and abroad, which were conferred upon him for his scholarship. The library which he left to the American Academy is of sustaining interest. Bowdoin College was named for him.

1781   Arrival in New York of most famous of American furniture makers, **Duncan Phyfe.** His furniture shows influence of French Empire style, Sheraton, and Hope. Less than 10 years before, Phyfe had emigrated with his family from Scotland to America. At 16 he was apprenticed to a cabinet maker from Albany. When he had learned his trade he moved to New York and set about opening the

(Column 1 continued)

1779 Mar. 3 British victorious at **Brier Creek,** Ga., where 300 Americans under Gen. Ashe were lost.

1779 July 15 **Stony Point,** N.Y. seized by Gen. Anthony Wayne. More than 600 British killed or taken prisoner.

1779 July 26 Congress awarded **1st decoration to a foreign national** to Lt. Col. François Louis Teisseidre de Fleury. He was presented with silver medallion for his part in attack on fort at Stony Point, N.Y., July 15, 1779, when he commanded part of the American attack forces himself

(Continued in next column)

(Column 1 continued)

and captured British flag. He was only foreigner so honored during Revolutionary War.

1779 Sept. 23 **Bonhomme Richard** defeated and captured *Serapis,* a British man-of-war. *Bonhomme Richard,* commanded by John Paul Jones, was lashed fast during battle to *Serapis,* which finally struck its colors after 3 hours of brutal fighting.

1779 Oct. 9 **Count Pulaski,** Polish officer in American service, mortally wounded in unsuccessful attack upon Savannah, Ga.

SCIENCE; INDUSTRY; ECONOMICS; EDUCATION; RELIGION; PHILOSOPHY.

SPORTS; FASHIONS; POPULAR ENTERTAINMENT; FOLKLORE; SOCIETY.

1780–1784

1780 Col. Benjamin Hanks of Litchfield, Conn., who had already cast the 1st brass cannon and the 1st bells in America, constructed and mounted the clock for the Old Dutch Church in New York city, the **1st town clock** in the country.

1781 Dec. 31 Congress established the **Bank of North America.** Under Articles of Confederation Congress could not tax, so the Bank of North America was founded with a capitalization of $400,000 to supply government with money.

1782 Opening of **Harvard Medical School** signalized movement in America to end dependence upon Europe for professional training of American students.

1782 Growth of **rationalism** in America reflected in fact that Princeton College could claim only two church members in its student body.

1782 Apr. **Washington College** chartered in Chestertown, Md. Established under Episcopalian auspices, Washington College awarded its 1st degrees in 1783.

1782 Oct. **Washington and Lee University** 1st chartered in Lexington, Va., as

1780 Nov. 3 days of **racing** on Hempstead Plains, Long Island, included: Gentleman's Purse, Ladies' Subscription, and race run by women riders. Gentlemen fond of fox hunting met daily at dawn at Loosely's King's Head Tavern.

1780 Clause in the Massachusetts constitution indited to declare that **scientific associations** should be encouraged.

1781 18th-century French traveler to **Annapolis** reported on splendor of this Southern city. Fine women, elegant horses, coaches, sumptuous dinners and balls. He noted that "A French hair dresser is a man of importance among them, and it is said, a certain dame here hires one of that craft at a thousand crowns a year salary."

1782 Worcester (Mass.) town meeting **opposed a state liquor excise** on the grounds that the tax was "contrary to

1781 Mar. 15 Cornwallis defeated American force led by Gen. Greene at **Guilford Court House** in N.C. Heavy losses suffered by both British and Americans.

1781 July 11 Thomas Hutchins designated **Geographer of the U.S.** On May 4 he had been appointed Geographer of the Southern Army, which he had joined after he had returned from England where he had been charged with high treason for passing information to sympathizers of the American Revolution. After the war Hutchins was employed by several states to lay out their boundaries.

1781 Sept. 5 French fleet, under command of De Grasse, entered Chesapeake Bay and engaged **British fleet** under command of Admiral Graves. De Grasse drove British back to New York, precluding any possibility of aid to Cornwallis at Yorktown, Va.

1781 Sept. 8 New London, Conn., seized and burned by Gen. Benedict Arnold, now with British. He then took Fort Griswold and was responsible for death of many American soldiers after their surrender.

1781 Sept. 9 Gen. Greene forced to withdraw at **Eutaw Springs,** S.C., after assault upon British under Col. Stewart.

1781 Oct. 9 Yorktown, Va., surrounded by American and French troops, who began shelling British position.

1781 Oct. 19 Cornwallis surrendered at **Yorktown,** Va., to Washington and Lafayette. Capitulation, which yielded about 8000 British prisoners, brought war virtually to end.

1782 Virginia legislature, under urging by Thomas Jefferson, enacted bill making it lawful for any man "by last will and testament or other instrument in writing sealed and witnessed, to emancipate and set free his **slaves."**

1782 June 20 Great Seal of the U.S. adopted. It was 1st used Sept. 16, 1782, on a document granting Gen. Washington

joiner's shop on Broad Street which was in business in 1792.

1782 1st Bible printed in U.S. at Philadelphia by Robert Aitken. British copyright laws prevented earlier printing of English Bible and thus printing had to be held off until colonies were virtually independent.

1782 Noah Webster's *Speller* published. For short time it supplanted *New England Primer* as principal text for early grades of public school. *Speller* included stories, aphorisms, maxims of ethical training.

1782 Fortune of **Gilbert Stuart** skyrocketed with reception of his painting *The Skater*. Originally intended as portrait, idea of skater struck him when sitter suggested that they leave cold studio and go skating in St. James's Park, London. Unconventionality of composition and masterful handling won him hundreds of commissions for portraits.

1782 1st U.S. flag shown in England appeared in a painting by John Copley. At work on a portrait, he introduced ship in background flying Stars and Stripes.

1782 Once considered greatest American poem, *M'Fingal* by **John Trumbull** was lively debate on revolutionary matters.

1782 Extremely popular book on early American life about time of Revolution was *Letters from an American Farmer* by **Hector St. John de Crevecoeur.** A well-born Frenchman, Crevecoeur settled in New York, from which he collected his famous impressions of New World. Letters are idyllic, reflecting "noble savage" views of 18th century. Book reprinted 5 times in English, appeared in 3 French editions, and 2 German translations. Crevecoeur travelled extensively in America, became a naturalized citizen, was an experienced woodsman and farmer. *Letters from an American Farmer* contains 12 letters which reflect, in warm and vivid detail, his knowledge of farm life, animals, and the geography of the colonies. He believed in the

SCIENCE; INDUSTRY; ECONOMICS; EDUCATION; RELIGION; PHILOSOPHY.	SPORTS; FASHIONS; POPULAR ENTERTAINMENT; FOLKLORE; SOCIETY.

Liberty Hall Academy. Liberty Hall Academy had developed from Augusta Academy, founded in 1749 about 15 miles southwest of what is now Staunton, Va. Liberty Hall, established under Presbyterian auspices, became Washington Academy in 1789, Washington College in 1813, and Washington and Lee University in 1871.

the genius of a free people." Liquor was, said the meeting, "absolutely necessary" for the morale of farm workers.

1783 1st Protestant Episcopal bishop in America, Dr. Samuel Seabury, elected by 10 of his fellow ministers at Woodbury, Conn.

1782 Use of the **scarlet letter** for adulterers discontinued in New England.

1784 1st motor boat demonstrated to Gen. Washington by its inventor, James Rumsey. Designed for use in rapids, Rumsey's boat utilized force of river against boat to propel it forward through variable action of setting poles. 2 years later he succeeded in propelling boat with use of steam.

1782 Less than ½ as much **printed matter** published as in 1775.

1784 *Empress of China* sailed from Sandy Hook to Canton, China, around Cape Horn with cargo of ginseng root for which Chinese were willing to pay enormous prices. Voyage lasted year and was very profitable. **Trade route** enabled American commerce to recover from crippling British blockade during Revolutionary War. By 1789, 18 American merchantmen were plying their way through harbor of Canton. Salem, Mass., had become main terminus of China trade.

1782 Publication of *Plocacosmos or the Whole Art of Hair Dressing* exercised great influence on **American hair styles.** It was practical book with many rules for all classes of persons, interspersed with homilies.

1784 1st publication of *Inquiry into the Effects of Spiritous Liquors on the Human Body and Mind* by Dr. **Benjamin Rush,** authoritative support for early temperance drives in America, supplemented religious arguments with scientific facts. In spite of his addiction to antiquated categories of thought, Rush commands interest as one of the early investigators of the relationships between bodily and mental ills. His roles of physician and social re-

1783 **Enrollment at Yale,** the highest in U.S. colleges, reached 270.

1783 It took Jefferson 5 days to travel by **public transportation** from Philadelphia to Baltimore.

93

POLITICS AND GOVERNMENT; WAR;
DISASTERS; VITAL STATISTICS.

BOOKS; PAINTING; DRAMA;
ARCHITECTURE; SCULPTURE.

authority to consult with British about prisoner exchange. On Sept. 15, 1789, Congress declared that the Great Seal was to be the official seal of the U.S. and that it was to be kept in custody of the Sec. of State. Since then there have been 6 dies of the Seal officially cut and used.

1782 Aug. 7 The **Badge of Military Merit** (the **"Purple Heart"**) instituted by George Washington. Only 3 men of the Continental Army are known to have received award. It came into disuse after Revolution, but was revived in Feb. 1932.

1782 Dec. 5 Birth of **Martin Van Buren** in Kinderhook, N.Y. He was the 1st president to be U.S. citizen at birth. All previous presidents had been born during colonial times.

1783 **Slavery** made illegal in Massachusetts by judicial interpretation of State Constitution of 1780, in which text stating that all men were "born free and equal" was construed as legal nullification of slavery. This year also saw **slave trade** outlawed in Maryland.

1783 The **Know Ye Men** came to denote advocates of paper money policy in Rhode Island. They were so called because one of their pamphlets on issue began with words "Know ye men."

1783 Sept. 3 **Peace treaty** with Britain signed, thus ending Revolutionary War. American independence recognized by British and boundaries of Republic agreed upon with Great Lakes and Florida to north and south, and Mississippi R. to west. Franklin, John Jay, and John Adams were American agents during peace negotiations in Paris.

1783 Dec. 24 **Gen. Washington** resigned his commission as Commander in Chief of American Army.

1784 **Slavery** abolished in Connecticut and Rhode Island.

1784 Nov. 24 **Zachary Taylor,** 12th president, born in Orange Court House, Va.

simple life of Rousseau and popularized the ideas of the physiocrats that the goodness of man was to be traced from his connection with the soil. He apotheosized the new man who was to come from the experiment.

1783 May 30 *Pennsylvania Evening Post,* published by Benjamin Towne, began publication in Philadelphia, Pa. It was **1st daily newspaper** in U.S.

1784 Arrival in America of British painter **Robert Edge Pine,** bringing with him 1st cast of Venus de Medici, which shocked many citizens of Quaker Philadelphia. During Revolution he became known for his portraits of contemporary leaders: Gen. Gates, Charles Carroll, Baron Steuben, and Gen. Washington.

1784 **Joel Barlow,** poet of Connecticut, appointed to "Americanize" hymns of Dr. Isaac Watts, most popular religious music of 18th century. His versions criticized by some for being too far from Watts's originals.

1784 Single surviving church of Franciscan missions in Arizona and most ambitious of all Spanish colonial churches, **San Xavier del Bac,** begun at Tucson; completed 1797. Height of Spanish-Mexican baroque style in U.S.

1784 Apr. 1 **Theater performances** revived in Philadelphia with reopening of Southwark Theater under direction of Lewis Hallam. He delivered a *Monody to the Memory of the Chiefs who have fallen in the Cause of American Liberty.*

1784 May **1st magazine** to appeal to women, *Gentlemen and Ladies' Town and Country Magazine,* appeared in Boston. It included fiction and advice to young ladies; but even so magazine only issued 8 numbers.

1784 June Boinod & Gaillard, booksellers of Philadelphia, Pa., issued prospectus for **1st French newspaper** in U.S., *Le Courrier de l'Amérique.* Presumably the paper was published for a short time, although no copies exist today.

SCIENCE; INDUSTRY; ECONOMICS; EDUCATION; RELIGION; PHILOSOPHY.

SPORTS; FASHIONS; POPULAR ENTERTAINMENT; FOLKLORE; SOCIETY.

former overlapped, and it is difficult to separate them in any consideration of his work. But his *Inquiry into the Effects of Spiritous Liquors* and his generally enthusiastic support of the movement against alcohol has earned him, among the many "firsts" which are his credits, the title of father of American temperance.

1784 David Landreth of Philadelphia, Pa., founded what was probably **1st seed business** in U.S., although Price family of Flushing, Long Island, preceded him as nurserymen.

1784 Nov. **St. John's College** chartered in Annapolis, Md., under Episcopalian auspices. 1st degree awarded in 1793. Saint John's, under the name of King William's School, dates back originally to 1696. William Paca who, as governor of Maryland, had laid the cornerstone at Washington College the year before, was an early supporter of the change. He was joined by Samuel Chase, Charles Carroll and Thomas Stone, who were all on the Board of Visitors and Governors.

1784 Nov. 18 1st American Episcopal bishop, **Samuel Seabury,** consecrated by nonjuring Scottish bishops of Aberdeen and Moray in contravention of wishes of Archbishop of Canterbury.

1784 Dec. 24 **Methodist Church** organized in America in Christmas conference in Baltimore. At same time Francis Asbury elected **1st Methodist bishop** in North America. Methodist Church not formally separated from Church of England until 1791.

1783 May 13 **Society of Cincinnati** founded by officers of American Revolutionary army. Membership restricted to eldest male descendant of original Revolutionary soldier. George Washington was first president-general and Gen. Alexander Hamilton second.

1784 **Society of the Friendly Sons of St. Patrick** organized in New York by Irish veterans of American Revolution; a century later Society acquired new vigor from U.S. sympathies with cause of Irish independence, and it still exists in mid-20th century.

1784 **Nocturnal deer hunting expeditions** in Carolinas became misdemeanor because of accidental slaughter of many domestic cows and horses.

1784 New Haven town meeting approved the return of **Tories** to business and to the general life of the community.

POLITICS AND GOVERNMENT; WAR;   BOOKS; PAINTING; DRAMA;
DISASTERS; VITAL STATISTICS.   ARCHITECTURE; SCULPTURE.

1785-1789

1785 **Slavery** made illegal in New York.

1785 Mar. 10 **Thomas Jefferson** appointed Minister to France, and **John Adams** appointed Minister to England.

1785 May 20 Continental Congress act provided that section no. 16 of each township in Western Reserve be set aside for support of public schools; this was **1st federal land grant for schools.**

1785 July 6 Thomas Jefferson proposed in Congress the establishment of a **coinage system** based on the Spanish milled dollar. He proposed a gold piece of value $10; a dollar in silver, a tenth of a dollar in silver; and a hundredth of a dollar in copper. This proposal was adopted by Congress, and on Aug. 8, 1786, a full plan of coinage was enacted.

1786 **Slavery** outlawed in New Jersey.

1786 Maj. Samuel Shaw of Massachusetts appointed U.S. consul to China. Shaw established himself in Canton, China, and was reappointed to his post in 1790. He was **1st consul** to be appointed in U.S. foreign service.

1787 Jan. 25 Daniel Shays led 1100 men in attempt to seize Springfield, Mass., arsenal, but militia, commanded by Gen. Shepherd, routed insurgents. This action, known as **Shays's Rebellion,** resulted when penniless farmers were imprisoned for nonpayment of debts.

1787 May **Federal Constitutional Convention** met in Philadelphia. It was in session until Sept. 17. Every state except Rhode Island sent delegates. On June 21, 1788, the Constitution had been ratified by sufficient number of states to become effective.

1787 July 13 **Northwest Ordinance** enacted by Congress under Articles of Confederation included provision barring slavery from the territory and, in general, contained provisions in which the number of

1785 Phenomenal international success of American painter **John Copley** seen in his commission to paint *Children of George III.*

1785 **Rocky Hill Meeting House,** finest extant example of a late Colonial meeting house in Massachusetts, built at Amesbury.

1786 1st time in **American theater** that plays enjoyed extended runs. Hallam's American Company, performing in New York city, gave 7 performances of Sheridan's *The School for Scandal* and 18 of John O'Keefe's *The Poor Soldier.* This year also saw **1st U.S. performance of Hamlet** in New York city at John Street Theater by Hallam and Henry Group.

1786 *The Worcester Collection of Sacred Harmony,* which became one of most popular **hymn books** of the time, 1st appeared at Worcester, Mass.

1786 May **1st musical periodical** in America, *American Musical Magazine,* was collection of tunes and hymns published and edited by Daniel Read in New Haven, Conn.

1786 Sept. The **Columbian Magazine** appeared, one of most important periodicals of early American times. In 1790 its name changed to *Universal Asylum and Columbian Magazine.* It died in Dec. 1792.

1787 *A Select Collection of the Most Favorite Scots Tunes,* compiled by Alexander Reinagle, published in New Haven, Conn.; it was one of earliest books of **secular music** published in the U.S.

1787 **Old Erasmus Hall High School,** built in Brooklyn; excellent example of early Georgian style.

1787 Jan. The **American Museum** published, most important American magazine of 18th century. Its contents were especially rich in early American material. It died in Dec., 1792.

1785–1789

1785 **1st dispensary** in America, the Philadelphia Dispensary, established by Dr. Benjamin Rush.

1785 New American attitude toward the **Negro** stated by Gov. James Bowdoin before assembly of American Academy of Arts and Sciences. Bowdoin stated that inferior accomplishments of free Negroes were due not to any innate ignorance in race but to lack of educational opportunities afforded them.

1785 **1st Unitarian Church** in America established out of change in Episcopalian service in King's Chapel by minister, James Freeman, Harvard graduate. Part of liturgy treating of mystic trinity of Father, Son, and Holy Ghost omitted and single or "unitarian" conception of God substituted.

1785 **Regular stage routes** linking New York city, Boston, Albany, and Philadelphia initiated. Trip from Boston to New York consumed 6 days with coaches traveling from 3 A.M. until 10 P.M.

1785 State of Virginia authorized **1st American turnpike,** known as Little River Turnpike.

1785 Jan. 27 **University of Georgia** in Athens, Ga., chartered as state university with no denominational ties. Oldest state university in America, it awarded its 1st degrees in 1804.

1785 Oct. 1 *MacPherson's Directory for the City and Suburbs of Philadelphia,* printed by Francis Bailey, published; it was **1st directory** of an American city.

1785 Pennsylvania legislature revokes charter of **Bank of North America.** Enemies charged bank with responsibility for commercial depression. When things did not get better, supporters of bank rebutted that trade was bad because charter had

c1785 Description by printer of Boston indicates a **style of dress for men:** "He wore a pea-green coat, white vest, nankeen small clothes, white silk stockings, and pumps fastened with silver buckles which covered at least half the foot from instep to toe. His small clothes were tied at the knees with ribbon of the same colour in double bows, the ends reaching down to the ancles. His hair in front was loaded with pomatum, frizzled or craped and powdered. Behind, his natural hair was augmented by the addition of a large queue called vulgarly a false tail, which, enrolled in some yards of black ribbon, hung half-way down his back."

1785 Phrase **"Facing the music"** entered into popular talk from theater jargon. It originally characterized difficulty an actor "faced" when stepping before footlights.

1785 The protests of reformers and better heating of houses weakened the arguments in favor of **bundling,** early American courting custom which sanctioned occupancy of same bed by fully clothed couple. The custom quickly became obsolescent, lingering only in backwoods sections, such as western Pennsylvania where last instances of bundling were reported in 1840's.

1785 **Canton ware** became very popular in America. Imported from potteries located near Canton and Ch'ing-te-chen, China.

1785 **George Washington** retired from active hunting, giving away his valuable kennel of hounds, which he had renewed after Revolutionary War. Washington enjoyed riding to hounds, and between 1783 and 1785 often went on 3 hunts a week during season.

1785 One of leading props of aristocracy, **primogeniture,** or preserving of large

free persons was used to determine the various stages of self-government.

1787 Dec. 7 The 1st state, **Delaware,** ratified the Constitution.

1787 Dec. 12 **Pennsylvania** ratified Constitution and became 2nd state of the Union.

1787 Dec. 18 **New Jersey** ratified Constitution and became 3rd state of the Union.

1788 Jan. 2 **Georgia** ratified Constitution and became 4th state of the Union.

1788 Jan. 9 **Connecticut** ratified Constitution and became 5th state of the Union.

1788 Feb. 6 **Massachusetts** ratified Constitution and became 6th state of the Union.

1788 Mar. 21 **Fire** destroyed more than 800 buildings in New Orleans, La.

1788 Apr. 28 **Maryland** ratified Constitution and became 7th state of the Union.

1788 May 23 **South Carolina** ratified Constitution and became 8th state of the Union.

1788 June 21 **New Hampshire** ratified Constitution and became 9th state of the Union. With this ratification Constitution became effective. Constitution was not declared in effect until Mar. 4, 1789.

1788 June 25 **Virginia** ratified Constitution and became the 10th state of the Union.

1788 July 26 **New York** ratified Constitution and became 11th state of the Union. For a time North Carolina and Rhode Island refused to ratify; but, since the Constitution was now effective, they were eventually forced to accept it.

1789 **Federalist Party** formed by those who had supported ratification of Constitution. They were considered pro-English and enjoyed considerable support until 1800 when Jefferson, Republican, defeated their candidate. Party disappeared c1820. Hamilton was their leader.

1787 Apr. 16 **1st American comedy** to be performed on regular stage by company of professional actors was *The Contrast,* by Bostonian Royall Tyler, at John Street Theater in New York; it became immediate success. **1st stage Yankee** in America appeared as hero in this prodemocratic play that ridicules aristocratic values while extolling rustic virtues of hero.

1787 Oct. 27 1st paper appeared in what is regarded as greatest American work on political theory, **The Federalist.** Written variously by Alexander Hamilton, James Madison, and John Jay, work was completed on Apr. 4, 1788, and printed immediately. Purpose was to gain support for ratification of Constitution; it presents argument for republican rather than democratic form of government, in which individual is protected by checks from oppression by strong factions.

1788 Together with earlier volume printed in 1786, publication of *Miscellaneous Works of Freneau* marks emergence of greatest American poet to date. Some memorable poems appearing in these volumes are: "To the Memory of the Brave Americans," "The Hurricane," "The Indian Burying Ground." "The Wild Honey Suckle" considered **Philip Freneau**'s finest poem.

1788 1st American edition of famous English dictionary, **The Royal Standard English Dictionary,** by William Perry. It was published at Worcester, Mass.

1788 Tremendous **New Orleans fire** virtually wiped out old French and Spanish style of architecture. 2nd fire in 1794 completed process. Territory purchased by U.S. in 1803, whereupon Federal and Greek revival styles predominated.

1789 Nationalism which the Revolution boosted found expression in **Noah Webster**'s *Dissertation on the English Language.* He sought to set up American

SCIENCE; INDUSTRY; ECONOMICS; EDUCATION; RELIGION; PHILOSOPHY.

SPORTS; FASHIONS; POPULAR ENTERTAINMENT; FOLKLORE; SOCIETY.

been lost. In 1787 Republicans rewon legislature and rechartered bank. It was 1st bank owned and operated by and for merchants, acquired capital and influence so quickly that it became center of political rivalry and ambition.

1785 Representatives of 26 trades convene in Boston and form **Association of the Tradesmen** and Manufacturers of the Town of Boston. Association grew out of demands of manufacturers, mostly small artisans engaged in shop and home production, for legislative protection against foreign competition.

1786 **1st steamboat in America,** built by John Fitch, sailed on Delaware R. On Aug. 22, 1787, Fitch ran his 2nd and improved boat on Delaware at 3 mph. It used a system of upright paddles at the sides of the boat.

1786 U.S. founded the **1st U.S. Indian reservation.**

1786 **1st recorded strike** in U.S. called by printers of Philadelphia, Pa. Printers were successful in obtaining $6-a-week wage.

1786 Oct. 20 Prof. Samuel Williams of Harvard College headed party of students to observe total eclipse of sun at Penobscot Bay; believed to have been 1st such **astronomical field trip** in America.

1787 Growing American belief in **education of women** seen in publication of *Thoughts on Female Education,* by Dr. Benjamin Rush. Important argument was that to have well-educated children depends on well-educated mothers.

1787 1st noncleric appointed president of any English or American college, Dr. **William Samuel Johnson,** president of Columbia College from 1787 to 1800. He was son of 1st president (1753–1763) of King's College (later Columbia College), **Samuel Johnson.**

estates by yielding them intact to oldest son, abolished in Virginia Legislature largely through efforts of Thomas Jefferson.

1786 Aug. 17 **David Crockett,** legendary frontiersman, Congressman, and one of defenders of Alamo, born in Hawkins County, Tenn.

1787 August Tenche Coxe saluted growth of **American Manufactures** in speech before an assembly in Philadelphia: ". . . we now make ourselves . . . meal of all kinds, ships and boats, malt liquors, distilled spirits, potash, gun-powder, cordage, loaf-sugar, paste-boards, cards and paper of every kind, books in various languages, snuff, tobacco, starch, cannon, muskets, anchors, nails, and very many other articles of iron, bricks, tiles, potters ware, millstones, and other stone work, cabinet work, trunks and windsor chairs, carriages and harness of all kinds, cornfans, ploughs and many other implements of husbandry, saddlery and whips, shoes and boots, leather of various kinds, hosiery, hats and gloves, wearing apparel, coarse linens and woolens, and some cotton goods, linseed and fish oil, wares of gold, silver, tin, pewter, lead, brass and copper, clocks and watches, wool and cotton cards, printing types, glass and stoneware, candles, soap and several other valuable articles, with which the memory cannot supply us at once."

1788 New era in **furniture design** in America initiated with publication of George Hepplewhite's *Cabinetmaker and Upholsterer's Guide* in England. Trend was away from rococo designs of Chippendale towards subtler, more graceful lines. Book was familiar to most furniture manufacturers in America.

1788 May Famous gray stallion, **Messinger,** believed to be original sire of fine breed of trotting horses, 1st in America, arrived from England. He was buried with military honors on Jan. 8, 1808.

1789 Beginning of **social courtesy** that was soon to spread elsewhere seen in fol-

GEORGE M. SMILEY MEMORIAL LIBRARY
CENTRAL METHODIST COLLEGE
FAYETTE, MISSOURI 65248

1789 Mar. 4 **1st session of Congress of U.S.** held, but only 9 of 22 senators and 13 of 59 representatives had arrived. House had its 1st quorum Apr. 1, the Senate Apr. 5.

1789 Apr. 6 U.S. Senate having, after long delay, achieved quorum, **1st Congress was formally organized.** House had achieved quorum on Apr. 1.

1789 Apr. 15 Election of William L. Smith of South Carolina to U.S. House of Representatives contested by his opponent, David Ramsay, said to be **1st contested election** in U.S. Smith, born in Charleston, S.C., spent most of his youth abroad; Ramsay claimed he had not been U.S. citizen for required 7 years. Smith's election was sustained by 1 vote.

1789 Apr. 30 **George Washington** inaugurated 1st President of U.S., holding office for 7 years 10 months. He belonged to Federalist Party.

1789 June 1 Pres. Washington signed **1st legislation enacted by Congress.** It was an act to legalize certain oaths.

1789 July 27 Congress created the **U.S. State Department. Thomas Jefferson** became 1st Secretary of State in Feb. 1790.

1789 Aug. 7 **U.S. War Department** created. Gen. **Henry Knox** was chosen by Gen. Washington for the 1st Secretary of War. At this time the regular army amounted to 840 men, who supervised public lands and guarded the Indian frontier.

1789 Sept. 2 Congress created **U.S. Treasury Department.** 1st U.S. Treasurer was **Alexander Hamilton.**

1789 Sept. 26 Congress confirmed John Jay's appointment as **1st Chief Justice of the U.S. Supreme Court.** He had been appointed by Pres. Washington. He served for 6 years.

1789 Sept. 26 Pres. Washington appointed **Samuel Osgood Postmaster General of the U.S.** He resigned Aug. 1791 because of the government's removal to Philadelphia.

language, republican in nature as opposed to language of royalist England. The *Dissertations* grew out of a series of lectures which Webster had given in Baltimore 4 years before. They called for a revision of native speech as radical as the suggestions with which Bernard Shaw was to dazzle later generations. Webster had the ear, eye and mind of Franklin behind him, but he never realized these early ambitions for the language. He did not, however, outgrow his nationalism, and the link which he forged between language and loyalty has left an inheritance of memorable maxims: "a *national language* is a band of *national union*"; "as independent in *literature* as she is in *politics*—as famous for *arts* as for *arms.*"

1789 **1st American novel,** *The Power of Sympathy; or The Triumph of Nature,* by **William Hill Brown;** written "to expose the dangerous Consequences of Seduction and to set forth the advantages of female Education."

1789 **Capitol** at Richmond, Va., built from plans by Thomas Jefferson, generally considered 1st building of Classic Revival in U.S.

1789 **Methodist Book Concern** established in New York city by Methodist Church to publish religious material and further Christian education. It is today the oldest book publishing house in continuous operation in the U.S.

1789 Jan. **1st American sectarian magazine,** *Arminian Magazine,* which lasted nearly 2 years, published. Edited by Bishops Coke and Asbury of Philadelphia. This month also saw appearance of **1st juvenile magazine,** *Children's Magazine,* in Hartford, Conn. It issued only 3 numbers.

1789 Mar. 2 Pennsylvania repealed law prohibiting **performance of plays.** Attitude of all colonies went through similar change.

SCIENCE; INDUSTRY; ECONOMICS; EDUCATION; RELIGION; PHILOSOPHY.	SPORTS; FASHIONS; POPULAR ENTERTAINMENT; FOLKLORE; SOCIETY.

1787 **1st cotton factory** in New England established at Beverly, Mass., under management of John Cabot and Joshua Fisher.

1787 Pennsylvania **Society for the Encouragement of Manufactures** and Useful Acts organized. Society supported protective tariff, inventions and research. Committee on Manufactures, chosen by subscribers to manufacturing fund, agreed to promote cotton manufacturing, ordered two English carding and spinning machines. By end of 1788 factory put out 10,000 yards of cotton and linen. New York, Boston and Baltimore established similar societies in same year, were soon followed by other cities.

1787 Mar. 10 **Franklin and Marshall College** 1st chartered as Franklin College in Lancaster, Pa., under German Reformed auspices. College merged in 1850 with Marshall College, which had been chartered in 1836 at Mercersburg, Pa. 2 branches of Franklin and Marshall in Lancaster and Mercersburg combined in Lancaster, Pa., in 1853.

1787 Dec. **Cokesbury College,** 1st Methodist college in U.S., opened. College was named for bishops Thomas Coke and Francis Asbury, 1st 2 Methodist bishops in U.S. Located 1st at Abingdon, Md., it moved later to Baltimore.

1789 *A Survey of the Roads of the United States of America,* compiled by Christopher Colles, published in New York city; book contained **1st known road maps** published in U.S.

1789 Jan. 23 **Georgetown College,** 1st Catholic college in U.S., founded in Washington, D.C. Founded by Fr. John Carroll. In 1805 the college came under the direction of the Society of Jesus.

1789 Apr. 23 Probably **1st Catholic newspaper in U.S.,** the *Courrier de Boston,* appeared. It lasted until Oct. 15.

1789 July 4 **1st tariff bill** enacted by U.S. Congress set up protective duties on over 30 different types of commodities.

lowing announcement at performance in Park Theater, New York city: "The offensive practice to Ladies, and dangerous to the House, of smoking segars during the performance, it is hoped, every gentlemen will consent to an absolute prohibition of."

1789 Frequent appearance of **George Washington** in his box at John Street Theater in New York city during year lent respectability to theater but also caused disapproval of certain prominent citizens.

1789 **1st organized temperance group** in America formed by 200 farmers in Litchfield county, Conn. Pledged not to partake of alcoholic beverages during farming season.

1789 Apr. 23 1st committee formed in House and Senate to devise suitably lofty **style of address** for president of U.S. Sen. Izard proposed address of "Excellency" while Sen. Lee considered "Highness."

1789 May 7 Pres. Washington attended a ball at the Assembly Rooms, New York city; this was the **1st Inaugural Ball.**

1789 May 12 **Society of Tammany** held its 1st meeting in New York. Name derived from ancient and wise chief of the Delaware Indians, Tammany, and Society was essentially anti-Federalist in character. Chief founder and 1st Grand Sachem was William Mooney.

1789 Oct. 7 Visitation of **devil** reported by *Hampshire Gazette.* A Connecticut man, imprisoned for theft, told his guards that he was awaiting devil, with whom he had made a pact. While talking he spread gunpowder over floor. ". . . when the time arrived . . . that the Devil was to call him—he by some means conveyed fire to the powder, by which means the room appeared to be in flames, and while the guards were in the greatest consternation and surprise—*The Devil carried off the Prisoner!"*

1789 Nov. 26 **Thanksgiving Day** celebrated for 1st time as national holiday. Pres. Washington, at instance of Congress,

101

POLITICS AND GOVERNMENT; WAR; DISASTERS; VITAL STATISTICS.	BOOKS; PAINTING; DRAMA; ARCHITECTURE; SCULPTURE.

1789 Sept. 26 Pres. Washington appointed **Edmund J. Randolph Attorney General of the U.S.** In 1794 he became Secretary of State when Jefferson retired.

1789 Nov. 21 **North Carolina** ratified Constitution and became 12th state of Union.

1789 Apr. 11 Famous Federalist newspaper, **Gazette of the United States,** appeared. It was edited by John Fenno.

1790–1794

1790 Feb. 11 **1st emancipation petition** submitted to Congress by Quakers through their Society of Friends.

1790 Mar. Sizable **French colony** founded at Gallipolis, Ohio, by emigrants who had to come to America in response to glowing claims of Scioto Company. The Scioto Company, named for river in Ohio, was a venture in land speculation organized in 1787 for purchase of holdings beside the Ohio and Scioto Rivers. It proved a disastrous undertaking and is classified among the great American swindles. Of 218 French immigrants, about 150 settled at Gallipolis, the rest at Marietta where a subsidiary of the Scioto Company had another claim. The settlers were in for a miserable time. They were left stranded without supplies, there were legal doubts as to the validity of their holdings, the company itself went bankrupt and was finally charged with fraud. But one of the superb accidents of history makes it memorable. Through the Scioto Company Joel Barlow, the 1st "American Milton," "Hartford Wit," teacher, chaplain, businessman, journalist, and lawyer (unsuccessful), took up the loose slack of his life and left for Europe to huckster lands to the unsuspecting French. For the most part he was a failure. His enterprise, *La Compagnie du Scioto,* expired in 1789. Left adrift in Europe, Barlow immersed himself in the revolutionary ferment, established himself on intimate terms with leading European intellectuals, introduced himself to a colorful career with the American state department, and after a transatlantic lifetime of fame and good works, died in 1812 as minister to France.

1790 **Duncan Phyfe,** Scotch immigrant in New York, opened his shop to well-to-do homemakers, concentrating on fine workmanship. He charged $25 each for chairs, as much as $300 for great pier table.

1790 Printing began on Dobson's **Encyclopaedia,** magnificent American edition in 18 volumes of *Encyclopaedia Britannica.* For task special types were prepared and countless engravings of fine workmanship made on Pennsylvania paper. Printing required 7 years, cost of venture being covered by subscription. When completed, hailed as greatest achievement of press in America up to that time.

1790 Publication of *The Contrast,* a play by **Royall Tyler.** It was comic satire of Americans who continued to ape British customs, and 1st American comedy to be produced and performed in public.

1790–1791 **John Adams** wrote *Discourses on Davila* which proposed classical view of social order. Adams advocated a utopia ruled by wealthy, powerful and talented, and his theory was regarded as a reaction towards monarchism.

c1791 **Alexandre Reinagle** composed 4 sonatas for pianoforte. Though influenced by Haydn and Carl Philipp Emanuel Bach, sonatas show genuine individuality and are among earliest compositions of real merit done in America. Not published during Reinagle's lifetime, manuscripts were found among effects of his daughter many years later. But undoubtedly he performed them at concerts in Philadelphia.

1791 Major influence on American furniture design was **Thomas Sheraton's**

SCIENCE; INDUSTRY; ECONOMICS; EDUCATION; RELIGION; PHILOSOPHY.	SPORTS; FASHIONS; POPULAR ENTERTAINMENT; FOLKLORE; SOCIETY.

1789 Dec. 11 **University of North Carolina** chartered in Chapel Hill, N.C., as State University. 1st degrees awarded in 1798.

had proclaimed it a day of thanksgiving for the Constitution. Anti-Federalists protested that his proclamation violated states' rights.

1790–1794

1790 **Oldest lighthouse** still in operation, the Portland (Maine) Head Lighthouse, ordered built by Pres. Washington.

1790 Wide use of **Wilderness Road** by early American pioneers reflected in fact that of Kentucky's 75,000 population, more than 90% had traversed Road on their way to Blue Grass State. Road was created largely by wear of constant travel and followed a route from Fort Chissel, Va., through Cumberland Gap to Kentucky and Tennessee. Road links from Philadelphia and Richmond, Va., merged at Fort Chissel enabling settlers from Pennsylvania, Maryland, Virginia, Carolinas, and Georgia to enter West.

1790 Samuel Slater erected **1st cotton mill** in U.S. at Pawtucket, R.I. Slater had been an apprentice of Sir Richard Arkwright in England.

1790 **1st Catholic Bible** in America printed by Mathew Carey, 1st prolific publisher of Catholic works.

1790 **Trinity Church,** burned during Revolutionary War, rebuilt and rededicated by Bishop Provoost of Episcopal Church with Pres. George Washington attending ceremony. From then on, 1st President had special pew reserved for him, distinctively ornamented and covered by baldachin.

1790 Anti-Trinitarian position taken by **Universalist convention** meeting in Philadelphia under leadership of the Rev. Elhanan Winchester and Dr. Benjamin Rush. Meeting declared that Jesus was human intermediary between man and God rather than son of God.

c1790 Followers of **horse racing** began to take interest in blood and breed of horses. The offspring of *Medley,* an earlier champion, *Belair, Gimcrack,* and *Calypso* won repeatedly at races.

1790 **New York city,** state capital, population 30,000, 5 markets. Gov. George Clinton moved into Government House to save $750 rent which he was paying for his own house.

1790 Philadelphia: High Street became **Market Street,** a symbolic concession to the ascendency of commerce in American life.

1790 Anonymous, the indestructible **wandering minstrel,** was as prolific this year as in any other. 5 years before John Keats was born, anonymous sang of a shape as immortal as any on a Grecian urn:

"In Wall-street oft I view that beaut'-
ous form
Which does my heart with soft emotions warm."

1790 "Not worth a continental" expressed feeling felt toward **continental currency** issued by Congress at end of Revolution. 200 million dollars' worth of paper money shrank rapidly in value until it took $40 to buy 1 silver dollar.

1790 Relentless activity of Society for Alleviating the Miseries of the Public Prisons, led by such Pennsylvanians as Tenche Coxe, William Howard, and Benjamin Rush produced important changes in **prison conditions** in Pennsylvania, in-

1790 Mar. 1 Congress authorized **1st U.S. census,** completed on Aug. 1. Population placed at 3,929,625 including 697,-624 slaves and 59,557 free Negroes. Most populous state was Virginia, at 747,610, and largest city Philadelphia, 42,444. Center of U.S. population was 23 miles east of Baltimore. Population was about equally divided between New England and Middle States, and the South. Massachusetts was only state to report no slaves.

1790 Mar. 26 **Federal naturalization act** passed. It provided uniform rules for naturalization after 2 years of residence.

1790 Mar. 29 **John Tyler,** 10th president, born in Greenway, Va.

1790 Apr. 10 **1st patent law passed.** It provided a 3-man board with the power to grant patents. Board members included secretaries of state and war, and attorney-general. 1st incumbents were Thomas Jefferson, Henry Knox, and Edmund Randolph.

1790 Apr. 17 **Benjamin Franklin** died in Philadelphia at age of 84. Of him, Lord Jeffrey, editor of *Edinburgh Review,* wrote: "In one point of view the name of Franklin must be considered as standing higher than any of the others which illustrated the Eighteenth Century. Distinguished as a statesman he was equally great as a philosopher, thus uniting in himself a rare degree of excellence in both these pursuits, to excel in either of which is deemed the highest praise."

1790 May 29 **Rhode Island** ratified Constitution and became 13th state of the Union.

1790 May 31 **1st U.S. copyright act** signed by Pres. Washington. Protected plays, maps, and books. Term of protection was for 14 years, with right of renewal for another 14 years. Title page had to be deposited in the clerk's office of the local U.S. district court. Credit for the success of agitation in behalf of a copyright is generally attributed to Noah Webster. Until the 18th century copyright had remained, on the whole, a matter of common

Cabinet-maker and Upholsterer's Drawing Book, widely read by American furniture makers. Sheraton's designs followed the delicate tradition of Hepplewhite.

1791 **1st opera house** in New Orleans, the Théâtre de St. Pierre, began tradition that was to mark New Orleans as opera center of U.S. until the Civil War.

1791 Early interpretation of American landscape is **William Bartram's** *Travels through North and South Carolina, Georgia, East and West Florida.* Nature exalted to a religion, and popularity of work was evident from borrowings from it by such Romantic writers as Chateaubriand, Wordsworth, and Coleridge.

1791 Popular essay dealing with political and educational matter is *The Prompter* by **Noah Webster.** Written in simple, workaday prose of Franklin, essay went through 7 editions before 1800.

1791 Mar. In Boston **1st printed orchestral score** in America, **"The Death Song of an Indian Chief."** It was inserted in March issue of *The Massachusetts Magazine.*

1792 1st appearance of celebrated actor **John Hodgkinson** on American stage with American Company in Philadelphia.

1792 Cornerstone of **Capitol** laid in Washington, D.C. Building completed about 1830 though it was in use before then. Designed by William Thornton on lines of English country mansions in Palladian mode. Work also 1st begun this year on **White House,** from plans by James Hoban. Sumptuous example of post-Colonial architecture, modeled after palace of Duke of Leinster in Ireland. Rebuilt 1818; restored 1951.

1792 **Raynor Taylor,** former teacher of Alexander Reinagle and director of Sadler's Wells Theatre in London, arrived in America and set himself up in Baltimore as "music professor, organist and teacher of music in general." He later be-

SCIENCE; INDUSTRY; ECONOMICS; EDUCATION; RELIGION; PHILOSOPHY.

SPORTS; FASHIONS; POPULAR ENTERTAINMENT; FOLKLORE; SOCIETY.

1790 July 31 **U.S. Patent Office** opened. It is said a dozen men from Connecticut were waiting at door. At any rate, more men from Yankee Connecticut have registered patents than from any other state. 1st U.S. patent to Samuel Hopkins, of Vermont, for new method of making pearlash and potash.

1790 Aug. 4 Congress authorized interest-bearing **government bonds.** 6% bonds were sold to refund federal debt.

1790 Aug. 15 **1st Roman Catholic bishop in U.S.,** Father John Carroll, consecrated at Lulworth Castle, England. He was selected by Pope Pius VI, who also chose Baltimore as the 1st Episcopal See in America. Bishop Carroll held his 1st synod Nov. 7, 1791.

1790 Dec. 21 **Cotton mill** of Almy, Brown, and Slater began operations in Pawtucket, R.I., using British industrial methods. Samuel Slater had come to America with up-to-date familiarity with new machinery invented in Britain by Arkwright, Crompton, and Hargreaves. His factory manned by children between 4 and 10 years old. Slater was 1st American industrialist to break down production process into simple component parts, thus enabling his child laborers to outproduce most skilled artisan.

1791 Massachusetts Historical Society, **1st historical association** in U.S., founded by Jeremy Belknap, Boston clergyman and historian; society was organized to collect important historical documents.

1791 Beginning of **Philadelphia carpet industry** with the manufacture of Turkish and Axminster carpets by William Peter Sprague.

1791 Nov. 3 **University of Vermont** chartered in Burlington, Vt. It has only recently become the official university of the state. 1st degrees awarded in 1804.

1791 Dec. 12 Main branch of 1st **Bank of the U.S.** opened in Philadelphia with

cluding greater privacy, adequate clothing, religious instruction, separation of different types of criminals, and protection of rights of prisoners from avaricious keepers.

1790 Introduction in Walnut St. Prison, Philadelphia, of **Pennsylvania system of prison management** based on concept of absolute solitary confinement, which was supposed to promote moral regeneration by means of enforced meditation. Pennsylvania system was opposed to **Auburn system** (initiated by state penitentiary in Auburn, N.Y., in 1816), which permitted congregation of prisoners during the day. At night, however, Auburn prisoners slept in separate cells. In general, Auburn system prevailed in U.S.

1790 **High heels** went out of fashion in America to be replaced by sandal-like footwear, with low quarters and with bows and ribbons instead of buckles.

1790 Apr. 21 **Benjamin Franklin** buried in Christ Church yard, Philadelphia. The funeral drew 20,000 spectators, the largest gathering of U.S. citizens to date.

1790 June 30–July 7 *The Connecticut Journal* advertised exhibition of 2 Arabian **camels,** calling them "the greatest natural Curiosity ever exhibited to the Public on this Continent." It is not certain, however, that these were 1st camels ever exhibited in America. Samuel Sewall reported appearance of dromedary, or Arabian camel, in 1714.

1790 July 14 Americans celebrated 1st anniversary of storming of **Bastille** as expression of their revolutionary sentiments. Main public ceremony of event held in Philadelphia. After a few years, Bastille Day was not celebrated in any formal manner except by French societies and those interested in France and her language. A special observance of Bastille Day in America was arranged on July 14, 1918, by committee organized by William Howard Taft.

| POLITICS AND GOVERNMENT; WAR; DISASTERS; VITAL STATISTICS. | BOOKS; PAINTING; DRAMA; ARCHITECTURE; SCULPTURE. |

law and protection ebbed and flowed with the tides of political fortune. But, in 1710, the English Parliament passed the Statute of Anne and set the pattern of copyright which has since prevailed in England and the U.S. The Statute provided for a period of coverage up to 28 years, and became standard in the colonies as well as in England. After the Revolution, however, the various states were lax about establishing copyright prerogatives and the federal government was completely powerless to control abuse. When Webster was ready to publish his unprecedented *American Spelling Book* he soon discovered that he would have no say in the disposition of his work. He began a tour of the states campaigning in behalf of new legislation. The man and the matter came to the attention of Washington. It provided a springboard for theory in behalf of a strong federal government and bound Webster in sympathy with the cause of Madison. Legislation followed in 1790, when maps, charts and books came under protection for a period of 14 years, with a similar period provided for renewal privileges. Subsequent regulation has reinforced the pattern of this law.

1790 Capt. Robert Gray docked the *Columbia* in Boston harbor, completing the **1st trip around the world on an American boat.**

1791 Aristocratic view of government advocated by **John Adams** in his *Discourses on Davila.* Conservative, Adams feared oppression by democratic majority and wanted checks to insure rule of rich and well-born.

1791 Mar. Incendiary pamphlet which attacks monarchy and argued strongly for democracy was American Thomas Paine's **The Rights of Man.** Incisive in his attack, Paine was tried for treason in England and forced to flee to France, where he played role in French Revolution before returning to U.S.

1791 Mar. 3 Congress passed **1st internal revenue law.** 14 revenue districts were created and a tax of 20 to 30 cents a gallon put on distilled spirits. Legislatures of

came associated with Reinagle and New Theatre in Philadelphia.

1792 **Hugh Henry Brackenridge** began publication of *Modern Chivalry.* Brackenridge was a type of American Cervantes, wrote rollicking satire of the manners of his contemporaries.

1792 **Benjamin West** appointed president of Royal Academy of London. West, an American-born artist, settled in England in 1763 and remained there until his death in 1820. He was noted as the foremost portrait painter of his day.

1792 Apr. 24 Beginnings of **American farce** can be seen in J. Robinson's *The Yorker's Strategem, or Banana's Wedding.* A New Yorker disguises himself as bumpkin and under name of Banana woos and wins West Indian heiress. Play introduces Negro characters (not American) for 1st time on stage.

1792 Oct. 12 **1st memorial to Christopher Columbus** in America dedicated at Baltimore, Md. Built of English brick, coated with cement, it was put up at North Ave. and Bond St.

1792 Dec. 5 **1st theater** in Boston closed and its manager, Joseph Harper, arrested by sheriff. Called The New Exhibition Room in an attempt to circumvent Boston's ban against theaters, it had just been built this year.

1793 *The Rural Harmony,* collection of songs by **Jacob Kimball,** published. Kimball was one of native-born musicians of post-Revolutionary period who tried to compete with immigrant professionals. He died eventually in almshouse at Topsfield, Mass.

1793 **Famous early anthology,** *American Poems, Selected and Original,* selected by Elihu Hubbard Smith, published at Litchfield, Conn. Anthology was devoted largely to "Connecticut Wits," Trumbull, Barlow, Dwight, and Hopkins, who were friends of Smith.

106

additional branches scattered through main urban centers in America. Bank served federal government as its fiscal representative and through its possession of specie backing for currency acted as bank of last resort.

1792 **Russian Orthodox Church** initiated missionary program in Alaska, then owned by Russia. Resident bishop in Sitka co-ordinated missionary work.

1792 Englishman Dr. Hugh Smith published in America his **Letters to Married Women,** *on Nursing and the Management of Children.* Later there appeared in U.S. *Letters to Married Ladies, to which is added, a Letter on Corsets, and Copious Notes by an American physician.* Both books went through many American editions, the latter having 3 editions by 1835.

1792 James Woodhouse of Philadelphia, Pa., organized **Chemical Society of Philadelphia,** one of the earliest scientific societies in America.

1792 **1st important wooden truss bridge,** type invented to suit American needs, completed by Colonel Ewel Hale at Bellows Falls, Vt. Wood was plentiful, but rafts and barges were impeded by pile bridge or rows of arches. Two spans of 175 ft. each rested on an island.

1792 May 17 Organization of **New York Stock Exchange** at the Merchants Coffee House, New York city.

1793 **Famous American geography,** the *American Universal Geography; or, a View of the Present State of All the Empires, Kingdoms, States and Republics in the Known World, and of the United States of America in Particular.* Illustrated with Maps. By Jedidiah Morse of Boston. Morse was a famous geographer, and in 1797 he published what was probably the 1st American gazetteer, *The American Gazetteer, exhibiting, in Alphabetical Order, a much more full and accurate Account, than has been given, of the States, Provinces, Counties, Cities, Towns . . . on the American Continent, also of the West-Indies Islands,*

1791 Benjamin Thompson, native of North Woburn, Mass., made **count of the Holy Roman Empire** by Charles Philip Frederick, Duke of Bavaria. Thompson was an American scientist; but, since he was considered pro-British, he was in 1776 evacuated from Boston with the British troops and sent to England. He always considered himself a British citizen. Sarah Thompson, his daughter, became **1st American woman to be a countess.** His title, **Count Rumford,** was derived from Rumford, N.H.

1791 Jan. 1 Pres. Washington initiated custom of giving reception on **New Year's Day** after his inauguration. Custom was continued by 1st Democratic president, Thomas Jefferson, and remained in practice until Jan. 1, 1934, when it was suspended by Pres. Franklin D. Roosevelt who, because of his handicap, found it too difficult to stand in receiving line of reception for too long a time.

1792 Apr. 1 **1st New Church sermon** in America delivered by the Rev. James Wilmer in Baltimore. New Church was made up of followers of teachings of great Swedish mystic, Emanuel Swedenborg.

1792 June 1 **Statehood Day** in Kentucky commemorates admission of Blue Grass state to statehood on this date.

1792 Oct. 12 1st celebration of **Columbus Day** in America held in New York city under auspices of Society of St. Tammany. St. Tammany had been chosen as patron saint in spirit of ridicule since he was Indian savant. Ridicule was directed at such societies as those of St. George, St. Andrew, and St. David.

| POLITICS AND GOVERNMENT; WAR; DISASTERS; VITAL STATISTICS. | BOOKS; PAINTING; DRAMA; ARCHITECTURE; SCULPTURE. |

North Carolina, Virginia, and Maryland passed resolutions of disapproval shortly thereafter.

1791 Mar. 4 **Vermont** joined Union, becoming 14th state. It had ratified Constitution in Jan.

1791 Apr. 23 **James Buchanan,** 15th president, born in Cove Gap, Pa.

1792 **Attack on slavery** in Virginia led by George Mason, who likened slavery to slow poison that was corrupting future legislators with habits of despotism.

1792 **Republican Party** (anti-Federalists) formed. This party became present Democratic Party. It was formed to oppose Federalists, who were considered pro-English and against republican form of government. Jefferson, who was sympathetic toward French Revolution, became party leader. Republicans enjoyed overwhelming popularity until 1820.

1792 Jan. 12 Pres. Washington appointed Thomas Pinckney of South Carolina **1st U.S. minister to England.** His instructions desired him to express "that spirit of sincere friendship, which we bear to the English nation" and also to seek the liberation of American commerce from British restrictions.

1792 Apr. 2 Congress authorized **1st U.S. mint,** to be constructed at Philadelphia, Pa. David Rittenhouse, astronomer and mathematician, was chosen 1st director. Both silver and gold coins were minted, at a ratio of 15 to 1.

1792 May 8 Congress passed a **national conscription act** to require "each and every free able-bodied white male citizen of the republic" to serve in U.S. militia.

1792 June 1 **Kentucky** became 15th state. It was previously part of Virginia territory.

1792 Dec. 15 **Bill of Rights,** 1st 10 amendments to the Constitution, went into effect as Virginia provided necessary ratification. Approval had been needed by both houses of Congress and two thirds of states.

1793 Oldest American daily newspaper, **American Mercury,** founded. An anti-slavery paper, it threw its support behind Lincoln. In 1904 it was merged with *The Evening Globe,* and called *The Globe and Commercial Advertiser.* Finally acquired by Munsey, it was consolidated in 1923 with *The New York Sun,* which merged with *The New York World-Telegram* in 1950 to become *The New York World-Telegram and Sun.*

1793 Essay best reflecting humanitarian spirit of 18th century is *A Word of Remembrance and Caution to the Rich* by **John Woolman,** Quaker tailor of New Jersey. Advocating vast social reforms, abolition of slavery, etc., tract was reprinted by Fabians in 1898, who referred to Woolman as "the voice in the wilderness, the John the Baptist of the Gospel of Socialism."

1793 1st publication of *Letters from an American Farmer* by J. Hector St. John, better known by his pen name, **Crevecoeur.** Published in Philadelphia, this work offered personal view of growth of American nationality, combining through intermarriage the many nationalities of Europe.

1793 **Philip Freneau endorsed the French Revolution** in *On the Anniversary of the Storming of the Bastille.* Freneau continued to propagandize the cause of the revolution after the tempers of his contemporaries had begun to cool.

c1794 Most popular musician in Boston, **John L. Berkenhead,** blind pianist from London, became famous for his realistic renditions of *The Demolition of the Bastille,* one of pieces of descriptive music which flourished toward close of 18th century.

1794 Law of 1750 **prohibiting plays** in Boston repealed and **Boston Theater** opened under management of Charles Stuart Powell.

etc. This gazetteer went through many editions.

1793 Jan. 9 **1st balloon flight** in U.S. made at Philadelphia by J. P. F. Blanchard, a Frenchman, reaching an altitude of 5812 ft. in 46 min. and landing 23 days later in Depford Township, N.J.

1793 Feb. 22 **Williams College** in Williamstown, Mass., chartered. Its entrance requirements reflected current vogue for learning French, a result of close ties between France and America formed during Revolution. French was accepted as substitute for classical languages as prerequisite.

1793 May 25 Fr. Stephen Theodore Badin ordained in Baltimore, Md., the **1st Catholic priest** ordained in U.S. He was a refugee from French Revolution; after ordination he served in Kentucky where he dedicated the **1st Catholic chapel** in Lexington in 1800.

1793 Oct. 28 Eli Whitney of Mulberry Grove, Ga., filed application for patent on **cotton gin**; patent was granted 2 years later on Mar. 14, 1794. Cotton production mounted spectacularly after Whitney's invention, rising from 138,000 lbs. exported in 1792 to 17,790,000 lbs. exported in 1800. Whitney, however, received very little return for his invention. His machine was stolen by others in spite of patent, and powerful interests bore against him in his fight for royalties. In 1812 Congress refused to renew his patent.

1794 Major force in American mass education was Philadelphia artist, **Charles Willson Peale,** whose museum in Philadelphia began disseminating historical and scientific knowledge to less educated. Museum featured intellectual curios in tangible form with displays of wampum, tomahawks, scalps, and other antiquities against realistically painted backgrounds.

1794 One of **earliest American unions,** Federal Society of Journeymen Cordwainers, 1st organized in Philadelphia. It called strike this year and succeeded in raising wages of its members.

1793 Jean Pierre Blanchard made 1st successful **balloon ascent** in America at Philadelphia. Blanchard, a Frenchman, had previously crossed the English Channel in a balloon accompanied by an American Tory, Dr. John Jeffries, who had fled to England in 1779 and returned to U.S. in time for this other flight.

1793 **Brillat-Savarin,** French émigré, arrived in New York. Savarin supported himself by giving French lessons and playing in a theater orchestra. He ate in Little's Tavern and soon began to apply his gustatory art and continental tact to mitigating the English preference in American cooking.

1793 Lexington, Ky.: Town trustees ordered an end to **horse racing** in the streets. It was frightening the pedestrians.

1793 Method of **house numbering** in Philadelphia, with even numbers on one side of street and odd numbers on other, so intrigued Moreau de Saint-Mery, refugee from Terror in France, that upon his return to Europe he introduced practice in various European cities.

*c*1793 **Ricketts' Circus,** John Bill Ricketts, proprietor, gave performances at Philadelphia, Pa.; one performance on April 22nd, 1793, was seen by Gen. George Washington. Ricketts later moved his circus to New York, where he exhibited at Greenwich Theatre near the Battery in 1795.

1794 Widely read attack on **woman's inferior status** by Mary Wollstonecraft entitled *A Vindication of the Rights of Women* had great influence in advanced intellectual circles in America.

POLITICS AND GOVERNMENT; WAR;

DISASTERS; VITAL STATISTICS.

BOOKS; PAINTING; DRAMA;

ARCHITECTURE; SCULPTURE.

1793 Mar. 4 **Pres. Washington** inaugurated for his 2nd term. John Adams was his vice-president.

1793 Apr. 22 Pres. George Washington issued **proclamation of neutrality.** It warned Americans to avoid aiding either side in the European war between Great Britain and France.

1794 Early **anti-federalist** movement spearheaded by John Taylor of Caroline, Va., who argued dangerous evils of protective tariffs, chartered banks, and large corporations in his *Enquiry into the Principles and Tendency of Certain Public Measures.*

1794 Feb. 28 Sen. **Abraham Alfonse Albert Gallatin** of Pennsylvania, later Sec. of Treasury, barred from Senate after dispute concerning election. His seat was declared void because he had not fulfilled 9-year residence requirement for election to Senate. Gallatin had incurred enmity of Federalists and Alexander Hamilton when he introduced a motion demanding that the administration present a record of its finances.

1794 Apr. 22 Pennsylvania eliminated **capital punishment** except for 1st degree murder.

1794 Aug. 7 Pres. Washington issued a proclamation ordering out militia to put down **Whisky Rebellion** in Pennsylvania. Riots were a result of excise tax placed on whisky in 1791.

1794 Aug. 20 Gen. Wayne routed 2000 Indians, killing and wounding many, on Miami R. in Ohio. This victory virtually ended **Indian War,** which had started at northwest frontier in 1790 and was preceded by costly defeats to Gen. St. Clair and Gen. Harmer.

1794 Nov. 19 **Jay Treaty** concluded between England and U.S. Widely denounced in America because it continued to allow British the right to search U.S. ships and impress American seamen on the grounds that they were actually of British birth and citizenship.

1794 During Philadelphia theater season **dramatic criticism** 1st begins to take shape in America.

1794 Continuing **Dutch influence** in English New York reflected in publication of some 50 books in New York in Dutch language between 1708 and 1794.

1794 **Benjamin Franklin's** *Autobiography,* among most widely read books in English, considered greatest autobiography written by an American.

1794 *The Harmony of Maine,* songs by **Supply Belcher,** published at Boston. Belcher, known as "the Handel of Maine," was politician, schoolteacher, and tavernkeeper on northern frontier, as well as composer of simple hymns and Fugues which attained great popularity among rural audiences.

1794 **American novel** *Charlotte Temple* by Suzanne Rowson. This highly successful sentimental "seduction" novel 1st published in England 1791; but it had no success until published in Philadelphia 3 years later. Beginning episodes in England, but last tragic scenes in New York. Often considered 1st American novel.

1794 1st part of deistic *The Age of Reason* by **Thomas Paine,** written with frequently faulty logic but with unmistakable fervor and conviction. Especially popular with common people, who resented religious as well as political tyranny, *The Age of Reason* has perhaps done as much to change men's thinking as nearly any other American book. On Dec. 27, 1793, Paine had been thrown into Paris prison for his opposition to French Reign of Terror. Rest of book completed under shadow of guillotine and published on his release in 1795.

1794 Feb. 17 **New Theatre** in Chestnut Street, Philadelphia, opened with performance of Samuel Arnold's opera *The Castle of Andalusia.* Opening had been long delayed by yellow fever epidemic which raged in Philadelphia in 1793.

110

SCIENCE; INDUSTRY; ECONOMICS; EDUCATION; RELIGION; PHILOSOPHY.

1794 Richard Allen, Negro and former slave, founded **1st independent Methodist Church for Negroes** at Philadelphia, Pa. Allen became 1st bishop of **African Methodist Episcopal Church** in 1816, when 16 Negro congregations united to form the new denomination.

1794 **1st important turnpike** in America completed between Philadelphia and Lancaster. Large profits of sponsoring company led to construction of many such roads throughout America, often in areas where they were not necessary. Lancaster Turnpike was 1st macadam road in U.S. —62 miles long.

1794 **One of earliest American canals** built to circumnavigate South Hadley's falls on the Connecticut R. in Massachusetts. Its lift operated by means of inclined planes and cables powered by the current. At about the same time the famous Middlesex Canal was constructed (its 1st section opened in 1804). It was thought the best American canal until the Erie Canal was opened. The Middlesex Canal was 27 miles long, and it cost about $3.50 for a standard barge to go its length. The sizes of the barges were fixed by regulations. The barges were pulled by horses.

1794 June 24 **Bowdoin College** chartered in Brunswick, Me., under Congregational auspices. 1st degrees awarded in 1806.

1794 Sept. 10 **University of Tennessee** 1st chartered as Blount College in Knoxville, Tenn. Established under Presbyterian auspices, Blount College became state university in 1806 through federal grant providing for two state universities, one in eastern part of state and other in western. Blount College chosen as eastern member and, in 1807, renamed East Tennessee College. College became East Tennessee University in 1840 and University of Tennessee in 1879. 1st degrees awarded in 1806.

SPORTS; FASHIONS; POPULAR ENTERTAINMENT; FOLKLORE; SOCIETY.

1794 Use of **powder** on men's hair went out of fashion after being worn for over 100 years. Hair still worn in queue, tied with black ribbon.

1794 **Penal reform** undertaken in Pennsylvania resulted in decrease in number of crimes for which capital punishment was decreed.

1794 Charles Bulfinch started to build attached houses on Tontine Crescent in Franklin Place, Boston. Houses, done in the "Federal style," mark the beginnings of 1st, or Roman, phase of the **Classic Revival in architecture.**

1794 **Cornelius Vanderbilt,** the future "Commodore," born on Staten Island, N.Y. 4th son of a Dutch squatter, Van Der Bilt, there is no record of a golden spoon in his layette.

1794 **Barber-hairdresser,** specializing in men's wigs, hired out in Philadelphia for 22 shillings a month.

1794 Philadelphians saluted one another as "citizen," demonstrating their sympathy for the **French Revolution.**

1794 Nov. 21 The Sign of the Black Bear in Philadelphia advertised a performance there of guillotining of Louis XVI, describing its climax as point at which "the head falls in a basket, and the lips, which are first red, turn blue." Spectacle was significant index of American political opinion regarding **French Revolution.** Supporters of Thomas Jefferson and his party flocked to applaud revolutionary event "performed to the life by an invisible machine without any perceivable assistance."

1795–1799

1795 1 of earliest and most spectacular land frauds in American history, **Yazoo Land Frauds,** rocked Georgia. Yazoo lands located in what is now Mississippi and Alabama, and owned by Georgia. Georgia legislature granted 35 million acres of this land for settlement to 4 companies at price of $500,000. When it was discovered that every legislator but 1 had interest in grants when he passed on measure, James Jackson left U.S. Senate to run for State legislature to reclaim lands from companies for State of Georgia. Although contract was repealed by new legislature elected in 1796 and led by Jackson, original grants could never be overturned in Courts. Unanimous Supreme Court Decision delivered by Chief Justice Marshall upheld contract and declared that Georgia legislature had acted unconstitutionally in nullifying a contract. In 1810, U.S. Congress passed bill appropriating up to $8,000,000 to settle original Yazoo claims which Georgia refused to honor.

1795 Indian Factory system established by federal government to assist Indians in their dealing with white traders. Under supervision of "factors," system was designed to get fair prices for products of Indians.

1795 Jan. 29 **Naturalization Act** passed. It required residence period of 5 years and renunciation of allegiances and titles of nobility as prerequisites to citizenship.

1795 Nov. 2 **James K. Polk,** 11th president, born in Pineville, N.C.

1796 May 19 Congress enacted **game protection law** to restrict white encroachments on Indian hunting grounds. Act provided fines or jail for hunting game in Indian territory.

1796 June 1 **Tennessee** became 16th state.

1796 Sept. 17 Document which has had tremendous effect upon American

1795 1 of best of post-Revolutionary public buildings, **Massachusetts State House,** built in Boston from designs by Charles Bulfinch.

1795 Feb. 16 **Gothic melodrama** found expression on American stage in Dunlap's *Fontainville Abbey,* adapted from 1 of Mrs. Radcliffe's books. On Oct. 31, 1796, he followed with *The Mysterious Monk.*

1795 May 22 1st native Negro to appear on American stage is character Sambo in *The Triumphs of Love, or Happy Reconciliation* by **John Murdock,** gifted barber. Play also treats Quakers on stage for 1st time.

1796 1st New York appearance of actor **Joseph Jefferson** with American Company. He was progenitor of long line of celebrated actors of 19th century.

1796 Most famous portrait of "Father of his Country" is **Gilbert Stuart's** *George Washington,* known as "Athenaeum" head. Stuart made numerous tries before this successful result. Nothing but head of president can be seen, character being derived only from features. This likeness is accepted one and has become familiar to millions. Head was placed in Boston Athenaeum, and later permanently loaned to the Boston Museum of Fine Arts.

1796 Mock epic poem singing virtues of American dish, cornmeal mush, *The Hasty Pudding,* is most popular work of **Joel Barlow.**

1796 1st complete American edition of William **Shakespeare's** *Plays.* Shakespeare has ever since remained among most popular authors, his *Plays* being 1 of 7 works to sell over 2½ million copies.

1796 1st publication of **Thomas Paine's** *Agrarian Justice,* imbued with faith of 18th century French *philosophes* in rational basis for perfectibility of social institutions.

| SCIENCE; INDUSTRY; ECONOMICS; EDUCATION; RELIGION; PHILOSOPHY. | SPORTS; FASHIONS; POPULAR ENTERTAINMENT; FOLKLORE; SOCIETY. |

1795–1799

1795 **1st library** in Kentucky founded at Lexington, reflecting city's cultural ascendancy in early frontier region.

1795 **Comte de Volney** visited U.S. where his work, *The Ruins: or, A Survey of the Revolution of Empires* had been favorably received and translated by Jefferson and Joel Barlow. *The Ruins* is a study in the philosophy of history and the cultivated deism of the author greatly appealed to American intellectuals. Unfortunately, Volney's arrival was followed closely by the crisis with France. He was charged with spying for France in behalf of the restitution of Louisiana and forced to leave for home the next year. Volney is an interesting figure in the evolution of American utopianism. In 1792 he had associated himself with Corsica where the restoration of Gen. Paoli the year before had reintroduced on the island the spirit of reform and experiment which made Corsica and her government a stronghold of 18th century liberalism. It was a mutual sympathy of ideals and plans which later drew Volney to America.

1795 Feb. 25 **Union University** chartered in Schenectady, N.Y., as Union College. Founded under Presbyterian auspices, Union College awarded its 1st degrees in 1800. College became University in 1873.

1796 **1st important suspension bridge** in U.S. built between Uniontown and Greensborough, Pa., over Jacobs' Creek. Bridge, no longer standing, based on principle of suspension developed mainly by James Finley of Fayette County, Pa.

1796 View that **slavery** was inconsistent with high moral purpose of Bill of Rights upheld by St. George Tucker, professor of law in William and Mary.

1796–1797 **John Fitch** made 1 last effort to convince New Yorkers that he had something in his steamboat. On Collect Pond, where the Tombs stood on Cen-

1796 Reforms in **criminal code** of Virginia reduced number of crimes for which capital punishment was decreed as sentence.

1796 1st experiments with **gas illumination** attempted in Philadelphia.

1796 **Billiards** frequently played in South according to contemporary reports. Francis Baily noted dozen tables in Norfolk alone.

1796–1799 **Louis Philippe,** who was to be proclaimed "king of the French" by the deposed Charles X in 1830, was living in a 1 room flat over a bar in Philadelphia. He managed, however, to travel in the best of circles where he met the daughter of William Bingham, banker, then U.S. Senator from Pennsylvania and husband of Washington's most colorful and celebrated hostess, Anne Willing Bingham. Louis Philippe proposed marriage to the young Miss Bingham, but the Senator stepped in and said "no" on the ground that she was not good enough for Louis if Louis were king, and too good for him if he were not. There is no record of Miss Bingham as an actress though, if she took after her mother, she was at least the rival of Grace Kelly in beauty. As things stood, the Senator was undoubtedly discreet. Louis Philippe did return and become king, and that high station remained for some time beyond the aspirations of middle class daughters. Nor did Senator Bingham, who had founded the Bank of North America and for whom the city of Binghamton, N.Y., was named, overvalue his daughters. One married the Comte de Tilly and the other, Alexander Baring, Baron Ashburton, the English financier and banker. Louis Philippe lived to fall between the father's both qualifications when he was dethroned in 1848.

1796 Harried travelers along the **Philadelphia-Baltimore roads** complained of

foreign policy is **George Washington's** *Farewell Address.* Delivered before Congress, address warned against America's involvement in foreign disputes and thus paved way for isolationist policy of 19th century.

1797 Mar. 4 **John Adams** inaugurated 2nd president. He remained in office 4 years, and was the last Federalist president to be elected.

1797 May 15 Congress convened in **1st special session,** called by Pres. Adams to debate crisis in French-American relations. American envoy to France, Charles Cotesworth Pinckney, had left France after being insulted by French foreign minister; situation deteriorated rapidly and caused growing concern in U.S.

1798 Severe **yellow fever** epidemic in New York caused 2086 deaths in population of 50,000.

1798 **Anti-Jacobin reaction** in America reflected in Harvard commencement speech saying of French Revolution that "it has . . . annihilated society."

1798 Pioneer **Daniel Boone** received grant of 850 acres of land from Spanish government in Femme Osage district of Louisiana Territory.

1798 **1st Secretary of Navy** appointed by Pres. Adams. He was Benjamin Stoddert, and he found himself with a weak navy in a time of trouble with France. Within 2 years he acquired 50 ships, planned for a marine corps, naval hospital, and dock yards.

1798 Jan. 8 **11th amendment** adopted. It stipulates that Federal courts shall not have jurisdiction over litigations between individuals from one state against another state.

1798 Apr. 3 **XYZ Affair** reported to Congress by Pres. Adams, disclosing refusal of French secretary of foreign affairs, Talleyrand, to receive U.S. representatives unless bribe paid and loan granted. Famous expression "Millions for defense, but not one cent for tribute," originated in this affair.

1796 1 of earliest instances in U.S. of Adam influence from England, **Harrison Gray Otis House,** built in Boston; later became headquarters of The Society for the Preservation of New England Antiquities.

1796 *The Archers, or the Mountaineers of Switzerland,* **early and perhaps 1st American opera,** staged in New York city. An adaptation of Friedrich von Schiller's *William Tell,* it was composed by William Dunlap and Benjamin Carr.

1796 June **William Dunlap** entered into partnership with Lewis Hallam and actor Hodgkinson, beginning long career as producer of plays for American Company.

1796 Dec. 19 1st and only performance of *Edwin and Angelina,* opera by French immigrant **Victor Pelissier,** produced at the New York Theater. It is based on *Edwin and Angelina* by Oliver Goldsmith.

1797 Most ambitious of colonial buildings in California, main church at mission **San Juan Capistrano,** begun; completed 1806. Designed by Isidoro Aguilar, stonemason from Mexico, it had 120-ft. bell tower, many carved ornaments. Destroyed in earthquake of Dec. 8, 1812, its ruins are still favorite visiting place.

1797 Feb. 17 Dramatic spectacle provided in last act of **John Daly Burk's** play *Bunker Hill,* in which real attack was staged. Play was revived often on July 4th celebrations.

1798 Patriotic fervor stirred up in poem "Hail, Columbia," **by Joseph Hopkinson,** at time when war with France was impending.

1798 Influence of Gothic vogue and pre-Byronic hero of European fiction seen in novels by American **Charles Brockden Brown.** In *Wieland* ventriloquism and superstition play big parts; in *Ormond* (1799) and *Edgar Huntly* (1799) diabolical heroes, sleep-walking, Indian massacres, etc., assume much importance.

1798 Apr. Remarkable dramatic tour-de-force is *Female Patriotism, or the Death*

tre Street, he sailed a steamboat built-for-four in which he made use of a screw propeller. He had no takers and was undoubtedly told to get himself a horse.

1797 1st instruction booklet for students of **experimental chemistry** in America published by Dr. James Woodhouse in Philadelphia.

1797 **1st glassworks** in early American Midwest established in Pittsburgh by O'Hara and Craig.

1797 **1st American patent** for clock taken out by Eli Terry for his newly devised method of employing wooden works in his clocks. Clocks were sold rather cheaply—$18 to $70; sales so great that he became 1st to use water power to cut parts.

1797 **1st medical periodical** in U.S. appeared. It was *The Medical Repository,* edited by Dr. Samuel Latham Mitchill, who directed it for 16 years.

1797 June 26 1st U.S. patent for **plow** issued to Charles Newbold of N.J. After expending his entire fortune in developing practical plow of cast iron, Newbold was unable to sell it to farmers because of their fear of harmful effect of iron on soil. Thomas Jefferson had made 1st studies of plows in America and had designed a moldboard plow according to distinctive requirements of American soil but Jefferson never applied for patent.

1798 1st professional and important **nursing instruction** given. Dr. Valentine Seaman lectured on anatomy, physiology, obstetrics, and pediatrics. Later he published an outline of these lectures, which constituted probably the 1st attempt in U.S. at a nursing text.

1798 June George Logan, worried about the imminence of **war with France,** sailed on peace ship to do what he could, as a private citizen, to prevent the outbreak of hostilities. Logan, erstwhile doctor, active Pennsylvania politician, friend to Jefferson, was a lifelong Quaker. His mission to France was expression of his religious pacifism. He was further influ-

chasms 6–10 feet deep along the way. They were lucky when their vehicles did not overturn. It sometimes took a stagecoach 5 days to make a trip.

1797 Early American novelist, Charles Brockden Brown, made a special plea for cultural, social, political and economic **liberation of women** in *Alcuin,* novel that held that men and women had more in common than they had at issue.

1797 Philadelphia put the Schuylkill R. to work supplying **water.** There were 3 underground tunnels for distributing water around the city. They ran into a tower in the center of the city. This was 1st attempt of the kind in U.S.

1798 **Breeding of horses** in U.S. began in earnest in 1798. This year, *Diomed,* great English champion who had won Epsom Derby in 1780, was brought to U.S. by Col. John Hoomes of Virginia. *Diomed* sired many famous American horses, including *Eclipse* and *Lexington.*

1798 *Sporting Magazine* of England reported that large **hawk** that had been shot in Yorkshire had attached to its leg brass band inscribed, "Belonging to the Governor of New Halifax, America, A.D. 1762."

1798 June 18 The expression, **"Millions for defense, but not one cent for tribute,"** entered American political language at banquet at O'Eller's Tavern in Philadelphia in honor of John Marshall, one of presidential envoys to French Foreign Minister Talleyrand. Honored by Federalists for refusing to consider an indirect request for a bribe by one of Talleyrand's agents, Marshall listened to 16 toasts in honor of his part in the XYZ affair. 13th toast, proposed by Robert

POLITICS AND GOVERNMENT; WAR; DISASTERS; VITAL STATISTICS.

BOOKS; PAINTING; DRAMA; ARCHITECTURE; SCULPTURE.

1798 June 18   Amendments to **Naturalization Act of 1795** adopted, requiring residence period of 14 years and declaration of intention for 5 years. This is 1 of 4 acts collectively known as Alien and Sedition Acts.

1798 June 25   **Alien Act** passed, granting president power for 2 years to deport any alien he might deem dangerous to country's safety. This was 2nd of 4 acts known as Alien and Sedition Acts.

1798 July 6   **Alien Enemies Act** passed. It provided for apprehension and deportation of male aliens who were subjects or citizens of hostile country. This was 3rd act of 4 known collectively as Alien and Sedition Acts.

1798 July 7   1st case of outright **abrogation of a treaty** by U.S. occurred when Congress pronounced U.S. "freed and exonerated from the stipulations" of treaties of 1778 with France.

1798 July 14   **Sedition Act** passed. It provided for arrest and imprisonment of any person, citizen or alien, who attempted to impede lawful processes of government, foment insurrection, or write, publish, or utter any false or malicious statement about president, congress, or government of U.S. This was 4th and last of Alien and Sedition Acts. In point of import, rather than of time, it is, however, the Alien Act, the 2nd of the series, which was the most important. These acts reflect the panic of the Federalist Party in the face of the XYZ Affair, the general conflict with France, and the growing strength and aggression of the Republican Party. They were weapons to curb the power of domestic opponents, resulted in confusion and injustice, brought the Federal Party into contempt, to political defeat, and final dissolution.

1799   **Spanish census** counted 42,375 inhabitants, ⅔rds white, in settlements of lower Louisiana.

1799 Dec. 14   **George Washington** died at age of 67. He is buried at Mount Vernon, Va.

of Joan d'Arc by **John Daly Burk**, produced at Park Theater, New York. He was able to instill real Elizabethan vigor in his lines. Spirit of liberty breathes through entire play.

1798 Dec. 10   Great vogue for domestic dramas of German writer **Kotzebue** seen in success of adaptation by William Dunlap in New York of *The Stranger. Lovers' Vows, Count Benyowski* follow in 1799. *False Shame* (1799), *Force of Calumny* (1800), *Count of Burgundy* (1800), *Virgin of the Sun* (1800), etc.

1799   1st newspaper outside Washington to give verbatim reports of Congressional debates, **Baltimore American** begun. Paper had long life of 130 years.

1799   Compilation of **Lindley Murray Readers.** They were accepted for 4 generations as standard authority on English grammar.

1799   1 of few remaining examples of country mansions that were built in upper Manhattan during 18th century, **Gracie Mansion,** constructed in what is now Carl Schurz Park. Was acquired as official residence for mayors of New York city in 1942.

1799   **St. Mark's in-the-Bouwerie** built on site of former farm of Gov. Stuyvesant. One of New York's architecturally best small churches.

1799   **Bank of Pennsylvania** in Philadelphia built from plans by Benjamin H. Latrobe, 1 of chief architects in "Greek Revival." In this building he used Ionic hexastyle portico which led toward heavy, monumental concept of public buildings.

1799 Apr. 1   **1st quarterly review** in America was *American Review and Literary Journal,* edited and composed mainly by Charles B. Brown. In 1801 this review followed by *Literary Magazine and American Register.* In 1808 this replaced by *American Register, or General Repository of History, Politics and Science.*

1799 Dec. 20–30   New York city's theaters closed because of **Washington's** death.

enced by natural sympathy of Republican party, of which he had become member, for France. Despite personal threats from Federalists he equipped himself for the mission and set sail. With assistance from Lafayette, himself in German exile, he got into France and presented his pleas to Talleyrand after U.S. relations with France had been severed and the last representative had left. Logan is credited with having influenced the course of peace, but he was strongly censured at home for his action, which brought about passage of Logan Act and prohibition against interference by private citizens in normal diplomatic procedure for conducting relationships with foreign governments.

1798 Eli Whitney adapted suggestions of Le Blanc for **manufacture of interchangeable parts** for arsenal production of firearms supplied to U.S. government. The long series of misunderstandings which hampered success of cotton gin made Whitney turn to firearms manufacturing as a means of livelihood.

1798 Early geological researches in New York state performed by **Dr. Samuel L. Mitchill,** physician, who accurately catalogued various rock strata of eastern New York.

1798 **1st American vessel** constructed on Lake Ontario some 3 miles from Rochester. *Jemima* was relatively small, some 30 tons.

1798 Dec. 14 Patent awarded to David Wilkinson of Rhode Island for machine that cut **screw threads.** In Aug. 1848, Congress awarded Wilkinson $10,000 for his invention.

1799 1st recorded use of the word "scab" in labor-management conflicts came in strike of shoemakers in Philadelphia. Word was striker's abusive reference to workers hired at establishments during a strike. At same time the **"paid walking delegate"** was born. It was duty of "paid walking delegate" to inspect struck establishments for presence of "scabs" and to take necessary measures.

Goodloe Harper, Federalist Congressman from South Carolina, was famous "Millions for defense, but not one cent for tribute." Although statement was correctly attributed to Harper in Philadelphia's *American Daily Advertiser* on June 20, expression came to be identified with Charles Cotesworth Pinckney, one of American envoys to whom bribe request had been directed. Pinckney shortly before his death denied ever having made statement; but because expression seemed more apt as diplomatic reply than as forensic toast, legend persisted.

1798 After his dismal failure as a steamboat salesman, John Fitch began to experiment with model trains. He is said to have built the **1st free-moving railway steam engine in miniature.**

1799 **Boy of 14** graduated from Rhode Island College. Childish precocity was frequent during colonial times. Infants of 3 were sometimes taught to read Latin as soon as English. Timothy Dwight was able to read Bible at 4.

1799 Dec. 14 **"First in war, first in peace, first in the hearts of his countrymen,"** automatically associated with George Washington, was 1st said as part of Henry Lee's funeral oration before Congress, after Washington's death. "Light-Horse Harry" had served under Washington in Revolution and became close personal friend. He was father of Robert E. Lee, great Confederate general.

1800

2nd U.S. census recorded population of 5,308,483, including 896,849 slaves. This represented ten-year gain of 1,379,269, and gain of 199,168 slaves. Center of U.S. population was 18 miles southwest of Baltimore, a westward shift from 1790, and reflects the growth of the frontier. Total population of U.S. in 1800 was less than population of New York city in 1950.

High tension of **political campaign** of 1800 reflected in statements of clergymen hostile to Jefferson that his election would mean the confiscation of every Bible in New England. Jefferson was widely thought to be deist but most evidence indicates that he was closer to Unitarianism than to deism.

1st of 4 resolutions in Virginia Assembly proposed **African resettlement** of Negro slaves held in state. Resolution reflected antislavery attitudes in South at this time even among influential slaveholders. Subsequent similar resolutions were passed in 1802, 1805, and 1816.

Jan. 7 Millard Fillmore, 13th president, born in Locke, N.Y.

May 7 Law enacted by Congress divided Northwest Territory, creating **Indiana Territory** out of western section. The provisions of the Treaty of Paris, 1783, which ended the Revolutionary War, defined boundaries of U.S. Among other concessions, Britain agreed to a line through the Great Lakes which formally placed the Old Northwest Territory above the Ohio in U.S. control. The states which laid claim to parts of the region ceded their territories by 1785, in anticipation of the Northwest Ordinance of 1787. The act of 1800 split the Northwest Territory into 2 territories, Indiana and Ohio. Successive acts in 1805 and 1809 created what is now the state of Indiana.

June Washington became new capital of U.S. when government departments began to move into new buildings. 1st Con-

Sofas and settees made in **Sheraton and Directoire style** enjoyed monopoly of public taste during this period. Workshop of Duncan Phyfe turned out many superb examples.

Well known cabinetmaker **Michael Allison** began producing cabinets of distinctive craftsmanship in New York city.

Source of many legends and anecdotes about George Washington was **Parson Weems's** popular *Life of Washington* published. Keyed to popular taste, there were 9 editions by 1809. In 1806 Weems inserted episode of the cherry tree and hatchet. Mason Locke Weems won distinction in a number of fields. He was one of the 1st 2 Anglican divines ordained in U.S. after the requirement of an oath of allegiance to English crown was suspended. He was, by avocation, a bookseller and paced out a prodigious path through the colonies over the course of 31 years. As an author he combined all of his talents. He knew the formula for best sellers and never missed the opportunity to edify as well as enlighten.

1st American painter to show genuine feeling for nature, **Ralph Earl,** earned his living as itinerant portrait limner. His *Looking East from Leicester Hills* shows large landscape as viewed from open window. Painting commissioned by landowner, who probably desired to "immortalize" his holdings.

Death of **Washington** occasioned countless poems which were collected in *Hymns and Odes Composed on the Death of General George Washington.* Among contributors were Thomas Paine, C. B. Brown, Richard Alsop.

1st edition of **New Testament** printed in Greek in U.S. is Η Καινη Διαθηκη—*Novum Testamentum* of Isaiah Thomas of Worcester, Mass.

Mission of Our Lady of the Rosary

SCIENCE; INDUSTRY; ECONOMICS; EDUCATION; RELIGION; PHILOSOPHY.	SPORTS; FASHIONS; POPULAR ENTERTAINMENT; FOLKLORE; SOCIETY.

1800

Establishment by Act of Congress of **Library of Congress,** which was at 1st housed in Capitol. In 1897 it was moved into its own building, which is largest and most costly library building in world.

Jacob Albright of Lebanon County, Pa., organized a religious movement whose members were at 1st called "Albrights." In 1816 they adopted the designation **"Evangelical Association."**

1st genuine canal in U.S., Santee Canal, completed in S.C., linking Santee R. with headwater of Cooper R., which flowed into harbor of Charleston. Canal was built by Christian Senf, Swedish engineer imported for the job, with help of 110 laborers, both slaves and freemen, men and women. Canal was 22 mi. long with 10 locks that raised and lowered water 103 ft. Completed canal cost $1,000,100, but ultimately failed because of inadequate supply of water at summit level.

Famous strike in early U.S. history was sailors' strike in New York. Sailors demanded rise in wages from $10 to $14 per month. They actively agitated throughout city, urging other seamen to join in demonstrations. Strike was broken with arrest of its leader for disturbing the peace and inciting to riot.

1st shoemaker in America to make **separate shoes** for the right and left foot was William Young, who resided at 128 Chestnut Street in Philadelphia.

Church of the United Brethren in Christ organized. Movement had originated among Mennonites in Lancaster County, Pa., in 1766. Martin Boehm and Philip W. Otterbein, Mennonite clergymen, had influenced the early founders.

1st cowpox vaccination in U.S. performed by Dr. Benjamin Waterhouse at Philadelphia.

July **1st recorded Methodist camp meeting** held at Logan County, Ky., near Gaspar R. Church.

"Johnny Appleseed" legend born. Rare instance of folk tale having well authenticated basis in fact is the story of John Chapman, known as "Johnny Appleseed," who chose the life of a benign itinerant and wandered up and down pioneer settlements in Ohio Valley, distributing religious tracts and scattering appleseeds wherever he went. His career lasted 50 years. Chapman was born not long before the works of Swedenborg were introduced in U.S., and he grew up when the new doctrines were beginning to be popularized. Whatever his connections with the New Jerusalem Church, it was Swedenborg's effort to reconcile the world of spirit with the physical science which dominated the religious temperament of Chapman. There are many reports of the eagerness with which Chapman would declaim from Swedenborg to anyone who was willing to listen. Undoubtedly he was impressed also with Swedenborg's great sympathy for the natural world and made the distributions of seeds and sermons part of a single religious crusade. Chapman was also a frontier Paul Revere: he is said to have made nightrides to warn Americans of Anglo-Indian raids during the War of 1812. His interest in horticulture was not restricted to his celebrated apples. He also introduced and encouraged the raising of many useful medicinal herbs.

4-tined forks came into common use in American homes at about this time. 2- or 3-tined forks had been more customary.

Working conditions of actors reflected in hiring of Mrs. Merry as "Star" for American Company performing in New York. Her salary was $100 a week plus a "benefit." This benefit was usually the 3rd performance of the play, the actor receiving a share of the proceeds.

Gouging, popular frontier sport, reached peak of popularity in Ohio Valley. Ultimate goal was gouging out of an opponent's eye with the thumbnail. Thumbnails

POLITICS AND GOVERNMENT; WAR;

DISASTERS; VITAL STATISTICS.

BOOKS; PAINTING; DRAMA;

ARCHITECTURE; SCULPTURE.

gress to sit in Washington convened on Nov. 17. John Adams, 1st president to live in Executive Mansion, moved in also in Nov. Jefferson was 1st president to be inaugurated there when he was sworn into office Mar. 4, 1801. U.S. considered 1st nation in world to design a city exclusively for its capital.

Oct. 1 By secret treaty of San Ildefonso Spain ceded **Louisiana Territory** to France. In 1762 Spain was given Louisiana by France through the provisions of the Treaty of Fontainebleau. It was Napoleon, with his projects for a new French colonial empire, who inspired the agreement at San Ildefonso.

built at Battery Park, New York; attributed to John McComb. One of few remnants of day when lower Broadway was neighborhood of fine residences.

1st number of **Musical Journal,** weekly published and edited by Benjamin Carr, appeared in Philadelphia. Carr announced he would publish "a regular supply of new music from Europe" and would draw on "the assistance of Men of Genius in this Country."

July 9 Opening of **1st summer theater** in New York, Mount Vernon Gardens on Broadway and Leonard Street. Performances began at 9 P.M., tickets selling for 4 and 5 shillings.

1801

Jan. 20 **John Marshall** appointed Chief Justice of U.S. Supreme Court. He became one of greatest judges in U.S. history, establishing Supreme Court as final authority in determining state and federal powers.

Feb. 11 Tie in electoral votes between Jefferson and Burr announced. This tie led to adoption in 1804 of **12th amendment,** which requires that electors cast separate ballots for president and vice-president. Prior to adoption of 12th amendment candidate receiving most votes became president; he with 2nd highest became vice-president.

Feb. 17 After 36 ballots, House of Representatives elected **Thomas Jefferson** and **Aaron Burr** as president and vice-president over John Adams. On Feb. 11 Electoral College had split, 73 votes each for Jefferson and Burr.

Mar. 4 **Thomas Jefferson,** 3rd president of U.S., became 1st to be inaugurated in Washington, D.C. He held office for 8 years, and was 1st of Republican (later Democratic) Party elected to presidency.

May 14 Yusuf Karamanli, Pasha of Tripoli, opened **Tripolitan War** by symbolic act of ordering his soldiers to cut down flagpole at U.S. consulate.

Leading magazine of decade, **Port Folio,** founded by Joseph Dennie of Philadelphia. Federalist in sympathy, Dennie leaned to British literature and culture, printing verses of Wordsworth and Thomas Moore very early.

City Hall at Charleston, S.C., 1 of best examples of post-Colonial, "studied" architecture, built from plans by Manigault.

Newspaper which enlisted some of foremost editorial writers of 19th century, **New York Evening Post,** established. Under editorship of W. C. Bryant, 1829–78, it was Free-soil and supported Lincoln. After Civil War Carl Schurz and E. L. Godkin steered paper in its attack on local corruption. After passing through many hands it finally became *New York Post* in Mar. 1934.

Feb. 11 **Romanticism** in its Byronic aspects expressed in Dunlap's *Abaellino, the Great Bandit,* adapted from German of Johann Heinrich Daniel Zschokke. Play held boards for 25 years and was translated into many languages.

| SCIENCE; INDUSTRY; ECONOMICS; EDUCATION; RELIGION; PHILOSOPHY. | SPORTS; FASHIONS; POPULAR ENTERTAINMENT; FOLKLORE; SOCIETY. |

Sept. **Famous bridge,** the Cayuga bridge, spanned 1¼ miles and was wide enough to allow 3 wagons to pass abreast. Represented expenditure of $150,000 for Manhattan Company of New York, which financed it.

Nov. 1 **Middlebury College** chartered in Middlebury, Vt. 1st degrees awarded in 1802.

1800–1819 Renewed interest in **German culture** in America spurred by the Rev. William Bentley of Salem, whose *Impartial Register,* released periodically over two decades, reported on cultural, intellectual, and scientific advances made in Germany.

were grown long for this purpose. This style of fighting imported from England into South and spread westward.

Ball game, which later became **baseball,** played by boys using cricket balls but not cricket bats.

Apr. 3 **Martha Washington** granted franking privilege. Special act of Congress allowed her to receive and send all mail free of charge. The distinction, pleasant as it is to recall, is somewhat tarnished by the thought that Martha Washington lived to enjoy her privilege only 2 years. Franking, extended to veterans of the Revolution, became so widespread that a complete revision of practice was soon necessary.

1801

Longest **suspension bridge** of time opened over Merrimac River near town of Newburyport, Mass., with span of 244 ft. Although not 1st ever built in America, this is oldest suspension bridge in America still standing.

"Plan of Union" adopted by Congregationalists and Presbyterians to combine their resources in bringing religion to frontier settlements. This proved one of the most fruitful policies in American church history. The rush to Western lands had grown beyond the organizational resources of the churches. Settlements were scattered and poorly serviced. To make the most of available resources, the Plan of Union permitted Congregationalist ministers to serve in Presbyterian churches and vice versa.

Growing importance of **insurance** in U.S. economy seen in incorporation of the Columbian Insurance Company of New York.

American Company of Booksellers organized in New York city. It was promoted especially by Philadelphian publisher Matthew Carey. The Organization sponsored 5 book fairs between 1802 and 1806.

Oct. 19 **1st aqueduct water** for Philadelphia delivered.

Hardwater crackers 1st began to appear in New England. Josiah Bent of Milton, Mass., constructed a Dutch oven in his home, in which the 1st crackers were probably made. He peddled the crackers himself, and they soon became widespread in New England. Eventually they enjoyed international favor.

Johnny Appleseed arrived at Licking County, Ohio, with bag of appleseeds which he had collected at cider mills in New York and Pennsylvania. His planting of appleseeds became one of strangest missions in American history. It has been estimated that Johnny Appleseed's travels yielded fruit-bearing trees over area of 100,000 sq. mi. His real name was John Chapman.

Mar. 4 Thomas Jefferson coined expression, **"entangling alliances"** in his 1st inaugural address: "Peace, commerce, and honest friendship with all nations—entangling alliances with none." These words have been commonly attributed to George Washington; but, although he supported the idea expressed, there is no record of his having used this precise phraseology.

1802

Jan. 29 Virginian John Beckley designated **1st librarian of Congress.** He had been Clerk of the House of Representatives.

Feb 6 Act of Congress provided for protection of American vessels against **Tripolitan cruisers** by empowering president to arm existing vessels. Act did not explicitly declare war, but ambiguously mentioned that U.S. might use force at sea but not against ports of Tripoli.

Mar. 16 Congress enacted bill to establish **U.S. Military Academy** at West Point, N.Y. Academy was officially opened on July 4.

Apr. 30 **1st enabling act** passed by Congress authorized people of eastern division of Northwest Territory to hold convention and frame constitution in order to become state. Precedent set in Ohio's gaining of statehood was then followed for admission of rest of states.

Banjo clock 1st appeared in American homes. Designed by Simon Willard, famous clockmaker of Roxbury, Mass., banjo clock was constructed so as to hang on wall against which it was supported by small gilt bracket.

Benjamin West completed his enormous composition, *Christ Healing the Sick,* which he planned to donate to Philadelphia Hospital. Picture caused sensation in London, and when British Institution offered 3000 guineas for it, he sold it, and painted duplicate for hospital.

Upper-class dominance of American culture reflected in unusual machinery employed to establish **American Academy of Arts** in New York city. Shares of stock in organization were sold as if academy were industrial concern.

Apr. Library of Congress issued **1st catalogue of books,** entitled *Catalogue of Books, Maps, and Charts, Belonging to the Library of the Two Houses of Congress.*

1803

Jan. 11 **James Monroe** appointed by President Jefferson Minister Plenipotentiary and Envoy Extraordinary to France and Spain to purchase New Orleans and Floridas. American minister at Paris, Robert Livingston, was surprised when offered whole of Louisiana territory.

Feb. 19 Ohio became 17th state. Since slavery had been outlawed in Northwestern Territory by Northwest Ordinance in 1787, Ohio was 1st state in which **slavery** was forbidden by law from its beginning. Vermont had outlawed slavery since the adoption of its Constitution July, 1777, some 6 months after its declaration of independence as a state.

Mar. John Sibley set out to explore **Red River** as far as present site of Shreveport, La.

Popular essayist of period, **William Wirt,** published his *Letters of a British Spy.* His interest ranged widely—from essays on oratory, education, politics to papers on early Virginian history. By 1814 work had gone through 5 editions; before its publishing history ended, the editions ran to 12. It appeared 1st as a series in a Richmond paper. Wirt did not sign his name to the articles, but his identity was pretty much an open secret. He followed the fashion of 18th century social commentators by posing as a foreigner observing the customs of a supposedly strange society.

Social and political satire formed the basis of **Thomas G. Fessenden**'s *A Terrible Tractoration,* which ridiculed medical quackery, vivisection, animal cross-

SCIENCE; INDUSTRY; ECONOMICS; EDUCATION; RELIGION; PHILOSOPHY.

SPORTS; FASHIONS; POPULAR ENTERTAINMENT; FOLKLORE; SOCIETY.

1802

New American Practical Navigator by **Nathaniel Bowditch,** famous seaman and mathematician who devised method of computing longitudes with sextant, measuring angular distances between certain fixed stars and moon. Guide attained international recognition and went through 60 editions.

Abel Porter & Co., early **brass-working factory,** organized in Waterbury, Conn. Porter set up rolling mill operated by horse power and initiated brass industry in Waterbury.

Jan. 9 **Ohio University** 1st chartered in Athens, Ohio, as American Western University. Became Ohio University in 1804. 1st degrees awarded in 1815.

Jan. 15 **Washington and Jefferson College** 1st chartered as Jefferson College in Canonsburg, Pa. 1st degrees awarded in 1802. In 1865 joined Washington College, chartered in Washington, Pa., 1806.

Nov. 18 **1st sheet copper** produced in U.S. in Boston.

100 Merino sheep brought from Spain by Col. David Humphreys, U.S. Minister to Spain. They were brought on the sloop *Perseverance,* and were the 1st in U.S. The Merino sheep, specialized for its fine wool, was long a Spanish monopoly. It was just at the time that Humphreys was sent to Spain that the Merino was being exported to other countries. Merino strains bred in U.S. were among the finest in the world.

1st hotel in America, Union Hotel, built at Saratoga, N.Y., by Gideon Putnam. There were, of course, many taverns and inns before this. A public building designed primarily for lodging instead of entertainment defines a hotel.

New York State passed law forbidding **public races.** Only races in state were held by private Jockey Clubs.

Expectation, powerful horse owned by Colonel Tayloe, won sweepstakes at Richmond, doing 2 miles in 3:47. After race, he was sold to Col. Alston for $4000.

1803

1st tax supported public library founded in Salisbury, Conn. It was started by gift from Caleb Bingham, Boston publisher, and was continued by grants of town monies.

German pietist group, **Harmonists,** more popularly known as Rappites after their leader, George Rapp, established communal settlement near Pittsburgh which they called Harmony.

Glove-manufacturing begun in Gloversville, N.Y., by Ezekiel Case. Town became noted for business of making gloves and mittens.

Road building in Midwest spurred by allotment of 5% of net proceeds of sale of public lands within state of Ohio. Act took effect at time of granting statehood to Ohio.

Doctor, setting up practice, advertised that he would be only too glad to wait upon the public but that his first concern is for "his friends in particular."

Racehorse *Peacemaking* set **30 year record** running 2 miles in 3 min. 54 sec.

John Randolph fluttered Philadelphia circles with his announcement that he had fathered an illegitimate child.

Subscription to Philadelphia periodical *Port Folio* cost $5 per year. It was suggested that the price would be negligible if readers organized themselves into **reading clubs.**

POLITICS AND GOVERNMENT; WAR; DISASTERS; VITAL STATISTICS.	BOOKS; PAINTING; DRAMA; ARCHITECTURE; SCULPTURE.

Apr. 30 **1st territorial expansion** was through purchase of tract of land, some 828,000 sq. mi. in extent, known as **Louisiana Purchase.** It was bought from France for 80,000,000 francs (about $15 million); but this price included 20,000,000 francs for assumption of American claims against France. Purchase increased national territory about 140%. Following states comprise original territory: Missouri, Nebraska, Iowa, Arkansas, North and South Dakota, most of Louisiana, Kansas, Minnesota, Montana, and Wyoming, and parts of Colorado and Oklahoma.

May 23 Captain Edward Preble commissioned as commander of 3rd squadron to be sent against **Tripoli.**

breeding, and scientific theories of such naturalists as Buffon and Dr. Erasmus Darwin. His *Democracy Unveiled* (1805) attacked Jefferson, and his *Pills, Poetical and Philosophical* (1809) again satirized medical profession.

New York City Hall, one of best of late Georgian buildings, erected from plans made by John McComb.

Feb. 4 1st example on American stage of French *mélodrame* type play was **Dunlap's** adaptation, *The Voice of Nature,* from a play by L. C. Caigniez, *Le Jugement de Salomon.* Type is free from strict observance of cause and effect, and exaggerates passion and sentiments.

1804

Feb. 16 **Lt. Decatur** burned *Philadelphia* while it was docked in Tripoli. American ship had been captured by Tripolitan gunboats when it ran onto reef.

Mar. 26 1st official notice of U.S. government's intention of moving **Indians** living East of Mississippi R. to the West of the river appeared in the Louisiana Territory act, which divided the Territory and gave it a government.

May 14 **Expedition of Meriwether Lewis and William Clark,** organized under Pres. Jefferson, started from St. Louis to explore Louisiana Territory. They went up the Missouri R., then headed west to the Columbia R., which they explored to its mouth, reaching the Pacific Nov. 8, 1805.

July 11 **Alexander Hamilton** fatally wounded in pistol duel with Aaron Burr. Burr had promoted disunion and establishment of a northern Confederacy. Hamilton fought his attempt for presidency in 1800, and again in 1804. Burr challenged Hamilton who deliberately misfired before Burr aimed with intent to kill.

Sept. 25 **12th Amendment** to Constitution ratified, providing in part that voters shall "name in their ballots the person

Flight of **American artists** to Europe marked by presence this year of Washington Allston and John Vanderlyn in Rome where they encountered Washington Irving, Samuel Coleridge, and Joseph Turner. Henry James later used Allston's career to demonstrate that art "withers" in America.

"The Hermitage," now national shrine, 1st built by Andrew Jackson and his wife as 3-room cabin in Tennessee wilderness.

Romanticism introduced in American painting by tremendous representation of *The Deluge* by **Washington Allston.** A young man of 25 in Paris, he studied works of masters which Napoleon had collected. Scene depicts wild surge flinging naked bodies on shore. Allston's biography reads like the classic romance of expatriate American artist who "finds" himself in Europe. His well-placed but philistine family did everything possible to discourage signs of talent in the young boy. In secret, Washington nourished his inclination, rebelled against being a doctor, declared himself for art and sailed for London in 1801. After his return in 1818 he lost his European inspiration and began to decline.

Impressive, authoritative biography of 1st president appeared, **John Marshall's**

SCIENCE; INDUSTRY; ECONOMICS; EDUCATION; RELIGION; PHILOSOPHY.	SPORTS; FASHIONS; POPULAR ENTERTAINMENT; FOLKLORE; SOCIETY.

May Benjamin Latrobe presented report to American Philosophical Society concerning **U.S. improvements in construction of steam engines.** Report was answer to request by Philosophical Society of Rotterdam for information about state of American advance in field of engineering. On eve of success of steamboat the Latrobe report, academic and aloof, was still summing up arguments for and against steam engine. Latrobe himself was no impassioned partisan, was typical of dim horizon of spokesmen of his period. Within 5 years steam engine was perfected and operating.

Sept. 29 **1st Roman Catholic Church** built in Boston formally dedicated.

British Government ruled that **British ships crossing to America** must allow 43 ft. of space for each passenger. Traffic was so heavy that it would soon have been necessary to stand the bunks on end.

Apr. John James Audubon banded phoebes, thus becoming the 1st person in U.S. to **band birds** for scientific reasons.

1804

Major contributions to scholarship and establishment of enduring historical records effected by **The New-York Historical Society,** founded mainly through efforts of wealthy merchant named John Pintard. Pintard actually had the habits of wealth more than wealth itself when he embarked on his spectacular career of promoting cultural institutions. He lost his money through a bad investment, but was able to reestablish himself to the point of being free to do what became his vocation. He is credited with having encouraged the start of the Massachusetts Historical Society and other similar groups before he undertook the N.Y. Historical Society, which was organized to gather historical records of U.S. and New York state. Among his other "firsts" are included the General Theological Seminary, the American Bible Society, and an improved method of keeping the vital statistics of New York city.

Oliver Evans, famous U.S. inventor, was commissioned by Philadelphian Board of Health to build **steam engine** for dredging and cleaning city docks. 5-hp engine propelled scow 12 ft. wide and 30 ft. long. When completed weighed 15½ tons and was driven from its construction shed 1½ mi. on wheels. Thus it was **1st known "au-**

1st recorded importation of bananas to U.S. arrived on schooner *Reynard*. It was not until after Civil War that 1st important shipments of bananas to New York city began.

"Coonskin Library" founded in Marietta, Ohio. This unique institution came into being when settlers along Ohio R. bartered coonskins for books from Boston merchants.

1st agricultural fair held. It took place in Washington, D.C. There existed before this time various societies which promoted agriculture, commerce, and the arts. These groups distributed literature, some bulletins being exclusively devoted to agriculture.

Beginning of French Empire and period of style which dominated continental and American **house furnishings** in 1st decades of 18th century. Simple neo-classic taste of revolutionary era replaced by more haughty vision of imperial temper. New French styles influence American design, producing furniture lavishly fitted out with marble, brass and mahogany. Most American pieces, however, were not so lush as French originals. They are remarkable for use of elaborate decorative carvings of

voted for as President and in distinct ballots the person voted for as Vice-President." In election of this year, electors for 1st time voted separately for president and vice-president. Previously, persons having 2nd largest number of votes of electoral college became vice-president.

Nov. 23 **Franklin Pierce,** 14th president, born in Hillsborough, N.H.

Dec. 5 In 1st election with separate ballots for president and vice-president **Thomas Jefferson** re-elected by electoral vote of 162 to 14. His opponent was Charles C. Pinckney. **George Clinton** was elected vice-president.

Life of Washington. In 5 volumes, book reflects Federalist prejudices of author. Shorter biographies of Washington were written by Aaron Bancroft (1807) and David Ramsay (1807).

St. Stephen's Catholic Church built in Boston, only extant church in Boston designed by Charles Bulfinch. Sometimes called New North Church.

Boston, Mass., booksellers joined to publish *The Catalogue of All the Books Printed in the United States. . . .* One of the earliest **book catalogues** issued in America.

1805

Mar. 4 Pres. **Jefferson** inaugurated for his 2nd term. George Clinton succeeded Aaron Burr as vice-president.

Apr. 26 Eaton seized Derna, a city in Tripoli. This was major victory of **Tripolitan War,** which was concluded with treaty of peace on June 4th.

Apr. 27 1st engagement of **U.S. armed forces** in North Africa occurred at capture of city of Derna. This victory under U.S. Consul to Tunis, William Eaton, was favorable turning point in U.S. relations with all Barbary states. Eaton collected rabble army in Egypt, accompanied by Lt. Presley N. O'Bannon and his 7 marines, who were only organized U.S. group in Eaton's command. Phrase "To the shores of Tripoli" in U.S. Marine Corps official song refers to this campaign.

June 4 **Peace treaty** signed with Tripoli, granting U.S. Navy freedom to sail in Mediterranean unmolested. Additional terms were an exchange of prisoners, $60,-000 ransom for extra American prisoners, and relinquishment of claims by Tripoli for tribute from Tripoli. Treaty was favorable to American interests.

Aug. 9 **Zebulon Montgomery Pike,** commanding 20 men, set out to find source of Mississippi R. His reports, derived in part from talk with Indians and in part

Founding of our oldest, still existing, art institution, the **Pennsylvania Academy of Fine Art,** by Charles Willson Peale. In 1801 New York Academy had been founded, but it survived only 4 years.

Growing French influence on American culture reflected in vogue of **French Directoire** style furniture.

Early account of American Revolution with particular emphasis on participating actors is *Rise, Progress and Termination of the American Revolution* by Mrs. **Mercy Warren.** Many anecdotes of Revolutionary figures spring from this mine of sketches.

One of early students of Benjamin West, **Matthew Pratt,** died in Philadelphia. During his early life he spent considerable effort and skill painting wooden signboards, which were still to be seen after Civil War. He studied with West for 2½ years, immortalizing his sojourn by his painting *The American School,* which shows West instructing 4 pupils.

Gore Place, built at Waltham, Mass., finest New England example of late Georgian or Federal architecture in private residences.

1 of first public buildings to reflect Gothic Revival in U.S. architecture, **Cathedral** at Baltimore, begun from plans by Benjamin Latrobe.

SCIENCE; INDUSTRY; ECONOMICS; EDUCATION; RELIGION; PHILOSOPHY.	SPORTS; FASHIONS; POPULAR ENTERTAINMENT; FOLKLORE; SOCIETY.

tomobile," and was driven down Center Street much to amusement of Philadelphians. Evans offered to bet onlooker $3000 that he could make steam-driven vehicle that would go faster than any horse in world. Drive belt was shifted from land wheels to paddle wheels, and scow went steaming down river against wind, leaving behind all sail boats. Despite this demonstration, public was not very impressed with principle of steam engine.

foliage and scrolls, with legs often shaped to resemble animal legs, including paws.

2 patents granted for **"galluses,"** which are not to confused with "galoshes." Galluses were used to keep one end of trousers up rather than to keep the other end dry. Like the man who wears both belt and braces, 2 patents on suspenders in 1 year testify that certain early Americans must have had a longing for security.

1805

1st important shipment of ice from New England made by Frederick Tudor. He exported it to Martinique. Shipping ice to the East, especially to India, became a prosperous business for "Yankee" traders.

1st anti-Trinitarian book written and published in U.S., **Hosea Ballou's** *Treatise on the Atonement,* established theological system of Universalism based on all-loving God. In this system, Jesus united man with God by His precepts and crucifixion but was not part of and did not alter unalterable deity. In New Hampshire, Ballou made the confession of faith which sums up the theological argument of his later works. He affirmed the fatherhood of God and the freedom of man's will, with the sacrifice of Christ an example of the perfection which man can attain by turning away from sin. This is called "salvation by character" because of the burden which it places upon the function of voluntary choice.

1st appeal to courts by struck employer resulted in the conviction of leaders of the Philadelphia Society of Cordwainers for criminal conspiracy for purpose of increasing their wages. Conviction was secured under English common-law doctrine.

Dec. 14 **University of South Carolina** 1st chartered as South Carolina College in

In concluding 2nd part of *Modern Chivalry,* Hugh Henry Brackenridge put his finger on the vice of ambition which he named the "poison of public virtue." His **satiric view of his contemporaries** ends gravely: "In the American republic, we retain yet a great deal of the spirit of monarchy. . . . The first lesson I would give to a son of mine would be to have nothing to do with public business, but as a duty to his country. . . . They should be warned to beware of flatterers, whose object is not to serve them, but themselves. The demagogue in a democracy, and the courtier in a monachy, are identical. . . ."

Mar. 4 Jefferson's **Second Inaugural Address** called attention to the discontinuance of "internal taxes," and went on to record an idyllic word-picture of American taxpayer: "The remaining revenue on the consumption of foreign articles, is paid cheerfully by those who can afford to add foreign luxuries to domestic comforts, being collected on our seaboards and frontiers only, and incorporated with the transactions of our mercantile citizens. . . ."

Apr. 27 **1st time U.S. Standard raised** over fort of Old World occurred when party of marines and bluejackets landed

POLITICS AND GOVERNMENT; WAR; DISASTERS; VITAL STATISTICS.	BOOKS; PAINTING; DRAMA; ARCHITECTURE; SCULPTURE.

from pure personal speculation, were not very reliable.

Feb. 22 **Dunlap's theater** in New York city closed, Dunlap himself having become bankrupt. Early American theater was at best precarious enterprise.

1806

Western expansion reflected in early plan for what later became **Erie Canal** across New York state. It was projected by Jesse Hawley.

Law passed in Virginia stipulating that any **Negro** who had become a freedman must leave state within the year.

Aaron Burr's empire planned. He and his followers meant to carve out independent state from land then owned by either Spain, U.S., or both. Plot collapsed when Pres. Jefferson ordered Burr arrested later that year.

Apr. 18 Congress passed **act prohibiting importation of many British products** in protest against seizure of American ships and impressment of American sailors by British.

May 16 **European coast blockaded.** Charles James Fox, British foreign secretary, formally closed all ports from Brest to Elbe River.

July 15 **Zebulon Pike** began his exploration of southwestern territory. He traveled up Missouri R., through Kansas and southern Nebraska to New Mexico, through Rio Grande Valley and on to Mexico City. Pike 1st saw on Nov. 15 famous **Pike's Peak** in what is now Colorado.

Byronic note was struck in dramas of young playwright-painter from South Carolina, **John Blake White.** His *Foscari, or the Venetian Exile* presented in Charleston. *The Mysteries of the Castle* (1806), *Modern Honor* (1812), and *Forgers* (1825) also exploit romantic vein.

Noah Webster's *Compendious Dictionary of the English Language* represented retreat from Webster's earlier attempts to Americanize English language. Although many supporters of a purely American tongue, divorced from the British tongue, continued to agitate for linguistic changes, Webster's compromises with the mother tongue and its traditions became the accepted standards of language in U.S. The *Dictionary* was the culmination of a series of his works, beginning in 1783 with *The Grammatical Institute of the English Language* which included readers, spellers, and grammars that had enormous circulation in America.

Exhuming of **1st mastodon skeleton** depicted in a painting of about this time by Charles Willson Peale. He had made find in a marsh in New York state, and his painting reveals excitement of event.

Nov. 15 **1st college magazine** appeared, the Yale University *Literary Cabinet*.

1807

Mar. 2 Congress passed act prohibiting **African slave trade** and importation of slaves into any place within jurisdiction of U.S. after Jan. 1, 1808.

Sept. 1 **Aaron Burr** acquitted of treason charges by circuit court at Richmond, Va., on ground he was not present when overt act was committed. Pres. Jefferson, having been warned of Burr's activities in

Extremely effective series of essays entitled *Salmagundi* printed in New York, authors being **J. K. Paulding, William Irving,** and **Washington Irving.** Carrying on the essay style of 18th century, pieces were mildly satirical; they afford wonderful glimpses of New York at this period. Hundreds of imitations followed in short order. Marks beginning of literature now

Columbia, S.C. Established as state college, South Carolina College awarded its 1st degrees in 1806.

at Derna, Tripoli, after city was bombarded by *Hornet, Nautilus,* and *Argus.* This engagement was in war against Barbary pirates.

1806

1st industry-wide strike in U.S. resulted when 200 journeymen shoemakers in New York city, suspecting that struck employers were having their work done in other establishments, obtained nationwide strike order from Journeyman Cordwainers' Society of Baltimore. Leaders of strike were indicted for criminal conspiracy in their attempt to secure higher wages.

Lancastrian system of education introduced in America in a New York city school. System provided for use of pupil-teachers who, having once learned their lessons from either other pupil-teachers or single master teacher, would pass on their knowledge to pupils beneath them. Founded in England by Joseph Lancaster, who emigrated to America in 1818 to supervise his ideas, system was economical and very popular with wealthier citizens in America who preferred Lancastrian schools to tax-consuming public schools.

Early attempt in U.S. to **popularize scientific knowledge** for lower, less-educated classes embodied in *The Wonders of Nature and Art* by Smith and Mease. Net effect of book of this nature was to break monopoly of knowledge held largely by well-to-do classes in America.

Gas street Lighting introduced in U.S. by David Melville, who constructed lamps on Pelham St., Newport, R.I. But there were legal complications, and the project was a failure for Melville.

1st picture of **football game** on American soil showed Yale students kicking ball under stern eye of Puritan Yale president Timothy Dwight. Football had been kicked around at Yale for 45 years by this time.

Some **expressions** that Webster included in his *Compendious Dictionary* were "lengthy," "sot," "spry," "gunning," "belittle," and "caucus." These Americanisms were denounced as "wigwam" words, and dictionary was criticized as containing vulgar New Englandisms.

Andrew Jackson fought a duel with Charles Dickinson in Kentucky. Several of Jackson's ribs were broken, and Dickinson was killed.

June 5 **1st horse** to trot a mile in under 3 min. was *Yankee,* covering distance in 2.59.

1807

Major institution fostering scholarship in America, **Boston Athenaeum,** founded out of old Anthology Society. It combined functions of exclusive subscription library limited to the commercial, professional, and academic citizens of Boston, social meeting place for these groups, superior reference library, and museum of natural history.

Publication of *Life of Washington* by **Aaron Bancroft** is both proof and refutation of Emerson's claim that between 1790 and 1820 "there was not a book, a speech, or a conversation, or a thought" in Massachusetts. Bancroft was minor historian of merit, scholarly but uninspired. His scholarship was only a secondary occupation. Like his generation he was content with

129

respect to annexation of Spanish territory, had already issued warning on Nov. 27, 1806, to all citizens against joining any expedition against Spanish territory. Burr was arrested in Alabama Feb. 19, and indicted June 24 on charges of treason.

Dec. 22 **Embargo Act** signed by President. Britain and France had refused to recognize neutral rights and had hampered American shipping. Act was a retaliatory measure based on Jefferson's idea of commercial exclusion; U.S. exports were prohibited to Britain and France. This attempt to force France and England to remove restrictions on U.S. trade was considered by many "cure that killed" since it seriously crippled American commerce.

called the **Knickerbocker movement,** with Washington Irving and Paulding 2 of its most important leaders. Due to temperament of authors, who were indifferent to current events, politics and public figures, *Salmagundi* sketches remained charming embroidery rather than basic fabric of American literature. But they are the lasting memorial of old days of New York and they established vogue of metropolitan wit which continues to present day.

1st satirization of **American college type** seen in character of Dick Dashaway in comedy of A. B. Lindsley, *Love and Friendship, or Yankee Notions,* performed in New York. Dick was fop, contrasted with other Yankee characters.

1808

Apr. 17 **Bayonne Decree** issued by Napoleon. It ordered seizure of all U.S. vessels entering French and Italian ports, and all ports of Hanseatic towns. U.S. was helpless before this legalized piracy since the French took the position that all American shipping in those waters was British masquerading under false registration, hence subject to seizure. And if they were not, then, because of the Embargo Act, they were there illegally and should be confiscated as favor to U.S. government. Through Bayonne Decree, Napoleon became richer by some $10 million worth of U.S. ships and cargo.

Dec. 7 **James Madison elected president** by electoral vote of 122 to 47. He defeated Charles Cotesworth Pinckney of South Carolina, Federalist candidate, and George Clinton, Eastern Republicans' nominee from New York, who received only 6 ballots. Clinton won vice-presidency from Federalist Rufus King of New York by vote of 113 to 47. James Monroe of Virginia had been nominated by Southern "Old Republicans" but withdrew from race.

Dec. 29 **Andrew Johnson,** 17th president born in Raleigh, N.C.

Beginning of New York city as an **American art center** came in founding of the New York Academy of Fine Arts. Robert R. Livingston, U.S. ambassador to France, was 1st president. Academy's European orientation made it popular with New York aristocracy.

Position of New Orleans as America's **operatic capital** strengthened by construction of Théâtre d'Orleans at cost of $100,000.

1st publication in America of **Lord Byron's** *Poems.* Selling slowly in beginning, these *Poems* became popular after poet's death in the cause of Greek independence, which made him a hero to Americans. Eventually his poetry sold hundreds of thousands of copies.

Apr. 6 1st play dealing with Indians to reach American stage, *The Indian Princess, or La Belle Sauvage* by **James N. Barker,** staged in Philadelphia. It dealt with Pocahontas, a theme to be repeated in countless plays of the 19th century.

SCIENCE; INDUSTRY; ECONOMICS; EDUCATION; RELIGION; PHILOSOPHY.	SPORTS; FASHIONS; POPULAR ENTERTAINMENT; FOLKLORE; SOCIETY.

Robert Fulton's **steamboat** *Clermont* made its 1st run to Albany from New York, traveling at about 5 mph for about 30 hours. Initial trial of *Clermont* took place earlier in spring when it crossed Hudson R. from New York to New Jersey. In same year Jefferson wrote him about the torpedoes which Fulton was proposing as chief defense of harbors. But Jefferson could not see gambling the safety of the nation on the success of a single weapon, as Fulton tended to advocate. Fulton had also proposed the development of submarines, and Jefferson noted how effective torpedoes launched from a submarine would be. Jefferson encouraged Fulton in his researches and experiments.

competence. With him New England dreamed of the past rather than the future. The lethargy of her intellectual life merely epitomized the general social lull.

Feb. 27 **Henry Wadsworth Longfellow** born in Portland, Me. His birthday has been honored by public schools throughout America with appropriate exercises. Among earliest records of such a celebration is biennial report of superintendent of schools in West Virginia in 1905. Historical Society of Cambridge, Mass., celebrated centenary of Longfellow's birth in 1907 with addresses by William Dean Howells, Charles W. Eliot, Charles Eliot Norton, and Thomas Wentworth Higginson.

1808

American Law Journal, probably **earliest legal periodical** in U.S., founded in Baltimore, Md., by John Elihu Hall, professor of rhetoric at Univ. of Maryland. Continued until 1817.

Big contribution to scientific tradition in America made by publication of 1st volume of **Alexander Wilson's** *American Ornithology,* a work not only of great scholarship but of unusual interest to the layman because of its attractive illustrations and recurring analogies to human nature.

Feb. 11 **Anthracite coal burned for 1st time in an open grate.** Experiment conducted by Judge Jesse Fell in his home at Wilkes-Barre, Pa. Anthracite was too hot a fuel for most domestic stoves of period. It was at this time considered generally worthless, except for some small manufacturing and forging concerns.

Dec. 12 **1st Bible Society** in U.S. formed in Philadelphia. Its 1st president was the Rev. William White.

Great popularity of **horse racing** in America seen in widespread mourning in Virginia for death of a famous race horse named *Diomed.*

George W. Campbell of Tennessee and Barent Gardenier of New York, both U.S. congressmen, duelled with pistols at Bladensburg, Md. Gardenier had attacked Campbell in abusive speech on floor of Congress. It was **1st recorded duel** between Congressmen and **1st duel on famous dueling grounds at Bladensburg.** Gardenier, though dangerously wounded, recovered.

Oct. 30 Arrival of schooner *Betty* at Marblehead under command of Skipper **Benjamin Ireson** formed prologue to an episode which has entered into traditional lore of New England. Ireson was accused of sailing away from a sinking ship because he feared losing his own vessel. Men and women of Marblehead tarred and feathered him, and executed "Skipper Ireson's Ride," which Whittier was to dramatize in his famous poem.

POLITICS AND GOVERNMENT; WAR; DISASTERS; VITAL STATISTICS.

BOOKS; PAINTING; DRAMA; ARCHITECTURE; SCULPTURE.

1809

Henry Clay from Kentucky filled unexpired term in the Senate, but resigned after a year and was elected to the House because he wanted to be closer to the people. He advocated protective tariff and internal improvement. He ran for president in 1824, and when Pres. John Q. Adams was elected, Clay was made secretary of state. He ran again in 1832, was candidate for the Whig Party in 1844. During this campaign when warned that direct statement on slavery question would lose him antislavery vote, he answered, "I would rather be right than president."

Feb. 12 **Abraham Lincoln,** 16th president, born in Hodgenville, Ky.

Mar. 1 **Embargo Act** repealed because it was considered highly detrimental to American economic interest.

Mar. 1 **Non-Intercourse Act** signed by Jefferson in retaliation for English and French interference with American commerce. It closed ports of U.S. to France and England and outlawed their imports. It was repealed when loss in customs revenue appeared detrimental.

Mar. 4 **Thomas Jefferson** retired to private life at Monticello impoverished after 44 years of nearly continuous public service.

Mar. 4 **James Madison** inaugurated 4th president. He served in office for 8 years and belonged to the Republican Party.

1st American humorous masterpiece, *History of New York* by **Washington Irving.** This was 1st American book to impress Europe as literature. It was a tongue-in-cheek history of Dutch New Amsterdam. With subsequent editions it became best seller. Irving wrote under pseudonym Diedrich Knickerbocker. It has been said that the descendants of the old Dutch settlers were put out by treatment Irving gave their ancestors. Actually, the Dutch patroons were 1 target among many. Irving had as good a time with Jefferson, the Republicans, the Yankees, the Swedes, European literature, and the kind of historians who wrote the things which did please the children of the Dutch. He also possessed the redeeming quality of being able to laugh at himself.

Family Group, a new look in **American painting,** completed by **Charles Willson Peale** of Philadelphia. Peale was one of 1st American painters to apply the objectives of the new science to art. He was intensely interested in the Natural History Museum and developed a technique of natural representation. He executed many portraits of Washington, as well as of other leading personalities of the day, with none of the glosses of romantic idealization.

Old West Church, which later became Cambridge Street Branch of Public Library, built in Boston by Asher Benjamin.

1810

3rd U.S. census recorded population of 7,239,881, a gain of 1,931,398 over 1800. Negro population rose by 481,361 to 1,378,110; but of this total, 186,746 were free citizens, a group omitted in 1800 census. Center of population moved north and west to a point 40 miles northwest of Washington, D.C.

Park Street Church built in Boston by Peter Banner, with capitals on tower carved by Solomon Willard.

Organization of the Society of Artists of the United States. Painters revealed their contempt for American milieu by remarking that American art began when Benjamin West sailed for Europe.

132

| SCIENCE; INDUSTRY; ECONOMICS; EDUCATION; RELIGION; PHILOSOPHY. | SPORTS; FASHIONS; POPULAR ENTERTAINMENT; FOLKLORE; SOCIETY. |

1809

1st screw-cutting machine in U.S. designed and produced by Abel Stowel in Massachusetts.

1st successful sea voyage by a steamboat made by John Stevens' *Phoenix,* which sailed from New York city to Philadelphia. Stevens had designed a screw propeller in 1802. He was one of America's most important early inventors, and he was influential in the formation of 1st federal patent laws.

Boston Crown Glass Company incorporated. Company had been in business since 1792, when it made 1st successful window glass in U.S. Glass was said to be superior to any imported product. Charter of incorporation suspended company taxes and freed employees from army service.

Feb. 17 **Miami University** chartered in Oxford, Ohio as a state university. 1st degrees conferred in 1826.

Feb. 25 Jefferson wrote to **Henri Gregoire** thanking him for sending copy of *Literature of Negroes.* Gregoire wanted to refute contention of Jefferson, expressed in *Notes on Virginia,* that Negroes were mentally and physically inferior to whites. He presented evidence that Jefferson's opinions were based on limited acquaintance with behavior of Negroes. Jefferson acknowledged that his conclusions had been tentative and drawn solely from what he had observed in Virginia. He recognized the social value of Gregoire's work.

2 of most aristocratic families of New York and Virginia merged with the wedding of Gouverneur Morris and Anne Cary Randolph. Of all the wealthy families in New York the Morrises alone were not engaged in trade.

Those who were in search for some **common sense about rheumatism** were a ready market for Hamilton's "Essense and Extract of Mustard: for rheumatism, gout, Palsy, Swelling, Numoness, etc."

May 31 *The New York Post* carried an **advertisement for a performance** to be given at the New Theater. It was to be a benefit for Master Payne, and the play was the tragedy of *Hamlet,* with Payne as Hamlet. The feature was followed by a "musical afterpiece" called the "Agreeable Surprise." Doors opened at a quarter past six, with curtain rising at quarter past seven.

Oct. 31 George Hicks of Brooklyn offered through *The New York Post* a reward of $25 for **return of "Negro** woman named Charity and her female child . . . 25 years of age, 5 feet high, of a yellowish complexion . . . has lost the use of one of her fingers, occasioned by a fellon (sic), took with her several suits of clothes."

Nov. 1 Exhibit featured **Grand Panorama,** a view of New York and surrounding country "as seen from an eminence in the neighborhood of the Park." Admission was 50¢ and children paid half price. A $2.00 lifetime ticket was also available.

1810

Thomas Campbell and his father, Alexander, Presbyterians of Brush Run, Pa., founded **Campbellite Church of Christ.** Opposed to open communion, they adopted Baptist forms of worship but were later rejected by Baptist church. Formed own sect, **Disciples of Christ,** in 1827; founded **Bethany College** in 1840.

Connecticut Moral Society begun to combat "Sabbath-breakers, rum-selling, tippling folk, infidels and ruff-scruff" among the Protestant clergy. Rev. Lyman Beecher was charter member.

Lottery at Union College, 1st of kind, in which the winning ticket stood chance of drawing up to $100,000.

133

POLITICS AND GOVERNMENT; WAR; DISASTERS; VITAL STATISTICS.	BOOKS; PAINTING; DRAMA; ARCHITECTURE; SCULPTURE.

Elbridge Gerry, who gave his name to device of **gerrymandering,** elected governor of Massachusetts. Under him, the state legislature passed measures to redistrict state for election of state senators to insure Republican (present Democratic Party) majority. The device received approval from Thomas Jefferson himself.

Mar. 23 **Rambouillet Decree** signed by Napoleon ordering seizure and confiscation of all American shipping in any French port. However, when he learned of Macon's Bill No. 2, he instructed Foreign Minister, Duc de Cadore, to inform Washington that he would revoke Berlin and Milan decrees provided U.S. enforce nonintercourse with England. This seemingly straightforward move on Napoleon's part was clouded by the **Decree of Trianon,** signed the same day (Aug. 5) as the **Cadore Letter,** which ordered confiscation of all U.S. vessels in French ports between May 30, 1809 and May 1, 1810. Pres. Madison, unaware of Napoleon's duplicity, acted on the Cadore note and issued an order to resume trade with France. This move forced British to revoke their Orders in Council June 23, 1812.

May 1 **Macon's Bill No. 2** passed by Congress. It was a substitute measure, designed to take the place of the Non-Intercourse Act which was to expire later that year. Introduced by Nathaniel Macon of North Carolina, it authorized the president to restore trade with both England and France despite their antagonistic commercial policies. The lever of the bill was a provision that if one nation removed her offensive decrees before Mar. 3, 1811, the president had the power to break off all trade with the other.

Oct. 27 **West Florida annexed** by Pres. Madison. Territory included area from Mississippi R. to Perdido R. Proclamation authorized military occupation as part of the Orleans Territory.

Self-conscious America found voice in **Charles Ingersoll,** who in his *Inchiquin, The Jesuit's Letters* supplied varied data to prove excellence and greatness of this new country. Growing tension with Britain and storm of European criticism of America gave rise to need for native apologists.

Tremendous American popularity of *Scottish Chiefs* by **Jane Porter** ushered in the better novels of Walter Scott. Miss Porter and Scott wrote in reaction to the novels of sensibility and high life and to the Gothic novels characteristic of the 18th century. *Scottish Chiefs* is a romantic adventure story that was still popular 100 years after its 1st publication.

1st western theater season launched in Lexington, Ky., beginning a long tradition of dramatic presentations, which have consisted mainly of contemporary melodramas and farces.

At about this time Johann Christian Gottlieb Graupner organized the **1st regular orchestra in U.S.** at Boston. It was the Phil-harmonic Society, and it played its last concert Nov. 24, 1824, at the Pantheon, Boylston Square, Boston. See 1842, II.

George Frederick Cooke, famous British actor, arrived for 1st time in U.S. Cooke was a rival of Kemble at Covent Garden. In U.S. he played at most of the principal northern cities, and was reviewed everywhere with great enthusiasm.

Jefferson, retired from public life, confided to correspondent that he hoped to recoup money which being President had cost him by converting **Monticello** to large-scale farming. He intended to profit from advice of his scientific son-in-law, Thomas Mann Randolph, whom he credited with inventing technique of horizontal plowing of hills to prevent erosion by draining water.

Formation of the **American Board of Commissioners for Foreign Missions.** At first a Congregational group, it became interdenominational in 1812. Began American missionary organization, and marked the beginning of wide American missionary effort.

Growth of **higher education** in America reflected in establishment of 7 new colleges during decade beginning in 1810, making total of 37 institutions of higher learning in U.S.

June 23 Prominent in U.S. finance and high society, **John Jacob Astor** organized Pacific Fur Company.

July 1st number of the **1st agricultural magazine** in U.S., the *Agricultural Museum,* published in Georgetown, D.C. It lasted until May, 1812.

July 12 **Trial of members of Journeymen Cordwainers,** a trade union, accused of conspiring to raise their wages by calling a strike, began on July 12 in New York city. They were found guilty and fined one dollar each plus costs because: "Even to do a thing which is lawful in itself, by **conspiracy,** is unlawful." This decision followed precedent established in an 1806 trial of bootmakers in Philadelphia. In 1842 Supreme Court of Massachusetts reversed this trend by clarifying legal meaning of "conspiracy" to exclude unions.

Contemporary remedies:

For asthma: take ½ oz. senna, ½ oz. flour of sulphur, 2 drams ginger, ½ dram pounded saffron, and mix up in 4 oz. honey.

For consumption: take yolks of 2 new-laid eggs and beat in three tablespoons rosewater, then mix well in ½ pt. (English) of milk fresh from the cow and sweeten with syrup of capillaire and a little nutmeg grated over. Take this mixture early every morning.

N.B.: In using any medicine, do it with confidence and the battle is more than half won.

Popular lyric of the day:

"Swan's sing before they die . . .
        t'were no bad thing,
    Should certain persons die before
        they sing."

Oct. 1 **Important county fair,** Berkshire Cattle Show, in Pittsfield, Mass. From this fair grew **1st permanent agricultural association** in U.S. It wasn't until about the turn of the century that amusement park features were added to agricultural fairs. **Texas State Fair** of Dallas is the largest state fair in country, with an attendance of over 2 million people in a 2 week period in 1955.

Dec. 10 1st unofficial **heavyweight champion** of U.S., Tom Molineaux, freed slave from Virginia beaten in 40th round by Tom Cribb, English champion, in fight at Copthall Common, England.

POLITICS AND GOVERNMENT; WAR; DISASTERS; VITAL STATISTICS.	BOOKS; PAINTING; DRAMA; ARCHITECTURE; SCULPTURE.

1811

Jan. 15 Secret act passed authorizing Pres. Madison to take possession of East **Florida.** He appointed George Matthews and John McKee to execute act, which was not published until 1818. Annexation could only occur with consent of inhabitants or if foreign power attempted occupation.

Feb. 11 Pres. Madison prohibited **trade with Britain,** 3rd time in 4 years that such action was taken in hope of effecting repeal of Orders in Council, by which Britain placed her own restrictions on neutral commerce.

Apr. 12 Colonists from New York under Capt. Thorn found **1st permanent colony** in Pacific Northwest. They landed at Cape Disappointment, Wash., after voyage around Cape Horn on *Tonquin.* John Jacob Astor stood behind the colony.

Nov. 7 Battle against Indians won at Tippecanoe River in Indiana by **William Henry Harrison.** It was meant as chastisement to marauding Indians under Tecumseh. Victory frustrated formation of powerful Indian confederation and was therefore decisive. Many Indians crossed to Canada to fight later with British.

Dec. 16 **Worst quake** in American history rocked Ohio–Mississippi valleys. Tremors felt over an area of 301,656 sq. mi. Earth's surface sank or was raised from 5 to 25 feet in 30,000-sq. mi. district. Incalculable loss of life and property.

Notable success in fiction was **Isaac Mitchell's** *Alonzo and Melissa,* strange blend of sentimental novel of late 18th century and romantic Gothic tale. For almost 40 years this book read by countless Americans.

Romanticism à la Scott enlisted most poets of this decade. 1st noteworthy imitation of him was **Eaglesfield Smith's** *William and Ellen.* **J. M. Harney's** *Crystalina* (1812) deals with Scottish Highlands; **Washington Allston's** *The Paint Rug* added burlesque to imitation; **R. C. Sands'** *Bride of Vaumond* (1817) and **H. H. Wright's** *The Fall of Palmyra* (1816) borrowed profusely from Scott.

Early efforts to promote closer **cultural ties** with Latin America recorded in Congressional report by Congressman and Dr. Samuel Latham Mitchill of New York, recognized authority on Spanish and Portuguese literature in Latin America.

1812

Whites driven out of Lake Michigan region by Indians in **Fort Dearborn massacre.** Whites retreated along trail which, a few years later, became Indiana Avenue in Chicago.

Tradition of urbane, cosmopolitan portraiture maintained in this period by American artist **Thomas Sully.** His study of *Samuel Coates* standing by his desk with quill in his hand has all the charm and

| SCIENCE; INDUSTRY; ECONOMICS; EDUCATION; RELIGION; PHILOSOPHY. | SPORTS; FASHIONS; POPULAR ENTERTAINMENT; FOLKLORE; SOCIETY. |

1811

1st steamboat to sail down Mississippi R. owned by a Mr. & Mrs. Roosevelt. After "mishaps" (earthquake at New Madrid, Mo., birth of baby to Mrs. Roosevelt) boat reached New Orleans on Jan. 12, 1812, and caused a sensation. Boat then made regular New Orleans-Natchez run, charging $18 and $25 for downstream and upstream trip respectively.

Popular interest in science and art marked opening of **The American Museum** in New York city. On display were stuffed and live animals, paintings, etc. Lectures given to public. In 1841 Barnum purchased contents and used them in his own museum.

The Maternal Physician; A Treatise on the Nurture and Management of Infants, from the Birth until Two Years Old, Being the Result of Sixteen Years' Experience in the Nursery. Illustrated by extracts from the most approved medical authors. By an American matron. Probably begins **literature of child care** in America.

Important road in early Illinois, the **Kaskaskia and Cahokia Road** 1st charted. Road has remained in service to present time.

John Stevens' steamboat *Juliana* constructed for **ferry service** on Hudson R. Because they held monopoly rights, Fulton and Livingston threatened lawsuits, and Stevens gave up his plan.

Jan. 28 Increasing monopoly of **fur trade** in U.S. indicated by formation of South West Company with a ⅔ interest controlled by John Jacob Astor.

Competitive rowing races came into prominence at this time. Race between *Knickerbocker* of New York and *Invincible* of Long Island from Harsimus, N.J., to Battery attracted thousands. Race was won by *Knickerbocker*.

Mrs. and Miss Andrews opened apartments to teach **painting on velvet** at 65 Maiden Lane, New York city.

Nathaniel Dearborn published 1st edition of *Singsters Repository of ballads collected from New Yorkers*. It sold for 25¢ a copy.

Dec. 12 Opening of J. Delacroix's **Vauxhall** for the winter season in New York city. Advertisements announced that there was a "large" saloon for more than 200 people; a tea room for 100; card rooms and dressing rooms; choicest liquors. It was to be an establishment "for the accommodation of genteel company" and would be open on fair days only.

1812

American missionaries begin work in Bombay. Supported by American Board of Commissioners for Foreign Missions, 283 American missionaries were active in Orient by 1848.

Samuel Wilson, a meat-packer in Troy, N.Y., became the original **"Uncle Sam."** He was called "Uncle" Sam to distinguish him from a younger Samuel Wilson from the same town. Soldiers began to call the

POLITICS AND GOVERNMENT; WAR; DISASTERS; VITAL STATISTICS.

BOOKS; PAINTING; DRAMA; ARCHITECTURE; SCULPTURE.

Feb. 15 **William Hunt** arrived at Astoria, Ore. He had started from St. Louis to establish route and fur trading post at Columbia R. for John Jacob Astor. He crossed much unexplored territory, and last part of his route was almost identical with later Oregon Trail.

Mar. 3 **1st foreign aid act** ever passed by Congress authorized $50,000 for relief of Venezuelan victims of severe earthquake. Congressional opposition was based on constitutional question of whether such an act was permitted under legislative provisions of Constitution. James Monroe reportedly observed in 1820 that Congress had no express authority, but rather an implied power, from Constitution for such an act.

Mar. 14 Congress authorized **1st issue of U.S. war bonds** valued at $11,000,000. 1st of 6 war loans floated during War of 1812.

Apr. 8 **Louisiana** declared a state, 18th of Union, from territory ceded by France under Treaty of Paris.

May 14 Annexation by congressional act added **West Florida territory** to territory of Mississippi and to nation.

June 1 Pres. Madison recommended that **war** be declared on Britain in a message to Congress. Among injuries suffered at hands of British which Pres. Madison cited were blockade of foreign and American ports and impressment of American seamen.

June 18 Congress declared war against Great Britain. This is known as **War of 1812.**

July 1 Congress doubled **tariff on imports** as means of obtaining additional funds for prosecution of war.

Aug. 16 **Gen. Hull** surrendered to British at Detroit, making no attempt to defend city though attacking force was inferior in number to his own. Hull was court-martialed 2 years later for yielding without resistance.

Aug. 19 **"Old Ironsides"** (*Constitution*) defeated British ship *Guerrière* off Nova

suavity of the school of Benjamin West. Sully was born in England but came to U.S. as boy.

Polemical book, trenchant in its political satire, *The Diverting History of John Bull and Brother Jonathan* by Hector Bull-Us **(James K. Paulding)**, 1st comic history of U.S. Tracing the history of Anglo-American relationships from the Revolution to the War of 1812, it attacks the sea policy of the English, impressment of American seamen, English attitude toward emigration.

1st American painter to study at Paris instead of London or Rome was **John Vanderlyn.** His painting of nude *Ariadne* was favorably received in Paris, though it shocked Americans. In 1808 Vanderlyn had received praise of Napoleon for his *Marius.*

One of most interesting Classic Revival churches, **Monumental Church** of Richmond, Va., built on octagonal design with columned portico. Classic Revival was characterized by adaptation of architectural models of Greece and Rome. It was concrete expression of how Revolutionary patriots actually saw the great work that they were doing. They wanted American things done in an American way. But the American way was, in their minds, subordinated to their sense of what things were ideally meant to be. In effect, in keeping with the pattern of 18th century thought, this meant a return to classical standards. Jefferson drew up a platform for a native architecture which is a typical statement of what the men of his day were thinking. He was himself deeply impressed by the work of the Italian master, Palladio, and the ancient Roman models which the Italian imitated came to represent for him an approach to perfection. The whole Classic

Dr. **Benjamin Rush** published 1st work on mental disorders. It was entitled *Medical Inquiries and Observations upon the Diseases of the Mind.*

War of 1812 stimulated rapid expansion of **banking institutions** in America, with 120 banks receiving charters between 1812 and 1815.

1st American insurance company primarily involved with **life insurance,** the Pennsylvania Company for Insurance on Lives and Granting Annuities, incorporated in Philadelphia.

William Monroe of Concord, Mass., began **lead pencil** manufacture with own formula for using ground lead.

Academy of Natural Sciences of Philadelphia, dedicated to the advancement of the natural sciences, founded. It was immediately popular and generously supported. Within 2 years the original membership of 7 was doubled, 33 correspondents were making contributions, and a program of lectures on plants and insects was scheduled. The public was admitted in 1828, 2 years after the museum had been expanded by the addition of another building. Among today's 140,000 volumes, those presented by original donors maintain place of historic importance.

May 26 **Hamilton College** chartered in Clinton, N.Y. under Presbyterian auspices. 1st degrees conferred in 1814.

June 30 Congress authorized **Treasury notes** in an issue not to exceed $5 million. It was the 1st of 5 war issues.

July 23 William Ellery Channing, as an apostle of **modern pacificism,** weighed the negativism of New England toward the War of 1812 in a deliberative sermon which cautioned loyalty toward the just acts of good government. "It is the time," he said, "to be firm without passion." He denounced attempts which had been made to stifle opposition and criticism in the name of patriotism. "The sum of my remarks is this. It is your duty to hold fast and to assert with firmness those truths and

meat "Uncle Sam's" because of the stamp "U.S." on provision boxes.

Term **"Coodies"** applied derisively to faction of Federalist Party that urged support of War of 1812, highly unpopular with majority of party. Term derived from series of prowar articles written by Gulian Crommelin Verplanck under pen name *Abimeleck Coody.* Verplanck was a distinguished editor, author, and Shakespearean scholar of his time. Epithet "King Coody" was applied to Congressman and later Chief Justice of U.S. Supreme Court Roger Brooke Taney of Maryland.

Samuel J. Mills, sponsored by the Connecticut and Massachusetts Missionary Societies, making 1st of 2 celebrated **tours of the hinterland,** confirmed the suspicions of the East about its backdoor neighbors. He surveyed "the nakedness of the land" and "the heartrending report reached the ears of the Church." "South of New Connecticut, few Bibles or religious tracts have been received for distribution among the inhabitants. The Sabbath is greatly profaned and but few good people can be found in any one place . . . within 30 miles of the falls of the Ohio. . . . We found the inhabitants in a very destitute state; very ignorant of the doctrines of the Gospel; and in many instances without Bibles, or any other religious books. The Methodist preachers pass through this country, in their circuits, occasionally. There are a number of good people in the Territory, who are anxious to have Presbyterian ministers amongst them. They likewise wish to be remembered by Bible and Religious Tract Societies. . . ." ". . . At New Orleans . . . the greater part of the inhabitants are French Catholics, ignorant of almost every thing except what relates to the increase of their property; destitute of schools, Bibles and religious instruction. In attempting to learn the religious state of the people, we were frequently told, that they had no Bibles, and that the priests did not allow of their distribution among them."

| POLITICS AND GOVERNMENT; WAR; DISASTERS; VITAL STATISTICS. | BOOKS; PAINTING; DRAMA; ARCHITECTURE; SCULPTURE. |

Scotia. The *Constitution* was captained by Isaac Hull.

Oct. 9 **2 British ships,** *Detroit* and *Caledonia,* captured by surprise on Lake Erie in early morning by Lt. Elliott. He was later forced to set fire to the *Detroit.*

Oct. 13 **Gen. Van Rensselaer** defeated in the battle of Queenstown Heights, Canada, by British and Indians. About 1000 U.S. troops were killed or wounded. British Gen. Isaac Brock was killed during engagement.

Dec. 2 James Madison defeated De Witt Clinton in **presidential elections** by an electoral vote of 128 to 89. Elbridge Gerry defeated Jared Ingersoll for the vice-presidency by an electoral vote of 131 to 86.

Dec. 29 U.S. frigate **Constitution** destroyed **Java,** British frigate, in sea fight off coast of Brazil. "Old Ironsides" was under command of Capt. Bainbridge.

Revival endorsed his preference. The 1st phase (1789–1820) was a Roman Revival, characterized by simple lines, sparse decoration and superb discipline. The Greek Revival (1820–1860) introduced greater structural variety and a liberal use of Greek columns, mantletrees and doors.

Apr. 13 American sense of inferiority in **drama** seen in history of *Marmion,* a dramatization of Scott's poem by American James N. Barker. Fearing public would stay away, the producer listed the play as written by an Englishman, Thomas Mortan. Piece was a success until public discovered real identity of author. From then on it ceased to attract.

1813

Feb. 24 **British ship** *Peacock* captured by *Hornet,* commanded by Capt. James Lawrence.

Mar. 4 **Pres. Madison inaugurated** for his 2nd term. Elbridge Gerry succeeded George Clinton as vice-president.

Apr. 27 British surrendered **York, Canada,** to Americans, who were commanded by Gen. Pike.

June 1 Capt. **Lawrence** cried, "Don't give up the ship," to his crew as he lay mortally wounded aboard the *Chesapeake,* which was subsequently defeated and captured by British frigate *Shannon.*

Aug. 14 *Pelican* captured **American ship** *Argus* off English coast. *Argus* had brilliant record since beginning of war, having captured 27 British merchant ships.

Sept. 4th **British ship** *Boxer* defeated and captured off Maine by *Enterprise* commanded by Capt. William Burrows.

Sept. 10 Capt. Oliver Hazard Perry defeated and captured **British fleet** under

Founding of **1st religious weekly** in America, *Religious Remembrancer.*

Strong Whig supporter, **Boston Daily Advertiser,** started under editorship of Nathan Hale. In 1917 it was purchased by Hearst and combined with *Boston Record.*

Appearance of poet of real stature seen in publication of **Washington Allston's** 1st book *The Sylphs of the Season.* Painter as well as poet, he was praised by such writers as Coleridge, Southey, and Wilkie Collins. Wordsworth thought him greatest artist of age.

Padre Narciso Durán, choirmaster at San José Mission in California, compiled **choir book** for use in Catholic Missions in Southwest. Most choirs were composed of Indians, who adapted religious music to growing folk tradition.

Enormous popularity of Sir Walter Scott in England duplicated in America

| SCIENCE; INDUSTRY; ECONOMICS; EDUCATION; RELIGION; PHILOSOPHY. | SPORTS; FASHIONS; POPULAR ENTERTAINMENT; FOLKLORE; SOCIETY. |

principles on which the welfare of your country seems to depend, but do this with calmness, with a love of peace, without ill will and revenge."

Oct. 24 Significant contributions to American culture foreshadowed in founding of **American Antiquarian Society,** organization of prominent Worcester citizens, most notably Isaiah Thomas, famous publisher of instructional and devotional works. Society dedicated itself to preservation of native historical materials for the benefit of America's future historians. Indian relics, precolonial manuscripts, and old imported books were scrupulously preserved.

Dec. 29 **University of Maryland** chartered as state university in Baltimore, Md. It was organized around the College of Medicine of Maryland, founded in 1807. In 1920 the Maryland State College was formally merged with it.

Gerrymandering entered the national vocabulary of political abuse through the tactics of the Massachusetts legislature in sponsoring a bill to rig the contests for senatorial offices by a systematic reapportionment of the electoral districts within the state. In 1812 the senatorial districts corresponded to the areas of the counties. When the Republicans got control of the legislature they appealed to a provision of the state contitution which invested the legislature with the power of determining electoral districts. Elbridge Gerry, the governor, signed the bill into a law. The districts followed no regular lines. One resembled a salamander or, in the words of a Federalist, a "Gerrymander."

Aug. 19 **Lucy Brewer,** serving under name of Nicolas Baker, participated as member of crew of *Constitution* in naval battle with British *Guerrière*. She served 3 years aboard *Constitution* and successfully disguised her sex during entire time.

1813

Jethro Wood patented **iron plow,** 19th patent for a plow issued in America. Wood's plow was extremely popular in Eastern farm lands but proved inadequate for stickier soil of the Midwest.

William Ellery Channing, world famous Congregationalist Unitarian minister, founded the **Christian Disciple,** liberal Protestant magazine as challenge to more conservative **The Panoplist,** Protestant newspaper published by the Rev. Jedidiah Morse, father of Samuel F. B. Morse, inventor of telegraph. Conflict between these 2 publications mirrored conflict between liberal and conservative Protestantism that has continued in America to the present time. By nature Channing resisted any attempt to define his ideas within the logical limits of a dogma. Nor did he particularly relish the notoriety which his ideas gained for him. 6 years passed before he was, in a sermon, to define his position as Unitarian. But the ferment within the religious life of New England con-

1st blackout of American town happened about this time in St. Michaels, Md. When British forces sailed into bay townspeople doused lights and set up lanterns in trees outside the village. The British shot at these lanterns.

Celebrated "witch" **Moll Pitcher** died in Lynn, Mass. Her fame had spread throughout country and hundreds went to her for prophecy, love potions, and knowledge of lost things. She is reputed to have presided at conventions of witches at Lynn. Every time she visited another community she entered into its folklore.

Craps 1st introduced to U.S. by Bernard Xavier Philippe de Marigny de Mandeville, rich playboy of New Orleans, La. It was an adaptation of "hazards," a French

Barclay on Lake Erie. Perry accepted surrender of British aboard his flagship *Lawrence,* which he left when it was crippled during battle. His famous message, "We have met the enemy and they are ours: two ships, two brigs, one schooner, and one sloop," was sent after this battle.

Oct. 5   Gen. Harrison defeated Proctor, British general, at **Battle of the Thames,** Canada. Tecumseh, Shawnee Indian chief and ally of the British, was killed during the engagement.

with the sale of 5 million copies of **Waverley Novels** within a decade. **J. K. Paulding** published a verse parody, *The Lay of the Scottish Fiddle,* counting on audience already familiar with allusions to work of Scott. The Romantic period in American literature was beginning with a flourish, and it soon rivaled revolution in English letters, of which Scott was among founders. It characterized an era which did not end until Civil War.

1814

Jan. 3   Proposal for **peace negotiations** from England reached Washington.

Mar. 29   Creek Indian War ended as Gen. Andrew Jackson defeated Creeks under Chief Weatherford at decisive battle of Horseshoe Bend, Ala., where nearly 900 of 1000 Indians engaged were killed. Creeks had fought with British against Americans in War of 1812.

Aug. 24   British, under General Ross, captured **Washington** and set fire to Capitol, White House, and Navy yard.

Sept. 11   Comm. Thomas Macdonough defeated British fleet on **Lake Champlain,** while Sir George Prevost's attack on a **Plattsburg** fort was repulsed by Gen. Macomb.

Dec. 15–Jan. 4, 1815   **Hartford Convention,** held in secret sessions, expressed strong states' rights principles in a time of national emergency. Delegates were from New England states where War of 1812 was especially unpopular. Backed by New England Federalists, Convention proposed various limitations of Federal power over states, and even advocated dissolution of Union if the existence of states themselves was threatened by inability of Federal Government to offer proper protection. Distorted reports were circulated throughout country, and the secrecy of meetings lent credence to charges of treason. Arrival of news of Peace of Ghent and Battle of New Orleans drowned re-

Report of famous Lewis and Clark expedition given by **Meriwether Lewis** in his *History of the Expedition.* Lewis, private secretary to Jefferson, gave exciting, often racy, account of dangers, encounters with Indians, trappers, missionaries. The report, by Nicholas Biddle and Paul Allen, was actually a digest of the unedited journals of Lewis and Clark. It was published with a preface by Jefferson in which the career of Lewis was told in succinct but memorable detail. In 1806 Jefferson had himself given advance notice of the findings of the expedition in his *Message from the President of the United States, Communicating Discoveries Made by Captains Lewis and Clark.* Lewis had entertained the desire to arrange the publication of the material. But, immediately after the expedition and his retirement from the army, Jefferson appointed him governor of the Louisiana Territory. He was kept so busy with the affairs of his office that he never found the time to finish his revision before his mysterious death in an inn in Tennessee. Clark, in spite of his own political obligations, did contribute to the edition of the journals, but final discretion was left to his editors and the complete papers remained unpublished until 1903.

1st American-born sculptor of note, William Rush, carved full-length statue in wood of George Washington. Rush made his name as the sculptor of wooden bowsprits.

SCIENCE; INDUSTRY; ECONOMICS; EDUCATION; RELIGION; PHILOSOPHY.	SPORTS; FASHIONS; POPULAR ENTERTAINMENT; FOLKLORE; SOCIETY.

tinued. In 1815 there was a flurry of excitement about a heresy within the Congregational Churches. It resulted in the formulation and use of the label Unitarian to distinguish the liberal element from the conservative. In the name of reason, the liberals proposed that Christ was not of the same nature as God but was sent as a moral teacher rather than as a divine mediator between heaven and earth. It was not until 1819, however, that Channing publicly identified himself with this position.

dice game, which Marigny had played in English coffee-houses. American name derived from Johnny Crapaud, soubriquet for Louisiana Creoles. Crapaud later syncopated to Craps. Marigny lost most of his wealth playing the game.

1814

1st large **library network** west of Alleghanies established from several circulating libraries in Pittsburgh, forming Pittsburgh permanent library.

1st factory in world to manufacture **cotton cloth** by power machinery enclosed in 1 building constructed in Waltham, Mass., by Boston Manufacturing Company. Company formed in 1813 by Francis Cabot Lowell, Boston importer who had observed power machinery in British textile plants and who had violated British laws by smuggling secretly drawn sketches of machinery out of country. With financial backing of his brother-in-law, Patrick Tracy Jackson, and mechanical skill of machinist Paul Moody, Lowell secured charter for Boston Manufacturing Company at capitalization of $300,000. Machinery used in Waltham factory and all subsequent enterprises of company came to be known as Lowell-Moody machinery. This machinery now quite different from English models upon which it had been originally based.

Oct. 29 **1st steam-powered warship,** *Demologos,* launched in New York harbor. Designed and constructed by Robert Fulton, ship was officially christened *Fulton the First.*

Cost of education at Harvard was about $300 a year. John Thornton Kirkland became president in 1810 and continued innovations which determined liberal bent of college's subsequent history. He made it possible for poor students to meet fees by opening a number of small jobs at which they could work and earn extra money. He also supervised grants and scholarships, as well as an annual subsidy of $2500 which Massachusetts donated to encourage gifted but needy students. In Kirkland's time Harvard had reputation of being poor man's school, because he did so much to make it easy for students to make ends meet in one way or another. Yet the tradition of gentility was already apparent, since whole aim of college was to create same kind of gentlemen who were described in prospectuses of Cambridge and Oxford. Students attended classes 5 days a week from 6 A.M. to 4 P.M., with an hour between the sessions. Campus social life was encouraged by Kirkland. He contributed to beginnings of some of most famous clubs, the Hasty Pudding, the Porcellian, the Hermetic Society, the Speaking Club. There were extracurricular pleasures in parties and dances, and the college was far enough outside of Boston to provide the pastimes of both city and country life.

May 17 **Norwegian Independence Day** celebrated by Americans of Norwegian

| POLITICS AND GOVERNMENT; WAR; DISASTERS; VITAL STATISTICS. | BOOKS; PAINTING; DRAMA; ARCHITECTURE; SCULPTURE. |

sults of Convention in ridicule, and signaled the end of the Federalist Party's influence in American affairs.

Dec. 24 **Peace treaty** signed with Great Britain at Ghent. Territory taken during war was to be returned and commissions were to settle disputed boundaries in Northeast.

Apr. 13 Words to U.S. **national anthem** written by Francis Scott Key while detained on British warship bombarding Fort McHenry near Baltimore. Poem was known as "Defense of Fort M'Henry," and was set to music of "Anacreon in Heaven," official song of Anacreonic Society of London.

1815

Jan. 8 **Battle of New Orleans** fought 2 weeks after armistice signed at Ghent. U.S. troops under command of Gen. Andrew Jackson inflicted at least 2000 casualties on British.

Feb. 11 News of **Treaty of Ghent** reached New York city.

Mar. 3 Congress declared war against **Algiers.** Bey of Algiers had molested American ships and insisted upon payment of tribute to his country.

June 17 Com. Decatur captured **Algerian frigate** *Mashouda.* Hammida, renowned Algerian admiral, was killed during this engagement by cannon shot.

June 19 Com. Decatur's squadron captured *Estido,* **Algerian brig,** off Cape Palos.

July 3 **Treaty with Algiers** concluded. No more payments of tribute were to be demanded by Dey of Algiers and all Americans reduced to slavery were to be released without ransom.

Dec. 5 In a **message to Congress,** Pres. Madison asked improvements in armed forces, creation of national currency, construction of roads and canals, and establishment of a national university. This was strong divergence from creed of his predecessor, Jefferson, who urged careful guard over **rights and powers of states.**

1st edition of **Benjamin Franklin's** *Autobiography* edited by Parson Weems appeared in America. In 1791 1st installment had been issued in Paris; in 1793 sections 2 and 3 had appeared in London. It was not until 1868 that definitive edition was published.

Poet of American Revolution, **Philip Freneau,** fulfilled his patriotic duty with publication of his *Poems on American Affairs,* concerned mostly with War of 1812 and reflecting his unmitigated hatred for British. Most poems commemorate sea battles, bearing titles like "The Battle of Lake Champlain," "On the Capture of the Guerrière," "On British Commercial Depredations."

May Founding of **North American Review** in Boston. In short time it became leading review in America, throwing tremendous weight upon literary scene. Articles generally written in orderly, scholarly fashion.

July 4 Cornerstone for **Washington Monument** in Baltimore laid. It was 1st public monument to George Washington, and was designed by Robert Mills, advocate of Greek Revival in U.S. architecture.

1816

Jan. 1 **Public debt** stood at $127,335,-000, or more than a million dollars for the 1st time. It amounted to about $15 per person.

Historical novel enjoyed vogue during decade, **Samuel Woodworth's** *Champions of Freedom.* In true romantic tradition spirit of Washington is made to appear

SCIENCE; INDUSTRY; ECONOMICS; EDUCATION; RELIGION; PHILOSOPHY.	SPORTS; FASHIONS; POPULAR ENTERTAINMENT; FOLKLORE; SOCIETY.

Publication of a translation of Madame de Staël's *De l'Allemagne.* Interest in this work, an enthusiastic endorsement of **German culture,** foreshadowed the dominant position which German thinking was to play in the intellectual life of 19th century America.

descent to commemorate adoption of national constitution by Norwegian subjects of Sweden on this date.

1815

Library of Congress acquired Thomas Jefferson's extensive collection of rare and significant books. This acquisition helped replace volumes lost in fire ignited by British in War of 1812.

Rise of U.S. **whaling industry** made greater amounts of whale oil and tallow for illuminating purposes available to U.S. homes.

Most colorful mode of transportation during this period was the **Conestoga wagon** with its lively colors, its 4-to-6-horse team festooned with bells. It carried load of several tons, stretched some 60 ft.

Mar. 1 **Georgetown College** 1st chartered as College of Georgetown in Washington, D.C., and 1st degrees were conferred in 1817. 1st college in America established under Catholic auspices, it had been founded in 1789 at the suggestion of John Carroll. In 1805 school was transferred to Society of Jesus, and in 1844 it was renamed and incorporated as Georgetown College.

From 1815 to the Civil War one of the archetypical **styles of American glassware was Ohio** which, as a general name, was applied to both the blown and molded glass produced in the Midwest. Three of the leading factories which made this glassware were located in Mantua, Kent, and Zanesville, all cities of Ohio, and the name of the glass was derived from these busy centers. Ohio was also used to identify the glass factories in the neighboring regions of West Virginia and western Pennsylvania.

Boston Society for the Moral and Religious Instruction of the Poor established. It promoted Sunday school education in city.

Jan. 8 **Jackson Day,** or Old Hickory's Day, became legal holiday in Louisiana after famous battle of New Orleans in which Andrew Jackson won major victory over British invasion forces led by General Pakenham, Duke of Wellington's brother-in-law. General Pakenham, 2 of his generals, and 2000 of his troops killed in unsuccessful assault on Jackson's improvised defenses near New Orleans. This last battle of War of 1812 actually fought after signing of peace. Jackson Day has also been commemorated by Democratic Party as occasion for partisan gatherings and celebrations.

1816

Divinity School at Harvard College organized as separate branch, introduced non-denominational theological study in U.S. In 1819 it became a separate administrative

New mile record in horse racing set by *Timoleon.* Time was 1:47.

Freak summer in New England brought

145

POLITICS AND GOVERNMENT; WAR; DISASTERS; VITAL STATISTICS.

BOOKS; PAINTING; DRAMA; ARCHITECTURE; SCULPTURE.

Mar. 16 James Monroe nominated for presidency by Congressional Republican (Democratic) Caucus. His opponent was William H. Crawford of Georgia whom he defeated by a vote of 65 to 54.

Mar. 20 Power of **Supreme Court** further consolidated in the case of *Martin v. Hunter's Lessee,* which gave Court jurisdiction over Virginia's state court.

Mar. 20 Draft of **tariff bill** presented and later passed kept virtually same tariff on imports that had been added to raise money for war expenses. Measure was continued for protection of domestic manufacturers and eventual lessening of need for foreign goods.

Dec. 4 James Monroe elected president, thus continuing "Virginia Dynasty." He defeated Federalist candidate, Rufus King, by Electoral College vote of 183 to 34. Monroe's running mate was Daniel D. Tompkins of New York.

Dec. 11 Indiana admitted as state, 19th of Union. 5 years before, Harrison laid the platform of his presidential campaign of 1840 by routing the Indians under Tecumseh in the battle of Tippecanoe. The Indians made one last major raid in 1812, then chose to sell out to the whites and move beyond the Mississippi. In June 1816 a constitution for the new state was drafted in the 1st Indiana state capital, Corydon. In 1825 the state capital was moved to Indianapolis.

to *dramatis personae,* among whom are Andrew Jackson, pirate Lafitte, and heroes of Lake Erie.

1st hand printing press constructed in America by George Clymer of Philadelphia, Pa.

Extremely popular book of verse—3 editions in one year—was **John Pierpont's** *Airs of Palestine.* With "correctness" of disciple of Pope, he traced influence of music upon Jewish history, extending it further to pay tribute in verse to Chateaubriand, "the poetic pilgrim of the West."

1st formal study of American speech, **John Pickering's** *Vocabulary.* It was dictionary of some 500 distinctly American words and phrases, and reflected rising cultural differences between America and England. But, although changes in vocabulary and spelling were extensive and continued to accumulate, American language never achieved independence from mother tongue that some of its partisans had expected.

American Bible Society founded in New York city. The purpose of the organization is to increase the circulation of texts of the Bible. Through the society the best available translations of the Bible have been distributed across the earth. It emphasizes distribution of the Bible to the poor. The Society was incorporated in 1841 and has developed into a worldwide organization with a large membership and many auxiliaries.

1817

Jan. 7 2nd Bank of U.S. opened in Philadelphia, Pa.

Mar. 1 Congress established office of **Supreme Court reporter.** Bill proposed that reporter receive annual salary of $1000 and that he could sell reports for

Widespread literacy of Americans noted by traveler William Cobbett, who saw that farmers read much more than peasants of Europe.

Surprising resistance of many Southern planters to **lingual changes** reported by

unit with a president and 4 professors.

Significant judicial decision in history and development of U.S. **higher education** rendered by U.S. Supreme Court Chief Justice, John Marshall, who held against New Hampshire State Legislature in its attempt to make privately chartered Dartmouth College a state university. Marshall held that college charter was legal contract that could not be violated or superseded by legislative action. Decision spurred building of state universities.

Feb. 6 Probably **1st railroad charter** granted in U.S. made by New Jersey legislature to Col. John Stevens for a railroad between Delaware and Raritan rivers. Project was never developed.

Feb. 14 **University of Virginia** 1st chartered as Central College in Charlottesville, Va. State-sponsored Central College became University of Virginia in 1819. 1st degrees awarded in 1849.

Apr. 10 **2nd national bank** established for period of 20 years with capital of $35,000,000, $28,000,000 of which to be sold in shares of $100 each to private stockholders and remaining $7,000,000 to be subscribed by federal government.

Apr. 11 **1st Negro bishop** in America, the Rev. Richard Allen, ordained to head newly organized African Methodist Episcopal Church.

June Baltimore, Md., became 1st city in U.S. to inaugurate a **gas company;** Gas Light Company of Baltimore was organized to provide coal gas for lighting city streets.

Dec. 13 **1st savings bank** in U.S. organized in Boston as The Provident Institution for Savings.

10 inches of snow on June 6. July and August were no better, with half an inch of ice spread over Vermont and New Hampshire. This year was entered into records as "year in which there was no summer."

Memorable phrase **"Our country, right or wrong"** delivered by Com. Stephen Decatur at Virginia dinner, commemorating his successful expedition against pirates of Barbary Coast. Called on to propose toast he said, "Our Country! In her intercourse with foreign governments may she always be in the right; but our country, right or wrong."

In **1st "pugilistic encounter"** in America, Jacob Hyer beat Tom Beasley in grudge fight and called himself America's 1st champion, being so recorded. Bare knuckles, London Prize Ring Rules.

Peace Society of Massachusetts established as result of an antiwar sermon by the Rev. William Ellery Channing. Channing was not complete pacifist, however, since he conceded necessity of waging war in self-defense or in defense of a moral principle.

June 22 **Grand Encampment of Knights Templar** started in New York city; De Witt Clinton elected Grand Master.

1817

1st insane asylum in America established at Frankford, Pa.

Significant force in early frontier education, **American Tract Society,** began to circulate vast quantities of religious literature via circuit riders, often supplying a family

Negro boy William Read blew up ship in Boston harbor because he was not permitted to take part in **Election Day** festivities. This occasioned humorous jingle:

"Who blew up the ship?
Nigger, why for?

147

| POLITICS AND GOVERNMENT; WAR; DISASTERS; VITAL STATISTICS. | BOOKS; PAINTING; DRAMA; ARCHITECTURE; SCULPTURE. |

personal profit. He had to publish complete reports promptly. Need for such an office grew from misunderstandings based on incomplete knowledge of Supreme Court cases.

Mar. 3 **Alabama Territory** formed. It was piece cut out of Mississippi Territory.

Mar. 3 **Bonus Bill vetoed.** On Dec. 23, 1816, John C. Calhoun had introduced bill setting aside $1½ million bonus paid by Bank of U.S. for internal improvements such as canals and highways. Pres. Madison vetoed measure (his last official act) on constitutional grounds.

Mar. 4 **James Monroe** inaugurated 5th President, ushering in **"The Era of Good Feeling."** This phrase was originated by editorial writer on Boston *Columbian Centinel* in June, 1817.

Apr. 28–29 **Bush-Bagot Agreement** signed by England and U.S. It limited naval power on Great Lakes to police force.

Nov. 20 **Seminole War** (1817–1818) began when settlers attacked Florida Indians, and Indians retaliated by raiding isolated Georgia homesteads. American feeling was that Spain had incited Seminoles against white settlers.

Dec. 10 **Mississippi** admitted as state, 20th of Union.

James K. Paulding, who was astonished that these planters opposed changes even in England, preferring 18th-century prose and language styles of Milton, Newton, Locke, and Addison to 19th-century innovations of Byron, Herschel, and Stewart.

Best seller *Lalla Rookh* by English poet **Thomas Moore,** which was popular for 100 years.

Founding fathers of republic immortalized by **John Trumbull** in his famous *Signing of the Declaration of Independence.* Countless thousands of prints and copies have made this scene familiar to all Americans.

Aug. 29 *Philanthropist,* **abolition newspaper,** published by Charles Osborn in Mt. Pleasant, Ohio. An 8-page weekly, it lasted to 1820.

Sept. For the 1st time American poetry gained European attention and applause with printing of "Thanatopsis" by **William Cullen Bryant** in *North American Review.* Its appearance was "much as if a classic temple had been exorcised from the wilderness by the strains of a new Amphion." Its still reflections on death and nature created entire school of American poets.

1818

Laws extending **suffrage** adopted in Connecticut largely as result of challenging suffrage laws of Western states and territories.

Attorney General 1st granted assistance of clerk and office location. He had been little more than legal advisor to executive branch. Department of Justice not established until 1870.

Jan. The *James Monroe* sailed from New York city and *Courier* from Liverpool bound for opposite ports. This was initiation of **regular monthly trips** on

Famous American painter, **Washington Allston,** returned to America from England, and, from this time on he was unable to develop his career. Between this year and his death, July 9, 1843, Allston labored over his monumental canvas *Belshazzar's Feast,* which he was never able to complete to his satisfaction. Though his inability to complete this picture and to continue his career was much due to obsessions about personal perfection, he nevertheless saw himself trapped by American business culture. As frustrated American artist, he became, after his death, symbol

SCIENCE; INDUSTRY; ECONOMICS; EDUCATION; RELIGION; PHILOSOPHY.	SPORTS; FASHIONS; POPULAR ENTERTAINMENT; FOLKLORE; SOCIETY.

with only books it possessed, and hence sole means by which children could be taught to read.

Thomas Gilpin produced the **machine-made paper** in U.S. near Wilmington, Del. For 1st time custom-made paper was available.

Isaac Mason financed the Plumsock Rolling Mill in Pennsylvania. It was a very important early **mill** which produced rolled iron.

Mar. 24 **Allegheny College** chartered in Meadville, Pa., under Presbyterian auspices. 1st degrees granted in 1821. College shifted to Methodist affiliation in 1833.

July 4 Construction of **Erie Canal** begun under governor of New York state, De Witt Clinton, elected in spring of this year. Canal was to affect vitally development of New York, city and state, bringing Great Lakes trade to Atlantic.

> 'Cause he couldn't go to 'lection
> An shake paw-paw."

Paw-paw was a game of chance with sea shells used as dice.

Cup plates became rage at about this time. They were miniature plates with center cavity about size of cup bottom used as dainty but practical perch for cups while drinker sipped his beverage from his saucer. Cup plates were decorated with lavish attention to detail, came in great variety of patterns which fairly catalogued or chronicled taste of the period. They were introduced 1st as chinaware. The development of glass industry, especially of glass press, made them even more plentiful and popular and, considering their use, necessary. Cup plates lasted as long as it was considered polite to drink from saucer but went out of vogue before Civil War.

Aug. 18 Wild accounts of **sea serpent** off coast of Gloucester, Mass., led to formation of committee to investigate. Reports described strange undulating creature, 3 ft. in diameter and from 70 to 100 ft. long. It had long tongue that shot out from its gaping mouth. Completely oblivious to sounds or sights, it was even unaffected by gunshots.

1818

West Point Foundry established at Cold Spring, N.Y., across Hudson from the U.S. Military Academy. Beginning as small forge, foundry became Union's main source of artillery pieces and projectiles, producing in course of Civil War over 3000 heavy cannon and 1,600,000 shells. Gouverneur Kemble, a leading American ironmaster and operator of foundry, was largely responsible for quality and quantity of ordnance produced at foundry.

Benjamin Silliman began *American Journal of Science,* oldest American **scientific periodical.** Silliman was pioneer in

1st recorded trotting contest occurred when *Boston Blue* did the mile in less than 3 minutes, winning his supporters $1000.

1st mention of **bowling at pins** made in *Rip Van Winkle,* Washington Irving's story of Dutch settlers in New York. Bowling at pins, as well as lawn bowls, probably popular for some years by this time.

Apr. 4 **13 stripes** on U.S. flag made constant by law. Upon admission of new state to Union another star to be added to flag.

149

POLITICS AND GOVERNMENT; WAR; DISASTERS; VITAL STATISTICS.	BOOKS; PAINTING; DRAMA; ARCHITECTURE; SCULPTURE.

scheduled dates between distant ports. 4 ships formed Black Ball Line.

May 27 Fall of Pensacola, Fla., to Gen. Andrew Jackson terminated **First Seminole War.** Alexander Arbuthnot and Robert Ambrister, British subjects, sentenced by Jackson to death for inciting Seminoles to hostility against U.S.

Oct. 20 Convention signed between Britain and U.S. gave **fishing rights** to American seamen off parts of Newfoundland and coast of Labrador. U.S. renounced any such activities within 3 miles of any other British territory. Also boundary between Canada and U.S. between Lake of the Woods and crest of Rocky Mountains fixed at 49th parallel. No boundary decided upon further west, and Oregon was declared open territory for 10 years.

Dec 3 **Illinois** admitted as state, 21st of Union.

for sensitive man wrecked on American materialism.

The Executive Mansion in Washington, D.C., restored. It had been burnt by the British in 1814. To cover the scorch marks the Mansion was painted white, and this gave rise to its popular name, the **"White House."**

Walter Scott's best seller *Rob Roy.* Scott's tremendous popularity produced 1st real competitive publishing in U.S. Publishers went to great lengths to be 1st to "pirate" new English works.

1st lithograph made in U.S. drawn on stone by Bass Otis; it was portrait of Rev. Abner Kneeland for use as frontispiece in book of sermons.

Dec. 3 Tremendous success of American play in England, new tragedy, *Brutus, or the Fall of Tarquin* by **John Howard Payne.** Star in play was Kean. In America play was staged for 75 years and starred such actors as J. B. Booth, Edwin Forrest, John McCullough, and Edwin Booth.

1819

This year saw country in state of **financial panic.** State banks closed and much western property was turned over to Bank of the U.S. Immigration slowed to trickle for almost decade.

Feb. 13 **Tallmadge amendment** added to bill for Missouri statehood. Amendment was 1st great trial of Constitution on domestic issue. Proposed that all children born in Missouri would be free at age of 25, and further introduction of slavery prohibited. Question raised was whether Congress had right to impose restrictions on new states which Constitution did not impose on original commonwealths. Tallmadge amendment was dropped.

Feb. 22 Spain ceded Florida to U.S. with signing of **Adams-Onés Treaty.** U.S. agreed to assume claims of American citizens against Spain amounting to $5 million. Florida and parts of Alabama, Louisi-

2nd Bank of the U.S. built in Philadelphia; architect, Benjamin Latrobe. He introduced Doric portico of Parthenon into his plans, thus making it central part of Greek Revival in U.S.

Poet of great promise, **Joseph Rodman Drake,** emerged in pages of *New York Evening Post* with satirical series, *The Croaker Papers,* in which he collaborated with Fitz-Greene Halleck. In many poems he urged exploitation of national themes. "Look with creative eye on Nature's face," he wrote in "To a Friend"; "no more . . . laud your lady's eyes." His poems, "The American Flag," "The Culprit Fay," and "Niagara" are well-known.

Romantic feeling for nature admirably captured by **Allston** in his *Moonlit Landscape,* canvas flooded with aura of mystery. Coleridge said of him that he alone was able to capture true aspects of nature, "not the dead shapes, the outward letter,

SCIENCE; INDUSTRY; ECONOMICS; EDUCATION; RELIGION; PHILOSOPHY.

SPORTS; FASHIONS; POPULAR ENTERTAINMENT; FOLKLORE; SOCIETY.

American geological research, held chair of natural science and chemistry at Yale from 1802–1853. He edited *Journal of Science* for 26 years, was one of great popularizers of science through spoken as well as written word.

Peter Durand introduced **tin can** in America. Durand, an Englishman, hit upon idea of sealing hot perishable foods in suitable containers and took out patent on process in 1810. He put tin at top of list of recommended materials for containers. Glass had already been used for similar purpose in France by François Appert, author of *Art of Preserving Animal and Vegetable Substances for Many Years,* published 1810.

Works of **New England Glass Company** of Cambridge, Mass. began operations. Company made major contribution to developing glass industry of nation.

Sept. 20 1st manufacture of **patent leather** in the U.S. by Seth Boyden at Newark, N.J.

Vogue of thin muslin dresses, which were also low-cut and flatteringly fitted, stimulated a great deal of solicitous speculation. There was considerable concern for the women who went out attired in these dresses. Was the fashion in the best interests of the ladies' health? Were they not even in physical danger from fire? It was also wondered whether such dresses did not reflect upon the virtue of the wearer.

Among the popular vocalists giving **recitals** were Mr. Philips who intoned, among other selections, "Behold in his soft expressive face," "Robin Adair," and "Lilla come down to me"—at the New York Theater.

The City Hotel in New York featured the exhibition of the Albiness until Feb. 5.

1819

Significant advance in American higher education effected with opening of **Norwich University** in Vermont, specializing in technical training, neglected in most colleges of time with important exception of West Point Military Academy.

Ebenezer Brown, began **Methodist mission** in U.S.; assigned by Methodist Board to convert French-speaking population of New Orleans, La. Mission failed. Later (1829) Brown established textile business at Troy, N.Y., and manufactured 1st detachable collars made in U.S.

Ezra Daggett and Thomas Kensett of New York city began to can fish as a business venture. Probably **1st canning business** in U.S.

Thomas Jefferson founded **University of Virginia** in accordance with his ideas on religious freedom. Chapel attendance made voluntary for 1st time in American college

Apr. 26 American chapters of **Society of Odd Fellows** begun in U.S. with Washington Lodge No. 1 at Baltimore, Md., under charter granted by Duke of York Lodge, England. Grand Lodge of Maryland and U.S. founded 1821.

June 1 Mme. Adolphe, noted European **tightrope performer,** has American debut at Anthony Street Theater, New York.

New York Picture Gallery for the display and sale of art opened. It advertised showings of old and modern pictures, sculptures and bronzes.

Feb. 5 1st nighters in New York city caught *Rob Roy M'Gregor,* or *Auld Lang Syne,* and after the play, the interludes *Dr. Last's Examination* and the comic ballet of *Little Red Riding Hood.* The **double-feature program** is of long standing!

ana, and Mississippi comprised original territory.

Mar. 2 **1st immigration law** enacted by Congress established rules and procedures for passenger ships bringing immigrants to U.S., most important of which was numerical registry of immigration. Thus it became possible to compile accurate statistics on immigration in following years.

Dec. 14 Alabama admitted as state, 22nd to join Union.

but the life of nature revealing itself in the phenomenon."

Washington Irving's *Sketch Book* immediate best seller, and among more popular American books of all time. With this book Irving established himself as one of most loved and certainly 1st purely literary genius in America.

St. Paul's Church, Augusta, Ga., excellent example of Southern architecture of Greek Revival, built from plans by unknown architect.

1820

Population—9,638,453. Center of population: 16 miles east of Moorefield, W. Va.

Group of Democrats known as Albany Regency introduce big-time **machine politics** to U.S. Martin Van Buren was among the leaders of the group, which controlled New York politics for 2 decades.

Capt. Nathaniel Brown Palmer and crew of 6 sight antarctic peninsula, later called Palmerland; believed to have been **1st discovery of Antarctica.** Palmer commanded sloop *Hero* out of Stonington, Conn.

Feb. 6 1st organized **emigration of Negroes** to Africa from U.S. begun with group of 86 sailing from New York to Sierra Leone.

Feb. 17 Sen. Thomas' **compromise amendment** to a bill to admit Maine and Missouri to statehood (Missouri Compromise) adopted. It prohibited introduction of slavery into any state formed from territory of Louisiana north of 36° 30', except Missouri.

Mar. 3 Missouri Compromise passed. Voting in Congress for 1st time followed geographical lines. Arkansas was to be slave state; Maine free; Missouri to be permitted constitution without restriction of slavery; but Compromise held provision forever prohibiting slavery north of 36° 30'.

Imitations of Byron in deed and poetry were legion during this decade, best poem in Byronic vein being *Fanny* (1819) by **Fitz-Greene Halleck.** Rollicking imitation of *Don Juan*, poem sets out to satirize New York life in all its aspects—finance, women, society, etc.

Great **literary theme** of '20's was romantic treatment of the Indian. There was *Frontier Maid, or the Fall of Wyoming* (1819); *Yamoyden* (1820) by Eastburn and Sands; *Logan, an Indian Tale* (1821) by Samuel Webber; *The Land of Powhatten* (1821) by a Virginian; *Ontwa, Son of the Forest* (1822) by Henry Whiting; etc.

Grove Street Houses in Greenwich Village show early 19th-century New York style, before emergence of Greek Revival.

Dawning of Music in Kentucky, or the Pleasures of Harmony in the Solitudes of Nature, by **Anton Philip Heinrich,** published. 2 years earlier, Heinrich had emigrated from Hamburg, Germany, but his book was call for nationalistic music. Among Heinrich's compositions were: *The Columbiad; Grand American National Chivalrous Symphony; Jubilee; Yankee Doodliad;* etc.

One of greatest of all best sellers, *Ivanhoe* by **Walter Scott,** had sold over 2½ million copies in America. Scott and Charles Dickens were 2 most republished authors in America.

SCIENCE; INDUSTRY; ECONOMICS; EDUCATION; RELIGION; PHILOSOPHY.	SPORTS; FASHIONS; POPULAR ENTERTAINMENT; FOLKLORE; SOCIETY.

and no religious professions were required of faculty.

Apr. 2 *American Farmer,* **1st successful agricultural journal** in U.S., founded in Baltimore, Md., by John Stuart Skinner. Became widely popular and continued operation until 1897.

May 26 **1st American steamboat** to cross Atlantic left Savannah bound for Liverpool, and made crossing in 25 days, all but 7 on steam.

New York Evening Post carried offer of 6 cents reward for a lost, strayed, or stolen 19 year old **apprentice** blacksmith.

Feb. G. Geib advertised his **Patent Analytical Grammatical** system of teaching the composition and practice of music. Lessons were $30 a quarter. Money refunded if not satisfied. Geib thoughtfully bonded himself for $1,000 against failures.

1820

Drive of American middle classes for more reading material seen in establishment of **Mercantile Library Association** and **Apprentices' Library Association,** both in New York city, followed shortly thereafter by formation of similar libraries in Boston and Philadelphia.

Maj. **Stephen Long's expedition** to area below Missouri R., suggested by War Secretary John C. Calhoun, resulted in discovery of 60 rare or previously unknown animals, hundreds of new insects, and many unknown plants.

Major advance in public scholarship effected by establishment of **1st state supported libraries** in America, in New York and New Hampshire.

James Fenimore Cooper estimated 8000 **college graduates** in population of 10 million.

Thomas Blanchard stepped up evolution of **interchangeable machine parts** with invention of special lathe to finish off wooden stocks of firearms. Stocks could be cut out in rapid order and used with standardized metal parts of guns. Success with lathe encouraged Blanchard to apply his invention to more general industrial uses.

Elihu Emree began publication of *Emancipator* at Jonesboro, Tennessee. Year before, he had started crusade against slavery with a weekly paper, the *Manumission In-*

During this decade **1st football games** appeared in American colleges. It was form of hazing used especially at Yale and Harvard. Sophomores and freshmen were supposed to kick ball around, but sophomores generally kicked freshmen instead. These "games" were banned during 1830's because of large number of injuries.

Famous chair factory started by Lambert Hitchcock at Hitchcockville (now Riverton), Conn. Factory produced chair parts which were sent to South Carolina for assembly. "Hitchcock chair" thus became very popular in South. In 1823 chair was completely manufactured in Hitchcockville.

Expression **"Half horse and half alligator"** used on frontier to characterize rough and tumble individuals. Often term was used to designate Badmen who thrived in raw communities beyond Alleghenies.

In beginning of 1820 John C. Calhoun reported to John Quincy Adams that he noticed that **popular attitudes and actions** deserved careful attention. The panic of 1819 had wrought great changes in economic status. Period of wild speculation had ended with wholesale foreclosures by banks, with much property in South and West reverting to national bank. There were, said Calhoun, "enormous multitudes in deep distress" who were disenchanted with Government, alert to main chance and

Mar. 6 **Missouri Enabling Act** passed authorizing people of Missouri to draw up constitution and form state government.

Mar. 15 **Maine** admitted as state, 23rd to join Union.

Mar. 22 **Stephen Decatur,** hero of Tripolitan war, shot and killed in duel with James Barron.

June 6 Expedition of **Maj. Stephen Long** set out from Pittsburgh to explore region below Missouri R. and Rocky Mts. Only important geographical discovery of expedition was the course of Canadian R., later important part of route to New Mexico.

Dec. 6 James Monroe defeated John Quincy Adams in **presidential election,** by 231 electoral votes to 1. Daniel D. Tompkins re-elected vice-president.

Jan. Famous taunt hurled at American culture by English critic **Sydney Smith** widely circulated in America. Observed Smith: "In the four quarters of the globe, who reads an American book? or goes to an American play? or looks at an American picture or statue?"

Nov. 27 Celebrated actor of 19th-century American stage **Edwin Forrest** made his debut at Walnut Street Theater, Philadelphia, as young Norval in Home's *Douglas.* Not quite 15, his performance was not greeted with unusual enthusiasm.

1821

Indian Factory system abolished. It was established to enable Indians to obtain fair prices in their trading with white men, but political pressures from white traders caused its dissolution.

William Becknell of Missouri pioneered **Santa Fe Trail,** opening route for commerce with northern Mexico, and eventually providing outposts for settlers.

Genius of Universal Emancipation, **antislavery publication,** 1st issued in Ohio by Benjamin Lundy, who articulated widespread hope of resettling Negroes in Africa.

Mar. 5 Pres. **Monroe** inaugurated Mar. 5th for his 2nd term. Daniel D. Tompkins was his vice-president.

Aug. 10 **Missouri** admitted as state, 24th to join Union.

Sept. Treaty concluded by which **Seminole Indians** agreed to retire to center of Florida peninsula, an almost uninhabitable territory. They were to move west 20

Publication of *Boston Handel and Haydn Society Collection of Church Music,* compiled by **Lowell Mason,** banker in Savannah, Ga., achieved immediate success; collection went through 21 editions, and was largely responsible for Mason's change from banking to music for his career.

Best seller *Kenilworth* by **Walter Scott.** Scott's colorful adventure novels constitute most important literary fact of 1st third of 19th century.

Possibly 1st great American novel, **James Fenimore Cooper's** *The Spy.* It sold more than 3 editions in 1 year. It is romance of Revolution, set in Westchester County, N.Y., neutral territory.

Dec. 24 Greatest piece of sculpture in America at this time, *Statue of Washington* by **Antonio Canova,** installed in State House at Raleigh, N.C.—a backwoods town. Washington, dressed like a Roman,

SCIENCE; INDUSTRY; ECONOMICS; EDUCATION; RELIGION; PHILOSOPHY.	SPORTS; FASHIONS; POPULAR ENTERTAINMENT; FOLKLORE; SOCIETY.

telligencer. Embree was forced to convert to a monthly and renamed his publication the *Emancipator.* It was popular and powerful organ of agitation which categorically denounced slavery and slaveholding as evils. Embree, a convert to Quakerism, was strongly influenced by argument of Friends that all men are entitled to exercise freedom given them by God.

Henry Schoolcraft, pioneer American geologist, was member of expedition prospecting for **lead** in country around Lake Superior.

June 19 **Colby College** 1st authorized to confer degrees by 1st legislature of Maine. As Maine Literary and Theological Institution it had already been chartered Feb. 27, 1813, by General Court of Massachusetts. 1st degrees were awarded in 1822.

"looking out anywhere for a leader." This proved shrewd political insight into factors which were ushering in age of Jackson.

Apr. 12 Congressman John Randolph of Roanoke, Va., popularized term **"dough-face,"** according to a report in *New Brunswick Times.* Term applied to Northern congressmen who voted with Southern slave-holding interests. John Quincy Adams continued to use term with same reference until 1843.

1821

1st girls' high school founded by Emma H. Willard at Troy, N.Y., as Troy Female Seminary. An early feminist, Mrs. Willard devised curriculum considered, at that time, unusually rigorous for women. Seminary became model for both European and American attempts at higher education for women.

First natural gas production in U.S. from well at Fredonia, New York.

Feb. 6 **George Washington University** 1st chartered as Columbian College in Washington, D.C. Established under Baptist auspices, college awarded 1st degrees in 1824. Columbian College became Columbian University in 1873 and George Washington University in 1904.

May English Classical School, later called English High School, opened in Boston, Mass., **1st high school** in U.S.

May 31 Cathedral of the Assumption of the Blessed Virgin Mary, Baltimore, Md., **1st Catholic cathedral** in U.S., dedicated by Archbishop Maréchal. Cornerstone had been laid in 1806.

During next decade and a half **coffee** came into general use in America. But temperance movements directed heavy campaigns against it, and in some quarters it was considered an aphrodisiac.

New York State relaxed laws against **public horse racing,** permitting tracks to open in Queens County. This led to building of Union Course on Long Island.

Charles Taylor Caldwell sailed to Europe with $10,000 allocated by Kentucky for purchase of **library** for Transylvania University. While in Europe, Caldwell became familiar with principles of phrenology and returned to America to put his knowledge into practice in Lexington, Louisville, and

POLITICS AND GOVERNMENT; WAR; DISASTERS; VITAL STATISTICS.	BOOKS; PAINTING; DRAMA; ARCHITECTURE; SCULPTURE.

years from date of treaty, and U.S. was to pay them annuities and assure them protection and care.

holds tablet with inscription in Italian: "Giorgio Washington al popoli degli Stati Uniti; Amici e Concittadini . . ."

1822

Mar. 8 Pres. Monroe, in a message to Congress, urged recognition of **Latin American republics** La Plata (Argentina), Brazil, Chile, Peru, Colombia, Mexico, and Federation of Central American States. Congressional Act (May 4) provided for diplomatic recognition of these states.

April 27 **Ulysses S. Grant,** 18th president, born in Point Pleasant, Ohio.

May 4 Pres. Monroe vetoed bill appropriating money for repair of Cumberland Road and authorizing **toll charges.** Monroe asserted that federal government did not have right to operate and hold jurisdiction over public road or any internal improvements. Bill did not pass over his veto.

May 30 **Vesey Slave Plot** uncovered and suppressed in Charleston, S.C., with aid of informer. Plot organized by Denmark Vesey, emancipated Negro, and involved large group of Negro city workers. 37 participants were executed.

Oct. 4 **Rutherford B. Hayes,** 19th president, born in Delaware, Ohio.

Best seller *The Pilot* by **James Fenimore Cooper.**

Washington Irving continued his quest among beauties of antiquity with his *Bracebridge Hall.* Like *Sketch Book* it is made up of sketches, stories, essays, many of which romanticize English countryside. "The Stout Gentleman" is one of best stories in collection.

Mine of information for historian of early 19th century is **Timothy Dwight's** *Travels in New England and New York.* A Calvinist minister, president of Yale College, he presented unflattering picture of provincial and frontier life in prose that is heavy and diffuse.

St. Luke's Chapel built at Hudson and Grove Sts., New York. Was first known as St. Luke's-in-the-Fields.

1823

Dec. 2 Pres. Monroe formulated policy of isolation in his annual message to Congress. Statement, which became known as **Monroe Doctrine,** declared that any attempt by Europeans to colonize Americas or interfere with internal affairs of Western Hemisphere would be interpreted as act of aggression. It further stated that U.S. would remain aloof from European quarrels. In substance, this was foreign policy advocated by John Quincy Adams, Monroe's Secretary of State.

1st American minstrel Edwin Forrest, who blackened his face to play part of Negro Ruban in farce by Sol Smith, *Tailor in Distress.* Later both Edwin Booth and John S. Clarke took part in "Negro" minstrelsy.

Hudson River school of landscape painting formed about this time. Thomas Cole and Asher B. Durand were among those artists who were noted for their lush, highly romanticized landscapes.

May 8 Most popular song by an American, **"Home Sweet Home,"** written by John Howard Payne and composed by Henry Bishop for his opera *Clari,* presented today at the Covent Gardens in London.

Dec. 18 **University of Alabama** chartered as state university in Tuscaloosa, Ala. 1st degrees granted in 1832.

other Western communities. He became known as "American Spurzheim." (Spurzheim was Viennese inventor of phrenology.)

1822

Rise of **protectionist sentiment** in American industrial circles reflected in Mathew Carey's *Essays on Political Economy,* which advocated both protective tariffs and federal expenditures for internal improvements to equalize federal treatment for all interests in economy.

1st patent for making of **false teeth** awarded to C. M. Graham.

Apr. 10 Charter granted to Geneva College, Geneva, N.Y., later **Hobart College.** Hobart offered 1st non-classical course in U.S.; called "English Course," it offered to equip "the Agriculturist, the Merchant, and the Mechanic" with a "practical knowledge of what genius and experience have discovered."

June 26 Thomas Jefferson expressed his faith in ultimate triumph of **Unitarianism** in America in letter to Dr. Benjamin Waterhouse of Harvard. "I trust that there is not a young man now living who will not die a Unitarian."

Football at Yale College prohibited by Pres. Timothy Dwight, who ordered any violations to be reported and violators to be penalized by fine not to exceed a half dollar.

May Noah Ludlow, comedian, sang **"The Hunters of Kentucky"** before enthusiastic audience at New Orleans consisting mostly of river boatmen. Song turned famous Battle of New Orleans into a Jacksonian legend. 5th stanza goes:

But Jackson, he was wide awake,
And wasn't scared at trifles;
For well he knew what aim to take,
With our Kentucky rifles;
So he led us down to Cypress swamp,
The ground was low and mucky;
There stood John Bull, in martial pomp,
And here was old Kentucky.
Oh! Kentucky, the hunters of Kentucky,
The hunters of Kentucky.

1823

1st preparation of **hydrofluoric acid** in America by Benjamin Silliman, professor of chemistry at Yale.

Major defense of American culture against derogatory criticism of British intellectuals made by **Charles J. Ingersoll** before American Philosophical Society in lecture entitled *Discourse Concerning the Influence of America on the Mind,* in which he accepted challenge of British critics by comparing American culture with European and finding that average intellect in America far surpassed corresponding intellect in Europe, and that America's great contribution to world civilization had been self-government.

May **1st great horse racing event** in America was between *American Eclipse* from North and challenger *Sir Henry* from South for tremendous purse of $20,000. 100,000 spectators jammed Union Course on Long Island to see *American Eclipse* take 2 out of 3 heats, doing 4-mile stretch in 7:49 and 8:24. Victory of northern horse spread gloom throughout South.

1824

Gateway through Rocky Mountains discovered. South Pass, Wyo., found by Jedediah Strong Smith of Rocky Mountain Fur Company.

Feb. 14 **Last Congressional nominating caucus** convened and named William H. Crawford of Georgia as its candidate for president.

Mar. 2 Federal control of **interstate commerce** established by *Gibbons v. Ogden* steamboat case argued before Supreme Court.

Apr. 17 **U.S.–Russian territorial treaty** signed. Russia acknowledged 54° 40′ parallel as southern limit of her territory, and abandoned some of her claims to territory in northern Pacific.

Aug. **1st nominating convention** held at Utica, N.Y. For 1st time electors of nominees for office were elected by popular vote. Nominations for president and state candidates had been made in caucus, but this method was soon replaced by the convention. Utica convention nominated candidates for offices of governor and lieutenant governor.

Dec. 1 In **presidential elections** no electoral majority was reached, John Quincy Adams receiving 84 votes; Andrew Jackson, 99; William H. Crawford, 41; Henry Clay, 37. John C. Calhoun was elected vice-president. On Feb. 9, 1825, John Quincy Adams chosen by House of Representatives.

Gothic tale as developed by German romanticists found American expression in **Washington Irving's** collection of tales and sketches, *Tales of a Traveler*. Noteworthy among stories are "Adventure of the German Student" and "The Devil and Tom Walker."

Another famous story of Indian captivity published, *The Life of Mary Jemison* by **James E. Seaver.** Mary Jemison lived with Delaware Indians for almost 70 years, married 2 Indian husbands, and, as told to Seaver, hers was one of most interesting accounts of Indian life.

Meeting House at Deerfield, Mass., built from plans by Isaac Damon, most popular country architect of New England in early 19th century. Very good example of his rather monumental style.

Mar. 12 Successful play based on Indian warfare and witch trials of early New England history, **James N. Barker's** *Superstition,* performed at Chestnut Theater in Philadelphia. Preceded by year a similar treatment in Hawthorne's famous story, "The Grey Champion."

May 27 Best comedy from pen of **John Howard Payne,** *Charles the Second, or the Merry Monarch,* adapted from original French play, as he was to do in his *Richelieu* (1826). He also wrote *'Twas I* (1825), and *The Lancers* (1826).

1825

Fire in Library of Congress caused irreparable loss. This was 2nd such fire in less than 15 years.

"The Albany Regency" began to come into long-lasting prominence as a group of political leaders in Democratic Party in New York state who had served in Albany, state capital, in some administrative capacity. Leaders in so-called regency

Development of **stage Yankee** began. Type found its epitome in Jonathan Ploughboy of Samuel Woodworth's *The Forest Rose,* which opened this year. James E. Hackett, actor, made the "Yankee" famous. Under various titles—Uncle Ben, Solomon Swap, Industrious Doolittle, Jonathan Doubikins—type became stock role for comedian.

1824

1st recorded strike in U.S. involving **women employees** occurred in Pawtucket, R.I., where male and female weavers struck together against proposed decrease in wages and increase in hours.

Jan. 24 **Kenyon College** 1st chartered in Gambier, Ohio, as the Theological Seminary of the Protestant Episcopal Church. 1st degrees were awarded in 1829. Seminary became Kenyon College in 1891.

May 25 **American Sunday School Union** established in Philadelphia to promote and co-ordinate Sunday school activity in America. Representatives of many denominations from upward of 15 states were represented in organization which absorbed similar local associations in Philadelphia, Boston, and New York. American Sunday School Union was 1st significant national organization in its field and has remained major Sunday school organization in America.

Oct. 3 **Rensselaer Polytechnic Institute** at Troy, N.Y., established. It was one of the 1st engineering schools founded in this country.

Estimated crowd of 50,000 witnessed **boat race** in New York harbor for a purse of $1000. Crew of victorious craft, *Whitehall,* became civic heroes and received tumultous ovation on their appearance at Park Theater.

Frances Wright, well-known personality and lecturer of day, arrived from Scotland to stump country, spreading gospel of free thought, labor, public education, antislavery and women's rights.

Aug. 2 **Emancipation Day** commemorated by Negroes of Illinois since on this date slavery was abolished in state.

1825

1st significant strike in U.S. for **10-hour day** called in Boston by 600 carpenters.

1st technical innovation in making of glass since ancient times, **mechanical pressing,** introduced into American factories. Change resulted in production of intricately designed glassware. Famous glassworks established this year by Deming

During next 10 years emigration to U.S. of economic victims of industrial revolution in England created large number of "paupers," who overtaxed inadequate poor laws written in 18th century.

Guidebooks for American travel became available. Stagecoach travelers for 1st time had a guide to the whole country, *The American Traveller* by Daniel Hewett. 1st

| POLITICS AND GOVERNMENT; WAR; DISASTERS; VITAL STATISTICS. | BOOKS; PAINTING; DRAMA; ARCHITECTURE; SCULPTURE. |

were Martin Van Buren, William L. Marcy, Silas Wright, John A. Dix, all past or future governors, Azariah C. Flagg, Benjamin F. Butler, Edwin Crosswell, and Michael Hoffman. This group enjoyed great influence in state and national politics for about 30 years.

Proposal of 8 northern state legislatures that all **slaves** in America be emancipated at federal expense summarily rejected by Southern states.

Jan. 3 New Harmony, Ind., **1st secular utopian society** in U.S., founded when Robert Owen bought 20,000 acres; community grew to 900 individuals. Owen left group in 1827, and it discontinued shortly after.

Feb. 29 **John Quincy Adams chosen president** by House of Representatives, being favored by 13 of 24 states. Andrew Jackson had received most votes at regular election, but this was not a majority in 4-way race that included Henry Clay and William Crawford as candidates. Therefore, final selection devolved on House for 2nd time.

Feb. 12 **Creek Indian treaty signed.** Tribal leaders agreed to turn over all their lands in Georgia to government and promised to migrate to West by Sept. 1, 1826. Treaty was rejected by most Creeks.

Mar. 4 **John Quincy Adams,** 6th president, inaugurated. He was a Republican and held office for 4 years.

Mar. 7 **1st minister to Mexico named.** He was Joel R. Poinsett. His appointment was approved by Senate on following day.

Mar. 24 **1st American settlers allowed in Mexican state of Texas-Coahuila.** State passed colonization law permitting immigration.

Dec. 25 **Commercial treaty signed with Central American Confederation.**

Sensational murder in Kentucky produced countless stories, novels, and plays during century. Col. Beauchamp of Frankfort killed Col. Sharpe when he discovered that the latter had seduced his wife before he, Beauchamp, had married her. Tried and convicted, he attempted suicide in his cell; but he was unsuccessful and was finally hanged. T. H. Chivers' drama *Conrad and Eudora* (1834) and Edgar Allan Poe's *Politian* (1835) both use incident, with story placed in another country and century; Charlotte Barnes Conner used it in her play *Octavia Brigaldi* (1837); novelist William G. Simms' border romance *Beauchampe* (1842) used original locale; and John Savage employed it in his play *Sybil* (1858).

John Pierpont's *Readers* came into use this year, especially in public schools of New England. John Pierpont was greatgrandfather of John Pierpont Morgan, Jr.

1st poems of **Henry W. Longfellow** appeared in *United States Literary Gazette,* most noteworthy being "Autumnal Nightfall," "Woods in Winter," "The Angler's Song," and "Hymn of the Moravian Nuns." His 1st poem, "The Battle of Lovell's Pond," appeared in the *Portland Gazette,* Nov. 17, 1820.

June 27 **Daniel Webster's** name spread far and wide after his famous "Bunker Hill Oration." Other early speeches, "The Dartmouth College Case" (1818) and "The Landing of the Pilgrims" (1820), were never surpassed by his later polemical oratory.

Nov. 8 New York Drawing Association, which later became **National Academy of Design,** organized in New York city. Samuel F. B. Morse, who was one of active founders, chosen 1st president.

Nov. 29 **Regular Italian opera** introduced to New York at Park Theater with performance of *Il Barbiere di Siviglia.* Company was led by famous tenor Signor

160

| SCIENCE; INDUSTRY; ECONOMICS; EDUCATION; RELIGION; PHILOSOPHY. | SPORTS; FASHIONS; POPULAR ENTERTAINMENT; FOLKLORE; SOCIETY. |

Jarves at Sandwich, Mass., noted for their production on large scale of pressed glass.

"Suffolk System" initiated by Suffolk Bank in Boston. System required rural banks to maintain deposits in Suffolk Bank as security for Suffolk Bank in negotiating their notes. This system created banking phenomenon known as "pyramiding," a dangerous situation in which a run on relatively few banks could launch a national bank panic. Immediate effect, however, was the termination of discounts on rural bank notes.

Amasa Holcomb of Southwick, Mass., began at about this time to manufacture reflecting and achromatic **telescopes,** probably the 1st made in America.

Homoeopathy introduced in America by Dr. Hans Burch Gram from Germany. System of homoeopathy was invention of Samuel Hahnemann, who was, in 1820, forbidden by law to practice his treatments, but was protected and encouraged to continue research by Duke Ferdinand of Anhält-Köthen. The homoeopathic formula for cures states that a sick person can be cured by a medicine which can produce similar symptoms of disease in a healthy person. It was radical departure from established theory, but persecution of Hahnemann drove him from place to place and indirectly assured rapid propagation of his ideas.

Feb. 21 Amherst College chartered in Amherst, Mass., although classes actually began Sept. 19, 1821 under the Rev. Zephaniah Swift Moore, who later acted as institution's 1st president.

Oct. 26 Erie Canal officially opened at Buffalo, N.Y., and 1st boat began trip from Buffalo to Albany, then down Hudson R. to New York city and the Atlantic. 544-mile route was lined with cannon to celebrate occasion. From Albany to New York city boat carried Gov. Clinton. Erie Canal was longest canal in world up to

newspaper in America especially devoted to coach interests, *American Traveller* of Badger and Porter, appeared in Boston. This year also saw publication of popular travel booklet, "The Fashionable Tour."

Legend of **Tom Walker and the Devil** born from tale in Washington Irving's *Tales of a Traveler,* published this year. Like countless other "devil tales," this describes bargain Tom Walker and his wife strike with Old Nick when he promises them treasure of Capt. Kidd.

Organization of **New York Trotting Club,** which constructed racing course on Long Island, 1st especially devoted to trotting.

1st U.S. gymnasium established at Northampton, Mass., by Charles Beck, disciple of Friedrich Jahn, founder of 1st "turnplatz" in Germany. Widespread popular interest in German gymnastics was also stimulated by Charles Follen, refugee student leader from Germany who introduced the sport in Boston. Follen later taught at Harvard.

Frances Wright, British visitor to U.S., began her public lectures on political equality, radical theology, and women's rights, setting significant example for later American feminists.

Glassware in cheap, standardized sets appeared for 1st time on American counters. It marked transition from blowing to pressing glass. The mechanical press introduced new method of stamping out molds in glassmaking factories, brought quicker, less expensive, more uniform product. Housewives eagerly bought the new pieces to fill up their cabinets with ornamental necessities. At first, glassware made on presses was heavy, though thickness was balanced by patterns visually worked out in tiny raised dots giving appearance of fragility. In 1825 opening of famous James works at Sandwich, Mass., gave additional impulse to flood of new wares. These

POLITICS AND GOVERNMENT; WAR; DISASTERS; VITAL STATISTICS.	BOOKS; PAINTING; DRAMA; ARCHITECTURE; SCULPTURE.

Garcia, and cast included Signorina Maria Garcia, afterwards famous Mme. Malibran.

1826

Free Mason **William Morgan** of Batavia, N.Y., kidnaped and persumably killed because he was said to have revealed secrets of that order. Morgan's supporters subsequently founded the **Anti-Masonic Party.**

Fugitive Slave Act of 1793 largely nullified by a Pennsylvania law which made kidnaping a crime. Pennsylvania statute declared unconstitutional by the Supreme Court in 1842 in case of *Prigg v. Pennsylvania.* Decision further stated that states could not be obliged to enforce fugitive slave laws through state officers. This led to a series of personal liberty laws in Northern states, forbidding states to assist in returning fugitives.

Nashoba founded by Frances Wright as planned community in which Negroes could be trained and subsequently colonized in Africa. Located near Memphis, Tenn., the Nashoba colony was in operation until 1828.

Jan. 24 Creek Indians signed **Treaty of Washington.** It nullified previous treaty and ceded less territory to the government. It also granted the Indians the right to stay on their lands until Jan. 1, 1827.

Apr. 8 Henry Clay and John Randolph fought **duel** over Randolph's charges that Clay had entered into a deal with John Quincy Adams over the Panama Congress vote. Neither man was harmed.

June **Panama Congress,** called by Simon Bolívar, provided 1st test of Adams administration. Adams had sent a special message to the Senate naming 2 delegates to the Congress. A coalition in the Senate led by John C. Calhoun and Martin Van Buren opposed U.S. attendance mainly on the grounds that U.S. participation broke with traditions of independence and neu-

Edward Everett stirred a New England audience with his impassioned tribute in memory of Adams and Jefferson. Regarded as one of the foremost speakers of his day, he was called upon for public celebrations at Concord, Plymouth, Cambridge, Charlestown, etc.

Most popular of **James Fenimore Cooper's** novels, *The Last of the Mohicans* among most widely read books, selling over 2 million copies. "Leatherstocking Tales" are still popular, even in England and Europe, especially France.

Always popular poem, "The Old Oaken Bucket," written by **Samuel Woodworth.** Other important poetry of this year was 24 poems by **William Cullen Bryant,** among them his "Summer Wind," "An Indian at the Burial of His Fathers," "Monument Mountain," and "A Hymn."

Great vogue of the **Annuals** began. An annual was an ornamental publication bound in beautiful leather and exquisitely printed, used mostly as a gift for ladies. A whole school of poetasters contributed each year to these publications.

American debut of famous actor **William Charles Macready** at Park Theater, New York.

Famous character actor of 19th century American theater, **James H. Hackett,** made debut at Park Theater, New York city. He was to be well-known for his characterization of Yankees, of Nimrod Wildfire and Rip Van Winkle.

Quincy Market, area east of Faneuil Hall, laid out in Boston, with façades designed by Alexander Parris, who used individual granite slabs to form piers and

SCIENCE; INDUSTRY; ECONOMICS; EDUCATION; RELIGION; PHILOSOPHY.	SPORTS; FASHIONS; POPULAR ENTERTAINMENT; FOLKLORE; SOCIETY.

that time and established commercial supremacy of New York state vis-à-vis West, a supremacy that the state has never surrendered.

pieces, called Sandwich after their place of origin, were associated with pressed glass in particular and soon became collectors' items. Sandwich factory was operated until 1888.

1826

1st railway steam locomotive in America was run on small circular track by its builders, Colonel John Stevens and his sons, Robert and Edward.

1st overland expedition to California made by Jedediah Strong Smith. With 17 men Smith left Salt Lake City in August, 1826, and crossed through the Mohave Desert to California 3 months later. He spent the next 4 years on similar exploratory missions in these states and in Oregon.

James Kent published 1st volume of *Commentaries on American Law.* Kent, a lawyer and jurist, was considered in his day to be the American counterpart of Blackstone, and his *Commentaries* have often been compared with the English *Commentaries* of Blackstone. The comparison is not accurate. Kent had no intention of revising Blackstone for Americans. The schemes of the two commentaries differed essentially, and compare merely because both attempt a general study of law and both are in 4 volumes. Kent's *Commentaries* grew out of a series of lectures which he gave at Columbia Coll.

Feb. 7 **Western Reserve University** 1st chartered as Western Reserve College in Hudson, Ohio. Established under the joint auspices of Presbyterian and Congregational groups, college awarded its 1st degrees in 1830. Western Reserve College moved to Cleveland in 1882 and became Western Reserve University in 1884. 1st college in America to be established under sponsorship of two denominations.

Mar. 9 **Lafayette College** in Easton, Pa., chartered under Presbyterian auspices. 1st degrees granted in 1830.

Apr. 1 Capt. Samuel Morey of Orford,

Charles Follen, Harvard Coll. instructor, introduces **physical education** into college education. He taught the Friedrich Jahn system. He also taught German litterature and was a preacher and lecturer in Boston.

The Lyceum movement, begun by Josiah Holbrook in Millbury, Mass., south of Worcester, gave opportunity to new kind of circuit crank. Lyceums were intended to instruct and entertain with ideas and facts about art, science and public affairs, with the goal of contributing to general welfare by raising the level of intelligence of citizens. But early lyceums were usually short of ready cash and could not fill their programs as they wished because fees of topflight speakers were too high. Consequently the lyceums were forced to take what they could get. Any politician, theorist, dreamer, quack who loved to hear himself talk was guaranteed a captive audience. The platform quickly became substitute for cracker barrel, and lyceums languished while waiting their time of glory.

Jan. 17 The Franklin Typographical Society of Boston, group organized to assist needy printers, arranged 1 of earliest celebrations of **Benjamin Franklin's** birthday.

Feb. 13 **1st national temperance group,** The American Temperance Society, founded. *The National Philanthropist,* 1st journal entirely devoted to temperance, was founded this year by the Rev. William Collier, Baptist missionary.

June 30 Memorable phrase **"Independence now and Independence forever"** uttered by John Adams 4 days before he

163

POLITICS AND GOVERNMENT; WAR; DISASTERS; VITAL STATISTICS.

BOOKS; PAINTING; DRAMA; ARCHITECTURE; SCULPTURE.

trality. Southern Senators joined in the opposition since certain republics would be present at the Congress which were under the control of Negroes. The Senate finally approved the mission and dispatched 2 delegates, neither of whom ever arrived; Richard C. Anderson died en route, John Sergeant had gone as far as Mexico when the Congress adjourned.

July 4 **Thomas Jefferson** and **John Adams** died on this, the 50th anniversary of the Declaration of Independence, which they both had helped to frame.

Aug. 22 **Exploration expedition,** under command of Jedediah Smith of the Rocky Mountain Fur Company, left Great Salt Lake with 15 men for Southwest. His greatest contribution was the mapping of the area.

lintels rather than blocks laid up as ashlar.

Best painting of **Samuel F. B. Morse,** later inventor of telegraph, portrait of *Lafayette.* The beloved Frenchman stands surrounded by a motley array of busts, urns, flowers, and domed by a sunset sky.

During theatrical season 1825–1826 Signor Garcia, a celebrated European tenor, tried to introduce permanent company of **Italian opera** in New York city. He rented Park Theater for 2 nights a week, raised admission prices to $2 top for boxes, $1 for pit.

Oct. 23 **Bowery Theater,** which had largest stage in New York at the time, built for most popular musical and minstrel shows. Continued as melodrama and vaudeville theater for over 100 years.

1827

Fort Leavenworth built. It was constructed as a strong point for military units patrolling Sante Fe trade route. The site of Leavenworth is on the direct line of the route followed by Lewis and Clark on their expedition in 1804. Leavenworth became a permanent settlement when the Santa Fe Trail started to take the load of traders passing through the area and needed some kind of a fort for protection. From 1825 to 1854 the traders began to form a town around the fort which was finally defined and established by a group of Missouri squatters in 1855 as 1st incorporated town of Kansas. Leavenworth was named for Henry Leavenworth, who founded it.

Feb. 2 Supreme Court gave president final authority to call out **militia.** The decision was handed down in the case of *Martin v. Mott.*

Feb. 28 **Woolens Bill** stalled by Senate. Bill, which increased tariffs on raw and manufactured wool, was passed by the House but was tabled in the Senate by the tie-breaking vote of Vice-Pres. Calhoun. Rejection of bill stimulated high-tariff forces in the manufacturing centers

Unique American contribution to painting and science was **John James Audubon's** *The Birds of America,* a series of 1065 pictures of birds in their natural habitat, accurately shown in water color and crayon. His monumental work was not completed until 1838 with the 5th volume, *Ornithological Guide.*

1st poetry of **Edgar Allan Poe,** *Tamerlane and Other Poems,* printed in Boston. Little attention was aroused by the slim volume. In 1829 a second volume, *Al Aaraaf, Tamerlane and Minor Poems,* also went unnoticed.

Scholarly and literary journal **American Quarterly Review** founded in Philadelphia by Robert Walsh. Contributions touched upon travel, biography, law, political economy, Egyptian hieroglyphics, etc. Such writers as Ticknor, Bancroft, and Paulding appeared in it.

The Prairie, best seller by **James Fenimore Cooper.** Cooper's "tales" owed some of their success to their clean adventure, the people's growing pride in America, and popular reaction against the novel of sensibility.

N.H., received one of first patents for **internal combustion engine,** probably 1st made in U.S. His design was for a 2-cylinder engine.

Nov. 1st American **lyceum** formed at Millbury, Mass., by Josiah Holbrook. 100 additional local branches were formed within 2 years; by 1834 nearly 3000 local branches were distributed in nearly every state. These local lyceums were voluntary associations devoted to lectures, discussion, and plays presented for purpose of popular education. State and national organizations were developed, but these large units had short lives, the last national convention having been held in 1839. Lyceum bureaus provided lecturers and other talent to local communities until well into the 20th century.

died. He had been asked to propose a toast for the celebration of Independence Day and offered the following: "It is my living sentiment, and by the blessing of God it shall be my dying sentiment,—Independence now and Independence forever!"

Aug. 2 Stirring sentence **"Sink or swim, live or die, survive or perish, I give my hand and my heart to this vote"** delivered by Daniel Webster in speech eulogizing John Adams. Adams was imagined as uttering this phrase during the debate over the adoption of the Declaration of Independence, when some delegates expressed fear.

1827

1st state high school law passed. It was enacted by Massachusetts and called for a tax-supported high school in every community of 500 families or more. An additional clause made the study of U.S. history mandatory.

Arthur Tappen founded New York **Journal of Commerce.** 1st number announced that the newspaper would be free from "immoral advertisements" and "regardful of the Sabbath."

Classic statement of **industrial economy** made by German, Friedrich List, in his *Outlines of American Political Economy.* His opinion was that a nation's wealth could be measured more by the extent of its industrial output than by the commodities it had on hand for commercial transactions. This view harmonized with the shift in the New England economy from trade and commerce to light and heavy industry, which placed it in desperate competition with foreign producers for American market.

Distinguished German contribution to American culture, begun by refugee scholar Francis Lieber, was **Encyclopaedia Ameri-**

Thanksgiving Day as national holiday 1st urged by Mrs. Sarah J. Hale in pages of the *Ladies' Magazine,* of which she was editor and founder. The publication, **1st woman's magazine,** was founded this same year in Boston, Mass.

French-American students organized a procession of street maskers on Shrove Tuesday, thus initiating the **1st Mardi Gras** celebration in New Orleans.

2nd handbook for American sportsmen, *American Shooter's Manual* published in Philadelphia. It considered new sport of shooting on the wing, offering much practical advice.

Theaters in New York city were plagued with fires, inadequate houses, crowded bookings. Bowery Theater, showplace of the season before, was destroyed by fire. The Chatham played out the season, then closed for alterations. The Park Theater was running Signor Garcia's Grand Opera Company 2 nights weekly, forcing the

POLITICS AND GOVERNMENT; WAR; DISASTERS; VITAL STATISTICS.	BOOKS; PAINTING; DRAMA; ARCHITECTURE; SCULPTURE.

of the North; at the same time the South was in general against high tariff because it disturbed world markets on which its agricultural economy depended. Tariff questions led to an emphasis of sectional differences in U.S., and was in part the reason for increasing dissension between North and South.

Mar. 2 Congress raised the salary of **Postmaster General** to same as that received by heads of other departments. This was the 1st indication of the growing importance of the Post Office, and the recognition of it by Congress.

July 30 **Higher tariffs** demanded by protectionists at convention at Harrisburg, Pa. Delegates from 13 states attended.

Aug. 6 Joint occupation of **Oregon** agreed to by U.S. and Great Britain. Treaty renewed the commercial agreements made in 1818.

Nov. 15 **Creek Indians ceded remaining territory** to U.S. The area included all their lands in Georgia.

First completely American song-hit, *The Minstrel's Return from the War* by John Hill Hewitt, called the Father of the American Ballad. Most composers of early songs, like Philip Peil ("Hail Columbia") were not American born.

Freedom's Journal, 1st U.S. Negro newspaper, published in New York city. Edited by John Brown Russwurm and Samuel E. Cornish, it suspended publication in 1830.

Feb. 7 Mme. Francisquy Hutin, famed French danseuse, introduced **ballet** to U.S. with *The Deserter,* staged at Bowery Theater, New York city. Mme. Hutin's light and scanty drapery so shocked the American taste that every woman in the lower tier of boxes immediately left the theater.

Dec. **Mrs. Frances Trollope** arrived in U.S. on a visit from England. She later wrote *Domestic Manners of the Americans,* one of 1st of a long series of books by English authors who criticized American tastes and customs.

1828

Democratic Party formed. Essentially it was an extension of the Republican (Jeffersonian) Party (formed May 13, 1792), and it advocated Jeffersonian principles, promoting equality and standing against special privilege. Andrew Jackson became the 1st president nominated by the new Democrats.

National Republican Party formed during John Quincy Adams' term of office. Bitterness between Adams and his followers, and Andrew Jackson and his Party, increased to such a point that the former organized. The National Republican Party advocated a strong nationalistic program including a national bank, protective tariffs, and internal improvements financed by the federal government. Sometimes referred to as Clay's American System. National Republican Party later became the Whig Party.

Celebrated novelist **Nathaniel Hawthorne's** 1st work, *Fanshawe,* appeared. A short novel, it draws upon Hawthorne's experience as an undergraduate at Bowdoin College.

Publication of **Noah Webster's** monumental *American Dictionary of the English Language,* a labor of more than 20 years. Webster spent much time in England gathering material for his work; he completed it while resident at Cambridge.

Washington Irving turned from Knickerbocker settings to Spanish romance in his *History of the Life and Voyages of Christopher Columbus* and his *Conquest of Granada* (1829). Irving's international point of view earned him the title "Ambassador-at-large from the New World to the Old."

| SCIENCE; INDUSTRY; ECONOMICS; EDUCATION; RELIGION; PHILOSOPHY. | SPORTS; FASHIONS; POPULAR ENTERTAINMENT; FOLKLORE; SOCIETY. |

cana, organized along German principles of research and scholarship.

May Josiah Warren of Cincinnati, Ohio, founder of philosophical anarchism in U.S., opened **"equity" store** to prove his theory of "labor for labor." Sold goods almost at cost; store closed in 2 years. Warren was something of an inventor, having devised a speed press which, since he had failed to patent it, was in part incorporated in the famous Roe presses. His ingenuity was again displayed in his construction of a press and his making of type for the publication of his *The Peaceful Revolutionist*, a periodical which lasted less than a year. Though an extreme individualist and a disbeliever in all government, he established in the 1850's "Modern Times," a town on Long Island. "Modern Times" was a center for philosophical anarchists and for others who believed in extreme individualism.

Park company to barnstorm at the Broadway Circus on those nights. But shows did go on. The Lafayette Theater was rebuilt and hailed as biggest and best in the States. It may have been indication of high ambitions of the Lafayette that the stage lighting and machinery were manipulated from above.

July 23 **1st swimming school** in America opened in Boston, Mass. It was taught by placing a belt "around the bodies, under the arms, attached to a rope and pole, by which the head and body are kept in the proper position in the water, while the pupil is learning the use of his limbs." The school was attended by many notables, including John James Audubon, the naturalist, and John Quincy Adams. The latter is reputed to have done some diving from the 6-foot board when he was 61.

1828

Total value of **gold** mined in America up to this time amounted to $110,000 and was derived from small deposits in North Carolina.

New England's transition from commercial to industrial economy reflected dramatically in political shift of Daniel Webster to advocacy of high tariffs and supported statistically by Willard Phillips, Boston business man, lawyer, and editor, whose *A Manual of Political Economy* skillfully identified the needs of New England industrialists with the economic good of the entire nation.

1st significant American production of **china** begun at factory of American Pottery Manufacturing Company in Jersey City. Up to this time, china had been supplied almost entirely from producers in France, Germany, England, and China.

Thomas Dartmouth Rice 1st sings **"Jim Crow."** Rice took the tune, which became America's 1st international song hit, from old Negro who worked near the Louisville Theater, Louisville, Ky. Rice himself became known as "Jim Crow" Rice, and the term passed into the language as a synonym for the Negro.

American Peace Society established. Society maintained close relations with similar organizations in Europe and repeatedly petitioned Congress and the state legislatures to set apart an annual day for peace prayers.

Phrase **"Tariff of Abominations"** used to characterize excessively high protective tariff pushed through Congress by efforts of Henry Clay. Southerners, led by Calhoun, felt that the law discriminated against

POLITICS AND GOVERNMENT; WAR; DISASTERS; VITAL STATISTICS.

BOOKS; PAINTING; DRAMA; ARCHITECTURE; SCULPTURE.

May 19 Tariff of Abominations passed by Congress and signed by Pres. Adams. This was a severe defeat for the Jacksonian Democrats who dominated House Committee on Manufacturers and who had framed the bill for defeat. The issue underlying the measure was the economic rivalry between the Northern mercantile interests and the Southern agricultural economy.

Dec 3 Andrew Jackson elected president by 647,231 popular votes and 178 electoral votes as against 509,097 popular votes and 83 electoral votes for John Quincy Adams. John C. Calhoun was re-elected vice-president by 171 electoral votes. The election was swung by Martin Van Buren of New York on the understanding that his power in that state would be bolstered by a free exercise of "Spoils System."

Dec. 19 South Carolina legislature adopted set of 8 resolutions declaring the **Tariff of Abominations** oppressive, unjust, and unconstitutional. The motion was supported by the legislatures of Georgia, Mississippi, and Virginia. These resolutions caused publication of the *South Carolina Exposition and Protest* by John C. Calhoun. In it, Calhoun rejected nationalism and identified himself with the economic and political interests of the South.

First Church (Unitarian) at Quincy, Mass., built by Alexander Parris from local granite. Usually called the "Stone Temple."

Founding of **National Academy of Design** by Samuel F. B. Morse. Taking issue with John Trumbull, then president of American Academy of Fine Arts, he formed a more democratic organization, one which was to become the most influential in American art.

1st theatrical version of famous **Rip Van Winkle** story presented in Albany, N.Y. It was written by an unknown playwright. On Oct. 30, 1829, a version by John Kerr was acted in Philadelphia with great success. Role of Rip was much later the most famous part played by Joseph Jefferson who revised play to fit his own conceptions.

Feb. 21 Printing press arrived at the headquarters of Cherokee Council in Echota, Ga., where half-breed, Sequoyah, invented Cherokee alphabet. Publication began of the *Cherokee Phoenix*, the **1st Indian newspaper** on the continent, edited by a full-blooded Cherokee, Elias Boudinot. The redwood trees, the Sequoias, are named in honor of the inventor.

1829

Workingmen's Party formed in New York allying itself with similar organization in Philadelphia. Their candidates were defeated on a platform of free public education and a program of protection of mechanics against prison contract labor. The Jacksonians exploited the party for their purposes.

"Spoils System" introduced into national politics by Pres. Andrew Jackson. Contrary to popular belief he did not make wholesale political appointments and removals. During his 1st year in office only

Flourishing period of **scrimshaw**, art of making pictures on or carving teeth or jaw of sperm whale. Busks for corsets, chessmen, vases, cutlery, etc. were carved; historical scenes often etched. Hobby filled long lonely hours on whaling cruises.

1st history of American literature in book form **Samuel L. Knapp**'s *Lectures on American Literature*. Although he dealt only with poets and authors who had died, his book was comprehensive compared to previous summaries.

1st recorded strike of **factory workers** occurred in textile plant in Paterson, N.J. Strike was doubly significant because of the 1st recorded summoning of the militia to end labor violence. The workers' agitation for a 10-hour day failed of its purpose and the strike ended.

Jan. 24 **Indiana University** 1st chartered in Bloomington, Ind., as Indiana College. State supported, Indiana College granted its 1st degrees in 1830 and became university in 1838. Basis of Indiana College was founding of a State Seminary in Jan. 20, 1820, by the General Assembly.

July 4 Construction begun on **Baltimore & Ohio RR.** Though Mohawk & Hudson RR was chartered earlier, Baltimore & Ohio was 1st to begin operations. President of company was Charles Carroll, a signer of Declaration of Independence.

Dec. 30 **Hanover College** chartered by General Assembly of Indiana. It had been founded by Rev. John Finley Crowe under Presbyterian auspices in 1827 as a seminary to train ministers in the "wilderness," 1st degrees awarded in 1834.

one region (the South) in favor of another (North and West).

America's **1st archery club** formed by group of famous artists. The United Bowmen of Philadelphia was formally organized by Franklin Peale, Titian Ramsey Peale, Samuel P. Griffith, Jr., Thomas Sully, and others. Initiation fee was $5 and dues 50¢ per month. Members wore Lincoln green frock coats with gold trim, broad straw hats decorated with 3 black ostrich plumes. It held annual tournaments, awarded silver trophies until disbanded in 1859. Forerunner of National Archery Association founded in 1879. Field archery national association founded in 1939 now has over 800 clubs and 10,000 members.

Growth and transformation of **New York city** noted by James Fenimore Cooper, who observed that less than 500 buildings were still standing that antedated 1783. Continual razing and rebuilding has remained notable characteristic of city even to present day, resulting in international comment upon the physical energy it represents.

Boots, with side lacing and decorative fringes at the top, 1st came into vogue as woman's footgear.

1829

1st volume of **Encyclopaedia Americana,** edited by Francis Lieber, published in Philadelphia, Pa. It was 1st American encyclopedia. Lieber, a political exile from Germany, resided 1st in England, then in America, in each place with hopes of establishing himself in education. When these ventures fell through, he worked as a newspaperman until, through a German friend, he was encouraged to plan an American edition of the Konversations-Lexikon of Brockhaus. With the help of friends in Boston he succeeded in coming to terms

Earliest recorded **"Fat Ladies"** in America were Deborah and Susan Tripp, who at the ages of 3 years and 5 years and 10 months, respectively, weighed 124 pounds and 205 pounds, respectively.

Aug. **American Turf Register and Sporting Magazine,** 1st American publication of its kind, founded by John Stuart Skinner in Baltimore, Md. Magazine devoted to improvement of thoroughbred horses, racing, hunting, shooting, fishing and the habits of American game.

169

| POLITICS AND GOVERNMENT; WAR; DISASTERS; VITAL STATISTICS. | BOOKS; PAINTING; DRAMA; ARCHITECTURE; SCULPTURE. |

about 9 per cent of office holders were replaced.

"Kitchen Cabinet" instituted by Pres. Jackson. This was a small group of unofficial political advisers whom Jackson's opponents scornfully named the "Kitchen Cabinet." Its height of influence was between 1829 and 1831.

American Society for Encouraging Settlement of Oregon Territory organized in Boston, Mass.

Mar. 4 Andrew Jackson, 7th president, inaugurated. He was the 1st president of the Democratic Party and served 2 terms in office. His was probably the most conspicuous of all inaugurations. In his democratic way he invited the tremendous crowds present to the White House where refreshments were served. The famous invasion of the premises and the mud stains on satin chairs caused much comment; tubs of punch were set on the White House lawns to entice people outside.

Aug. 25 Pres. Jackson offered to purchase **Texas** from Mexico, but the offer was refused.

"The Chanting Cherubs" carved at about this time by **Horatio Greenough** for James Fenimore Cooper. Work was poorly received because nude cherubs shocked American taste.

Mar. 26 Growing tendency to write melodrama seen in work of **Richard Penn Smith.** His *Disowned, or the Prodigals,* adapted from the French, has all the trappings: villain Malfort, out to win virgin Pauline and her fortune; Gustavus, the hero, who loves a widow, Amelia, instead of Pauline; Bertrand, the villain's accomplice, who unsuspectingly stabs his sister Amelia, etc.

Sept. 14 Spectacle offered at Bowery Theater in New York presented **Peters the Antipodean,** who walked on the ceiling with his head down and lifted from stage 16 men and 10 coach wheels. It is not recorded how he did these feats.

1830

Population—12,866,020. Center of population: 19 miles west-southwest of Moorefield, W. Va.

During this decade suppression of revolutions in Europe and upswing in American prosperity caused sharp increase in **immigration.** Factual guidebooks about America began to appear for the 1st time. These guides checked many of the wild tales about U.S. that had been circulated in Europe by professional recruiters of immigrants.

1st **covered wagons** made trek from Missouri R. to Rocky Mts. They were led by Jedediah Strong Smith and William Sublette of the Rocky Mountain Fur Company.

Hudson River School, most prominent school of painting before Civil War, a group motivated, like Barbizon group of France, by desire to paint directly from nature. School exploited beauties of Hudson Valley. Foremost in this group Thomas Doughty (1793–1856), Thomas Cole (1801–1848), Asher Durand (1796–1886) and J. F. Kensett (1818–1872).

Limner painting flourished during this period, as illustrated by works of **William Prior.** He traveled extensively along the Atlantic Coast painting portraits in native American style, which ranged from a very flat, shadowless linear representation (with high foreheads and wide-open eyes) to more lifelike techniques, all depending on

SCIENCE; INDUSTRY; ECONOMICS; EDUCATION; RELIGION; PHILOSOPHY.	SPORTS; FASHIONS; POPULAR ENTERTAINMENT; FOLKLORE; SOCIETY.

with Carey, Lea and Carey, Philadelphia publishers. His edition ran to 13 volumes.

Fellenberg Manual Labor Institution, probably **1st manual training school** in U.S., opened in Greenfield, Mass. James H. Coffin, founder, later won renown as mathematician and meteorologist.

Mar. 2 New England Asylum for the Blind incorporated at Boston, Mass., the **1st school for the blind in U.S.** It was founded by Dr. John Dix Fisher, and in Aug. 1832, it opened under direction of Dr. Samuel Gridley Howe. In 1839 it was renamed Perkins Institution and Massachusetts Asylum (now School) for the Blind, and is at present located in Watertown, Mass.

July 23 Patent issued to William A. Burt of Mt. Vernon, Mich., for **1st typewriter,** called "typographer." It proved unworkable, however.

Oct. 17 **Delaware and Chesapeake Canal** formally opened. Canal linking Delaware River and Chesapeake Bay was 14 miles long and cost some $2,250,000, which was shared by the U.S. government, the state governments of Delaware, Maryland, and Pennsylvania, and by various private citizens.

1st fancy dress ball of record in New York society held at the house of Madame Brugière at Bowling Green.

Mike Fink, "king of the keelboatmen," 1st appeared in print in *The Western Souvenir* in article by Morgan Neville, "The Last of the Boatmen." Mike Fink was born in Fort Pitt in 1770, was renowned in his youth as an Indian scout and the most accurate shot in Pittsburgh. In due course, he joined the boatmen on the Mississippi. He was called the "Snag" on the Mississippi and the "Snapping Turtle" on the Ohio. R. Bernard DeVoto has described his legendary figure as one in which "Casanova, together with Paul Bunyan, merges into Thor."

Oct. 16 Tremont Hotel in Boston, **1st modern hotel** in America, opened with a $1-a-plate dinner attended by such notables as Daniel Webster and Edward Everett. Hotel was famous for its 8 water closets, probably the 1st such conveniences included in any public building in U.S. Tremont Hotel was the largest in the world with 170 bedrooms; it was the most elegant hotel in America at the time. Architects of luxury hotels for the next few decades generally used the Tremont House as their model.

1830

Canal mileage in America amounted to 1277 compared to only 73 m. of railroads. By 1840 there were 3326 m. of canals as against 2818 m. of railroads. By 1850 there were 3698 m. of canals as against 9021 m. of railroads. In 1830 New York was 1st in canals with 546 m. while Pennsylvania had virtually all railroads, 70 out of 73 miles. In 1840, Pennsylvania seized 1st place with 954 m. of canals, keeping its lead in rail mileage with 576 m. In 1850, Pennsylvania retained its lead in canal mileage with 954 m. while yielding rail leadership to N.Y. with its 1361 m.

Largest library west of the Alleghenies located in Transylvania University, which possessed some 2000 volumes.

John Nepomuk Maelzel came from successful tour of Europe with exhibition of his generally useless inventions, such as: a universal orchestral instrument called a "panharmonicum," an automatic trumpeter, speaking dolls, tiny birds that flew out of little boxes, an act called the "Conflagration of Moscow," and a mechanical chess player. Although Edgar Allan Poe and other observant Americans exposed the mechanical chess player as a hoax directed by human intelligence, Maelzel's exhibitions attracted large crowds in America for many years.

Sam Patch became national hero during this decade by a series of daring, well advertised leaps from bridges and banks of

Chicago laid out at Fort Dearborn.

Congress enacted **Removal Bill** under which eastern Indians were to be resettled in the Oklahoma Territory.

"Cotton Whigs" applied to Northern members of Whig Party, who, being responsive to the mercantile interests of the North, opposed any attempt to widen sectional differences and thus to endanger the cotton market.

Jan. 19–27 **Webster-Hayne debates** took place. They began when Sen. Samuel A. Foot offered a resolution restricting the sale of public lands in the West. Thomas Hart Benton, a Senator from Missouri, replied by declaring that eastern interests were trying to check the prosperity of the West and was supported in this contention by Robert Y. Hayne of South Carolina, who defended states' rights as opposed to federal interference. Hayne stated that "the very life of our system is the independence of the states, and that there is no evil more to be deprecated than the consolidation of this government." Daniel Webster of Massachusetts replied by criticizing the tendency of some senators "to habitually speak of the union in terms of indifference, or even of disparagement." The debate then evolved into a discussion of the powers of the Constitution and the nature of the Union. In his speech of Jan. 26–27 Webster declared that the states are sovereign only in that area where their power is not qualified by the Constitution, and that the Constitution and the government were sovereign over the people.

Apr. 6 Mexico forbade further **colonization of Texas** by U.S. citizens. It also prohibited the importation of Negro slaves.

May 28 **Indian Removal Act** signed by Pres. Jackson. It called for the general resettlement of Indians to lands west of the Mississippi.

July 15 Treaty concluded in which Ter-

price sitter could pay. Today his "cheap" works, being more primitive, are more highly thought of. Many **anonymous folk paintings** of this period also reveal this primitivism. *The Quilting Party* (c1840), *Portrait of a Woman* (c1830), *The Buffalo Hunter* (c1830), and *Meditation by the Sea* (c1860) all reveal a crudeness of color and flatness of surface that derives from early colonial painting. Even sculpture of period is highly imitative, as illustrated by pieces exhibited about this time in the Boston Athenaeum by **John Frazee** of New Jersey. Like 18th century neo-classic artists he wrapped his figures in Roman drapery, and his desire to be faithful often made his busts ugly.

Early novelist of the frontier, **Timothy Flint,** published his last novel, *Shoshonee Valley.* As in his earlier works, *Francis Berrian* (1826), *Arthur Clenning* (1828), and *George Mason* (1829), pioneer ways and mores are the dominant note; salmon fishing, buffalo hunting, Indians—friendly and hostile—the noble savage, the pure white man, the schemers and villains, all are here.

Indian plays flooded American stage before Civil War. Among the more famous were the anonymous *Indian Wife* (1830), *Pontiac, or the Siege of Detroit* by General Alexander Macomb, and *De Soto* by George Miles (1852). Besides these, approximately 50 plays about Indians appeared between 1825 and 1860.

Approximately 8200 **makers of fancy chairs** in America supplied population of 12,700,000. Chairs of Adam, Sheraton, Directoire, and Empire style were in great demand.

Trinity Church at Wall Street, New York city, built from designs by Richard Upjohn. Original church on the site was built in 1698. The wealthiest church in New York, it still holds large portions of lower Manhattan real estate received in a grant from Queen Anne in 1705.

Row of houses on **Washington Square North** built with uniform façades de-

Robert L. Stevens invented the **T-rail,** major innovation in the development of the railroad. Stevens, a Promethean figure in American engineering, made significant contributions to steamships and weapons as well as to railroad engineering. He established the Hoboken ferry line between New York and New Jersey, the 1st scheduled steamship ferry system in the world. Through his family holdings he became president of the Camden and Amboy Railroad. It was this interest in railroad operations which stimulated him to design the T-rail. The T-rail, which designates the shape of the vertical cross section of Steven's rail, became standard on all American tracks. Stevens completed the task of joining the rail sections by inventing, at the same time, the "iron tongue" (the plate which fastens rail end to rail end), the "hook-headed spike" (a special spike which fastens the rail to the ties), and the accessory bolts and nuts to fasten sections of rail together.

American Institute of Instruction, oldest educational association in U.S., founded at Boston, Mass. Francis Wayland, president of Brown Univ., chosen 1st president. Organized for "diffusion of useful knowledge in regard to education."

Apr. 6 **Church of Jesus Christ of the Latter Day Saints,** known as **Mormon Church,** founded at Fayette, N.Y., by Joseph Smith, with 30 original members. *Book of Mormon* published in July, at Palmyra, N.Y., had been dictated by Smith; it contained history of New World from Biblical times, showing colonization of America by outcasts from Tower of Babel and Jerusalem. Smith said that the angel Moroni had come to him in 1823 and told him of a Bible of the west which Smith finally located in 1827. It consisted of golden tablets inscribed in the "reformed Egyptian tongue," together with a pair of miraculous spectacles which enabled Smith to decipher the writing.

Dec. Robert Dale Owen's *Moral Physiology,* 1st American book on **birth control,** published. Approximately 25,000 copies

waterfalls. His 1st great triumph was a 90-ft. jump into the Passaic R. from the bridge at Paterson, N.J. He began touring country after this success, and was well paid for his efforts. His next spectacular achievement was a drop into Niagara Falls from the highest point on Goat Island, a drop of more than half the height of the falls. His last and fatal leap was into the Genesee Falls from the Genesee R., "a distance of 125 feet."

Exceptional endurance shown in **walking feat,** in which Joshua Newsam of Philadelphia covered 1000 m. in 18 days.

"Town Ball," based on English game, "Rounders," popular in New England. Several teams in Boston.

"Graham boarding houses" made their appearance in their decade in several eastern cities. They emulated the principles of Sylvester Graham, whose name is now linked to the present-day cracker. Graham, a lecturer on temperance, advocated, besides total abstinence, the following rules of diet and deportment: "Graham" bread, aged 12 or more hours before being eaten, light clothing, hard mattresses, daily exercises, baths taken at least 3 times a week, cheery dispositions at meals, and "roughage" of fruits and vegetables. Graham subsequently added chastity as one of his principles.

"Trail of Tears" came to describe forced march of Eastern Indians to western lands allotted to them. Thousands of Indians died on these long treks.

Jan. 27 Impassioned phrase **"Liberty and Union, now and forever, one and inseparable!"** delivered by Daniel Webster in his debate with Sen. Hayne of South Carolina before Congress. Webster supported view that Union, or the federal government, is stronger than any individual state.

Feb. 11 Continued interest in **cock**

ritory of Sac and Fox Indians ceded to U.S.

Sept. **Anti-Masonic Party** held at Philadelphia its 1st national convention. It was a temporary and inconsequential party.

Oct. 5 **Chester A. Arthur,** 21st president, born in Fairfield, Vt.

Dec. 6 **Pres. Jackson** in his annual message opposed federal grants for internal improvements unless national in scope.

signed by Martin Thompson. Excellent example of Greek Revival.

Sept 16 Perennial favorite **"Old Ironsides"** written for the Boston *Daily Advertiser* by **Oliver Wendell Holmes.** Stirred by the notice that the frigate *Constitution* was to be destroyed, he dashed off this impassioned ballad, which became so popular that the order for the destruction of the ship was rescinded.

1831

Rising tension in America over **slavery** seen in the resolution of the Georgia Senate, offering a $5000 reward for the apprehension and conviction in a Georgia court of the editor and publisher of *The Liberator*.

Jan. 1 1st issue published of **The Liberator,** abolitionist newspaper published by William Lloyd Garrison in Boston.

Mar. 4 **John Quincy Adams** began term as 1st ex-president to serve in Congress. He represented Plymouth, Mass., district in House of Representatives for 8 terms.

June 27 Agreement reached between **Black Hawk,** leader of Sac Indians, and Gen. Gaines. Under pressure from white squatters, who had taken over Sac Indian territory on Rock R., near the Mississippi R., the Sacs agreed to move west of the Mississippi R. Once there they starved and so, under the leadership of Black Hawk, they returned to cultivate their corn fields.

July 4 **James Monroe** died at age of 73. He is buried at Richmond, Va.

Aug. **Negro insurrection** led by Nat Turner during which about 55 white persons were killed in Virginia and possibly 100 Negroes; 20 Negroes executed.

Sept. 26 **Anti-Masonic Party** convened at Baltimore, Md.; William Wirt of Maryland nominated for president. Wirt polled

Gramercy Park, one of few private parks in U.S., established in New York in order to attract wealthy residents and maintain an exclusive neighborhood.

Girard College, most complete example of Greek Revival style in U.S., built in Philadelphia, Pa., from plans by Thomas U. Walter. Building has complete peripheral colonnade of Corinthian columns. Was so inappropriate that it helped end Greek Revival in U.S.

June 21 Great fire in State House of Raleigh, N.C., destroyed famous statue of **George Washington** by Canova. Loss was felt throughout the states, and immediately Congress was spurred to commission a statue of the 1st president.

July 4 **"America,"** composed in ½ hr. by Dr. Samuel Francis Smith, Baptist minister, was introduced in services at Park Street Church, Boston, Mass. Smith took the tune from a German song-book and did not know that it was the same as the British national anthem.

Sept. 26 Romantic drama in America found best expression in *The Gladiator* of **Robert Montgomery Bird.** With Forrest in the hero's role the play had tremendous New York success. It deals with the revolt of Spartacus. Abolitionist sentiment and hate for tyranny dominate the piece.

"Death to the Roman fiends," cries
    Spartacus, "that make their
    mirth
Out of the groans of bleeding misery!

174

were sold in regular and pirated editions despite the refusal of respectable newspapers and magazines to carry its advertisements.

Dec. 16 **Mississippi College** chartered in Clinton, Miss., under partial state auspices. College passed under Presbyterian sponsorship in 1842 and under Baptist sponsorship in 1850. 1st degrees granted in 1854.

fighting indicated by a great main held in Harrisburg, Pa., in which $100 was put up for each fight.

Sept. 18 Race between horse and **"Tom Thumb,"** 1st locomotive built in America, won by horse. Locomotive pulled 40 passengers over 9-mile course from Riley's Tavern to Baltimore, but sprang leak in boiler and failed to finish.

1831

Mechanical reaper invented by Cyrus McCormick. McCormick relied on principles of earlier inventions, especially cutter and reel principle of reaper made by Henry Ogle, an Englishman. Previous American reapers had been made by Jeremiah Bailey (1822) and Obed Hussey (1830).

Joseph Henry devised the **electric bell.** In his demonstration that it was possible to magnetize iron at a distance, Henry made use of a magnet which vibrated the armature of an intensity battery, causing a bell, placed at the other end of a mile of insulated copper wire, to strike. The electric bell was among the 1st pieces of electrical equipment in the home.

Dr. Samuel Guthrie, working in laboratory at Sacketts Harbor, N.Y., synthesized "Chloric ether" or **chloroform;** his discovery antedated almost simultaneous discoveries in France and Germany.

Apr. Timothy Bailey of Cohoes, N.Y., perfected **powered knitting machine,** used following year in factory run by Bailey and Egbert Egberts.

Apr. 18 **New York University** 1st chartered as the University of the City of New York. Established mainly by Presbyterian interests, the university issued its 1st degrees in 1833. University of the City of New York became New York University in 1896.

May 26 **Wesleyan University** chartered in Middletown, Conn. Established under

1st use of term **"Old Glory"** to designate U.S. flag made by New England seaman, William Driver. Before setting sail for the Orient he had the flag unfurled and, moved, he said, "I name thee Old Glory!" The term caught on during the Civil War, when Union troops commonly employed it.

Jan. 1 Powerful abolitionist sentiment, **"I will not retreat a single inch, and I will be heard,"** forms opening statement of William Lloyd Garrison's new paper *The Liberator.* "I will be as harsh as truth and as uncompromising as justice, on this subject [slavery]. I do not want to think or write with moderation. No! No!" His uncompromising stand brought him and his followers immeasurable trouble. Even in Boston he was maligned, threatened, and beaten. Were the editor someone other than **William Lloyd Garrison** it could be said that *The Liberator,* understaffed and operating on a shoestring, overcame almost unsurmountable obstacles in going to press. But his early experiences, from the time that he began his anti-slavery crusade in Boston in 1829, were a series of obstacles that would have defeated a less inspired man. They are as good an index of the manners and tempers of his fellow Americans as of his own. In 1830 Garrison was convicted of libel and imprisoned. He was threatened with bodily harm. The state of Georgia offered $5,000 for his arrest.

Apr. 25 One of great comedy types of American literature, **frontier man,** 1st seen in James K. Paulding's play *The Lion of*

POLITICS AND GOVERNMENT; WAR; DISASTERS; VITAL STATISTICS.	BOOKS; PAINTING; DRAMA; ARCHITECTURE; SCULPTURE.

7 electoral votes against 219 cast for Andrew Jackson in election of 1832.

Nov. 19 **James A. Garfield,** 20th president, born in Orange Township, Ohio.

Dec. National Republican Party was 1st important political party to convene a **nominating convention.** It selected Henry Clay as presidential candidate.

Ho, slaves, arise! It is your hour to kill!
Kill and spare not—for wrath and liberty!
Freedom for bondmen—freedom and revenge!"
(Shouts and trumpets—The guards and gladiators rush and engage in combat, as curtain falls)

By 1853 the play had more than 1000 performances in America and England.

Oct. 13 **Riots** occurred at Park Theater when Joshua R. Anderson, English actor who had strongly criticized America, made his appearance on stage.

1832

1st Asiatic cholera epidemic in U.S. occurred. It 1st appeared on June 28 in New York city and soon spread to other large cities throughout Northeast. New York city alone reported 2251 deaths. In the Mohawk Valley thousands died from it. During a 12-day period beginning Oct. 25 more than 6000 perished in New Orleans. Some corpses weighted with bricks and stones were thrown into the river while others were heaped in long trenches. During the next decade disease swept the Indian Nations of the Great Plains, drastically reducing their numbers and their ability to resist the advance of white settlers. This is one of the main reasons why the period of the great Indian wars did not begin until the 1860's.

Apr. 6 **Black Hawk war** began when Sacs, led by Black Hawk, massacred white settlers near Rock R., Ill. The war started because Black Hawk had recrossed the Mississippi R. in order to plant corn in the Sacs' old corn fields. Panicky settlers killed an Indian holding truce flag, and Black Hawk, enraged, began killing white settlers.

May 21 **Democratic Party,** formerly known as "Republican Delegates from the Several States" and called both Republican and Democratic, formally adopted present name at convention in Baltimore,

Old Merchant's House built in New York, fine example of urban architecture of its time. Today it is a museum with all original furnishings preserved.

American debut of famous English actress **Fanny Kemble** with her father Charles at Park Theater, New York.

Performance of **Richard Brinsley Sheridan**'s *Pizarro* at Columbus, Ga., utilized band of Creek Indians as "extras" representing the Peruvian army. They were paid 50¢ and a glass of whiskey a head. Indians made their stage entrance the occasion for a genuine war dance culminating in the scalping, or wig removing, of King Ataliba, the demolition of the sets, and the frightened exit of the feminine "extras," who played the virgin roles.

"Clare de Kitchen" copyrighted by George Willig, Jr., Baltimore music publisher. It was made popular by Thomas Dartmouth ("Jim Crow") Rice, a noted minstrel singer who used several versions. It is a nonsense song about animals, chiefly a blind horse.

176

SCIENCE; INDUSTRY; ECONOMICS; EDUCATION; RELIGION; PHILOSOPHY.

SPORTS; FASHIONS; POPULAR ENTERTAINMENT; FOLKLORE; SOCIETY.

Methodist auspices, university granted its 1st degrees in 1833.

Aug. **Adventist movement** born in doctrines of William Miller, Baptist farmer from New England, who preached that the exact time of Christ's return to the earth and His final judgment could be determined by passages from *Daniel* and *Revelation.* The date of the second coming was set at March 21, 1843, and as this day approached, thousands were swept by an emotional frenzy. When the day passed uneventfully and a year passed without change, Miller's once united followers divided into several Adventist groups.

the West at Park Theater in New York city. Col. Nimrod Wildfire was described as "a raw Kentuckian recently elected to Congress." Although the playwright denied that he was satirizing Davy Crockett, who was approaching the end of his 2nd term in Congress, the suspicion persisted that Col. Nimrod Wildfire was a stage parody of Crockett himself. The play has not survived except for a speech which was printed in several periodicals.

Dec. 10 A popular weekly **racing sheet,** *Spirit of the Times,* founded by William Trotter Porter. Its stated purpose was to raise reputation of racing and other sports.

1832

"Science" of phrenology introduced to America in Boston by Johann Kaspar Spurzheim of Vienna, a disciple of the founder of phrenology, Dr. Franz Joseph Gall, of Swabia and Vienna. Phrenology was based on the premise that a man's moral character and intellectual capacity could be determined by the shape of his cranium. Many distinguished Americans, like John Quincy Adams, questioned the claims of this science; but others, like Daniel Webster and Andrew Jackson, endorsed phrenology, especially after phrenologists had rendered flattering analyses of the crania of these distinguished men.

Cleveland was connected to Ohio R. at Portsmouth by **Ohio and Erie Canal.** Construction of canal took 7 years, with malaria and shortage of funds crippling the year-round labor of some 2,000 workers. Canal, opened in 1833, gave Ohio farmers an outlet to Mississippi R. and to the markets of the South.

Launched from Baltimore, Md., 1st of the famous **American clipper ships,** the *Ann McKim.* Her structure was revolutionary, and her type was eventually preferred to those of all other sailing ships.

Oranges and **lemons** entered American diet. They had been a delicacy for the rich before the 1st shipment of cargo direct from Sicily. Oranges and lemons have both been traced to Asia. It was not until the conquests and migrations of the Arabs that the fruit became of major agricultural consequence. The Arabs planted lemon trees in Spain during their occupation. Columbus is credited with planting **1st orange tree** in New World. It was distributed by the Spaniards throughout the regions they explored and settled. Neither the orange nor the lemon became of commercial importance here until later.

William A. Alcott's famous *The Young Man's Guide,* a moralistic book of manners for every personal and domestic situation, 1st published.

Growing spirit of **feminism** in America spurred by publication of Lydia Maria Child's *History of Woman,* the 1st work in America to treat women in a completely distinctive way.

One of leading large **land holdings** in America, Charles Carroll's, with some 80,000 acres scattered in Maryland, Pennsylvania, and Virginia broken up on his death.

1st sports editor in U.S., William Trotter Porter, was given that position and title

POLITICS AND GOVERNMENT; WAR; DISASTERS; VITAL STATISTICS.

BOOKS; PAINTING; DRAMA; ARCHITECTURE; SCULPTURE.

Md. Convention nominated Pres. Andrew Jackson for a 2nd term and nominated Martin Van Buren of New York for vice-president.

May 9 **Treaty of Payne's Landing,** a prelude to 2nd Seminole War (1836–42). Under pressure from white settlers in Florida, some chiefs agreed to migrate to country allotted Creeks west of the Mississippi R. But unexpected opposition from tribes developed, and it was the whites' attempt to force Indians to obey this treaty that eventually brought on the war.

July 10 Bill to renew **Bank of U.S. Charter** vetoed by Pres. Jackson, who charged that the bank was a monopoly and saw the danger of its being principally controlled by foreigners who owned about $8,000,000 of the bank's stock.

Aug. 2 **Black Hawk's tribe** massacred at the mouth of the Bad Axe R. by Illinois militia led by Gen. Atkinson. Old men, women, and children were all destroyed without regard for pleas of mercy or truce flags.

Aug. 27 **Black Hawk** surrendered to government authorities by the Winnebago Indians, thus ending the Black Hawk War.

Nov. 24 South Carolina passed **Ordinance of Nullification,** an order nullifying in that state the existing tariff laws of U.S. It stated that no appeal from the ordinance would be allowed in the U.S. Supreme Court or any court beyond those of the state. This was an extreme application of the principle of States' rights.

Dec. 5 **Andrew Jackson re-elected president** by 687,502 popular votes and 219 electoral votes, as opposed to 530,189 popular votes and 49 electoral votes for Henry Clay. Martin Van Buren was elected vice-president.

Dec. 10 **Proclamation** by Pres. Jackson asserted the supremacy of U.S. law over the Commonwealth law, and defined an act of rebellion as any nullification by a state of a federal law.

Famous boys' classic *Swiss Family Robinson* by **Johann Rudolph Wyss** 1st published in U.S. Has sold at least a million copies in America.

Very popular poetess **Hannah F. Gould** published edition of her *Poems.* Generally short, her verses are full of sentimentalities and fancies, excellently adapted to the "souvenir" or "gift book" vogue of the times.

Collected *Poems* of **William Cullen Bryant** includes such favorites as "O Fairest of the Rural Maids," "The Death of the Flowers," "June," "A Forest Hymn," "Hymn to Death," "A Meditation on Rhode Island," and "To a Fringed Gentian."

Literary Remains, the posthumous writings of **John Gardiner Brainard,** published. Brainard was a popular poet who wrote light and humorous verses in ballad form. John Greenleaf Whittier admired his work and edited his final papers.

The Heidenmauer by **James Fenimore Cooper** published. It was 1 of 3 novels in which Cooper employed European backgrounds to complement his theme. In these novels, which were partially apologies for the American way of life, he illustrated the deficiencies of feudalism and aristocracy in Europe.

June 17 Yankee type exploited in plays of **Joseph Stevens Jones.** His *Liberty Tree,* produced this year, contains Bill Ball; his *Green Mountain Boy* (1833) a character named Jedediah Homebred; his *People's Lawyer* (1839) the well known Solon Shingle; his *Silver Spoon* (1852) the Honorable Jefferson S. Batkins. Actor George Handel Hill excelled in these parts.

SCIENCE; INDUSTRY; ECONOMICS; EDUCATION; RELIGION; PHILOSOPHY.

SPORTS; FASHIONS; POPULAR ENTERTAINMENT; FOLKLORE; SOCIETY.

John Ireland Howe of Derby, Conn., invented machine to make **pins.** Similar machine had been in use in England since 1824.

Feb. 2 **Denison University** 1st chartered in Granville, Ohio, as Granville Literary and Theological Institution. Established under Baptist auspices, Institution awarded its 1st degrees in 1840. It became Granville College in 1845 and Denison University in 1856. Denison University formed an administrative tie with Shepardson College in 1900.

Feb. 6 1st printed suggestion for a **transcontinental railroad** advanced in the *Emigrant,* a weekly newspaper published at Ann Arbor, Mich.

Apr. 7 **Gettysburg College** 1st chartered in Gettyburg, Pa., as Pennsylvania College of Gettysburg. Founded under Lutheran auspices, college awarded its 1st degrees in 1834. The Pennsylvania College of Gettysburg became Gettysburg College in 1921. Gettysburg College was 1st Lutheran sponsored institution of higher learning in America.

Nov. 26 New York & Harlem RR, New York city, began operation with **1st street-car** in world. Built by John Stephenson, it was the "John Mason," a horse-drawn car which ran on lower 4th Ave.

Dec. 28 **St. Louis University** chartered in St. Louis, Mo., under Catholic auspices. 1st Catholic university west of the Alleghenies, St. Louis University awarded its 1st degrees in 1834.

after he sold his newspaper *The Spirit of the Times* to *The Traveller.*

Calisthenics prescribed for urban women in *Atkinson's Casket,* a suggestion which reflected growing fear of the physical deterioration of city dwellers. Illustrated exercises stressed muscular development of the arms and shoulders, but, above all, the back. Exercises were of the swinging variety.

Jan. 21 Sen. William Learned Marcy of N.Y. originated expression **"To the victors belong the spoils,"** in a speech defending the system of party patronage initiated under the Democrats against the attack of Henry Clay. The entire sentence reads, "They see nothing wrong in this rule, that to the victor belong the spoils of the enemy."

Apr. 1 **Robert the Hermit,** of Massachusetts, one of the most colorful and famous hermits in American history, died in his hermitage near the Washington Bridge at Seekonk, Mass. Robert was a bonded slave, born of African mother and probably an Anglo-Saxon father, at Princeton, N.J. He obtained his freedom, was swindled out of it and shipped abroad to a foreign slave market, escaped to America, was parted from his 1st wife by force, was rejected by his 2nd wife after a long voyage at sea, and, in general, was buffeted about before withdrawing from the society of men to his lonely dwelling.

July 9 A resolution, proposed by Henry Clay, that congress and president proclaim a **National Fast Day,** so that the nation might officially pray for relief of a cholera epidemic, was defeated after a bitter debate. The opposing Democrats held that "prayer and humiliation" should be "prompted by the devotion of the heart, and not the bidding of the state." Pres. Jackson had already declined on the principle of separation of church and state, following Jefferson's example. However, other presidents both before and after Jackson have proclaimed days of thanksgiving and prayer.

179

POLITICS AND GOVERNMENT; WAR; DISASTERS; VITAL STATISTICS.

BOOKS; PAINTING; DRAMA; ARCHITECTURE; SCULPTURE.

1833

Mar. 2 Pres. Jackson signed 2 bills; **Clay's new tariff of 1832,** which caused extensive trouble between the federal government and South Carolina, and a **"force act,"** authorizing the president to enforce the collection of tariff by use of the army and navy if necessary.

Mar. 4 **Pres. Jackson** inaugurated for his 2nd term. Martin Van Buren succeeded John C. Calhoun as vice-president.

Mar. 4 1st Regiment of Dragoons organized at Fort Jefferson, Mo., under command of Col. Henry Dodge. Cavalry had been used as early as Revolutionary War, but this was **1st regular cavalry unit of U.S. Army.**

Mar. 15 South Carolina convention revoked its **Ordinance of Nullification.**

Mar. 18 South Carolina passed ordinance to nullify **"force act."**

Mar. 20 U.S. signed **commercial treaty** with Siam at Bangkok.

Aug. 20 **Benjamin Harrison,** 23rd president, born in North Bend, Ohio.

Sept. 21 U.S. signed **commercial treaty** with Sultan of Muscat.

Sept. 23 William J. Duane, **Secretary of Treasury, removed from office** because he refused to withdraw government deposits from Bank of the U.S. Roger B. Taney was appointed by Pres. Jackson to take his place.

Oct. 1 Public deposits withdrawn from the **Bank of the U.S.** in accord with executive order. The funds were redeposited in a number of state banks, known as "pet banks."

1st colossal work done in marble by an American sculptor, the statue of George Washington by **Horatio Greenough,** was commissioned this year by the government. It is a half-draped, seated figure of Washington, which weighed so much that the floor of the Capitol could not hold it. It was placed outdoors, but rapidly deteriorated, whereupon it was placed in Smithsonian Institution where it may now be seen. Because of its classically draped figure, which was thought unsuitable for Washington, Greenough's masterpiece was received with much jocose criticism and indignation.

Edgar Allan Poe's story "MS Found in a Bottle" won prize of $50 in a competition for the *Baltimore Saturday Visiter.* More important it brought Poe in contact with J. P. Kennedy who helped him find work on the *Southern Literary Messenger.*

Noah Webster bowdlerized the **Bible,** omitting many verses altogether and substituting *breast* for *teat, in embryo* for *in the belly, smell* for *stink, to nurse* or *to nourish* for *to give suck,* and so on.

1st American appearance of celebrated Irish actor **Tyrone Power** at Park Theater, New York.

Father of American sculpture, **William Rush** of Philadelphia, died. Working in wood and clay, he reflected in his work the neoclassical influence. Work includes feminine allegories, personifications of Tragedy and Comedy to be seen at the Actors' Home outside Philadelphia, the *Nymph of the Schuylkill* in Fairmount Park, Philadelphia.

One of earliest **"blackface" songs,** "Sambo's Address to He' Bred'rin" or "Ching a Ring Chaw," published in Boston. Its lyrics urge Negroes to emigrate

180

1833

Massachusetts last state to **disestablish its church.** From this date on, legal separation of church and state has been complete in America.

1st large-scale effort at **paternalism** in industry seen at Kensington Glass Works in Philadelphia founded by Thomas Dyott, who had already established 1st large patent medicine business in U.S. Beset by drunken glass blowers he experimented with prohibition and moral indoctrination of his employees. Ostensibly as moral gesture, he put many little children to work as apprentices to help mold their character. He was 1st glass manufacturer to keep men employed 12 months out of year, although he had them work 11 hours a day, closing day with singing and prayer.

Tax supported public library established at Peterborough, N.H., under leadership of Rev. Abiel Abbot. It charged a small membership fee, and is considered oldest public library in U.S. Library of Congress, however, was established in 1800 by Act of Congress.

Samuel Colt perfected **successful revolver.** He began production at Patent Arms Manufacturing Company, Paterson, N.J.

1st steel plow produced in America by John Deere, blacksmith from Grand Detour, Ill. He hit upon the idea while visiting a sawmill where he noticed that a steel blade shone where it had been subjected to friction. He proceeded to make a plow out of a discarded circular saw blade. This improvised plow was self-scouring and solved the problem of the sticky midwestern soil that resisted the traditional iron plows. Great lumps of mud had adhered to these iron plows impeding their progress. Deere sold his 1st plow for $10 and moved to Moline, Ill., where he built a factory. The John Deere plow became famous throughout the West as the "singing plow." It became a familiar item in the wagon trains of farmers emi-

Henry Perrine introduced **avocado trees** from Mexico on his farm in Florida. Spaniards probably had brought them much earlier, however.

Introduction of **flies** in angling noted this year. Jerome Van Crowninshield Smith's *Fishes of Massachusetts* reported that the angler "enjoys the sport and exults in its success, according as it requires an exertion of his skill. . . . There are not only individuals of whom we speak, but others who availing themselves of all the information to be acquired from books and experience, are fully aware that fly-fishing is the perfection of angling."

Rudimentary form of **baseball** played in Philadelphia by Olympic Ball Club. Home plate was situated between 2 bases. Like cricket, a ball hit behind the batter was considered a "hit," and runners struck by the ball were "out."

George Fibbleton, who advertised himself as "Ex-Barber to His Majesty, the King of England," invented a **shaving machine** shortly after opening his barber shop in New York city. The machine was ineffective, causing more damage to the face than the beard.

1st publication of the *Sketches and Eccentricities of Col. David Crockett, of West Tennessee* helped launch the legend of **Davy Crockett** throughout America. The author was ostensibly Davy himself, but there is some doubt that he wrote unaided.

Congressional Temperance Society established in Washington, D.C., by the nation's legislators for the purpose of discouraging "the use of ardent spirit and the traffic in it, by example and by kind moral influence." The Society declined in vitality shortly after its founding until in 1842 it was suddenly revived by John H. W. Hawkins, a crusading temperance lecturer who, in the 1st 10 years of his crusading activity, traveled more than

| POLITICS AND GOVERNMENT; WAR; DISASTERS; VITAL STATISTICS. | BOOKS; PAINTING; DRAMA; ARCHITECTURE; SCULPTURE. |

Dec. 4 **American Antislavery Society** formed as merger of abolitionist groups from New York and New England, the former headed by merchants Arthur and Lewis Tappan and the latter by the famous publisher, William Lloyd Garrison. It was a national organization which recognized sovereignty of individual states on slave regulation, but wanted to stop slave trade and to abolish slavery in the District of Columbia and in the territories.

Dec. 26 Henry Clay introduced two censure resolutions in senate on the question of withdrawing deposits from the **Bank of the U.S.** Both were directed at Pres. Jackson.

to "Hetee" (Haiti) where they will be free and wealthy.

Lowell Mason founded **Boston Academy of Music** to instruct both children and music teachers.

Sept. 3 Beginnings of **mass journalism** in U.S. appeared with the 1st issue of the *New York Sun,* which sold for a penny, the 1st penny paper in New York.

Nov. 16 Opening of newly constructed **Italian Opera House** at Leonard and Church Sts., New York city, partly sponsored by various leaders of New York society who subscribed to season boxes at prices up to $6000. Admission prices to 1st performance, a Rossini opera, were $1.50 for box, $2 for sofa seats, $1 for pit, and 75¢ for gallery.

1834

English Poor Law overhauled, throwing thousands of people off relief and into the overcrowded labor markets of the farms and cities. This spurred **English emigration** to America.

Whig Party organized. Chiefly made up of National Republicans and all who opposed "King Andrew." The name "Whig," which was also the designation of an English political party, was suggested by a cartoon that appeared in a New York newspaper showing Andrew Jackson in crown and royal robes. The Party terminated in 1852.

Feb. 17 **Territorial claims** between Spain and U.S. settled by Van Ness convention signed at Madrid.

Mar. 28 **Henry Clay's censure resolutions** adopted by senate. They were directed at Pres. Jackson for removing public deposits from the Bank of the U.S.

"**Zip Coon**" performed in New York by Bob Farrell, who claimed to have composed the song; others disputed the claim. The tune probably derived from folk or Negro sources. Later it became popular as "Turkey in the Straw," a fiddle tune, and passed again into folklore.

Source of most of our information concerning early American painters comes from the *History of the Rise and Progress of the Arts of Design in the U.S.* by **William Dunlap,** the Vasari of American art. After studying under West he returned to New York, only to desert painting for business. Instrumental in founding American Academy of Fine Arts and National Academy of Design.

One of the most popular of historical romances, *The Last Days of Pompeii* by **Edward Bulwer-Lytton.**

Merchants' Exchange built in Philadelphia, Pa., from plans by William Strick-

grating to California and Oregon in the 1850's.

Oberlin Collegiate Institute, Oberlin, Ohio, begins. 1st American college to admit women students on equal terms with men. Awarded 1st degrees in 1837, became Oberlin College in 1850.

Feb. 5 **University of Delaware** 1st chartered as Newark College in Newark, Del. 1st degrees were awarded in 1836. Newark College became Delaware College in 1843 and the University of Delaware in 1921. Established under Presbyterian auspices, the college was an educational battleground for conflicting interests in Delaware. The Presbyterian groups fought to have the college accepted as the state college while maintaining a degree of denominational control. An opposing faction fought for a completely nonsectarian state university. The controversy mounted in intensity until the Civil War, after which the nonsectarian forces gained power enough to pass the college to state control.

100,000 miles and spoke on at least 2500 separate occasions.

New **Opera House** at Leonard and Church Streets in New York city was something entirely new to Americans. There was a second balcony of boxes which ran all around the back of the house, painted white with decorations in gold, red and blue. The upholstery of the divans and orchestra seats was in blue, and the floors were carpeted from wall to wall. It was, all in all, a fitting abode for the Muses who peered from pastel bowers in the domed ceiling as though waiting to welcome visits from the ladies of the city. To attract women to the theater was the purpose behind the sumptuous decor of the Opera House. A certain gentility attached even to the purchase of tickets—there was no charge for ordering seats in advance. But beauty and thrift were, in this case, small compensation for the main drawback of the Opera House. Unattended ladies could not come because the neighborhood had a very bad reputation.

1834

Arthur Brisbane returned to U.S. with ideas for establishing **utopian community** on the plan projected in Charles Fourier's *Traite de l'Association Domestique-Agricole.* Brisbane was sympathetic to the Fourierian program of dignifying the laboring classes by making their work attractive. He later organized a society and publicized the theories of Fourier in addresses and articles, many of which were bought by Horace Greeley for the New York *Tribune.*

Electric motor constructed by Thomas Davenport. Davenport, a Vermont blacksmith, recognized the versatility of Joseph Henry's electro-magnet and saw that it could be adapted to an electric power machine. He connected 4 electro-magnets to a battery and set them up on a wheel which rotated rapidly when current was turned on. This is the same basic design of the standard electric motor of today.

In keeping with the trend towards heightened elegance in theatrical decor, the **Park Theater** in New York city was completely renovated for the coming season. William Shakespeare was decidedly the theme of the new decorations. All of the details complemented the portrait of Shakespeare which graced the center of the proscenium. On the fronts of the boxes there were reproductions of scenes from his plays, as well as replicas of the buildings which he immortalized in passing, including his house, the Globe, Falcon Inn and Charlecot Hall. The old mirrors which had stood on either side of the stage were replaced with figures of Tragedy and Comedy. The theater gleamed with colors of gold and crimson on a cream-colored ground.

Myth of **Davy Crockett** augmented by publication of his "autobiography," *A Narrative of the Life of David Crockett.*

POLITICS AND GOVERNMENT; WAR; DISASTERS; VITAL STATISTICS.	BOOKS; PAINTING; DRAMA; ARCHITECTURE; SCULPTURE.

Apr. 15 Pres. Jackson formally protested **Clay's censure resolutions.** He succeeded in having them removed from senate journal the following year.

June 15 **Fort Hall,** 1st settlement in Idaho, founded by N. J. Wyeth. It was on the Snake R.

June 24 Roger B. Taney, serving as Sec. of Treasury on a recess appointment from Pres. Jackson, rejected by Senate when formally proposed for the office. Again in 1835 Taney was rejected when nominated for Associate Justice of Supreme Court, but in 1836 he was confirmed as **Chief Justice.**

June 28 Famous **16 to 1 ratio** between silver and gold authorized by **2nd Coinage Act.** Gold strikes in California unbalanced intended valuation of gold and led to fantastic profits for the miners.

June 30 **Department of Indian Affairs** established by act of Congress.

July 4 **Anti-abolition riots** broke out at antislavery society meeting in New York city.

Oct. **Proslavery rioting** erupted in Philadelphia, Pa. with about 40 homes in the Negro community being destroyed.

Oct. 28 **Seminole Indians** ordered to evacuate Florida. The government acted under a treaty signed May 9, 1832.

land. Good example of Greek Revival at its most ornate.

Firm of **Currier & Ives,** "Publishers of Cheap and Popular Pictures," founded by Nathaniel Currier, who took his bookkeeper, James Merritt Ives, into partnership with him. The company became the largest and most prosperous of many publishers of cheap lithographs.

George Bancroft saw 1st volume of his monumental *History of the United States* off the press. Busy as a diplomat and statesman, he spent more than 50 years on the work, spending a fortune copying documents. Unlike later volumes, the 1st is oratorical in style, conforming to the taste of the time.

Perhaps 1st American to explore Greece (1806), **Nicholas Biddle,** built his home at Andalusia, Pa., with full Doric peristyle, one of few in U.S.

July 10 Birth of **James McNeill Whistler** in Lowell, Mass. Later in life when his birthplace was brought up in conversation, he remarked, "I shall be born when and where I want, and I do not choose to be born in Lowell."

1835

Gen. **Sam Houston** made commander of Texan army. A Virginian by birth, he had been governor of Tennessee.

Theodore Dwight Weld of Oberlin College began conducting an active and effective campaign against **slavery.** Oberlin became 1st college to accept Negroes as students.

Jan. 30 Pres. Jackson attacked in **1st attempt on life of a U.S. president.** Richard Lawrence fired twice while Jackson was attending funeral of Warren Ransom Davis,

Monumental *Letters and Papers of Washington* edited and published by **Jared Sparks,** McLean professor of history at Harvard. The 1st volume is a detailed life of 1st president.

William Ellery Channing published his *Slavery,* an influential tract of the abolitionist cause.

Collected Works of **James Kirke Paulding** published, a literary event of the year. Among these are his 2 novels written during the decade, *The Dutchman's Fireside* (1831), a novel of 18th Century Albany,

Cyrus McCormick patented early model of his famous **reaper.** Although 20 patents for reapers in the U.S. preceded his, McCormick's persistent experimentation and technical improvements made his product pre-eminent in its field. He did not market his patented model until certain defects were eliminated. He sold his 1st reapers in 1841, 2 in all, produced 4000 in 1856, and 23,000 in 1857. McCormick's reapers revolutionized American agriculture and had a material influence on the outcome of the Civil War.

Jan. 15 **Wabash College** 1st chartered as Wabash Manual Labor College in Crawfordsville, Ind. Established under Presbyterian auspices, college awarded its 1st degrees in 1838, became Wabash College in 1851. The College had been founded by 4 ministers and 5 laymen in 1832.

May 8 **University of Delaware** had its collegiate beginnings in the opening of Newark College (Delaware College, 1843), Newark, Del., under a charter granted by the General Assembly of Delaware on Feb. 5, 1833. It was merged with Newark Academy, a preparatory school, which traced its founding to the Rev. Francis Alison in 1743. On Mar. 28, 1921, name was changed to University of Delaware when it was combined with The Women's College, an affiliate.

He is featured as a great bear hunter and congressman. Interspersed are tales, tall talk, and yarns. In many respects the book was an answer to a previous one which had characterized Crockett as "fresh from the backwoods, half-horse, half-alligator, a little touched with the snapping-turtle."

George Orson Fowler became 1st American **professor of phrenology.** Although the title was self-awarded, Fowler demonstrated his mastery of the "science" in highly profitable fashion, clearing $40 on his 1st lecture-demonstration. Fowler made phrenology in America both popular and dignified.

Americans began to eat **tomatoes** about this time. They had been considered poisonous and had been used ornamentally as "love apples."

Possibly 1st **"hurdle race"** run in America took place at the Washington, D.C., Jockey Club. 6 fences were distributed over the mile stretch, the winner being awarded a plate valued at £100.

1st printed rules for **"baseball"** appeared in Robin Carver's *The Book of Sports.* Rules for game called "Rounders" copied verbatim from English book. Little resemblance to modern baseball.

Oldest club for gentlemen in America, **Philadelphia Club,** 1st formed as the Adelphi Club.

1835

Failure of **wheat crop** in Western farming areas caused a severe economic crisis in that region with an attendant strain on banking and loan facilities.

Samuel F. B. Morse invented the **telegraph.** Morse's model was severely limited and inefficient simply because he was unfamiliar with the advances made in electromagnetism by his contemporaries. It had about the same applicability as a phone with a range of 40 ft. When he applied the results of more recent research, he ex-

Association of Delegates from Benevolent Societies of Boston presented 1st report on conditions in that city. Joseph Tuckerman pioneered in the formation of this Association and of the **Society for the Prevention of Pauperism,** organized in Boston in this year. His premise was that low wages and the uncertainties of seasonal work, together with other economic evils, had to be remedied before any successful sound reform could be made.

1st appearance of the temperance stories of **Lucius Manlius Sargent,** who became

| POLITICS AND GOVERNMENT; WAR; DISASTERS; VITAL STATISTICS. | BOOKS; PAINTING; DRAMA; ARCHITECTURE; SCULPTURE. |

congressman from South Carolina, but both shots hung. Lawrence was later found insane.

May 20 **Democratic nominating convention,** meeting at Baltimore, Md., chose Martin Van Buren and Richard M. Johnson of Kentucky as its national ticket. **Daniel Webster** had been nominated in January by a Massachusetts **Whig caucus.** The same month, **Hugh L. White** was picked by anti-Jacksonian Democrats in Tennessee. In December of this year, the **anti-Masonic Party,** meeting at Harrisburg, Pa., named William Henry Harrison of Ohio and Francis Granger of New York as its candidates.

July 8 **Liberty Bell** cracked while it tolled for the death of Chief Justice John Marshall.

Oct. 21 **William Lloyd Garrison,** the noted abolitionist, rescued from a Boston mob of some 2000 people. He was lodged for safety in the Leverett Street Jail on the night of Oct. 21. The mob was angered by his preaching "that all men are created equal. . . ."

Nov. **2nd Seminole War** begun by Osceola, leader of Florida Seminoles, who refused to abide by the terms of the Removal Bill which dictated that they move on to the West.

Nov. 24 **Texas Rangers** authorized by Texas Provisional Government. One of earliest state police forces in U.S.

and *Westward Ho!* (1832), a popular romance.

Extremely popular woman novelist of New England, **Catherine Maria Sedgwick,** published *The Linwoods,* a domestic novel set against the historical background of the Revolution. Although characters like General Washington are introduced, the essential tenor of the book is that of the homely virtues, piety, respect, domesticity. Her novel *Home* also printed this year went through 15 editions by the end of the decade.

Distinctive cultural pattern of poor white farmers in the South emerged in humorous dialect sketches by **Augustus B. Longstreet,** a noted Georgia humorist with a scholarly approach to his source material: vulgar jokes, local expressions, and uninhibited revival meetings.

Newspaper which was strongly proSouthern, the **New York Herald,** started by J. G. Bennett. In 1869 it astounded world by sending Stanley to Africa to find Livingstone. In 1924 it was merged with the *New York Tribune* to form the *Herald Tribune.*

Washington Irving bought and remodeled a Dutch farmhouse near Tarrytown, N.Y., creating 1 of 1st Gothic Revival buildings in U.S. Called **"Sunnyside,"** it is a favorite spot for tourists today.

St. Philip's Church, Charleston, S.C., known as "the Westminster Abbey of South Carolina" because of the number of distinguished men buried in its cemetery, built in the most ornate tradition of the Greek Revival.

1836

Mar. 2 **Texas** declared itself an independent republic. 2 weeks later it wrote a constitution and organized a government, which sent commissioners George Childress and Robert Hamilton to Washington, where their authority was not accepted because U.S. was unwilling to recognize the Republic of Texas.

Mar. 6 **The Alamo,** a fortified mission

Return of **American painters** from classical imitations of 18th century to study of American landscape is revealed in work of Thomas Cole (1801–1848). In his *Oxbow of the Connecticut* painted this year, nature is depicted in her wildness: a storm brews in the background bending the trees lining the river. Romanticism marks all of Cole's works.

tended the range of his telegraph system to 10 miles.

Democracy in America, a classic exposition of the theory and practice of democracy, published in Belgium by **Alexis de Toqueville.** It was the result of his visit to U.S. as representative of French government. He used America as model for the ideal democratic state of the future in which the liberal aims of the 19th century would be justified and fulfilled.

Col. James Bowie, later killed at Alamo, invented **"Bowie knife,"** according to popular legend.

Feb. 9 **Illinois College** chartered in Jacksonville, Ill., under joint auspices of Congregational and Presbyterian groups. 1st degrees were awarded in 1835.

Feb. 14 **Marietta College** chartered in Marietta, Ohio, under Congregational auspices. 1st degrees awarded in 1838.

Nov. 23 Patent issued to Henry Burden of Troy, N.Y., for **horseshoe-manufacturing machine.** Machine became widely popular and made virtually all horseshoes used by Union troops during Civil War.

Dec. 21 **Oglethorpe University** 1st chartered in Milledgeville, Ga., as Oglethorpe College. Founded under Presbyterian auspices, college awarded 1st degrees in 1839. Oglethorpe College was moved from Milledgeville to Atlanta, Ga., in 1913 when it became Oglethorpe University.

the most popular writer on this subject in America. No temperance stories were as widely circulated or so often reprinted in the next 25 years.

Growing **urbanization** of American life blamed by *The People's Magazine* for the creation of a new type of young man, unhealthy, badly postured, pale and nervous.

American House in Boston opened by Lewis Rice with **1st gas lighting** in American hotel history for both the guest rooms and the upstairs halls.

Nearly 30 thousand spectators saw famous **10-m. foot race** at Union Course, L.I. An offer made in New York of $1000 to any man who could run 10 miles in less than an hour drew 9 contestants. Henry Stannard of Killingsworth won, covering the 1st mile in 5:36, last mile in 5:54, and the entire course in 59:44. Great jubilation as Stannard leaped on a horse and triumphantly retraced his winning course.

Apropos the **Temperance Movement** the Rev. Charles Giles declared that 56,000 people in U.S. were destroyed by drink annually and that "500,000 drunkards are now living in our blessed America, all moving onward to the dreadful verge. What a scene of immolation."

1836

1st incorporation law in U.S. passed by Connecticut.

A First and Second Reader compiled by **William Holmes McGuffey** published for use in public schools. Series grew to include 6 readers. The series was revised 5 times, last in 1901; they were still in use in U.S. schools in 1927. Except in New

Popular phrase **"Tippecanoe and Tyler too"** adopted by public during campaign for 9th presidency. William Henry Harrison, the candidate, had engaged the Indians at Tippecanoe, beaten them off, and thus became identified with the place. John Tyler was his running mate.

Apt tag **"Boston is a state of mind"** sprang up with the founding of New Eng-

at San Antonio, Tex., where less than 200 Texans were garrisoned, captured by Santa Anna, who had led 3000 troops across the Rio Grande from Mexico. Every Texan in the mission was killed.

Apr. 21 Texan army under Gen. Sam Houston defeated Mexican army under Santa Anna at **Battle of San Jacinto R.** War was concluded by this battle and Texas thus earned its independence from Mexico.

May 25 Resolutions passed **House of Representatives** concerning slavery and right of petition. It was made a house rule that agitation on the slavery question should be arrested, therefore all petitions on that subject would be tabled without discussion or action. The House thus asserted the power to control its own procedure.

June 12 **Edmund Roberts** of New Hampshire died on an American vessel at Macao, China, during an oriental plague. He was the pioneer of American diplomacy in the Far East, having negotiated treaties with and visited in Muscat, Siam, and Annam.

June 15 **Arkansas** admitted as state, 25th to join Union.

June 28 **James Madison** died at the age of 85. He is buried at Montpelier, his estate in Virginia.

July 2 Act passed reorganizing the **Post Office Department,** ordering that any postmaster intentionally keeping mail from an addressee would be fined and imprisoned and lose all rights ever to serve as postmaster. The act grew out of the struggle concerning the use of the mails for abolition literature.

July 11 **Specie circular** issued ordering federal land agents to accept only gold or silver for public lands sold. As a result the sale of public lands fell sharply, and in spite of Jackson's good intentions the circular precipitated the financial panic of 1837.

Emergence of **Shobal Vail Clevenger** as a sculptor of the West, formerly an apprentice stonecutter in the shop of David Guion of Cincinnati.

Building of **Washington Monument,** Washington, D.C., begun from plans by Robert Mills. It is outstanding for its absolute lack of ornament in a period when taste was becoming more and more flowery.

Hodges-Field House, one of best examples of Greek Revival architecture in U.S., built in North Andover, Mass.

Prolific short story writer from Knickerbocker New York, **James Kirke Paulding,** collected a series of his tales dealing with Nieuw Amsterdam, entitled *The Book of Saint Nicholas.* Favorites like "Cobus Yerks," "Claas Schlaschenschlinger" were included.

Collected edition of the early poems of **Oliver Wendell Holmes** revealed his jocose vein that points back to the light verse writers of the 18th century. Poems like the "Ballad of the Oysterman," "My Aunt," reflect this light touch, while the element of pathos is seen in the ever popular "The Last Leaf."

Maria Monk's book of scandal, *Awful Disclosures of Maria Monk, as Exhibited in a Narrative of Her Suffering During a Residence of Five Years as a Novice, and Two Years as a Black Nun, in the Hotel Dieu Nunnery at Montreal.* The book, now proved a hoax, quickly sold hundreds of thousands.

William Ellery Channing, influential Unitarian minister, published *The Abolitionist,* a powerful statement of his position on the moral implications of slavery.

Celebrated actor **James E. Murdoch** makes his New York debut at Richmond Hill Theater. He was already well known as a road star.

The use of Spanish themes in drama is seen in the *Court of Love* by **James N. Barker.** Story of play is based on picaresque French novel **La Folie Espagnole** by Pigault-Lebrun.

England, *McGuffey's Readers* were the standard elementary school textbooks for nearly a century.

Transcendental Club, with Emerson, Bronson Alcott, George Ripley, Henry Hedges, Orestes Brownson, Theodore Parker, Margaret Fuller, W. H. Channing, Hawthorne, the Peabody sisters and James Freeman Clark as participants, began as casual discussion group. The group convened frequently enough to maintain an identity, but the note of informality was never lost. The club was always impromptu, without officers, office, or schedule, and membership waxed and waned with the seasons. A result of the Transcendental Club was the beginning, in 1840, of the Transcendentalist organ, *The Dial.*

Jan. James G. Birney published 1st issue of **The Philanthropist,** an anti-slavery newspaper, at New Richmond, Ohio. *The Philanthropist* was 1 of the most radical organs of the period, and it soon infuriated the North as well as the South. Birney was chosen executive secretary of the American Anti-Slavery Society the next year, and he moved to New York to continue his agitation for reform. He believed he could accomplish his objectives by political action, was nominated by the Liberty Party for the presidency, and assisted as vice-president to World's Anti-Slavery Convention in England in 1840. Birney was born in Kentucky, had been himself a slaveholder. His wholesale rejection of his heritage was among the most spectacular records of the early days of abolitionism.

Jan. 9 **Spring Hill College** chartered in Spring Hill, Ala., under Catholic auspices. 1st Catholic college in the deep South, Spring Hill issued its 1st degrees in 1837. It had been founded in 1830.

Jan. 30 **Franklin College** 1st chartered as Indiana Baptist Manual Labor Institute in Franklin, Ind. Renamed Franklin Col-

land's Transcendental School. Proud of its intellectual rather than physical or geographical position, New England accepted term as complimentary, although many have used it derisively.

Stirring war cry **"Remember the Alamo"** sounded by Texans at the battle of San Jacinto, where the army of Santa Anna was routed and revenge taken for its massacre of the previous year. The Alamo, a fort in San Antonio, had been besieged for a month, and after having been taken, its defenders were slaughtered. Among dead were Davy Crockett and James Bowie.

South recovered honor in a return South-versus-North **horse race** (see 1823) when its entry *John Bascombe,* belonging to Col. Crowell of Alabama, defeated *Post Boy* at the Union Course, L.I., doing the 4-mile stretch in 7:49 and 7:51½.

William A. Alcott, 1 of most influential and most prolific arbiters of manners in America, published *The Young Woman's Guide* and *The Young Mother,* in which he upheld traditional moral standards. His *The Young Wife* (1837) and *The Young Husband* (1838) extended the scope of his moralistic approach to manners of the marriage relationship.

Ernestine L. Rose, Polish woman living in New York, circulated a **feminist's petition** requesting the state legislature to grant married women the right to hold property in their own names. Her petition obtained only 5 signatures.

Pledge of **total abstinence** became official policy of Protestant ministries; but even before official pressure was exerted, over 300,000 ministers had been enrolled under this pledge.

The Rev. Thomas P. Hunt enlisted children in the **Temperance crusade** via Cold Water societies. Hunt approached children mainly through Sunday Schools, furnished them with pledge cards and set them loose on the nonabstainers to obtain signatures.

POLITICS AND GOVERNMENT; WAR; DISASTERS; VITAL STATISTICS.	BOOKS; PAINTING; DRAMA; ARCHITECTURE; SCULPTURE.

Sept. 1 **1st American settlement in northern Oregon** founded by 2 missionaries, Marcus Whitman and H. H. Spalding.

Oct. 22 **Sam Houston** sworn in as 1st president of Republic of Texas. Served until 1841 and later became U.S. Senator from Texas.

Nov. 21 **77 lives lost** when the *Bristol,* an English ship, coming into New York harbor, was wrecked near Far Rockaway.

Dec. 7 **Martin Van Buren** elected president with popular vote of 761,549. Other candidates received the following popular votes: Harrison, 549,567; White, 145,396; Webster, 41,287. None of the four vice-presidential candidates received a majority of the electoral votes. The Senate, for the 1st and only time, had to choose, and named Richard M. Johnson to the office.

Adaptation of foreign plays characteristic of **early American drama.** Richard Penn Smith typified this trend: his *Daughter,* produced in Philadelphia this year, was a literal adaptation of a play by Laroche; his *Actress of Padua* was based on Hugo's *Angelo, Tyran de Padoue; The Bombardment of Algiers* (1829) on a French play by Frédéric du Petit-Méré.

Ralph Waldo Emerson published *Nature.* He had visited with Carlyle in England 4 years before, where he was strongly impressed by the school of thought which derived from Kant and German idealism. When he returned to the U.S. he married, settled in Concord, began work on American edition of Carlyle's *Sartor Resartus,* and started his lifelong definition of himself. *Nature* was a premature but seminal prospectus of the objectives of the Transcendentalist movement.

1837

Beginnings of wave of **Scandinavian immigration** foreshadowed by arrival of Ole Rynning in Illinois. His *True Account of America for the Information and Help of Peasant and Commoner* encouraged many of his countrymen to migrate.

American Peace Society formally condemned all war.

Jan. 1 **Distribution bill** took effect. It was a measure designed to relieve the government of the surplus money collected in the period of financial boom. The federal books were to be balanced, a working capital of $5,000,000 was to be set aside, and the rest of the funds were to be distributed among the states in 4 installments. But the financial panic hit the nation, and the 4th installment was never made.

Jan. 26 **Michigan** admitted as state, 26th to join Union.

Feb. Ships' captains required to file **a report on each immigrant** as he landed. The Supreme Court in the case of *New*

New England historian **William H. Prescott** published his famous *The History of Reign of Ferdinand and Isabella,* which had an immediate success. It has been translated into many languages. It is distinctive in its capture of the pageantry of the times. Above all it is written as a superb narrative.

Famous plea for American arts and letters, often regarded as our literary Declaration of Independence, **Ralph Waldo Emerson's** *American Scholar* address. Although many previous writers and speakers had dealt with the same theme, Emerson's handling of the subject lifted it to the area of philosophy.

English visitor **Harriet Martineau** wrote a favorable account of her impressions of this country in her *Society in America,* which had great vogue in England and France. Even she, however, remarked that "If the American nation be judged by its literature, it may be pronounced to have no mind at all."

SCIENCE; INDUSTRY; ECONOMICS; EDUCATION; RELIGION; PHILOSOPHY.	SPORTS; FASHIONS; POPULAR ENTERTAINMENT; FOLKLORE; SOCIETY.

lege in 1843, college awarded its 1st degrees in 1847. The College had been founded in 1834.

Mar. 23 **U.S. Mint** produced its 1st coins to be made by steam power. This new press had been designed by Franklin Beale.

June 17 North American Academy of the Homoeopathic Healing Art, **1st of type** in world, chartered at Allentown, Pa. Founded by Constantine Hering, it offered degree of Doctor of Homoeopathia.

Dec. 10 **Emory University** 1st chartered as Emory College in Oxford, Ga. Established under Methodist auspices, Emory College granted its 1st degrees in 1841, became Emory University in 1915, and moved to Atlanta, Ga., in 1919.

Mar. 2 **Texas Independence Day,** a legal holiday in Texas, commemorates the drafting and signing of a Declaration of Independence from Mexico on this date.

Apr. 21 **San Jacinto Day,** a holiday in Texas commemorates the battle of San Jacinto.

May 31 **Astor Hotel** opened in New York city. Built by John Jacob Astor on a plot facing City Hall Park, it was the most impressive hotel in the U.S. and the most fashionable meeting place in New York.

July 4 **1st women to cross North America,** Narcissa Prentiss Whitman and Eliza Hart Spalding, reached Oregon in party organized by American Board of Commissioners for Foreign Missionaries. Success of this missionary expedition stimulated emigration to northwest territories.

1837

Expansion of **credit facilities** in U.S. between 1834 and 1837 facilitated by charters for 194 new banks.

William W. Gerard made significant contribution to American medicine with his clinical tests of **typhus** and **typhoid fever.** By these tests, he succeeded in differentiating the 2 dread diseases.

Jan. 10 **DePauw University** 1st chartered in Greencastle, Ind., as Indiana Asbury University. Established under Methodist auspices, university granted 1st degrees in 1840, became DePauw University in 1884.

Feb. 15 **Knox College** 1st chartered in Galesburg, Ill., as Knox Manual Labor College under the joint auspices of Congregational and Presbyterian groups. 1st degrees were granted in 1846. Knox Manual Labor College became Knox College in 1857.

Mar. 18 **University of Michigan** chartered in Ann Arbor as a state university. It had been preceded by the founding of

P. T. Barnum convinced a credulous public that Joyce Heth, a woman weighing only 46 lbs., was the nurse who brought George Washington into the world and was, hence, 161 years old. A crowd of 10,000 people flocked to see her at Niblo's Garden in New York city. An autopsy performed after her death revealed her to be only half as old as Barnum had claimed. She was Barnum's 1st successful hoax.

Temperance stories began to enjoy a wide vogue in American magazines. "Plot" of these stories generally emphasized the evils of drink on the part of sinning husbands against innocent wives and children, who often died of sorrow. Sentimental stories of this stripe began to replace such didactic pieces on temperance as Lyman Beecher's *Six Sermons.* Temperance annuals and gift books soon became common items in American bookshops.

A Manual of Politeness for Both Sexes, published this year, expressed its position on the disposition of ladies' knees: "To cross them one over the other, and to em-

191

POLITICS AND GOVERNMENT; WAR; DISASTERS; VITAL STATISTICS.	BOOKS; PAINTING; DRAMA; ARCHITECTURE; SCULPTURE.

York v. Miln upheld a state law to that effect.

Feb. 6 Resolution passed in the House asserted that **slaves** do not possess the right of petition secured to people of U.S. by the Constitution.

Mar. 3 **Supreme Court membership** increased from 7 to 9 by act of Congress.

Mar. 3 Pres. Jackson recognized the **Republic of Texas** with the approval of Congress.

Mar. 4 **Martin Van Buren** inaugurated 8th president and 1st to be born after the signing of the Declaration of Independence. Conscious of this fact, Van Buren deferentially mentioned it in his inaugural, "Unlike all who have preceded me, the Revolution that gave us existence as one people was achieved at the period of my birth; and while I contemplated with gratified reverence that memorable event, I feel that I belong to a later age and that I may not expect my countrymen to weigh my actions with the same kind and partial hand."

Mar. 18 **Grover Cleveland,** 22nd and 24th president, born in Caldwell, N.J.

May 10 **Panic of 1837** began when New York banks suspended all specie payment. This year saw 618 banks fail. The ensuing depression lasted for about 7 years.

Nov. 7 **Elijah P. Lovejoy killed** by proslavery rioters at Alton, Ill. His antislavery printing plant had previously been wrecked.

Dec. 8 **Wendell Phillips** delivered his 1st abolition speech in Faneuil Hall, Boston, Mass. It was a protest against the murder of Elijah P. Lovejoy.

Dec. 29 The **Caroline Affair** resulted in murder of an American by a Canadian militiaman. Canadian insurrectionists led by William Lyon Mackenzie had taken refuge on Navy Island on Canadian side of Niagara R. Small American steamboat *Caroline* had been turned over to him as a supply transport by American sym-

Current taste for historical fiction measured by weighty novel by **William Ware,** *Zenobia,* a heavily documented tale of Rome, written in the epistolary style. Ware followed this with *Aurelian* (1838) and *Julian* (1841).

Popular novel of the backwoods pitched in a melodramatic vein was *Nick of the Woods* by **Robert Montgomery Bird.** In contrast to Cooper, he saw the Indian as a vicious, dirty, unforgiving, unforgetting "varmint," who had to be exterminated. Book has gone through more than 25 editions in this country.

Earliest collection of **Nathaniel Hawthorne's** tales appeared under the title *Twice-Told Tales.* Dipping deep into chronicles and histories of colonial New England and adding symbolic overtones, he achieved some of the finest moral allegory ever written.

1st book of **Charles Dickens** published in America, *The Pickwick Papers,* inaugurating an unmatched popularity. Even in recent times Dickens still sells better than other standard authors.

Masterpiece of the Hudson River School, **Thomas Cole's** *In the Catskills.* A resident of village of Catskill on the Hudson, artist romanticized rural setting. Here, in a clearing surrounded by trees, two figures rest by a winding stream that loses itself in the foliage of the background. In the rear the mountains rise gently.

New York, a city of 300,000, opened this season with 8 operating **theaters;** Bowery, Broadway, Franklin, National, Niblo's, Olympic, Park, Vauxhall Gardens. For concerts there were the Castle Garden and the Richmond Hill Circus.

Mar. 20 Romantic comedy, which later inspired at least 1 novel and another play, *The Prophet of St. Paul's* by **David Paul Brown,** opened in Philadelphia. Famous historical novel *When Knighthood Was in*

SCIENCE; INDUSTRY; ECONOMICS; EDUCATION; RELIGION; PHILOSOPHY.

SPORTS; FASHIONS; POPULAR ENTERTAINMENT; FOLKLORE; SOCIETY.

a University of Michigan in 1817, but this institution never taught course on a collegiate level. University opened its doors in 1841, and 1st degrees were awarded in 1845.

Apr. 20 Massachusetts Senate enacted law to establish **state board of education** probably 1st such in U.S. Horace Mann, then president of Senate, served as secretary of board until 1848.

Sept. Samuel Finley Breese Morse filed for patent on his **telegraph.** It was not granted until 1844.

Nov. 8 **Mt. Holyoke Seminary** opened. 1st college in U.S. intended specifically for women, it had been founded in previous year by Mary Lyon. Accommodated 80 students; the next year 400 were turned away for lack of room. Mount Holyoke established higher standards for admission than had formerly been demanded of women. A girl had to be 16 to begin schooling and entrance examinations were required. The course of instruction ran to 3 rather than 2 years, and it included rudimentary training in home economics: the student cooked and cleaned and spent Monday, their "Recreation" day, polishing up the school. Diplomas were granted to seniors who successfully passed a final year of chemistry, astronomy, geology, rhetoric, logic, moral philosophy, natural theology, and ecclesiastical history. The 1st year enrollment was 116, of whom 3 graduated at the 1st commencement, Aug. 23, 1838.

Dec. 22 **Mercer University** chartered in Penfield, Ga., under Baptist auspices. University granted its 1st degrees in 1841, was moved to Macon, Ga., in 1871.

Dec. 29 Patent awarded to Hiram Avery and John Avery Pitts of Winthrop, Me., for their invention of a combined **portable thresher and fanning mill.** Eventually Hiram moved to Chicago where he manufactured "Chicago-Pitts" threshers, which were widely used throughout grain

brace them with the hands joined, is deemed vulgar."

Amos Lawrence became a well known model of the virtuous merchant by his practicing of moral hygiene. Lawrence gave up tea and coffee in 1832, fish, meat, and gravies in 1835, and butter in 1836. Lawrence conducted regular family prayers, conscientiously observed the Sabbath, and contributed to many worthy charities. In the midst of his piety, Lawrence prospered as a landlord and businessman to such an extent that his example was cited as evidence of the rewards of good living.

Telling phrase **"The Almighty Dollar"** coined by Washington Irving in his book *The Creole Village* to symbolize crass materialism and the preoccupation with gain. The phrase appears in a sentence: "The Almighty Dollar, that great object of universal devotion throughout our land."

1st convention of **American Moral Reform Society** held in Philadelphia adopted a resolution pledging "to practise and sustain the principles of Moral Reform in the United States, especially Education, Temperance, Economy, and Universal Liberty." Convention also praised George Thompson, the English Abolitionist and Benjamin Lundy, Quaker leader in the antislavery movement. Resolutions were adopted against the custom of mourning clothes for the dead and against the pomp and ceremony of funerals on the grounds that this fashion imposed an unfair burden on the poor.

Nathaniel Hawthorne reported that young officers at the Charlestown Navy Yard, Mass., had adopted the **mustache,** a fashion which had arrived from England.

Typical 19th century American view on **women riding horseback** presented in Donald Walker's *Exercises for Ladies*, which held that horseback riding tended to consolidate unnaturally the bones of the lower part of the body, causing difficulties in the

pathizers, but Canadian militiamen captured and burnt boat at night, killing an American in course of attack. Canadian was later acquitted and trouble between U.S. and Canada was averted.

Flower (1898) by Charles Major draws its substance from this play.

1838

By this time the **Underground Railroad,** a system of escape routes for Southern slaves, was well established. From about 1830 to 1860 perhaps 500–1000 slaves fled North each year. Some states, such as Connecticut, Pennsylvania, New York, Vermont, and Ohio passed Personal Liberty Laws which impeded the enforcement of Federal Fugitive Slave Law of 1793. Perhaps Quakers of Pennsylvania initiated system which reached from Kentucky and Virginia across Ohio, and from Maryland across Pennsylvania to New York and New England.

Congress declared that all U.S. railroads were to be **legal carriers of the mails.** The day of the stage, which had previously been the mail route, declined after 1838 when a presidential message went by rail from Philadelphia to New York 1 hour more quickly than it took the stagecoach on the same route.

Most banks resumed **specie payment.**

Jan. 5 Pres. Van Buren issued **neutrality proclamation** forbidding Americans to take sides in the Canadian revolt. This was a direct outcome of the *Caroline* affair. On Jan. 13 Canadian rebels, who had been operating from Navy Island against Canada, surrendered to U.S. Sentiment in U.S. was at this time anti-British, and there were numerous border violations. Pres. Van Buren issued 2nd neutrality proclamation on Nov. 21, and ordered swift punishment of Americans who violated border.

Feb. 14 John Quincy Adams presented before the House **350 petitions against slavery and annexation of Texas.**

Apr. 25 **Steamer Moselle exploded** on Ohio R. near Cincinnati killing 100.

May 18 Congress approved voyage to survey South Seas under command of Lt.

John Greenleaf Whittier joined abolition movement with his volume of verse, *Ballads and Anti-Slavery Poems.* Noteworthy among the pieces are "To William Lloyd Garrison," "The Hunters of Men," "The Slave Ships," "Stanzas for the Time," "Toussaint L'Ouverture," "Hymn," the extremely popular "Stanzas," and "The Moral Warfare."

Best of the novels of Southerner **John P. Kennedy,** *Rob of the Bowl,* published. Set in Maryland in the days before the Revolution, it is a romantic piece à la Scott, with incidents of smuggling, piracy, and love against a background of religious dispute.

James Fenimore Cooper, upon his return from Europe, turned to social criticism in his *The American Democrat.* Though believing in equality of rights, he could not accept equality of conditions. The dangers of democracy from a social point of view are cogently represented.

Thomas Cole, a popular painter of romantic landscapes, wrote in his diary: "I am out of place . . . ; there are few persons of real taste; and no opportunity for the true artist to develop his powers. The tide of utility sets against the fine arts." This attitude was common among American artists for several generations. Most known American **artists** were in Europe. An

194

SCIENCE; INDUSTRY; ECONOMICS; EDUCATION; RELIGION; PHILOSOPHY.	SPORTS; FASHIONS; POPULAR ENTERTAINMENT; FOLKLORE; SOCIETY.

producing belt for more than a half century.

performance of future womanly duties (not mentioned by the author).

1838

John and Lyman Hollingsworth, brothers of South Braintree, Mass., created **manila paper** from hemp sails, canvas, etc. Their experiments were stimulated by Panic of 1837, which left them with no money and no stock for their paper business. Patent was issued to them in 1843.

Apr. 23 Establishment of **first transatlantic steamship service** with the arrival in New York city of the *Great Western* after less than 16 days at sea. The day before the *Sirius* arrived, taking 17½ days from Great Britain. The ships, both British, were steam-sail packets and for the next generation Great Britain led the world in transatlantic steamer service. First regular service not established until 1840.

Chauncey Jerome of Bristol, Conn., first used **standardized brass clock works;** soon was manufacturing 600 clocks a day. His 1-day brass clock sold for $2, compared to $40 for wooden clock, and became widely used.

Pennsylvania had approximately 2500 miles of **turnpikes,** which cost $37,000,000.

Jan. 12 Joseph Smith fled from Kirtland, Ohio, to escape arrest after failure of Mormon bank. With his associate, Sydney Rigdon, Smith relocated in Far West on the Missouri frontier where a pilot Mormon community had lately been set up. Many of the Kirtland converts deserted him. He punished them with a formal public excommunication. From this time Smith became more aggressive and determined

Comment **"Here she goes; there she goes!"** enjoyed great popularity through advertising stunt. In front of the Bradshaw Hotel in Harlem a man sat and in unison with a large pendulum clock repeated the sentence over and over. Crowds of course collected, and soon Bradshaw's became the most popular gathering place in the city. A play, *The Old Clock; or, Here She Goes—There She Goes,* was produced at the Franklin Theater this year.

A new craze among the ladies of New York city was **rolling hoops** on the Washington Parade Ground.

New York Herald printed 130 inches of advertisements, of which 54 were devoted to doctors and their **quack remedies.** *Boston Transcript* surveyed on the same date contained 224 inches of which 134 were devoted to medical panaceas.

George Combe, celebrated English exponent of **phrenology,** came to America for a 2-year lecture tour. Combe succeeded in making phrenology fashionable with both lectures and textbooks which were stamped with intellectual authority.

Jan. *The American Monthly Review* sounded a "modern" complaint against **U.S. newspapers:** "The newspaper now is a lame thing, and quite uniform from New York to Maine, Arkansas and Mississippi."

Jan. 26 Temperance agitation continued. Tennessee became 1st state to pass prohibition laws, making it a misdemeanor to sell alcoholic beverages in taverns and stores. Later this year political storm erupted in Massachusetts when a law was passed prohibiting sale of alcoholic beverages (except for "medicinal or mechanical" purposes) in quantities less than 15 gallons. Next state-wide election deposed the incumbent governor, Edward Everett,

POLITICS AND GOVERNMENT; WAR; DISASTERS; VITAL STATISTICS.	BOOKS; PAINTING; DRAMA; ARCHITECTURE; SCULPTURE.

Charles Wilkes. Expedition left Hampton Roads, Va., on Aug. 18, 1838, for 4-year exploratory voyage, during which Antarctic Continent was sighted.

June 12 **Iowa** Territory formed from Wisconsin Territory.

June 14 **Steamer Pulaski exploded** off coast of North Carolina killing 140 persons.

Oct. 12 **Texas** withdrew annexation request.

Dec. Remaining **Cherokee Indians** forcibly ejected from Georgia by federal troops.

Dec. 3 **1st abolitionist Congressman** entered House. He was Joshua R. Giddings of Ohio.

Dec. 11 The **"Atherton Gag"** adopted by House. It was a resolution entered by Charles G. Atherton of New Hampshire to eliminate discussion of slavery in the House. Adopted as a House Rule, it was also known as the **"gag rule."**

indication of their reception in London was shown in the following newspaper comment, referring to the Pall Mall Exhibit in which many Americans were represented: "The cognoscenti first stared, then wondered, and finally admired."

Boston School Committee, under urging from Lowell Mason, authorized public schools to include **music** as a branch of instruction. Mason was appointed 1st Superintendent of Music in an American public school system.

1839

American Slavery As It Is, an antislavery work written by **Theodore** and **Angelina Weld,** offered a documentary report on the evils of slavery with material culled from Southern newspapers and the eyewitness testimony of ex-slaves and abolitionists.

Amistad incident occurred. Negro slaves, being transported from Africa on a Spanish ship, mutinied and were captured by a U.S. warship. They were declared free by U.S. Supreme Court in a decision handed down 2 years later.

Feb. 12 **Aroostook "War"** began with seizure of Rufus McIntire, a land agent sent to the Aroostook region between New Brunswick, Canada, and Maine, to expel Canadian lumberjacks who had entered the disputed area. The boundary question had been an Anglo-American issue since 1783 and had never been satisfactorily settled despite a decision handed down by the neutral King of Netherlands in 1827. After McIntire's arrest, Maine

Formation of **American Art Union** in New York city stimulated popular appreciation of classics in fine arts. Union's activities were financed by subscription and paintings, purchased by excess funds, were raffled off to subscribers on Christmas night. This feature violated New York State's anti-lottery laws and led to dissolution of organization.

Returning from a stay in Europe, **Henry Wadsworth Longfellow** published a prose romance, *Hyperion,* and his 1st collection of verse, *Voices of the Night.* His reception as a poet was still not warm.

1st book in English language about California, *California* by Englishman **Alexander Forbes.** A businessman, he stopped off at Yerba Buena (San Francisco) on a voyage to Pacific and saw possibilities of new land. He urged British government to take over territory before Russians or American settlers pushed into it. To make

to oppose force with force. This policy soon brought him into conflict with the other Missouri settlers, who needed little provocation to fight with the Mormons. The settlers took up arms and drove the Mormons from Missouri. They retreated to Illinois, then to Iowa. The next major step brought them finally to Utah.

Dec. 26 Wake Forest College chartered in Wake Forest, N.C. Founded under Baptist auspices in 1834, it granted its 1st degrees in 1839.

Dec. 28 Greensboro College 1st chartered as Greensborough Female College in Greensborough, N.C. Sponsored by Methodist groups, Greensborough Female College awarded its 1st degrees in 1913 when it became Greensboro College for Women. It was renamed Greensboro College in 1920.

who had signed the controversial statute. Pres. Eliphalet Nott of Union College declared to his students that such a large number of drunkards had died from **internal fires** caused by alcoholic fumes "that I presume no person of information will be found to call the reality of their existence [eternal fires] into question."

Dec. 15 *The New York Mirror* echoed, somewhat feebly, a **wise saying** of Benjamin Franklin's *Poor Richard's Alamanac:* "Keep your head cool by temperance, your feet warm by exercise, rise early and go soon to bed; and if you are inclined to get fleshy, keep your eyes open and your mouth shut."

Mar. 3 *The New York Mirror* printed the following **program for a dinner conversation:** "When you are seated next a lady, you should be only polite during the first course; you may be gallant in the second; but you must not be tender till the dessert."

1839

Samuel F. B. Morse, painter and inventor, brought from Paris **1st photographic equipment** in U.S. Morse had learned the process from Daguerre, and he made the 1st daguerreotype portraits in America.

1st state normal school in U.S. instituted in Lexington, Mass., largely through the efforts of Horace Mann, 1st secretary of the Massachusetts State Board of Education.

Vulcanized rubber 1st made by Charles Goodyear. This was the 1st really successful attempt to make rubber non-sticky and solid at high temperatures.

Report on *Elementary Instruction in Europe* by **Calvin Stowe,** published in *Common Schools and Teachers' Seminaries.* The report was prepared for Ohio state legislature. Stowe, husband of Harriet Beecher Stowe, visited schools in England,

Col. Abner Doubleday is said to have laid out **1st baseball diamond** at Cooperstown, N.Y. 1st rules, including dimension of diamond, were not established until 1845.

Josephine Amelia Perkins achieved notoriety as **1st lady horsethief** of record in America by a confession which was published with the following description of herself, "A young woman, who, in early life was deservedly esteemed for her exemplary behavior, yet for three years last past (friendless and unprotected) has been unhappily addicted to a criminal propensity, more singular and surprising in its nature (for one of her sex) than can be found on record; in the commission of which, she has been four times detected, twice pardoned on account of her sex, once for reasons of supposed insanity, and the fourth and last time, convicted and sentenced to two years imprisonment in Madison county jail, Kentucky. Annexed

POLITICS AND GOVERNMENT; WAR; DISASTERS; VITAL STATISTICS.

BOOKS; PAINTING; DRAMA; ARCHITECTURE; SCULPTURE.

and New Brunswick called out their militia, and the Nova Scotia legislature appropriated war funds. Congress authorized a conscription of 50,000 men and voted $10 million toward the prosecution of this action. War was averted when Gen. Winfield Scott arranged a truce and agreed to refer dispute to a boundary commission. The issue was settled in 1842 by the Webster-Ashburton Treaty.

Feb. 20 **Dueling prohibited** in District of Columbia by act of Congress.

Apr. 11 **U.S. citizens granted arbitration rights** on claims **against Mexico** through treaty concluded in Texas.

Sept. 25 France became 1st European nation to recognize **Texas independence.** The 2 countries signed a commercial treaty.

Nov. 13 1st National Convention of the **Liberty Party,** an antislavery party, at Warsaw, N.Y., nominated James G. Birney of New York for the presidency. Birney, a former Kentuckian and slaveholder, wielded strong political influence in western New York and Ohio valley. Francis J. Lemoyne was nominated for the vice-presidency.

Dec. 4–7 **William Henry Harrison nominated for presidency** by Whig national convention meeting at Harrisburg, Pa. John Tyler of Virginia was named vice-presidential candidate.

territory more accessible, he suggested cutting a canal across Isthmus of Panama.

Classic adventure story for boys, *The Green Mountain Boys* by **Daniel P. Thompson.** In less than 30 years, 50 American editions were issued. Has sold nearly a million copies in America.

Present **Trinity Church** of New York erected on site of 2 previous churches of that parish. A prominent example of the Gothic revival in America. Trinity Church and Chapel were designed by **Richard Upjohn** who became 1st president of the future American Institute for Architecture. Trinity was a pacemaker of the style which dominated American architecture through its next major development. The Gothic Revival was popularized in the successful works of **Andrew Downing,** a landscape gardener from Newburg-on-the-Hudson, who had made architecture his hobby and then his passion, and who published *A Treatise on the Theory and Practice of Landscape Gardening* (1841) and *Cottage Residences* (1842). The impact of Downing's ideas was tremendous. For 2 more decades parks, gardens, houses, and monuments were literally cut to the bias of his personal taste. Downing was ridiculed in the *Broadway Journal* by Edgar Allan Poe and, more seriously, in the studies in beauty and form in architecture by Horatio Greenough, but the Gothic tide was not stopped.

1840

Population—17,069,453. Center of population: 16 miles south of Clarksburg, W. Va.

Approximately 40,000 **Indians** from the Five Civilized Nations of the East were resettled in Indian Territory by this time. Most of the tribes were organized into self-governing republics with written constitutions and laws.

Republic of Texas recognized as an individual nation by U.S., Great Britain, Holland, and Belgium.

Forerunner of 20th century documentary film, **panorama type painting** that flourished during this period. Canvases were rolled on one or two drums and unfolded yard by yard to the spectator, often taking an hour and a half for the presentation. Famous panoramic painter was **John Banvard.** His Mississippi R. scenic series was advertised as 3 miles long and it depicted 1200 miles of scenery.

During this period **miniature painting** was in vogue (just before the emergence of

Germany, and France, and returned with his report, which he delivered to the legislature in 1837. It became the basis for the free common school system of Ohio. Like many of his contemporaries, Stowe was particularly impressed by what he saw in Germany. He was an advocate of better schools, higher salaries for teachers, and advanced educational techniques. Because his plan encompassed an extension of state control over local school boards, it became a center of controversy. Ohio, however, took up the campaign and was soon followed by New York, Connecticut, Massachusetts and Michigan.

Jan. 7 Washington Mining Company, **1st silver-mining concern** in U.S., chartered in North Carolina to work newly-discovered Silver Hill Mine near Lexington, N.C. Company began mining operations in 1842.

Feb. 11 University of Missouri chartered in Columbia, Mo., as the University of the State of Missouri. State supported, the university issued its 1st degrees in 1843, became the University of Missouri in 1913.

is a well-written Address to Parents and Children." Miss Perkins was born in Devonshire, England, in 1818, stole her 1st horse from her father to make an elopement 117 miles away in Portsmouth. Through a series of misadventures, she landed in America without any money, cover, and only the clothes on her back. Her career in horse stealing began at that time.

Sale of alcoholic beverages in quantities less than a gallon prohibited in Mississippi.

William Mitchell reopened the Olympic Theater in New York city as a cut-rate house which specialized in the production of **burlettas** and **musical novelties.** The price of boxes was 50¢, and seats went for 25¢. This liberal policy pleased particularly the men of the city, who made the Olympic a "fashionable resort" and "honored it with their constant patronage for the next ten years."

1840

2818 miles of railroad track in U.S.

Early astronomical observatory in America constructed at Harvard by William Cranch Bond.

1st normal trans-Atlantic steamer service inaugurated by British and North American Royal Mail Steam Packet Company (now the Cunard Steamship Company).

John William Draper took **1st photograph of the moon.** Draper, a physicist and

Full impetus of **temperance** movement swept through Northern states during this decade. Maine voted itself dry in 1846 and was followed by all the other New England States except Massachusetts. In their wake came Ohio, Delaware, Tennessee, Indiana, Illinois, Michigan, Wisconsin, Iowa, and Minnesota. However, except in Maine and Vermont, prohibition did not last long in any of the above states. Prohibition was generally removed either in the courts or by legislative repeal. The temperance movement survived, however,

POLITICS AND GOVERNMENT; WAR; DISASTERS; VITAL STATISTICS.

BOOKS; PAINTING; DRAMA; ARCHITECTURE; SCULPTURE.

Capt. Gabriel J. Rains, serving in campaign against Seminole Indians, began to experiment with **1st land mines.** In 1862 at Yorktown and Williamsburg, he left shells with percussion fuses planted in road behind retreat of Union forces to stop advance of McClellan's troops. Rains claimed credit for detonating devices only.

Presidential campaign reflected social consciousness of period. The Whigs, who had no clear-cut program, waged their campaign on a question of personalities. A Democratic newspaper, the Baltimore *Republican,* attempted to dismiss Harrison's qualifications by remarking "that upon condition of his receiving a pension of $2000, and a barrel of cider Gen. Harrison would no doubt consent to withdraw his pretentions, and spend his days in a log cabin on the banks of the Ohio." The Whigs turned this remark into political gold by using the symbols of cider and log cabin to present Harrison as simple man of the people. In the campaign itself they used such now-familiar paraphernalia as campaign hats, effigies, floats, bonfire rallies, and movable log cabins with the doors left freely open; they even distributed coonskin hats and barrels of cider. Their campaign song featured the words "Tippecanoe and Tyler Too," and "Van, Van is a used up man." Van Buren was pictured as opulent aristocrat lavishly entertaining his friends and political cronies in "the Palace," as the White House was then called. They underscored this point by distributing "golden" spoons at many of their political rallies.

Jan. 8 Resolution passed making it a standard rule of the House that no petition or resolution concerning the **abolition of slavery** "shall be received by this House, or entertained in any way whatever."

Jan. 13 **140 persons** died when the steamboat *Lexington* caught fire near Eaton's Neck, N.Y.

Jan. 19 **U.S. expedition** to the southern oceans led by Capt. Charles Wilkes laid claim to the continent of Antarctica for U.S.

daguerreotype). Often portraits were expensively painted on ivory. Prominent in this type of painting were Alexander H. Emmons, James Sanford Ellsworth, T. H. Wentworth, and Josiah Brown King.

During the '40's and '50's several books enjoyed large sales because of their shocking contents. Included are **Eugène Sue's** *The Mysteries of Paris* (1843); **George Lippard's** *The Quaker City* (1844), which had 30 editions in 4 years; and 2 nonfictional books by the celebrated French historian, **Jules Michelet:** *L'Amour* (1859) and *La Femme* (1860).

American classic *Two Years Before the Mast* by **Richard Henry Dana, Jr.,** published. The book drew on the author's experience as a sailor (1834–36). A sensitive man, he was revolted by the cruelty, especially the flogging, aboard ship, and was instrumental in having it outlawed.

James Fenimore Cooper returned to frontier in his novel *The Pathfinder,* a tale set during the period of the French and Indian War. Most of the action centers near Fort Oswego on Lake Ontario.

Most popular writer of the '40's, **Nathaniel Parker Willis,** published a collection of his stories, *The Romance of Travel.* The best paid magazine writer of the period, at one time he was receiving $100 a month from 4 magazines for his stories and sketches. His poetry and plays—wordy, ornate, and diffuse—were acclaimed. He was also the most popular playwright of the period. His *Bianca Visconti* (1837) in blank verse was acted by Josephine Clifton in New York city. His *Tortesa the Usurer* (1839), written for actor James W. Walleck, enjoyed tremendous success here and abroad.

1st publication of **Edgar Allan Poe's** *Tales.* Poe's works did not sell until after his death. His 10 published works earned him not more than a few hundred dollars.

SCIENCE; INDUSTRY; ECONOMICS; EDUCATION; RELIGION; PHILOSOPHY.

astronomer at New York University, also had the distinction of being 1st photographer to capture a human subject with the subject's eyes open. Draper's photograph of the moon was not impressive by later standards, but it foreshadowed America's unique role in the development of photography: its use in astronomy.

"Milking" the railroads by juggling the intricate investment structure became a common practice during this period although not on a scale comparable to the gigantic financial manipulations which occurred after the Civil War.

Dr. Willard Parker opened **1st clinic in an American College** at College of Physicians and Surgeons, New York city. Parker also performed **1st cystotomy** in U.S.

American Society of Dental Surgeons, significant dental organization, founded by Henry H. Hayden and Chapin A. Harris in Baltimore, Md.

Leading antireligious magazine, **The Beacon,** 1st appeared in New York city, linking the rights of labor to the repudiation of all religious doctrines. Typical effort of the times to popularize such rejections of organized religion as deism and agnosticism was made by appealing at the same time for greater social justice.

Mar. 2 **Bethany College** chartered in Bethany, W. Va., under the auspices of the Disciples. 1st degrees granted in 1844.

SPORTS; FASHIONS; POPULAR ENTERTAINMENT; FOLKLORE; SOCIETY.

despite these setbacks and renewed its active campaign after the Civil War.

Washingtonian Temperance Society formed in Baltimore, Md., quite casually by 6 convivial artisans who were inspired by the reports of the arguments of a Temperance lecturer in a nearby hall. Society eventually evolved into a series of meetings in which former drunkards related their experiences before and after taking the pledge of abstinence. This organization was the American archetype of Alcoholics Anonymous, and was based on the same principle, reform of drunkards by ex-drunkards. Within 3 years, the Society claimed half a million intemperate drinkers, and 100,000 habitual drunkards had reformed under the auspices of the Washingtonian Society and had attested to this fact on Washingtonian cards. A convert relating his own experience explained, "A few leaders in the ranks of intemperance having signed the Pledge, it appeared to be a signal for the mass to follow; and on they came, like a torrent sweeping everything before it. It was for weeks the all-absorbing topic."

Growing poverty in New York city caused organization of more than 30 relief agencies in city.

World's Anti-Slavery Convention in London refused to admit several women delegates who had been sent to the Convention by American antislavery societies. Mrs. Lucretia Mott, 1 of the rejected delegates, became a leading champion of women's rights in America.

1st use of the expression **O.K.** It alluded to "Old Kinderhook," Martin Van Buren's birthplace, and was the name of a Democratic club in New York city.

Hydropathy introduced into America at this time as a health "fad" after the popu-

POLITICS AND GOVERNMENT; WAR; DISASTERS; VITAL STATISTICS.

BOOKS; PAINTING; DRAMA; ARCHITECTURE; SCULPTURE.

Apr. 14 Famous speech by Whig Congressman **Ogle** of Pennsylvania, later published as a campaign document was *Speech on the Regal Splendor of the President's Palace.* Speech helped destroy political career of Martin Van Buren by its revelation of sumptuous luxuries in the White House with which most of the people had been unfamiliar.

May 5 **Martin Van Buren nominated for presidency** by Democratic national convention meeting at Baltimore, Md.

Dec. 2 **William Henry Harrison elected president** by popular vote of 1,275,017 as against 1,128,702 popular votes for Van Buren. The Liberty Party candidate, James G. Birney, drew 7,059 votes. John Tyler became vice-president.

Founding of **The Dial,** a famous quarterly meant to be the mouthpiece of the Transcendental Club. Under the editorship of Margaret Fuller, it ran until 1844, receiving material from writers like Emerson and Thoreau.

Theme of **Benedict Arnold** and his treason was popular in drama. During 40's and 50's most prominent handlings were Joseph Breck's *West Point* (1840); Horatio Hubbell's *Arnold* (1847); James R. Orton's *Arnold* (1854); Elihu G. Holland's *Highland Treason* (1852); W. W. Lord's *André* (1856).

1841

1st covered wagon train arrived in California via the Oregon Trail, Humboldt R., and the Sierras.

International cause célèbre resulted when Negro slaves aboard the *Creole* seized the ship on the high seas and sailed to Nassau where they took sanctuary. British government refused to surrender them. (Slavery had been made illegal in Britain and the colonies of the British Empire in 1833.) Rep. Joshua Giddings of Ohio made a speech on the House floor in which he asserted that the Negroes were free on the high seas since state laws on slavery did not apply there. Giddings was censured by the House and not permitted to finish his speech. He resigned and was overwhelmingly re-elected by the voters of his district. He then returned to Congress and finished his speech.

Mar. 4 **William Henry Harrison,** 9th president, inaugurated. He became the 1st Whig president, but died after 1 month in office.

Apr. 4 **William Henry Harrison** died at the age of 68. He is buried at North Bend, Ohio. John Tyler thus became the

1st appearance of **Emerson's** *Essays* (1st series). In the beginning they had only a small sale; but, with the advent of the "cheap libraries" of the 1870's and 1890's, the *Essays* reached best-seller status. *Essays* (2nd series) appeared in 1844. Transcendentalism found its best expression in these essays.

Humorist **T. B. Thorpe** sprang into popularity with his tall tale of the Southwest, *Big Bear of Arkansas.* The broad exaggeration, the contrived contrasts of characters, and the unbelievable world of frontier Arkansas show the artistry of an apparent folktale.

Last of the "Leatherstocking Tales," *The Deerslayer,* issued from the pen of **James Fenimore Cooper.** The hunter is shown in his youth, skillful in the hunt, resourceful, tough, and sinewy. Above all he is virtuous, sincere, and unspoiled by civilization. When asked about his church, he replies: "I'm in church now; I eat in church, drink in church, sleep in church. The 'arth is the temple of the Lord. . . ."

Possibly the world's 1st detective story was **Edgar Allan Poe's** *The Murders in the*

SCIENCE; INDUSTRY; ECONOMICS; EDUCATION; RELIGION; PHILOSOPHY.	SPORTS; FASHIONS; POPULAR ENTERTAINMENT; FOLKLORE; SOCIETY.

Mar. 4 **University of Richmond** 1st chartered in Richmond, Va., as Richmond College. Founded by Baptist groups in 1830, college issued its 1st degrees in 1849, became a university in 1920.

lar "water cures" of Vincent Priessnitz in Europe had impressed American travelers. By the 1850's there were some 27 hydropathic sanitoriums in America. Establishments like the one at Saratoga became a gathering point for the members of high society.

1st international cricket match in which a U.S. team participated took place in Toronto, where an underrated New York club beat the Toronto club by the slim margin of 1 point. Stakes for the match were $500 a side.

Mar. 31 **10-hour day** established by executive order for all federal employees engaged on public works. It had long been a goal for U.S. labor.

1841

Earliest commercial use of oil in U.S. by Samuel M. Kier and others who began about this time to skim "rock oil" from surface of streams in northwestern Pennsylvania, renamed it "Seneca Oil," and sold it as patent—or "Indian"—medicine. The "Kickapoo Indian doctor" became a ubiquitous traveler in all U.S. areas.

Famous sermon by the Rev. **Theodore Parker** entitled "The Transient and Permanent in Christianity" caused sensation at South Boston Unitarian Church where it was delivered and led ultimately to Parker's expulsion from the Unitarian order. Parker held that the ritualistic elements of Christianity are transient expressions of particular churches in particular periods in history. The permanent quality of Christianity derived, as Parker put it, from the rational truth of the teachings of Jesus rather than from His personal authority.

The Brook Farm Association organized by George Ripley, William E. Channing, and a number of fellow New England Unitarians, later designated Transcendentalists. Ralph Waldo Emerson refused to join,

Phrase **"Old Fuss and Feathers"** coined by soldiers to designate and characterize Gen. Winfield Scott. A stickler for army dress and etiquette, he used to parade before his troops with a feathered hat.

Jacob Hyer's son, Tom, claimed his father's unofficial **boxing championship** and was challenged by John McCluster. Tom Hyer, who weighed 205 pounds, defeated McCluster in short order.

Dorothea Dix began a long, energetic campaign to secure better care for paupers and insane. By 1854, she had influenced the legislatures of 11 states to remove the insane from jails and almshouses and place them under medical care in the proper asylums. A congressional law sponsored by Miss Dix and providing for the maintenance of insane asylums on 12,225,000 acres of public lands passed both Houses of Congress, but was vetoed by Pres. Pierce in 1854 on constitutional grounds.

Horace Greeley founded the **New York Tribune** with capital backing of $1000. But his ideals were compensatingly high. He promised to exclude from his pages "the

POLITICS AND GOVERNMENT; WAR;
DISASTERS;   VITAL   STATISTICS.

BOOKS;   PAINTING;   DRAMA;
ARCHITECTURE;   SCULPTURE.

10th president, and the 1st vice-president to succeed to the office by the death of the president. He remained in office 3 years and 11 months.

June 12   Act calling for **Fiscal Bank of the U.S.** (practically a revival of the 2nd Bank of the United States) introduced into Senate. It was passed by both houses and later vetoed by Pres. Tyler. A 2nd Fiscal Bank bill was passed by Congress and again vetoed by the President on Sept. 9.

June 27   American whaling vessel *John Howland* rescued 5 shipwrecked Japanese, including boy named Manjiro Nakahama. All but boy put ashore at Honolulu. Boy was taken to New Bedford, Mass., in 1844 and thus became **1st Japanese immigrant in U.S.** Resided at home of Capt. William A. Whitfield at Fairhaven, Mass., for several years and eventually returned to Japan where he acted as interpreter for Matthew Perry in 1854.

Aug. 9   **175 persons killed** when steamship *Erie* burned on Lake Erie.

Aug. 19   **Uniform bankruptcy system** made law by Congress.

Sept. 11   **Pres. Tyler's entire cabinet resigned,** with exception of Secretary of State, Daniel Webster, because of Tyler's bank bill veto.

Rue Morgue. Practically all the ingredients are present: the eccentric detective, his stupid companion or straight-man, the unimaginative or blind policemen, the surprise solution, the explanation, etc.

Henry Wadsworth Longfellow made tremendous leap forward with publication of his *Ballads and Other Poems,* in which he displays his spirited narrative technique in a form endeared to the romantics. Poems like "The Skeleton in Armor" and "The Wreck of the Hesperus" have become almost part of the American folk heritage. In 7 years the collection went through 10 editions.

Andrew Jackson Downing published his *Treatise on the Theory and Practice of Landscape Gardening.* Downing attacked the Greek Revival movement and spoke out for romantic houses and gardens. His book exerted a great influence on American taste and gave a boost to the still rudimentary profession of domestic architecture in America.

Hibernian Hall, Charleston, S.C., built at heyday of Greek Revival. Its hexastyle Ionic portico one of the best in U.S.

1842

1st expedition of John Frémont, who was placed at the head of a party sent to explore the route to Oregon beyond the Mississippi R. to as far as South Pass in Wyoming. Frémont's preliminary expedition took place in 1841 when he traced the headwaters of the Des Moines R.

Apr. 18   Thomas W. Dorr chosen governor of Rhode Island by voters who under legal constitution were denied vote. Legal government was headed by Gov. Samuel W. King, whose regime declared the Dorr party in a state of insurrection and imposed martial law. Both parties appealed to Pres. Tyler for help, who answered it

New York Philharmonic Society founded through efforts of Ureli C. Hill, its 1st president. Charles Edward Horn, composer, and Henry Christian Timm and William Scharfenberg, European-born musicians, were also among original founders.

Charles Dickens visited America. Idolized as America's favorite author, Dickens was given an unparalleled reception in U.S.

Earlier success as novelist of the sea induced **James Fenimore Cooper** to write 2 tales of the sea, *The Two Admirals* and *The Wing-and-Wing.* These were followed by *Afloat and Ashore* (1844), *The Crater*

though he visited Farm on several occasions. Farm, which was purchased by group for the practical application of its ideas, was sold after 7 years of unprofitable operation.

Oct. 29 Bishop John Hughes urged state support of **parochial schools** in New York and encouraged political action by Catholic voters to achieve this end. The entire issue of Catholic education and Catholic influence in America was argued against a background of riots, religious bigotries, and the rise of the frankly anti-Catholic Native American Party. The house of Bishop Hughes was attacked in 1842 as tension rose between "native" American groups which were predominantly Protestant and the growing stream of predominantly Catholic immigrants.

Dec. 29 **Howard College** chartered in Marion, Ala., under Baptist auspices. College awarded its 1st degrees in 1848, moved to Birmingham, Ala., in 1887.

unmoral and degrading Police Reports, Advertisements, and other matters which have been allowed to disgrace the columns of our leading Penny Papers," and to exert every effort to render the *Tribune* "worthy of the beauty approved of the virtuous and refined, and a welcome visitant to the family fireside."

In his *America: Historical, Statistic and Descriptive,* James Buckingham characterized upstate New York **society** as frugal and staid, but he found New York city speculative, extravagant, and loaded with *nouveaux riches.*

In commenting on current fashion, *Godey's Lady's Book* noted the vogue for tight sleeves for **ladies' dresses** and predicted that the style would last and "again exhibit the beautiful contour of a lady's arm." Yet bare limbs were not proper. Ladies who attended summer resorts were warned against "brocade breakfast dresses" with sleeves and necklines so short that they caused brothers to blush "through the tediousness of three courses and dessert."

1842

John Bennet Lawes invented process for making superphosphate from rock phosphate and sulphuric acid, thus producing **1st commercial artificial fertilizer.**

Samuel Colt, inventor of the famous Colt 45 revolver, began a series of experiments with **explosive underwater mines** and their electrical detonation.

Massachusetts Supreme Court decision in the case of Commonwealth v. Hunt upheld **legality of labor unions** and **right of workers to strike** in order to obtain a closed shop, higher wages, shorter working hours, and better working conditions. It

Sons of Temperance founded at Teetotalers' Hall in New York city with these objectives: to protect its members from intemperance, to elevate their characters, and to provide mutual aid in case of sickness. The Sons of Temperance were financed by dues and an initiation fee and practiced many of the secret rituals of Masonic organizations. This secret aspect of the organization drew fire from John Marsh of the American Temperance Union, who objected to the exclusion of nonmembers at the meetings of the Sons of Temperance.

Annual mortality rates, as published in

was Federal Government's duty to support legal state authority. Dorr's supporters began military action, and on May 18 made an unsuccessful attempt to seize state arsenal. Dorr later gave himself up to state authorities, was tried and sentenced to life imprisonment; but the next year he was fully pardoned. Reforms in state constitution quickly followed **The Dorr Rebellion.**

May 31 Henry Clay resigned from Senate after 40 years as a public official. A defeat of Whig party in the mid-term congressional elections and the failure of his party's program in Congress led to Clay's departure.

June 25 Reapportionment Act passed. It provided that all congressmen were to be elected by districts equal in number to each state's quota of representatives.

Aug. 9 Webster-Ashburton treaty signed by Britain and settled northeast boundary of U.S. which had been in dispute and had caused unrest. The treaty ended border incidents with Canada and ended also a popular American hope of freeing Canada from Great Britain.

Aug. 30 Tariff Act passed by Congress. It restored the generally high protective level of 1832.

Dec. 1 Midshipman Philip Spencer, son of Sec. of War, hanged for **mutiny** on board *U.S.S. Somers;* he and 2 enlisted men were guilty of planning to turn their ship to piracy. Commander Mackenzie, who ordered the hanging, was court-martialed and acquitted.

(1847), *Jack Tier* (1848), and *Sea Lions* (1849).

1st American publication of *Poems* by **Alfred Tennyson.** A 1-volume edition eventually sold over 1½ million copies.

Outstandingly popular anthology of period, **Rufus Wilmot Griswold's** *Poets and Poetry of America* 1st published.

1st "cheap" publishing in America. Because of low postal rates for newspapers and recent development in printing, novels were published in a newspaper format, selling for as low as 6¼ and 12½¢. This forced regular publishers to produce cheap "paperbacks." These newspaper "extras" lasted only 4 or 5 years, having been killed off by the more handy paperbacks.

Feb. 14 The Park Theater in New York city contributed to the triumphant tour of Charles Dickens through America by holding a grand "Boz" Ball in his honor. It was a select affair, with the pedigree of every "guest" rigorously checked by a committee beforehand. The tickets to the ball sold for $10 each, which was a preliminary insurance that the utterly unwanted would not be there. The affair was a sellout. Between dances the record crowd was entertained and edified with representations of scenes from the popular works of Dickens. After the ball, the decorations were left up, for the management had realized that other audiences might like to see them. He arranged for 2 additional balls, with somewhat cheaper admission; the crowds continued to come.

1843

U.S. sent **1st diplomatic representative to Hawaiian Islands.** He was George Brown.

Jan. 29 William McKinley, 25th president, born in Niles, Ohio.

May 1 Thomas Oliver Larkin became **U.S. consul** and confidential agent to California. He served in Monterey from 1844 to 1848 when California was ceded to the U.S. by Mexico.

"Old Dan Tucker" copyrighted by Millet's Music Saloon, New York city. Claims to the song were made by various composers, including Henry Russell, Dan Emmett, and others. The tune had been familiar for 10 years before it was copyrighted; its great popularity in minstrel shows for 4 decades was due to Dan Emmett's performances of it.

An American historical and literary

was held further that individual members of unions could not be indicted collectively for the illegal actions of other union members. This decision was one of the most significant acts in the reversal of traditional judicial hostility to labor organizations.

Mar. 3   Gov. John Davis of Massachusetts signed 1st law to regulate **work day for children** under 12 years. They were limited to 10 hour day. But law only applied to "manufacturing establishments" and was not enforceable. **1st effective child labor law** was enacted by Massachusetts in 1879.

Mar. 7   **Ohio Wesleyan University** chartered in Delaware, Ohio. Founded under Methodist auspices, university granted its 1st degrees in 1846.

Mar. 30   Dr. C. W. Long of Jefferson, Ga., used sulphuric ether to produce **anaesthesia** during operation for cystic tumor on James Venable. During next 5 yrs., Long used anaesthesia several times, including its use for his wife during childbirth. He did not publish his findings until 1849, however, when others had already used anaesthetics, and hence did not receive credit for its discovery.

Apr. 12   Charter granted to Mutual Life Insurance Company of New York, **1st mutual life insurance society** in U.S. Charter often called the "Magna Carta" of American insurance.

Godey's Lady's Book, were broken down by cities. In Boston the rate was 1 in 45, in Philadelphia 1 in 42.3, and in New York city 1 in 37.83.

Pelerine, watered silk and velvet **cardinals** and **scarves** were very popular with the women. But it was not considered good taste to wear the cardinal with a dress of the same color.

E. P. Christy claimed that he organized his minstrels in 1842, a year before his rivals, **The Virginia Minstrels,** opened at the Chatham Theater in New York city. Actually it was another 4 years before **The Christy Minstrels** debuted at Mechanics Society Hall. The American audiences who applauded the minstrels cared little about the "how's" and "why's" of the acts they applauded. They wanted entertainment, not history. The ruling passion of the theater was, for the next 2 decades, the spirit of burlesque. The minstrel merely led by a step a company of clowns, which included the Yankee, the frontiersman, the Indian, the Irishman. The trend was clear to William Mitchell, the English impresario of burlesque, who reopened the Olympic Theater in 1839, and he created a loud, mocking, and completely American comedy.

May 20   Greatest of the **intersectional horse races** took place at Union Course, L.I., between *Fashion* (entry from North) and *Boston* (entry from South) for a purse of $20,000. Thousands of people swamped the course to see *Fashion* break all records by doing the 4 miles in 7:32.

1843

North American Phalanx established in Monmouth County, N.J. This community, which based its constitution on the ideas of Albert Brisbane, had the longest life of any of the utopian communities of the Fourierist type, in which goods produced were the property of the group, but private property and inheritance were not abolished. This Phalanx was finally dissolved in 1854.

New word **millionaire** coined by newspapers in their reports of the death of Pierre Lorillard, banker, landlord, and tobacconist. His fortune of a million dollars was notable at this time, but within 5 years such personal wealth became much less rare, and "millionaire" was being printed without italics.

Association for Improving the Condition of the Poor of New York City founded

| POLITICS AND GOVERNMENT; WAR; DISASTERS; VITAL STATISTICS. | BOOKS; PAINTING; DRAMA; ARCHITECTURE; SCULPTURE. |

May 2 **Oregon** settlers determined to form local government at meeting at Champoeg, and prepared a constitution modeled upon that of Iowa.

May 22 Over 1000 settlers left Independence, Mo., on their way to **Oregon.**

May 29 2nd and most fruitful **Frémont expedition,** under John Frémont, left Kansas City. The outward journey yielded an accurate survey of the emigrant route to Oregon, the return corrected many errors in the concept of the geography of California. He discovered the nature of the Great Basin, and probably 1st used that term to describe the independent system of lakes and rivers divided from the ocean by the mountains. Frémont made a great contribution to geographical knowledge.

June **American Republican Party** formed at New York largely through the efforts of the **Native American Association,** an organization of an anti-Catholic, anti-Irish-immigrant nature. This party evolved into the **Native American Party** in 1845, but it died as a result of Mexican War. It was revived in 1853.

Aug. 23 Mexican president, Santa Anna, warned U.S. that any attempt to annex **Texas** would be considered "equivalent to a declaration of war against the Mexican government."

Aug. 31 The abolitionist **Liberty Party** named James G. Birney as its presidential candidate at a convention in Buffalo, N.Y. Thomas Morris of Ohio was named for the vice-presidential position on the slate.

classic is **William Hickling Prescott's** *The Conquest of Mexico,* a monumental work for which he had practically to import a library. Concerned always with style, he had a passion for the fact, making his work authoritative as well as beautiful. In 1847 he added *The Conquest of Peru* to his history of Spanish America. It has sold in hundreds of thousands of copies.

Extremely popular humorist **William Tappan Thompson** collected his pieces and published them as *Major Jones's Courtship.* A semiliterate Georgia planter, Major Jones sends a series of letters to the editor of a journal. These are full of everyday happenings, weddings, military service—all in dialect. In time book went through more than 20 editions.

Dan (Daniel Decatur) Emmett, who later wrote "Dixie," formed **1st minstrel troupe** in New York city. A quartette of blackface singers and musicians, the group played in several Bowery theaters, and established many of the basic routines followed by later minstrel shows.

John G. Whittier continued his verse descriptions of New England in his *Lays of My Home,* containing such distinctive pieces as "The Merrimack," "Cassandra Southwick," "The Funeral Tree of the Sokokis," "Extract from 'A New England Legend,'" and "St. John."

New York debut of the **Virginia Minstrels** made at the Bowery Amphitheater. Composed of Daniel Decatur Emmett, Billy Whitlock, Frank Brower, and Dick Pelham, the Virginia Minstrels became the 1st "blackface" entertainers to achieve widespread popularity.

Dec. 25 **1st matinee** is offered at Mitchell's Olympic Theater in New York city.

1844

Oregon boundary question resulted in serious Anglo-American friction. The previous year the Oregon boundary had been unofficially set at 54° 40′ by many Americans.

Theme of the American Revolution, often including the representation of Washington, Franklin, Ethan Allen, Nathan Hale, etc., was popular on stage during this period. Marked success was achieved

Unsuccessful typewriter, called "Chirographer," invented by Charles Thurber of Norwich, Conn.

American medical science gained international stature with the publication of "The Contagiousness of Puerperal Fever" by **Dr. Oliver V'endell Holmes** in *The New England Quarterly Journal of Medicine.*

Benjamin T. Babbitt introduced **1st soap powder** at about this time. Became immediately successful; "Babbitt's Best Soap" was known throughout U.S.

Largest telescope available purchased by subscription for Harvard Astronomical Observatory. In March a comet appeared in the daytime and aroused such interest and comment that a subscription for fitting out the observatory with the latest astronomical equipment was proposed. There had been a steady growth of effort to establish an American astronomy. The purchase of the telescope indicated that lectures and public addresses by scientists were having the intended effect. After these early successes, astronomy never failed to win public support. **Harvard Observatory** was begun through the initiative of William Cranch Bond, who had made observations for some years at his home and then moved to Dana House in 1839. A main branch of the Harvard Observatory is still maintained at Cambridge.

Oct. 11 **New York Clearing House** opened with 38 member banks at 14 Wall St. It was organized by Francis W. Edmonds.

Dec. 30 **Cumberland University** chartered in Lebanon, Tenn., under Presbyterian auspices. 1st degrees awarded in 1843. It had been founded in 1842.

after an investigating committee had reported that existing relief societies in the city were derelict in their duty because of their failure to learn the "wants, capacities, and susceptibilities" of the poor by visiting at their homes. The Association for Improving the Condition of the Poor of New York City was a comprehensive group which integrated the programs of the myriad private agencies before it. It was later copied in other cities, notably Brooklyn, Baltimore, Boston, and Chicago.

Rowing introduced to Harvard when William Weeks, a student, bought and outfitted a shell. Yale set up boat and crew in 1844. In 1852 Harvard defeated Yale crew in a regatta on Lake Winnepesaukee.

Jan. **Dorothea Dix** published her *Memorial to the Legislature of Massachusetts,* which contained a scathing indictment of the treatment of the insane.

July 12 Joseph Smith, leader of the Mormon Church, announced that a divine revelation had sanctioned the practice of **polygamy.** This announcement caused bitter feeling both within the Mormon ranks and between Mormons and non-Mormons around Nauvoo, Ill., where Smith's followers were settled at this time.

1844

Alphadelphia Phalanx established on some 3000 acres in Kalamazoo County, Mich., with a membership of almost 500. Internal dissension caused the dissolution of this utopian community within 3 years.

Famous political phrase, **"Fifty-four Forty or Fight,"** adopted as campaign slogan by forces supporting James K. Polk for the presidency. It dealt with the Oregon controversy between Great Britain

| POLITICS AND GOVERNMENT; WAR; DISASTERS; VITAL STATISTICS. | BOOKS; PAINTING; DRAMA; ARCHITECTURE; SCULPTURE. |

Series of riots in Philadelphia between Catholics and non-Catholics. Before order could be restored, 24 persons were dead, 2 Catholic churches were burned, and extensive damage had been done to other Catholic property.

Mar. 6 John C. Calhoun appointed Secretary of State.

Apr. 12 Texas Annexation Treaty signed by U.S. and Texas. It provided for the admission of Texas as a territory.

Apr. 27 Martin Van Buren and Henry Clay opposed annexation of **Texas** without the consent of Mexico.

May 1 Henry Clay nominated as presidential candidate by Whig national convention in Baltimore, Md. Theodore Frelinghuysen of New Jersey was named vice-presidential candidate.

May 27 Tyler Democrats named John Tyler for president at convention in Baltimore, Md. Tyler withdrew from the race on Aug. 20.

May 27 Democratic National Convention opened at Baltimore. It was the 1st convention at which a "dark horse" candidate won. After 8 ballots, all candidates but James K. Polk withdrew, leaving him the nomination. George M. Dallas of Pennsylvania was nominated for the vice-presidency. It was also the 1st convention reported by telegraph.

June 8 Texas Annexation Treaty voted down by Senate.

June 26 Pres. **John Tyler** and Miss **Julia Gardiner** were married at Church of the Ascension, New York city. Tyler was 1st American president to marry during his term of office.

July 1–27 Henry Clay, in the so called **"Alabama letters,"** stated that he had no objection to the annexation of Texas if it could be done "without dishonor, without war."

July 3 Treaty signed at Canton by Caleb Cushing and a representative of the Emperor's government by which the status

by N. H. Bannister in *Putnam, the Iron Son of '76;* by Oliver Bell Bunce in *Love in '76* (1857); by J. G. Burnett in *Blanche of Brandywine* (1858).

"Lubly Fan" copyrighted by Cool White. Song was later used by Christy Minstrels as "Bowery Gals," and after that by the Ethiopian Serenaders as "Buffalo Gals," in which form it entered folklore.

Stephen Foster's 1st published song, "Open Thy Lattice, Love," published by George Willig of Philadelphia. Based on a poem by George Pope Morris, it was a sentimental and genteel ballad of no value.

Strongly feminist book which brought its author nationwide attention was **Margaret Fuller's** *Woman in the Nineteenth Century.*

1st American publication of *The Three Musketeers* by Frenchman **Alexandre Dumas.** At least 1,000,000 copies sold in America. *The Three Musketeers* and *The Count of Monte Cristo* were published in cheap, popular editions, as well as library editions, from the beginning.

Charles Dickens' *A Christmas Carol,* marked by very low sales in the beginning, eventually topped all Dickens' titles, selling over 2,000,000 copies in U.S.

Home of James F. D. Lanier built in Madison, Ind., at cost of $40,000—an extraordinary sum at the time. Full Greek Revival style, with tetrastyle Doric colonnade.

Ralph Waldo Emerson published *Essays, Second Series.* Among the essays were included Experience, Gifts, New England Reformers, The Poet, Character, Politics, Nature, and Manners. It proved a more popular book than the 1st series of essays, but it has not enjoyed an equal critical reputation. The most notable of the essays was Experience, in which Emerson, declaring that sin is the result of ignorance, reaffirmed the Hellenistic credo.

The Dial suspended publication. Founded in 1840, *The Dial* never proved a popular publication and 16 issues did not, from the circulation reports, indicate that it ever

SCIENCE; INDUSTRY; ECONOMICS; EDUCATION; RELIGION; PHILOSOPHY.

Stuart Perry of New York city invented a **gas engine;** it was a non-compression cylinder engine which used turpentine for fuel.

Association of Medical Superintendents of American Institutions for the Insane established. Association was later renamed the **American Psychiatric Association.**

Jan. 15 University of Notre Dame chartered in Notre Dame, Ind., under Catholic auspices. 1st degrees were awarded in 1849. It was founded in 1842 by Rev. Edward Frederick Sorin, C.S.C., and 6 Brothers of the Congregation of Holy Cross.

Feb. 24 University of Mississippi chartered as a state university in Oxford, Miss. Its 1st session began on Nov. 6, 1848. Its 1st degrees were issued in 1851.

May 24 1st telegraph message, "What hath God wrought?" sent from U.S. Supreme Court room in Washington, D.C., to Baltimore, Md., by Samuel F. B. Morse, the inventor of the telegraph.

June 15 Charles Goodyear patented the **vulcanization process for rubber,** which he had discovered accidentally in 1839 when he dropped a mixture of rubber and sulphur on a hot stove and discovered a thin line of charred material. Goodyear correctly deduced that a certain amount of heat could affect rubber in such a way that it would not become sticky in warm temperatures.

June 27 Founder of Mormonism, **Joseph Smith,** and his brother, Hiram Smith, murdered by a mob in Carthage, Ill.

Sept. 19 Mesabi iron range, near Lake Superior, discovered accidentally by a group of government surveyors headed

SPORTS; FASHIONS; POPULAR ENTERTAINMENT; FOLKLORE; SOCIETY.

and the U.S., many Americans feeling the country should press American claims to the 54′ 40°th parallel. Settlement was finally made on the 49th parallel, everything north becoming part of Canada, everything south part of U.S. Northwest.

1st private bath in American hotel introduced at the New York Hotel. **1st bridal suite** in American hotel introduced at the Irving House in New York city.

Moses Yale Beach, owner of the *New York Sun,* published 1st practical **guide book of credit standings and marriage possibilities** entitled, *The Wealth and Biography of the Wealthy Citizens of New York.* Booklet ran through 10 somewhat revised editions by 1846 and was revised twice more in the following 10 years. The 1846 edition had approximately 850 names in its select list out of a total New York city population of 400,000.

1st female manikin ever exhibited in America employed by Paulina Wright in her public lectures on the physiology of women before women audiences.

New York Prison Association established "to take into consideration the destitute condition of discharged convicts." Female department, "The Home," was opened in 1845 to provide for the practical education of released women convicts.

International track meet took place at Hoboken, N.J., in which John Gildersleeve of New York outran Britishers in a 10-mi. race for a purse of $1000; his time, 57:01½. Enthusiastic crowd of 25,000 broke into grounds more than once.

Celebrated news hoax fabricated by Edgar Allan Poe and printed literally in the *New York Sun* reported a balloon crossing of the Atlantic bringing passengers from Europe to America. The hoax was a great success.

211

POLITICS AND GOVERNMENT; WAR; DISASTERS; VITAL STATISTICS.	BOOKS; PAINTING; DRAMA; ARCHITECTURE; SCULPTURE.

of Americans in China was so clearly fixed that other nations later asked the same considerations.

Dec. 3 Gag rule lifted by the House under resolution offered by John Quincy Adams.

Dec. 4 James K. Polk elected president by a popular vote of 1,337,243 as against 1,299,068 for Clay and 62,300 for Birney.

would. Yet it was of crucial importance in the history of New England Transcendentalism and has had an influence upon American life and letters which is totally belied by its size and life span. It remains a primary source for an understanding of the cultural views of the Transcendentalists. As editor, Margaret Fuller drew upon an outstanding list of contributors, among them Emerson and Thoreau.

1845

Jan. 23 Congress enacted law to establish **uniform election day for presidential elections.** Previously states had set their own election days. Act named the first Tuesday after the first Monday in November as election day, and 1st national election fell on Nov. 4.

Mar. 1 Texas annexed by joint resolution in last session of Tyler's administration. This was the 1st time, in foreign relations, that a joint resolution was employed instead of a treaty. The whole of Texas and parts of Oklahoma, New Mexico, Kansas, and Colorado made up the original Texas territory.

Mar. 3 Florida admitted as a state, 27th to join Union.

Mar. 4 James K. Polk, 11th president, inaugurated. He was a Democrat and served 1 term as president.

Mar. 6 Mexican minister to Washington formally **protested annexation of Texas** and prepared to leave the country.

Mar. 28 Diplomatic relations between U.S. and Mexico **broken off** by Mexican government.

Spring **John Frémont** left on his 3rd expedition, this time directly to California. It was on the eve of the Mexican War, and when he reached California, Frémont gave moral support to the Bear Flag War when Americans in Northern California revolted from Spain. Frémont has been nicknamed the "Pathfinder" for his brilliant explorations.

June 8 Andrew Jackson, 7th president

1st publication of *The Raven and Other Poems* by **Edgar Allan Poe.** Poe died in obscurity and poverty, but his works eventually reached best seller lists. Among these are *Tales,* 12 short stories also published this year. Poe did most of his work during this decade.

Western life realistically portrayed in collection of short stories by **Caroline M. Kirkland,** *Western Clearings.* Her bent for local color led her into detailed discussions of politics, teaching, boating on the rivers, speculation for land, etc.

American best seller *The Wandering Jew* by Frenchman **Eugène Sue.**

Mar. 24 Comedy of social satire attained prestige and great vogue with success of **Anna Cora Mowatt's** *Fashion,* story of a *nouveau riche* family and the social aspirations of the wife. Introduction of foreign characters heightened international contrasts. This latter aspect influenced many plays: *Nature's Nobleman* (1851) by **Harry Watkins** set an English earl in America; *The Golden Calf* (1857) by **Mrs. Sydney Bateman** contrasted the English, French, and Americans and satirized snob-

SCIENCE; INDUSTRY; ECONOMICS; EDUCATION; RELIGION; PHILOSOPHY.	SPORTS; FASHIONS; POPULAR ENTERTAINMENT; FOLKLORE; SOCIETY.

by William A. Burt. Burt observed that his compass was deviating 87 degrees from normal and upon investigating the soil found evidence of large deposits of iron ore.

July 29 Foundation of the **New York Yacht Club** on board the schooner *Gimcrack* docked off the Battery. John C. Stevens elected commodore. It was the 1st yacht club in America.

1845

1st written examinations in American elementary schools initiated in Boston.

Industrial Congress of the United States, one of earliest labor organizations in America, organized in New York city. The Congress organized local congresses of labor, reform, and cooperative groups throughout the country. By 1856, however, the organization had weakened through internal confusion and was invaded by Tammany political forces.

Dr. William Keil founded communal settlement of **Bethel** in Shelby county, Mo. He led 500 German immigrants into this haven and established his Church of the Living God as a successful enterprise. Keil held autocratic power, and his subjects seldom received any money for their efforts; but all their needs were satisfied—food, clothing, shelter, education for their children, and all the benefits of a free living.

Feb. 1 **Baylor University** 1st chartered in Independence, Tex., under Baptist auspices. 1st degrees awarded in 1855. University moved to Waco, Tex., in 1886 when it merged with Waco University.

Mar. 11 **Wittenberg College** chartered in Springfield, Ohio, under Lutheran auspices. 1st degrees awarded in 1851.

Oct. 10 Official opening of the **U.S. Naval Academy.** It combined at 1 site,

Temple of Honor established in New York city as a combination Temperance society and Protestant fraternal order. Mr. William L. Stacey, who became Most Worthy Templar of the National Temple in 1849, described the Temple as "all that is excellent in older associations with additional advantages." Temple practiced "unceasing and universal abstinence." No one was admitted to membership who did not acknowledge the existence of God. Embellished with passwords and colorful ceremonial costumes, the Temple of Honor flourished most in the plantation regions of the South.

John Bartholomew Gough, 1 of most successful of all temperance lecturers, was receiving an average income of $14.42 from each speaking engagement, as compared with a $4 fee, or thereabouts, which his colleagues in the cause were receiving.

Cartwright devised 1st formal rules for playing **baseball.** Most significant differences from rules applied at present were: game was terminated when 1 team made 21 aces (runs); the ball had to be pitched underhand (today, ball may be pitched underhand, overhand, or sidearm, almost always the 2 latter); only 1 base was allowed when the ball bounced off the playing field; a ball caught on the 1st bounce was out.

of U.S., died at the age of 78. He was the 1st president to belong truly to the common people, and his popularity originated from his strength as an army general. He is buried at "The Hermitage," Tenn.

June 15 **Texas assured of U.S. protection** if she agreed to annexation. Tangible evidence was given to the Texans when Gen. Zachary Taylor was ordered to defend a line "on or near the Rio Grande."

Nov. 10 **John Slidell** sent to Mexico by Pres. Polk as minister plenipotentiary to restore peaceful relations between the countries. On Dec. 20, Mexican government refused to see him.

Dec. 29 **Texas** admitted as state, 28th to join Union.

bery and craze for money; *Americans in Paris* (1858) by **William Henry Hurlbert** dealt with American couples in France.

June 4 **1st American grand opera,** *Leonora,* composed by William Henry Fry, was presented at author's expense at the Chestnut Street Theater in Philadelphia. It lasted for 12 nights. Written in the grandest Italian tradition, it was nevertheless given in English. It was not a success.

1846

Feb. 10 **Westward migration of Mormons** from anti-Mormon terror in Nauvoo, Ill., began. It was organized by Brigham Young after the murder of Joseph Smith, founder of Mormonism.

Apr. 25 **American soldiers taken prisoner** by Mexican Army in disputed Texas territory.

Apr. 27 1st example in U.S. of **termination of a treaty** by notification of the contracting party occurred when Congress authorized the president to give, at his discretion, notice to Britain of the abrogation of the treaty providing for joint occupation of the Oregon Territory.

Apr. 30–May 1 **Mexican Army** crossed Rio Grande, and on May 3 placed Fort Texas under siege. On May 8 battle of Palo Alto, 1st important engagement of **Mexican War,** took place. Mexicans were repulsed. On May 9 Gen. Taylor won the battle of Resaca de la Palma, driving Mexicans across Rio Grande. On May 18 Taylor crossed Rio Grande and occupied Matamoros.

May 4 Michigan legislature enacted law abolishing **capital punishment,** 1st state to do so. Law became effective Jan. 1,

Napoleon and his Marshals by **Joel T. Headley** had 50 editions in 15 years.

Margaret Fuller published her collected writings as *Papers on Literature and Art.* Margaret Fuller, up to, and even past, her time, was the most formidable bluestocking in American history. She was notorious for her support of the rights of women, for her militant intellect, her knowledge of German, and her understanding of philosophy, all of which, it was said, made her the mental equal of any man. She has been called the best-equipped American critic up to 1850, but her writings have had as limited and select an audience as *The Dial,* which she edited 1840–42. Hawthorne probably used her as the fabulous original for Zenobia in *The Blithedale Romance.*

Henry Wadsworth Longfellow published *The Belfry of Bruges and Other Poems.* It was like all of Longfellow's volumes of this period, spectacularly popular; but it is not generally regarded today as one of his best.

Two original units of **Essex Company mills built of granite** at Lawrence, Mass. Excellent examples of high standards of

Annapolis, Md., a group of schools previously located in the port cities of New York, Boston, Philadelphia, and Norfolk. 1st graduation exercises held on June 10, 1854.

Dec. 20 **Baldwin-Wallace College** 1st chartered in Berea, Ohio, as the Baldwin Institute under Methodist auspices. Institute became Baldwin University in 1854, awarded its 1st degrees in 1858, and joined with German Wallace College in 1914 to form Baldwin-Wallace College.

Aug. Term **"Manifest Destiny"** employed for 1st time in an article by John Louis O'Sullivan in the *United States Magazine and Democratic Review* in support of the annexation of Texas. He wrote: "Our manifest destiny [is] to overspread the continent allotted by Providence for the free development of our yearly multiplying millions."

1846

Smithsonian Institution authorized by Congress in 1846 upon receipt of a bequest of 100,000 pounds from James Smithson, an English chemist and mineralogist.

1st rotary printing press devised and produced by Richard M. Hoe, capable of turning out 8000 papers an hour.

Erastus Brigham Bigelow founded **1st gingham factory** in U.S. at Clinton, Mass.

American Association for the Advancement of Science established.

Jan. **Commercial Review of the South and Southwest** began publication in New Orleans. Edited by James Dunwoody De Bow, the periodical gave an outstanding picture of the social and economic life of the antebellum South. De Bow had trouble getting his review started. Circulation remained small and forced its suspension the following year. But he was able to borrow additional funds, and it resumed publication, continuing, with the largest number of subscribers of any Southern magazine, until 1880.

Feb. 5 **Bucknell University** 1st chartered in Lewisburg, Pa., as the University at Lewisburg. Established under Baptist auspices, university issued its 1st degrees

Publication of *Mince Pie for the Million* related for 1st time many of **tall stories of the frontier,** including "Skinning a Bear," "The Death Hug," and "A Sensible Varmint," the latter involving the ubiquitous Davy Crockett. Stories were written in frontier dialect with colorful misspellings and generally involved animals, particularly bears and game animals, like the raccoon (spelled rakkoon in "A Sensible Varmint").

John Bartholomew Gough, popular temperance lecturer, began his campaign for a **"Prohibition"** amendment to the Constitution. Gough had himself been a drunkard and had been on the wagon now for 4 years.

Eastern Exchange Hotel, **1st public building heated by steam,** opened in Boston.

New York State Constitution abolished the right of a landlord to live in **feudal style** on a manor where he required his tenants to buy at his store and to apply for written permission to entertain a guest at home for the day.

The **exodus of the Mormons** from Nauvoo, after the animosity of their Illinois neighbors had erupted into virtual war,

POLITICS AND GOVERNMENT; WAR; DISASTERS; VITAL STATISTICS.

BOOKS; PAINTING; DRAMA; ARCHITECTURE; SCULPTURE.

1847. Treason against the state, however, was still considered a capital crime.

May 13 Mexican War began with U.S. declaration of war. War measures passed over Whig opposition, which increased as the War progressed.

June 14 Bear Flag Revolt began with proclamation by group of California settlers of the Republic of California. Name came from the "Republic's" standard, which included the name of the Republic, a grizzly bear, and a star, on a field of white cloth. Capt. Frémont lent moral support to revolt. On Aug. 17 Com. Stockton issued proclamation declaring the annexation of California by the U.S., and establishing himself as governor.

June 15 Oregon Treaty signed. It established the boundary (49th parallel) between U.S. and British Northwest Territory. Idaho, Oregon, and Washington, and parts of Montana and Wyoming comprised U.S. acquisition. This was a compromise from the campaign slogan of Polk in 1844: "Fifty-four Forty or Fight."

Aug. Wilmot Proviso designed by David Wilmot of Pennsylvania to be tacked to the bill in which Pres. Polk asked for $2,000,000 to buy additional territory from Mexico. The proviso provided that slavery should never exist in this territory, an unnecessary stipulation because the territory was totally unsuited to slavery. It caused much ill feeling, did not pass.

Sept. 25 Monterey captured by forces under command of Gen. Taylor after battle of 4 days.

Dec. 28 Iowa admitted as state, 29th to join Union.

industrial architecture in 1st half of 19th century.

Grace Church, designed by James Renwick, built at Broadway and 10th St., New York. One of 1st Gothic Revival churches in U.S.

1st novel of **Herman Melville,** *Typee,* published. It is a romance of the South Seas, recounting the actual experience of the author on an island in the Marquesas. He contrasts the brutal life aboard ship with the simple, uncivilized humanity of the Polynesians.

Great art of **Nathaniel Hawthorne** seen in his collection of short stories, *Mosses from An Old Manse.* Together with an earlier collection, *Twice-told Tales, Second Series* (1842), all the themes for which he is known were touched upon: isolation, secret guilt, spiritual arrogance, the search for perfection.

Feb. 9 1st play to introduce **mountain folk type** of North Carolina and Georgia, *The Hoosier at the Circus* by a playwright named Carrol.

Apr. 27 Virginia Minstrels of Albert Christy opened at Palmo's Opera House in New York city. Christy's minstrels were acknowledged to have brought minstrelsy to its highest peak of maturity as an entertainment form.

1847

Jan. 16 Oregon Bill providing for territorial government of that area passed the House. It excluded slavery under the restrictions of the Northwest Ordinance and was tabled in the Senate.

Feb. 22–23 Gen. **Zachary Taylor** de-

Robert Ball Hughes, American sculptor, cast **1st life-sized bronze statue** in U.S. A likeness of the astronomer Nathaniel Bowditch, it was placed on his grave in cemetery at Mt. Auburn, Cambridge, Mass. In 1886 the original casting was replaced by

in 1851. University of Lewisburg became Bucknell University in 1886.

Mar. 26 Colgate University 1st chartered in Hamilton, N.Y., as Madison University. University renamed Colgate in 1890. It had been founded Mar. 5, 1819, under Baptist auspices.

Apr. 10 Fordham University 1st chartered in Fordham, N.Y., as St. John's College. Established 1841 under Catholic auspices, college granted its 1st degrees in 1846, became Fordham University in 1907.

Apr. 13 One of the most famous eastern railroads, **The Pennsylvania Railroad,** chartered.

June 17 Grinnell College chartered in Davenport, Iowa, as Iowa College under the joint auspices of Congregational and Presbyterian interests. 1st degrees issued in 1854. College was moved to Grinnell, Iowa, in 1859 and renamed Grinnell College in 1909.

Sept. 10 1st **sewing machine** in U.S. with an eye-pointed needle patented by Elias Howe, the acknowledged father of the modern sewing machine.

Oct. 16 1st public demonstration of anesthesia by William T. G. Morton, Boston dentist, who administered sulphuric ether during an operation performed by John Collins Warren at the Massachusetts General Hospital. A neck tumor was removed. Earlier on Sept. 30 Morton had painlessly removed an ulcerated tooth from a patient anesthetized by ether.

came on the heels of a hard winter of preparation. They had turned all of their homes into workshops and equipped 12,000 wagons to carry their families and belongings. Beginning in February, small groups, who were ready for the road, began to leave Nauvoo. They crossed the Mississippi by flatboats. Later in the month the river froze over and subsequent groups were able to cross on the ice. By the end of the month, 2,000 men, women and children were in Iowa and ready to go on. The sprawling caravan was broken down into companies of 50 wagons. The leading parties advanced slowly, setting up resting spots all along the route where the tired men and cattle could recover from the ravages of ice, snow and rain. By the middle of May, 16,000 Mormons had crossed the Mississippi. The stragglers cleared out of Nauvoo by September. Through the fall and following winter, the main body of the wagon train was, from fear of the winter and the Indians on the plain ahead, bogged down in the bottom lands of the Missouri, near Council Bluffs.

Orson Squire Fowler published *Matrimony; or, Phrenology and Physiology applied to the Selection of Congenial Companions for Life.* This book sold well, and was noted for its motto on the title page: "Natural waists or no wives."

June 19 1st recorded baseball game in history played at Elysian Field, Hoboken, N.J., between the New York Nine and the Knickerbockers. The New York Nine won, 23–1, but Davis, their pitcher, was fined 6 cents for swearing at the umpire. Alexander Joy Cartwright, founder of Knickerbockers, wrote rules for the game, which are still followed in large part today.

1847

Jan. 15 Lawrence College chartered as Lawrence Institute in Appleton, Wis. Founded under Methodist auspices, institute became Lawrence University in 1849, issued its 1st degrees in 1857, and became Lawrence College in 1908.

Union of high society and opera in New York city typified by subscribed construction of the Astor Place Opera House, a very ostentatious structure in which a huge, gaudy chandelier blocked out a view of the stage from the 50¢ balcony seats.

POLITICS AND GOVERNMENT; WAR; DISASTERS; VITAL STATISTICS.	BOOKS; PAINTING; DRAMA; ARCHITECTURE; SCULPTURE.

feated Gen. Santa Anna at the battle of Buena Vista.

Feb.–Mar. **Cannibalism** broke out in starved camps of Donner party caught by snow slides in the Rockies. The bodies of the recently dead were devoured when provisions were exhausted and starvation seemed imminent. Impassable terrain along a new trail, "Hastings' Cut-off," proved disastrous for the party.

Mar. 9 Gen. Winfield Scott landed on beaches south of **Vera Cruz** with force of 10,000 troops. At that time Vera Cruz was most powerful fortress in Western Hemisphere. This was **1st large-scale amphibious operation** in U.S. military history. After 2 weeks spent in securing his position, Scott began siege of Vera Cruz Mar. 22. Fortress surrendered Mar. 27, and was occupied Mar. 29.

Apr. 8 Gen. Scott moved toward **Mexico City.**

Apr. 15 Nicholas P. Trist appointed commissioner to negotiate **peace with Mexico.**

Apr. 18 Gen. Winfield Scott on his way to Mexico City, met and defeated a Mexican force of about 13,000 at **Cerro Gordo.**

June 6 **Peace negotiations** with Mexico begun through the British minister, Charles Bankhead.

July 22 **1st Mormon emigrants** arrived in Utah, settling what later was to become Salt Lake City.

Aug. 20 Gen. Winfield Scott defeated a Mexican army of 20,000 at **Churubusco.**

Sept. **Native American Party** convention at Philadelphia, Pa., nominated Gen. Zachary Taylor for president and Henry A.S. Dearborn of Massachusetts for vice-president.

Sept. 8 Gen. Winfield Scott defeated an estimated 12,000 Mexicans at battle of **Molino del Rey.**

Sept. 13 Gen. Winfield Scott took possession of fortified hill of **Chapultepec,** last obstacle before Mexico City.

another made in Paris by Gruet Jeune. A plaster cast is in Boston Athenaeum.

Famous mystical poem on death is **Edgar Allan Poe's** "Ulalume," which was composed after the death of his young wife. In a dialogue with his soul Poe tried to console himself, but was only confronted with the finality of the grave.

Herman Melville continued his fictional treatment of the South Seas with *Omoo,* a tale set on the island of Tahiti. Romantic characters like beachcombers, consuls, mutinous sailors, native dancers, etc., are introduced.

An idyllic tale in verse, *Evangeline,* by **Henry Wadsworth Longfellow.** Based on an account told to the poet by Nathaniel Hawthorne, the story concerns the fate of 2 lovers in French Acadie, who are separated when the French are expelled from Nova Scotia. It is a tale of ideal, virginal love that maintains itself through disappointments and frustrations.

Most prolific of Southern playwrights, **Nathaniel H. Bannister,** died impoverished in New York. His plays usually reflect romantic vogue for foreign settings: *Gaulantus* (1837); *England's Iron Days* (1837) uses Anglo-Saxon times; *Gentleman of Lyons* (1838).

The "Wedgwood of America," **Christopher Webber Fenton,** founded United States Pottery. His ability to sketch led him to produce variegated forms and designs in ceramics: cow-shaped creamers, water pitchers shaped like dachshunds, lions, cats, etc. He also used new materials.

Unitarian Church of Lexington, Mass., built by Isaac Melvin. Good example of mid-19th century ornate style.

Plymouth Church of the Pilgrims, an example of late meeting house style, built in Brooklyn, N.Y. Noted chiefly as the

218

SCIENCE; INDUSTRY; ECONOMICS; EDUCATION; RELIGION; PHILOSOPHY.

Jan. 18 **Taylor University** chartered in Fort Wayne, Ind., as Fort Wayne Female College. Established under Methodist auspices in 1846, college became Fort Wayne Methodist Episcopal College some time between 1852 and 1855, moved to Upland, Ind., in 1893 when it was renamed Taylor University.

Feb. 16 **Tulane University** of Louisiana chartered in New Orleans as University of Louisiana. Partially supported by the state, university awarded its 1st degrees in 1857, assumed its present name in 1884. Tulane traces its history to Sept. 25, 1834, when a group of physicians 1st published plans for the Medical College of Louisiana, which opened Jan. 5, 1835. 1st degrees for medicine conferred in this region Mar., 1836.

Feb. 25 **State University of Iowa** chartered in Iowa City, Iowa, as a state university. 1st degrees granted in 1858.

Apr. 16 Congress turned over Washington-Baltimore telegraph line to newly-founded Magnetic Telegraph Company of Maryland, the **1st telegraph company** in U.S.

May 1 **Smithsonian Institution** formally dedicated in Washington.

May 7 **American Medical Association** organized in Philadelphia. The previous year representatives of all national medical societies and schools attended a national medical convention in New York city and appointed the following year for a second convention. The A.M.A. grew out of the discussions and decisions of the Philadelphia convention.

July 1 Congress authorized **1st issue of adhesive postage stamps.**

July 24 **Brigham Young**, with a party of 143, reached the valley of Great Salt Lake. The flight of Joseph Smith from Missouri to Illinois ended with a quarrel among the factions of the **Mormon Church,**

SPORTS; FASHIONS; POPULAR ENTERTAINMENT; FOLKLORE; SOCIETY.

Vermont law guaranteed to the wife full ownership of real estate held by her at the time of her marriage or gained by gift or bequest afterward. Husband's consent was still necessary, however, if the wife wished to sell or transfer ownership of this property. Still, this marked a slight improvement in the **legal status of women.**

George V. Callendines, author of *The Geometrical Regulator, or Circular Transfer; being a Scientific Guide for Draughting, Balancing and Cutting Pantaloons,* was wroth with **tailors.** Not 1 in 20 of them, Callendines declared, knew how to fold a new pair of pantaloons correctly.

Felix O.C. Darley published a pamphlet in which he described a strange freak from Texas named Eli Bowen who was born without legs, lived with bears, snakes, and wolves in the woods, to which he would escape when approached by strangers. He overcame his shyness eventually to become a well-paid **circus freak.**

Discovery of a comet by Maria Mitchell with the attendant recognition and prestige of later researches made her the **idol of many women** of this period.

Lyman Cobb published his *The Evil Tendencies of Corporal Punishment as a Means of Moral Discipline in Families and Schools* in which he listed some 60 arguments against the traditional educational practice of **flogging boys and girls.** Cobb, an advanced educator, even announced that he didn't want his pupils to suffer over tedious reading. His views were widely held by those turning against the old fashion "school of the rod."

Horace Bushnell, pastor of North Church, Hartford, Conn., argued in his *Discourses on Christian Nurture* that a child who was loved enough would not have a sinful nature. *The Discourses* quickly became a controversial subject.

True Politeness; a Hand-book of Etiquette for Ladies, a popular **etiquette manual** of this period, inveighed against the *double entendre* on the part of the woman, "especially when perpetrated in the pres-

Sept. 14 Gen. Winfield Scott entered Mexico City. Battalion of U.S. Marines began guard of "halls of Montezuma."

Nov. Liberty Party nominated John P. Hale for president and Leicester King for vice-president at their convention in New York city. Hale later withdrew from the race in favor of Martin Van Buren.

Nov. 19 Collision of steamers *Talisman* and *Tempest* caused the death of 100 persons on the Ohio R.

Nov. 22 200 Dutch immigrants died as a result of fire aboard the *Phoenix* on Lake Michigan near the end of a 4000-mi. journey.

church of Rev. Henry Ward Beecher (1813–87) and as a center of abolitionist activity before the Civil War.

Sept. 11 "Susanna," by Stephen Foster, performed for 1st time at a concert in the Eagle Saloon, Pittsburgh. It became Foster's 1st widespread success, being taken up by minstrel troupes and carried to the west coast by '49ers.

1848

1st representative to Vatican appointed. He was Jacob L. Martin.

Purchase of Cuba from Spain suggested by Pres. Polk. He offered $100 million.

Free-Soil Party organized at a convention in Buffalo, N.Y. It urged the prohibition of slavery in the new territory added to the Union after the Mexican War. The party nominated Martin Van Buren of New York and Charles F. Adams of Massachusetts, but they were defeated by Zachary Taylor and Millard Fillmore.

3 Chinese immigrants reached San Francisco; they, the 1st, had sailed on the *Eagle*. During next 2 years several Chinese laborers who had escaped from Peru reached the West coast, and immigration from China increased. By 1852 number of Chinese in U.S. was estimated at 18,000.

Jan. 24 Gold discovered at Sutter's Mill, near Sacramento, Calif., resulting in the great "gold rush" of 1849.

Feb. 2 War with Mexico ended with signing of **Treaty of Guadalupe-Hidalgo.** U.S. casualties included 1721 dead and 4102 wounded. 11,155 died of disease. Total cost of war was $97½ million. Mexico ceded Texas to the Rio Grande, New Mexico, and upper California in return for which Mexico was granted $15 million.

Membership in **American Art Union** had grown to the point where the annual lottery distributed more than 450 paintings, for which the artists had been paid $40,907.

Edgar Allan Poe published *Eureka.* *Eureka* was not a popular work. Subtitled *A Prose Poem,* it proved among the most obscure of Poe's writings and was not calculated to please the public taste, which was soon to reject Melville's *Moby Dick.* Poe, at the height of the style which revolutionized the use of the exclamation point, essayed a philosophical explanation of the origin and nature of the universe. He was an avid, if uncritical, reader of scientific literature, and tried to put all his knowledge in *Eureka.* The result was more successful as poetry than as science, but was not insignificant as an effort to see the world steadily and whole. Poe was deeply impressed by Newton's theory of the oneness of the universe, and he was trying to achieve a glimpse of the essential unity underlying all things.

The Oak Openings, a novel about Indians and bearhunting beside Lake Michigan, published by **James Fenimore Cooper.** The novel, which did not attain the popularity it merited, drew upon the author's

the imprisonment of Smith by order of the Illinois governor, and his assassination by a mob, which stormed the jail at Carthage and shot him and his brother to death. Brigham Young was chosen to succeed Joseph Smith as leader of the Mormons. Hostility towards the Church continued and violence increased. Young was compelled to begin the Western trek of The Latter-Day Saints, which is, in fact and in legend, among the great epics of the American West. When Salt Lake City was established Young returned to lead the rest of the eastern Mormons from Council Bluffs, Iowa, to their permanent headquarters in Utah.

ence of men." Manual continued, "it is, in general, bad taste for ladies to kiss each other in the presence of gentlemen with whom they are but slightly acquainted." Ladies were warned also, "Never sing more than one or two songs consecutively," and, "Be very cautious of giving a gentleman a letter of introduction to a lady,—it may be the means of settling the weal or woe of the persons for life."

July 26 Moses Gerrish Farmer demonstrated a **miniature electric train** in Dover, N.H. Children were charged a penny a ride. In 1851 Farmer devised for Boston the 1st electric fire alarm system.

1848

New York newspaper group organized **The Associated Press.** A.P. was a result of the impatience of Moses Beach, publisher of *The New York Sun,* with the established news lines. He experimented with ways of getting the news faster, including the use of carrier pigeons. Reports from the Mexican War came in so slowly that he finally set up his own express. The arrangement was successful enough to convince other New York publishers to carry the expense of a private news gathering service. The Associated Press followed from this original proposition.

Brussels Peace Congress, organized by Elihu Burritt, convened in Belgium. Burritt, editor of the abolitionist-temperance (a familiar team in that period) organ, *Christian Citizen,* went to England in 1846 to promote the **League of Universal Brotherhood.** He traveled widely and interviewed many notable figures, soliciting support for a peace congress and setting up local groups of agitators. The Brussels congress was followed by periodic conventions in other major European cities. Burritt attended them all and advanced his proposals for an international court of arbitration. In this period of revolution, wars, and rumors of war, Burritt won

John Humphrey Noyes, a reformer from Vermont, established the **Oneida Community** near Seneca Lake in New York as an experimental community. This settlement was unique among American Utopias in that it eventually based its economy primarily on manufacturing rather than agriculture. Noyes insisted upon full equality of the sexes. The women cut their hair and wore bloomer costumes which symbolized their freedom from restrictive fashions. Noyes wished to eliminate competition entirely and substitute a co-operative way of life. He was an able manager and his community prospered to such an extent that in 1881 when the experiment was abandoned, the community was reorganized as a corporation, the Oneida Community, Ltd., which manufactured a number of products and concentrated eventually on silverware.

Baseball rules altered to provide that a runner was out at 1st base if ball was held by a fielder on the bag before the runner could reach it.

New York State granted to women property rights equal to those of men. This was most significant improvement in **woman's legal status** up to this time but New York's example was not copied elsewhere.

| POLITICS AND GOVERNMENT; WAR; DISASTERS; VITAL STATISTICS. | BOOKS; PAINTING; DRAMA; ARCHITECTURE; SCULPTURE. |

This territory now includes California, Arizona, Nevada, Utah, parts of New Mexico, Colorado, and Wyoming.

Feb. 23 John Quincy Adams, 6th president of U.S., died at age of 80. He was a foreign minister under Washington, a U.S. Senator, Secretary of State under Monroe, and president from 1825 to 1829. He was U.S. Representative for Massachusetts from 1831 till his death.

May 22–26 Democratic National Convention nominated Lewis Cass of Michigan for presidency at convention in Baltimore, Md. His running mate was William O. Butler of Kentucky.

May 29 Wisconsin admitted as state, 30th to join Union.

June 2 Liberty League, an abolition organization, named Gerrit Smith of New York as their presidential candidate at a convention in Rochester, N.Y. Charles E. Foote of Michigan was named to vicepresidency.

June 3 Senate approved treaty with New Granada (now Colombia) by which U.S. was assured travel rights in that region in return for a guarantee that the neutrality of the route would be maintained. This right of way across the **Isthmus of Panama** was invaluable to American commerce.

June 7–9 Whig National Convention at Philadelphia, Pa., nominated Gen. Zachary Taylor of Louisiana for the presidency and Millard Fillmore of New York for the vice-presidency.

June 22 The Barnburners, an antiadministration splinter group of the Democratic Party, withdrew from the National Convention at Baltimore, Md., and met at Utica, N.Y. They named for their ticket Martin Van Buren of New York and Henry Dodge of Wisconsin.

July 27 Clayton Compromise passed by Senate. It organized the territories of Oregon, New Mexico, and California on what was basically an antislavery government.

experiences the year before during a trip to the borderlands of the West.

James Russell Lowell had an *annus mirabilis* with publication of 3 major poetical works. *The Biglow Papers* (First Series) consist of 9 poems which humorously voice opposition to the war with Mexico and the annexation of Texas. The Yankee dialect of Ezekiel and Hosea Biglow immediately caught popular fancy. *A Fable for Critics* in the tradition of Pope's *Dunciad* and Byron's *Vision of Judgment* dealt with contemporary writers and critics. He also published *Poems: Second Series* and *The Vision of Sir Launfal.*

American publication of *Wuthering Heights* by **Emily Brontë.** Not very popular at first, but eventually sold about 1,000,000 copies. Probably movie dramatization in 1939 accounts in great part for its tremendous sales. The recent Pocket Book edition has sold 700,000 copies.

American publication of the immediately popular *Jane Eyre* by **Charlotte Brontë.** A classic story of the love between a governess and her married master was sensational literary material in these days. It has sold at least 1,000,000 copies. Movie version in 1944 increased sales tremendously.

Famous *Shoes of Fortune and Other Tales* by **Hans Christian Andersen** 1st published in U.S. These are the 1st of those stories which eventually constituted Andersen's classic *Fairy Tales.*

Cast-iron building, designed by James Bogardus who originated the method of construction, built in New York. Castiron front covered masonry walls.

1st Congregational Church, from designs by **Richard Bond,** built at Haverhill, Mass. Interesting for its precise detail in the Gothic Revival manner.

wide attention and sympathy on both sides of the Atlantic.

John Humphrey Noyes established **Perfectionist Community** at Oneida, New York. The colony attempted to revive the communism of the early Christian communities; but, under the spell of Noyes' private revelation of the nature of the deity, it subscribed to such unconventional marital and extramarital arrangements that they were soon forced by public opinion to pull up stakes and camp out in Canada.

Power loom to weave Brussels and tapestry carpets invented by Erastus B. Bigelow.

Jan. 3 **Girard College** in Philadelphia opened its doors. It was a free home, secondary school, and junior college for fatherless boys, founded by Stephen Girard.

Mar. 10 Augustinian College of **Villanova** chartered in Villanova, Pa., under Catholic auspices. 1st degrees awarded in 1855. College has come to be called more simply, "Villanova," but official designation still stands on its documents.

June 27 Probably 1st **"air conditioning"** installed in theater. Broadway Theater Bill had following notice: "The public is respectfully informed that an Extensive Apparatus for the Perfect Ventilation of the Entire Building is now in operation. The Steam Power by which it is impelled, being capable of conveying to the Audience part alone, 3000 Feet of Cool Air per minute, thus rendering the Establishment during the hottest and most crowded nights in all respects comfortable. The machinery patented by Mr. J. E. Coffee."

July 26 **University of Wisconsin** chartered in Madison, Wis., as a state university. 1st degrees granted in 1854.

Sept. **American Association for the Advancement of Science** founded. The charter of the association expressed a determination to "advance science in the New

John B. Curtis of Bangor, Me., manufactured **1st chewing gum commercially sold** in U.S. Curtis later traveled as a drummer throughout western territories and is reputed to be 1st commercial traveler for an Eastern firm in the West.

Jan. 24 **Discovery of gold** on the estate of John Sutter made California and broke Sutter. From the day that he began the settlement of Nueva Helvetia, at the juncture of the American and Sacramento Rivers, Sutter prospered. He built up a princely seat where everything he touched burst into flower. Then gold was found. The workers on the estate left to look for gold. Every kind of adventurer squatted on his lawns. In 4 years he was ruined. For the rest of his life, Sutter petitioned the state and federal governments for aid, and finally died while the bill he sought was being argued in the House of Representatives. The defeat of Sutter was also the defeat of a civility which California could not then afford to cherish. The boom was on, and other men with different visions were needed. Nowhere was the reversal more evident than in the list of the literary personalities who began or established their careers in the wake of the gold rush. Mark Twain, Joaquin Miller, Bret Harte, Ambrose Bierce, George Horatio Derby, Charles Warren Stoddard, Edward Rowland Sill were all in the ranks of the uprooted who sought and found inspiration in the volatile new atmosphere. The printers of California were kept busy, for there was much to be said and many voices. Culture came to California overnight, like riches. Amid the clamor there was little dissent from the prevalent eager refrain. A single strong dismissal jars the record. The Mormon Church in Salt Lake City, having heard the reports about gold in California, cautioned its children to hoard up other riches: "The true use of gold is for paving streets. . . . When the Saints shall have preached the gospel . . . and built up cities enough, the Lord will open up the way for a supply of gold to

| POLITICS AND GOVERNMENT; WAR; DISASTERS; VITAL STATISTICS. | BOOKS; PAINTING; DRAMA; ARCHITECTURE; SCULPTURE. |

The bill was tabled by the House the following day.

Aug 24 200 Americans lost their lives off Carnarvonshire, North Wales when the *Ocean Monarch* caught fire.

Nov. 7 Gen. Zachary Taylor won **presidential election** with vote of 1,360,101. Cass received 1,220,544 votes; Van Buren, 291,263. This was the 1st election held on a uniform election day under the Elections Act of 1845.

Feb. 15 Vogue for plays dealing with city life—"crooks," firemen, showgirls, etc.—introduced by **A Glance at New York** by Benjamin A. Baker, with central character Mose the foreman. In episodic fashion aspects of city were put on boards, even to the display of firemen at work. In short order there appeared a *Mose in California* and a *Mose in Philadelphia*.

1849

Feb. 28 The first shipload of ocean traveling **gold seekers** arrived at San Francisco.

Mar. 3 **Department of the Interior created** in federal government to meet the needs and demands of Western settlers who wanted new policies on the administration of public lands and Indians, policies which would enable the white settlers to exploit the lands more easily. Originally named the Home Department.

Mar. 3 **Minnesota** established as a territory. Slavery was prohibited.

Mar. 5 **Zachary Taylor,** 12th President, inaugurated. He was the 2nd and last Whig to be voted to the Presidency. He died after 1 year and 4 months in office.

Mar. 10 **Missouri legislature** took the position that "the right to prohibit slavery in any territory belongs exclusively to the people thereof."

May 17 More than 400 buildings and 27 steamships destroyed in **St. Louis, Mo., fire.**

June 15 **James K. Polk** died at the age of 53. He is buried at Nashville, Tenn.

Sept. 1–Oct. 13 **California convention,** meeting in Monterey, drew up a constitution prohibiting slavery and requested admission to the Union.

Oct. British naval vessel seized **Tigre Island** off the west coast of the Isthmus of

1st publication of Thoreau's **Civil Disobedience,** an antiauthoritarian work in which is expressed a fear of the tyranny of the state in a democracy.

2nd Publication of *Poems* by **John G. Whittier.** But this favorite American poet did not become popular until after the Civil War. The famous poem "Snow-Bound" was important in securing Whittier's reputation.

May 10 **Spectacular riot** erupted outside the Astor Place Opera House where the celebrated British actor, Macready, was performing. Angry crowds reacted both against the snobbish requirements of dress for admission to the theater and Macready's scornful public utterances on the vulgarity of American life. His feud with the popular American actor, Edwin Forrest, who asserted the cause of the masses both in his stage roles and in his public statements, only added to the indignation of the common citizens. Clubs, paving stones, and brickbats were used to shatter the windows of the theater during Macready's performance. Troops were summoned and when order could not be re-

World" in every possible way. The association developed as a joint endeavor of American and Canadian scientists.

Nov. 1 **1st medical school for women** opened with enrollment of 12. It was promoted by Samuel Gregory, a pioneer in medical education for women. Known as the Boston Female Medical School, it was merged in 1874 with the Boston University School of Medicine.

the perfect satisfaction of his children. . . . Let them not be over-anxious, for the treasures of the earth are in the Lord's storehouses."

July 19 1st convention of record in world to meet for purpose of discussing **rights of women** assembled at Seneca Falls, N.Y., and adopted a Declaration of Sentiments written in the prose style of the Declaration of Independence and following a feminist line.

1849

American Horologe Company, later the Waltham Watch Company, established at Roxbury, Mass. It was the 1st permanently successful American watch business.

Safety pin patented by Walter Hunt of New York city.

Elizabeth Blackwell became **1st woman in U.S. to receive medical degree;** in 1853 she and her sister founded Infirmary for Women and Children in New York city.

Feb. 13 **Otterbein College** chartered in Westerville, Ohio, as Otterbein University under United Brethren auspices. 1st degrees granted in 1857. University became Otterbein College in 1917. It had been founded in 1847.

Feb. 27 **William Jewell College** chartered in Liberty, Mo., under Baptist auspices. 1st degrees granted in 1855.

Nov. 22 **Austin College** chartered in

Jan. **Amelia Bloomer,** celebrated American feminist, published 1st issues of *Lily,* a journal devoted to the causes of temperance and women's rights.

In Philadelphia a Mr. Peabody opened a shop where he did portraitures in cameo. Peabody had a great success, which was 1 of the last in his line of work. The **cameo portrait** was soon due to be displaced by the daguerreotype.

There were at least 6 periodicals which were exclusively spiritualist publications. In the next decade **spiritualism** caught on well enough to become a national cult. The seance quickly became prevalent.

The American Fistiana published. It was a history of **American boxing** which listed the main events of the 40 years previous and gave an account of the $10,000 purse match between Sullivan and Hyer.

The Great Chinese Museum opened on Broadway between Spring and Prince Streets, New York city. It was the only museum of its kind in the country. All of the typical features of Chinese life were displayed, including a large number of life-size Chinamen of all classes who presided over a collection of hundreds of Chinese paintings, homes and house furnishings, models of pagodas, temples and bridges, and specimens of Chinese manufactures.

Feb. 7 Tom Hyer, unofficial **American heavyweight champion,** met Yankee Sullivan, an Englishman who was touring the

POLITICS AND GOVERNMENT; WAR; DISASTERS; VITAL STATISTICS.	BOOKS; PAINTING; DRAMA; ARCHITECTURE; SCULPTURE.

Panama. Great Britain disavowed the seizure, but the situation between U.S. and Britain became explosive.

stored by their presence, they were ordered to fire, killing approximately 20 rioters and wounding many more.

1850

7th U.S. Census set population of the 31 states of the union at 23,191,876. America's center of population located 23 miles southeast of Parkersburg, W. Va.

Number of immigrants to America in 1850 totaled 369,980.

Jan. 29 Henry Clay introduced 8 resolutions in Congress from which eventually came the famous **Compromise of 1850,** perhaps the most important American historical event of the year. Neither the proslavery nor the antislavery elements in Congress commanded enough strength to enact their legislation, so the Compromise was an attempt to settle their differences. 5 Bills, which constitute the Compromise, were eventually passed.

Mar. 7 **Daniel Webster** supported Clay's Compromise in a speech to the Senate in which he accepted the **Fugitive Slave Bill.** Whittier had Webster in mind when he wrote in his poem "Ichabod,"

"All else is gone; from those great eyes
The soul has fled;
When faith is lost, when honor dies
The man is dead."

Apr. 19 **Clayton-Bulwer treaty** signed. U.S. and Great Britain agreed to the neutrality of a projected canal to be built across Central America. Both governments contracted to act as joint protectors over the territory, while neither was to establish any military post on, or assume control over, any part of Central America.

May 22 **Rescue expedition** sailed to Arctic in search of **Sir John Franklin,** an English explorer who was lost in an attempt to find the Northwest Passage. Henry Grinnell bore expense of fitting out two vessels, the *Advance* and the *Rescue,* which sailed under command of Lt. De Haven. Though Grinnell Land was dis-

Louis Moreau Gottschalk, American pianist and composer, toured French provinces, Switzerland, and Savoy; was widely acclaimed.

Founding of **Harper's Magazine** in New York. It promised "to place within the reach of the great mass of American people the unbounded treasures of the periodical literature." Most of the contributions were serializations of the English novels of Dickens, Thackeray, and Eliot. In most cases *Harper's* paid the author more than the English publishers did.

A study of the role of the great man underlies **Emerson's** series of essays entitled *Representative Men.* Influenced perhaps by Carlyle, he discusses the lives and works of Plato, Swedenborg, Montaigne, Shakespeare, Napoleon, and Goethe. Self-reliance is the keynote of their careers, to which is added insight and honesty.

Classic novel *The Scarlet Letter* by **Nathaniel Hawthorne** a best seller from the beginning. 4000 copies sold in first 10 days; 2nd printing immediately sold out. Its then daring subject matter accounted in part for its immediate success.

Significant novel of the period, *White-Jacket,* by **Herman Melville** revealed the inhuman treatment of sailors on U.S. warships.

Early American genre painter who, like Washington Irving, characterized country life was **William Sidney Mount.** *Who'll Turn the Grindstone* reveals him at his best. A father points a fist at his awestruck boy. Details of farm are sketched in. Mount was a popular painter, known as much for his portraits as for his country scenes of Nassau County, Long Island, N.Y.

SCIENCE; INDUSTRY; ECONOMICS; EDUCATION; RELIGION; PHILOSOPHY.	SPORTS; FASHIONS; POPULAR ENTERTAINMENT; FOLKLORE; SOCIETY.

Huntsville, Tex., under Presbyterian auspices. 1st degrees issued in 1850. College moved to Sherman, Tex., in 1876.

country taking on all comers, and knocked him out. This was Hyer's last fight as no one else challenged him.

1850

Cholera epidemic swept through the Middle West after having passed through the South in the previous year. Cholera broke out in Europe for 1st time in 19th century. It had caused serious epidemics in Asia in the past, but did not reach the West until it was carried by shipping lines after the Asian epidemics of 1826 and 1837. It appeared 1st in Marseilles, then gradually spread through the continent. From New Orleans it fanned out in a similar way through U.S. and was checked in successive advances only by seasonal cold.

Aaron Lufkin Dennison established factory to manufacture **1st commercial 8-day watch.** Mainspring was too long, however, and model was abandoned in favor of 36-hour watch.

1st agricultural binder in U.S. invented by John E. Heath.

James N. Richmond, glassmaker of Cheshire, Mass., built glass house which attracted visitors from many areas. Later Richmond became 1st to make **plate glass** in America.

Fares for **immigrants** to America dropped as low as $10, but living conditions in the steerages of ocean vessels remained atrocious until late in the century.

1st proposal for creation of a **park** in New York city large enough to provide a healthy atmosphere for all the citizens, such park considered as a "central park."

Growing accessibility of American **newspapers** reflected in rise of annual distribution of papers for each person in America to 22 as compared with 8 in 1828.

Nicholas Pike, introduced 8 pairs of Eng-

Madame Restell, a notorious **abortionist** in New York, advertised herself as a "woman's physician," thus discouraging many women from entering the study of medicine.

Girls hired as clerks for 1st time in America by department stores in Philadelphia.

Mrs. Amelia Bloomer, editor of the *Lily*, woman's rights and temperance paper, began to wear **"bloomers,"** which were full trousers gathered at the ankle under a loose knee-length skirt. Bloomers had been worn before, having been originated by Mrs. Elizabeth Smith Miller. By Spring of 1851 they had become very popular costume for active women despite protests against immodesty.

Phrase, **"Sold down the river"** entered American idiom. Slaves on the older plantations, where treatment was relatively good and where affection for the land and the owner often developed, contrasted their situation with that of slaves on the Mississippi and in the Deep South. To be sold down the river meant being cut off from family and home—a dreadful fate. Term later was used to characterize any summary action that left out feelings of those affected.

Memorable phrase **"I would rather be right than be President"** uttered by Henry Clay in Congress during his impassioned plea for the Compromises proposed by him between the slavery and free factions. Bitter because of his failure to achieve the presidency, he threw off his famous remark when taunted by his colleagues.

18,456 people sheltered in 8,141 cellars in New York city. By 1856 tenements had been built to house some of these unfortunates.

227

POLITICS AND GOVERNMENT; WAR; DISASTERS; VITAL STATISTICS.	BOOKS; PAINTING; DRAMA; ARCHITECTURE; SCULPTURE.

covered, expedition was unsuccessful in its main purpose.

May 25 **New Mexico,** impatient for statehood, formed own state government. Convention set boundaries of state, banned slavery, applied for statehood.

June **2 successive fires** in San Francisco destroyed property to the amount of several million dollars. Losses believed cause of panic in San Francisco market in Sept.

June 17 **300 lives lost** when steamer *Griffith* burned on Lake Erie.

July 1 **1st overland mail delivery** west of the Missouri R. organized on the basis of a monthly delivery from Independence, Mo., to Salt Lake City, Utah.

July 8 **Overland gold rush** to California through Fort Laramie involved 42,300 emigrants and 9,720 wagons between Jan. 1 and July 8. Reflecting gold rush of 1849–50, more than 9/10 of the population of California were male. Even 9 years later proportion of men to women was 6 to 1.

July 9 Pres. **Zachary Taylor** died. Vice-president **Millard Fillmore** became president on July 10th. Taylor was the 2nd and last of the Whig party to be elected to the presidency.

Sept. 9 **California admitted** as a free state, the 31st state to be admitted, and giving the free states a majority in the Senate. This was one of the bargains of the **Compromise of 1850** and a concession to the North.

Sept. 9 **Texas and New Mexico Act** passed. The Act established the Texas boundaries, authorized payment of $10,-000,000 for relinquishing her claims to territories beyond the new state lines, and established the boundaries of New Mexico territory. As a concession to the South, New Mexico would be a free or a slave state according to her constitution upon admission to the Union. This option plan was part of **Compromise of 1850.**

Sept. 9 **Utah Act** established territorial boundaries of Utah. It was to be a free

Painting which gave subsequent generations their conception of history is *Washington Crossing the Delaware* by German-born American painter, **Emanuel Leutze.** Done while he was in Germany, faces of boatmen are more German than American, and the river used as a model is the Rhine rather than the Delaware. But fortitude and courage are communicated in the figures, the moral being the essential worth of the painting.

Celebrated clown and pantomimist, George L. Fox, made his New York debut. Greatest fame achieved in later years with burlesques of Hamlet and Macbeth, thoroughly enjoyed by Edwin Booth.

Famous stage Yankee, John Edmond Owens, also made his debut this year in New York as Mr. Fright in *Crimson Crimes.* In later years, Mr. Owens' Yankee roles were particularly well liked in England.

1st publication of *Weekly Oregonian* in Portland, Ore., and of *Deseret News* in Salt Lake City, Utah. The latter was a publication of the Mormon Church.

Final design of **U.S. Capitol** by Thomas U. Walter reflected influence of Greek Revival in American architecture.

Mar. 18 Romantic tragedy represented in play by **Charles James Cannon** *The Oath of Office,* set in 15th century. Other high-flown period pieces of time are **James Pilgrim's** *Robert Emmet* (1853), **Samuel Y. Levy's** *Italian Bride* (1857) and **Julia Ward Howe's** *Leonora* (1857), *Hyppolytus* (written 1864).

July 22 Vogue of plays dealing with urban life occasioned productions of many plays contrasting rich and poor. **S. D. Johnson** in his *New York Fireman and Bond Street Heiress* plays up this aspect. A Philadelphia play (1850) is entitled *Democracy and Aristocracy.*

SCIENCE; INDUSTRY; ECONOMICS; EDUCATION; RELIGION; PHILOSOPHY.	SPORTS; FASHIONS; POPULAR ENTERTAINMENT; FOLKLORE; SOCIETY.

lish sparrows; these were **1st English sparrows** in U.S. The birds died, and 2 years later Pike imported a 2nd group successfully.

Aid to Roman Catholic churches and missions in America by the Lyon Propaganda, a French missionary group organized in 1822 to help American Catholics, amounted to 9,000,000 francs.

Secretly formed **anti-Catholic organization,** "The Supreme Order of the Star-Spangled Banner," one of the forerunners of the American or Know-Nothing Party, agitated against rising immigration of Irish and German Catholics and activities of foreign Catholic missionary groups in America.

1st large federal land grant for railroad construction provided a right of way on land in Illinois, Mississippi, and Alabama, for railroad from Chicago to Mobile.

New speed record for sailing ships, 13 days from Boston Light to the Equator, set by the *Stag-Hound,* a clipper designed by Donald McKay.

Jan. 2 **1st U.S. commercial treaty** with Salvador approved.

Jan. 21 **Westward migration** of the Florida Indians, mutually agreed upon. This removed most Indians from the Atlantic seaboard though a few have remained on isolated reservations.

Mar. 4 **John Calhoun's last formal oration** in U.S. Senate. He gave an account of the regional tensions in the various religions over slavery.

Mar. 11 Incorporation of 1st regularly organized school for the medical education of women, the **Woman's Medical College of Pennsylvania.** Classes began Oct. 12.

Apr. 27 Collins Line inaugurated **1st standard transatlantic schedule** between

The Turnverein, or Turners, gymnastic societies among German immigrants, combined as single organization in Cincinnati. The Turnverein was started in Germany by Friedrich John as a politico-athletic society to foster patriotism in German youth. It came under suspicion and was disbanded, but a revival was authorized after 1848. The German immigrants brought the institution to America, where it was soon functioning as a physical, social, and political culture center.

Most prevalent **American habits,** according to English travelers, were bragging, tobacco chewing, and spitting. American industry and hospitality were also mentioned frequently in the many accounts of America rendered by English visitors, many of whom stayed on.

Estimated 2000 **professional gamblers** were active on the river boats during this period.

Tammany Hall obtained the political loyalty of many immigrants to New York city by its charitable services.

Federal Indian policy at this time was summed up in the weary dictum that it was "cheaper to feed the Indians for a year than fight them for a day."

Approximately 40 **communal settlements** derived in greater or less degree from the plans of social reconstruction propounded by Brisbane and Fourier were founded in America in the decade between 1840 and 1850.

Spring fashions emphasized a "decided tendency to depart from simplicity in dress and adopt ornamental elegance of middle ages." Bonnets, mantles, dresses were trimmed with puffings of net, lace, flowers.

Apr. Amelia Bloomer reported in her magazine, *Lily,* the tragic consequences of a **drinking contest** between 2 bar habitués in Auburn, N.Y. 2 contestants had each rapidly consumed 3 pints of Irish whisky, after which the defending champion had sunk to the floor and died.

or slave state according to the constitution it adopted upon admission to the Union. Part of the Compromise of 1850, this was a concession to the South.

Sept. 18 **Fugitive Slave Bill** passed. Known as the second Fugitive Slave Law (a first, enacted on Feb. 1, 1793, was largely circumvented in the North), this severe legislation required the return of escaped slaves to their owners. Fugitives were not permitted a jury trial, they could not testify in their own behalf, and the commissioners earned $10 if their decision favored the claimant but only $5 when it favored the fugitive. This law was part of the Compromise of 1850, a concession to the South.

Sept. 20 **Slave trade** abolished in the District of Columbia. This was a concession to the North in the Compromise of 1850.

Sept. 28 Brigham Young, Mormon leader, named **1st governor of the territory of Utah** by the president.

Sept. 28 **Flogging outlawed** in the Navy and Merchant Marine.

Oct. 25 **Southern Rights Association** formed to achieve united opposition to antislavery action.

Aug. 19 **Celebrated low comedian,** William Davidge, made American debut at Broadway Theater, New York city, as Sir Peter Teazle in Sheridan's *The School for Scandal.* He became noted for Shakespearean roles, Dogberry, Touchstone, Holofernes, and later introduced Gilbert and Sullivan's Dick Deadeye from *H. M. S. Pinafore.*

Sept. 9 Famous actor **Edwin Booth** made his New York debut at age of 15 at National Theater.

Sept. 11 **Jenny Lind,** the "Swedish Nightingale," gave 1st American performance in Castle Garden Theater, New York city. P. T. Barnum, her American promoter, had auctioned seats for the performance; auctioneer sold out theater in 2 sessions for total of $17,864.05. A hatter named Genin paid $225 for 1st ticket and became a celebrity; he was accused by other New York hatters of "luxury and idleness."

Dec. 3 **New theater,** Brougham's Lyceum (afterwards Wallack's Theater) opened in New York city. Price scale was: $5 private boxes; $1 orchestra stalls; 50¢ dress circle and parquet; 25¢ family circle.

1851

Feb. 15 Mob rescue in Boston of Shadrach, a **fugitive slave.** Attempts to put into effect the Fugitive Slave Law of 1850 caused much bitterness in the North and increased abolitionary sentiment. Many states (Vermont, 1850; Connecticut, 1854; Rhode Island, 1854; Massachusetts, 1855; Michigan, 1855; Maine, 1855 and 1857; Kansas, 1858; and Wisconsin, 1858) passed *Personal Liberty Laws,* which in large part were designed to circumvent Fugitive Slave Law. These laws aroused much controversy and contributed a great deal to the split between North and South which led to the Civil War. South Carolina cited these laws as one of her grievances justifying her secession from the Union. Other out-

Probably the foremost paper in U.S., **The New York Times,** started as a Whig paper under editorship of H. J. Raymond. During Civil War it strongly supported Lincoln and his policies, while after the war it fought the Tweed Ring and Tammany. In 1896 it was purchased by A. S. Ochs and finally A. H. Sulzberger acquired it in 1935.

Study of inherited curse upon a house forms theme of Hawthorne's **The House of the Seven Gables.** Set in Salem, elements of the Gothic are provided in the form of moving portraits and the romantic device by which the curse is removed from the house.

SCIENCE; INDUSTRY; ECONOMICS; EDUCATION; RELIGION; PHILOSOPHY.

SPORTS; FASHIONS; POPULAR ENTERTAINMENT; FOLKLORE; SOCIETY.

British Isles and U.S. The Collins steamers were the biggest and fastest ships afloat. They established standards of design and outlay which determined American steamship building through the following decades. Their steamer was constructed from the plans of John Willis Griffiths, a naval architect, who lopped off the bowsprit of the traditional steamer and cut a vertical stern. It opened a new era in American passenger ships and marked a great anniversary in world steamship development.

June 1 Of 10,540 officers and men in U.S. Army only ⅓ were **native born.** 6,638 seamen and marines were at sea. Of U.S. Navy total of 7,500 men, ⁹/₁₁ were native born.

June 23 **1st U.S. commercial treaty** with **Borneo** concluded.

July 8 **1st Mormon kingdom** in U.S. (and the last) established on Big Beaver Island in Lake Michigan as the Kingdom of St. James by its leader and crowned king, James Jesse Strong.

Nov. 25 1st U.S. **commercial treaty with Switzerland** concluded.

Mrs. Bloomer ended her tirade against this exhibition with a sympathetic thought for the dead man's mother and sister, "for we know they mourn as those who have no hope."

July **500 ships deserted** in San Francisco's bay. Sailors left to find their fortunes in California's newly discovered gold fields.

July 25 **Gold discovered** in Rogue R., Ore., providing new prospecting territory for the excess "49ers" of California's gold rush.

Aug. 21 **New record** for shortest time crossing the Atlantic, 10 days, 4½ hours, made by American steamer, *Pacific,* arriving in New York from Liverpool.

Oct. 23–24 **1st national convention** of women advocating woman suffrage held in Worcester, Mass. On July 19 in Seneca Falls, N.Y., **1st Woman's rights convention** in history met at home of Mrs. Elizabeth Cady Stanton.

1851

1st electric fire alarm system in America installed in Boston by Dr. William P. Channing and Moses Gerrish Farmer.

1st American chapter of **Young Men's Christian Association** organized in Boston. 24 such chapters had already been formed in Great Britain.

Jan. 28 **Northwestern University** chartered in Evanston, Ill., as North Western University under Methodist auspices. "North" and "Western" combined in 1867.

Jan. 29 **Ripon College** chartered in Ripon, Wis., as Brockway College under the joint auspices of Congregational and Presbyterian groups. College became Ripon

New emphasis on children in social work led to the founding of the **Asylum for Friendless Boys** in New York city. Asylum was reorganized in 1853 into a semimunicipal institution, the Juvenile Asylum, to which courts were empowered to commit not merely young vagrants but children who had been grossly neglected, abused, or exploited by their parents. This civic statute constituted the 1st legal challenge to the supremacy of the family head in determining a child's life.

1st evaporated milk made by Gail Borden of Brooklyn, N.Y.; Borden had observed difficulties of children who could not obtain milk on board ship and pro-

231

POLITICS AND GOVERNMENT; WAR; DISASTERS; VITAL STATISTICS.	BOOKS; PAINTING; DRAMA; ARCHITECTURE; SCULPTURE.

standing rescues or attempted rescues include James Hamlet in New York city (1850), Thomas Simms in Boston (1851), "Jerry" M'Henry in Syracuse, N.Y. (1851), Anthony Burns in Boston (1854), two Garner families in Cincinnati (1856), and the Oberlin rescue (1858).

Mar. 3 Congress authorized **coinage of 3¢ pieces.** At same time **cheaper postage** rates were set by Congress. A half ounce could now be sent up to 3000 miles for 3¢.

May 3 **Conflagration** destroyed 2500 buildings in San Francisco, Calif. Property damage estimated at $12,000,000.

June 2 **Maine passed prohibition law.** It forbade the manufacture and sale of alcoholic beverages of all kinds throughout the state.

July 23 **Sioux Indians** turned over all their land in Iowa and most of their territory in Minnesota to U.S.

Aug. 24 **Lopez expedition,** a group unauthorized by the federal government, formed for the purpose of taking Cuba by force, dissolved with the death of Lopez and the dispersement of his men by Spanish troops at Havana. Gen. Narciso Lopez was a leader of Spanish refugees agitating for the liberation of Cuba, which, they claimed, was on the verge of revolution against Spanish rule. Lopez attracted a group of Americans in New Orleans who thought that Cuba could be annexed to the U.S. and thus become a ripe field for speculation. They issued bonds against the success of the Lopez mission and organized a band of recruits, who were led on by promises of plunder. The *Pampero,* with a vest-pocket army of 500, many mere boys, sailed from New Orleans on Aug. 3. Both Pres. Taylor and Fillmore had forbidden the expedition and pledged the security of Spanish property. The illegal voyage, with no possible support, ended in complete disaster. Col. William Crittenden of Kentucky

Powerful novel of the sea and the cosmos is Herman Melville's monumental **Moby Dick.** Ostensibly a whaling story, it raises the struggle of Captain Ahab and the whale to the level of man's conflict with the irreducible evil in the universe.

Francis Parkman began his famous study of French settlement in the New World with his history of the Indians, *The Conspiracy of Pontiac.* Painstaking scholarship is combined with consuming love for the forest to produce a monumental chronicle.

Famous statue *Greek Slave* by **Hiram Powers** exhibited this year in London at the Crystal Palace. It had been completed in 1843 after which at least 6 marble copies were made. It was the most celebrated statue of its day, and its nudity shocked American taste.

"Old Folks at Home" composed by Stephen Foster. Foster, noting the prejudice against "Ethiopian songs" and wanting to preserve his name for more genteel compositions, sold the first-performance rights to E. P. Christy, famous minstrel, and allowed Christy's name to appear on the published music as composer. Song is commonly known by its 1st line, " 'Way down upon the Swanee River . . ."

American composer and pianist **Louis Moreau Gottschalk** toured Spain. Compositions which were written or 1st conceived during this tour include: *Midnight in Seville, Manchega, The Siege of Saragossa,* etc.

Andrew J. Downing commissioned at an annual salary of $2500 to **landscape** the public gardens near the Capitol and the White House grounds in Washington, D.C.

Horace Greeley, editor of the *New York Tribune,* began serial publication of **Karl Marx'** *Revolution and Counter-Revolution.* The articles were collected in 1896 and republished as *Revolution and Counter-*

College in 1864. 1st degrees awarded in 1867.

Feb. 13 University of Minnesota established by Territorial Act, but it did not begin instruction until 1868. 1st degrees granted in 1873. It is now one of the largest of American universities.

Feb. 13 Heidelberg College, founded in 1850, was chartered in Tiffin, Ohio, under German Reformed auspices. 1st degrees awarded in 1854. College was a university between 1890 and 1926.

Feb. 18 Westminster College chartered in Fulton, Mo., as Fulton College under Presbyterian auspices. College became Westminster College in 1853, issued degrees in 1855.

Mar. 1 Milwaukee-Downer College chartered in Milwaukee, Wis., as the Female Normal Institute and High School. Established under the joint auspices of Congregational and Presbyterian groups, Institute awarded its 1st degrees in 1851. Institute became Milwaukee Female College in 1853, Milwaukee College in 1876, and Milwaukee-Downer College through a merger with Downer College in 1897.

May 6 1st patent in America for ice-making machine awarded to John Gorrie. He died in 1855 from a nervous breakdown largely brought on by his failure to raise capital for the manufacture of the machine.

May 15 Longest railroad line in the world up to this time, the Erie Railroad, opened with a 483-mile route between Piermont, N.Y., on the Hudson and Dunkirk, N.Y., on Lake Erie.

July 10 College of the Pacific chartered in Santa Clara, Calif., as California Wesleyan College. Established under Methodist auspices, college renamed University of the Pacific in 1852, granted its 1st degrees in 1858, transferred to San Jose, Calif., in 1871, integrated with Napa College of Napa, Calif., in 1896, and became the College of the Pacific in 1911. College of the Pacific transferred to Stockton, Calif., in 1924.

duced his product to fill the need. Production began in 1861 and the business grew into the Borden Milk Company of today.

Horace Greeley won prize essay-contest in Palmer's *Business Men's Almanac* for 1851 with article entitled "The Philosophy of Advertising." Greeley contended that the days of large profits were all but gone. "The general diffusion of intelligence and the improvement of the facilities for direct exchanges between producer and consumer render extensive and regular trade on the basis of small sales and large profits impossible."

All 21 of the enormously popular **Temperance** stories of Lucius Manlius Sargent reprinted in a single volume with the following preface: "The perusal of some of these narratives is well known to have turned the hearts of many persons of intemperate habits, from drunkenness and sloth, to temperance and industry. Many years have passed since their first publication, in separate numbers. It may not be uninteresting to the children of parents, once intemperate, to cast their eyes upon these pages, whose influence, under the blessing of Heaven, has preserved them from a miserable orphanage."

Wendell Phillips made a famous, if pessimistic, observation on human improvement, while addressing a rally for women's rights. Said Phillips, "Every step of progress the world has made has been from scaffold to scaffold and from stake to stake."

The phrase **"Go West, young man, go West,"** originated as the title of an editorial by John B. L. Soule, editor of the Terre Haute *Express.* Horace Greeley, the editor of the New York *Tribune,* who had been deeply impressed with the West on his travels, reprinted the piece with full credit to Soule, and later in a letter to a friend repeated the advice adding: "and grow up with the country." Phrase has since been attributed to Greeley because of his prominence in national affairs.

and his company of volunteers were caught and shot. Lopez was publicly executed in Havana. 162 prisoners, at least ½ of them Americans, were sent to Spain. When news of the rout reached New Orleans, a mob attacked the Spanish consulate there, tore the Spanish flag to shreds, and mutilated the portrait of the Spanish queen. Congress was forced to pay $25,000 indemnities for the damage done in New Orleans before the Americans were released by Spain.

Dec. 1 **Charles Sumner** filled the seat in U.S. Senate for Massachusetts vacated by **Daniel Webster.** Sumner kept the seat until his death 23 years later, was the Senate leader for abolition and union.

Dec. 24 ⅔ of the collection of the **Library of Congress destroyed by fire.**

Revolution in Germany. They were actually a joint production by Friedrich Engels and Marx. In 1848 Marx had met Charles Anderson Dana, managing editor of the *Tribune,* in Cologne. 3 years later he began to send features to Dana on questions of European politics. But he did not know enough English to write with ease and asked Engels to help him. Most of the material which was republished in 1896 was composed by Engels. Marx was paid £2 per article and covered a great number of topics, including discussions of Panslavism and the Crimean War.

Sept. 14 **James Fenimore Cooper** died. His last novel, *The Ways of the Hour,* an unsuccessful attempt at a murder mystery, was published this year.

1852

Young America movement at peak of power and influence. George N. Sanders of Kentucky, the mouthpiece of the group, began a series of articles in the January issue of the *Democratic Review* which attacked the political opponents of Stephen A. Douglas. He outlined a program which he claimed would unite Americans behind worthy leaders and open the world to her commerce and culture. He labeled his proposals a part of "Young America." Sanders argued that the bickering factions in the U.S. could be induced to cooperate if they were given a European controversy to divert them. He urged the U.S. to take the initiative in the crusade for freedom by identifying herself with the liberal revolutions of the century. It would provide an entrance to European hearts and ports and ready outlets for ideals and surplus products. "Young America," as a movement, dated from 1840. It was essentially an attempt to establish a common meeting-ground above sectional dissensions. To the end, the movement remained heterogeneous, though most of the members were Democrats. It was too weak to last long

Western paper, **Missouri Democrat,** established. It strongly urged emancipation.

Leading **newspaper** in Cleveland, the *Leader,* established by Joseph Medill. Later it merged with the *Plain Dealer,* which had been founded in 1845, a newspaper which achieved fame through the columns of C. F. Browne, author of "Artemus Ward" series.

Stephen Foster composed "Massa's in de Cold Ground" and in 1853 "My Old Kentucky Home." In the latter, he dropped Negro dialect for straightforward English, thus allowing more widespread popularity for the song.

Rev. A. C. Coxe, popular clergyman, railed against Hawthorne's **The Scarlet Letter.** "Let this brokerage of lust be put down at the very beginning," he said in recommending that the book be banned. Many others agreed with him.

Most provocative book in America, **Uncle Tom's Cabin** by Harriet Beecher Stowe

SCIENCE; INDUSTRY; ECONOMICS; EDUCATION; RELIGION; PHILOSOPHY.	SPORTS; FASHIONS; POPULAR ENTERTAINMENT; FOLKLORE; SOCIETY.

Aug. 12 Patent for a **practical sewing machine** granted to Isaac Merrit Singer, who very quickly organized the I. M. Singer & Company. Unique feature of Singer's machine was its continuous stitching feature; but Elias Howe, whose machine was then the most popular, initiated a royalty suit against Singer for producing a machine based in part on Howe's own machine. Singer lost and was forced to make a settlement of $15,000; but his machine had in the meantime achieved a leading position. It was improved in the next decade by additional patented devices.

Dec. 16 Hiram Hayden of Waterbury, Conn., received **1st patent for a process of shaping brass into bowls.** Dishes of brass fastened to spinning dies, were pressed, or "rolled" to the shape of the die.

Sculling match which excited much popular interest took place around Bedloe's Island, the contestants being William Decker of the East R. and James Lee of the North R. Crowds, betting heavily, gathered at Battery to see Decker win by 300 yds.

June 3 **1st baseball uniforms** worn by New York Knickerbockers. Outfits consisted of straw hats, white shirts, and blue full-length trousers.

Aug. 22 **Schooner-yacht America** unexpectedly won over 14 British vessels in 60-m. yacht race around the Isle of Wight. The trophy won became known as "The America's Cup." The *America* was skippered by Commodore John C. Stevens, wealthy Hoboken financier and yachtsman. Cup has remained in America ever since. Last race was in 1937.

1852

1st adequate safety device for **hydraulic elevators** developed by Elisha Graves Otis of New York. This permitted the practical design of passenger elevators and thus the development of skyscrapers.

Alexander Bonner Latta invented **1st effective fire engine,** a "steam" engine. Built in Cincinnati, Ohio, its chief feature was a boiler made of 2 square chambers, the inner one a fire-box, the outer a space for water and steam. The machine could shoot as many as 6 jets.

Massachusetts enacts 1st effective **school attendance law,** requiring all children between ages of 8 and 14 to attend school at least 12 weeks a year, 6 of them consecutive.

Jan. 15 Sampson Simson and 8 associates incorporate Jews' Hospital in New York city, **1st Jewish hospital** in U.S. Later it became Mt. Sinai Hospital.

Apr. 21 **Tufts College** chartered in

Godey's began featuring paragraphs with the heading, **"Employment of Women,"** recording most recent entries of women into the world of business and industry. *Godey's,* itself, was staffed largely by women, in both editorial rooms and pressrooms.

Trend toward **women teachers** in public schools reflected in following figures: In Boston, 6000 out of 8000 teachers were women; in Brooklyn, 103 out of 120 teachers were women; and in Philadelphia, 699 teachers were women in a staff of 781.

Caroline Fry Marriage Association advertised in the Tribune "CHEAP WIVES for poor and deserving young men . . . particular attention paid to the proper matching of temperaments." **Matrimonial agencies** were becoming popular at about this time.

Word **"lingerie"** came into general circulation, replacing such phrases as "white work," "white sewing," and "the under wardrobe."

POLITICS AND GOVERNMENT; WAR; DISASTERS; VITAL STATISTICS.	BOOKS; PAINTING; DRAMA; ARCHITECTURE; SCULPTURE.

and it disappeared after some minor literary apologies. "Young America" did, however, belong in the mainstream of effort to evolve a typically American pattern of democratic values.

June 1–6 Franklin Pierce of New Hampshire nominated as presidential candidate by **Democratic National Convention** in Baltimore, Md. His running mate was William R. King of Alabama. The convention adopted a platform that favored the Compromise of 1850 as a solution to the slavery problem.

June 16–21 **Whig National Convention** nominated Winfield Scott of New Jersey for the presidency in Baltimore, Md. Vice-presidential nominee was William A. Graham of North Carolina. The candidates were committed to a strict enforcement of the Compromise of 1850.

Aug. 11 **Free Soil National Convention** met in Pittsburgh, Pa. Taking as their keynote, "slavery is a sin against God and a crime against man," they nominated a ticket of John P. Hale of New Hampshire for the presidency and George W. Julian of Indiana for the vice-presidency.

Nov. 2 **Franklin Pierce elected President,** receiving 1,601,474 votes. Winfield Scott received 1,386,578, and John P. Hale, 156,149 votes. Electoral vote was 254 to 42.

published in Boston and created a storm that helped to drive nation to the "irrepressible conflict." The Dred Scott decision and the Fugitive Slave Law were to inflame the Abolitionist sentiment. The emotional tone of the novel combined with this sentiment to produce unswerving convictions.

Craft of **limning portraits** best exemplified in life of Isaac Augustus Wetherby (1819–1904), who traveled West making a living where he could with his pen and brush. He lithographed caricatures of Democratic Party and sold them at 7¢ apiece. In Iowa in 1856 he offered to paint for both parties at a price. He experimented in early daguerreotypes, drew heads for itinerant phrenologists and patent medicine retailers, illustrated temperance books, and painted portraits from life and death.

Sept. 6 **Gala occasion** at Castle Garden, New York city, to commemorate introduction of drama to America in 1752 at Williamsburg, Va. Most prominent players in nation performed in *Merchant of Venice* and David Garrick's *Lethe*.

Nov. 30 William H. Fry began series of lectures on **music**, illustrated by selections performed by a chorus and orchestra of 80 members, at the Metropolitan Hall, New York city. In the last lecture of the series, he made a vigorous plea for American music and American composers.

1853

More that 5000 killed by **yellow fever** epidemic in New Orleans, La., during next 2 years. A few cases of fever were reported in the spring in New Orleans, but epidemic proportions were not reached un-

Feminine sentimentality rampant in the verse of the decade; one of its foremost practitioners, **Fanny Fern,** published her *Fern Leaves from Fanny's Portfolio,* which sold 100,000 copies in one year. She was

| SCIENCE; INDUSTRY; ECONOMICS; EDUCATION; RELIGION; PHILOSOPHY. | SPORTS; FASHIONS; POPULAR ENTERTAINMENT; FOLKLORE; SOCIETY. |

Medford, Mass., under Universalist auspices. 1st degrees awarded in 1857.

May 9 **1st Plenary Council of all Roman Catholic Bishops and Arch-Bishops** in U.S. and territories held at Cathedral of Baltimore, Md.

Oct. The Rev. Thomas Gallaudet founded **St. Ann's Church for deaf mutes** in New York city; 1st service held in chapel at University of the City of New York. In 1859 church moved to building on W. 18th St.

Oct. 6 American Pharmaceutical Association, **1st nation-wide pharmaceutical association** founded in Philadelphia, Pa.; Daniel B. Smith chosen president. Total membership today: 26,299.

Nov. 5 **American Society of Civil Engineers** established in New York city. First called American Society of Engineers and Architects, it did not hold its 1st annual meeting until 1869 when membership was 160. Membership today is 38,000.

Nov. 21 **Duke University,** founded in 1838 as Union Institute, was chartered in Randolph County, N.C., as Normal College. Established under Methodist auspices, it awarded its 1st degrees in 1853, was renamed Trinity College in 1859. It transferred to Durham, N.C., in 1892, and in 1924 it became Duke University upon receipt of large endowment from James B. Duke.

Jan. 28 Famous sentence, **"Eternal vigilance is the price of Liberty,"** uttered by abolitionist Wendell Phillips in an address before the Massachusetts Anti-Slavery Society. A great orator, he was in constant demand as a speaker before antislavery groups. Phillips misquoted "The condition upon which God hath given liberty to man is eternal vigilance . . . ," made in a speech by John Philpot Curran in 1790.

May 25 Stephen Foster wrote to E. P. Christy, leader of the Christy Minstrels, saying that he now wished to put his own name on the **"Ethiopian" songs** which he had written and offered to pay back the money that he had taken from Christy for allowing "Old Folks at Home" to appear under the minstrel leader's signature. He had "sold" his authorship of the song for a reported $500. Christy was unwilling to have the attribution changed and "Old Folks at Home" was legally his until 1879.

Apr. 6 1st use of word **"telegram"** in a notice in the Albany *Evening Journal.* It read in part: "A friend desires us to give notice that he will ask leave . . . to introduce a new word. . . . It is 'telegram,' instead of 'telegraphic dispatch' or 'telegraphic communication.' " English refused to accept this piece of "Yankee slang" until 1857 when *Times* used word in a heading over official British dispatch.

Aug. 3 Yale and Harvard held **1st intercollegiate rowing race** on 2-mi. course at Lake Winnepesaukee, N.H. Harvard won by 4 lengths.

1853

James Renwick of New York city produced **1st terra cotta** in U.S. Renwick, professor of Natural Philosophy and Experimental Chemistry at Columbia, suggested its use as paving material.

U.S. Secretary of State, William L. Marcy, warned all members of the American **diplomatic service** that they must not wear medals or knee breeches under any circumstances.

POLITICS AND GOVERNMENT; WAR; DISASTERS; VITAL STATISTICS.	BOOKS; PAINTING; DRAMA; ARCHITECTURE; SCULPTURE.

til mid-summer. 200 deaths were recorded in week ending July 16. Vicksburg, Miss., lost ⅙ of her population in same epidemic.

Gadsden Purchase negotiated for $10 million. Southern Arizona and New Mexico, the territory acquired, was the last addition to the present U.S. boundaries. The treaty with Mexico was completed by the end of the year. The Mexican president endorsed amendments which were added to the treaty by the U.S. Senate. The following year Congress passed the necessary legislation, and on June 30, 1854, the treaty was mutually ratified. According to the final terms the U.S. received the Mesila Valley, about 20 million acres of land, and was able to adjust the disputed U.S. Mexican boundary. The land was considered unfertile, but it was coveted as the route for the Southern Pacific Railroad. The final result of the treaty made it unnecessary for the U.S. to protect Mexico from Indian invasions.

The Native American or "Know Nothing" Party formed. Its adherents were greatly concerned by the steadily growing number of immigrants. It would exclude anyone not native born from holding federal, state, or municipal offices, and urged the repeal of naturalization laws. "Know Nothing" became unofficial name because its followers' response to any question regarding policy was, "I don't know." This was not because of ignorance but secrecy.

Feb. 21 **Silver content of all coins** except silver dollar **reduced.** The Coinage Act was passed to keep smaller coins in circulation. It also provided for the minting of $3 gold pieces.

Mar. 2 **Territory of Washington** formed. It was separated from the Oregon Territory.

Mar. 3 **Transcontinental railroad survey** authorized by Congress. $150,000 was appropriated to find the most practical railroad route across the country. Survey was to be conducted by the War Department.

Mar. 4 **Franklin Pierce, 14th president,** inaugurated. He was a Democrat and

followed by a whole group of "botanical" poetesses, including Fanny Forester, Grace Greenwood. This era, known as the "Feminine Fifties," is noted for the number of women writers of best sellers who were more popular than such famous names as Nathaniel Hawthorne, Ralph Waldo Emerson, Herman Melville, and Walt Whitman. The 1st dime novelist was Mrs. **Ann Sophia Stephens,** whose *Malaeska* initiated the Beadle Dime Novels in 1860. This novel was 1 of the 2 best sellers among Beadle's series: the others, **E. S. Ellis'** *Seth Jones* (1860).

Building of Harper & Bros., publishers of New York, burned with a loss of $1,500,000, the **largest fire loss** suffered by one U.S. business firm up to that time.

Crystal Palace built in New York to house 1853 Exhibition. Constructed of cast iron and glass, it had the largest dome erected in the U.S. up to that time, and was hailed as the reintegration of engineering and decoration in a new national style of architecture.

The Bryan Gallery of Christian Art opened in a loft on Broadway, New York city, by Thomas Jefferson Bryan, a wealthy art collector who tried to stimulate public taste. The collection included works by Dürer, Van Eyck, Mantegna, Velasquez, etc. Bryan charged 25¢ admission. In an introduction to the catalogue of the Bryan Gallery of Christian Art, Richard Grant White describes the **popular art** of the day: "Floras and Doras, with big eyes and little mouths, big arms and little hands, big busts and little waists, big bustles and little feet; manikin men, all forehead and favoris; portraits of homely old women flattered, in Books of Beauty, into a conventional prettiness and unnatural youth, far more repulsive than their own actual comeliness: such are the works of art which 'sell.'"

Frontier humor of the Southwest best exemplified in Joseph Glover Baldwin's *Flush Times in Alabama and Mississippi,* a series of descriptive pieces dealing with the roaring life of the newly opened region.

| SCIENCE; INDUSTRY; ECONOMICS; EDUCATION; RELIGION; PHILOSOPHY. | SPORTS; FASHIONS; POPULAR ENTERTAINMENT; FOLKLORE; SOCIETY. |

Improvement of the **sluicing process** by E. E. Matteson came in handy in California gold fields and later in the Klondike.

College of the City of New York, founded in 1847 as the Free Academy, was incorporated this year.

Crystal Palace Exhibition of the Industry of All Nations held in New York city to demonstrate American inventions and industrial progress. Called a World's Fair, it was inspired by the London Exhibition of 1851. The building which housed the exhibit was impressive enough to be referred to as Aladdin's palace.

Jan. 12 **Baltimore & Ohio railroad** completed to Ohio R., and its 1st trains began run from Baltimore to Wheeling, W. Va. For 1st time Chicago was connected by track to East, with terminals in New York city and Boston. Railways increased from 7500 miles of track in 1850 to 29,000 in 1860.

Jan. 12 **Willamette University** chartered in Salem, Ore., under Methodist auspices. 1st degrees issued in 1859. It had been founded in 1842.

Feb. 12 **Illinois Wesleyan University** chartered in Bloomington, Ill., under Methodist auspices. 1st degrees awarded in 1853. It had been founded in 1850.

Feb. 22 **Washington University** chartered in St. Louis, Mo., as Eliot Seminary. Established under Unitarian auspices, seminary became Washington University in 1857, awarded 1st degrees in 1862.

Mar. 31 **Louisiana State University** chartered in Alexandria, La., as the Louisiana State Seminary of Learning and Military Academy. State-supported, the seminary awarded its 1st degrees in 1869, moved to Baton Rouge, La., in 1870 when it was renamed Louisiana State University.

Apr. 1 **Ohio Wesleyan Female College** chartered in Delaware, Ohio. Combined with Ohio Wesleyan University in 1877.

Apr. 13 **Loyola College** chartered in Baltimore, Md., under Catholic auspices.

Mount Vernon Ladies' Association organized by Anne Pamela Cunningham for the purpose of purchasing George Washington's plantation home. Edward Everett donated all his fees from his Lyceum lecture on the moral qualities of Washington. This came to more than ⅛ of the required $200,000. The Mount Vernon Ball at the Boston Theater in 1859, sponsored by Mrs. Harrison Gray Otis, provided the final $10,000. **Mount Vernon** was dedicated in that year and Mrs. Cunningham made the presentation speech describing the acquisition as "the sacred heritage of America's children."

Feb. Paulina Wright Davis and Mrs. Caroline H. Dall, early American **suffragettes,** began publication of their magazine, *Una,* in Washington, D.C.

Dinah Taylor wrote the following description in an 1853 issue of Amelia Bloomer's **feminist magazine,** *Lily:* "Woman is the great and grand Archimedian lever, whose fulcrum is childhood, whose weight is the world, whose length is all time, whose sweep is vast and endless eternity."

Amelia Bloomer, celebrated American feminist, reported on the emergence of **women waitresses** in this fashion: "Stopping over night at the Delavan House in Albany, we were very agreeably surprised on entering the dining-room for supper to see about a dozen young women in attendance on the tables. This was something new. When we visited the house last winter the waiters were all men, as is usual in such places. Now not a man was to be seen in that capacity; but in place of their heavy tread, and awkward motions, was woman's light footfall and easy, graceful movements. In a conversation with the proprietor we learned that the change was made in May . . . entirely satisfactory . . . the only objectors being a few women . . . preferring black men."

239

| POLITICS AND GOVERNMENT; WAR; DISASTERS; VITAL STATISTICS. | BOOKS; PAINTING; DRAMA; ARCHITECTURE; SCULPTURE. |

served 1 term in office.

May 31 2nd Grinnell Expedition on the *Advance* left New York city under command of Elisha Kent Kane, who had sailed with Lt. De Haven in 1st Grinnell Expedition in 1850. Ship remained ice bound for 21 months in Kane Basin. Entire party abandoned ship on May 25, 1855, for spectacular retreat to Upernivik, Greenland, in 83 days, a trek famous in Arctic exploration. Here Kane and party were rescued by relief expedition.

July 8 Trade opened with Japan as a result of show of force by Com. Matthew C. Perry (brother of the Perry of Lake Erie fame) when he entered Yedo Bay with an armed squadron, and his credentials were received by the Mikado. Japan had refused almost all foreign intercourse for 2 centuries.

Dec. 24 240 of 700 passengers **lost at sea** from the steamer *San Francisco* which foundered on its way to California.

Jan. 8 1st equestrian statue cast in U.S. It was of *Gen. Andrew Jackson* in Lafayette Square, Washington, by the inexperienced sculptor Clark Mills. Jackson is seen raising his cap high while the horse rears on legs which are placed directly in center of body, thus giving the whole piece a very precarious balance.

Feb. 11 Formal American debut of **Louis Moreau Gottschalk** took place at Niblo's Garden, New York city. Only 24 years old, Gottschalk was widely acclaimed, offered a long-term contract by P. T. Barnum (which he refused), and embarked on a concert career under the management of Max Strakosch.

Aug. 15 Attitude in New York toward the Negro reflected in notice issued by Purdy's Theater during its successful run of *Uncle Tom's Cabin*. Respectable colored people would be accommodated in a comfortable parquet, set off from the rest of the house. A special entrance would be provided, admittance being 25¢.

1854

Republican Party formed at Jackson, Mich. It originated as a reaction against the Kansas-Nebraska Act and attracted antislavery men from all parties. High tariffs and the transcontinental railroad were planks in its platform. Lincoln became 1st president it elected, and the party remained in power for 6 administrations. It was the only 3rd party to become a major party. A preliminary organizational meeting was held in Ripon, Wisc., Feb. 28, 1854. It included Free-Soilers, Whigs, and anti-slavery Democrats. It was here that the name "Republican" was 1st suggested.

Mar. 31 The **Treaty of Kanagawa** signed by Perry with Japan. The U.S. was permitted a consulate and American ships were permitted to enter certain Japanese ports for limited trade.

Apr. 26 Massachusetts Emigrant Aid Society founded by Eli Thayer. Organized

Benjamin Shillaber's *Life and Sayings of Mrs. Partington,* a humorous book popular for many years.

1st newspaper in Nebraska territory, the *Nebraska Palladium,* started in Iowa.

Long popular **The Lamplighter,** a novel by Maria Susanna Cummins, published. 40,000 copies sold in 1st 8 weeks; 100,000 in 1st decade.

Tremendously popular book for the vast unthinking audience, *Tempest and Sunshine* by Mary Jane Holmes published. It sold about 1,000,000 copies. Usually constructed around domestic disputes and tragedies, Mrs. Holmes's novels were read by America's growing mass of uncritical readers.

American classic and most famous work of Henry Thoreau is **Walden,** a series of

SCIENCE; INDUSTRY; ECONOMICS; EDUCATION; RELIGION; PHILOSOPHY.	SPORTS; FASHIONS; POPULAR ENTERTAINMENT; FOLKLORE; SOCIETY.

1st degrees awarded in 1853. It had been founded in 1852.

June 3 **Central College** chartered in Pella, Iowa, under Baptist auspices. 1st degrees awarded in 1861. University passed from Baptist to Dutch Reformed control in 1916.

Sept. **Antioch College,** which unconventionally welcomed both male and female students equally, began operation. The 1st president of this non-sectarian school was Horace Mann.

Sept. 15 **1st national librarians' convention** convened at newly incorporated College of the City of New York. Presiding officer was Charles Jewett, the librarian of the Smithsonian Institute.

Intercity baseball rivalry, which was to have a long history in New York, marked by a game between an All-New York team and an All-Brooklyn 9. New York won 2 out of 3 matches.

1st newspaper story on baseball appeared in New York *Mercury* written by Sen. William Cauldwell, paper's owner and editor.

Oct. 12 John C. Morrissey, who claimed the **heavyweight boxing championship** was challenged by Yankee Sullivan. Sullivan led for 36 rounds, but during a rest period, climbed out of the ring to take on a few Morrissey supporters who had been heckling him. He failed to get back into the ring on time and the referee awarded the decision and the title to Morrissey.

1854

Paper collar invented by Walter Hunt.

Astor Library opened in New York city. John Jacob Astor left $40,000 in his will to be used for the establishment of the Astor Library. He had never been formally educated, but was so completely the self-educated man that he maintained a lifelong interest in literature and science, and he counted many celebrities from these fields among his friends. Fitz-Greene Halleck and Washington Irving are said to have been instrumental in persuading Astor to grant the funds for the library.

Boston Public Library opened to public. The library was founded 2 years before, but it was not immediately ready for public use. The library is credited with having inaugurated the basic practice for American libraries when the board recommended that popular books be kept in large enough supply to fill the demands of many

Embattled words **"popular sovereignty"** introduced in the slavery issue by Sen. Stephen A. Douglas during the debate on his bill to organize the territory of Nebraska into separate territories. He advanced the principle that each territory had the right to choose whether to accept or outlaw slavery within its borders. "Popular sovereignty," originated by Lewis Cass, was called "squatter sovereignty" by opponents.

Phrase, **"Beecher's Bibles,"** introduced to characterize the Sharps rifles shipped to the settlers of Kansas after the passage of the Kansas-Nebraska Act. Determined to keep the territory "free," Northerners rushed in thousands of guns, which Beecher had once designated as moral agencies greater than the Bible.

William Stuart of Connecticut became one of most **notorious counterfeiters** in

241

| POLITICS AND GOVERNMENT; WAR; DISASTERS; VITAL STATISTICS. | BOOKS; PAINTING; DRAMA; ARCHITECTURE; SCULPTURE. |

to encourage antislavery emigration to Kansas, it was renamed (Feb. 21, 1855) New England Emigrant Aid Society as its membership spread. Lawrence, Kansas, was settled this year by immigrants sent by the Society. Town was named for Amos Lawrence, backer of the expedition.

May 26 The Kansas-Nebraska bill passed; it repealed the Missouri Compromise, gave popular sovereignty or the freedom of choice for all territories or states on the question of slavery. Bill was widely condemned by abolitionists and people in general in North and West.

June 2 Most dramatic fugitive slave case came to an end when Anthony Burns, a fugitive slave, was led through the streets of Boston to the Long Wharf and a trip back to the South. The streets had to be guarded with thousands of troops and policemen. The buildings were draped in black, the church bells tolled. It is said that Boston had not experienced such excitement since the Revolution. In a few months Burns was sold to a friendly master who in turn sold him to people in Boston interested in setting him free. It cost U.S. government at least $100,000 to return this one fugitive slave to South.

June 5 Canadian Reciprocity Treaty opened the U.S. market to Canadian agricultural products, timber, and fish, and in return American fishermen received new privileges in Canadian waters, and freedom of operation in the Great Lakes and the St. Lawrence R.

July Land office opened in Kansas.

Oct. 18 Drafting of the **Ostend Manifesto** by Pierre Soulé, U.S. minister to Spain, at Ostend, Belgium, in consultation with John Y. Mason and James Buchanan, U.S. ministers to France and Great Britain respectively. Manifesto declared that, in order to preserve slavery, U.S. should obtain Cuba, and that, if Spain should not be willing to sell, then "by every law human and divine, we shall be justified in wresting it from Spain, if we possess the power." Soulé resigned when Sec. of State

essays on 2 years spent close to nature and away from civilization. The book's theme is the philosophy of simplicity and insistence that happiness is not to be had by the feverish pursuit of wealth. Excellent descriptions of plants, birds, and animals are interspersed with reflections on life.

William Grayson published a poetical reply to Harriet Beecher Stowe, *The Hireling and the Slave.* The poem, in heroic couplets, contrasted the wretched life of the wage slaves of the North with the ideal life of Negroes on Southern plantations. The best parts of the poem dealt with the daily routine of the Negroes at work and play. Like many Southern poets Grayson was an inferior and belated echo of 18th century English diction and form.

New York theatrical seasons 1853–54, 1854–55 were notable for the appearances of many **new American plays.** Among the productions were: *Anna* and *The Brewery,* both by H. J. Conway; *Uncle Tom's Cabin; Camille, or The Fate of a Coquette,* translated by Jean Davenport; *The Fox Hunt or, Don Quixote the Second, Masks and Faces, Andy Blake, To Parents and Guardians,* and *The Young Actress* by Dion Boucicault; *The Game of Love* and *Love and Murder* by James Brougham; and *A Gentleman from Ireland* by Fitz James O'Brien.

1st publication of the often revised **The Life of P. T. Barnum, Written by Himself.** 1 of 1st American "success" stories, *The Life* has probably sold ½ million copies.

1st "fire-proof" building in U.S., Harper & Bros. publishing headquarters in New York city, built from wrought-iron beams set in masonry walls.

Influential book on architecture, *A Home for All, or the Octagon Mode of Building,* by O. S. Fowler, also a noted phrenologist. After its publication, many U.S. houses built on round or octagonal plans.

| SCIENCE; INDUSTRY; ECONOMICS; EDUCATION; RELIGION; PHILOSOPHY. | SPORTS; FASHIONS; POPULAR ENTERTAINMENT; FOLKLORE; SOCIETY. |

concurrent readers without neglecting the regular catalogue of books of a more limited nature. This policy permitted the development of the libraries of manuscripts and rare books for which Boston Public Library is world famous. The original building was replaced in 1893 with a new structure which was another 1st for the Boston Public Library—the 1st major embodiment of the classical principles evolved by the Chicago Exhibition of 1893, the start of a new era of architectural style.

Railroad Suspension Bridge built over Niagara gorge by John A. Roebling, later famous for building Brooklyn Bridge.

Pennsylvania State College, State College, Pa., chartered by the Pennsylvania Legislature as the Farmers High School of Pennsylvania. It opened in 1859, and became Pennsylvania State College in 1847. **Michigan State Agriculture College** was also chartered this year, and held its 1st classes in 1857. These 2 colleges were the **1st agricultural schools in U.S.**

Jan. 13 **Pacific University** chartered in Forest Grove, Ore., as Tualatin Academy and Pacific University. It had been founded 1849 under the joint auspices of Presbyterian and Congregational groups. University awarded its 1st degrees in 1863, became Pacific University in 1922.

Feb. **Cornell College** chartered in Mt. Vernon, Iowa, as the Iowa Conference Seminary under Methodist auspices. It had been founded the previous year. Seminary became Cornell College in 1855, granted its 1st degrees in 1858.

May 6 1st American company concerned with **transatlantic cable communication** formed by Cyrus W. Field.

American history with the publication of his *Life,* a vivid account of crime which has become a collector's item.

Little Katy; or, The Hot Corn Girl was a **successful temperance play.** Play opened with a happy successful home. The husband began to drink, gamble, and to recoup his losses, he committed forgery and was apprehended. His wife began to drink, while toiling at her sewing needle, the rum destroying her maternal feelings. Little Katy is driven into the street to sell "hot Corn" and catches her death from pneumonia.

Superb trotting horse, Flora Temple, broke all records by running the mile at Kalamazoo, Mich., in 2:19½—1st time a horse had run below 2:20. News flashed immediately throughout nation by telegraph made her a national legend.

Children's Aid Society in New York city opened a lodging house for boys and integrated it with an Industrial School and "Boys' Meetings" which stressed religious education.

Baseball rules stipulated exact weight and size of the baseball for 1st time. Ball had to weigh between 5½ and 6 oz. and have a diameter of between 2¾ and 3½ in.

Growing interest in **baseball** indicated by the establishment of many clubs. The Eagle and the Empire of New York; the Excelsior of Brooklyn. By 1855 Morrisania had the Union Club, while Brooklyn added the Atlantic and the Eckford.

Oct. 31 *Nebraska Palladium* reported that "the number of females at present holding office of Post Master is 128." An interesting aspect of this story in the *Palladium* was the report that the **women**

POLITICS AND GOVERNMENT; WAR; DISASTERS; VITAL STATISTICS.	BOOKS; PAINTING; DRAMA; ARCHITECTURE; SCULPTURE.

William Marcy, who had ordered the conference to establish policy toward Cuba, disavowed Soulé's statements.

Nov. 13 Upwards of 300 deaths caused by **wrecking of emigrant ship** *New Era* off New Jersey coast. The ship was on its way to New York city from Bremen.

Oct. 2 Famous landmark in New York city, the **Academy of Music,** opened at 14th Street and Irving Place with a season of opera.

1855

Increased immigration reflected by the fact that the New York state Immigration Commission leased Castle Garden at the tip of Manhattan as a reception center for expected immigrants. In 1854, some 400,-000 immigrants had landed in the U.S.

William Walker landed company of men in Nicaragua, overthrew government, and set himself up as ruler. Walker, fitfully a lawyer, doctor, newspaper editor, had seized Lower California in 1853, and made himself, by proclamation, president. When his regime collapsed, he was afterwards tried, and acquitted, by a San Francisco Court for breaking neutrality laws. He went to Nicaragua at request of a revolutionary party and became leader of the rebellion. By 1856 he was again a president, and his state was recognized by U.S. He was forced out of power through the maneuvers of Cornelius Vanderbilt, who resented Walker's interference in Nicaraguan administration of the Accessory Transit Company. Walker was executed in 1860 by a Honduras court when a new invasion of Nicaragua failed.

Jan. 16 **Nebraska's 1st territorial legislature** met at Omaha "City."

Feb. 24 Pres. Pierce signed act creating **1st U.S. Court of Claims.** Previously citizens could remedy claims against Federal government only by petitioning Congress.

Mar. 30 **Kansas elected its 1st territorial legislature** in a setting of armed violence. Some 5000 "Border Ruffians" invaded the territory from western Missouri and forced the election of a pro-slavery legislature. Andrew H. Reeder, 1st territorial governor of Kansas, reluctantly

Israel Potter: His Fifty Years of Exile published by **Herman Melville.** *Israel Potter,* with an American Revolutionary War background, is notable for portraits of Benjamin Franklin and John Paul Jones, and for a colorful description of a naval battle.

Famous *Familiar Quotations,* compiled by **John Bartlett,** 1st published. "Bartlett's Quotations" has been often revised, the 14th edition having appeared in 1968.

Powerful organ of Tammany Hall in New York, the **Daily News,** established by W. D. Parsons. Strongly opposed to Civil War, it led all American newspapers in circulation until 1901, the year of its demise.

A famous temperance book, **Ten Nights in a Bar-Room and What I Saw There** by T. S. Arthur, published. Before 1880, *Ten Nights* had probably sold 100,-000 copies. This temperance classic was often dramatized.

One of the slowest books to reach the best seller list, **Leaves of Grass** by Walt Whitman, published. In the 1940's a book club distributed over ¼ million copies in 5 years. It appears in many reprint series.

Considered by many the best of all historical romances, **The Cloister and the Hearth** by Charles Reade, 1st published in U.S.

Longfellow reached peak of his fame with the publication of "**The Song of Hiawatha,**" a vast collection of Indian myths built around the character of Hiawatha. Using the meter of the Finnish epic the

SCIENCE; INDUSTRY; ECONOMICS; EDUCATION; RELIGION; PHILOSOPHY.	SPORTS; FASHIONS; POPULAR ENTERTAINMENT; FOLKLORE; SOCIETY.

Sept. 15   **1st newspaper in Kansas,** the *Kansas Weekly Herald,* began publication at Leavenworth.

post masters received the same pay as the men. No other occupation could make that claim at this time.

1855

American Journal of Education, **1st national publication of the teaching profession** in America, published by Henry Barnard. In 1867 Barnard became **1st U.S. commissioner of education.**

Railway completed across the Isthmus of Panama.

"Old Spanish" lighthouse built at Point Loma, San Diego, Calif., **1st Pacific coast lighthouse.** Said to have been highest lighthouse in world, it was built after American occupation of California in 1851 and hence is misnamed.

Jan. 1   George H. Bissell and Jonathan J. Eveleth, New York city law partners, formed **1st oil business** in U.S., the Pennsylvania Rock Oil Co. Spring oil from Cherrytree Township, Venango County, Pa., had been analysed by Prof. Benjamin Silliman of Yale who found that 8 products could be extracted from the oil by commercially feasible processes. Bissell and Eveleth, who had previously leased the property, went into business to use the oil from the spring.

Jan. 25   **Iowa Wesleyan College** chartered in Mt. Pleasant, Iowa, as Iowa Wesleyan University. Founded under Methodist auspices, university awarded its 1st degrees in 1856, became a college in 1912. It had been founded in 1842.

Feb. 6   **Eureka College** chartered in Eureka, Ill. under the auspices of the Disciples. 1st degrees granted in 1860.

Feb. 10   **Kalamazoo College** chartered in Kalamazoo, Mich. under Baptist auspices. 1st degrees presented in 1855. It had been established in 1833 as a "literary institute."

Mrs. Anna McDowell began publishing *The Woman Advocate* which supported the cause of **feminism** in America.

Mrs. Sarah J. Hale launched a campaign in the columns of *Godey's* against the use of the word "female" in reference to women in public activity. This campaign became one of the minor objectives of **feminism** in America.

Phrase **"Cotton is king"** came into prominence. The phrase is taken from the title of a book, *Cotton is King, or the Economical Relations of Slavery,* by David Christy. At this time export of cotton amounted to ½ of total exports of the U.S. Its value was more than $100,000,000 annually.

Vogue for **horseback riding** among ladies of America widespread. In Boston and New York numerous riding academies were set up to help women adjust to side saddle. A newspaper editorial commented: "A lot of cynical old fogies . . . have recently been startled . . . by the rushing, galloping, slashing, and dashing exploits of the lady equestrians at the agricultural fairs. This jocund spectacle like everything else that is new . . . does not suit the still veins of these respectable old goats. . . . But still the ladies go on riding. . . ."

By 1855 the outline of the present **railroad system of the East** was already in existence. It was possible to make a trip between most of the large cities, but the schedules and conveniences of the lines were still pretty far removed from what is now the average American expectations of the proper way to run railroads. There was, for example, only a single train a day

245

POLITICS AND GOVERNMENT; WAR; DISASTERS; VITAL STATISTICS.

BOOKS; PAINTING; DRAMA; ARCHITECTURE; SCULPTURE.

allowed the election in order to prevent widespread bloodshed.

June 5 **National Council of Native American Party** met at Philadelphia and changed its name to the **American Party.** Control of the party was achieved by Southerners and proslavery men which eventually resulted in the death of this "Know-Nothing" Party.

July 31 Andrew H. Reeder, **territorial governor of Kansas, removed from office** by Pres. Pierce. He was charged with participating in land speculation, but was actually eased out because of his antislavery views. He was succeeded by Wilson Shannon of Ohio, a proslavery man.

Sept. 5 **Kansas territorial legislature repudiated** by proslavery settlers at a convention held in Big Springs. Arms were sent them from the North, and an army was formed called the Free State Forces. John Brown allied himself with this army.

Oct. 23 **Topeka Constitution,** drawn up by Kansas Free State Forces, set up a governor and a legislature. This meant that Kansas now had dual government. Topeka Constitution outlawed slavery.

Nov. 26 **"Wakarusa War"** threatened Lawrence, Kansas when some 1500 "Border Ruffians," camped on Wakarusa R., advanced on the town. They held off their attack, however, when they learned the town was heavily defended by Free State forces. The "war" was ended by Gov. Shannon without bloodshed.

Kalevala, he created atmosphere by stringing together many Indian words and names. The poem marks the epitome of the glorification of the noble savage.

Children's classic, *Age of Fable; or, The Beauties of Mythology* by Thomas Bulfinch, published.

Plates and rights of **Noah Webster's Elementary Spelling Book** (called by many generations of schoolboys the "Blue-Back Speller") taken over by D. Appleton & Co., N.Y. Originally published in 1783, the book sold 1,000,000 or more copies a year for 40 years after Appleton took it on.

Stephen Foster wrote "Come Where My Love Lies Dreaming."

Sept. 27 George F. Bristow's **opera,** *Rip Van Winkle,* opened at Niblo's Theatre, New York City; it ran for 4 weeks. Critic Richard Storrs wrote: "Sebastopol has fallen, and a new American opera has succeeded in New York!" This was 2nd American opera publicly performed.

Oct. 9 Patent awarded to Joshua C. Stoddard of Worcester, Mass., for invention of **steam calliope.** Stoddard later extended his scope to invention of hay-tedder and horse-rake.

1856

Feb. 22 1st national meeting of **Republican Party** took place at Pittsburgh, Pa. It met to plan a national presidential nominating convention to be held in June.

Feb. 22 **National Convention of Know-Nothing Party** met at Philadelphia and nominated ex-Pres. Millard Fillmore for the presidency and Andrew J. Donelson of Tennessee for the vice-presidency. Know-

One of America's most endearing poems, Whittier's **"The Barefoot Boy,"** included in his *The Panorama and Other Poems* published this year. Avoiding the slavery issue in this poem, Whittier turned to memories of his own boyhood and created a masterpiece of local color.

Long popular novel *John Halifax, Gentleman,* by **Dinah Maria Mulock Craik,** 1st published. It is still being reissued.

SCIENCE; INDUSTRY; ECONOMICS; EDUCATION; RELIGION; PHILOSOPHY.

SPORTS; FASHIONS; POPULAR ENTERTAINMENT; FOLKLORE; SOCIETY.

Feb. 10 Important change in **U.S. citizenship laws** provided that all children born abroad of U.S. citizens were assured of citizenship.

Apr. 28 **Santa Clara University** chartered in Santa Clara, Calif., under Catholic auspices. 1st degrees issued in 1857. It had been founded Mar. 19, 1851, as Santa Clara College, a name it kept until 1912.

Apr. 31 **College of California** chartered in Oakland, Calif., under denomination control of Congregational and Presbyterian interests. 1st degrees awarded in 1864. It was 1st institution in California to establish full and separate courses on the model and scale of the leading colleges of the East.

Sept. 17 **1st public library** in Massachusetts supported by tax money, the Boston Public Library, formally dedicated. It was founded largely as a result of activities of Edward Everett and George Ticknor. A public library at Wayland, Mass., was founded by an endowment in 1850 by Pres. Francis Wayland of Brown University.

Oct. 17 **1st American conference of rabbis** met at Medical College in Cleveland, Ohio. Isidor Kalisch, a reformist rabbi, called meeting and was elected chairman. Some lay leaders also attended.

Dec. Church of St. John Nepomucene dedicated in St. Louis, Mo., **1st American Bohemian Church** in U.S.

out of Washington that connected with other trains on the way to Boston. It included changes and stopovers in Baltimore, Philadelphia, and New York, which varied in length from ½ hour in Baltimore to 9 hours in New York. The total traveling time of the run was 35½ hours. What might possibly strike the fancy of the contemporary American would be the price of the fare. The whole trip from Washington to Boston cost $11.60.

July 4 **Prohibition** became effective in New York State. Called upon to enforce the law in New York city, Mayor Fernando Wood, personally opposed to the statute, issued instructions to the police which have become classics of the art of nonenforcement. In part, they read: "Whether liquors exhibited in your presence . . . are intoxicating liquors . . . you must judge with great circumspection, and be careful to avoid seizing any thus exempt. An error in this regard may lay you liable to severe personal responsibility . . . Keeping liquor with intent to sell or give away, is not an offense fully within the scope of the eye. . . . You can not see the violation . . . for an intent can not be seen. . . . These violations . . . do not . . . compel you to arrest or seize without complaints." This anomalous situation of law enforcement was disposed of by the judiciary who declared the statute unconstitutional in March, 1856. 12 states and 2 territories had prohibition by end of 1855.

1856

1st kindergarten in America opened in Watertown, Wis., under the guidance of Mrs. Carl Schurz, Jewish wife of the prominent German refugee and leading Republican figure in the Lincoln and Hayes administrations. Mrs. Schurz was an ardent disciple of Friedrich Froebel, the progressive educator in Thuringia, whose theories, including that of the kindergarten, had great influence on American education.

Early indication that **baseball** was already considered a national pastime is the following passage from the sporting paper *Spirit of the Times:* "With the fall of the leaf and the diminution of the daylight, many of the out-of-door sports and pastimes come to a close for the season. The manly and exhilarating pastimes of Base Ball, Cricket, Foot Ball, and Racket are not playable. . . . We feel a degree of

247

| POLITICS AND GOVERNMENT; WAR; DISASTERS; VITAL STATISTICS. | BOOKS; PAINTING; DRAMA; ARCHITECTURE; SCULPTURE. |

Nothing Party was officially called the American Party.

May 21 **Lawrence,** Kansas, sacked by "Border Ruffians" and pro-slavery Kansas men. Loss was not great, but act inflamed Northern sentiment, and in retaliation **John Brown,** with 4 sons and 3 companions, massacred 5 pro-slavery men along Pottawatomie Creek on May 24.

May 22 **Sen. Charles Sumner of Massachusetts severely beaten** by cane-wielding Preston S. Brooks, a member of the House from South Carolina. Sumner had made a speech on the Senate floor the day before pertaining to the admission of Kansas to the Union in which he referred to Sen. Butler of South Carolina, a proslavery opponent of admission, in these terms: "the Senator touches nothing which he does not disfigure with error, sometimes of principle, sometimes of fact. He shows an incapacity for accuracy, whether in stating the Constitution, or in stating the law, whether in details of statistics or the diversions of scholarship." Sumner also delivered derogatory comments about South Carolina. Rep. Brooks, Sen. Butler's nephew, felt personally affronted, caned Sumner in the Senate chamber, was arrested and fined $500, which he later paid. Expulsion proceedings in the House failed but Rep. Brooks resigned anyway. However, he was triumphantly re-elected to Congress from his district in the next election. He later challenged a Northern Congressman to a duel which was never held. Sen. Sumner was so severely injured that he spent 4 years recovering from the assault.

June 2 **Anti-slavery section of the Know-Nothing Party** met in New York city and nominated John C. Frémont of California for the presidency and W. F. Johnston of Pennsylvania for the vice-presidency.

June 2–5 **National Convention of the Democratic Party** met at Cincinnati and nominated James Buchanan of Pennsylvania for the presidency and John C.

Vogue for **romantic** and emotional subjects in **painting** is met by Thomas P. Rossiter, who returned from extended stay in France. Titles of his paintings reflect demand of day: *The Last Hours of Tasso; The Parting between Ruth, Orpha, and Naomi; The Return of the Dove to the Ark; Morn, Noon and Evening in Eden.*

Dred, A Tale of the Great Dismal Swamp, published by **Harriet Beecher Stowe.** Dred was popular both in the U.S. and in Europe, but it did not rival *Uncle Tom's Cabin.* The problem of slavery was projected in a utopian setting on a Canadian farm where an abolitionist educated his slaves towards gradual emancipation. *Dred* was significant attempt to emphasize the economic as well as the moral evil of slavery. The author demonstrated the wastefulness of slavery when compared with free labor market of the North.

George William Curtis published 1st part of *Prue and I* (1856–57), satirical essays about life in New York city which imitated *Salamagundi* by Washington Irving. Curtis, a former student at Brook Farm, essayist, and editor, also delivered address against slavery, *The Duty of the American Scholar to Politics and the Times,* this year.

Ruskin, famous English art critic, has this to say of **American painting:** "I have just been seeing a number of landscapes by an American painter of some repute; and the ugliness of them is Wonderful. I see that they are true studies and that the ugliness of the country must be unfathomable." But Ruskin also attacked British art.

Classic history in the vein of Prescott is John L. Motley's monumental *Rise of the Dutch Republic,* acclaimed as the definitive study on the fight for freedom in The Netherlands. Style—glowing with color—is combined with hard fact.

Protracted stay in England provided **Emerson** with material for his **English Traits.** More relaxed than in his *Essays,* he comments keenly and amusingly on the British. Emerson culled some notes from

1st railroad in California built, from Sacramento to Folsom.

This period saw the development and wide use of **"caloric" engines,** invented by John Ericsson. The name was Ericsson's own: the engines were propelled by hot air. Too large for locomotive use they nevertheless were sold for stationary industrial service. Later Ericsson designed and constructed the *Monitor.*

Western Union founded through the consolidation of unstable western telegraph lines. Ezra Cornell suggested the present name of the Company, which was adopted Apr. 1, 1856. 10 years later Western Union moved from Rochester, N.Y., to New York city.

George Fitzhugh, most influential of defenders of southern slavery, published editorial **defense of slavery** in Richmond *Enquirer* which derided the doctrine of "universal liberty." Fitzhugh denied the efficiency of laissez faire, which derived from the economics of Adam Smith, as a norm for the economic good of society. Like the socialist utopians he pointed to the degradation of the working classes of the North. The remedy could, he said, be witnessed in the progressive paternal economy of Southern slavery where the right of society to rule men according to their abilities was outstandingly realized.

Dr. Joseph F. Berg, pastor of Second Reformed Dutch Church of Philadelphia, published *The Stone and the Image, or The American Republic, the Base and Ruin of Despotism.* Dr. Berg argued that America was the **Promised Land of the Bible.**

Jan. 8 **Borax** found for 1st time in U.S. by Dr. John A. Veatch at spring in California.

Mar. 15 **Haverford College** chartered in Haverford, Pa., as the Haverford School Association. It had been founded by the Society of Friends in 1833, the **1st college established in U.S. by the Quakers.** It

old Knickerbocker pride at the continued prevalence of Base Ball as the National game in the region of the Manhattanese."

1st condensed milk plant established at Torrington, Conn., by Gail Borden. This plant was not successful, so Borden opened the 1st commercial condensed milk plant at Burrville, Conn., in 1857. The Civil War gave great impetus to the industry. In 1851 Gail Borden won the Great Council Medal at the Great International Exposition, London, for his development of a 1 lb. meat biscuit containing nutritional qualities of 5 lbs. of meat and 10 oz. of flour. Borden was 1st American food producer to win such honor.

1st recorded observance of **Children's Day** held in the Universalist Church of the Redeemer in Chelsea, Mass., by the Rev. Dr. Charles H. Leonard who conducted a special service for the children of the parish. Since that time, it has been the custom in American Protestant churches to observe Children's Day on the 2nd Sunday in June each year.

Planche or Lively Fairies, a lavish, multi-act **pantomine,** opened in New York city. *Planche* was a London original and was literally floated across the Atlantic. Several thousand dollars were spent in importing the London sets and organizing the show for the New York première.

William Andrus Alcott published *The Home Book of Life and Health* which became the most popular and most authoritative **"doctor book"** of the American home.

The New York Times carried this **advertisement:** "Two well-educated young men would like to make acquaintance of two young ladies, with a view to matrimony. They must be well-educated, of loving temperament, and above all religiously disposed." The young men, a lawyer and a theologian respectively, declared that they were each financially able to support a wife and gave their forwarding address as: Columbians, Box #272, Union-Square Post Office, New York city.

Freeman Hunt wrote *Wealth and Worth.*

| POLITICS AND GOVERNMENT; WAR; DISASTERS; VITAL STATISTICS. | BOOKS; PAINTING; DRAMA; ARCHITECTURE; SCULPTURE. |

Breckinridge of Kentucky for the vice-presidency.

July 17 66 children killed on a Sunday-school outing in a railroad disaster outside Philadelphia, Pa.

June 17–19 National Convention of the Republican Party met in Philadelphia and nominated John C. Frémont of California for the presidency and William L. Dayton of New Jersey for the vice-presidency.

Aug. 1 House refused to seat either pro-slavery or Free State territorial delegates from Kansas. **"Bleeding Kansas"** was without any settled government, and raids between the 2 elements continued, with an estimated 200 killed and $2 million in property destroyed between Nov., 1855, and Dec., 1856.

Aug. 10 400 drowned at a ball on Last Island, La. Winds drove waves over the Gulf resort inundating the island.

Sept. 17 National Convention of the Whig Party met in Baltimore and endorsed candidates of the Know-Nothing Party.

Nov. 4 James Buchanan and John C. Breckinridge defeated John C. Frémont and William L. Dayton in the **presidential elections** by an electoral vote of 174–114. Popular vote: Buchanan, 1,838,169; Frémont, 1,335,264; Fillmore, 874,534.

Dec. 28 Woodrow Wilson, 28th President, born at Staunton, Va.

the journal of his trip to England in 1833, when, completely unknown, he yet managed to interview Wordsworth, Landor, and Carlyle. But the major part of *English Traits* was based upon his observation during his second visit in 1847. England was, he found, the "best of all actual nations," though it was "no ideal framework."

Extraordinarily **popular 2nd-rate novel,** *Lena Rivers,* by Mary Jane Holmes published. Sold about 1,000,000 copies. About this time American readers began to separate into very marked levels of literary tastes.

Mar. 1 New York Philharmonic Society Orchestra performed Second Symphony in D Minor by George F. Bristow, 1 of the few orchestral works by a **native-born composer** to be presented during the mid-19th century.

July 4 Early equestrian statue, masterpiece of the sculptor, is the bronze *Washington* of Union Square, New York city, by Henry Kirke Brown of Massachusetts. Subscriptions for the work were derived from merchants who contributed $400 each. Work catches spirit of nobility and leadership in its subject.

Aug. 18 Copyright law passed by Congress which gives author of a play "along with the sole right to print and publish the said composition, the sole right also to act, perform, or represent the same."

1857

Jan. 15 State Disunion Convention met at Worcester, Mass. Most fiery speech was delivered by William Lloyd Garrison who declared, "No union with slave holders."

Feb. 21 Foreign coins declared no longer legal tender by Act of Congress.

Mar. 3 Foreign duties lowered to level of about 20% by Tariff Act, and free list enlarged.

Mar. 4 James Buchanan, 15th presi-

Atlantic Monthly founded in Boston under the editorship of James Russell Lowell. All the famous New England writers contributed to it. Holmes's *The Autocrat of the Breakfast Table* was printed in it.

Russell's Magazine founded in Charleston, S.C., with Paul Hamilton Hayne as editor. A literary journal, it achieved distinction during its 3 years of life, especially presenting studies of Southern life and literature, but also considering more general matters in science, poetry, travel,

SCIENCE; INDUSTRY; ECONOMICS; EDUCATION; RELIGION; PHILOSOPHY.

SPORTS; FASHIONS; POPULAR ENTERTAINMENT; FOLKLORE; SOCIETY.

granted its 1st degrees in 1856. Haverford School Association became Haverford College in 1875.

Mar. 26 **1st street trains** in New England began running between Boston and Cambridge. They were drawn by steam engines.

Apr. 3 **St. Lawrence University** chartered in Canton, N.Y., under Universalist auspices. 1st degrees awarded in 1863.

Apr. 21 **1st railroad bridge** over Mississippi R. opened with the 1st crossing of a locomotive. Bridge ran between Rock Island, Ill., and Davenport, Iowa.

Oct. 7 Cyrus Chambers, Jr., Pennsylvanian inventor, awarded patent for **1st practical folding machine** to fold book and newspaper sheets mechanically. Installed in Bible printing house of Jasper Harding & Son, Philadelphia, Pa., it proved defective for use in printing fine Bibles but was practical, rapid, and economical in folding almanacs. Chambers, a prolific inventor, built a gold and silver steam engine weighing less than ½ oz.; constructed of 150 parts with screws invisible to naked eye, it was pronounced a marvel of the age.

Dec. 20 **Newberry College** chartered in Newberry, S.C., under Lutheran auspices. 1st degrees granted in 1869. College transferred to Walhalla, S.C., in 1868 but returned to Newberry in 1877.

Hunt, an experienced financial editor, was leading defender of the American business ethos against the champions of the arts and sciences. He argued that commerce had taken such a commanding position in the modern world that the concept of culture had to be broadened to include business. He predicted that the study of business would soon be developed and pursued not merely as a technique but as a culture on par with medicine and law.

Editorial by George Fitzhugh in Richmond *Enquirer* drew the parallel between slavery and liberty which Lincoln later used as the source for his **"House Divided" speech.** Fitzhugh declared that the slave system of the South and the free labor market of the North were mutually antagonistic and would eventually come into conflict with each other. This sentiment was echoed by Lincoln in his great speech of June 16, 1858, in which he declared: " 'A house divided against itself cannot stand.' I believe this government cannot endure permanently half slave and half free."

Lake Michigan linked with Mississippi and Ohio Rivers by completion of **Illinois Central Railroad** between Chicago and Cairo, Illinois. Illinois granted the Illinois Central over 2½ million acres of land in 1851, the largest grant ever made to an American railroad up to that time. The Chicago-Cairo line became, on completion, the longest in the U.S.

1857

1st patent for a **postmarking and stamp-canceling machine** granted.

Mar. 3 **1st U.S. subsidy of overseas cable** voted by Congress, paying company formed by Cyrus W. Field $70,000. Project was also supported by England, and private resources on both sides of Atlantic. Laying of cable from Ireland to Newfoundland begun this year, but it broke some several hundred miles out from Valentia, Ireland. It was decided to use 2 ships, beginning from the middle of the

Central Park, ½ mi. wide and 2½ mi. long, laid out in Manhattan by Frederick Law Olmsted and Calvert Vaux on plans which followed the romantic and naturalistic ideas of the time.

Charity balls invented in New York city to enable society to pay its respects to its charitable obligations with gaudy displays of its wealth. **1st annual Charity Ball** given at the Academy of Music. Ball, an annual social fixture, has been installed in the Waldorf Astoria in recent years.

251

POLITICS AND GOVERNMENT; WAR; DISASTERS; VITAL STATISTICS.

BOOKS; PAINTING; DRAMA; ARCHITECTURE; SCULPTURE.

dent, sworn into office. He was a Democrat and served 1 term in office.

Mar. 6 The decision in the **Dred Scott case** by the Supreme Court under Chief Justice Taney was a setback for the abolitionist cause. Dred Scott, a slave, had been taken into free territory, and maintained that he was therefore free when taken back to slave territory. The court ruled that a Negro was no citizen of the U.S. and therefore could not sue in the courts.

May 1 Massachusetts adopted amendment to state constitution requiring **literacy test** in order to vote. Connecticut had adopted a similar law 2 years earlier, but not as a constitutional amendment.

Aug. 24 **Financial panic** precipitated by failure of the New York city branch of the Ohio Life Insurance Company. 4932 businesses failed this year; by 1859 another 8000 failed. It was primarily the result of over-speculation in railway securities and real estate.

Sept. 11 **Mountain Meadows Massacre** resulted in the death of 120 emigrants headed for California. They were killed in Utah by Indians incited by the Mormon fanatic, John D. Lee. Lee's justification was that he was retaliating for Pres. Buchanan's order removing Brigham Young as governor of Utah.

Sept. 15 **William H. Taft,** 27th President, was born in Cincinnati, Ohio.

Oct. 5 Kansas elected **Free-State legislature** under Gov. Robert J. Walker. Elections were held under supervision; thousands of fraudulent pro-slavery votes were rejected.

Oct. 19 **Lecompton Constitutional Convention** met in Kansas to prepare constitution for popular approval. It was rigged by pro-slavery elements in such a way that slavery could not be eliminated from territory even by a negative majority vote. "Free-Staters" consequently refused to vote, and the constitution, permitting slavery, won approval on Dec. 21. Free-State Party, however, succeeded in

and literary criticism. Among its supporters and contributors were William Gilmore Simms, Henry Timrod, and Basil Gildersleeve.

The Impending Crisis of the South: How to Meet It, by Hinton Rowan Helper, 1st published. It was the most controversial non-fiction book of era, since it asserted that slavery had brought to economic and moral ruin large numbers of Southern whites. Though written by a North Carolinian, it was banned in South. 68 House Republicans endorsed and circulated condensed version of book; in Dec., 1859, John Sherman was denied House Speakership because he had endorsed book.

Harper's Weekly founded under the editorship of George William Curtis.

Aurora Leigh by Elizabeth Barrett Browning **condemned** in Boston as "the hysterical indecencies of an erotic mind."

Finest single granite commercial edifice in Boston's dock area, the Custom House, built according to severe style of an earlier period.

Studio Building, New York's 1st structure designed for artists' studios, built by Richard Morris Hunt.

Oct. **Exhibition of Pre-Raphaelite paintings** organized in New York. Paintings made a great impression upon young artists and public, who had been avidly following the writings of Ruskin in pirated editions. Painters turned to detailed study of nature.

Oct. 10 1 of the most productive and original of early **American sculptors,** Thomas Crawford, died. Most of his life was spent in Rome where he had gone to study with Thorvaldsen. Noteworthy works are the *Bronze Doors* of the Senate Portico, sculptural studies of *James Otis* and *Beethoven, Washington Monument* in Richmond, and the *Armed Freedom* which crowns dome of Capitol. Novelist Francis Marion Crawford was his youngest son.

Dec. 8 *The Poor of New York,* by Irish actor-playwright **Dion Boucicault,**

Atlantic and traveling in opposite directions. After 3 more failures, a copper wire 1950 miles long was laid between Trinity Bay and Valentia, the ships both arriving at their destination on Aug. 5, 1858. Queen Victoria sent 1st message on Aug. 16, 1858, to Pres. Buchanan. Feat was considered a glorious achievement until cable failed to work in very short time, perhaps due to faulty insulation. Finally, in 1866 Field succeeded in laying cable, using the largest steamship of the time, the *Great Eastern.*

May **Channing Home,** hospital for poverty-stricken women, opened in Boston, Mass., under guidance of Harriet Ryan Albee. Became one of best-known charity hospitals in U.S., one of 1st to accept tubercular patients. Home and Mrs. Albee were subjects of poems by Oliver Wendell Holmes, James Russell Lowell, and Ralph Waldo Emerson.

James Edward Allen Gibbs of Mill Point, Va., a farmer, perfected the single-thread loop-stitch **sewing machine.** Though he relied on previous inventions of others, his machine was 1st to achieve practical success. Later improvements made by James Willcox of Philadelphia, Pa., and machine became known as the Willcox and Gibbs.

June 23 Patent awarded to William Kelly for inventing process by which pig

1st pageant of decorated floats in the **New Orleans Mardi Gras** instituted by the Mystic Krewe of Comus, a clandestine organization established in that year.

Growing popularity of **"variety" performances** at eating places. Admission fee at many places was 12¢.

1st baseball association formed. 25 amateur baseball clubs became National Association of Baseball Players. Within 2 years Association doubled in size.

New **baseball rule** fixed the length of a game at 9 innings and provided that an interrupted game would be legal after 5 innings.

The America's cup presented to the New York Yacht Club as a perpetual challenge cup by its owners, Messrs. J. C. Stevens, Edwin A. Stevens, Hamilton Wilkes, J. Beekman Finley, and George L. Schuyler.

Thomas Wentworth Higginson, addressing the National Woman's Rights Convention at New York, attacked American women of letters who refused to risk their popularity by contributing to the **feminist movement.** Observed Higginson, "The first obstacle . . . is the feminine. I feel a sense of shame for American literature, when I think how our literary women shrink, and cringe, and apologize, and dodge, to avoid being taken for 'strong-minded women.'"

Prioress, owned by Richard Ten Broeck, won English Cesarewitch Handicap. Race ended in dead-heat and *Prioress* won run-off against *El Hakim* and *Queen Bess* at end of day's program. Time for the 2-mile 468-yard course was 4:15. *Prioress* was **1st U.S. horse to race in Europe.**

Oct. 6 **American Chess Association** organized at 1st American Chess Congress, New York city. A. B. Meek of Alabama elected president. Committees formed "On the Chess Code," "On An American Chess

| POLITICS AND GOVERNMENT; WAR; DISASTERS; VITAL STATISTICS. | BOOKS; PAINTING; DRAMA; ARCHITECTURE; SCULPTURE. |

convening state legislature, which set another election, this time permitting an unequivocal vote. On Jan. 4, 1858, constitution lost by an overwhelming vote. 3 years previously, Stephen Douglas had converted a simple bill for the government of Kansas and Nebraska into the subtle Kansas-Nebraska Bill. With the support of Pres. Pierce and the Southern leaders, Douglas effectively repealed the Missouri Compromise by making it the choice of the people of Kansas to decide at any time whether they wanted slavery in the state. In the Lecompton Convention the same Southerners reversed their stand.

opened in New York city during Panic of 1857, an event which was incorporated into the play. Boucicault wrote many plays, among them *London Assurance* (produced in London Mar. 4, 1841, before he immigrated to U.S.), *The Octoroon* (1859), dealing with love of a white man for a colored girl, and *Rip Van Winkle* (1865), in which famous actor **Joseph Jefferson** played with so much success. Boucicault is credited with inaugurating the "road system." It was the result of his efforts to secure a law which guaranteed dramatist sole right to "act, perform, or represent" his play.

1858

Mar. 23 Senate voted to allow Kansas into the Union under **Lecompton Constitution** after it had been rejected by Kansas. The House, however, voted to resubmit the Constitution to a popular vote.

May 4 **Lecompton Constitution** resubmitted to the people of Kansas under the **English Bill,** a compromise measure proposed by W. H. English of Indiana. It offered admission to Kansas plus a bonus of a large grant of public land, provided she accept the Lecompton Constitution.

May 11 **Minnesota admitted as state,** 32nd to join Union.

June 8 **Anglo-American accord** reflected by memorandum to U.S. from the British Foreign Secretary in which he formally disclaimed any right to search vessels in peacetime. Slave or suspected slave trade vessels had been repeatedly searched by the British, and many incidents had occurred in the unrest over the Panama Isthmus.

June 13 **Steamship Pennsylvania blew up** causing the death of 160 persons on the Mississippi R., near Memphis, Tenn.

Aug 2 The federal government submitted the **Lecompton Constitution** to the people of Kansas for popular vote for 3rd time. It was rejected and the territory be-

Sales of **Lowell Mason's** *Carmina Sacra,* published in 1841, exceed 500,000 copies, making it the **most popular book of music** in U.S. Mason had been editor of the famous *Boston Handel and Haydn Society Collection of Church Music,* which was published in 1821 and which enjoyed remarkable success. Considering the nature of sacred music, collections sold extraordinarily well. Mason's collection *The Hallelujah* sold 150,000 copies in 5 years.

St. Patrick's Cathedral, New York city, begun; completed 1879. A late example of the Gothic Revival in U.S. architecture, designed by James Renwick.

Wit and humanity of Oliver Wendell Holmes combined to produce his most popular work, **The Autocrat of the Breakfast Table.** A brilliant conversationalist, he found a perfect form in the framework of free talk on any subject that comes to mind: trees, books, sports, poetry, painting, intellect, etc.—all is grist for the "autocrat." Poems, too, are interspersed, among which are "The Chambered Nautilus" and "The Deacon's Masterpiece."

Longfellow revealed his gift as a storyteller in his classic **The Courtship of Miles Standish,** a verse account of a bit of Puritan history of the domestic kind. Miles Standish, John Alden, and Priscilla have become living traditions to millions

254

SCIENCE; INDUSTRY; ECONOMICS; EDUCATION; RELIGION; PHILOSOPHY.	SPORTS; FASHIONS; POPULAR ENTERTAINMENT; FOLKLORE; SOCIETY.

iron is converted to **steel**. Method depends on blowing air through molten pig iron. Actually Henry Bessemer of England had been granted a U.S. patent for essentially same process in 1856, but Kelly proved he had developed method as early as 1851. Kelly was therefore declared the original inventor, and Bessemer's patent was refused renewal.

Association," and "On the Problem Tourney."

Oct. 6 Paul C. Morphy, 20-year-old chess wizard from New Orleans, La., won American chess championship at 1st American Chess Congress in New York city. Left the next year to tour Europe and won many foreign tournaments. Morphy is recognized as **1st American international chess** master.

1858

New Jerseyite Richard Esterbrook developed **1st successful steel pens;** all previous attempts had failed. Esterbrook Pen Company today produces over 216,000,000 pens a year.

1st horsecar in Philadelphia went into operation. As in New York, where the invention began regular passenger runs in 1852, the horsecar soon began to replace the older omnibus. The horsecar, which ran on wheels, effected a minor revolution in city planning, for the tracks were permanent and inflexible. Boston adopted a horsecar line in 1852, Chicago in 1859.

Religious Revival, beginning in New York and Philadelphia, swept across the country. The revival has been associated with the financial panic of 1857. Actually, the religious history of 19th century America was marked by emotionalism and the camp-meeting, so characteristic of outdoor evangelism, had been established as early as 1830. The revival of 1858 was accompanied by daily prayer meetings in every major city, and conversions to the various churches reached unprecedented numbers. The revivalist spirit soon caught on in Europe, and Ireland, Scotland, and Wales joined in the movement.

Jan. 6 **University of the South** char-

Spirited phrase, **"Pike's Peak or Bust,"** adopted as the rallying cry of gold-rushers pushing across the plains towards the Rockies where gold had been discovered in 1857. Denver became a boom town as more than 35,000 Easterners flooded Colorado.

H. C. Wright's *The Unwelcomed Child; or, the Crime of an Undesigned and Undesired Maternity* was popular book on **birth control.** It indicated growing frankness about sexual matters in American society.

National Association of Baseball Players organized to include 16 New York city clubs. Association adopted, with a few changes, rules which had been created by New York Knickerbocker Baseball Club, including standardized measurements for ball and bat, distance between bases, etc. Many of these rules still in force today.

Apr. 12 **1st billiard championship** of U.S. held at Fireman's Hall, Detroit, Mich. Michael J. Phelan defeated John Seereiter in match lasting 9½ hours. It was witnessed by "genteel" audience including a few ladies.

June 16 **"A house divided against itself cannot stand,"** pronounced by Abraham Lincoln in accepting his nomination

came nonslaveholding. It did not enter the Union until 1861.

Aug. 21 1st of 7 **Lincoln-Douglas debates** took place. They were part of the campaign for a Senate seat from Illinois.

Oct. 9 Stage on **1st overland mail service** to Pacific coast reached St. Louis, Mo. Mail was transferred to train at St. Louis for remainder of journey to east coast.

Oct 27 **Theodore Roosevelt**, 26th president, born in New York city.

through this work. In London 10,000 copies were sold on the 1st day of its appearance. Longfellow's popularity is revealed by the fact that over 300,000 of his books were sold by 1857.

John Gorham Palfrey, former editor and publisher of the *North American Review,* began publication of his 5 volume study of the *History of New England.* Palfrey was a pioneer in the creation of an American historiography.

1859

Comstock Lode discovered in Nevada. It was the 1st major silver strike in country.

Feb. 14 **Oregon admitted as state,** 33rd to join Union.

Mar. 7 **Fugitive Slave Act** declared constitutional by Supreme Court. This was the case of *Ableman v. Booth* which reversed an earlier decision handed down by the Wisconsin Supreme Court.

May 12 Vicksburg Commercial Convention urged reopening of African **Slave Trade.** An Act passed in 1820 forbade the further importation of Negro slaves from Africa. The Vicksburg Convention took the position that all laws, state and Federal, restricting the slave trade should be repealed.

July 5 **Kansas constitutional convention** convened at Wyandotte, Kans. The chief issue was whether the state should be free or slave. On Oct. 4 an anti-slavery constitution was ratified by a vote of 10,421 to 5530.

Oct. 16 **John Brown seized the arsenal at Harpers Ferry, W.Va.** He wanted to establish an abolitionist republic in the Appalachians, and to fight slavery with fugitive Negroes and abolitionist whites. On Dec. 2 he was hanged at Charlestown, Va., for murder, conspiracy, and treason against Virginia. In the South he was thought of as a murderer and traitor who

"Dixie," or as first known, "I Wish I Was in Dixie's Land," composed by Dan Emmett as a "walk-around" for Bryant's Minstrels. The song was later claimed by both sides during Civil War, but eventually became associated almost completely with the Confederacy. Emmett was a Northerner from Ohio.

One of the most **popular novels,** *The Hidden Hand,* by the famous E. D. E. N. Southworth published. Nearly all of the more than 50 books of Mrs. Southworth sold over 10,000 copies. Her books were the most marketable of those of any American authoress. *The Hidden Hand* sold almost 2,000,000 copies.

1st newspaper in South Dakota, the *Democrat,* published at Sioux Falls. Later it was called the *Northwestern Independent.* At this time there were very few settlers in the Sioux Valley, and in 1862 homes were abandoned after outbreak of Sioux Indians in Minnesota.

A Tale of Two Cities by Charles Dickens published. Ranks 3rd in American popularity of Dickens' books. 16 books by Dickens may be considered **American best sellers.**

Excitement stirred in salon of New York where 2 pieces of **sculpture,** the *Coquette* and the *Fisher Girl* by William Barbee, were exhibited. One critic writing of the *Fisher Girl* remarked, "We unhesitatingly pronounce the carving of that fishing-net

| SCIENCE; INDUSTRY; ECONOMICS; EDUCATION; RELIGION; PHILOSOPHY. | SPORTS; FASHIONS; POPULAR ENTERTAINMENT; FOLKLORE; SOCIETY. |

tered in Sewanee, Tenn., under Episcopalian auspices. 1st degrees granted in 1873.

Aug. 16 **1st cable message** is sent across the Atlantic Ocean.

Oct. 9 **1st cross-country mail delivery** took 23 days and 4 hours from San Francisco to St. Louis. Westbound stage, leaving at same time, took 24 days, 20 hours, and 35 minutes.

for the senate. He was referring to the nation torn in two by slavery.

July 20 **1st admission charge to a baseball game** (50¢) levied for the contest between Brooklyn and the New York All Stars at Fashion Race Course in Long Island. 1500 spectators saw New York defeat Brooklyn by a score of 22–18.

Oct. 25 Phrase **"An irrepressible conflict,"** used in relation to the slavery issue, was 1st employed by William Henry Seward in a speech delivered in Rochester, N.Y.

1859

Dr. Elias Samuel Cooper founded **1st West coast medical school** as medical department of University of the Pacific, Santa Clara, Calif. Later became Cooper Medical College.

Founding of **Cooper Union** in New York city, significant addition to facilities for mass education. The school offered free courses in practical subjects to working people of all races, colors, and creeds.

Massachusetts Institute of Technology established at Cambridge, Mass. 1st classes met in 1865.

Fifth Avenue Hotel, New York city, installed **1st passenger elevator** in U.S. hotel. Many patrons still preferred stairs.

John Francis Appleby, 18 year old hand on Wisconsin farm, made a model of a machine which bound the sheaves of grain as they were cut by the reaper. Not until 20 years later was the **Appleby Knotter** put into mass production. But, once it caught on, it was rapidly introduced across the world, and is today used to bind the greater part of all grain wherever grown.

Apr. 23 **1st newspaper in Colorado,** the *Rocky Mountain News,* issued from the town of Auraria, absorbed in later-day Denver.

July Prof. Moses G. Farmer illuminated parlor of his home at Salem, Mass., with electric lights in **1st demonstration of electric home lighting** in the world. Cur-

The Dime Book of Practical Etiquette published by Erastus F. Beadle. Its popularity revealed the preocupation with manners that pervaded most American life.

George W. Henry of Oneida, N.Y., known to his contemporaries as **Henry the Holy Shouter,** published his "Shouting: Genuine and Spurious in all Ages of the Church . . . Giving a History of the Outward Demonstrations of the Spirit, such as Laughing, Screaming, Shouting, Leaping, Jerking and Falling under the Power." Mr. Henry advocated a violent form of revivalism and went back to the Old Testament to cite Church Fathers who leaped and sang with joy over their conversion to God.

John C. Heenan claimed **heavyweight boxing championship** after the retirement of John C. Morrissey. No one ever disputed his claim in America so he left for England to find opponents. After his departure, Joe Coburn and Mike McCoole both claimed the American title.

Apr. 12 Michael Phelan of New York city became **1st national billiard champion** by defeating John Seerciter of Detroit, Mich., in 2,000-point match for $15,000 stake. Game was 4-ball carom on 6-pocket table.

June 30 Charles Blondin, French **tightrope walker, crossed Niagara Falls on 1100-ft. cable** suspended 160 ft. above falls. On July 4 he crossed blindfolded pushing

POLITICS AND GOVERNMENT; WAR; DISASTERS; VITAL STATISTICS.	BOOKS; PAINTING; DRAMA; ARCHITECTURE; SCULPTURE.

deserved the gallows, but in the North his gibbet was described as "the cross of a martyr." In Concord, Thoreau, who had dined with Brown 2 years before and heard him address a town hall meeting when the plan for the raid was already in his head, wrote with reference to John Brown: "When a government puts forth its strength . . . to kill the liberators of the slave, what a merely brute . . . force it is seen to be.'" Lincoln was philosophical, and brooded over the fates of historical zealots who had taken it upon themselves to end oppression. Longfellow sounded a prophetic and, as it happened, an echoing, note: "This will be a great day in our history, the date of a new revolution. . . . As I write, they are leading old John Brown to execution. . . . This is sowing the wind to reap the whirlwind, which will soon come."

one of the most perfect triumphs of the chisel, that we have ever beheld. . . ."

Henry David Thoreau wrote "A Plea for Captain John Brown," a consideration of the slavery question.

History of the Reign of Philip the Second, King of Spain, completed by **William Hickling Prescott.**

"Out of the Cradle Endlessly Rocking," among the greater lyrics of **Walt Whitman,** written.

The Minister's Wooing, a romantic novel with setting in Puritan New England, published by **Harriet Beecher Stowe.**

Mar. 26 George F. Bristow's Third Symphony, in F sharp, performed by the New York Philharmonic Society Orchestra. Bristow, though far from being a genius, was the most **noted American composer** of the mid-19th century.

1860

Population—31,443,321. Center of population: 20 miles south by east of Chillicothe, O. 448,070 free negroes; 3,953,760 slaves.

Feb. 27 Abraham Lincoln made famous address at Cooper Union, New York city. He indicated that no compromise with slavery was possible. Speech introduced Lincoln to Easterners.

Mar. 9 1st Japanese embassy to a foreign power, led by Niimi Masaoki, reached San Francisco aboard *Powhatan.* Embassy reached Washington Apr. 25 and remained in U.S. 6 weeks.

Apr. 3 1st relay on pony express mail service left St. Joseph, Mo.; arrived Sacramento, Calif., Apr. 13. Cost at first was $5 a half oz., later reduced to $1. Service discontinued Oct., 1861, when transcontinental telegraph opened.

Apr. 23 National Convention of the Democratic Party met at Charleston, S.C. On Apr. 30 delegates from South walked out over dispute about platform. Remainder, led by Stephen Douglas, sup-

Appearance of **1st Beadle Dime Novel.** By 1865, this series had sold over 4 million copies. Ended in 1897, the Beadle books constituted 1st of the cheap "paperbacks," popular in the last half of the 19th century. Famous characters: Deadwood Dick, Calamity Jane, Kit Carson. In orange jackets, the books were read extensively by soldiers in camp. Originally Beadle's Library had 386 titles; it was soon increased to 630. In 1870 a new series, Beadle's "Pocket Novels," was begun. Literary fare in these novels consists of tales of the West, of the Indian, the pioneer, the gunman, history in the making, etc. In general, the moral tone of these books was high. It was in the later decades that drinking and profanity cropped up as dominant themes.

A best seller, *Rutledge,* by Mrs. Miriam Coles Harris, described the pitfalls of a girl making her way in the serious business of love. It remained popular for a half a century.

Last completed romance of **Nathaniel Hawthorne** is *The Marble Faun.* Laid in

rent, supplied by Voltaic battery, was conducted to 2 lamps on mantelpiece. Strips of platinum provided resisting and lighting medium. Device produced best artificial light then known but was much more expensive than gaslight.

Aug. 27 Edwin Laurentine Drake sunk **1st successful oil well** in U.S. Drilling to depth of 69 feet, he showed for 1st time that petroleum could be drawn from its underground pools.

Sept. 1 George M. Pullman's **1st sleeping car** made its 1st run. It was a converted coach. Around 1864 he built the *Pioneer,* 1st modern sleeping coach, which had most of the features of privacy and service that characterize the Pullmans of today.

wheelbarrow; on Aug. 19 he carried a man on his back; on Sept. 14, 1860, he crossed the wire on stilts. He was 1st man to perform the trick, though many others followed later.

July 1 Amherst defeated Williams, 66 to 32, in the **1st intercollegiate baseball game** in history.

July 26 Harvard won **1st intercollegiate regatta** over Yale and Brown at Lake Quinsigamond, Worcester, Mass. Race, in 6-oared shells, was 3 miles; 1st planned for previous year, race was postponed when Yale stroke, George E. Dunham, drowned.

Oct. 3 **International cricket match** took place in Hoboken between an All-England 11 and an All-U.S. 22 from Philadelphia and New York. The English team was victorious by a score of 64 runs and an inning, after a match that lasted 3 days.

1860

1st kindergarten in English—a German kindergarten had previously operated in Wisconsin—established in Boston by Miss Elizabeth P. Peabody. A student of Friedrich Froebel, German educator, Miss Peabody introduced the Froebel system in her school, but after 7 years decided her training was insufficient and returned to Germany for further study. She was an original member of the Transcendental Club and a friend of Emerson's.

U.S. Department of Education survey showed a total of 321 high schools in all the country; more than half were in 3 states: Massachusetts, New York, Ohio.

Charles Darwin's *Origin of Species,* published in 1859, appeared in America on eve of Civil War when press was preoccupied with politics. Louis Agassiz of Harvard, brilliant Swiss-American naturalist, rejected Darwin's contentions, holding that all species were immutable from the time of creation. Agassiz' position was challenged by his Harvard colleague, botanist Asa Gray, who defended Darwinism as an enrichment of the plan of divine creation.

Olympia Brown admitted to St. Lawrence University, becoming **1st woman in America to be permitted to study theology in full fellowship with men.**

Prices for shaves, haircuts, and curling raised in Tony Delight's in Chicago, 1 of the most famous tonsorial enterprises in America. Shaves went up from 5¢ to 6¢, haircuts from 10¢ to 12¢, and curling from 15¢ or 20¢ to 25¢. Shampoos were now priced at 25¢.

Intercollegiate rowing contests became institutionalized. This year's Regatta saw Harvard, Yale, and Brown striving for the prize, with Harvard winning.

Game of **croquet,** which is well adapted to female participation, introduced from England and enjoyed a large following. Much of its popularity might be attributed to its incidental values as a courting device.

"7th-Inning Stretch" became common at baseball games. It refers to the custom of

ported Constitutional decisions and Congressional non-interference in slavery issue of territories. Convention adjourned May 3 without making nomination.

May 9 **National Convention of the Constitutional Union Party** met in Baltimore and nominated John Bell of Tennessee for the presidency and Edward Everett of Massachusetts for the vice-presidency. Party was composed of remnants of the Whig and American parties.

May 16–18 **National Convention of the Republican Party** met in Chicago and nominated Abraham Lincoln for the presidency and Hannibal Hamlin of Maine for the vice-presidency.

June 18–23 **Democrats** reassembled at Baltimore and nominated Stephen A. Douglas of Illinois for the presidency and Herschel V. Johnson of Georgia for the vice-presidency.

June 28 **Democratic seceders** of the Charleston convention met at Baltimore and nominated John C. Breckinridge of Kentucky for the presidency and Joseph Lane of Oregon for the vice-presidency. Platform supported slavery in the territories.

Sept. 7–8 **Almost 400 perished** when steamship *Lady Elgin* collided with schooner *Augusta* on Lake Michigan. Edward Spencer, a student of Northwestern University, entered the icy waters 16 times to bring back 17 victims of the collision. A bronze tablet on the university campus memorializes his heroism.

Nov. 6 Abraham Lincoln and Hannibal Hamlin won **presidential elections** by an electoral vote of 180 for Lincoln to 72 for Breckinridge, 39 for John Bell, and 12 for Stephen A. Douglas. Popular vote: Lincoln, 1,866,252; Douglas, 1,375,157; Breckinridge, 849,781; Bell, 589,581. News of Lincoln's election was reported as early as Nov. 8.

Dec. 18 **Last-minute compromise** proposed by Sen. Crittenden of Kentucky offered proslavery legislation if the southern states would stay in the Union. But fur-

Rome, the story is a close study of sin growing out of love. He makes full use of his setting, delighting in descriptions of the Eternal City to the extent that the book has often been termed "a guide-book to Rome."

"Old Black Joe," last of Stephen Foster's "plantation songs," published. Foster, in bad financial condition and suffering from alcoholism, moved to New York city and began to write sentimental potboilers—as many as 46 songs in 1 year. He died in Bellevue Hospital, New York city, on Jan. 13, 1864.

Extremely popular marble statue of *Puck* by **Harriet G. Hosmer** made fortune for her. Originally purchased by Prince of Wales, piece was in such great demand that sculptress had to keep 20 Italian stone-cutters busy in her studio.

Ralph Waldo Emerson published *The Conduct of Life.* Emerson reached the fullest perfection of his powers with this work, which was based upon a series of lectures given previously in Pittsburgh and Boston. He emerged as an astute social commentator as well as a moral philosopher. The discoveries of science and the theory of evolution, the uses of wealth, the importance of culture, faith and art, and a reavaluation of the position of the Transcendentalists were among the topics of *The Conduct of Life.*

John Greenleaf Whittier published *Home Ballads,* a minor collection of lyrics.

Henry Timrod, South Carolina poet-tutor, published *Poems,* a collection of his nature poetry. Timrod became the poetic voice of the South during the Civil War, but his reputation rests on the collection of his poems published after his early death in 1867.

Paul Hamilton Hayne published *Arolio, A Legend of the Island of Cos.* Hayne, a Charlestonian lawyer, had his greatest success as a poet with the sonnet. *Arolio* was, despite his preference for the legendary past, among his minor works.

1st repeating rifle in U.S. produced by Oliver F. Winchester, whose name identified his weapon across the continent.

Feb. 15 Wheaton College chartered in Wheaton, Ill., as the Illinois Institute. Established under Methodist auspices, Institute awarded its 1st degrees in 1860, passed under Congregational control in 1861 when it became Wheaton College. It is now not affiliated with any denomination.

Feb. 22 Shoemakers in Lynn, Mass., **struck** for higher wages and recognition of union, choosing Washington's Birthday as symbol of their demand for freedom. The strike, which followed the introduction of new machinery in the shoe industry, soon spread to include 25 towns and 20,000 shoemakers. The workers protested because boys and girls were being introduced to work the new machines, cutting the salary of skilled men to $3 a week. The Mechanics' Association, formed in 1859 at Lynn, organized the strike, but the effort to win general union recognition was largely frustrated.

Mar. 20 St. Stephen's College chartered in Annandale, N.Y. under Episcopalian auspices. 1st degrees granted in 1861. It was rechartered 1935 as Bard College and became coeducational in 1944.

Apr. 14 1st permanent settlement in Idaho established by Mormon emigrants and called Franklin.

May 10 Morrill Tariff Bill passed by the House of Representatives. The tariff became law in March, 1861. It called for the issue of a loan, and payment of treasury notes, as well as for revision of the tariff. It became the regulator of the imports, and was superceded only by the McKinley Bill which was passed by the 51st Congress in 1890.

May 28 The American Peace Society, which was founded in 1828 by William Ladd, met without quorum. The society, dedicated to arbitration and peace, would not countenance even a defensive war. In its early years it had spread quickly, and the waning of its popularity before Civil

spectators standing up in their seats and stretching just before the home team comes to bat in the 7th inning. The custom serves 2 functions, 1 practical and 1 superstitious. The spectator not only relieves his cramped muscles but he brings good luck to his team as well because of the traditional luck of the number "7" in dice.

The press hailed the **strike of shoemakers** in Massachusetts as a virtual revolution. "Rebellion among the workers in New England," "Revolution at the North," were among the warnings which greeted readers over their morning coffee. Some of the newspapers were shocked by the part of the women workers in the strike and bewailed the effects of the feminist movement. The church, in general, supported the strikers, while the New England manufacturers threatened the German and Irish immigrants, who formed the bulk of the strikers, with legislative retaliation which would take away their voting privileges. On April 10, the manufacturers signed a demand for a 10% increase in wages and 1,000 workers returned to their jobs in Lynn. The strike petered out a few weeks later, with the strikers' demand for a union unrecognized.

1st organized baseball game in San Francisco played.

Yale met Harvard in **1st inter-collegiate billiards match.**

A **$5 chemistry set,** the "Youth's Chemical Cabinet," was advertised in *The New York Times* as being "perfectly safe in the hands of youth." The set included directions for experiments, none of which called for strong acids or other "deleterious or dangerous articles."

Mink muffs were advertised in *The New York Times.* They were on sale for $10, regular price $14.

The New York Times carried a no-

| POLITICS AND GOVERNMENT; WAR; DISASTERS; VITAL STATISTICS. | BOOKS; PAINTING; DRAMA; ARCHITECTURE; SCULPTURE. |

ther concessions were impossible with the agitation that had grown between the South and the North. Lincoln opposed Critten-den Compromise.

Dec. 20 South Carolina became 1st state to secede from the Union. Action was taken as a consequence of Lincoln's election.

On Dec. 22 **South Carolina** appointed 3 commissioners to arrange with Pres. Buchanan and Congress for delivery of public lands to state, and on Dec. 27, after Ft. Moultrie had been abandoned by Maj. Robert Anderson, the state seized it and Castle Pinckney. On Dec. 30 South Carolina troops seized U.S. arsenal at Charleston.

Period before the Civil War has been called the **"Golden Day" of American art.** The appellation, where it has application, belonged chiefly to literature. There was little painting of note, and sculpture fared even worse. The Hudson River school, which specialized in landscape painting, was the notable exception to the general mediocrity of painting.

Mar. 29 Irish setting and character used by **Dion Boucicault** in 1 of his smash hits, *Colleen Bawn*. Other plays based on Ireland are *Arrah-na-Pogue* (1864), *The O'Dowd* (1873), *The Shaughraun* (1874), *Cuishla Machree* (1888).

1861

Jan. 9 **Star of the West,** unarmed Federal supply ship, fired upon by South Carolina State battery at Charleston harbor; command to fire given by Francis Wilkinson Pickens, Governor of state. Ship had been sent under orders from President Buchanan to supply and reinforce Federal garrison at Ft. Sumter, S.C.

Jan. 9 **Mississippi** became 2nd state to secede from the Union.

Jan. 10 **Florida convention** voted for secession from the Union. "United States" was changed to "Confederate states" in their constitution.

Jan. 11 **Alabama** convention **adopted ordinance of secession.**

Jan. 19 **Georgia convention passed secession** proposal, thus becoming 5th state to leave the Union.

Jan. 26 **Louisiana convention adopted secession** ordinance, becoming the 6th state to leave the Union.

Jan. 29 **Kansas admitted as a state,** 34th to join the Union. She entered as a free state.

Feb. 4 **Confederate States of America formed** at Montgomery, Ala. President was Jefferson Davis of Mississippi; Alex-

Best seller *East Lynne* by Englishwoman Mrs. Henry Wood. Usually published in cheap editions, this famous domestic melodrama has sold at least 1,000,000 copies.

Outbreak of Civil War occasioned **closing down of many theaters.** Niblo's Garden and the Bowery in New York, the Boston Theater, and some in Philadelphia and Richmond were closed.

"All Quiet Along the Potomac Tonight" appeared as one of the **hit tunes** of the Civil War. Composed by James Hewitt, northern musician then living in the South.

Early example of **Impressionism** in American painting seen in the *Delaware Water Gap* by George Inness. He sums up his notion of the painter's craft by saying, "The purpose of the painter is simply to reproduce in other minds the impression which a scene has made upon him. A work of art does not appeal to the intellect. It does not appeal to the moral sense. Its aim is not to instruct, not to edify, but to awaken an emotion."

Aug. 15 **Events of Civil War quickly dramatized** on New York stage: *Bull Run* by Charles Gayler presented less than a month after the event itself. Other plays dealing with war are *Capture of Fort*

SCIENCE; INDUSTRY; ECONOMICS; EDUCATION; RELIGION; PHILOSOPHY.

SPORTS; FASHIONS; POPULAR ENTERTAINMENT; FOLKLORE; SOCIETY.

War was an indication of the shift in popular sentiment regarding the justice of the approaching conflict. In Jan. 1861, the society sent a plea to 500 newspapers, advising a more temperate presentation of the issues which were leading the country towards war.

June 23 Congress enacted bill to establish **Government Printing Office.** Later the government bought an existing commercial press in Washington, D.C. Today Government Printing Office is largest printing establishment in world with plant valued at over $20,000,000.

tice of an **Exhibition of the Great Paintings.** The chefs-d'oeuvre on display were Thomas B. Thomp's "Niagara As It Is!"; the "last and greatest" of William Page, "Moses on Mount Horeb"; Thomas Rossiter's "three great paintings," "Miriam," "Noah," and "Jeremiah." An exhibition of famous sculptures was also promised, which included "The Dead Pearl Diver," "The Fisher Girl," and "Flora."

Oct. 4 **The Prince of Wales,** bored by a reception at the White House, slipped off with the niece of President Buchanan, Harriet Lane, to the gym of Mrs. Smith's Institute for Young Ladies, where the prince and his partner played ten-pins.

1861

University of Colorado, Boulder, Colo., chartered as University of Boulder. It became a state school in 1877.

University of Washington, Seattle, Wash., established as Territorial University of Washington. 1st classes held same year. Present name adopted 1889.

Yale University, 1st American institution to offer effective course of **graduate study,** awarded 3 Ph.D. degrees, 1st given in U.S.

Jan. 18 **Vassar College** chartered in Poughkeepsie, N.Y. as Vassar Female College. Established by Baptist interests, Vassar Female College opened in 1865 and awarded its 1st degrees in 1867, the same year it dropped the "Female" from its name. Founder was Matthew Vassar.

Apr. 20 Thaddeus Sobieski Coulincourt Lowe, inventor and balloonist, made **record balloon voyage** from Cincinnati, Ohio, to coast of South Carolina in 9 hrs. On Oct. 1 he was appointed by Pres. Lincoln commander of newly-formed Army Balloon Corps.

Aug. 5 **1st income tax** law passed by Congress. It was levied to aid in financing the Civil War.

Feat of walking accomplished by Edward P. Weston, who did the distance of 478 miles from Boston to Washington in 208 hours. Union army studied this feat to determine how far troops could be made to travel on forced marches.

Sensation in England was the Seneca Indian **foot racer, Deerfoot,** who, running in breechcloth and moccasins, outdistanced every available English runner. Greatest crowds ever to attend a meet, including the royal family, flocked to see him run.

1st baseball trophy offered by newspaper, *New York Clipper.*

Mar. 4 In his **Inaugural Address** Lincoln began with the sentiment which has since become an integral part of the literature, as well as the history of America: "This country, with its institutions, belongs to the people who inhabit it. Whenever they shall have grown weary of the existing government, they can exercise their constitutional right of amending it, or their revolutionary right to dismember or overthrow it." He concluded: "We are not enemies, but friends. We must not be enemies. . . . The mystic chords of memory . . . will yet swell the chorus of the Union, when again touched, as they surely

| POLITICS AND GOVERNMENT; WAR; DISASTERS; VITAL STATISTICS. | BOOKS; PAINTING; DRAMA; ARCHITECTURE; SCULPTURE. |

ander H. Stephens of Georgia was vice-president. Both were chosen on Feb. 9.

Feb. 9 Confederate Provisional Congress asserted that all laws under the U.S. Constitution which were not inconsistent with the constitution of the Confederate States would be recognized.

Feb. 13 Col. Bernard John Dowling Irwin conducted **1st Medal of Honor action** as part of Indian campaign at Apache Pass, Ariz. The medal awarded because the Colonel led his troops to victory over Indian detachment, was not given until Jan. 24, 1894.

Feb. 18 Jefferson Davis inaugurated president of Confederacy. Confederate capital 1st established in Montgomery, Ala., where Davis lived at 626 Washington St., in building known as White House of the Confederacy; capital later was moved to Richmond, Va.

Feb. 23 Texas voted in favor of secession after state convention recommended it on Feb. 1. She was 7th state to join Confederacy.

Mar. 2 Creation of the Nevada and Dakota territories by a division of the territory of Utah.

Mar. 4 Confederate Convention, meeting at Montgomery, Ala., chose "Stars and Bars" as official **Confederate flag.** Flag had 7 stars and 3 stripes, and was raised over Confederate Capitol at Montgomery. Later after similarity between Union and Confederate flags created confusion at Battle of Bull Run, Confederate Army adopted battle flag consisting of red field and blue cross of St. Andrew with 13 stars.

Mar. 4 Abraham Lincoln inaugurated president of what was no longer the *United* States.

Mar. 9 Confederate Congress enacted **coinage bill** authorizing issuance of treasury notes in denominations up to $1 million and not less than $50.

(Continued in next column)

Donelson (1862) by Harry Seymour; *How to Avoid Drafting* (1862) anonymous; *A Supper in Dixie* (1865) by William C. Reynolds; *The Guerrillas* (1862) by James D. McCabe, Jr.; *Grant's Campaign* (1865) by John Poole; *The Color Guard* (1870).

Elsie Venner, a novel by **Oliver Wendell Holmes,** published. Like "The Deacon's Masterpiece," *Elsie Venner* is critical of Calvinism. Holmes used his novel to support the determinism which dominated the intellectual life of his day.

(Column 1 continued)

Mar. 11 Confederate Congress in session at Montgomery, Ala., adopted **Constitution** unanimously; it declared sovereignty of states and forbade passage of any law to prohibit slavery.

Apr. 12 Civil War broke out when Fort Sumter, Charleston, S.C., was fired upon by Fort Moultrie. Gen. Beauregard, Confederate, ordered the action when Maj. Anderson at Fort Sumter refused to surrender.

Apr. 13 Maj. Anderson **surrendered Fort Sumter** to the Confederates when provisions ran out. He and his men were allowed to return north.

Apr. 15 Pres. Lincoln declared existence of an "insurrection" and issued 1st call for **volunteer troops;** he asked for 75,000 for 3 months' service.

Apr. 17 Virginia convention voted for secession from Union as a result of Lincoln's call for troops. The proposal was put before the people of Virginia on May 23 and passed. Virginia was 8th state to leave Union.

Apr. 19 Troops of 6th Massachusetts Regiment marching en route to Washington, D.C., stoned by mobs in Baltimore, Md.; 4 soldiers killed. Incident constituted **1st casualties of Civil War.**

(Continued in next column)

SCIENCE; INDUSTRY; ECONOMICS; EDUCATION; RELIGION; PHILOSOPHY.

Oct. 4 U.S. Navy authorized construction of armored turreted warship, **Monitor.** Invented and made by John Ericsson, vessel was launched in Long Island waters.

Oct. 24 Pres. Lincoln in Washington, D.C., received **1st coast-to-coast telegram,** sent from Sacramento, Calif. The transcontinental line had been joined at Ft. Bridger, Utah.

Dec. 24 **Waco University** chartered in Waco, Tex. University became part of Baylor University in 1886.

(Column 1 continued)

Apr. 19 **Pres. Lincoln ordered blockade of Southern ports,** thus preventing the importation of greatly needed war supplies.

May 6 **Arkansas seceded from the Union,** the 9th state to join the Confederacy.

May 20 **North Carolina,** in convention, **voted to secede from the Union,** the 10th state to join the Confederacy.

May 21 Richmond, Va., made **Capital of the Confederate States.** Virginia at this time was the most populated of the Southern states.

June 8 **Tennessee seceded from Union,** the 11th state to join the Confederacy.

July 21 Gen. McDowell defeated at **Bull Run,** near Manassas, Va., by the Confederates. McDowell delayed the attack 2 days, thus allowing Confederate Gen. Beauregard, who was apprised of the imminent arrival of federal troops, to call upon reinforcements. Their arrival on the 21st gave the Confederates a numerical advantage over the Federals.

July 25 **Use of volunteers sanctioned** by Congress to assist in putting down the rebellion in the South. A bonus of $100 was paid to those who volunteered for at least 2 years.

(Continued in next column)

SPORTS; FASHIONS; POPULAR ENTERTAINMENT; FOLKLORE; SOCIETY.

will be, by the better angels of our nature."

June 10 **Dorothea Dix,** famous penal and hospital reformer, appointed **superintendent of women nurses,** in which post she served as head of hospital nursing for the Union Army.

Aug. **Summer camp** for boys, perhaps 1st in country, founded at Welch's Point, Milford, Conn., by Frederick William Gunn, founder and head of Gunnery School at Washington, Conn.

(Column 1 continued)

Aug. 10 **Battle of Wilson's Creek** won by the Confederates under Gens. Price and McCulloch. Gen. Lyon, who commanded the outnumbered Union forces, was killed during the battle.

Sept. 13 In what was perhaps **1st real naval engagement** of the Civil War Lt. John Henry Russell raided navy yard at Pensacola, Fla., in order to destroy privateer *Judah,* which was protected by Confederate shore batteries and 1000 men. Russell succeeding in burning ship after sharp encounter with enemy at night. He was thanked personally by Pres. Lincoln and given special recognition by the Navy department for his gallantry.

Oct. 21 Union troops defeated at **Ball's Bluff,** Leesburg, Va. Some 1900 Union soldiers were killed during the engagement.

Nov. 1 Gen. Scott succeeded by Gen. McClellan as **Commander in Chief of the Federal Armies.** Scott went into retirement the previous day at the age of 75.

Nov. 7 **Forts Beauregard and Walker captured** by Union forces under Gen. Sherman and Comm. duPont. Port Royal Sound, where the 2 forts were located, was subsequently used as a base of operations from which attacks along southeastern coast originated.

POLITICS AND GOVERNMENT; WAR;   BOOKS;   PAINTING;   DRAMA;

DISASTERS;   VITAL   STATISTICS.   ARCHITECTURE;   SCULPTURE.

1862

Feb. 8 Union Forces captured Roanoke Island, N.C. Gen. Wise and his Confederate garrison of 2675 men were made prisoners.

Mar. 6 Battle of Pea Ridge, Ark., began and continued for 2 days. A Confederate attack was repulsed by the Federals under Gen. Curtis. Gens. McCulloch and McIntosh of the Confederate army were killed.

Mar. 8 The Virginia (Merrimac) sank 2 Union frigates, the *Cumberland* and the *Congress* at Hampton Roads, Va.

Mar. 9 Sea battle between Union vessel **Monitor** and Confederate **Merrimac** occurred off Hampton Roads, Va., 1st encounter between fully armored warships. *Monitor* won the engagement.

Apr. 6–7 Battle of Shiloh or Pittsburg Landing, Tenn., was fought. The Union army of Tennessee, under Gen. Grant and the Confederate army of Mississippi under Gens. Albert Johnston and Beauregard waged a furious and mutually destructive battle against each other, but the engagement ended indecisively. Gen. Albert Johnston was killed.

May 1 Farragut took possession of New Orleans after a battle on the Mississippi R. with Confederate vessels.

May 20 Homestead Act, enacted the day before by both houses of Congress, signed by President Lincoln. Law entitled any citizen or intending citizen, 21 years old or older and head of a family, to acquire 160 acres of the public domain by settling on it for 5 years and paying $1.25 per acre.

May 31–June 1 Confederates repulsed in the **Battle of Seven Pines** (or Fair Oaks) near Richmond, Va. The arrival of Gen. Sumner with reinforcements decided the victory in favor of the Federals. Confederate Gen. Joseph Johnston was badly wounded in the engagement.

One of **America's foremost satirists,** Charles Farrar Browne, issued his *Artemus Ward, His Book,* a series of humorous commentaries on contemporary affairs, recounted in the warm style of a Will Rogers. The passions and foibles of men are his butt; rarely does he take a strong partisan stand.

Posthumous **novel of the Rockies** is Theodore Winthrop's *John Brent.* It features the adventures of three men and a girl, with a horse, Don Fulano, whose likes have rarely been seen. Pictures of the Mormons, bravos of the frontier, etc. fill out the tale. Winthrop's career as a novelist was cut off by the war; he was killed early in the battle of Great Bethel.

1st newspaper published in Idaho was the *Golden Age* of Lewiston.

Study of American landscape with the close fidelity of French realists is Albert Bierstadt's *Guerrilla Warfare.* Most of Bierstadt's works, large panoramas of Western mountain ranges, are empty of human feeling.

Famous best seller, *Parson Brownlow's Book,* by Parson William G. Brownlow, an ardent Unionist, published. A denunciation of the Confederate cause, this book sold 100,000 copies in 3 months. The Parson's violent oratory during his countrywide tours helped boost sales throughout Civil War. In 1865 he was elected governor of Tennessee, and in 1869 he became a U.S. senator.

Apr. New York Legislature passed law against resorts and restaurants where **"Variety" programs** were staged and where liquor was served by "waitresses."

Dec. 8 Giant of **post-Civil War playwrights,** Augustin Daly, began career with

1862

Medical department of University of the City of New York set up a **clinic for children,** under direction of Dr. Abraham Jacobi. Jacobi was founder of *American Journal of Obstetrics* and president of A.M.A.

John D. Rockefeller, 23 years old, invested $4000 of his savings in an "oil-refining" partnership.

Prof. Louis Elsberg of University of City of New York opened **1st public clinic for throat diseases.** He was 1st American laryngologist, having studied in Vienna, and 1st to demonstrate laryngoscope in America.

Famous American balloonist, Thaddeus Lowe, performed significant **aerial reconnaissance** for Union forces by photographing Confederate ground emplacements around Richmond, Va., at a height of 1000 ft. **1st use of cameras to produce panoramic shots of military positions.**

Violent influence in U.S. labor relations was secret organization known as the **"Molly Maguires,"** an American development of the anti-landlord Ancient Order of Hibernians in Ireland.

May 15 Federal government established **Dept. of Agriculture.** Previously it was a part of the Patent Office. Department attained cabinet rank in 1889.

July 1 Pres. Lincoln signed bill incorporating the Union Pacific Company and subsidizing it with federal funds so that it might construct a line from Nebraska to Utah to meet the Central Pacific and thus form a **transcontinental railroad.**

July 2 Pres. Lincoln signed **Morrill Act** granting public land to states for establishment of agricultural colleges; the act created the "land grant" colleges which exist in most states today.

Aug. 28 **1st work of Bureau of Printing and Engraving** begun with 5 employees,

War did not diminish interest in the **trotting races.** A new track established in New York city at 144 St. between 7th and 8th Aves.

1st enclosed baseball field opened at Union Grounds, Brooklyn, N.Y.

Alexander T. Stewart, a drygoods merchant, built a store at Broadway and 10th Street, New York city, which quickly became a landmark and was a forerunner of the department store. The building, designed by John Kellum, was later purchased by John Wanamaker and expanded into the famous **department store,** which stood, until it was destroyed by fire in 1956.

July 16 Popular Civil War slogan, **"We Are Coming, Father Abraham, Three Hundred Thousand More,"** appeared in the marching song by James Sloan Gibbons published in the New York *Evening Post.* Lincoln had urged Congress to raise an army of a half a million; the song was written to aid in the call for volunteers.

July 30 Term, **"Copperhead,"** used extensively for 1st time. It appeared in the Cincinnati *Gazette* and referred to the Indiana state Democratic Convention where some Southern sympathy was manifested.

Dec. 29 Walt Whitman wrote from Washington to tell his mother the news about his brother, George, whom he had visited in **camp.** He had a hard time locating his brother's outfit, and his pocket had been picked while he was changing cars in Philadelphia. But he found George safe and promoted to a captain of the 51st New York Volunteers, stationed at Falmont, Va., near Fredericksburg. George Whitman was sharing a tent with a Captain Francis, and Walt lived in with them: "There were 5 of us altogether, to eat, sleep, write, etc., in a space twelve feet square. George is about building a place,

POLITICS AND GOVERNMENT; WAR;
DISASTERS; VITAL STATISTICS.

BOOKS; PAINTING; DRAMA;
ARCHITECTURE; SCULPTURE.

June 1 Gen. **Robert E. Lee** appointed Confederate commander of armies of Eastern Virginia and North Carolina.

July Maj. Gen. David Hunter organized 1st South Carolina Regiment, the **1st organized Negro troops of the Civil War.** It later became 33rd U.S. Colored Infantry.

July 1 **Public debt** rose to $524,176,-412.13 and exceeded $500 million for 1st time. 1 year before it had been only $90 million; one year later it exceeded $1 billion.

July 1 Congress enacted **antipolygamy measure** aimed at Mormon practices in Utah. Previous antipolygamy legislation had been enacted as far back as 1847, largely under the leadership of Justin Smith Morrill.

July 1 **"7 Days' Battle"** ended with the Battle of Malvern Hill where retreating Union forces repulsed the Confederates, allowing them to withdraw to Harrison's Landing. Gen. McClellan commanded the Union forces while Gen. Lee led the Confederates.

July 11 Maj. Gen. Halleck appointed **Commander in Chief** of all U.S. land forces.

(Continued in next column)

adaptation of play by German von Mosenthal which he called *Leah the Forsaken.* Besides his original plays, Daly was responsible for 90 adaptations from the French, German, and English.

(Column 1 continued)

July 12 Congress authorized **Medal of Honor** for gallantry in action; 2000 medals were struck for presentation to Federal non-commissioned officers and privates.

July 22 1st draft of **Emancipation Proclamation** submitted to Cabinet by Pres. Lincoln. On June 17 Congress had freed all slaves in U.S. territories. Lincoln was persuaded to keep Proclamation quiet for a time, and so it was not made public until after Battle of Antietam. Circulated by press Sept. 23 under title Preliminary Emancipation Proclamation, it took effect Jan. 1, 1863, and affected only areas in rebellion.

July 24 **Martin Van Buren** dead at the age of 79. He is buried at Kinderhook, N.Y.

(Continued in next column)

1863

Henry Ward Beecher, famous clergyman of the Plymouth Congregational Church in Brooklyn, journeyed to England on a lecture tour during which he defended the Union position before English audiences often sympathetic towards the South.

Congress enacted bill establishing **free delivery of mail in cities.**

Jan. 1 **Lincoln issued Emancipation Proclamation.** This was distinctly a war measure and did not cover the states that had not seceded from the Union (Missouri, Delaware, Kentucky, and Maryland) nor did it prevent the South from reinstituting slavery after their readmission

Close relationship of **Whistler** to French Impressionists—Manet, Degas, Legros—seen in his **Little White Girl** shown at Salon des Refusées. Picture was well received, and thereafter he saw Paris as one of his 2 European havens, the other being London.

Most influential **labor paper** of Civil War, *Fincher's Trades' Review,* established in Philadelphia, Pa.

1st newspaper to be printed in Wyoming was the *Daily Telegram,* published at Fort Bridges.

Although engrossed in his translation of Homer, Bryant published a number of

SCIENCE; INDUSTRY; ECONOMICS; EDUCATION; RELIGION; PHILOSOPHY.	SPORTS; FASHIONS; POPULAR ENTERTAINMENT; FOLKLORE; SOCIETY.

who undertook task of sorting notes and affixing the seal to them.

Nov. 4 Patent issued to Richard Jordan Gatling for "revolving gun battery," the **1st machine gun**; it shot 350 rounds a minute. Gatling offered his invention to Union Army, but Ordnance Department did not accept it until 1866.

half hut and half tent, for himself. Every captain has a tent, in which he lives, transacts company business . . . has a cook, (or a man of all work,) and in the same tent mess and sleep his lieutenants, and perhaps the first sergeant. They have a kind of fire-place—and the cook's fire is outside on the open ground. . . ."

(Column 1 continued)

Aug. 9 Union forces defeated at **Cedar Mountain**, Va., by Confederates under Gen. Jackson. 314 Federals were killed and almost 1500 wounded. The Confederates lost 229 killed and some 1000 wounded.

Aug. 18 Chief Little Crow led **Sioux uprising** in Minnesota. There were many massacres (350 whites killed), but Indians defeated by Col. Henry Sibley at Wood lake Sept. 23.

Aug. 30 Union troops, under Gen. Pope, defeated in the **2nd Battle of Bull Run** and were forced to retreat to Washington. The Confederates were led by Jackson, Lee, and Longstreet.

Sept. 15 **Harpers Ferry**, W. Va., captured by "Stonewall" Jackson. Tremendous

(Continued in next column)

(Column 1 continued)

quantity of materials and 12,500 men were captured.

Sept. 17 Gen. Lee's **invasion of the North** halted by Gen. McClellan at the **Battle of Antietam**, Md. Bloodiest day of Civil War: Union, 2108 killed, 9549 wounded; Confederate, 2700 killed, 9029 wounded.

Nov. 5 Pres. Lincoln relieved **Gen. McClellan** as commander in chief of Northern forces and appointed Gen. **Ambrose E. Burnside** to succeed him.

Dec. 13 Union troops defeated at **Fredericksburg**, Va., by Gen. Lee. The Federals, under Gen. Burnside, suffered 12,653 killed and wounded while the Confederates lost 5309 men.

1863

University of Massachusetts, Amherst, Mass., chartered as Massachusetts Agricultural College. 1st classes met in 1867. Name was changed to Massachusetts State College in 1931; present name adopted in 1947.

Ebenezer Butterick of Sterling, Mass., invented **1st paper dress patterns** sold in U.S. At 1st he used heavy paper but changed to tissue paper in 1864. Patterns were immediately successful; 6 million sold in 1871.

Travelers Insurance Company founded in Hartford, Conn., as **1st travelers' accident insurance company** in U.S. 1st pre-

Famous actress, Adah Isaacs Menken, scored spectacular triumph in Virginia City, Nev., with her performance in *Mazeppa, or The Wild Horse,* at the climax of which she was strapped to the side of a wild horse and, in a flimsy gauze garment, driven up a mountain trail. The mining audiences stood on their chairs and wildly cheered. Virginia City was so electrified that it named a new mining district the Menken and established a Menken Shaft and Tunnel Company. Miss Menken departed from Virginia City with bars of bullion, silver ingots, and certificates of mining stock donated by her many admirers.

into the Union. Hence the 13th amendment abolishing slavery constitutionally.

Feb. 24 Territory of Arizona formed from New Mexico.

Feb. 25 Office of Comptroller of the Currency established by Congress. Hugh McCulloch was 1st to hold the post. He was appointed May 9, 1863.

Mar. 3 Territory of Idaho carved from 4 existing territories—Washington, Utah, Dakota, and Nebraska.

Mar. 3 1st national conscription act passed which called for the enrollment of all male citizens and aliens who had declared intention to become citizens between 20 and 45 years of age. Conscripts could be exempted from military service by a payment of $300 or by substitution.

May 2 Gen. Thomas "Stonewall" Jackson mortally wounded by his own men during the **Battle of Chancellorsville**, Va., when he was mistaken for an enemy as he returned from a night reconnaissance.

June 20 West Virginia admitted as a state, the 35th to join the Union.

June 27–July 4 Gen. Robert E. Lee defeated at **Gettysburg** by the Union army under Gen. Meade. Many in both armies were killed, and in November, when Lincoln made his famous Gettysburg Address, the battlefield was made a national cemetery.

July 4 Gen. Pemberton capitulated at **Vicksburg,** Miss. to Gen. Grant, surrendering his entire garrison of over 29,000 men.

July 8 Confederate Gen. Gardner surrendered **Port Hudson,** Miss., and his garrison of 5500 men to Gen. Banks after a siege of 6 weeks.

July 13–16 Antidraft riots broke out in New York city where almost 1000 persons were killed or wounded before federal troops restored order.

Sept. 19–20 Union Gen. Rosencrans defeated at **Chickamauga,** Ga., by Gen. Bragg. The Federals lost some 16,000 in

(Continued in next column)

wartime poems entitled *Thirty Poems.* Other poets also turned to themes of patriotism and war: George Henry Boker produced a volume *Poems of the War* (1864); Whittier, *In War Time* (1864); Herman Melville, *Battle Pieces and Aspects of War* (1866).

The narrative skill of Longfellow is wonderfully employed in the series of stories in verse, **Tales of a Wayside Inn** (Part I). Using the convention of Chaucer and Boccaccio, he and 6 associates gather at an inn in Sudbury, Mass., and recount such favorites as "Paul Revere's Ride," "The Saga of King Olaf," "The Legend of Rabbi Ben Levi," and "The Birds of Killingworth."

June 1 Striking example of **freedom of the press** despite the difficulty of events and the attitude of the newspaper occurred when the Chicago *Times*, a violently anti-Lincoln newspaper, was suppressed by General Burnside. The order was revoked 3 days later by Pres. Lincoln personally.

Nov. 19 One of the immortal speeches of all times, **"The Gettysburg Address,"** delivered on the bloodstained field by Abraham Lincoln. Simple diction, rhythmic sentences, and perfect ordering of material added to the sense of the tragic give this brief address the universal appeal it will always maintain. Lincoln spoke at ceremonies dedicating a national cemetery.

Dec. Edward Everett Hale's **Man Without a Country** published by *Atlantic Monthly.*

(Column 1 continued)

killed and missing; the Confederates about 18,000.

Nov. 23–25 Union forces under Grant defeated Confederates at **Chattanooga,** Tenn. The Union army suffered 5815 casualties while the Confederates under

(Continued in next column)

| SCIENCE; INDUSTRY; ECONOMICS; EDUCATION; RELIGION; PHILOSOPHY. | SPORTS; FASHIONS; POPULAR ENTERTAINMENT; FOLKLORE; SOCIETY. |

mium received was 2¢ for insuring a Hartford banker while walking from postoffice to home. Company was founded by James G. Batterson.

Rise of railway brotherhoods began with organization of Railway Locomotives Engineers.

Jan. Noninterference in the internal affairs of **Confederate churches** behind the Federal lines demanded of the military by Abraham Lincoln in a letter to the commanding general of the Union forces at St. Louis, Mo.

Mar. 2 Congress authorized railway gauge of 4 ft. 8½ in. for the Union Pacific Railroad. This act rejected Pres. Lincoln's recommendation of 5 ft. as the gauge. **Congressional gauge** has become the generally accepted measure in most of the world's railways.

Mar. 3 Congress chartered in Washington **National Academy of Sciences** as a private, non-profit organization to promote science and investigate scientific problems for the government. Academy includes 518 members today.

Apr. 14 **Continuous roll printing press** patented by William Bullock, who developed his invention in Pittsburgh, Pa.

May 1 **New York Hospital for Ruptured and Crippled Children** opened in New York city; 1st orthopedic hospital in U.S. In 1940 institution was renamed Hospital for Special Surgery.

Dec. 1 Samuel D. Goodale of Cincinnati, Ohio, secured patent for stereoscopic apparatus to show scenes in motion. Operated by hand, it was forerunner of modern **"peep-show"** devices.

(Column 1 continued)

Gen. Bragg, lost some 7000 men in killed and wounded.

Dec. 8 **Proclamation of Amnesty and Reconstruction** offered full pardon to all Southerners who voluntarily took a "prescribed oath."

New baseball regulation provided that both balls and strikes were to be called.

Roller skating introduced to America by James L. Plimpton. He invented the 4-wheel skate, which worked on rubber pads.

1st attempt to "steal a base" made by Eddie Cuthbert of Philadelphia when Keystones played against Brooklyn Atlantics.

Sport of **racquets** greatly encouraged by the construction of excellent courts on West 13th Street, New York city and the engagement of Frederick Foulkes of England as a professional player. In 1867 an international match with England was staged, in which William Gray, the champion of the British Isles, beat the American entry.

A letter by Walt Whitman to Nat and Fred Gray gave some vivid glimpses of **life at the front:** "I . . . have seen warlife, the real article—folded myself in a blanket, lying down in the mud with composure—relished salt pork and hard tack —have been on the battlefield among the wounded, the faint and the bleeding . . . have gone over with a flag of truce the next day to help direct the burial of the dead. . . ." Whitman also visited the army hospitals: "These Hospitals, so different from all others—these thousands, and tens and twenty of thousands of American young men, badly wounded, all sorts of wounds, operated on, pallid with diarrhoea, languishing, dying with fever, pneumonia, etc."

Jan. 1 **Emancipation Day** commemorated as a holiday by Negroes as it was on this date that Pres. Lincoln issued his Emancipation Proclamation.

May 5 Joe Coburn knocked out Mike McCoole in a 63-round **American boxing championship** bout held at Charleston, Md. Coburn announced his retirement in 1865 and McCoole claimed the title.

Oct. 3 **Thanksgiving Day** proclaimed by Pres. Lincoln as a national holiday to be observed on the last Thursday in November.

1864

Motto, "In God We Trust," appeared on U.S. coin for 1st time; it was used on the 1864 2¢ piece.

Feb. 7 **Union Gen. Seymour entered Jacksonville,** Fla., and attempted to reconvert the state to Union allegiance.

Feb. 20   Gen. Seymour beaten at **battle of Olustee, Fla.,** by Confederates under Gen. Finegan. Some 2000 Union troops were killed or wounded.

Mar. 10   **Gen. Ulysses S. Grant named Commander in Chief** of the Federal armies, replacing Gen. Halleck.

Apr. 12   Confederates, led by Maj. Gen. Forrest, stormed and captured **Fort Pillow** on Mississippi R. in Tennessee. The next day Forrest's troops massacred the Negro troops in the Union garrison.

Apr. 17   Gen. Grant discontinued **prisoner of war** exchange, stating the practice served to prolong the conflict and mitigated against a speedy Union victory.

Apr. 20   **Rations** of Confederate captives reduced by War Department as a counterstroke to mistreatment of Union prisoners.

May 5–6   **Battle of Wilderness** ended indecisively as the armies of Lee and Grant wrought mutual destruction upon each other near Chancellorsville, Va. Because of the thick forest growth, most of the fighting was done at close hand and resulted in a high number of casualties.

May 12   In **battle of Spotsylvania,** Va., Gen. Hancock gained a salient and captured Confederate Gen. Edward Johnson and about ⅔ of his troops.

May 26   **Territory of Montana** formed from Territory of Idaho.

June 3   Lee repulsed **Grant's assault at Cold Harbor,** Va., where the Union army suffered heavy casualties.

June 7   **Republican party** nominated Abraham Lincoln for Presidency, Andrew

1st newspaper to be published in North Dakota, the *Frontier Scout,* started at Fort Union.

1st newspaper in the Montana Territory, the *Montana Post* begun.

Adaptation of *Le Papillon* of Sardou by **Augustin Daly** initiated host of adaptations of plays by this prolific Frenchman: *King Carrot* (1872), *Folline* (1874), *Odette* (1882), *The Golden Widow* (1889) —all by Daly.

Death of famous teacher of fine calligraphy, Platt Rogers Spencer. Teacher at early age, he helped found boys' schools of New York and New England where expert penmanship (Spencerian writing) was taught. Young gentlemen were impressed with idea that fine handwriting could be key to success.

With the opening of Japan in 1854, **artistic influences** began to flow **from Far East.** 1 of best works showing acquaintance with art of Japanese print is Whistler's *La Princesse du Pays de la Porcelaine.*

What has been considered by some critics the **"best and most interesting statue** that Central Park contains," the *Indian Hunter,* completed by John Quincy Adams Ward after a long trip among Indians of West and Northwest. Vitality and tenseness are admirably conveyed through figure of boy and dog.

Ranking among the **finest equestrian statues** in the U.S. is the *Washington* of the Boston Public Gardens, by Thomas Ball of Boston. Since there were no funds for the casting, Ball kept the statue until July 3, 1869, when it was finally unveiled.

Bayard Taylor published *John Godfrey's Fortunes,* an autobiography.

1864

1st college for deaf mutes, Gallaudet College in Washington, D.C., granted right by Congress to confer degrees. School had been founded about 1857 by Edward Gallaudet, son of famous educator of the deaf, Thomas Hopkins Gallaudet.

University of Kansas, Lawrence, Kans., established. 1st classes met in 1866.

1st Baptist social union in America composed entirely of laymen established in Tremont Temple, Boston. Forerunner of many such lay groups formed in the following decade, it reflected growing influence of businessmen in church affairs, particularly in the administrative posts.

George Presbury Rowell began **1st successful U.S. advertising agency.** His 1st job was the preparation of a theatrical program for the holiday season in Boston. Later he published an important newspaper directory.

1st significant plan for underground transit in America proposed by Hugh B. Willson who established a company for that purpose in New York city with a capitalization of $5,000,000. His request for a franchise was rejected by the N.Y. State Legislature.

William, John, and George Hume and Andrew S. Hapgood built **salmon cannery,** probably 1st in U.S., next to the Sacramento R., Washington, Calif. It failed, but they built another the next year at Eagle Fish, Wash., which became a success and led to the spread of salmon canneries in the northwest.

Rising living costs spurred **formation of unions** in next 10 years, 26 in all. There were about 300,000 union men in 1872.

Feb. 17 **1st successful submarine attack** made by Confederate underwater craft, the *Hunley* against Union ship *Housatonic,* anchored in Charleston Harbor, S.C. All 9 members of the crew of the *Hunley* were lost in the action. The *Housa-*

Abraham Lincoln coined a **new political expression** in his campaign of 1864 when he observed, ". . . it was not best to swap horses while crossing the stream, and . . . I am not so poor a horse that they might not make a botch of it in trying to swap."

John Morrissey, ex-prize fighter, built **race track** at Saratoga, N.Y., and organized 1st race meets there. He named 1st stakes race The Travers after local family; it is still run today, the oldest race of its kind in U.S.

1st American croquet club founded. It was the Park Place Croquet Club of Brooklyn, N.Y.

Feb. 19 Washington Lodge, No. 1, of **Knights of Pythias** organized in Temperance Hall, Washington, D.C., by 13 charter members. Organization today totals more than 350,000 members.

May 11 Gen. Grant's stubborn determination to push on to Richmond reflected in his memorable statement, **"I propose to fight it out on this line if it takes all summer."**

June **1st professional baseball player** was Al Reach, who accepted money from Philadelphia Athletics to leave Brooklyn Atlantics.

Aug. 5 Fiery phrase **"Damn the torpedoes! Go ahead!"** hurled forth by Adm.

Johnson for Vice-Presidency, at national convention held in Baltimore, Md.

June 15–18 Gen. Grant repulsed by Lee and Beauregard at **Petersburg, Va.** Union losses during the 3-day engagement numbered more than 8000 in killed, wounded, and missing.

June 19 Confederate cruiser **Alabama sunk** off Cherbourg, France, by the U.S.S. *Kearsarge* commanded by Capt. Winslow.

July 5 Horace Greeley received letter with a **Confederate proposal for peace** negotiations to be held in Canada. Greeley forwarded the letter to Pres. Lincoln.

July 18 Horace Greeley sent on **peace mission to Canada** to meet Confederate ambassadors. Lincoln instructed him that any treaty which included the restoration of the South to the Union and the renunciation of slavery would be acceptable. The Confederates would not accept these conditions.

Aug. 29 **Democratic National Convention** at Chicago, Ill., nominated Gen. McClellan for President and George H. Pendleton of Ohio for Vice-President. Party's platform attacked Lincoln's conduct of the war, declared it to be a failure.

Sept. 2 Gen. **Sherman occupied At-**

(Continued in next column)

The Nasby Papers, a collection of the acerb writings of **David Ross Locke,** who delighted readers with the witty opinions of Petroleum V. Nasby, published. Petroleum V. Nasby epitomized the backwoods humor which became art in the hands of Mark Twain.

(Column 1 continued)

lanta, Ga., after the city was evacuated by Gen. Hood on the previous day.

Oct. 19 **Confederates defeated at Cedar Creek,** Va., in the last battle of the Shenandoah Valley. The Union forces were commanded by Gen. Sheridan.

Oct. 31 **Nevada admitted as a state,** 36th to join Union.

Nov. 8 Abraham Lincoln defeated Gen. McClellan in **presidential elections.** His popular majority was only 400,000 votes out of the 4 million votes cast. He defeated Democratic candidate Gen. McClellan by an electoral vote of 212–21.

(Continued in next column)

1865

Jan. 15 **Fort Fisher,** N.C., fell to the Union forces under a joint sea and land assault. The entire garrison of 2000 men was captured, among whom was Maj. Gen. Wm. H. C. Whiting, mortally wounded. This gave the Federals control of Cape Fear R. and meant the blockade of the last Confederate port.

Feb. 3 **Lincoln met with Confederate peace commissioners** aboard the *River Queen* in Hampton Roads, Va. Negotiations were deadlocked because the Confederates insisted upon Southern autonomy.

Feb. 6 Pres. Jefferson Davis named

Famous children's story, Hans Brinker; or, The Silver Skates, by Mary Mapes Dodge became, after a slow start, a best seller.

American humorist and apostle of horse sense **Henry W. Shaw** (Josh Billings) collected his **Sayings.** His aphorisms, spelled out in the semiliterate vernacular, fascinated the public and earned him the title of "Aesop and Ben Franklin condensed and abridged." Typical of his aphorisms is the following: "The muel iz haf hoss and haf Jackass, and then kums tu a full stop, natur diskovering her mistake."

SCIENCE; INDUSTRY; ECONOMICS; EDUCATION; RELIGION; PHILOSOPHY.	SPORTS; FASHIONS; POPULAR ENTERTAINMENT; FOLKLORE; SOCIETY.

tonic was sunk, but her crew suffered no casualties.

June 30 Congress passed new **Internal Revenue Act** which increased taxes on many items, including tobacco, and introduced a 2nd income tax. Tax on incomes was 5% on incomes between $600 and $10,000, 10% on incomes over $10,000.

July 4 **Spur to immigration to U.S.** caused by passage of federal emigrant contract labor act, guaranteeing 12-month wage contracts for emigrants.

David Glasgow Farragut to his flagship attacking Confederate forces in Mobile Bay. The Southerners had set a ring of torpedoes (mines) before the harbor, causing the Northern ships to hesitate in their attack.

(Column 1 continued)

Nov. 16 Gen. Sherman began his **march to Savannah**, Ga., with an army of about 60,000. His troops lived off the country and destroyed communications and remaining Confederate installations.

Nov. 25 Confederate underground set fire to Barnum's Museum and the Astor House in an **attempt to destroy New York city.**

Dec. **Salmon P. Chase appointed Chief Justice of the Supreme Court.** His most significant achievements came when he held the office of Secretary of the Treasury under Lincoln. He was partly responsible

(Continued in next column)

(Column 1 continued)

for saving the country from financial ruin with the **Legal Tender Act** which he sponsored in 1862, by which 150,000,000 greenbacks were issued. The phrase **"In God We Trust"** on the national coins was by order of Chase.

Dec. 22 Gen. **Sherman captured Savannah**, Ga., after besieging the city for 10 days. During the march from Atlanta to Savannah, Sherman lost just a little over 2000 men.

1865

Yale University opened **1st Department of Fine Arts** in U.S. college. Under direction of Prof. John F. Weir, the Yale School of Fine Arts began with 4 students.

Purdue University, West Lafayette, Ind., chartered as Indiana Agricultural College. 1st classes met in 1874. Present name adopted in 1869.

Cornell University incorporated at Ithaca, N.Y. School taken over by Ezra Cornell in 1866. 1st classes held 1868.

University of Maine, Orono, Me., established as Maine State College of Agricul-

Beards became fashionable for distinguished men after the Civil War. Every president from Grant to Chester Arthur was fittingly bewhiskered. Cleveland's clean-shaven face both caused and reflected a shift of taste away from beards.

Clara Barton placed in charge of a government-sponsored search of missing soldiers of the Civil War. During the Civil War, Miss Barton had organized hospital services for sick and wounded Union troops.

Interest in **baseball** took a tremendous

| POLITICS AND GOVERNMENT; WAR; DISASTERS; VITAL STATISTICS. | BOOKS; PAINTING; DRAMA; ARCHITECTURE; SCULPTURE. |

Gen. Robert E. Lee **General in Chief of the Confederate Army.** The office was created by Confederate Congress, dissatisfied with the record of the Army under Davis in 1864.

Feb. 17 **Columbia, S.C., set afire** and almost completely destroyed as the Confederates evacuated the city threatened by Gen. Sherman's army. Responsibility for the starting of the conflagration is still disputed.

Mar. 2 Gen. R. E. Lee dispatched a letter to Gen. Grant requesting that a **conference be held to iron out differences between North and South.** Lincoln rejected the proposal, demanding the surrender of the Confederates before such negotiations took place.

Mar. 3 **Freedmen's Bureau** founded to provide education and advancement for Negroes. Congressional bill authorized Bureau for 1 year only after end of Civil War, but Congress of 1866 extended the term indefinitely over Pres. Johnson's veto. Bureau was finally discontinued in 1869.

Mar. 4 **Pres. Lincoln inaugurated** for his 2nd term. Andrew Johnson succeeded Hannibal Hamlin as vice-president.

Mar. 13 **Slaves made subject to military call to duty** for the Confederate Army by virtue of a bill signed by Pres. Davis.

Apr. 1 Gen. Sheridan routed Confederates under Gen. Pickett at **Five Forks,** Va. Some 5000 Confederate prisoners were taken.

Apr. 2 Gen. Lee advised Pres. Davis to **evacuate Richmond** and informed him that he must withdraw from Petersburg, Va. Davis left the city that night with his Cabinet, retreating to Danville, and Confederate army began evacuation of Petersburg.

Apr. 3 **Maj. Gen. Weitzel entered Richmond** and extinguished fires started by Confederate troops. Union troops also occupied Petersburg.

Apr. 9 **Gen. Lee capitulated to Gen. Grant.** Terms of surrender were nego-

Politics and humor are combined in **David R. Locke's** *Divers Opinions of Yours Trooly,* Petroleum V. Nasby. As in his earlier books, which Lincoln loved to read, Locke represented Nasby as a corrupt, stupid, semiliterate, copperhead preacher. He was the straw man that Locke used as a means to get across his own political point of view.

Mark Twain captured a large reading public with his artistic tall tale **"The Celebrated Jumping Frog of Calaveras County."** Taking the folk-tale of Smiley and his pet, he puts it into a comic frame; the story made him famous overnight.

Experience as a nurse in Washington during the Civil War provided Walt Whitman with information and inspiration for his moving book of poems, *Drum Taps,* later incorporated into the **Leaves of Grass.** Such favorites as "O Captain! My Captain!" and "Beat! Beat! Drums!" were included.

Francis Parkman continued his study of the French in the New World with his **Pioneers of France in the New World.** Authoritative, beautifully written, the book still remains the master in the field.

Leading Democratic newspaper in the Far West, the **San Francisco Examiner,** begun by William Moss. Hearst purchased paper in 1880 and turned its policy towards sensationalism.

California paper which called for reform in state and city politics, demanding at times a new constitution, the **San Francisco Chronicle,** founded by the De Young family. It later gave hearty support to theories of Henry George.

Mastery of George Inness as a **landscape painter** is revealed in his huge canvas, *Peace and Plenty.* Though containing many details in the wide vista, there is a singular unity of mood provided by suffused lighting. His formalism,

SCIENCE; INDUSTRY; ECONOMICS; EDUCATION; RELIGION; PHILOSOPHY.

SPORTS; FASHIONS; POPULAR ENTERTAINMENT; FOLKLORE; SOCIETY.

ture and the Mechanical Arts. 1st classes met in 1868. Present name adopted in 1897.

University of Kentucky, Lexington, Ky., established as Agricultural and Mechanical College of Kentucky University. 1st classes were held same year. Name was changed to Agricultural and Mechanical College of Kentucky in 1878, to State University of Kentucky in 1908; present name adopted in 1916.

Number of dollars in circulation in U.S. rose to 1,081,540,514, more than double the number in 1860, as federal government inflated currency to pay costs of Civil War.

Fredonia Gas Light and Water Works Company, Fredonia, N.Y., became **1st American company to sell natural gas.** Small natural gas wells had been brought in at Fredonia in 1821, and the gas had been piped to the Fredonia Hotel where it was used for lighting and cooking.

Free delivery of mail provided in all cities with populations of at least 50,000.

1st woman professor of astronomy in America, Maria Mitchell, began teaching at Vassar in 1865.

May 2 **1st Fire Department with paid firemen** established in New York city by an act of the State Legislature.

The Nation founded by **James Miller Mc Kim.** *The Nation,* a weekly magazine, quickly established a reputation as a leading liberal voice in politics, literature and art. Wendell Phillips Garrison, the son-in-law of Mc Kim, was long an editor and carried on the crusades for which his namesakes, and *The Nation,* were famous. The 19th century editorials of the magazine were directed toward revision of the tariff and civil service, and against the corrupt politics of the age of the Moguls.

Louis Agassiz began a 19 months ex-

upsurge after the Civil War. This year saw 91 clubs included in the National Association of Base Ball Players. In 1866 Arthur P. Gorman was named president of the organization, and in 1867 237 teams were represented.

John Wesley Hyatt received patent for a **composition billiard ball,** and was awarded $10,000 prize by a billiard ball manufacturer who up to this time had to use expensive ivory. Hyatt, one of most prolific inventors of his time, later discovered the process by which celluloid is made, thus creating a revolution in American industry. He invented many other things including a type of roller-bearing still in use, a water filter, a sugar-cane mill, etc.

Mar. 4 Many of the people who heard Lincoln deliver his **Second Inaugural address** were observed to have tears in their eyes. It was a silent audience, befitting a solemn occasion made only more solemn by the things which Lincoln called upon his hearers to remember. The war was not over, but there was room for hope, if not certainty. Lincoln began by saying that the occasion did not call for such an extended address as he delivered at his 1st inaugural. The audience was as familiar as he with the progress of the war. But he asked his listeners to relive with him the forebodings of 4 years before, when both sides were rushing towards war, though "neither party expected the magnitude or duration which it has already attained. Neither anticipated that the cause of the conflict might cease before the conflict itself should cease. Each looked for an easier triumph and a result less fundamental and astonishing. Both read the same Bible and pray to the same God. Each invokes His aid against the other. It may seem strange that any man should dare to ask a just God's assistance in wringing bread from the sweat of other men's faces; but let us judge not, that we be not judged." He ex-

277

POLITICS AND GOVERNMENT; WAR; DISASTERS; VITAL STATISTICS.

BOOKS; PAINTING; DRAMA; ARCHITECTURE; SCULPTURE.

tiated and agreed upon at Appomattox Court House.

Apr. 14 Abraham Lincoln, **1st President to be assassinated,** shot at Ford's Theater, Washington, D.C., by John Wilkes Booth, an actor. The President died on Apr. 15, age 56. He is buried at Springfield, Ill.

Apr. 15 Andrew Johnson, 17th president, inaugurated. He succeeded to the presidency upon the death of Lincoln, serving 3 years and 10 months in office, the remainder of Lincoln's 2nd term.

Apr. 27 1700 dead in the **worst ship disaster in U.S. history.** The steamer *Sultana* exploded on the Mississippi R. with 2300 on board, 2134 of whom were Union soldiers returning from Confederate prison camps.

Apr. 29 Commercial restrictions removed from most parts of the Southern states, except Texas, by an executive order.

May 10 Jefferson Davis apprehended at Irwinville, Ga. by contingent of Gen. Wilson's cavalry, led by Lt. Col. Benjamin Pritchard.

Aug. 14 Mississippi convention **passed ordinances voiding the secession ordinance** of 1861 and prohibiting slavery in the state.

Nov. 9 North Carolina voted the secession ordinance of 1861 null and void, **prohibited slavery** in the state, and elected officers to the U.S. Congress.

Dec. 2 Alabama became the 27th state to ratify anti-slavery amendment, which thereby gave the amendment the ratification required for adoption of ⅔ of the states.

Dec. 4 "**Joint Committee on Reconstruction**" appointed by Pres. Johnson to make a survey of the Southern states and determine whether they were entitled to representation in Congress.

Dec. 18 13th amendment adopted, abolishing slavery.

often compared to Poussin, is best revealed in his *Evening at Medfield, Mass.* (1875), where an afterglow is made to embrace solid forms of tree and shrub.

Series of paintings depicting the plight of boys away at the front during the Civil War was **Prisoners from the Front** by **Winslow Homer,** who at the age of 25, was engaged by *Harper's Weekly* as a special correspondent and artist.

Actor-producer-playwright **David Belasco** began career as playwright with a romantic play *Jim Black, or the Regulator's Revenge,* written at the age of 12.

Main buildings of Vassar, designed by James Renwick, reflected the influence of French taste in **American architecture.** The age which succeeded to the Romantic era adopted variety without developing a definite style of its own. The result was a fashion that turned to novelty for the sake of novelty. In the maze of forms which characterize the Civil War period, the French touch can be felt even where it is not immediately seen. Imitation was, however, usually frank, and sometimes blatant. Washington, Boston, Philadelphia and Detroit, all modeled public buildings upon the style then current in France. Renwick followed the fashion of his times and wove French themes into the buildings which he designed.

Apr. 15 All New York theaters closed until Apr. 26 because of death of **Abraham Lincoln.**

July 21 Possibly the **finest expression of American patriotism** in verse was James Russell Lowell's *Ode Recited at the Harvard Commemoration.* On the broad grounds of the college, Lowell paid tribute to the men who had served in the war. One section, "Our Martyr Chief," is a moving tribute to Lincoln.

SCIENCE; INDUSTRY; ECONOMICS; EDUCATION; RELIGION; PHILOSOPHY.

SPORTS; FASHIONS; POPULAR ENTERTAINMENT; FOLKLORE; SOCIETY.

pedition, with his wife and 6 assistants, to study the natural history of Brazil and add to his collection of specimens. Agassiz, who had become a naturalized American citizen, began his career at the University of Munich where, at 21, he published *The Fishes of Brazil.* The study was based upon a collection brought back to Germany by an expedition to Brazil in 1821. Agassiz always cherished the ambition to go to Brazil and see the natural life of the country at 1st hand. The trip was financed by Nathaniel Thayer of Boston and was so facilitated by parties in both the U.S. and Brazil that it turned into something of a triumphal tour. A journey to Brazil, published in 1868, recounted the day to day experiences of the expedition.

Opening of the **Union stockyards** in Chicago, Illinois, led, within the decade, to the phenomenal growth of Chicago to world's greatest meat-producing and meat-packing center. Cincinnati, Ohio, had been at the top of the meat industry for over 20 years, and Chicago was just emerging as a rival when the Union stockyards combined the various yards of the city into a common, efficient center and stepped up production to the point where the output of Cincinnati was soon surpassed. The appearance of the Union stockyards was matched by consolidation of companies within the industry, which also accelerated the pace of production. Chicago, as a railroad center, was in the direct line of livestock shipments from the western ranches and had immediate access to all the principle railroad lines of the country.

Dec. 24 **The Ku Klux Klan** 1st formed in the law office of Thomas M. Jones in Pulaski, Tenn. Name evolved from Greek *kyklos* (circle), suggested by John B. Kennedy, broken up into the more euphonious Ku Klux by James R. Crowe, who added the word Klan as a reflection of the predominant Scotch-Irish population of the area.

pressed the common hope that the war would soon end, and bade his hearers to continue what they had begun: "With malice toward none, with charity for all, with firmness in the right, as God gives us to see the right, let us strive on to finish the work we are in, to bind up the nation's wounds, to care for him who shall have borne the battle, and for his widow and orphans; to do all which may achieve and cherish a just and lasting peace among ourselves and with all nations." The address was not followed by any demonstration, either public or personal, to indicate to Lincoln whether it had been effective. He felt himself that it was among the best which he had written and delivered, and he expressed this sentiment in a letter to Thurlow Weed thanking Weed for a few words of congratulation.

Apr. 26 **Confederate Memorial Day,** a legal holiday in Mississippi, born of the visit of Mrs. Sue Landon Vaughn, descendant of John Adams, 2nd president of the U.S., with other ladies to the military cemetery in Vicksburg, Miss.

May 5 **1st railroad train hold-up** took place at dawn at North Bend, Ohio, when Ohio and Mississippi train was derailed by gang. Male passengers robbed and express car looted.

June 19 **Emancipation Day** established in Texas by proclamation of Gen. Robert S. Granger, commander of the Texas military district, who officially notified the Negroes that they were free.

1866

Cholera epidemic decimated many U.S. cities. About 200 a day died in St. Louis, Mo., during the height of epidemic.

Feb. 19 New Freedmen's Bureau Bill passed by Congress. The law authorized military trials for those accused of depriving newly freed Negroes of their civil rights. Pres. Johnson vetoed the bill on the grounds that it violated the 5th Amendment, and that the legislation affected 11 Southern states not represented in Congress. The veto served to widen the rift between Congress and the President. Legislators retaliated by overriding the veto on July 16.

Apr. 2 Insurrection declared over by Presidential proclamation in following states; Georgia, South Carolina, Virginia, North Carolina, Tennessee, Alabama, Mississippi, Louisiana, Arkansas, and Florida. On Aug. 2 the President announced that insurrection was at an end in Texas, and that civil authority existed in the U.S.

Apr. 9 Civil Rights Act passed over Pres. Johnson's veto. It granted citizenship to all persons born in U.S., except Indians; declared the same civil rights for all citizens and provided for the punishment of persons who prevented the free exercise of these rights. The 14th Amendment was proposed when the constitutionality of the first section of this act was questioned.

May 16 Congress authorized issuance of a 5¢ coin, known as a **"nickel."** Piece was minted of copper and nickel with not more than 25% nickel.

July 4 1500 buildings destroyed by **fire** in Portland, Me. Property loss estimated at $10,000,000.

Most famous poem of **John Greenleaf Whittier,** "Snow-Bound" written. Drawing on his own youth and memories of home life in rural New England, he paints a warm, inviting genre picture of a homestead buried in snow: all is here—the blazing hearth, the family members, the sparkling snowbanks, the schoolmaster, etc.

Young **William Dean Howells** collected his impressions of Venice and published them as *Venetian Life.* Consul in this Italian city throughout the Civil War, he observed closely life about him and was able to capture the flavor of Latin life and literature.

Confederate novelist **John Esten Cooke** harked back to the chivalry of antebellum Virginia and the emerging catastrophe in *Surry of Eagle's Nest.* Often vivid pictures of Southern leaders and of battles were evoked. In *Hilt to Hilt* and *Mohun*—both written in 1869—he continued in the same vein.

1st American publication of Lewis Carroll's classic *Alice's Adventures in Wonderland.* An estimated 2 million copies or more have been sold in America. The original manuscript was sold in 1928 for $75,250.

1st course in **architecture** at an American college opened at Massachusetts Institute of Technology.

Commission for statue of Lincoln given to **Larkin G. Mead,** a New Hampshire sculptor. Price of monument was $200,000, thus surpassing all other monuments built to date in U.S. Completed work was unveiled in 1874 at Springfield, Ill., and used as tomb for the assassinated president.

Dec. 29 Interesting performance of **Othello** took place at Winter Garden, New York city. Bogumil Dawison, Polish actor, played part of Othello in German; Edwin Booth played Iago to him in English;

SCIENCE; INDUSTRY; ECONOMICS; EDUCATION; RELIGION; PHILOSOPHY.	SPORTS; FASHIONS; POPULAR ENTERTAINMENT; FOLKLORE; SOCIETY.

1866

University of New Hampshire, Durham, N.H., founded as New Hampshire College of Agriculture and Mechanic Arts at Hanover, N.H. 1st classes held in 1868. Moved to present site in 1893, adopted present name in 1923.

Apr. 1 **Western Union,** with capital of about $40,000,000, absorbed the U.S. Telegraph Co., with $6,000,000 worth of shares. This was on 10th anniversary of the day that Western Union was named. The absorption of U.S. Telegraph made Western Union 1st complete monopoly servicing all parts of the country, with uniform rates.

Apr. 10 **American Society for the Prevention of Cruelty to Animals,** 1st such organization in U.S., chartered in New York city. Inspired by Royal S.P.C.A. in England, it was founded by Henry Bergh, its 1st president.

July 27 Steamship *Great Eastern* reached U.S. completing final laying of the **Atlantic cable** between Britain and U.S. The final cable-laying voyage of the Great Eastern took 2 weeks, July 13–July 27. The previous year, it had attempted to complete the cable, only to have it break in mid-ocean. Success came after 12 full years of effort. Cyrus Field chartered his company May 6, 1854, with Peter Cooper, Moses Taylor, Marshall Roberts, and Chandler White on the board of directors. 600 men worked on the 1st line, which had to be cut at sea because of a gale. 7 more efforts were needed before the cable was completed. The line of 1858 was able to carry message, but was probably badly insulated, and went out after 3 weeks of operation.

Aug. 20 1st **National Labor Congress** met at Baltimore, Md., and met annually in different cities for several years.

Aug. 29 Public invited to view the famous **Mt. Washington Cog Railroad** built at Mt. Washington, N.H. The invention of Sylvester Marsh of N.H., the railroad

1st Young Women's Christian Association in U.S. opened at Boston, Mass. The organization had its beginnings in England.

Expression **"40 acres and a mule"** gained currency during the Reconstruction period. Many freed Negroes had their hopes built up by the promises that Congress would divide up the Southern estates and distribute acreage to each freed slave. Expression came to characterize vain expectations foisted upon Negroes by reconstructionists.

Brooklyn's team, the Atlantics, played the Athletics of Philadelphia for the unofficial **baseball championship** of U.S. Enthusiastic crowd smashed its way to the field, causing game to be halted and finally moved to Long Island. Brooklyn defeated the Athletics 27 to 10.

1st deliberate **bunt** in baseball laid down by Dickey Pearce of Brooklyn Atlantics.

James Gordon Bennett's 107 ft. schooner, the *Henrietta,* won **1st transoceanic yacht race.** The *Henrietta* engaged 2 other schooners in a race from Sandy Hook, N.J., to the Isle of Wight. Her time was 13 days, 21 hours, 45 minutes.

600 "more or less" **public balls** were held in New York city in 1866. The cost of the balls was estimated at $7,000,000, and the average cost of a gown was computed to be $1,000, not including jewelry.

Feb. 12 1st formal observance of **Lincoln's birthday** held in the Capitol of the U.S. with most of the high government officials, including Pres. Johnson, in attendance.

June 17 **New York City Athletic Club** founded.

Sept. 15 *Scientific American* reported that there were "more men in New York today whose **annual incomes reach $100,-000** than there were twenty-five years ago of those whose entire possessions amounted to as much."

Nov. 20 1st national encampment of

POLITICS AND GOVERNMENT; WAR; DISASTERS; VITAL STATISTICS.	BOOKS; PAINTING; DRAMA; ARCHITECTURE; SCULPTURE.

Oct. 3 **250 lives lost** when the *Evening Star,* a steamer on its way to New Orleans from New York city, foundered at sea.

Madame Methua-Scheller played Desdemona alternately in English and German.

1867

1st tenement-house law in America enacted in New York. Despite supplementary laws enacted in 1879, 1887, and 1895, housing conditions became worse instead of better because of both inadequate enforcement of the laws and increasing pressures of population.

Oakes Ames, Representative from Massachusetts, bought off Col. H. K. McComb and at the same time revealed to him the names of the politicians behind the **Crédit Mobilier of America.** In 1872, McComb turned these names over to the New York *Sun;* and their publication and the resulting Congressional investigation created the most flagrant political scandal of the period. Ames, a director of the Union Pacific Railroad, was also a member of the House committee which authorized the railroad to issue bonds that the government actually stood pledged to redeem. Railroad construction began, but soon stopped for lack of funds. A 2nd company, the Crédit Mobilier, was formed to continue the construction, and in payment it received the stock and bonds of the railroad. While the railroad company went to ruin, the profits of the Crédit Mobilier mounted. During the presidential campaign of 1872 McComb revealed the set-up to the public, and the House made its sensational report on Feb. 18, 1873.

Jan. 8 Negroes given the right of **suffrage** in Washington, D.C., by a bill passed over Pres. Johnson's veto.

Feb. 25 Survey for a **canal** at Darien, Panama, connecting the Atlantic and Pacific Oceans provided for by a resolution adopted by Congress.

Mar. 1 **Nebraska** admitted as a state, 37th to join Union.

Mar. 2 **1st reconstruction Act** passed

A best selling 2nd-rate novel, **St. Elmo,** by Augusta Jane Evans. A long love affair, attacks on the rich, and the success story of a poor girl are elements that appealed to the average reader. *St. Elmo* sold about 1 million copies. Towns, streets, and babies were given this popular name.

Poet-musician **Sidney Lanier** published chaotic war novel, *Tiger Lilies.* In his depiction of the life of the soldier his realism is sharp, but he rambles on art, romanticism, and music.

Popular humorist of the Southwest, **George W. Harris,** collected tales built around his hero Sut, in *Sut Lovingood Yarns.* Sut, a "nat'ral born durn'd fool" is a prankish roughneck who takes advantage of the foibles of mankind. His enemies are mercilessly treated, and he makes no bones about picking his "victims" even from the White House.

Sculptor who achieved great popularity in the U.S. for his group statuary, **John Rogers,** at the Paris Exposition offered 3 groups in bronze, *One More Shot, Taking the Oath,* and the *Wounded Scout*—scenes of the Civil War. Earlier his realism was reflected in groups like *Checkers up at the Farm* and the *Football Game.*

Founding of the American Society of Painters in Water Color, now called the **American Water Color Society,** by Samuel Colman and John D. Smillie, two young painters. Colman was the Society's 1st president.

Brete Harte published *The Lost Galleon and Other Tales,* a 1st volume of poems with characteristics of his later writings.

Miss Ravenel's Conversion from Secession to Loyalty, realistic novel of Civil War, published by **John William De For-**

was the 1st mountain-climbing railroad in the world and remained the steepest. Work on it was finished in 1869.

the **Grand Army of the Republic** comprising Union veterans of the Civil War held at Indianapolis, Ind.

1867

Main goal of labor unions, the **8-hour day** enacted in Illinois, New York, and Missouri, but it was not enforced.

Howard Theological Seminary (now Howard University) chartered in Washington, D.C., and named after Gen. Oliver O. Howard, its 1st president. It was 1st predominantly Negro college to offer comprehensive university facilities.

Major contribution to education in the postwar South made by **George Peabody** with a fund of $3,500,000. The Peabody fund hastened the construction of town and city schools and provided for the training of teachers.

West Virginia University, Morgantown, W. Va., established as Agricultural College of West Virginia. 1st classes held 1868, the year present name was adopted.

Johns Hopkins University chartered at Baltimore, Md. 1st classes met in 1876.

University of Illinois, Urbana, Ill., founded as Illinois Industrial University. 1st classes met in 1868. Present name adopted in 1885.

James Cruikshank's **Primary Geography** published; it became the chief school geography during the last 3 decades of 19th century. Of the U.S. it said: "There are now more than 30,000,000 of people and the United States are the freest, most enlightened, and powerful government on earth."

Cigarettes began to appear in America. Cigarette production had been formerly confined to Europe. Their production in America did not, however, become a major source of revenue until the 1880's.

Christopher Latham Sholes constructed **1st successful typewriter** and first used word "typewriter." Patent was issued to him,

"**Now is the time for all good men to come to the aid of the party**," slogan created by Charles Weller, a court reporter, to test efficiency of 1st practical typewriter (invented by his friend, Christopher Sholes).

Ruthless won the **1st annual Belmont Stakes.** Jockey was F. Morris; time was 3:05 for winnings valued at $1850. Race held at Jerome Park, N.Y., from 1867 to 1889; at Morris Park, N.Y., from 1890 to 1905; and at Belmont Park, N.Y., from 1906 to the present time. In the beginning the distance was 1⅝ miles, but it has been changed from time to time. Belmont Stakes is the oldest of the 3 classic American races.

When the quarrels of the insiders in the **Crédit Mobilier** scandal began to bubble and boil, Oakes Ames, the prime mover of the scandal, took out 343 shares of stock and palmed them off "where they will do most good." He had politicians in high places in mind for his plums, and, when the scandal broke, his choice turn of phrase quickly became popular.

Harper's New Monthly Magazine published an account by George Ward Nichols of a visit to the city of Springfield, Mo., where he met and interviewed **"Wild Bill" Hickok.** Nichols swore that he recorded only what "William Hitchcock" (as Nichols called him) told him, that the facts were confirmed by witnesses, and that he himself did not doubt their truth. The article fitted nicely into the literature of the "tall tale," which had been growing ever taller and more popular since the century began. The author painted vivid portraits of Springfield and James Butler Hickok. Springfield was, he found, "not a burgh of extensive dimensions," though it was the local crossroads. The people, "strange, half-civilized," came to Spring-

over Pres. Johnson's veto. The bill imposed martial law upon the Southern states, which were split into 5 districts, and provided for the restoration of civil government as soon as the said states were reorganized into the Union and passed the 14th amendment.

Mar. 2 **Tenure of Office Act** passed. In substance, it denied power to the President to remove officials who had been appointed by and with the consent of the Senate. This act was ruled unconstitutional by the Court of Claims in 1926 by the Myers v. U.S. case.

Mar. 5 1000 **Negroes'** votes rejected at Alexandria, Va., when they attempted to exercise suffrage rights granted them under Reconstruction Act.

Mar. 23 **2nd Reconstruction Act** passed over Pres. Johnson's veto. It provided for the registration of all qualified voters who were subsequently to decide readmittance into the Union.

Mar. 30 U.S. agreed to purchase **Alaska** from Russia for $7,200,000. Senate ratified treaty on Apr. 9. Transfer of territory took place on Oct. 18. Despite price of about 2¢ an acre, purchase was ridiculed. However, value of land was proved after discovery of gold in the Klondike region in 1896.

July 19 **3rd Reconstruction Act** passed over Pres. Johnson's veto. The bill was essentially a restatement of the 2 previous Acts except for the added provision that the 15th amendment must also be ratified before the Southern states could be reorganized with the Union.

est. De Forest, writing from his own military experiences, produced what has been rated the best novel of the Civil War.

Horatio Alger published *Ragged Dick* in *Student and Schoolmate* magazine. It was the beginning of the most popular series of stories for boys in the history of American literature. Alger spread the myth of the poor boy who, by virtue and industry, fights his way to the top of the pile. All of his fortunate young heroes had an avid following, though none ever again rivaled the popularity of Ragged Dick.

Katherine, a narrative poem by **"Timothy Titcomb"** published. Titcomb was the nom-de-plume of J. G. Holland, whose poem sold 30,000 copies in 1st 3 months of publication.

James Redpath established a **central booking office** and introduced order into the helter-skelter system of hiring speakers for the lecture circuits. He made it possible for local committees to fill their engagements through the national agency which he set up.

Aug. 12 Melodrama which held stage in New York and London for many years, *Under the Gaslight* by **Augustin Daly** opened in New York. Play has all trappings of type: villain who binds hero to railroad tracks, pure heroine harried by a blackmailer, wounded soldier, etc.

Dec. 2 **Charles Dickens** gave his 1st reading in New York city. This was his 2nd visit to the U.S. He read in a New York theater in December. Before box-office opened, people were standing in 2 lines, almost a mile long, waiting for tickets. Scalpers were asking $20 for a ticket. In 1867, 31 different editions of Dickens' collected works were published.

1868

Ku Klux Klan formulated its revised constitution, which declared that the organization was to be guided by the principles of chivalry, humanity, mercy, and patriotism. The Southern States were to

Short story which had immediate phenomenal success is "The Luck of Roaring Camp" by **Bret Harte.** Written for the California *Overland Monthly*, it proved a sensation in the East. *Atlantic Monthly*

Samuel W. Soulé, and Carlos Glidden on June 23, 1868.

Abilene, Kan., became a leading cattle terminal through the foresight of J. G. McCoy, a Chicago cattle dealer, who built a cattle yard in the town. He had selected Abilene as the closest point to the intersection of the Texas cattle trail and the railroad. The most celebrated trail from Texas to Abilene was established by a half-breed Cherokee Indian cattle driver named Jesse Chisholm. His "Chisholm Trail" became part of the folklore of the West.

Pullman Palace Car Company incorporated by **George Pullman.** Within 2 years, he was operating 48 cars on 3 different railroads with an investment in rolling stock amounting to $1,000,000.

Patrons of Husbandry, or **Grangers,** established by Oliver H. Kelley as a fraternal organization of farmers and any citizens interested in agriculture. It later became a militant political group.

1st elevated railroad in America began operation in New York city. Built by the West Side Elevated Railroad Co., its single track ran from Battery Place through Greenwich St. and 9th Ave., to 30th St.

Mar. 7 Technological unemployment in U.S. shoe industry led to the founding of **Order of the Knights of St. Crispin.** Order's main objective was the protection of seniority rights against cheaper competition of beginners.

Oct. 25 Maimonides College, 1st rabbinical college in U.S., opened in Philadelphia, Pa. It closed in 1873 from lack of support. A 2nd Maimonides College opened in New York city in 1927.

field to market. "Men and women dressed in queer costumes; men with coats and trousers made of skin" so thick with dirt and grease as to defy identity of the animals which grew them. Homespun was common. The men were, said Nichols, so lazy that their highest ambition seemed to let their hair and beards grow. They lolled in front of the shops which lined either side of the main street, or even lay on the wooden sidewalks. There were some still wearing army blue—the liveliest men of the lot. Everyone wore a pistol. Springfield contrasted vividly with Hickok, who finally came riding up for his appointment with Nichols. Hickok was 6′ 1″ tall in moccasins. He wore a deerskin shirt, which hung "jauntily" over his shoulders, revealing a "remarkable" breadth and depth of chest. Around his "small round waist" were 2 Colt navy revolvers on a belt. His toes turned inwards when he walked. On his head was a large sombrero. He had thin, sensitive lips, not-too-square jaw, slightly prominent cheekbones.

Record for long-distance walking set by **Edward P. Weston,** who did the distance from Portland, Me., to Chicago in 26 days, and won for his efforts $10,000.

Jan. 23 East R. frozen over after a series of heavy snowstorms. Thousands crossed the river on foot.

Mar. 30 Seward Day in Alaska commemorated the purchase of Alaska from Russia through a treaty signed by Secretary of State Seward. Phrase **"Seward's Folly"** adopted by those who thought the purchase of Alaska from Russia by Sec. of State William Henry Seward, for the price of $7,200,000, an extravagant blunder. Alaska was also ridiculed as an "Arctic waste" and an "icebox."

1868

University of Minnesota, Minneapolis, Minn., chartered. 1st classes met in 1869.

Open-Hearth Process in the American steel industry introduced from England by

Susan B. Anthony founded suffragette newspaper, *The Revolution.* It adopted the motto, "The true Republic—men, their rights and nothing more; women, their rights and nothing less."

be its empire with the Grand Wizard as the supreme leader and its body of officers to be designated "ghouls." In reality, the order was formed to intimidate the Negro and carpetbagger and regain white supremacy in the South.

Feb. 21 Edwin M. Stanton removed from office as Secretary of Department of War by Pres. Johnson, who was later impeached for violation of the Tenure of Office Act.

Mar. 11 4th Reconstruction Act passed. Under its provisions a majority of the votes actually cast would decide the adoption or rejection of a state constitution, whereas the provisions of the Second Reconstruction Act required a majority of the registered voters. The measure was taken to counter the intimidation of the Negro by the Ku Klux Klan and disenfranchised whites to keep him away from the polls.

Mar. 13 Andrew Johnson's **impeachment** trial opened. He was charged with violation of the Tenure of Office Act.

May 16 Impeachment proceedings against Pres. Johnson closed with an acquittal. Johnson had been charged with taking law into his own hands, abusing his veto power, and other irregularities, none of which could be substantiated.

May 20–21 Republican National Convention at Chicago, Ill., nominated Gen. Ulysses S. Grant for the Presidency and Schuyler Colfax of Indiana for the Vice-Presidency. At the same meeting, the convention adopted the name of "National Republican Party."

June 1 James Buchanan died at the age of 77. He is buried at Lancaster, Pa.

June 25 Congress provided **8-hour day** for laborers and workmen employed by the government. Concept of 8-hour day was still something of a novelty, although ineffectual 8-hour laws had already been passed in a few states.

June 25 Congressional representation granted to North Carolina, South Carolina, Louisiana, Georgia, Alabama, and Florida

offered him a lucrative contract and he moved triumphantly to the East, where he exploited the vein of the romantic western tale.

Wilkie Collins' famous mystery classic *The Moonstone,* published serially in *Harper's Weekly.* Some have thought it the finest mystery ever written.

The most popular girls' story in American literature, *Little Women* by **Louisa May Alcott,** has sold over 2,000,000 copies in the U.S. Before Miss Alcott's death *Little Women* netted her about $200,000. She was also a prolific writer of juveniles. In the same year as *Little Women,* she turned out *Morning-Glories and Other Stories, Kitty's Class Day, Aunt Kipp, Nelly's Hospital,* and *Psyche's Art.* It is part of the folklore of *Little Women* that the author was asked by her publisher to write a book for girls. Louisa May Alcott influenced the trend of juvenile literature in America by avoiding didacticism in her popular novel and tempering the pervasive sentimentality of this type of fiction by using characters who were drawn from life.

The New England Tragedies, part III of *Christus—A Mystery,* completed by **Henry Wadsworth Longfellow.** The writing of *Christus* occupied Longfellow for more than 20 years. In 1851, he finished *The Golden Legend,* which was based upon the typical miracle tales of medieval literature, with a Prince as hero who is, like Faust, under the power of Lucifer. *The Golden Legend* became Part II of *Christus.* Part I, *The Divine Tragedy,* was published in 1871. It was a dramatization of the Gospel story, which included a miracle play called "The Nativity." *The New England Tragedies* was based upon incidents in American colonial history which the author turned into 2 5-act plays, "John Endicott" and "Giles Corey of the Salem Farms." In spite of his long and intense efforts, *Christus* was not a literary success and it

Abram S. Hewitt in Trenton, N.J. Process expanded steel production by making more ore available through the extraction of sulphur and phospherus.

2 patents for **typewriter** granted to Christopher Sholes, Samuel Soulé, and Carlos Glidden. For 5 years afterwards, Sholes worked to complete his machine. He did not succeed. In 1871, he applied for and received additional patent for improvements which he had added to his original invention. 2 years later he sold his rights to the Remington Arms Company for $12,000. Remington mechanics quickly converted Sholes' invention into a marketable product. Sholes had produced a crude machine in 1867. The Remington Company had a perfected model by 1873. Sholes carried on with ideas for improvements of the typewriter, took out another patent in 1875, but finally turned all of his work over to Remington, which marketed the machine as the "Remington typewriter."

Philip and Herman Armour enlarged the original Chicago Grain Commission of **H. O. Armour and Company** by the addition of a pork-packing plant. It became Armour and Company in 1870.

$2 million left by Walter Loomis Miller for establishment of a free public reference library in Chicago. Miller, merchant, banker, founded the **Young Men's Library Association** in 1841, which became the nucleus of the Chicago public library system. He was president of the Historical Society in 1863. The money which he provided for the **Newberry Library** was drawn from undeveloped real estate. It represented ½ of his estate. The Newberry Library has, through its collection, become world famous; it concentrates upon the fields of history, music, literature and philology.

Carolina Severance completed the organization of the **New England Woman's Club.** Julia Ward Howe, a founder of the club, served as president for 18 years, beginning in 1871. The objective of the

1st **baseball uniforms** introduced by Cincinnati Red Stockings. Featuring knickerbockers, they were ridiculed at first.

General Duke won the 2nd annual **Belmont Stakes.** Jockey was R. Swim; time was 3:02 for winnings valued at $2800.

Great vogue for **ice skating** led to the meeting of an American skating congress in Pittsburgh, whose purpose was to formulate regulations for the sport and also to give encouragement to its spread.

New sport of **velocipeding** (cycling) attained great vogue in America 3 years after it had been perfected in Paris. Schools for all ages and both sexes are set up throughout the large cities; newspapers report on the vogue seriously and in caricature. The fact that women could participate added greatly to its rapid spread.

Benevolent Protective Order of Elks formed in New York city.

The New York Times carried on a campaign against the **regulations of the custom-house** which made it compulsory for all passengers on arriving boats to stay on board until all the baggage was removed to the docks. The homecoming of passengers was also inconvenienced because guests were not permitted to go on board to greet their friends. These trials were compounded by a delay on the docks where none of the baggage was sorted until the whole lot had been taken off the ships.

Sunday sermons of Henry Ward Beecher were so popular that they reappeared in print in the papers on Tuesday mornings and sold for as much as 5¢.

The seniors of Amherst College passed a resolution which condemned **"hazing"** of underclassmen.

May 30 **Decoration Day** celebrated nationally for 1st time. Day was chosen by

| POLITICS AND GOVERNMENT; WAR; DISASTERS; VITAL STATISTICS. | BOOKS; PAINTING; DRAMA; ARCHITECTURE; SCULPTURE. |

by omnibus bill which was passed over Pres. Johnson's veto.

July 4–9 Democratic National Convention at New York city nominated Horatio Seymour of New York for the Presidency and Francis P. Blair, Jr., of Missouri for the Vice-Presidency.

July 28 14th Amendment adopted granting citizenship to Negroes. It also validated debts incurred during the war between the states, but denied the responsibility of any debts incurred in aid of conspiracy or insurrection against the U.S.

Oct. 21 San Francisco, Calif., rocked by severe **earthquake** causing the loss of about $3,000,000 in property damage.

Nov. 3 Gen. Ulysses S. Grant defeated Horatio Seymour in **Presidential election.** His popular majority was a scant 306,000 out of 5,715,000 votes, although his margin in the electoral college count was 214-80. The Negro vote, which totalled over 700,000 decided the election for Grant.

Dec. 3 Treason **trial of Jefferson Davis,** president of Confederacy, began in Richmond, Va., before Circuit Court Judges Salmon P. Chase and John C. Underwood. Charge was dropped on Feb. 15, 1869, after Pres. Johnson's proclamation of general amnesty.

Dec. 25 Unqualified **amnesty** granted to all who participated in the "insurrection or rebellion" against the U.S. by a Presidential proclamation.

was too complicated and lifeless to win popular favor.

Harriet Beecher Stowe published *Men of Our Times,* and *The Chimney Corner.*

Bayard Taylor wrote *The Golden Wedding: A Masque.*

Hiram Powers completed his celebrated sculpture *Clytie.*

Charles A. Dana, who had served as managing editor of the *New York Tribune* under Horace Greeley, became editor of the New York *Sun.*

1 of the largest daily newspapers of the East, **Atlanta Constitution,** started by W. A. Hemphill.

Newspaper which maintained liberal Republican point of view, the **Louisville (Ky.) Courier-Journal,** established. It was to support Greeley for president and later the establishment of League of Nations. In 1939 Herbert Agar became editor.

1869

Major contribution to knowledge of the West made by John Wesley Powell, a 1-armed casualty of the Civil War, and the 1st white man to navigate the stretch of the Colorado R. that runs treacherously through the Grand Canyon for over 1000 mi. of torrents and dangerous rapids. Powell later became director of the U.S. Geological Survey.

Feb. 6 1st caricature of **"Uncle Sam"** with chin whiskers appeared in *Harper's*

St. Anne's Church, designed by Renwick and Sands, built in Brooklyn, N.Y. Large and confused example of the worst of **Italian Gothic revivals** in U.S.

Plight of dramatist, who could not publish plays unless given permission by producer, reflected in reply of actor-producer Forrest to heir of Robert Montgomery Bird, who asked for permission to print his father's plays: Forrest writes: "The heirs of the late Dr. R. M. Bird have

SCIENCE; INDUSTRY; ECONOMICS; EDUCATION; RELIGION; PHILOSOPHY.	SPORTS; FASHIONS; POPULAR ENTERTAINMENT; FOLKLORE; SOCIETY.

N.E.W.C. was to concentrate and promote the efforts of women to win recognition for their rights.

Rise of **Railroad Brotherhoods** continued with union of Railway Conductors.

Political rebuffs of **labor** led National Labor Union to concentrate on political organization.

Equitable Life Assurance Society, built in New York, is 1st office building in world to contain an **elevator.**

George Westinghouse invented the **air brake,** 1st used on passenger trains this year.

Jan. 16 William Davis, fish-market owner of Detroit, Michigan, granted patent for **refrigerator car.** Davis, wanting to increase his area of sales, had worked for many years to develop his "ice box on wheels." He used his new invention for the transportation of fish and fruit. He also designed 1st railroad refrigerated car, which was built in 1869.

Mar. 23 **University of California** chartered in Berkeley, Calif., by merger with the College of California under provisions of the Morrill Land-Grant College Act of 1866. The trustees of the College of California, which was 1st California institution to adopt the educational standards of the leading colleges of the east, turned over the rights and sites of the college of the state, giving University of California the grounds at Berkeley. 1st classes on Berkeley campus met in 1873.

John A. Logan, National Commander of Grand Army of the Republic, for decoration of Civil War graves. Previously, however, local communities had appointed many decoration days on different occasions.

Oct. 1 The **Rochester Agricultural Fair** in upstate New York brought 50,000 visitors to the city. 40,000 attended the fair on Oct. 1, for a record $11,000 in gate receipts.

Oct. 1 *The New York Times* apologized to readers for increasing the number of its pages from a convenient 8 to a cumbersome 12. There was such a demand for **advertising space** that the newspaper was compelled from time to time to introduce the additional pages.

Nov. 11 1st **amateur track and field meet** (indoors) held by the New York Athletic Club. The New York A.C., which had been organized Sept. 8th, later held outdoor meets, established rules for the conduct of meets, built the 1st cinder track, and continues, to this day, to promote track and field and other sports.

1869

University of Nebraska chartered at Lincoln, Nebr. 1st classes held in 1871.

1st state board of health in U.S. founded in Massachusetts.

Little known but very significant Edison invention was the **electric voting machine,** 1st used in an election in 1892.

Henry J. Heinz and L. C. Noble established **food-packing company** at Sharpsburg, Pa. 1st item was grated horse-radish.

Susan Brownell Anthony became president of the National Woman Suffrage Association.

Arabella Mansfield admitted to the Iowa bar as the **1st woman lawyer** in America since Mistress Margaret Brent, colonial attorney for Cecilius Calvert, Lord Proprietor of Maryland in the 1640's.

"Battery" 1st employed in baseball parlance to describe the combination of pitcher

POLITICS AND GOVERNMENT; WAR; DISASTERS; VITAL STATISTICS.	BOOKS; PAINTING; DRAMA; ARCHITECTURE; SCULPTURE.

Weekly. Figure had been used without whiskers by cartoonists for several years and had evolved ultimately from Revolutionary caricature of "Brother Jonathan." After 1869 "Uncle Sam" became stock device of political cartoonists.

Mar. 4 **Ulysses S. Grant,** 18th president, **inaugurated.** He was a Republican and served for 2 terms.

Apr. 10 Before being readmitted to the Union Georgia, Mississippi, Texas, and Virginia were required to ratify the **15th Amendment.** This amendment states that suffrage shall not be denied or abridged because of race, color, or previous condition of servitude.

Sept. 1 **Prohibition party organized** during the National Prohibition Convention in Chicago. The convention was called by the National Temperance Convention in Cleveland.

Sept. 6 **108 miners killed** by suffocation in a coal mine disaster at Avondale, Pa.

Oct. 8 **Franklin Pierce died** at the age of 64. He is buried at Concord, N.H.

Oct. 27 **200 persons died** when the steamer *Stonewall* caught fire on the Ohio R. near Cairo, Ill.

Dec 10 **1st woman suffrage** in U.S. granted by Wyoming Territory.

neither right, title, nor any legal interest whatever in the plays written by him for me. . . . These plays are my exclusive property, by right of purchase, and for many years by the law of copyright."

Harriet Beecher Stowe developed local color admirably in her series of sketches entitled *Oldtown Folks.* Referring to her own memories of Litchfield, Conn., and that of her husband, she painted a picture of New England life, paving the way for Sarah Orne Jewett and Mary Wilkins Freeman.

Mark Twain made use of his tour of Europe and the Near East in his extremely popular and humorous "guide book," **Innocents Abroad.** A collection of articles he had sent from abroad, the book irreverently pokes fun at Old World institutions; shrines, paintings, customs. Historical facts are often distorted, exaggeration is manifest everywhere. At least it is an excellent satire on the sentimentalism associated with the Grand Tour.

Statue, *West Wind* by Thomas Gould, created a sensation in America. Figure of young girl surrounded by drapery was thought to be a reproduction of a statue of famous Italian Canova. Gould was commissioned to make 7 replicas of the work.

1870

Population—39,818,449. Center of population: 48 miles east by north of Cincinnati, O.

Harper's Weekly published 1st political

Great impetus given to **vaudeville** in New York by the team Harrington and Hart. Impersonating a male and female combination they travestied all phases of

Heinz eventually had a widespread commercial success.

1st summer university course offered by Dean Shaler of Harvard University. It consisted of lectures in geology and was taken as recreation, rather than for credit. 1st formal summer course in education for public school teachers consisted of a 6-week series of lectures held at Martha's Vineyard, Mass., in 1878.

The Noble Order of the Knights of Labor established at Philadelphia, Pa. 9 original members, all garment-cutters, were headed by Uriah S. Stephens. This secret order was formally organized in 1871.

Jan 23 **1st state bureau of labor in** U.S. organized in Massachusetts.

Feb. 15 **University of Nebraska** obtained its charter. It opened in 1871.

May 10 **1st transcontinental railroad** in U.S. completed at Promontory Point, Utah, with the link-up there of the Central Pacific Railroad from the West and the Union Pacific Railroad from the East.

June 8 1st U.S. patent for suction-principle **vacuum cleaner** awarded to I. W. McGaffey of Chicago, Ill.

Sept. 24 Financial manipulators Jay Gould and James Fisk ruined thousands of gold speculators in **"Black Friday" in Wall Street** incident. In an attempt to corner the gold market, the 2 men tried to keep Pres. Grant from selling government gold, and assured the public that they had been successful. However, Grant ordered sale of $4 million in gold, forcing down the price from 162 to 135.

Dec. 6 **1st national Negro labor group** in America, the Colored National Labor Convention, met in Washington, D.C.

and catcher. Term derived from telegraphy where combination of transmitter and receiver formed a battery.

Fenian won the 3rd annual **Belmont Stakes.** Jockey was C. Miller; time was 3:04¼ for winnings valued at $3350.

Poughkeepsie (N.Y.) Ice Yacht Club formed, 1st such society in U.S. It was followed by New Hamburgh and Hudson River Ice Yacht Clubs as sport grew in popularity.

Jan. Sentence, **"The only good Indian is a dead Indian,"** is credited to Gen. Philip H. Sheridan, 1 of the North's great cavalry officers during the Civil War. Sheridan is said to have made the statement in reply to Comanche Chief Toch-a-way's remark, "Me good Indian," when they met at Fort Cobb, Mo.

Mar. 15 **1st professional baseball team** was Cincinnati Red Stockings who announced regular payments to players and began a successful 8-month tour of East and Middle West.

June 15 American boxing champion, Mike McCoole, won on a foul in 9th round from Tom Allen of England in what was probably **1st international bare knuckles boxing match** at St. Louis, Mo.

Nov. 6 **1st intercollegiate football** game played at New Brunswick, N.J. Rutgers beat Princeton 6–4 in a game more like soccer than football as it is played today. There were 25 men on each team and no running with ball was allowed.

1870

1st comprehensive organization of a **graduate program of studies** initiated at Yale and Harvard.

Great Atlantic and Pacific Tea Com-

The **Woman's Journal,** the official organ of the National Woman Suffrage Association, founded by Lucy Stone, who guided its policies until her death in 1893.

cartoon to use **donkey as symbol for Democratic Party.** Cartoon, by Thomas Nast, was called "A Live Jackass Kicking a Dead Lion."

Jan. 26 Virginia granted readmission to representation in U.S. Congress provided that the members of the Legislature take an oath agreeing never to amend their constitution to deny the Negro the right of suffrage, the right to hold office, or their educational privileges.

Feb. 23 Mississippi granted readmission to representation in U.S. Congress. The provisions were the same as those contained in the bill admitting Virginia, except that the representatives were permitted an affirmation instead of an oath.

Feb. 25 1st Negro in Congress took his seat. He was Hiram R. Revels, U.S. senator from Mississippi. 1st Negro member of the House was J. H. Rainey, representative from South Carolina, who also entered Congress this year.

Mar. 30 Texas granted readmission to representation in U.S. Congress. The provisions were the same as those contained in the bill admitting Mississippi.

Mar. 30 15th amendment adopted. It stipulated that no state shall deprive any citizen of the right to vote because of race, color, or previous condition of servitude.

Apr. 27 61 killed and 120 injured when the floor of the Supreme Court room in Richmond, Va., collapsed.

June 22 Act to create **Justice Department** under direction of the Attorney General passed by Congress. It supervises all government police, the F.B.I., and Bureau of Prisons.

July 15 Georgia granted readmission to representation in U.S. Congress.

Aug 1 Women voted for 1st time in

city life: baseball, politics, army, navy, Negro, German, Italian.

1st publication in America of Omar Khayyám's **Rubáiyát,** in the famous version by Edward FitzGerald. Little Blue Books sold about ¼ million copies at 5¢; Pocket Books about same number at 25¢. But there have been countless editions of 1 or another of FitzGerald's versions.

Founding of **Scribner's Monthly,** the leading periodical of the 70's. Unlike other literary magazines, it gave preference to American writers, printing contributions by Edward Eggleston, Joaquin Miller, Bret Harte, and Frank Stockton.

A perennial favorite "boy's book" is Thomas B. Aldrich's **The Story of a Bad Boy.** Semi-autobiographical, the book provides a fresh and simple account of boyhood, eschewing the moralizing that characterized most juvenile fiction.

Introduction of a new mode of **painting on glass** by John La Farge in his *Battle Window* in Memorial Hall, Harvard University. He employed countless varieties of glass to catch and reflect light in different forms. What is today referred to as American glass is an outgrowth of his experimentation.

Corcoran Art Gallery, Washington, D.C., incorporated by Act of Congress. William C. Corcoran, a financier, had given $300,-000 to build the gallery, which was completed in 1859. During the Civil War it had been used for military purposes. Corcoran also gave $1,000,000 to build a collection, as well as 79 paintings from his own collection.

Mecca for American painters was no longer London, Rome, or Düsseldorf, but Paris. Painters like Hunt, La Farge, Whistler drew their influence from the prominent French schools.

SCIENCE; INDUSTRY; ECONOMICS; EDUCATION; RELIGION; PHILOSOPHY.	SPORTS; FASHIONS; POPULAR ENTERTAINMENT; FOLKLORE; SOCIETY.

pany organized "for the purpose of importing and distributing pure and reliable teas and coffees and subjecting the purchaser to but one profit from the foreign factor." Company grew into the largest single chain of grocery stores in U.S. in terms of volume of business. The company's early advertising stressed the fact that it could provide bargains by eliminating middlemen from grocery sales.

Stevens Institute of Technology established at Hoboken, N.J. 1st classes held in 1871.

Syracuse University established at Syracuse, N.Y. 1st classes met in 1871.

Wellesley College founded as Wellesley Female Seminary. 1st classes began 1875.

Ohio State University at Columbus, Ohio, chartered as Ohio Agricultural and Mechanical College. 1st classes met 1873. Present name adopted 1877.

Loyola University, Chicago, Ill., chartered as St. Ignatius College. Change to present name was made the same year. 1st classes met in 1869, year before official chartering.

This decade saw the emergence of the **refrigerated railroad car** as an important factor in the commercial development of certain industries. Pioneer development of refrigerated car is credited to Gustavus Franklin Swift, who in the 1870's began to ship dressed beef from Chicago to the East, the 1st time this had been done successfully. He employed a railroad car in which fresh air was forced over ice and then circulated through the storage compartments. George Henry Hammond also pioneered at about this time in the use of refrigerated cars, shipping meat from Omaha and from Hammond, Ind.

Growth of unions in America reflected in membership of 300,000.

John D. Rockefeller and his brother, William, were principal organizers of **Standard Oil Company**, with 2 refineries in

Craze for **roller skating** spread throughout America as it did throughout world. By 1863, 4 rollers had been added to "parlor skates" and a young skater, William H. Fuller, developed art of figure skating, which he displayed on a tour around the world.

One of the most **popular spectator sports** was walking. Gilmore's Gardens in New York City would usually sell out when famous heel-and-toers raced there. About 1900, bicycle riders replaced the walkers in popularity.

2 popular sports were cricket and baseball. Cricket was generally favored in the press because of its gentility.

Famous international boat race took place in New York between British yacht *Cambria* and host of entries from New York Yacht Club. Race was won by an American boat, the *Magic*. More than 100,000 crowded the shores to follow the regatta, and the bay was dotted with ships of all descriptions.

Pimlico race track built in Baltimore, Md., by a group of racing enthusiasts who were encouraged by the success of the course at Saratoga Springs, N.Y., in 1864.

Kingfisher won the 4th annual **Belmont Stakes.** Jockey was W. Dick; time was 2:59½ for winnings valued at $3750.

Atlantic City **boardwalk** completed, 1st in America.

May 10 Jem Mace of England, who claimed **world heavyweight boxing championship** upon retirement of Tom King, also of England, fought Tom Allen, another claimant, in a 10-round bout near Kennersville, La. Mace was declared winner.

Columbia, Princeton and Rutgers were playing their earliest **football matches.**

America in a Utah election. The legislature had passed a women's suffrage bill on Feb. 12.

Aug. 14 Adm. David G. Farragut died at Portsmouth, N.H., at the age of 69.

Oct. 4 Benjamin Helm Bristow appointed **1st U.S. Solicitor General** by Pres. Grant.

Oct. 12 Gen. Robert E. Lee died at Lexington, Va., at the age of 63. He was a graduate of West Point and the Commander in Chief of the Confederate Army during the Civil War.

Dec. Gov. William Woods Holden, highly unpopular "scalawag" governor of North Carolina, impeached by state legislature. It was **1st impeachment of state governor** in the U.S. He was replaced by Gov. Tod R. Caldwell.

Saratoga, by Bronson Howard, produced on New York stage. Howard was the only U.S. dramatist of the 19th century who was able to earn his living solely from his writing for the stage.

Feb. 14 Frontier burst upon stage with popular *Kit the Arkansas Traveler,* by T. B. DeWalden. It was followed by *Horizon* (1871) by Augustin Daly; *Davy Crockett* (1872) by Frank Murdock; *The Gilded Age* (1874) by Mark Twain and C. D. Warner; *The Two Men from Sandy Bar* (1876) by Bret Harte; and *The Danites in the Sierras* (1877) by Joaquin Miller.

1871

Feb. 21 District of Columbia provided with territorial government. Several systems of government were tried, the one in present use having been adopted in 1878.

Feb. 28 Law passed providing for Federal supervision of **elections** in any city having more than 20,000 inhabitants. The measure was taken primarily to protect the Negro voter in the South.

Mar. 3 Indian Appropriation Act passed. It made all Indians national wards and nullified all Indian treaties.

Mar. 4 Pres. Grant established **1st civil service commission,** headed by George William Curtis of New York city. Unwillingness of Congress to make additional appropriations rendered the commission ineffective.

May 8 Treaty of Washington signed between U.S. and Great Britain at Washington, D.C. It provided for arbitration for the *Alabama* claims by an international tribunal to meet at Geneva. The

Best seller *The Hoosier Schoolmaster* by Edward Eggleston, a classic of regional literature. Eggleston's *The Circuit Rider* and *Roxy* are better novels, but they have never had the circulation of the *Schoolmaster,* which has probably sold ½ million copies.

The "Good Gray Poet," **Walt Whitman,** still generally ignored and often maligned by the public, augmented his body of poetry with the publication of *Passage to India,* including the famous title poem and 72 others. A broadening of his scope and subject matter is seen: the cosmic and spiritual breaks through the limitations of the American scene and embraces all peoples and lands.

America's most famous naturalist, **John Burroughs,** issued his popular bird study, *Wake-Robin.* An invitation to ornithology, the book imparts some of the vivid interest the author cultivates as a bird watcher. Outdoor life in New England and New

Cleveland and a selling agency in New York.

Jan. 2 Construction of the **Brooklyn Bridge** began. It spanned the East R. from Park Row, Manhattan, to Sands and Washington Sts., Brooklyn.

Feb. 9 **U.S. Weather Bureau** established by Congress. Originally part of the Signal Corps, it became part of the Department of Agriculture on July 1, 1891. On June 30, 1940 it was transferred to the Commerce Department.

July 12 U.S. patent for discovery of process by which **celluloid** is produced awarded to John W. Hyatt, Jr., and Isaiah S. Hyatt of Albany, N.Y. Discovery of celluloid was significant advance in the science of photography as later developed by George Eastman.

Dec 16 **Colored Methodist Episcopal Church** of America established at Jackson, Tenn., by Bishop Paine.

The game which was played was technically soccer.

Yale and Harvard met in a **crew race** on a circular course at Worcester, Mass. Yale came in 1st, but was disqualified for having run into Harvard.

Aug. 16 Fred Goldsmith demonstrated that the **curve ball** was not an optical illusion before a large crowd at Capitoline Grounds, Brooklyn. Goldsmith set up 3 poles in a straight line and hurled a ball that went to the right of the 1st pole, to the left of the 2nd, and to the right of the 3rd.

1871

Greater **emphasis on science** in U.S. education reflected in publication of an official Yale pamphlet entitled *The Needs of the University*. Without renouncing the virtues of classical education, the authorities at Yale admitted the utility of laboratory courses in the material sciences.

Daily Illini published at the University of Illinois became **1st undergraduate daily newspaper** in America.

Smith College chartered at Northampton, Mass. 1st classes met in 1875.

James Freeman Clarke's *Ten Great Religions* (2 vols., 1871–83), reflected growing American awareness of religions other than Christianity. By 1886, Clarke's book had run through 21 editions.

Spencer Fullerton Baird appointed **U.S. Commissioner of Fish**. Directed the establishment, in the same year, of U.S. Bureau of Fisheries.

Andrew Smith Hallidie invented **underground continuous moving cable** and me-

Late war revived interest in rifle shooting and led to formation of **National Rifle Association** this year. Shooting at a target replaced shooting for a game prize.

1st professional baseball association organized, National Association of Professional Baseball Players, which replaced the amateur National Association.

New **baseball rule** permitted the batter to call for a high or low pitched ball as he desired. This rule was rescinded in 1887.

Harry Bassett won the 5th annual **Belmont Stakes**. Jockey was W. Miller; time was 2:56 for winnings valued at $5450.

Henry James made a trip to **Niagara Falls**, sailing down from Toronto across Lake Ontario, and recorded his impressions in an early travel essay. Much of what he felt is still the common reaction of visitors to the Falls, and the most "modern" of all of his descriptions is something which has evidently been said since the 1st shop went up along the cliff and

| POLITICS AND GOVERNMENT; WAR; DISASTERS; VITAL STATISTICS. | BOOKS; PAINTING; DRAMA; ARCHITECTURE; SCULPTURE. |

treaty also renewed Canadian-American fishing arrangements in the North Atlantic.

July 12 52 persons killed and many wounded in **riot** between the Irish Catholics and the Irish Protestants in New York city.

July 30 Over 100 killed when boiler exploded aboard the **Staten Island ferryboat** *Westfield* in New York.

Sept. 4 70 citizens appointed at a mass meeting at Cooper Institute, New York city, to investigate the fraudulent practices of **Tammany Hall** led by William (Boss) Tweed. By the end of the year he had been twice arrested and released on bail.

Oct. 8 Upwards of **600 killed** and 350 homes destroyed when the entire community of Peshtigo, Wis. was razed by fire. About 50 persons seeking refuge in brick building were completely consumed by the intense flames.

Oct. 8–11 More than 250 died in the **Chicago fire.** It devastated an area of 3½ sq. mi., left 98,500 persons homeless, and consumed 17,450 buildings. Property loss was estimated at $200,000,000. The original draft of Lincoln's Emancipation Proclamation was also destroyed with the burning of the Chicago Historical Society.

York provided him with another volume in 1875, *Winter Sunshine*. In *Birds and Poets* (1877) he relates birdlore to literary creation.

1st novel of **William Dean Howells,** *Their Wedding Journey*, is a combination of travelogue and book of manners. In a book that moves leisurely, he traces the honeymoon journey of the Marches (family used in later novels) to Niagara, Montreal, Quebec, dealing lightly with their newly established relationship. Other novels of the decade are *A Chance Acquaintance* (1873), *A Foregone Conclusion* (1875), *The Lady of the Aroostook* (1879), and *The Undiscovered Country* (1880). In all these Howells reveals his delightful art of representing the domestic and "uneventful."

Probably the best-known painting by an American is **Whistler's** *Mother*, entitled unpretentiously *Arrangement in Gray and Black*. He remarked relative to the latter title that no one would have an interest in the identity of the sitter. Actually millions since have identified the canvas with their feelings for their own mothers.

Lenox Library, New York city, built from plans by Richard Morris Hunt, who was 1 of 1st Americans to study at the Ecole des Beaux-Arts in Paris and was influential in introducing French architecture to U.S.

Patent issued to Balthaser Kreischer, New York manufacturer, for 1st **hollow tile design.** Hollow tile was both light and fireproof, came into extensive use for industrial buildings.

1st **Grand Central Station** opened in New York city, with tracks running into huge vault of open, webbed wrought iron. Later demolished to make way for present terminal.

1872

1st recorded political speech of William Jennings Bryan delivered to Democratic rally in Centralia, Ill., when he was 12

Best seller appeared, *Barriers Burned Away*, by Edward Payson Roe, a remarkably popular writer whose books had a

SCIENCE; INDUSTRY; ECONOMICS; EDUCATION; RELIGION; PHILOSOPHY.	SPORTS; FASHIONS; POPULAR ENTERTAINMENT; FOLKLORE; SOCIETY.

chanical **gripper** for underside of streetcars, preparing the way for introduction of cable car in San Francisco and other cities by 1873.

Mar. 27 **University of Arkansas** founded as Arkansas Industrial University at Fayetteville, Ark. 1st classes met in 1872.

May 1 **Legal Tender Act** declared constitutional by Supreme Court decision in *Knox vs. Lee.* The Legal Tender Act, passed in 1862, when national credit was ebbing, had ultimately authorized the issue of $450 millions in treasury notes, making them legal tender for all private debts and public dues, except import duties and interest on public debt. The Supreme Court, reduced to 7 members, declared the Legal Tender Acts unconstitutional on Feb. 7, 1870, in the case of *Hepburn vs. Griswold,* on the grounds that they exceeded any delegated or implied powers of Congress, violated the spirit of the Constitution and deprived creditors of property without due process of law. Pres. Grant made nominations to the empty Supreme Court posts on the same day the decision was handed down, and, 4 days later, the Supreme Court voted to reargue the issues. The decision of May 1, 1871, found the power to issue legal tender implied in the expressed powers to coin money and wage war. It also declared that the Constitution does not forbid Congress to impair contracts, but only the States. Whether Pres. Grant actually "packed" the court is still a moot point among historians.

began to sell souvenirs to tourists: "There is every appearance that the spectacle you have come so far to see is to be choked in the horribly vulgar shops and booths and catchpenny artifices which have pushed and elbowed to within the very spray of the Falls, and ply their importunities in shrill competition with its thunder. You see a multitude of hotels and taverns and stores, glaring with white paint, bedizened with placards and advertisements, and decorated by groups of those gentlemen who flourish most rankly on the soil of New York and in the vicinage of hotels; who carry their hands in their pockets, wear their hats always and every way, and, although of a stationary habit, yet spurn the earth with their heels. A side glimpse of the Falls, however, calls out your philosophy; you reflect that this may be regarded as one of those sordid foregrounds which Turner liked to use, and which may be effective as a foil; you hurry to where the roar grows louder, and, I was going to say, you escape from the village. In fact, however, you don't escape from it; it is constantly at your elbow, just to the right or left of the line of contemplation. It would be paying Niagara a poor compliment to say that, practically she does not hurl away this chaffering by-play from her edge; but as you value the integrity of your impression, you are bound to affirm that it suffers appreciable abatement from such sources. You wonder, as you stroll about, whether it is altogether an unrighteous dream that with the slow progress of taste and the possible or impossible growth of some larger comprehension of beauty and fitness, the public conscience may not tend to confer upon such sovereign places of nature something of the inviolability and privacy which we are slow to bestow, indeed, upon fame, but which we do not grudge at least to art."

1872

Russian Orthodox Church transferred its Episcopal See from Sitka, Alaska, to San Francisco. The purchase of Alaska by the

Susan B. Anthony tested the 14th Amendment by leading a group of women to cast ballots in the presidential election.

POLITICS AND GOVERNMENT; WAR; DISASTERS; VITAL STATISTICS.

BOOKS; PAINTING; DRAMA; ARCHITECTURE; SCULPTURE.

years old. Audience, at first mocking, was captured by boy's oratorical genius; afterwards he was carried through town on shoulders of cheering men.

1st Negroes chosen as delegates to a major party convention participated in the Republican National Convention in Philadelphia which renominated President Grant for re-election. Speeches were delivered from the rostrum by 3 of the Negroes, William E. Gray of Arkansas, B. B. Elliott of South Carolina, and John Roy Lynch of Mississippi.

Earliest recorded use of the word **"mugwump"** occurred in Indianapolis *Sentinel.* Beginning Mar. 23, 1884, the New York *Sun* began to use the word to describe Republicans who were against James G. Blaine; in the course of a series of editorials the word became widely known. It was roughly the equivalent of the later political classification, "egghead."

New American political party formed out of National Labor Union, called the **National Labor Reform Party,** prepared for presidential election with nomination of Judge David Davis of Illinois at its convention in Columbus, Ohio whose subsequent withdrawal from the race dealt a death blow to both the Party and the Labor Federation that had spawned it.

Feb. 22 1st national nominating convention of the **Prohibition Party** held at Columbus, Ohio. James Black of Pennsylvania was nominated for president and the Rev. John Russell of Michigan for vice-president.

May 1 1st National Convention of the **Liberal Republican Party** held at Cincinnati, Ohio, and nominated Horace Greeley for the presidency and B. Gratz Brown for the vice-presidency. Same slate was nominated by Democratic convention on July 9.

May 23 **Workingmen's National convention** at New York city nominated Ulysses S. Grant for president, and named Henry Wilson as their vice-presidential candidate.

combined sale of 4 to 5 million copies. Roe's books often centered on a sensational public catastrophe. The great Chicago fire of 1871 was the foundation for *Barriers Burned Away.*

A boisterous, exciting book of the Far West is Mark Twain's "record of several years of variegated vagabondizing," **Roughing It.** Here is the rough-and-tumble, exaggerated life of the Nevada miners, the stagecoach days on the Overland Trail, the tall tales, the hilarious optimism, the desperadoes and pioneers. Twain also includes chapters on his stay in Hawaii.

The *North American Review* declared that the true fiction writer must idealize what he finds. In the end, the *Review* judged, **idealist fiction** would be the true realistic fiction, since all truth was not to be found in facts alone. The American writer, in particular, said the *Review,* must look beyond his native land, which had neither depth nor antiquity, to the uncharted fields of the imagination.

Masterpiece of the sculptured works of William H. Rinehart is his marble nude *Clytie,* which enjoys prominent position in the Peabody Institute of Baltimore. Its naturalism is in direct opposition to the neoclassical representations of the nude.

First Baptist Church, originally New Brattle Square Church, built in Boston by H. H. Richardson, 1 of his 1st truly distinguished works.

Work begun on **Old Art Museum,** Boston, huge example of Victorian Gothic in U.S. architecture. 1st domestic terra cotta

U.S. ended the official influence of the Russian Orthodox Church in that possession.

Jehovah's Witnesses organized by Charles Taze Russell, a layman member of the Presbyterian Church. First called "Russellites," "International Bible Students," and "Millennial Darwinists," they officially became Jehovah's Witnesses in 1931 and in 1939 were incorporated in New York as the "Watch Tower Bible and Tract Society."

Eadweard Muybridge, English photographer, conducted early experiments in **photographing moving objects** in a project sponsored by U.S. government. Later he photographed a running horse by tripping a series of cameras synchronized by electric circuits with 12 clocks, and in 1881 he invented the zoopraxiscope, forerunner of the moving picture, for the projection of animal pictures on a screen.

University of Oregon at Eugene and Portland, Ore., established. 1st classes held in 1876.

Contract signed between Pennsylvania Railroad and South Improvement Company, a Rockefeller interest, which called for secret rebates and drawbacks; later became the most celebrated example of **pernicious business practices** among large corporations.

1st mercantile corporation in U.S. formed. It was the Simmons Hardware Company, which was controlled by Edward Campbell Simmons of St. Louis, Mo.

Montgomery Ward & Company, 1st mail order house in U.S., opened for business in Chicago, Ill. 1st catalogue was only a single page. Founder was Aaron Montgomery Ward.

Popular Science Monthly founded by **Edward Livingston Youmans.** Youmans

She was immediately arrested, found guilty, and fined $100. Defiantly she refused to pay the fine—and never would. Her reward came 14 years after her death in 1906 when in 1920 the 20th Amendment was finally adopted.

Yellowstone Park Timberland Reserve established to set apart the region for the enjoyment of the public. Designated the 1st Federal Forest Reserve by Congress in 1891. The early history of Yellowstone shades back into the popular yarns spun out of the romantic fervor for the American West, and disappears imperceptibly into mist. John Colter, who was with Lewis and Clark, is credited with reaching the region in 1806, but his report of his adventures and the things he saw merely set the pattern for the fantastic stories about Yellowstone in the years to come. The government finally sent exploratory parties to the area in 1859 and 1870. The reports of these expeditions were widely read and became the grounds for the act of Congress which established Yellowstone Park as a public park. Yellowstone is the oldest and biggest of the national parks. The area of the park was originally marked off as 3,348 square miles. In subsequent years, the boundaries of Yellowstone were substantially increased, and the Shoshone National Forest, a timber and land reserve, has been added.

New baseball rule permitted the pitcher to snap his delivery of the ball. However, the pitcher was still restricted to an underhand, below-the-waist motion. Present day regulations for size of ball also set this year: not less than 5 nor more than 5¼ oz., and not less than 9 nor more than 9¼ in. in diameter.

Joe Daniels won the 6th annual **Belmont Stakes.** Jockey was J. Rowe; time was 2:58¼ for winnings valued at $4500.

Apr. 10 **Arbor Day,** a festival of tree

POLITICS AND GOVERNMENT; WAR; DISASTERS; VITAL STATISTICS.	BOOKS; PAINTING; DRAMA; ARCHITECTURE; SCULPTURE.

July 9 Democratic National Convention at Baltimore, Md., named Horace Greeley and B. Gratz Brown for the presidency and vice-presidency.

Nov. 5 Gen. Ulysses S. Grant defeated Horace Greeley in the **Presidential elections** by an electoral vote of 286 to 66. Pres. Grant was returned to office by a popular vote of 3,597,132 against 2,834,-125 for Greeley.

Nov. 9 Fire which killed 13 persons and destroyed $75,000,000 in property started in Boston, Mass. The fire raged for 3 days, burning 65 acres.

used. The museum hewed closely to the aesthetic principles of John Ruskin. The period after the Civil War was deeply influenced by the dictums of Ruskin, who stanchly defended and promoted medieval architecture against the "immoral" forms of the Renaissance. He was so successful in his campaign that Victorian Gothic is also known as Ruskinian.

1873

The Farmers' Alliance, which soon became a national farmers' welfare organization, began with small, local, meetings. It grew into a statewide group in Texas in 1876, and a nationwide alliance in 1887, when all the state groups which had been formed by that date joined into a cooperative union. The program of the alliance soon concentrated upon such issues as free silver, greenbacks, national railroads, the curtailment of speculation, and decentralized banking, emphasizing the common grievances of the straightened farmlands. When the alliance joined with the **Knights of Labor** in 1889, these issues were discussed on a broader basis and became the major radical demands of the final ¼ of the century.

Feb. 12 Routine **coinage act** of Congress omitted all silver currency, because silver was so scarce it brought more as bullion than as dollars. 3 years later, when Nevada mines were producing unprecedented quantities of silver, mine owners demanded government buy their product for coinage; coinage act became known as **"The Crime of '73."**

Mar. 3 "Salary Grab Act" passed doubling the president's salary and raising the pay of congressmen, the cabinet and the Supreme Court.

Mar. 3 Act passed prohibiting the

Romantic concern with landscapes reached a peak in *Home of the Heron* by **George Inness.** He believed, along with the French school of Corot, that greatness lies in the area of the emotions, not in that of fact. Effect of Inness on younger painters was great. Sentimentalism that mars their paintings persisted until well into the 20th century.

A famous best seller, *Around the World in Eighty Days,* by **Jules Verne** exceeded the million mark in sales.

Probably the most intellectual painter that America has produced was **Thomas Eakins.** In his early work, *Turning Stake Boat,* depicting a number of sculls on a flat surface of water, he confessed using trigonometric tables to fashion perspective, and studying refraction to get the exact shimmer on the water. His attitude, like that of Renaissance painters, is often scientific rather than aesthetic.

Longfellow completed his cycle of *Tales of a Wayside Inn,* drawing subject matter for his narratives from foreign and indigenous sources. The "Bell of Atri" is set in Abruzzi; others are set in New Hampshire, Alsace, Kambalu, Casal-Maggiore, Pennsylvania, the Pyrenees.

Sidney Lanier composed *Field-larks and Blackbirds; Swamp Robin; Danse des*

was among the American disciples of Herbert Spencer and became Spencer's American publisher. He began the *International Scientific Series* in 1871, which specialized in popular presentations of the best scientific ideas. The *Popular Science Monthly,* which became the *Scientific Monthly,* was the mouthpiece for Youmans' eager and earnest appeals to extend scientific education in America.

planting, inaugurated in the state of Nebraska through the efforts of Julius Sterling Morton, later Secretary of Agriculture. In 1885, April 22 was officially designated as Arbor Day by the State Legislature. Other states followed suit: Michigan and Minnesota (1876), Ontario, Canada (1887), and New York (1888).

Nov. 5 **Conviction of William Marcy "Boss" Tweed** in New York city ended the reign of one of the most corrupt political groups in the history of the United States, known as the "Tweed Ring."

1873

1st national grouping of Jewish congregations organized as the **Union of American Hebrew Congregations.** 2 years later, this group founded Hebrew Union College in Cincinnati, oldest rabbinical seminary in U.S. A conference in Cleveland in 1855 had resulted in a breach between the Eastern and the Western rabbis and their division was not bridged until 1879. The Union of American Hebrew Congregations, therefore, consisted of congregations only from the South and the West. There was no institution in the U.S. similar to the seminary, and the organization of the faculty and student body involved pioneer, and even novel, planning.

Rise of **Railroad Brotherhoods** continued with organization of firemen.

Epidemics of yellow fever, cholera, and smallpox swept through many Southern cities.

Cable street car, invented by Andrew S. Hallidie, 1st used in San Francisco, Calif.

1st major institution of **nursing education** founded at Bellevue Hospital, N.Y., based its teaching on the theories of Florence Nightingale.

Free delivery of mail provided in all cities with a population of at least 20,000.

Memorial Day became a legal holiday in New York, the 1st state so to act. Rhode Island followed suit in 1874; Vermont in 1876; New Hampshire in 1877; and Wisconsin in 1879. Memorial Day is now legally observed in all the states of the North and in all the territories.

Famous decision by **President White of Cornell:** "I will not permit 30 men to travel 400 miles to agitate a bag of wind." when refusing Cornell football players permission to meet Michigan at Cleveland.

Bookmakers 1st appeared at U.S. race tracks. 1st few were English but Americans soon learned the skill, and the days of informal wagering between owners or between spectators were over.

The **Fair Grounds race course** was opened in New Orleans, La., to operate on a system of prolonged meetings patterned after John Morrissey's races begun in Saratoga Springs in 1864.

The No. 1 national idols during the 1870's were **riflemen.** More than 100,000 people attended one national rifle shooting tournament held at Creedmoor, Long Island, N.Y. in 1873. No. 2 in the hearts of their countrymen were **oarsmen.** As many as 60,000 men, women, and children lined the banks of the Harlem River in New York city to watch and wager on the sculling contests.

sending of **obscene literature** through the mails. The bill was sponsored by Anthony Comstock, secretary of the Society for Suppression of Vice. Comstock, formerly a dry-goods store clerk, joined the YMCA and began to agitate for a New York vice society. He drew his inspiration from a London society which had, for 75 years, been engaged in ferreting out and bringing to trial whoever and whatever offended against orthodoxy.

Mar. 4   Pres. **Ulysses S. Grant inaugurated** into office for his 2nd term. Henry Wilson succeeded Schuyler Colfax as vice-president.

Sept. 18   **Panic of 1873** precipitated by the failure of Jay Cooke & Co., a banking house involved in financing the Northern Pacific railroad. Over 5000 businesses failed in the depression that followed.

Sept. 20   **New York Stock Exchange** closed. The same day the secretary of treasury reissued $26-million of legal tenders. 10 days later the exchange reopened.

Oct. 31   American steamer **Virginius captured** by the Spanish gunboat *Tornado* while transporting supplies to Cuban revolutionary forces. 8 U.S. citizens from the steamer were subsequently executed in Cuba by the Spanish authorities.

Nov. 19   **William "Boss" Tweed** convicted on 204 charges of fraud. He was sentenced to 12 years in prison and fined $12,550.

Moucherons—all compositions for the flute.

A favorite book of adventure for boys, *Twenty Thousand Leagues Under the Sea* by **Jules Verne** was published. At least a million copies have been sold.

Thomas Bailey Aldrich published *Marjorie Daw,* a long short story, or novelette, written in the form of the epistolary novel. It was a popular and critical success and has been consistently ranked above the more ambitious novels of the author.

Mrs. Skaggs' Husband and other stories by **Bret Harte** published, among the best of his writing for this period. *The Head of Sandy Bar,* a favorite story, was included in the volume.

Edward Eggleston published *The Mystery of Metropolisville.* In the preface to his novel, Eggleston wrote a literary manifesto which declared that he considered the novel, as a form, a proper vehicle for contributing to the history of civilization in America. The novel was an illustration of this thesis. Though his intention was quite clear, it did not amount to a complete defense of the author's technique. In his pursuit of history, Eggleston became so bogged down in realistic detail that it was difficult to decide where fact left off and fiction began.

1874

Mar. 8   **Millard Fillmore** died at the age of 74. He was buried at Buffalo, N.Y.

Apr. 15   **War between Joseph Brooks and Elijah Baxter** broke out in Arkansas, with Brooks taking possession of the State capitol though he had lost the election for governor to Baxter.

May 15   Pres. Grant issued proclamation recognizing **Elijah Baxter** as governor of Arkansas after the state legislature had

1st American edition of **Lorna Doone** by R. D. Blackmore. Still selling, this famous romance has sold nearly a million copies.

Corruption and speculative fever of post-Civil War America epitomized in **The Gilded Age,** a novel by Mark Twain and Charles Dudley Warner. In the character of Colonel Sellers "the grandfather of all American boosters" is represented, "with

| SCIENCE; INDUSTRY; ECONOMICS; EDUCATION; RELIGION; PHILOSOPHY. | SPORTS; FASHIONS; POPULAR ENTERTAINMENT; FOLKLORE; SOCIETY. |

May 1 **1st penny post cards** in U.S. issued.

Aug. 18 1st American conquerors of **Mt. Whitney,** highest mountain in U.S., John Incas, C. D. Begole, and A. H. Johnson, recorded climb.

Oct. 27 Illinoisan Joseph F. Glidden, received patent for improvement in **barbed wire;** his product became widely popular, and is basis of its manufacture today.

Nov. 27 5 mile **Hoosac Tunnel,** longest tunnel in world at that time, excepting Mount Cenis Tunnel in Swiss Alps, run through the Hoosac Mountains in Massachusetts at cost of $10 million. As early as 1825, Massachusetts, realizing the commercial importance of a route through the Green Mountains, inquired about the prospects of a tunnel. Work began Sept., 1858. The tunnel, which gave Massachusetts an entree to the rich Hudson Valley trade of New York city, was 26 ft. wide and 23–26 ft. high. A double railroad accommodated the trains of the Fitchburg Railroad.

Sales at a general store in Philadelphia, Ind., one Saturday included: "eggs, tablecloths, calico, flour, lard, tacks, blankets, muslin, batting, shoes, socks, sugar, crackers, cheese, coffee, thread, cigars, collars, spices, screws, castor oil, shawls, axle grease, matches, and fish."

Survivor won the 1st annual **Preakness Stakes,** at Pimlico, Md., paying 11–1. Jockey was G. Barbee; time was 2:43 on a slow track for winnings valued at $1800. Preakness Stakes is one of the 3 classic races in American racing. It is associated with the Kentucky Derby and the Belmont Stakes in importance, and a horse which has won all three has earned the Triple Crown of American racing. Preakness Stakes has been run over varying distances. See 1889, 1894, 1901, 1908, 1909, 1910, 1911, 1925, IV.

Springbok won the 7th annual **Belmont Stakes.** Jockey was J. Rowe; time was 3:01¾ for winnings valued at $5200.

Sept. 23 Tom Allen of England, who claimed **world's heavyweight boxing championship** after retirement of Jem Mace, fought Mike McCoole near St. Louis, Mo. Allen won and was declared world champion.

Oct. 19 Yale, Princeton, Columbia, and Rutgers met at 5th Avenue Hotel, New York city, to draft 1st code of rules for **football.** Rules chosen were more like soccer than modern football and were abandoned in a few years in favor of the "Boston Game" played at Harvard.

1874

Opening of **New York Cooking School** reflected new American attitude toward cooking as a worthy field of study.

Chautauqua movement founded by Lewis Miller, an Ohio industrialist, and John H. Vincent, a Methodist clergyman, as an annual summer meeting for the training of Sunday-school teachers. The movement derived its name from the site of its meetings on the shores of L. Chautauqua,

Rugby football introduced on American campus in a match between Harvard and McGill University of Canada. Canadian rules for the game greatly interested the sports-minded of America and were instrumental in development that led to modern football.

Philadelphia Zoological Gardens, Philadelphia, Pa., opened; it was **1st public zoo** in U.S.

303

disallowed the gubernatorial claims of Joseph Brooks.

May 16 More than **100 drowned** and millions of dollars in property lost when the Ashfield reservoir dam collapsed above Williamsburg, Mass., inundating Mill River Valley.

June 20 Territorial government abolished in the **District of Columbia** and replaced by a commission.

June 20 Congress created a **Life-saving Medal** to be awarded by Treasury Department to those who risked their own lives to rescue persons "from the perils of the sea within the United States or upon any American vessel." In 1878 Treasury Department organized Life Saving Service, later incorporated in Coast Guard.

July 1 Country greatly excited by sensational **kidnapping of Charles B. Ross,** 4-year-old boy, from his home at Germantown, Pa. Abductors demanded $20,000 ransom. Child was never found.

Nov. 7 *Harper's Weekly* published **1st cartoon to use elephant to symbolize Republican Party.** Entitled "Third Term Panic," the cartoon by Thomas Nast showed Republican concern that Pres. U. S. Grant would be elected for a 3rd term on the Democratic ticket.

Nov. 25 Convention held at Indianapolis, Ind., to form **Greenback Party.** Members were chiefly farmers from South and West who sought an inflation of currency to ease farm debts. At nominating convention on May 17 Peter Cooper of New York was chosen candidate for the presidency.

Dec. 7 About **70 Negroes killed** when they attacked the court house at Vicksburg, Miss. Negroes became riotous over the intimidation and ejection of a carpetbag sheriff by the whites of Vicksburg.

his dreams of an immediate future gilding a present of poverty-stricken, whiskey-soaked, rough-and-tumble frontier."

Distinctive type of American public sculpture began with erection of **Soldiers' and Sailors' Monument** on Boston Common by Martin Milmore. This consists of a heavy base crowned by an allegorical figure of Liberty or Victory or other personifications, beneath which statues of men are ranged.

1st use of **pneumatic foundation caissons** in bridge construction occurred in Eads Bridge over the Mississippi at St. Louis.

Francis Parkman completed *The Old Régime in Canada,* a volume in his great cycle of histories about the struggle of the English and the French for the dominion of North America.

The Circuit Rider, a major novel by **Edward Eggleston,** published. The circuit rider was a pioneer preacher whose pulpit was the saddle of his horse. He rode out and visited outlying communities without churches. The career was synonymous with hardship. Eggleston, with his novel, made the circuit rider a permanent character of American literature.

In commemoration of the death of his friend, **Louis Agassiz, James Russell Lowell,** then in Italy, wrote the elegy, "Agassiz," the most outstanding of his poems about the intimate tragedies of his life.

Henry Wadsworth Longfellow published *The Hanging of the Crane,* an ambitious long poem not generally classed among his best.

SCIENCE; INDUSTRY; ECONOMICS; EDUCATION; RELIGION; PHILOSOPHY.

N.Y. The meetings gradually expanded their educational scope both in the range of subject matter and in the size of the student body.

University of Nevada, Reno, Nev., established at Elko, Nev. It provides the only facilities for higher education in the state.

Osteopathy, a new medical discipline, developed by Dr. Andrew T. Still of Baldwin, Kan.

Patents for barbed wire issued independently to Joseph Farwell Glidden and Jacob Haish, both of De Kalb, Ill.

Outlines of Cosmic Philosophy by **John Friske,** published. It was long considered the outstanding exposition and defense of the ideas of Herbert Spencer. Fiske advanced his own theory of the important distinction between the long relative infancy of the human being as compared with the short infancy of the other animals.

First steel arch bridge to span Mississippi, built by James Eads, opened at Saint Louis. The construction was in process for 7 years. Immediately afterwards, Eads began work on the South Pass of the **Mississippi delta,** to clear the river of mud and improve navigability. He built jetties of willow mattress which turned the current so that it cut through and washed out the bars of silt blocking the mouth of the river and made the port of New Orleans deep enough for ocean vessels.

Stephen Field of New York city invented the **3rd rail** which revolutionized municipal rail transportation by providing a convenient source of electric power.

Woman's Christian Temperance Union, called the WCTU, established at Cleveland, Ohio, as outcome of women's crusade against liquor traffic in Midwestern states. Mrs. Annie Wittenmyer was elected the 1st president.

Mar. 22 1st **Young Men's Hebrew Association** in U.S. organized in New York city. 1st president was Lewis May.

SPORTS; FASHIONS; POPULAR ENTERTAINMENT; FOLKLORE; SOCIETY.

Culpepper won the 2nd annual **Preakness Stakes,** paying 8–1. Jockey was M. Donohue; time was 2:56½ on a muddy track for winnings valued at $1900.

Saxon won the 8th annual **Belmont Stakes.** Jockey was G. Barbee; time was 2:39½ for winnings valued at $4200. From this year to 1889 distance was 1½ miles.

Mary Ewing Outerbridge, young U.S. tourist, brought **lawn tennis** to America from Bermuda. She set up her net on grounds of Staten Island Cricket and Baseball Club, where she and a friend played 1st game in U.S.

Ohio women began the **whiskey war,** an effort to eradicate the liquor trade. They stood in front of liquor stores and, with prayers and songs, denounced the sale of intoxicants. The movement had sympathetic response in other states, but met strong resistance and began to subside the following month.

The **potato bug,** which was discovered in the Rocky Mountains in 1824, reached the states along the Atlantic coast. It is also known as the Colorado beetle. The female beetle lays batches of 500–1000 orange eggs in clusters on the back of leaves where the larva have a ready supply of food. The potato bug, which does great damage to potato crops when uncontrolled, is indigenous to the U.S.

Aug. 21 **Henry Ward Beecher** sued for $100,000 by Theodore Tilton, who accused the famous preacher of committing adultery with his wife. The trial attracted nation-wide publicity and controversy, especially since the jury handed down a split decision, 9–3, in favor of the defendant, Beecher. A special investigating committee made up of members of his congregation, the Plymouth Church, Boston, Mass., had previously exonerated Beecher of the charge after having interviewed 36 witnesses, including Tilton.

| POLITICS AND GOVERNMENT; WAR; DISASTERS; VITAL STATISTICS. | BOOKS; PAINTING; DRAMA; ARCHITECTURE; SCULPTURE. |

1875

Jan. 14 Specie Resumption Act passed providing for the redemption of fractional currency for specie to begin Jan. 1, 1879. Circulating greenbacks were to be reduced to $300,000,000.

Jan. 30 Hawaiian Reciprocity Treaty signed. It provided that no Hawaiian territory be turned over to any 3rd power.

Mar. 1 The Negro guaranteed equal rights in public places by **Civil Rights Act.** The law further prohibited exclusion from jury duty.

Mar. 3 Congress passed a **homestead law** for desert land in Lassen County, Calif. It extended privileges of Homestead Act of 1862 by granting individuals the right to own 4 times more land and liberalizing absentee ownership requirements.

May 7 200 lives lost when the *Schiller,* a steamship en route from New York to Hamburg, went aground at Scilly Islands.

May 27 120 people burned to death when the French Catholic Church in South Holyoke, Mass., was consumed by fire.

July 31 Andrew Johnson died at the age of 66. He is buried at Greenville, Tenn.

Nov. 4 236 persons drowned off Cape Flattery, Washington, when steamer *Pacific* sank after a collision.

Dec. 4 William "Boss" Tweed escaped from prison at Ludlow St., New York city, and fled to Cuba.

Dec. 15 The House overwhelmingly passed **anti-3rd-term resolution.** It was directed against Pres. Grant's 3rd term ambi-

Vogue for small plaster statuary groups from casts by **John Rogers** reached its height. Most of Rogers' groups were narrative in intent, depicting such scenes as *The Checker Players, The Slave Market,* etc. Rogers cast and sold the reproductions himself, selling more than 100,000 altogether.

Masterpiece of realism in the style of Gérôme and Bonnat is Thomas Eakins' *Gross Clinic.* Objectivity with which Eakins approaches subject corresponds to scientific objectivity of doctor who is the subject.

An **inspired piece of sculpture** of Lincoln is the famous *Emancipation* in Lincoln Park, Washington, by Thomas Ball. A replica was set up in Boston in 1877. Lincoln is shown with his hand lifted over a kneeling slave.

The perspicuity and psychological realism of Henry James is seen in his early collection of short stories, **A Passionate Pilgrim and Other Tales,** containing such stories as the title piece, "The Madonna of the Future," and "Madame de Mauves." The international theme runs through most of these tales.

Economic and political corruption of period, with particular reference to **Credit Mobilier scandal,** fictionalized by J. W. DeForest in **Honest John Vane.** The hero of the title, being elected Congressman on the virtue of his honesty, gives in to pressure of lobbyists and is instrumental in using national funds for the enrichment of private individuals.

Prof. J. K. Paine, who had taught music

1875

Northwestern Interstate Collegiate Association established to promote **collegiate debating** between various colleges. Association was among the earliest groups in America to co-ordinate intercollegiate debating activities.

Hebrew Union College, one of oldest rabbinical seminaries in U.S., founded in Cincinnati, Ohio. 1st president was Isaac Mayer Wise. College opened with enrollment of 9 men.

Luther Burbank set up a **plant nursery** in Santa Rosa, Calif., in which he developed new strains of berries, fruits, vegetables, grains, and grasses.

Henry Bergh became 1st president of the new **Society for the Prevention of Cruelty to Children.** In 1866, Bergh had incorporated the Society for the Prevention of Cruelty to Animals after a long and lonely crusade. The Society for the Prevention of Cruelty to Children was organized with the help of Eldridge T. Gerry, and quickly became the major society, though Bergh remained more intimately associated with the effort to eliminate wanton cruelty to animals.

Mar. 15 1st American cardinal, Archbishop John McCloskey of New York, invested as such in St. Patrick's Cathedral.

Sept. 10 American Forestry Association founded in Chicago. Dr. John A. Warder, an early conservationist, played a leading role in the organization.

Nov. 17 Theosophical Society of America founded in New York city by Mme. Helena Petrovna Blavatsky. The following were the chief objects of the society when formed: to unite humanity in universal brotherhood without race or creed distinctions; to encourage the study

Formation of the **Coaching Club** reflected popularity of 4-in-hand coach driving as a fad of the American upper classes. Expense of maintaining horses and purchasing custom-built coach put this hobby out of the reach of persons with only average incomes.

1st appearance of **football uniform** at match between Harvard and Tufts.

Baseball glove introduced by Charles G. Waite, 1st baseman for a Boston team. Glove was unpadded.

Tom Ochiltree won the 3rd annual **Preakness Stakes,** Jockey was L. Hughes; times was 2:43½ on a slow track for winnings valued at $1900.

Calvin won the 9th annual **Belmont Stakes.** Jockey was R. Swim; time was 2:42¼ for winnings valued at $4450.

May 17 **1st Kentucky Derby** held at Churchill Downs, Ky., the winner being *Aristides,* ridden by Jockey Lewis for a purse of $2850.

Nov. 23 **National Railroad Convention** held at Saint Louis for 2 days beginning Nov. 23. The citizens of Saint Louis were the formal sponsors of the convention and issued invitations after a mass meeting which also drew up the entertainment program. 869 delegates, representing 31 states and territories, attended. It was claimed as largest formal delegation ever convened in the West. The assembly hall was decorated with banners which read: "Westward the Star of Empire Takes Its Way," "Twenty Millions of People seek an acceptable Route to the Pacific," "There is the East—There is India," and "The Grange Railway—The Texas Pacific." **Jefferson Davis,** chairman of the Mississippi Delegation, declined a seat on the dias, after a protest that, if all the Command-

| POLITICS AND GOVERNMENT; WAR; DISASTERS; VITAL STATISTICS. | BOOKS; PAINTING; DRAMA; ARCHITECTURE; SCULPTURE. |

tions, although he had reluctantly disclaimed any intention of running in a statement made May 29 of this year.

at Harvard University since 1862, appointed to **1st chair in music** at an American university.

1876

Southern Congressmen, in an almost solid bloc, won enough Northern support to enact the repeal of the *Southern Homestead Act*. The Southern Homestead Act of 1866, designed to prevent the domination of the public lands in the South by speculators, monopolists and former Confederates, preserved 47½ million acres of the public lands in Alabama, Arkansas, Florida, Louisiana and Mississippi exclusively for homesteaders, by ruling out cash purchases and the rights of pre-emption. The act, applying to public lands of the South alone, aimed to insure that the freedman would get a chance to his promised 40 acres and a mule. When the Southerners returned to the Senate and the House they joined in a concerted effort to force the repeal of the Southern Homestead Act. The opposition held firm for 10 years. The repeal of the act opened the way for speculators to snatch up the rich Southern timberlands. Most of the dealers turned out to be from the North. They did not, as their Southern allies said they would, use the lands to contribute to the general development of the South, but held on to them and kept them from competing with Northern industry and agriculture.

Mar. 2 **Impeachment** proceedings against Secretary of War William W. Belknap recommended by House committee on the grounds of malfeasance in office. He was later acquitted by Senate Court of Impeachment.

May 17 2nd national convention of the **Prohibition Party** held in Cleveland, Ohio. Green Clay Smith, of Kentucky, was nominated for president and Gideon T. Stewart, of Ohio, was nominated for vice-president.

May 18 **Greenback Party** held its 1st

Mark Twain's **best seller,** *The Adventures of Tom Sawyer,* originally published by subscription only. The most popular of Twain's books, *Tom Sawyer* has sold over 2 million copies.

Mark Twain's **The Adventures of Tom Sawyer** excluded from the children's room of the Brooklyn Public Library and banned altogether by Denver Public Library.

The **still popular Helen's Babies** by John Habberton. The title continues: *Some Account of their ways, Innocent, Crafty, Angelic, Impish, Witching, and Repulsive. Also a Partial Record of Their Actions During Ten Days of Their Existence, by Their Latest Victim.* The book was at once a success.

Roderick Hudson, a novel by **Henry James,** published. *Roderick Hudson* is the story of an American sculptor who is overwhelmed as an artist and as a man by his exposure to the culture of Europe.

Clarel, a narrative poem in 2 volumes, written by **Herman Melville.** The author sought his inspiration from the impressions of his recent trip to the Holy Land.

William Dean Howells published *A Days Pleasure and other Sketches,* a collection of essays.

William Cullen Bryant composed 2 of his most memorable poems, *A Lifetime* and *The Flood of Years.*

Sidney Lanier composed the Centennial Ode, *Psalm of the West,* which commemorated the hundred years of American history since the Revolution.

Joel Chandler Harris began to work for the **Atlanta Constitution.** He stayed with the newspaper for 24 years and published the Uncle Remus series in its pages.

of Eastern cultures; to investigate unexplained laws of nature and the psychical powers latent in man.

ing Generals from either side of the late war were to sit in the Place of Honor, there would not be enough room.

1876

Formation of **American Chemical Society** reflected growing specialization of American scholarship in science. The society was incorporated in 1877, reorganized in 1891, in order to permit national participation, and finally incorporated under a federal charter in 1937. The purpose of the society was to encourage the broadest and most liberal advancement of all the branches of chemistry; to promote research; to raise the standards of practice and ethics among chemists; to add to and to disseminate chemical knowledge; and to promote scientific interests, towards the betterment of public welfare and education.

1st photograph of the solar spectrum taken by John William Draper, a physicist and astronomer at New York University, who was credited in 1840 with the **1st photograph of the moon.**

Mimeograph device invented by Thomas A. Edison, in his laboratory at Menlo Park, N.J. The machine employed a stencil for making impressions. The impressions were inserted into a set frame and ink was applied. It was probably 1st practical duplicating machine.

New York Society for Ethical Culture established by Dr. Felix Adler. In the same year Adler founded 1st free kindergarten in New York city in connection with his Ethical Culture School.

Johns Hopkins University founded with **1st adequately equipped physical laboratories** in U.S.

Lampoon published at Harvard became **1st undergraduate humor magazine** in America.

Central Park completed along the design of its planners, Frederick Law Olmsted and Calvert Vaux, as a growing part of New York city, to be expanded as the

Polo brought to America by James Gordon Bennett, famous publisher of New York *Herald.* Sport was launched at Dickel's Riding Academy, New York city.

1st fraternity house in U.S. opened at Williams College, Williamstown, Mass. It was occupied by a chapter of Kappa Alpha Society.

Catcher's mask used in baseball invented by F. W. Thayer, of Harvard University.

Professional baseball entrenched in America with the formation of the National League. League was composed of the following teams: the Athletics of Philadelphia; Hartford; Boston; Chicago; Cincinnati; Louisville; St. Louis; and the Mutuals of New York. 1st president of the League was Morgan G. Bulkley. 1st pennant winner was Chicago with a season record of 52 wins and 14 losses.

1st American amateur to run **100 yds. in 10 secs.** was Horace H. Lee of Pennsylvania.

"Tenderloin" section of New York city (24th to 40th Sts. between 5th and 7th Aves.) so named by Police Captain A. S. Williams who is reported to have said, on being transferred to the West 30th St. precinct: "I've been having chuck steak ever since I've been on the force, and now I'm going to have a bit of tenderloin." The expression was taken up by the press and soon became the term applied to the gay wicked sections of any city.

Algerine won the 10th annual **Belmont Stakes.** Jockey was W. Donohue; time was 2:40½ for winnings valued at $3700.

I.C.A.A.A. (Intercollegiate Association of Amateur Athletes of America) founded at Saratoga, N.Y., by delegates from 14 U.S. colleges participating in crew and track events held on July 20–21. Or-

POLITICS AND GOVERNMENT; WAR; DISASTERS; VITAL STATISTICS.	BOOKS; PAINTING; DRAMA; ARCHITECTURE; SCULPTURE.

national convention at Indianapolis, Ind. The convention named Peter Cooper of New York for president and Samuel F. Perry of Ohio for vice-president.

June 14–16 **Republican national convention** named Rutherford B. Hayes of Ohio for president. His running mate was William A. Wheeler of New York.

June 25 **Gen. George A. Custer** and every 1 of the 265 men of the 7th Cavalry slaughtered by Sitting Bull's Sioux Indians at the Battle of Little Big Horn in Montana.

June 27–29 Democrats named **Samuel J. Tilden** of New York and Thomas A. Hendricks of Indiana as their presidential ticket at their national convention in St. Louis, Mo.

July 25 Free and **unlimited coinage of silver** proposed in a bill introduced in the House by Richard P. Bland of Missouri.

Aug. 1 **Colorado admitted as a state,** 38th to join Union.

Nov. 7 **Presidential election** gave Tilden a popular vote plurality of 250,000. Republicans refused to concede on the grounds that the returns from Florida, Louisiana, South Carolina, and Oregon were in dispute. Tilden needed the electoral vote of those states in order to win. On Dec. 6, 2 different sets of electoral returns were reported from the 4 states.

Nov. 23 **William "Boss" Tweed** delivered to authorities in New York city to serve his prison sentence after his capture in Spain.

Dec. 5 **Worst theater fire** in New York occurred at Brooklyn Theater, when 289 of 1200 in the audience were killed.

Dec. 5 Pres. Grant delivered his **speech of apology** to Congress ascribing his errors while President to inexperience. His fail-

The One Fair Woman, a novel by **Joaquin Miller,** published.

James Russell Lowell composed **An Ode for the Fourth of July, 1876.** He also published **Among My Books: Second Series.**

The Spagnoletto, a verse tragedy set in Italy in the age of the Baroque, written by **Emma Lazarus,** author of the sonnet inscribed on the base of the Statue of Liberty.

Charles Dudley Warner, editor of the *American Men of Letters Series* of biographies of American literary figures, published *My Winter on the Nile,* a book of travel sketches based on his trip to Africa and the Middle East the year before.

Chicago Daily News founded by Melville E. Stone and William Dougherty. In 1931 it was purchased by Frank Knox and T. D. Ellis.

Excellent evocation of the sea and the joy of racing before the wind produced by **Winslow Homer** in his painting, *Breezing Up.*

1st commission given to a major artist for the purpose of **mural decoration** presented to John La Farge by architect of Trinity Church, Boston. The church, being an adaptation of Romanesque architecture, provided ample wall space for the painter to display his native techniques.

Gigantic statue of *Daniel Webster* now standing in Central Park, the work of Thomas Ball, unveiled. 14 feet in height, the statue was cast in Munich. Popularity of work brought Ball orders for statues of Josiah Quincy and Charles Sumner.

Excellent piece of **public statuary** is the bronze *Chancellor Robert R. Livingston* in Statuary Hall, Washington, by Erastus D. Palmer of Albany. Exhibited at the Centennial Exposition at Philadelphia, it received a medal of the 1st class.

Nature of sculpture changed in America

city expanded, mainly because of its health-giving function.

World's largest **cantilever bridge** constructed for Cincinnati Southern Railway. Designer Charles S. Smith's bridge was influential in the spread of the cantilever principle for long-span construction.

Dewey Decimal Systems of classification originated by Melvil Dewey. The Dewey system permits subdivision and expansion of file entries without the necessity of rearrangement. Dewey divided knowledge into 9 classes and assigned a number to each. They were (1) philosophy; (2) religion; (3) sociology; (4) philology; (5) natural science; (6) useful arts; (7) fine arts; (8) literature; and (9) history. These 9 classes were broken down into 9 subdivisions, numbered 1–9, and each subdivision was further separated into 9 sections. The Dewey Decimal System was intended for use by the American Library Association, which was established in the same year, Dewey being one of the original founders.

Josiah Willard Gibbs published 1st half of "On the Equilibrium of Heterogeneous Substances" in the *Transactions of the Connecticut Academy of Arts and Sciences.* This work is among the great theoretical achievements of science. Starting with the given thermodynamic theory of homogeneous substances, Gibbs worked out the thermodynamic theory of heterogeneous substances, and established the basis of later research in what has come to be called the science of physical chemistry. The 2nd half of this classic memoir was published in 1878.

Charles Sanders Peirce, the inventor of *Pragmatism,* the most typical of American philosophies, formulated his famous original *Pragmatist maxim:* "Consider what effects, that might conceivably have practical bearings, we conceive the object of our conception to have. Then, our conception of these effects is the whole of our conception of the object."

ganization was earliest significant intercollegiate sports association in U.S. Amherst, Bowdoin, Brown, CCNY, Columbia, Cornell, Dartmouth, Harvard, Princeton, Trinity, Union, Wesleyan, Williams, and Yale were original members.

Shirley won the 4th annual **Preakness Stakes,** paying 2–1. Jockey was G. Barbee; time was 2:44¾ on a good track for winnings valued at $1950.

Jan. 1 **Philadelphia Mummers' parade** organized in its present form in celebration of the American centennial. The parade was sponsored mainly by the Silver Crown New Year's Association. The Mummers' parade dates back to early colonial times. It combines the boisterous Swedish custom of celebrating the New Year with the English tradition of the Mummers' play in which St. George slays the dragon. The city of Philadelphia did not officially recognize the parade until 1901, when 42 fraternal organizations received permits to stage a parade for which prizes were awarded for costumes, music, and comic antics.

Apr. 2 In **1st official National League baseball game** Boston beat Philadelphia, 6–5, with Jim O'Rourke getting the 1st hit.

May 15 *Vagrant* won 2nd **Kentucky Derby** at Churchill Downs, Ky. in 2:38¼ for a purse of $2950. Jockey was Swim; owner was W. Astor.

May 23 Joe Borden pitched **1st no-hitter** in the history of the National League. The Boston pitcher lost his effectiveness soon after and ended the season as the club's groundskeeper.

June 6 Dr. Walter Fleming, assisted by Charles T. McClenachan, organized the **Imperial Council of the Ancient Arabic Order of Nobles of the Mystic Shrine** for the U.S.A., a Masonic order.

Sept. 7 Joe Goss of England defeated Tom Allen in 27 rounds at Covington, Ky. The victory earned Goss the **world's heavyweight boxing championship.**

Nov. Juliet Corson of New York city

311

ures, he said, were "errors of judgment, not of intent."

Dec. 12 Prohibition amendment to the constitution introduced for the 1st time. It was proposed before the House in a bill brought out by Henry W. Blair of New Hampshire.

Dec. 29 84 killed when the Pacific Express plunged into a gorge in Ashtabula, Ohio. The accident occurred when the bridge spanning the gorge cracked in the center as the passenger train passed over it.

after famous Centennial of 1876 at Philadelphia. American sculptors were able to study works of Europeans who had turned away from neoclassical style. Among artists exhibited: Cordier, Cain, Dalou, De Groot, Rodin, Vincotte.

Feb. 28 Excellent monument to a revolutionary hero is the statue of *Ethan Allen* by Larkin G. Mead, which is today placed in the National Hall of Statuary in the Capitol. It depicts Col. Allen as he demanded the surrender of Fort Ticonderoga.

1877

Anti-Chinese riots broke out in California. Incited by Workingmen's Party formed by Denis Kearney as protest at the use of cheap Chinese labor.

Rutherford B. Hayes, 19th president, **inaugurated.** He was a Republican and served 1 term.

Jan. 2 Carpetbag government ended in Florida when George F. Drew, Democrat, was inaugurated as governor.

Jan. 29 Electoral Count Act passed. It provided a commission of 15 to judge "as to which is the true and lawful electoral vote" from those states where more than one return in the election of 1876 was recorded.

Mar. 2 Rutherford B. Hayes declared president at 4:10 A.M. He defeated Samuel J. Tilden by a congressional vote of 185 to 184. William A. Wheeler was declared vice-president.

Apr. 10 Carpetbag government ended in South Carolina when Federal troops evacuated Columbia.

Apr. 24 Carpetbag rule ended in Louisiana. This was the last Southern state to regain control of its internal government.

June–Oct. Nez Percé Indians went to war with U.S. in Idaho. The war ended

American provincialism, its Puritanical objections to the nude, highlighted in Eakins' painting, *William Rush Carving the Allegorical Figure of the Schuylkill River.* Besides the artist and nude, a chaperone is shown seated with her knitting. Eakins' insistence on drawing from nude caused demand for his resignation. Unable to cope with strong American prejudices, he eventually gave up painting of nudes.

Famous libel suit against Ruskin grew out of exhibition of Whistler's *The Falling Rocket.* Writing of Whistler, the great critic, Ruskin, remarked, "His ill-educated conceit so nearly approached imposture. I have seen and heard much Cockney impudence before now, but never expected to hear a coxcomb ask two hundred guineas for flinging a pot of paint in the public's face." Whistler sued for libel and was awarded 1 farthing.

New York musical comedy team of Harrigan and Hart presented a number called "Walking for Dat Cake," an imitation of ante bellum plantation "cakewalks." The **cakewalk** soon became a popular feature of all minstrel shows; syncopated cakewalk tunes, taken more or less accurately from Negro sources, later developed into "ragtime" music.

Fine study of cultural contrasts is provided in the novel **The American** by Henry James—best of his early books. Here

Mar. 7 1st U.S. patent for the **telephone** awarded to Alexander Graham Bell.

Oct. 6 **American Library Association established** in Philadelphia by a group of leading public and university librarians for the purpose of supplying "the best reading for the largest number at the least expense." Melvil Dewey, author of the preceding quotation, librarian at Columbia, and originator of the Dewey decimal system, F. W. Poole of the Chicago Public Library, and Charles Cutter of the Boston Athenaeum were prominent founders of the Association.

opened **1st U.S. cooking school** at her residence in St. Marks Pl.

Nov. 23 At invitation of Princeton, delegates from Yale, Harvard, Rutgers, Columbia, and Princeton met at Massasoit House, Springfield, Mass., to discuss **rules for football.** Princeton had recently adopted Harvard's rules which in turn were chiefly based on the rules of the British Rugby Union, and these were adopted by all colleges represented at the meeting. Intercollegiate Football Association, 1st such organization in U.S., grew out of the meeting.

1877

Sharp decline in **labor union influence** saw number of national unions dwindle from 30 to 9 and membership drop from 300,000 to 50,000.

Thomas Edison patented the **phonograph.**

Charles Elmer Hires began making and distributing his **root beer;** popularity of his product led to a business which today extends throughout the world.

Asaph Hall made a major contribution to astronomy with his detection of the **2 satellites of Mars** from the Naval Observatory in Washington. This discovery was ranked as the most significant since the discovery of Neptune in 1846.

1st interconnection of lines by a **telephone switchboard** was made in Boston. A crude system of metal blocks and plugs at a burglar alarm office permitted connection of lines from several outside stations. The first regular exchange went into operation the following year in New Haven.

July 17 Most **serious strikes** of period began over wage cuts on Baltimore and Ohio Railroad and spread to lines east and west until a violent situation erupted in 4 cities, Baltimore, Pittsburgh, Chicago, and St. Louis. Federal troops were dispatched by President Hayes to restore

1st annual dog show held at Gilmore's Garden in New York sponsored by the Westminster Kennel Club. Setters of the English, Irish, and Gordon type, pointers, spaniels, mastiffs, St. Bernards, terriers, and poodles were all well represented.

New baseball rule exempted hitter from time at bat if he was walked. This rule affected the scoring of a batter's average rather than actual play. Another new rule stipulated that a substitute player could replace a starting player only before the 4th inning. **National League baseball pennant winner** was Boston with a record of 31 wins, 17 losses.

Cloverbrook won the 5th annual **Preakness Stakes.** Jockey was C. Holloway; time was 2:45½ on a slow track for winnings valued at $1600.

Cloverbrook won the 11th annual **Belmont Stakes.** Jockey was C. Holloway; time was 2:46 for winnings valued at $5200.

May 22 *Baden Baden* was the winner of the **3rd Kentucky Derby,** held at Churchill Downs, Louisville, Ky. He won $3300 running the 1½ miles in 2:38 on a fast track, under jockey Walker.

POLITICS AND GOVERNMENT; WAR; DISASTERS; VITAL STATISTICS.	BOOKS; PAINTING; DRAMA; ARCHITECTURE; SCULPTURE.

when Federal troops captured Chief Joseph and evacuated the Indians to a reservation.

June 15 Henry O. Flipper became **1st Negro to graduate from the U.S. Military Academy** at West Point.

Nov. 23 Halifax fisheries commission awarded $5,500,000 to England for **U.S. fishing rights** in the North Atlantic. The commission was created by the Treaty of Washington.

Dec. 26 Workingmen's Party reorganized as **Socialist Labor Party** at a convention held in Newark, N.J.

Christopher Newman, the American, is invested with the finest traits of America which are contrasted with the more urban and sophisticated traits of "Europe."

May 1st appearance of the most successful of the **"cheap libraries,"** George Munro's Seaside Library. Munro published a novel a day in this cheap quarto form.

June 1 Founding of the **Society of American Artists** by Saint-Gaudens, Wyatt Eaton, Shirlaw, and Miss Helena De Kay. New society was formed to exhibit work of new artists who were being held back by Academy of Design.

1878

5000 died during a **yellow fever** epidemic in Memphis, Tenn. Annie Cook, who operated a brothel in the city, discharged her prostitutes to provide hospital quarters for yellow fever patients. She later died of the fever contracted while caring for patients.

4000 died in New Orleans during the **yellow fever** epidemic.

Jan. 10 **Women's Suffrage Amendment** introduced by Senator A. A. Sargent in the exact words of its final form.

Jan. 14 **Supreme Court** declared that any state law requiring a railroad to provide equal accommodations for all passengers regardless of race or color was unconstitutional.

Jan. 17 **Commercial treaty** with Samoa signed. Pago Pago harbor reserved for a coaling station for U.S. Naval vessels.

Feb. 22 National convention met at Toledo, Ohio, to form **Greenback-Labor Party.** Ohio workers had previously (1877) founded National Party, while workers in other states had already joined Greenback Party. New party was a fusion of both elements. At 1st national convention, held June 9–10, 1880, at Chicago, Ill., new party chose James B. Weaver of Iowa and

Survey of American theater buildings showed that 1 of every 4 theaters burned down within 4 years of being built. The average life of any theater building was 12 years. Gas lighting, inflammable scenery, few proper exits combined to make theater-going a dangerous pastime.

The Leavenworth Case, a famous mystery novel by **Anna Katharine Green,** her 1st novel. It has long been a best seller.

Formation of 1 of America's respected newspapers, the **St. Louis Post-Dispatch** by Joseph Pulitzer through combining the St. Louis *Post* and *Dispatch.* A crusader against local corruption, it achieved further note by throwing its support behind Bryan for president.

1st successful **Sunday edition** of daily newspaper published by the *Philadelphia Times.*

Foremost among American sculptors of animals, **Edward Kemeys** exhibited his group *Bison and Wolves* at the Paris Salon. Returning to New York he later produced the *Still Hunt* of Central Park, New York, the *Wolves* of Fairmount Park, Philadelphia, *Panther and Deer, Raven and Coyote.*

Melodrama found expression in 2 plays by Bronson Howard written this year: *The Banker's Daughter* and *Only a Tramp.* The latter concerns a weak man who by his drinking forces his wife to leave him and

SCIENCE; INDUSTRY; ECONOMICS; EDUCATION; RELIGION; PHILOSOPHY.	SPORTS; FASHIONS; POPULAR ENTERTAINMENT; FOLKLORE; SOCIETY.

order in Pittsburgh and Martinsburg, W. Va.

Oct. **American Humane Association** formed at Cleveland, Ohio, by representatives of various societies for prevention of cruelty to animals. Delegates were particularly concerned about transport of livestock to slaughterhouses; called upon cattlemen and railroad companies to develop a cattle car which would provide facilities for water and food.

June 14 **Flag Day** observed throughout U.S. for 1st time to celebrate 100th anniversary of selection of U.S. flag.

Aug. 29 **Death of Brigham Young** marked the end of an era in the development of Mormonism. Henceforth, tensions between Mormon doctrines and the laws and customs of non-Mormons were reduced.

1878

Conflict of religious fundamentalism and the new scientific attitude reflected in dismissal of geologist **Alexander Winchell** from Methodist-sponsored Vanderbilt University for his scientific contradictions of Biblical chronology.

Patent for **phonograph** awarded to Thomas A. Edison.

Post-Civil War **deflation of currency** reached its lowest point; average man had only half as many dollars as in 1864.

End of activities by the **Order of the Knights of St. Crispin.**

Albert A. Michelson published his 1st paper in the *American Journal of Science,* which he called *On a Method of Measuring the Velocity of Light.* It was devoted to a method for determining the velocity of light, a project which occupied him for the rest of his life, and made him the international authority on all questions relating to the subject. Michelson was equally concerned with experiments on the interference of light, helped clear the way for the discoveries of **Einstein,** and, with Edward Morley, established the basic equipment and theory in spectroscopy.

Report on the Lands of the Arid Region of the U.S., a monograph by **John Wesley Powell,** published. In 1869, with a party of 11 men, Powell successfully navigated the gorges of the Green and Colorado Riv-

Publication of *The Social Etiquette of New York* indicated rising social aspirations of many Americans. Other books of etiquette were *The P.G., or, Perfect Gentlemen,* published in 1887 and *Success in Society,* published in 1888.

1st bicycles, called "wheels," manufactured in U.S. Consisted of one very large wheel, with pedals connected, and a small wheel attached to the first by a curved "backbone." Dangerous to ride, because if rider shifted his weight too far forward, he would take a "header."

Revival of interest in archery led to formation of **National Archery Association** which remains the governing body for U.S. archers today.

Duke of Magenta won the 6th annual **Preakness Stakes,** paying 2–5. Jockey was C. Holloway; time was 2:41¾ on a good track for winnings valued at $2100.

Duke of Magenta won the 12th annual **Belmont Stakes.** Jockey was L. Hughes; time was 2:43½ on a muddy track for winnings valued at $3850.

Forerunner of the **Wild West Shows** was the exhibition of Dr. W. F. Carver, who came to New York from California to show his art of firing balls from the back of a racing horse.

National League baseball pennant winner was Boston with a season record of 41 wins and 19 defeats.

| POLITICS AND GOVERNMENT; WAR; DISASTERS; VITAL STATISTICS. | BOOKS; PAINTING; DRAMA; ARCHITECTURE; SCULPTURE. |

B. J. Chambers of Texas for the presidency and vice-presidency respectively.

June 11 **District of Columbia** given permanent constitution by Congress. 3 commissioners (2 residents and an officer in army engineers) recommend governing legislation to Congress. Residents have no direct voice in either local or national government.

Nov. 5 **Democrats** won control of both houses of Congress for 1st time since 1858 after mid-term elections.

Dec. 17 **Greenbacks** reached par value on Wall Street exchange for the 1st time since 1862.

marry his employer. Robbery and murder play a part in the play.

Henry James published *The Europeans,* a novel about a brother, Felix Young, and his sister, Eugenia (Baroness Münster), who visit their New England cousins, the Wentworths, and experience some difficulty in adjusting to their new environment.

The Revenge of Hamish, and *The Boy's Froissart* published by **Sidney Lanier.** *The Revenge of Hamish* is a border tale, rated among the major poems by the author. *The Boy's Froissart,* a boy's book, was 1 of a series which included *The Boy's King Arthur* (1880), *The Boy's Mabinogian* (1881), and *The Boy's Percy* (1882). Lanier considered these children's stories as hack work, but here the judgment of time has been against him.

Sarah Orne Jewett published *A Book of Stories for Children.*

1879

Clarence King appointed director of newly created **U.S. Geological Survey** in Dept. of Interior. King had helped to organize the Survey and was noted for his insistence on high scientific standards.

Jan. 1 Government resumed **specie payment** for 1st time since it was suspended in 1861. Lack of specie payment had kept currency in unsettled state, partly contributing to Panic of 1873, and its approaching resumption caused much apprehension that the government could not provide enough coin to meet the overwhelming demand that was expected. Mints had been kept open after hours to produce additional coinage, and there was much surprise when little currency was presented by the public for redemption. This showed the extent to which public confidence in government fiscal policies had been restored since Civil War. Payment of specie has been maintained ever since.

What is thought to be 1st written indication of a demand for a **native American style in building,** an article titled "Originality in American Architecture," published in *American Architect.*

Bust of Emerson modeled from life by New England sculptor Daniel Chester French. Face combines strength and vigor in general form with delicacy and sensitiveness in details. Other works by French are *John Harvard* (1882), *General Cass* (1888) and *Thomas Starr King* (1890).

Masterpiece of local color fiction is the collection of short stories of New England, **Old Friends and New** by Sarah Orne Jewett. Making free use of dialect, she ranges widely over her limited sphere, tempering her realism with warm sympathy. Favorites include "A Lost Lover," "Miss Sydney's Flowers," and the "Last Supper."

Most popular work of Henry James is the short novel **"Daisy Miller."** In a few pages he sets up a contrast between the typical American girl—naïve, innocent,

316

ers. In 1875 he published *Explorations of the Colorado River of the West*, in which he pointed out that the Uinta canyons were caused by rivers cutting through rock which was being gradually elevated.

Jan. 1st national organization of **Knights of Labor** established.

Jan. 28 1st regular **telephone exchange** opened at New Haven, Conn., earliest in U.S.

Aug. 21 Convention of lawyers at Saratoga, N.Y., met to create **American Bar Association,** 1st important national association of lawyers. James O. Broadhead was chosen president.

Oct. 15 **1st electric light company** formed. It was The Edison Electric Light Company, and was located at 65 Fifth Avenue, New York city.

May 21 *Day Star* won the 4th **Kentucky Derby** at Churchill Downs, Louisville, Ky. He won $4050 on a good track in 2:37¼, under jockey Carter.

Oct. 10 Earliest American **jockey record** was Jimmie McLaughlin's riding of winners in all 3 races in Nashville, Tenn. One of the races was run in 2 heats, of which McLaughlin won both.

Oct. 27 Celebrated $3,000,000 robbery of the Manhattan Savings Institution in N.Y. was credited to gang-leader, **"Western" George L. Leslie.** Although 2 of his accomplices were convicted of the robbery, Leslie was never brought to trial because of lack of evidence. New York Chief of Police Walling attributed four-fifths of the bank hold-ups in America to Leslie, whose career was terminated by his murder in 1884.

1879

1st public street lighting installed in Cleveland, Ohio, by Charles F. Brush. Wabush, Ind., was 1st city to be completely lighted by electricity (Mar. 31, 1880).

Richard Henry Pratt founded **Carlisle Indian School** at Carlisle, Pa., one of the most successful schools for Indians in U.S. In 1881 it became a federal school when Congress voted an appropriation to pay Pratt's salary. Pratt retired in 1904, and thereafter school declined until its abandonment in 1918.

Archaeological Institute of America, an association of scholars and students, established in Boston, Mass., with Charles Eliot Norton as 1st president. It was 1st important U.S. archaeological association.

1st intercity telephone communications established between Boston and Lowell, Mass.

Phrase **"The public be damned"** given nationwide prominence after William H. Vanderbilt flung it at a reporter. Wishing to get rid of a reporter who insisted that the public was waiting for his reported interview, Vanderbilt brusquely drove him off with this phrase, which when printed further aroused public against railroad barons. Vanderbilt controlled the New York Central Railroad.

Interest in **fox hunting** revived among wealthy of New York and New England after the Civil War. Reporting on last hunt of season at Newport, newspaper wrote, "all Newport mustered at the meet, the road to Southwick's Grove being literally choke-full of vehicles of every sort, shape, size, and description."

New baseball rule allowed a batter to reach 1st base after receiving 9 balls. The requirements for a "walk" to 1st base were reduced to 8 balls in 1880, 7 in 1881, 6 in 1884, raised to 7 again in 1885, reduced to 5 in 1887, and 4 in 1889. This

| POLITICS AND GOVERNMENT; WAR; DISASTERS; VITAL STATISTICS. | BOOKS; PAINTING; DRAMA; ARCHITECTURE; SCULPTURE. |

Feb. 15 **Women attorneys** won right to argue cases before U.S. Supreme Court by act of Congress.

Mar. 1 Bill restricting **Chinese immigration** vetoed by Pres. Hayes as violation of Burlingame Treaty of 1868. Chinese exclusion was particularly favored in California for economic, rather than social, reasons, "Chinese cheap labor" having been especially feared on the Pacific coast. On May 7 Californians adopted a new constitution which had, as one of its clauses, a provision forbidding employment of **Chinese labor.**

Summer **Ute Indians** in Colorado staged armed uprising. Purely a local action, it was quickly controlled and a treaty signed whereby the entire nation was evacuated to reservation in Utah.

and good—and Continental society with its formalized patterns and complexities. The "international theme" is seen at its clearest.

Jan. 13 Beginning of the famous cycle of **Mulligan plays,** in which Mulligan, the courageous, often drunken and disorderly Irish grocer and his wife Cordelia are shown in various aspects of New York life, took place in *The Mulligan Guard Ball* by Edward Harrington. Following this we have the *Mulligan Guard Chowder,* the *Mulligan Guard Surprise,* and *Mulligan Guard's Christmas,* etc.

June 16 **Gilbert and Sullivan** introduced to New York city with performance of *H.M.S. Pinafore* at Bowery Theater.

Sept. Famous **Progress and Poverty,** by Henry George. The reasons for its popularity can be determined from its subtitle: *An Inquiry Into the Cause of Industrial Depressions, and of Increase of Want with Increase of Wealth. The Remedy.* Translated into at least 10 languages, *Progress and Poverty* has sold over 700,000 copies in the U.S. alone.

1880

Population—50,155,783. Center of population: 8 miles west by south of Cincinnati, Ohio. (West Kentucky). New York became 1st state to exceed 5 million population.

Mar. 1 **Excluding Negroes from jury duty** was held unconstitutional by Supreme Court. The authority for the decision was based on section 5 of the 14th amendment and advised jury commissioners that they were forbidden to administrate their offices in such a way that they would effectually discriminate in the selection of jurors on racial grounds.

Bellaman House, 1st of H. H. Richardson's influential shingled houses, built in Cohasset, Mass.

1st performance of **John K. Paine**'s Second Symphony given at Boston, where audiences went wild with enthusiasm. Paine, professor of music at Harvard University, wrote themes imitative of the popular German motifs of the time.

1st portion of **Metropolitan Museum of Art** opened in New York. The largest art museum in U.S., it contains paintings of all European schools, classical and European sculpture; antiquities of Egypt, As-

SCIENCE; INDUSTRY; ECONOMICS; EDUCATION; RELIGION; PHILOSOPHY.

SPORTS; FASHIONS; POPULAR ENTERTAINMENT; FOLKLORE; SOCIETY.

Radcliffe College, Cambridge, Mass., established as adjunct to Harvard University, incorporated as The Society for the Collegiate Instruction of Women in 1882, chartered under its present name in 1894.

Frank W. Woolworth established his 1st successful **5-and-10-cent store** at Lancaster, Pa. Earlier, in Utica, N.Y., he had failed with a similar store, but by 1911 he owned more than 1000 stores throughout the U.S.

The First Church of Christ, Scientist, in Boston organized by Mary Baker Eddy, discoverer and founder of Christian Science. Mrs. Eddy was the author of the Christian Science textbook *Science and Health with Key to the Scriptures,* published in 1875.

May 8   1st U.S. patent application for a gasoline-driven **automobile,** was filed by George B. Selden, patent lawyer of Rochester, N.Y. Because of Selden's changes and his delays in answering Patent Office objections, the patent for his horseless carriage was not issued until Nov. 5, 1895.

Oct. 21   **Electric light** finally perfected by Thomas A. Edison in his laboratories at Menlo Park, N.J. He found that a carbonized filament of cotton would last for about 40 hours.

last requirement for a base on balls has persisted until the present time.

Spendthrift won the 13th annual **Belmont Stakes,** paying 1–1. Jockey was Evans; time was 2:48¾ on a slow track for winnings valued at $4250.

Harold won the 7th annual **Preakness Stakes,** paying 1–6. Jockey was L. Hughes; time was 2:40½ on a fast track for winnings valued at $2550.

May 20   Lord Murphy won the **5th annual Kentucky Derby** held at Churchill Downs, Louisville, Ky. His time was 2:37 on a fast track under jockey Schauer, and earned $3550.

June 24   **1st Childs Cup** won by University of Pennsylvania in 9:23. The cup was presented this year by George W. Childs of Philadelphia, Pa. Columbia, Pennsylvania, and Princeton are the only schools eligible to win the cup. Cornell and Navy occasionally participate by invitation, but if they win, may not claim the prize. The Childs Cup is the oldest trophy in sprint racing; was limited to 4-oared crews until 1887; 8-oared crews since 1889 (there was no competition in 1888).

Fall   Providence won the **National League baseball pennant** with a season record of 55 victories, 23 defeats.

1880

Formation of **American Society of Mechanical Engineers** reflected rising specialization of American scholarship in science.

Commissioner George Railton and 7 women workers from British **Salvation Army** arrived in Pennsylvania to found American branch. Organization grew, and in 1904 Evangeline Booth, daughter of founder, was put in charge of U.S. branch; in 1934 she became General of the International Salvation Army.

Illiteracy in America estimated at 17 per cent of the population, a decrease of 3 per cent over the previous decade.

Increasing vogue of **women participating in sports** during this decade. Besides tennis, archery and croquet, they went in for riding, cycling, swimming, boat racing, fencing, and skating. Woodcuts of the period even show women bowling.

"Gold brick" swindle introduced into New York city by Reed Waddell, who was originally from Springfield, Ill. It is estimated that Waddell amassed more than ¼ of a million dollars in 10 years through the sale of gilded lead bricks and counterfeit currency.

Edwards Heirs fraud initiated by Dr. Herbert H. Edwards of Cleveland, Ohio,

319

| POLITICS AND GOVERNMENT; WAR; DISASTERS; VITAL STATISTICS. | BOOKS; PAINTING; DRAMA; ARCHITECTURE; SCULPTURE. |

Apr. National Farmers' Alliance organized at Chicago, Ill. It was the forerunner of the Peoples' Party. The National Farmers' Alliance was formed because the Grange had put itself in jeopardy through its political activity. The intention of the Alliance was to unite farmers against discriminatory legislation. It was an open union, without central organization, and, as a result, offered little upon which to establish a national union, except such common bonds as the transportation problems.

May 6 Ulysses S. Grant's nomination for the presidency opposed by **Republican anti-third-term convention** that met in St. Louis, Mo.

June 8 James A. Garfield of Ohio nominated for the presidency by **Republican national convention** at Chicago, Ill. Chester A. Arthur of New York was named as his running mate. Sen. Blanche Kelso Bruce of Mississippi became **1st Negro chairman of a major party national convention** by presiding temporarily over the Republican National Convention.

June 9 National Convention of the Greenback Labor Party nominated James B. Weaver of Iowa and B. J. Chambers of Texas for the presidency and vice-presidency at their convention in Chicago, Ill.

June 17 3rd National Convention of the Prohibition Party held at Cleveland, Ohio. Neal Dow, of Maine, was nominated for the presidency, and the Rev. H. A. Thompson, of Ohio, for the vice-presidency.

syria, Iran; collections of lace, furniture, woodwork, etc.

Glorification of the American girl found expression in paintings of Paris-trained young men, who were forced to avoid the nude because of prevailing prejudices. In works of Abbott Thayer and Thomas Dewing, young girls are presented as angels, fairies, allegories of virginity, *Spirit of the Water Lily,* etc.

Last decade of the **great poets of New England.** Longfellow published his last volume of poems *In the Harbor* (1882); Whittier brought out his collected *Poems* (1888); Lowell printed *Heartease and Rue* (1888); Holmes published *The Iron Gate* (1880) and *Before the Curfew* (1888).

Mark Twain again exploited contrast of European and American life for humor in *A Tramp Abroad,* the record of a walking tour through Germany, Italy, and Switzerland. Like *Innocents Abroad,* the book pokes fun at European institutions, art, history, society.

1st appearance of *Five Little Peppers and How They Grew* by **Margaret Sidney** (Harriet Mulford Stone Lothrop). This favorite children's classic was followed by the less popular *Five Little Peppers Midway, Five Little Peppers Grown up,* etc.

Ever popular historical romance of Rome, *Ben Hur* by **Lew Wallace** published. Its fame spread rapidly, the romance being reprinted countless times. The cinema of the 20th century exploited the colorful scenes of the arena and catacombs.

Henry Adams exposed the chicanery and corruption of Washington during the Grant Administration in his novel, *Democracy.* The capital is seen through the eyes of a Mrs. Lightfoot Lee, who closes the novel after a flight to Europe with the indictment, "In all my experience I have

320

Bryn Mawr College, Bryn Mawr, Pa., established. 1st classes held 1885.

Mileage of U.S. railroads had increased to total of 93,671, covering all the then settled parts of the country.

Large-scale cultivation of corn, wheat, potatoes, and hay on Southern farms during this decade reflected greater **diversification of crops** and a swing away from previous reliance on 1 or 2 basic crops like cotton and tobacco. New markets were opened for wine grapes from North Carolina, watermelons from Georgia, peanuts and apples from Virginia, and an array of subtropical fruits from Florida, notably oranges, lemons, and pineapples.

1st major gold strike in Alaska led to the rapid development of the small Alaskan village of Juneau.

Major improvements in **plumbing facilities** for the home effected during this decade, largely through the pressures of city and state inspection codes of health and safety.

At about this time **1st municipal electric lighting plant** established in New Britain, Conn., by Charles Leonard Newcomb.

1st successful roll film for cameras patented by George Eastman of Rochester, N.Y. In 1885 he placed on market his 1st commercial film, cut into strips and sealed in a box camera which was returned to factory for removal and developing. Introduction of daylight loading film came in 1891, and the 1st pocket Kodak in 1895.

Safety razor devised by Kampfe Bros. of New York city.

House paint manufactured for 1st time from standard formulae. The Cleveland, Ohio, Sherwin-Williams Company, began

who claimed he was a descendant of Robert Edwards, the alleged owner of 65 acres of valuable property on Manhattan Island in 1770. This property included the site of the Woolworth Building. Dr. Edwards founded the International Edwards Heirs Association to institute litigation for the return of the property to its rightful owners. Applicants for the inheritance were subject to an enrollment fee of $26.00 while a pretended genealogical investigation of each applicant was conducted by a carpenter named Milo Pressel. By the time the U.S. Post Office Department exposed the hoax, a sum of $10,000 had been deposited in the name of the Association.

Orange Blossom, a pseudonym for Joseph M. Mulholland of Washington, Pa., became famous as the by-line for implausible stories which were printed as serious news items. Mulholland's most spectacular hoax was his account of a flaming meteor which landed in western Pennsylvania setting fire to a huge area. In later years, his stories came to be printed as short works of the imagination which were not to be taken literally.

"Charley Horse" became common parlance for a muscle strain in the leg. Two Chicago baseball players, Billy Sunday and Joe Quest, generally credited with coining the expression after a horse they backed in a race pulled up lame near the finish line.

"Hot corner" became baseball parlance for 3d base. Term was coined by Ren Mulford, a writer of this period, who watched a game in which the Cincinnati 3d baseman Hick Carpenter fielded several sharply hit balls in his direction.

New baseball rule stipulated that a batter was out if he was hit by a batted ball.

Grenada won the 14th annual **Belmont Stakes,** paying 2–5. Jockey was L. Hughes; time was 2:47 on a good track for winnings valued at $2800.

Grenada won the 8th annual **Preakness Stakes,** paying 1–4. Jockey was L. Hughes;

| POLITICS AND GOVERNMENT; WAR; DISASTERS; VITAL STATISTICS. | BOOKS; PAINTING; DRAMA; ARCHITECTURE; SCULPTURE. |

June 22–24 Gen. Winfield S. Hancock of Pennsylvania and William H. English of Indiana composed the ticket named by the **Democratic National Convention** in Cincinnati, Ohio.

Nov. 2 James A. Garfield defeated Gen. Winfield S. Hancock in the **presidential election** by an electoral vote of 214–155. Popular vote: Garfield, 4,449,-053; Hancock, 4,442,035; Weaver, 308,-578; Dow, 10,305.

Nov. 17 Immigration treaty signed with China at Peking. Called the **Chinese Exclusion Treaty,** it gave U.S. the right to "regulate, limit, or suspend" but not to exclude completely the entry of Chinese nationals.

found no society which has had elements of corruption like the United States."

Plantation life and the folk tale immortalized in **Joel Chandler Harris'** unforgettable *Uncle Remus, His Songs and His Sayings.* Creating a mouthpiece in Uncle Remus, Harris recounts in dialect numerous Negro folk tales. These had phenomenal success in America as well as abroad.

Feb. 4 Transition from older romantic tradition in playwrighting to the simpler written realistic drama seen in works of **Steele MacKaye.** His *Hazel Kirke* which opened in New York is a domestic drama. In *Paul Kauver* (1887) he reverts to older melodramas using French Revolution as setting.

Nov. 8 Celebrated French actress, **Sarah Bernhardt,** made her American debut at Booth's Theater. During the season she performed Dumas' *La Dame aux Camélias* and 3 other plays.

1881

James A. Garfield, 20th president **inaugurated.** He was a Republican and died after 6 mos., 15 days in office. Vice-president Arthur succeeded him.

Jan. 24 Supreme Court declared **Federal Income Tax Law of 1862 constitutional** in the case of *Springer v. U.S.* Counsel for Springer charged that the tax was a direct tax and could be collected only if it was distributed among the states according to population. The Supreme Court denied that there was precedent for the charge. A direct tax had never been levied by the government, said the Court, except upon real estate and slaves. In the case of the slaves, it was partially because some states regarded them as real estate, partially because the tax lessened the assessment upon real estate in the same area

Establishment of the **Century Magazine,** the new name of *Scribner's Monthly,* under the guidance of Richard Watson Gilder. A great literary force during the '80's and '90's it published the writings of such men as William Dean Howells, Josh Billings, F. Marion Crawford, and Joel Chandler Harris.

Boston & Albany Railroad station at Auburndale, Mass., built from designs by H. H. Richardson. Generally thought to be the best of the many suburban stations designed by Richardson.

Novelist **Henry James** produced 1 of his most popular works, *The Portrait of a Lady.* Through his heroine Isabel Archer, the innocent American girl who is "educated" by Europe, he lifts the international

322

SCIENCE; INDUSTRY; ECONOMICS; EDUCATION; RELIGION; PHILOSOPHY.

SPORTS; FASHIONS; POPULAR ENTERTAINMENT; FOLKLORE; SOCIETY.

producing an all-purpose paint for wood from an unvarying formula. This production method was later applied to the production of stains, varnish stains, varnishes, and enamels.

Jan. 27 Thomas A. Edison received patent for his **incandescent lamp,** which was made with a carbonized cotton thread for the filament. The 1st public demonstrations of lamp had been held Dec. 31, 1879, at Edison's laboratories at Menlo Park, N.J. The 1st commercial installation of these lamps was made in the steamship *Columbia* of the Oregon Railroad and Navigation Company. Equipment was in use for 15 years before ship was overhauled.

Oct. 4 **University of Southern California** founded 1880 at Los Angeles, Calif. 1st classes met same year.

time was 2:40½ on a good track for winnings valued at $2000.

Mar. 12 Inspector Thomas Byrnes of the New York city police established a **"Dead Line"** at Fulton St., south of which any known criminal would be arrested on sight. Byrnes was attempting to stem a wave of bank robberies.

May 18 *Fonso* was the winner of the **6th annual Kentucky Derby.** He ran the 1½ miles in 2:37½ under jockey G. Lewis, winning $3800.

June 5 Famous sentence, **"He will hew to the line of right, let the chips fall where they may,"** used by Sen. Roscoe Conkling of New York in nominating U. S. Grant for 3rd term presidency. Grant did not win the nomination, Garfield being selected by the Republican delegates in Chicago.

June 21 Paddy Ryan, an American, defeated Joe Goss in the 87th round of a fight for the **world's heavyweight boxing championship** held near Colliers Station, W. Va.

Fall Chicago won the **National League baseball pennant** with a season record of 67 victories, 17 defeats.

1881

Formation of the **American Institute of Christian Philosophy** in New York represented an attempt to integrate science with the Bible by the dissemination of appropriate literature.

1st summer camp in America for the use of city children successfully established at Squam Lake, N.H. This 1st success encouraged the founding of similar camps in New England, New York, Pennsylvania, and other states.

Thomas A. Edison directed construction of **1st central electric-light power plant** in world at Pearl St., New York city. Operation began with 1 generator.

Rising academic prestige of business reflected in founding of the **Wharton School**

New baseball rule increased the distance of the pitcher from home plate from 45 ft. to 50 ft. A short-lived rule provided that a pitcher be fined for hitting a batter deliberately with a pitched ball. This rule was abolished in 1882.

United States Lawn Tennis Association born at meeting of the leaders of the Eastern clubs where tennis was played. A pattern of play was set and adopted all over the world. National championship was held at Newport, R.I., Aug. 31. Richard D. Sears won the 1st men's singles crown.

Saunterer won the 15th annual **Belmont Stakes,** paying 5–2. Jockey was T. Costello; time was 2:47 on a heavy track for winnings valued at $3000.

Saunterer won the 9th annual **Preakness**

323

| POLITICS AND GOVERNMENT; WAR; DISASTERS; VITAL STATISTICS. | BOOKS; PAINTING; DRAMA; ARCHITECTURE; SCULPTURE. |

without diminishing the returns to the national treasury, and was permitted in deference to the desires of the South. It was questionable, besides, whether the validity of such taxes had ever been adjudicated. Since slavery was now abolished, the question could not subsequently arise. There was, therefore, no evidence that any tax like that in the Springer Case had ever been regarded by Congress as a direct tax.

July 2 **President Garfield shot** in a Washington, D.C., railroad station by Charles J. Guiteau, a disgruntled office seeker. Garfield died 2 mos. later from the effects of the bullet wound. He is buried in Cleveland, Ohio. Guiteau was hanged in Washington June 30, 1882. Garfield survived for 11 weeks after he was shot, and was treated in Washington and at Elberon, N.J. The doctors' reports were frequent, but uninformative, and no trial was made to determine whether the President had been rendered so unfit to fulfill his office that a replacement was needed. Garfield died Sept. 19, 1881, without ever leaving his bed.

Sept. 20 **Chester A. Arthur,** 21st President, **inaugurated.** He succeeded to the presidency upon the death of Garfield serving 3 yrs., 5 mos. in office. Arthur was a Republican.

Nov. 22 **Pan-American movement** launched by Sec. of State James G. Blaine when he invited Latin-American states to Washington for a congress to be held in 1882. But Blaine's successor Frederick T. Frelinghuysen revoked invitations, and meeting was never held.

theme to its height. Psychological insight is coupled with sketches of social life and with an abundance of living secondary characters to create a fascinating piece of fiction.

High flown romantic drama still held stage despite inroads of realism. Prominent among romantic plays were *Victor Durand* (1881) by Henry Guy Carleton, *Monsieur* (1887) by Richard Mansfield, *Napoleon Bonaparte* (1896) by Lorimer Stoddard, *Judith and Holofernes* (1904) by Thomas Bailey Aldrich.

Counterpart of Henry James and Edith Wharton in painting was **Mary Cassatt.** Excessive refinement and scrupulosity in social behavior are excellently caught in her *Mother and Child Driving.*

Excellent example of portrait art of **Eastman Johnson** seen in his *Two Men,* a representation of Samuel Rowse and Robert W. Rutherford in deep conversation. Trained in Düsseldorf, Eastman returned a finished painter, never at a loss for commissions.

Independence of artist from patron keynoted in work of **John Singer Sargent.** Courage to paint what he sees, without need to flatter or be deferential, marks his early canvases. His portrait of English writer "Vernon Lee" catches the "reality" of his subject in a manner unsurpassed in the 19th century.

Whitman's **Leaves of Grass removed from circulation** in Boston but next year it was republished in Philadelphia.

June 1 New playwright of stature introduced to New York audiences with his play, *The Professor,* was **William Gillette,** better known as an actor. Play is a close study of character—almost psychological. *Esmeralda,* written with Frances Hodgson Burnett (1881) and *The Private Secretary* (1884) also underscore realism.

1882

French Ensor Chadwick, naval officer and historian, appointed **1st U.S. Naval Attaché.** He served in London until 1889.

Excellent delineation of ordinary people was forte of **William Dean Howells** in his tragic problem novel, *A Modern In-*

| SCIENCE; INDUSTRY; ECONOMICS; EDUCATION; RELIGION; PHILOSOPHY. | SPORTS; FASHIONS; POPULAR ENTERTAINMENT; FOLKLORE; SOCIETY. |

of **Finance and Economy** within the University of Pennsylvania.

University of Connecticut established as Storrs Agricultural School at Storrs, Conn. Name was changed to Storrs Agricultural College in 1893, to Connecticut Agricultural College in 1899, to Connecticut State College in 1933, to its present name in 1939.

Loganberry developed by Judge James H. Logan of Santa Cruz, Calif. He crossed Texas early blackberry with wild California blackberry to produce the fruit.

Clara Barton organized **American National Red Cross** at Washington, D.C.; federal charter was granted in 1900.

By 1881 all of the major **elevated railroads in Manhattan** were completed. The 1st El in New York had been finished in 1869. During the following decade, the progress of the elevated was at a standstill. It has been said that it took New Yorkers at least that long to get used to the shock of the original. But the men who were to lay the iron arteries up and across Manhattan Island were only biding their time. Led by Cyrus W. Field, they mapped out the island and, in 1878, went to work. In 3 years, the burden of the job was over. If the Els ran through vacant lots and outlying areas, it was not because the planners had forgotten that people who take trains usually expect to arrive somewhere. These foresighted men had allowed for imaginary neighborhoods which would soon become real through the magic of transportation.

July 4 **Tuskegee Institute** established at Tuskegee, Ala., as Tuskegee Normal and Industrial Institute. 1st classes met the same year.

Stakes, paying 3–2. Jockey was W. Costello; time was 2:40½ on a good track for winnings valued at $1950.

Coney Island, which had been a deserted sand bank 4 years before, was already internationally famous. The nucleus of Coney Island was Cable Beach. In the early days, Rockaway, Manhattan Beach and Brighton Beach were all apt to be in the minds of people who referred to Coney Island. But Cable Beach was the beach with the awesome boardwalk wading on steel girders ¾ of a mile into the sea; it had the hotel which had been carted piece by piece from the Philadelphia Centennial and resurrected at Sea Beach; it had the museums and the sideshows, orchestras, rides, sandy beaches and salt sea air which attracted New Yorkers by the hundreds of thousands. From the beginning it was Cable Beach which had to become the 1, the only and the original Coney Island.

The *home* of **William Kissam Vanderbilt,** on the corner of Fifth Avenue and 52nd Street, completed at a total cost of $3 millions. It marked the beginning of the great and often grotesque buildings erected by American millionnaires in imitation of the castles and palaces of Europe.

May 17 *Hindoo* won the **7th annual Kentucky Derby,** at Churchill Downs, Louisville, Ky. He earned $4410 in this race running a fast track in 2:40 under jockey J. McLaughlin. Hindoo was one of the 1st great American race horses, going on to win 18 out of 20 races this year.

Fall Chicago won the **National League baseball pennant** with a season record of 56 victories, 28 defeats.

Oct. 15 *American Angler,* owned and edited by William C. Harris, published in Philadelphia, Pa. It was the **1st American fishing journal.**

1882

Prof. **Granville Stanley Hall** of Johns Hopkins University, Baltimore, Md., appointed to a special lectureship in psychol-

Rival baseball organization formed as **American Association** which flourished for some years, introducing some innovations

| POLITICS AND GOVERNMENT; WAR; DISASTERS; VITAL STATISTICS. | BOOKS; PAINTING; DRAMA; ARCHITECTURE; SCULPTURE. |

Mar. **Mississippi floods** make 85,000 people homeless.

Mar. 22 **Edmunds law** enacted by U.S. Congress to supplement existing **antipolygamy statutes** directed against the Mormon community in the Utah territory.

Mar. 31 U.S. Congress voted a **special pension** for the widows of Presidents Polk, Tyler, and Garfield. The pension amounted to $5000 a year. This initiated a custom in Congress to vote similar pensions to widows of subsequent presidents.

May 6 **1st Chinese Exclusion Act** barred Chinese labor from entering U.S. for 10 years. The act was regularly renewed, and was still on the books in 1920.

May 22 **Korean independence** recognized and a commercial treaty signed.

July 26 **Geneva Convention** of 1864 for the care of war wounded accepted by U.S. Miss Clara Barton, founder of American branch of Red Cross, did much to promote public sentiment in favor of joining Geneva Convention. Senate had consented Mar. 16.

Aug. 2 Congress overrode President's veto on the **Rivers and Harbors Bill,** thus authorizing over $18 million for public works.

Aug. 3 Congress approved 1st act to **restrict immigration.** Law kept from country paupers, convicts, and defectives, and imposed a tax on all incoming immigrants. Tax was 1st set at 50¢ each but was later increased.

Nov. 7 The **Democratic Party** swept into power in New York State, with **Grover Cleveland** elected **governor.** The rise of

stance. Collecting a handful of characters, each with a tragic flaw, he traces the history of a marriage that leads to divorce and the gradual disintegration of a character. Fine picture of journalistic Boston is included as background.

Mark Twain expressed his hatred of oppression and injustice in juvenile romance *The Prince and the Pauper.* Monarchism and the insidious power of the priesthood are blamed for the economic and social evils during the reign of Edward VI.

1st American best seller with a pro-Catholic sentiment, *L'Abbé Constantin* by the Frenchman Ludovic Halévy. Idyllic and completely Catholic, this book has become a classic.

1st appearance of the very popular **Lovell's Library.** John W. Lovell was the leading publisher of the cheap "regular" sized book, selling at 10 to 20¢ each. For a time there was a new title every day, bearing a date like a newspaper. Lovell eventually issued Lovell's Popular Library, cloth bound at 50¢, and Lovell's Standard Library, at $1 a copy.

Newspaper characterized by sensationalism, the **New York Morning Journal,** begun by Albert Pulitzer. Sold to Hearst in 1895, it was renamed the *New York Journal* and supported Bryan and the free silver movement. Under editorship of Arthur Brisbane it clamored for war with Spain and the independence of Cuba.

Lafcadio Hearn published his 1st book, *One of Cleopatra's Nights.* It was a collection of short stories which the author had translated from the French of **Théophile Gautier.**

Mr. Isaacs, a novel by **Francis Marion Crawford,** published. The author, who, in his polyglot and ubiquitous career, had

SCIENCE; INDUSTRY; ECONOMICS; EDUCATION; RELIGION; PHILOSOPHY.

SPORTS; FASHIONS; POPULAR ENTERTAINMENT; FOLKLORE; SOCIETY.

ogy and given $1000 to establish psychological laboratory. William James at Harvard University had previously organized a laboratory for work in "psycho-physics," but Johns Hopkins almost immediately took the lead.

University of South Dakota, Vermillion, S.D., chartered as University of Dakota. 1st classes held same year. Present name adopted 1891.

Henry Adams published a biography, *John Randolph,* which reflected his sustained interest in the lives and motives of the founding fathers of the U.S. He had written *The Life of Albert Gallatin* in 1879, and edited the Gallatin papers. He was preparing his multi-volumed *History of the United States during the Administrations of Jefferson and Madison.*

Helen Hunt Jackson, popular novelist and poet, author of *Ramona,* the perennially favored novel about the conflict between the Indian and the white man in America, turned her attention to another burning question of the times and published *The Training of Children,* a manual of child care.

Founding of the **American School of Classical Studies** at Athens encouraged the study of the classics by Americans. The cultural success of this enterprise led to the establishment of a similar institution in Rome in 1885.

New Yorker Henry W. Seely patented electric **flatiron.**

Formation of **American Forestry Association** reflected growing specialization of American scientific scholarship.

Electric fan developed by Schuyler Skaats Wheeler.

Nation's **1st hydro-electric plant** built at Appleton, Wis., where **1st electric streetcar appeared** in 1886.

Jan. 2 Most famous American **cartel,** the Standard Oil Trust, 1st organized.

The **"trust"** invented by Samuel C. T. Dodd, lawyer for the Standard Oil Com-

into league rules later adopted by National League. It formed working agreement with National League in 1886, but had bad season in 1891 and disbanded.

There were no **handball** courts in the U.S. in 1882 when Phil Casey, one of Ireland's great handball players, migrated to Brooklyn, N.Y. Casey soon built one and opened a school, introducing a new sport into the U.S. with the help of some fellow immigrants from the British Isles.

National Croquet Association formed, to revise and standardize rules of game.

Boxing achieved nationwide popularity through efforts of world bare-knuckle champion, John L. Sullivan, who toured the U.S. putting on boxing exhibitions, with gloves under the Marquis of Queensberry rules, and offering $500 to any man who could last 4 rounds with him. Bare-knuckle fighting had been frowned upon by respectable people until this time.

William Horlick, Racine, Wis., produced the **1st malted milk.** He used a mixture of the extract of wheat and malted barley to which milk had been added; the whole was then evaporated to a powder. Horlick began to manufacture his product commercially in 1883, and he used the name "malted milk" for the 1st time in 1886. Originally malted milk was primarily a supplemental food for infants and the sick.

U.S. Intercollegiate Lacrosse Association founded. Members were Harvard, Princeton, and Columbia; Yale and NYU admitted the following year.

Vanguard won the 10th annual **Preakness Stakes,** paying 1–7. Jockey was W. Costello; time was 2:44½ on a good track for winnings valued at $1250.

Forester won the 16th annual **Belmont Stakes,** paying 1–5. Jockey was J. McLaughlin; time was 2:43 on a fast track for winnings valued at $2600.

U.S. lawn tennis men's singles champion, Richard D. Sears.

| POLITICS AND GOVERNMENT; WAR; DISASTERS; VITAL STATISTICS. | BOOKS; PAINTING; DRAMA; ARCHITECTURE; SCULPTURE. |

the preacher's son had been sudden and spectacular. The year before he was a lawyer in Buffalo, secure but not conspicuously ambitious. He was offered the party candidacy for mayor, and accepted. He won not so much because he was so good, as because his Republican opponent was so bad. In office he made a reputation by prosecuting graft and became a dark horse in a deadlock between warring factions of the Democratic Party in the next gubernatorial nominations. The Republican Party was also split. For Cleveland the waters of politics had parted like the Red Sea, and, within 2 years, he passed through to the White House, conspicuously dry.

once spent 2 years editing the *Indian Herald* in India, gave an exotic but firsthand insight into the lives of the British nabobs of India. Crawford always wrote with a romantic flourish and the background of *Mr. Isaacs* found him at his dazzling best.

Anne, a novel by **Constance Fenimore Woolson,** published. Constance Woolson has been claimed to be the 1st American writer of realistic fiction. She was popular with the public and with the critics, and was as celebrated for her short stories as for her novels. For the setting of *Anne* she drew upon her knowledge of the Great Lakes and of the East, where she moved with equal ease.

Nov. 6 Famous British actress **Lily Langtry** made appearance in Fifth Avenue Theater in Shakespeare's *As You Like It.*

1883

Southern Immigration Association formed. The organization promoted European immigration to the South. At the same time the Northern Pacific railroad dispatched agents to Europe and England with a view to encouraging immigration to the Northwest.

Jan. 10 **Fire** consumed the Newhall House causing the death of 71 persons in Milwaukee, Wis. This was the worst hotel fire in U.S. history until Dec. 7, 1946, when the Winecoff Hotel fire in Atlanta, Ga., caused 121 deaths.

Jan. 16 **Pendleton Act** passed establishing the **Civil Service Commission.** The legislation was intended to replace the spoils system by a merit system. It took the assassination of President Garfield by a disappointed office-seeker to make clear the necessity for the change.

Mar. 3 **Postage** reduced to 2¢ per ½ oz. by act of Congress. On the same day the **"Mongrel Tariff" Act** was passed by Con-

Highest masonry building in U.S., Monadnock Building, erected in Chicago. All 16 stories rest entirely on masonry walls, which are 15 ft. thick at the base.

Newspaper which was to revolutionize journalism, the **New York World,** acquired by Joseph Pulitzer. Jingoistic in its demand for war with Spain, sensational in its crusade for reform, it became the foremost paper in New York. In 1931 it was purchased by Scripps-McRae and formed into *World-Telegram.*

The Breadwinners, anonymously published novel by diplomat John Hay, was largest serial success of any U.S. work until that time.

Ladies' Home Journal established. Magazine reflected broadening range of interests shared by women. Magazine founded by Cyrus H. K. Curtis and popularized in 1889 by a Dutch-American editor named Edward W. Bok.

328

pany. He used the laws governing trust funds to create a monopolistic organization within the oil industry which would evade the antimonopoly laws of the time. In effect, Rockefeller and his associates became "trustees" of the stock and management of many previously rival companies.

Feb. 2 1st organization of Catholic fraternal group, the **Knights of Columbus,** at New Haven, Conn.

Aug. 16 **Radcliffe College,** then known as the Harvard Annex, obtained a charter for the education of women at Cambridge, Mass.

Dec. 11 1st use of **incandescent lighting** for a theatrical presentation effected in the Bijou Theater in Boston at a performance of Gilbert and Sullivan's *Iolanthe.* Performance was illuminated by some 650 incandescent bulbs.

Feb. 7 **John L. Sullivan** won the American heavyweight championship when he defeated Paddy Ryan in 9 rounds at Mississippi City. This contest was fought with bare knuckles.

May 16 The 8th annual **Kentucky Derby** at Churchill Downs, Louisville, Ky. was won by *Apollo.* He won $4500 running on a good track in 2:40¼ under jockey Hurd.

June 24 Only major league baseball umpire ever expelled for dishonesty, Richard Higham, was expelled from National League.

Fall Chicago won the **National League** baseball **pennant** for the 3rd time in a row with a season record of 55 victories, 29 defeats.

Sept. 25 **1st major league baseball double-header** (2 games for the price of 1) held between Providence and Worcester.

1883

Famous book *Dynamic Sociology* by **Lester Frank Ward,** which initiated the development of evolutionary sociology in U.S. Though Ward was well known in the fields of geology, biology, psychology, and anthropology, he made his biggest and most lasting contributions to sociology. He also wrote *The Psychic Factors of Civilization* (1893), *Outlines of Sociology* (1898), *Pure Sociology* (1903), and *Applied Sociology* (1906).

Lewis E. Waterman began experiments to produce **fountain pen.** The 1st to apply principle of capillary attraction, he produced a practical pen the next year and founded the Ideal Pen Company. The venture was so successful that he incorporated in 1887 as L. E. Waterman Company.

Formation of the **Modern Language Association** reflected growing specialization in American scholarship.

George Kinney won the 17th annual **Belmont Stakes,** paying 1–12. Jockey was J. McLaughlin; time was 2:42½ on a fast track for winnings valued at $3070.

Jacobus won the 11th annual **Preakness Stakes.** Jockey was G. Barbee; time was 2:42½ on a good track for winnings valued at $1635.

William Frederick "Buffalo Bill" Cody organized his **1st Wild West show.** 1st performance may have occurred at North Platte, Neb., on July 4.

G. M. Hendrie of Springfield, Mass., won the **1st recorded bicycle race.** It was called a race for the championship although only 2 riders participated. Hendrie later became famous as an automobile and motorcycle builder.

U.S. lawn tennis men's singles champion, Richard D. Sears.

May 1 1st **National League** baseball game played; Philadelphia beating Providence, 4–3.

May 23 The 9th annual **Kentucky**

POLITICS AND GOVERNMENT; WAR; DISASTERS; VITAL STATISTICS.	BOOKS; PAINTING; DRAMA; ARCHITECTURE; SCULPTURE.

gress. Excise taxes were removed from everything but liquor and tobacco, but an unsystematic increase in protective tariffs was made in spite of recommendations to the contrary by a special tariff committee. Act was an attempt to reduce American surpluses.

Mar. 3 Foundation of modern navy made by act of Congress that authorized the Secretary of the Navy to build 3 steel cruisers and 1 dispatch boat.

Oct. 15 Supreme Court declared **Civil Rights Act of 1875** unconstitutional except where it related to jury duty and interstate travel. The original act had granted Negroes equal rights in public places.

Nov. 18 Standard time established. 4 zones were demarcated by the railroad. In 1918 Congress gave its supervision to Interstate Commerce Commission.

The famous semiautobiographical *Life on the Mississippi* by **Mark Twain** published. The *Life* did not sell enough to be considered a best seller until as late as the 1940's when Bantam Books published a "paper-back" edition, reissued in 1956.

James Whitcomb Riley's *The Old Swimmin' Hole and 'Leven More Poems* published, 1 of the few books of poetry to reach best seller status. 3 of his most famous poems are "The Old Swimmin' Hole," "An Old Sweetheart of Mine," and "Little Orphant Annie."

Benjamin Franklin Keith opened his 1st theater in Boston, Mass. Keith introduced the 1st continuous performances in U.S., thus inaugurating **vaudeville.** His success as a showman grew until at his death in 1914 400 theaters bore his name and Keith's vaudeville circuit provided much of the best entertainment in the country.

May 24 Brooklyn Bridge opened in New York city. Designed by John A. Roebling, it is one of the finest suspension bridges in the world.

1884

Equal Rights Party formed by a group of suffragettes who nominated Mrs. Belva A. Lockwood of Washington, D.C., for President. Mrs. Lockwood, a woman lawyer, was renominated in 1888. She was the 1st woman candidate for the presidency.

Feb. 9 700 killed by a tornado that swept across the Southern states.

May 14 Anti-Monopoly Organization of the United States, a 3rd party, founded at convention in Chicago. Former Union general Benjamin F. Butler of Massachusetts was nominated for the presidency.

Francis Parkman continued his mammoth history of French and English relations in North America with *Montcalm and Wolfe,* a study of the French and British generals who decided the fate of the continent through their trials of luck and skill.

Sarah Orne Jewett published *A Country Doctor.* She was the daughter of Dr. Theodore Jewett, a country doctor in Maine, who is the doctor in the title of her book.

Three Villages, a travel book by **William Dean Howells,** published.

330

SCIENCE; INDUSTRY; ECONOMICS; EDUCATION; RELIGION; PHILOSOPHY.

SPORTS; FASHIONS; POPULAR ENTERTAINMENT; FOLKLORE; SOCIETY.

Feb. 23 The University of North Dakota chartered at Grand Forks.

Feb. 27 Patent issued to Oscar Hammerstein, operatic impresario and uncle of the librettist of the same name, for **1st practical cigar-rolling machine.**

Mar. 24 1st telephone service between New York and Chicago initiated.

Sept. 15 1st classes at the **University of Texas** held at Austin.

Sept. 21 1st direct telegraph service between Brazil and the U.S. established.

Derby was won by *Leonatus,* ridden by jockey W. Donohue. The track was heavy, the time 2:43, winnings $3760.

June 2 1st baseball game played under electric lights in Fort Wayne, Ind. Fort Wayne beat Quincy, 19–11, in 7 innings.

June 16 1st Ladies' Day baseball game staged by the New York Giants. On Ladies' Day, both escorted and unescorted ladies were admitted to the park free of charge.

Fall Boston won the **National League baseball pennant** with a season record of 63 victories, 35 defeats.

Oct. 22 1st annual New York Horse Show opened at Gilmore's Gardens, New York city, organized by National Horse Show Association of America. Show included 165 exhibitors and 299 horses; many work horses, including fire-engine horses, police mounts, draught horses, etc., were shown. Show was immediately popular and became an annual event. After 1913 character of show altered; working breeds were no longer allowed, and show was limited to show horses, gaited horses, etc.

Dec. 4 Sons of the American Revolution organized in New York to keep alive the patriotic spirit of the men who fought for American independence. Membership was restricted to male descendants of those men who saw active service in the Revolutionary War.

1884

American Historical Association created by conference of historians at Saratoga, N.Y. Organization was granted a national charter by act of Congress; its annual reports are published by the government.

Memorial Hospital for the Treatment of Cancer founded in New York city, one of the few hospitals in America devoted exclusively to cancer treatment and research.

American Institute of Electrical Engineers founded. It was the parent organization of all trade associations in the American electrical industry.

Sarcastic term **"mugwump"** had great currency during this election year. It was used to designate the liberal wing of the Republican Party that bolted and threw its weight behind Democratic Grover Cleveland. Origin of term is hazy. It goes back to Algonquin word meaning "Big Chief." Actually it is meant to satirize the intellectual element in the Party.

Humorous **campaign slogan** aimed at Grover Cleveland was "Ma, Ma, where's my Pa?"—a reference to his admission of having sired a child out of wedlock. To this

| POLITICS AND GOVERNMENT; WAR; DISASTERS; VITAL STATISTICS. | BOOKS; PAINTING; DRAMA; ARCHITECTURE; SCULPTURE. |

Butler, an active politician, had been both a Democrat and a Republican. The party platform called for many liberal measures, including a graduated income tax. On May 28 Butler was also endorsed by National Greenback Labor Party and resulting coalition was called People's Party.

May 28 National Convention of the Greenback Party at Indianapolis, Ind., nominated Gen. Benjamin F. Butler of Massachusetts for the presidency and Alanson M. West of Mississippi for the vice-presidency.

June 3–6 National Convention of the Republican Party at Chicago, Ill., named James G. Blaine for the presidency; Gen. John A. Logan of Illinois for the vice-presidency.

June 6 "Mugwumps" or independent Republicans walked out of national convention in Chicago, Ill., when party nominated James G. Blaine. They felt he would not support civil service reform. On June 16, they held a convention of their own in New York city, pledging support to the Democratic party if a liberal candidate were named.

June 27 U.S. Bureau of Labor created as part of Dept. of Interior. Separate Dept. of Labor was not authorized until 1913.

July 8–11 National Convention of the Democratic Party at Chicago, Ill., nominated Grover Cleveland, governor of New York, for the presidency. Thomas A. Hendricks of Indiana was named for the vice-presidency.

July 23 4th National Convention of the Prohibition Party held in Pittsburgh, Pa. John P. St. John of Kansas was nominated for the presidency, and William Daniel of Maryland for the vice-presidency.

July 30 National Convention of the Labor Party met at Chicago, Ill., and supported the slate named by the Democrats earlier in the month.

Aug. 5 Cornerstone laid of **Statue of Liberty**'s pedestal at Bedloe's Island in

Louise Imogen Guiney, poet and essayist, published her 1st book of poems, *Songs at the Start.*

Francis Marion Crawford published *A Roman Singer* and *To Leeward,* each with an Italian setting.

1st true **steel-skeleton construction** used in W. L. Jenney's Home Life Insurance Building in Chicago. Walls and masonry as well as floors hung on structural framework, permitting skyscraper-type construction.

Great popularizer of **Darwinism** in America was **John Fiske,** who published 2 books: *Excursions of an Evolutionist* and *The Destiny of Man Viewed in the Light of His Origin.*

Chef-d'œuvre of **Mark Twain** and a true world classic is *The Adventures of Huckleberry Finn,* an excellent study of life along the Mississippi R. before the Civil War. In the picaresque character of Huck, he in part relives his own boyhood, and in the mighty river he sees a thread holding together a varied, multicolored world of scapegraces, actors, rivermen, etc. The book is also a glorification of the "tall tale" and western folklore.

One of the most popular short stories of all time is "The Lady or the Tiger?" by **Frank R. Stockton.** A story as well as a conundrum, its perennial appeal has never diminished.

One of the finest sets of illustrations for a book of poetry is **Elihu Vedder's** plates for the *Rubáiyát.* True to the text, he develops intellectual rather than sensuous side of painting, never taking reader away from essential philosophy of text.

332

SCIENCE; INDUSTRY; ECONOMICS; EDUCATION; RELIGION; PHILOSOPHY.	SPORTS; FASHIONS; POPULAR ENTERTAINMENT; FOLKLORE; SOCIETY.

One of earliest **glider flights** made in U.S., perhaps the 1st, made by John Joseph Montgomery. He launched his glider from a 300-ft. hill near Otay, Calif., and covered a distance of 600 ft.

Rapid growth of **telephone service** in New York city and impracticality of endless telephone poles on the city streets led to municipal order that all telephone wires be placed underground. The extension of the telephone in 1884 was marked by the beginning of the **1st long-distance line** between Boston and New York.

Home Insurance Building, 10 stories high, erected in Chicago, was a marvel of science as well as of art. It used the steel frame, and, with respect to height, was thought to have gone about as far as they could go. It brought the term *skyscraper* into currency.

Mar. 12 **Mississippi Industrial Institute and College,** 1st state-supported women's college, chartered at Columbus, Miss. It was renamed the Mississippi State College for Women in 1920.

May 29 **Bureau of Animal Industry** authorized by Congress as a section of U.S. Dept. of Agriculture. It had been organized by Dr. Daniel Elmer Salmon the previous year; he became head of the bureau and held post until 1905.

June **James Buchanan Eads,** noted American hydraulic and bridge engineer, received Albert Medal from the British

query the Democrats would reply "Gone to the White House, ha, ha, ha."

Knights of Labor voted to observe **Labor Day** on 1st Monday in September. For several years the Knights had agitated for the observance of the holiday, and it had 1st been celebrated on Dec. 28, 1869. Oregon became 1st state to recognize Labor Day officially in 1887.

Huguenot Society of America established by descendants of French Huguenots who had fled to America. **Huguenot Day** is celebrated on Apr. 13 in commemoration of the signing of the Edict of Nantes in 1598 by King Henry IV of France.

New baseball regulation removed all restrictions on the manners in which pitchers could hurl the ball. Pitcher was compelled, by another rule of this year, to take only 1 step before delivering his pitch.

1st baseball championship of America won by Providence of the National League at the Polo Grounds, N.Y. The Providence team swept a 3-game series from the Metropolitans of New York who won the American Association title.

1st Negro to play baseball in a major league was Moses Fleetwood Walker of Toledo in the American Association.

Greyhound racing introduced at Philadelphia, Pa.

Panique won the 18th annual **Belmont Stakes,** paying 11–10. Jockey was J. McLaughlin; time was 2:42 on a good track for winnings valued at $3150.

Knight of Ellerslie won the 12 annual **Preakness Stakes,** paying 3–5. Jockey was S. H. Fisher; time was 2:39½ on a fast track for winnings valued at $1905.

U.S. lawn tennis men's singles champion, Richard D. Sears.

May 16 10th annual **Kentucky Derby** won by *Buchanan* at Churchill Downs, Louisville, Ky.; the time, 2:40¼ on a good track, the winnings $3990. The jockey was Isaac Murphy, one of the great American jockeys. Murphy, a Negro, won 4

New York Harbor. The pedestal, which holds the Bartholdi statue, is 151 ft. high.

Oct. 6 **Naval War College** established by Navy Department at Newport, R.I. 1st superintendent was Commander Stephen Bleecker Luce, who had been instrumental in creating the college.

Nov. 4 Grover Cleveland defeated James G. Blaine in the **presidential election** by an electorate vote of 219–182. Popular count was: Cleveland, 4,911,017; Blaine, 4,848,334; Butler, 175,370; St. John, 150,-369.

Nov. 4 **"Bob" M. La Follette** elected for 1st time to Congress from Wisconsin on the Republican ticket; 1 of the most fiery politicians in U.S.

Masterpiece of realism which caused a scandal when exhibited at the Salon in Paris is **John Singer Sargent's** *Madame X.* The subject, Mme. Gautreau, Paris' most celebrated beauty, is presented exactly as she was—shallow, egocentric, immodestly garbed. The public was shocked; Mme. Gautreau became hysterical; Sargent forced to move to London.

Nov. 8 **1st newspaper syndicate** in U.S., McClure's Syndicate, founded by Samuel Sidney McClure.

1885

Feb. 25 Act of Congress prohibits unauthorized **fencing of public lands** in the West. On Aug. 17, President Cleveland re-enforced the act with orders to remove all illegal enclosures. Five years before, Carl Schurz, then Secretary of the Treasury, had conducted an investigation into **public land abuses** and pressure was mounting steadily to curb the railroad and cattle interests who were exploiting the weak post-war management of the Western lands. By fencing in all water sources, special interests were concentrating great holdings. They reacted to the strictures of 1885 by forcing W. A. J. Sparks from his presidential appointment as Land Commissioner. The agitation for reform persisted and eventually won out.

Feb. 26 Congress, as result of lobbying by the Knights of Labor, **prohibited the importation of contract labor.**

Mar. 3 U.S. Post Office established **special delivery service.**

Mar. 4 **Grover Cleveland,** 22nd president, inaugurated. He was a Democrat.

July 1 **Postal rates** lowered to 2c. per oz. by act of Congress. 2nd class postage reduced to 1c. per lb. Continued deficit in post office department resulted.

Fictional masterpiece of **William Dean Howells** is *The Rise of Silas Lapham,* the story of a self-made businessman of Vermont who, coming to Boston, finds himself. Nowhere is the American businessman handled more sympathetically. Incidental to the story of regeneration are the fine study of female sensibility and the contrast of classes in mid-19th-century Boston.

The Adventures of Huckleberry Finn banned by Public Library in Concord, Mass., as "trash and suitable only for the slums." Concord Free Trade Club retaliated by electing **Mark Twain** to honorary membership.

Gen. **Ulysses Simpson Grant's** *Memoirs* appeared, written largely to pay off his debts and published posthumously. 312,000 sets were sold in 2½ years. Mrs. Grant's first check was for $200,000; in all she received nearly $500,000.

Marshall Field's wholesale store built in Chicago from plans by H. H. Richardson. One of Richardson's most important large structures, it had an influence on Sullivan and later Chicago architects.

Asbestos curtains, as protection against the hazard of fire, came into use in theaters in larger U.S. cities. Theater mana-

334

Society for the Encouragement of Arts, Manufactures, and Commerce; the 1st time an American had been so honored. Eads was famous for many of his ambitious projects. In 1861 he built the 1st iron-clad warship. In 1874 he built an arched steel bridge across the Mississippi at St. Louis, and in 1879 he deepened the mouth of the river by building a series of jetties out into the sea. He won the Albert Medal for a scheme to widen the Mississippi as far as the Ohio R.

American Derbies and 3 Kentucky Derbies in addition to many other important races during the 1880's, often riding inferior horses.

Fall Providence won the **National League baseball pennant** with a season record of 84 victories, 28 defeats.

Oct. 9 Alliterative phrase **"Rum, Romanism, and Rebellion,"** used by Dr. Samuel D. Burchard in a speech to a meeting of clergymen supporting James G. Blaine. This vicious attack on Catholics and the Democratic party was taken up by the newspapers and led to the victory of Grover Cleveland.

1885

American Economic Association organized at Saratoga, N.Y. It published *American Economic Review*. American Economic Association formed as a revolt of young German-trained economists against **determinist economics**. The members of the AEA, 186 in number at the start, were philosophical moderates. They were impressed by the scientific climate of the latter part of the century and declared that laissez faire principles of the previous generation were "unsafe in politics and unsound in morals." They argued that the state must contribute "positive aid" as "an indispensable condition of human progress," but their program was a middle course between both laissez faire and the German political philosophy and tolerated a wide spectrum of political opinion, with emphasis upon the problem of the relationship between individual welfare and state control. The AEA claimed indifference to political positions as such. Members included Profs. Henry C. Adams, John B. Clark, Woodrow Wilson, Carrol Wright, Andrew Carnegie.

Furnaces for **garbage disposal** began to be introduced in many cities, particularly in the land-locked Middle West, as a health measure. It had been discovered that

Harper's Bazaar sized up the the **fashion picture** of the season: " 'Moyen âge' is the term used to describe the new fashions in the spring of 1885. Scarfs, handkerchiefs, wide ribbons and fabrics are emblazoned to imitate medieval banners. Vieux rouge (old red) is showing two tones while the new blue is called, vieille blouse usée, the color of workmens' shirts. Much beige and cream color and bright gold is being shown. Flowers and scarfs are replacing feathers on hats. Combinations of two materials with long drapery and plain lawn skirts are being used in both suits and dresses."

Tyrant won the 19th annual **Belmont Stakes,** paying 10–9. Jockey was P. Duffy; time was 2:43 on a good track for winnings valued at $2710.

Tecumseh won the 13th annual **Preakness Stakes,** paying 2–5. Jockey was J. McLaughlin; time was 2:49 on a heavy track for winnings valued at $2160.

U.S. lawn tennis men's singles champion, Richard D. Sears.

Jan. 17 The Old Time Printers Association of Chicago began celebrating **Benjamin Franklin's** birthday. Regarded as 1 of the founding fathers of American printing, Franklin has been honored by printing

POLITICS AND GOVERNMENT; WAR; DISASTERS; VITAL STATISTICS.

BOOKS; PAINTING; DRAMA; ARCHITECTURE; SCULPTURE.

July 23 **Ulysses S. Grant died** at the age of 63. He is buried at Riverside Park, New York city. **The funeral of General Grant** was a day of national mourning. The body had been brought to New York on a special train shrouded in black curtains. Fittingly, it rained. The corpse was accompanied by the New York militia from the station to the City Hall, where it was laid in state. The people of the city who wished to pay their last respects gathered in a line a mile long. For 2 solid days, by night and day, they filed past the crypt. The line was unbroken and seemed never to grow shorter. On the day of the funeral, 24 black horses drew the huge hearse through the streets to the tomb on Riverside Drive. The way was thronged with spectators, many of whom had been waiting in place all night. They had climbed to the tops of buildings, of telephones, and had rented standing space on the balconies and in the windows looking down on the route. The funeral procession passed by and below them. General Hancock rode in front, with the general staff, followed by wave after wave of militia. Then came the battalion from Virginia which Grant had defeated, still pursued by Grant's own battalion, which marched behind. The hearse came next. President Cleveland rode behind the hearse, in a coach also drawn by black horses. After him the carriages of celebrities stretched on and on, more than 500 in procession. The family of General Grant came last, the women of his house swathed in long black veils. A vine from Napoleon's tomb at St. Helena had been planted at the tomb. There, with the symbol of the conqueror, Grant was laid to rest.

Dec. Pres. Cleveland, in his Message to Congress, recommended **suspension of the compulsory coinage of silver dollars**, which had been authorized by law passed in Feb., 1787. He expressed fear that the coinage of silver would result in the replacement with silver of all the gold which the Government owned.

gers were proud of the innovation, had artists paint "Fireproof Asbestos Curtain" on the novelties in fancy lettering, and ran curtain up and down a half dozen times before each performance.

Turning point in career of **Winslow Homer** came when he started painting land and seascapes in Maine. These pictures usually centered around some human situation, as seen in such paintings as *Life Line, Undertow, Eight Bells, All's Well.*

American painting finds its way into the barroom with the realistic representations of **Michael Harnett.** His *After the Hunt* fascinated crowds in Paris, and was purchased by a New York saloonkeeper. Painting shows dead game and hunter's paraphernalia hanging from a wooden door. Objects are so "real" that many a tippler stretched a hand out for the painted jug.

American sculptor who utilized classic themes and represented his figures ideally was **John Donoghue.** Working in Chicago, he was pointed out by Oscar Wilde as a promising talent and went to Rome. This year he fashioned his masterpiece, *Young Sophocles Leading the Chorus after the Battle of Salamis.* Before his death by suicide in July, 1903, he produced *Hunting Nymph* (1886), *Kypris* (Columbian Exposition), and a *Saint Paul.*

1st work of a gifted sculptor from the West is the *Tired Wrestler* by **Douglas Tilden.** In similar vein he later fashioned the *Baseball Player*, the *Young Acrobat*, and the *Football Players*. In 1895 he worked on the *Mechanics' Fountain* in San Francisco.

After period of itinerant piano-playing, **Scott Joplin** arrived in St. Louis and began career of playing in honky-tonks along Chestnut and Market Streets. Joplin, a Negro from Texarkana, Tex., had classical training, but his interest was in **Negro ragtime music.** He became 1 of the chief performers and composers of rags in America.

336

swine fed with garbage from the cities contracted a disease called trichinosis which could be transmitted to consumers of the diseased meat.

Josiah Strong, an apostle of **imperialism,** published *Our Country.* Strong used the theory of Darwin to support his thesis that the Anglo-Saxon, selected by God to be his brother's keeper, had discovered his destined home in America. Because of this innate superiority, there could be no limit set upon the territorial expansion of the U.S., for this would be tantamount to interfering with the will of providence. Strong was a Congregational minister and wrote his book to raise money for the missions. The identification of patriotism with millennial religion enjoyed tremendous vogue. And the ideas of Strong were among the most quoted of their day.

Dr. **Edward Livingston Trudeau** opened **Adirondack Cottage Sanatorium** for **tuberculosis patients** at Saranac Lake, New York, first in U.S. It was a small one-room cottage with two cots, porch, a wood stove, wash-stand, kerosene lamp and two chairs. Twelve years before, Trudeau, then a young New York country doctor, had withstood a siege of tuberculosis. He attributed his recovery to the cold dry climate of the Adirondacks and worked out a regimen for pulmonary ailments which emphasized rest and fresh air and the segregation of patients by wards.

Ottmar Mergenthaler invented **linotype machine.** The linotype sets molds of letters into lines from which whole lines of type are cast. Whitelaw Reid 1st used linotype in 1886 on the *New York Tribune.*

Bryn Mawr College for Women opened at Bryn Mawr, Pa., under sponsorship of Quakers. School noted for its pioneer work in the field of graduate education for women.

Mar. 12 **University of Arizona** chartered.

Nov. 11 **Stanford University** at Palo Alto, Calif., chartered.

associations in many of the major American cities.

Jan. 24 The **New Orleans Exposition** was found to be the most extensive fair of its kind ever held in America, ⅓ again as large as the Centennial Exhibition at Philadelphia. Austria, Belgium, England, France, China, and Japan all maintained exhibits in the Main Building, and the Smithsonian Institute had a display of "almost every survival of prehistoric times." Every department of the government had a display set up, as did each of the countries of South America. But many Americans thought that "the importance of the Exposition will be in the unrivalled collection of American products and resources."

Feb. 21 **Washington Monument** dedicated some 37 years after the laying of its cornerstone. Monument cost $1,300,000, soared to a height of 585 ft. 5⅛ in., the top of which could be reached by both an elevator and a stairway of 898 steps.

May 14 Winner of the 11th annual **Kentucky Derby** was *Joe Cotton* in 2:37¼ on a good track under jockey Henderson; earnings $4630.

June 5 **Famous political sentence** "If nominated, I will not accept. If elected, I will not serve," written by General William T. Sherman in reply to message asking him to accept nomination for presidency. Sherman, a man of 65, had lived to see the difficulties of the presidency as experienced by Gen. Grant.

Fall Chicago won the **National League baseball pennant** with a season record of 87 victories, 25 defeats. The **baseball championship series** ended in a tie between Chicago, the National League winners, and St. Louis of the American Association. In the 7-game series both teams won 3 games each and 1 game ended in a draw.

Dec. 20 William B. Curtis, phenomenal **weight-lifting strongman,** reported to have hoisted 3,239 lbs., "with harness."

1886

Jan. 19 Presidential succession Act passed. It provided that, in the event of removal, death, resignation, or inability of the president and the vice-president, the heads of the executive departments in the order of the creation of their offices would succeed to the presidency.

Apr. 8 Free coinage of **silver bill** introduced into the House by Richard P. Bland. It was defeated.

May 4 Shocking **Haymarket Massacre** occurred at Haymarket Square, Chicago when police dispersed a meeting of left-wing labor leaders. A bomb was hurled at the law officers, prompting them to open fire on the crowd. 7 police were killed, 70 police and other participants injured.

May 10 Supreme Court declared that an **alien** is a person and further ruled that any municipal ordinances discriminating against Chinese laundries violated the 14th amendment. The decision was handed down in the case of *Yick Wo v. Hopkins.* The same day the court ruled that a corporation was to be considered a person and was entitled to protection afforded under the 14th amendment.

June 19 Trial of accused **Haymarket** assassins lasted 2 months, resulted in many convictions and 7 death sentences although identity of actual bomb thrower was never established. Of the 7 sentenced to die, 4 were subsequently hanged; 3 went to prison, were later pardoned.

June 30 Congress approved legislation recognizing the **Division of Forestry,** which had been established in 1881 in the Department of Agriculture. Dr. B. E. Fernow, a professional forester, was put in charge. Division was result of an agency established in 1876 for the study of American forests, and their probable future supply of timber.

Sept. 4 Apache Indian chief, **Geronimo,** captured by Federal troops under

Henry James ventured into the world of class war with his *Princess Casamassima,* a tale of the ferment underlying the placidity of social and economic life in London. It is the story of a proletarian youth and his contact with the world of riches and beautiful things.

Cosmopolitan Magazine founded in Rochester, N.Y. Moving to New York city next year, it attained a large circulation through its printing of popular reading material.

The very successful **Little Lord Fauntleroy** by Frances Hodgson Burnett published. This book helped set a fashion in boys' clothes.

Whistler elected president of the Royal Society of British Artists. Failing to achieve re-election he said, "The artists had come out and the British had remained."

William Dean Howells published *Indian Summer,* a bright novel about 2 middle-aged romances, set in Florence. *Tuscan Cities,* a travel book, was also published. The farce play, *The Garroters,* rounded out a prolific and varied year.

Roland Blake, a novel by the pioneer of psychological analysis, **S. Weir Mitchell,** published.

Henry (H. C.) Bunner, editor of *Puck,* published *The Midge,* a characteristically delicate novel about a doctor and an orphan in New York.

The Monarch of Dreams, a tale by **Thomas Wentworth Higginson,** published.

Jan. 4 *The Little Tycoon,* by **Willard Spenser,** produced in Philadelphia, one of the 1st comic operas to be written by an American composer.

338

1886

Cheap process for extracting **aluminum** from its ore invented by Charles Martin Hall. His electrolytic method caused the price of aluminum to drop from $5 a lb. in 1888 to 18¢ a lb. in 1914.

"Andover Controversy" typified relentless conflict between liberal and orthodox religious forces in America at this time. Controversy erupted in the Andover Theological Seminary, a Congregational institution in Massachusetts, with the trial of 5 professors charged with theological liberalism, and the finding by the board of visitors that 1 of the 5 was guilty of the charge. The celebrated trial had been preceded by several years of acrimonious disputes within the Seminary.

1st settlement house in America, the Neighborhood Guild in New York, established by Dr. Stanton Coit. Settlement houses provided many social services for the poorer inhabitants of the cities.

"Whisky Trust" formed on model of Standard Oil Trust. Included 80 distilleries, of which all but 12 were closed down; profits were distributed *pro rata*.

Period of labor unrest, especially marked by great strike of railroad workers (Mar.–May) on the Gould system in the Middle West, promoted by the Knights of Labor. Strike failed; but it helped publicize the 8-hour day, a goal of the Knights of Labor. Haymarket Massacre in Chicago and Pres. Cleveland's message to Congress reflected labor unrest.

Mar. 4 **University of Wyoming** chartered at Laramie, Wyo.

Apr. 22 **1st presidential labor message** delivered to Congress by Pres. Cleveland.

1st international polo match took place between an English 4 and an American at Newport, R.I. and was a gala occasion. Both teams were colorfully dressed in satin with leather boots. The grounds were lined with the social set of New England and New York. The visiting team, more practiced, easily swept the match 10 to 4 and 14–2.

Inspector won the 20th annual **Belmont Stakes**, Jockey was J. McLaughlin; time was 2:41 on a fast track for winnings valued at $2720.

The Bard won the 14th annual **Preakness Stakes,** paying 13–5. Jockey was S. H. Fisher; time was 2:45 on a good track for winnings valued at $2050.

U.S. lawn tennis men's singles champion, Richard D. Sears.

Jan. 1 **1st Tournament of Roses** in Pasadena, Calif., staged by the Valley Hunt Club which had been founded by Charles Frederick Holder, a distinguished naturalist. Mr. Holder suggested that the members of the Valley Hunt Club decorate their carriages with the natural flowers of California on New Year's Day and that after a parade of these carriages, a program of athletic events be devised to round out the day. Holder's floral motif has remained a characteristic feature of the Tournament to this day.

May 14 *Ben Ali,* the favorite, won the 12th annual **Kentucky Derby.** Time was 2:36½ on a fast track for winnings valued at $4890. Jockey was P. Duffy.

June 2 Pres. **Grover Cleveland** and Miss **Frances Folsom** married at White House. The ceremony was held in the Blue Room.

Fall Chicago won the **National League baseball pennant** with a season record of

POLITICS AND GOVERNMENT; WAR; DISASTERS; VITAL STATISTICS.

BOOKS; PAINTING; DRAMA; ARCHITECTURE; SCULPTURE.

Gen. Miles in Arizona, thus ending last major Indian war.

Sept. 16 National convention of **Anti-Saloon Republicans** held in Chicago, Ill.

Oct. 12 250 died in a **flood** along Texas Gulf Coast. The gulf waters were whipped onto the mainland by gale winds.

Oct. 28 **Statue of Liberty** unveiled and dedicated by Pres. Cleveland in a ceremony on Bedloe's Island. The 225-ton, 152-ft.-high copper statue was presented to the U.S. by France in commemoration of 100 years of American independence.

Nov. 18 **Chester A. Arthur died** at the age of 56. He is buried at Albany, New York.

Feb. 22 1st important drama concerned with the Civil War was **William Gillette's** *Held by the Enemy*, which opened in Brooklyn. Play describes conflict of 2 soldiers who are in love with a Southern belle in an occupied Southern city. In *Secret Service* (1895) Gillette again reverted to South and Civil War and makes use of spy episode.

Aug. 19 1st English-speaking dramatic company to tour the continent in 300 years led by **Augustin Daly.** Reception in Berlin and Paris was not very enthusiastic.

1887

Free delivery of mail provided in all communities with a population of at least 10,000.

Jan. 20 **Pearl Harbor** leased from Hawaii as a naval station.

Feb. 3 **Electoral Count Act** fashioned to avoid disputed national elections. It made individual state responsible for its own electoral returns, forced Congress to accept result, except in the case of irregularity.

Feb. 4 **Interstate Commerce Act,** giving Federal government right to regulate all transportation and business extending beyond state lines, passed by Congress. Law grew out of agitation attending the midwestern reaction against exorbitant railroad rates. **Interstate Commerce Commission** established. Powers of the commission subject of much controversy in the press. It was regarded as government's 1st large-scale invasion of private property; it was probably the government's 1st regulatory commission.

Feb. 8 Congress passed **Dawes Severalty Act,** which reflected a more tolerant attitude toward the American Indian. It provided for division of Indian lands among Indian families, 160 acres per

Controversy over Rodin's style in sculpture centered about a massive block by American **George Grey Barnard** called *Brotherly Love.* 2 figures are seen emerging from a block of roughly hewn stone. A critic remarked: "Like a second Rodin he has the cleverness of leaving . . . statues half in the rough. Mr. Barnard ought to leave this last mannerism to those who possess less talent." Great portrait statue is the famous *Lincoln* by **Augustus Saint-Gaudens,** now standing in Lincoln Park, Chicago. Lincoln stands with bowed head before the chair he has just risen from.

Popular melodrama *She* by Englishman Sir **Henry Rider Haggard.** It was immediately imitated by *He, It, Me, Her,* etc. *She,* and Rider Haggard's equally popular *King Solomon's Mines,* both have sold more than ½ million copies in America.

Journalist-poet **Eugene Field** endeared himself to Americans by his moving poem

SCIENCE; INDUSTRY; ECONOMICS; EDUCATION; RELIGION; PHILOSOPHY.	SPORTS; FASHIONS; POPULAR ENTERTAINMENT; FOLKLORE; SOCIETY.

In it, he proposed a federal commission to arbitrate and adjust labor disputes.

Dec. 8 **American Federation of Labor** organized at Columbus, Ohio. Chief aim of federation was to protect legislative interests of founding unions. Samuel Gompers, 1st president, had been a New York cigar-maker. The new federation grew out of the Federation of Organized Trades and Labor Unions which had been organized in 1881.

90 victories, 34 defeats. St. Louis of the American Association won the **baseball championship** of America, defeating the Chicago team, winners of the National League title, 4 out of 6 games.

Oct. At 1st annual Autumn Ball of Tuxedo Club, Tuxedo, N.Y., Griswold Lorillard wore a tailless dress coat, thereafter called a **"tuxedo."** So far as is known, this was 1st appearance of such a garment in the U.S. The Tuxedo Club, a sporting and social club, had been founded the previous year by Pierre Lorillard.

1887

U.S. Congress enacted **Edmunds-Tucker law**, which was directed against the Mormon community in Utah. Law provided for federal confiscation of all church land in the territory not used specifically for church functions. This act aroused resentment and defiance from the Mormon elders, but it served ultimately to curb the power of the Mormon Church in Utah.

Lick Observatory completed at Mt. Hamilton, Calif.

Marine Biological Laboratory founded at Woods Hole, Mass.

1st successful electric trolley line built by Frank J. Sprague in Richmond, Va.

"Sugar Trust" formed. Later became known as American Sugar Company. Originally included 18 refineries, of which 11 were immediately closed down. The next year, the margin between crude and refined sugar rose from .787¢ (a competitive profit) to 1.258¢.

Clark University established at Worcester, Mass. 1st classes held in 1889.

Saying **"Put up or shut up"** used in a sense not associated with sports in the Louisville *Courier Journal.* Originally a challenge to bet, it came to designate any assertion to show proof.

American law enforcement improved by the introduction of the **Bertillon System** of identifying criminals. Devised originally for the Paris police and 1st used in America by the Illinois police, it was characterized by a more exact procedure of recording all the physical measurements of the criminal's body.

Probably **1st real golf club** in the U.S. was the Foxburg Golf Club, founded in Foxburg, Pa., as a result of John Mickle Fox's trip to Scotland where he learned the game. Foxburg Golf Club is still in existence. There were clubs calling themselves "golf clubs" in Savannah and Charleston as far back as 1795 and '96, but there is no record of their members ever playing golf.

Hanover won the 21st annual **Belmont Stakes**, paying 1–20. Jockey was J. McLaughlin; time was 2:43½ on a heavy track for winnings valued at $2900.

POLITICS AND GOVERNMENT; WAR; DISASTERS; VITAL STATISTICS.	BOOKS; PAINTING; DRAMA; ARCHITECTURE; SCULPTURE.

family. This land was to be held in trust by the U.S. for 25 years to prevent exploitation. Act was 1st of many which sought to encourage Indians to adjust to a new world, and, at the same time, tried to protect them from avaricious elements in the country at large.

Mar. 2 Hatch Act called for establishment of an agricultural experiment station in each state that held a land-grant college.

Mar. 3 American Protective Association founded in Clinton, Iowa; became very powerful as anti-Catholic, pro-isolationist movement.

Aug. 10 Train wreck at Chatsworth, Ill., killed about 100 people. A burning bridge, hidden by knoll, crumbled when the train passed over it. 800 people from Illinois, Iowa, and Wisconsin were making excursion to Niagara Falls. In commemoration the ballad, "The Bridge Was Burned at Chatsworth," was written.

"Little Boy Blue." Success following the printing of this poem led him to publish *Culture's Garland* (1887) and *A Little Book of Western Verse* (1889).

Nov. 1 1st play written by the combination **David Belasco-Henry C. DeMille** was *The Wife,* which opened in New York and scored a great success. Further collaboration produced *Lord Chumley* (1888), *The Charity Ball* (1889), and *Men and Women* (1890).

1888

Australian secret ballot 1st used in America in local elections in Louisville, Ky. The secret ballot, adopted in Australia as early as 1858, came to be referred to in America as "Kangaroo voting." Henry George, famed proponent of the single land tax, was among the earliest American public figures urging adoption of the Australian ballot. South Carolina became the last state to adopt the secret ballot in 1950.

Feb. 19 Mount Vernon, Ill., virtually destroyed by **cyclone.** 35 persons lost their lives.

Feb. 22 Industrial Reform Party met in Washington, D.C. and nominated Albert E. Redstone, of California for the presidency, and John Colvin, of Kansas, for the vice-presidency.

Mar. 12 400 lives were lost and millions of dollars of property was destroyed during the 36-hour **blizzard** which struck New York city. The city was virtually isolated from the world when the heavy snows

Of great ethnological and artistic value are the reliefs depicting Indian heads produced about this time by **Olin Levi Warner.** These are the fruits of a long trip the sculptor took through the West. Use of aboriginal themes in sculpture is also characteristic of **John J. Boyle.** In *The Stone Age,* modeled this year, an Indian woman is shown defending her children from a powerful eagle. An earlier work, *The Alarm,* shows a male Indian figure with a long pipe in his hand.

Famous fantasy, *Looking Backward 2000–1887* by **Edward Bellamy,** recounts the observations of a man who, waking after a sleep of 113 years, studies the changes in government, society, morals, etc. 200,000 copies were sold by Jan., 1890, and in 1945 a publisher put out an edition of 100,000 copies.

Walt Whitman continued to augment his *Leaves of Grass* and fight the battle for American poetry. In a prose piece "A Backward Glance O'er Travel'd Roads,"

342

SCIENCE; INDUSTRY; ECONOMICS; EDUCATION; RELIGION; PHILOSOPHY.

SPORTS; FASHIONS; POPULAR ENTERTAINMENT; FOLKLORE; SOCIETY.

Theodore Roosevelt appealed to the reputations of 2 of his spiritual brothers when he proposed that, in honor of Davy Crockett and Dan'l Boone, a club, the *Boone and Crockett Club,* be formed, for the **protection of big game.** Since 1883, he had been putting money into Dakota ranch lands. He gave up the investments in 1887, but the contact with the wide open spaces only stimulated his interest in nature and, in 1888, he wrote his western experiences into *Ranch Life and the Hunting Trail.*

Apr. 19 **Catholic University of America** chartered in Washington, D.C.

Dunbine won the 15th annual **Preakness Stakes,** paying 4–1. Jockey was W. Donoghue; time was 2:39½ on a fast track for winnings valued at $1675.

U.S. lawn tennis men's champion, Richard D. Sears; **1st U.S. women's champion,** Ellen F. Hansell.

Mar. 2 **American Trotting Association** organized at Detroit, Mich.

May 11 Montrose won the 13th annual **Kentucky Derby,** paying 10–1. Jockey was I. Lewis, time 2:39¼ on a fast track for winnings valued at $4200.

May 26 1st day of **legal betting** at tracks in New York state.

Fall Detroit won the **National League baseball pennant** with a season record of 79 victories, 45 defeats.

Sept. 5 **Labor Day** 1st observed as legal holiday in New York.

1888

Nikola Tesla developed the **induction motor.** Although many experiments had been made in this direction before his discovery, Tesla, a Croatian immigrant, was the 1st man to perfect the motor capabilities of the electric dynamo.

Formation of the **Geological Society of America,** the **American Society of American Church History,** the **American Folklore Society,** the **American Mathematical Society,** and the **National Statistical Association** reflected the growing specialization in American scholarship.

Chautauqua College of Liberal Arts established to offer institutional incentive to ambitious students already enrolled in the summer programs of the Chautauqua movement. A bachelor's degree in liberal arts could be attained in this relatively unique institution by a 4-year course combining study via residence, extension, and correspondence.

By this year the following industries were organized in one or another form of

Political slogan **"As Maine goes, so goes the nation"** adopted by the Republican party after the election of Benjamin Harrison. State elections in Maine are held weeks before national elections and so they are used as gauges for predicting the results in the national balloting.

Track records as they stood this year:

100 yd. dash	—10 sec. flat
220 yd. dash	—22 sec.
¼ mi.	—47¾ sec.
½ mi.	—1:55⅖
1 mi.	—4:21⅖
10 mi.	—52:58⅜

New York won the **baseball championship,** defeating the St. Louis team 6 games to 4.

Major league record for most consecutive games won by a pitcher in a season set by Tim Keefe of New York. He won 19 straight games.

Refund won the 16th annual **Preakness Stakes,** paying 4–1. Jockey was F. Little-

343

| POLITICS AND GOVERNMENT; WAR; DISASTERS; VITAL STATISTICS. | BOOKS; PAINTING; DRAMA; ARCHITECTURE; SCULPTURE. |

halted transportation and disrupted communications. Messages to Boston had to be relayed via England.

May 15 **National convention of Equal Rights Party** held at Des Moines, Iowa. Belva Lockwood, of Washington, was nominated for the presidency and Alfred Love, of Philadelphia, for the vice-presidency. Mr. Love subsequently declined, and Charles Stuart Wells was substituted.

May 16 **National convention of Union Labor Party** held at Cincinnati. A. J. Streeter, of Illinois, was nominated for the presidency, and Charles E. Cunningham, of Arkansas, for the vice-presidency.

May 17 **National convention of United Labor Party** held at Cincinnati. Robert H. Cowdrey of Illinois was nominated for the presidency, and W. H. T. Wakefield of Kansas for the vice-presidency.

May 31 **National convention of Prohibition Party** held at Indianapolis. Gen. Clinton B. Fisk of New Jersey and Rev. John A. Brooks of Missouri were nominated for the presidency and the vice-presidency, respectively.

June 4 **Electrocution** replaced death by hanging as capital punishment in New York state. Gov. Hill signed a bill which went into effect Jan. 1, 1889.

June 5 **National convention of the Democratic Party** held at St. Louis. Grover Cleveland was renominated for the presidency, and Allen G. Thurman of Ohio was nominated for the vice-presidency.

June 25 Benjamin Harrison of Indiana was nominated for the presidency and Levi P. Morton of New York for the vice-presidency on the 8th ballot at the **National convention of the Republican Party** at Chicago.

July 29 **Yellow fever epidemic** broke out in Jacksonville, Fla., and persisted until Dec. 7. Over 4500 cases were reported and more than 400 persons died.

printed this year, he states: "Without stopping to qualify the averment, the Old World has had the poems of myths, fictions, feudalism, conquest, caste, dynastic wars, and splendid exceptional characters and affairs, which have been great; but the New World needs the poems of realities and science and of the democratic average and basic equality, which shall be greater."

Famous mural painting done in style of Renaissance is the *Ascension* of **John La Farge**, painted in the chancel of the Church of the Ascension, New York city. Nobility and expert workmanship characterize this vast undertaking.

Boston Public Library (Main Branch, Copley Square) begun from designs by McKim, Mead, and White. Exterior was based on Alberti's Tempio Malatestiano at Rimini.

The Wreck of the Hesperus, a choral work by **Arthur Foote,** presented in Boston; enthusiastically received by audience. Foote was one of a group known as "New England Academicians" or "Boston Classicists," whose theories were largely Brahmsian and who dominated American music from 1880 to World War I.

Very popular book which extolled the virtues of Americans compared to Europeans, *Mr. Barnes of New York,* by **Archibald Clavering Gunter.** A romantic adventure story, *Mr. Barnes* is a badly written melodrama; but it has probably sold ½ million copies.

Edward MacDowell arrived in the U.S. after having studied for 12 years in Germany; he became the 1st American composer of "serious" music to be as highly regarded as his European contemporaries.

Best seller in America *A Romance of Two Worlds* by **Marie Corelli,** an Englishwoman whose real name was Mary Mackay, daughter of poet and newspaper man Charles Mackay. Her 2nd novel *Thelma,* published in America in 1887, earned her English and American reputation. All Marie Corelli's novels are highly melo-

344

SCIENCE; INDUSTRY; ECONOMICS; EDUCATION; RELIGION; PHILOSOPHY.

SPORTS; FASHIONS; POPULAR ENTERTAINMENT; FOLKLORE; SOCIETY.

combination, loosely called "**trusts**": oil, whisky, sugar, glass, copper, rubber, coal, beef, reaping and mowing machinery, gas, lead, threshing machines, ploughs, steel rails, steel and iron beams, wrought-iron pipe, iron nuts, stoves, school slates, castor oil, linseed oil.

George Eastman of Rochester, N.Y., perfected **box camera** and **roll film.** He proceeded to manufacture the Kodak No. 1, which made amateur photography feasible and widely popular.

Chinese laborers who left the U.S. were prohibited to return by an act of Congress aimed at a more stringent exclusion of Chinese from America. The law cancelled provisions in the act of 1882 which permitted Chinese to return to the U.S. under certain conditions, and now held that no Chinese laborer resident in the U.S. who left the U.S. and did not return before passage of the act could return in the future.

American Commonwealth by **James Bryce** published. With de Tocqueville's *Democracy in America* this study remains a classic view by a foreigner of the way American society works. Viscount Bryce, an eminent historian, jurist and statesman, an enthusiastic traveler and mountain climber, served as British ambassador in Washington 1907–1913.

Critical Period of American History by **John Fiske** published. Fiske, an early exponent of the theory of evolution, attracted more people to his history lectures than any other such speaker in American history. He established his reputation as a philosopher, and interpreted the ideas of Comte, Darwin, and Herbert Spencer. In the later part of his career he turned to history. *The Critical Period of American History,* among his best interpretative works, studied the beginning of the American Republic, under the Articles of Confederation and the early years of the Constitution, 1783–1789.

Henry C. Lea's *History of the Inquisition in the Middle Ages,* 1 of few historical

field; time was 2:49 on a heavy track for winnings valued at $1185.

Sir Dixon won the 22nd annual **Belmont Stakes,** paying 2–5. Jockey was J. McLaughlin; time was 2:40¼ on a fast track for winnings valued at $3440.

U.S. lawn tennis men's singles champion, Henry W. Slocum Jr.; **women's singles champion,** Bertha L. Townsend.

Jan. 21 Unscrupulous promoters attempting to take over amateur athletics thwarted by formation of **Amateur Athletic Union of the U.S.** A.A.U.'s aim has been to preserve "sport for sport's sake." Its high ideal and success in attaining it is respected all over the world. It now includes 42 amateur associations and many allied members, and supervises activities of millions of amateur athletes.

March 13 The spring season in New York city had been brazenly false. For Easter, the city was bright and gay, and straw hats were in evidence everywhere. Then, overnight, the **snow fell.** For the next 2 days the city was paralyzed. The elevated trains and the streetcars stopped running. The snow was more than knee high, obliterating the sidewalks and even the intersections of the streets. While the snow lasted, the city was thrust back to a primitive time when people crept and slid their ways through mountains and valleys of snow and ice. There was no

345

There were similar epidemics throughout the South at this time.

Aug. 15 **National convention of American Party** held at Philadelphia. James L. Curtis of New York was nominated for the presidency, and James R. Greer of Tennessee was nominated for the vice-presidency.

Nov. 6 Benjamin Harrison and Levi P. Morton defeated Grover Cleveland and Allen G. Thurman in the **presidential elections.** Electoral vote was 233 to 168. Popular vote: Cleveland, 5,540,050; Harrison, 5,444,337; Fisk, 250,125; Streeter, 146,897; Cowdrey, 2,808.

Dec. 24 **Mississippi Steamboat fires** killed 55 persons over holidays. Steamer *Kate Adams* burned on this day, killing 25, and steamer *John H. Hanna* burned Dec. 26, killing 30.

dramatic, fantastic, full of grotesque ideas and suggestions, and sold well. She and Mrs. Humphry Ward were England's 2 most popular women writers in America during the *fin de siècle* period.

Controversial best seller *Robert Elsmere* by **Mrs. Humphry Ward,** granddaughter of Rugby's Dr. Arnold and niece of Matthew Arnold. The book discusses religious problems suggested by the Oxford Movement. Published in England and the U.S. the same year, 9 American editions were brought out in 1 year. It has probably sold a million copies in the U.S.

Casino at Newport, R.I., built from plans by McKim, Mead & White, forerunners in the adaptation of modern French styles to U.S. architecture.

May 1st public recitation by DeWolf Hopper of "**Casey at the Bat**" at Wallack's Theatre, New York city.

1889

New Jersey passed law authorizing the **incorporation of "holding companies"** within its jurisdiction; device was later much used to circumvent the provisions of the Sherman Anti-Trust Law. As a result New Jersey became the home of most giant corporations.

Jan. 28 **Transit workers strike** tied up virtually all of New York city's surface transportation. Strike ended in a few days when the workers realized their efforts were futile.

Feb. 11 **1st secretary of agriculture,** Norman J. Colman, appointed by Pres. Cleveland. Department of Agriculture had been raised to Cabinet rank on Feb. 9.

Mar. 2 **1st antitrust law** passed by Kansas State Legislature. North Carolina, Tennessee, and Michigan followed the same year; South Dakota, Kentucky, and Mississippi the next year; North Dakota, Oklahoma, Montana, Louisiana, Illinois, Minnesota, Missouri, and New Mexico in 1891.

Bitter satire on the romantic handling of the Middle Ages is **Mark Twain's** novel *A Connecticut Yankee at King Arthur's Court.* In obvious contrast to such writers as Tennyson, he shows that life of feudal England, especially as revealed in chivalry, was brutal and immoral, that tyranny of the aristocracy made life a veritable hell for the common people.

One of New York's finest pieces of public sculpture, the *Nathan Hale* of City Hall Park, fashioned by **Frederick MacMonnies.** The patriot is shown fettered and proud, ready to pronounce his famous "I only regret that I have but one life to lose for my country." Exhibited in Salon of 1901 with another work of artist, the portrait of *James L. T. Stranahan,* which won artist a "2d medal."

Edward Bok became editor of the *Ladies' Home Journal;* kept position until 1919, by which time circulation had risen

SCIENCE; INDUSTRY; ECONOMICS; EDUCATION; RELIGION; PHILOSOPHY.

SPORTS; FASHIONS; POPULAR ENTERTAINMENT; FOLKLORE; SOCIETY.

studies of the period which went beyond purely American interests, published.

June 13 Establishment of a **Department of Labor** without Cabinet status, by an act of Congress. In 1903 it was reduced to status of bureau, this time (see 1884) in the Department of Commerce and Labor. On Mar. 4, 1913, Congress created a Department of Labor headed by a Cabinet member.

July 27 **1st electric automobile**, designed by Philip W. Pratt, demonstrated in Boston. It was a tricycle driven by storage batteries, and was built by the Fred W. Kimball Company of Boston.

Oct. 1 Beginnings of **federal labor arbitration** marked by Congressional authorization of a commission to mediate labor disputes between interstate railroads and their workers.

coal, no milk, no newspapers, no telephones, and the mails definitely did not go through. All the stores and all the offices shut down and rescuers dug everywhere to find the bodies of victims buried and lost in the snow.

May 14 *Macbeth II*, an 8–1 shot, ridden by jockey Covington, won the 14th annual **Kentucky Derby**. Time, 2:34½ on a fast track for $4780.

Fall New York won the **National League baseball pennant** with a season record of 84 victories, 47 defeats.

1889

New emphasis on social doctrines of Jesus Christ advanced by group of ministers meeting in Boston as the **Society of Christian Socialists.** Group led by Washington Gladden, Josiah Strong, Prof. Richard T. Ely, David Jayne Hill, and E. Benjamin Andrews believed that socialism was a logical development of Christianity and that the concentration of wealth in America was inimical to the teachings of Christ.

J. Walker Fewkes, who had been commissioned by Mrs. Mary Hemenway to study Indian folklore along the Passamaquoddy River in Maine, became the 1st scholar to use a **phonograph to record Indian music and speech.**

Hull House, famous settlement house, established in Chicago by Jane Addams. Like other settlement houses of this period, Hull House was patterned after Toynbee Hall in London.

Barnard College, New York city, established as part of Columbia University. 1st classes met the same year.

General Federation of Women's Clubs founded, uniting the many influential clubs that flourished throughout the U.S. The relatively easy access American women had to higher education gave them community interests that, stimulated by increased leisure for the housekeeper, found an outlet in women's clubs, which often held considerable political and social power.

"Safety" bicycle manufactured for 1st time on a large scale. It was generally the same as bicycles today, having 2 wheels of equal size with saddle above and between them. It replaced dangerous "wheels" with one very large and one very small wheel. Cycling became most popular activity, causing traffic and parking problems very severe for the times.

"Texas Leaguer" became baseball parlance for a weak hit just over the heads of the infield but short of the outfield players. Term was 1st used to describe the short hits of Arthur Sunday, a player from the Texas League, who was able to maintain

Mar. 4 **Benjamin Harrison,** 23rd president, inaugurated. He was a Republican and served 1 term.

Apr. 22 Official opening of famous **Oklahoma land rush,** begun with firing of starter's gun; thousands of settlers set off in search of land. More than 20,000 people were lined up on the border at noon, the hour appointed for the rush forward into unstaked territory. For many years squatters and cattlemen had been invading the Oklahoma territory, though they had been expressly enjoined by law to keep out. The years before the Land Rush were punctuated by sharp set-to's with the Indians, who had been promised the western half of the territory in return for the other rights they had surrendered, and found themselves even there pressed by the invaders. But the clamor for permission to settle was unabated and the day was finally set by the congressional act. The towns along the frontier filled with eager people. Only the circle of marshalls ringed around the territory kept them from rushing in at once. The temptation was all the stronger because of rumors that some of the marshalls were in cahoots with friends who had been quietly slipped in during the night. At noon, the appointed hour, the crowd, on horseback, in wagons, waited tensely at the borders. The bugle sounded, and the starter's gun. The cavalry let the people through. From every direction, they poured into the territory. Guthrie had been designated the city of the territory. It became a boom town within an hour. The claims office was flooded with applications by people who wanted plots in the city. But the rumors had been true after all. By 10 A.M., 2 hours ahead of schedule, Guthrie had been a city. The marshalls had played the crowd false.

May 31 Famous **Johnstown Flood,** in which 2295 persons died when dam above Johnstown, Pa., broke after heavy rains had swelled the Conemaugh R. Flood destroyed 4 valley towns before drowning

from 440,000 to 2,000,000. Introduced intimate tone in women's publications, answers to letters, departments on health, marriage, cooking, etc. Also published outstanding authors of the day.

Schlesinger Building, the best of the Chicago buildings designed by Louis Sullivan, built. Later became Carson, Pirie, Scott Store.

Edward MacDowell performed his *Second Piano Concerto* in New York, his 1st great success after his return to the U.S.

Theodore Roosevelt published 2 volumes of the *Winning of the West,* a popular history of the early settlements west of the Alleghanies. The completed history ran to 4 volumes.

Henry James published *The Liar,* among his most accomplished short stories.

Chita, A Memory of Last Island, written by **Lafcadio Hearn.**

Sant' Ilario, 2nd novel of a trilogy, published by **Francis Marion Crawford.** With *Saracinesca* (1887) and *Dr. Orsino* (1892), *Sant' Ilario* forms a cycle of novels set in 19th century Italy.

Eugene Field published *A Little Book of Western Verse,* a collection of verses.

The Poems of Emma Lazarus published.

SCIENCE; INDUSTRY; ECONOMICS; EDUCATION; RELIGION; PHILOSOPHY.

SPORTS; FASHIONS; POPULAR ENTERTAINMENT; FOLKLORE; SOCIETY.

University of New Mexico established at Albuquerque, N.M. 1st classes met in 1892.

1st Bessemer Steel I beams in U.S. produced by Jones & Laughlin of Pittsburgh, Pa., making possible rapid construction of steel-skeleton, skyscraper-type buildings.

1st movie film developed in America by Thomas A. Edison on a base devised by George Eastman.

Singer Manufacturing Company of Elizabethport, N.J., produced and marketed 1st electric sewing machine known in U.S.

Tower Building, probably 1st steel-skeleton building in New York city, built at 50 Broadway. In his plans, Bradford Gilbert, the architect, specified a building with 11 stories, 129' high and 21'6" wide. The Tower Building was 1st building in the world in which the total weight of walls and floors was carried through girders and columns to the foundations. The New York Building Department altered the city building code to permit such a novel construction.

John Crerar, wealthy merchant left $2½ millions in his will for the establishment of the **John Crerar Library** in Chicago. Crerar, who was a power in railroads and banking, bequeathed the bulk of his estate to charities, churches, missions, and scholarship. He also desired "a colossal statue of Lincoln," later executed by St. Gaudens. The John Crerar Library specializies in scientific and technical refererence works.

Jan. 30 **University of Idaho** chartered at Moscow, Idaho. 1st classes met in 1892.

June **1st systematic theory of philanthropy** in U.S. appeared in the *North American Review* in an article by Andrew

a batting record of .398 with the help of these "Texas Leaguers."

1st all-American football team selected by Walter Camp, who picked 11 players as best in their positions. His selections appeared annually in *Collier's Weekly* until Camp's death in 1925, when Grantland Rice took over. Now selections are made by board of outstanding football coaches.

Erie won the 23rd annual **Belmont Stakes,** paying 7–5. Jockey was W. Hayward; time was 2:47 on a good track for winnings valued at $4960.

Buddhist won the 17th annual **Preakness Stakes,** paying 1–30. Jockey was H. Anderson; time was 2:17½ on a fast track for winnings valued at $1130. This year the distance was 1¼ miles. There were no races between 1889 and 1894.

U.S. lawn tennis men's singles champion, Henry W. Slocum Jr.; **women's singles champion,** Bertha L. Townsend.

Jan. 19 Georgia made **Robert E. Lee's birthday** a legal holiday. Virginia followed in 1890. This date is now legally commemorated in Alabama, Arkansas, Florida, Kentucky, Louisiana, Mississippi, North Carolina, South Carolina, Tennessee, and Texas, as well as in Georgia and Virginia. Lee was born in 1807.

Jan. 24 **$500,000 robbery** of the Connecticut Mutual Life Insurance Company by Joseph A. Moore, an Indianapolis agent, announced.

May 9 Armstrong's *Spokane*, ridden by Kiley, won the 15th annual **Kentucky Derby.** *Spokane*'s time was 2:34½, the record for this race as a 1½-mi. run (the length of the race was shortened to 1¼ mi. in 1896). The track was fast and the winner earned $4970.

June 5 Career of boxer **James J. Corbett,** a young bank clerk, began with his

POLITICS AND GOVERNMENT; WAR; DISASTERS; VITAL STATISTICS.	BOOKS; PAINTING; DRAMA; ARCHITECTURE; SCULPTURE.

Johnstown in 30 feet of water. Every Johnstown survivor lost a relative or friend in this tremendous disaster.

June 10 **United Confederate Veterans** organized at New Orleans for the purpose of uniting all Confederate veteran organizations. John B. Gordon, governor of Georgia, was elected the 1st General of the Association.

Oct. 2 **International Conference of American States** began in Washington, D.C., in effect 1st inter-American conference held in U.S. Convened to discuss formation of an American customs union.

Nov. 2 **North and South Dakota** admitted as states, the 39th and 40th to join the Union.

Nov 8 **Montana** admitted as a state, the 41st to join the Union.

Nov. 11 **Washington** admitted as a state, the 42d to join the Union.

Dec. 6 **Jefferson Davis**, ex-president of the Confederate States of America, died in New Orleans. He was 1st buried in New Orleans, but in 1893 his remains were transferred to Richmond, Va.

Personally Conducted, a travel book, published by **Frank Stockton.**

The Charity Ball, written by **David Belasco** and **Henry De Mille,** performed.

July 12 At a concert of American music at the Paris Exposition conducted by Van der Stucken, performances given of works by **Edward MacDowell, Dudley Buck, George W. Chadwick, Arthur Foote, Henry Holden Huss, Margaret Ruthven Lang, John K. Paine,** and **Frank Van der Stucken.**

Sept. 9 Civil War, and its conflict of patriotisms, was the theme for most successful of **Bronson Howard's** plays, *Shenandoah,* which was produced by Charles Frohman in New York.

1890

Population—62,947,714. Center of population; 20 mi. east of Columbus, Ind.

"Melting pot" character of New York city reflected in statistics which revealed half as many Italian New Yorkers as Neapolitans in Italy, as many German New Yorkers as were to be found in Hamburg, twice as many Irish New Yorkers as Dubliners, and 2½ times as many Jews as were living in Warsaw.

William Jennings Bryan elected to Congress on Democratic ticket in a heavily Republican district of Nebraska, his 1st public office.

Foremost sculptor of American Indian, especially equestrian, was **Cyrus E. Dallin,** who said he was prompted in this direction by a view of Buffalo Bill in Paris. *The Signal of Peace* received honorable mention at Paris Salon. Other Indian figures were *The Medicine Man* and *Massasoit.*

1st American publication of the famous children's classic *Black Beauty* by **Anna Sewell.** Though appearing many years earlier in England, *Black Beauty* did not have an American sale until it was published by the American Humane Education Society, whose founder, George T. Angell, was a

| SCIENCE; INDUSTRY; ECONOMICS; EDUCATION; RELIGION; PHILOSOPHY. | SPORTS; FASHIONS; POPULAR ENTERTAINMENT; FOLKLORE; SOCIETY. |

Carnegie entitled "Wealth." Carnegie combined a defense of the free enterprise system as a manifestation of natural law with an exhortation to businessmen to donate their wealth to worthy causes as the best means of adjusting the inequities of capitalism.

Oct. 7 Seth Low chosen president of Columbia College. He was a merchant, educator and publicist, and was elected mayor of New York city in 1901.

Nov. 11 1st Congress of the Roman Catholic laity of the U.S. assembled at Baltimore.

Dec. 14 Founding of the **American Academy of Political and Social Science** in Philadelphia. This year also saw formation of the **American Physical Association** and the **American Dialect Society.** These organizations reflect the necessity for greater specialization in American scholarship.

defeat of Joe Choyinski in 27 bloody rounds. Corbett finished the battle with a left hook, a blow he is said to have invented.

July 8 Last bare-knuckle championship fight, between John L. Sullivan and Jake Kilrain at Richburg, Miss. Sullivan defeated Kilrain after 75 grueling rounds, and claimed the world's championship since Kilrain had fought a draw with the champion of England, Jem Smith. After this bout boxing with gloves and under Marquis of Queensberry rules was introduced.

Fall New York won the **National League baseball pennant** with a season record of 83 victories, 43 defeats. Team then won the **baseball championship** for the 2nd consecutive year, defeating Brooklyn of the American Association.

Nov. 14 Journalist **Nellie Bly** (Elizabeth Cochrane) started on her famous journey around the world for the New York *World*, which took her 72 days, 6 hrs., and 11 mins., at that time a record. She completed her trip Jan. 25, 1890, thus beating the record set in Jules Verne's famous fictional story, *Around the World in Eighty Days.* In 1888 she had herself committed to insane ward at Blackwell's Island, New York, to report on treatment of insane.

1890

Growth of **child labor** in the South reflected in fact that some 23,000 children were now employed in the factories of the 13 Southern states. Adoption of traditional "family system" of employment from agriculture mainly responsible for high number of children employed.

How the Other Half Lives, a grim report on poverty in American cities and industrial towns by **Jacob A. Riis,** published; conditions described by Riis were a shock to many people, and the book was an important factor in labor reforms, slum clearance, new building codes, etc.

Charles D. Warner wrote at about this time famous observation, **"Everybody talks about the weather, but nobody does anything about it,"** in the Hartford *Courant.* Remark has been erroneously attributed to Mark Twain.

Phrase **"How the other half lives"** became popular through the title of book by Jacob A. Riis. Theodore Roosevelt, reading the book, became closely associated with Riis, and they both worked toward bettering housing conditions in cities.

Smoking became more accepted for males at social functions during this dec-

POLITICS AND GOVERNMENT; WAR; DISASTERS; VITAL STATISTICS.

BOOKS; PAINTING; DRAMA; ARCHITECTURE; SCULPTURE.

Feb. 4 Senate ratified the **Samoan treaty** with Germany and Great Britain. This treaty placed Samoan Islands under the joint control of the 3 powers, and thus provided the U.S. with a fueling station for its growing Pacific fleet.

Feb. 10 **Mormons** suffer 1st defeat in the municipal elections at Salt Lake City, Utah.

Feb. 10 U.S. opened to **general settlement** 11 million acres of Sioux territory that had been ceded to government in 1889.

Feb. 24 Chicago chosen as the site for the **World's Columbian Exposition** by the House of Representatives. The fair was to commemorate the 400th anniversary of the discovery of America in 1492.

Mar. Sen. John Sherman, Ohio, introduced antitrust bill. It passed July 2 with perhaps less opposition than any other public bill ever introduced in Congress. It was called the **Sherman Anti-Trust Act,** and it declared illegal "every contract, combination in the form of trust or otherwise, or conspiracy, in restraint of trade or commerce among the several States, or with foreign nations."

Apr. 14 Resolution of the Pan-American Conference held in Washington between Oct. 2, 1889, and Apr. 21, 1890, established the **Pan-American Union.**

May 2 **Oklahoma Territory** created by act of Congress. It was last territory in continental area of U.S., and was made by cutting into Indian Territory. It was later increased in size.

May 24 Trip around the world completed by **George Francis Train.** The journey took 67 days, 13 hr., 3 min. and 3 sec. This time bettered Nellie Bly's record.

July 3 **Idaho** admitted as a state, the 43d to join Union.

July 10 **Wyoming** admitted as a state, the 44th to join Union. As a territory it gave women the vote in 1869. It thus became **1st state to grant woman suffrage.**

July 13 Upwards of 100 persons were

vigorous crusader against cruelty to animals. In 2 years the Society circulated over 200,000 copies; American sales have been about 2½ million copies.

American naval officer **Alfred Thayer Mahan** published provocative history, *The Influence of Sea Power upon History, 1660–1783.* At a time when European nations were competing in naval strength, this book was generally received as authoritative.

1st printing of collected *Poems* of **Emily Dickinson** 4 years after her death. Here a new note is struck in American prosody and poetic thought. Many of the poems are fragments, many unrhymed, all of them full of self-communion, charm, and subtlety.

1st publications in America of **Rudyard Kipling,** who had just become a great English success. *Barrack-Room Ballads, Plain Tales from the Hills, Soldiers Three, The Story of the Gadsbys,* and *Mine Own People.* These books were Kipling's biggest American successes since they were "pirated" just before the International Copyright agreement went into effect, and were consequently sold in cheap editions.

William Dean Howells employed a large canvas in his "sociological" novel of New York *A Hazard of New Fortunes.* His longest and most complicated novel, it shows his characters laboring under the strain of a streetcar strike.

The Kreutzer Sonata, a book by **Leo Tolstoi,** forbidden by U.S. Post Office Department. Great controversy ensued. Theodore Roosevelt denounced Tolstoi as a "sexual and moral pervert."

Wainwright Building, St. Louis, built from designs by Louis Sullivan, who has

SCIENCE; INDUSTRY; ECONOMICS; EDUCATION; RELIGION; PHILOSOPHY.

SPORTS; FASHIONS; POPULAR ENTERTAINMENT; FOLKLORE; SOCIETY.

Illiteracy in America estimated at 13.3% of the population, a decrease of 3.7% over the preceding decade.

1st U.S. patent for a **pneumatic hammer** awarded to Charles B. King. Hammer was exhibited at Columbian Exposition of 1893.

1st publication of **William James'** *Principles of Psychology,* which revolutionized study of psychology in U.S. Rejected concept of mind as separate entity, and considered all human thought and action as behavior of nervous system.

John W. Burgess' *Political Science and Comparative Constitutional Law* charted a new course in American political science by rejecting passive notions of natural rights for historic and legal analysis of the potentialities of social and political institutions. **W. W. Willoughby's** *An Examination of the Nature of the State* expresses the same spirit in its analysis of government.

Establishment of **Sequoia and Yosemite National Parks** by the federal government assisted the cause of conservation in America by preserving native species of animal and plant life against the depredations of hunters and timber interests.

Cyanide process of extracting **gold** from low-grade ore invented by 2 metallurgists (MacArthur and Forrest). Annual production of gold in U.S. more than doubled within 8 years, undermining arguments for the free coinage of silver. Value of **silver** produced in the U.S. for the year rose to $57,242,100, more than 5 times the value produced in 1865. Rapid inflation of silver, as opposed to deflation of gold, in post-Civil War period led to currency issues in politics, rise of William Jennings Bryan, formation of such "3d parties" as Greenbackers, populists, Silverites, etc.

Monopoly in U.S. tobacco production achieved with formation of **American To-**ade, but the social tabu against women smoking in the company of men still persisted.

Composition of "The Washington Post March" (1889), a fast march in 6/8 time, by John Philip Sousa led to the invention of the **"2-step,"** a lively dance which remained popular for 10 or 15 years and replaced in popularity the older dances, i.e. waltz, polka, lancers, gallop, Portland fancy, quadrille, reel, etc.

Very popular joke at this time when **cable cars** and **trolley cars** 1st replaced horse cars had incredulous Chinaman watching a newfangled trolley and saying, "No pushee, no pullee; but goee like hellee allee samee."

"Baltimore Chop" became baseball parlance for a batted ball which bounced so high in the infield that the hitter could reach 1st base before the ball could be fielded and thrown. Term originated with the Baltimore Orioles, who were adept at securing this tricky hit.

Burlington won the 24th annual **Belmont Stakes,** paying 6–1. Jockey was S. Barnes; time was 2:07¾ on a fast track for winnings valued at $8560. From this year to 1892 the distance was 1¼ miles.

U.S. lawn tennis men's singles champion, Oliver S. Campbell; **women's singles champion,** Ellen C. Roosevelt.

May 14 Isaac Murphy rode his 2d **Kentucky Derby** winner when he brought Corrigan's *Riley* in 1st in the 16th running of classic race. Time was 2:45 on a heavy track; winnings were $5460.

| POLITICS AND GOVERNMENT; WAR; DISASTERS; VITAL STATISTICS. | BOOKS; PAINTING; DRAMA; ARCHITECTURE; SCULPTURE. |

drowned when a **tornado** swept over Lake Pepin, Minn.

July 14 Congress passed **Sherman Act** requiring government to purchase 4,500,-000 oz of silver per month and issue paper notes against it. A compromise with the "free coinage of silver" interests in the West. Act repealed 1893.

Aug. 8 **Strike** on the New York Central and Hudson River R.R. called by the Knights of Labor. It lasted until Sept. 17.

Sept. 3 **Single Tax platform** adopted by Single Tax National League of the U.S. at a conference in Cooper Union, New York. Henry George acted as chairman.

Oct. 1 Congress passed **McKinley Tariff Act** which raised tariffs to highest level yet known in U.S. Among other items it taxed opium at $10 per lb. if manufactured for smoking.

Oct. 1 Creation by act of Congress of the **Weather Bureau** in the Department of Agriculture. Previously weather information had come from the Signal Corps.

Nov. 1 Mississippi adopted a new constitution and became **1st state to restrict Negro suffrage,** effected by means of the "understanding" clause, which requires ability to read and understand Constitution.

Dec. 15 **Sitting Bull,** chief of the Sioux Indians, killed in a skirmish with soldiers in South Dakota.

been called the "father of modern architecture" and "the inventor of the skyscraper."

Charles ("Buddy") Bolden formed his own band in New Orleans. A cornetist, Bolden was one of the pioneers of instrumental jazz, and most of the early jazz musicians of New Orleans played at one time or another in his band.

May 19 Career of an American playwright who excelled in characterization began in New York city with production of *Beau Brummell* by **Clyde Fitch.** He followed this in Dec. with study of a French actor *Frédéric Lemaître.*

May 30 Cornerstone of the **Washington Memorial Arch** in Washington Square, New York city, laid.

June 9 *Robin Hood,* a comic opera by **Reginald De Koven,** produced in Chicago by a company called The Bostonians. De Koven later wrote many other comic operas, but none achieved the success of *Robin Hood,* which contained his two most popular songs, "Brown October Ale" and "Oh, Promise Me."

1891

Mar. 3 Office of **Superintendent of Immigration** created. This period saw great growth in immigration, but its character was different from that of earlier periods. Increase in Latin and Slavic stock most notable change, and at this time organized labor favored immigration restrictions. Much study of problems and several reports presented to Congress.

Mar. 3 **Circuit Courts of Appeal** created by act of Congress. This relieved the

1st appearance of **George M. Cohan,** at the age of 13, with his family in *Peck's Bad Boy.* He later became one of the most loved personalities of the American stage.

Probably one of the most moving and enigmatic sculptured figures in America is **Saint-Gaudens'** monumental figure for the tomb of Mrs. Adams in Rock Creek Cemetery, Washington, D.C., called *Grief* or *Death* or the *Peace of God.* With a face

bacco Company by James B. Duke, sponsor of Duke University in Durham, N.C.

Pyramiding of wealth in U.S. caused estimates of 1 per cent of the people possessing more wealth than the other 99 per cent.

Formation of the **Association of Economic Entomologists** and the **American Dante Society** reflected the growing specialization of American scholarship.

Jan. 23 **Fastest time** for an American train claimed for the Atchison, Topeka & Santa Fe Railroad which carried Nellie Bly from La Junta to Chicago at 78.1 mph.

Mar. 10 **Blair education bill** defeated in the Senate. Bill provided for common schools financed by U.S. Government.

May 1 **Bank of America** at Philadelphia failed, and caused the failure of several other banks, as well as the American Life Insurance Company of Philadelphia.

Oct. 6 Mormon Church, Salt Lake City, discontinued its sanction of **polygamy.** Thereafter most of the embarrassing cases that arose of Mormons in conflict with federal law were men who had married polygamously before 1890 and did not know what to do with their plural wives.

Aug. 6 **1st electrocution** took place at Auburn Prison, Auburn, N.Y. Executed prisoner was William Kemmler who murdered Matilde Zieigler on Mar. 29, 1889.

Fall Brooklyn won the **National League baseball pennant** with a season record of 86 victories, 43 defeats. **Baseball Championship of America** ended in a tie between the Brooklyn and Louisville teams. Of the 7 games played both teams won 3 games each and 1 game was played to a draw.

Nov. 29 1st **Army-Navy football game** was played at West Point, N.Y. The score, Navy 24, Army 0. This was the 1st game in what became an annual game between the 2 service academies (missing 1909, '17, '18, '28, '29). Usually held in Philadelphia's Municipal Stadium, it now draws over 100,000 privileged spectators and is viewed by millions on a nation-wide television broadcast.

1891

University of Chicago, Chicago, Ill., chartered in 1891. 1st classes met in 1892.
California Institute of Technology founded as Throop Polytechnic Institute in Pasadena, Calif. 1st classes met same year. Name was changed to Throop College of Technology in 1913, to present name in 1920.
Zipper patented by Whitcomb L. Judson.
Rise of monopoly in U.S. sugar industry

Basketball invented by Dr. James A. Naismith, physical education insructor at YMCA Training College (now Springfield College) in Springfield, Mass., as an indoor substitute for baseball and football. It retains the speed and competitiveness while eliminating the extreme violence of football. It is now the most widely attended spectator sport in U.S.

Congress authorized construction of 3 **federal penitentiaries,** the 1st non-military

POLITICS AND GOVERNMENT; WAR; DISASTERS; VITAL STATISTICS.

BOOKS; PAINTING; DRAMA; ARCHITECTURE; SCULPTURE.

Supreme Court of some of its appellate jurisdiction.

Mar. 4 Congress passed **International Copyright Act,** which gave British, French, Belgian, and Swiss authors copyright protection in U.S. Previously American publishers had freely pirated works by foreign authors, thus cutting off book market from native authors and depriving foreign authors of their rightful royalties. Copyright was later extended to include most other countries of the world.

Mar. 14 **Lynching** of 11 Sicilian immigrants who had been indicted for the murder of the Irish chief of police of New Orleans caused an international crisis, the recall of the Italian minister, and an indemnification by the federal government. Mob of citizens was incensed by the acquittal of 3 of the suspects. Incident served to restrain subsequent official encouragement of immigration and to cause satisfaction with failure of previous attempts to lure immigrants into the South.

May 19 **People's or Populist Party** launched in Cincinnati, Ohio. Farmers in the West and South were in desperate economic plight, and backers of new party, thinking Eastern bankers were hoarding gold, advocated free coinage of silver. High railroad rates also hurt farmers, and so they advocated government ownership of railroads. Free silverites captured Democratic Party in 1896, but lost election by 600,000 votes.

Sept. 22 900,000 acres of Indian land in Oklahoma opened for **general settlement** by a presidential proclamation. Land had been ceded to U.S. by Sauk, Fox and Potawatomi Indians.

Oct. 16 **Mob at Valparaiso, Chile, attacked American sailors** from *U.S.S. Balti-*

hidden by a mantle the figure poses more questions than it answers.

Masonic Temple in Chicago, one of the earliest "modern" buildings, built from designs by Burnham and Root, disciples of the Romanesque Revival of H. H. Richardson. It was 20 stories high and the tallest building in U.S. at the time.

As strange a writer as a man, **Ambrose Bierce** published his *Tales of Soldiers and Civilians* in San Francisco (it was reprinted in New York under the title *In the Midst of Life,* 1898). It has since been reprinted several times. It includes 26 grim tales of the Civil War, of the ghastly, the supernatural. Chief stories are "A Son of the Gods," and "A Horseman in the Sky."

Jan. *The Light that Failed,* 1st novel by **Rudyard Kipling,** published in *Lippincott's Magazine. The Light* is by no means Kipling's greatest novel, but its sales in America were the largest because it was circulated in cheap editions, made possible by lack of copyright agreements. Kipling's better books, such as the *Jungle Books, Captains Courageous,* and *Kim,* were protected by copyright, and, though popular, never enjoyed the sales of his earlier books. This illustrates, no matter what the disservice to the author, how cheap publishing in America insured a tremendous circulation of literature, both good and bad, to a very large number of people.

Apr. 1 1st pastoral play in America is *Alabama* by **Augustus Thomas.** Using characters "symbolically" to represent regional points of view, he emphasized the theme of a reunited nation rising after the Civil War.

Apr. 4 **Edwin Booth** played *Hamlet* in Brooklyn, his last performance before going into retirement.

May 5 New **Carnegie Hall** in New York city opened. It was built and endowed by Andrew Carnegie.

356

SCIENCE; INDUSTRY; ECONOMICS; EDUCATION; RELIGION; PHILOSOPHY.

promoted by both formation of **American Sugar Refining Company** by Henry Havemeyer and by a favorable protective tariff.

1st sun photography in America made possible by the invention of the spectroheliograph by George E. Hale of the University of Chicago.

Publication of *Gospel Criticism and Historical Christianity* by Pres. **Orello Cone** of Buchtel College reflected new liberal interpretations of the Bible and Christianity, interpretations that came into conflict with the views of fundamentalist religious leaders, such as the famous evangelist, Dwight Moody. Publication of **Washington Gladden's** *Who Wrote the Bible* also reflected new liberal approach to the Scriptures. Book was extremely successful with both the lay public and religious leaders. Although questioning the absolute infallibility of the Bible, Gladden's work became a text for Bible Classes and Young Men's Christian Associations. Its discovery of hitherto neglected literary, spiritual, and ethical values in the Bible served to rekindle popular interest in it.

1st important national committee of educators, the Committee of Ten on Secondary School Studies, formed. In 1893 it reported a need for greater diversification of subject matter in the country's schools.

May 19 Charter granted to **Rice Institute** in Houston, Tex.

Aug. 24 1st patent in America for a **motion picture camera** filed by Thomas Edison.

Oct. 16 **1st correspondence school in U.S.** opened by Thomas Jefferson Foster, editor of Shenandoah *Herald.* Now known as the International Correspondence School, Scranton, Pa., it was begun to teach mining methods to workers in the

SPORTS; FASHIONS; POPULAR ENTERTAINMENT; FOLKLORE; SOCIETY.

prisons built by federal government. They were located at Ft. Leavenworth, Kans.; Atlanta, Ga.; and McNeil's Island, Puget Sound, Wash.

New baseball rule permitted the insertion of a substitute player at any time during a game, removing restriction imposed in 1877 which allowed a substitute to enter the game only before the 4th inning.

Foxford won the 25th annual **Belmont Stakes,** paying 8–1. Jockey was E. Garrison; time was 2:08¾ on a fast track for winnings valued at $5070.

U.S. lawn tennis men's singles champion, Oliver S. Campbell; **women's singles champion,** Mabel E. Cahill.

Bob Fitzsimmons became **1st American boxer to hold 3 international titles;** he held middleweight, light heavyweight, and heavyweight crowns.

May 13 Isaac Murphy rode his 3d **Kentucky Derby** winner (2d straight) when he brought the favorite *Kingman* in 1st. Slow time of 2:52½ on a good track. Winnings were $4680.

Fall Boston won the **National League baseball pennant** with a season record of 87 victories, 51 defeats.

Oct. 18 **1st International 6-day bicycle race** in the U.S. run in the old Madison Square Garden in New York city. Riders used high wheelers and worked alone, pumping until exhausted, then resting, then starting again to total 142 hours. 1st winner was "Plugger Bill" Martin. Record under one-man rules was established in 1898 by Charlie Miller at Madison Square Garden; he rode 2,093.4 miles. Most of

more. 2 were killed, several wounded; war became imminent because of Chile's delay in making settlements, which she finally did to the amount of $75,000 to the injured and heirs of the dead.

Nov. 9 Longest consecutive run of any play up to this time was **Charles H. Hoyt's** farce about San Francisco, *A Trip to Chinatown,* which ran 650 times. Hoyt's satirization of types is best seen in *A Temperance Town* (1893) where he depicts an old soak; *A Runaway Colt* (1895), a satire on baseball; and *Stranger in New York* (1897).

1892

Jan. 1 **Ellis Island** in New York harbour became receiving station for immigrants. On Nov. 12, 1954, it was closed after 62 years of operation in which 20 million immigrants were processed.

Feb. 29 Convention signed by U.S. and Great Britain submitting to arbitration the right of U.S. to prohibit **pelagic hunting of fur seals in the Bering Sea.** On Aug. 15, 1893, the award favored Great Britain. This concluded a long controversy which had at times resulted in the seizure of Canadian vessels for killing of seals on the open sea.

Apr. 12 **$25,000 indemnity** paid by the U.S. Government to the families of the Italian subjects lynched at New Orleans.

May 5 Additional restrictive legislation on **Chinese immigration** enacted by Congress, providing registration of Chinese laborers and deportation regulations for those not specifically authorized to remain. It was called the Geary Chinese Exclusion Act, and extended existing exclusion laws another 10 years.

May 27 31 persons lost their lives and 2 towns completely destroyed when a **cyclone** ripped through Kansas.

Winslow Homer's genius in creating a mood excellently seen in his painting *Coast in Winter,* where the white-foamed breakers off the Maine shore dash in fury towards the snow-covered sands and rocks.

Realism in stage sets, the study of the character of real, simple people make **James A. Herne's** *Shore Acres* a modern play. His *Reverend Griffith Davenport* (1899) and *Sag Harbor* (1900) also stress same vein.

"Daisy Bell," the "bicycle built for two" song, written to celebrate the great rise in popularity of cycling as the American pastime.

Mrs. Humphry Ward's popular *The History of David Grieve* published.

The Adventures of Sherlock Holmes, which appeared this year, was the 1st Sherlock Holmes publication to receive wide attention in the U.S. *The Sign of the Four, A Study in Scarlet,* and *The Adventures* are the 3 top sellers of Sir **Arthur Conan Doyle** in America. Since 1900 the country has seen a continuing "craze" for Sherlock Holmes. The theater, movies, radio, and television have continually revived his adventures until perhaps no other fictional character surpasses him in popularity.

Reliance Brass Band formed in New Orleans by **Jack "Papa" Laine.** Laine, a white musician, was one of 1st to imitate Negro styles of "hot" music; his later or-

SCIENCE; INDUSTRY; ECONOMICS; EDUCATION; RELIGION; PHILOSOPHY.	SPORTS; FASHIONS; POPULAR ENTERTAINMENT; FOLKLORE; SOCIETY.

belief that this would increase the safety of the coal mines.

Dec. 29 **1st important radio patent** awarded Thomas Edison for a "means of transmitting signals electrically . . . without the use of wires."

his competitors ended in hospitals, ill from exhaustion.

Nov. 21 Yale won the **Intercollegiate football championship,** defeating Harvard 10 to 0 at Hampden Park, Springfield, Mass.

Nov. 28 **Army** defeated Navy at Annapolis, Md., by a score of 32 to 16 at their 2d annual contest.

1892

Labor unrest, reflected in many strikes and much violence, characterized the year, especially in Pennsylvania, Tennessee, Wyoming, and Idaho. Unrest in Tennessee was result of employment of convict labor. Pres. Harrison issued orders against strikers, especially in West, and Federal troops were used to enforce court injunctions.

1st comprehensive work on bacteriology in this country, *A Manual of Bacteriology,* published by Lt. Col. George Miller Sternberg (the following year to become Surgeon-General of the army with the rank of brigadier general).

Famous **heresy trial** of Prof. Charles A. Briggs dramatized the conflict within religious circles of the "higher criticism," which involved a more liberal approach to religious questions. Prof. Briggs was a noted exponent of the higher criticism from his theological chair in Union Theological Seminary. His appointment to the new chair of Biblical theology resulted in nationwide protests from Presbyterian leaders. More than 70 Presbyteries joined in denouncing the appointment and despite the recommendation of the N.Y. Presbytery that in the interest of church harmony no action be taken, the General Assembly of the Presbyterian Church suspended Prof. Briggs from the ministry on the charge of heresy. The decision served to widen the controversy with one clergyman in Albany resigning in sympathy for Briggs and another, Prof. H. P. Smith of the Lane

1st use of the tag, **"The 400,"** made by Ward McAllister in reference to the Astor ballroom, which had capacity of 400 persons and could therefore contain all of High Society.

Expression **"Diamond Horseshoe"** came into prominence to describe 35 newly constructed parterre boxes in the Metropolitan Opera House, for which their owners paid $60,000 apiece.

Illinois Legislature made the anniversary of **Lincoln's birthday,** Feb. 12, a legal holiday. The legislatures of New Jersey, New York, Washington, and Minnesota followed suit in 1896.

George W. G. Ferris designed **Ferris Wheel.** He built his 1st the next year for Columbia Exposition. 40 passengers could be carried 250 ft. high in its 36 cars.

Expression **"Garrison finish"** born when jockey Ed "Snapper" Garrison came from the rear of the field and won the Suburban Handicap at Sheepshead Bay by 3 in.

Patron won the 26th annual **Belmont Stakes,** paying 6–5. Jockey was W. Hayward; time was 2:17 on a muddy track for winnings valued at $6610.

U.S. lawn tennis men's singles champion, Oliver S. Campbell; **women's singles champion,** Mabel E. Cahill.

Jan. 29 Kansas Republicans began celebrating **Kansas Day** as both a political and a state holiday. Kansas was admitted into

359

POLITICS AND GOVERNMENT; WAR; DISASTERS; VITAL STATISTICS.	BOOKS; PAINTING; DRAMA; ARCHITECTURE; SCULPTURE.

June 7–11 **Republican National Convention** met in Minneapolis and nominated Pres. Harrison as the presidential candidate and Whitelaw Reid of New York for the vice-presidency.

ganization, Jack Laine's Ragtime Band, was probably the **1st white Dixieland jazz band.**

Formation of **American Fine Arts Society** by combination of Society of American Artists, the Art Students' League, and the Architectural League. New group housed on 57th Street, New York, much of the expense having been defrayed by George W. Vanderbilt.

June 21–23 **Democratic National Convention,** in session at Chicago, nominated Grover Cleveland as the presidential candidate and Adlai Ewing Stevenson of Illinois for vice-presidency.

Antonín Dvořák, Bohemian composer, came to New York city in response to invitation to direct the National Conservatory of Music. Dvořák was particularly interested in nationalistic movements in music, especially as allied to interests in folklore, independence, romanticism, etc.

June 29–July 1 **Prohibition National Convention** met at Cincinnati and nominated John Bidwell, of California, for the presidency, and James B. Cranfill, of Texas, for the vice-presidency.

"After the Ball Is Over," perennially favorite song in U.S., composed by Charles K. Harris, one of the most successful songwriters of the '90's and early 1900's. "After the Ball" very popular during Columbian Exposition of 1893 in Chicago.

Cartoons of little bears and tigers, drawn by **Jimmie Swinnerton** for the San Francisco *Examiner,* were forerunners of the comic strip.

July 4–5 **People's (Populist) Party National Convention** met at Omaha and nominated James B. Weaver, of Iowa, for the presidency, and James G. Field, of Virginia, for vice-presidency.

Charnley House, generally thought to be the 1st home designed by **Frank Lloyd Wright,** built in Chicago. Wright made the plans while still working in the firm of Adler & Sullivan.

Aug. 28 **Socialist Labor Party,** meeting at New York, nominated Simon Wing, of Massachusetts for the presidency, and Charles H. Matchett, of New York for vice-presidency.

In the Midst of Life, short stories by **Ambrose Bierce,** published. The collection includes some of the starkest and most harrowing tales in American literature. "Chickamauga," the battlefield as seen through the eyes of a deaf child creeping through the forest; "A Son of the Gods," an ironic tale of the will of men to die; "An Occurrence at Owl Creek Bridge"; "One of the Missing" and "The Eyes of the Panther" are among the memorable stories of the volume. *The Monk and the Hangman's Daughter,* a story of medieval madness, was published the same year.

Oct. 15 **Crow Indian reservation** in Montana opened to settlers by a presi-

360

SCIENCE; INDUSTRY; ECONOMICS; EDUCATION; RELIGION; PHILOSOPHY.

SPORTS; FASHIONS; POPULAR ENTERTAINMENT; FOLKLORE; SOCIETY.

Theological Seminary in Cincinnati, being suspended for supporting Briggs's position. In 1900 Briggs became an Episcopal clergyman. As a result of his suspension Union Theological Seminary severed Presbyterian connections and became nonsectarian.

Boll weevil, of Mexican or Central American origin, 1st seen in Texas; pest spread widely and has caused as much as $200,000,000 damage a year to U.S. cotton crops.

E. E. Barnard made a significant contribution to **astronomy** with his detection of the 5th satellite of Jupiter from the Lick Observatory in California.

Formation of the **American Psychological Association** reflected growing American specialization in scientific scholarship.

Rhode Island University, Kingston, R.I., chartered as Rhode Island College of Agriculture and Mechanical Arts. 1st classes held same year. Present name adopted 1951.

University of Chicago integrated the summer session with the academic year. This policy was prompted by Pres. William Rainey Harper, one-time supervisor of the summer meeting of the Chautauqua movement. 1st classes at University.

1st College of Osteopathy in U.S. established at Kirksville, Mo.

Nikola Tesla developed **1st motor** that could be driven by alternating current.

Aug. 20 Tolls established on the **Sault Ste. Marie Canal** by a proclamation issued by Pres. Harrison in retaliation for similar measures taken by Canada.

Sept. **1st gasoline automobile** made in U.S. built by Charles and Frank Duryea, bicycle designers and toolmakers, at Chicopee, Mass. They were afraid of ridicule if they tested the vehicle publicly, hence tested it during this month indoors. It was barely a success, and they built a better car with a more powerful motor the next year.

Sept. An **electric automobile,** made by William Morrison of Des Moines, Iowa,

the Union by an act signed on Jan. 29, 1861.

Mar. 18 **Jockeys** prohibited from using anything but a whip and a spur on a horse during a race. Ruling prompted by the discovery that jockey Cook used an electric spur while riding *Gyda* at Guttenburg, N.J. Cook was ruled off the track.

May 11 18th annual **Kentucky Derby** won by the favorite, G. J. Long's *Azra,* ridden by jockey Clayton. Time, 2:41½ on a heavy track; value, $4230.

June 3 **Jefferson Davis' birthday** 1st observed as an official holiday in Florida. Date has since been made a legal holiday in Alabama, Georgia, Louisiana, Mississippi, South Carolina, Tennessee, and Texas. It is a Memorial Day in Arkansas. Jefferson Davis was born in 1808.

Fall Boston won the **National League baseball pennant** with a season record of 102 victories, 48 defeats.

Sept. 7 **1st heavyweight boxing champion** under the Marquis of Queensberry rules requiring gloves and 3-minute rounds was **James J. Corbett** when he knocked out the great John L. Sullivan in the 21st round at New Orleans, La. Sullivan was world bare knuckle champion and there are claims that he was 1st champ under Marquis of Queensberry rules because of previous fight with gloves.

Oct. 5 **Dalton gang** of robbers virtually wiped out at Coffeyville, Kan., while attempting to rob a bank.

Oct. 20–23 Magnificent ceremonies dedicated the **World's Columbian Exposition** at Chicago. There were also imposing celebrations in Brooklyn, N.Y. Vice-Pres. Levi Morton gave the opening address in Chicago. John Philip Sousa, who had resigned from the Marine Corps that year and organized his own band, conducted. The exhibition was the result of a public

POLITICS AND GOVERNMENT; WAR; DISASTERS; VITAL STATISTICS.	BOOKS; PAINTING; DRAMA; ARCHITECTURE; SCULPTURE.

dential proclamation. The territory covered 1,800,000 acres.

Oct. 28   **Great fire** in Milwaukee, Wis., destroyed $5,000,000 worth of property over 26 acres.

Nov. 8   Grover Cleveland and Adlai E. Stevenson defeated Benjamin Harrison and Whitelaw Reid in the **presidential elections** by an electoral vote of 277–145. James B. Weaver received 22 electoral votes. Popular votes: Cleveland, 5,554,414; Harrison, 5,190,802; Weaver, 1,027,329; Bidwell, 271,058; Wing, 21,164.

Joel Chandler Harris published *Nights with Uncle Remus,* another in his popular series of the Uncle Remus stories.

Richard Harding Davis saw *The West from a Car-Window,* a travel book.

James Whitcomb Riley published *Green Fields and Running Brooks,* a book of verses.

Don Orsino, final novel of the *Saracinesca* trilogy, published by **Francis Marion Crawford.**

The Tiddleywinks' Poetry Book, a juvenile, by humorist **John Kendrick Bangs,** published.

Aug. 27   **Metropolitan Opera House** in New York city almost totally destroyed by fire.

Dec. 27   Construction begun on **Cathedral of St. John the Divine,** planned as largest church in U.S. Still incomplete. Begun in Romanesque style, but new plans adopted in 1911 shifted emphasis to pure Gothic. 600-ft. nave occupies 3 blocks of New York city.

1893

Jan. 17   **Rutherford B. Hayes** died at the age of 70. He is buried in Fremont, Ohio.

Jan. 17   **Revolution in Hawaii** deposed Queen Liliuokalani and a provisional government was formed. Action taken with connivance of U.S. minister John L. Stevens.

Feb. 1   U.S. established a protectorate in **Hawaii** when American minister Stevens raised the American flag at Honolulu and landed U.S. Marines.

Feb. 15   **Hawaiian annexation treaty** submitted to Senate. It had already been signed by provisional government of Hawaii, but on Mar. 9 Pres. Cleveland

Frank Lloyd Wright's 1st completely independent commission was the Winslow residence built this year in Chicago.

Transportation Building of Columbian Exposition in Chicago designed and built by **Louis Sullivan,** one of his 1st and most influential projects in creating a modern style.

Sculpture at the Columbian Exposition in Chicago highlighted by the contributions of **Daniel Chester French.** His relief *The Angel of Death and the Young Sculptor* depicted a winged figure lightly touching the half-turned artist; the enormous *Republic* meant to represent America sculpturally. But the sculptural jewel of the Chicago Columbian Exposition was the great fountain of the Court of Honor,

SCIENCE; INDUSTRY; ECONOMICS; EDUCATION; RELIGION; PHILOSOPHY.	SPORTS; FASHIONS; POPULAR ENTERTAINMENT; FOLKLORE; SOCIETY.

appeared on streets of Chicago. Owner called on police to help him make his way through crowds of curious spectators.

Oct. 3 **University of Idaho** 1st opened to students. It had been chartered Jan. 30, 1889, by the Territorial Legislature, and is thus 18 months older than the State itself.

Nov. 20 Famous **Homestead strike** declared over by the Amalgamated Association. It had been called because of pay cuts and because management refused to recognize union, but the majority of workers at the Carnegie Mills returned to work as nonunion men. One of bloodiest strikes in American labor history, 10 persons had been killed and many wounded on July 6 when strikers fired on Pinkerton detectives hired by management. On July 9 state troopers had been ordered by Gov. Pattison of Pennsylvania to Homestead where they stayed 95 days to keep order.

Dec. 2 **Jay Gould**, millionaire railroad magnate, died of consumption in New York city at the age of 56, leaving an estate of $72,000,000.

Dec. 19 **University of Oklahoma** opened at Norman, Okla.

demand for some fitting commemoration of the discovery of America. On April 25, 1890, Congress passed an act which authorized an "exhibition of the arts, industries, manufactures, and products of the soil, mine and sea." Pres. Harrison recommended a sum of "not less than $10 millions" be allotted for the fair. The estimate of expenditures has been given as over $22 millions. The fair was set out on an area of 644 acres, with the Exposition itself covering 150 acres. There were 50 acres of concessions and 55 acres of State, Transportation, Electric, Arts and Liberal Arts buildings. It officially opened May 1, 1893.

Nov. 26 **Navy** defeated Army at West Point in their annual football game by a score of 12 to 4.

Dec. 31 **Great American race horse** was *Hindoo,* who by the end of 1892, after 3 years of racing, had won 31 of 36 starts and never finished out of the money (less than 3d).

1893

Frederick J. Turner made famous contribution to American historiography, "The Significance of the Frontier in American History," an address delivered before the American Historical Association.

Leo H. Baekeland perfected the process by which Velox paper was produced. Although not immediately successful, Baekeland received $1,000,000 for his patent from George Eastman in 1899. With this money, Baekeland constructed a private laboratory in which he made his monumental discoveries in plastics.

Expiration of Bell patent on the telephone terminated monopoly of Bell Company on telephone service in America. Many small companies took advantage of

Conservative estimate of number of visitors to **Court of Honor** at Columbian Exposition in Chicago was 12,000,000—one out of every 6 people in U.S.

Dance called the **"hootchy-kootchy"** originated with so-called "Egyptian Dancers" on the Midway at the Chicago Columbian Exposition. A couple of decades later, same dance was called the "shimmy."

America's contribution to field and track events, the **relay race,** 1st held by the University of Pennsylvania.

Ice hockey introduced to the U.S. at Yale and Johns Hopkins University. Hockey 1st played in Canada in Kingston, Ont., by Royal Canadian Rifles of the Imperial Army in 1855. In 1875, McGill

| POLITICS AND GOVERNMENT; WAR; DISASTERS; VITAL STATISTICS. | BOOKS; PAINTING; DRAMA; ARCHITECTURE; SCULPTURE. |

withdrew it from Senate and it was never ratified.

Mar. 1 Congress authorized the creation of rank of ambassador under **Diplomatic Appropriation Act,** which stipulated that American ministers shall enjoy a rank similar to that of ministers from countries to which they are accredited. By 1920, 15 legations had been raised to ambassador rank.

Mar. 4 **Grover Cleveland,** 24th president, inaugurated for 2d time. Adlai Stevenson was inaugurated vice-president. Cleveland was a Democrat and served 1 term. He was immediately faced with the currency problem. Amount of paper money in circulation 5 times as great as gold in U.S. Treasury, although all paper notes were theoretically redeemable in gold.

Mar. 10 **Tremendous fire** in Boston destroyed nearly $5,000,000 in property. Several lives were lost.

Mar. 26 **Illegal immigration of Chinese** for cheap labor typified by discovery of 67 "bootleg" immigrants entering Portland, Ore., from Vancouver, Can.

Apr. 3 Thomas Francis Bayard appointed **U.S. Ambassador to Great Britain,** the 1st time that ambassadorial rank had been conferred in the U.S. foreign service.

Apr. 13 American protectorate in **Hawaii** came to an end, when Comm. Blount ordered U.S. troops to withdraw.

May 15 **Geary Chinese Exclusion Act** declared constitutional by the Supreme Court.

July 17 American Minister Stevens was accused of heading a group of conspirators, who promoted the revolution in **Hawaii.** Charge was made by Blount in a report to Secretary Gresham.

Aug. 10 1st Chinese deported from San Francisco for nonregistration under the **Chinese Exclusion Act.**

designed and executed by **Frederick MacMonnies.** On the recommendation of Saint-Gaudens he was given $50,000 to carry it out. The result was stupendous: 27 colossal figures are combined around a great white ship, on top of which Columbia sits enthroned; Sculpture, Architecture, Music, etc., surround her.

Première of **Antonín Dvořák's** *New World Symphony* given in New York. Dvořák, though a Bohemian who had been in the U.S. only a year, produced the most "American" composition of the 19th century. Though no theme of the symphony is specifically imitated from folk music, many are close to the spirit of plantation songs and Indian melodies.

Both **Nellie Melba** and **Emma Calvé** made their 1st appearances in U.S. Foreign musicians toured U.S. more frequently as a result of new interest in "Classical" music stimulated by Columbian Exposition.

1st building in New York to rise higher than Trinity Church steeple, the **Manhattan Life Insurance Building,** erected on basis of 17 stories plus tower. Trinity had been highest structure for 52 years. Within another 10 it was almost completely overshadowed.

Famous horror story *The Strange Case of Dr. Jekyll and Mr. Hyde* by **Robert Louis Stevenson** published in America. Stage and screen versions have helped this favorite to sell in the hundreds of thousands.

Realistic portrayal of the ugly and sordid in the naturalistic novel of **Stephen Crane,** *Maggie: A Girl of the Streets.* Completely objective, reportorial in manner, Crane presents episode after episode in the life of a New York girl victimized by her surroundings.

Best selling woman's rights novel *The Heavenly Twins* by **Sarah Grand** (Mrs.

SCIENCE; INDUSTRY; ECONOMICS; EDUCATION; RELIGION; PHILOSOPHY.

SPORTS; FASHIONS; POPULAR ENTERTAINMENT; FOLKLORE; SOCIETY.

expiration to establish telephone service in areas which the Bell Company had failed to cover.

American University, Washington, D.C., chartered by Congress. 1st classes met in 1914.

Montana State University, Missoula, Montana, chartered. 1st classes held in 1895.

Mormon Temple dedicated at Salt Lake City. The site of the temple was selected by Brigham Young 6 years before work began in 1853. The massive temple, of white granite, which looks from a distance to be marble, was erected at a cost between $6–$12 millions. It was lavishly appurtenanced, from sky-blue ceiling to marble tiled and seasoned oak floors.

Lillian D. Wald, social worker, founded **Livingston Street Settlement** in New York city. The settlement, which grew into the famous **Henry Street Settlement,** began when Lillian Wald set up a nursing center in the slums of the lower East Side. She had studied at the New York Hospital Training School for Nurses and at Woman's Medical College, and became interested in the social background of sickness. In 1895, Jacob Schiff, the banker, gave her staff larger quarters on Henry Street. It was popularly known as the Nurses' Settlement.

Jan. 4 Official amnesty announced by Pres. Benjamin Harrison for all previous violators of **antipolygamy Act** with stipulation that law must be observed from that day onward. Announcement applied chiefly to Mormon elders.

Feb. 1 Famous early **film studio** constructed in West Orange, N.J., by Edison laboratories. It was a small structure pivoted so that it could turn with the sun.

June 26 India, following several major European countries, abandoned bimetallism in its currency; same day value of U.S. silver dollar fell from 67¢ to below

University students formulated the rules of hockey.

Rise of **bicycling** as a popular diversion in America indicated by the increase of bicycles in use from some 20,000 in 1882 to over 1,000,000 in 1893.

1st national fly casting tournament held at the Chicago World's Fair (Columbian Exposition) by the newly formed Chicago Fly Casting Club. Accuracy, Accuracy Fly, Delicacy Fly, Long-distance Bait, and Long-distance Fly events were held at distances of 75, 80, and 85 ft. The club held national tournaments in 1897, 1903, and 1905. In 1906 a permanent organization, the National Association of Scientific Angling Clubs, was formed in Racine, Wis., and held a national tournament in 1907. This organization, still strictly amateur, is now the governing body of fly casting as the National Association of Angling and Casting Clubs.

Anti-Saloon League organized at Oberlin, Ohio, by representatives of temperance societies and evangelical organizations. League's goal was prohibition of liquor in Ohio.

New baseball rule established the distance between the pitcher and home plate at 60 ft. 6 in. This distance has remained the same up to the present time.

Comanche won the 27th annual **Belmont Stakes,** paying 20–1. Jockey was W. Simms; time was 1:53¼ on a fast track for winnings valued at $5310. This year and next the distance was 1⅛ mi.

U.S. lawn tennis men's singles champion, Robert D. Wrenn; **women's singles champion,** Aline M. Terry.

May 1 **World's Columbian Exposition** officially opened in Chicago by Pres. Cleveland.

May 10 19th annual **Kentucky Derby** won by favorite *Lookout* in 2:39¼ on a fast track under jockey Kunze, winning $4090.

June 14 1st official observance of **Flag Day** outside of school ceremonies occurred

POLITICS AND GOVERNMENT; WAR; DISASTERS; VITAL STATISTICS.

BOOKS; PAINTING; DRAMA; ARCHITECTURE; SCULPTURE.

Aug. 13 $2,000,000 in property destroyed and some 1500 persons made homeless by fire in Minneapolis.

Aug. 24 1000 lives lost and a great deal of property damage inflicted by a terrible **cyclone** which ripped through Savannah and Charleston.

Sept. 7 1st American agreement with Canada for surveillance of **illegal immigrants** into U.S. through Canadian ports on Pacific Coast concluded.

Sept. 16 **Cherokee Strip,** between Kansas and Oklahoma, opened for "land rush" settlement. More than 100,000 persons rushed into area of 6,000,000 acres that had been purchased from Cherokees in 1891.

Sept. 17 **Yellow fever** cases reached epidemic proportions in Brunswick, Ga.

Oct. 2 Some 2000 persons killed by a disastrous **cyclone** which raged along the Gulf coast of Louisiana.

Nov. 7 Colorado adopted **woman suffrage.**

Frances Elizabeth M'Fall) shocked current American sensibilities by its discussions of tabooed subjects, such as syphilis. Mrs. M'Fall was an important British suffragette later the Mayoress of Bath.

Jan. 23 World-famous actress **Eleonora Duse** made her American debut at Fifth Avenue Theater in *Camille.*

Aug. 7 Play of locality developed successfully by **Augustus Thomas.** His *In Mizzoura* draws on local color of character and place. *Arizona* (1899), depicting life on a Far Western ranch, lifts Western melodrama to level of real dramatic art. *Colorado* (1911) turns to the mountain regions for inspiration.

Oct. 23 Popular melodrama that ran for 27 consecutive seasons in New York and on the road, *In Old Kentucky* by **Charles T. Dazey** opened in New York city. Play makes use of fights, murder, horse racing, the conflict of mountaineers and plainsmen.

1894

Defeated in his bid for a Senate seat, **William Jennings Bryan** became editor of the Omaha, Neb., *World-Herald,* a position which gave him, in addition to his heavy and perpetual program of speeches, an influential role in the political development of the West.

Jan. 8 **Fire** at the Chicago World's Fair destroyed virtually all the buildings with property damages estimated at $2,000,000.

Jan. 17 U.S. Treasury offered **bond issue** of $50,000,000 to replenish gold reserve. Since this issue did little good, the Treasury offered a second bond issue Nov. 13 of another $50,000,000.

Jan. 30 **Suspected corruption** in the Police Department of New York city prompted the New York State Senate to pass a resolution authorizing an investigation.

Best known work of sculptor **George Grey Barnard** is his *Two Natures* completed this year and now in the Metropolitan Museum. Work was suggested by line of Victor Hugo: "Je sens deux hommes en moi." 2 figures grapple, one standing over the prostrate form of the other. Which represents "good" and which "evil" poses an enigma to public.

Famous American female painter is **Mary Cassatt,** whose *La Toilette* was exhibited this year in Paris. Daughter of a wealthy businessman, she gave up life of a society girl and went to Paris to learn to paint. Fell early under influence of Manet and Impressionists such as Degas. Her paintings were of simple realistic subjects, such as that of a mother and child.

Publication of **Anthony Hope's** best seller, *The Prisoner of Zenda,* a historical

60¢ in gold, precipitating the **Panic of 1893,** one of the worst in history. Financial panic was felt, however, as early as May 5 when securities fell suddenly on New York Stock Exchange. There was financial panic in Chicago on June 5. On June 29 money panic was averted in New York by a loan of $6,000,000 by Clearing House banks. On Aug. 7 Pres. Cleveland called extra session of Congress to consider crisis.

Aug. 1 Populists and Republicans met in Chicago and formed **National Bimetallic League.** 810 delegates from 42 states attended the convention. The convention demanded free coinage of silver at 15½ or 16 to 1, for which they would agree to repeal of the Sherman Law. The delegates sought banking reforms and a repeal of the tax on national bank circulation.

Dec. 24 **Henry Ford** completed construction of his 1st gasoline engine that ran successfully. His first motor car was assembled in 1896.

in Philadelphia by order of the mayor, who ordered that the flag be displayed over every public building in the city pursuant to a resolution of the Colonial Dames of the State, whose president, Mrs. Elizabeth Duane Gillespie, was directly descended from Benjamin Franklin.

Fall Boston won the **National League baseball pennant** with a season record of 86 victories, 44 defeats.

Oct. 30 **World's Columbian Exposition** at Chicago officially closed.

Nov. 30 Princeton defeated Yale by a score of 6 to 0 at New York to win the **Intercollegiate Football Association championship.**

Dec. 2 At Annapolis, Md., **Navy** beat Army, 6–4, in their 4th annual football classic.

1894

Saranac Laboratory for the treatment of tuberculosis founded by Dr. Edward Livingston Trudeau, himself a victim of the dread disease.

Unique nonideological development typical of organized U.S. labor foreshadowed by American Federation of Labor in formal **repudiation of socialism.**

1st large, well-run Southern railroad organized by J. P. Morgan as the **Southern Railroad Company.** It connected Atlantic coast points, and linked the Gulf of Mexico to the Ohio R.

Apr. 4 **Rising U.S. unemployment** reflected in the formation of Kelly's "industrial army" of unemployed for a march on Washington *à la Coxey.* That these were hard times is seen in price of wheat, which dropped to 49¢ a bushel after averaging

Highest batting average ever compiled in one season by a major league baseball player was Hugh Duffy's .438. He was a member of the Boston Nationals in 1894.

New baseball rule replaced the pitching box with a slab 12 x 4 in. Other rules stipulated that a foul bunt was to be considered a strike and player who sacrificed was not to be charged with a time at bat for scoring purposes.

Henry of Navarre won the 28th annual **Belmont Stakes,** paying 1–10. Jockey was W. Simms; time was 1:56½ on a fast track for winnings valued at $6680.

Assignee won the 18th annual **Preakness Stakes,** paying 4–1. Jockey was F. Taral; time was 1:49¼ on a fast track for winnings valued at $1830. From this year until 1900 the distance was 1⅟₁₆ mi.

POLITICS AND GOVERNMENT; WAR; DISASTERS; VITAL STATISTICS.

BOOKS; PAINTING; DRAMA; ARCHITECTURE; SCULPTURE.

Jan. 30 **U.S. flag** fired upon by the Brazilian revolutionists in Rio de Janeiro harbor.

Feb. 13 **13 miners buried alive** in a cave-in at the Gaylord mine in Plymouth, Pa.

Mar. 17 **Chinese Exclusion Treaty** again signed in which China agreed to exclusion of Chinese laborers from U.S. Senate ratified treaty Aug. 13.

Mar. 30 Pres. Cleveland vetoed the **Bland Bill** to coin silver bullion.

Apr. 5 **11 men killed** when a riot broke out among striking miners at Connellsville, Pa.

Apr. 24 **37 miners killed** in disastrous mine accident at Franklin, Wash.

Apr. 30 **"Coxey's Army,"** lead by Jacob Sechler Coxey, marched from Ohio to Washington, D.C., to "take control of the government"—or at least to demonstrate in favor of legislation for emergency work projects to help unemployed. On May 1 he stood on the steps of the Capitol and declared to the president the wishes of the people. Coxey's plans were thwarted when the Capitol guards arrested him for trespassing.

June 21 **Democratic Silver Convention** held in Omaha, Neb., attended by 1000 delegates. William Jennings Bryan led the convention to adoption of a free-coinage plank on silver ratio of "16 to 1."

Aug. 1 $3,000,000 worth of property destroyed by **tremendous fire** in Chicago, Ill.

Aug. 8 **Hawaiian Republic** officially recognized by the U.S. Government. On May 31 U.S. had recognized that Hawaii should enjoy its own government and that interference from any foreign power would be considered unfriendly to U.S. On July 4 the Republic of Hawaii had been proclaimed and an extremely progressive Constitution adopted.

Aug. 18 Congress created **Bureau of Immigration.**

romance of a dashing Englishman caught up in the palace intrigues of a mythical Balkan kingdom. There have been repeated stage and movie versions of it in America, and a paperback publisher of 1946 sold at least ¼ million copies. This English author's full name was Sir Anthony Hope Hawkins.

Tremendously popular *Trilby,* a vivid, sentimental, well-written novel of Bohemian life, by **George du Maurier,** a successful black-and-white artist, a Frenchman who had become an English citizen. Heroine's name became very popular in America; streets, a town, shoes, food, etc., were named Trilby.

Perhaps most influential book on economics ever published in U.S., *Coin's Financial School,* by **William Hope Harvey,** issued by the author in Chicago. Made up of cartoons and dialogues, it presented mostly false interpretations of banking, finance, and currency; was wholly accepted by Bryan and free silver agitators. Its success reflects the great American interest in coinage and related problems during the last few years of the 19th century. By 1895 *Coin's Financial School* had sold 300,000 copies, and was selling at rate of 5000 a day.

"The Sidewalks of New York" written and composed by Charles Lawler, a buck-and-wing dancer in out-of-the-way music halls who later went blind. Song was popular in '90's, but even more popular when revived by Democratic Party during National Convention in 1924, when Al Smith was a candidate for the nomination for the presidency.

William Dean Howells created a Utopia in his *A Traveler from Altruria.* Against the current background of labor disputes and depression, he presented his imaginative land where collectivism has removed economic and social suffering, where all men participate equally in the work of the community, and where there is no caste.

Still popular dog story, *Beautiful Joe* by **Margaret Marshall Saunders,** published.

368

SCIENCE; INDUSTRY; ECONOMICS; EDUCATION; RELIGION; PHILOSOPHY.

SPORTS; FASHIONS; POPULAR ENTERTAINMENT; FOLKLORE; SOCIETY.

better than $1.00 a bushel between 1865 and 1873. It was lowest price up to that point.

Apr. 20 136,000 **coal miners struck** for higher wages at Columbus, Ohio. This, like the year before, is a season of labor unrest.

May 11 Beginning of the famous **Pullman strike** in Chicago. Money panics of 1893 and 1894 caused Pullman Palace Car Company to reduce wages; workers struck amid much violence and bloodshed. Mobs of the worst classes in Chicago pillaged and burned railway cars.

June 26 American Railway Union, under leadership of Eugene Debs, later founder of the Social Democratic Party in America, boycotted the servicing of Pullman cars as sympathy gesture for **Pullman strikers.** This caused **general railway strike,** and on July 2 U.S. government ordered Debs to call off strike on grounds of interference with interstate commerce and postal service. Railway strike paralyzed 50,000 miles of Western railroads.

July 2 **Injunction** against railroad strikers issued by the U.S. Court.

July 3 Pres. Cleveland ordered U.S. troops to Chicago on constitutional grounds that **Pullman strike** interfered with U.S. mails and interstate commerce and to enforce federal court injunctions brought against Pullman strikers.

July 6 2 men killed and several injured when U.S. deputy marshals fired upon **railroad strikers** at Kensington, near Chicago.

July 10 **Eugene Debs,** leader of American Railway Union, indicted for criminal conspiracy and contempt of court. On Dec. 14 he was sentenced to 6 months' imprisonment. Debs' famous court trial involved defense attorney Clarence Dar-

Jockey Club incorporated in Feb. as a result of a meeting of trainers and owners the previous year. Club's purpose was to "encourage the development of the Thoroughbred horse" and "establish racing on such a footing that it may command the interest as well as the confidence and favorable opinion of the public."

U.S. lawn tennis men's singles champion, Robert D. Wrenn; **women's singles champion,** Helen R. Helwig.

May 15 20th annual **Kentucky Derby** won by the favorite, *Chant,* ridden by jockey Goodale. Time was 2:41 on a fast track for winnings valued at $4020.

June 16 **Squeeze play** 1st employed in baseball by George Case and Dutch Carter, players on the Yale team, in a game against Princeton. Squeeze play is a batting maneuver in which, with a runner at 3d and with less than 2 out, the batter bunts the ball slowly to the infield, enabling the runner on 3d to come home safely. It was introduced in the major leagues in 1904 by Clark Griffith. There are 2 types of squeeze play now in use. One type is called the "delayed" squeeze, in which the runner on 3d does not move toward the plate until the ball has been bunted. The other, more dramatic, type is called the "suicide" squeeze, in which the runner on 3d breaks toward home plate with the delivery of the pitcher.

June 28 Congress approved resolution to make **Labor Day** a legal holiday.

POLITICS AND GOVERNMENT; WAR; DISASTERS; VITAL STATISTICS.	BOOKS; PAINTING; DRAMA; ARCHITECTURE; SCULPTURE.

Aug. 27 **1st graduated income tax law** passed by predominantly Democratic Congress, after much acrimonious debate. Denounced by Sen. Sherman (Ohio) as "socialism, communism, devilism." Law was declared unconstitutional in the next year by the Supreme Court. It was part of the Wilson-Gorman Tariff Act, which became law without signature of Pres. Cleveland.

Sept. 1 **Fire** killed 500 persons at Hinckley, Minn., and 18 neighboring towns. Flames were swept along by hurricane. 500 fled in train from burning Hinckley station.

Dec. 14 New York police department **bribe disclosures** made when Police Capt. Creedon confessed to having paid $15,000 for his captaincy.

Dec. 29 40 persons killed by **fire** during a Christmas festival at Silver Lake, Ore.

This book has possibly sold over 1,000,000 copies in the U.S.

Wealth Against Commonwealth, an impassioned attack on "trusts," written by **Henry Demarest Lloyd.** Became an exceedingly popular book.

July 26 Economics and politics brought into the theater by the plays of **Augustus Thomas.** *New Blood* opened today in Chicago during the great Pullman strike. It presents conflict between labor and capital. *The Capitol,* set in Washington, deals with lobbyists, coal strikes, railroad pools, religion, and government. Thomas wrote more than 60 plays, most of them social comedies. His most famous play is *The Witching Hour* (1907). Lionel Barrymore appeared in his most serious popular play, *The Copperhead* (1918), which deals with the Civil War.

1895

Feb. 8 U.S. Treasury bought with bonds $62 million in **gold** from banking houses of Morgan and Belmont. Gold reserves had fallen to $41 million. Revival of business activity in 1896 eased seriousness of further falls in gold reserve; but gold hoarding did not cease until after election of 1896 when future of gold standard was assured.

Feb. 24 **Revolt against Spanish rule** broke out in Cuba. On June 12 Pres. Cleveland called on U.S. citizens to avoid giving aid to insurgents. Part of cause of rebellion was panic of 1893 which caused severe economic depression in Cuban sugar industry. Repressive measures taken by Spanish aroused American sympathy, which was inflamed to war pitch by the "yellow journalism" of William Randolph Hearst's New York *Journal* and Joseph Pulitzer's *New York World.*

Mar. 5 A minority of the House Demo-

Fin de siècle best seller lists were noted for historical fiction and romances, which dominated the literary scene for about a decade. Some of the more famous titles were: *The Prisoner of Zenda* (1894), *Graustark* (1901), *Quo Vadis* (1896), *When Knighthood Was in Flower* (1899), *Dorothy Vernon of Haddon Hall* (1902), *Janice Meredith* (1899), *To Have and to Hold* (1900), and the justly famous masterpiece *The Red Badge of Courage* (1895).

One of most famous of American editors, **William A. White** purchased the *Emporia Gazette* of Kansas and aroused nation by editorial, "What's the Matter with Kansas?" A committeeman for Progressive Party in 1912, White set the pattern of the newspaper toward a liberal Republican point of view which it maintained.

Statue of Shakespeare modeled for the Library of Congress by **Frederick MacMonnies.** Desiring it to be as authentic as possible, he followed the bust of the

370

row, who at this time 1st came into national prominence.

July 16 Many Negro miners killed when they were attacked by disgruntled strikers in Alabama.

July 20 U.S. troops withdrawn from Chicago. On Aug. 3 **Pullman strike** called officially over by American Railway Union. Strike failed.

Sept. 4 12,000 tailors struck in New York city in protest against the task work and sweating systems.

Fall Baltimore won the **National League baseball pennant** with a season record of 89 victories, 39 defeats.

Dec. 22 United States Golf Association formed at a meeting of 5 golf clubs from Long Island, Brookline, Mass., Rhode Island, and Chicago. Many clubmen had felt the necessity for a national organization to conduct championships, to standardize rules of play, and settle questions of amateur status. U.S.G.A. held its **1st amateur championship** in 1895 at Newport, R.I. C. B. Macdonald won over the 32 entrants. **1st open championship,** held the next day, was won by Horace Rawlins.

1895

George Westinghouse made significant contribution to American industry by his construction of **huge power generators** at Niagara Falls. 1st generator capable of a widespread distribution of hydroelectric power.

Establishment of the **Yerkes Observatory** by the University of Chicago enabled American astronomers to achieve preeminence with the help of the most powerful refracting telescopes in the world. The Observatory is located at Lake Geneva, Wisc.

Jan. 14–Feb. 2 Trolley railroad strike in Brooklyn, N.Y., accompanied by riots which forced intervention of New York and Brooklyn militia.

Jan. 22 1st meeting of National Association of Manufacturers held at Cincinnati, Ohio; attended by representatives of several hundred manufacturing firms.

1st noticeable tendency to **shorten women's skirts** came in bicycling costumes. Skirts were shortened an inch or 2 from the ankle and the hems weighted with lead.

1st drawings by Charles Dana Gibson appeared in reproductions. **"Gibson Girl"** became ideal of most Americans. "Gibson Man" more responsible than any other single factor for the disappearance of mustaches and for the shoulder padding in well-tailored coats.

1st movies were made in obscure circumstances. Some of the early names were: kineopticon, animatograph, cinematograph, nickelodeon, biograph.

New baseball regulation established the infield "pop fly" rule, which provided that when runners were on 1st and 2d, or on 1st, 2d, and 3d, with less than 2 out, any fly ball which could be caught by an infielder was declared automatically out even before it was caught. This rule was intended to protect the runners from force plays made possible by a fielder inten-

POLITICS AND GOVERNMENT; WAR; DISASTERS; VITAL STATISTICS.	BOOKS; PAINTING; DRAMA; ARCHITECTURE; SCULPTURE.

crats issued an appeal for the **free coinage of silver** at ratio of 16–1. Appeal was framed by Reps. Richard P. Bland of Missouri and William Jennings Bryan of Nebraska. This year saw several free silver conventions in the South and West, the most notable being held in Salt Lake City on May 15 with delegates from 17 states and territories.

Mar. 18 **Emigration of U.S. Negroes** to Liberia continued with departure of 200 from Savannah, Ga.

Sept. 27 **Irish National Convention** held at Chicago where physical force was discussed as a means of achieving freedom for Ireland from Great Britain.

Nov. 5 Territory of Utah adopted constitution that called for **woman suffrage.** Constitution came into effect Jan. 4, 1896, the day Utah entered the Union.

Nov. 6 40 persons killed by **boiler explosion** in the building of The *Evening Journal* at Detroit.

Dec. 21 Congress authorized Pres. Cleveland to appoint **Venezuelan Boundary Commission.** On July 20 Sec. of State Richard Olney asked Great Britain to arbitrate boundary dispute with Venezuela, basing U.S. interference on Monroe Doctrine. On Nov. 26 Lord Salisbury replied that dispute was not concern of U.S. But on Feb. 2, 1897 Venezuela and Great Britain agreed to arbitrate, and Commission was dissolved.

bard at Stratford and the Droeshout portrait. Others of his works in Congressional library are the personifications of *Humanities* and the *Intellect.*

"You've Been a Good Old Wagon but You've Done Broke Down," by Ben R. Harney, a white musician, published in Louisville, Ky. Although it was not called a rag, it contained authentic ragtime figures. Tune later became a standard one in New Orleans jazz repertoire.

"The Purple Cow," very early poem by **Gelett Burgess,** appeared in the 1st number of *The Lark,* amateur magazine of humor and light comment patterned after the *Chap Book.* Poem became probably the most widely known piece of verse in America.

Symphonic Sketches, by **George W. Chadwick,** begun. Chadwick, though a member of the "Boston Classicists," nevertheless took a livelier view of contemporary America than most of his fellow composers. His *Sketches* include "A Vagrom Ballad" which is based on hobo themes.

1st number of the *Philistine,* edited and mostly written by **Elbert Hubbard,** published at Aurora, N.Y. Known as "The Sage of Aurora," Hubbard was a disciple of William Morris. His best-known work was an essay called "Message to Garcia," (1899) which sold over 80,000,000 copies.

One of earliest skyscrapers, in which steel frame superseded solid masonry construction, built in Chicago: **Reliance Building,** designed by Burnham & Root.

Oct. **Stephen Crane's** American classic *The Red Badge of Courage.* This very realistic novel of the Civil War did not immediately reach its popularity because current taste was for sentimental historical fiction. But for the past 40 years *The Red Badge* has sold about 10,000 copies annually.

SCIENCE; INDUSTRY; ECONOMICS; EDUCATION; RELIGION; PHILOSOPHY.	SPORTS; FASHIONS; POPULAR ENTERTAINMENT; FOLKLORE; SOCIETY.

May 20 **Income tax clauses** of 1894 Tariff Act declared null and void by the Supreme Court by a vote of 5 to 4.

May 27 Supreme Court declared that Federal injunction preventing strikers from **interfering with interstate commerce** is legitimate.

June 11 1st U.S. patent for a **gasoline-driven automobile** by a U.S. inventor was issued to Charles E. Duryea. On June 26 of the previous year, a U.S. patent had been granted for a motor car developed in Germany by Karl Benz.

Nov. 2 **1st contest between self-propelled vehicles** in U.S. held at Chicago, Ill. A Benz motor wagon, imported and improved by Oscar Bernhardt Mueller, was only car to finish the race.

Nov. 5 Patent No. 549,160, filed in 1879, was issued to George B. Selden for his gasoline-driven automobile. Alleged infringements of the **Selden patent** brought about the most celebrated litigation in the history of the auto industry. In 1899 Selden assigned exclusive license for his motor car to the Electric Vehicle Company. Suits initiated by this company led, in 1903, to the formation of the Association of Licensed Automobile Manufacturers, which began to collect royalties from the industry for the Selden patent. The fledgling Ford Motor Company and a few other manufacturers not affiliated with the A.L.A.M. refused to pay the royalties, and suit was brought against the Ford company and one other in New York in 1903. The court upheld the validity of Selden's patent on Sept. 15, 1909. Ford appealed and the N.Y. Court of Appeals on Jan. 9, 1911, again ruled in favor of the Selden patent. But it was a pyrrhic victory for Selden and the Electric Vehicle Company: the patent was held to be restricted to the particular construction it described, and every important auto manufacturer used a motor significantly different from that of Selden's patent.

tionally dropping the pop fly. Other rules classified foul tips as strikes, restricted the length of a bat to 42 inches, and increased the size of the pitcher's slab from 12 x 4 in. (1894) to 24 x 6 in.

Belmar won the 29th annual **Belmont Stakes,** paying 6–1. Jockey was F. Taral; time was 2:11½ on a heavy track for winnings valued at $2700. This year the distance was 1¼ mi.

Belmar won the 19th annual **Preakness Stakes,** paying 3–1. Jockey was F. Taral; time was 1:50½ on a fast track for winnings valued at $1350.

U.S. lawn tennis men's singles champion, Fred H. Hovey; **women's singles champion,** Juliette P. Atkinson.

May 6 21st annual **Kentucky Derby** won by the favorite *Halma,* ridden by J. Perkins. Time was 2:37½ on a fast track for winnings valued at $2970.

Aug. 31 **1st "professional" football game** played in Latrobe, Pa., when Latrobe's team of profit-sharing players met the Jeannette, Pa., team. Latrobe hired a substitute quarterback, John Brallier, for $10 expenses, making him the game's **1st professional player.**

Fall Baltimore won the **National League baseball pennant** with a season record of 87 victories, 43 defeats.

Sept. 9 **American Bowling Congress** formed in Beethoven Hall, N.Y., to revive waning interest in once popular sport. Bowling alleys and matches had been taken over by gamblers and ruffians. Teams of businessmen or workers were often physically beaten in revenge after they had won their matches. The A.B.C. became the ruling body of bowling, standardized rules and equipment and planned national tournaments. Modern tenpin game became standard.

| POLITICS AND GOVERNMENT; WAR; DISASTERS; VITAL STATISTICS. | BOOKS; PAINTING; DRAMA; ARCHITECTURE; SCULPTURE. |

1896

Jan. 4 Utah admitted as a state, the 45th to join Union.

Feb. 28 House of Representatives passed resolution favoring the **granting of belligerent rights** to the Cuban revolutionists and urging president to offer his good offices to obtain peace. Senate passed resolution Apr. 6. Spain rejected offer May 22. Gen. Valeriano ("Butcher") Weyler arrived in Cuba Feb. 10, and began suppressing revolt ruthlessly.

May 18 Jim Crow Car Law of Louisiana declared constitutional by the Supreme Court in famous case *Plessy v. Ferguson,* which stated the "separate but equal doctrine." Thus segregation was legal if equal facilities were offered to both races. U.S. Supreme Court reversed this doctrine in a series of civil rights decisions May 17, 1954; May 31, 1955; Nov. 7, 1955. Chief Justice Earl Warren said in 1st of these decisions that the separate but equal doctrine had no place in the field of public education and maintained that separate facilities were inherently unequal.

May 27 Tornado caused 400 deaths in St. Louis and East St. Louis. Upwards of 120 were injured and more than 5000 were left homeless as the twister, which was preceded by rain and winds up to 120 mph, swept through the cities.

May 27–28 National Convention of the Prohibition Party met at Pittsburgh and nominated Joshua Levering of Maryland for the presidency and Hale Johnson of Illinois for the vice-presidency.

June 18 Republican National Convention held in St. Louis, Mo., where William McKinley of Ohio was nominated for the presidency and Garret A. Hobart of New Jersey was nominated for the vice-presidency.

Sarah Orne Jewett continued her sharp delineation of a dying Maine community in her collection of short stories, *The Country of the Pointed Firs.* Willa Cather regarded this book as one of the best written in America.

Mark Twain made an excursion into historical romance with his moving *The Personal Recollections of Joan of Arc by the Sieur Louis de Conte.* Against the background of cruelty, tyranny, and superstition he sets up the splendid girl of Orleans, with the immaculate, intelligent, and unselfish qualities which Twain idealized.

Book which created a furor was **Harold Frederic's** *The Damnation of Theron Ware,* a realistic study of religious hypocrisy. It tells the story of a Methodist minister of half-faith whose character deteriorates throughout the novel. Small-town Methodism is shown in its most unattractive side.

New York *World* began publication of "The Yellow Kid," by R. F. Outcault, generally thought to be the forerunner of modern **comic strips.** The Yellow Kid was a boy dressed in a bright yellow, sack-like garment. Outcault soon began to use words printed on the shirt, thus making the 1st time that a comic cartoon caption had appeared inside the frame of the picture.

1st exploits of "Mr. Dooley," written by **Finley Peter Dunne,** began to appear about this time in Chicago newspapers; became widely popular during Spanish-American War and remained so during 1st 2 decades of 20th century.

Edward MacDowell appointed head of Music Department at Columbia University. He stimulated interest in native American music through his use of Indian and Negro melodies in orchestral compositions.

1896

William Ashley Sunday (known as **Billy Sunday**) began his evangelical career. He had been a professional baseball player and had worked with the YMCA beginning 1891. Ordained Presbyterian minister Apr. 15, 1903; died 1935. Said to have preached to more people than any other Christian and to have been greatest single influence in promoting Prohibition.

Establishment of the **New York Aquarium** provided both a diversion for the public and an invaluable source for research for American ichthyologists.

⅞ths of America's wealth controlled by only ⅛th of its people.

Massachusetts Supreme Court, with Oliver Wendell Holmes dissenting, **denied workers the right to picket,** however peacefully. Holmes wrote at the time that his dissent probably would shut him off from all chances of further advancement as a judge.

Production of Duryea Brothers, automobile manufacturers, rose to 10 cars for the year. They were the outstanding figures in early U.S. automotive "industry" and easily won most of the road races in 1894, 1895, and 1896 with their cars.

Appellate Division of New York court **rejected plans to build a subway** in New York city, quoting St. Luke: "Which of you, intending to build a tower, sitteth not down first and counteth the cost, whether he have sufficient to finish it?" The argument was that an underground railroad would overtax the city's finances.

"Book" matches became popular in the U.S. for 1st time. They had been invented

"**Dorothy Dix**" (Mrs. Elizabeth M. Gilmer) began her column of personal advice in the *New Orleans Picayune*. This was **1st popular "advice to the lovelorn" feature** in a daily newspaper.

U.S.G.A. amateur championship won by H. G. Whigham at Shinnecock Hills, N.Y. He defeated J. G. Thorp 8 and 7. **Open championship** won by James Foulis with a score of 152.

Hastings won the 30th **Belmont Stakes,** paying 8–5. Jockey was H. Griffin; time was 2:24½ on a fast track for winnings valued at $3025. From this year to 1925 (except for 1904 and 1905) the distance was 1⅜ mi.

Margrave won the 20th annual **Preakness Stakes,** paying 4–5. Jockey was H. Griffin; time was 1:51 on a fast track for winnings valued at $1350.

U.S. lawn tennis men's singles champion, Robert D. Wrenn; **women's singles champion,** Elisabeth H. Moore.

Apr. 6 **1st modern Olympic Games** in Athens, Greece, dominated by a small group of Americans who arrived just as the roll of athletes for the 1st events was being called on April 6th. The U.S. team, out of condition from the long ocean trip, with no time to rest or limber up, won 9 of the 12 events. James B. Connolly, who won the 1st event, the hop, step, and jump, was the 1st Olympic champion to be crowned in 15 centuries. Revival of the games was brought about by the untiring efforts of a young French baron, Pierre de Coubertin of Paris. His plan, to hold international contests every 4 years, has

POLITICS AND GOVERNMENT; WAR; DISASTERS; VITAL STATISTICS.

BOOKS; PAINTING; DRAMA; ARCHITECTURE; SCULPTURE.

July 4–9 **National Convention of the Socialist Labor Party** met in New York city and nominated Charles H. Matchett of New York for the presidency and Matthew Maguire of New Jersey for the vice-presidency.

July 11 **Democratic National Convention,** meeting at Chicago, nominated William Jennings Bryan of Nebraska, a "dark horse," for the presidency. The day before, Bryan had, in his famous "Cross of Gold" speech, united the "Silverite" wing of the party and had taken the convention by acclaim. Platform advocated "free and unlimited coinage of both silver and gold at the present legal ratio of sixteen to one." Arthur Sewall of Maine was nominated for the vice-presidency.

July 22–24 **National Silver Republican Convention** held at St. Louis and nominated the Democratic candidates for the presidency and the vice-presidency. These western Republicans, under leadership of Sen. Henry M. Teller, had bolted the Republican Party when it had adopted a gold plank.

July 25 **People's Party National Convention** held at St. Louis, Mo., and William J. Bryan was nominated for the presidency and Thomas E. Watson of Georgia for the vice-presidency.

Sept. 2–3 **National Convention of the National Democratic Party** ("Sound Money" Democrats) met at Indianapolis and nominated John M. Palmer of Illinois for the presidency and Simon P. Buckner of Kentucky for the vice-presidency.

Oct. 1 **Rural free postal delivery** established.

Nov. 3 McKinley and Hobart defeated Bryan and Sewall in the **presidential elections,** by an electoral vote of 271–176. McKinley and the Republicans scored 7,104,779 popular votes; Bryan and the Democrats 6,502,925. Republicans retained control of both houses of Congress. Palmer received 133,148; Levering, 132,007; Matchett, 38,274.

"There'll Be a Hot Time in the Old Town To-Night," an adaptation of an old "coon song," written by Theodore A. Metz. 2 years later, during Spanish-American War, it became favorite song of American troops; was revived by AEF during World War I.

George E. Bissell's *Colonel Abraham de Peyster* completed. It now stands in the grassy square at Bowling Green. In 1902 a nominating committee composed of prominent sculptors named this work as one of New York city's finest pieces of sculpture.

Jan. 28 Best seller about a Carolina backwoods community, *The Jucklins,* by **Opie Read,** who wrote it to pay a gambling debt. It immediately sold over 100,000 copies. It is good regional literature, written by a man who knows his people.

Aug. 15 An editorial called "What's the Matter with Kansas?" appeared in the small-town Emporia, Kans., *Gazette.* Was reprinted in every important paper in the U.S., used as campaign literature by McKinley, and made the reputation of its author, **William Allen White,** overnight.

Oct. Remarkable best seller (in English translation) *Quo Vadis,* by **Henryk Sienkiewicz,** a Polish historical novelist. This novel's combination of religious themes and lurid sensationalism appealed to popular taste, and its total sale probably has been in the neighborhood of 2,000,000.

376

in 1892 by Joshua Pusey, an attorney, and in 1895 the Diamond Match Company bought his patent. At 1st they proved unpopular; but this year a famous brewery ordered 10 million "books" for advertising, and their future was secured.

Model airplane designed by Samuel P. Langley flew 1½ min. and traveled ½ mi. over the Potomac; model weighed 26 lb., had 14 ft. wingspan, was powered by a miniature steam engine.

Jan. 29   1st use in U.S. medical history of **X-ray treatment for breast cancer** made by Emil H. Grube.

June 4   At 2 A.M. in a brick workshed in Detroit, Henry Ford and his associates completed assembly of the **1st Ford automobile.** The road test of the car was delayed an hour or so because genius had overlooked one detail: the car was wider than the shed door and the men had to use the back of an axe to knock bricks out of the framework.

Aug. 12   **Discovery of gold** on Klondike Creek, about 3 mi. from Dawson in the Yukon territory of Northwest Canada. This sparked 2d great gold rush in U.S. history, the **Klondike Stampede** of 1897–98. News of strike reached U.S. in June, 1897, and within month thousands had left their homes. In 1898 there were about 18,000 people in the Klondike area. Total gold production from 1885–1929 exceeded $175 millions.

Sept. **Rose Hawthorne Lathrop,** 2nd daughter of Nathaniel Hawthorne, founded free home for destitute cancer victims in New York city. She and her husband, George Parsons Lathrop, were converted to Catholicism, and she later joined a Dominican community of nuns at Sherman Park, N.Y. As Mother Mary Alphonsa she became director of the Rosary Hill Home, a charitable organization.

been carried out, whenever a war did not interfere.

Apr. 23   **1st moving picture** on a public screen exhibited at Koster and Bial's Music Hall in New York city. The program consisted of two blonde girls performing the umbrella dance, a view of the violent surf breaking on a beach, a comic boxing exhibition between a tall, thin comedian and a short, fat one, a bit of comic allegory entitled, "The Monroe Doctrine," a moment of movement in a popular farce repeated again and again, and, finally, a performance of the skirt dance by a tall blonde. The program proved fascinating to all its viewers. Edison's associate, W. K. L. Dickson, hailed the technology of the motion picture exhibition as "an object of magical wonder, the crown and flower of nineteenth century magic." *The New York Times* of Apr. 24, reviewing the exhibition, found it "all wonderfully real and singularly exhilarating."

May 12   This year the **Kentucky Derby** was shortened to 1¼ miles and the favorite, M. F. Dwyer's *Ben Brush,* made the new distance in 2:07¾ on a good track to win the 22d Derby and $4850. Jockey was W. Simms.

July 7   Stirring sentence, **"You shall not crucify mankind upon a cross of gold,"** delivered by William Jennings Bryan at the Democratic National Convention. The reference is to the "gold faction," which opposed the free coinage of silver.

Fall Baltimore won the **National League baseball pennant** with a season record of 90 victories, 39 defeats.

Nov. **1st U.S. hockey league,** the Amateur Hockey League, organized in New York city. 1st league game was played a month later. Sport spread through the U.S., hockey teams playing in New England, Philadelphia, Pittsburgh, Chicago, and Washington, D.C.

| POLITICS AND GOVERNMENT; WAR; DISASTERS; VITAL STATISTICS. | BOOKS; PAINTING; DRAMA; ARCHITECTURE; SCULPTURE. |

1897

Jan. 12 National Monetary Conference met at Indianapolis, Ind., and endorsed existing gold standard. Commission appointed which later in year offered Congress plan for monetary system. With the free silver issue finally settled U.S. entered into decade of prosperity.

Feb. 2 Fire destroyed the Pennsylvania State Capitol at Harrisburg.

Mar. 2 Pres. Cleveland vetoed immigration bill that required a literacy test. He called it a "radical departure from our national policy."

Mar. 4 William McKinley, 25th president, inaugurated. He was a Republican and died by assassination after serving 6 months of his 2d term.

May 5 Greater New York city charter signed by governor; it went into effect Jan. 1, 1898. Total area: 326 square miles; total population: 3,400,000.

May 24 Congress voted $50,000 for **relief of Americans in Cuba.** Concessions made later this year by liberal Sagasta ministry in Spain, which included the recall of Gen. Weyler and release of imprisoned Americans, satisfied neither side in **Cuban rebellion.**

July 7 Republican Congress passed **Dingley tariff bill,** an upward revision of most categories. It was the highest tariff the U.S. had ever imposed.

July 14 $750,000 in gold, **1st large Klondike shipment of gold,** arrived in San Francisco. Another shipment of $800,000 arrived in Seattle July 17.

Extraordinary best seller *In His Steps* by **Charles M. Sheldon,** a minister of the Central Congregational Church of Topeka, Kan. It had been serialized in a magazine in 1896. In order to bring young people to the Sunday afternoon service the Rev. Mr. Sheldon gave a serialized fiction account from the pulpit of what people would do if they pledged themselves for a year to think and do as Jesus might do, each week ending at a moment of suspense. Eventually published, *In His Steps* had a worldwide sale. It has possibly sold 2,000,000 copies in the U.S. alone, and, since it was published in at least 20 foreign languages, it has sold several millions abroad.

New voice in American poetry was **Edwin Arlington Robinson,** who published a volume of verse *The Children of the Night,* containing many of his most famous lyrics. "Cliff Klingenhagen," "Richard Cory," "Credo" are among the many well-known poems. He had previously published *The Torrent and The Night Before* (1896).

"On the Banks of the Wabash," one of most popular songs ever written in America, composed at about this time by Paul Dresser. Later adopted as state song of Indiana. Dresser's real name was Dreiser; he was brother of Theodore Dreiser, who wrote the 1st draft of the lyric for the song.

Finest example of a U.S. public building which follows the principles of design taught in the 19th century at the Ecole des Beaux Arts, the **New York Public Library,** begun on Fifth Avenue from plans by Carrère and Hastings. It was finished in 1911.

1898

Jan. 25 U.S. battleship **Maine** arrived at Havana on a friendly visit. The real purpose of the Maine was to protect American life and property.

Unsuccessful court action brought against booksellers handling Gabriele D'Annunzio's *The Triumph of Death* by the Watch and Ward Society of Boston.

SCIENCE; INDUSTRY; ECONOMICS; EDUCATION; RELIGION; PHILOSOPHY.	SPORTS; FASHIONS; POPULAR ENTERTAINMENT; FOLKLORE; SOCIETY.

1897

1st subway in U.S., the Boston subway, completed.

Entire faculty of the Kansas Agricultural College dismissed on the ground that it did not support the political doctrines of populism.

Growing influence of osteopathy in U.S. reflected in formation of the **American Osteopathic Association.**

Feb. 17 **National Congress of Mothers** organized in Washington, D.C., by Mrs. Theodore W. Birney. Next year it became the National Congress of Mothers- and Parent-Teacher Associations, and in 1924 the National Congress of Parents and Teachers. Total membership in 1955: 9,409,282.

July 2 **Strike of coal miners** in Pennsylvania, Ohio, and West Virginia put 75,000 men out of work.

Sept. 10 More than 20 men killed when **coal mine strikers** were fired upon by deputy sheriffs at Hazelton and Latimer, Penn.

Sept. 11 **Coal miners' strike** ended in Pennsylvania, Ohio, and West Virginia. Miners won 8-hr. day, semimonthly pay, abolition of company stores, and biennial conferences.

Citizens of Cheyenne, Wyo., held **1st annual Frontier Day** at Fair Grounds; celebration has since become a 5-day wild west show, held annually in Frontier Park.

U.S.G.A. amateur championship won by H. G. Whigham at Chicago, G. C., Wheaton, Ill. He defeated W. R. Betts, 8 and 6. **Open championship** won by Joe Lloyd with a score of 162.

Scottish Chieftain won the 31st annual **Belmont Stakes,** paying 9–5. Jockey was J. Scherrer; time was 2:32¼ on a fast track for winnings valued at $3550.

Paul Kauvar won the 21st annual **Preakness Stakes,** paying 6–1. Jockey was Thorpe; time was 1:51¼ on a sloppy track for winnings valued at $1420.

U.S. lawn tennis men's singles champion, Robert D. Wrenn; **women's singles champion,** Juliette P. Atkinson.

Mar. 17 **"Gentleman Jim" Corbett,** one of the most popular champion prizefighters ever known in U.S., defeated by "Bob" Fitzsimmons on St. Patrick's Day in a 14-round contest. Corbett added the term, **"Solar plexus,"** to the prizefighting vocabulary. It was 1st boxing match photographed by a moving picture camera.

May 4 23d **Kentucky Derby** won by J. C. Cahn's *Typhoon II,* ridden by F. Garner. Time was 2:12½ on a heavy track for winnings valued at $4850.

Fall Boston won the **National League baseball pennant** with a season record of 93 victories, 39 defeats.

1898

Establishment of the **National Association of State Dairy and Food Departments,** an organization of public health officials from all the states which had them at that

Impassioned phrase **"Remember the Maine"** became war cry of Americans urging war with Spain. The battleship *Maine* had been destroyed by an undetermined

Feb. 9 De Lôme letter, written by Spanish minister to U.S., Señor Dupuy de Lôme, published in Hearst's New York *Journal.* This private letter was stolen by Cuban revolutionists from mails in Havana It characterized Pres. McKinley as "weak" and questioned his political integrity. Señor de Lôme immediately resigned.

Feb. 15 American battleship **Maine** blown up in Havana harbor; 260 seamen lost. U.S. sympathies were already strong for Cuba in the revolt against Spanish tyranny; the *Maine* disaster made U.S. intervention inevitable, though the cause of the sinking was never established.

Apr. 5 Pres. McKinley **recalled U.S. consuls** in Cuba.

Apr. 11 Pres. McKinley asked Congress for authorization to use armed force to compel **Spanish evacuation of Cuba;** did not mention *Maine* disaster in his message. On Apr. 19 Congress adopted resolutions declaring Cuba independent and directing the president to use forces of the U.S. to put an end to Spanish authority in Cuba.

Apr. 20 President signed the resolutions of Congress and an **ultimatum** was cabled to Spain through minister Woodford. But Woodford's passports were returned to him on Apr. 21 before he could deliver message.

Apr. 22 U.S. instituted a **blockade** of all Cuban ports.

Apr. 22 1st prize of the Spanish-American War taken by gunboat *Nashville,* which captured the Spanish ship, *Buena Ventura.*

Apr. 22 Volunteer Army Act, which permitted the organization of 1st Volunteer Cavalry, or **"Rough Riders,"** under command of Col. Leonard Wood and Lt. Col. Theodore Roosevelt.

Apr. 23 President issued a call for **125,000 volunteers** to fight in the war with Spain.

National Institute of Arts and Letters established by the American Social Science Association "for the furtherance of literature and the fine arts in the United States."

Stephen Crane showed his mastery of the short story in a published collection, *The Open Boat and Other Stories,* of which the title story is his masterpiece. In a telling objective fashion it is the story of a handful of men bobbing desperately on the ocean after the loss of their ship. Though simple men, their refusal to surrender to fate marks them as godlike.

"The Rosary," words by Robert Cameron Rogers and music by Ethelbert Nevin, published; it remained the most popular song in U.S. for more than 25 years, reaching its peak of sales 1911–16.

Bayard Building, designed by Adler and Sullivan, built in New York. Good example of low-relief work in terra cotta, favored by Louis Sullivan.

Tearing Down the Spanish Flag, one of the earliest dramatic scenes in an American film. J. Stuart Blackton directed the incident in a 10 x 12 room with the building next door as the background. While an operator manipulated the camera, Blackton tore down the Spanish flag from a pole and raised the American flag in its place. Blackton reported in a lecture at the University of Southern California in 1929 that the audiences "went wild."

Sept. 23 Famous and ever popular *David Harum,* published at $1.50. Its author, **Edward Noyes Westcott,** died 6 months before this best seller was published. It has sold well over a million copies. A mildly humorous novel of rural life, *David Harum* introduced the fad for what publishers called "b'gosh fiction."

Oct. Cyrano de Bergerac opened with Richard Mansfield in the lead at the Garden Theatre in New York. One of the most immediately popular plays ever presented in the U.S. Its author was Edmond Rostand, a Frenchman.

SCIENCE; INDUSTRY; ECONOMICS; EDUCATION; RELIGION; PHILOSOPHY.	SPORTS; FASHIONS; POPULAR ENTERTAINMENT; FOLKLORE; SOCIETY.

time; it became one of the primary advocates of a national pure food and drug law and of a federal department for food inspection.

Biltmore Forest School opened by Dr. Carl A. Schenck in Biltmore, N.C. School offered a 1-year course in forestry plus a 6-months course of field training. The school, which closed in 1914, was the 1st forestry school in U.S.

Nome, Alaska, founded as the result of a gold strike on the Seward Peninsula. Nome was named for a misspelling of a nearby cape on a map. The cape was referred to actually as "no name."

Battleship *Oregon,* essential to U.S. naval force in Gulf of Mexico during Spanish-American War, took 67 days (Mar. 19 to May 24) to sail from San Francisco to Key West. Trip was the most important factor in arousing Americans to the necessity of building a **canal** across the Panamanian isthmus.

June 1 **Erdman Arbitration Act** authorized governmental mediation between interstate carriers and their employees. It forbade interstate carriers to discriminate or blacklist union laborers. But on Jan. 27, 1908, the Supreme Court held the provision against discrimination unconstitutional according to 5th amendment. On July 15, 1914, Congress replaced Erdman Act by the Newlands Act, which set up a mediation board.

Oct. 12 13 persons were killed and 25 wounded in United Mine Workers' **strikers'**

explosion while docked in Havana. The American public was led to believe that it had been blown up by agents of Spain. This feeling easily fell in with American resentment against Spanish rule of Cuba.

U.S. lawn tennis men's singles champion, Malcolm D. Whitman; **women's singles champion,** Juliette P. Atkinson.

U.S.G.A. amateur championship won by Findlay S. Douglas at Morris County G.C., Morristown, N.J. He defeated W. B. Smith, 5 and 3. **Open championship** was won by Fred Herd at Myopia Hunt Club, Hamilton, Mass., with a score of 328.

Bowling Brook won the 32d annual **Belmont Stakes,** paying 7–2. Jockey was F. Littlefield; time was 2:32 on a heavy track for winnings valued at $7810.

Sly Fox won the 22d annual **Preakness Stakes,** paying 8–5. Jockey was W. Simms; time was 1:49¾ on a good track for winnings valued at $1500.

May 1 Adm. Dewey's exploits in the Battle of Manila Bay commemorated as **Dewey Day** by the Dewey Congressional Medal Men's Association, comprising the officers and enlisted men who participated in the battle. In recent years, the festivities have been concentrated in the Philadelphia Navy Yard where Admiral Dewey's flagship was kept after it was decommissioned in 1922. Congress authorized award of **"Dewey Medal,"** a campaign decoration, to all officers and men who served under Dewey in Battle of Manila Bay.

May 4 24th **Kentucky Derby** won by J. E. Madden's *Plaudit.* Time was 2:09 on a good track for winnings valued at $4850. This was jockey Simms's 2d Derby winner (1st was *Ben Brush* in 1896).

381

| POLITICS AND GOVERNMENT; WAR; DISASTERS; VITAL STATISTICS. | BOOKS; PAINTING; DRAMA; ARCHITECTURE; SCULPTURE. |

Apr. 24 Spanish refusal to comply with demands of U.S. Congressional resolution concerning Cuban independence precipitated **Spanish-American War.** Spain recognized state of war Apr. 24; U.S. declared on Apr. 25 that state of war had existed since Apr. 21 when Spain broke diplomatic relations with U.S.

May 1 **Naval engagement** between American and Spanish fleets in Manila Bay ended with destruction of Spanish forces by Com. Dewey. Spanish casualties were heavy: 381 killed, while Americans counted only 8 men wounded.

May 25 Pres. McKinley called for **75,000 more volunteers** to help in the war against Spain.

May 25 **1st troop expedition to Manila** set sail with some 2500 men from San Francisco.

May 28 Supreme Court declared that native **citizenship** is without respect to race or color, and that a child born of Chinese parents in this country is a U.S. citizen and cannot be deported under Chinese Exclusion Act.

June 10 **War Revenue bill** passed by Congress and signed by the president on June 13. Bill authorized the government to make a loan up to $400 million and place a tax on liquor, tobacco, flour, and other items. Actually government sold only $200 million dollars of 3% bonds.

June 11 **About 600 marines landed** at Guantanamo, Cuba, and made contact with the enemy the next day.

June 12–14 **17,000 Americans embarked** under Gen. Shafter at Key West, Fla., to attempt an invasion of Santiago.

June 15 **Battle at Guantanamo Bay** in Cuba where the U.S. marines repulsed a Spanish force.

(Continued in next column)

Nov. 7 1st appearance in U.S. of **Madame Schumann-Heink,** in Chicago. Her New York debut was at the Metropolitan Opera House Jan. 9, 1899.

(Column 1 continued)

June 15 Joint resolution for the **annexation of Hawaii** adopted by the House of Representatives and was passed by the Senate on June 17. Signed by president July 7.

June 20 Pacific island of **Guam** surrendered to Capt. Glass on the U.S.S. *Charleston.* Spanish commander on the island obviously had not heard of war, for the previous day when Capt. Glass fired on the island a message was sent to the *Charleston* with an apology for not having returned the salute—there was no ammunition on the island.

June 22 Gen. Shafter's **invasion forces** landed at Daiquiri, 15 miles from Santiago. American casualties were 1 killed and 4 wounded.

June 24 Spaniards defeated at the battle of **Las Guásimas,** Cuba, in 1st land battle of the war. Engagement fought by Gen. Joseph Wheeler, Cols. Leonard Wood and Theodore Roosevelt, commanding 1000 regular troops and the "Rough Riders," who had pushed ahead of main army.

July 1–2 Americans, suffering heavy casualties, took **El Caney** and **San Juan.** "Rough Riders" participated in the attack.

July 3 **Spanish fleet,** under Adm. Cervera, destroyed by American warships in an attempt to escape from Santiago.

July 8 Adm. Dewey occupied **Isla Grande** in Subig Bay, near Manila. German gunboat, *Irene,* which had attempted to frustrate American operations, was forced to withdraw.

(Continued in next column)

SCIENCE; INDUSTRY; ECONOMICS; EDUCATION; RELIGION; PHILOSOPHY.	SPORTS; FASHIONS; POPULAR ENTERTAINMENT; FOLKLORE; SOCIETY.

riot at Virden, Ill., which broke out when employers attempted to replace the striking miners with Negro miners.

Fall Boston won the **National League baseball pennant** with a season record of 102 victories, 47 defeats.

(Column 1 continued)

July 17 Gen. Toral **surrendered Santiago and 24,000 Spanish troops** to Gen. Shafter. There were 5462 American casualties during the war, but less than 400 were actually killed in battle or died of wounds. More than 90 per cent of the American casualties were caused by disease.

July 21 **Final sea battle on Cuban coast** took place in the harbor of Nipe. Port taken by 4 U.S. warships after heavy bombardment.

July 25 American troops under Gen. Miles landed on **Guanica,** Puerto Rico, and took possession of the town after a brief encounter with the Spanish.

July 26 Spanish government asked for **peace terms** through the French Ambassador.

July 28 Town of **Ponce** surrendered to Gen. Miles. It was the 2d largest city of Puerto Rico.

July 31 Spanish attack repulsed by Americans under Col. Greene at **Malate,** near Manila. Both sides suffered heavy casualties.

Aug. 1 Some **4200 sick American soldiers** in Cuba, more than 3000 of whom had **yellow fever.**

Aug. 7 T. Roosevelt, the **"Rough Riders,"** and other troops left Santiago for Montauk Point, L.I., in order to escape sickness.

Aug. 9 Americans, under Gen. Ernst, defeated a Spanish force at **Coamo,** Puerto Rico.

(Continued in next column)

(Column 1 continued)

Aug. 9 Spanish government **formally accepted peace terms.**

Aug. 12 **Hostilities halted by protocol** in which Spain was to give up Cuba, cede Puerto Rico and 1 of Ladrone Islands to U.S. American forces were to occupy Manila pending a decision of peace treaty. See Dec. 10. Agreement signed at 4:30 P.M., which was 5:30 A.M., Aug. 13 in the Philippines. U.S. forces were engaged in **battle for Manila,** which surrendered after a short fight. This put an end to almost 100 years of rebellion against Spanish rule (11 revolts between 1807–72). The Philippines were "not to exploit but to develop, to educate, to train in the science of self-government," as Pres. McKinley said. On July 4th, 1946, this promise was fulfilled.

Sept. 9 **U.S. Peace Commissioners** appointed. Headed by Judge W. R. Day. They sailed for France on Sept. 17.

Nov. 8 **Theodore Roosevelt** nominated and elected to governorship of New York on Republican ticket. He was chosen by Republican bosses for his outstanding record with "Rough Riders" and because Republican Party needed a strong candidate to overcome evil effects of Erie Canal swindles the previous year.

Dec. 10 **Treaty ending Spanish-American War** signed in Paris. U.S. acquired Puerto Rico, Guam, and Spain relinquished claim to Cuba. See Aug. 12. Treaty was ratified by Congress Jan. 9, 1899. U.S. paid Spain $20 million for the Philippines.

1899

Feb. 4 Filipinos, under Aguinaldo, attacked the American forces at Manila, beginning a **battle** lasting several days. During the engagement 57 Americans were killed and 215 wounded, while some 500 Filipinos were killed, 1000 wounded, and 500 were made prisoners. This was the beginning of a **rebellion** against American rule that lasted until Mar. 23, 1901, when Aguinaldo was captured by Gen. Frederick Funston at Palawan, Luzon.

Feb. 10 **Peace treaty** with Spain signed by the president.

Mar. 30 Gen. MacArthur occupied **Malolos,** Luzon, Philippine Islands, forcing Gen. Aguinaldo to withdraw to Tarlac. Gen. MacArthur was the father of the famous Gen. Douglas MacArthur of World War II.

Apr. 27 More than 40 persons were killed and over 100 injured by a **tornado** which swept across northern Missouri.

Apr. 28 **Terms of armistice** proposed by Filipino peace commission to Gen. Otis who rejected them and demanded unconditional surrender.

May 18–July 29 **1st Hague Peace Conference.** Called by Czar Nicholas II of Russia. Its only signal success was the establishment of the Permanent Court of International Arbitration, strongly advocated by U.S. Arbitration was not to be considered compulsory.

June 12 Some 250 persons killed at New Richmond, Wis., by a **tornado** which tore through Minnesota and Wisconsin.

Nov. 24 Gen. Otis reported **Central Luzon** under U.S. control and that the president of the Filipino Congress, the Filipino secretary of state, and the treasurer were made prisoners. Only small, isolated bands of insurgents still continued to fight.

Dec. 2 **Samoan partition treaty** signed at Washington with Germany and England.

American **Winston Churchill's** best seller *Richard Carvel,* a historical novel dealing with the Revolutionary period. Churchill, because he was patriotic and because he took pains to depict the grand sweep of historical forces, was during this period the most popular novelist of middle-class American readers.

Charles Major's best seller *When Knighthood Was in Flower* belongs squarely in the tradition of historical romance, which dominated the fin de siècle novels. Major also wrote best selling *Dorothy Vernon of Haddon Hall* (1902). Both novels deal with 16th-century England.

John Stillwell Stark, music publisher, heard **Scott Joplin** playing piano at Maple Leaf Club in Sedalia, Mo. Stark persuaded Joplin to write down one of his tunes, and it was published under the title, "**Maple Leaf Rag.**" The tune became an immediate popular success and introduced the vogue for ragtime among white musicians and listeners throughout the U.S.

Song which typifies '90's for later generations, "**She Was Only a Bird in a Gilded Cage,**" composed. Not as popular at the time as other songs.

Jan. 15 "The Man with the Hoe," a poem by **Edwin Markham,** California school teacher, published in San Francisco *Examiner*. Within one week it had been reprinted by successive newspapers across the country to New York. The antitrust forces called it "the cry of the Zeitgeist," and it was the most popular poem in the U.S. by far. Poem was a social protest which pictured a farmer made brutal by hard work.

July 18 **Death of Horatio Alger, Jr.,** author of the "Alger Books," all about boys who, against great odds, struggled to success. He wrote 135 such books, their combined sales probably exceeding 16,000,-

| SCIENCE; INDUSTRY; ECONOMICS; EDUCATION; RELIGION; PHILOSOPHY. | SPORTS; FASHIONS; POPULAR ENTERTAINMENT; FOLKLORE; SOCIETY. |

1899

1st experimental U.S. mail collection by motor made by a Winton truck in Cleveland. 126 stops along 22 mi. of streets were made in 2 hrs. and 27 min., less than half the 6 hrs. time for a horse-drawn wagon. But the Post Office did not set up a motor vehicle division for 15 years.

John Dewey caused an upheaval in educational circles with the publication of *The School and Society*. Some of his key concepts were "learning by doing," instrumentalism, and the necessary shaping of man's environment by the fullest development through education of his native capacities.

Feb. 14 Congress authorized **voting machines** for federal elections if desired by the individual states.

Mar. Congress created an **Isthmian Canal Commission** to study plans for building interocean canal in Central America.

Apr. 24 $3.50 a day for underground miners and a closed shop was asked for **striking miners** at Wardner, Idaho. Employers refused to grant the closed shop. On Apr. 29 miners blew up mills and destroyed mining property estimated at $250,-000.

July 1 **The Gideons,** Christian Commercial Men's Association of America, organized by 3 commercial travelers at Janesville, Wis. 1st Gideon Bible was placed in Superior Hotel, Iron Mountain, Mont., in Nov. 1908.

Oct. 14 From the *Literary Digest:* "The ordinary 'horseless carriage' is at present a luxury for the wealthy; and altho its price will probably fall in the future, it will never, of course, come into as common use as the bicycle."

Dec. 22 Death of **Dwight L. Moody,** great evangelist of latter 19th century. Had

New baseball rule required a pitcher to complete a throw to 1st base if he had motioned in that direction to pick a runner off.

U.S. lawn tennis men's singles champion, Malcolm D. Whitman; **women's singles champion,** Marion Jones.

U.S.G.A. amateur championship won by H. M. Harriman at Onwentsia Club, Lake Forest, Ill. He defeated Findlay S. Douglas, 3 and 2. **Open championship** was won by Willie Smith at Baltimore, G.C. with a score of 315.

Half Time won the 23d annual **Preakness Stakes,** paying 1–1. Jockey was R. Clawson; time was 1:47 on a fast track for winnings valued at $1580.

Jean Bereaud won the 33d annual **Belmont Stakes,** paying 5–2. Jockey was R. Clawson; time was 2:23 on a fast track for winnings valued at $9445.

McKinley became **1st president to ride in an automobile** by taking a trip in a Stanley Steamer.

May 4 Only 3 horses ran in this year's **Kentucky Derby,** the 25th. Winner was the favorite, A. H. and D. H. Morris' *Manuel,* ridden by jockey F. Taral. Time was 2:12 on a fast track for winnings valued at $4850.

June 9 James J. Jeffries became **world heavyweight boxing champion** after knocking out Bob Fitzsimmons in 11th round at Coney Island, N.Y.

Fall Brooklyn won the **National League baseball pennant** with a season record of 88 victories, 42 defeats.

POLITICS AND GOVERNMENT; WAR; DISASTERS; VITAL STATISTICS.	BOOKS; PAINTING; DRAMA; ARCHITECTURE; SCULPTURE.

Samoan Islands were to be partitioned between the U.S. and Germany with U.S. receiving Tutuila with Pago Pago, its harbor.

000 copies. Among the more successful titles are *Ragged Dick, Luck and Pluck, Tattered Tom* (Tom was a girl).

1900

Population—75,994,575. Center of population: 6 mi. southeast of Columbus, Ind.

Number of Americans served by **rural free delivery** was 185,000; by 1924 number rose to 6,500,000.

Mar. 6–7 Social Democratic Party's national convention held at Indianapolis, Ind. **Eugene V. Debs** of Indiana was nominated for president, and Job Harriman of California for vice-president.

Mar. 14 Congress passed an act making **gold** the single **standard** of currency in the U.S. Made possible by increased gold production in South Africa and Klondike fields, the act put an end to the free silver controversy, although William Jennings Bryan and the Silverites continued to be active for 10 years more.

May 1 More than 200 men killed in a **mine explosion** at Scofield, Utah.

May 10 **Populist** (Fusion) **National Convention** held at Sioux Falls, S.D. William J. Bryan was nominated for the presidency and Charles A. Towne for the vice-presidency.

May 10 National convention of the **Populist** (middle-of-the-road) **Party** nominated Wharton Barker for the presidency, and Ignatius Donnelly for the vice-presidency at Cincinnati, Ohio.

May 14 Sanford Ballard Dole became **1st governor of Hawaii.** Dole had been born in Honolulu of American missionary parents. Since Hawaii was a territory, he was appointed by Pres. McKinley.

June 2–8 National convention of the **Socialist Labor Party** nominated Joseph P. Maloney for the presidency and Valentine Remmel for the vice-presidency at New York city.

In addition to the current liking for sentimental domestic novels the beginning of the 20th century saw a great demand for **adventure stories** dealing with the great outdoors. Pres. Roosevelt greatly influenced Americans in this sort of reading. His own books, *African Game Trails* (1910) and *The Winning of the West* (1889–96) were popular. Such writers as Jack London, Rex Beach, Robert W. Service, Owen Wister, Zane Grey, and Edgar Rice Burroughs capitalized on this popular taste. At the same time **reform books** were fairly successful. Among them are Frank Norris' *The Pit* (1903), American Winston Churchill's *Coniston* (1906), Upton Sinclair's *The Jungle* (1906), William Allen White's *A Certain Rich Man* (1909), and Vaughan Kester's *The Prodigal Judge* (1911). In this year 28 books and more than 150 magazine articles were devoted to the growth and menace of the "trusts"— by far the greatest political question of the day.

Beginning with the 20th century publishers realized for the 1st time that sales of **novels** well into the millions were possible. This reflects the vast American reading public and, although popular taste has never been highly literary, several of the more successful books may be considered classics.

1st novel by **Theodore Dreiser,** *Sister Carrie,* tentatively issued and then removed from sale by publisher. An unflinching naturalistic novel, it tells of the sordid rise of a girl and the deterioration of a man.

American sculptor signalized at Paris Exposition was **Hermon Atkins MacNeil,** whose figures of American Indian life won him a silver medal. Some of his Indian

SCIENCE; INDUSTRY; ECONOMICS; EDUCATION; RELIGION; PHILOSOPHY.

SPORTS; FASHIONS; POPULAR ENTERTAINMENT; FOLKLORE; SOCIETY.

great influence. With Ira D. Sankey, wrote many popular hymns: "The Ninety-and-Nine," "Hiding in Thee," "Where Is My Wand'ring Boy," etc.

Dec. 2 Army defeated Navy, 17–5, in the annual **Army-Navy football game** held at Franklin Field, Philadelphia, Pa.

1900

Survey of **Protestant religious sects** in U.S. at end of 19th century showed reformed and evangelical denominations in vast majority: 6,000,000 Methodists; 5,000,000 Baptists; 1,500,000 Lutherans; 1,500,000 Presbyterians; 350,000 Mormons; 80,000 Christian Scientists.

Illiteracy in America reached a new low of 10.7% of the population, a decline of 2.6% from 1890 and a decline of 9.3% from 1870.

International Ladies' Garment Workers Union established. At the time the average working week in the trade was 70 hours. Jacob A. Riis reported that **women sewing at home** for the clothing industry were earning 30¢ a day at best.

Infancy of **telephone service** in U.S. reflected in figure of 1,335,911 telephones in use.

Cigarette production in U.S. reached the 4,000,000,000 mark. Cigars, pipes, and chewing tobacco were much more popular than cigarettes, which were considered effete.

Survey indicated less than 8000 **automobiles** in U.S., and less than 10 mi. of **concrete pavement.**

Wright brothers, Orville and Wilbur, built their 1st full-scale **glider,** after several years of reading and experimenting with models. Glider incorporated their idea of "warped wings," predecessor of ailerons, the first successful device for lateral control of a flying airship. Glider was flown as a kite at Kitty Hawk, N.C., in Sept.

1st quantity-production **automobile factory** established by Olds Company in Detroit with capitalization of $350,000. Assembled one model only from parts

Only 12,572 dozen pairs of **silk stockings** sold in U.S., one pair to 2000 people. In 1921 18,088,841 pairs sold, one to each 6 persons.

Automobile was strictly a luxury. Most of the 76,000,000 Americans did their independent traveling with the help of horses and mules (there were approximately 18,-000,000) or on bicycles (about 10,000,-000). There were only 4000 automobiles, often denounced in the press as "an expensive luxury for the man who does not need one. It is well named the 'devil-wagon.' "

New **baseball rule** introduced the 5-sided home plate which is still used.

Biggest boost to the popularity of tennis was the putting up of the **Davis Cup** by Dwight F. Davis for competition in tennis between U.S. and England. Competition soon opened to teams of all nations. Thus, tennis, a game for the few in the 1870's and 1880's, became a game for the masses by the 1950's. This year the U.S. team won the cup. In 1901 there was no competition.

U.S. lawn tennis men's singles champion, Malcolm D. Whitman; **women's singles champion,** Myrtle McAteer.

U.S.G.A. amateur championship won by Walter J. Travis at Garden City G.C., N.Y. He defeated Findlay S. Douglas, 2 up. **Open championship** was won by Harry Vardon of England at Chicago G.C. with a score of 313.

Ildrim won the 34th annual **Belmont Stakes,** paying 7–2. Jockey was N. Turner;

POLITICS AND GOVERNMENT; WAR; DISASTERS; VITAL STATISTICS.

BOOKS; PAINTING; DRAMA; ARCHITECTURE; SCULPTURE.

June 21 **Republican National Convention** in Philadelphia nominated Gov. Theodore Roosevelt of New York, much against his own will, to run as Vice-Presidential candidate with William McKinley. Roosevelt felt he was being sidetracked from politics and would have been but for McKinley's assassination. One of most vigorous political campaigns ever conducted in U.S. put on by Roosevelt, who visited 24 states, traveled 21,000 miles, and made 700 speeches. McKinley conducted a "front porch campaign," never stirring from his home.

June 21 **Amnesty granted Filipino insurgents** by a proclamation issued by Gen. MacArthur.

June 27–28 National Convention of the **Prohibitionist Party** nominated John G. Woolley for the presidency, and Henry B. Metcalf for the vice-presidency at Chicago.

June 30 326 died when piers and steamship caught **fire** at Hoboken, N.J. Total damage was $10,000,000.

July 5 **Democratic National Convention** met in Kansas City, Mo., nominated William Jennings Bryan of Nebraska for presidency, Adlai E. Stevenson of Illinois for the vice-presidency. Platform denounced "colonial policy" of the Republican administration. Only opposition to Bryan had been from Admiral George Dewey, whose candidacy "blew up" when public disapproved his marriage to a Catholic lady.

Sept. 8 **Circular hurricane** killed 6000 at Galveston, Tex. Winds up to 120 mph drove Gulf waters over land. Afterwards looters were found with ringed fingers which they had cut from the swollen hands of the dead. Property damage amounted to $20,000,000. To assure quicker, more effective aid in future, 1st form of commission city government established.

Sept. 18 **1st direct primary** in U.S. tried in Minneapolis, Minn. Aroused considerable interest throughout country.

Nov. 6 Pres. McKinley and Theodore Roosevelt won the **presidential elections.**

pieces are *The Moqui Runner, A Primitive Chant,* and *The Sun Vow.* Returning to U.S. he did *President McKinley* for the McKinley Memorial in Columbus, Ohio, and a relief of General Washington for the Washington Arch on Washington Square, New York city.

During this period mysticism found expression in the paintings of **Albert Pinkham Ryder,** who spent most of his life in an unkempt, cluttered New York studio. Born into a seafaring family, he painted many marine subjects. His *Toilers of the Sea* pictures a dark sail silhouetted against a wan moon and clouds, the whole atmosphere giving off an aura of ghostliness and mystic strangeness.

Most **popular song** of the year was "Good-Bye, Dolly Gray," a war-time song about a soldier departing for the Philippines. This and "In the Good Old Summer Time" (1902), were among the best known songs of the 1st decade of the 20th century.

"The White Rats" formed as a union of actors patterned after the similarly named actors' organization in London. Union was established as a counterforce against a recently formed association of vaudeville managers whose main function was to keep actors' wages down via the "gentleman's agreement." As a result of the surprise appearance of "The White Rats," many vaudeville theaters shut down. Others retaliated against the actors' union by exhibiting motion pictures as the sole attraction. Thus, indirectly, "The White Rats" had a great influence on the development of motion pictures as a mass medium.

Spectacular **motion picture reportage** of American disasters in Bayonne, N.J., and Galveston, Tex., recorded in 2 on-the-spot films entitled *Destruction of the Standard Oil Company Plant at Bayonne,* and the *Galveston Cyclone.*

July 2 Remarkable best seller **Eben Holden** by Irving Bacheller. A book of

388

SCIENCE; INDUSTRY; ECONOMICS; EDUCATION; RELIGION; PHILOSOPHY.	SPORTS; FASHIONS; POPULAR ENTERTAINMENT; FOLKLORE; SOCIETY.

bought in quantity from other manufacturers. Made 400 cars first year, 1600 in the second; 4000 in the third. Paid 105% in cash dividends in 1st 2 years, the real beginning of the automotive industry.

Largest railroad of its time, the New York Central, controlled 10,000 mi. of track through 5 terminals in New York, Cincinnati, Boston, Chicago, and St. Louis. **Spectacular railroad growth** in 4 decades reflected in following figures: average freight weight, up from 15,000 tons to 100,000 tons; running time between New York and Chicago, down from 50 hrs. to 24 hrs.; and cost per ton of freight cut from $2 to 73¢.

Jan. 2 1st **autostage** appeared on Fifth Avenue, New York city. It was an electric bus seating 8 persons inside, 4 outside. Fare was 5¢.

Jan. 25 In last case involving **polygamous marriage** in Congress, the House of Representatives votes 268 to 50 to unseat Congressman-elect Brigham H. Roberts of Utah. He had 3 wives and an undetermined number of children.

Mar. 5 **"Hall of Fame"** founded for purpose of commemorating great Americans. First substantial gift amounting to $250,000 given by Mrs. Finley J. Shepard. New members are voted on every 5 years by a committee of 100 men and women from all the states. To be elected a nominee must have been dead at least 25 years, have been a citizen of the United States and receive ⅗ majority. Any citizen may make a nomination. A bust of the person nominated is placed in the open air colonnade at New York University known as the "Hall of Fame."

Mar. 24 **New Carnegie Steel Company** incorporated in New Jersey with capitalization of $160,000,000, making it one of largest and most talked-about corporations in U.S. Apr. dividend payments of **Standard Oil Company** for 1st quarter of 1900 amounted to $20,000,000; 15% was ordinary quarterly dividend, the rest extra.

time was 2:21½ on a fast track for winnings valued at $14,790.

Hindus won the 24th annual **Preakness Stakes,** paying 15–1. Jockey was H. Spencer; time was 1:48⅖ on a fast track for winnings valued at $1900.

Jan. 29 **New baseball league** formed in Chicago. **American League** demanded recognition as major league, which was refused by National League until 1903 when National, American, and minor leagues joined forces as "Organized Baseball" and set up a ruling body known as National Commission.

Mar. 18 **Maud S.,** one week less than 26 years old, died. Race track queen longer than any other horse of her generation, beloved by millions. Her record for mile was 2:08.75, made at Cleveland, Oct. 20, 1891. Owned by Robert Bonner, who had bought her from William H. Vanderbilt for $40,000.

Spring Mrs. **Carry Nation** initiated her antiliquor crusade when she led a group of women through Kansas. Many liquor-selling establishments were either damaged or destroyed by them.

Apr. 15 1st well-organized **automobile race** in U.S. held at Springfield, L.I. Won by A. L. Riker with an electric car; he covered 50 mi. in 2 hr., 3 min.

Apr. 30 At 3:52 A.M. railroad engineer **Casey Jones died** at the throttle slowing down his crashing "Cannonball" to save his passengers' lives. Memory perpetuated in ballad and folk tales. In April, 1950, U.S. Postal Service issued stamp bearing his name and likeness.

May 3 26th annual **Kentucky Derby** won by the favorite, C. H. Smith's *Lieutenant Gibson,* ridden by jockey J. Boland.

POLITICS AND GOVERNMENT; WAR; DISASTERS; VITAL STATISTICS.	BOOKS; PAINTING; DRAMA; ARCHITECTURE; SCULPTURE.

Popular vote: McKinley, 7,219,530; Bryan, 6,358,071; Woolley, 209,166; Debs, 94,768; Barker, 50,232. Electoral vote: McKinley, 292; Bryan, 155.

Dec. 29 State Department announced that all negotiations for the purchase of Danish West Indies (Virgin Islands) had been completed; only an appropriation from Congress was needed to bring about transfer. However, this did not occur for another 17 years.

folksy humor and country life, *Eben Holden* was in part inspired by the very popular *David Harum.* Bacheller's book sold 50,000 copies in 3 mos.; 300,000 by Christmas. It has probably sold over 750,-000 copies in the U.S.

1901

Socialist Party organized by merger of Social Democratic Party under Eugene V. Debs and reformist section of Socialist Labor Party under Morris Hillquit.

Feb. 2 U.S. Army Dental Corps created by Congress.

Feb. 2 Army Nurse Corps organized as branch of U.S. Army.

Mar. 2 Platt amendment adopted by Congress. It was a series of provisions which the Cubans had to append to their new constitution before U.S. would withdraw its troops. In effect, amendment established a quasi-protectorate over Cuba. Amendment was abrogated May 29, 1934.

Mar. 4 Pres. McKinley inaugurated for his 2d term. Theodore Roosevelt was his vice-president.

Mar. 13 Benjamin Harrison died at the age of 67. He is buried at Indianapolis, Ind.

Mar. 23 Emilio Aguinaldo, leader of Philippine insurgents, captured by American patrol under command of Brigadier-General Frederick Funston in province of Isabela, Luzon.

Apr. 19 Rebellion in the Philippines ended by proclamation. It had been the most unpopular "war" ever fought by U.S., many Americans believing that insurgent Filipinos should be given their independence.

American Winston Churchill's popular historical novel, *The Crisis,* dealing with events of the Civil War. One of the elements that help to account for the popularity of Churchill's novels was his interesting characterizations of historical figures. *The Crisis* introduces Lincoln and Grant.

Most powerful novel of the decade was Frank Norris' epic of the wheat fields in California, *The Octopus.* 1st of a projected trilogy (which was never finished), it tells of the struggles between the farmers of the San Joaquin Valley and the Railroad Trust. Social and economic forces, Nature herself, are represented as the determining factors in molding men's lives. *The Pit* (1903) carries the epic of wheat to the grain markets of Chicago, where the "bulls" and "bears" wrestle with one another.

Best seller Graustark by George Barr McCutcheon. This stirring romance promoted the thesis that American males are the most handsome and daring in the world. Graustark, like Anthony Hope's Zenda, was a mythical Balkan kingdom. The hero, Grenfall Lorry, wooes its Princess, Yetive. Total sales over 2,500,000.

Combination of Impressionism and a Venetian love of pageantry marks paintings of Maurice Prendergast. Returning from Paris, where he was the 1st important American painter to recognize the genius of Cézanne, he painted many beach scenes.

390

Largest quarterly dividend ever declared by corporation up to this time.

Sept. 17 Strike of 112,000 miners in coal fields sent **price of anthracite** in New York from $1 to $6.50 per ton. Strike ended Oct. 25 with a settlement favorable to the workers.

Nov. 15 **Carnegie Institute of Technology,** more popularly known as Carnegie Tech, established by steel millionaire and benefactor, Andrew Carnegie.

Time was 2:06¼ on a fast track (best yet); value: $4850.

Fall Brooklyn won the **National League baseball pennant** with a season record of 82 victories, 54 defeats.

1901

Report of Yellow Fever Commission read to Pan-American Medical Congress at Havana. Commission reported experiments definitely proving for 1st time that **yellow fever** is transmitted by mosquito (Stegomyia Calopus). Theory had been held for 20 years by Dr. Carlos Finlay of Havana, but he had been unable to offer definite proof and had been ridiculed by medical profession. Commission sent by U.S. government to Cuba after Spanish-American war included Walter Reed, Aristides Agramonte, Jesse W. Lazear, James Carroll. Drs. Lazear and Carroll both died from effects of yellow fever contracted during experiments.

New York in a Blizzard, one of the **1st panoramic films** made in America, described in the Edison Catalogue of 1901–1902. "Our camera is revolved from right to left and takes in Madison Square, Madison Square Garden, looks up Broadway from South to North, passes the Fifth Avenue Hotel, and ends looking down 23rd Street West." Panoramic films were made practicable by a new device on motion picture cameras, which made it possible to rotate the camera, or "pan" it. Thus, the "panning" or panoramic shot came into existence as one of the most significant and most lasting developments in camera technique.

2d full-scale **glider** built by Wright brothers and flown as a kite at Kitty Hawk,

U.S. lawn tennis men's singles champion, William A. Larned; **women's singles champion,** Elisabeth H. Moore.

U.S.G.A. amateur championship won by Walter J. Travis at Atlantic City, N.J. He defeated W. E. Egan, 5 and 4. **Open championship** won by Willie Anderson at Myopia Hunt Club, Hamilton, Mass., with a score of 331.

Commando won the 35th annual **Belmont Stakes,** paying 7–10. Jockey was H. Spencer; time was 2:21 on a fast track for winnings valued at $11,595.

The Parader won the 25th annual **Preakness Stakes,** paying 9–20. Jockey was Landry; time was 1:47⅕ on a heavy track for winnings valued at $1605. From this year until 1907 distance was 1 mi. and 70 yd.

Apr. 29 27th annual **Kentucky Derby** won by F. B. Van Meter's *His Eminence* ridden by jockey J. Winkfield. Time was 2:07¾ on a fast track for winnings valued at $4850.

Aug. 21 **"Iron Man" Joe McGinnity** expelled from the National League for stepping on umpire Tom Connolly's toes, spitting in his face, and punching him. McGinnity was reinstated later because of fans' pleas after receiving stiff fine and official rebuke.

POLITICS AND GOVERNMENT; WAR;
DISASTERS; VITAL STATISTICS.

BOOKS; PAINTING; DRAMA;
ARCHITECTURE; SCULPTURE.

May 3 Jacksonville, Fla., **conflagration** consumed 1700 buildings, caused $11,000,-000 damage, and made 10,000 homeless.

May 27 Supreme Court decision on the so-called **"Insular Cases"** stated that territories acquired as a result of Spanish-American War were neither foreign countries nor part of the U.S. Point was important in establishing a tariff policy toward Puerto Rico and the Philippines.

Sept. 6 **Pres. McKinley** shot during public reception at the Pan-American Exposition in Buffalo, N.Y., by Leon F. Czolgosz, thought by most to be a half-crazy anarchist. Doctors at first thought McKinley would recover; he had received 2 bullets in the stomach, and the wounds seemed to be healing. But gangrene set in.

Sept. 14 **William McKinley** died at the age of 58. He is buried at Canton, Ohio. **Theodore Roosevelt** sworn in as 26th president in same house in Buffalo where body of McKinley awaited transportation to his home. He served McKinley's remaining term of 3 years, 5 months, and was elected for another term in 1904.

Nov. 18 **Hay-Pauncefote Treaty** signed, abrogating Clayton-Bulwer Treaty. British consented to American control of the Isthmian Canal. Senate ratified treaty Dec. 16.

His water color *East River* now hangs in the Museum of Modern Art.

Works in sculptural portraiture of **Herbert Adams** exhibited at the American Exhibition and received high praise. Here were seen his *Portrait of a Young Lady, Rabbi's Daughter,* and *Julia Marlowe.*

March **"High Society,"** composed by Porter Steele; it later was adopted by jazz musicians of New Orleans as a standard tune for "hot" treatment.

Mar. 21 It was reported in *Life* that **"Uncle Tom's Cabin** is today the greatest money-maker of any attraction on the stage of New York City." It was true as well of every other city in the U.S. But 10 years later it was seldom played.

Oct. 7 Real romantic flavor evident in plays of **Booth Tarkington.** *Monsieur Beaucaire,* which opened in Philadelphia tells story of French nobleman of 18th century who comes in contact with English society. *The Man from Home* (coauther Harry Leon Wilson—1908) sets an American in Sorrento; *Getting a Polish* (1910) similarly places an American widow in Paris; *Mr. Antonio* (1916) contrasts a simple Italian organ-grinder with Pennsylvania community.

1902

Traditional blue **uniforms of U.S. Army** discarded in favor of olive drab, despite protests of sentimentalists who remembered "the boys in blue." Experience during Spanish-American War had taught that blue is decidedly too good a target.

Jan. 24 Treaty with Denmark for purchase of **Dutch West Indies** signed. U.S. Senate approved treaty, but Danish Rigsdag rejected it. In 1917, after Danish plebiscite favored sale (Dec. 14, 1916), the islands St. Croix, St. Thomas, and St. John, all part of the **Virgin Island** group, were finally purchased for $25 million.

Mar. 6 **Permanent Bureau of the Census office** established.

National Educational Association adopted **simplified spellings** for 12 words, viz.: program, tho, altho, thoro, thorofare, thru, thruout, catalog, prolog, decalog, demagog, pedagog.

1st of the last great novels of **Henry James** is *The Wings of the Dove,* the story of the dying American girl Milly Theale, who is caught up in the mercenary scheme of an English girl.

Vogue for outdoor life encouraged by **Theodore Roosevelt's** *Outdoor Pastimes of an American Hunter.* He was followed by such writers as **Stewart Edward White,** who wrote 4 novels in the decade stressing the active life in the open air. **John Muir**

SCIENCE; INDUSTRY; ECONOMICS; EDUCATION; RELIGION; PHILOSOPHY.

SPORTS; FASHIONS; POPULAR ENTERTAINMENT; FOLKLORE; SOCIETY.

N.C. Built on basis of tables by Otto Lilienthal, German scientist, who worked out ratio of wing area to forward motion required to sustain flight, glider crashed; Wrights, much discouraged, returned to Dayton, and later worked out new tables.

Jan. 4 **Andrew Carnegie** sold his interest in the Carnegie Steel Company and spent the next 20 years distributing his wealth in benefactions amounting to $350 million.

Jan. 10 1st great **oil** strike in Texas launched a fabulous era in the Southwest. The Spindletop claim near Beaumont, Tex., owned by Anthony F. Lucas, blew in on this date to open the door to savage financial struggles over oil that have persisted to this day.

Mar. 12 **1st extensive public library system** in New York city made possible by a gift of $5,200,000, providing for 39 branches, from Andrew Carnegie. Department now has 69 branches.

Fall Pittsburgh won the **National League baseball pennant** with a season record of 90 victories, 49 defeats.

Fall Chicago won the **1st American League baseball pennant** with a season record of 83 victories, 53 defeats.

Sept. 2 Popular saying **"Speak softly and carry a big stick"** employed by Theodore Roosevelt a few weeks after his acceptance of the presidency. Sentence, emphasizing the need for strong official policy, caught the fancy of the entire nation and "the big stick" proved to be a Godsend to cartoonists.

Oct. 18 One of most talked-of luncheons ever given in U.S., Pres. Roosevelt's to Negro educator **Booker T. Washington.** There was widespread Southern resentment.

Nov. 30 **Army** defeated Navy in their annual football contest by a score of 11 to 5. The game was held at Philadelphia, Pa.

1902

Feb. Announcement by Dr. Charles Wardell Stiles of the discovery of the **hookworm.** He declared "poor whites" in South were neither lazy nor innately slovenly, but were suffering on a wide scale from debilitating effects of the parasite. Antihookworm campaign begun throughout South, widely supported by Rockefeller Foundation.

Survey showed that **average wage** of shopgirls in North and West Ends of Boston was $5 to $6 a week.

Mar. 10 1st decisive act of **Pres. Theodore Roosevelt,** 3 months after the assassination of McKinley, was his announcement that the government would prosecute

U.S. lawn tennis men's singles champion, William A. Larned; **women's singles champion,** Marion Jones.

U.S.G.A. amateur championship won by L. N. James at Glen View G.C., Golf, Ill. He defeated E. M. Byers, 4 and 2. **Open championship** won by Lawrence Auchterlonie at Garden City G.C., N.Y., with a score of 307.

Old England won the 26th annual **Preakness Stakes,** paying 9–5. Jockey was L. Jackson; time was 1:45⅘ on a sloppy track for winnings valued at $2240.

Masterman won the 36th annual **Belmont Stakes,** paying 13–5. Jockey was J.

| POLITICS AND GOVERNMENT; WAR; DISASTERS; VITAL STATISTICS. | BOOKS; PAINTING; DRAMA; ARCHITECTURE; SCULPTURE. |

Apr. 29 **Chinese Exclusion Act** extended to prohibit immigration of Chinese laborers from the Philippine Islands.

May 20 U.S. flag lowered from government buildings in **Cuba** and replaced with flag of new Cuban government. Cuban independence achieved 4 years after end of Spanish-American War.

June 17 **Reclamation Act** passed by Congress. Beginning of conservation in U.S., it gave president authority to retain public lands as part of public domain. Beginning of the federal park system. Act also provided a fund obtained from sale of public lands to irrigate arid Western areas.

June 28 **Isthmian Canal Act** passed by Congress. It authorized the financing and building of a canal across the Isthmus of Panama. If president could not obtain concession from Panama Canal Company of France (which he eventually did for $40,000,000) and could not negotiate a proper treaty with Colombia, act authorized canal through Nicaragua. Treaty difficulties were obviated by revolt of Panama from Colombia Nov. 1903, and the new republic immediately granted a 10-mi.-wide strip of land for a canal.

July 1 **Philippine Government Act** passed by Congress. It declared the Philippine Islands an unorganized territory, its inhabitants citizens of the islands. It authorized a commission, appointed by the president, to govern territory. On July 4 president issued an order establishing civil government and granting full amnesty to all political prisoners.

Sept. 3 **Pres. Theodore Roosevelt** escaped serious injury near Pittsfield, Mass., when the coach he was riding in collided with a trolley car. Secret Service agent Craig was killed in the accident, while the President suffered but minor injuries.

staged his fight for national parks (1901) and **John Burroughs** turned out many articles and books during the decade.

Florodora, phenomenally successful musical, closed in New York after 547 performances. Most popular feature was its famous sextet, of six beautiful girls and their escorts, who sang "Tell Me, Pretty Maiden."

One of most popular **"coon songs"** of the year was Hughie Cannon's "Bill Bailey, Won't You Please Come Home," which was later taken up by Negro jazz musicians in the South.

Violence is not the only note struck by representatives of "Ashcan" school of painting. In **Robert Henri's** *New York Street in Winter,* evening falls over snow covered street lined by tenements. Mood is that of sadness and nostalgia.

Report of the **McMillan Commission** for the reconstruction of Washington, D.C. In general, followed up original 18th century designs of L'Enfant. Created Mall from White House to Lincoln Memorial, which required removal of Pennsylvania R.R. and building of Union Station.

Apr. *The Virginian* by **Owen Wister,** a story of outdoor life in Wyoming noted for its humor and good writing. It was reprinted 14 times in 8 months; in 2 years it had sold 300,000 copies. Its total sales have been well over a million.

Nov. 3 Study of character, especially with emphasis on people possessing a strong single virtue or vice, characterizes major works of playwright **Clyde Fitch.** *The Stubbornness of Geraldine,* which opened this night, is a study of fidelity; *The Girl with the Green Eyes* (1902) probes jealousy; *The Truth* (1906) deals with lying.

SCIENCE; INDUSTRY; ECONOMICS; EDUCATION; RELIGION; PHILOSOPHY.	SPORTS; FASHIONS; POPULAR ENTERTAINMENT; FOLKLORE; SOCIETY.

the Northern Securities Company, a J. P. Morgan interest, under the Sherman Anti-Trust Law. McKinley had let the law lie dormant, despite the rapid growth of holding companies under his administration.

May 12 **Strike of anthracite coal miners** began in Pennsylvania. 140,000 miners were idle. It was called by United Mine Workers after union president John Mitchell's suggestion of arbitration had been refused by mine operators. Miners had requested a 20% increase in wages and an 8-hr. day.

June 15 Time of Chicago–New York run reduced by **New York Central Railroad** to 20 hr.

July 30 **Intervention of militia** required to restore order among rioting anthracite miners at Shenandoah, Pa.

Aug. 12 **International Harvester Company** became incorporated in New Jersey with a capital of $120 million. It controlled 85% of production of agricultural machinery.

Sept. Wright brothers' 3d **glider,** built according to new calculations of pressures, drift, and resistance, flown successfully at Kitty Hawk, N.C. During September and October nearly 1000 flights were made, several more than 600 ft.

Oct. 16 Commission named by Pres. Roosevelt to settle **anthracite coal miners' strike.** Judge George Gray appointed head of commission. On Oct. 21 John Mitchell of United Mine Workers declared **strike at an end** after workers had accepted commission's arbitration at a convention in Wilkes-Barre, Pa. Refusal of coal operators to accept arbitration at beginning of strike aroused much popular opinion against big trusts, and consequently Pres. Roosevelt's announced policy of enforcing antitrust laws, which former Pres. McKinley had largely ignored, was given considerable popular support.

Bullman; time was 2:22½ on a fast track for winnings valued at $13,220.

1st postseason bowl football game was held at the Tournament of Roses. Michigan defeated Stanford, 49–0.

May 3 28th annual **Kentucky Derby** won by T. C. McDowell's *Alan-a-Dale,* ridden by jockey J. Winkfield (his 2d straight Kentucky Derby win). Time was 2:08¾ on a fast track for winnings valued at $4850.

Aug. 8 **Davis Challenge Cup** won by the American team defeating the British 3 matches to 2 at the Crescent Athletic Club grounds, in Brooklyn, N.Y.

Aug. 19 **National Lawn Tennis Championship** was won by W. A. Larned, who defeated R. F. Doherty in the final round, at the Casino, Newport, R.I.

Aug. 31 Mrs. Adolph Ladenburg, at Saratoga, N.Y., rode astride her horse, created considerable stir in press. She wore a **split skirt** and declared it much more comfortable and no more immodest than riding costumes for side-saddle use.

Fall Pittsburgh won the **National League baseball pennant** with a season record of 103 victories, 36 defeats.

Fall Philadelphia won the **American League baseball pennant** with a season record of 83 victories, 53 defeats.

Nov. 29 **Army** defeated Navy, 22–8, in their annual football classic at Franklin Field, Philadelphia.

1903

Wisconsin adopted **1st mandatory primary election system;** in 1905 system was extended to include choice of delegates to national nominating conventions. By 1948 primary system in one form or another had been adopted by 45 states.

Jan. 22 **Hay-Herrán Treaty** (Panama Canal) signed with Colombia. The U.S. Senate ratified it on Mar. 17, but on Aug. 12 the Colombian Senate rejected it.

Feb. 14 Pres. Roosevelt signed law creating **Department of Commerce and Labor,** the 9th Cabinet office. In 1913, Department was divided into 2 separate departments.

Feb. 23 Supreme Court, in *Champion v. Ames,* declared Congress has right to prohibit transmission of **lottery tickets** from one state to another. 1st declaration of a federal police power exceeding that of the individual states; led to federal regulation of food, drugs, narcotics, etc.

May 1 New Hampshire, after 48 years of complete **prohibition,** enacted a system of licenses for liquor sales.

May 31 More than **200 persons drowned** and some 8000 made homeless when the Kansas, Missouri, and Des Moines Rs. overflowed causing the destruction of $4 million in property.

Nov. 2 Pres. Roosevelt ordered **warships to Panama** to maintain "free and uninterrupted transit" across isthmus. This insured success of revolution, which was engineered in part by officers of the Panama Company and in part by native groups, all with tacit approval of Roosevelt's administration. Separatist movement in Panama was directed against Colombia.

Nov. 3 Quickest recognition ever offered a foreign country by U.S. came

Drama in blank verse given impetus by works of **Percy MacKaye.** His *Canterbury Pilgrims,* published this year, imaginatively employs Chaucer's characters in poetic adventures. Set to music by Reginald De-Koven, it opened at Metropolitan in 1917. *Fenris the Wolf* (1905), *Jeanne d'Arc* (1906), *Sappho and Phaon* (1907), etc., continued lyrical vein.

Henry James published his chef-d'oeuvre, *The Ambassadors,* the story of Americans in Paris, the quintessence of the "international" novel. James's technique is now involved and complex but perfected. Character analyses and personal relationships are presented in almost "metaphysical" subtlety.

Jack London's greatest success, *The Call of the Wild,* 1st published in the *Saturday Evening Post* as a serial. His next most popular book *The Sea-Wolf* appeared in 1904. Both books rely on larger-than-life adventure and on physical brutality; but, still popular today, they are often considered American classics.

"Autobiography" of **Helen Keller,** *The Story of My Life,* one of the most remarkable books to appear during the year. Miss Keller, a blind deaf-mute, is famous for her success in rising above her handicaps and for her help in the rehabilitation of handicapped children.

Joseph Pulitzer announced his intention of establishing a **Graduate School of Journalism** at Columbia University. Funds of $2 million were provided in his will. He did not die until 1911.

Larkin Administration Building, an office structure, built at Buffalo, N.Y., from plans by **Frank Lloyd Wright.** One of his earliest buildings, it was a forerunner of much recent architectural design.

Williamsburg Bridge, 2d important suspension bridge across the East R., opened in New York city.

1903

University of Puerto Rico at Rio Pedras, P.R., chartered. 1st classes held in 1900 when institution was a normal school.

1st film exchange in America established by Harry J. Miles and his brother, Herbert. Film exchange became economic foundation of the motion picture industry because it enabled producers to sell their product to one big buyer who could pay high prices. More than 100 film exchanges had been established by 1907 in 35 cities throughout the U.S. This led to the opening of thousands of new motion picture theaters and daily changes of program became customary.

Pelican Island near east coast of Florida designated as **1st federal wildlife refuge** by Pres. Theodore Roosevelt.

1st male motion picture star made his debut in *The Great Train Robbery.* He was known variously as Max Aronson, "Broncho Billy," Max Anderson, and G. M. Anderson. Film is said to be **1st with plot.**

Henry Ford organized and became president of the **Ford Motor Company.**

Heavier-than-air flying machine, built by Samuel P. Langley, tested from a houseboat in the Potomac. On takeoff, wing hit houseboat stanchion and machine crashed. Langley was subjected to much public ridicule for his efforts. In 1914 the machine was "reconditioned" and flown. It was a 14 ft. model, and flew without a pilot.

Mar. 21 Report of the Anthracite Coal Strike Commission, appointed by Pres. Roosevelt to investigate conditions in **mining industry,** favored miners. Report established principle that "no person shall be refused employment, or in any way discriminated against, on account of mem-

The Passion Play was one of the longest motion pictures exhibited in America up to this time. It ran for 2150 ft., or nearly 36 min. This running time contrasted sharply with that of the average films of the year which ran between 3 and 4 min. (Film was projected at that time at the rate of 60 ft. per min.) *Passion Play* reflected popularity of religious themes in early films.

U.S. lawn tennis men's singles champion, Hugh L. Doherty of England; **women's singles champion,** Elisabeth H. Moore.

U.S.G.A. amateur championship won by Walter J. Travis at Nassau G.C., Glen Cove, N.Y. He defeated E. M. Byers, 5 and 4. **Open championship** won by Will Anderson at Baltusrol G.C., Short Hills, N.J., with a score of 307.

Flocarline won the 27th annual **Preakness Stakes,** paying 8–1. Jockey was W. Gannon; time was 1:44⅘ on a fast track for winnings valued at $1875.

Africander won the 37th annual **Belmont Stakes,** paying 3–5. Jockey was J. Bullman; time was 2:23⅕ on a fast track for winnings valued at $12,285.

Apr. 27 Opening of **Jamaica Race Track** in Long Island, N.Y., was attended by many notable figures from the world of entertainment and gambling, including Lillian Russell, a reigning glamour queen of the time, "Diamond Jim" Brady, and "Bet-a-million" Gates. Although not the oldest track in New York it is one of the most famous and well attended in the U.S. On Memorial Day in 1945 it drew the largest crowd in the history of New York racing: 64,670.

May 2 29th annual **Kentucky Derby** won by C. R. Ellison's *Judge Himes,* who paid off at 12–1. Time was 2:09 on a fast

POLITICS AND GOVERNMENT; WAR; DISASTERS; VITAL STATISTICS.	BOOKS; PAINTING; DRAMA; ARCHITECTURE; SCULPTURE.

when **Republic of Panama** was recognized 3 days after it was proclaimed. Roosevelt's opponents openly hinted that he was involved in the Panamanian revolution in order to speed negotiations for the Panama Canal.

Nov. 18 **Hay-Bunau-Varilla Treaty** negotiated, giving the U.S. full control of a 10-mi. strip of land in Panama in return for $10,000,000 in gold plus a yearly payment of $250,000.

Dec. 30 **Disastrous fire** in Iroquois Theatre, Chicago, during a performance by Eddie Foy, killed 588 people. Public reaction led to new theater codes in most American cities: more fire walls, better and more exits, unobstructed alleyways, noninflammable scenery, etc.

Mar. Vogue for **"Nantucket"** limerick hit U.S. newspapers, eliciting many variations and sequels. Original went:

There once was a man from Nantucket
Who kept all his cash in a bucket;
But his daughter, named Nan,
Ran away with a man,
And as for the bucket, Nantucket.

June 17 1st performance of *Babes in Toyland,* by **Victor Herbert,** in Chicago. Became one of the best-known operettas in America.

Oct. Famous story for girls *Rebecca of Sunnybrook Farm* by **Kate Douglas Wiggin.** It has sold well over 1,000,000 copies in the U.S., and has been translated into several foreign languages. Like all books that belong to this school of sentimental domestic fiction, *Rebecca* is marked by cheerful optimism, homespun philosophy, and a happy ending.

1904

Jan. 4 **Citizens of Puerto Rico** are not aliens, ruled the United States Supreme Court. And neither may they be refused admission to the continental limits of the U.S., though they are not classified as citizens.

Feb. 7–8 **Tremendous fire** in Baltimore, Md., destroyed 2600 buildings in an 80-block area of the business district. Fire burned for about 30 hours, which made it the biggest fire since the great Chicago fire of 1871. Loss estimated at $80 million.

Feb. 29 **Panama Canal** Commission appointed by Pres. Roosevelt. The 7-man board was charged with construction of the waterway. On Apr. 22, 1904, Panama Canal property transferred to U.S. by agreement signed at Paris. J. F. Wallace named engineer in chief of the project on May 10, 1904.

May 5 **National Convention of the Socialist Party** met in Chicago and nominated Eugene V. Debs of Indiana for the presidency and Benjamin Hanford of New York for the vice-presidency.

1st building designed entirely for **poured concrete construction,** Unity Temple, built in Chicago from plans by Frank Lloyd Wright.

Conception of superman as delineated by Nietzsche fictionalized in **Jack London's** tale of the sea *The Sea-Wolf,* in which the domineering individual—Captain Wolf Larsen—is shown in his complete disregard of accepted values.

Lincoln Steffens' magazine articles exposing municipal corruption collected in book form under the title, *The Shame of the Cities*—one of the most popular books in the "literature of exposure."

Novel, *Freckles,* by **Gene Stratton Porter,** the most successful American writer of sentimental domestic fiction. 5 of her books are considered best sellers: *Freckles, A Girl of the Limberlost* (1909), *The Harvester* (1911), *Laddie* (1913), and *Michael O'Halloran* (1915). Mrs. Porter probably made $2 million from

SCIENCE; INDUSTRY; ECONOMICS; EDUCATION; RELIGION; PHILOSOPHY.	SPORTS; FASHIONS; POPULAR ENTERTAINMENT; FOLKLORE; SOCIETY.

bership or non-membership in any labor organization."

July 4 **1st Pacific cable** opened. Pres. Roosevelt sent a message around the world; it came back to him in 12 min.

May 23–Aug. 1 **Packard automobile** arrived in New York, completing 52-day journey from San Francisco. It was the 1st time a gasoline-driven automobile had made the trip under its own power.

Dec. 17 **1st successful flight** of a large sized heavier-than-air machine made at Kitty Hawk, N.C., by Orville and Wilbur Wright.

track for winnings valued at $4850. Jockey was H. Booker.

Oct. 1–13 Boston, of the American League, won the 1st annual **World Series** for baseball's world championship, by beating Pittsburgh, of the National League, 5–3. In 1904 New York, of the National League, refused to play Boston, of the American League.

Nov. 28 **Army** defeated the Navy in their annual contest by a score of 40 to 5 at Franklin Field, Philadelphia.

Dec. 16 **1st female ushers** in New York city employed by Majestic Theatre.

1904

Yellow fever study in Panama Canal area begun by William C. Gorgas. Eradication of the disease made possible the construction of the canal.

National Tuberculosis Association organized.

National Child Labor Committee formed to promote child labor laws.

1st exhibition of a Diesel engine in America at the St. Louis Exposition. Engine based on the plans of the German inventor, Rudolf Diesel.

Cigarette coupons 1st came into use as "come-ons" of new chain tobacco stores.

1st speed law passed by New York state: 10 mph in closely built-up districts; 15 in villages; 20 in open country.

Mar. 11 Shield from the New Jersey end of the **Morton Street Tunnel** touched that of the New York end. A few moments

Vogue for **jiu-jitsu** started by Pres. Roosevelt, who had a Japanese instructor call regularly at the White House.

New baseball rule limited the height of the pitching mound to 15 in. above the plate.

U.S.G.A. amateur championship won by H. Chandler Egan at Baltusrol G.C., Short Hills, N.J. He defeated Fred Herreshoff, 8 and 6. **Open championship** won by Will Anderson at Glen View, G.C., Golf, Ill., with a score of 303.

U.S. lawn tennis men's singles champion, Holcombe Ward; **women's singles champion,** May G. Sutton.

Delhi won the 38th annual **Belmont Stakes,** paying 3–2. Jockey was G. Odom; time was 2:06⅗ on a fast track for winnings valued at $11,575. This year the distance was 1¼ mi.

Bryn Mawr won the 28th annual **Preakness Stakes,** paying 3–2. Jockey was E. Hildebrand; time was 1:44⅕ on a fast track for winnings valued at $2355.

POLITICS AND GOVERNMENT; WAR; DISASTERS; VITAL STATISTICS.

BOOKS; PAINTING; DRAMA; ARCHITECTURE; SCULPTURE.

June 16 Steamship **General Slocum** caught fire and burned in New York Harbor. Total loss estimated at 900 lives.

June 21–23 **National Convention of the Republican Party** held at Chicago and nominated Theodore Roosevelt for the presidency and Charles W. Fairbanks, of Indiana, for the vice-presidency.

June 29–30 **National Convention of the Prohibition Party** met at Indianapolis, Ind., where Dr. Silas C. Swallow of Pennsylvania was nominated for the presidency, and George W. Carroll, of Texas, for the vice-presidency.

July 2–8 **National Convention of the Socialist Labor Party** met in New York and nominated Charles H. Corregan of New York, and William W. Cox, of Illinois, for the presidency and vice-presidency, respectively.

July 4–5 **National Convention of the People's Party** held at Springfield, Ill., and nominated Thomas E. Watson of Georgia, for the presidency and Thomas H. Tibbles of Nebraska for the vice-presidency.

July 6–9 **National Convention of the Democratic Party** was held in St. Louis where Alton B. Parker of New York was nominated for the presidency and Henry G. Davis of West Virginia, for the vice-presidency. Upon nomination Parker announced to the convention that he regarded the gold standard as irrevocably fixed. The convention replied that this issue was not involved in the party's campaign.

Nov. 8 Theodore Roosevelt and Charles W. Fairbanks defeated Alton B. Parker and Henry G. Davis in the **presidential elections** by an electoral vote of 336–140. Popular vote: Roosevelt, 7,628,-834; Parker, 5,884,401; Eugene Debs, 402,-460; Silas C. Swallow, 259,257; Thomas E. Watson, 114,753; Charles H. Corregan, 33,724. Election of Theodore Roosevelt on Republican Ticket was most overwhelming victory since Horace Greeley's disas-

her books, 19 of which have sold nearly 9,000,000 copies.

Arthur Farwell undertook a nationwide lecture tour to stimulate interest in American music and to bring new Russian and French influences to bear on American audiences. Farwell often played his own compositions based on Indian themes, and he made a notable collection of folk music from the Southwest.

Metropolitan Opera Company's production of Wagner's **Parsifal** much criticized. W. J. Henderson, critic, said audience was more interested in 45-sec. kiss than in Lord's Supper. Eleanor Franklin called the performance "profanity, sacrilege, blasphemy, and a gigantic outrage."

Henry Gilbert composed a Symphonic Prelude to *Riders to the Sea,* the drama by the Irish playwright, John Synge. Later the Prelude was expanded to a work for full orchestra.

Instruction Book No. 1 for Rag-Time, by **Axel Christensen,** published. Admitting that only accomplished pianists could play ragtime properly, Christensen nevertheless undertook to teach the rudiments in 20 lessons. Book became widely popular.

Tour de force of sculpture is the *Mares of Diomedes* by **Gutzon Borglum.** 6 wild ponies gaunt from hunger are shown stampeding. In later life Borglum interested himself in "Jumboism," or the art of carving figures out of mountains.

Ethel Barrymore achieved great popularity in *Sunday,* in which she improvised the famous line, "That's all there is, there isn't any more."

American Academy of Arts & Letters founded by the National Institute of Arts & Letters. Academy's membership, limited to 50, is chosen from among members of Institute.

Sept. 3 Dramatization of **Mrs. Wiggs of the Cabbage Patch** opened in New York

later William G. McAdoo, president of New York and New Jersey Railroad, stepped through, becoming 1st man to cross the North R. on dry land.

Mar. 14 Famous milestone in U.S. government's relations with business culminated in Supreme Court decision ordering the dissolution of the **Northern Securities Company.** Theodore Roosevelt's reputation as a trust-buster rested largely on the prosecution of this case and the angry comments he drew from J. P. Morgan as a result.

Apr. 15 **"Hero fund"** of $5,000,000 set aside by Andrew Carnegie for those who endanger their lives to rescue others, and for the survivors of those who lose their lives while attempting rescues.

May 23 German, French, Belgian, and Dutch steamship companies announced cut in **steerage rates** to $10. This was to compete with British lines carrying immigrants to U.S.

July 25 **Textile strike** involving 25,000 workers in Fall River, Mass., begun. It ended successfully when mills granted wage demands on Jan. 8, 1905.

Sept. 9 **1st use of mounted police** in New York city.

Oct. 19 **American Tobacco Co.** formed by a merger of its 2 subsidiaries, Consolidated, and American & Continental.

Oct. 27 **New York city subway,** 1st underground and underwater railway in the world, began operation. Construction had been supervised by Alexander Ector Orr, who became known as the "father of New York's subways." It ran from City Hall to West 145th St.

Nov. 2 Miss **Evangeline Booth** appointed commander of the Salvation Army of the U.S.

Dec. 10 **Bethlehem Steel Corporation** founded in New Jersey.

Dec. 21 Corporations involved in **in-**

The New York Giants, National League champions, **called off the World Series.** Incensed by the abuse which Ban Johnson, president of the American League, had heaped upon him when he switched from the Baltimore Americans in 1903, Manager John McGraw got even by refusing to let the Giants meet Boston, the American League leaders, for the post-season series. It took all of the persuasion of owners, managers, players and fans to smooth the incident over. By that time it was too late for the games to be played.

Apr.–May Frank J. Marshall, of Brooklyn won the **international masters' chess tournament,** held at Cambridge Springs, Pa., and at St. Louis, Mo., without the loss of a single game. Among the contestants were Lasker, the world's champion and Pillsbury, U.S. champion, as well as champions of France, England, Russia, and Austria.

May 2 30th annual **Kentucky Derby** won by Mrs. C. E. Durnell's *Elwood,* who paid 10–1. Time was 2:08½ on a fast track for winnings valued at $4850. Jockey was F. Prior.

May 5 **1st "perfect" major league game** pitched when Cy Young of Boston Americans did not allow a single Philadelphia player to reach 1st base.

May 14 **1st Olympic Games held in America** opened as part of the St. Louis Exposition in St. Louis, Mo. U.S. won 21 events in this, the 3d Olympiad of the modern era.

Sept. 28 Woman arrested in New York city for smoking a **cigarette** while riding in an open automobile. "You can't do that on Fifth Avenue," said arresting policeman.

Oct. 8 **Automobile racing began** in America with 1st **Vanderbilt Cup race** sponsored by William K. Vanderbilt. Cup won by A. L. Campbell in foreign-built Mercedes before 25,000–30,000 spectators. He beat 17 other starters after 10 laps around 28.4-mi. course.

POLITICS AND GOVERNMENT; WAR; DISASTERS; VITAL STATISTICS.	BOOKS; PAINTING; DRAMA; ARCHITECTURE; SCULPTURE.

trous campaign of 1872. Missouri went Republican for the 1st time since the Civil War.

city. Mabel Taliaferro played "Lovey Mary," and Will T. Hodge played "Mr. Stubbins of Bagdad Junction."

1905

While Commissioner in the Philippines, **William Howard Taft,** who weighed 354 pounds, fell ill. Sec. of War Elihu Root cabled to ask how he was. Taft replied he was fine, had just ridden 25 miles on horseback. Root cabled back: "How is horse?" Later Supreme Court Justice Brewer said: "Taft is the politest man in Washington; the other day he gave up his seat in a street-car to three ladies." Taft himself made jokes about his fatness and as a result became one of the most popular men in U.S. of his time.

Jan. 21 **Protocol** signed with Santo Domingo which gave the U.S. complete charge of customs finances with the purpose of satisfying European creditors of Santo Domingo. Meanwhile, the U.S. was also to guarantee the territorial integrity of the republic. Though the U.S. Senate refused to ratify the protocol, Pres. Roosevelt made a temporary arrangement with Santo Domingo which put into effect the essence of the protocol. This was an example of Roosevelt's corollary to Monroe Doctrine in action.

Feb. 20 Virginia City, Ala., **mine disaster** killed 112.

Mar. 4 **Pres. Theodore Roosevelt** inaugurated Mar. 4 for his 2d term. Charles W. Fairbanks was his vice-president.

Apr. Writing against **woman suffrage** in the *Ladies' Home Journal,* Grover Cleveland said that "sensible and responsible women do not want to vote. The relative positions to be assumed by man and woman in the working out of our civilization were assigned long ago by a higher intelligence than ours."

June 8 Pres. Roosevelt urged Russia and Japan to **end hostilities** in a note sent to both governments. He suggested that a

Chronicler of fashionable society in New York, **Edith Wharton,** published *The House of Mirth.* A close disciple of Henry James, she analyzed the subtle relationships and refinements of an oversophisticated, artificial world of people.

Theodore Roosevelt wrote an essay, published in *The Outlook,* in appreciation of the poem, "The House on the Hill," by **Edwin Arlington Robinson.** Resulting publicity made Robinson one of more popular American poets. Through Roosevelt's intercession Robinson was given a post in the New York Customs House in this year.

Impetus given to American playwriting by formation this year of famous playwriting class conducted at Harvard by Prof. **George Pierce Baker.** Baker's "Dozen," as his class was called, eventually included such famous playwrights as Sidney Howard, Edward Sheldon, Philip Barry, Eugene O'Neill, and S. N. Behrman.

Popular song of the year was **"Everybody Works but Father."** It was only partly a comic reference to father's laziness; women were beginning to work on a large scale, often driving men out of their jobs in offices and factories.

Oct. 3 Wild West, with its color, violence and "improbabilities," exploited by **David Belasco** in a series of plays. 1st and most popular, *The Girl of the Golden West,* opened in Pittsburgh and ran for 3 years. The final scene in which the wounded hero's blood drips down on the sheriff from the attic where he is hidden was taken from life. Puccini set this play to music, and it opened on Dec. 10, 1910, at the Metropolitan with Caruso singing the role of Dick Johnson, the hero. It was 1st opera based on an American theme. Belasco continued western subjects in *The Rose of the Rancho* (1906).

402

SCIENCE; INDUSTRY; ECONOMICS; EDUCATION; RELIGION; PHILOSOPHY.	SPORTS; FASHIONS; POPULAR ENTERTAINMENT; FOLKLORE; SOCIETY.

terstate trade recommended to be placed under federal control by James R. Garfield, Commissioner of Corporations.

Nov. 26 **Army** beat the Navy by a score of 11 to 0 in the annual football contest at Franklin Field, Philadelphia.

1905

Congestion of **slum population** in New York city reached a density ratio of 1000 persons an acre in some sections, exceeding the population ratio of Bombay.

Ladies' Home Journal, conducting **exposé of patent medicines,** proved that Mrs. Winslow's Soothing Syrup, a medicine for soothing teething babies, contained morphine and was labeled "poison" in Great Britain.

1st cigarette testimonials by stars of the entertainment world employed comedians Fatty Arbuckle and Harry Bulger and dramatic actor John Mason in advertisements praising the qualities of Murads.

Number of **automobiles** registered in U.S. rose to 77,988, as compared with only 300 a decade earlier. Automobile was still considered a useless toy by most people, however.

Feb. 20 State has power to enact **compulsory vaccination law,** ruled the Supreme Court in case of *Jacobson v. Massachusetts.*

Apr. 17 Important Supreme Court Decision affecting labor held that **state laws limiting working hours** per day or week were unconstitutional.

June 7 Highest recorded **retail price for real estate** at that time paid for No. 1 Wall Street in New York city. Plot containing 1250 sq. ft. sold for $700,000.

June 11 Pennsylvania Railroad inaugurated an **18-hour train** between New York and Chicago, the "fastest long-distance train in the world." On June 18, New York Central Railroad also inaugurated 18-hour service with the "Twentieth Century Ltd." Both trains suffered wrecks within a week, and 19 lives were lost.

1st Rotary Club founded by Paul Percy Harris, a Chicago lawyer. Name derived from early practice of meeting at each member's home in rotation. Clubs soon spread to other cities and National Association of Rotary Clubs established in 1910. Overseas branches were established, and in 1922 name was changed to Rotary International. Each club contains a representative from each business or profession in its locality.

New world heavyweight boxing champion, Marvin Hart, knocked out Jack Root in 12 rounds in final bout of elimination tourney to fill championship vacated by James J. Jeffries' retirement.

Drastic rules revisions made this season by the Rules Committee of Football as a result of Pres. Roosevelt's threat to abolish football after he had seen a newspaper picture of a badly mangled football player. Changes included the legalization of the forward pass and the elimination of certain dangerous scrimmage plays.

U.S.G.A. amateur championship won by H. Chandler Egan at Chicago G.C., Wheaton, Ill. He defeated D. E. Sawyer, 6 and 5. **Open championship** won by Willie Anderson at Myopia Hunt Club, Hamilton, Mass., with a score of 314.

U.S. lawn tennis men's singles champion, Beals C. Wright; **women's singles champion,** Elisabeth H. Moore.

Cairngorm won the 29th annual **Preakness Stake,** paying 9–5. Jockey was W. Davis; time was 1:45⅘ on a fast track for winnings valued at $2200.

POLITICS AND GOVERNMENT; WAR; DISASTERS; VITAL STATISTICS.	BOOKS; PAINTING; DRAMA; ARCHITECTURE; SCULPTURE.

peace conference be held in the near future.

May 11 Upwards of 100 persons killed and 141 others injured when a **tornado** struck Snyder, Okla.

July 22 Beginning of **severe yellow fever epidemic** in New Orleans. It lasted into Oct., but was finally brought under control by U.S. government antimosquito campaign. In Aug. federal authorities took charge. There were 3000 cases, about 400 deaths.

July 11 Russia and Japan accepted Pres. Roosevelt's proposal for a **peace parley** and the president chose Portsmouth, N.H., as the site for the conference.

Sept. 5 **Treaty of peace** signed by representatives of Russia and Japan at Portsmouth, N.H.

Oct. 23 Romantic drama of period seen in plays of **Edwin Milton Royle.** *The Squaw Man* had tremendous success on New York and London stage this season. It deals with a British nobleman transplanted to Wyoming and his love for an Indian squaw. In *Launcelot and Elaine* (1921) Royle dramatized Tennyson's poem, using many of the latter's lines.

Oct. 31 **Police censorship** of George Bernard Shaw's *Mrs. Warren's Profession.* Play ordered closed after one performance at the Garrick Theater in New York city. **Anthony Comstock,** self-appointed protector of public morals in New York, had complained and called the play "reekings." Shaw retaliated by coining word "Comstockery." Comstock took case against *Mrs. Warren's Profession* to court, but play was held not actionable.

1906

Feb. 2 Col. George B. M. Harvey, editor of *Harper's Weekly,* proposed **Woodrow Wilson** for next U.S. president at a dinner at the Lotos Club, New York city.

Mar. 1 **Woodrow Wilson,** president of Princeton University, speaking before the North Carolina association, said: "Nothing has spread socialistic feeling in this country more than the use of the automobile." This was before Ford's mass-produced cars became available to the ordinary pocketbook.

Apr. 18 **Earthquake** destroyed San Francisco. Loss of life and property has never been accurately estimated; damage from fire, looting, etc., as great as that caused by quake. By far the most damaging earthquake in U.S. history. All available **automobiles** commandeered by the military to aid the 500,000 homeless victims by rushing the injured to hospitals, carrying the aged to safety, lugging dynamite, delivering messages. An editorial: "Hereafter the people of San Francisco

Bitter novel of political chicanery is **Winston Churchill's** *Coniston,* the study of "boss rule" in a state legislature. He traces the vicious control that Jethro Bass has upon the public representatives, and shows how he channels funds to his pockets, how he secures privileges for the railroads, and how he seats a governor. This American author is not to be confused with the famous British statesman.

Zane Grey's *The Spirit of the Border* started him on his long career as a writer of colorful but often violent "Westerns." *The Spirit* and *Riders of the Purple Sage* (1912) were his most popular books. Altogether he wrote 54 novels, and his total sales may well go over 15 millions.

Telling indictment of the meat-packing industry is **Upton Sinclair's** novel *The Jungle,* an exposé of the ruthless methods of industry in breaking the body and spirits of its workers. He also offers sections exposing the tainted meat put on the market and started a scandal that helped lead to federal control.

July 7 Controversial **I.W.W., the Industrial Workers of the World,** established in Chicago as a reaction against the more conservative American Federation of Labor.

Nov. 8 **Electric lamps** placed in railroad train for 1st time on Chicago & North Western's "Overland Ltd." from Chicago to California.

Dec. 30 Last of 57 public hearings on **scandals in life insurance business** held under chairmanship of **Charles Evans Hughes.** Hughes had been appointed by governor after New York state legislature ordered an investigation of reported malfeasance in Equitable Life Assurance Society; dramatic hearings, involving many of New York's richest financiers, 1st brought national attention to Hughes. Investigation had begun on Sept. 6 and it led to many reforms.

Tanya won the 39th annual **Belmont Stakes,** paying 11–5. Jockey was E. Hildebrand; time was 2:08 on a fast track for winnings valued at $17,240. This year the distance was 1¼ miles.

May 10 For the 2d time since its inception, only 3 horses ran in the **Kentucky Derby.** Winner was the favorite, S. S. Brown's *Agile,* ridden by jockey J. Martin. He ran the 1¼ miles in 2:10¾ on a muddy track, earning $4850.

Oct. 9–14 New York, NL, defeated Philadelphia, AL, 4–1 in the 2d annual **World Series.**

Dec. 2 **Army** and **Navy** tied in their classic football contest, 6–6, at Princeton, N.J.

1906

Monsignor John A. Ryan's influential *A Living Wage,* which condemned any social system that could not give workers security, ordinary comforts, and recreation.

Mar. 12 **Witnesses in antitrust proceedings** might be compelled to give testimony against their corporations and produce papers and documents that might prove pertinent to the case, according to a U.S. Supreme Court ruling. Decision came in the case of *Hale v. Henkel.*

Apr. 18 **Famous trial for heresy** in the U.S. opened at Batavia, N.Y. Rev. Algernon Sidney Crapsey, rector of St. Andrew's Protestant Episcopal Church, Rochester, N.Y., had been a "high church" clergyman, but under influence of Marx and Renan became a "rationalist," preached against the divinity of Christ, etc. Trial before an ecclesiastical court with full detachments of secular and clerical lawyers on both sides attracted much attention throughout U.S. and England, with daily accounts in all newspapers. De-

Pres. Roosevelt declared Devil's Tower, Wyoming the **1st national monument** of the U.S. A tower of rock, it tapers from 1000 ft. at the base to 275 ft. at the top.

U.S. lawn tennis men's singles champion, William J. Clothier; **women's singles champion,** Helen Homans.

U.S.G.A. amateur championship won by E. M. Byers at Englewood, N.J., G.C. He defeated G. S. Lyon, 2 up. **Open championship** won by Alex Smith at Onwentsia Club, Lake Forest, Ill., with a score of 295.

Burgomaster won the 40th annual **Belmont Stakes,** paying 2–5. Jockey was L. Lyne; time was 2:20 on a fast track for winnings valued at $22,700. Distance reverted to 1⅜ mi. and was not changed again until 1926.

Whimsical won the 30th annual **Preakness Stakes,** paying 9–5. Jockey was W. Miller; time was 1:45 on a fast track for winnings valued at $2355.

will regard the automobile as a blessing, rather than a nuisance."

June 11 Congress enacted **Employer's Liability Act;** Supreme Court found it unconstitutional in 1908.

June 29 Railroad Rate bill, giving federal government authority to set rates for interstate shipments, passed by Congress. Was preceded by 60 days of debate, most of it violently acrimonious; bill's opponents feared federal encroachment on states' rights and/or private property.

June 30 Pure food and drug act prohibited the sale of adulterated foods and drugs and demanded an honest statement of contents on labels. Dr. Harvey W. Wiley was mainly responsible for pointing up the necessity for this act. On the same day a meat inspection act was passed by Congress. It was the result of the **Reynolds and Neill report** (June 4), which revealed shockingly unclean conditions in meatpacking plants. Act required sanitary conditions and federal inspection for all plants dealing in interstate commerce.

Aug. 23 Tomás Estrada Palma, 1st president of Cuba, requested U.S. intervention to quell a **revolt** arising from election disputes. Pres. Roosevelt held off, but finally sent troops, took over Cuban government for 13 days in October. Order finally restored.

Sept. 22 18 Negroes and 3 whites killed and many injured in **anti-Negro riots** which broke out in Atlanta, Ga. City was placed under martial law. One of worst race riots in U.S. history.

Sept. 29 Platt Amendment applied in Cuba when the U.S. assumed military control. Sec. Taft was Provisional Governor.

Nov. 4 Charles Evans Hughes elected governor of New York. Election largely a result of popularity derived from his in-

Master of the short story **O. Henry** collected many of his tales of New York city and published them under the title *The Four Million.* A technician employing surprise endings, suspense, and humor, he wrote more than 250 stories in the decade beginning 1899, chronicling in his mixture of laughter and tears the lives of the masses in the city.

Ruth St. Denis captivated New York audiences with her "modern" dances, including several "Hindoo dances."

Alla Nazimova, famous Russian actress, played in New York city with a company of Russian actors; her English version of *Hedda Gabler* was especially well received by the critics. This was her English-speaking debut in New York; she had been acting Russian roles the year before.

George M. Cohan produced *Forty-Five Minutes from Broadway,* one of his most successful musicals, with Fay Templeton in a leading part.

Season marked the height of **George Bernard Shaw's** popularity in New York; 6 of his plays were on the New York stage during the season: *Caesar and Cleopatra; Arms and the Man; Man and Superman; John Bull's Other Island; Mrs. Warren's Profession* (raided by police on charge of indecency); *Major Barbara.*

"King Porter Stomp" written by famed New Orleans ragtime piano player, **Ferdinand "Jelly Roll" Morton.** Morton gave the St. Louis ragtime style of Scott Joplin a heavy beat. Among his other ragtime compositions were: "The Pearls," "Kansas City Stomps," "Chicago Breakdown," "Black Bottom Stomp," "Buddy Carter's Rag," "The Perfect Rag," and many others.

Geraldine Farrar made her American debut, after having played with great success in Berlin opera.

Oscar Hammerstein opened his 2nd Manhattan Opera Company in New York (1st in 1892), in competition with the Metropolitan Opera Company. His purpose was to produce a preponderance of

fendant was found guilty of heresy and unfrocked on December 5.

Apr. 28 New York Legislature passed complete legislative program to **reform life insurance business;** the result of investigations the previous year by Charles Evans Hughes. Laws provided for "mutualizing" stock companies, prohibited speculative investment of insurance company funds, forbade companies to hold stock in banks or trust companies, etc.

June 10 **1st Church of Christ Scientist** dedicated in Boston. Ceremony attended by thousands of followers of the new denomination.

June 21 Speaking in Congress, James R. Mann read a partial list of **adulterations** found in food; he included: "*Coffee.* Colored with Scheele's green, iron oxide, yellow ochre, chrome yellow, burnt umber, Venetian red, tumeric, Prussian blue, indigo; adulterated with roasted peas, beans, wheat, rye, oats, chicory, brown bread, charcoal, red slate, bark, date stones."

Aug. William Jennings Bryan, returning from Europe, proposed **government ownership of railroads** to the Democrats who assembled to greet him at Madison Square Garden, N.Y. Cheers turned to silence in the definitely chilly reception of the idea.

Aug. 13 **Pennsylvania Railroad** announced that all coaches henceforward

Feb. 23 Tommy Burns defeated Marvin Hart in 20 rounds at Los Angeles, Calif. and claimed the **heavyweight title.** James J. Jeffries, who retired in 1905 because he could find no worthy adversary, refereed the fight.

Mar. 17 Word **"muckraker,"** taken from a passage in John Bunyan's *Pilgrim's Progress,* 1st used in its modern meaning by Pres. Roosevelt in an address to the Gridiron Club, Washington, D.C. "Muckrakers" were authors of "literature of exposure," who in the decade beginning 1903 helped stimulate reform by exposing unpleasant sides of American life. The more famous of them included Lincoln Steffens, Ida M. Tarbell, Ray Stannard Baker, and David Graham Phillips. As an example, Upton Sinclair's *The Jungle* helped passage of the Meat Packing Act of 1906.

Apr. U.S. won **Olympic Games** at Athens with 75 points against England's 41 and Sweden's 28.

May 2 32d annual **Kentucky Derby** won by the favorite, G. J. Long's *Sir Huon,* ridden by R. Troxler. Time was 2:08⅘ on a fast track for winnings totaling $4850.

Oct. 9–14 Chicago, AL, defeated Chicago, NL, 4–2 in the 3d annual **World Series.**

Nov. 28 Philadelphia Jack O'Brien became claimant for the **heavyweight championship** when he fought a 20-round draw with Tommy Burns in Los Angeles, Calif. Burns' claim to the title derived from his defeat of Marvin Hart, who was named champion by retired champion James Jeffries after knocking out Jack Root, the only other contender for the title.

Dec. 1 **Navy** beat the Army by 10 to 0 in their annual football contest at Franklin Field, Philadelphia.

Dec. 29 1st annual convention of the

| POLITICS AND GOVERNMENT; WAR; DISASTERS; VITAL STATISTICS. | BOOKS; PAINTING; DRAMA; ARCHITECTURE; SCULPTURE. |

vestigations of life insurance scandals. He became a vigorous reformer in many fields.

Nov. 9 1st time a U.S. President left the country while in office occurred when Pres. Roosevelt sailed on battleship *Louisiana* to visit the Isthmus of Panama and inspect the Canal. He returned on Nov. 26.

Dec. 12 Oscar S. Straus of New York city appointed Secretary of Commerce and Labor by Pres. Roosevelt. Straus was **1st Jew to receive a cabinet appointment.**

French and Italian works, in contrasts to the "Met's" emphasis on German opera. Manhattan Company lasted until 1910, when Hammerstein sold out to the Metropolitan, agreeing not to produce opera for 10 years.

Apr. 12 *A Sabine Woman* (retitled *The Great Divide*, 1910), serious drama of the Southwest by **William Vaughn Moody,** acted by Henry Miller and Margaret Anglin. Critics called it "a new mark in the American drama."

1907

Jan. 26 Congress enacted **law prohibiting campaign contributions** by corporations to candidates for national offices.

Feb. 8 Treaty with Santo Domingo signed. It provided for the collection of customs by U.S. agent with the purpose of satisfying foreign and domestic creditors. The Senate ratified the treaty on Feb. 25. This is essentially the same treaty which the Senate refused to accept in 1905.

Feb. 12 Steamer **Larchmont** foundered in Long Island Sound causing 131 deaths.

Feb. 26 General Appropriations Act passed. It increased the salaries of the cabinet members, the speaker of the House, and the vice-president to $12,000, and granted salary increases to senators and representatives to $7500.

Mar. 14 Japanese laborers excluded from continental U.S. by presidential order.

Mar. 14 Inland Waterways Commission appointed by Pres. Roosevelt. It was to study related problems of forest preservation and commercial waterways. Theodore E. Burton was designated chairman.

Mar. 21 U.S. Marines landed in **Honduras** to protect life and property from revolutionary hazards.

June 15–Oct. 15 2nd Hague Peace Conference. It had originally been proposed by **Pres.** Roosevelt in 1904, but Russo-Japa-

Vogue for the cynical, Oriental philosophy of **Omar Kháyyám** reached its height at about this time in the U.S. Many thousands of de luxe editions in limp leather bindings sold; a favorite book for the parlor table in hundreds of thousands of homes.

Great intellectual and spiritual autobiography is the **Education of Henry Adams.** Adams had fallen prey to the skepticism and loss of faith chronicled by so many thinkers during the *fin de siècle.* Life assumed a meaningless, chaotic pattern for him, and his searches in politics, science, religion, travel did not resolve his basic maladjustment to the times. It was not published until 1918.

Three Weeks, a romantic novel by **Elinor Glyn.** Story relies heavily on illicit sex, and part of its popularity stemmed from its suppression in Boston. 50,000 copies distributed in 3 weeks; hundreds of thousands altogether. Mrs. Glyn wrote other daring romances. She also is responsible for the term **"It"** (sex appeal).

1st American production of Franz Lehár's **The Merry Widow,** which played off and on for years and contained the very popular "Merry Widow Waltz."

Plaza Hotel in New York city built on designs by Henry Hardenbergh. A striking example of the idea of luxury current in U.S. during early 20th century.

SCIENCE; INDUSTRY; ECONOMICS; EDUCATION; RELIGION; PHILOSOPHY.	SPORTS; FASHIONS; POPULAR ENTERTAINMENT; FOLKLORE; SOCIETY.

would be made of steel, wooden coaches would be abandoned.

Dec. 24 Reginald A. Fessenden, private radio experimenter, broadcast **1st known program of voice and music** in U.S. In the same year he established 2-way wireless communication with Scotland.

Intercollegiate Athletic Association held. Formed as an educational organization to establish sound requirements for intercollegiate athletics, in 1910 it changed its name to the **National Collegiate Athletic Association.** In 1931 it set definite "Standards for the Conduct of Intercollegiate Athletics," with which all members were required to comply as a condition of membership. It strengthened its enforcement powers in 1951 and is now the rules-making body for all intercollegiate athletics.

1907

William D. ("Wild Bill") Haywood, president of Western Miners Union, acquitted of murder of ex-Governor Frank Steunenberg of Idaho. Trial, with Clarence Darrow for defense counsel and William E. Borah for prosecuting attorney, was most widely known "cause" in the labor-capital disputes of the times.

Prof. Albert Abraham Michelson, head of Physics Department at Univ. of Chicago, awarded **Nobel Prize in physics.** Michelson, America's 1st Nobel laureate, was known particularly for his studies of the speed of light, carried out with apparatus designed and built by himself.

University of Hawaii established as College of Agriculture and Mechanic Arts at Honolulu, Hawaii. 1st classes met in 1908. Name was changed to College of Hawaii in 1911, to present name in 1920.

1st public presentation of primitive talking and colored motion pictures in Cleveland, Ohio. Chromophone process employed in film consisting of a little grand opera, a bull fight with naturalistic sound effects, and a political speech accompanied by vocal derision.

Mar. 9 Death of **John Alexander Dowie.** Dowie, a Scot who came to U.S. by way of Australia, established Zion's Restoration Host, a sect which grew to more than 100,000 members with headquarters at Zion, Ill. He founded the city, the tabernacle, and industries worth more

Florence Lawrence began screen career at Vitagraph Company. She joined the Biograph Company when D. W. Griffith became director, and soon was known as "the Biograph girl." Then she made her appearance for the Independent Motion Picture Company, where she was called "the IMP." Miss Lawrence was probably the 1st motion picture actress to be treated as a star, and her career is usually regarded as the beginning of the star system.

U.S.G.A. amateur championship won by Jerome D. Travers at Euclid Club, Cleveland. He defeated Archibald Graham, 6 and 5. **Open championship** won by Alex Ross at Philadelphia Cricket Club, Chestnut Hill, Pa., with a score of 302.

U.S. lawn tennis men's singles champion, William A. Larned; **women's singles champion,** Evelyn Sears.

Don Enrique won the 31st annual **Preakness Stakes,** paying 15–1. Jockey was G. Mountain; time was 1:45⅘ on a slow track for winnings valued at $2260.

Peter Pan won the 41st annual **Belmont Stakes,** paying 7–10. Jockey was G. Mountain; winnings were valued at $22,765.

May **Mother's Day 1st observed** in Philadelphia through the efforts of Miss

POLITICS AND GOVERNMENT; WAR; DISASTERS; VITAL STATISTICS.	BOOKS; PAINTING; DRAMA; ARCHITECTURE; SCULPTURE.

nese War interfered. Establishment of World Court, advocated by U.S., was unsuccessful. Conference stipulated that armed force must not be used against American nations for the collection of debts owed foreign creditors.

July 20   30 persons lost their lives and 70 injured in a **train wreck** near Salem, Mich., on the Père Marquette Railroad.

July 28   Great **fire** at Coney Island, N.Y. destroyed some $1,500,000 worth of property.

Sept. 17   **Oklahoma** adopted new constitution, which included a prohibition article.

Nov. 16   **Oklahoma** admitted as a state, 46th to join Union.

Dec. 6   361 men killed in one of the worst **coal mine disasters** in our history, when a mine exploded in Monongah, W. Va.

Dec. 19   **Coal mine explosion** caused the death of 239 persons in Jacobs Creek, Pa.

Robey House, one of Frank Lloyd Wright's earliest designs, built in Chicago. Showed the broad low roofs and horizontal lines of Wright's "prairie" houses.

Jan. 22   1st American performance of Richard Strauss' opera **Salomé,** based on drama by Oscar Wilde at the Metropolitan Opera House in New York city. While critics violently disputed the merits of the music, other citizens were shocked by the sensational plot. Metropolitan cancelled further performances and Boston, urged on by the New England Watch and Ward Society, prevented Mary Garden from singing the role there.

Nov. 18   Theme of the macabre, the "extra-" human, employed with great success by **Augustus Thomas** in *The Witching Hour,* a play which revolves around the power of hypnotism. *The Harvest Moon* (1909) concerns the power of the suggestion of evil over a young girl; *As a Man Thinks* (1911) deals with mental healing.

1908

Feb. 18   **Gentlemen's Agreement** with Japan reached through a note sent to the American ambassador which acknowledged Roosevelt's order of Mar. 14, 1907, and agreed not to issue any more passports to Japanese laborers for emigration to the U.S.

Mar. 28   More than 60 miners killed by an **explosion and cave-in** at the Union Pacific Coal Company's mines at Hanna, Wyo.

Apr. 2–3   **People's Party National Convention** met at St. Louis, Mo., and nominated Thomas E. Watson, of Georgia, for the presidency and Samuel W. Williams, of Indiana, for the vice-presidency.

Apr. 12   **Chelsea, Mass.,** virtually destroyed by fire, leaving more than 10,000

Songs showing the increasing **suggestiveness of popular music,** especially from musical dramas, were: "Mary Took the Calves to the Dairy Show" (1909); "This Is No Place for a Minister's Son" (1909); "If You Talk in Your Sleep, Don't Mention My Name" (1910).

Mary Roberts Rinehart's *The Circular Staircase* published. Of all her numerous books this mystery story is her top best seller.

Best seller *Anne of Green Gables,* a book for girls, by **Lucy M. Montgomery,** a Canadian writer. She wrote several popular sequels.

Censorship of Elinor Glyn's *Three Weeks* instituted in Boston by the Watch and Ward Society's successful prosecution of book salesman.

| SCIENCE; INDUSTRY; ECONOMICS; EDUCATION; RELIGION; PHILOSOPHY. | SPORTS; FASHIONS; POPULAR ENTERTAINMENT; FOLKLORE; SOCIETY. |

than $10,000,000. Was insane before his death.

May 1st "fleet" of **taximeter cabs**, imported from Paris, arrived in New York.

June 6 **Dropsie College for Hebrew and Cognate Learning,** a post-graduate college for Rabbinical and Biblical studies, chartered in Philadelphia, Pa.

Oct. 21 **Currency panic of 1907** began with run on Knickerbocker Trust Company, of New York. Run lasted 1½ days, until bank's reserves gave out. Other banks throughout country were forced to close. Panic brought to an end when J. Pierpont Morgan and a group of businessmen combined resources to import $100,000,000 in gold from Europe.

Sept. 12 **Lusitania,** largest steamship in the world, arrived in New York on maiden voyage. Set speed record of 5 days, 54 minutes, between Queenstown and New York.

Anna M. Jarvis, who arranged a special mother's service in a church, requesting that those attending the service wear a white carnation. The custom spread rapidly until, by 1911, every state in the Union was participating in Mother's Day exercises held on the 2d Sunday in May.

May 6 33d annual **Kentucky Derby** won by J. Hal Woodford's *Pink Star,* paying 15–1. Time was 2:12⅗ on a heavy track for winnings valued at $4850. Jockey was A. Minder.

Oct. 8–Oct. 12 Chicago, NL, defeated Detroit, AL, 4–0 in the 4th annual **World Series.** 1st game ended in tie score.

Nov. 30 **Navy** defeated Army 6 to 0 in the 11th annual football classic at Franklin Field, Philadelphia.

Dec. 2 **Tommy Burns** knocked out Gunner Moir in 10 rounds at London, England. Burns was the sole legitimate claimant to the **heavyweight championship** of the world, and this bout clinched his title.

1908

U.S. Navy established **Nurse Corps** and appointed Esther Voorhees Hasson as 1st superintendent. In 1947 corps became a staff corps and nurses were made commissioned officers.

Unemployment resulting from Panic of 1907 still continued. Bowery Mission reported 2000 more than usual applied daily for free breakfasts. Newspapers were full of "situation wanted" advertisements which stated willingness to accept wages well below prevailing standard.

1st great skyscraper in America, the 47-story Singer Building, built in New York city. It was soon eclipsed by the 50-story Metropolitan Tower and the 60-story Woolworth Building erected in 1913.

Transatlantic steerage rate from Genoa to New York reduced to $12.

"**Directoire**" or "sheath" gown imported from Paris. Police had to rescue 1st women to wear one in Chicago. Very narrow skirts without petticoats became the style, along with enormous "Merry Widow" hats, huge dotted veils, boned collars, and "fish-net" stockings.

Irving Brokaw, who had studied **figure skating** in Europe, returned to U.S. and popularized the new sport. Through his efforts 1st national figure skating tournament was held in 1914 in New Haven, Conn.; singles winners were Theresa Weld of Massachusetts and Norman N. Scott of Montreal. During World War I sport declined but it revived quickly during twenties.

New baseball rule prohibited pitchers from soiling new baseballs.

U.S.G.A. amateur championship won by Jerome D. Travers at Garden City, N.Y.,

people homeless and destroying some $10,-000,000 in property.

Apr. 30 Worcester, Mass., voted for local **prohibition;** became the largest dry city in the country (pop. 130,000). 76 saloons were closed, 2000 men thrown out of work. On the same day 17 cities and 249 smaller towns also went dry in Massachusetts.

May 10–17 **Socialist Party's National Convention** held at Chicago, Ill., where Eugene V. Debs, of Indiana, was nominated for the presidency and Benjamin Hanford, of New York, for the vice-presidency.

May 25 **$13 million remitted** to China. This sum was about half of the indemnity China was required to pay U.S. as result of Boxer Rebellion. Money was set aside for education of Chinese students in U.S.

May 28 Congress passed a bill which provided for the regulation of **child labor** in the District of Columbia. It was hoped that this legislation would serve as a model for the rest of the country.

June 16–20 **National Convention of the Republican Party** held at Chicago, Ill., where William H. Taft of Ohio was nominated for the presidency on the 1st ballot, and James S. Sherman of New York for the vice-presidency. When Chairman Henry Cabot Lodge spoke in praise of Pres. Roosevelt, delegates began a demonstration which lasted 45 min., breaking all previous records for both parties.

June 24 **Grover Cleveland died** at the age of 71. He is buried at Princeton, N.J.

July 4 **Socialist Labor Party's National Convention** held at New York city nominated Martin R. Preston of Nevada who was serving a jail sentence in the Nevada Penitentiary for murder, for the presi-

Formation of the **"Ash Can School"** by group of painters who turned away from "Art for Art's Sake" and, in this era of "muckraking," began to portray life of proletariat in New York city. Group, made up predominantly of ex-newspaper illustrators, led by teacher Robert Henri, included John Sloan, George Luks, William Glackens, Everett Shinn, George Bellows. Art critics were willing to grant that the paintings of the school reflected something of the tensions of the 20th century, but they clearly considered Henri, Luks, and Bellows to be morbid and extreme. **Frank Jewett Mather** of *The Nation* wrote of them that there "was more green, yellow and red sickness about their position than positive talent."

Company from the **Irish National Theatre** of Dublin produced in New York *The Rising of the Moon, The Birthright,* and other Irish plays.

Mme. Luisa Tetrazzini made her 1st appearance in New York city with the Manhattan Opera Company. She had appeared in San Francisco in 1904.

Rex Beach, called "The Victor Hugo of the North," contributed to the school of "he-man" adventure fiction *The Barrier* (1908), *The Silver Horde* (1909), and *The Net* (1912).

Isadora Duncan danced a series of scenes from Gluck's *Iphigénie en Aulide,* reproducing the postures of Greek dancers as studied from ancient statues and pottery. The "poor" years which she had spent studying Greek art in the British Museum, the financial collapses of her temple of dancing near Athens and her school of the dance near Berlin, were now being rewarded with riches and fame. On this 2nd American tour, Isadora was high on the rising crest of her career.

Mischa Elman, violinist, made his 1st

Julia Ward Howe, author of "The Battle Hymn of the Republic," became **1st woman member of the American Academy of Arts and Letters.**

Carl M. Wheaton, Newtonville, Mass., announced **lethal gas** could be used as an effective weapon and offered the Army his formula, the result of 9 years of experimenting.

Sky advertising introduced in America as plane flew over Broadway towing a box kite rigged with a dummy on a trapeze and a banner advertising a theatrical attraction.

Feb. 3   Supreme Court ruled that the **Anti-trust law** applies to **labor combinations** as well as to capital combinations and declared union boycotting illegal in the *Loewe v. Lawlor,* Danbury Hatters case.

Apr. 13   New England Methodist Episcopal Conference voted to **remove ban** on dancing, card-playing, and theater-going.

May 13–15   **Conservation conference** was held at the White House and was attended by the Governors of 44 states and territories to discuss the conservation of national resources. On June 8 **National Commission for the Conservation of Natural Resources** was appointed by Pres. Roosevelt, with a body of 57 to be headed by Gifford Pinchot.

June 12   The *Lusitania* established a **trans-Atlantic record crossing** from Queenstown, Ireland, to New York, a trip of 2780 miles, in 4 days, 15 hr.

Sept. 17   **Orville Wright** crashed in his airplane at Ft. Myer while conducting a series of experiments. Accident occurred when a propeller blade broke and the plane fell 150 ft. to ground, injuring Wright seriously and killing his passenger, Lt.

G.C. He defeated Max Behr, 8 and 7. **Open championship** won by Fred McLeod at Myopia Hunt Club, Hamilton, Mass., with a score of 322.

U.S. lawn tennis men's singles champion, William A. Larned; **women's singles champion,** Mrs. Maud Bargar-Wallach.

Colin won the 42d annual **Belmont Stakes,** paying 1–2. Jockey was J. Notter; winnings were valued at $22,765.

Royal Tourist won the 32d annual **Preakness Stakes,** paying 1–2. Jockey was E. Dugan; time was 1:46⅖ on a fast track for winnings valued at $2455. This year the distance was 1$\frac{1}{16}$ miles.

Jan. 21   **Smoking for women** in public places made illegal in New York city by the passage of the Sullivan Ordinance.

Feb. 12   Great **around-the-world automobile race** from New York city to Paris by way of Alaska and Siberia sponsored by the *New York Times* and *Le Matin* began at 11 A.M. when 6 cars, French, German, Italian, and American, left New York for Albany. Muddy roads, snow and ice, timber wolves, and gasoline shortages were just a few of the obstacles overcome by the 2 cars that arrived on July 30 in Paris: 1st, the huge German "Protos" driven by Lt. Koepens and the American "Thomas Flyer" with George Schuster at the wheel. German team was penalized for shipping their car to Seattle by rail, so the Americans were declared the winner. The only other entrant to finish, the Italian "Zust," arrived 2 weeks later. All New York turned out to greet the winners and Pres. Roosevelt received them at the White House on August 20.

May 5   24–1 long shot, *Stone Street,* won the 34th annual **Kentucky Derby** in 2:15⅕ on a heavy track, to win $4850 for his owner, C. E. Hamilton. A. Pickens was the jockey.

413

| POLITICS AND GOVERNMENT; WAR; DISASTERS; VITAL STATISTICS. | BOOKS; PAINTING; DRAMA; ARCHITECTURE; SCULPTURE. |

dency, and Donald L. Munro of Virginia for the vice-presidency. Because Preston was under the constitutional age as well as a convict, he was ineligible, and August Gilhaus of New York was nominated in his place.

July 7–10 Democratic Party's National Convention met at Denver, Colo. William J. Bryan of Nebraska was nominated for the presidency, and John W. Kern of Indiana was chosen as nominee for the vice-presidency.

July 15–16 Prohibition Party's National Convention met at Columbus, Ohio, and Eugene W. Chafin of Illinois was nominated for the presidency, and Aaron S. Watkins of Ohio for the vice-presidency.

July 27 Independence Party's National Convention held at Chicago, Ill., and nominated Thomas L. Hisgen of Massachusetts for the presidency, and John Temple Graves of Georgia for the vice-presidency. This was the party of William Randolph Hearst, who acted as temporary chairman during the convention.

Oct. 1 2¢ postage rate between the U.S. and Great Britain became effective.

Nov. 3 William H. Taft and James S. Sherman defeated William Jennings Bryan and John W. Kern in the **presidential elections** by an electoral vote of 321–162. Popular votes: Taft, 7,679,006; Bryan, 6,409,106; Eugene Debs, 420,820; Eugene Chafin, 252,683; Thomas L. Hisgen, 83,-562; Thomas E. Watson, 28,131; August Gilhaus, 13,825.

Nov. 28 More than 100 miners entombed when an **explosion** caused supporting structure in the Marianna Mine at Monongahela, Pa., to collapse.

American appearance at Carnegie Hall, New York, Oct.

The Trail of the Lonesome Pine by **John Fox, Jr.,** a best seller of the year. A native of the wild Cumberland Mts., Fox wrote his own experience as a vigilante into his picturesque novel.

Aug. 8 Percy MacKaye turned from verse plays to satire of contemporary themes in his *Mater,* a comedy dealing with politics. More successful is his *Anti-Matrimony* (1910), a clever piece satirizing cult of Ibsen, Hauptmann, and Shaw by young intellectuals; *Tomorrow* (1913) takes up problem of eugenics and marriage.

Aug. 26 Antonio ("Tony") Pastor died. As actor and manager, he was known as "father" of the music hall. He had opened "Tony Pastor's Opera House" in New York in 1865. He initiated vaudeville road shows and imported talent from London music halls.

Nov. 12 Career of playwright **Edward Sheldon** began with *Salvation Nell,* in which the heroine rises out of the depths of moral degradation to a newfound life. *The Nigger* (1909) depicts the "education" of a Southern gentlemen in racial tolerance through his own degradation; *The Boss* (1911), *The High Road* (1912) concern politics and the reformation of characters.

Dec. 24 Early film censorship spearheaded in New York by the Society for the Prevention of Crime which persuaded Mayor George B. McClellan to revoke the licenses of 550 movie houses. Managers were permitted to reapply for their licenses only after they signed an agreement not to give Sunday performances or show immoral films.

414

Thomas W. Selfridge, of the U.S. Signal Corps. Selfridge was **1st person killed in airplane accident.** Wright brothers, still using their original machine, though with improvements, had made thousands of flights, had remained in air as much as 38 min. and covered as much as 24 mi., but their work was still unknown in America to all but a few hundred observers and disbelieved by public at large. This year Wilbur Wright went to Europe to make tests for the French, and there vast crowds watched his flights. On Sept. 21 he set new air duration record over Le Mans, France—1 hr., 31 min., and 25 sec. in air for flight of 61 mi.

Oct. 1 Introduction of Henry Ford's famous **Model T automobile.** It cost $850 but in 1926 the price, because of efficient manufacturing, had dropped to $310, which included self-starter and other improvements.

Dec. **1st Red Cross Christmas seals** for campaign against tuberculosis sold. Raised $135,000.

Dec. 2 **Federal Council of the Churches of Christ in America** established in Philadelphia. 30 Protestant denominations were represented.

Dec. 21 At **tariff hearings** before House Ways and Means Committee, Andrew Carnegie said, on Dec. 21: "Take back your protection; we are now men, and we can beat the world at the manufacture of steel."

Dec. 27 Followers of Prophet **Lee J. Spangler** gathered atop South Mountain, near Nyack, N.Y., to await the end of the world; they wore white dresses "specially made for the occasion."

Aug. 29 **American Olympic team** honored in New York city upon its return from London where it distinguished itself in the track and field events by winning 15 firsts out of a possible 28. Praising of the team's achievements by Pres. Roosevelt brought them the attention and admiration of the country.

Sept. 23 Greatest dispute in baseball in decisive game at Polo Grounds, N.Y., of Chicago–New York pennant race. In last of 9th, score tied at 1–1, 2 out, New York was at bat with 2 men on. Bridwell hit safely to center field, scoring runner. Chicago players, however, claimed that when **Fred Merkle,** man on 1st, saw the winning run score, he started to walk toward the clubhouse without touching 2d base, invalidating play. Johnny Evers, Chicago 2d baseman, tried to get the ball, to tag Merkle out. But fans streamed onto the field, and bedlam reigned. Days later Pres. Pulliam of National League decided to call the game a tie. Fans invented the terms "boner" and "bonehead" to apply to Merkle's play.

Oct. 10–14 Chicago, NL, defeated Detroit, AL, 4–1 in the 5th annual **World Series.**

Oct. 30 Death of **Mrs. William Waldorf Astor** virtually ended old-style "society" in New York. She had ruled Eastern society with an iron hand; attendance at "Mrs. Astor's Ball" had been the test of social position.

Nov. 28 **Army** triumphed over Navy 6 to 4 in their 14th annual football contest at Franklin Field, Philadelphia.

Dec. 26 **"Jack" Johnson,** Negro stevedore from Galveston, Tex., fought and defeated the **world heavyweight champion,** "Tommy" Burns of Canada, at Sydney, Australia. Retired champion James J. Jeffries of California was immediately besieged with suggestions that he re-enter the ring and bring championship back to white race. At first he declined, but 2 years later he fought Johnson and was defeated.

1909

National Association for the Advancement of Colored People founded to promote the rights and welfare of American Negroes.

Jan. 28 2nd military occupation of Cuba by U.S. troops ended. Last troops left island Mar. 31.

Feb. 19 Revised Homestead Act permitted entry on twice as many acres of grazing land where irrigation would not work.

Feb. 21 American battleship fleet arrived at Hampton Roads, Va., completing the round-the-world cruise. Next day the fleet was reviewed by Pres. Roosevelt.

Mar. 4 William H. Taft, 27th President, inaugurated. He was a Republican and served 1 term.

Mar. 23 Theodore Roosevelt sailed for Africa on a scientific expedition under the patronage of the Smithsonian Institution.

Apr. 6 Robert Edwin Peary discovered **North Pole.** Peary, his Negro servant, and 17 Eskimos made final dash from advance base and reached latitude 90 degrees north for 1st time in recorded history.

May 22 700,000 acres of government land opened to **settlers** by the President in the states of Washington, Montana, and Idaho.

July 12 Income tax (16th) amendment submitted to the states for ratification after the Senate adopted a resolution to that effect. This became the 16th amendment to the Constitution.

Aug. 5 Payne-Aldrich Tariff Act signed by Pres. Taft. Act was so frankly protective that the President was the object of a great deal of criticism. The next month, when in speech at Winona, Minn., the President referred to the bill as the best tariff legislation ever enacted by the Republican Party, Taft's critics became more numerous and more abusive.

Jack London's tempestuous life on the Pacific coast formed the basis of a semi-autobiographical novel, *Martin Eden.* Here is the story of a laborer, a seaman, who drives himself mercilessly to the heights of authorship and fame, but after overcoming all obstacles finds himself "burned out" and gives up his life to the sea.

American modern sculpture perhaps began with stay of Paul Manship at American Academy in Rome, which he left in 1912. Eschewing decorative, impressionistic and "literary" sculpture of 19th century, he put all his emphasis on design, making the details subordinate to the whole.

Savage realism represented in the painting *Both Members of This Club* by **George Bellows.** A wonderfully drawn Negro boxer ploughs into his opponent who is sagging, while crowd shouts with glee.

"Texas" Guinan, unknown young actress, played 1-night stands in the West in a musical called *The Gay Musician.*

W. C. Handy, Negro band leader in Memphis, Tenn., wrote campaign song for E. H. Crump in municipal election campaign. Originally called "Mister Crump," the song was published as "Memphis Blues" 3 years later; it was the **1st blues to be written down and published** as such.

"Buddy" Bolden, chief among New Orleans jazz musicians, committed to an insane asylum. His place was taken by Freddie Keppard, cornet player and leader of the Olympia Band, which included such musicians as Louis "Big Eye" Nelson, Sidney Bechet, Willy Santiago, Zue Robertson, and Joe "King" Oliver.

John McCormack, famous Irish tenor, 1st came to U.S. He popularized "Mother Machree" (1910) and "When Irish Eyes Are Smiling" (1912).

Mar. 15 Conflict of love and the dedicated life forms the theme of **William**

SCIENCE; INDUSTRY; ECONOMICS; EDUCATION; RELIGION; PHILOSOPHY.	SPORTS; FASHIONS; POPULAR ENTERTAINMENT; FOLKLORE; SOCIETY.

1909

Henry Ford produced 19,051 **Model T Fords.** He led the auto industry in production and sales by building only 1 model, the "universal" car, which "customers could have any color as long as it was black."

1st notable animated cartoon shown in America, *Gertie the Dinosaur,* consisted of 10,000 drawings by Winsor McCay, a cartoonist for the *New York American.*

1st wireless message from New York to Chicago sent.

1st production of bakelite, which had been invented by Leo H. Baekeland, constituted important advance in U.S. plastic industry.

Mar. Glenn H. Curtiss motor works at Hammondsport, N.Y., taken over by Herring-Curtiss Company; 1st airplane produced, probably the **1st commercially manufactured airplane** in U.S., was sold to New York Aeronautical Society for $5,000.

Mar. 30 **Queensboro Bridge** opened for traffic in New York city.

July 25 French aviator Louis Blériot flew his plane across the English Channel and landed at Dover; 1st time any traveler had reached Britain who did not come by water. Hailed in the U.S. press as the **greatest air achievement of the time.**

July 27 Orville Wright made a **new flight duration record** remaining in the air 1 hr. 1 min. and 40 sec. and carrying a passenger.

Aug. 7 **Lincoln penny,** designed by Victor D. Brenner, issued by Philadelphia Mint. Replaced the Indian-head penny which had been in circulation for 50 years.

Suntanned, even redfaced, **Outdoor Girl** replaced the soft, white **Gibson Girl** when women took up automobile driving. "Automobile wrinkles" were soothed by the application of raw, freshly cut cucumbers. New field was opened for hungry fashion designers: special clothes for motoring, including a long veil to keep a lady's hat in place.

U.S.G.A. amateur championship won by R. A. Gardner at Chicago, Ill., G.C. He defeated H. Chandler Egan, 4 and 3. **Open championship** won by George Sargent at Philadelphia, Pa., Cricket Club with a score of 290.

U.S. lawn tennis men's singles champion, William A. Larned; **women's singles champion,** Hazel V. Hotchkiss.

Effendi won the 33rd annual **Preakness Stakes,** paying 20–1. Jockey was W. Doyle; time was 1:39⅘ on a fast track for winnings valued at $3225. This year the distance was 1 mi.

Joe Madden won the 43d annual **Belmont Stakes,** paying 11–5. Jockey was E. Dugan; time was 2:21⅗ on a slow track for winnings valued at $24,550.

Feb. 12 100th anniversary of **Lincoln's birth** attracted an estimated 1,000,000 New Yorkers to the exercises held in that city. Among the speakers were Booker T. Washington, Mayor George B. McClellan, son of the Civil War general who opposed Lincoln in the election of 1864, and Lyman Abbott, pastor of Plymouth Church in Brooklyn. Chicago celebrated the Lincoln centennial with 50 public meetings sponsored by as many separate organizations.

Mar. 7 **Arbor Day** made a state holiday by the Legislature of California in honor of Luther Burbank. His birth date officially chosen although it had previously

POLITICS AND GOVERNMENT; WAR; DISASTERS; VITAL STATISTICS.

BOOKS; PAINTING; DRAMA; ARCHITECTURE; SCULPTURE.

Sept. 1 **Dr. Frederick Cook,** of Brooklyn, claimed to have reached the North Pole on Apr. 21, 1908. After having read the records, University of Copenhagen refused to acknowledge the claim, declaring there was insufficient proof.

Nov. 13 259 persons killed by an **explosion** at the St. Paul mine at Cherry, Ill.

Nov. 18 U.S. warships and troops ordered to **Nicaragua** after it was reported that 500 revolutionists, with 2 Americans among them, were executed by dictator Zelaya. On Dec. 18 American troops stopped hostilities, supporting cause of revolutionists.

Vaughn Moody's *The Faith Healer,* which opened in St. Louis. Ulrich Michaelis, a religious healer, wanders into a Midwestern community and performs "miracles," but loses his power when he succombs to love.

Sept. 4 *The Fortune Hunter,* play by well-known dramatic caricaturist **Winchell Smith,** opened in New York city. *The Fortune Hunter* contains a number of typical small town types; *The Boomerang* (1916) concerns a doctor and nurse; *Thank You* (1921) presents delightful picture of board of trustees for a church.

1910

Population: 91,972,266. Center of population: Bloomington, Ind.

Farm population in America continued its steady decline with 32,077,000 farm inhabitants in 1910; 30,529,000 in 1930; and 25,058,000 in 1950. **Little immigration to** South in 19th and early 20th centuries reflected in the 2.5% of the Southern population which was at this time foreign born.

By now the following states have adopted **prohibition:** Maine (1858), Kansas (1880), North Dakota (1889), Georgia (1907), Oklahoma (1907), Mississippi (1908), North Carolina (1908), Tennessee (1909).

Last 5 years saw worst period for **mine disasters** in U.S. history. From 1906–1910 inclusive there were 84 coal mine disasters which killed 2494 miners. Most of these accidents were explosions. 1907 was worst year with total of 919 fatalities, and Dec. 1907 saw 702 fatalities.

Mar. 17 Bill introduced in House of Representatives by George W. Norris of Nebraska to have the **Committee on Rules** elected by the House rather than appointed by the Speaker, passed Mar. 19 by a combination of Democrats and Republican "insurgents." New ruling made struc-

Pennsylvania Station, New York city, built from plans based on the Tepidarium of the Baths of Caracalla in Rome, opened. Remains one of the most spacious structures in U.S.

Dominant voice in the "New Poetry" movement, **Ezra Pound,** published his 1st volume of criticism *Spirit of Romance.* Here he adumbrated themes that were to interest him for many years: the barrenness of American culture, the need for absolute criteria for evaluating art, the concept of the "mask" in the poet.

Completed grade-school education had been earned by less than half of the population over 25 years. Only about 4% of the population acquired college diplomas.

The Rosary by **Florence M. Barclay,** a best seller that reached a half million copies in 3 years. Book still sells today.

1st opera by an American to be produced at the Metropolitan Opera House, *The Pipe of Desire,* by **Frederick Converse,** given in New York city.

Popular song of the year, **"A Perfect Day,"** composed and written by Mrs. Carrie Jacobs Bond, a boardinghouse keeper, who became rich as the result.

418

SCIENCE; INDUSTRY; ECONOMICS; EDUCATION; RELIGION; PHILOSOPHY.	SPORTS; FASHIONS; POPULAR ENTERTAINMENT; FOLKLORE; SOCIETY.

Aug. 26 1st convention of the **National Conservation Congress,** with 37 states represented, met at Seattle, Wash. Charles W. Eliot presided.

Sept. 27 3,000,000 acres of public lands in the West withdrawn by Pres. Taft for **conservation** purposes.

Dec. 31 Manhattan Bridge, 3d span across the East R., opened to traffic in New York city.

been celebrated informally since 1886 by the planting of trees. Luther Burbank was still alive in 1909 when he was honored. An Arbor Day had been 1st observed in Nebraska Apr. 10, 1872. It is now observed (on different days) in every state of the Union, District of Columbia, and Puerto Rico.

May 5 Winner of the 35th annual **Kentucky Derby** was the favorite, J. B. Respess's *Wintergreen*, ridden by V. Powers. Time for 1¼ mi. was 2:08⅕ on a slow track for winnings valued at $4850.

Oct. 8–16 Pittsburgh, NL, defeated Detroit, AL, 4–3 in 6th annual **World Series.**

1910

Illiteracy in America reached a new low of 7.7% of the population, a decline of 3.0% from 1900 and a decline of 12.3% from 1870.

Reed College established at Portland, Ore. 1st classes held 1911.

Andrew Carnegie established the **Carnegie Endowment for International Peace** with a fund of $10,000,000, following his donation of funds for the Temple of Peace at The Hague. He lived to see both projects collapse in 1914.

Beginning of modern fundamentalist movement in American religious history inspired by publication of a booklet entitled *The Fundamentals: A Testimony to the Truth,* which declared 5 basic truths of Christianity: the inerrancy of the Scriptures, the Virgin birth, the physical resurrection of Christ, the vicarious atonement, and the physical 2d coming of Christ.

"Taylorization" became a byword of American industrialism and a synonym for scientific management of labor and machinery in the factory. Frederick W. Taylor championed industrial efficiency in such pamphlets as *A Piece Rate System* and *Shop Management.*

Hugh Chalmers offered a **Chalmers car** as 1st prize for the leading batter in the Major Leagues. He was rather hurt when the winner, Ty Cobb, sold his prize immediately. This was one of the many publicity stunts dreamed up by automobile manufacturers. Some were unbelievable, such as the story, presented as a news item, that Henry Ford raced a thunderstorm home, getting into his garage just as the rains came. Phrase **"tom-tom beater"** was coined to describe these early automobile publicity men.

F. R. Steel caught a **Chinook salmon** weighing 83 lbs. out of the Umpqua R. in Oregon. This was for a long time the largest fresh water fish ever snared by rod and reel. On May 22, 1949, however, Roy A. Groves snared a blue catfish in the James R., S.D., weighing 94 lbs., 8 oz., and on Dec. 2, 1951, G. Valverde caught an alligator gar in Rio Grande R., Tex., weighing 279 lbs.

U.S.G.A. amateur championship won by W. C. Fownes, Jr., at the Country Club, Brookline, Mass. He defeated W. K. Wood 4 and 3. **Open championship** won by Alex Smith at Philadelphia, Pa., Cricket Club with a score of 298.

POLITICS AND GOVERNMENT; WAR; DISASTERS; VITAL STATISTICS.	BOOKS; PAINTING; DRAMA; ARCHITECTURE; SCULPTURE.

ture of House much freer and in effect deposed Speaker Joseph G. Cannon of Illinois from his position of complete power.

Mar. 19 Municipal corruption in Pittsburgh disclosed by the confession of ex-Councilman Klein in which 60 other municipal officers were implicated.

Mar. 26 Criminals, paupers, anarchists, and diseased persons forbidden entrance to U.S. by an **amendment to the immigration act of 1907.**

Apr. 23 $30,000,000 in crops and property destroyed in the Middle West by intense cold spell.

Apr. 25 Charles Evans Hughes, governor of New York state, appointed to Supreme Court by Pres. Taft.

June 18 Mann-Elkins act placed telegraph, telephone, and cable companies under the jurisdiction of the I.C.C., and authorized the commission to suspend railroad rate increases pending investigations and court decisions. Established Commerce Court.

June 20 Senate passed bill enabling **New Mexico** and **Arizona** to form state constitutions and state governments.

June 25 Postal Saving Bank system established by an act of Congress.

June 25 Mann Act, popularly called the "White slave traffic act," passed by Congress. Prohibited the interstate or foreign transportation of women for "immoral purposes." Grew out of much public agitation over "white slavery," especially the importation of European girls to work in American bordellos.

Aug. 31 Famous **"new nationalism" speech** delivered by Theodore Roosevelt at Osawatomie, Kan. He proclaimed the **"square deal"** as his policy, which included graduated income tax, control of the trusts, labor protection, conservation, and an adequate army and navy.

Sept. 7 International Court of Arbitration at The Hague settled long dispute over **Newfoundland Fisheries.** U.S. retained

Regionalism in American theater given impetus by founding of the Dakota Playmakers by Prof. Frederick H. Koch at the University of North Dakota. Community plays, such as the *Pageant of the North West* (1914) and *Shakespeare the Playmaker*, grew out of this institution.

1st place of entertainment catering exclusively to a **Negro audience** established at the New Palace Theater in New York city.

Minor British comedian named **Charlie Chaplin** was the leading performer in a vaudeville act at the Colonial called "Karno's Wow Wows."

The Bungalow Book, a Short Sketch of the Evolution of the Bungalow from its Primitive Crudeness to its Present State of Artistic Beauty and Cozy Convenience, Illustrated with Drawings of Exteriors, Floor Plans, Interiors, and Cozy Corners of Bungalows Which Have Been Built from Original Designs, by **Henry L. Wilson,** published. Went through 5 editions and was immensely popular.

1st exhibition of "moderns" in America took place with opening of Alfred Stieglitz's "291." This show of the **Younger American Artists** at the Stieglitz Photo-Secession Gallery at 291 Fifth Avenue brought forward works by Max Weber, John Marin, Abraham Walkowitz, William Zorach, Gaston Lachaise, Bernard Karfiol, Joseph Stella, etc.

Feb. 14 Albert E. Thomas's *Her Husband's Wife* opened in Philadelphia. Thomas's plays dealt principally in social comedy. *The Rainbow* (1912), *Come Out of the Kitchen* (1916), *Just Suppose* (1920), and *Only 38* (1921) all concern domestic human relations.

July 20 Christian Endeavor Society of Missouri began **censorship campaign** to ban all motion pictures which depicted kissing between people who were not relatives.

420

SCIENCE; INDUSTRY; ECONOMICS; EDUCATION; RELIGION; PHILOSOPHY.

SPORTS; FASHIONS; POPULAR ENTERTAINMENT; FOLKLORE; SOCIETY.

The **Brush,** "Everyman's Car," produced to sell for $485, about ½ the price of a Ford. It had a good record for durability and gasoline economy, and in 1912 the price was lowered to $350; but it soon disappeared, while the Ford led the industry for 17 years.

Survey showed average **manufacturer of farm implements** was capitalized at $400,-439. In 1850 average capitalization of farm implement manufacturers had been $2,674. During same period, number of such manufacturers fell from 1,333 to 640 in U.S.

1st American aviation meet held at Los Angeles. Audiences, ranging each day from 20,000 to 50,000, watched air pioneers Louis Paulhan from France and Glenn H. Curtiss, an American, smash most of the air speed records of the meet. In spite of popularity of show and great desire among many men to fly, in 3 years only 5 airplanes had been sold to private individuals.

Throughout the world **30 aviators killed** by accidents during the year; 3 of them were Americans.

Jan. 19 **Southern Health Conference** formed at Atlanta, Ga., for the purpose of combating **hookworm disease.**

Jan. 24 Judge Landis began an investigation of the **beef trust** at Chicago concerning the raising of meat prices and the National Packing Company.

Mar. 16 Barney Oldfield recorded the **fastest speed ever traveled by man** at the time when he covered a mile at a speed equivalent to 133 mph in a Benz car at Daytona Beach, Fla.

May 16 **U.S. Bureau of Mines** established as part of Dept. of Interior, with Dr. Joseph Austin Holmes as 1st director.

May 18 **Halley's comet** passed the sun. It had been predicted that the earth would pass through the tail of the comet, with

U.S. lawn tennis men's singles champion, William A. Larned; **women's singles champion,** Hazel V. Hotchkiss.

Layminster won the 34th annual **Preakness Stakes,** paying 8–1. Jockey was R. Estep; time was 1:40⅗ on a fast track for winnings valued at $3300. This year the distance was 1 mi.

Sweep won the 44th annual **Belmont Stakes,** paying 1–10. Jockey was J. Butwell; time was 2:22 on a fast track for winnings valued at $9700. Race was not run in 1911 and 1912.

Feb. 8 **Boy Scouts** of America chartered at Washington, D.C. William D. Boyce, a Chicago publisher, was largely responsible for their formation. Boyce obtained the idea from an experience in London with a helpful English Scout and firsthand observation of the English movement founded by Sir Robert Baden-Powell, an English army officer.

Mar. 17 **Camp Fire Girls** organized by Dr. and Mrs. L. H. Gulick, Mr. and Mrs. E. Thompson Seton, and others. It was incorporated in 1912. After 20 years there were more than 200,000 members in U.S. It now has 392,000 members in U.S.

May 10 The winner of the 36th annual **Kentucky Derby** at Churchill Downs, Louisville, Ky., was the favorite W. Gerst's *Donau,* ridden by jockey F. Herbert. His time was 2:06⅖ on a fast track (the fastest so far), and his winnings totaled $4850.

June **Father's Day** celebrated for 1st time in Spokane, Wash. Initiated by Mrs. John B. Dodd, it was backed by Ministerial Association and Y.M.C.A. Today it is celebrated on 3rd Sunday of June.

July 4 Heavyweight Champion **Jack Johnson** defeated Jim Jeffries in 15 rounds at Reno, Nev. Jeffries, who had retired from the ring in 1905 because there were no challengers, was prevailed upon by the public to return to the ring and challenge

POLITICS AND GOVERNMENT; WAR; DISASTERS; VITAL STATISTICS.	BOOKS; PAINTING; DRAMA; ARCHITECTURE; SCULPTURE.

right to buy water and bait in Newfoundland, and a commission was established to settle disputes over fishing regulations. One of the most successful cases of international arbitration in a difficult issue.

Nov. 8 **Democratic Congress** elected for 1st time since 1894 by a country dissatisfied with Republican Pres. Taft's vacillating policies toward tariff and other matters. **1st socialist ever sent to Congress** was Victor L. Berger, a Representative from Milwaukee. In the same election **Franklin Delano Roosevelt** from Dutchess County was elected to the New York state Senate. **Presidential preferential primary** by popular vote was adopted by Oregon and **woman suffrage** was adopted by constitutional amendment in Washington state.

Sept. 10 Master of comedy-farce **George M. Cohan** presented his *Get-Rich-Quick Wallingford* on New York stage, a highly successful satire of "success" drive in America. *Seven Keys to Baldpate* (1913) contains a treasury of types: politicians, crooks, reporters, etc.; *The Miracle Man* (1914) and *The Song and Dance Man* (1923) again play up exaggerated type character.

Oct. 24 1st out-of-town performance of **Victor Herbert's** *Naughty Marietta* given at Syracuse, N.Y. 1st Broadway performance 2 weeks later on Nov. 7th.

Dec. 10 Puccini's opera, **The Girl of the Golden West** staged by Metropolitan Opera Company. The most talked-of production of the season.

1911

Jan. 21 **National Progressive Republican League** formed in Washington, D.C., by Sen. Robert M. La Follette. Sen. Jonathan Bourne of Oregon was elected president. Organization's chief aim was the promotion of popular government (direct primaries, direct election of delegates to national conventions, amendments to state constitutions providing for the initiative, referendum, and recall) and enactment of progressive legislation.

Mar. 7 20,000 U.S. troops ordered to Mexican border. Conditions in **Mexico** continued to be chaotic; fighting sometimes occurred so close to border that crowds of U.S. citizens gathered to watch. Troops recalled June 24.

Apr. 14 Pres. Taft send a message to the **Mexican Government** demanding that fighting cease along the American border.

May 1 U.S. Supreme Court ruled that **forest reserves** were subject to the authority of the federal government and not that of the States.

Aug. 22 **Arizona statehood** vetoed by Pres. Taft on grounds that its constitution permitted recall of judges, which he considered a threat to independence of judici-

Best seller *Mother* by **Kathleen Norris**. It has sold at least 1½ million copies. T. R. Roosevelt, struck by its campaign possibilities, publicly endorsed this sentimental book.

Stark tragedy of New England life is **Edith Wharton's** short novel, *Ethan Frome*. In a bare style she tells of the lonely life of the hero and his frustrated attempt at escape through death.

"Alexander's Ragtime Band" composed by **Irving Berlin**. Although not strictly speaking a "rag," it was the 1st song to popularize the "ragtime" manner outside the limited area of the Mississippi Delta.

Jan. 23 Most talked-of production of the season was Rostand's *Chantecler* at the Knickerbocker Theatre, New York city. Title role, that of a cock, was assigned to **Maude Adams,** a choice the critics ridiculed.

Apr. 19 Prewar romantic vogue seen in the success of *Kismet* by **Edward Knoblock,** which set the atmosphere of Arabian

SCIENCE; INDUSTRY; ECONOMICS; EDUCATION; RELIGION; PHILOSOPHY.	SPORTS; FASHIONS; POPULAR ENTERTAINMENT; FOLKLORE; SOCIETY.

dire results for all. Farmers went into their cyclone cellars; many workers stayed home in the belief that their last day on earth should be spent with their families. But nothing happened.

June 24 Act of Congress required that **radio equipment** be installed in all American passenger ships that leave U.S. ports.

Nov. 14 **1st plane takeoff from the deck of a U.S. warship** made by Eugene Ely at Hampton Roads, Va.

Johnson. The fight was a disappointment to the 18,000 spectators in the arena for Jeffries, who was the betting favorite, was completely outclassed. After 15 rounds the one-sided fight was stopped and Johnson declared the winner. Crowd unsympathetic with Negro victor. After match, Johnson's mother said, "He said he'd *bring home the bacon,* and the honey boy has gone and done it," thus adding a new phrase to the vernacular.

Oct. 17–23 Philadelphia, AL, defeated Chicago, NL, 4–1 in 7th annual **World Series.**

Nov. 26 **Navy** defeated Army, 3–0, in their annual classic at Franklin Field, Philadelphia.

1911

Roosevelt Dam on Salt R., Ariz., completed at cost of $3,890,000. It was one of the important conservation projects undertaken by the federal government under Pres. Roosevelt's direction.

G. W. McCoy and C. V. Chapin identified 1st specifically American disease, **tularemia.** Also called deer fly fever, it is found among rabbits and other wild animals and was discovered 1st in Tulare County, Calif. Disease can be transmitted to humans and is somewhat similar to undulant fever and the plague.

Feb. Henry Leland, head of the Cadillac division of General Motors, demonstrated the **1st electric self-starter,** perfected by Dayton's Charles Franklin Kettering (invented by Clyde J. Coleman in 1899), and a new automobile era began. Now millions of women could look forward to driving, as soon as they shortened their skirts.

May 15 Supreme Court ordered the **Standard Oil Company** to be dissolved. Court's decision established the principle that trusts were unlawful only if they engaged in "unreasonable" restraint of trade, thus adding a word to the original law.

U.S.G.A. amateur championship won by Harold H. Hilton at Apawamis Club, Rye, N.Y. He defeated Fred Herreshoff, 1 up in 37 holes. **Open championship** won by John J. McDermott at Chicago G.C. with a score of 307.

U.S. lawn tennis men's singles champion, William A. Larned; **women's singles champion,** Hazel V. Hotchkiss.

Watervale won the 35th annual **Preakness Stakes,** paying 13–10. Jockey was E. Dugan; time was 1:51 on a fast track for winnings valued at $2700. From this year until 1924 the distance was 1⅛ mi.

Record for **most baseball games pitched by one pitcher** set when Cy Young finished his career after pitching 906 games in his 21 years in the major leagues (516 in the national, 390 in the American). Young also secured record for the **most games won by a single pitcher** in the major leagues—511 of the 906 games he pitched.

May 13 Winner of the 37th annual **Kentucky Derby** was R. F. Carman's *Meridian,* who cut 1⅖ sec. from the previous

423

| POLITICS AND GOVERNMENT; WAR; DISASTERS; VITAL STATISTICS. | BOOKS; PAINTING; DRAMA; ARCHITECTURE; SCULPTURE. |

ary. After removing provision, Arizona was admitted to Union, after which it reinstated this provision.

Oct. 16 **National Conference of Progressive Republicans** held at Chicago. Sen. Robert M. La Follette chosen as its nominee for the presidency.

Dec. 18 Pres. Taft informed Russia of the **abrogation of the treaty of 1832** because of Russia's refusal to recognize U.S. passports in the hands of Jews, clergymen of certain evangelical denominations, and others. On Dec. 21 a joint resolution abrogating the treaty was ratified by Congress.

Dec. 23 **Theodore Roosevelt** announced in letter that he had decided to run for presidency on Republican ticket.

Nights on modern stage. Otis Skinner played the part of Hajj, the beggar, who is caught up in intrigues of Bagdad.

Sept. 26 Opening of **George Broadhurst's** play *Bought and Paid For,* which illustrates his tendency to build climax around one scene—here the breaking down of a door by a husband to get his young wife, who rejects his advances because of his drinking. Heightened melodrama of prewar American theater best seen in Broadhurst's plays, which include *The Man of the Hour* (1906) and *The Price* (1911).

1912

Jan. 6 **New Mexico** admitted as state, 47th to join Union.

Jan. 22 U.S. troops began **occupation of Tientsin,** China, for the protection of American interests.

Feb. 14 **Arizona** admitted as state, 48th to join Union.

Apr. 14–15 Steamship **Titanic** struck iceberg and sank. Ship had insufficient lifeboats; about 1502 lost. Company blamed for poor equipment and for ordering ship to speed through dangerous waters.

May 17 **National Convention of the Socialist Party** held at Indianapolis where Eugene Debs of Indiana was nominated for the presidency and Emil Seidel of Wisconsin for the vice-presidency.

June 5 U.S. marines landed in **Cuba** to protect American interests.

June 18 **Republican National Convention,** meeting in Chicago, violently split between followers of Pres. Taft and followers of ex-Pres. Theodore Roosevelt. It was the noisiest and most disorderly convention known to that time. Taft forces won parliamentary control of the conven-

Problem novel of domestic life is **Dorothy Canfield's** *The Squirrel Cage,* a protest against the stifling life in which men are consumed by money-getting and women by social obligations.

Famous receptacle for "new poetry," **Poetry: A Magazine of Verse,** founded by Harriet Monroe in Chicago. Contributors have included Ezra Pound, Richard Aldington, Hilda Doolittle, Vachel Lindsay, Carl Sandburg, Amy Lowell, T. S. Eliot, Hart Crane.

Theodore Dreiser's important novel *The Financier* published, which traces the life of a predatory businessman, Frank Cowperwood, who eventually rises to a position of great wealth. Dreiser's *The Titan* (1914) continues Cowperwood's story. Hero is modeled on Charles T. Yerkes, Philadelphia magnate.

Excellent practitioner of modernism in sculpture **Gaston Lachaise** began at about this time work on his bronze *Standing Woman.* Always fascinated by roundness of forms and their rhythmic relationships, he achieved here a fine glorification of the human body.

424

SCIENCE; INDUSTRY; ECONOMICS; EDUCATION; RELIGION; PHILOSOPHY.	SPORTS; FASHIONS; POPULAR ENTERTAINMENT; FOLKLORE; SOCIETY.

May 29 U.S. Supreme Court ordered that the **American Tobacco Company** be dissolved as a monopoly and in violation of the Sherman Anti-Trust Act.

Sept. 17–Nov. 5 **1st cross-country flight** made by Calbraith P. Rodgers, consuming 82 hr. 4 min. in flying time.

Nov. 10 Andrew Carnegie established the **Carnegie Corporation** of New York with an initial endowment of $125,000,000, the 1st of the great foundations for scholarly and charitable endeavors. Previous smaller "funds" Carnegie had established are: Carnegie Institute of Pittsburgh, 1896, $24 million; Carnegie Institute of Washington, 1902, $22 million; Carnegie Foundation for the Advancement of Teaching, 1905, $15 million; and Carnegie Endowment for International Peace, 1910, $10 million.

year's time, running the 1¼ mi. in 2:05 on a fast track, under jockey G. Archibald, to win $4850.

Sept. 4 Frank A. Gotch successfully defended his **World's wrestling championship** against George Hackenschmidt of Russia at Chicago, Ill. Gotch achieved the 2 necessary pin falls in 19:50.4 sec., and showed complete mastery over Hackenschmidt, who tried to explain his poor showing by claiming a knee injury.

Oct. 14–26 Philadelphia, AL, defeated New York, NL, 4–2 in 8th annual **World Series.**

Nov. 25 **Navy** defeated Army, 3–0, in their annual classic at Franklin Field, Philadelphia.

1912

Vitamin discoveries in America begun by Prof. Elmer V. McCollum of Yale who, while studying dietary deficiencies, discovered the curative values of 2 food chemicals designated as vitamins A and B.

Jan. 12 **Famous strike of textile workers at Lawrence, Mass.**, over a reduction of wages following introduction of new hour's law. Lasted more than 2 months; noted for its violence and growing power of the I.W.W. (Industrial Workers of the World), which came into prominence among sweated textile workers in the East for the 1st time.

Jan. 22 **Florida East Coast Railroad** between Key West and mainland opened for passenger traffic for 1st time. Passenger and freight service through to New York city initiated this year. Service not very successful, partly because of storms. After bad hurricane damage in 1935, line was abandoned, and in 1938 converted into Overseas Highways.

Mar. 14 The Department of Justice be-

Spreading fad for **"ragtime"** introduced at about this time a series of **"animal dances,"** which scandalized the conservative and were execrated in press and pulpit. Among them were: *fox trot, horse trot, crab step, kangaroo dip, camel walk, fish walk, chicken scratch, lame duck, snake, *grizzly bear, *turkey trot, *bunny hug. (*Asterisk denotes those which achieved more or less widespread popularity.)

Life magazine listed the **slang phrases of the year** as: Flossy. Beat it! Peeved. Sure! Classy. It's a cinch. What do you know about that? Fussed. Speedy. Peachy. Nutty. Getting your goat.

Theodore Roosevelt, 4 years after retiring from government office, said, **"My hat is in the ring"**—thus announcing his candidacy for the presidency in 1912 and originating a phrase which has been popular in American politics ever since.

James Thorpe, an American Indian from the little Indian college, Carlisle, won both the decathlon and the pentathlon at the 1912 Olympics held in Stockholm, Sweden,

POLITICS AND GOVERNMENT; WAR;

DISASTERS; VITAL STATISTICS.

BOOKS; PAINTING; DRAMA;

ARCHITECTURE; SCULPTURE.

tion through the election of their candidate for convention chairman, Elihu Root, and through the seating of their delegates in disputed delegations. Taft was nominated. Roosevelt immediately announced the formation of the **Progressive Party**, a 3d party, and was asked to assume leadership at meeting June 22. At a convention Aug. 5, the Progressive Party was formally established and Roosevelt was nominated for the presidency, Hiram Johnson of California for the vice-presidency. Also called the **Bull Moose Party**, the Progressives voted a platform which included woman suffrage, direct primaries, and other advanced measures.

June 25–July 2 **National Convention of the Democratic Party** met at Baltimore, Md., and nominated Woodrow Wilson of New Jersey for the presidency and Thomas R. Marshall of Indiana for the vice-presidency.

July 10–12 **National Convention of the Prohibition Party** met at Atlantic City, N.J., and nominated Eugene W. Chafin of Arizona for the presidency, and Aaron S. Watkins of Ohio for the vice-presidency.

Aug. 24 **Parcel post system** authorized. It was put into service Jan. 1, 1913.

Oct. 14 **Theodore Roosevelt shot** from a distance of 6 ft. by John Schrank of New York. Incident occurred in a Milwaukee hotel during Roosevelt's campaign tour. Bullet struck a bulky manuscript and entered Roosevelt's chest; in spite of the wound, Roosevelt insisted on delivering his speech before he was taken to a hospital.

Nov. 5 Woodrow Wilson and Thomas R. Marshall defeated both the Progressive Party candidates and the Republican Party candidates in the **presidential elections** by an electoral vote of 435 to 88 for Roosevelt and 8 for Taft. Popular votes: Wilson, 6,293,454; Roosevelt, 4,119,538; Taft, 3,484,980; Debs, 900,672; Chafin, 206,275. Roosevelt carried 6 states, Taft 2.

Formation of **New York Stage Society** by a group of prominent New Yorkers was a serious-minded attempt to represent the best of the old and the new on the stage.

John M. Synge's *Playboy of the Western World* presented in Boston, Philadelphia, and New York; in each city its performance was the occasion of public disorders.

Popular song of the year was **"Waiting for the Robert E. Lee,"** which was chosen 40 years later as the best song of the 1st half of the 20th century by a group of composers and musicians.

Feb. 5 Women's role in the "new" society of the 20th century perhaps found its best dramatic treatment in the plays of **Rachel Crothers**. *He and She,* 1st staged this year, deals with a woman's struggle to maintain home and enjoy career at same time; *A Man's World* (1909) concerns the double standard; *Young Wisdom* (1914) discusses trial marriages; *Ourselves* (1913) deals with the new woman; *Nice People* (1920) centers around youthful immorality; *As Husbands Go* (1931) compares American and European husband. Perhaps her most famous play is *Susan and God* (1937). This pokes light fun at the Oxford movement.

Mar. 14 **Brian Hooker**'s opera, *Mona,* opened. It is a poetic drama (set to music by Horatio Parker) that takes place in 1st century Britain. Containing excellent dramatic poetry, it won the $10,000 prize offered by Metropolitan Opera Company. In 1915 his opera *Fairyland* won prize of American Opera Association. In 1915 *Morven and the Grail* appeared. Hooker is known for his excellent translation of *Cyrano de Bergerac.*

Nov. 4 Highly successful attempt to employ conventions of Chinese stage to American drama is *The Yellow Jacket* by **George Cochrane Hazelton, Jr.** Use of property man and chorus caught fancy of American audiences.

426

gan **action against the merger** of the Southern Pacific and Union Pacific Railroads. The Union Pacific had acquired 46% of the stock of the Southern Pacific and the court ruled that, in such a large corporation, where the stockholders were so scattered, this constituted a minority large enough to control the operations of the corporation. Since there was evidence of competition between the railroads before the merger, the court also declared that the ability to stifle competition was tantamount to stifling competition.

May 1 As a result of *Titanic* disaster Federal inspectors ordered that all steamships carry enough **lifeboats** to hold all passengers.

June 19 **8-hour day labor law** extended by act of Congress to all workers under Federal contract.

Aug. 24 Congress passed, with Pres. Taft's approval, a bill allowing **rebates of Panama Canal tolls** to American coastwise ships. Much indignation aroused in England and the Continent; foreign governments claimed a violation of the Hay-Pauncefote Treaty. The law was repealed under Pres. Woodrow Wilson in 1914.

Oct. 1 New York state passed **a 54-hour week labor law.**

Oct. 10 **Nobel Prize** in medicine and physiology presented to Alexis Carrel "in recognition of his works on vascular suture and the transplantation of blood vessels and organs." Alexis Carrel was born in Lyons, France, on June 28, 1873. He came to America in 1904 and in 1906 began his prize-winning experiments on blood vessels at the Rockefeller Institute for Medical Research in New York. Carrel was the 1st American to be honored in the field of medicine and physiology.

Oct. 30 Sec. of Treasury MacVeagh ordered the use of **common drinking cups** prohibited on all interstate railroad trains.

and was proclaimed the "world's greatest athlete." Later, Thorpe's medals and honors were taken from him when it was learned that he had played semiprofessional baseball as part of a summer job while in college.

U.S.G.A. amateur championship won by Jerome D. Travers at Chicago, Ill., G.C. He defeated Charles Evans, Jr., 7 and 6. **Open championship** won by John J. McDermott at Buffalo, N.Y., C.C. with a score of 294.

U.S. lawn tennis men's singles champion, Maurice E. McLoughlin; **women's singles champion,** Mary K. Browne.

Colonel Holloway won the 36th annual **Preakness Stakes,** paying 23–10. Jockey was C. Turner; time was 1:56⅘ on a slow track for winnings valued at $1450.

Mar. 12 **1st patrol of Girl Guides,** forerunners of the **Girl Scouts,** formed by Daisy Gordon and 10 other young girls in an unused stable owned by Miss Gordon's aunt, Mrs. Juliet Low of Savannah, Ga.

May 11 Winner of the 38th annual **Kentucky Derby** was favorite, H. C. Hallenbeck's *Worth,* ridden by C. H. Shilling. The time was 2:09⅘ on a muddy track; the value to the winning owner was $4850.

July 12 1st showing in America of **Sarah Bernhardt** in the French-made *Queen Elizabeth.* This film, more than any other up to that time, gave motion pictures the prestige accorded to an art.

Oct. 8–16 Boston, AL, defeated New York, NL, 4–3 in 9th annual **World Series.** 2d game ended in a tie.

Nov. 30 **Navy** defeated Army, 6–0, in their annual football classic Franklin Field, Philadelphia.

1913

Feb. 14 **Immigration Bill** with literacy test provisions vetoed by Pres. Taft.

Feb. 24 U.S. Supreme Court ruled the **Mann White Slave Act** constitutional.

Feb. 25 **16th amendment adopted.** It granted power to Congress to levy and collect taxes on incomes without apportionment to the states.

Mar. 1 **Webb-Kenyon Interstate Liquor Act** passed over Pres. Taft's veto. It stated that no liquor could be shipped into states where its sale was illegal. 1st nationwide victory of Anti-Saloon league.

Mar. 4 **Woodrow Wilson,** 28th president, inaugurated. He was a Democrat and served 2 terms.

Mar. 21–26 So-called **"Dayton Flood"** raged in Miami Valley, Ohio, killing more than 400 people. Property damage has been estimated at $100,000,000. In 1925 5 dams were completed across upper Miami R. and its tributaries at a cost of $32,000,000. These dams provide protection against floods 40% greater than that of this year, and 20% greater than any floods estimated to be possible. More than 200 more killed by floods along Indiana R. and elsewhere in West and South as result of heavy rains which swept area for 5 days.

Apr. 8 **Pres. Wilson appeared before Congress** to deliver his message on tariff revision. 1st president to address Congress personally since John Adams, and it re-established precedent set by Thomas Jefferson.

May 2 Official recognition of new **Chinese Republic** extended by Pres. Wilson.

May 19 **Webb Alien Land-Holding Bill** signed by Gov. Johnson of California in the face of objections by Pres. Wilson and Japan. In effect, new law excluded the Japanese from ownership of land.

May 31 **17th amendment** adopted. It provided for **popular election of U.S.**

O Pioneers! by **Willa Cather** published, her 1st important novel. It is a story of a 2d generation American woman Alexandra Bergsen, who, through courage, diligence, and sacrifice, triumphs over the barren land and creates fields of wheat and corn.

1st exhibition of sculpture by **Paul Manship** in New York. Public presented with new art. Modeling is smooth, archaic in style; draperies are flat and all irregular outlines are done away with. Young sculptors were greatly influenced by the new technique.

Alamo restored to its original form as a monastery and maintained as a patriotic shrine by the civic authorities of San Antonio.

Woolworth Building, tallest building in the world of its time, built in New York, reaching 792 ft. from the ground. Considered a "wonder" by New Yorkers when it was 1st built.

Dancing couple, idolized during the war years and into '20's, the **Vernon Castles,** made their American debut in an English musical show, *The Sunshine Girl.*

Feb. *Pollyanna* by **Eleanor H. Porter** published. Its sales have been more than a million, and its name has become part of our standard English.

Feb. 2 One of most spacious public buildings in U.S., **Grand Central Terminal,** built in New York city in the eclectic Classic style popular after the Columbian Exposition of 1893, opened officially.

Feb. 10 Tremendous success greeted **Edward Sheldon** in his play *Romance,* which tells the story of the love of an American clergyman for an Italian opera singer. Play ran in London for 1128 performances. It subsequently played in Australia, New Zealand, South Africa, India, Egypt, Norway, Sweden. In 1923 it was staged in Paris.

SCIENCE; INDUSTRY; ECONOMICS; EDUCATION; RELIGION; PHILOSOPHY.

SPORTS; FASHIONS; POPULAR ENTERTAINMENT; FOLKLORE; SOCIETY.

1913

Jan. **Garment workers' strike** began in New York city, taking about 150,000 workers off their jobs. In Feb. strike spread to Boston. It ended in New York city on Mar. 12 and in Boston Apr. 21 with wage concessions, reduced hours, and recognition of union.

Jan. 11 Pres.-elect Woodrow Wilson declared that **business monopoly** must come to an end. Statement was made before the Chicago Commercial Club.

Feb. 25 **Silk workers' strike** in Paterson, N.J. Directed by the I.W.W., it was in protest to improved machinery. It was abandoned at end of 5 months.

Mar. 4 Act of Congress divided **Department of Commerce and Labor** into 2 departments having Cabinet status. At same time it approved act establishing **U.S. Board of Mediation and Conciliation** to adjust labor disputes.

Mar. 22 **Wireless message** sent from Arlington, Md., to Eiffel Tower, Paris.

May 14 John D. Rockefeller donated $100 million to the **Rockefeller Foundation** chartered by the New York State Legislature. Contribution was reckoned to be the largest single philanthropic act in history.

Summer Henry Ford set up his **1st assembly line** for the production of relatively low-priced Model T's with a revolutionary high wage for his workers of $5 a day. Between 1909 and 1924, the price of the Model T dipped from $950 to $290. Ford engineers had adopted the meat packers' conveyor belt system and soon 1000 Fords were turned out per day.

July 1 **Lincoln Highway Association** formed. A group interested in promoting road construction, the Association selected an automobile route between New York city and San Francisco. It constructed "seed" sections of ideal highway at various places to stimulate road building. When

Major league record for the **most consecutive shutout innings pitched in 1 season** set by Washington's great pitcher Walter Johnson in 1913, when he pitched 56 consecutive innings, allowing no runs.

U.S. lawn tennis men's singles champion, Maurice E. McLoughlin; **women's singles champion,** Mary K. Browne.

U.S.G.A. amateur championship won by Jerome D. Travers at Garden City, N.Y., G.C. He defeated J. G. Anderson, 5 and 4. **Open championship** won by Francis Ouimet at The Country Club, Brookline, Mass., with a score of 304. Francis Ouimet, only 20, beat a field which included 2 great English golfers, who had been conceded the match. Ouimet and golf made the headlines.

Buskin won the 37th annual **Preakness Stakes,** paying 7–5. Jockey was J. Butwell; time was 1:53⅗ on a fast track for winnings valued at $1670.

Prince Eugene won the 45th annual **Belmont Stakes,** paying 3–1. Jockey was R. Troxler; time was 2:18 on a fast track for winnings valued at $2825.

Feb. 27 Ex-Pres. Theodore Roosevelt coined the expression **"lunatic fringe"** in referring to certain of his too zealous supporters. Roosevelt, writing to Sen. Henry Cabot Lodge, observed that the various groups with whom he had been associated "have always developed among their members a large lunatic fringe."

May 10 91–1 long shot, T. P. Hayes's *Donerail,* won the 39th annual **Kentucky Derby.** These were the longest odds ever paid on a winner of this race, a $2.00 mutual ticket on *Donerail* paying $184.90 to win. His time was the fastest yet, 2:04⅘ on a fast track; his prize money amounted to $5475. Jockey was R. Goose.

June 30 **Reunion at Gettysburg** of thousands of veterans of Union and Con-

429

POLITICS AND GOVERNMENT; WAR; DISASTERS; VITAL STATISTICS.

BOOKS; PAINTING; DRAMA; ARCHITECTURE; SCULPTURE.

senators. Previously, senators were chosen by their state legislatures. It thus reduced the power and status of state governments and increased popular control of the federal legislature.

Aug. 27 Pres. Wilson announced his policy of **"watchful waiting"** in respect to Mexico. Mexican reactionary Gen. Victoriano Huerta had seized power after assassination of Pres. Madero on Feb. 22. Neither Taft nor Wilson would recognize Huerta (whose government did not enjoy popular support) despite pressure brought on them by American business interests. (Pres. Madero's government had seized American business holdings in Mexico.) On Nov. 7 Wilson requested Huerta's abdication, and later in month announced a policy of material support of Huerta's opponents.

Oct. **Floods** in southern Texas caused $50 million worth of damage and 500 fatalities.

Dec. 10 Elihu Root won the 1912 **Nobel Peace Prize.**

Feb. 17 **International Exhibition of Modern Art,** known as the "Armory Show," opened at 69th Regiment Armory, Lexington Avenue, New York city. It included both American and European works, centering mainly on post-Impressionists. Marcel Duchamp's "Nude Descending a Staircase" became the most controversial painting of the show and was lampooned widely by newspaper cartoonists because of its cubistic and kinetic representation.

Apr. **Max Eastman** published *The Enjoyment of Poetry,* which went through 6 editions during the decade.

Sept. 12 Great exponent of community drama and the masque as an art form, **Percy MacKaye,** presented *Sanctuary, A Bird Masque* at Meriden, N.H., to celebrate opening of Meriden Bird Club. *Caliban, by the Yellow Sands* (1916) was written to celebrate Shakespeare's Tercentenary; 2500 persons helped stage it at the stadium of the College of the City of N.Y.

1914

Jan. 27 Permanent Civil government established in the **Panama Canal Zone** by an executive order. George W. Goethals was named 1st governor and received the confirmation of the Senate on Feb. 4.

Apr. 9 Small party of **U.S. Marines,** landing at Tampico, Mex., to obtain supplies, were **arrested** and detained for 1½ hours by Mexican authorities. Their release was followed by an apology from Mexican commander at Tampico and expression of regret by Pres. Huerta, but U.S. commander, Admiral Mayo, demanded a special salute to the U.S. flag by the Mexican troops.

Apr. 11 Refusal of Pres. Huerta of Mexico to salute the U.S. flag in reparation for the detention of U.S. marines at Tampico led to a **breach of diplomatic relations.**

Apr. 14 Pres. Wilson **ordered American fleet to Tampico Bay,** Mexico, as re-

Booth Tarkington attained great success with his boy's book *Penrod.* He followed his success with *Penrod and Sam* (1916) and *Seventeen* (1916).

1st "Tarzan" book, *Tarzan of the Apes,* by **Edgar Rice Burroughs.** He immediately followed it with *The Return of Tarzan.* 1st Tarzan movie was produced in 1917. There have been 25 Tarzan books altogether, and they have been translated into many languages. *Tarzan of the Apes* has sold over 1½ million copies in the U.S., and over 5 million elsewhere.

Vachel Lindsay established himself with the publication of his *The Congo and Other Poems.* His conception of poetry as a species of choral ode was borne out by his own examples. Much of his fame spread through his own recitation of his rhythmic pieces.

| SCIENCE; INDUSTRY; ECONOMICS; EDUCATION; RELIGION; PHILOSOPHY. | SPORTS; FASHIONS; POPULAR ENTERTAINMENT; FOLKLORE; SOCIETY. |

U.S. route numbers came into use about 1925, Lincoln Highway Association began to curtail its function. Actually the route has been changed often, and today there is no officially designated Lincoln Highway between East and West Coast.

Aug. 26 World's largest power dam, Keokuk Dam, opened across Mississippi R. from Keokuk, Iowa, to Hamilton, Ill.

Oct. 3 Underwood-Simmons tariff act reduced duties on 958 articles, increased 86, and left the duty of 307 articles unaltered.

Oct. 10 Waterway across the Isthmus of Panama completed when Gamboa Dike blown up. Pres. Wilson set off the explosion by pressing electric button at the White House.

Dec. 23 Federal Reserve System established by the Glass-Owen bill which divided the country into 12 reserve districts. All national banks were required to become members of the reserve system while all others could join if they wanted.

federate armies to commemorate the great battle on its 50th anniversary.

July 25, 26, 28 The United States Tennis team won the **Davis Cup** in the challenge round against the British Isles, at Wimbledon, England, 3 matches to 2.

Oct. 7–11 Philadelphia, AL, defeated New York, NL, 4–1 in 10th annual **World Series.**

Nov. 1 1st Army-Notre Dame football game, in which little known Notre Dame defeated powerful Army by constant use of forward pass, did a great deal to popularize the game by proving that a small, clever team could defeat a large, powerful one. This encouraged small schools to play the game.

Nov. 29 Army defeated Navy, 22–9, in their annual football classic. It was held this year at the Polo Grounds, New York city.

1914

Nobel Prize in chemistry presented to Theodore William Richards "for his exact determinations of the atomic weights of a great number of elements." Richards was 1st American to be honored in this category. He corrected the atomic weights of several elements which had been erroneously measured. His investigation of the atomic weights of oxygen and hydrogen led ultimately to the discovery of "heavy hydrogen," an indispensable component of modern atomic research. In his description of his prize-winning work, Richards confessed he was especially thrilled when he discovered that iron in the earth had the same atomic weight as iron from a meteorite. This discovery gave him "an added realization of the unity of the universe."

Death rate in Canal Zone, Panama, had dropped to 6 per 1000 as against 14.1 per 1000 in the U.S. When work on Canal began in 1904, area was among most un-

Propaganda from both sides during early stage of World War I tried to swing U.S. opinion. Atrocity stories, almost all of them later disproved, were circulated by both sides. Many rumors appeared in American press and were believed because strict German and British censorship of all news dispatches from Europe had made all U.S. newspapers unreliable as regards the war. The most persistent rumor was that a large Russian army had left Archangel and, traveling by way of Scotland and England, joined the Allied forces on the western front. There was never the slightest truth in it, although U.S. newspapers carried many "eye-witness accounts" of bearded Russian soldiers in Glasgow or London or Calais.

Cotillion, once "the most fashionable dance of society," took 2d place about this time to the **waltz** and **2-step** in American ballrooms. Cotillion was a colorful, elabo-

POLITICS AND GOVERNMENT; WAR; DISASTERS; VITAL STATISTICS.	BOOKS; PAINTING; DRAMA; ARCHITECTURE; SCULPTURE.

sult of incident involving arrest of U.S. troops.

Apr. 16 2d "Coxey's Army" organized at Massillon, Ohio, to march on Washington. Made up of unemployed workers, it was headed by "General" Jacob S. Coxey.

Apr. 19 Pres. Wilson, in special message to Congress, asked authority to use **U.S. armed forces** "to obtain from General Huerta and his adherents the fullest recognition of the rights and dignity of the United States." After considerable debate, approval was given by both houses on April 22.

Apr. 21 U.S. fleet seized the custom house at Vera Cruz, Mexico, and marines occupied the city. Detachment was sent to exact an apology from Pres. Huerta of Mexico for the arrest of several U.S. Navy men. U.S. losses: 4 dead; 20 wounded.

Apr. 22 Mexico severed **diplomatic relations** with U.S. when Huerta returned passports to Nelson O'Shaughnessy, U.S. Chargé d'affaires.

Apr. 25 So-called "ABC" countries—Argentina, Brazil, Chile—offered to **arbitrate U.S.-Mexico dispute.** Pres. Wilson quickly accepted. While mediation commission was meeting, crisis dissolved when Gen. Huerta was forced to resign presidency of Mexico on July 15.

July 28–Aug. 6 Outbreak of **World War I** in Europe occurred. Americans caught in France and Germany took any means to reach London, often leaving money and possessions behind. In New York, the largest neutral port in the world, merchant and passenger ships of all belligerent nations anchored, fearful to chance crossing the Atlantic without naval protection.

Aug. 4 U.S. made formal **proclamation of neutrality** in war between Austria and Serbia, Germany and Russia, Germany and France. On Aug. 5 proclamation extended to include war between England and Germany. Pres. Wilson offered his good offices to warring nations in effort to promote peace.

"Trees," by **Joyce Kilmer,** published; became one of the most quoted poems in America.

Publication abroad of **Robert Frost's** 1st book, *North of Boston,* brought his immediate recognition as an important writer.

Novelty of twin beds and the tan~o added to great popularity of farce *Twin Beds* by **Salisbury Field** and **Margaret Mayo,** which recounts the story of a young wife who is caught up in the whirls of the new dance craze.

Establishment of **Whitney Studio Club,** which led to formation of Whitney Museum. Club was a social gathering place for moderns and at same time provided a gallery for work.

John Alden Carpenter composed his descriptive suite for orchestra, *Adventures in a Perambulator,* a work with "modern" tendencies.

Feb. 13 The American Society of Composers, Authors and Publishers, most often known by its initials, **ASCAP,** organized at a meeting of more than 100 composers and their associates at the Hotel Claridge, New York city. Victor Herbert, one of the chief persons responsible for calling the meeting, was made director and vice-president.

May 29 1st poems by **Edgar Lee Masters** published in *Reedy's Mirror.* Later the collection called *Spoon River Anthology* was published, and Masters became one of the best known American poets.

Aug. 19 Dramatic device of the "flashback" introduced on the stage in **Elmer Rice's** 1st play *On Trial.* Often used in the moving picture, this device gave theater another dimension.

Dec. 8 *Watch Your Step,* a "syncopated musical show" with music and lyrics by **Irving Berlin,** produced in New York.

432

| SCIENCE; INDUSTRY; ECONOMICS; EDUCATION; RELIGION; PHILOSOPHY. | SPORTS; FASHIONS; POPULAR ENTERTAINMENT; FOLKLORE; SOCIETY. |

healthy in the world. Fight against yellow fever and malaria had been won by Gen. William Gorgas, whose antimosquito campaigns had been pushed through in spite of official opposition.

Jan. 3 **Direct wireless connection** established between U.S. and Germany.

Jan. 13 Litigation over the **patents for balancing airplanes** settled by the U.S. Circuit Court of Appeals in favor of the Wright brothers and against Glenn Curtiss.

Jan. 20 **Marriage law of Wisconsin** based on eugenic principles was declared unconstitutional by the Circuit Court. Law was enacted in 1913.

Apr. 10 **Successful heart surgery** upon an animal announced by Dr. Alexis Carrel. He said the operation was performed while he suspended blood circulation for several minutes.

May 8 **Smith-Lever Act** passed by Congress. It provided federal funds for state agricultural colleges to establish instructional and advisory programs for farmers.

May 18 **Panama Canal** opened to barge service.

May 30 **Lassen Peak** in California, long supposed extinct, began to emit steam and ash. On June 8 and 14 steam rose to height of 10,000 ft. above crest. It is only active volcano in U.S.

July 29 **Cape Cod Canal** opened connecting Cape Cod Bay and Buzzards Bay.

rate dance which required the frequent changing of partners and the presentation of costly favors. It was often considered the climax of a ball.

1st great football stadium, the Yale Bowl, seating almost 80,000, opened, reflecting the increasing popular interest in football. After World War I crowds increased and many large stadia were erected throughout the U.S., some costing millions.

U.S.G.A. amateur championship won by Francis Ouimet at Ekwanok C.C., Manchester, Vt. He defeated Jerome D. Travers, 6 and 5. **Open championship** won by Walter Hagen at Midlothian C.C., Blue Island, Ill., with a score of 290.

U.S. lawn tennis men's singles champion, R. Norris Williams II; **women's singles champion,** Mary K. Browne.

U.S. lost the **Davis Cup** matches to Australia at matches held at the West Side Tennis Club, Forest Hills, N.Y.

Holiday won the 38th annual **Preakness Stakes,** paying 21–5. Jockey was A. Schuttinger; time was 1:53⅘ on a fast track for winnings valued at $1335.

Luke McLuke won the 46th annual **Belmont Stakes,** paying 9–5. Jockey was M. Buxton; time was 2:20 on a fast track for winnings valued at $3025.

Apr. Mack Sennett began production of **1st 6-reel motion picture.** A comedy entitled *Tillie's Punctured Romance,* it starred Marie Dressler and Charlie Chaplin.

May 7 Resolution introduced by Thomas Heflin of Alabama passed both houses of Congress and provided that the 2d Sunday in May be designated **"Mother's Day."** Pres. Wilson on May 9 issued a proclamation calling on public to display the U.S. flag on that day as an expression "of our love and reverence for the mothers of our country."

May 9 Winner of the 40th annual **Kentucky Derby,** H. C. Applegate's *Old*

Aug. 15 **Panama Canal** formally opened.

Sept. 26 **Federal Trade Commission** established to prevent monopolies and preserve competition in commerce. Pres. Wilson said the bill was meant "to make men in a small way of business as free to succeed as men in a big way and to kill monopoly in the seed." Commission was to incorporate and supersede the Bureau of Corporations.

Nov. 23 **U.S. forces** left Vera Cruz.

1915

Jan. 2 U.S. Senate passed bill to require **literacy tests** for all immigrants; vetoed by Pres. Wilson on Jan. 28.

Jan. 26 **Rocky Mountain National Park** established by act of Congress.

Jan. 28 Congress established **U.S. Coast Guard.** Coast Guard was formed by combining Revenue Cutter Service and Life Saving Service.

Feb. 23 Nevada **"easy divorce"** law requiring 6 months' residence signed by Gov. Boyle.

May 7 Steamship **Lusitania,** Queen of the Cunard fleet, sunk without warning off Ireland by German submarine. Of 1924 aboard, 1198 were drowned, including 63 infants. Number of Americans drowned was 114. Indignation aroused in U.S. by the sinking made American entry into war against Germany inevitable.

May 13 U.S. sent protest to Germany against the sinking of the *Lusitania* and other submarine incidents. This is known as **1st Lusitania note.**

May 28 **Germany's reply** to the U.S. note of protest justified the sinking of the *Lusitania* as a measure of self-defense, asserting that the ship was armed with cannon and carried a cargo of munitions and arms.

May 31 In a note to Secretary Bryan British Ambassador declared that the **Lusitania** was not armed when attacked by the German submarine, nor was it ever armed.

This was the 1st of many musicals written by Berlin. His phenomenal career continued with other ragtime musical comedies: *Stop! Look! Listen!* and *The Century Girl* (1916) began the parade that grew to a flood in the 20's.

Family Limitation, pioneer work on birth control by **Margaret Sanger,** brought to court by New York Society for the Suppression of Vice. Book found to be "contrary not only to the law of the state, but to the law of God." Mrs. Sanger jailed as a result.

Novel of protest reached a climax in **Ernest Poole's** *The Harbor,* a study of the New York waterfront with its amalgam of foreign-born, illiterate masses, mobsters, and bosses. He sympathetically pointed out how such conditions led to the formation of labor organizations and to subsequent strikes.

Strange chronicle of assorted lives in a small town appears in *Spoon River Anthology* by **Edgar Lee Masters.** Outwardly a series of short poems in the form of postmortem confessions, the book reveals the violence, dishonesty, and criminal, sex-dominated lives of the inhabitants.

Publication of poems of **Robert Frost,** *A Boy's Will* and *North of Boston,* established him as a major poet. In conventional form, his poetry depicts various aspects of New England rural life—the stony hills, the neglected or abandoned farms, the lonely scattered inhabitants.

Early exponent of modernism in American painting was **John Marin.** Following the French Expressionists like Matisse and Rouault, he distorted color and form to represent interior nature of things. In his watercolor *Woolworth Building* the mass of brick sways, and he defended this by

SCIENCE; INDUSTRY; ECONOMICS; EDUCATION; RELIGION; PHILOSOPHY.	SPORTS; FASHIONS; POPULAR ENTERTAINMENT; FOLKLORE; SOCIETY.

Distance between New York and Boston was reduced by 70 mi.

July 31   Cables received early in the morning announced the closing, because of the outbreak of war, of the **London Stock Exchange.** Every other important stock exchange in the world followed suit.

Rosebud, ran the 1¼ mi. in the fastest time yet, 2:03⅗ on a fast track under jockey J. McCabe, winning $9125, another high for this race.

Oct. 9–13   Boston, NL, defeated Philadelphia, AL, 4–0 in 11th annual **World Series.**

Nov. 28   **Army** defeated Navy 20–0 in their annual football classic at Franklin Field, Philadelphia.

1915

Automobile owners found that many people were willing to pay for a short ride and so the **taxicab** was born. Price was a nickel, or **"jitney,"** and the term soon became legal for the cars. Drivers were known as "hackers" or "hackies" in the East, "cabbies" in the Midwest. Intercity bus lines sprang from regular jitney service.

Important discovery in **vitamin research** made by Joseph Goldberger of the U.S. Public Health Service in determining that pellagra was caused by certain vitamin deficiencies.

Jan. 25   **Major legal setback for labor** rendered with Supreme Court decision announced on Jan. 25th that a state law (Kansas) forbidding an employer from requiring nonunion membership for his employees was unconstitutional.

Jan. 25   **1st transcontinental telephone call** made by same 2 men who had made original telephone conversation in 1876. Alexander Graham Bell, speaking from New York, said to Dr. Thomas A. Watson in San Francisco: "Mr. Watson, come here, I want you." In 1876, Watson had been in the next room.

May 24   Invention of **"telescribe"** to record telephone conversations announced by Thomas A. Edison.

June 3   **United States Steel Corporation** ruled lawful and not in violation of

Humorous quip **"What this country really needs is a good five-cent cigar"** originated with Indiana-born Thomas R. Marshall, vice-president under the Wilson presidency. During one of the tedious debates in the Senate he threw forth this bit of cogent advice.

Modern major-league record for the **most bases stolen in 1 season** is 96, set by Ty Cobb in 1915. Cobb holds more records than any player in the history of baseball, but this record is most indicative of his fiery aggressive play.

National tennis championship site now **Forest Hills,** New York. National women's tennis championships moved here in 1921.

The Finn won the 47th annual **Belmont Stakes,** paying 7–5. Jockey was G. Byrne; time was 2:18⅖ on a fast track for winnings valued at $1825.

Rhine Maiden won the 39th annual **Preakness Stakes,** paying 6–1. Jockey was D. Hoffman; time was 1:58 on a muddy track for winnings valued at $1275.

U.S.G.A. amateur championship won by Robert A. Gardner at C.C. of Detroit, Grosse Point Farms, Mich. He defeated J. G. Anderson 5 and 4. **Open championship** won by Jerome D. Travers at Baltusrol G.C., Short Hills, N.J., with a score of 297.

U.S. lawn tennis men's singles champion, William M. Johnston; **women's singles champion,** Molla Bjurstedt.

In Cambridge, Mass., Norman Taber of the U.S. **ran the mile in 4:12.6,** nearly 2 seconds under the old record.

POLITICS AND GOVERNMENT; WAR; DISASTERS; VITAL STATISTICS.

BOOKS; PAINTING; DRAMA; ARCHITECTURE; SCULPTURE.

June 9   U.S. asked Germany to take steps to avoid future attacks on American ships. This is known as **2d Lusitania note.**

July 2   **Bomb destroyed** U.S. Senate reception room. It had been placed there by Erich Muenter, alias Frank Holt, a German instructor at Cornell University.

July 3   **J. Pierpont Morgan shot** by Erich Muenter at Glen Cove, L.I. Morgan represented the British Government in war contract negotiations. 3 days later on July 6 Muenter committed suicide.

July 8   **German reply** to Pres. Wilson's note of June 9 declared that properly marked ships of neutral countries could cross the seas unmolested by German submarines.

July 15   U.S. Secret Service men captured a portfolio belonging to Dr. Heinrich F. Albert, the contents of which proved Albert the head of a **German propaganda and espionage ring** of major proportions. Portfolio was examined on July 24 and its contents turned over by Sec. of the Treasury William G. McAdoo to the New York *World* for publication. Several German-Americans, including George Sylvester Viereck, were implicated, along with German consuls, members of the German Embassy staff, and officials of the Hamburg-American Steamship Line.

July 21   **3rd Lusitania note** dispatched to Germany by Pres. Wilson warning that any future violation of U.S. rights would be regarded as "deliberately unfriendly."

Aug. 5   **Latin-American Conference** to debate means of ending unrest in Mexico opened at Washington, D.C.; attended by Argentina, Brazil, Bolivia, Chile, Guatemala, Uruguay, and U.S.

Sept. 16   **Haiti became U.S. protectorate** under terms of a treaty signed with that country. U.S. Senate approved Feb. 28, 1916.

Oct. 19   U.S government recognized **Gen. Venustiano Carranza as President of Mexico.** Next day an embargo was placed on the shipment of arms to Mexico, except to territories controlled by Carranza.

saying, "Are the buildings themselves dead? . . . I see great forces at work, great movements, the large buildings and the small buildings."

Painting which was attacked mercilessly by the conservatives when exhibited in America is **Max Weber's** *Chinese Restaurant.* Closely associated with Matisse, Rousseau, and other European moderns, he adds to their technique the influence of Oriental art.

At Wallack's Theatre in New York, American audiences were introduced to the brilliant repertory productions of **Harley Granville-Barker** and the stagecraft of **Gordon Craig,** in plays by Shaw and Shakespeare. Late in the year, Granville-Barker staged productions of Euripides' *The Trojan Women* and *Iphigenia in Tauris* (translations by Gilbert Murray) before audiences of 7,000–10,000 in college stadiums.

Feb.   Foundation of **Neighborhood Playhouse** in Grand Street, New York City, which devoted itself to fostering new American and European experimental drama.

Feb.   Famous theater company which gave tremendous impetus to modern drama, the **Washington Square Players,** founded, one week after 1st production of Neighborhood Playhouse. Operating at Bandbox Theater on 57 Street, New York City, group continued until war. In 1919 it was organized as the **Theater Guild.**

Nov. 14   Educator **Booker T. Washington** died. The son of a mulatto slave and a white man, he became an effective writer and lecturer on interracial matters. In 1881 he founded Tuskegee Institute, which emphasized industrial training as the best means to advance Negroes. Among his many books, the most important was his autobiography *Up From Slavery.*

Summer   Beginning of one of America's most significant theater groups, the **Provincetown Players** in Massachusetts. Organized by a colony of artists from Greenwich Village, the group improvised a stage for early productions of Eugene O'Neill.

436

| SCIENCE; INDUSTRY; ECONOMICS; EDUCATION; RELIGION; PHILOSOPHY. | SPORTS; FASHIONS; POPULAR ENTERTAINMENT; FOLKLORE; SOCIETY. |

the antitrust law by the District Court of New Jersey.

July 1 **Telephone rate reduced to 5¢** in New York City.

July 13 **Workmen's Compensation bill** ruled valid by the New York Court of Appeals.

July 16 **1st warships to pass through Panama Canal,** the *Missouri, Ohio,* and *Wisconsin,* made successful passage during U.S. fleet maneuvers.

July 27 **1st direct wireless service** between U.S. and Japan effected.

Aug. 17 **Leo M. Frank,** convicted murderer of Mary Phagan, one of his factory workers, was lynched at Marietta, Ga. Frank was sentenced to death after a sensational trial, and appeals up to the Supreme Court proved futile. Outgoing Gov. Slaton inflamed the state by commuting Frank's sentence to life imprisonment; the killing followed shortly thereafter. Outside the South it was widely believed that because he was a Jew Frank was a victim of hate.

Oct. 15 American bankers, organized under J. P. Morgan & Company, agreed to lend British and French governments $500,000,000—the **largest loan floated in any country** up to that time.

Oct. 21 **1st transatlantic radiotelephone** communication was made, from Arlington, Va., to the Eiffel Tower.

Oct. 27 **New record established for the seaplane** in U.S. by Oscar A. Brindley, flying 544 mi. above California coast in 10 hours.

Nov. 1 Supreme Court declared unconstitutional Arizona's **anti-alien law** that required 80% of a firm's employees be native-born Americans.

Dec. 4 Long dormant **Ku Klux Klan** revived in Georgia under a new charter granted by the state.

Dec. 10 **1 millionth automobile** produced by Ford plant in Detroit.

Feb. 8 **The Birth of a Nation** opened at Clune's Auditorium in Los Angeles. Most brilliant film made up to that time, it aroused bitter protests from Northern liberals for its sympathic treatment of the Ku Klux Klan during Reconstruction. Negro leaders objected to its lurid racism. It was produced from a scenario based on *The Clansman,* by Thomas Dixon.

Feb. 20 **Panama-Pacific International Exposition** opened at San Francisco.

Apr. 5 **Jess Willard** of Kansas took the **heavyweight championship** from Jack Johnson in a 23-round bout at Havana, Cuba. They fought under a blazing sun and it is not clear whether heat exhaustion or a blow from Willard felled Johnson; his descent to the canvas was described as a slow sinking.

May 8 Only filly to win the **Kentucky Derby** was H. P. Whitney's *Regret,* which took the 41st running of the Churchill Downs classic in 2:05⅗ on a fast track to win $11,450. Jockey was J. Nutter.

July 24 The excursion steamer *Eastland* capsized at her pier in Chicago, killing 852 people.

Oct. 8–13 Boston, AL, defeated Philadelphia, NL, 4–1 in the 12th annual **World Series.**

Oct. 9 Driving a Stutz at 102.6 mph, Gil Anderson won the Astor cup and set a **new auto speed** record at Sheepshead Bay, N.Y.

Nov. 7 In Chicago, 40,000 men paraded in protest against the **closing of saloons** on Sunday.

Nov. 27 **Army** defeated Navy 14–0 in their annual football classic, held this year at the Polo Grounds, New York City.

Dec. Pacifist slogan **"Out of the trenches and back to their homes by Christmas"** invoked by Henry Ford in his short-lived plan to end the holocaust in Europe.

Dec. 18 Pres. Wilson married Mrs. Edith Bolling Galt, in Washington.

437

POLITICS AND GOVERNMENT; WAR; DISASTERS; VITAL STATISTICS.

BOOKS; PAINTING; DRAMA; ARCHITECTURE; SCULPTURE.

1916

Jan. 7 German note to Washington declared that a strict adherence to international law in **submarine warfare** would be henceforth followed.

Mar. 9 Mexican revolutionary general, **Francisco "Pancho" Villa,** led band of 1500 guerrillas across border and attacked Columbus, N.M., killing 17 Americans. U.S. troops pursued Mexicans, killed 50 on U.S. soil, 70 more in Mexico. Brig.-Gen. John J. Pershing ordered to Mexico to capture Villa.

Mar. 15 Senate unanimously passed the resolution to bring the **Army** to full strength.

Mar. 15 U.S. military expedition of 6000 men began the pursuit of **Villa** and his brigands, entering Mexico under the command of Brig.-Gen. John J. Pershing and Col. Dodd.

Apr. 18 Pres. Wilson, in a strong note to Germany, said that unless the series of **U-boats attacks** which began with the sinking of the *Lusitania* and continued through several additional attacks on passenger liners were immediately discontinued, diplomatic relations between U.S. and Germany would be severed.

May U.S. Marines landed in **Santo Domingo** to settle internal violence. Occupation continued until 1924.

May 4 In reply to U.S. note of Apr. 18, Germany pledged not to attack any **merchant vessels** without warning and without giving passengers a chance to escape.

June 3 **National Defense Act** passed. It increased the standing Army to 175,000, National Guard to 450,000.

June 10 **Republican National Convention** nominated Charles Evans Hughes of New York and Charles Warren Fairbanks of Indiana for the presidency and the vice-presidency respectively.

June 14–16 **National Democratic**

Publication of **Carl Sandburg's** *Chicago Poems* focused attention on Midwestern writing and created much controversy among readers and critics. In this and in the subsequent *Cornhuskers* (1918), *Smoke and Steel* (1920) and *Slabs of the Sunburnt West* (1922) he ranges over the entire American landscape: cities, cemeteries, fields and flowers, prairies, and steel.

Edwin Arlington Robinson published his book of verse, *The Man Against the Sky,* and was immediately acclaimed as a foremost poet. His earlier works were then reprinted and in the '20's he won the Pulitzer prize 3 times. Robinson introduced many character types, including psychological studies of failures.

Censorship in New York City caused suppression of Theodore Dreiser's *The Genius.*

Edgar Varèse, one of the most uncompromising of experimentalist composers, settled in the U.S., after having been rejected for service in the French Army.

Dixieland Jass Band opened at Schiller's Cafe in Chicago. Composed of Dominique La Rocca, Eddie Edwards, Henry Ragas, Alcide "Yellow" Nunez, and Tony Sbarbaro, it achieved great popularity and, with somewhat different personnel, went to New York the following year, where it was billed as The Original Dixieland Jass Band.

Among events marking the **tercentenary of Shakespeare's death,** the Drama Society paid a fitting tribute with their Century Theatre production of *The Tempest* in the Elizabethan manner; Beerbohm Tree brought from England a 4-hour production of *Henry VIII,* more notable for its pageantry than fidelity to the original; James K. Hackett was a failure as Macbeth, but with Thomas A. Wise as Falstaff, he did a creditable production of *The Merry Wives of Windsor.* The nadir of the celebration was reached late in May with Percy Mac-

1916

National Research Council organized by National Academy of Sciences.

Important advance in the prevention of internal blood clotting made by a Johns Hopkins medical student with the discovery of **heparin,** a substance that acted as a temporary anticoagulant of the blood. Need for more lasting method of anticoagulation with less frequent injections led to discovery of **dicumarol.**

Theory behind "progressive education" formulated by **John Dewey** in his *Democracy and Education.* According to him, intelligence is to be seen as an instrument for changing one's environment and should be trained accordingly. Subject matter should be adjusted to the child, not the child to the subject matter. Distinction between cultural and vocational training should be abolished.

Submachine gun invented by Brig. Gen. John Taliaferro Thompson; hence gun was known as "Tommy gun."

Automobile production soared about 80% over 1915, and the output of new cars and trucks passed the million mark for the 1st time. The average price for a new car was just over $600, and it was estimated there were now about 3.5 million cars on the highways.

Jan. 24 **Federal income tax** ruled constitutional by a decision handed down by the U.S. Supreme Court in the case *Brushaber v. Union Pacific Railroad Co.*

Jan. 25 **U.S. exports for 1915** surpassed all previous figures, totaling $3,555,-000,000 and showing an excess of $1,772,-309,538 over imports.

Jan. 28 Pres. Wilson named **Louis D. Brandeis** to the Supreme Court. The appointment was confirmed June 1; he was sworn in June 3, the first Justice who was a Jew.

Feb. 29 **Child labor legislation** in South Carolina raised minimum age of

D. W. Griffith bewildered movie audiences with his film **Intolerance,** in which sequences dealing with Babylon, the Crucifixion, St. Bartholomew's massacre, and the killing of modern strikers were joined by a repeated scene suggested by Whitman's line "Out of the cradle endlessly rocking." Other memorable films of the year were a spectacular production of Jules Verne's *20,000 Leagues Under the Sea,* and *Joan the Woman,* in which opera star Geraldine Farrar depicted events in the life of Joan of Arc.

5 more states voted themselves "dry" this year: Michigan, Montana, Nebraska, South Dakota, and Utah. **Prohibition** was now law in 24 states with approximately 32.5 million people.

Major league record for the **most shutouts** pitched in 1 season set by Grover Cleveland Alexander of Philadelphia Phillies, who pitched 16 shutout games.

Friar Rock won the 48th annual **Belmont Stakes** paying 5–2. Jockey was E. Haynes; time was 2:22 on a muddy track for winnings valued at $4100.

Damrosch won the 40th annual **Preakness Stakes,** paying 13–2. Jockey was L. McAfee; time was 1:54⅘ on a fast track for winnings valued at $1380.

U.S. lawn tennis men's singles champion, R. Norris Williams II; **women's singles champion,** Molla Bjurstedt.

U.S.G.A. amateur championship won by Charles Evans Jr. at Merion Cricket Club, Haverford, Pa. He defeated Robert A. Gardner, 4 and 3. **Open championship** won by Charles Evans Jr. at Minikahda Club, Minneapolis, Minn., with a score of 286. No competition in 1917–18.

Jan. 1 **1st permanent annual Rose Bowl football game** held between Washington State College and Brown University, Washington State winning 14–0. In 1923 this annual game was officially desig-

Convention met at St. Louis and renominated Pres. Woodrow Wilson and Vice-Pres. Thomas R. Marshall.

June 16   Gen. J. J. Pershing advised by Gen. Jacinto Trevino, Commander of the Northern Army of Carranza, that any further movement of American troops into **Mexico** would be interpreted as hostile.

June 17   American troops re-entered **Mexico** and an ultimatum was issued by the Carranza consul at Brownsville, Tex., asserting that they would be attacked unless withdrawn.

June 20   Secretary Lansing's note to Carranza government asserted that American troops would not be withdrawn from **Mexico** until order was restored on the border.

June 21   Capt. Charles T. Boyd killed when Carranza troops attacked an American force at Carrizal, **Mexico.** Americans lost 17 in killed and wounded while 38 Mexicans were killed, among whom was Mexican commander, Gen. Gomez.

July 22   **Bomb thrown during a Preparedness Day parade** in San Francisco killed 10, wounded 40. In 1917 labor leader Tom Mooney was sentenced to hang and Warren K. Billings got life imprisonment for the deed. Pres. Wilson commuted Mooney's sentence to life imprisonment in 1918, but because of confessions of perjured testimony at the trial the case was an international *cause célèbre* for many years. On Jan. 7, 1939, Mooney was pardoned by Gov. Olson of California, and Billings was released later in the year.

July 28   U.S. accepted **Mexican proposal** to submit differences to a commission in a note to the Carranza government sent by acting Secretary of State Frank L. Polk.

Aug. 4   Treaty for the purchase of the **Danish West Indies** for $25,000,000 signed between U.S. and Denmark.

Nov. 7   Woodrow Wilson, having campaigned on an antiwar-but-prepared-

Kaye's presentation of his new masque, *Caliban by the Yellow Sands,* in the stadium of N.Y.'s City College.

One of most popular dramas of the season in New York City was **Edna Ferber's** *Our Mrs. McChesney,* a play about a lady drummer in the petticoat line; the role was played by Ethel Barrymore. Miss Barrymore's brother John was seen in Galsworthy's *Justice,* directed by B. Iden Payne; Madame Strindberg directed a production of her husband's *Easter* for the Stage Society of New York; and Margaret Anglin revived Oscar Wilde's *A Woman of No Importance.*

American growing interest in **ballet** and artistic dancing made a success of visiting *Ballet Russe* company under direction of Diaghilev, with music by Stravinsky and others. Era also saw great popularity of Pavlova, Ruth St. Denis, Ted Shawn.

New York Building Code revised to allow skyscraper construction to unlimited height provided setbacks, depending on width of adjacent streets, were incorporated in the design on ¾ of ground area.

The **Massachusetts Institute of Technology** moved to its present location on the banks of the Charles River, Cambridge, into magnificent new buildings designed by William Wells Bosworth.

Mar. 2   The Philadelphia Symphony Orchestra gave **Gustav Mahler's** 8th Symphony its American première, employing 8 soloists, a mixed chorus of 800, a children's choir of 150, and an augmented orchestra of 110. Critics complained the piece lacked sustained inspiration, found the musical ideas did not justify the employment of such an enormous technical apparatus.

Mar. 20   Successful dramatist of the '20's, **Zoë Akins** began career with 1-acter *Magical City,* which recounts effect of New York City upon a young girl. *The Varying Shore* (1921) traces the history of a professional mistress; *Greatness* (1922) tells story of an opera singer and her do-

children employed in mills, factories, and mines from 12 to 14 years.

Apr. 26 **Military training** in public schools voted down by the New York City Board of Education.

July 11 Pres. Wilson signed **Shackleford Good Roads Bill,** which authorized federal government to turn over $5,000,-000 to states for roadbuilding programs; only states willing to contribute equal amounts could benefit. Law remained in force 5 years, with increases each year in the amounts spent

July 17 **Federal Farm Loan Act** established land bank system which provided for loans to farmers who needed money for maintenance or improvement.

July 18 *The Official Gazette,* London, published the names of 80 **U.S. firms blacklisted under England's trading-with-the-enemy act.** The U.S. charged that Britain had repeatedly violated the rights of neutrals; that our ships were convoyed to British ports and searched at leisure, the mails rifled, and trade secrets filched; that U.S. exporters to European neutrals had to submit lists of their customers for British approval, which lists were then passed to British competitors.

Aug. 16 U.S. and Canada established **migratory bird treaty** to protect insect-destroying birds in North America.

Aug. 25 **National Park Service** established as part of the Dept. of Interior.

Sept. 1 **Keating-Owen Act** prohibited interstate shipment of goods manufactured by children under 14 years of age. In 1918 the Supreme Court declared this law unconstitutional.

Sept. 3 Pres. Wilson signed Adamson bill which provided that **8-hour day** be standard for most railroad workers. Bill had been hurriedly passed through both houses of Congress to stave off nationwide railroad strike called for Sept. 4. Strike was averted, but the President was severely criticized and accused of wooing labor during an election year.

nated "Rose Bowl Game," and its success encouraged other cities and organizations to sponsor postseason "bowl games." Now there are more than a dozen such games held annually, the major ones drawing from 80,000 to over 100,000 spectators.

Apr. 10 **1st professional golf tournament** held at the Siwanoy course in Bronxville, N.Y., by the Professional Golfers' Association of America, which had been formed Jan. 17. Professional golfers made very little money due to the scarcity of tournaments. In 1935, the top money-maker was Johnny Revolta, who made $9543. The rest of the year's prize money, $135,000, was divided among 226 other players. By 1945, chiefly due to the efforts of promoter Fred Corcoran, the prizes had increased considerably. Byron Nelson, that year's top money winner, made $52,541.

May 13 Winner of the 42nd annual **Kentucky Derby** was J. Sanford's *George Smith,* ridden by J. Loftus. Time, a new record, was 2:04 on a fast track; winnings, $9750.

June 15 **Boy Scouts of America** incorporated by a bill signed by President Wilson.

July 30 German saboteurs set off huge explosions of ammunition on the docks of **Toms River Island** near Jersey City, N.J. On Jan. 17 the following year they are believed to have destroyed a munitions plant at Kingsland, N.J. In 1922 the U.S. lost a suit to recover damages through an international claims commission, but after new hearings in 1939, the German government was ordered (in 1940) to pay a total of $50 million.

Sept. 30 **Longest winning streak in modern baseball history** was stopped at 26 games, when the N.Y. Giants were beaten by the Boston Braves, 8–3, in the 2nd game of a doubleheader.

Oct. 7–12 Boston, AL, defeated Brooklyn, NL, 4–1 in the 13th annual **World Series.**

POLITICS AND GOVERNMENT; WAR; DISASTERS; VITAL STATISTICS.	BOOKS; PAINTING; DRAMA; ARCHITECTURE; SCULPTURE.

ness platform, won the **presidential election** from Republican candidate Charles Evans Hughes. Election returns were close, and for 3 days the outcome was uncertain. Final electoral score: Wilson, 277, Hughes, 254. Popular vote: Wilson, 9,128,837; Hughes, 8,536,380.

Dec. 18 Pres. Wilson addressed identical **peace notes** to all the belligerent powers. He said that the U.S. was as vitally interested in peace as the warring nations and that steps should be taken not only to end the war but "to secure the future peace of the world."

mestic problems. The heroine of *Déclassée* (1919), played by Ethel Barrymore, was victim of a scandal.

May 20 Bill authorizing **motion picture censorship** vetoed by Gov. Whitman of New York.

Nov. 13 The Metropolitan Opera opened its season with the 1st complete production in America of Bizet's *The Pearl Fishers.*

1917

Jan. 17 U.S. and Denmark ratified the American purchase of the **Virgin Islands** for $25 million.

Jan. 22 In "Peace without victory" speech Pres. Wilson outlined his famous **ten points**, or conditions, under which he would urge the U.S. to enter a world federation. World federation would be designed to prevent future wars.

Jan. 28 **Gen. Pershing** ordered home from Mexico after nearly a year of fruitless searching for Pancho Villa among mountains.

Jan. 31 German Ambassador von Bernstorff delivered to the U.S. Department of State a note saying that effective the next day, Feb. 1, **submarine assaults** against all neutral and belligerent shipping would be renewed.

Feb. 3 Pres. **Wilson severed diplomatic relations with Germany.** On same day **U.S. liner Housatonic** was sunk after warning was given by German submarine.

Feb. 5 **Immigration Act** passed over veto. It excluded Asiatic laborers (unless protected by special treaties).

Feb. 24 British Secret Service men, who had intercepted and decoded a message from the German Ministry of Foreign Affairs to the German Ambassador in Mexico, handed it to U.S. Ambassador in

Pulitzer Prizes: U.S. history, *With Americans of Past and Present Days* by J. J. Jusserand, Ambassador of France to the U.S.; biography, *Julia Ward Howe* by Laura E. Richards and Maude Howe Elliott, assisted by Florence Howe Hall.

Edwin Arlington Robinson turned to the Arthurian legends in his *Merlin.* Unlike Tennyson, he gives the cycle a 20th century point of view by studying the individual psychologies of his characters. He continued his cycle with *Lancelot* (1920) and *Tristram* (1927).

Poetic credo and practice of **Imagists** formulated in **Amy Lowell's** *Tendencies in Modern American Poetry.* Through her efforts the "school" was organized. She gave much encouragement to poets like John Gould Fletcher and H.D.

Hamlin Garland's **A Son of the Middle Border** published. This was an autobiographical narrative about westward migration, a frankly realistic picture of the hard lot of Western farmers. It was followed by 14 more semi-historical studies, including the Pulitzer Prize-winning *A Daughter of the Middle Border* (1921).

Sinclair Lewis, who had been considered one of the most promising young American writers, disappointed critics with this 3rd novel, *The Job: An American Novel.*

| SCIENCE; INDUSTRY; ECONOMICS; EDUCATION; RELIGION; PHILOSOPHY. | SPORTS; FASHIONS; POPULAR ENTERTAINMENT; FOLKLORE; SOCIETY. |

Oct. 16 Margaret Sanger, Fania Mindell, and Ethel Burne opened the 1st **birth control clinic,** at 46 Amboy St., Brooklyn.

Dec. 21 Volume of trade on the **N.Y. Stock Exchange** reached a 15-year high following Secretary of State Robert Lansing's statement that the U.S. was being drawn into the war.

Oct. 24 Battling Levinsky outpointed Jack Dillon in a 12-round fight in Boston and proclaimed himself the **light-heavyweight champion.** He lost the title in 1920 to Georges Carpentier.

Nov. 25 **Army** defeated Navy in their annual football classic, 15–7, at the Polo Grounds, New York City.

1917

Irving Langmuir performed epoch-making experiments in molecular chemistry, determining molecular measurements with an accuracy and precision that became models for later researchers.

University of Alaska founded as Alaska Agricultural College and School of Mines at College, Alaska. 1st classes held in 1922. Present name adopted in 1935.

The **Columbia School of Journalism** nominated the 1st candidates for the **Pulitzer Prize.** Joseph Pulitzer had endowed the Columbia School of Journalism, specifying that the annual interest on the endowment be allotted to awards for outstanding contributions to the several fields of American letters. The 1st list of prize candidates was submitted to the trustees of Columbia College in 1917. A Pulitzer Prize is awarded yearly to the best novel, play, poetry, biography, history, and journalism.

Creative Intelligence, with contributions by **John Dewey** and others, published.

Helium was first produced in quantity this year, at 3 experimental plants in Texas. They produced about 200,000 cubic ft. of the gas, but not quickly enough to be put to use in military balloons in France. At the war's end, most of the gas was awaiting shipment from New Orleans' docks.

Expression **"Pie in the Sky"** came into usage from song adopted for I.W.W. movement. Originally a hobo song, it promises the downtrodden that after a life of eating hay, they will have their "pie in the sky."

U.S. lawn tennis men's singles champion, R. Lindley Murray; **women's singles champion,** Molla Bjurstedt.

Hourless won the 49th annual **Belmont Stakes.** The jockey was J. Butwell. The winning 3-year-old carried 126 pounds and earned $5,800.

Kalitan won the 41st annual **Preakness Stakes,** paying 10–1. Jockey was E. Haynes; time was 1:54⅗ on a fast track for winnings valued at $4800.

Jan. 1 2d annual **Rose Bowl** game at Pasadena, Calif., saw Oregon defeat Pennsylvania by a score of 14 to 0.

Jan. An **anti-prostitution drive** in San Francisco attracted huge crowds to public meetings this month. At one event attended by 7000 citizens, 20,000 were turned away. In a conference with the Rev. Paul Smith, the most outspoken foe of vice, 300 prostitutes made a plea for toleration, explaining they had been forced into a life of sin by poverty. When the Reverend Smith asked if they would take "honest work" at $8 to $10 a week, the la-

Great Britain. Called the **Zimmermann note,** it instructed the German Ambassador to offer Mexico an alliance as soon as war broke out between Germany and U.S.

Mar. 2   Passage of the **Jones Act** made Puerto Rico a U.S. territory and U.S. citizens of its inhabitants.

Mar. 5   **Pres. Wilson** inaugurated for his 2d term. Thomas R. Marshall was his vice-president.

Mar. 8   Senate adopted **cloture rule,** permitting majority to terminate debate. Each senator may be permitted to speak for an hour after rule is invoked.

Mar. 9   Pres. Wilson announced that the Attorney-General had decided the President has in his own right authority to **arm merchant vessels** and that he would proceed to do so immediately.

Apr. 2   Pres. Wilson delivered his **war message** to a hastily convened Congress. On same day Rep. Jeannette Rankin, Republican from Montana, became **1st woman member in the House** (from 1917–19; 1941–43). She cast the sole votes against U.S. participation in both World War I and II.

Apr. 6   Pres. Wilson signed a joint resolution of Congress proclaiming a **state of war** with Germany. Congress had met in extraordinary session Apr. 2, and the resolution was passed by the Senate and the House on Apr. 4 and Apr. 5 respectively.

Apr. 24   **Liberty Loan Act,** a war finance measure, authorized Sec. of the Treasury McAdoo to issue for public subscription $2 billion of $3\frac{1}{2}\%$ convertible gold bonds.

May 18   **Federal conscription of troops** for armed services approved by Congress. **Selective Service Act** required registration of all men between 21 and 30 inclusive.

June 26   1st **American troops** arrived in San Nazaire, France, under Maj. Gen. William L. Sibert.

The book offended because it was an unidealized depiction of the U.S. business world, and because it treated realistically the subject of women in business, with the resultant conflicts between career and marriage. His *The Innocents,* also published this year, was a sentimental picture of an elderly couple and of village life.

The great French actress **Sarah Bernhardt,** now 72, began what was to be her last tour of the U.S. Although she was unable to move about without assistance (her leg had been amputated in 1915 following aggravation of an old stage injury), she thrilled audiences with remarkably youthful portrayals, among them, Portia in Shakespeare's *The Merchant of Venice.*

"Storyville" or "The District," a section of New Orleans set aside for organized vice, closed at the insistence of the U.S. Navy. The closing tended to drive jazz musicians, who had made a living in the honky-tonks and sporting houses, out of New Orleans.

Original Dixieland Jass Band opened at Reisenweber's Restaurant in New York city. In the same year, this group made the **1st jazz recordings,** including "Tiger Rag," "Reisenweber Rag," "Barnyard Blues," "At the Jazz Band Ball," "Ostrich Walk," "Bluin' the Blues," "Clarinet Marmalade."

Hell Gate Bridge, a cantilevered steel arch spanning the Harlem River, built for railroad service in New York. It was one of the most striking nonsuspension bridges in the world.

Ornithologists noted that the **starling,** which had been introduced successfully in New York at the turn of the century, was spreading all over the U.S. and becoming a pest.

Apr. 14   **Committee on Public Information,** headed by George Creel, was created by executive order to control the censorship of news and propaganda releases.

Oct. 27   In New York Russian violinist **Jascha Heifetz,** 16, made his American debut. Critics without exception pro-

SCIENCE; INDUSTRY; ECONOMICS; EDUCATION; RELIGION; PHILOSOPHY.

SPORTS; FASHIONS; POPULAR ENTERTAINMENT; FOLKLORE; SOCIETY.

There were 4,842,139 **motor vehicles** registered in the U.S., 435,000 of them trucks; in all the other nations of the world it was estimated there were only 719,246. This year alone, 1,795,840 passenger cars and 181,348 commercial vehicles were made here, and there were 25,500 garages and 13,500 repair shops to service them. The average price of a new car was $720.

Feb. 23 **Federal Board for Vocational Education** created by the Smith-Hughes Act. In order to stimulate the development of studies in trade and agricultural schools, the government ruled that the expenditures of the various states in these fields would be supplemented by grants from the federal government equal to the amounts spent by the states.

Mar. 3 Congress approved the **1st excess profits tax,** to help pay for increased military spending. It was a progressive tax, from 20% to 60% on all corporate profit in excess of 7% to 9% of capital. The law was repealed Oct. 3 by the Revenue Act of 1917.

Mar. 19 **8-hour day** for railroad workers agreed upon by railroad managers in co-operation with the defense program, thus relieving the threat of a railroad tie-up. But labor gained by keeping the same pay scale.

Apr. 4 **Price of wheat** per bu. passed $2 on the Chicago Board of Trade for 1st time in a normal market. On May 11th, when price reached $3.25, trading was discontinued.

Apr. 19 **Price of cotton** reached 21¼¢ per lb. on New York Exchange, the highest price since the Civil War.

Aug. 18 **1st 2-way radiotelephone communication** between a plane and the ground, and 2 days later between 2 airborne planes, was established at Langley Field, Va.

Sept. 5 Anti-war activities of the **I.W.W.** prompted simultaneous raids on the organization's headquarters in 24 cities.

dies laughed derisively. This lost them public sympathy, and the police shortly thereafter closed about 200 houses.

Apr. 2 Memorable sentence **"The world must be made safe for democracy"** sounded by Woodrow Wilson in his address to Congress in which he asked for a declaration of war against Germany. The latter had notified U.S. that she would begin her unrestricted submarine warfare. Wilson tried to make clear the motive for our entry into the conflict: the need to check the might of an arbitrary power.

May 2 The **1st double no-hit 9-inning baseball game** in the major leagues was played in Chicago. Jim Vaughn of the Cubs and Fred Toney of Cincinnati both pitched the full game without allowing a hit. The Reds scored in the 10th to win 1–0.

May 12 1st imported horse to win the **Kentucky Derby** was Billings and Johnson's *Omar Khayyam,* who won the 43d running of the Churchill Downs classic in 2:04⅘ on a fast track to win $16,-600.

June 23 Ernie Shore joined the select company of **perfect-game pitchers** (no hits, no runs, no man reached 1st base), as he led Boston to a 4–0 victory over Washington.

July 4 Famous phrase **"Lafayette, we are here"** delivered by Col. Charles E. Stanton, speaking in General Pershing's stead at the tomb of the French nobleman.

Aug. 19 1st baseball game played in New York's **Polo Grounds** resulted in the arrest of managers John McGraw of the Giants and Christy Mathewson of the Cincinnati Reds for violating New York Blue Law prohibiting Sunday ball playing.

Aug. 28 In Washington, 10 **suffragette** pickets were arrested in front of the White House. 4 of them received 6-month penitentiary sentences on Oct. 16. On Nov. 10 picketing was resumed and 41 women were arrested. The leaders received sentences of 6 days to 6 months in prison.

445

| POLITICS AND GOVERNMENT; WAR; DISASTERS; VITAL STATISTICS. | BOOKS; PAINTING; DRAMA; ARCHITECTURE; SCULPTURE. |

July 4 **1st U.S. training field** for military aviators opened at Rantoul, Ill. Other fields opened shortly thereafter at Dayton, Ohio, and Mount Clemens, Mich.

July 14 House of Representatives voted unanimously to appropriate $640,-000,000 for **military aviation program.**

Nov. 3 Small contingent of U.S. infantrymen suffered a setback in France in the **1st engagement** in which American soldiers participated.

Nov. 30 **"Rainbow (42d) Division"** arrived in France with every state in the Union represented.

claimed him the equal of the greatest living masters, both in technique and maturity of conception. He became a U.S. citizen in 1925.

On Broadway Jesse Lynch William's play *Why Marry?* opened in the Fall. The comedy, a close study of the institution of marriage, was to win a Pulitzer prize for its author the next year, the first play to be so honored. In 1922 Lynch wrote a companion play *Why Not?* that was followed in 1925 by *Lovely Lady.*

1918

Jan. 8 Pres. Wilson addressed to Congress a "statement of the **War Aims and Peace Terms** of the United States." Speech listed the famous **"14 points"** which he felt to be indispensable to a just peace. It was translated and distributed to German soldiers and civilians throughout middle Europe by the Office of Public Information.

Mar. 7 **Distinguished Service Medal for U.S. Army** authorized by Pres. Wilson. A bronze medallion with ribbon, it is awarded to Army officers and men who have performed "exceptionally meritorious service."

Apr. 14 Lt. Douglas Campbell shot down his 5th German aircraft, thus becoming the **1st American-trained "ace."**

May 16 **Sedition Act** provided heavy penalties against those who hindered war effort by making false statements, obstructing enlistment, and talking against production of war materials, American form of government, the Constitution, the flag, etc. Enforcement chiefly aimed at Socialists and pacifists.

June 25 **Belleau Wood** cleared by

Pulitzer Prizes: novel, *His Family* by Ernest Poole; drama, *Why Marry?* by Jesse Lynch Williams; U.S. history, *A History of the Civil War 1861–1865* by James Ford Rhodes; biography, *Benjamin Franklin, Self-Revealed* by William Cabell Bruce; poetry, *Love Songs* by Sara Teasdale.

Henry Adams' **The Education of Henry Adams** was published posthumously. Conceived as a companion piece to *Mont-Saint-Michel and Chartres* (1913), the volume decried the multiplicity of our mechanized society (symbolized by the dynamo). He saw the 13th century (symbolized by the Virgin) as the era when man most successfully reconciled the forces of science and religion.

A study of 3 generations of a family in Indianapolis written by **Booth Tarkington** in *The Magnificent Ambersons.* From 1873 to 1916 the course of the family fortune is traced from wealth to poverty against the background of a community growing from a town into a city.

Willa Cather broadened her canvas and created a masterpiece of prairie life in her novel *My Ántonia*, the story of Ántonia Shimerda and the community she lives in,

446

SCIENCE; INDUSTRY; ECONOMICS: EDUCATION; RELIGION; PHILOSOPHY.	SPORTS; FASHIONS; POPULAR ENTERTAINMENT; FOLKLORE; SOCIETY.

Federal agents seized documents and books and made 10 arrests.

Oct. 1   **2d Liberty Loan Drive** for $3 billion at 4%. It was over-subscribed by half by Nov. 15, end of drive.

Oct. 13   In New York City, Mayor John P. Mitchel dedicated the **Catskill Aqueduct** at ceremonies in Central Park. The aqueduct and its various dams and reservoirs had been under construction for 12 years, and cost $177 million.

Nov. 13   The Federal Fuel Administrator ordered all electric advertising signs shut off on Sunday and Thursday of each week.

Oct. 6–15   Chicago, AL, defeated New York, NL, 4–2 in 14th annual **World Series.**

Nov. 6   New York State adopted a constitutional amendment granting **suffrage** to women. The suffragist victory gave added impetus and prestige to movements in other states.

Dec. 18   The **Prohibition Amendment** was submitted to state legislatures, after the Senate accepted minor House changes in the resolution. It had passed the Senate Aug. 1, the House Dec. 17. The 36th ratification was secured Jan. 16, 1919, and on Jan. 29 the Secretary of State declared it ratified.

1918

Last state to pass **compulsory school attendance law** was Mississippi in 1918.

United Lutheran Church organized through the doctrinal agreement of 45 hitherto divided synods.

Phrase on businessmen's lips during the last year of World War I was: **"Change from a debtor to a creditor nation."** It was assumed the dollar would replace the pound in international trade, and that the balance given to U.S. by the production of war goods for the Allies would never be upset.

In 1918 there were a million more **women employed** than in 1915. On Sept. 30 Wilson told the Senate that woman suffrage was a "vitally necessary war measure." But Senate lacked enough strength to carry proposal (Oct. 1).

Apr. 6   **3d Liberty Loan Drive** begun with goal of $3 billion at 4.5% interest.

May 13   **1st airmail stamps** were issued by the Post Office Dept., in denominations of 6¢, 16¢, and 24¢.

May 15   **1st airmail service** was inaugurated, with regular flights scheduled between New York City and Washington, D.C.

French box car inscription **"Hommes 40-Chevaux 8"** (40 Men, 8 Horses) provided source of inestimable humor to doughboys. After the war, reminiscences of these crowded conveyances led to the formation of the Forty and Eight Society, a part of the American Legion which devotes itself to fun and high jinks.

42d annual **Preakness Stakes** was run in 2 sections this year. *War Cloud*, ridden by jockey J. Loftus, won the 1st on a sloppy track, paying 17–10. Time was 1:53⅖ for winnings valued at $12,250. *Jack Hare, Jr.*, ridden by C. Peak, won the 2nd on a good track, paying 9–10. Time was 1:53⅖ for winnings valued at $11,250.

Johren won the 50th annual **Belmont Stakes,** paying 11–5. Jockey was F. Robinson; time was 2:20⅖ on a fast track for winnings valued at $8950.

U.S. lawn tennis men's singles champion, R. Lindley Murray; **women's singles champion,** Molla Bjurstedt.

Jan.   Mare Island Marines defeated Camp Lewis by a score of 19 to 7 in the 3d annual **Rose Bowl** football game.

Jan. 10   House of Representatives adopted the Susan B. Anthony resolution

POLITICS AND GOVERNMENT; WAR; DISASTERS; VITAL STATISTICS.

BOOKS; PAINTING; DRAMA; ARCHITECTURE; SCULPTURE.

brigade of U.S. Marines and troops of the 2d Division after 2 weeks of bitter fighting in which 1654 German prisoners were taken and U.S. losses amounted to 285 officers and 7585 men killed.

July 18–Aug. 6 Aisne-Marne Offensive launched by more than 250,000 Americans joined with selected French units in response to German attack of July 15 on both sides of Rheims **(2d Battle of the Marne).** Offensive marked the turning point of the war, and succeeded in driving German line back to the Vesle.

Sept. 26–Nov. 11 Battle of the Meuse-Argonne, involving 1,200,000 U.S. troops. Objective was the cutting of the German supply line, the Sedan-Mézières railroad, which would force a general German withdrawal. Armistice of Nov. 11 brought American advance to a halt after having succeeded in reaching the railroad.

Oct. 5 Prince Max of Baden, a "moderate" who had recently been appointed Imperial Chancellor of Germany, wrote to Pres. Wilson and asked him to "take a hand in the restoration of **peace.**" Note said that Germany was willing to accept the "14 points" Wilson had set forth in his message to Congress on Jan. 8. In his reply of Oct. 15 Pres. Wilson said that armistice must be arranged by military authorities, that German armies must stop their illegal and inhuman practices, and that arbitrary government must cease in Germany.

Oct. 20 Germany in a note to Pres. Wilson accepted his conditions for **peace negotiations.**

Oct. 23 Pres. Wilson's note to Germany declared that he would forward German **armistice terms** to the Allies for consideration. Delay in armistice was caused by Allied reluctance to accept Wilson's 14 points as a basis of negotiation, and by Wilson's reluctance to deal with German government.

made up of Bohemian, Scandinavian, French, and Russian settlers. Out of a tragic life she emerges as the mother of a brood of children who were to help make a thriving, upstanding community.

Early instalments of *Ulysses* by **James Joyce,** published in the *Little Review,* were burned by Post Office Department. The complete novel, generally regarded as the greatest 20th-century novel in the English language, was published in Paris in 1922 by the expatriate American publisher and bookseller Sylvia Beach. It was banned from the U.S. until 1933.

Some of the **war plays** which held the New York stage during the season were: *Where Poppies Bloom,* with Marjorie Rambeau; *Billeted,* with Margaret Anglin; *Under Orders* by Berte Thomas, with Effie Shannon and Shelley Hull; *The Better 'Ole,* a play built around the cartoons by British artist Bruce Bairnsfather.

Among the more **memorable stage performances** this year, Walter Hampden impressed critics and the public as the best American Hamlet since Edwin Booth, and John Barrymore starred in a version of Count Leo Tolstoi's *The Living Corpse,* retitled *Redemption.*

Mme. Nazimova played in 3 Ibsen revivals, *The Wild Duck, Hedda Gabler,* and *A Doll's House.*

Lightnin', by Winchell Smith and Frank Bacon, opened on Broadway, destined for one of the longest runs (1291) in the history of the U.S. stage.

Regional drama emphasized in the repertory of the Carolina Playmakers, which had its inception at the University of North Carolina under supervision of Prof. Frederick H. Koch. Dramas generally deal with themes and subject matter of historical or folk significance to the South.

1st building under new **New York Building Code** built at 27 W. 43 St. It showed setbacks which became dominant feature of New York skyline.

Among the **notable buildings** completed

448

| SCIENCE; INDUSTRY; ECONOMICS; EDUCATION; RELIGION; PHILOSOPHY. | SPORTS; FASHIONS; POPULAR ENTERTAINMENT; FOLKLORE; SOCIETY. |

May 28   **American Railroad Express Company** organized under federal supervision by an enforced merger of the Adams, American, Wells-Fargo, and Southern Express Companies. Move was encouraged by the government in order to improve the shipment of war goods.

May 31   Secretary of War Newton D. Baker ordered that **conscientious objectors** be granted leave from military service, without pay, to join in agricultural pursuits.

June 3   The U.S. Supreme Court declared unconstitutional the **Federal Child Labor Law** of 1916, on the grounds that it violated rights reserved to the states under the 10th Amendment, and because Congress, in blocking interstate shipments of goods made by under-age children, had exceeded its powers to regulate interstate commerce.

July 4   As a special demonstration of patriotic fervor, the holiday was celebrated with launchings of nearly 100 ships at ports throughout the country.

July 26   **Sugar ration** reduced to 2 lbs. per person per month, by edict of U.S. Food Board.

Aug. 9   All automobile manufacturers ordered by the War Industries Board to convert to 100% **war work** before Jan. 1, 1919.

Aug. 29   Labor Department statistics revealed an increase in the **cost of living** in New York between July, 1917, and July, 1918, of 17%.

Sept. 10   1st Chicago-New York **airmail trip** to be completed in 1 day showed overall time for transportation of mail 12 hr. 55 min. Flying time was 10 hr. 5 min.

Oct.   **Influenza epidemic** reached its height. Disease had first appeared in early September in Boston, New York, and Phil-

to submit the **woman suffrage** constitutional amendment to the states for ratification. Resolution failed to pass the Senate, in spite of support by Pres. Wilson.

Jan. 26   2 **"wheatless,"** 2 **"porkless,"** and 1 **"meatless"** day a week arranged by Food Administrator Hoover. Moreover there was 1 "meatless" and 1 "wheatless" meal each day.

Feb. 15   **Vernon Castle** was killed in a plane crash at Fort Worth, Tex. Before the war he and his wife, Irene, were the nation's most famous dance team, originators of the 1-step, the turkey-trot, the Castle walk, and many other steps which remained popular for many years. Castle had shot down 2 German planes during service with the Royal Flying Corps, and at his death he was giving flying instructions to fledgling American pilots.

Mar. 31   **Daylight Saving Time** went into effect throughout the country, in accordance with an act passed by Congress on Mar. 19.

May 11   One of the great American race horses, *Exterminator,* known affectionately as "Old Bones," won the 44th annual **Kentucky Derby.** He ran the muddy track in 2:10⅘ and won $14,700 for his owner, W. S. Kilmer. His jockey was W. Knapp.

July 14   **Quentin Roosevelt,** youngest son of the former President, was shot down and killed during a battle with an enemy plane.

Sept. 1   **Baseball season** cut short by order of the Sec. of War, Baker. World Series started early, Sept. 5th, Boston Red Sox winning first game, 1–0, on pitching of Babe Ruth.

Sept. 5–11   Boston, AL, defeated Chicago, NL, 4–2 in the 15th annual **World Series.** Each member of the Boston team received $1,102.51 as his share of the Series receipts. This is the all-time low payoff to players of the winning team.

449

POLITICS AND GOVERNMENT; WAR; DISASTERS; VITAL STATISTICS.

BOOKS; PAINTING; DRAMA; ARCHITECTURE; SCULPTURE.

Nov. 4   Austria accepted terms of armistice and ordered the **demobilization** of the Austro-Hungarian army. Peace news was joyously received in Vienna.

Nov. 7   **Armistice** reported in New York newspapers, after erroneous United Press dispatch from France. City broke into wild demonstrations. Later in day, report was denied by the Secretary of War.

Nov. 9   **Kaiser Wilhelm II** abdicated.

Nov. 11   3:00 A.M. News of **German surrender** reached U.S. by Associated Press flash. Long before dawn, fire whistles, factory whistles, air-raid sirens were turned on, bonfires built, parades organized; riots developed in several cities when huge crowds of soldiers and sailors celebrated too enthusiastically. Armistice celebration was the greatest single nationwide demonstration ever known in U.S. Total mobilized forces, 4,355,000; total deaths, 126,-000; total wounded casualties, 234,300; total prisoners and missing, 4500; total casualties, 364,800.

Nov. 18   Wilson announced that he would attend the **Peace Conference** in person. Many in U.S. criticized the announcement as a sign of Wilson's "egotism."

this year were the Commodore and Pennsylvania hotels and St. Bartholomew's Church, in New York City.

Dance in Place Congo, a symphonic poem scored for ballet, presented at the Metropolitan Opera House, New York City. The composer, **Henry Franklin Belknap Gilbert,** was one of the chief advocates of "American" music as opposed to European. His symphonic poem was based on Creole themes from New Orleans, and brought him national recognition.

Feb. 8   1st issue of **The Stars and Stripes,** Army newspaper, published.

Feb. 12   All Broadway **theaters closed** in New York City in a move to save coal.

Sept. 14   **Eugene V. Debs,** 4-time Socialist candidate for the presidency, was sentenced to 10 years' imprisonment for violating the wartime espionage and sedition law. He had been arrested June 30 for allegedly seditious statements against recruiting at Canton, Ohio. His sentence was commuted by Pres. Harding in 1921.

Dec. 14   **Puccini's** trio of 1-act operas, *Il Tabarro, Suor Angelica,* and *Gianni Schicchi* (collectively called *Il Trittico*), was given its world première at the Metropolitan Opera.

1919

Jan. 18   **Peace Conference** opened in Paris. For Pres. Wilson it was the beginning of a fight to preserve the principles of his "14 points" against the demands of the other victorious Allies. On many important points he failed to do so.

Jan. 29   **18th amendment ratified** prohibiting liquor traffic in the U.S. It was the 1st amendment to place a time limit on ratification (7 years) and the only one that has been repealed.

Feb.   Congress established **Navy Dis-**

Pulitzer Prizes: novel, *The Magnificent Ambersons* by Booth Tarkington; drama, no prize; U.S. history, no prize; biography, *The Education of Henry Adams* by Henry Adams; poetry, *Old Road to Paradise* by Margaret Widdemer, and *Corn Huskers* by Carl Sandburg.

Romantic operetta held its own well into the '20's and '30's. *Apple Blossoms* by Fritz Kreisler and Victor Jacoby scored a success with the dancing of the Astaires; *Rose Marie* (1924) the combined efforts of Otto Harbach, Oscar Hammerstein II,

adelphia. By mid-October death rate in these cities had risen over 700%. Doctors were baffled. Epidemic spread to 46 states, killed between 400,000 and 500,000 altogether. Many war plants shut down, telephone service was cut in half, the draft call was suspended in several cities. Panic spread rapidly, newspapers were filled with rumors, outlandish theories, long lists of the dead. Epidemic relaxed and disappeared in 1919; it left many afflicted with Bright's disease, cardiac diseases, and tuberculosis.

Oct. 19   The **4th Liberty Loan drive** ended. Treasury officials estimated that 20 million persons, over half of the adult population, had bought bonds.

Nov. 27   The Navy's newest seaplane, the giant NC-1, broke **the record for number of passengers carried in any type of aircraft** when it flew from Rockaway, N.Y., with 50 men aboard.

Dec. 8   An anti-submarine device, a huge steel net stretched underwater across the Narrows in New York Harbor since the beginning of the war, was removed.

Oct. 21   **Typewriting speed record established** by Margaret B. Owen in New York City. She typed 170 words in a minute. She had no errors.

Nov. 1   A 5-car train on the Brighton Beach **subway** line was derailed and crashed into supporting structures of the tunnel at Malbone St., Brooklyn. The wooden cars were virtually demolished, killing nearly 100 persons and injuring as many. The motorman, a dispatcher pressed into service during a strike, said his brakes failed.

Nov. 9   **Charlie Chaplin** announced that he had married actress Mildred Harris at Los Angeles, Calif., on Oct. 23.

Nov. 21   Pres. Wilson signed the **Wartime Prohibition Act,** which banned the manufacture and sale of any intoxicating liquors, except for export, from June 30, 1919, until the troops had been demobilized. This year 5 more states enacted prohibition laws—Texas, Florida, Nevada, Ohio, and Wyoming.

Dec. 16   **Jack Dempsey** knocked out Carl Morris in 14 seconds at New Orleans. On July 27, at Harrison, N.J., he had stopped Fred Fulton in 18 seconds.

1919

Behaviorism in America found its most positive expression in *Psychology from the Standpoint of a Behaviorist,* by Dr. John B. Watson. His theory that human behavior could be determined entirely by environmental factors aroused both fellow psychologists and the general public.

Father Divine's Peace Mission movement gained national attention through its communal activities at Sayville, Long Island. Viewed literally as God in the flesh by his followers, Father Divine combined fundamental evangelism with a concrete

U.S. lawn tennis men's singles champion, William M. Johnston; **women's singles champion,** Mrs. Hazel Hotchkiss Wightman.

U.S.G.A. amateur championship won by S. D. Herron at Oakmont, Pa., C.C. He defeated Robert T. (Bobby) Jones, Jr., 5 and 4. **Open championship** won by Walter Hagen at Brae Burn C.C., West Newton, Mass., with a score of 301.

Sir Barton won the 51st annual **Belmont Stakes,** paying 7–20. Jockey was J. Loftus;

POLITICS AND GOVERNMENT; WAR;
DISASTERS; VITAL STATISTICS.

BOOKS; PAINTING; DRAMA;
ARCHITECTURE; SCULPTURE.

tinguished **Service Medal,** corresponding to similar decoration for meritorious service in the Army.

Feb. 14 Pres. Wilson presented the completed draft of the covenant of the **League of Nations** to the Peace Conference and then embarked at Brest on Feb. 15 for the U.S. Later he returned to Europe again, and remained at the Peace Conference until it ended on June 28. He arrived in New York city the last time on July 8.

Mar. 10 U.S. Supreme Court upheld conviction of **Eugene V. Debs,** Socialist party leader and Presidential candidate, for violating Espionage Act through statements made in a speech at Canton, Ohio, in June, 1918. Debs began to serve a 10-year prison sentence on April 13.

Mar. 15 Delegates representing 1000 units of the AEF met in Paris and formed the **American Legion.**

June 28 **Treaty of Versailles** signed but never came into force because of the Senate's failure to ratify it.

July 10 Covenant of the **League of Nations** with the Versailles Treaty placed before U.S. Senate for ratification by the President, declaring that acceptance of the treaty would assure future peace.

Aug. 31 **Communist Labor Party** of America founded at Chicago, Ill. Party adopted platform of 3rd International, including badge of hammer and sickle encircled by strands of wheat. Party motto was: "Workers of the world unite!"

Sept. 3 Pres. Wilson gave the 1st speech of a nationwide tour on behalf of the **Peace Treaty** and the League of Nations at Columbus, Ohio. Tour was undertaken against the advice of his friends and his doctors; he was obviously ill, suffering from what was then called "brain fag." On Sept. 26 he suffered a **stroke** during his

Rudolph Friml, and Herbert Stothart is a colorful romance of Canadian Mounties; *If I Were King* (1925) with music by Friml enlisted the singing of Dennis King to portray life of the rascal poet-thief François Villon; *The Desert Song* (1926) with music by Sigmund Romberg is set in Morocco during the Riff war.

The New Symphony Orchestra founded by **Edgar Varèse.** Later Varèse resigned when the board of directors refused to follow out his original plan of concentrating on the performance of modern music.

Strange excursion through the world of fantasy, allegory, and escape is **James Branch Cabell's** ironic reworking of the Faust story in *Jurgen, a Comedy of Justice.* Time and space are reshuffled to bring to the reader figures from past and present and from heaven, hell, and earth.

Naturalism is the keynote of the collection of short stories by **Sherwood Anderson,** *Winesburg, Ohio.* In these studies of gnarled and frustrated lives, he shows the stormy instinctive force that lies beneath the veneer of "average" people, and how it explodes or is sublimated with all its consequent effects.

Novel of the East and West is **Joseph Hergesheimer's** masterpiece *Java Head.* Set in Salem in the 1840's, it recounts the reaction of an Oriental beauty, Taou Yuen, to the Puritan community and the impact of that community upon her basic philosophy.

Abraham Lincoln, drama by British playwright, **John Drinkwater,** played in New York with Frank McGlynn in the leading role. It was praised by critics as the most serious and best done play of the season.

The White Peacock, originally a piano composition by **Charles T. Griffes** based on a poem by Fiona Macleod (William Sharp), presented in a version orchestrated for ballet at the Rivoli Theatre, New York city. It aroused considerable enthusiasm among followers of music and dance.

452

SCIENCE; INDUSTRY; ECONOMICS; EDUCATION; RELIGION; PHILOSOPHY.

SPORTS; FASHIONS; POPULAR ENTERTAINMENT; FOLKLORE; SOCIETY.

social philosophy stressing racial equality and economic co-operation.

Elihu Root, Nicholas Murray Butler, and **Stephan Duggan** contributed their efforts to the establishment of the **Institute for International Education.** The institute was sponsored by the **Carnegie Endowment for International Peace.** The provisions of the original policymakers declared that the function of the institute was primarily as a liaison between students interested in opportunities for international education and "the persons who may make these opportunities available." In 1949, the institute received support from the Departments of State and Army, the Office of Education, the Economic Cooperation Administration, UNESCO, the Carnegie and Rockefeller foundations, 115 American colleges and universities, and 260 foreign colleges and universities. The headquarters of the institute in New York city is at 1 E. 67 Street.

July 1 **Daily air mail service** begun between New York and Chicago.

July 14 **Trade with Germany** resumed when the U.S. Department of State authorized the issuance of export and import licenses.

July 21 Goodyear Tire and Rubber Company **balloon,** the "Wing Foot," crashed into Illinois Trust and Savings Bank at La Salle and Jackson Sts., Chicago, Ill. 12 killed, 28 hurt.

July 23 **Hogs** on the hoof brought $23.50 per hundredweight at the Chicago stockyards, the highest price known until that time.

Sept. 9 Union of policemen in Boston called **strike,** and 1117 out of 1544 patrolmen walked off jobs. Many merchants locked up their shops, but looting occurred on a wide scale. New police were hired and strike put down. Gov. Calvin Coolidge told AFL president Samuel Gompers: "There is no right to strike against the public safety by anybody, anywhere, any time," a sentence that became famous.

time was 2:17⅖ on a fast track for winnings valued at $11,950.

Sir Barton won the 43d annual **Preakness Stakes,** paying 7–5. Jockey was J. Loftus; time was 1:53 on a fast track for winnings valued at $24,500.

Jan. 1 Great Lakes Naval Training Station defeated Mare Island Marines by a score of 17 to 0 in the 4th annual **Rose Bowl** football game.

Mar. 18 **The Order of De Molay** established in Kansas City, Mo., by Frank S. Land, who started out with the idea of a boys' club. This club was later named after Jacques De Molay, the last grand master of the Order of Knights Templars, who was burned at the stake in Paris on Mar. 18, 1314. This day was established by the American Order as Devotional Day. The Order of De Molay, although not officially a Masonic Order, has a ritual that is similar to that of freemasonry and is closely co-ordinated with Masonic lodges in each area.

May 10 1st horse to win the **Kentucky Derby** and then go on to win the Preakness and the Belmont Stakes, gaining the mythical "Triple Crown," was *Sir Barton,* who won the 45th Kentucky Derby in 2:09⅘ on a muddy track to win his owner, J. K. L. Ross, $20,825. This was the 2d Kentucky Derby winner for jockey J. Loftus.

July 4 Jack Dempsey became **Heavyweight Champion of the World** when he scored a technical knockout over Jess Willard after 3 rounds of a scheduled 12-round match at Toledo, Ohio. Willard, who held the title since he defeated Jack Johnson in 1915, was 37 years old, weighed 243 lbs., and was 6 ft. 6½ in. tall. Dempsey was 24 years old, weighed 187 lbs., and was 6 ft. 1 in. tall.

Oct. 1–9 Cincinnati, NL, defeated Chicago, AL, 5–3 in the 16th annual **World Series.**

453

POLITICS AND GOVERNMENT; WAR; DISASTERS; VITAL STATISTICS.	BOOKS; PAINTING; DRAMA; ARCHITECTURE; SCULPTURE.

speaking tour while en route to Wichita, Kan., and had to return to Washington.

Nov. 19 **Versailles Treaty** failed ratification in the Senate by a vote of 55 to 39.

Aug. 7 **Actors' strike** resulted in the closing of 12 theaters in New York city and others in Boston, Philadelphia, and Chicago. The actors pressed for the recognition of the Actors' Equity Association.

1920

Population, 105,710,620. Center of population: 8 mi. south-southeast of Spencer, Owen Co., Ind. For 1st time a decline in **rural population** to less than 50% of the total population. The actual number of farm residents had dwindled to less than 30%.

Apr. 15 Frank Parmenter and Alexander Berardelli, paymaster and guard for a shoe factory in South Braintree, Mass., shot and killed; payroll they were carrying was seized by murderers. 3 weeks later **Nicola Sacco** and **Bartolomeo Vanzetti,** workmen of Brockton, Mass., were arrested and charged with the crime.

May 5–10 **National Convention of the Socialist Labor Party** met in New York city and nominated W. W. Cox of St. Louis for the presidency and August Gillhaus of Brooklyn for the vice-presidency.

May 8–14 **National Convention of the Socialist Party** met at New York city and nominated Eugene V. Debs of Indiana for the presidency for the 5th time and Seymour Stedman of Ohio for the vice-presidency. Debs, who had been found guilty of violating the Espionage Act, was serving a 10-year prison sentence.

June 8–12 **National convention of the Republican Party** at Chicago nominated Warren G. Harding of Ohio for the presidency and Calvin Coolidge, governor of Massachusetts, for the vice-presidency. Final nomination was decided on the 10th ballot.

June 12 National Convention formed **Farmer Labor Party** in Chicago. It derived from a section of the National Labor

Pulitzer Prizes: novel, no prize; drama, *Beyond the Horizon* by Eugene O'Neill; U.S. history, *The War with Mexico* by Justin H. Smith; biography, *The Life of John Marshall* by Albert J. Beveridge; poetry, no prize.

Thoroughgoing satire of American small town is *Main Street* by **Sinclair Lewis.** Everything characteristic of the narrowness, hypocrisy, stupidity, drabness, and overweening pride of Gopher Prairie, Minn., is indicted. Novel created a sensation from coast to coast.

Fictional chronicler of the "flapper" age, the postwar disillusioned '20's, **F. Scott Fitzgerald,** published his 1st novel *This Side of Paradise.* Tremendous success of this novel gave him the means to embark on a life of big parties and madcap living, which he used as background for most of his later novels.

Edith Wharton pursued her study of New York society in *The Age of Innocence.* Set in the 1870's, the book traces the struggle of Newland Archer to break out of the narrow conventions of his society background.

Journalist and authoress **Zona Gale** published *Miss Lulu Bett,* a novel of rural life in the Middle West, reflecting the postwar reaction against the cold conventionalism of middle-class, small-town life.

The Great Impersonation by **E. Phillips Oppenheim** published. This well-known adventure story has sold more than a million copies.

Influx of theatrical greats after the war —probably drawn by wealth to be gained— made New York the **leading theatrical city** of the world. Prominent among foreigners on these shores were Reinhardt, Duse, Ba-

Nov. 20 Inauguration of Tucson, Ariz., Municipal Airport, the **1st municipal airport** in U.S. Field located south of Tucson is still in use.

Nov. 29 Navy defeated Army, 6–0, in the annual **Army-Navy** game held at the Polo Grounds, New York city.

1920

Illiteracy in America reached a new low of 6.0% of the population, a decline of 1.7% from 1910 and a decline of 14.0% from 1870.

Graduate school of geography organized at Clark University. Wallace Walter Atwood, formerly professor of physiography at Harvard University, had become president of Clark and had organized the school of geography with himself as director. It was the **1st graduate school of geography** in the U.S.

Life expectancy in U.S., as determined by Bureau of Public Health, was 54.09 years; in 1901 it had been 49.24 years.

Pragmatic philosophy of **John Dewey** found militant expression in his *Reconstruction in Philosophy*. Metaphysics is attacked as the product of an aristocratic class, a philosophy of escapism which does not come to grips with practical problems of a democratic society.

Albert A. Michelson measured for 1st time the diameter of a star with the aid of the interferometer which he had invented in 1880. He demonstrated that the diameter of Alpha Orionis is 260 million miles.

Rail mileage in America reached its all-time peak at 253,000 as contrasted with 31,000 mi. of railroads in existence at the close of the Civil War. Since 1920, railroad mileage has been on the decline.

Wheat prices reached a new high of $2.33 per bushel.

As the "Roaring Twenties" began the **motor car** was "a definite element in our standard of living." By 1923, about 15 million cars, were registered. 1 out of every 4 families in the U.S. was involved in an automobile transaction every year.

Term **"smoke-filled room"** came into usage as a designation for party-machine-made choices during the race between Harding, Hiram Johnson, Frank O. Lowden, and General Leonard Wood. After a constant deadlock, Harry M. Daugherty, a politician from Ohio, told press: "The convention will be dead-locked, and after the other candidates have gone their limit, some twelve or fifteen men, worn out and bleary-eyed for lack of sleep, will sit down about two o'clock in the morning around a table in a smoke-filled room in some hotel and decide the nomination. When that time comes, Harding will be selected."

Boxing fully legalized in New York state when "Walker Law" passed. Success of boxing in New York led to legislation legalizing boxing in other states.

U.S.G.A. amateur championship won by Charles Evans, Jr., at Engineers C.C., Roslyn, N.Y. He defeated Francis Ouimet, 7 and 6. **Open championship** won by Ted Ray of England at Inverness Club, Toledo, Ohio, with a score of 295.

U.S. lawn tennis men's singles champion, William T. Tilden II; **women's singles champion,** Mrs. Molla Bjurstedt Mallory.

Man o' War won 52d annual **Belmont Stakes,** paying 1–20. Jockey was C. Kummer; time was 2:14⅕ on a fast track for winnings valued at $7950.

Man o' War won 44th annual **Preakness Stakes,** paying 4–5. Jockey was C. Kummer; time was 1:51⅗ on a fast track for winnings valued at $23,000.

Davis Challenge Cup won by U.S. at Aukland, New Zealand with U.S. defeating Australia 5–0.

Party. In 1924 Farmer Labor Party joined forces with Progressive Party led by Robert La Follette.

June 28–July 5 **Democratic National Convention,** assembled in San Francisco, nominated Gov. James M. Cox of Ohio for the presidency. Other chief candidates for the nomination had been A. Mitchell Palmer, Attorney-General in President Wilson's Cabinet, and ex-Sec. of the Treasury William G. McAdoo. Franklin D. Roosevelt of New York was chosen for vice-presidency.

July 13–16 **National Convention of the Farmer-Labor Party** met at Chicago in its 1st nominating convention and chose Parley P. Christensen of Utah for the presidency and Max S. Hayes of Ohio for the vice-presidency.

July 21–22 **National convention of Prohibition Party** met at Lincoln, Neb., and nominated Aaron S. Watkins of Ohio for the presidency.

Nov. 2 **Warren Harding,** who had conducted a "front porch campaign" on the slogan, **"Back to normalcy,"** won the presidential election; Republican majorities returned to both houses of Congress. The electoral vote was 404 to 127 for Cox and Roosevelt. Popular vote: Harding, 16,152,-200; Cox, 9,147,353; Debs, 919,799; Watkins, 189,408; W. W. Cox, 31,175; Christensen, 26,541.

lieff, Mei Lan-fang, the Moscow Art players.

Outstanding **dramatic success** of the season was *The Jest,* a play set in medieval Florence; John and Lionel Barrymore were in the cast.

Musical extravaganza, **Sally,** the combined efforts of Guy Bolton, Clifford Grey, Joseph Urban, and Jerome Kern broke all box office records by grossing $38,985 in one week. Edward Sheldon wrote the play.

Some **popular songs** of 1920 were: *Japanese Sandman; Margie; Avalon; Whispering.*

Feb. 2 Significant note struck in theater with presentation of *Beyond the Horizon,* 1st long play by **Eugene O'Neill,** at Morosco Theater in New York. In the study of two brothers who love the same girl, he sounds the theme which is dominant throughout his work, namely that the greatest boon to human beings is their illusions.

Nov. 1 Conventions of theater are cast aside in powerful production of *The Emperor Jones* by **Eugene O'Neill.** In 8 scenes the theme of reversion to the primitive is startlingly developed in the career of a Negro car porter who comes to the West Indies. Effect is heightened by use of tom-toms throughout piece.

1921

Jan. 13 51% of **U.S. population** centered in cities and towns of more than 2500, according to census bureau.

Mar. 4 **Warren Gamaliel Harding,** 29th President, inaugurated. He was a Republican and died after 2 years in office.

Apr. 2 Prof. **Albert Einstein,** physicist, arrived in New York from Europe, and

Pulitzer Prizes: novel, *The Age of Innocence* by Edith Wharton; drama, *Miss Lulu Bett* by Zona Gale; biography, *The Americanization of Edward Bok* by Edward Bok; poetry, no prize; U.S. history, *The Victory at Sea* by William Sowden Sims in collaboration with Burton J. Hendrick.

Some **dramas** on Broadway in 1921:

SCIENCE; INDUSTRY; ECONOMICS; EDUCATION; RELIGION; PHILOSOPHY.	SPORTS; FASHIONS; POPULAR ENTERTAINMENT; FOLKLCRE; SOCIETY.

There were 1 million less cars than telephones, only 7 million less than dwelling places.

Jan. 17 **Samuel Gompers** again chosen president of the Pan-American Federation of Labor at Mexico City.

Jan. 18 Public school teachers made subject to dismissal for active membership in the **Communist Party** by a ruling handed down from Acting New York State Commissioner Frank B. Gilbert.

July 20 **Air mail service** between New York and San Francisco begun. The mail-carrying planes arrived in California on Aug. 8th.

June 5 **Merchant Marine Act** passed by Congress as an incentive to American shipping. Act specified that government-owned ships be sold to American shipping companies. The Merchant Fleet Corporation was empowered to supply loans to American shippers and to operate unsold government vessels.

Nov. 2 Radio station KDKA, originally an experimental station operated by Westinghouse Electric and Manufacturing Company in East Pittsburgh, Pa., began the **1st regular broadcasting service** by putting on the air the returns of the Harding-Cox election.

Dec. 10 **Woodrow Wilson** received Nobel Peace Prize for 1919.

Jan. 1 Harvard edged out Oregon by a score of 7 to 6 in the 5th annual **Rose Bowl** football game.

Apr.–Sept. U.S. won 1st place in the **Olympic Games** held in Belgium, scoring 212 points, 1st 9 times, 2d 12, 3d 9, 4th 10, 5th 9, and 6th 5. The 2d place team was Finland with 105 points.

May War Department officially adopted **shoulder insigne,** called "patch," to distinguish different Army units in battle. Practice, though officially frowned upon before this, had already been adopted by a number of divisions.

May 8 Paul Jones, a 16–1 long shot, won the 46th annual **Kentucky Derby** in 2:09 on a slow track, winning $30,375 for his owner, R. Parr. Jockey was T. Rice.

Sept. 28 Chicago grand jury indicted 8 members of **Chicago White Sox** for "throwing" World Series between White Sox and Cincinnati Reds in 1919. Trial, next July, ended in acquittal; afterwards jury carried 8 players on their shoulders.

Oct. 5–12 Cleveland, AL, defeated Brooklyn, NL, 5–2 in the 17th annual **World Series.**

Oct. 30 **Ku Klux Klan** paraded in Jacksonville, Fla. Sudden, rapid growth of Klan in 1920 aroused much attention in press.

Nov. 8 **Judge K. M. Landis,** of Chicago, appointed Baseball Commissioner by a joint decision of both major leagues.

Nov. 20 **Navy** defeated Army, 7–0, in their annual contest at the Polo Grounds, New York city.

1921

Wide-spread **wage cuts** announced by many large industries. 43,000 employees of the New York Central railroad suffered a 22½% cut; clothing workers accepted a 15% reduction. On Sept. 30, a national conference on unemployment advised manufacturers, retailers to cut prices, proposed a program of public works to provide jobs.

Nobel Prize in physics awarded to Al-

U.S. tennis team successfully defended the **Davis Cup** by defeating the Japanese team 5–0. The U.S. singles players were William T. Tilden and William M. Johnston; Richard Norris Williams 2d and Watson M. Washburn made up the doubles team.

Grey Lag won the 53d annual **Belmont Stakes,** paying 2–1. Jockey was E. Sande;

POLITICS AND GOVERNMENT; WAR; DISASTERS; VITAL STATISTICS.

BOOKS; PAINTING; DRAMA; ARCHITECTURE; SCULPTURE.

on Apr. 15th, during a lecture at Columbia University on his theory of Relativity, he introduced "time" as the 4th dimension.

Apr. 25 Congressman **Andrew Volstead,** author of Prohibition enforcement statute, introduced a bill to prohibit the sale of beer to the sick on medical prescriptions.

May 19 **1st generally restrictive immigration act** in America initiated the quota system, which restricted immigration in any given year to 3% of the number of each nationality reported in the Census of 1910. Total number of immigrants allowed to enter in any given year was set at 357,000.

June 3 Arkansas R. overflowed as a result of a **cloudburst** causing property damage estimated at $25 million, $15 million of which represented losses in Pueblo, Col., which was largely destroyed by the flood. More than 1500 persons were reported either killed or missing.

June 10 Congress authorized the office of **Comptroller General** of the U.S., and the **Bureau of the Budget** as part of the treasury department. 1st comptroller general was John Raymond McCarl who took office on July 1.

June 20 1st woman to preside in the House of Representatives in American history was Miss **Alice Robertson** of Oklahoma. She occupied the chair for 30 min.

July 2 **State of war** between U.S. and the German government declared at an end by a joint resolution of Congress. The resolution also claimed all rights, reparations, or indemnities entitled to the U.S. under the Treaty of Versailles.

Aug. Wave of lawlessness swept South, most of it associated with the **Ku Klux Klan.** Whippings, brandings, tarrings, destruction of property directed against "nigger-lovers," although no motive could be found for some of the violence.

Aug. 25 **Treaty of Peace** with Germany signed in Berlin with stipulation that none of the provisions of Joint Resolution of

The Prince and the Pauper, with William Faversham; *Miss Lulu Bett,* a dramatization of her own novel by Zona Gale; *The Circle,* W. Somerset Maugham's play, with John Drew and Mrs. Leslie Carter; *Dulcy,* with Lynn Fontanne (Connelly-Kaufman), *The Gold Diggers,* with Ina Claire; *Anna Christie,* a Pulitzer Prize drama by Eugene O'Neill which caused much comment, starring Pauline Lord; *A Bill of Divorcement,* with Katharine Cornell; *Goat Alley,* with an all-Negro cast; *Blossom Time,* a musical founded on the life of Franz Schubert; *Music Box Revue,* a lavish musical by Irving Berlin; *The Perfect Fool,* written, staged, and acted by Ed Wynn; and *Alias Jimmy Valentine* and *Bought and Paid For,* 2 revivals.

U.S. **censorship** of early literature on contraception reflected in conviction of New York state physician for selling Marie C. Stopes's *Married Love.*

Some **popular songs** of 1921 were: *If You Would Care for Me; Look for the Silver Lining; Kitten on the Keys; I Never Knew; Blue Moon; Down in Chinatown.*

American Prix de Rome for musical composition awarded to **Howard Hanson.**

Spring Edith M. Hull's shocking romance, **The Sheik,** published chronicling the love adventures of a beautiful girl carried off into the desert by an Arab chieftain. Valentino starred in the silent movie version. *The Sheik* was very popular, and produced a host of imitators. They include Joan Conquest's *Desert Love,* Louise Gerard's *A Son of the Sahara,* and a parody called *The Shriek* by Charles Somerville.

Aug. 13 1st comedy by successful team of **George S. Kaufman** and **Marcus C. Connelly,** *Dulcy,* opens in New York. *To the Ladies* (1922) continued presentation of eccentric characters. *Beggar on Horseback* (1924) is a satire on contemporary world presented in form of dream sequence.

Oct. 10 Impact of **Ibsen** on American theater seen in host of domestic dramas:

bert Einstein for his discovery of the theory that explained the photoelectric effect. Albert Einstein was a German citizen at this time but was later driven out by the Nazi government and entered America.

Death rate per 100,000 in U.S. was 1,163.9. In 1900 it had been 1,755.

Jan. 3 Significant Supreme Court Decision on **labor unions** delivered the opinion that labor unions could be prosecuted for restraining interstate trade.

Apr. 30 Henry Ford announced **crisis in his business over;** Ford Motor Company assets rose to $345,140,557. 6 months previously, Ford had 175,000 finished surplus automobiles; he closed his plants and forced the surplus upon unwilling dealers, when an upsurge of buying saved the day.

May 20 Pres. Harding presented to Mme. Curie, codiscoverer of radium, a capsule of **radium** worth $100,000, the gift of American women.

June 25 **Samuel Gompers** chosen President of the American Federation of Labor for the 40th time. He polled more than twice as many votes (25,022) as John L. Lewis (12,324), his opponent in the election.

July 21 Possibilities of **concentrated bombing** shown by army test directed by Gen. William Mitchell in which former German battleship *Ostfriesland* was sunk by aircraft. Test was held off Hampton Roads, Va. Many at the time believed the demonstration vindicated Gen. Mitchell's belief in the superiority of air power over sea power.

Aug. 16 Department of Labor released estimate of **unemployment** throughout U.S. at 5,735,000, the greatest unemployment of the postwar depression.

time was 2:16⅖ on a fast track for winnings valued at $8650.

Broomspun won the 45th annual **Preakness Stakes,** paying 1–1. Jockey was F. Coltiletti; time was 1:54⅕ on a slow track for winnings valued at $43,000.

U.S. lawn tennis men's singles champion, William T. Tilden II; **women's singles champion,** Mrs. Molla Bjurstedt Mallory.

U.S.G.A. amateur championship won by Jesse P. Guilford at St. Louis, Mo., C.C. He defeated Robert A. Gardner, 7 and 6. **Open championship** won by James M. Barnes at Columbia Club, Chevy Chase, Md., with a score of 289.

Jan. 1 California defeated Ohio State by a score of 28 to 0 in the 6th annual **Rose Bowl** football game.

May 7 The winner of the 47th annual **Kentucky Derby** was E. R. Bradley's *Behave Yourself,* who ran the 1¼ mi. in 2:04⅕ on a fast track to win $38,450. C. Thompson was the jockey.

May 12 **Hospital Day** 1st observed on the birth date of Florence Nightingale. On the 100th anniversary of her birth in 1920, Matthew O. Foley, the editor of a hospital magazine in Chicago, advanced Hospital Day as a fitting tribute to the famous English nurse.

July 2 Jack Dempsey–Georges Carpentier championship heavyweight fight, **1st prize fight with a million dollar gate,** held at Jersey City, N.J. Dempsey won by knock-out in 4th round.

Aug. 3 Judge K. M. Landis, Commissioner of Baseball, ruled that the **Chicago White Sox** players charged with throwing games during the World's Series and regular season, though acquitted, would not be permitted to play again.

Oct. 5–13 New York, NL, defeated

| POLITICS AND GOVERNMENT; WAR; DISASTERS; VITAL STATISTICS. | BOOKS; PAINTING; DRAMA; ARCHITECTURE; SCULPTURE. |

Congress of July 2, 1921, or of the Versailles Treaty be vitiated by this treaty.

Nov. 12 Washington Conference for the Limitation of Armament opened in Washington, D.C., with delegates from Japan, England, France, and Italy, as well as U.S. Conference ended Feb. 6, 1922, produced treaties establishing fixed ratio of naval armaments among the 5 powers, and assigned rights of all powers in the Pacific.

Dec. 23 Pres. Harding commuted the sentences of **Eugene V. Debs** and 23 others convicted under the Espionage Act, release of prisoners to take effect on Christmas Day. Debs had served 2 years and 8 months of his 10 year sentence for allegedly seditious statements made at Canton, Ohio, in 1918.

Arthur Richman's *Ambush,* opening in New York, studies the sordid life of a clerk and the burdens imposed on him by wife and child; Owen Davis' *The Detour* studies a woman who tries to make up for her mistake in marriage by choosing a better life for her daughter. In *Icebound* (1923) Davis examines a family in Maine.

Nov. 2 Powerful drama of the waterfront which catapulted **Eugene O'Neill** to international fame is *Anna Christie,* produced in New York and shortly afterward in London, Berlin, Sweden, Norway, Denmark, Barcelona, Vienna, Moscow, Italy, and the Orient.

Nov. 11 At Arlington, Va., burial ceremony held at tomb of **Unknown Soldier.**

1922

Feb. 6 Nine-Power Treaty signed. The contracting countries agreed to respect the territorial integrity of China. Essentially, this was a subscription to the open-door policy of America.

Feb. 6 Naval limitation treaty signed by U.S. the British Empire, France, Italy, and Japan, limiting the sea power of the contracting countries. The treaty was to remain in force until Dec. 31, 1936.

Feb. 27 Woman Suffrage (19th) Amendment to the Constitution declared constitutional by a unanimous decision of the Supreme Court.

Apr. 15 Sen. John B. Kendrick of Wyoming introduced a resolution that called upon Sec. of the Interior, Albert B. Fall to explain if, and why, the **"Teapot Dome"** oil lands in Wyoming, which had been set aside by the Senate for the use of the Navy, were being leased secretly to the Mammoth Oil Company, which was controlled by Harry F. Sinclair. This was the 1st formal action, taken rather per-

Pulitzer Prizes: novel, *Alice Adams* by Booth Tarkington; drama, *Anna Christie* by Eugene O'Neill; U.S. history, *The Founding of New England* by James Truslow Adams; biography, *A Daughter of the Middle Border* by Hamlin Garland; poetry, *Collected Poems,* Edwin Arlington Robinson.

U.S. Post Office officials burned 500 copies of *Ulysses* by **James Joyce.** Work could not be copyrighted, hence author could not benefit from publication of hundreds of bowdlerized, pirated editions.

Sinclair Lewis continued his satire of small town life and psychology in *Babbitt.*

Lincoln Memorial completed in Washington, D.C., a temple-form Doric structure in the best tradition of the Greek revival in U.S. public architecture.

Some **popular songs** of 1922 were: *Song of Love; April Showers; My Man; Say It with Music; Hot Lips; Rose of the Rio Grande.*

SCIENCE; INDUSTRY; ECONOMICS; EDUCATION; RELIGION; PHILOSOPHY.

SPORTS; FASHIONS; POPULAR ENTERTAINMENT; FOLKLORE; SOCIETY.

Oct. 5 Radio station WJZ, Newark, N.J., **broadcast 1st play-by-play of World Series baseball game.** Graham McNamee announced game between Giants and Yankees directly from Polo Grounds in New York city.

Nov. 2 Founding of **American Birth Control League** in New York city under the leadership of Mrs. Margaret Sanger. It was a combination of the National Birth Control League, which she had founded in 1914, and the Voluntary Parenthood League, founded by Mrs. Mary Ware Dennett in 1919.

New York, AL, 5–3 in the 18th annual **World Series.**

Nov. 5 Armistice Day proclaimed a legal holiday by Pres. Harding.

Nov. 26 Navy defeated Army, 7–0 in the annual **Army-Navy football game** held at the Polo Grounds, New York city.

Dec. Knee-length skirts for women became the standard fashion by the end of 1921, causing much comment in the press. Following joke was typical:
Policeman: "Lost your mamma, have you? Why didn't you keep hold of her skirt?"
Little Alfred: "I cou-cou-couldn't reach it."

1922

1st fruitful radar research in America conducted by Dr. Hoyt A. Taylor and Leo C. Young of the U.S. Naval Research Aircraft Laboratory in Washington, D.C.

Number of **postage stamps** used by Americans was 14,261,948,813; in 1900 they used 3,998,544,564.

1st successful use of **Technicolor** process made by Herbert T. Kalmus; was not to become widely used on motion pictures in Hollywood until almost 20 years later.

Feb. 21 Semi-dirigible, the *Roma,* which had been purchased from the Italian government, exploded after hitting high tension wires at Hampton Roads Army Airbase, killing 34 of its 45-man crew. Despite continued disasters, advocates of lighter-than-air craft did not give up their programs.

May 12 20-ton meteor fell near Blackstone, Va., causing a 500-sq. ft. breach in the earth. Loud explosion and gigantic

U.S. won the **Davis Cup** for the 3d consecutive year defeating Australia in the challenge round 4 to 1, the U.S. doubles team (W. T. Tilden 2d and V. Richards) losing the only match. W. M. Johnston and W. T. Tilden 2d played the singles matches for the U.S.

Pillory won the 54th annual **Belmont Stakes,** paying 6–1. Jockey was C. H. Miller; time was 2:18⅘ on a fast track for winnings valued at $39,200.

Pillory won the 46th annual **Preakness Stakes,** paying 11–1. Jockey was L. Morris; time was 1:51⅗ on a fast track for winnings valued at $51,000.

U.S. lawn tennis men's singles champion, William T. Tilden II; **women's singles champion,** Mrs. Molla Bjurstedt Mallory.

U.S.G.A. amateur championship won by Jess W. Sweetser at The Country Club, Brookline, Mass. He defeated Charles Evans, Jr., 3 and 2. **Open championship** won by Gene Sarazen at Skokie C.C., Glencoe, Ill., with a score of 288.

Jan. 1 Washington and Jefferson Col-

461

functorily, of the investigation which led to the "Teapot Dome" scandals. Sen. Kendrick's information had come to him from one of his constituents, a small businessman in Wyoming.

May 13   Otto L. Wiedfeldt, 1st **German Ambassador** to the U.S. after World War I, arrived in New York.

May 26   Pres. Harding signed the bill providing for the creation of a **Federal Narcotics Control Board.**

Sept. 22   Federal law (Cable Act) declared that women no longer would be deprived of **citizenship** upon marriage to an alien.

Oct. 3   Mrs. W. H. Felton became **1st U.S. woman Senator** when Georgia's governor selected her on death of Sen. Thomas E. Watson. Her term extended to only 1 day.

Nov. 7   In **mid-term election,** Republicans retained majorities in both houses, but lost heavily nevertheless, dropping 70 seats in the House, 7 in the Senate. Forecasters predicted a swing to the Democrats in 1924.

Louis Armstrong, young cornetist, brought from New Orleans to Chicago to join Joseph "King" Oliver's Creole Jazz Band.

Mar. 9   Naturalistic theater found voice in **Eugene O'Neill's** *The Hairy Ape,* where the struggle of emerging consciousness is symbolized in the powerful figure of Yank, the stoker, representative of the force that gives birth to civilization.

May 23   Play with longest run of any in American stage history to this date, **Abie's Irish Rose,** by Anne Nichols, opened in New York. Closed Oct. 22, 1927, running up a total of 2327 performances. Describing the love of a Jewish boy and an Irish girl, play touches upon theme of racial prejudice, especially in characters of two fathers. Like *Uncle Tom's Cabin,* it is an important social document.

Oct. 30   Play which is to have perennial success on stage, on screen, and as a musical, **Seventh Heaven** by Austin Strong, opened in New York. A romantic melodrama, it tells story of Diane and Chico and their love during the war years. Helen Menken played role of Diane.

1923

Jan. 10   **U.S. occupation troops** on the Rhine in Germany ordered to return by Pres. Harding.

Mar. 5   Both Montana and Nevada enacted country's 1st **old age pension** grants. The Montana pension allotted a monthly $25 to qualified septuagenarians.

Apr. 9   **Minimum wage law** for women and children in the District of Columbia was ruled unconstitutional by the U.S. Supreme Court by a vote of 5 to 3.

May 4   New York state Assembly passed an act repealing the state's **prohibition** enforcement act. Despite Pres. Harding's warning that federal authorities would have to take over the enforcement of

Pulitzer Prizes: novel, *One of Ours* by Willa Cather; drama, *Icebound* by Owen Davis; U. S. history, *The Supreme Court in United States History* by Charles Warren; biography, *The Life and Letters of Walter H. Page* by Burton J. Hendrick; poetry, *The Ballad of the Harp-Weaver; A Few Figs from Thistles;* 8 Sonnets in *American Poetry, 1922, A Miscellany* by Edna St. Vincent Millay.

Innovator in poetry was **E. E. Cummings,** whose 1st volume *Tulips and Chimneys* reveals his idiosyncratic style—unorthodox handling of punctuation and typography. His important war novel *The Enormous Room* was published in 1922.

Some of the **plays** that appeared on

flames seen for miles around accompanied the crash.

Radio station WEAF, New York, broadcasted **1st commercially sponsored program** in U.S.

June 14 Pres. Harding's dedication of the Francis Scott Key Memorial in Baltimore was broadcast by radio, the **first use of radio made by a president of the U.S.** The first official governmental message was not broadcast, however, until Dec. 6, 1923.

Sept. 12 House of Bishops of the U.S. Protestant Episcopal Church voted 36–27 to delete the word "obey" from **marriage service.**

Oct. 14 1st **mechanical switchboard** installed in New York city telephone system; exchange was called "Pennsylvania."

Nov. 15 Dr. Alexis Carrel of the Rockefeller Institute announced his discovery of **leucocytes** or white corpuscles, the agents in the blood which prevent the spread of infection in animal tissue.

lege and California University played to a scoreless tie in the 7th annual **Rose Bowl** football game.

May 13 The winner of the 48th **Kentucky Derby** was B. Block's *Morvich*, the favorite, who ran the 1¼ mi. in 2:04⅗ on a fast track, winning $46,775. A. Johnson was the jockey.

Aug. 28 **Oldest American international team golf match,** Walker Cup match between U.S. and Great Britain, established with opening play at National Golf Links of America, Southampton, N.Y. U.S. team won on 2nd day, 8 to 4.

Oct. 4–8 New York, NL, defeated New York, AL, 4–0 in the 19th annual **World Series. 1st radio broadcast** of a baseball game direct from the field was Graham McNamee's announcing of this Series.

Oct. 20 Lt. Harold Harris became 1st member of **Caterpillar Club** by parachuting from defective airplane during test flight at McCook Field, Dayton, Ohio. Caterpillar Club is composed of those who have escaped death by means of a parachute.

Nov. 25 Army defeated Navy, 17–14, in the annual **Army-Navy football game** at Philadelphia, Pa.

1923

Nobel Prize in physics presented to Robert Andrews Millikan "for his work on the elementary electric charge and on the photoelectric effect." Millikan conducted his prize-winning experiments in the physics department of the University of Chicago between 1906 and 1916. He was America's 2d distinguished physicist after Michelson, winning the Hughes Medal of the Royal Society of London, the Comstock Prize of the National Academy of Sciences, and the Edison Medal of the American Institute of Electrical Engineers.

More cars built this year than had been produced in the 1st 15 years of the industry (1900–15). About 15 million passenger cars were in use in the U.S., and

Political slogan **"It won't be Long now"** made the rounds in the Louisiana gubernatorial elections and brought to public notice a new boisterous figure, Huey Long. The opposition to this 30-year-old upstart coined the phrase. Long ran 3d in the election.

U.S. won the **Davis Cup** for the 4th year in succession by defeating the Australian team in the challenge round 4 matches to 1, W. M. Johnston (U.S.) losing the first singles match to J. O. Anderson (Austr.) W. T. Tilden 2d and R. N. Williams were the other 2 members of the U.S. team.

U.S. lawn tennis men's singles champion,

prohibition in states which did not do the job themselves, Gov. Alfred E. Smith signed the act. This was thought by many to have been the beginning of the end of prohibition.

May 9 Prescriptions for whisky by physicians not limited under **prohibition** law, declared Judge John C. Knox of U.S. District Court in New York.

Aug. 2 **Pres. Harding died** at a hotel in San Francisco, Calif., at the age of 58. He had been taken ill at Grant's Pass, Ore., on July 28, reportedly from ptomaine poisoning. Final medical report cited apoplexy as the cause of death.

Aug. 3 Vice-Pres. **Calvin Coolidge** sworn in as President by his father at 2:30 A.M. in Plymouth, Vt., where the news of Pres. Harding's death reached them.

Sept. 15 **Oklahoma placed under martial law** by Gov. J. C. Walton because of terrorist activities of the Ku Klux Klan, which had become a powerful political force in mid-West politics. At about this time several newspapers began exposing the Klan and its secret, "night-riding" activities.

Oct. 16 Law making mandatory educational and **literacy test** for new voters sustained by the New York State Court of Appeals.

Oct. 25 1st meeting of Senate subcommittee to investigate **Teapot Dome** oil leases held under chairmanship of Sen. Thomas J. Walsh of Montana. Walsh had used the 18 months since his appointment as chairman to study the case, and during that time public interest in it had died down; it was quickly reawakened by the hearings Walsh conducted.

Dec. 6 1st of Pres. Coolidge's annual messages to Congress announced support for U.S. adherence to **World Court** and

Broadway during 1923 were: several productions by the Moscow Art Theater, "jammed with the elite"; *Polly Preferred*, with Ina Claire; *The Laughing Lady*, with Ethel Barrymore; *Humoresque*, by Fannie Hurst, with Laurette Taylor; *Poppy*, with Madge Kennedy and W. C. Fields; *The Swan*, a comedy by Ferenc Molnar, with Eva LeGallienne, Basil Rathbone, and Philip Merivale; *Laugh, Clown, Laugh*, with Lionel Barrymore; Peggy Hopkins Joyce and Joe Cook in Earl Carroll's *Vanities*. In October Eleonora Duse paid her final visit to U.S.

Most popular **musical comedy** of the season was *No! No! Nanette*, with music by Vincent Youmans. It contained the songs "Tea for Two" and "I Want to Be Happy."

Some **popular songs** of 1923 were: *Yes, We Have No Bananas; Barney Google; Kiss in the Dark; Tea for Two; I Want to Be Happy; Sonny Boy; Linger Awhile.*

Wolverine Orchestra organized in Chicago by Leon "Bix" Beiderbecke, one of the early northern white jazz musicians whose work became most important in the development of jazz.

Vote conducted by editors and critics of *Film Daily* determined the following 10 **motion pictures** were the best of 1923: *Covered Wagon; Robin Hood; Safety Last; Little Old New York; Merry-Go-Round; Green Goddess; Rosita; Hunchback of Notre Dame; Scaramouche; Down to the Sea in Ships.*

Feb. 19 1st play of prominent playwright **Philip Barry**, *You and I*, opened in New York. Play is concerned with conflict of demands of love and art.

Mar. **German expressionism** adapted to American stage in 2 plays that appeared this month: *The Adding Machine* by Elmer Rice and *Roger Bloomer* by John Howard Lawson. Both satirize American middle class, business mores.

| SCIENCE; INDUSTRY; ECONOMICS; EDUCATION; RELIGION; PHILOSOPHY. | SPORTS; FASHIONS; POPULAR ENTERTAINMENT; FOLKLORE; SOCIETY. |

New York, New Jersey, Pennsylvania, and Maryland combined had more autos than all the rest of the world outside the U.S.

DuPont Corporation began production of **"cellophane"** cellulose film through the purchase of American rights to the Swiss patent of Jacques F. Brandenberger. Swiss factories had been producing cellophane since 1912.

1st chinchillas imported into the U.S. —founding new **fur industry**—consisted of 7 male and 4 female animals.

Jan. **William Jennings Bryan** continued to stir up controversy over evolution by addressing a group of ministers in St. Paul, Minn. The theory of evolution, he said, is a "program of infidelity masquerading under the name of science." Debate taken up by newspapers, who gave names of "Fundamentalist" and "Modernist" to the 2 sides.

Mar. 13 Process for producing **sound motion pictures** unveiled by Dr. Lee de Forest in New York city. Called "Phonofilm," new device provided sound on film; show included performance of an orchestra on film.

Oct. 6 **Air speed records** broken by Naval Lt. A. L. Williams, ex-New York Giant baseball pitcher, who averaged 243.76 mph. over the 125-mi. course of the Pulitzer Trophy contest. His plane was a Curtiss racer.

Nov. 6 Patent issued to Col. Jacob Schick for **1st electric shaver.** Schick received several additional patents, and in 1931 he established his own company, the Schick Dry Shaver Company, Inc., at Stamford, Conn.

Dec. 6 Broadcast of Pres. Coolidge's message to both houses of Congress the **1st radio transmission of a presidential communication.** Transmission was so clear

William T. Tilden II; **women's singles champion,** Helen N. Wills.

U.S.G.A. amateur championship won by Max R. Marston at Flossmoor, Ill., C.C. He defeated Jess W. Sweetser, 1 up. **Open championship** won by Robert T. (Bobby) Jones, Jr. at Inwood, N.Y., C.C., with a score of 296.

Vigil won the 47th annual **Preakness Stakes,** paying 9–2. Jockey was B. Marinelli; time was 1:53⅗ on a fast track for winnings valued at $52,000.

Zev won the 55th annual **Belmont Stakes,** paying 4–5. Jockey was E. Sande; time was 2:19 on a good track for winnings valued at $38,000.

Jan. 1 Southern California defeated Pennsylvania State by a score of 14 to 3 in the 8th annual **Rose Bowl** football game.

Jan. 4 **Emile Coué,** popular psychologist, arrived in New York and was greeted by thousands of cheering admirers. He established a clinic in New York and made a speaking tour through the country. He was the originator of a system of curing mental ills through autosuggestion, part of which included saying, "Every day in every way I am getting better and better."

Apr. 18 **Yankee Stadium** in New York city opened. It became the home park of the New York Yankees of the American League.

May 19 One of the great American jockeys, Earle Sande, won his 1st **Kentucky Derby** when he rode Rancocas Stable's *Zev* to victory in the 49th Churchill Downs classic, winning $53,600. Time, 2:05⅖ on a fast track.

Sept. 14 **Dempsey-Firpo fight** held at the Polo Grounds, New York city, in which Dempsey knocked out the challenger in the 2d round and retained his heavyweight championship. In the 3 min. 57 sec. of fighting time there was a total of 11 knockdowns, the most famous of which occurred in the 1st round when Firpo knocked the champion completely out of the ring.

Oct. 10–15 New York, AL, defeated

POLITICS AND GOVERNMENT; WAR; DISASTERS; VITAL STATISTICS.	BOOKS; PAINTING; DRAMA; ARCHITECTURE; SCULPTURE.

prohibition enforcement. Coolidge believed strongly in government noninterference in business and in lower taxes.

May 23   1st time in New York an acting group was found guilty under a law which prohibited the presentation of **immoral plays**. *God of Vengeance* by **Sholem Asch** was the play ruled objectionable.

1924

Feb. 3   **Woodrow Wilson** died at his house in Washington, D.C. He had been completely inactive for more than 4 years, suffering from paralysis and failing memory.

Mar. 18   House of Representatives passed **Soldiers' Bonus Bill,** providing for paid-up 20-year annuities for most veterans, at a cost of $2,000,000,000. Only veterans entitled to less than $50 adjusted compensation were paid in cash. Bill passed by Senate April 23, vetoed by Pres. Coolidge May 15, repassed over the veto May 17 by House and May 19 by Senate.

Mar. 18   **Worst tornado** in U.S. history obliterated 35 towns in Illinois, Indiana, Tennessee, Kentucky, and Missouri, killing 800 people, injuring 3,000, and leaving 15,000 homeless.

May 11–13   **National Convention of the Socialist Labor Party** met in New York and nominated F. T. Johns of Oregon for the presidency and Verne L. Reynolds of Maryland for the vice-presidency.

June 5   National Convention of the **Prohibition Party** met at Columbus, Ohio, and nominated H. P. Faris of Missouri for the presidency and Miss Marie C. Brehm of California for the vice-presidency.

June 12   **Republican National Convention** at Cleveland nominated Calvin Coolidge and Charles G. Dawes of Illinois for the presidency and vice-presidency respectively.

June 19   **National Convention of the Farmer-Labor Progressive Party** met at St. Paul, Minn. and nominated Duncan MacDonald, a miner of Illinois, for the presidency, and William Bouck, a farmer of Washington, for the vice-presidency. On

Pulitzer Prizes: novel, *The Able McLaughlins* by Margaret Wilson; drama, *Hell-Bent Fer Heaven* by Hatcher Hughes; U.S. history, *The American Revolution— A Constitutional Interpretation,* by Charles Howard McIlwain; biography, *From Immigrant to Inventor* by Michael Idvorski Pupin; poetry, *New Hampshire: A Poem with Notes and Grace Notes* by Robert Frost.

The Student Prince, an operetta by **Sigmund Romberg,** produced in New York city.

Some **popular songs** of 1924 were: *Big Butter and Egg Man; Lady, Be Good; Indian Love Call; Rose Marie; I'll See You in My Dreams; Yes, Sir, That's My Baby; Sweet Georgia Brown.*

Rose Marie, an operetta by **Rudolf Friml,** produced in New York city. It contained Friml's 2 most popular songs, "Indian Love Call" and "Rose Marie, I Love You."

Cumulative effect of **Eugene O'Neill's** one-act dramas of the sea felt in staging of *S.S. Glencairn* by Provincetown Players.

The 10 best **motion pictures** of 1924, as determined by the editors and critics of *Film Daily,* were: *Thief of Bagdad; Beau Brummel; Ten Commandments; America; Sea Hawk; Secrets; Girl Shy; Monsieur Beaucaire; Marriage Circle; Abraham Lincoln.*

Feb. 12   *Rhapsody in Blue,* famous composition by **George Gershwin,** 1st per-

SCIENCE; INDUSTRY; ECONOMICS; EDUCATION; RELIGION; PHILOSOPHY.	SPORTS; FASHIONS; POPULAR ENTERTAINMENT; FOLKLORE; SOCIETY.

that technicians in St. Louis, Mo., telephoned Washington to ask about occasional rustling noise and were told it was caused by president turning the pages of his address.

New York, NL, 4–2 in the 20th annual **World Series.**

Nov. 24 Navy and **Army** tied, 0–0, in their annual football classic this year at the Polo Grounds, New York city.

1924

After a series of price decreases, the price of Ford cars hit their lowest point: $290 (without self-starter). Price for the Model T had originally (1909) been $950.

1st notable study of curriculum-making in U.S. made by Franklin Bobbitt in his book *How to Make a Curriculum.*

Test run for **transcontinental air mail** made in 27 hr. from New York to San Francisco. Best time in 1848 was three mo. (by ship to Panama, overland across the Isthmus, ship to San Francisco); in 1869 7½ days by railway.

Jan. 1 Radios in U.S. homes were over 2,500,000. 5 years earlier, in 1920, there were not more than 5,000 receiving sets in U.S., most of them in the hands of expert technicians.

Mar. 31 U.S. Supreme Court declared unconstitutional a law of the state of Oregon requiring all children of grammar-school age to attend **public schools.** Law aimed chiefly at Catholic and Lutheran parochial schools.

May 21 Theory of Evolution ruled untenable by the General Assembly of the Presbyterian Church at San Antonio, Texas.

May 27 Methodist Episcopal General Conference, meeting at Springfield, Mass.,

Popular campaign slogan was **"Keep Cool with Coolidge."** Despite the storm and unrest prevailing during 1923, Coolidge remained calm and unperturbed. Republicans played up this placidity in the campaign.

National football champion, Notre Dame, played 9 games and won them all under the guidance of coach Knute Rockne, who had been a member of the 1913 Notre Dame team which upset Army.

U.S.G.A. amateur championship won by Robert T. (Bobby) Jones, Jr., at Merion Cricket Club, Haverford, Pa. He defeated George Von Elm, 9 and 6. **Open championship** won by Cyril Walker at Oakland Hills C.C., Birmingham, Mich., with a score of 297.

U.S. lawn tennis men's singles champion, William T. Tilden II; **women's singles champion,** Helen N. Wills.

U.S. Tennis Team successfully defended the **Davis Cup** for the 4th year in succession by defeating the Australian team in the challenge round 5 matches to 0. William T. Tilden 2d, Vincent Richards, and William M. Johnston made up U.S. team.

Nellie Morse won the 48th **Preakness Stakes,** paying 12–1. Jockey was J. Merimee; time was 1:57⅕ on a heavy track for winnings valued at $54,000.

Mad Play won the 56th annual **Belmont Stakes,** paying 2–1. Jockey was E. Sande; time was 2:18⅘ on a good track for winnings valued at $42,880.

Jan. 1 Washington and Navy played to

467

| POLITICS AND GOVERNMENT; WAR; DISASTERS; VITAL STATISTICS. | BOOKS; PAINTING; DRAMA; ARCHITECTURE; SCULPTURE. |

July 10th, MacDonald and Bouck stepped aside, and William Z. Foster and Benjamin Gitlow became the nominees for president and vice-president.

June 30 Ex-Sec. of Interior Fall, Henry Sinclair, and Edward Doheny and his son indicted on charges of conspiracy and bribery, the result of **"Teapot Dome"** hearings. After a long series of trials, mistrials, and appeals, Fall was found guilty and sent to jail for 1 year in July, 1931.

July 4 **National Convention of the Conference for Progressive Political Action** nominated U.S. Senator Robert M. La Follette of Wisconsin for the presidency and on July 18 U.S. Senator Burton K. Wheeler of Montana for the vice-presidency.

July 9 **Democratic National Convention,** meeting in New York city, nominated on 103d ballot John W. Davis of West Virginia for the presidency, and Charles W. Bryan of Nebraska, brother of William Jennings Bryan, for the vice-presidency.

July 10 **National convention of the Workers' Party** met at Chicago and nominated William Z. Foster of Illinois for the presidency and Benjamin Gitlow of New York for the vice-presidency. Workers' Party was communist.

Nov. 4 Calvin Coolidge defeated John W. Davis in the **presidential elections** by an electoral vote of 382–136. 13 electoral votes went to Robert M. La Follette and Burton K. Wheeler. Popular vote: Coolidge, 15,725,016; Davis, 8,385,503; La Follette, 4,822,856; Faris, 57,520; Johns, 36,429; Foster, 36,386.

formed. It was one of the 1st attempts by a Tin Pan Alley writer to incorporate the structures and idioms of popular music into a symphonic work.

May 15 Theme of miscegenation forms the basis of **Eugene O'Neill's** *All God's Chillun Got Wings.* Paul Robeson acted the role of Jim Harris, the Negro who aspires to rise above his race by marrying Ella Downey, a white girl.

Sept. 3 **Unromantic treatment of war** is the theme of *What Price Glory?* by Maxwell Anderson and Laurence Stallings.

Nov. 11 Powerful drama of New England, emphasizing lust and Puritanism and sordid family relations, is *Desire Under the Elms* by **Eugene O'Neill,** which like his other plays enjoyed immediate international fame, being acted in Prague, Berlin, etc.

Nov. 24 Melodrama which concerns small people in everyday life is *They Knew What They Wanted* by **Sidney Howard.** Using the framework of the Tristan myth, he tells the story of a middle-aged wine grower in California and his love for a younger woman. Play was awarded Pulitzer Prize.

1925

85% of U.S. **population** lived in "registered" areas, that is, areas covered by accurate vital statistics record. In 1900, only 40% of the population had been so covered.

Charles Gates Dawes won this year's **Nobel Peace Prize** (which he shared with Sir Austen Chamberlain). In 1923 he had

Pulitzer Prizes: novel, *So Big* by Edna Ferber; drama, *They Knew What They Wanted* by Sidney Howard; U.S. history, *A History of the American Frontier* by Frederic L. Paxson; biography, *Barrett Wendell and his Letters* by M. A. DeWolfe Howe; poetry, *The Man Who Died Twice* by Edwin Arlington Robinson.

468

SCIENCE; INDUSTRY; ECONOMICS; EDUCATION; RELIGION; PHILOSOPHY.

SPORTS; FASHIONS; POPULAR ENTERTAINMENT; FOLKLORE; SOCIETY.

gave up the ban on dancing and theater attendance.

June 2 Struggle against **child labor in** U.S. took form of proposed amendment to the Constitution. But by 1950 only 26 of the necessary 36 states had ratified amendment.

June 15 Ford Motor Company announced its 10 millionth automobile had been manufactured. Ford took 7 years to make his 1st million cars; 132 working days to make his 10th million.

Oct. 15 Dirigible ZR-3, a German airship, completed flight from Friedrichshafen to Lakehurst, N.J. It was renamed the *Los Angeles* when taken over by U.S. Navy.

Nov. 30 Transmission of photographs from London to New York by **wireless telegraph** demonstrated by the Radio Corporation of America. 20 to 25 min. were consumed for the transmission of each photograph.

a 14–14 tie in the 9th annual **Rose Bowl** football game.

May 17 50th annual **Kentucky Derby** won by Mrs. R. M. Hoots's *Black Gold.* Time was 2:05⅕ on a fast track; the value, $52,775; jockey was J. D. Mooney.

July 13 For 8th consecutive time, U.S. team took 1st place in **Olympic Games,** held at Paris, with 255 points.

July 21 After a sensational trial, **Nathan Leopold** and **Richard Loeb** sentenced to life imprisonment for the kidnapping and murder of Bobby Franks. 2 intelligent and well-educated young men, Leopold and Loeb had decided to kill someone apparently just to see what it would feel like and picked a young boy at random. After 12 years in prison, Loeb was killed by a fellow inmate, Jan. 28, 1936. Leopold applied for parole in 1953 but was refused.

Oct. 4–10 Washington, AL, defeated New York, NL, 4–3 in the 21st annual **World Series.**

Nov. 29 Army defeated Navy, 12–0, in their classic contest, this year at Baltimore Stadium.

Dec. 31 Greatest cup performer and perhaps the most popular horse ever to race in America, **Exterminator,** ended his 8th and final year of racing with a record of 50 wins in 100 starts and $252,996.00 in total earnings. "Old Bones" had won the 1918 Kentucky Derby as a last-minute substitute. He went on to a great career which included winning the Saratoga Cup 4 years in succession.

1925

Survey of U.S. business showed that only 89 firms in the whole country had been in the same family for 100 years or more.

15 of the **automobile manufacturing companies** that started before 1905 were still in existence: Apperson (1901); Buick (1903); Cadillac (1902); Ford (1903);

"Banjo Hit" coined by Snooks Dowd of the Jersey City team to describe a fly ball weakly hit into the outfield which landed safely for a base hit. Term referred to sound of ball against the bat resembling the plucking of a banjo string.

Charleston became popular dance step with both professional entertainers and the

469

POLITICS AND GOVERNMENT; WAR; DISASTERS; VITAL STATISTICS.

BOOKS; PAINTING; DRAMA; ARCHITECTURE; SCULPTURE.

been named chairman of the committee to study the German budget with a view to the payment of war reparations. The committee submitted a plan (since known as the Dawes plan) for the reorganization of German finances. This plan went into effect Sept. 1, 1924, and won for Dawes the celebrated award.

Jan. 5 Mrs. William B. (Nellie Tayloe) Ross inaugurated governor of Wyoming, **1st woman governor in American history.**

Mar. 4 **Pres. Calvin Coolidge** inaugurated for his 2d term. He had served 2 years previously when he succeeded to the presidency after Harding's death in 1923.

Mar. 23 Senate ratified **Isle of Pines** Treaty, which provided that the island shall belong to the Republic of Cuba; the treaty had been pending in the Senate since 1904.

May 5 Arrest of **John T. Scopes** in Dayton, Tenn., for violation of the state law which forbade the teaching of the theory of evolution. This led to the famous Scopes trial, July 10–21, in which Scopes, who was defended by Clarence Darrow and Dudley Field Malone, was convicted and fined $100. William Jennings Bryan, who served as one of the prosecuting attorneys, died July 26 as a result, it is said, of the trial. High point of trial came on July 20, when Bryan agreed to go on the witness stand himself and was questioned by Darrow on the points of the "Fundamentalist" doctrine; Bryan was completely humiliated by Darrow's insistence on the absurdities of a strict reading of the Bible. Trial attracted more attention than any other legal proceeding in U.S. history. Verdict was eventually reversed on a technicality by the Tennessee Supreme Court.

Oct. 28–Dec. 17 Famous court martial of **"Billy" Mitchell,** Army colonel who

Sinclair Lewis turned from satire to a novel dealing with the quest for truth, *Arrowsmith.* It is the story of Martin Arrowsmith, an idealistic young man whose love for medical research drives him from the Midwest to New York, and finally to sacrifice his pleasant life with its wealth and social amenities.

Most popular novel of **Theodore Dreiser,** *An American Tragedy,* is a study of biological determinism. It tells the story of Clyde Griffiths, a weak youth who drifts into a dilemma from which he cannot extricate himself and commits an "inevitable" crime. He murdered the girl.

Fictional cross section of New York provided in novel, *Manhattan Transfer,* by **John Dos Passos.** Countless characters are introduced, but since the treatment is so kaleidoscopic, few are remembered. The dominant aim seems to be the presentation of a whole social organism, the individual being subsumed in the whole.

F. Scott Fitzgerald wrote his masterpiece *The Great Gatsby,* the epitome of the illusions of the "roaring '20's." Here are the palatial mansions on Long Island, the expensive parties, prohibition, frustrated love affairs, and entangled marriages; here is the beginning of that "crack-up" that is dealt with more directly in his next novel, *Tender Is the Night* (1934).

Poet-critic and guiding spirit of the "New Poetry," **Ezra Pound,** issued *A Draft of XVI Cantos,* the 1st of a series of long and involved poems to which he added many more in subsequent years. Here is the fruit of theory and scholarship. Subject matter is drawn from ancient times, the Renaissance, China and Japan, Colonial America, and modern times. The style is highly complex.

Founding of America's most sophisticated magazine, **The New Yorker.**

Aaron Copland awarded the 1st **Guggenheim Fellowship** given to a composer for his experiments with the use of jazz in "serious" compositions.

470

SCIENCE; INDUSTRY; ECONOMICS; EDUCATION; RELIGION; PHILOSOPHY.

SPORTS; FASHIONS; POPULAR ENTERTAINMENT; FOLKLORE; SOCIETY.

Franklin (1900); Haynes (1896); Locomobile (1899); Maxwell (1904); Olds (1897); Overland (1902); Packard (1902); Peerless (1900); Pierce-Arrow (1901); Stearns (1900); Studebaker (1898). Over 1000 had failed.

William Green elected President of the American Federation of Labor, succeeding the Federation's founder, the late Samuel Gompers.

1st dry ice manufactured commercially made by the Prest-Air Devices Company, Long Island City, N.Y.

DuPont Corporation began production of **industrial alcohol** in the steady diversification of the chemical industry in America.

National Spelling Bee initiated by the *Louisville* (*Ky.*) *Courier Journal*. Since 1939, the annual event has been sponsored by the Scripps-Howard newspapers.

Antitoxin for **scarlet fever** prepared by George Frederick and Gladys Henry Dick of Chicago.

Jan. 24 New Yorkers witnessed a **total solar eclipse** for the 1st time in over 3 centuries.

Feb. 2 Relays of dog teams at last reached Nome, Alaska, with antidiphtheria serum to combat epidemic. **Gunnar Kasson,** who made the final lap, arrived blind and nearly dead from cold.

Apr. 1 Dillon, Read & Company, New York banking house, purchased the Dodge Brothers automobile company for $146,000,000, **largest cash transaction** in U.S. industrial history to that time.

May 13 Florida House of Representatives passed bill requiring **daily Bible readings** in all public schools.

Sept. 3 **Shenandoah,** U.S. Army dirigible, wrecked in a storm near Ava, Ohio,

general public. It was introduced originally in cabarets but it spread throughout the country as no previous dance of the '20's had been able to do. Even children danced it for pennies in side streets and in front of theaters at intermission. The Charleston was a very active dance, featuring exuberant side kicks which contrasted sharply with the wriggling movements of the shimmy and other jazz dances.

U.S.G.A. amateur championship won by Robert T. (Bobby) Jones, Jr., at Oakmont, Pa., C.C. He defeated Watts Gunn, 8 and 7. **Open championship** won by Willie Macfarlane at Worcester, Mass., C.C. with a score of 291.

U.S. lawn tennis men's singles champion, William T. Tilden II; **women's singles champion,** Helen N. Wills.

Coventry won the 49th annual **Preakness Stakes,** paying 22–1. Jockey was C. Kummer; time was 1:59 on a fast track for winnings valued at $52,700. From this year the distance has been 1¾₆ mi.

American Flag won the 57th annual **Belmont Stakes,** paying 9–20. Jockey was A. Johnson; time was 2:16⅖ on a fast track for winnings valued at $38,500.

National football champion was Dartmouth, coached by Jesse B. Hawley. They were undefeated and untied in 8 games.

Jan. 1 Notre Dame defeated Stanford by a score of 27 to 10 in the 10th annual **Rose Bowl** football game.

May New vogue for **crossword puzzles** reached a peak.

May 16 Earle Sande returned to racing when he drove home his 2d **Kentucky Derby** winner, **Flying Ebony** in the 51st annual Churchill Downs classic at Louisville, Ky. This was Sande's 1st mount after months spent in a hospital recuperating from a bad spill the year before at Saratoga Springs, N.Y. Not expected to ride for a long time, if ever, Sande rose from a hospital bed, arrived in Louisville after riders had been hired for the favored

471

| POLITICS AND GOVERNMENT; WAR; DISASTERS; VITAL STATISTICS. | BOOKS; PAINTING; DRAMA; ARCHITECTURE; SCULPTURE. |

advocated greatly expanded air force and made predictions about air power that have since come true. He accused military high command of "incompetency, criminal negligence, and almost treasonable administration of national defense." He was found guilty, and suspended for 5 years without pay or allowances. Later Pres. Coolidge upheld the suspension, but restored the allowances and granted Mitchell half pay. He resigned from the army 2 weeks later.

Nov. 3 **James J. Walker** elected Mayor of New York city by overwhelming majority.

Some **popular songs** of 1925 were: *Show Me the Way to Go Home; Collegiate; Thanks for the Buggy Ride; Don't Bring Lulu.*

Ten best **films** of 1925 as determined by editors and critics of *Film Daily* were: *Gold Rush; Merry Widow; Phantom of the Opera; Kiss Me Again; Unholy Three; Last Laugh; Lost World; Don Q, Son of Zorro; The Freshman; Big Parade.*

Jan. 11 Premiere performance of **Aaron Copland**'s Symphony for Organ and Orchestra, commissioned by Nadia Boulanger, given by the New York Symphony, Walter Damrosch conducting. In an opening speech, Damrosch said: "If a young man at the age of 23 can write a symphony like that, in 5 years he will be ready to commit murder."

1926

Congress passed **Air Commerce Act,** providing for Bureau of Air Commerce. Bureau assumed jurisdiction over safety of civil aviation, including licensing of aircraft and pilots. Previously federal government had had no connection with civil aviation except through appropriations for the air mail service.

Jan. 27 A resolution adopted by the U.S. Senate consented to United States membership in the **World Court** with 5 reservations. The vote was 76 to 17. All reservations were acceptable to members of World Court except part of one which related to advisory opinions. Consequently, and in spite of offers of additional agreements, U.S. would not join. On Dec. 9, 1929, Pres. Hoover permitted U.S. chargé d'affaires in Switzerland to sign protocol of adherence to World Court, but it was defeated in Senate in 1935 in spite of Pres. Roosevelt's support.

Feb. 26 Pres. Coolidge signed the **Revenue Act,** which provided for reductions in income taxes, surtaxes, and taxes on passenger cars, and abolished many nui-

Pulitzer Prizes: novel, *Arrowsmith* by Sinclair Lewis; drama, *Craig's Wife* by George Kelly; U.S. history, *The History of the United States* by Edward Channing; biography, *The Life of Sir William Osler* by Harvey Cushing; poetry, *What's O'Clock* by Amy Lowell.

Novel of postwar disillusion is **Ernest Hemingway's** *The Sun Also Rises.* Here is represented that lost generation, cut off from all national and emotional ties, wandering in France and Spain.

History book which attained wide usage as a text in American colleges is *The Making of the Modern Mind* by **Herman Randall.** A student of Dewey and Robinson, he undertook to study the social and material background of the thoughts of such men as Dante, Hegel, Marx, etc.

Need for protection of their rights led playwrights to organize the **Dramatists' Guild** as part of the Authors' League.

Virgil Thomson, working under the influence of Parisian composers, completed his *Sonata da chiesa* (church sonata) for E flat clarinet, C trumpet, viola, F horn, and trombone. The 2d movement incor-

with loss of 14 lives. In spite of this and similar disasters, advocates of lighter-than-air craft continued to support their cause against the airplane.

Oct.   **Florida land boom** reached a peak in Fall of 1925, said to exceed any gold rush or other business stampede in U.S. history.

Oct. 16   Texas State Text Book Board prohibited the discussion of the **evolutionary theory** in any of its school textbooks.

Dec. 29   Board of Trustees of Trinity College in North Carolina agreed to change name of institution to **Duke University** in order to meet terms of $40,000,000 trust fund established by James B. Duke, tobacco millionaire.

mounts, and had to accept G. A. Cochran's horse, which wasn't given much of a chance. Sande rode *Flying Ebony* in 2:07¾ on a muddy track to win $52,950.

Sept. 12   The U.S. won the **Davis Cup** for the 6th year in succession by defeating the French team 5 matches to none in the challenge round at Philadelphia. W. T. Tilden 2d and W. M. Johnston won the singles matches for the U.S. and R. N. Williams and Vincent Richards were the victors in the doubles match.

Oct. 7–15   Pittsburgh, NL, defeated Washington, AL, 4–3 in the 22d annual **World Series.**

Nov. 28   **Army** defeated Navy, 10–3, in their annual contest, at the Polo Grounds, New York city.

1926

1st successful treatment of **pernicious anemia** applied by 2 Boston doctors, George R. Minot and William P. Murphy, with the imposition of a liver diet for the victims of the previously mysterious and fatal disease. Minot and Murphy, along with Dr. George H. Whipple, received the Nobel Prize in 1934 for their work on the disease.

Right of city boards of education to grant schoolchildren one hour each week from regular curriculum for **religious instruction** widely challenged. In test case involving White Plains schools, New York court granted the recess. Appeal was planned.

Sarah Lawrence College, Bronxville, N.Y. established as Sarah Lawrence College for Women. 1st classes met in 1928. Present name adopted in 1947.

Plans announced for the construction of a bridge across the Hudson River to Manhattan. Terminal sites decided upon were Fort Lee in New Jersey, and Fort Washington on Manhattan. The bridge was later called the **George Washington Bridge.**

1st woman to swim the English Channel was **Gertrude Ederle** of New York. 19 years old, she accomplished the difficult feat in 14 hr. 31 min.

National football champion was Stanford, coached by Glenn (Pop) Warner. They were undefeated and untied in 10 games.

Display won the 50th annual **Preakness Stakes,** paying 19–1. Jockey was J. Maiben; time was 1:59⅖ on a fast track for winnings valued at $53,625.

Crusader won the 58th annual **Belmont Stakes,** paying 7–10. Jockey was A. Johnson; time was 2:32⅕ on a sloppy track for winnings valued at $48,550. From this year until the present the distance has been 1½ mi.

U.S. lawn tennis men's singles champion, Réné Lacoste of France; **women's singles champion,** Mrs. Molla Bjurstedt Mallory.

U.S.G.A. amateur championship won by George Von Elm at Baltusrol G.C., Short Hills, N.J. He defeated Robert T. (Bobby) Jones, Jr., 2 and 1. **Open championship**

POLITICS AND GOVERNMENT; WAR; DISASTERS; VITAL STATISTICS.	BOOKS; PAINTING; DRAMA; ARCHITECTURE; SCULPTURE.

sance taxes. Income tax publicity clause was also abolished.

Apr. 29 Debt Funding agreement signed by U.S. and France providing for the repayment of France's wartime debt to the U.S. of about $4 billion over a period of 62 years, 60.3% of which debt was canceled.

May 9 Rear Adm. Richard E. Byrd and Floyd Bennett made **1st successful flight over North Pole.**

May 10 A detachment of U.S. marines landed at Bluefields, **Nicaragua,** following outbreak of insurrection there. The force, under Rear Adm. Julian L. Latimer, was withdrawn June 5.

May 18 Hugh S. Gibson represented U.S. at the Preparatory Commission for the **Disarmament Conference** which opened at Geneva.

July 2 **Army Air Corps** created by act of congress.

July 2 **Distinguished Flying Cross** commissioned for anyone who, "while serving in the armed services, distinguishes himself by heroism or extraordinary achievement while participating in aerial flight." Charles A. Lindbergh, decorated June 11, 1927, was 1st to receive medal.

July 10 **31 lives lost** at Lake Denmark, N.J., when U.S. Naval ammunition depot exploded after lightning struck a magazine. Sporadic explosions occurred for several days and damage reached $93 million.

Sept. 18 Disastrous **hurricane** swept Florida and the Gulf States, causing the death of 372 persons and the injury of over 6000. Some 5000 homes were destroyed by the storm, leaving almost 18,000 families homeless. Property damage was estimated at more than $80 million.

Oct. 25 **U.S. Supreme Court** ruled that the President had the power to remove executive officers from their positions. The decision nullified the act of 1876,

porates a tango, which provoked considerable comment.

Ferdinand **"Jelly Roll" Morton** began series of recordings made with his Red Hot Peppers in Chicago. The records, some of the most important in the history of jazz, include: "Black Bottom Stomp," "Smoke House Blues," "Original Jelly Roll Blues," "Doctor Jazz," etc. The band consisted of George Mitchell, Omer Simeon, Kid Ory, Johnny St. Cyr, John Lindsay, and Andrew Hilaire.

Some **popular songs** of 1926 were: *Horses; That's Why Darkies Were Born; Play Gypsy; One Alone; Desert Song; Blue Room; When Day Is Done; I Found a Million-Dollar Baby in a Five and Ten Cent Store; Bye Bye Blackbird; In a Little Spanish Town.*

Jan. 23 Symbolism on the stage admirably reflected in **Eugene O'Neill's** *The Great God Brown,* where character traits are externalized by use of masks.

Feb. 19 *Skyscrapers,* a ballet scored by **John Alden Carpenter** upon commission from Diaghilev, produced at the Metropolitan Opera House in New York city. Notable for its use of jazz idioms, it evoked much comment among concertgoers.

Apr. Beginning of the **Book-of-the-Month Club** paved the way for a literal revolution in book selling and publishing. At the end of the 1st year 40,000 subscribers were enrolled, a number which later increased to the hundreds of thousands.

May 5 **Sinclair Lewis** declined the $1000 Pulitzer Prize award for 1925 for his novel **Arrowsmith,** declaring that all such prizes tend to make writers "safe, polite, obedient and sterile." Lewis urged all novelists to refuse such awards if they wished to remain free from constricting standards.

Dec. 20 Profound psychological study of inverted mother-love is **Sidney How-**

Widespread depression in automobile industry prompted Henry Ford to introduce **8-hour day, 5-day week.** American industrial leaders shocked, but the proposition was warmly received by the AFL as a means to check overproduction and limit unemployment.

1st air mail service between New York city and Boston inaugurated.

Feb. 9 Teaching of the theory of **evolution** prohibited in the public schools of Atlanta, Ga., by a decision handed down by the Board of Education.

Mar. 7 1st successful trans-Atlantic **radio telephone** conversation held between New York and London at a demonstration by the American Telephone and Telegraph company, The Radio Corporation of America and the British General Post Office.

May 18 The kidnaping of **Aimee Semple MacPherson,** a successful revivalist, not too well known outside California, became front page news across the country and catapulted Mrs. MacPherson into national prominence. Her sudden, mysterious reappearance led the district attorney of Los Angeles to launch an investigation. He branded the kidnaping a hoax, precipitating a controversy with Mrs. MacPherson's many supporters. Even after all criminal charges against her had been dropped, Mrs. MacPherson carried her case to enthusiastic audiences both here and abroad.

June 20 **1st international Eucharistic Congress** in U.S. convened at Chicago. Cardinal John Bonzano was chosen Papal Legate *a latere* by Pope Pius XI.

July 5 **Strike** of subway employees in New York city began for higher wages and ended unsuccessfully for the workers on July 29. During the subway tie-up some 150,000 privately owned automobiles and several thousand buses carried New Yorkers to and from work.

July 26 **Sanctuary of Our Lady of Victory,** Lackawanna, N.Y., became 1st Cath-

won by Robert T. (Bobby) Jones, Jr., at Scioto C.C., Columbus, Ohio, by a score of 293.

Jan. 1 Alabama edged out Washington by a score of 20 to 19 in the 11th annual **Rose Bowl** football game.

May 15 The 52d annual **Kentucky Derby** at Churchill Downs, Louisville, Ky., won by Col. E. R. Bradley's Idle Hour Farm entry, *Bubbling Over* in 2:03⅘ on a fast track. First prize money amounted to $50,075. This was jockey A. Johnson's 2d Derby winner.

Aug. 5 Warner Theater, New York city, introduced **1st "talking movie."** Sound came from compatible phonograph records, not from the film track. Film was *Don Juan,* which featured John Barrymore.

Sept. 11 The United States Tennis team won the **Davis Cup** for the 7th year in succession defeating the French team in the challenge round 4 matches to 1, at the Germantown Cricket Club, Philadelphia, Pa. W. T. Tilden 2d lost the only match for the U.S., losing to J. R. Lacoste, 4–6, 6–4, 8–6, 8–6. W. M. Johnston, R. N. Williams, and V. Richards were the other members of the U.S. team.

Sept. 23 Gene Tunney became the **Heavyweight Champion** of the world by defeating defending champion Jack Dempsey by a decision in a 10-round fight held at the Sesquicentennial Stadium, Philadelphia. In spite of a rainstorm which lasted through the entire fight a record-breaking crowd was in attendance for the championship contest (118,736) and brought $1,895,723 in gate receipts, a record at the time and the 3d highest in boxing history. Tunney was 28 years old, weighed 189½ lbs. and was 6 ft. tall while the defending champion was 31 years old, weighed 190 lbs., and was 6 ft. 1½ in. tall.

Nov. 27 Army and Navy played to a 21–21 tie in the annual **Army-Navy football game** held at Soldiers Field, Chicago, Ill.

POLITICS AND GOVERNMENT; WAR; DISASTERS; VITAL STATISTICS.	BOOKS; PAINTING; DRAMA; ARCHITECTURE; SCULPTURE.

which required the consent of the Senate before such removals from office could be ordered.

ard's *The Silver Cord.* Mrs. Phelps, the mother, loves her sons with a passion that breaks their lives.

1927

Feb. 10 Pres. Coolidge called for **conference to limit naval armament.** It met in Geneva June 20. France and Italy refused to join; U.S., Great Britain, and Japan were represented. Great Britain and U.S. could not agree on cruiser restrictions, and conference ended in stalemate Aug. 4.

Mar. 7 **U.S. Supreme Court** ruled unconstitutional the Texas law which prohibited Negroes from voting in Democratic primary elections.

Apr. **Tremendous floods** in the Mississippi Valley inundated 4 million acres, causing property loss of $300 million. 600,-000 made homeless for many weeks, several hundred drowned.

Apr. 6 French Foreign Minister Aristide Briand proposed agreement for **outlawry of war.** On June 11 Secretary of State Frank B. Kellogg acknowledged Briand's proposal, which had already been supported by Pres. Nicholas Murray Butler and Prof. James T. Shotwell of Columbia University. On June 20 Briand submitted treaty draft, and on Dec. 28 Kellogg suggested that Briand's treaty be extended to include all nations of the world. This resulted in Kellogg-Briand Pact of 1928.

Apr. 17 Gov. Alfred E. Smith said: "I recognize no power in the institution of my Church to interfere with the operations of the Constitution of the United States or the enforcement of the law of the land," in response to an open letter from Charles C. Marshall asking the Governor where his allegiance would be in an issue which involved a conflict between the **Roman Catholic Church** and the Constitution of the U.S.

May 20–21 1st solo nonstop flight from New York to Paris was made by Capt. **Charles A. Lindbergh,** who flew the 3600 miles in his monoplane, the *Spirit of*

Pulitizer Prizes: novel, *Early Autumn* by Louis Bromfield; drama, *In Abraham's Bosom* by Paul Green; U. S. history, *Pinckney's Treaty* by Samuel Flagg Bemis; biography, *Whitman* by Emory Holloway; poetry, *Fiddler's Farewell* by Leonora Speyer.

A fictional tour-de-force is **Thornton Wilder's** *The Bridge of San Luis Rey,* the story of 5 persons killed when a bridge collapsed, and their relationship to a Divine Power that led them to the bridge at that moment.

A beautiful novel of the Southwest is **Willa Cather's** *Death Comes for the Archbishop.* In a series of episodes tied together by the figures of Bishop Jean Latour and Father Joseph Vaillant, she paints the desert country, the Spanish and Indian inhabitants, the spiritual struggles of the nascent church.

The Academy of Motion Picture Arts and Sciences, comprising all levels of studio personnel from actors to set designers, established to present annual awards, or "Oscars," to noteworthy achievements in the art of the motion picture.

Some **popular songs** of 1927 were: *Russian Lullaby; Old Man River; Tree in the Park; My Heart Stood Still; Hallelujah; Sometimes I'm Happy; My Blue Heaven; Rain; Let a Smile Be Your Umbrella; Blue Skies.*

1st outstanding Broadway success by **Richard Rodgers** and **Lorenz Hart** was the musical comedy, *A Connecticut Yankee.*

Hit the Deck, with music by Vincent Youmans, including the hit tune "Hallelujah," was the **popular musical** of the season on Broadway.

Jan. 28 Premiere performance of **Aaron Copland's** *Concerto for Piano and Orchestra* given by the Boston Symphony

SCIENCE; INDUSTRY; ECONOMICS; EDUCATION; RELIGION; PHILOSOPHY.	SPORTS; FASHIONS; POPULAR ENTERTAINMENT; FOLKLORE; SOCIETY.

olic Church in U.S. to be consecrated as a Basilica.

Oct. 2–10 St. Louis, NL, defeated New York, AL, 4–3 in the 23d annual **World Series.**

1927

Brookings Institution established in Washington, D.C. 1st president was H. G. Moulton; 1st board of trustees was practically a Who's Who of celebrated economic analysts.

New York University, New York city, set up 7 summer schools in European Universities, granting college credit for the courses. Classes were taught by American instructors.

New York subway system extended its operation between Times Square and Flushing, L.I.

Mechanical cotton picker developed by John D. Rust.

Development of 1st **national radio beacon** for air transportation announced. The beacon automatically informed the pilot if his machine was off course. This led to the refinement of an instrument that automatically kept the airplane on a preset course.

Nobel Prize in physics presented to **Arthur Holly Compton** "for his discovery of the effect named after him." Compton shared the award in physics with the Scottish physicist, Charles Thomson Rees Wilson, who was honored "for his discovery of the vapor condensation method of rendering visible the paths of electrically charged particles." Compton's prize-winning experiments with X-rays led ultimately to 1st experimental verification of Einstein's photon theory of light.

Jan. 7 Commercial **telephone service** opened between New York and London when Walter S. Gifford, president of the American Telephone and Telegraph Company, officially opened the line by saying "Hello, London."

2 major league records set when **Walter Johnson,** the Washington Senators' great pitcher, ended the last season of his 20-year career, having pitched 113 shutouts and struck out 3497 opposing batters.

1st **Golden Gloves** amateur boxing matches held, sponsored by New York *Daily News.* Spread to Chicago next year. Annual intercity and international Golden Gloves tournaments held now.

This year's **national football champion** was Illinois, coached by Bob Zuppke. Their record: 7 wins, no losses, 1 tie.

Bostonian won the 51st annual **Preakness Stakes,** paying 3–1. Jockey was A. Abel; time was 2:01⅗ on a good track for winnings valued at $53,100.

Chance Shot won the 59th annual **Belmont Stakes,** paying 2–7. Jockey was E. Sande; time was 2:32⅖ on a fast track for winnings valued at $60,910.

U.S. lawn tennis men's singles champion, René Lacoste of France; **women's singles champion,** Helen N. Wills.

U.S.G.A. amateur championship won by Robert T. (Bobby) Jones, Jr., at Minikahda Club, Minneapolis, Minn. He defeated Charles Evans, Jr., 8 and 1. **Open championship** won by Tommy Armour at Oakmont, Pa., C.C. with a score of 301.

Jan. 1 Alabama and Stanford battled to a 7–7 tie in the 12th annual **Rose Bowl** football game.

Mar. 3 **Prohibition Bureau** established as part of the treasury department by Prohibition Reorganization Act.

Mar. 20 **Albert Snyder** murdered by his wife, Ruth, and her lover, Judd Gray. The killers were executed at Sing Sing prison in Ossining, N.Y., on Jan. 12, 1928.

| POLITICS AND GOVERNMENT; WAR; DISASTERS; VITAL STATISTICS. | BOOKS; PAINTING; DRAMA; ARCHITECTURE; SCULPTURE. |

St. Louis. He arrived in Paris after 33½ hrs. in flight and was welcomed by some 100,000 people.

Aug. 2 **Pres. Coolidge** announced, "I do not choose to run for President in 1928." It had been generally assumed that he would seek re-election.

Aug. 27 **Nicola Sacco** and **Bartolomeo Vanzetti** executed in Massachusetts.

Sept. 29 Furious **tornado** which lasted but 5 mins. struck St. Louis, causing 87 deaths and the injury of 1500. More than 1000 houses were destroyed by the storm and estimates of property damage exceeded $50,000,000.

Oct. 10 U.S. Supreme Court ruled that the lease of the **Teapot Dome** oil reserve lands in Wyoming to the Mammoth Oil Company through former Sec. of Interior Albert B. Fall was fraudulently negotiated and therefore invalid.

Dec. 17 All 40 men aboard the **U.S. Submarine S-4** died as a result of a collision with the *Paulding,* a U.S. Coast Guard destroyer, as the sub attempted to surface off Provincetown, Mass. Divers said they heard tappings on the inside of the submarine and pleas for food and water for 3 days but were helpless to free the trapped men. On Jan. 4 the first bodies were removed but all the men were dead by that time.

with the composer at the piano. It is the last and most mature of Copland's experiments with symphonic jazz.

Jan. 31 Career of playwright **Robert E. Sherwood** began with comedy *The Road to Rome,* an earthy travesty of Hannibal's march on Rome. *Waterloo Bridge* (1930) tells story of a tragic wartime romance; *The Petrified Forest* (1935) acted by Leslie Howard was a great success. It places on stage a poet, and a gangster who alone is able to appreciate nobility of poet.

Apr. 10 *Ballet Mécanique,* scored by American composer **George Antheil,** produced at Carnegie Hall, New York city. Scored for 10 pianos, auto horns, buzz saws, cowbells, etc., the work made Antheil's "reputation" overnight. Much controversy raged round the work and the composer.

Dec. 27 **Show Boat** produced in New York by Flo Ziegfeld. With libretto by Oscar Hammerstein II adapted from Edna Ferber's novel of the same title (1926), and with music by Jerome Kern, it became an enormous success. Some of its songs were: "Old Man River," "Make Believe," "Can't Help Lovin' That Man," "My Bill," etc.

Dec. 27 Sparkling social comedy continued from pen of **Philip Barry.** *Paris Bound,* produced at this time, is a strong argument for the institution of marriage. *Holiday* (1928) continued his delightful art of persiflage amidst a wealthy Philadelphia family.

1928

Apr. 13–18 **The National Convention of the Socialist Party** held at New York city and nominated Norman Thomas of New York for the presidency and James H. Maurer of Pennsylvania for the vice-presidency.

May 27 **National Convention of the Workers' Party** (Communist) held at New York city and nominated William Z. Foster of Illinois and Benjamin Gitlow of New

Pulitzer Prizes: novel, *The Bridge of San Luis Rey* by Thornton Wilder; drama, *Strange Interlude* by Eugene O'Neill; U.S. history, *Main Currents in American Thought* by Vernon Louis Parrington; biography, *The American Orchestra and Theodore Thomas* by Charles Edward Russell; poetry, *Tristram* by Edwin Arlington Robinson.

The hard-boiled, swearing newspaper-

| SCIENCE; INDUSTRY; ECONOMICS; EDUCATION; RELIGION; PHILOSOPHY. | SPORTS; FASHIONS; POPULAR EN-TERTAINMENT; FOLKLORE; SOCIETY. |

Feb. 23 Federal Radio Commission established by Congress.

Apr. 7 1st successful demonstration of **Television** took place in New York, where Walter S. Gifford, Pres. of American Telephone and Telegraph Co., spoke with and saw Sec. of Commerce Herbert Hoover in his office in Washington.

Spring 15,000,000th **Ford Model T** car produced. Shortly after this the Model T was discontinued. It took 6 months to make the change to a new model, and cost the company $200,000,000, not counting the money lost through nonproduction.

June 28 1st successful airplane flight from San Francisco to Honolulu made by 2 Army Air Corps pilots, Lts. Lester J. Maitland and Albert F. Hegenberger.

July 29 Electric respirator, later called **"iron lung,"** installed at Bellevue Hospital, New York city. Devised by Drs. Phillip Drinker and Louis A. Shaw of Harvard University, the new device was hailed for its use in overcoming many kinds of respiratory failure.

Nov. 13 1st underwater vehicular tunnel in U.S. built beneath Hudson R. from New York to New Jersey. **Holland Tunnel** comprises 2 tubes, each large enough to carry 2 traffic lanes. The tunnel was opened to commercial traffic Nov. 13.

May 14 The winner of the 53d annual **Kentucky Derby** at Churchill Downs, Louisville, Ky., was H. P. Whitney's *Whiskery* ridden by jockey L. McAtee. The time was 2:06 on a slow track; the value was $51,000.

Sept. 10 France wrested the **Davis Cup** from the United States 3 matches to 2 at Philadelphia, the U.S. team winning 1 singles match and the doubles match. Prior to this year the United States had won the cup for 7 consecutive years.

Sept. 27 Home run record set when Babe Ruth hit his 60th home run of the season off Tom Zachary, Washington pitcher, in Yankee Stadium, New York city. Record approached but never equaled (58 by Jimmie Foxx in 1932, and 58 by Hank Greenberg in 1938).

Oct. 5–8 New York, AL, defeated Pittsburgh, NL, 4–0, in the 24th annual **World Series.**

Oct. 6 1st talking motion picture, in which the sound track was actually on the film, released. It was *The Jazz Singer,* starring Al Jolson.

Oct. 7 Tommy Loughran won the **Light Heavyweight title** by defeating Mike McTigue by a decision in a 15-round contest held at New York city.

Nov. 26 Army defeated Navy, 14–9 in the annual **Army-Navy football game** held at the Polo Grounds, New York city. No games played in 1928 and 1929.

1928

25th anniversary of 1st airplane flight celebrated in Washington, D.C., by the International Civil Aeronautics Conference. 137 delegates from 31 different countries attended. **Charles Lindbergh** was awarded the Harmon Trophy, papers and movies on the development of aeronautics were read and seen, and a tablet was placed at Kitty Hawk in commemoration of the **Wright** brothers.

This year's **national football champion** was the University of Southern California, coached by Howard Jones. Their record: 9 wins, no losses, 1 tie.

Vito won the 60th annual **Belmont Stakes,** paying 10–1. Jockey was C. Kummer; time was 2:33⅕ on a fast track for winnings valued at $63,430.

Victorian won the 52d annual **Preakness Stakes,** paying 9–1. Jockey was R. Work-

| POLITICS AND GOVERNMENT; WAR; DISASTERS; VITAL STATISTICS. | BOOKS; PAINTING; DRAMA; ARCHITECTURE; SCULPTURE. |

York for the presidency and vice-presidency, respectively.

June 12–15 National Convention of the Republican Party met at Kansas City, Mo., and on the 1st ballot nominated Herbert Hoover of California for the presidency. The next day Charles Curtis of Kansas was nominated for the vice-presidency, also on the 1st ballot.

June 26–29 National Convention of the Democratic Party met at Houston, Tex., and nominated Governor Alfred E. Smith of New York for the presidency on June 28 and Senator Joseph T. Robinson of Arkansas for the vice-presidency on June 29, each on the 1st ballot.

July 11 National Convention of the Farmer Labor Party met at Chicago and nominated George W. Norris of Nebraska for the presidency and Will Vereen of Georgia for the vice-presidency. Norris subsequently declined the nomination. Frank E. Webb became the party's candidate for presidency.

July 12 National Convention of the Prohibition Party met at Chicago and nominated William F. Varney of New York for the presidency and James A. Edgarton of Virginia for the vice-presidency.

Aug. 27 Kellogg-Briand Peace Pact subscribed to by 15 nations at Paris. Purport of the pact was the outlawing of wars and the settling of international controversies by arbitration. The pact was eventually signed by 62 nations. Frank B. Kellogg received Nobel Peace Prize for Kellogg-Briand Pact in 1929.

Nov. 6 Herbert Hoover and Charles Curtis elected president and vice-president, respectively, carrying 40 of the 48 states in a landslide Republican victory. They received 444 electoral votes to 87 for A. E. Smith and J. T. Robinson on the Democratic ticket. The popular vote was: Hoover, 21,392,190; Smith, 15,016,443; Thomas, Socialist, 267,835; Foster, Workers (Communist), 48,228; Reynolds, So-

man immortalized in the perennially revived play by **Ben Hecht** and **Charles MacArthur,** *The Front Page.* The role of the reporter was admirably acted by **Lee Tracy.**

Most widely read long poem of the decade is **Stephen Vincent Benét's** novel in verse, *John Brown's Body.* Mixing various verse forms, he tells the story of the abolitionist hero, evoking the time and personalities and intertwining fact with myth in this epic of the Civil War.

Philip Barry added *Holiday* to his growing list of Broadway comedy hits.

Buck in the Snow, a collection of poems by **Edna St. Vincent Millay,** published.

Mickey Mouse became a star overnight with *Plane Crazy,* 1st cartoon released by **Walt Disney Productions.** *Galloping Gaucho* and *Steamboat Willie* followed in the same year. *Steamboat Willie* introduced sound to the animated cartoon.

Ernest Bloch composed *America,* a symphony. Bloch, who characterized his music as an attempt to realize "the complex, glowing, agitated soul" that he felt pulsating through the Bible, won the $3,000 **Musical America** award with *America.*

George Gershwin composed *An American in Paris.*

Some **popular songs** of 1928 were: *Makin' Whoopee; Silver Moon; Rio Rita; Bill; Can't Help Lovin' That Man; Make Believe; Am I Blue?; Lover, Come Back to Me; You're the Cream in My Coffee; Crazy Rhythm; Button Up Your Overcoat.*

Excellent example of Ash Can School of painting is **John Sloan's** *Sixth Avenue and Third Street.* Artist depicts evening crowd walking beneath the "el" in the same manner as an earlier painter might have done a rural landscape.

Jan. 9 Symbolism on stage carried further by **Eugene O'Neill's** *Marco Millions,* in which blind materialism is represented by titular hero. *Lazarus Laughed,*

480

| SCIENCE; INDUSTRY; ECONOMICS; EDUCATION; RELIGION; PHILOSOPHY. | SPORTS; FASHIONS; POPULAR ENTERTAINMENT; FOLKLORE; SOCIETY. |

The scientific attack against "master race" doctrines in America spearheaded by *Anthropology and Modern Life* by Professor **Franz Boas** of Columbia University who argued that race and culture could not be correlated.

May 11 Station WGY, Schenectady, N.Y., began **1st program of scheduled television broadcasts.**

May 22 **Jones-White Act** passed by Congress provided a stimulus for **American shipping** in the form of production subsidies and favorable mail contracts. Despite this and other laws, American shipping continued to operate at a deficit.

May 25 **1st woman to fly the Atlantic,** Amelia Earhart, took off from Boston with 2 passengers in her airplane, "Friendship."

July 30 **1st colored motion pictures** in U.S. exhibited by George Eastman at Rochester, N.Y. The scenes in the original movies ran the gamut of colorful subjects, from goldfish, peacocks, scarlet-beaked doves, butterflies, flowers, Fifth Avenue fashion models, and just plain pretty girls in just plain pretty dresses. Among the viewers were Owen D. Young, Gen. Pershing, Kent Cooper, Roy Howard, David Lawrence, Mrs. Ogden Reid, and Adolph Ochs. Maj. Gen. James Harbord, president of RCA, and E. F. W. Alexanderson, a pioneer in television, predicted, on the strength of the showing, the application of color to television.

Sept. Pickwick Stages, Inc., bus manufacturers of Los Angeles, Calif., completed **1st "nite coaches"**—busses equipped with sleeping facilities for transcontinental travel.

Nov. 6 New York *Times* mounted **1st animated electric sign** in U.S. around top of Times Building, Times Square, New York city. Used to report election returns, it

man; time was 2:00⅕ on a fast track for winnings valued at $60,000.

U.S. lawn tennis men's singles champion, Henri Cochet of France; **women's singles champion,** Helen N. Wills.

U.S.G.A. amateur championship won by Robert T. (Bobby) Jones, Jr., at Brae Burn C.C., West Newton, Mass. He defeated T. Philip Perkins, 10 and 9. **Open championship** won by Johnny Farrell at Olympia Fields, Matteson, Ill., with a score of 294.

Jan. 1 Stanford edged out Pittsburgh by a score of 7 to 6 in the 13th annual **Rose Bowl** football game.

May 19 The winner of the 54th annual **Kentucky Derby** at Churchill Downs, Louisville, Ky., was the favorite, Mrs. J. Hertz's *Reigh Count,* ridden by jockey C. Lang. The time was 2:10⅖ on a heavy track; the value, $55,375.

July 21 **1st sound film** of more than 6000 ft. in length released by Warner Bros. Called *The Lights of New York,* it was presented at a gala premiere held at midnight, July 6, 1928, at the Strand Theater, New York city. The cast featured Helene Costello, Mary Carr, Cullen Landis, Gladys Brockwell, and Wheeler Oakman.

July 29–Aug. 12 The United States emerged with top honors in the 9th **Olympic Games** held at Amsterdam, Holland, scoring a total of 131 points, with 24 1sts, 21 2ds, and 17 3ds. Americans also established 17 new Olympic records, 7 of which are world records.

Oct. 4–9 New York, AL, defeated St. Louis, NL, 4–0 in the 25th annual **World Series.**

Oct. 20 Political phrase **"A Chicken in Every Pot,** a Car in Every Garage" used by Republicans in their election year advertisements. In 1932 Democrats made bitter reference to this promise, wrongly

POLITICS AND GOVERNMENT; WAR; DISASTERS; VITAL STATISTICS.	BOOKS; PAINTING; DRAMA; ARCHITECTURE; SCULPTURE.

cialist Labor, 21,181; Varney, Prohibition, 20,106; Webb, Farmer Labor, 6,391.

also produced this year, symbolizes the spirit of love as it conquers the symbol of Fear, represented by figure of Caligula.

1929

Frank Billings Kellogg won this year's **Nobel Peace Prize.** Award was primarily based on his contribution to the Kellogg-Briand Pact, which was a treaty signed by 15 nations Aug. 27, 1928, outlawing war.

Jan. 15 Kellogg-Briand Peace Pact passed the Senate by a vote of 85 to 1, Sen. John J. Blaine, of Wisconsin, casting the only negative vote.

Mar. 4 Herbert Hoover, 31st president, inaugurated. He was a Republican and served 1 term.

May 27 U.S. Supreme Court upheld the right of the president to prevent enactment of legislation by the **pocket veto,** thus sustaining the decision of the Court of Claims.

June 15 Agricultural Marketing Act authorized the establishment of a Federal Farm Board for promoting sale of agricultural commodities through agricultural cooperatives and stabilization corporations. Provisions were also made for the purchase of surplus farm products for storage and sale to foreign countries to maintain price levels; a $500 million revolving fund was set up to provide low-interest loans to the co-operating agencies to facilitate orderly marketing.

Sept. Just before **stock market crash,** 60% of U.S. citizens had annual incomes of less than $2000, which was estimated as the bare minimum to supply the "basic necessities of life."

Oct. 7 J. Ramsay MacDonald spoke before U.S. Senate in **1st speech by a British prime minister before Congress.** He was in U.S. to discuss naval armament.

Oct. 7 Trial of former Secretary of Interior **Albert B. Fall** began in the Su-

Pulitzer Prizes: novel, *Scarlet Sister Mary* by Julia Peterkin; drama, *Street Scene* by Elmer L. Rice; U.S. history, *The Organization and Administration of the Union Army, 1861–1865* by Fred Albert Shannon; biography, *The Training of an American. The Earlier Life and Letters of Walter H. Page* by Burton J. Hendrick; poetry, *John Brown's Body* by Stephen Vincent Benét.

Sinclair Lewis adapted the **international theme** for his new novel *Dodsworth,* the story of an American couple whose marital thread is broken during a trip to Europe. Incidental to the main plot is the series of contrasts between European and American life, in favor of the former.

1st novel of **Thomas Wolfe** is his masterpiece *Look Homeward, Angel,* a romantic novel of the South and a Whitmanesque evocation of American democracy. Autobiographical to a great degree, it tells the story of the youthful struggles of Eugene Gant, a highly sensitive and gifted boy, whose quest for adventure and experience runs up against the obstacles of his family and surroundings.

Beginning of the famous saga of Yoknapatawpha County is **William Faulkner's** *Sartoris.* Other novels in this cycle are *The Sound and the Fury* (1929), *As I Lay Dying* (1930), *Sanctuary* (1931), *Absalom, Absalom!* (1936).

Realistic, unheroic presentation of war is the keynote of **Ernest Hemingway's** *A Farewell to Arms,* the story of the love of Catherine Barkley, an English nurse, and Frederic Henry, an American caught up in the retreat from Caporetto.

Artist who excels in modernistic representations of flower patterns is **Georgia O'Keeffe.** Her *Black Flower and Blue Larkspur* at the Metropolitan was painted

SCIENCE; INDUSTRY; ECONOMICS; EDUCATION; RELIGION; PHILOSOPHY.	SPORTS; FASHIONS; POPULAR ENTERTAINMENT; FOLKLORE; SOCIETY.

was called the "zipper" from the way it encircled the building.

attributing it to the Republican candidate Herbert Hoover.

1929

First American experiment in the creation of a **garden community** attempted in Radburn, N.J., where all the health and safety hazards of urban life were circumvented to some extent by an intricate design and integration of homes, parks, schools, playgrounds, safe walks without traffic crossings, accessible swimming facilities, and natural surroundings for all the inhabitants. Design of the community stressed circular arcs intersecting via underpasses and overpasses and featured a more varied aesthetic shape to the whole community than was to be found in the rectangular concentrations of the big cities.

Middletown by Robert S. and Helen Lynd of Columbia University punctured small-town pretensions. Surveying the town of Muncie, Indiana, the Lynds pinpointed the tendencies toward conformity in our society.

Margaret Sanger's birth control clinic raided by New York police on complaint from Daughters of the American Revolution; 3 nurses and 2 doctors arrested; thousands of case histories confiscated. Case later dismissed as infringement of physician's lawful freedom of practice.

July **Milam Building**, San Antonio, Tex., completed. The most modern office structure of its time, it was noted especially for an attempt to air-condition the entire building.

Sept. Standard Statistics index of **common stock prices** reached an average of 216. Its climb was as follows: 100 during 1926; 114 by June, 1927; 148 by June, 1928; 191 by June, 1929. This increase represented the biggest bull market U.S. had ever known.

Sept. 24 Lt. James Doolittle piloted **1st "blind" airplane flight** at Mitchell Field,

This year's **national football champion** was Notre Dame, still coached by Knute Rockne who had led them to the mythical title in 1926. Their record: 9 wins, no losses, no ties.

Blue Larkspur won the 61st annual **Belmont Stakes**, paying 13–10. Jockey was M. Garner; time was 2:32⅖ on a sloppy track for winnings valued at $59,650.

Dr. Freeland won the 53d annual **Preakness Stakes**, paying 19–5. Jockey was L. Schaefer; time was 2:01⅖ for winnings valued at $52,325.

U.S. lawn tennis men's singles champion, William T. Tilden II; **women's singles champion,** Helen N. Wills.

U.S.G.A. amateur championship won by Harrison R. Johnston at Pebble Beach Course, Del Monte, Calif. He defeated Dr. O. F. Willing, 4 and 3. **Open championship** won by Robert T. (Bobby) Jones, Jr., at Winged Foot G.C., Mamaroneck, N.Y., with a score of 294.

Jan. 1 Georgia Tech edged out California by a score of 8 to 7 in the 14th annual **Rose Bowl** football game.

Feb. 14 The **"St. Valentine's Day Massacre"** took place when 6 members of Chicago's notorious Moran gang were lined up against a garage wall and shot down by a rival gang.

May 17 **Al "Scarface" Capone** sentenced to a year in prison at Chicago for

| POLITICS AND GOVERNMENT; WAR; DISASTERS; VITAL STATISTICS. | BOOKS; PAINTING; DRAMA; ARCHITECTURE; SCULPTURE. |

preme Court of the District of Columbia. He was accused of accepting $100,000 bribe from Edward L. Doheny in return for a lease of the Elk Hills naval oil reserve. On Oct. 25 the court declared him guilty as charged; he was sentenced to 1 year in prison and fined $100,000.

Oct. 24 Downward trend in **stock prices** which had prevailed for several weeks broke into outright panic. House of Morgan formed a buying pool to support the market by buying U.S. Steel at 205, and prices rallied briefly. But wave of selling began again; Oct. 29 was worst day, with over 16,000,000 shares dumped. Total of $30,000,000,000 in paper value lost in collapse of market and credit structure within 3 weeks.

this year. Also a landscape artist, she has been able to convey the vastness and loneliness of Texas and New Mexican space—an area she knows well.

Fifty Million Frenchmen, with songs and lyrics by **Cole Porter,** became that writer's 1st hit show.

Theatre Guild's production of *Strange Interlude,* a play by **Eugene O'Neill,** forbidden by Mayor Nichols of Boston on grounds of obscenity. Guild put on play in Quincy, a suburb, where thousands of Bostonians went to see it.

Construction begun on **Empire State Building,** New York city, tallest skyscraper in the world. Completed 1931.

1930

Population—122,775,046. Center of population: 3 mi. northeast of Linton, Greene Co., Ind.

Jan. 2 U.S. signed convention with Great Britain confirming U.S. ownership of the **Turtle Islands** located east of British North Borneo.

Jan. 13 Congress received 6 suggestions for legislation from President Hoover for the more efficient enforcement of the **Prohibition Amendment.**

Feb. 3 **Charles Evans Hughes** appointed Chief Justice of the United States Supreme Court by President Hoover to succeed retiring W. H. Taft. The appointment was confirmed Feb. 13.

Feb. 10 One of the largest rings of **bootleggers** since the Prohibition Amendment went into effect exposed at Chicago with the arrest of 31 corporations and 158 persons who, it was estimated, sold more than 7 million gal. of whisky to speakeasies all over the country, with total business of some $50 million.

Mar. 13 Trial of **Edward L. Doheny,** charged with bribing Albert B. Fall to obtain a lease for the Elk Hills naval oil re-

Pulitzer Prizes: novel, *Laughing Boy* by Oliver La Farge; drama, *The Green Pastures* by Marc Connelly; U.S. history, *The War of Independence* by Claude H. Van Tyne; biography, *The Raven* by Marquis James; poetry, *Selected Poems* by Conrad Aiken.

Number of southern writers, motivated by desire to press for regionalism in poetry and fiction, presented their views in a joint book, *I'll Take My Stand.* Such poets as **Allen Tate, John Crowe Ransom,** and **Robert Penn Warren** took their stand against the abstract and general in favor of the concrete, regional, and traditional; they deplored preoccupation with the dollar, and the domination of cold science and industry.

Copy of **James Joyce's** *Ulysses,* shipped from Paris to a prospective American publisher, Random House, seized in New York by Bureau of Customs on grounds of obscenity.

Rare example of political censorship in America resulted in Boston's banning of all the works of **Leon Trotsky.**

Painting which caught eye of entire na-

SCIENCE; INDUSTRY; ECONOMICS; EDUCATION; RELIGION; PHILOSOPHY.	SPORTS; FASHIONS; POPULAR ENTERTAINMENT; FOLKLORE; SOCIETY.

N.Y. He steered by instruments, which registered a radio signal.

Oct. 3 The stock market began its fatal decline that was to culminate in the **Great Depression.** Not even J. P. Morgan or John D. Rockefeller could halt the panicky wave of selling which reached its peak on Oct. 29 with the dumping of 16,400,000 shares on the exchange for any price they could bring.

Nov. Patent issued to Sebastiano Lando for **coin-operated vending machine** which could not be defrauded.

Nov. 29 Lt. Comdr. Richard E. Byrd completed **1st flight over South Pole.** Flight to pole and back from base at Little America, with stop at advance fueling station, lasted 19 hrs.

carrying a concealed weapon. He pleaded guilty to the charge.

May 18 The winner of the 55th **Kentucky Derby** at Churchill Downs, Louisville, Ky. was H. P. Gardner's *Clyde Van Dusen,* ridden by jockey L. McAtee. The time was 2:10⅘ on a muddy track; the prize, $53,950.

Oct. 8–14 Philadelphia, AL, defeated Chicago, NL, 4–1 in the 26th annual **World Series.**

1930

Nobel Prize in medicine and physiology awarded to Dr. **Karl Landsteiner** for discovery of human blood groups. Though born in Austria, he was 2d American to obtain the award in this field.

Student enrollment in federally supported **vocational classes** rose from 981,-882 in 1930 to 2,290,741 in 1940, and to 3,364,613 in 1950. In 1930, 188,311 students were enrolled in classes in agriculture, 618,604 in classes of trade and industry, and 174,967 in classes in home economics. In 1940, the distribution was 584,133 in agriculture, 758,409 in trade and industry, and 818,766 in home economics. In 1950, agriculture classes claimed 764,975, trade and industry classes claimed 804,602, and home economics classes claimed 1,430,366. The figures indicated an unusually rapid growth in the popularity of home economics courses with respect to the other areas of vocational education. This rapid growth reflected many trends in American life, including the relative decline of agriculture as an educational subject and the contributions of private corporations to industrial training.

Academy Awards were presented to *All Quiet on the Western Front* as the outstanding production of 1929 through 1930; to Norma Shearer as best actress for her portrayal of *The Divorcee,* and to George Arliss as best actor for his characterization of *Disraeli.* 1st award for sound recording presented to the Metro-Goldwyn-Mayer Studio for *The Big House.* This award reflected growing predominance of talking pictures.

Irish Sweepstakes, a lottery on behalf of several Irish hospitals, inaugurated, and soon became exceedingly popular in America. Within 5 years, it was the most successful lottery in the world.

This year's **national football champion** was once again Notre Dame, coached by Knute Rockne. Their record: 10 wins, no losses, and no ties.

1st A.A.U. James E. Sullivan Memorial Trophy for outstanding amateur athlete of the year won by golfer, Robert (Bobby) Jones. Award for amateur athlete who does most to advance cause of good sportsmanship.

| POLITICS AND GOVERNMENT; WAR; DISASTERS; VITAL STATISTICS. | BOOKS; PAINTING; DRAMA; ARCHITECTURE; SCULPTURE. |

serve, began at the Supreme Court of the District of Columbia. He was acquitted on Mar. 22.

Apr. 21 318 prisoners in the Ohio State Penitentiary at Columbus were burned to death when a fire broke out in the prison, which held about 4300 inmates. The penitentiary was built to accommodate 1500.

Apr. 22 **London Naval Treaty** signed in London by U.S., Great Britain, and Japan. France would not let Italy attain equal status with other powers, and both eventually refused to sign important provisions. It was a partially effective disarmament treaty effective until Dec. 31, 1936. The Senate confirmed the Treaty July 21.

May 7 The U.S. Senate turned down Pres. Hoover's nomination of Judge **John J. Parker** for the United States Supreme Court by a vote of 41 to 39. On May 20 the Senate unanimously consented to the appointment of **Owen J. Roberts**, a Philadelphia lawyer.

May 26 In a unanimous decision the U.S. Supreme Court ruled that purchasing intoxicating liquor does not constitute a violation of the **Prohibition Amendment.**

June 17 **Hawley-Smoot Tariff Act** signed by Pres. Hoover. It raised duties to a prohibitive level on 890 articles, especially favored farmers. It is said that this protective tariff legislation is in part responsible for the economic nationalism of the 1930's. On May 4 a petition of 1028 economists had been circulated in Washington protesting passage of Hawley-Smoot Act and urging presidential veto if it did pass.

July 3 **Veterans Administration** created by Veterans Administration Act which combined all federal agencies dealing with relief of ex-servicemen under the single department.

Sept. 9 Grave federal concern over **unemployment** reflected in State Depart-

tion was *American Gothic* by **Grant Wood.** For many years Wood had painted in traditional manner. While in Germany he studied Flemish and German primitives and, returning home, applied their technique to portrayal of Iowans. Originally intended as satire, feelings of artist changed to love in rendering people of his home.

A sculptor who carves in many media and aims to adapt form to the particularity of the medium is **Chaim Gross.** In his *Offspring,* carved out of American mahogany, he makes excellent use of grain in wood. Other works are *Alaskan Mail Carrier* (1936) and *The Fencing Boy* (1937).

Howard Hanson's 2d Symphony, *Romantic,* which he proclaimed an "escape from the rather bitter type of modern musical realism," achieved immediate success with popular audiences.

Hillman Houses, an early consumers' **co-operative housing project,** built in New York; developed by labor union.

Annual Festival of American Music inaugurated by the Eastman School of Music, University of Rochester, Rochester, N.Y., by Dr. Howard Hanson, director of the school, to promote contemporary American music.

Feb. 13 1930's marked prominence of **social drama,** often sheer propaganda. John Wexley opened the decade with *The Last Mile,* an impassioned protest against capital punishment. In *They Shall Not Die* (1934) he takes up the issue of the Scottsboro trial. *Stevedore* (1934) by George Sklar and Paul Peters brings the problem of racial prejudice on the boards in its account of a Negro who tries to gain admission to a white union. *Let Freedom Ring* (1935) by Albert Bein dramatizes the struggles to unionize in a mill town in Carolina. *If This Be Treason* (1935) by Reginald Lawrence and John H. Holmes takes up the banner for pacifism.

Apr. 14 Series play which studies the illusions of a group of people of various

SCIENCE; INDUSTRY; ECONOMICS; EDUCATION; RELIGION; PHILOSOPHY.

SPORTS; FASHIONS; POPULAR ENTERTAINMENT; FOLKLORE; SOCIETY.

Institute for Advanced Study established at Princeton, N.J., by an endowment from Louis Bamberger and his sister, Mrs. Felix Fuld. Albert Einstein became head of school in 1933.

Illiteracy in America reached a new low of 4.3% of the population, a decline of 1.7 from 1920 and a decline of 15.7% from 1870.

1 out of every 4.9 Americans owned an **automobile,** according to survey made this year.

Identification of Pluto by a photograph made at Lowell Observatory, Flagstaff, Ariz., confirmed calculations of Percival Lowell at Harvard in 1914. The planet was found Jan. 21, announced Mar. 13. With this confirmation, mathematical astronomy gained great prestige.

American Lutheran Church formed at Toledo, Ohio, by a union of 3 Lutheran groups: (1) Lutheran Synod of Buffalo; (2) Evangelical Lutheran Synod of Iowa; and (3) Evangelical Lutheran Joint Synod of Ohio. Membership of American Lutheran Church in 1952 was 767,261.

Wall Street Journal reported that there were 4000 or more **trade associations** in the U.S.

Production of **synthetic plastics** in America rose from 50 million lb. in 1930 to 250 million lb. in 1940.

Mar. 4 **Coolidge Dam,** Arizona, dedicated.

Mar. 30 Capt. Frank M. Hawks took off from San Diego, Calif., in **1st transcontinental glider flight.** He was towed by a biplane on a 500-ft. line. Reached Van Cortlandt Park, New York city, on Apr. 6. Hawks had flown 1st seaplane glider in U.S. 2 weeks earlier at Port Washington, N.Y.

May 11 Adler Planetarium, **1st planetarium in U.S.,** opened in Chicago.

Gallant Fox won the 54th annual **Preakness Stakes,** paying 1–1. Jockey was E. Sande; time was 2:00⅗ on a fast track for winnings valued at $51,925.

Gallant Fox won the 62d annual **Belmont Stakes,** paying 8–5. Jockey was E. Sande; time was 2:31⅗ on a good track for winnings valued at $66,040.

U.S. lawn tennis men's singles champion, John H. Doeg; **women's singles champion,** Betty Nuthall of England.

Jan. 1 Southern California defeated Pittsburgh by a score of 47 to 14 in the 15th annual **Rose Bowl** football game.

May 17 Earle Sande rode his 3d **Kentucky Derby** winner, the great *Gallant Fox,* who went on to win the Triple Crown. The time was 2:07⅗ on a good track; the prize, $50,725.

June 12 Max Schmeling of Germany became **Heavyweight Champion of the World** when he was awarded the victory over Jack Sharkey, who fouled him in the 4th round at New York city.

Sept. 27 **Robert Tyre "Bobby" Jones** became 1st golfer to win the 4 most important golf matches by taking U.S. Amateur Tournament at Philadelphia, Pa. Earlier in the year he had won British Open in England; British Amateur in Scotland; and U.S. Open in Minneapolis, Minn. On Nov. 17 Jones announced his retirement from competition and said that he was under contract to make golf films for a Hollywood producer.

487

ment order virtually prohibiting the immigration of laborers from abroad.

Dec. 2 In effort to aid unemployment Pres. Hoover asked Congress for an appropriation of from $100 to $150 million for construction of public works. On Dec. 20 Congress passed necessary legislation with an appropriation of $116 million. The President had announced in Oct. that there were 4½ million unemployed. In beginning of depression Hoover had tried to arrange relief on a self-help basis at local and state levels.

types collected in a house in Southern France is *Hotel Universe* by **Philip Barry.**

Sept. 29 Extremely successful attempt to revive blank verse on the stage is **Maxwell Anderson's** *Elizabeth the Queen,* which retells the love of England's queen for Essex and her desire to rule alone. *Mary of Scotland* (1933) recounts in verse the pathetic life of Elizabeth's rival.

Nov. 5 Nobel Prize in Literature bestowed on Sinclair Lewis for his novel *Babbitt.* Lewis was 1st American to receive the award.

1931

This year's **Nobel Peace Prize** was shared by Jane Addams and Nicholas Murray Butler, president of Columbia University. Miss Addams was charter member and president of the Woman's International League for Peace; Pres. Butler was famous for his support of the Kellogg-Briand Peace Pact. In 1928 he had succeeded in obtaining approval of this Peace Pact from Pope Pius XI.

Jan. 19 Wickersham Report stated that enforcement of the 18th Amendment was breaking down due to public apathy or hostility and lucrative profits made in illicit liquor. Recommended that enforcement should belong solely to federal government, and that certain revisions should be made in the Prohibition Amendment. Did not advocate repeal.

Feb. 24 Procedure for the adoption of the 18th Amendment (Prohibition) was ruled valid by the U.S. Supreme Court in a unanimous decision which reversed the ruling of Federal Judge William Clark of New Jersey.

Mar. 17 Mayor James J. Walker of New York charged with malfeasance and negligence of official duties and his re-

Pulitzer Prizes: novel, *Years of Grace* by Margaret Ayer Barnes; drama, *Alison's House* by Susan Glaspell; U.S. history, *The Coming of the War: 1914* by Bernadotte E. Schmitt; biography, *Charles W. Eliot* by Henry James; poetry, *Collected Poems,* Robert Frost.

Phenomenal bestseller is **Pearl S. Buck's** 1st novel, *The Good Earth,* the story of a generation of Chinese peasants. For 2 years the book was at the top of the sales list in bookstores; it was translated into many languages; and it finally won for its author the Nobel Prize in 1938.

Novel of perversion, violence, and degeneracy is **William Faulkner's** *Sanctuary.* Reprinted in an inexpensive edition, it became his best known work. Faulkner has often remarked that he meant the book to be a "shocker."

Willa Cather wrote another novel of the church in the new world, *Shadows on the Rock,* a beautifully written story of 17th-century Quebec. Here in a raw community where ambition and the good life are in conflict the church plays the major civilizing role.

New School for Social Research built on 12th St., New York city. Building designed specifically for adult education; a striking early example of modern architecture.

SCIENCE; INDUSTRY; ECONOMICS; EDUCATION; RELIGION; PHILOSOPHY.	SPORTS; FASHIONS; POPULAR ENTERTAINMENT; FOLKLORE; SOCIETY.

Sept. 3 Experimental **electric passenger train** installed by Thomas A. Edison on Lackawanna Railroad between Hoboken and Montclair, N.J.

Sept. 17 **Hoover Dam,** originally called Boulder Dam, begun at Las Vegas, Nev. Work was completed in 1936.

Dec. 11 **Bank of the U.S.** in New York city, with 60 local branches and 400,000 depositors, closed. More than 1300 banks throughout country were closed in these 1st months of the depression.

Oct. 1–8 Philadelphia, AL, defeated St. Louis, NL, 4–2 in the 27th annual **World Series.**

Dec. 13 Army defeated Navy, 6–0 in the annual **Army-Navy** football game held at Yankee Stadium, New York city.

1931

The discovery of an isotope of hydrogen with an atomic weight of 2 instead of 1 by **Dr. Harold C. Urey** of Columbia University was a significant milestone in the development of nuclear physics.

Radio interference from the Milky Way 1st detected by J. G. Lansky, a radio engineer for the Bell Telephone Laboratories. Lansky observed that a steady hissing sound began whenever his radio aerial was pointed toward the Milky Way. Although Lansky could not identify the exact source of the hissing, his observation helped establish the science of **Radio-Astronomy.** More sensitive radio equipment has since been able to identify Lansky's hissing sounds as the death rattles of stars which exploded many centuries ago.

Declining membership in **trade unions** reflected in membership figures for years of 1920, over 5 million; 1927, fewer than 4 million; and 1931, about 3,333,000.

General Council of Congregational and Christian Churches established at a meeting in Seattle, Wash., by union of National Council of Congregational Churches and General Convention of Christian Churches.

Jan. 7 **Unemployment** estimated at between 4 and 5 million by Col. Arthur Woods, head of President's Emergency Committee for Unemployment Relief.

Academy Awards were presented to *Cimarron* as the best production of 1930 through 1931; to Marie Dressler as best actress for her performance in *Min and Bill;* and to Lionel Barrymore as best actor for his portrayal in *A Free Soul.*

National football champion was Southern California, coached by Howard Jones. Their record: 9 wins, 1 loss, no ties. It was their 2d title.

Twenty Grand won the 63d annual **Belmont Stakes,** paying 4–5. Jockey was C. Kurtsinger; time was 2:29⅗ on a fast track for winnings valued at $58,770.

Mate won the 55th annual **Preakness Stakes,** paying 41–10. Jockey was G. Ellis; time was 1:59 on a fast track for winnings valued at $48,225.

U.S. lawn tennis men's singles champion, H. Ellsworth Vines Jr.; **women's singles champion,** Mrs. Helen Wills Moody.

U.S.G.A. amateur championship won by Francis Ouimet at Beverly C.C., Chicago, Ill. He defeated Jack Westland, 6 and 5. **Open championship** won by Billy Burke at Inverness Club, Toledo, Ohio, with a score of 292.

Jan. 1 Alabama defeated Washington

moval from office was urged in a statement of charges presented to Gov. Roosevelt by John Haynes Holmes, pastor of the Community Church, and Rabbi Stephen S. Wise. On Apr. 20 Walker denied charges in a statement to Gov. Roosevelt and on Apr. 28 the Gov. dismissed them as tenuous and unsubstantial.

June 20 Pres. Hoover proposed an international **moratorium** in war reparations and war debts. Hoover's 1st important act to break the international financial panic, it at 1st seemed successful; stock markets rallied, bankers and economists were enthusiastic. But soon the panic became worse than ever.

Sept. **Bank panic** spread in U.S. In September 305 banks closed; in October, 522. Fear that the U.S. would go off the gold standard led to gold hoarding throughout the country.

George Washington Bridge, connecting New York and New Jersey across Hudson R., completed. Main span 3500 ft. long. One of the most beautiful and simply designed bridges in U.S.

Mar. 3 Pres. Herbert Hoover, signed act making **"The Star-Spangled Banner"** U.S. national anthem. Francis Scott Key wrote words during bombardment of Ft. McHenry on night of Sept. 13, 1813.

Oct. 5 Play which employs the fable of Beauty and the Beast in its study of the marriage of a Jewish lawyer and a woman of fashion is *Counsellor-at-Law* by **Elmer Rice.** Since its opening it has been revived often on stage, screen, and radio.

Oct. 26 Masterly interpretation of a Greek legend in modern psychological terms is the dramatic trilogy, *Mourning Becomes Electra,* by **Eugene O'Neill.**

Dec. 26 Political satire is seen at its best in the musical *Of Thee I Sing* by **George Kaufman** and **Morris Ryskind.** *Let 'Em Eat Cake* (1933) proved a worthy sequel. In *First Lady* (1935) in which Kaufman collaborated with Katharine Dayton, we see a satire of a woman who wants her husband to become president.

1932

It was a trying year for the nation. Pres. Hoover tried desperately to stem the floodtide of depression by granting generous credit to industry and ordering a stern check on government spending. Not only did he reduce his personal salary by 20%, he persuaded his vice-president and 9 members of the Cabinet to accept similar cuts. Public works were planned to assuage the staggering unemployment problem. His program, however, was never realized, for the voters insisted upon a change of administration, electing Franklin D. Roosevelt to the presidency by what amounted to a Democratic landslide.

Number of **unemployed** in U.S. reached 13,000,000. National wages were 60% less

15,279 books of all kinds were published or reprinted; of these, 1996 were novels. The novelists' main preoccupation this year seemed to be with the problems of the South. William Faulkner published *Light in August;* Sherwood Anderson produced *Beyond Desire;* and Erskine Caldwell turned out *Tobacco Road.* Beyond these few, and John Dos Passos' *1919,* nothing of literary moment was offered to the public. In fact, a virtual paralysis had settled over the arts. Opera houses in Chicago and Philadelphia gave no performances. A number of new orchestral works were ventured, none with serious claim to stature. Painters looked elsewhere for inspiration, found it in the formalized primi-

| SCIENCE; INDUSTRY; ECONOMICS; EDUCATION; RELIGION; PHILOSOPHY. | SPORTS; FASHIONS; POPULAR ENTERTAINMENT; FOLKLORE; SOCIETY. |

Feb. New York World, best known liberal newspaper in U.S., suspended publication. Its editor, **Walter Lippmann,** joined staff of New York *Herald Tribune* and began to write his syndicated column, which immediately became popular throughout the country.

Mar. 20 **Birth control** defended by Federal Council of Churches of Christ in America.

May 1 **Empire State Building,** world's tallest, dedicated and opened to the public in New York city.

June 4 William G. Swan, stunt pilot, flew **1st rocket-powered glider** in U.S. at Atlantic City, N.J. Glider traveled 1000 ft. and reached height of 100 ft. It was staged as an entertainment for audience at Steel Pier.

June 23 **Wiley Post** and **Harold Gatty** took off from Roosevelt Field in their plane "Winnie Mae" to begin a trip around the world. They landed back at Roosevelt Field 8 days, 15 hr., and 51 min. later.

Oct. 5 Hugh Herndon and Clyde Pangborn landed at Wenatchee, Wash., after **1st nonstop flight across Pacific.** They flew from Sabishiro, Japan, a distance of 4860 mi., in 41 hrs. 13 min.

State by a score of 24 to 0 in the 16th annual **Rose Bowl** football game.

May 13 In the famous **"false start race,"** at Jamaica, N.Y., the entire field of horses went completely around the track before they were recalled. 1st and 2d in the false start were *Rideaway* and *Clock Tower;* in the official race *Clock Tower* came in 1st, *Rideaway* 2d.

May 16 *Twenty Grand* set a new **Kentucky Derby** record. The Greentree Stable entry, ridden by jockey C. Kurtsinger, ran the 1¼ mi. in 2:01⅘ on a fast track, winning $48,725.00. This record time held until 1941.

Oct. 1–10 St. Louis, NL, defeated Philadelphia, AL, 4–3 in the 28th annual **World Series.**

Dec. 12 Army defeated Navy, 17–7 in the annual **Army-Navy football game** held at Yankee Stadium, New York city.

1932

A trickling demands for goods, uncertain manufacturing conditions, and a wobbly stock market combined to make this one of the most unfavorable business years within memory. Labor, however, hailed its most important victory to date—passage of the Federal Anti-Injunction Law, or Norris-LaGuardia Act. The battle of the 5-day week was also being won, as Pres. Hoover ordered it to be standard for most government employees. With unemployment hovering at about 11 million, labor could make little headway in its demands for compulsory unemployment insurance. The single field of activity where there seemed to be a sense of progress was in the domain of science. Areas of work in-

That redoubtable "dry," John D. Rockefeller, spoke out for the repeal of the Volstead Act; both Presidential candidates asked for its erasure from the law books. With such powerful forces against it, the **experiment of Prohibition** was doomed. In the late summer and fall, principal topic of conversation, aside from the coming elections, was the most exciting baseball season in years. Fever pitch was reached when Jimmy Foxx threatened to eclipse Babe Ruth's home run record of 60; he failed to match it by 2. Tennis had a dazzling new name—16-year-old Frankie Parker, who mowed down veteran opposition wherever he played. Greatest blot on the nation's conscience was its fantastic

| POLITICS AND GOVERNMENT; WAR; DISASTERS; VITAL STATISTICS. | BOOKS; PAINTING; DRAMA; ARCHITECTURE; SCULPTURE. |

than in 1929; dividends 56.6% less. Total business loss during the year was $5 to $6 billions. 2½ years after market crash, **U.S. industry** as a whole was operating at less than half its maximum 1929 volume; total amount paid in wages 60% less than 1929 level.

Jan. 22 **Reconstruction Finance Corporation** established with $2 billions at its disposal to advance loans to failing banks, farm mortgage associations, building and loan societies, railroads, and insurance companies.

Mar. 1 **Charles A. Lindbergh, Jr.,** aged 20 months, was kidnaped from his parents' home at Hopewell, N.J. Baby's body was found on May 12, after $50,000 ransom had been paid. Outraged public opinion forced adoption of the death penalty in federal kidnapping cases.

Mar. 3 **20th ("Lame Duck") Amendment** to Constitution submitted to states for ratification. It provided for the convening of Congress on Jan. 3 and for the beginning of presidential and vice-presidential terms on Jan. 20.

Mar. 23 **Norris-LaGuardia Act** restricted the use of injunctions in labor disputes.

Apr. 30–May 2 **National Convention of the Socialist Labor Party** met at New York and nominated Verne L. Reynolds of New York for the presidency and J. W. Aiken of Massachusetts for the vice-presidency.

May 22–24 **National Convention of the Socialist Party** met at Milwaukee and nominated Norman Thomas for the presidency and James H. Maurer of Pennsylvania for the vice-presidency.

May 28 **National Convention of the Communist Party** met at Chicago and nominated William Z. Foster for the presidency and James W. Ford of Alabama, Negro leader from New York city, for the vice-presidency.

May 29 Arrival in Washington, D.C., of **"Bonus Army"** (about 1000 ex-service-

tivism of Mexican Diego Rivera and his compatriots. Architects choose to quarrel over the "International School" style rather than to build. The theater enjoyed only one real hit—Philip Barry's *The Animal Kingdom*.

Pulitzer Prizes: novel, *The Good Earth* by Pearl S. Buck; drama, *Of Thee I Sing* by George S. Kaufman, Morrie Ryskind, and Ira Gershwin; U.S. history, *My Experiences in the World War* by John J. Pershing; biography, *Theodore Roosevelt* by Henry F. Pringle; poetry, *The Flowering Stone* by George Dillon. **Musical received drama award for the 1st time.**

Ferde Grofé composes *Grand Canyon Suite,* which became a familiarly known piece of American music throughout the world.

One of most **popular songs** of the year was "Brother, Can You Spare a Dime."

Precisionism, or the use of austere line and proportion to convey a feeling of the architectural and mechanical, used by **Charles Sheeler** in his *River Rouge Plant,* a painting where tradition of American craftsmanship is combined with modern engineering design.

To the objective realism of early 20th century was added the note of satire and self-conscious interpretation best seen in paintings of **Grant Wood.** His *Daughters of the American Revolution* makes a wry commentary on an aspect of American life.

Romanticism found a representative in the painter, **Franklin C. Watkins.** By distorting forms, by strange wavering of lines, he is able to create mood. His painting *Soliloquy* shows how distorted face and body of subject work toward expression. Other noteworthy works are *Springtime* (1935), *The Sideboard* (1940), *Death in the Orchard* (1938).

Shabbiness and drabness of small town life in the Midwest, though often tinged with a sense of the tragic, is caught in the realistic paintings of **Charles Burchfield.** In *November Evening,* painted this year,

| SCIENCE; INDUSTRY; ECONOMICS; EDUCATION; RELIGION; PHILOSOPHY. | SPORTS; FASHIONS; POPULAR ENTERTAINMENT; FOLKLORE; SOCIETY. |

cluded cosmic rays, atomic physics spearheaded by the discovery of the neutron by James Chadwick, enunciation of the uncertainty principle, production of gamma rays. An isotope of hydrogen was announced; vitamin C was isolated and identified. Automation was fast becoming a specialty of its own with the construction of larger and more versatile computing machines.

Nobel Prize in chemistry awarded to **Irving Langmuir** "for his discoveries and investigations in surface chemistry." Langmuir conducted his prize-winning research on surface actions of glass, water, and metals at the Research Laboratory of the General Electric Company at Schenectady, N.Y. His research began quite practically on the actions of metal wires in electrical lamps. His discoveries have resulted in the longer service and more efficient operation of incandescent lamps. His study of the spreading effect of insoluble substances on water led to industrial applications for reducing light glare from glass surfaces. Langmuir's most recent application of his research is the controversial cloud-seeding process by which rain is artificially induced. Langmuir's dual objective in dousing clouds with dry ice or silver iodide is to cause rain in drought-stricken areas and to reduce and redirect the force of hurricanes.

1st polaroid glass devised by Edwin H. Land.

San Francisco–Oakland Bay Bridge begun. Total cost estimated at $70 million.

Wheat prices dropped to a new low of 32¢ a bu. This contrasted with peak prices of $2.33 a bu. in 1920.

Mar. 23 Significant gain for labor, of **Norris-LaGuardia Anti-Injunction Act,** signed into law. It prohibited injunctions as a means of maintaining anti-union employment contracts or to inhibit strikes, picketing, and boycotts.

crime wave. Citizens of Chicago this year shelled out some $145 million to racketeers. As if to compensate, Hollywood discovered the social message. Best example was *I Am a Fugitive from a Chain Gang,* starring Paul Muni.

Academy Awards presented to *Grand Hotel* as the outstanding production of 1931 through 1932; to Helen Hayes as best actress for her performance in *The Sin of Madelon Claudet,* and to Fredric March for his dual portrayal of *Dr. Jekyll and Mr. Hyde.* An additional award for acting was given to Wallace Beery for his performance in *The Champ.* 1st awards granted in short subject categories to Walt Disney for his animated cartoon, *Flowers and Trees,* to Mack Sennett for *A Wrestling Swordfish,* and to Hal Roach for *Laurel and Hardy in the Music Box.* A special award was presented to Walt Disney for his creation of Mickey Mouse.

Charles Urban Yeager introduced **"Bank Night"** into Colorado theaters. Later he copyrighted the idea, and it spread rapidly throughout the country.

Olympic Games were held in U.S., the winter events at Lake Placid, N.Y., and the summer events at Los Angeles. U.S. won 11 of the 23 events.

This year's national **football champion** was Michigan, coached by Harry Kipke. Their record: 8 wins, no losses, no ties.

U.S.G.A. amateur championship won by C. Ross Somerville at Baltimore, Md., C.C. He defeated Johnny Goodman, 2 and 1. **Open championship** won by Gene Sarazen at Fresh Meadow C.C., Flushing, N.Y., with a score of 286.

U.S. lawn tennis men's singles champion, H. Ellsworth Vines, Jr.; **women's singles champion,** Helen Hull Jacobs.

Faireno won the 64th annual **Belmont Stakes,** paying 5–1. Jockey was T. Malley;

493

POLITICS AND GOVERNMENT; WAR; DISASTERS; VITAL STATISTICS.

BOOKS; PAINTING; DRAMA; ARCHITECTURE; SCULPTURE.

men). In June other groups of veterans arrived from every section of country, swelling numbers of "army" to about 17,-000. Camped in open or in unused buildings near capital they intended to stay until Congress authorized the immediate cashing in full of soldiers' bonus certificates. Bill passed House June 15, but was killed in Senate June 17. Government provided money for veterans to return to their homes, but about 2000 refused offer and did not move. Finally on July 28 federal troops under Gen. Douglas MacArthur drove them out.

June 14–16 **National Convention of the Republican Party** met at Chicago and renominated on the 1st ballot Pres. Hoover for the presidency and Vice-Pres. Charles Curtis for the vice-presidency.

June 27–July 2 **Democratic National Convention** met in Chicago Stadium, Chicago, Ill. The chief candidates for the presidential nomination were Franklin D. Roosevelt, John Nance Garner, and Al Smith. On July 1 Franklin Roosevelt was nominated for the presidency. Deadlock was broken when John Nance Garner of Texas was persuaded to give his delegates to Roosevelt in return for the vice-presidential nomination. Roosevelt broke precedent by flying to Chicago to accept and made his famous "new deal" speech.

July 5–7 **National Convention of the Prohibition Party** met at Indianapolis and nominated William D. Upshaw of Georgia for the presidency and Frank S. Regan of Illinois for the vice-presidency.

July 10 **National Convention of the Farmer Labor Party** nominated Gen. Jacob S. Coxey, mayor of Massillon, Ohio, for the presidency.

Nov. 8 Democratic landslide elected **Franklin D. Roosevelt** President of the U.S. He carried all but 7 states, with 472 electoral votes to 59 for Herbert Hoover. Popular vote: Roosevelt, 22,821,857; Hoover, 15,761,841; Thomas, 881,951; Foster, 102,785; Reynolds, 33,276; Upshaw, 81,869; Coxey, 7309.

the isolation of building against a darkening sky, the solitary figure, the monotonous earth, speak of grandeur as well as of bleakness.

Jan. The **rhythmicon,** a machine invented by composer Henry Cowell and engineer Leon Theremin to reproduce all rhythmical combinations, however complex, presented in a concert at the New School for Social Research in New York city. The chief work on the concert program Cowell's *Rhythmicana* for orchestra and rhythmicon.

Mar. 28 Career of humorist **George M. Cohan** continued with his *Confidential Service,* a detective play which tells audience the culprit in 1st act. *Pigeons and People* (1933) and *Dear Old Darling* (1936) created delightful parts for this comedian-playwright.

Apr. 25 Relation of parent and child placed against background of the family was a popular theme of the '30's. **Rose Franken** began her career as playwright with *Another Language.* **Clifford Odets** followed with *Awake and Sing* (1935) and *Paradise Lost* (1935). **Lillian Hellman**'s 1st play, *The Children's Hour* (1934) studies a malicious child who wrecks a school by slander; while **Leopold Atlas** in his *Wednesday's Child* (1934) is concerned with a young boy who threatens to wreck a home.

Oct. 6 Delightful comedy of character is **Rachel Crothers'** *When Ladies Meet,* which studies 2 women—the wife and mistress of a man, and leads through bright dialogue to the scene of discovery on the part of the wife.

Oct. 31 Comedy of a small-town family who had once known a painter and thought him a ne'er-do-well, only to find themselves famous after his death is *The Late Christopher Bean* by **Sidney Howard.** In *Alien Corn* (1933) an artist is set against the atmosphere of a small Midwestern college.

494

SCIENCE; INDUSTRY; ECONOMICS; EDUCATION; RELIGION; PHILOSOPHY.

SPORTS; FASHIONS; POPULAR EN-TERTAINMENT; FOLKLORE; SOCIETY.

May 20 **Amelia Earhart** became 1st woman to cross the Atlantic in a solo flight when she landed near Londonderry, Ireland, 2026½ mi. from Harbor Grace, Newfoundland, her starting point. The flight took 13 hr. 30 min.

Fall Notable experiment of progressive education on college level began with opening of **Bennington College,** Vt. A school for women, it eschewed the orthodox methods of grading through credits and points. A similar project was **Teachers College,** Columbia University, New York city, where graduation was to be based on over-all knowledge acquired rather than on the completion of certain required courses.

Oct. 13 Cornerstone laid for new **Supreme Court Building** in Washington, D.C. Pres. Hoover, Chief Justice Charles Evans Hughes, and Guy A. Thompson, president of the American Bar Association, officiated.

Nov. 1st comprehensive study of relation between **medical practices** and needs completed as government project. The investigating group, the Committee on the Costs of Medical Care, suggested a modified socialization of medicine under state control, to be supported by health insurance payments or special taxation. The report left room for private cases. Immediate objections raised by the AMA, who called the plan "utopian," cumbersome, bureaucratic, and impersonal.

Dec. Vogue for **"Technocracy"** reached its height. Invented by Howard Scott, an amateur economist of Greenwich Village, New York city, and based in part on doctrines of Soddy and Veblen, it was a theory of price control based on units of energy. Its "scientific" and semimystical qualities gave the theory great popularity for a few months.

time was 2:32⅖ on a fast track for winnings valued at $55,120.

Burgoo King won the 56th annual **Preakness Stakes,** paying 16–5. Jockey was E. James; time was 1:59⅘ on a fast track for winnings of $50,375.

Jan. 1 Southern California defeated Tulane by a score of 21 to 12 in the 17th annual **Rose Bowl** football game.

Feb. 4 **Winter Olympic Games,** 1st held in U.S., opened at Lake Placid, N.Y., with ceremony led by Gov. Franklin D. Roosevelt.

May 7 The winner of the 58th annual **Kentucky Derby** was Col. E. R. Bradley's *Burgoo King,* ridden by E. James. Time was 2:05⅕ on a fast track; the prize, $52,-350.

June 21 **World Heavyweight Boxing Championship** won by Jack Sharkey, who took 15-round decision over Max Schmeling at New York, thus returning title to U.S.

July 2 Term **"New Deal"** introduced by Franklin D. Roosevelt in his speech accepting the nomination for the Presidency. Before the assembled delegates in Chicago, Roosevelt said: "I pledge you, I pledge myself, to a new deal for the American people. Let us all here assembled constitute ourselves prophets of a new order of competence and courage. This is more than a political campaign; it is a call to arms."

Sept. 28–Oct. 2 New York, AL, defeated Chicago, NL, 4–0 in the 29th annual **World Series.**

Oct. 13 **Kid Chocolate** knocked out Lew Feldman in round 12 of featherweight boxing championship match held at New York city. In 1934, Chocolate gave up the crown in order to box as a lightweight.

Dec. 3 **Army** defeated Navy, 20–0, in their annual contest at Franklin Field, Philadelphia.

495

1933

The change of administration deepened the economic crisis. Low-water mark was reached on inauguration day with a nationwide bank panic. In order to meet the situation, the administration demanded, and was given, unprecedented powers. These led to wide changes in the monetary system and to the creation of an army of federal agencies which regulated private industry and found jobs for millions on government-sponsored projects. While this program, known as the "New Deal," restored some confidence, its more radical measures came under furious conservative attack. Critics, however, failed to win popular support. In world affairs, our "good neighbor" policy paid dividends in fostering an era of Pan-American political and economic co-operation. The gravity of our internal problems muffled rumblings in Europe, merely took notice of sporadic warfare in the Far East, and the disintegration of the League of Nations.

1st woman cabinet member was Miss Frances Perkins, who was appointed Secretary of Labor by Pres. Franklin D. Roosevelt.

Feb. 6 20th amendment adopted. It abolished the lame-duck session and changed the Presidential inauguration date from Mar. 4 to Jan. 20. It also specified that the vice-president elect shall succeed to the presidency if the president-elect should die before inauguration.

Feb. 16 Senate voted to repeal the **Prohibition Amendment.** The House voted similarly on Feb. 20, and the issue was sent to the states for their action. On Dec. 5 21st Amendment was adopted with its ratification by Utah, 36th state.

Mar. 1 Bank holidays declared in 6 states, and by Mar. 4 bank panics reached greatest intensity. At 4:30 in the morning, Gov. Lehman of New York declared a bank holiday, and Gov. Horner of Illinois immediately followed suit.

In an undistinguished year for novels, American publishers studiously reflected a national taste for escape by underwriting such works as the monumental *Anthony Adverse* by Hervey Allen, and Kenneth Roberts' *Rabble in Arms.* More memorable were collections of short stories and poetry by such authors as Ernest Hemingway, Sherwood Anderson, Robinson Jeffers, and Archibald MacLeish. The theater, too, suffered a lackluster year despite offerings by "name" playwrights and stars. Most notable exception was Eugene O'Neill's *Ah, Wilderness!* Opera houses and symphonic societies curtailed their seasons and took no chances of alienating subscribers. A universally conservative climate enervated most painters and sculptors as well, even though they were unexpectedly showered with commissions from the Civil Works Administration. At one time, the government employed 2500 artists and 1000 architects, most of whom set to work decorating our public buildings with a rash of murals.

Pulitzer Prizes: novel, *The Store* by T. S. Stribling; drama, *Both Your Houses* by Maxwell Anderson; U.S. history, *The Significance of Sections in American History* by Frederick J. Turner; biography, *Grover Cleveland* by Allan Nevins; poetry, *Conquistador* by Archibald MacLeish.

The *Autobiography of Alice B. Toklas* by **Gertrude Stein** attracted a surprisingly large reading public for an author who was usually read only by a few devoted followers.

"Century of Progress" Exposition at Chicago was 1st large-scale expression of modern architectural aims and methods in the U.S.

Significant court decision handed down in New York involving **Erskine Caldwell's** novel, *God's Little Acre,* on one hand and the New York Society for the Prevention of Vice on the other. City Magistrate Ben-

1933

Encouraged by sympathetic legislation, especially the creation of the N.L.R.B., organized labor became more militant in making its demands—particularly its right to organize. The A.F.L. boasted 4 million members in 29,669 local bodies, and counted as allies the 1 million workers enrolled in the railroad brotherhoods. Science, meanwhile, confirmed the discovery (in 1932) of the positron (positive electron) and reduced to laboratory routine the transmutation of elements. Television pioneers were jubilantly hailing a new communication medium and pointed with pride to a 9-in. cathode ray screen already on the market. American education presented a more somber picture. 2000 rural schools failed to open in the fall. Over 1500 commercial schools and colleges were forced to suspend activities. Some 200,-000 certified teachers were unemployed, and it was estimated that 2,280,000 school age children were not going to school.

Nobel Prize in medicine and physiology presented to **Thomas Hunt Morgan** "for his discoveries concerning the function of the chromosome in the transmission of heredity." Morgan performed his most significant experiments as head of the California Institute of Technology in Pasadena, Calif. His prize-winning work was entitled *The Theory of the Gene* and dealt with the inherited characteristics of the *Drosophila* or fruit fly.

Average life expectancy, 59 years. This represented a gain of 10 years from the turn of the century.

American Newspaper Guild founded by Heywood Broun.

1st report of the **National Survey of School Finance,** authorized by Congress in 1931, was delivered and stated that one third of America's school children were receiving an inadequate education.

The financial depression damped most professional sporting activities with the exception of horse racing, which boomed as never before. State legislatures, recognizing the revenue value of track betting, compromised their erstwhile rigid morals and encouraged meets. Maryland this year earned some $66 million from racing revenues alone. League-leading baseball clubs played before packed parks, but the tailenders could not fill their stands, so had a rocky time. New rules made baseball a more exciting, hence more popular sport. Football contests enjoyed a 13% rise in attendance over last year—a popularity that extended to the professional game as well. People everywhere were talking about the repeal of Prohibition, Katherine Hepburn's performance in *Little Women,* and were imitating Mae West's mannerisms in *She Done Him Wrong,* the 2 most popular motion pictures of the day.

Academy Awards presented to *Cavalcade* as the outstanding production of 1932 through 1933; to Katherine Hepburn as best actress for her performance in *Morning Glory;* and to Charles Laughton for his portrayal of *Henry VIII.* Walt Disney obtained his 2d consecutive award in the short cartoon category, this time for his version of *Three Little Pigs.*

1st **totalizator** used at an American race track installed at Arlington Park, Chicago, Ill. This completely electrical device, invented and 1st built in U.S. in 1927, prints and issues betting tickets at the rate of 50 per min.; sorts, adds, and transmits totals to indicator boards, flashing new information every 90 sec. These machines are now in use at all major tracks run under the parimutuel system. According to the size of the track, from 100 to 350 vending machines operated by 400 to 900 men are used at each park.

This year's national **football champion** was, for the 2d straight year, Michigan,

POLITICS AND GOVERNMENT; WAR; DISASTERS; VITAL STATISTICS.

BOOKS; PAINTING; DRAMA; ARCHITECTURE; SCULPTURE.

Mar. 4 **Franklin D. Roosevelt** inaugurated as president in Washington, D.C. In his inaugural address, Pres. Roosevelt said: "The only thing we have to fear is fear itself"; and he went on to outline an aggressive policy in the emergency and said that he would ask for unusual powers if necessary.

Mar. 5 (Sunday) Pres. F. D. Roosevelt called a special session of Congress and proclaimed a **national bank holiday.**

Mar. 12 Pres. F. D. Roosevelt made the 1st of his **"fireside chats"** on a Sunday evening. His subject was the reopening of the banks during the following week.

Mar. 13 **Banks** across the country began to reopen. Before the end of the month over 75% of all banks again operating.

Mar. 31 **Civilian Conservation Corps** (CCC) was created by the Reforestation Unemployment Act to alleviate unemployment and initiate a reforestation program.

Apr. 19 Embargo placed on all gold shipments by executive order of Pres. F. D. Roosevelt. This in effect took U.S. off the **gold standard.**

May 12 **Agricultural Adjustment Act** created the AAA, which restricted the production of certain crops (to be determined by the farmer) and paid the farmer a bounty for his uncultivated acreage. The bounties were to be paid from the revenue obtained from a processing tax. The Supreme Court ruled the AAA unconstitutional in 1936.

May 12 Congress passed **Federal Emergency Relief Act** and an appropriation of $500 million for Federal Emergency Relief Administration (FERA).

May 18 **Tennessee Valley Act** passed establishing the TVA with the purposes of controlling Tennessee R. floods, instituting a reforestation program along the marginal lands in the Tennessee Valley, and developing rural electrification.

May 27 **Federal Securities Act** passed requiring the registration and approval of all issues of stocks and bonds.

jamin Greenspan exonerated the book of the charge of obscenity in a decision that stressed 3 criteria: (1) the consideration of the book as a whole rather than of isolated sections; (2) the aptness of coarse language in coarse characters; (3) that reactions of an average cross section of citizens were relevant to the determination of the case.

Original contribution of '30's to the theater was the **musical comedy,** where a good book is joined to good music and balanced performance. *As Thousands Cheer* by Irving Berlin and Moss Hart is a delightful comedy of newspaper world; Cole Porter's *Leave It to Me* (1938) is comedy of an American ambassador (Victor Moore) in Moscow; *Louisiana Purchase* (1940) by Irving Berlin and Morrie Ryskind again utilizes service of Victor Moore as a senator with aspirations to White House; Cole Porter's *Du Barry Was a Lady* (1939) is a musical that moves from New York night clubs to Versailles.

Roberta, with music by **Jerome Kern,** produced on Broadway, New York. Very popular, it contained such songs as "Smoke Gets in Your Eyes" and "The Touch of Your Hand."

Walter Piston, composer and professor at Harvard University, published *Principles of Harmonic Analysis,* one of the most influential textbooks on methods of modern composition.

Aaron Copland composed his *Short Symphony,* perhaps the best of his works done during the period of "austerity" which he entered after his experiments with jazz.

Sept. 26 Social drama is the keynote in plays of rising playwright **Sidney Kingsley.** *Men in White,* produced on this date, recounts the conflict of a doctor's duty and emotions, using the profession as a backdrop. *Dead End* (1935), a sociological drama, studies young gangs in an alley of New York and shows the patterns

| SCIENCE; INDUSTRY; ECONOMICS; EDUCATION; RELIGION; PHILOSOPHY. | SPORTS; FASHIONS; POPULAR ENTERTAINMENT; FOLKLORE; SOCIETY. |

Jan. 5 "Jones Parity Plan" for **agricultural bonuses** passed by U.S. House of Representatives.

Jan. 16 Electrification of **Pennsylvania Railroad** between New York city and Philadelphia, Pa., completed.

Feb. 25 *Ranger*, **1st U.S. aircraft carrier**, launched at Newport News, Va. Christened by Mrs. Herbert Hoover, ship was named after famous vessel commanded by John Paul Jones.

Mar. 7 **Credit** tightened by New York life insurance companies, which refused to grant further loans on insurance policies.

May 1 **"The Humanist Manifesto"** issued under the signature of 11 prominent college and university professors. Composed of 15 points, the manifesto sought to erase all distinctions between what was religious and what was human, between what was secular and what was sacred. All human activity was considered significant. The universe was considered self-existing rather than created and man was considered the product of evolutionary processes rather than of Divine Creation. Stressing happiness, well-being, and creativity for human beings, the manifesto took a strong stand against the capitalistic system as the vehicle of human aspirations.

May 18 The Muscle Shoals Bill, pioneer public power measure that authorized the government development of the **Tennessee R. Valley**, signed by Pres. Roosevelt.

May 27 **Century of Progress Exposition** opened at Chicago, Ill. Held in honor of centennial of founding of Chicago, it closed Nov. 12.

coached by Harry Kipke. Their record this year: 7 wins, no losses, 1 tie.

U.S.G.A. amateur championship won by George T. Dunlap, Jr., at Kenwood C.C., Cincinnati, Ohio. He defeated Max R. Marston, 6 and 5. **Open championship** won by Johnny Goodman at North Shore C.C., Glen View, Ill., with a score of 287.

U.S. lawn tennis men's singles champion, Frederick J. Perry of England; **women's singles champion,** Helen Hull Jacobs.

Hurryoff won the 65th annual **Belmont Stakes,** paying 15–1. Jockey was M. Garner; time was 2:32⅗ on a fast track for winnings valued at $49,490.

Head Play won the 57th annual **Preakness Stakes,** paying 9–5. Jockey was C. Kurtsinger; time was 2:02 on a slow track for winnings valued at $26,850.

Jan. 1 Southern California defeated Pittsburgh by a score of 35 to 0 in the 18th annual **Rose Bowl** football game.

Mar. 22 3.2 **percent liquor law** authorized the manufacture and sale of wines and beers containing 3.2% alcohol.

May 6 For the 2d straight year a horse owned and bred by Colonel E. R. Bradley won the **Kentucky Derby.** *Broker's Tip,* ridden by D. Meade, won the 59th annual racing classic at Churchill Downs, Louisville, Ky., in 2:06⅘ on a fast track, winning $48,925.

June 21 **World Heavyweight Championship** won by Italian giant, Primo Car-

POLITICS AND GOVERNMENT; WAR; DISASTERS; VITAL STATISTICS.

BOOKS; PAINTING; DRAMA; ARCHITECTURE; SCULPTURE.

June **Emergency Housing Division** created within the PWA to finance private construction of slum-clearing projects in U.S. cities.

June 16 **National Industrial Recovery Act** (NIRA) created. It established the **National Recovery Administration** and the **Public Works Administration.** Gen. Hugh Johnson was named administrator of the NRA and Harold L. Ickes in charge of the PWA. On this day Congress also passed the **Banking Act of 1933,** under which was established the **Federal Bank Deposit Insurance Corporation.**

Aug. 5 Pres. Roosevelt established **National Labor Board** authorized by the National Industrial Recovery Act, and appointed Sen. Robert F. Wagner of New York as chairman. Board was empowered to adjudicate collective bargaining disputes.

Nov. 8 **Civil Works Administration** set up with an initial appropriation of $400,000,000; 1st director was Harry L. Hopkins. The plan was intended to provide work for about 4 million unemployed or, in other words, to put ⅔ of families then receiving relief on self-sustaining basis.

which will make them the gangsters of tomorrow.

Oct. 2 Comedy of family life and the problems of adolescence is **Eugene O'Neill's** *Ah, Wilderness!* The role of Nat Miller, the father who grows to understand his son, was played by George M. Cohan in New York and Will Rogers in San Francisco.

Dec. 4 *Tobacco Road,* a play written by **Jack Kirkland** from the novel by **Erskine Caldwell,** produced in New York city. At first it failed to attract an audience, but soon its reputation spread among nontheater-goers, and it became the longest-running play on Broadway.

Dec. 6 Ban on *Ulysses,* by **James Joyce,** raised by Judge John M. Woolsey, who said: "[It is] a sincere and honest book . . . I do not detect anywhere the leer of a sensualist."

1934

Federal agencies continued to administer and control many phases of American life. A notable exception was the weather. Plagued by record cold snaps in February and searing heat in July, farmers watched their fields wither away in the most destructive drought the Midwest had ever seen. Rising agricultural prices afforded temporary relief for them, but not for city dwellers. Internal affairs were complicated by congressional and local elections. Republican orators had only 1 real issue—the dubious constitutionality of some of the more radical New Deal provisions. More orthodox methods were advocated; federal "boondoggling" had reached outrageous proportions, was seriously crippling the nation's financial resources, as witness 33 new government agencies, 24,303 new

2 major works of American fiction made 1934 a banner year. F. Scott Fitzgerald published *Tender Is the Night,* and John O'Hara contributed *Appointment in Samarra.* Generally, however, our novelists were cashing in on the vogues of regionalism and historical pastiche. The more adroit worked both veins simultaneously, emerging wealthy and renowned. Government-sponsored art projects encouraged the talented and the daubers indiscriminately, were responsible for the incredible number of some 15,000 works of art produced.

Pulitzer Prizes: novel, *Lamb in His Bosom* by Caroline Miller; drama, *Men in White* by Sidney Kingsley; U.S. history, *The People's Choice* by Herbert Agar; biography, *John Hay* by Tyler Dennett; poetry, *Selected Verse* by Robert Hillyer.

SCIENCE; INDUSTRY; ECONOMICS; EDUCATION; RELIGION; PHILOSOPHY.	SPORTS; FASHIONS; POPULAR ENTERTAINMENT; FOLKLORE; SOCIETY.

June 21 AFL announced that 1½ million of its members, thrown out of work because of the depression, had once more found **employment.**

June 22 **Illinois Ship Canal** formally opened. The waterway links the Great Lakes with the Gulf of Mexico.

Oct. 2 AFL took official stand for **6-hr. day** and **5-day week.**

Oct. 13 **AFL** voted to boycott all German-made products as a protest against Nazi antagonism to organized labor within Germany.

Nov. 7 16-year-year **Tammany** rule ended in New York city by a Fusion ticket headed by **Fiorello LaGuardia.**

nera, who knocked out Jack Sharkey at Long Island City Bowl.

July 6 American League defeated the National by a score of 4 to 2 in the **1st All-Star Baseball Game.** Contest was held at Comiskey Park in Chicago before 49,200 fans who paid $51,203.50 to get into the park.

Oct. 3–7 New York, NL, defeated Washington, AL, 4–1 in the 30th annual **World Series.**

Nov. 25 Army defeated Navy, 12–7 in the annual **Army-Navy football game** played at Franklin Field, Philadelphia, Pa.

Dec. 17 Chicago Bears defeated the New York Giants, 23 to 21, for the **1st National Professional Football League Championship.** Played at Chicago, Ill.

1934

Here and there breaks appeared in the depression cloud and people began to take new hope. Unemployment dropped by over 4 million; labor, which had claimed 58.3% of the national income in 1929, now earned 62.5%; business failures dropped sharply; the purchasing power of industrial workers went up by 25%; the AFL claimed 2 million new members. The near disastrous plight of the nation's schools was eased as capital outlay for education grew more generous. In their laboratories, scientists induced artificial radioactivity for the 1st time, extended the periodic table, tapped the sun's energy with 2 experimental solar motors, and enthusiastically predicted that man would soon harness atomic energy.

Nobel Prize in chemistry presented to

Dry forces stubbornly refused to concede defeat, renewed their campaign on the local level. However, they were powerless to stop the huge liquor industry from slowly lumbering into high gear. Distilleries, this year, satisfied an American thirst that took 35 million barrels of beer and 42 million gallons of hard liquor to slake. For the sports fan, the 2 most imposing figures in the country were Dizzy and Daffy Dean, brothers who rolled up 45 victories between them to pitch the St. Louis Cardinals into a world championship and the 1st $1 million World Series gate. Hollywood produced a dimpled darling who captured the heart of the world. Her name, Shirley Temple.

Academy Awards presented to *It Happened One Night* as the outstanding mo-

employees, and an increase in the national debt by nearly 20%. Few voters responded, for conditions were slowly improving; only 58 banks had failed in 1934—901 per year had been the average since 1921.

Jan. 1 **Dr. Francis E. Townsend** of Long Beach, Calif., announced his "Old Age Revolving Pensions Plan."

Jan. 31 Pres. Roosevelt signed the **Farm Mortgage Refinancing Act** which created the Federal Farm Mortgage Corporation. This institution was authorized to assist farmers in the payment of their mortgages by providing easier credit terms.

Mar. 24 **Tydings-McDuffie Act** granted independence to the Philippines and the Philippine legislature approved it on May 1. Complete independence would not be proclaimed until July 4, 1946.

Apr. 18 Legislature of **Puerto Rico** adopted resolution requesting statehood.

Apr. 28 Pres. Roosevelt signed the **Home Owners Loan Act** which supplemented the Home Owners Refinancing Act of 1933, both measures designed to stimulate home building.

June 6 Pres. Roosevelt signed the **Securities Exchange Act,** which provided for the creation of a Securities and Exchange Commission. The Act further provided for the licensing of stock exchanges and decreed that certain speculative practices were illegal.

June 12 Pres. Roosevelt signed the **Trade Agreements Act** by which he was authorized to cut tariffs by as much as 50% of the prevailing rates for those nations which accorded to U.S. the most favored nation treatment.

June 19 Congress passed **Communications Act** to establish Federal Communications Commission. New commission regulated all national and international communication by telegraph, cable or radio.

June 28 Pres. Roosevelt signed the **Federal Farm Bankruptcy Act** (Frazier-Lemke Act) which established a moratorium on farm mortgage foreclosures.

Merry Mount, an opera by **Howard Hanson,** produced by the Metropolitan Opera Company. It achieved a total of 9 performances.

The **hit musical** of the Broadway season was *Anything Goes,* with music by Cole Porter.

Catholic Legion of Decency began censorship of motion pictures. Though there were some protests from intellectual quarters, surprisingly little opposition was raised to the program.

Ever popular painting by a modern is *String Quartet* by **Jack Levine,** whose expressionistic art is used admirably to capture feelings of players.

Laurens Hammond, electric clock manufacturer of Chicago, Ill., created **1st pipeless Hammond organ,** marketed for 1st time the following year. New instrument produced sound by amplification of electrical modulations.

A painter of the cities, the thronging masses, the flop houses, theaters, beaches, etc., was **Reginald Marsh.** In *Negroes on Rockaway Beach* a mass of people is depicted in action, with the arrangement of the figures designed to emphasize the dramatic quality of the moment.

Jan. Modern miracle play in which split personality is externalized is **Eugene O'Neill's** *Days Without End.* John Loving, the hero, becomes whole only when he returns to the Catholicism of his youth.

Jan. 7 Deep study of the relationship of 2 mothers (the real and the adopted) to an illegitimate child gives **Zoë Akins** material for her play *The Old Maid,* which won the Pulitzer Prize in 1935. Play was adapted from Edith Wharton's novelette of the same name.

Jan. 26 **Roy Harris'** *First Symphony* performed by the Boston Symphony Orchestra under the direction of Serge Koussevitzky.

Feb. 8 Opera which is completely nonrepresentational and to most people incomprehensible is **Gertrude Stein's** *Four Saints*

| SCIENCE; INDUSTRY; ECONOMICS; EDUCATION; RELIGION; PHILOSOPHY. | SPORTS; FASHIONS; POPULAR ENTERTAINMENT; FOLKLORE; SOCIETY. |

Harold Clayton Urey "for his discovery of heavy hydrogen." Urey's discovery of heavy hydrogen in Dec., 1931, was followed almost immediately by the industrial production of this isotope of hydrogen, now called deuterium, and its oxide, "heavy" water. The 1st plant to manufacture deuterium and heavy water was located at Rjukan, Norway. Heavy water has been used with great success in slowing down neutrons in atomic piles.

Nobel Prizes in medicine and physiology for discovery of liver therapy against anemia awarded to **G. R. Minot, W. P. Murphy,** and **G. H. Whipple,** the 4th, 5th, and 6th Americans to be honored in this field.

Jan. 7   The Rev. **Dr. William Ashley (Billy) Sunday,** famous American revivalist, began an intensive 2-week revival campaign in New York city at the Calvary Baptist Church. Dr. Sunday, now 70, had not visited New York city for this purpose since 1917. At that time, he had evangelized for 10 weeks on Washington Heights. Many people looked upon "Billy" Sunday as the last of the old-fashioned forensic revivalists.

Mar. 13   Henry Ford made a confident gesture in the face of the depression by restoring the $5 a day **minimum wage** to 47,000 of his 70,000 workers.

May 23   Dr. Wallace H. Carothers, a research chemist in the **Du Pont** laboratories, succeeded in spinning a synthetic fiber that met exhaustive tests of durability. Carothers called this fiber "polymer 66" but it later became famous as **nylon.**

June 26   **Evangelical and Reformed Church** established in Cleveland, Ohio, by a union of the Reformed Church in the United States and the Evangelical Synod of North America. The 1st service of the newly combined churches was held on June 27.

tion picture of the year and to its stars, Claudette Colbert and Clark Gable as best actress and best actor, respectively. Walt Disney was honored for the 3d straight year in the cartoon category, this time for his version of *Tortoise and the Hare.*

This year's **National Football Champion** was Minnesota, coached by Bernie Bierman. Their record: 8 wins, no losses, no ties.

U.S. lawn tennis men's singles champion, Frederick J. Perry of England; **women's singles champion,** Helen Hull Jacobs.

U.S.G.A. amateur championship won by W. Lawson Little, Jr. at The Country Club, Brookline, Mass. He defeated David Goldman, 8 and 7. **Open championship** won by Olin Dutra at Merion Cricket Club, Haverford, Pa., with a score of 293.

Peace Chance won the 66th annual **Belmont Stakes,** paying 3–1. Jockey was W. D. Wright; time was 2:29⅕ on a fast track for winnings valued at $43,410.

High Quest won the 58th annual **Preakness Stakes,** paying 9–20. Jockey was R. Jones; time was 1:58⅕ on a fast track for winnings valued at $25,175.

Jan. 1   Columbia defeated Stanford by a score of 7 to 0 in the 19th annual **Rose Bowl** football game.

May 5   *Cavalcade* won the 60th annual **Kentucky Derby** with a whirlwind finish that held off J. H. Vanderbilt's fine *Discovery,* who chased *Cavalcade* home all year. The time was 2:04 on a fast track; the prize (much lower than usual); $28,-175. The jockey was M. Garner riding for Brookmeade Stable.

May 12   U.S. golfers defeated golfers of Great Britain in the International **Walker Cup Match** held at St. Andrews, Scotland. The score was 9 matches for the U.S. to 2 for Great Britain, and 1 match halved.

June 14   Max Baer scored a technical knockout over Primo Carnera, **World's**

503

| POLITICS AND GOVERNMENT; WAR; DISASTERS; VITAL STATISTICS. | BOOKS; PAINTING; DRAMA; ARCHITECTURE; SCULPTURE. |

June 28 **Federal Housing Administration** created by act of Congress to help home owners finance repairs and enlargements and to spur private building through federal mortgages.

July **Southern Tenant Farmers' Union** organized in Arkansas by a small group of white and Negro sharecroppers. It grew to 35,000 members, mostly in Arkansas and Oklahoma, by 1937 when it affiliated with the CIO.

July 22 **John Dillinger,** public enemy no. 1, shot by F.B.I.

Sept. 8 Some 130 persons died when a fire broke out on the ship, **Morro Castle,** near Asbury Park, N.J.

Nov. 6 By amendment to state constitution, Nebraska adopted **1st unicameral state legislature** in U.S. Amendment had been written by George W. Norris.

in Three Acts, with the music by Virgil Thomson, presented by the Society of Friends and Enemies of Modern Music at Hartford, Conn. Four acts are designated as follows:

"I—*Avila:* St. Theresa half indoors and half out of doors

II—Might it be mountains if it were not Barcelona

III—*Barcelona:* St. Ignatius and One of Two literally

IV—The Saints and Sisters reassembled and reenacting why they went away to stay."

Feb. 24 Highly moving account of an American businessman in Europe is **Sidney Howard's** dramatization of **Sinclair Lewis'** *Dodsworth,* which gave **Walter Huston** a magnificent vehicle for his talent. *Yellow Jack,* in which Howard celebrates scientific advancement, was produced later this year.

1935

Apparently, the gains registered in 1934 had a heady effect on the nation; labor and capital squared off for a no-holds-barred brawl. The New Deal suffered a stunning setback when the Supreme Court declared its cornerstone—the National Recovery Act—unconstitutional. This provided antiadministration forces with effective ammunition which they proceeded to use with vitriolic force, accusing the New Deal of being un-American, Bolshevistic, Communistic, and Socialistic, all in one breath. Rebellions—minor and major—destroyed the unity of the Democratic party line in Congress, making it difficult for Pres. Roosevelt to maintain control of his own supporters. In short, all the vested interests of the nation were engaged in a vicious, crackling feud.

Jan. 29 U.S. Senate refused to ratify American participation in the **World Court** by a vote of 52 to 36, some 7 votes short of the necessary ⅔.

Apr. 27 **Soil Conservation Act** created the Soil Conservation Service as a bureau of the Department of Agriculture.

The conflicting social forces at work were reflected in our literary production. The "proletarian" novel made its restless, angry appearance and found a receptive audience; a left-wing book club was founded. The trend even extended to that most conservative of all arts, the theater. Clifford Odets electrified audiences with his glorification of the "little man." Painters reacted sluggishly, continued to fill untold square feet of government-commissioned canvases with feeble blotches. A few more imaginative artists discovered American "primitivism" through a surprising interest in African Negro art. The government's Federal Music Project sponsored thousands of free concerts, employed some 18,000 musicians.

Pulitzer Prizes: novel, *Now in November* by Josephine Winslow Johnson; drama, *The Old Maid* by Zoë Akins; U.S. history, *The Colonial Period of American History* by Charles McLean Andrews; biography, *R. E. Lee* by Douglas S. Freeman; poetry, *Bright Ambush* by Audrey Wurdemann.

Thomas Wolfe beautifully employed his rich language and sense of pathos in his

SCIENCE; INDUSTRY; ECONOMICS; EDUCATION; RELIGION; PHILOSOPHY.	SPORTS; FASHIONS; POPULAR ENTERTAINMENT; FOLKLORE; SOCIETY.

July 16 Nation's **1st general strike** took place in San Francisco, Calif., as expression of support of 12,000 members of International Longshoremen's Association out on strike.

Oct. 1 Olivet College, Olivet, Mich., gave up all credits, grades, and other elements of traditional university education. Under new plan students were required only to pass general examinations and to be in residence for at least 3 years. Mornings were devoted to private study, group discussions, and individual conferences; afternoons to athletic activities, in which faculty participated; evenings to debates and other intellectual or aesthetic pursuits.

Heavyweight Champion, in the 11th round of a fight held before a crowd of 48,495 in New York city. Max Baer, the new champion, received about $40,000 for his efforts while the deposed champion, Carnera, received $122,000. Carnera, at 6 ft. 6½ in. and 260 lbs., was one of the biggest men ever to hold the Heavyweight Championship.

July 10 American League defeated the National by a score of 9 to 7 in the 2d annual **All-Star Game.** Contest was held in the Polo Grounds in New York city before 48,363 fans.

Oct. 3–9 St. Louis, NL, defeated Detroit, AL, 4–3 in the 31st annual **World Series.**

Dec. 1 Navy defeated Army, 3–0, in the annual **Army-Navy football** game held at Franklin Field, Philadelphia, Pa.

1935

Organized labor was in a furious mood over the Supreme Court's adverse decision on the NRA, and over management's attitude toward what it considered its basic rights. However, all energies could not be directed to the battle at hand, as labor found itself in the midst of a major civil war on the issue of craft unions vs. industrial unions. Chief opponents were John L. Lewis of the newly-organized Committee of Industrial Organizations and William Green, head of the AFL. Crisis was reached when Lewis resigned from the parent group and took his followers with him. Widespread unrest disturbed members of the DAR and the American Legion, who pressed state legislatures to pass laws requiring loyalty oaths from teachers. In all, 19 states put such measures on their books.

Largest salary earned during year in U.S. was that of William Randolph Hearst; 2d largest was Mae West's.

Annual **auto show** in New York city changed from Jan. to Nov. to even out employment and to ease slack winter sea-

Troubled times drew fresh blood into prohibition ranks, and soon many counties found themselves dry again. The highly charged emotional level of the people was reflected in an upsurge of lynchings in the South, a panting, eager interest in the details of the trial of Bruno Hauptmann, kidnapper of the Lindbergh baby. Film makers in Hollywood tried to divert the attention of the public with a raft of spectacular epics such as *Mutiny on the Bounty, A Midsummer Night's Dream, Lives of the Bengal Lancers,* and *A Tale of Two Cities.* At the same time, the industry managed to produce one of the finest films ever shown—*The Informer.* The death of Will Rogers was universally mourned.

Mutiny on the Bounty received the **Academy Award** as the outstanding film of the year. Bette Davis was chosen the best actress of the year for her work in *Dangerous* and Victor McLaglen was chosen best actor for his work in *The Informer.* John Ford was named best director for his direction of *The Informer.* Walt Disney won his 4th consecutive award in the field of the animated cartoon.

505

| POLITICS AND GOVERNMENT; WAR; DISASTERS; VITAL STATISTICS. | BOOKS; PAINTING; DRAMA; ARCHITECTURE; SCULPTURE. |

May 6 **Works Progress Administration** (WPA) instituted under authority of the Emergency Relief Appropriations Act.

May 11 **Rural Electrification Administration** established by Congress to build power lines and finance electricity production in areas not served by private distributors.

May 27 U.S. Supreme Court invalidated the NRA (**National Recovery Act**). The decision implied that any government attempt to legislate prices, wages, working conditions, etc., would be unconstitutional; this followed from the Court's very strict interpretation of "interstate commerce."

July 5 Pres. Roosevelt signed the **National Labor Relations Act** (Wagner-Connery Act). This act established the National Labor Relations Board, an organization that was empowered to determine appropriate collective bargaining units through elections the Board supervised at the request of the workers involved.

Aug. 14 Pres. Roosevelt signed the **Social Security Act** which established a Social Security Board to supervise the payment of old age benefits, such payments determined by the amount of money earned before the 65th birthday of the recipient.

Aug. 26 Pres. Roosevelt signed the **Public Utilities Act** (Wheeler-Rayburn Act). This act required all public utilities to register with the SEC and limited utility holding public corporations to 1st degree, simplest form of incorporation, unless the nature of the enterprise required greater complexity.

Sept. 8 **Huey Long,** powerful demagogue of Louisiana and national politics, shot to death in the corridor of the state capitol in Baton Rouge, La., by Dr. Carl Austin Weiss, Jr., young idealist.

2d novel about Eugene Gant, *Of Time and the River.* Here the young Southerner comes in contact with a huge world outside the South, the cosmopolitan world of New York city with its delights and terrors. In his next novel, *The Web and the Rock,* the city again is thoroughly evoked as a contrast to "the hills of home."

Poet-philosopher **George Santayana** published his only novel, *The Last Puritan,* a moving story of a New Englander whose strong Calvinist leanings cause him to break up when in contact with life.

Fictional study of the effect of environment upon youth is the trilogy, *Studs Lonigan,* by **James T. Farrell.**

Popularity of novelist **John Steinbeck** began with his publication of a collection of short stories called *Tortilla Flat* about the *paisanos* of Monterey.

Social propaganda found expression in **Clifford Odets'** play *Waiting for Lefty,* in which technique of minstrel show is used to launch an indictment against capitalism.

Poignant drama of lower middle class life in the Bronx is **Clifford Odets'** *Awake and Sing,* which made author immediately famous. In the same year Odets has *Till the Day I Die, Paradise Lost,* and *Waiting for Lefty* on New York stage.

Sept. 25 Powerful drama in verse inspired by the Sacco-Vanzetti case is **Maxwell Anderson's** *Winterset,* which tells the story of a boy who gives his life to clear his father's name. Stage set of a dark street under an immense bridge helped create atmosphere of portentous fate. In 1928 Anderson had handled more directly the Sacco-Vanzetti case in *Gods of the Lightning.*

Oct. 10 *Porgy and Bess,* an opera by **George Gershwin** based on the novel *Porgy* by Du Bose and Dorothy Heyward, opened at the Alvin Theater in New York, after a short trial run in Boston. It ran for 16 weeks, followed by a road tour of 3 months; was revived in 1938, 1942, 1952, and 1953; has played in many European opera houses. In 1955 *Porgy and Bess* traveled in Latin America and Russia.

SCIENCE; INDUSTRY; ECONOMICS; EDUCATION; RELIGION; PHILOSOPHY.	SPORTS; FASHIONS; POPULAR ENTERTAINMENT; FOLKLORE; SOCIETY.

son. Automobile manufacturers, this year, began to emphasize style innovations in order to stimulate sales.

Work completed on Federal hospital for narcotic addicts. It was **Public Health Service Hospital** at Leestown Pike, Lexington, Ky.

Automatic propeller that maintained constant engine speed under all conditions developed for use in airplanes.

Renewed national interest in combating **infantile paralysis** spurred by national epidemic and leadership of nation's most distinguished victim, Pres. Roosevelt.

General Federation of Women's Clubs, meeting in Detroit, reversed its stand on **birth control** and endorsed federal law allowing birth-control literature to pass through the mails.

Mar. 22   Gov. Herbert Lehman of New York signed bills to authorize the use of **blood tests** in court cases. Bills approved the introduction of blood types as evidence in criminal or civil cases.

June 10 **Alcoholics Anonymous** organized in New York city.

Aug. 9   Interstate Commerce Commission won jurisdiction over all interstate truck and bus traffic through **Motor Carrier Act** signed by Pres. Roosevelt.

Nov. 9   **CIO** (Congress of Industrial Organizations) established by John L. Lewis from elements expelled from AFL.

National College Football Champion was Southern Methodist. Their record: 12 wins, no losses, no ties.

U.S. lawn tennis men's singles champion, Wilmer L. Allison; **women's singles champion,** Helen Hull Jacobs.

Great Britain defeated the U.S. 5 to 0 in the challenge round of the **Davis Cup** International Matches.

U.S.G.A. amateur championship won by W. Lawson Little, Jr., at C.C. Cleveland, Ohio. He defeated Walter Emery, 4 and 2. **Open championship** won by Sam Parks, Jr. at Oakmont, Pa., C.C. with a score of 299.

Omaha won the 67th annual **Belmont Stakes,** paying 7–10. Jockey was W. Saunders; time was 2:30⅗ on a sloppy track for winnings valued at $35,480.

Omaha won the 59th annual **Preakness Stakes,** paying 9–10. Jockey was W. Saunders; time was 1:58⅗ on a fast track for winnings valued at $25,325.

Jan. 1   Alabama defeated Stanford by a score of 29 to 13 in the 20th annual **Rose Bowl** football game.

May 4   61st annual **Kentucky Derby,** won by Belair Stud's *Omaha* ridden by W. Saunders. He ran the 1¼ mi. in 2:05 on a good track and won $39,525 for his owners. He went on to win the Preakness and the Belmont Stakes and to gain the Triple Crown.

May 24   Reds and Phillies play **1st major league night game** at Crosley Field, Cincinnati, Ohio. Cincinnati 2; Philadelphia 1. Attendance: over 20,000.

June 13 **World's Heavyweight Championship** won by James J. Braddock over Max Baer on points in 15 rounds.

July 8   American League defeated the National by a score of 4 to 1 in the 3d annual **All-Star Game.**

Oct. 2–7   Detroit, AL, defeated Chicago, NL, 4–2 in the 32d annual **World Series.**

Nov. 30 **Army** defeated Navy, 28–6, in their annual contest at Franklin Field, Philadelphia.

507

1936

Despite attacks of the previous year, the administration received a healthy vote of confidence from the electorate as Pres. Roosevelt carried all but 2 states with the largest presidential vote cast up to that time. Democratic ranks closed, and party leaders hailed the advent of "good times." But it was bad times for farmers as another scorching drought created a vast dust bowl, sent thousands westward in search of more fertile land. Die-hard critics of the "New Deal" stressed the fact that there had been a $4 billion increase in public debt, and that, since its election in 1932, the Roosevelt government had swelled the debt by $12 billions. Countering these statistics was the impressive fact that during the same time, the national income had risen by $30 billions.

Mar. 2 Pres. Roosevelt signed **Soil Conservation and Domestic Allotment Act,** replacing the Agricultural Adjustment Act, which had been invalidated Jan. 6 by U.S. Supreme Court. The new measure provided benefit payments to farmers who practiced soil conservation in a cooperative program to withdraw land from use in the production of soil depleting crops, turning this land to soil conserving crops.

Apr. 25–28 **National Convention of the Socialist Labor Party** met at New York city and nominated John W. Aiken of Massachusetts for the presidency and Emil F. Teichert of New York for the vice-presidency.

May 5–7 **National Convention of the Prohibition Party** met at Niagara Falls and nominated Dr. D. Leigh Colvin of New York for the presidency and Sergeant Alvin C. York of Tennessee for the vice-presidency.

May 25 **National Convention of the Socialist Party** met in Cleveland and nominated Norman Thomas of New York for the presidency and George O. Nelson of Wisconsin for the vice-presidency.

The book business boomed, with a remarkable number of titles concerned with political matters. Far and away the most dramatic best seller was Margaret Mitchell's *Gone with the Wind.* The theater enjoyed one of the most distinguished seasons in years, was even more heartened by the founding of the Federal Theater Project under the WPA. As the depression eased, more concerts meant more new works performed, more musicians employed. 5300 artists in 44 states were under employment by the Federal Art Project of the WPA. They painted between 600 and 700 murals for government buildings, countless works in oil and water color. The demand so far outstripped the supply that some artists were turning out a finished work each week.

Pulitzer Prizes: novel, *Honey in the Horn* by Harold L. Davis; drama, *Idiot's Delight* by Robert E. Sherwood; U.S. history, *The Constitutional History of the U.S.* by Andrew C. McLaughlin; biography, *The Thought and Character of William James* by Ralph Barton Perry; poetry, *Strange Holiness* by Robert P. Tristram Coffin.

Impact of War reflected in 3 plays this year, which are strong in bitterness of denunciation: *Johnny Johnson* by **Paul Green** tells of treatment afforded a boy who took slogans of 1917 too seriously; *Bury the Dead* by **Irwin Shaw** is revolutionary in its protest.

Robert Frost adopted vein of moralizing and didacticism in his new book of verse, *A Further Range.* Many poems are to be "taken doubly," the reader being forced to watch for underlying morals. Noteworthy poems in this collection are "A Lone Striker," "The Golden Hesperidee," and "Two Tramps in Mud Time."

Foremost American dramatist **Eugene O'Neill** awarded Nobel Prize for literature.

1936

The nation's commerce was 12–15% higher in dollar totals than the previous year. Farm prices were up; metals were up; production of automobiles increased 20%. However, there were still 8 million unemployed. Labor warfare—against itself and against management—continued to be bitter, as unions discovered a new weapon in the sit-down strike. The education picture looked considerably brighter as fewer schools cried out for federal assistance. Teachers were granted slight increases in salaries; enrollment in lower grades dropped because of the falling birth rate; 35,000 illiterates were taught to read and write by CCC instructors; educators hailed a widespread interest in adult classes.

Nobel Prize in physics presented to **Carl David Anderson** "for the discovery of the positron." The American physicist shared the award with the Austrian scientist, Victor Francis Hess, who was honored "for the discovery of cosmic radiation." Anderson's prize-winning experiments were directly related to those of Hess in that they uncovered new aspects of nuclear physics for future scientists to ponder. Anderson's discovery of the positron confirmed experimentally previous theories about the structure of matter.

Dr. Alexis Carrel, helped by Charles A. Lindbergh, originated **perfusion pump,** called an artificial heart, at Rockefeller Institute, New York city.

The revolt against progressive education in America was led by Pres. **Robert Maynard Hutchins** of Chicago University in his controversial book, *The Higher Learning in America.* Hutchins wished to integrate an education that he believed had dissolved into mere factualism. His ideas never achieved the wide influence of Dewey's in educational circles.

Age of the **trailer** reached full swing. It was estimated that there were 160,000 trailers on the road, and observers on Jan.

More Americans attended athletic events this year than ever before. Football gate receipts were up 15%; there was a great increase in the popularity of basketball when it was included in the roster of Olympic Games for the 1st time. Movies enjoyed their most prosperous year since the depression, even though 4 out of 5 films were called financial failures by their producers. The industry turned out some 500 feature films; exhibitors imported about 200 more from Europe. Technicolor had definitely arrived, but few ventured to use the innovation. Biggest news story of the year was the abdication of King Edward VIII of England because of his love for an American woman, Mrs. Wallis Warfield Simpson.

Academy Awards presented to *The Great Ziegfeld* as the outstanding motion picture of the year, to its star, Luise Rainer as the best actress, and to Paul Muni for his portrayal of the title role in *The Story of Louis Pasteur.* 1st awards for supporting performances were given to Gail Sondergaard in *Anthony Adverse* and Walter Brennan in *Come and Get It.* Walt Disney was honored for the 5th consecutive year in the cartoon category, this time for *Country Cousin.* A special award was granted to the newsreel documentary series, *The March of Time,* "as a distinct novelty."

Expression **"The Nine Old Men"** to characterize the conservative attitude of the Supreme Court during the Roosevelt administration coined by columnists Drew Pearson and Robert Allen.

National Football Champion was, for the 2nd time (1934), Minnesota, coached by Bernie Bierman. Their record: 7 wins, 1 loss, no ties. This was the 1st year that the Associated Press conducted a poll of sports writers who selected 10 top teams in the nation. The No. 1 choice generally regarded as national champion.

POLITICS AND GOVERNMENT; WAR; DISASTERS; VITAL STATISTICS.

BOOKS; PAINTING; DRAMA; ARCHITECTURE; SCULPTURE.

June 9–12 **Republican National Convention,** meeting in Cleveland, unanimously nominated Gov. Alfred M. Landon of Kansas for the presidency. It chose Col. Frank Knox of Illinois for the vice-presidency. The Republicans were supported during their campaign by some conservative Democrats, among them Alfred E. Smith.

June 19 William Lemke of North Dakota announced his candidacy for the presidency on the **Union Party** ticket. Thomas C. O'Brien from Massachusetts was the vice-presidential candidate. Lemke was endorsed by the Rev. Charles E. Coughlin's "National Union for Social Justice," which held its 1st national convention in Cleveland on Aug. 14.

June 23–27 **Democratic National Convention** met in Philadelphia, Pa., and renominated Franklin D. Roosevelt by acclamation for the presidency. It chose John N. Garner for the vice-presidency. In general the platform took its stand on the administration's record. **American Labor Party** endorsed Roosevelt's candidacy.

June 24–28 National convention of the **Communist Party** met at New York city and nominated Earl Browder of Kansas for the presidency and James W. Ford of New York for the vice-presidency.

Nov. 3 Democratic landslide in **presidential election** carried every state except Maine and Vermont for Franklin D. Roosevelt. Congress became more than ¾ Democratic in both houses. Electoral vote: Roosevelt, 523; Landon, 8. Popular vote: Roosevelt, 27,751,612; Landon, 16,687,-913; Lemke, 891,858; Thomas, 187,342; Browder, 80,181; Colvin, 37,609; Aiken, 12,729. The campaign was one of the most bitter in American history. About 80% of the press opposed Roosevelt.

Advent of fascism and nazism and the defeat of loyalist Spain affected American playwrights and accounted for host of political dramas. This year saw **Victor Wolfson's** *Bitter Stream* and **Sinclair Lewis'** *It Can't Happen Here*—both eying European dictatorships with a view of their taking hold in America.

June *Gone With the Wind* by **Margaret Mitchell,** one of the top sellers in American publishing. It sold 1 million in 6 months, and it has probably sold over 3 million in the U.S., surpassing that other best seller, *Uncle Tom's Cabin.* In 1939 the movie version, costing $3,850,000, was released. It takes 3 hr. 45 min. to show, and may have earned $30 million in profits. Clark Gable and Vivien Leigh played the leading roles.

A sparkling comedy of escapism, loaded with eccentric characters and situations, is *You Can't Take It with You* by **George S. Kaufman and Moss Hart.**

On Your Toes, a musical comedy by **Richard Rodgers** and **Lorenz Hart,** was the hit of the Broadway season. The score included the realistic ballet, *Slaughter on Tenth Avenue.*

Novel project undertaken by WPA Federal Theater was presentation of the **Living Newspaper.** With a minimum of plot national and international news was presented dramatically. Prominent sequences were *Ethiopia, Triple-A Plowed Under, Injunction Granted.* In 1938 *One Third of a Nation* underscored housing plight of people.

Dec. 13 Première performance of **Samuel Barber's** First Symphony is given by the Augusteo Orchestra in Rome.

1937

The New Deal was definitely in a transition period. Through familiarity, its measures had lost a great deal of emotional and

The general uncertainty carried over to the nation's creative life, resulting in a limp, unproductive apathy. Federal support

SCIENCE; INDUSTRY; ECONOMICS; EDUCATION; RELIGION; PHILOSOPHY.

SPORTS; FASHIONS; POPULAR ENTERTAINMENT; FOLKLORE; SOCIETY.

1, 1937, counted an average of 25 trailers an hour crossing the state line into Florida. Some, like Roger Babson, predicted that soon half the population of the country would be living in trailers.

Lake Mead Reservoir (dam later renamed Hoover Dam) on the Colorado R. between Arizona and Nevada completed with a total capacity of over 10 trillion gallons of water, or 31,142,000 acre feet, making it the largest reservoir in America. It covers an area of 246 sq. mi.

Jan. 11 Management of General Motors took 1st aggressive action against **sit-down strike** of automobile workers at Fisher Body Plant No. 2, Flint, Mich. The strike was the 1st major sit-down strike in the U.S. Management ordered all heat in the plant buildings turned off, and police tried unsuccessfully to prevent union men on the outside from sending in food. Strikers continued to control the plant.

Feb. 3 National Guard massed to attack workers on **sit-down strike** at Fisher Body Plant No. 2, Flint, Mich., a General Motors company. **Struck workers** had been in control of the plant for several weeks. At the last minute, Walter Knudsen, General Motors head, agreed to recognize the United Automobile Workers and to negotiate for a union contract.

May 9 Airship *Hindenburg* landed at Lakehurst, N.J., after **1st scheduled transatlantic dirigible flight.** Built by German Zeppelin Transport Company, ship was 830 ft. long, 135 ft. in diameter; propelled by 4 1050 hp. Daimler Benz Diesel engines. It had a range of 8000 mi. On May 6, 1937, *Hindenburg* burst into flames while anchoring at Lakehurst, killing 36 persons.

June **S. S. Queen Mary,** from England, arrived in New York on her maiden voyage, the largest liner afloat.

Baseball's Hall of Fame established in Cooperstown, N.Y., by group of baseball leaders. Shrine and museum planned to honor "Immortals" of the game.

Granville won the 68th annual **Belmont Stakes,** paying 16–5. Jockey was J. Stout; time was 2:30 on a fast track for winnings valued at $29,800.

Bold Venture won the 60th annual **Preakness Stakes,** paying 9–5. Jockey was G. Woolf; time was 1:59 on a fast track for winnings valued at $27,325.

U.S. lawn tennis men's singles champion, Frederick J. Perry of England; **women's singles champion,** Alice Marble.

U.S.G.A. amateur championship won by John W. Fischer at Garden City, N.Y., G.C. He defeated Jack McLean, 1 up. **Open championship** won by Tony Manero at Baltusrol G.C., Short Hills, N.J., by a score of 282.

Jan. 1 Stanford defeated Southern Methodist by a score of 7 to 0 in the 21st annual **Rose Bowl** football game.

May 2 *Bold Venture* won the 62d annual **Kentucky Derby,** at Churchill Downs, Louisville, Ky., running the 1¼ mi. in 2:03⅗ on a fast track and winning $37,725 for its owner, M. I. Schwartz. Jockey was A. Hanford.

July 7 National League defeated the American by a score of 4 to 1 in the 4th annual **All-Star Game.** Contest was held in Boston before 25,556 fans and marked the 1st National League victory in this event after 3 defeats.

Sept. 30–Oct. 6 New York, AL, defeated New York, NL, 4–2 in the 33d annual **World Series.**

Nov. 28 Navy defeated Army, 7–0, in the annual **Army-Navy football game** held at Municipal Stadium, Philadelphia, Pa.

1937

Labor placed the administration in the awkward position of having to choose sides between warring factions. However,

While the government adopted no official position in the Spanish Civil War, the public took the conflict very much to heart,

511

dramatic impact. As administration forces tried to press on, more and more voices were raised against the program. Economic and political disputes rippled across the nation, aggravated to a degree by the unpleasant events in Europe and an uncertainty as how to handle them. It was a period of uneasy waiting; the depression had been conquered, the next step was not clear.

Feb. 5 After informing Congressional leaders at a special cabinet meeting in the morning, Pres. Roosevelt sent a message to Congress at noon recommending a revision of statutes governing the federal judiciary. Although the recommended revisions were ostensibly to provide more efficient and younger judges in all federal courts, it was charged that Roosevelt's chief aim was to "pack" the **Supreme Court,** which in the past had invalidated several important parts of the New Deal legislative program.

Mar. 1 Surprise announcement made that John L. Lewis, CIO head, and Myron Taylor, chairman of the board of United States Steel Corporation, had reached an agreement for the recognition of the **United Mine Workers.**

Mar. 1 Pres. Roosevelt signed the **Reciprocal Trade Agreement Act** which extended to June, 1940, the period in which he could negotiate foreign trade agreements under the provisions of the Trade Agreements Act of 1934.

May 1 Pres. Roosevelt signed **Neutrality Act** which prohibited the export of arms and ammunition to belligerent nations. Act also prohibited the sale of the securities of belligerent nations in the U.S. Act further prohibited the use of American ships for carrying munitions and military equipment into belligerent zones, insisting that all belligerents pay for certain specified non-military goods upon purchase and convey their purchases on their own ships.

of the arts served merely to keep its practitioners alive and working. Architects debated the merits of functional design, drew much of their inspiration from builders abroad.

Pulitzer Prizes: novel, *Gone with the Wind* by Margaret Mitchell; drama, *You Can't Take It With You* by Moss Hart and George S. Kaufman; U.S. history, *The Flowering of New England* by Van Wyck Brooks; biography, *Hamilton Fish* by Allan Nevins; poetry, *A Further Range* by Robert Frost.

Harlem River Houses, one of 1st public housing projects in New York, built from designs by many architects. They were 4- and 5-story walkups strung together.

Lincoln Tunnel, crossing Hudson R. at 38 St., in New York, built to supplement earlier Holland Tunnel. 2d tube added in 1945.

Pulitzer Prize winning novel (1938) of the decline of Boston's aristocracy was **John P. Marquand's** *The Late George Apley.* Told in the form of a memoir, it traces the history of a few generations, showing the impact of new immigration upon an older society.

John Steinbeck published his novelette of violence and pathos, *Of Mice and Men,* story of 2 farm hands and a girl. Distributed by the Book-of-the-Month Club, it became a great success. Shortly afterward dramatized, it had a long run on stage and screen.

Powerful novel employing new fictional devices is *U.S.A.* by **John Dos Passos.** Combining 3 earlier works: *The 42nd Parallel* (1930), *1919* (1932), and *The Big Money* (1936), he gives a vast picture of the U.S. and parts of Europe, showing how social forces work upon the lives of his characters. Use of "newsreel" and "camera eye" is an experimental feature of book.

Dramatic fantasy *High Tor* by **Maxwell**

SCIENCE; INDUSTRY; ECONOMICS; EDUCATION; RELIGION; PHILOSOPHY.

SPORTS; FASHIONS; POPULAR ENTERTAINMENT; FOLKLORE; SOCIETY.

despite internal difficulties, significant successes were won by unions in their efforts to organize companies and industries that had never before recognized them.

Nobel Prize in physics shared by **Clinton Joseph Davisson** and **Sir George Paget Thomson** "for the experimental discovery of the interference phenomenon in crystals irradiated by electrons." Joseph Davisson was born in Bloomington, Ill., on Oct. 22, 1881 and conducted most of his prizewinning experiments in the Bell Laboratories in New York. Thomson, a British physicist, conducted his own separate experiments on the interference phenomenon in crystals but emerged with much the same conclusions as did Davisson.

Golden Gate Bridge, San Francisco, Calif., dedicated.

National Cancer Institute founded.

Dr. E. C. Rosenow of Mayo Clinic announced that experiments leading to the development of a serum to prevent crippling effects of **infantile paralysis** were being carried on. Experiments were based on recent discovery that disease was caused by a transformed streptococcus germ.

New approach to **mental illness** revealed in Karen Horney's *The Neurotic Personality of Our Time,* which stressed cultural factors in place of the traditional factors of heredity.

During winter of 1936–37 more than 500,000 workers quit their jobs in wave of **industrial unrest;** many engaged in new, illegal **sitdown strikes.**

Mar. 29 **Minimum wage law for women** upheld by U.S. Supreme Court in decision of *West Coast Hotel v. Parrish.* The judgment reversed 2 previous rulings.

Apr. 12 **National Labor Relations Act** of 1935 upheld by U.S. Supreme Court.

May Government estimates showed nearly half a million **sitdown strikers** in U.S. since September, 1936.

May 6 Herbert Morrison conducted **1st Atlantic to Pacific radio program,** broadcasting his description of the landing and

offering a highly emotional support of the Loyalist side. American volunteers by the hundreds transported themselves to Spain where they joined the anti-Franco armies. There seemed to be a general need to repudiate the influence of fascism, and many Americans turned to foreign ideologies to find expression for this need. Membership in the Communist Party became, for many, not only a political duty, but a social obligation.

Arbitrary phrase **"I am the law"** became associated with Mayor Frank Hague of Jersey City. When questioned as to his right to prevent picketing on the street, he invoked the dictatorial phrase.

Academy Awards presented to *The Life of Emile Zola* as the outstanding film production of the year, to Luise Rainer as the best actress for her performance in *The Good Earth,* and to Spencer Tracy as the best actor for his portrayal in *Captains Courageous.* Alice Brady was named best supporting actress for her work in *In Old Chicago,* and Joseph Schildkraut was honored as best supporting actor for his performance in *The Life of Emile Zola.* Walt Disney received his 6th consecutive award for his cartoon, *The Old Mill.*

National football champion was Pittsburgh, coached by John Sutherland. Their record: 9 wins, no losses, no ties.

War Admiral won the 61st annual **Preakness Stakes,** paying 7–20. Jockey was C. Kurtsinger; time was 1:58⅖ on a good track for winnings valued at $45,600.

War Admiral won the 69th annual **Belmont Stakes,** paying 9–10. Jockey was C. Kurtsinger; time was 2:28⅗ on a fast track for winnings valued at $38,020.

U.S. defeated Britain 4 to 1 in the challenge round of the **Davis Cup** International Matches.

U.S. lawn tennis men's singles champion, J. Donald Budge; **women's singles champion,** Anita Lizana of Chile.

U.S.G.A. amateur championship won by Johnny Goodman at Alderwood G.C., Portland, Ore. He defeated Ray Billows, 2 up. **Open championship** won by Ralph

This became popularly known as the "cash and carry" clause.

July 22 Congress finally voted to return the **"Supreme Court bill"** to Committee, which in effect killed it. In the meantime, Justice Van Devanter had resigned from the Supreme Court, allowing Roosevelt to appoint a liberal justice (Hugo L. Black, appointed Aug. 12) and swing the balance in favor of New Deal.

July 22 Bankhead-Jones Act passed by Congress to establish the **Farm Security Administration.** The FSA was empowered to make 40-year loans at 3% to aid farm tenants, sharecroppers, and laborers.

Aug 26 Pres. Roosevelt signed the **Judicial Procedure Reform Act** which permitted Supreme Court justices and other federal judges to retire voluntarily and with full pension at the age of 70.

Sept. 2 Pres. Roosevelt signed the **National Housing** (Wagner-Steagall) **Act,** which created the U.S. Housing Authority for the purpose of administering loans to small communities and states for rural and urban construction.

Dec. 12 U.S. gunboat **Panay** sunk in Chinese waters by Japanese planes.

Anderson recounts in verse the strange visitations to a mountaintop overlooking the Hudson: bank robbers, criminal lawyers, ghosts of sailors of the *Half Moon,* etc.

Epoch-making event in history and rising prestige of radio occurred with signing of **Arturo Toscanini** as the conductor of the NBC Symphony Orchestra, created for him.

I'd Rather Be Right, a musical comedy satirizing Pres. Roosevelt, produced on Broadway with enormous success. The libretto was by **George Kaufman** and **Moss Hart;** the score by **Richard Rodgers** and **Lorenz Hart.**

Aug. 27 Premiere performance of **Aaron Copland**'s *El Salón Méjico* given in Mexico City.

Nov. Drama which illuminates the tragedy of American success drive is **Clifford Odets'** *Golden Boy*—the gifted Italian boy who deserts music for the quicker rewards of the prize ring.

Nov. 27 **Pins and Needles,** produced by Labor Stage, Inc., a group of garment workers, opened in New York. It became widely successful and broke all records for musical comedies. Its catchiest tune was "Sing Me a Song of Social Significance."

1938

A return of economic adversity led to an increase in government spending. This eased the situation a little, but led to a certain disillusionment with the New Deal. Congressional elections saw a sudden influx of Republican senators and representatives. However, the center of government activity and concern was swinging slowly in the direction of foreign affairs. The menace in Europe was evident, and for the 1st time, isolationism vs. limited intervention became an active national issue. There was widespread nervousness about the possibility of war, but few believed it likely.

Jan. 10 House of Representatives re-

It was an active year for both performing and creative arts, although little of distinction was produced. Authors rediscovered the historical novel and flooded the market with examples. Organization of 2 World Fairs, scheduled the following year at New York city and San Francisco, sent architects to their drawing boards and artists to their easels. Commissions were made subject to competition, and so the level of work done was somewhat more imaginative than it had been over the past few years.

Pulitzer Prizes: novel, *The Late George Apley* by John Phillips Marquand; drama, *Our Town* by Thornton Wilder; U.S. his-

SCIENCE; INDUSTRY; ECONOMICS; EDUCATION; RELIGION; PHILOSOPHY.	SPORTS; FASHIONS; POPULAR ENTERTAINMENT; FOLKLORE; SOCIETY.

explosion of dirigible *Hindenburg* at Lakehurst, N.J.

May 12 Broadcast of the coronation of King George VI was the **1st worldwide radio broadcast** heard in U.S.

May 24 Social Security Act of 1935 upheld by U.S. Supreme Court.

May 30 Workers striking against the Republic Steel Corporation in South Chicago, Ill., battled police. 10 strikers were killed and many more injured. Clash reflected bitter **labor-management controversies** in certain industries.

June 8 World's largest flower bloomed in the New York Botanical Gardens. It was the *Amorphophallus titanum* or giant calla lily, whose native home is Sumatra. The flower was 8½ ft. high, 4 ft. in diameter, and 12 ft. in circumference.

Aug. 1st signs of a **new business recession** became apparent in a selling wave on the stock markets. The retreat became sharper after Labor Day, and many stocks fell rapidly and far. On Oct. 19, the New York market was near demoralization, with total transactions of 7,290,000 shares —the largest since 1933.

Sept. 28 Bonneville Dam, Columbia R., Ore., officially dedicated by Pres. Roosevelt.

Guldahl at Oakland Hills C.C., Birmingham, Mich., with a score of 281.

Jan. 1 Pittsburgh defeated Washington by a score of 21 to 0 in the 22d annual **Rose Bowl** football game.

May 8 The Glen Riddle Farm's great champion, *War Admiral,* son of Man o' War, won the 63d annual **Kentucky Derby** at Churchill Downs, Louisville, Ky., May 8. His time was 2:03⅕ on a fast track and he won $52,050 under jockey C. Kurtsinger. *War Admiral* went on to win the Triple Crown.

June 22 World Heavyweight Boxing Championship won by Joe Louis, who knocked out James J. Braddock in 8th round at Chicago, on June 22. Louis was 2d Negro to hold title.

July 7 American League defeated the National by a score of 8 to 3 in the 5th annual **All-Star Game.** Contest was held in Washington before 31,391 fans and marked the 4th victory for the American League in 5 contests.

Oct. 6–10 New York, AL, defeated New York, NL, 4–1 in the 34th annual **World Series.**

Nov. 27 Army defeated Navy, 6–0, in the annual **Army-Navy football game** held at Municipal Stadium, Philadelphia, Pa.

1938

Heartened by government support, business conditions at the year's end were definitely healthier than at the start. Labor forces won 2 rousing victories—passage of the maximum hours and minimum wages bill and a long-sought measure that prohibited child labor in interstate industries. Isolated sitdown strikes still plagued industry, but public opinion seemed to swing against these tactics, so the unions stopped them entirely. Technological advances were steady; scientists everywhere were busy probing the nature and behavior of the atom.

Games Slayter and John H. Thomas of

Financially as well artistically, the motion picture industry suffered one of the worst years in its short history. Movie houses across the country reported a drop in attendance of about 40%. In desperation, film makers tried to entice the public with overblown spectaculars and remakes of past successes. Top money maker of the year was Walt Disney's *Snow White and the Seven Dwarfs,* the full-length animated color cartoon that made its creator a familiar name the world over.

Academy Awards presented to *You Can't Take It With You* as the outstanding film production of the year, to Bette Davis as the best actress for her portrayal

POLITICS AND GOVERNMENT; WAR; DISASTERS; VITAL STATISTICS.

BOOKS; PAINTING; DRAMA; ARCHITECTURE; SCULPTURE.

turned the **Ludlow Resolution** to committee. The resolution, calling for a **national referendum** to decide when and whether Congress should declare war, was a recurrent petition of Louis Ludlow, Representative from Indiana, who 1st sponsored the resolution.

Jan. 28 Pres. Roosevelt asked Congress for appropriations for building up **Army** and **Navy.** Naval expansion covered a 10-year period and included protection in both Pacific and Atlantic Oceans. It was provided for in the **Naval Expansion Act of 1938** passed on May 17.

Feb. 16 Pres. Roosevelt signed the second **Agricultural Adjustment Act,** which maintained the soil conservation program, provided acreage allotments, parity payments, marketing quotas, and commodity loans to farmers, and authorized crop insurance corporations and the "ever-normal granary" proposals of Henry A. Wallace, Secretary of Agriculture.

Mar. 2 **144 deaths** caused by floods and landslides in southern California. Thousands of homes destroyed. Nearly $60,000,000 in property lost.

Mar. 30 **Tornado** in Midwest killed 36 and caused widespread destruction. All but 2 buildings in South Rekin, Ill. (pop. 1500) were demolished.

Mar. 31 Herbert Hoover advised U.S. not to enter into **alliances** with openly antifascist European democracies since this course might lead to war. This was in part an answer to Pres. Roosevelt's speech of Oct. 5, 1937, in which Roosevelt urged collective international sanctions against aggressors. Public opinion did not go so far in respect to international co-operation as Roosevelt suggested.

May 17 **Billion dollar naval expansion,** to increase tonnage of major ships, cruisers, and carriers, over a 10 year period, provided for by the Vinson Naval act.

May 26 Formation of **House Committee to Investigate Un-American Activities** (Dies Committee). Martin Dies of Texas was its chairman.

tory, *The Road to Reunion, 1865–1900* by Paul Herman Buck; biography, *Pedlar's Progress* by Odell Shepard. *Andrew Jackson* by Marquis James; poetry, *Cold Morning Sky* by Marya Zaturenska.

Richard Wright's stories *Uncle Tom's Children* 1st published. In 1939 he won a Guggenheim fellowship and the Spingarn medal. One of the most important American Negro authors.

Scholarly and realistic dramatization of a great man's life is **Robert Sherwood's** *Abe Lincoln in Illinois,* awarded the Pulitzer Prize in 1939. Lincoln is presented as a man unsure of himself, unhappy and wavering. It is the firm will and purpose of Mary Todd which launches him on his career of greatness.

The lives, loves, deaths, and the pattern of life in a small New England village form the basis for *Our Town,* a thoughtful fantasy play by **Thornton Wilder.** Set on a bare stage, play makes use of a stage manager who moves pieces and people around at will.

William Faulkner published *The Unvanquished.*

James Branch Cabell wrote *The King Was in His Counting-House.*

Elizabeth Madox Roberts wrote her novel *Black Is My Truelove's Hair.*

Sinclair Lewis published *The Prodigal Parents.*

Robert Benchley kept them laughing with *After 1903—What?*

Ernest Hemingway wrote *The Fifth Column* and popularized the phrase which makes the title to his play.

The Selected Poetry of Robinson Jeffers published.

516

| SCIENCE; INDUSTRY; ECONOMICS; EDUCATION; RELIGION; PHILOSOPHY. | SPORTS; FASHIONS; POPULAR ENTERTAINMENT; FOLKLORE; SOCIETY. |

Newark, Ohio, perfected methods to manufacture **glass wool** or **fiberglass.**

John Dewey published *Logic: The Theory of Inquiry.*

John Dewey published *Experience and Education.*

Alfred North Whitehead published *Modes of Thought.*

George Santayana published *The Realm of Truth,* 4th volume of *The Realms of Being.* The other 3 volumes in the series were *The Realm of Essence* (1927), *The Realm of Matter* (1930), and *The Realm of Spirit* (1940).

Albert Einstein and **Leopold Infeld** published *The Evolution of Physics,* the most outstanding and lucid exposition of the history of physics.

Lewis Mumford published *The Culture of Cities,* a monumental study in the relationships between technology and culture, from the point of view of the changes in human life which were made necessary by the development of cities.

General Anthropology edited by **Franz Boas.**

Stuart Chase made "semantics" a household word with *The Tyranny of Words,* a study based on the work of **Ogden** and **Richards,** and **Korzybski.**

Patents for **nylon,** the pioneer synthetic, or "miracle," fabric, were issued. Commercial production began immediately. Du Pont manufactured toothbrushes with nylon bristles, the 1st nylon product marketed.

The long history of the development of the **combine,** which cuts, threshes, and cleans the grain while moving steadily across the field, gained another important chapter with the introduction of the **self-propelled combine.** Since 1935, the tractor driven combine had come into general use in America. The next step, the elimination of the tractor, was taken in 1938. Self-propelled combines, which come in different sizes, increased the adaptability of the combine and became a major factor in

of *Jezebel,* to Spencer Tracy as best actor for his performance in *Boys Town.* Fay Bainter was named best supporting actress for her performance in *Jezebel* and Walter Brennan was honored for his performance in *Kentucky.* George Bernard Shaw received an award for his screenplay for *Pygmalion.* Walt Disney was honored for the 7th consecutive year in the cartoon category, this time for his version of *Ferdinand the Bull.*

The National Safety Council recorded more than 32,000 **deaths in automobile accidents** for the year. About ⅓ of the fatalities involved pedestrians. Almost 9,000 deaths resulted from collisions between motor vehicles.

This year's **national college football champion** was Texas Christian, coached by Leo Meyer. Their record: 10 wins, no losses, no ties.

The Lambeth Walk became popular on American musical stages and dance floors although it had been performed as far back as 1909 by a dancer named Daphne Pollard.

U.S.G.A. amateur championship won by Willie Turnesa at Oakmont, Pa., C.C. He defeated B. Patrick Abbott, 8 and 7. **Open championship** won by Ralph Guldahl at Cherry Hills Club, Englewood, Colo., with a score of 284.

U.S. lawn tennis men's singles champion, J. Donald Budge; **women's singles champion,** Alice Marble.

U.S. defeated Australia 3 to 2 in the challenge round of the **Davis Cup** International Matches.

Pasteurized won the 70th annual **Belmont Stakes,** paying 8–1. Jockey was J. Stout; time was 2:29⅗ on a fast track for winnings valued at $34,530.

June 23 **Civil Aeronautics Act** approved. Act established the Civil Aeronautics Authority to supervise nonmilitary air transport in U.S.

June 24 **Wheeler-Lea Act** supplanted **Pure Food Act of 1906,** introducing more stringent regulation of foods, drugs and cosmetics.

June 25 Pres. Roosevelt signed the **Wage and Hours Act** which raised the minimum wage for workers engaged in interstate commerce from 25¢ to 40¢ an hour. Hours were limited to 44 per week the 1st year, to 40 after the 3d. Congress declared that it possessed the power in this act to ban the shipment in interstate commerce of products made by the unlawful exploitation of child labor.

July 17 Unable to obtain flight exit permit to Europe, Douglas G. Corrigan landed in Dublin and claimed that he had headed for California. Despite his illegal action **"Wrong-way Corrigan"** became a national hero.

Sept. 21 Tropical **hurricane** struck without warning in New England, taking an estimated 460 lives. Property damage estimated at $150 million.

Sept. 26 **President Roosevelt** sent **private memoranda** to Britain, France, Germany, and Czechoslovakia, recommending that the Sudetenland crisis, brought on by the German nationals in the Sudetenland, be arbitrated. The stage was now set for the accomplishment of the Munich Pact. Step by step, the German propaganda machine had won every major point. With assurance that all of the world wanted peace, Hitler prepared for the culminating, and most cynical, of his manoeuvres. Within a week after the Roosevelt notes went out, Hitler made a personal tour of the Czechoslovakian Sudetenland, and inspected the territory that had effectively been added to his domain.

Sept. 30 **Munich Agreement** signed by Hitler (Germany), Mussolini (Italy), Chamberlain (Great Britain), and Daladier (France). The Sudetenland and all important Czech military strongholds were

Selected Poems, by **John Gould Fletcher** published.

Land of the Free, a book of poetry by **Archibald MacLeish,** published.

Bestselling novel exploiting suspense and atmosphere is **Daphne Du Maurier's** *Rebecca,* the story of a 2d wife living in an English mansion haunted by memories of her husband's 1st wife. A Hollywood version of the story met with great success.

Comedy of adolescence made popular by Clifford Goldsmith in *What a Life,* where lovable character of **Henry Aldrich** is introduced.

Estimates showed that the **Music Appreciation Hour,** a program conducted by Walter Damrosch over a national radio network, was heard by 7,000,000 school children each week.

Modern master of sculpture in low relief is **Adolph Alexander Weinman.** Rhythm, stylization, a feeling of 3-dimensionality are conveyed beautifully in the doors he executed for the American Academy of Arts and Letters Building. Other works are the panels for the Morgan Library and the façade of the Municipal Building in New York.

Haggerty House, 1st work done in U.S. by **Walter Gropius** and **Marcel Breuer,** built in Cohasset, Mass.

The Cloisters, a branch of New York's Metropolitan Museum of Art, built at Ft. Tryon Park in upper Manhattan to house works of medieval art. Building incorporates parts of 5 different French cloisters ranging from the 12th to 15th centuries.

Dramatic fantasy bitter in tone and of cosmic proportions is **Philip Barry's** *Here Come the Clowns,* the story of a collection of assorted people in the Café des Artistes who work in a vaudeville show operated by James Concannen (who represents God). Their questionings, miseries, illusions, etc., are presented.

SCIENCE; INDUSTRY; ECONOMICS; EDUCATION; RELIGION; PHILOSOPHY.	SPORTS; FASHIONS; POPULAR ENTERTAINMENT; FOLKLORE; SOCIETY.

meeting the enormous food demands of the 2nd World War.

Nov. The Coast Artillery, then a branch of the U.S. Army, conducted exhaustive tests of the **radar system** which had been evolved by the Signal Corps in 1936. The Secretary of War had witnessed a special demonstration of the invention at Fort Monmouth in 1937.

Howard Hughes won the *International Harmon Trophy* for his flight around the world in the record time of 3 days, 19 hours, 14 minutes.

Civil Aeronautics Authority established as independent agency of federal government. Authority regulates the licensing of civil pilots, use of airways, rules of flight, development of new equipment for flying, etc.

Mar. The **stock market "Recession"** reached its lowest point. Most of the leaders had fallen 50 points or more since the preceding August. The Federal Reserve Board's Adjusted Index of Industrial Production fell to 76. On Apr. 14 Pres. Roosevelt asked Congress for additional aid to stimulate business recovery. This resulted in the **Emergency Relief Appropriation Act** of June 21.

Apr. 12 New York was 1st state to require **medical tests for marriage license applicants.** Measure, known as the Desmond-Breitbart law, was passed to prevent spread of syphilis. Law requiring all pregnant women to take blood test was passed on Mar. 13.

May 27 **Revenue Bill of 1938** passed by Congress on grounds that tax concessions were needed to stimulate business. It affected the taxes on corporations and was supported by growing opposition, both Republican and Democratic, to the New Deal.

Oct. 9 New $3¼ million **international bridge** between Port Huron, Mich., and Point Edward, Ont., Canada, over St. Clair R. dedicated.

Oct. 13 **William Green** re-elected president of the **AFL.** In his inaugural address,

Dauber won the 62d annual **Preakness Stakes,** paying 3–2. Jockey was M. Peters; time was 1:59⅖ on a sloppy track for winnings valued at $51,875.

Jan. 1 California defeated Alabama 13 to 0 in the **Rose Bowl** before a crowd of 90,000.

May 7 An 86–10 long shot, H. M. Woolf's **Lawrin** won the 64th annual **Kentucky Derby.** He ran the 1¼ mi. in 2:04⅘ on a fast track and won $47,050. He was ridden by Eddie Arcaro, who was to become one of modern racing's best and most popular jockeys.

July 6 National League defeated the American by a score of 4 to 1 in the 6th annual **All-Star Game.** Contest was held in Cincinnati before 27,067 fans.

Oct. 5–9 New York, AL, defeated Chicago, NL, 4–0 in the 35th annual **World Series.**

Oct. 30 **Orson Welles** staged his radio play "Invasion from Mars," based on H. G. Wells' *The War of the Worlds.* It caused widespread panic when listeners assumed his radio news reports of the invasion were true.

Nov. 2 **President Roosevelt** wrote to **King George VI** of England to express his pleasure that the projected **visit of the King and Queen** to Canada and the U.S. was now a certainty. He made suggestions for possible routes and schedules, and added some words of advice about what the American people would expect of their royal guests. He cautioned the King that the "essential democracy" of the royal couple would be the thing most likely to appeal to Americans. In particular, he urged the homely touch of a visit with the Roosevelts at Hyde Park. He outlined stopovers in Washington, New York, and Chicago, as well as at Hyde Park, but he did not think that it would be wise for the King and Queen to drive through the

POLITICS AND GOVERNMENT; WAR; DISASTERS; VITAL STATISTICS.	BOOKS; PAINTING; DRAMA; ARCHITECTURE; SCULPTURE.

yielded to Germany in an attempt to avoid European war. A Gallup poll taken in Oct. showed most Americans approved this appeasement.

Nov. 14–18 A sign of heightened international tension was the **recall of the American ambassador** to Germany for a conference in Washington. 4 days later, Hans Dieckhoff, German ambassador to the U.S., was recalled to Germany.

Dec. 6 Anthony Eden in a radio address in New York city warned Americans that the democracies shared common goals and faced common perils. Eden had recently resigned as British Minister of Foreign Affairs in a publicized policy disagreement with Prime Minister Neville Chamberlain, who had just signed Munich Agreement.

Amelia Goes to the Ball, a 1-act *opera buffa* composed by **Gian-Carlo Menotti** while he was a student at the Curtis Institute of Music in Philadelphia, produced by the Metropolitan Opera Company in New York.

Apr. 8 **Walter Piston's** First Symphony presented by the Boston Symphony Orchestra, the composer himself conducting.

May *The Incredible Flutist,* a ballet score by **Walter Piston,** performed by the Boston "Pops" Orchestra. The performance was a considerable success, and the ballet became Piston's best-known work.

1939

Prosperity, indeed, seemed just around the corner. Unfortunately, most of it was due to the tremendous volume of war orders that flooded the nation's factories. In any event, the administration could concentrate, for the 1st time, on the problems engendered by the approaching catastrophe in Europe. All sides agreed that war was unthinkable, but realized it was now inevitable. The principal question was how we were going to stay out of it. A policy of strict neutrality would have run counter to public feeling, which was strongly anti-German and anti-Italian; intervention would involve us. The debate ran its course as we, who had the power, refused to exercise it.

Jan. 12 **$535 million defense program** for next 2 years recommended by Pres. Roosevelt in a special message to Congress.

Mar. 14 **German forces invaded Czechoslovakia.**

June 8 **King George VI and Queen Elizabeth** of Great Britain arrived in Washington, D.C. They were the 1st British sov-

Our novelists were taking a long, fond look back on our nation's past. American historical novels were never so plentiful. The theater mourned the passing of the Federal Theater Project, but rejoiced in a sudden rebirth of interest in the legitimate stage. A shortage of New York city playhouses was felt for the 1st time. Painters seemed to be exploring 2 areas: the regional "American scene" which stressed people in relation to their land or locale; and a sudden discovery that art was a telling weapon in the hands of the social satirist and political propagandist.

Pulitzer Prizes: novel, *The Yearling* by Marjorie Kinnan Rawlings; drama, *Abe Lincoln in Illinois* by Robert E. Sherwood; U.S. history, *A History of American Magazines* by Frank Luther Mott; biography, *Benjamin Franklin* by Carl Van Doren; poetry, *Selected Poems* by John Gould Fletcher.

Great novel of social protest is **John Steinbeck's** saga of the "Oakies," *The Grapes of Wrath.* Here is the story of the migratory workers of Oklahoma who move into the groves of California, their plight, their misuse, their exploitation.

The **hit musical** of the Broadway season

SCIENCE; INDUSTRY; ECONOMICS; EDUCATION; RELIGION; PHILOSOPHY.	SPORTS; FASHIONS; POPULAR ENTERTAINMENT; FOLKLORE; SOCIETY.

Pres. Green asked the CIO to "return home" to the parent organization.

Oct. 27 Mayor **Frank Hague** of Jersey City, N.J., enjoined to grant **CIO** organizers their civil liberties. Action was taken by federal court.

Nov. 18 Newly formed Congress of Industrial Organizations, successor to **Committee for Industrial Organization,** elected **John L. Lewis** as its 1st president at meeting held in Pittsburgh, Pa.

Dec. 13 WPA administration announced that 2,122,960 were on **federal relief** as compared with 3,184,000 the previous year.

"narrow, crowded" streets of New York or Chicago.

Nov. 26 **Army** defeated Navy, 14–7, in their annual contest at Municipal Stadium, Philadelphia.

Dec. 11 New York Giants defeated Green Bay Packers 23–17 at New York city for the **National Professional Football Championship.**

1939

Business went through 3 distinct stages: (1) a gradual decline from 1938 levels; (2) an equally gradual recovery; and (3) a spectacular upsurge in the fall, attributable, of course, to the outbreak of war in Europe. By far the biggest news story of the year, although it received scant attention in the papers, was the announcement that scientists had succeeded in splitting uranium, thorium, and protactinium by means of a bombardment of neutrons.

Nobel Prize in physics presented to **Ernest Orlando Lawrence** "for the discovery and development of the cyclotron, and for the results obtained by its aid, especially with regard to artificially radioactive elements." Lawrence, born in Canton, S.D., performed his prize-winning experiments at the University of California. Lawrence's invention of the cyclotron provided nuclear scientists with an invaluable instrument with which to manufacture the heavy particles, alpha particles, protons, deuterons, important in the study of nuclear reactions.

Significant discovery of **Rh factor** in human blood by Dr. Philip Levine and Dr. Rufus Stetson of New York led to a clearer understanding of pregnancy and transfu-

The 2 World Fairs in New York city and San Francisco opened, and millions flocked to the expositions to get a glimpse of the wonders of the future. Astute observers noted the unreality of the enthusiasm, commenting wryly on the war in Europe that would soon engulf the world. However, everyone ignored these prophets of doom, instead lined up to take "death-defying" rides on the roller coaster, the parachute jump. With their European markets vanishing, film producers faced a bleak future, retrenched with a stringent economy wave. Even so, they managed to film one of the most expensive and successful pictures of all time, *Gone With the Wind.*

Academy Awards presented to *Gone With the Wind* as the best motion picture of the year, to Vivien Leigh, its star, as the best actress, and to Robert Donat as the best actor for his portrayal in *Goodbye, Mr. Chips.* Hattie McDaniel was named best supporting actress for her performance in *Gone With the Wind* and Thomas Mitchell was chosen best supporting actor for his portrayal in *Stagecoach.* Walt Disney was honored for the 8th consecutive year

| POLITICS AND GOVERNMENT; WAR; DISASTERS; VITAL STATISTICS. | BOOKS; PAINTING; DRAMA; ARCHITECTURE; SCULPTURE. |

ereigns to visit U.S. They remained 5 days, June 7–12.

July 1 Pres. Franklin D. Roosevelt established the **Federal Works Agency** as a consolidation of 5 existing agencies: Public Buildings Administration, Public Roads Administration, Public Works Administration, Works Projects Administration, and the U.S. Housing Authority.

Aug. 24 News of the **German-Russian nonaggression pact** reached U.S. newspapers. It was signed Aug. 23.

Sept. 1 **German armies invade Poland** without declaration of war. On Aug. 24 Pres. Roosevelt had cabled Germany, Poland, and Italy, urging arbitration, conciliation, or negotiation to avoid war. On Sept. 3 Great Britain and France declared war on Germany; on same day Belgium declared her neutrality and Pres. Roosevelt, in "fireside" chat, declared U.S. neutral.

Sept. 3 **30 Americans drowned** as British passenger ship, *Athenia*, sunk by submarine. The following day, Secretary of State Cordell Hull advised Americans to travel to Europe only under "imperative necessity."

Sept. 21 Congress, in special session convened by Pres. Roosevelt, urged by the President to repeal arms embargo provision of Neutrality Act of 1937. On Nov. 4 **Neutrality Act of 1939** was passed repealing prohibition of arms export and authorizing "cash and carry" sale of arms to belligerent powers.

Oct. 18 All **U.S. ports and waters**

was *Du Barry Was a Lady*, with music by Cole Porter.

Eve of new World War saw host of antifascist plays. *Key Largo* by **Maxwell Anderson** sees failure on part of intellectual to build up moral ideals; *The American Way* by **Kaufman and Hart** traces in cavalcade fashion life of a German immigrant couple in America; **Irwin Shaw's** *Gentle People* symbolically deals with "fascism" in Brooklyn; *Thunder Rock* by **Robert Ardrey** speaks out against self-isolation from world.

Popular writer of fantasy for the stage is **William Saroyan,** who began his dramatic career with *My Heart's in the Highlands*. Play collects a host of eccentrics in a Fresno house, who seem to interact in a strange and moving formlessness. *The Time of Your Life* (1939) collects the characters of Nick's saloon in San Francisco. *Love's Old Sweet Song* (1940) is a satire of the popular feeling for the Oakies. *The Beautiful People* (1941) tells the wistful tale of a poor family in California.

Highly successful comedy depicting life in a Victorian household is *Life with Father* by **Howard Lindsay** and **Russel Crouse.** Play is based on sketches written by Clarence Day, Jr., for the *New Yorker* magazine.

Johnson Wax Company administration building constructed at Racine, Wis., from plans by **Frank Lloyd Wright,** probably Wright's best known office structure.

Jan. 20 1st performance of **Charles Ives's** Second Piano Sonata, which had been composed between 1904 and 1915, given in Town Hall, New York city, by John Kirkpatrick. It is subtitled *Concord Sonata;* the separate movements are titled: Emerson, Hawthorne, The Alcotts, and Thoreau. It has been called the greatest music composed by an American, and also the most difficult composition for piano ever written. It took Kirkpatrick 2 years to learn it.

Feb. 24 **Roy Harris'** Third Symphony given its 1st performance by the Boston

sion complications that were hitherto unexplained.

A new form of radio reception, FM or **frequency modulation,** invented by Edwin H. Armstrong.

Sears Roebuck catalogue carried dresses "inspired by Schiaparelli." The next year (1940), Sears announced, "The traditional lapse between the acceptance of new fashions . . . in metropolitan centers and on farms apparently no longer exists."

The Law of Nations, an invaluable study of international law, published by **H. W. Briggs.**

Public Opinion, by **William Albig,** published. It was rated the best study of propaganda and censorship to date.

Feb. 27 Labor's most telling and controversial weapon, the **sitdown strike,** declared illegal by U.S. Supreme Court.

May 5 Domination of **United Mine Workers** and power of **John L. Lewis,** its head, indicated by the virtual stoppage of all soft coal production when the union and coal operators failed to reach agreement. Work was resumed on May 13 when a contract was signed.

May 10 The **Methodist Church,** after 109 years of division, **reunited,** with 8 million members. The conflict within the Methodist Church had been marked by 2 major crises. In 1830, the **Methodist Protestant Church** separated from the **Methodist Episcopal Church** over the question of episcopal authority and established a separate branch in which the layman had a voice in church government. The **Methodist Episcopal Church, South,** separated from the **Methodist Episcopal Church** in 1844, ostensibly over an administrative dispute, but probably over the slavery question. A Declaration of Union on May 10, 1939, unified American Methodism.

June 28 *Dixie Clipper,* Pan American Airways airliner, left Port Washington, Long Island, on **1st regular transatlantic passenger air flight** with 22 aboard;

in the cartoon category, this time for *The Ugly Duckling.*

National Football Champion was Texas A. and M., coached by Homer Norton. Their record: 10 wins, no losses, no ties.

Johnstown won the 71st annual **Belmont Stakes,** paying 1–8. Jockey was J. Stout; time was 2:29⅗ on a fast track for winnings valued at $37,020.

Challedon won the 63d annual **Preakness Stakes,** paying 6–1. Jockey was G. Seabo; time was 1:59⅘ on a muddy track for winnings valued at $53,710.

Australia defeated the U.S. 3 to 2 in the challenge round of the **Davis Cup** International Matches.

U.S. lawn tennis men's singles champion, Robert L. Riggs; **women's singles champion,** Alice Marble.

U.S.G.A. amateur championship won by Marvin Ward at North Shore C.C., Glen View, Ill. He defeated Ray Billows, 7 and 5. **Open championship** won by Byron Nelson at Philadelphia, Pa., C.C., with a score of 284.

Jan. 1 Southern California defeated Duke, 7 to 3, in the **Rose Bowl** before a crowd of 91,000 people.

May 6 Winner of the 65th annual **Kentucky Derby** was the favorite, Belair Stud's *Johnstown* ridden by J. Stout. He had been trained by "Sunny Jim" Fitzsimmons, who had trained 2 previous Derby winners, *Gallant Fox* and *Omaha. Johnstown* ran the 1¼ mi. in 2:03⅗ on a fast track, winning $46,350.

July 11 Baseball's 7th annual **All-Star Game** won by the American League, 3–1, at the Yankee Stadium in New York city.

POLITICS AND GOVERNMENT; WAR; DISASTERS; VITAL STATISTICS.	BOOKS; PAINTING; DRAMA; ARCHITECTURE; SCULPTURE.

closed to belligerent submarines by presidential order.

Nov. 30 **Russia invaded Finland.**

Symphony Orchestra, Serge Koussevitzky conducting. Although Harris had been known and recognized by critics and musicians before this, this was his 1st popular success, little short of sensational. The work was performed many times and soon recorded.

1940

No longer was the problem what could we do to avert war, but rather, how could we keep out of it and still substantially aid the forces of democracy. Realizing that America was at a major crisis point, Pres. Roosevelt decided to take the unprecedented step of running for a 3rd term. His rival was political newcomer, Wendell L. Willkie, whose rugged plain-spoken qualities made him an extremely powerful contender. Roosevelt won, largely because people felt it was better not to "change horses in midstream."

Population—131,669,275. Center of population: 2 miles southeast by east of Carlisle, Sullivan Co., Ind.

Apr. 7 **Socialist Party** chose Norman Thomas of New York for 4th time as its candidate for the presidency.

Apr. 12 Pres. Roosevelt signed the **Reciprocal Trade Agreement Act** which extended the life of the Trade Agreements Act of 1937 another 3 years.

Apr. 28 **National convention of the Socialist Labor Party** met in New York city and nominated John W. Aiken of Massachusetts for the presidency and Aaron M. Orange of New York for the vice-presidency.

May 10 **National convention of the Prohibition Party** met in Chicago and nominated Roger W. Babson of Massachusetts for the presidency and Edgar V. Moorman of Illinois for the vice-presidency.

May 28 **National Defense Advisory**

Book production was up, with 11,328 titles published. War novels, of course, led in popularity. The New York stage labored through a peculiarly uninspired season, relying principally on a slough of foreign importations. Musicologists noted a decided trend away from the ultramodernisms —the 12-tone system, for instance,—that had been intriguing composers. The art world reacted to the scores of European refugee painters who began to crowd our shores. Their work seemed less interested in nonobjective aesthetic values, more concerned with the individual. This tendency was carried over to architecture, where the more outstanding work was done on buildings designed for shelter, care of the sick, social services, recreation.

Pulitzer Prizes: novel, *The Grapes of Wrath* by John Steinbeck; drama, *The Time of Your Life* by William Saroyan; U.S. history, *Abraham Lincoln: The War Years* by Carl Sandburg; biography, *Woodrow Wilson. Life and Letters, Vols. VII and VIII* by Ray Stannard Baker; poetry, *Collected Poems* by Mark Van Doren.

Powerful and provocative novel of Negro life is **Richard Wright's** *Native Son,* a study of the mind of a Negro youth under the stress of adverse social surroundings. A play adapted from the book had considerable success on Broadway.

You Can't Go Home Again by **Thomas Wolfe** published. Critics found it more quietly written, better organized than his earlier works; all mourned his untimely death in 1938.

SCIENCE; INDUSTRY; ECONOMICS; EDUCATION; RELIGION; PHILOSOPHY.	SPORTS; FASHIONS; POPULAR ENTERTAINMENT; FOLKLORE; SOCIETY.

reached Lisbon, Portugal, 23 hrs. 52 min. later.

July 17 Proposed **Brooklyn-Battery bridge** over East R., New York city rejected by War Department on the grounds that it constituted a possible hazard to naval forces if bombed in wartime.

Oct. 25 **Nylon stockings** 1st went on sale in America.

Joe DiMaggio hit a home run for the winners.

Oct. 4–8 New York, AL, defeated Cincinnati, NL, 4–0 in the 36th annual **World Series.**

Dec. 2 Navy defeated Army, 10–0, in the annual **Army-Navy football game** held at Municipal Stadium, Philadelphia, Pa.

1940

Unemployment dropped dramatically, due to conscription of industrial workers, increased production. Labor suffered severe setbacks in its right to organize, in the matter of hours and wages. By and large, this was expected and accepted, as the labor force agreed sacrifice was necessary to maintain America's pledge to its sister democracies. The next step toward the atomic bomb was taken when science announced that a chain reaction was not only a possibility, but would soon become a reality.

American pioneer in antibiotics, Dr. Selman Waksman of Rutgers University, produced **1st of many antibotics developed in America, Antinomycin.** Found too poisonous for human patients.

Average **life expectancy** up to 64 years; an increase from 49 years in 1900.

Illiteracy in America reached a new low of 4.2% of the population, a decline of only .1% from 1930 but a decline of 15.8% from 1870.

Survey estimated that nearly 30 million American homes had **radios.**

Mar. 18 Board of High Education in New York city voted 11 to 1 against reconsidering the appointment of **Bertrand Russell,** the famous British philospher, as Professor of Philosophy in City College of New York. Russell had offended many prominent individuals with his published views on sex and marriage.

Apr. 20 **Electron microscope** 1st publicly tested at Radio Corporation of Amer-

The motion picture industry surprised itself and some of its critics by successfully tackling significant contemporary themes and by experimenting with new techniques. Examples include: *The Grapes of Wrath; The Philadelphia Story; The Great Dictator; The Long Voyage Home.* At the same time, a large section of the public wanted, and got, the wildly escapist films that seemed to be Hollywood's chief item of export.

Academy Awards presented to *Rebecca* as the outstanding motion picture of the year, to Ginger Rogers as the best actress for her portrayal of *Kitty Foyle,* to James Stewart as the best actor for his performance in *The Philadelphia Story,* to Jane Darwell as best supporting actress for her performance in *The Grapes of Wrath,* and to Walter Brennan as best supporting actor for his portrayal of *The Westerner.* Mr. Brennan became 1st actor to win award 3 times. Fred Quimby's *The Milky Way* won award in cartoon category, halting Walt Disney's string of consecutive awards at 8.

National football champion was Minnesota, coached by Bernie Bierman. Their record: 8 wins, no losses, no ties. This was 3d time for Minnesota (1934, 1936).

1st man to pole vault 15 feet was **Cornelius Warmerdam,** who 2 years later set new record when he vaulted 15 feet 7¾ inches. He retired from competition in 1943 after having vaulted 15 feet or higher 43 times.

In 1940: 8,500,000 people attended

Commission named by Pres. Roosevelt. The board of 7, headed by William S. Knudsen and Edward R. Stettinius, coordinated civilian, military defense protection.

June 2 **National convention of the Communist Party** met in New York city and nominated Earl Browder for the presidency and James W. Ford for the vice-presidency.

June 24–28 **National Convention of the Republican Party** met at Philadelphia and nominated Wendell L. Willkie of Indiana for the presidency and Charles L. McNary of Oregon for the vice-presidency.

June 28 **Alien Registration Act** (Smith Act) requiring the registration and fingerprinting of aliens and making it unlawful to belong to any organization advocating the overthrow of the U.S. government. It is the 1st U.S. law to sanction guilt by association. Registration showed approximately 5 million aliens.

July 15–19 **National Convention of the Democratic Party** met at Chicago, renominated on 1st ballot Franklin D. Roosevelt for the presidency and nominated Henry A. Wallace for the vice-presidency.

Sept. 3 U.S. Gave **50 over-age destroyers** to Great Britain in exchange for the privilege of 99-year leases on naval and air bases in Newfoundland and the West Indies.

Sept. 16 Congress enacted **1st peacetime** selective service for regular armed services. 900,000 selectees taken each year; all men between ages of 20 and 36 required to register. Length of service was extended to 18 months in Aug. 1941.

Nov. 5 Franklin D. Roosevelt and Henry A. Wallace defeated Wendell Willkie and Charles L. McNary in the **presidential elections** by an electoral vote of 449 to 82. Popular vote: Roosevelt, 27,-244,160; Willkie, 22,305,198; Thomas, 100,264; Babson, 57,812; Browder, 48,579; Aiken, 14,861.

A novel of affirmation of democracy and the worth of the individual is **Ernest Hemingway**'s *For Whom the Bell Tolls.* Set in Spain during the Revolution, it tells the story of Robert Jordan, an American who gives up his life in his fight against Fascism.

A college play with serious undertones is *The Male Animal* by **Elliott Nugent** and **James Thurber.** Here amidst satire of college types, the serious problem of freedom of thought and speech on the campus is debated.

Delightful farce recounting the adventures of 2 sisters who come to New York from Ohio to "crash the big town" is *My Sister Eileen* by **Joseph Field** and **Jerome Chodorov.** New York is also romanticized this year in **Elmer Rice**'s new play *Two on an Island.*

Powerful play which dramatizes the tyranny of a dictatorship over a scientist is **Robert Sherwood**'s *There Shall Be No Night.* Set in Finland, play became dated when Finns fought alongside Nazi Germany, and so the locale was changed.

For the 1st time since the two prizes were offered, the Pulitzer Prize committee and the New York Drama Critics' Circle gave their awards to the same play. It went to the *Time of Your Life* by **William Saroyan.**

Letter to the World, dance scored by Hunter Johnson, is presented in New York by **Martha Graham** and her company.

The 2 biggest **musical hits** on Broadway were *Du Barry was a Lady* by Cole Porter and *Louisiana Purchase* by Irving Berlin.

Popular **song hits** of the year were: "South of the Border," "Oh, Johnny," "Scatterbrain," "Careless," "In an Old Dutch Garden," "When You Wish Upon a Star," "Woodpecker Song," "Playmates," "I'll Never Smile Again," "Blueberry Hill," and "Only Forever."

1st large-scale urban college building of modern design, **Hunter College,** built in New York. A single building of 19 stories, it houses 5,650 day students.

| SCIENCE; INDUSTRY; ECONOMICS; EDUCATION; RELIGION; PHILOSOPHY. | SPORTS; FASHIONS; POPULAR ENTERTAINMENT; FOLKLORE; SOCIETY. |

ica laboratory in Camden, N.J. Instrument, about 10 ft. high and 700 lbs. in weight, magnified as much as 100,000 diameters. It had been developed by Dr. Ladislaus Marton and co-workers under the supervision of Dr. V. K. Zworykin.

Apr. 27 President and Fellows of Harvard University declared that the appointment of **Bertrand Russell** to the William James lectureship would not be affected by the dispute surrounding the British philosopher over his appointment to the faculty of City College of New York.

May 15 VS-300, experimental helicopter manufactured by Vought-Sikorsky Corporation, completed **1st successful helicopter flight** in U.S.

May 24 Oglethorpe University deposited a bottle of beer, an encyclopedia, and a movie fan magazine along with thousands of other objects in its **"Crypt of Civilization,"** which is not to be opened until the year 8113.

July 2 **Lake Washington Floating Bridge** opened to traffic at Seattle, Wash. Main portion of bridge floated on huge concrete pontoons. Built at cost of $8,294,-000, bridge is greatest floating structure ever built.

Oct. 24 **40-hour week,** part of Fair Labor Standards Act of 1938, went into effect.

Oct. 25 **John L. Lewis** continued his personal feud with the administration by urging labor to vote for a Republican president. He declared he would resign as CIO President if Pres. Roosevelt were re-elected.

Nov. 7 **Suspension bridge** over the Narrows at Tacoma, Wash., collapsed due to wind vibration. The bridge tumbled 190 feet into Puget Sound.

Nov. 21 True to his promise, **John L. Lewis** resigned as head of the CIO following Democratic victory at the polls. He was succeeded by **Philip Murray.**

racetracks in the U.S.; $408,500,000 was bet in pari-mutuel pools; $16,145,182 was gathered by states in revenue. By 1952 these figures had risen to: 26,434,903 attendance; $1,915,220,517.00 wagered; and $119,266,959.00 in revenue earned by states.

U.S. lawn tennis men's singles champion, W. Donald McNeill; **women's singles champion,** Alice Marble.

U.S.G.A. amateur championship won by Richard D. Chapman at Winged Foot G.C., Mamaroneck, N.Y. He defeated W. B. McCullough, 11 and 9. **Open championship** won by W. Lawson Little, Jr. at Canterbury G.C., Cleveland, Ohio, with a score of 287.

Bimelech won the 72d annual **Belmont Stakes,** paying 13–10. Jockey was F. A. Smith; time was 2:29⅗ on a fast track for winnings valued at $35,030.

Bimelech won the 64th annual **Preakness Stakes,** paying 9–10. Jockey was F. A. Smith; time was 1:58⅗ on a fast track for winnings valued at $53,230.

Jan. 1 Southern California defeated Tennessee, 14 to 0, in the **Rose Bowl** at Pasadena, Calif., before a crowd of 92,000 people.

May 4 A 35–1 long shot, Milky Way Farms *Gallahadion,* won the 66th annual **Kentucky Derby.** Under jockey C. Bierman he ran the 1¼ mi. in 2:05 on a fast track and won $60,150, the largest prize to that time.

July 9 The American League defeated the National League, 1–0, to win the 8th annual **All-Star Baseball Game.**

Oct. 2–8 Cincinnati, NL, defeated Detroit, AL, 4–3 in the 37th annual **World Series.**

Nov. 30 Navy defeated Army, 14–0, in the annual **Army-Navy football game** held at Municipal Stadium, Philadelphia, Pa.

527

1941

A divided, fearful nation responded to the disaster of Pearl Harbor with a single-minded unity it had not known since the dark days of 1933. A year of fence straddling and "peace at any price" had made our position of neutrality an extremely difficult one, especially since the moral weight of the people was solidly behind England and the British Commonwealth. By midyear it was fairly obvious that our role of self-appointed "arsenal of democracy" could not last long. We had spent $13 billion on lend-lease appropriations— all of it for war materials earmarked for use against the Axis, and had created some 35 separate agencies and offices that were practically war bureaus.

Feb. 3   U.S. Supreme Court upheld the **Federal Wage and Hour Law** unanimously. Law prohibited the use of children under 16 in mining and manufacturing and children under 18 in any dangerous occupation. Main provision of the law, however, was its regulation of minimum wages and maximum hours for industries engaged in interstate commerce.

Mar. 11   Pres. Roosevelt signed the **Lend-Lease Bill** which furnished a system by which the U.S. could lend goods and munitions to democratic countries in return for services and goods.

May 27   Pres. Roosevelt declared in a radio broadcast from the White House that there existed an **unlimited national emergency.** The proclamation came after a succession of sweeping victories in Europe by the German armies.

June 14   Pres. Roosevelt ordered the immediate freezing of all **German and Italian assets** in the U.S. and the freezing also of all assets belonging to invaded and occupied European countries.

June 16   U.S. State Dept. shut down the **German consulates** and Nazi propaganda organizations.

July 25   Pres. Roosevelt ordered an **embargo** on shipments of scrap iron and

Of all the art forms, the theater alone seemed concerned with the actuality of war. A number of propaganda plays were essayed by new as well as established writers. The unfortunate fact that their authors seemed to look upon the stage as a sort of soap box was accountable for their indifferent success—the pieces that tried to mirror the contemporary world were more peroration than play. Contrasted to this immaturity was the surprising nascence of a truly American painting style and musical awareness. New York City was no longer the sole arbiter of these arts; symphonic societies, ballet companies, opera houses, museums mushroomed across the nation, produced and exhibited works of differing quality but undismayed enthusiasm. Their vitality was such that it survived and even flourished under wartime conditions.

Pulitzer Prizes: novel, no prize; drama, *There Shall Be No Night* by Robert E. Sherwood; U.S. history, *The Atlantic Migration, 1607–1860* by Marcus Lee Hansen; biography, *Jonathan Edwards* by Ola Elizabeth Winslow; poetry, *Sunderland Capture* by Leonard Bacon.

John P. Marquand continued his study of the successful middle class in *H. M. Pulham, Esquire,* a novel of a New Yorker whose life falls into the rigid pattern set for him by his surroundings.

Protestant theologian and philosopher **Reinhold Niebuhr** published the 1st volume of his *Nature and Destiny of Man,* a strong argument for the supernatural quality of man. Evil and tragedy are seen as man's failure to set his "divine" self above his "natural" self.

Comedy which deals with question of maturity for a girl who is prevented from developing by a mother fixation is *Claudia* by **Rose Franken.** Play proved extremely popular, especially to matinee audiences made up predominantly of women.

Growing commercialism of New York stage made it difficult for a new playwright

1941

The nation's industry prepared for the gigantic job of retooling for an all-out war effort. Realizing that wartime is usually a time of inflation, the government prepared to curb prices and limit consumption. Numerous bureaus were created and given the jobs of organizing our vast economic potential for the struggle ahead. For the most part, the civilian population took the controls in their stride, convinced that it was all part of the price they had to pay to win the war. Sensing a wage freeze, labor attempted to win boosts before it was too late. There were some 4000 strikes this year, twice as many as last. Scientists became technicians as they sought to increase our arsenal of weapons. Federal educators prepared to meet the shortage of adequately trained personnel.

British pioneers in **penicillin** development, Sir Howard Florey and Dr. N. G. Heatley, flew to America to argue the necessity of large-scale production of the life-saving substance. American drug companies responded to their appeal with the result that penicillin soon became a household word in America.

Jan. 3 Government called for a **shipbuilding program** of 200 merchant vessels.

Jan. 7 Office of Production Management **(OPM)** created by executive order. The new agency to supervise defense production was 1st headed by industrialist William S. Knudsen and by associate director labor leader Sidney Hillman.

Jan. 22 Stoppage in Allis Chalmers plants signaled beginning of a wave of **defense industry strikes.**

Feb. 19 Construction of a 3rd set of locks for the **Panama Canal** was begun at Gatun.

Feb. 24 1st **industry-wide priority** schedule released by OPM. It affected aluminum and machine tools.

Feb. 26 **Strike** at Bethlehem Steel plants called by CIO. Subsequent settle-

"Remember Pearl Harbor" became the war cry of the man in the street, who used it more as a grim reminder than as an outburst of patriotism. World War I had been a lesson; it was a sober army that went into battle in 1941. Women's fashions reflected the general restraint, keeping to subdued colors and inconspicuous lines. Greatest furor of the year came when embargo on Japanese silk was announced. It caused a panic in the hosiery business and sent thousands of rioting women into shops to snatch up every available silk stocking.

Academy Awards presented to *How Green Was My Valley* as the outstanding motion picture of the year, to Joan Fontaine as best actress for her performance in *Suspicion,* to Gary Cooper as best actor for his portrayal of *Sergeant York,* to Mary Astor for her supporting performance in *The Great Lie,* and to Donald Crisp for his supporting performance in *How Green Was My Valley.* Walt Disney won his 9th cartoon award in 10 years, this time for *Lend a Paw.* He also received 2 special awards, 1 for his general contribution to the motion picture industry, and 1 for his part in the production of *Fantasia,* a film concert in which musical classics were accompanied by appropriate visualization.

This year's **National College Football Champion** was, for the 2nd straight time, 4 titles in all, Minnesota, coached by Bernie Bierman. Their record: 8 wins, no losses, no ties.

U.S. lawn tennis men's singles champion, Robert L. Riggs; **women's singles champion,** Mrs. Sarah Palfrey Cooke.

U.S.G.A. amateur championship won by Marvin Ward at Omaha, Neb., G.C. He defeated B. Patrick Abbott, 4 and 3. **Open championship** won by Craig Wood at Colonial Club, Fort Worth, Tex., with a score of 284. No competition 1942–45.

Whirlaway won the 73d annual **Belmont Stakes,** paying 1–4. Jockey was E. Arcaro; time was 2:31 on a fast track for winnings valued at $39,770.

gasoline to Japan and froze Japanese assets in the U.S.

Aug. 9–12 **Atlantic Charter** formulated by Pres. Roosevelt and Winston Churchill at a secret meeting off Newfoundland, Aug. 9–12. It contained 8 articles of agreement declaring the aims the 2 governments would pursue in the war.

Aug. 18 Pres. Roosevelt signed the **Selective Service Act Extension** which extended the period of service to not more than 30 months in time of peace and abolished the 900,000-man limitation of the Army.

Sept. 11 Pres. Roosevelt ordered attack "at sight" upon any **German or Italian vessel** met in U.S. defensive waters by American ships or planes. The order was issued after a number of American vessels had been sunk or fired upon by submarines.

Sept. 20 Pres. Franklin D. Roosevelt signed the **biggest tax bill** in American history for the purpose of raising a sum of $3,553,400,000. The tax bill provided for the following division of sources: Corporation and excess profits were to yield $1,382,100,060; individual income was to provide $1,144,000,000; capital stock tax was to produce $22,300,000; estates and gifts were to yield $157,600,000; and excise and miscellaneous taxes were responsible for $846,800.

Oct. 17 **U.S. destroyer Kearny** torpedoed by a German submarine off the coast of Iceland.

Oct. 31 **U.S. destroyer Reuben James** sunk by a German submarine. 100 lives were lost. Both U.S. and Germany did not consider hostilities as technical "war."

Dec. 7 **Pearl Harbor**, Hawaii, attacked by Japanese naval and air forces. American battleships the *Arizona, California, Oklahoma,* and *Utah* (an old target battleship) were sunk; the battleship *West*

to see his play produced. The **Experimental Theater**, sponsored by the Dramatists' Guild and Equity, and the **New Play Project** of the National Theater Conference started this year to encourage new plays.

Extremely effective war drama is *Watch on the Rhine* by **Lillian Hellman**, which sets a German resistance leader against the background of American complacency.

Unflinching depicter of American urban scenes, **Edward Hopper**, in his popular *Nighthawks*, depicts stray diners in an all-night restaurant. Contrast of light and shadow imparts a feeling of loneliness. It is life seen in a flash, a technique often employed by Hopper.

Subjective reality is keynote of **Louis O. Gugliemi's** *Terror in Brooklyn*. A group of female figures is encased in a vacuum-like bell jar on a lonely city street. Commenting on his own painting, he remarked, "I thoroughly believe that the inner world of subjective life is quite as real as the objective."

Extremely subjective painter is **Morris Graves**, who lived like a hermit on the west coast. His *Little-Known Bird of the Inner Eye* reveals the strange mixture of Japanese art and modernism. Nature, in the distorted singing bird, reflects simultaneously the inner mind of man.

Movement away from realism sharply punctuated by paintings of **Stuart Davis**. Geometry rather than æsthetics becomes the keynote in his canvases. For instance, in his *New York under Gaslight* time itself is destroyed, the gay Nineties being juxtaposed to skyscrapers. Form is paramount concern.

Feb. 21 Première performance of **Roy Harris'** 4th Symphony, the *Folk Song Symphony* for chorus and orchestra, given by the Boston Symphony Orchestra.

Mar. 8 Writer **Sherwood Anderson**, 64, died of peritonitis at Cristobal, Canal Zone. He had achieved fame in 1919 with the publication of *Winesburg, Ohio*, a collection of short stories with a common

| SCIENCE; INDUSTRY; ECONOMICS: EDUCATION; RELIGION; PHILOSOPHY. | SPORTS; FASHIONS; POPULAR ENTERTAINMENT; FOLKLORE; SOCIETY. |

ment according to OPM formula acclaimed as union's greatest victory to date.

Mar. 19 National Defense Mediation Board **(NDMB)** established to settle all labor disputes in defense industries. 1st chairman was Clarence A. Dykstra.

Mar. 22 **Grand Coulee Dam** in Washington began operations, 2 years ahead of schedule.

Apr. 11 **Ford Motor Company** signed its 1st contract with a labor union. This was settlement of a strike that began Apr. 2 when CIO called out 85,000 workers in the River Rouge plant. Ford closed the plant after rioting had injured 150.

Apr. 11 Office of Price Administration and Civilian Supply (OPACS, but better known as **OPA**) established with limited powers to recommend price control measures. 1st head was Leon Henderson.

Apr. 14 Steel industry granted 10¢ per hour **wage boosts** to prevent strikes.

Apr. 16 1st official act of OPA was to freeze **steel price** at levels of 1st quarter of current year. Industry co-operated.

Apr. 17 **Automobile industry** agreed to cut production by 20% beginning Aug. 1.

May 1 **U.S. Defense Savings Bonds and Stamps** went on sale.

May 16 General Motors granted 10¢ per hour **wage hikes** to ward off strikes. CIO, in turn, waived its demands for closed shop.

June 18 Water from the $200 million **Colorado Aqueduct** began flowing from taps in Los Angeles and other southern California cities. The aqueduct runs from Parker Dam on the Colorado River, 240 miles across the Mojave Desert and the San Bernardino Mts., generating in its descents power to lift its own water a total of 1617 ft.

July 24 A **no-strike agreement** for duration of national emergency signed by AFL building trade unions and OPM.

Whirlaway won the 65th annual **Preakness Stakes,** paying 11–10. Jockey was E. Arcaro; time was 1:58⅖ on a fast track for winnings valued at $49,365.

Jan. 1 Leland Stanford defeated Nebraska, 21 to 13, in the **Rose Bowl** at Pasadena, Calif., before a crowd of 91,500.

Jan. 6 Term **"4 Freedoms"** introduced by Pres. Roosevelt in his annual speech before Congress. These freedoms which he envisaged as the cornerstone of a new world are freedom of speech and expression, freedom of worship, freedom from fear, and freedom from want.

May 3 The present record time for the **Kentucky Derby** 2:01⅖, was made by Calumet Farms' *Whirlaway* with Eddie Arcaro up, in the 67th running of the Churchill Downs classic on May 3. The winner's prize was $61,275. *Whirlaway* went on to win the Preakness and the Belmont Stakes to take American racing's Triple Crown.

May 20 Pres. Franklin D. Roosevelt announced that **Thanksgiving** would be moved forward again to the last Thursday of November after a 2-year experiment with the next-to-last Thursday in November. Roosevelt had originally moved the holiday back one week to stimulate business activity.

June 2 Baseball's "Iron Man," **Lou Gehrig,** died in N.Y.C. Longtime first baseman for the Yankees, he had played in a record 2130 consecutive games.

July 8 The American League won the 9th annual **All-Star baseball game** at Detroit, beating the National League 7–5.

July 17 Cleveland pitchers Al Smith and Jim Bagby, Jr., halted the hitting streak of Yankee center fielder Joe DiMaggio. He had **hit safely in 56 consecutive games** from May 15 through July 16, a major-league record.

Sept. 23 A 6-ton granite monument

POLITICS AND GOVERNMENT; WAR; DISASTERS; VITAL STATISTICS.	BOOKS; PAINTING; DRAMA; ARCHITECTURE; SCULPTURE.

Virginia settled in shallow water and the *Nevada* ran aground. Damaged battleships were the *Pennsylvania, Maryland,* and *Tennessee.* Destroyers *Cassin, Downes,* and *Shaw,* and the layer *Oglala* were sunk or badly damaged. About 19 ships were sunk or damaged. About 3000 Americans lost their lives. Japanese lost 28 planes, 3 midget submarines.

Dec. 8   Congress voted for **war** against Japan. The 1 dissent was cast by Rep. Jeannette Rankin, as she did in 1917.

Dec. 10   Japanese invaded the **Philippines** at Luzon where Gen. MacArthur commanded the defending American and Philippine forces.

Dec. 11   Germany and Italy declared **war** against U.S. and Congress adopted a resolution recognizing a state of war between U.S. and these countries.

Dec. 22   **Wake Island** fell to the Japanese after a heroic stand by 400 U.S. Marines.

theme—youth in revolt against small-town conventions and respectability.

Mar. 17   In Washington, D.C., the **National Gallery of Art** opened its doors. The marble building, a gift of Andrew W. Mellon, was designed by John Russell Pope. It houses Mellon's art collection, as well as those donated later by Samuel H. Kress, Joseph E. Widener, and Chester Dale.

Apr. 11   **Arnold Schoenberg,** Viennese-born composer and creator of the 12-tone system of composing, became an American citizen. Schoenberg, now 66 years old, had come to U.S. in 1933 to escape persecution as a Jew under the Hitler regime in Germany.

May 4   At Staunton, Va., the **birthplace of Woodrow Wilson** was dedicated as a National Shrine by Pres. Roosevelt.

June 30   At Hyde Park, N.Y., the **Franklin D. Roosevelt Library** was dedicated by the President. He deeded the building, its contents, and the site to the federal government.

1942

American military pride was given a series of rude shocks this year as our forces were shoved from island after island in the Pacific. Chief defeat was the collapse of Bataan after a hopeless, heroic stand by last-ditch defenders on Corregidor. Relief from a long series of setbacks came in May when our naval fleet defeated a Japanese armada in the battle of the Coral Sea, and again in June when our torpedo bombers routed a 2d enemy task force in the Battle of Midway. At home, thousands of overage civilians flocked to Washington to man the army of special war offices that had been created to handle the mammoth war program.

Jan. 2   Japanese forces occupied **Manila,** forcing a withdrawal of MacArthur's Philippine army to Bataan.

Mar. 17   Gen. MacArthur left **Bataan** by presidential order when defense of the peninsula became hopeless. He with-

Far from destroying the American arts, World War II gave them an impetus they had not enjoyed for years. Producers scrambled for available playhouses, sold tickets at outrageous prices, gleefully counted their profits. Entertainment-hungry civilians and servicemen were given light escapist fare, which meant, in most cases, unclad ladies of the chorus keeping time to a loud pit orchestra. American literature seemed confused by world events, had not yet digested the impact of war. After the promising start of the previous year, hundreds of artists and musicians were absorbed by the armed forces, did not exhibit or compose. Architects became technicians instead of creative builders, bowing to the utilitarian demands of fast, cheap, prefabricated housing.

Pulitzer Prizes: novel, *In This Our Life* by Ellen Glasgow; drama, no prize; U.S. history, *Reveille in Washington* by Margaret Leech; biography, *Crusader in Crino-*

SCIENCE; INDUSTRY; ECONOMICS: EDUCATION; RELIGION; PHILOSOPHY.	SPORTS; FASHIONS; POPULAR ENTERTAINMENT; FOLKLORE; SOCIETY.

Aug. 3 **Gasoline curfew** begun at midnight in 17 eastern states. Curfew closed filling stations from 7 P.M. to 7 A.M.

Sept. 9 "**Imminent inflation**" predicted by Sec. of the Treasury Henry W. Morgenthau unless price controls became more stringent.

Nov. 1 The 950-ft. **Rainbow Bridge** was opened to traffic across the Niagara River, just below the falls. An ice jam destroyed the old bridge in January 1938.

Dec. 15 **No-strike policy** in war industries adopted by AFL executive council. Council also offered to make peace with CIO. On Dec. 23 an Industry-Labor conference pledged that there would be no strikes and lock-outs. All disputes were to be settled by peaceful means, and a War Labor Board was to be established to settle differences. Conference could not agree on question of closed shop.

Dec. 27 **Rubber rationing** announced by OPA. Measure decreased civilian consumption by 80%. Tire rationing was 1st rationing regulation.

over the site of a **time capsule** was unveiled in Flushing Meadow, Queens. A souvenir of the N.Y. World's Fair of 1939–40, the capsule contains artifacts and information about 20th-century culture. It is to be recovered A.D. 6939.

Oct. 1–6 New York, AL, defeated Brooklyn, NL, 4–1 in the 38th annual **World Series.**

Nov. 21 **1st woman to pay the death penalty in California** died in San Quentin's gas chamber. She was Mrs. Ethel Leta Juanita Spinelli, 52, alias "The Duchess," convicted slayer of 1 of her own gang.

Nov. 29 **Navy** defeated Army, 14–6, in their annual classic in Municipal Stadium, Philadelphia.

Dec. 7 Famous wartime phrase "**Praise the Lord and pass the ammunition**" pronounced by Howell M. Forgy, Chaplain on the U.S. cruiser *New Orleans*, which was attacked at Pearl Harbor by the Japanese. While sweating sailors kept up a continuous barrage, he kept their spirits up with this phrase.

1942

Stringent anti-inflation measures, such as rent ceilings, wage and price freezes were put into effect as the nation settled down to the grim business of war. Both AFL and CIO voluntarily agreed not to strike for the duration of the war and to submit all labor disputes to a federal mediation board. The powerful War Manpower Commission held dictatorial power over all essential workers and could, if the emergency warranted, mobilize every man and woman in the country. Hard hit by prevailing conditions were the colleges and universities, whose enrollments dropped off sharply. Adult education classes, however, increased in number and helped keep the schoolrooms at least partially filled.

Most talked-about man of the year was construction expert **Henry J. Kaiser,** whose 4 west coast shipyards by June had been assigned ⅓ of the U.S. shipbuilding program. His yard in Vancouver launched a 10,500-ton liberty ship in a record 4 days.

The motion picture industry faced a serious problem. Some 4000 of its most highly trained people were in the armed forces. This accounted for about 22% of total studio personnel. Yet the government expected the film companies to contribute to the general morale by keeping up production. Their plight was made still more difficult by a vanished European market. Quite naturally, they sought to cultivate new audiences in South America, made a number of films with Latin American backgrounds. Comedies—particularly the wild farces of Abbott and Costello—were the biggest box office draws of the year. Trends in fashion continued to follow the lines of 1941—this meant simplicity and economy of design. Crime rates across the nation jumped; officials claimed that draftable youth were having one "last fling" before entering the uncertainty of the army.

Academy Awards presented to *Mrs. Miniver* as the outstanding motion picture

drew to Australia where he was named commander in chief of the Southwest Pacific Command.

Mar. 27 Members of the armed forces were granted **free mail privileges.**

Apr. 9 **Bataan** peninsula fell to the Japanese after a heroic defense by a greatly outnumbered force. The military and civilian prisoners taken were to start the next morning on the infamous "Death March." Gen. Wainwright with about 3500 soldiers and nurses withdrew to Corregidor.

Apr. 10 **"Death March"** began at dawn. The American and Philippine prisoners taken at Bataan were forced to march 85 miles in 6 days with but one meal of rice during the period. At the end of the march, which was punctuated with atrocities, more than 5200 Americans and many more Filipinos had lost their lives.

Apr. 18 **Tokyo** bombed by a bomber group led by Maj. Gen. Doolittle. This was 1st American offensive blow in the Pacific.

May 4–8 Americans defeated the Japanese in the battle of the **Coral Sea**, inflicting heavy losses upon the Japanese fleet. This battle is significant for being the 1st naval engagement during which none of the surface vessels fired a shot. All the fighting was carried on by planes. U.S. loss: carrier *Lexington*, destroyer *Sims*, and a tanker. 7 Japanese warships, including 1 carrier, were sunk.

May 6 Gen. Wainwright surrendered **Corregidor** and remaining Philippine islands to Japanese under Gen. Yamashita.

May 14 Congress established **Women's Army Auxiliary Corps**; Oveta Culp Hobby chosen 1st commander. Name shortened to Women's Army Corps (WAC) in 1943.

June 4–6 Americans gained important victory over the Japanese at **Midway.** Americans repulsed an attempt to seize the island, sinking 17 Japanese ships including 4 aircraft carriers. Japan lost 275 planes, 4800 men. U.S. lost over 300 men and 2 ships.

line by Forrest Wilson; poetry, *The Dust Which Is God* by William Rose Benét.

James Gould Cozzens published one of his finest novels, *The Just and the Unjust*, which uses, as its background, a discussion of the American legal system in a small town.

Unique experiment was publication of *The Moon Is Down* by **John Steinbeck** as a novel at the same time as it was produced on the New York stage. Both versions met with public success, principally because the theme was topical and well handled; namely, the problem of moral resistance to Nazi occupation.

The Robe by **Lloyd C. Douglas** published, his most popular book. 2 more of his successes were: *Magnificent Obsession* (1929) and *Green Light* (1935). *The Robe* has probably sold over 2 million copies.

Immensely popular soldier chronicle, *See Here, Private Hargrove* by **Marion Hargrove,** published. These humorous sketches in 4 years sold over 2½ million copies.

Philosophical fantasy, profound and delightful at the same time, is **Thorton Wilder's** *The Skin of Our Teeth*, which in the symbolic character of Mr. Antrobus (played by Fredric March) traces the history of man, showing his foibles, his courage, his persistence, and survival value.

1st Broadway play to depict American soldiers in action in World War II was *Eve of St. Mark* by **Maxwell Anderson.**

Popular **hit songs** of the year included, "White Christmas," "Be Careful, It's My Heart," "I Left My Heart at the Stage Door Canteen," "The White Cliffs of Dover," "Praise the Lord and Pass the Ammunition," "Sleepy Lagoon," and "Blues in the Night."

Feb. 12 Artist **Grant Wood**, 50, died in Iowa City. He painted mostly American subjects, often sardonically. His most admired work is the portrait of a dour farm couple, *American Gothic* (1930).

SCIENCE; INDUSTRY; ECONOMICS: EDUCATION; RELIGION; PHILOSOPHY.	SPORTS; FASHIONS; POPULAR ENTERTAINMENT; FOLKLORE; SOCIETY.

Jan. 1 Complete **ban on retail sales of new passenger cars and trucks** was imposed by OPM (Office of Production Management).

Jan. 12 **National War Labor Board** (WLB) created by executive order. The new 12-man board, whose head was William H. Davis, supplanted the National Defense Mediation Board (NDMB). Its function was to maintain the flow of war materials by settling labor disputes.

Jan. 12 U.S. Supreme Court ruled unanimously that the **Georgia Contract Labor Act** violated the antislavery amendment to the Constitution. The Court stated as its opinion that "one who has received an advance on a contract for services which he is unable to repay is bound by the threat of penal sanction to remain at his employment until the debt has been discharged. Such coerced labor is peonage." This decision had a profound effect on labor relations, particularly in the South.

Jan. 16 **War Production Board** (WPB) established by executive order. In charge of the entire war production program, it supplanted the OPM, and was 1st headed by Donald M. Nelson.

Jan. 30 **Price Control Bill** signed, officially giving OPA power to fix all prices except farm products.

Feb. 9 **War Time** became effective throughout the nation.

Mar. 17 A **no-strike truce** announced by William Green of the AFL and Philip Murray of the CIO.

Apr. 18 **War Manpower Commission** established. The 9-man group was put under direction of Federal Security Administrator Paul V. McNutt.

Apr. 28 **Rents stabilized** by OPA. The ruling affected 86 million people, housed in 301 areas.

May 5 **Sugar rationing** begun.

May 15 **Gasoline rationing** in 17 Eastern states begun. Limit set was 3 gal-

of the year, to its star, Greer Garson, as the best actress, and to James Cagney as the best actor for his portrayal of George M. Cohan in *Yankee Doodle Dandy*. Teresa Wright was named best supporting actress for her work in *Mrs. Miniver* and Van Heflin was chosen best supporting actor for his performance in *Johnny Eager*. Walt Disney received his 10th award in 11 years in the cartoon category for his World War II-inspired effort, *Der Fuehrer's Face*.

Biggest **money-maker for movie theaters** was the comedy team of Bud Abbott and Lou Costello. Mickey Rooney, top attraction for past 3 years, fell to 4th place behind Clark Gable and Gary Cooper.

This year's **National College Football Champion** was Ohio State, coached by Paul Brown. Their record: 9 wins, 1 loss, no ties.

U.S. lawn tennis men's singles champion, Frederick R. Schroeder, Jr.; **women's singles champion,** Pauline M. Betz.

Alsab won the 66th annual **Preakness Stakes,** paying 1–2. Jockey was B. James; time was 1:57 on a fast track for winnings valued at $58,175.

Shut Out won the 74th annual **Belmont Stakes,** paying 7–2. Jockey was E. Arcaro; time was 2:29⅗ on a fast track for winnings valued at $44,520.

Jan. 1 Oregon State defeated Duke 20 to 16 in the **Rose Bowl** game, played for the 1st and last time at Durham, N.C.

Jan. 8 Memorable laconic statement **"Sighted sub, sank same"** radioed from the South Pacific by U.S.N. flyer David F. Mason. Noticing a surfaced Japanese submarine, he swooped down, deposited his depth charges, and then observed the strewn wreckage of the submarine on the water. His feat earned him the Silver Star.

June 28   1st land attack upon the Japanese in the South Pacific executed when a contingent of commandos assaulted Salamaua, **New Guinea,** at night.

July 30   **WAVES** organized as a women's reserve unit of the U.S. Naval Reserve.

Aug. 7   U.S. Marines occupied **Guadalcanal,** Solomon Islands.

Aug. 18   **"Carlson's Raiders"** landed on Makin with orders to destroy the radio station on the island. In 40 hrs. every Japanese (350) defender was killed, 1000 gallons of gasoline were set aflame, and the island was rendered militarily useless.

Sept. 15   **WASP,** U.S. aircraft carrier, sunk in battle of Guadalcanal.

Oct. 23   Japanese Sandai (2d) Div. opened an attack on Henderson Field, **Guadalcanal.** After 3 days of fierce fighting the veteran Japanese unit suffered its 1st defeat at the hands of a small Marine and Army force and Henderson Field was secure.

Nov. 7   American forces began landing in **French North Africa** with support of British naval and air units. Lt. Gen. Eisenhower commanded the 50 vessels and 400,000 troops employed in the operations.

Nov. 23   **SPARS** organized as a women's branch of the Coast Guard.

Nov. 28   Worst single fire of modern times in U.S., **Cocoanut Grove** night club in Boston burned; 487 deaths, mostly from asphyxia and trampling.

Apr. 14   *Social Justice,* a weekly published by Father Coughlin, was banned from mails; Attorney General Biddle charged the magazine violated the Espionage Act of 1917.

Apr. 14   *Solomon and Balkis,* a new opera by **Randall Thompson,** given a radio première from Harvard University, Cambridge, Mass.

May 1   Converse College was the scene of première of *A Tree on the Plain,* a new opera by **Ernst Bacon.**

May 29   **John Barrymore,** youngest member of the stage's "Royal Family," died in Hollywood at 60. He reached the peak of his stage career playing Hamlet; his film roles earned him the sobriquets "The Great Lover" and "The Great Profile."

June 22   First **V-mail** was sent overseas, from New York to London.

Aug. 3   Justice Dept. filed suit against American Federation of Musicians' president James C. Petrillo, charging the union's **ban on recorded music** for radio and jukeboxes violated antitrust act. Suit was dismissed in Chicago Oct. 12.

Oct. 16   *Rodeo,* a ballet with score by **Aaron Copland,** produced in New York by the Ballet Russe de Monte Carlo, with **Agnes de Mille.**

Dec. 28   Artur Rodzinski, conductor of the Cleveland Symphony Orchestra, became musical director and regular conductor of the New York Philharmonic-Symphony.

1943

An uncertain year dawned for our military forces. We were engaged in a seesaw battle in North Africa, and an agonizing, costly struggle in the Pacific, moving laboriously from one island to the next, attempting to take the initiative away from the Japanese. But as the months rolled by, war strategy became decidedly more offensive. Landings in the Solomons and in New Guinea increased our ability to fight an amphibious war, which seemed unavoida-

With younger men in the services, their more established seniors once more took up the burden of breaking new trails in music and art. Roy Harris, Aaron Copland, William Schuman all produced creditable, fresh, inventive works for the concert stage. Led by such painters as Thomas Hart Benton, American regionalism was discovered for about the 4th time this century. But it was not merely a reworking of old ideas that interested these men; instead

SCIENCE; INDUSTRY; ECONOMICS: EDUCATION; RELIGION; PHILOSOPHY.	SPORTS; FASHIONS; POPULAR ENTERTAINMENT; FOLKLORE; SOCIETY.

lons per week for nonessential driving. On July 22 the coupon system of rationing was initiated.

June 13   President Roosevelt established the **Office of War Information** to control dissemination of official news and propaganda; newsman Elmer Davis named as head.

July 23 $93 million **barge canal** across Northern Florida authorized by presidential signature.

Oct. 1   Robert Stanley, chief pilot for Bell Aircraft Corporation, flew XP-59, **1st American jet plane.** Test was made at Muroc Army Base, Calif.

Oct. 7   **United Mine Workers** (UMW) withdrew from CIO.

Nov. 1   Right Rev. Spence Burton enthroned Bishop of the Church of England, diocese of Nassau, Haiti. He was the **1st American to become a Bishop in the Church of England.**

Nov. 29   **Coffee rationing** begun.

Dec. 1   Nationwide **gasoline rationing** went into effect.

Dec. 2   **1st continuous nuclear reaction** demonstrated at Chicago, Ill., before scientists at Univ. of Chicago. Project known as the Argonne Project.

Dec. 4   **Works Progress Administration (WPA) abolished** by executive order.

Dec. 21   U.S. Supreme Court ruled Nevada divorces valid in all states.

Jan. 9   In 20th defense of his world heavyweight title, **Joe Louis** knocked out Buddy Baer in the 1st round.

Jan. 16   Movie star **Carole Lombard** (Mrs. Clark Gable), her mother, and 20 others were killed in a plane crash near Las Vegas, Nev.

Feb. 10   France's greatest ocean liner, the **Normandie,** the world's fastest, burned and capsized at her New York pier. Cause never discovered. The U.S. Naval officers investigating disaster rejected sabotage theory.

May 2   The winner of the 68th annual **Kentucky Derby** at Churchill Downs, Louisville, Ky., was the favorite, Greentree Stable's *Shut Out,* ridden by W. D. Wright. He ran the 1¼ mi. in 2:04⅖ on a good track to win $64,225.

July 6   The American League scored 3 runs in the 1st inning on home runs by Rudy York and Lou Boudreau to beat the National League, 3–1, in the 10th annual **All-Star game** at the Polo Grounds in New York City on July 6.

Sept. 30–Oct. 5   St. Louis, NL, defeated New York, AL, 4–1 in the 39th annual **World Series.**

Nov. 28   **Army-Navy football classic,** usually seen by 100,000 in Philadelphia, was played at Annapolis before less than 12,000 fans. By presidential order, tickets were sold only to residents within a 10-mile radius of the stadium.

1943

The CIO and AFL generally kept to the no strike pledges, making this a quiet year on the labor front. Principal exception was the United Mine Workers, whose president, John L. Lewis, led workers in defiance of the War Labor Board, claiming that working conditions and wages were impossible. A 48-hr. minimum work week was proclaimed by the President for all essential war industries in labor-scarce areas. The order was not contested. Colleges and

Much to the relief of the motion picture industry, more people than ever before decided to go to the movies. Top box-office attractions at motion-picture theaters, according to *Motion Picture Herald*'s poll, were Betty Grable, Bob Hope, Abbott and Costello, Bing Crosby, and Gary Cooper. General topics of conversation everywhere were the latest war news, the emergence of a new music called "jive" (which was not really new, only a bouncier, danceable

| POLITICS AND GOVERNMENT; WAR; DISASTERS; VITAL STATISTICS. | BOOKS; PAINTING; DRAMA; ARCHITECTURE; SCULPTURE. |

ble if we were to cross the many watery miles between Pearl Harbor and Tokyo. American troops in North Africa swept across the Mediterranean to Sicily, and then to the Italian mainland itself. To the north our bombers blanketed Europe, helped blast Nazi invasion ports in France.

1151 died and thousands were left crippled in U.S. during the **infantile paralysis** epidemic.

Jan. 14 Pres. Roosevelt arrived at **Casablanca** for a conference with Churchill and other Allied officials. The Allies planned their military strategy for 1943 and agreed to demand an unconditional surrender from the Axis nations.

Feb. 13 Women's unit attached to **U.S. Marine Corps.**

Feb. 20 U.S. Forces were beaten back at **Kasserine Pass,** Tunisia, by the Afrika Korps using their largest tank, the 62-ton Mark VI. On Feb. 25 American forces recaptured the pass.

Mar. 2–4 Major victory was gained by the U.S. in the battle of **Bismarck Sea** when an entire Japanese convoy of 22 ships was sunk by American bombers and over 50 Japanese planes were shot down.

May 7 American troops captured **Bizerte,** Tunisia; the British took Tunis.

May 12 **North African campaign** ended. Gen. von Arnim, commander of Axis forces after Rommel's flight to Europe, captured along with other enemy generals.

May 19 **Winston Churchill,** speaking before the U.S. Congress, declared that Japan would be utterly annihilated after the defeat of Hitler's armies.

May 30 **Attu, Aleutian Islands,** retaken by U.S. forces after intense fighting.

June 4 Maj. **Kermit Roosevelt,** son of former President Theodore Roosevelt and veteran of 2 world wars, was killed on active duty in Alaska.

July 10 **Sicily invaded** by Gen. Patton's 7th Army, Montgomery's 8th Army, and French and Canadian troops.

some painted with new, almost exotic lushness, others with an irresistible, defiant realism. The theater, too, found a new form—or rather, belatedly explored a very old one. Rodgers and Hammerstein elevated the musical comedy stage into a meaningful form with their remarkable production of *Oklahoma!* They proved, finally, that a musical need not be simply a tuneful girlie show, could have a dignity of its own as a valid expression of American life.

Pulitzer Prizes: novel, *Dragon's Teeth* by Upton Sinclair; drama, *The Skin of Our Teeth* by Thornton Wilder; U.S. history, *Paul Revere and the World He Lived In* by Esther Forbes; biography, *Admiral of the Ocean Sea* by Samuel Eliot Morison; poetry, *A Witness Tree* by Robert Frost. *Secular Cantata No. 2, A Free Song* by William Schuman won 1st Pulitzer Prize for a musical composition. Work is based on lines from Walt Whitman.

The year saw a rash of books about the war, mostly by war correspondents. Some of the better ones: *Battle for the Solomons,* by **Ira Wolfert;** *Guadalcanal Diary,* by **Richard Tregaskis;** *Here Is Your War,* by **Ernie Pyle;** *God Is My Co-Pilot,* by **Col. Robert L. Scott, Jr.;** and *Thirty Seconds Over Tokyo,* by **Capt. Ted W. Lawson.**

2 most popular fiction works of the year were *A Tree Grows in Brooklyn,* a lovingly and humorously told story of a slum family by **Betty Smith,** and *The Human Comedy,* a sentimental tale of Armenians in California by **William Saroyan.**

Extremely successful musical play that borders on folk opera is *Oklahoma!* by **Richard Rodgers** and **Oscar Hammerstein 2d.** Set in Oklahoma about 1900, it tells the story of the love of an Oklahoma girl for a cowboy. The tunes, "Oh, What a Beautiful Morning," "People Will Say We're in Love," "Poor Jud Is Dead," soon caught hold of all America.

SCIENCE; INDUSTRY; ECONOMICS: EDUCATION; RELIGION; PHILOSOPHY.	SPORTS; FASHIONS; POPULAR ENTERTAINMENT; FOLKLORE; SOCIETY.

universities were promised some relief by a plan that would send thousands of young men to school to be trained as officers for the Army and Navy.

Nobel Prize in medicine and physiology awarded to Edward A. Doisy "for his discovery of the chemical nature of vitamin K" and to Henrik Dam, the Danish biochemist, for the actual discovery of vitamin K. Doisy and his research colleagues in the St. Louis University School of Medicine succeeded in isolating vitamin K from alfalfa. Vitamin K has become an important factor in the prevention of postoperative bleeding in certain types of surgery.

Nobel Prize in physics presented to **Otto Stern** "for his contributions to the development of the molecular ray method and for his discovery of the magnetic movement of the proton." Otto Stern was born in Germany but emigrated to America in 1933 because of political pressure. Stern's prize-winning experiments established the foundations of the molecular beam method of studying the magnetic attributes of atoms and atomic nuclei. He thus gave further support to the wave theory of matter originally propounded by de Broglie.

Large-scale production of **penicillin in** America made possible by discovery of a mold on a cantaloupe in a fruit market in Peoria, Ill. This mold was found to yield 10 times as much penicillin as original mold discovered by Sir Alexander Fleming of England.

In **salvage drives** this year, 255,513 tons of tin cans, 43,919 tons of fats, 6 million tons of wastepaper, and more than 26 million tons of iron and steel scrap were collected for use in essential industries.

Jan. 5 **George Washington Carver,** chemurgist of Tuskegee Institute, died there. Born of slave parents, Dr. Carver gained fame as an agricultural expert; he developed hundreds of synthetic products from peanuts, cotton, and soybeans.

Jan. 18 U.S. Supreme Court found the **American Medical Association** guilty of violating antitrust laws on the grounds of preventing activities of co-operative

jazz) and the steady stream of star baseball players who were being drafted. Their departure made for a duller game, but the fans remained loyal.

As in several years past, the standard male garb of "hepcats" and young Negroes was the **zoot suit,** an ensemble made up of a long, one-button jacket with broad, padded shoulders and peaked lapels, high-waisted trousers that ballooned at the knees and gripped the ankles, a wide silk tie worn against a colored or striped shirt, a knee-length key chain, and a broad-brimmed hat.

The jitterbug was easily the most popular dance of the year, and variations on its basic routine (called the "Lindy hop") proliferated. In more strenuous forms of the dance, the young man swung his partner over his back, between his legs, etc. In a 9-page article, *Life* magazine hailed the Lindy hop as "the true national folk dance of America."

Academy Awards presented to *Casablanca* as the outstanding motion picture of the year, to Jennifer Jones as best actress for her portrayal in *The Song of Bernadette*, to Paul Lukas as best actor for his performance in *Watch on the Rhine*, to Katina Paxinou for her interpretation of Pilar in *For Whom the Bell Tolls*, and to Charles Coburn for his performance in *The More the Merrier*. George Pal received a special award for "his novel technique in producing Puppetoon shorts."

U.S. fashion designers were emancipated from the Paris tradition, produced clothes of simplicity in fabrics geared to wartime shortages. 2 silhouettes were featured; a slim straight, clinging line, caught at the waist by a belt, and a more bulky figure created by wool box coats and suits.

Outstanding basketball teams of the year were the University of Illinois, which won its 2nd straight Big Ten championship, and the University of Wyoming, Rocky Mountain conference champs who went on to win the N.C.A.A. tournament.

Stan Musial of the Cardinals and Spurgeon Chandler of the Yankees were named

POLITICS AND GOVERNMENT; WAR; DISASTERS; VITAL STATISTICS.

BOOKS; PAINTING; DRAMA; ARCHITECTURE; SCULPTURE.

July 19 **Rome** bombed by some 500 Allied planes. The highly strategic city with a network of railroads and freight yards had been spared for 4 years by the Allies because of its religious significance.

July 25 **Mussolini resigned** upon the insistence of King Victor Emmanuel.

Aug. 1 Rumania's **Ploesti** oil fields and refineries raided by U.S. bombers.

Aug. 15 **Kiska** retaken by American and Canadian units. The troops landed on the Aleutian Islands to find the Japanese gone.

Aug. 17 **Roosevelt** and **Churchill** met at Quebec where the Pacific campaign was worked out. Some Chinese representatives were also present during the conference, and there was some difficulty in arriving at an accord with the Russians over the future operations and postwar problems. Conference had begun Aug. 11 —ended Aug. 24.

Aug. 17 **Sicily** conquered, 37 days after its invasion. The Axis powers had lost 167,000 men during the campaign; the Allies lost 25,000 men.

Aug. 28 American troops secured **New Georgia**, Solomon Islands.

Sept. 3 **Italian mainland invaded** by Allies crossing the Strait of Messina.

Sept. 8 **Italy surrendered unconditionally** to the Allied powers. In Germany the surrender was considered a "betrayal."

Sept. 9 **Allies landed at Salerno, Italy.** Upwards of 700 Allied ships (American, British, Dutch, French, and Polish). Allied 5th Army was under the command of Gen. Mark Clark.

Sept. 17 Japanese base at Lae, **New Guinea** fell to the Allies.

Oct. 13. **Italy,** under Marshal Badoglio, declared war on Germany.

Oct. 19 **Moscow conference** opened when the foreign secretaries of Great Britain, U.S., and Russia and the Chinese ambassador in Moscow signed a Joint 4-Nation Declaration agreeing to collaborate in the surrender terms of the enemy and rec-

Deaths and Entrances, dance with musical score by Hunter Johnson, presented by **Martha Graham** and her company.

1st American performances of **Aaron Copland's** *A Lincoln Portrait* and *Piano Sonata.* **Paul Creston** received the New York Music Critics' Circle Award for his *1st Symphony.*

A good year for popular music, **song hits** included: "You'll Never Know," "As Time Goes By," "Brazil," "Comin' in on a Wing and a Prayer," "Taking a Chance on Love," "You'd Be So Nice to Come Home To," "That Old Black Magic," "Moonlight Becomes You," "I've Heard That Song Before," "Don't Get Around Much Any More," "All or Nothing at All," and "Pistol Packin' Mama."

Strong movement towards regionalism in painting spurred many artists to depict Middle Western scenes. Foremost in this direction are **Grant Wood, Thomas Benton,** and **John Steuart Curry.** Benton's *July Hay,* painted this year, strikes in the direction of folk art; it shows two farmers cutting hay in a swirling field of flowers and trees.

Among the younger painters brought forward for the 1st time in 1-man exhibitions, **Jackson Pollock** of Wyoming struck critics as the most individual.

Refugee artists, including Piet Mondrian, Marc Chagall, Fernand Léger, and Yves Tanguy, flourished in their new environment. The most striking of their productions were Mondrian's *Broadway Boogie-Woogie* and Chagall's *The Juggler.*

Mar. 28 Russian-born pianist, conductor, and composer **Sergei Rachmaninoff,** who made his home in the U.S. after World War I, died at 70 in Beverly Hills.

Apr. *One World* by **Wendell L. Willkie** published, written in 6 weeks. In 2 months it had sold over a million copies.

540

| SCIENCE; INDUSTRY; ECONOMICS: EDUCATION; RELIGION; PHILOSOPHY. | SPORTS; FASHIONS; POPULAR ENTERTAINMENT; FOLKLORE; SOCIETY. |

health groups. Action had been initiated Dec. 20, 1938.

Feb. 7 **Shoe rationing** begun. Limit set at 3 pairs per year for each civilian.

Feb. 9 **Minimum 48-hr. work week** in war plants ordered by Pres. Roosevelt.

Mar. 1 **Rationing** on all canned goods begun.

Mar. 25 Chester C. Davis appointed **U.S. Food Administrator** to combat widespread shortages.

Mar. 29 **Rationing** begun on meats, fats, cheese.

Apr. 17 27 million **essential workers frozen** at their jobs by order of War Manpower Commission.

May 1 **Coal mines seized** by government after 530,000 miners refused to obey WLB order to return to pits.

May 5 Fuel Administrator Harold L. Ickes given power to seize all **coal stocks** for use in war plants and for civilian purposes in case of emergency.

May 19 **United Mine Workers** (UMW) petitioned for membership in AFL.

May 22 *Collier's* magazine revealed that both Allied and Axis armed services were using **radar** detection devices. U.S. War and Navy departments disputed British claim to have discovered the principle.

May 27 **Office of War Mobilization** established. Its head, James F. Byrnes, was responsible for the conduct of the war on the home front.

June 10 **Current Tax Payment Bill** signed. This was the pay-as-you-go income tax law.

June 14 In a case brought by Jehovah's Witnesses, the Supreme Court reversed a 1940 decision and ruled that under the Bill of Rights, **school children**

most valuable baseball players, respectively, of the National and American leagues.

N.Y. Giants' relief pitcher Ace Adams set a new 20th-century baseball record of 70 games pitched. Only 1 of them was a complete game.

This year's **National College Football Champion** was, for the 1st time since 1930, Notre Dame, now coached by Frank Leahy. Their record: 9 wins, 1 loss, no ties.

The Heisman Memorial Trophy was awarded to Angelo Bertelli, Notre Dame quarterback named by sportswriters as the **outstanding collegiate football player of the year.**

U.S. lawn tennis men's singles champion, Lt. (j.g.) Joseph R. Hunt; **women's singles champion,** Pauline M. Betz.

Count Fleet won the 67th annual **Preakness Stakes,** paying 1–7. Jockey was J. Longden; time was 1:57⅘ on a good track for winnings valued at $43,190.

Count Fleet won the 75th annual **Belmont Stakes,** paying 1–15. Jockey was J. Longden; time was 2:28⅕ on a fast track for winnings valued at $35,340.

Jan. 1 Georgia defeated U.C.L.A., 9 to 0, in the **Rose Bowl** at Pasadena, Calif., before a crowd of 93,000.

Apr. 8 Detroit won the last of 4 straight games in the Stanley Cup finals, defeating Boston 2–0 to become National League **hockey champions.**

May 1 The winner of the 69th annual **Kentucky Derby** at Churchill Downs, Louisville, Ky., was the favorite, Mrs. J. Hertz's *Count Fleet,* J. Longden up. His time was 2:04 on a fast track; prize, $60,725. He went on to win the Triple Crown.

ognizing the need for an international organization to prevent future wars.

Nov. 2   Japan suffered its worst naval defeat at **Rabaul** when MacArthur, suspecting an attack from there upon Empress Augusta Bay, ordered a bombing mission. Nearly every ship in the harbor was either hit or sunk, about 94,000 tons of shipping.

Nov. 20   Americans made landings on Tarawa and Makin in the **Gilbert Islands.** On Nov. 22 landings were made on Abemama. Occupation of Gilbert Islands completed Nov. 23.

Nov. 22   **Pres. Roosevelt,** Prime Minister **Churchill,** and Generalissimo **Chiang Kai-shek** met in Cairo. They planned future military strategy against Japan and declared that when defeated, Japan would be stripped of all Pacific islands she had seized since 1914.

Nov. 28–Dec. 1   Roosevelt, Churchill, and Stalin met at **Teheran** where they agreed upon future war operations.

Dec. 24   Gen. **Eisenhower** was named Supreme Commander of the European invasion forces.

Altogether it has sold over 2 million, and has been translated into 16 languages.

May 5   **Postal-zone numbering system** was inaugurated in 178 cities. Postmaster general Frank C. Walker expected the use of numbers would speed up mail deliveries.

Nov. 22   **Lorenz Hart,** lyricist who collaborated with composer Richard Rodgers, died of pneumonia in New York. The team's musical comedy hits included *Connecticut Yankee* (1927), *The Boys from Syracuse* (1939), and *Pal Joey* (1940).

Dec. 11   Concert by the New York Philharmonic-Symphony opened the first season of the newly formed **City Center of Music and Drama** in New York City.

Dec. 17   Pres. Roosevelt signed into law a bill repealing the **Chinese Exclusion Acts,** and setting an annual immigration quota of 105 Chinese. The following day, Edward Bing Kan filed an application for citizenship in Chicago, and on Jan. 18, 1944, he became the 1st Chinese naturalized under the new law.

1944

After months of preparation and suspense, the country learned on June 6 that Western Europe had at last been invaded by the Allies. The public knew that fighting would grow more bitter and more costly as our armies drew closer to the Rhine, but now no one doubted the outcome. Similar successes in the Pacific led many to hope for victory within the year, despite repeated warnings by responsible leaders that the Axis war potential was still formidable.

Jan. 22   British and American troops made landings at **Anzio** and **Nettuno,** Italy.

Feb. 2   **Roi Island** in Marshalls taken by 4th Marine Div., while positions were secured on Namur and Kwajalein. For the 1st time Allied troops set foot on prewar Japanese territory.

The arts enjoyed an unparalleled boom year. Paper shortages forced publishers to experiment with soft-cover books; their success was overwhelming. Painters who managed to stay out of the army had a harvest year as a plentiful supply of money created new buyers. Since these collectors could not shop in the European market, our artists were doubly fortunate. With Broadway producers finding it was well-nigh impossible to be saddled with a flop, they crowded their wares into the playhouses and waited for the lines to form in front of the box office. Such a seller's market did not improve the quality of the offerings. Architects were still learning a new trade—that of the efficiency builder, since the criterion for a contract was the speed of construction. All their new ideas were confined to paper and reserved for the end of the war.

| SCIENCE; INDUSTRY; ECONOMICS: EDUCATION; RELIGION; PHILOSOPHY. | SPORTS; FASHIONS; POPULAR ENTERTAINMENT; FOLKLORE; SOCIETY. |

cannot be compelled to salute the flag if the ceremony conflicts with their religion.

June 20   Influx of 300,000 Southern whites and Negroes to war plants in the Detroit area produced tensions that exploded into widespread **race riots** in that city. In 2 days, 35 were killed, over 600 wounded, mostly Negroes. Police arrested over 1500 Negroes, less than 300 whites. Other serious race riots broke out this summer in Mobile (May 25), Los Angeles (June 4), Beaumont, Tex. (June 19), and N.Y.C.'s Harlem (Aug. 1).

July 19   **World's longest oil pipeline,** the "Big Inch," was dedicated. Its main line extends 1254 miles from Longview, Tex., to Phoenixville, Pa., crossing 30 rivers and nearly 200 smaller streams.

Oct. 17   At a special convention in N.Y.C., the **Young Communist League** declared itself dissolved. The 400 delegates organized a group called American Youth for Democracy, which offered membership to non-Communists.

Oct. 17   **Chicago's 1st subway** formally opened.

May 5   Film curator Howard L. Walls announced the **Library of Congress would preserve 5000 motion pictures** made from 1897 to 1917, including 75 Keystone comedies and all of D. W. Griffith's Biograph films.

June 16   Comedian **Charlie Chaplin,** 54, married Oona O'Neill, 18, daughter of playwright Eugene O'Neill. It was Chaplin's 4th marriage.

July 13   Baseball's 11th annual **All-Star Game** won by the American League, 5–3, at Philadelphia.

Oct. 5–11   New York, AL, defeated St. Louis, NL, 4–1, in the 40th annual **World Series.**

Nov. 27   **Navy** defeated Army, 13–0, at Michie Stadium, West Point.

Dec. 4   The federal government's 1st prosecution in recent years of a **Utah polygamy case** ended in the conviction of John Zenz, his wife, and son on charges of transporting a 15-year-old girl over state lines for "purposes of debauchery" after the elder Zenz "married" her in a religious ceremony.

1944

Industry had done such a remarkable job in producing war materials that the government was able to relax many of its priority regulations. Manufacturers took advantage of the temporary quiet by looking forward to consumer markets. Labor controls, however, remained in full effect, as did the many and varied curbs against inflation. Despite these checks, living costs rose nearly one third, engendering considerable unrest in the ranks of the unions. Institutions of higher education mourned the virtual end of the ASTP (Army Specialized Training Program). Some 110,000 out of 145,000 young men who had been enrolled in the nation's colleges were removed and sent to active service.

Nobel Prize in physics presented to **Isidor Isaac Rabi** "for his application of the resonance method to the measurement of the magnetic properties of atomic nuclei."

The movies enjoyed the greatest year in box office history. Receipts totaled between $1½ billions and $2 billions. European markets were beginning to open again as Hollywood films actually followed the advance of our troops on the continent. A decided change in the industry was the formation of more and more independent producing companies. Such established stars as Bing Crosby and Gary Cooper took advantage of the tax laws by appearing in films they made themselves. Fashions swung further from the severe, featuring bare midriffs, slim skirts, large hats. Victories on both fronts raised civilian morale, led to hopes that victory would soon be achieved.

Academy Awards presented to *Going My Way* as the best production of the year, to its star, Bing Crosby, as best actor, and to his co-star, Barry Fitzgerald as best

1944 *Pres.* FRANKLIN D. ROOSEVELT

POLITICS AND GOVERNMENT; WAR; DISASTERS; VITAL STATISTICS.	BOOKS; PAINTING; DRAMA; ARCHITECTURE; SCULPTURE.

Feb. 22   Parry Island fell to U.S. Marines, bringing all of the Marshall Islands under Allied control.

Mar. 6   Berlin attacked by 800 Flying Fortresses when 2000 tons of bombs were dropped on the German capital.

Apr. 22   U.S. troops invaded Netherlands New Guinea.

May 18   Cassino evacuated by the Germans after 2 mos. of bitter resistance.

May 19   Gustav line (Cassino-Anzio area) collapsed under heavy assault by Allied troops.

June 4   Germans were pushed out of **Rome** by Allied advanced tank units, Trinity Sunday. In deference to the religious holiday the American 5th and English 8th armies did not occupy the city until the next morning.

June 6   D-Day. The Allies invaded Europe and established beachheads on Normandy, France. The invasion, under the supreme command of Gen. Dwight D. Eisenhower, involved more than 4000 ships, some 3000 planes, and Allied troops eventually numbering over 4 million.

June 15   Southern Japan bombed by U.S. Superfortresses.

June 26–28   Republican Convention at Chicago nominated Thomas E. Dewey and John Bricker.

July 10   Saipan fell to Americans after 25 days of hard fighting. Upwards of 25,000 Japanese soldiers were killed while 2359 American lives were lost and more than 11,000 wounded.

July 18   U.S. 1st Army entered St. Lô. On same day Hideki Tojo, Japanese General, was removed from his post as Chief of the General Staff for his misman-

Pulitzer Prizes: novel, *Journey in the Dark* by Martin Flavin; drama, no prize; U.S. history, *The Growth of American Thought* by Merle Curti; biography, *The American Leonardo: The Life of Samuel F. B. Morse* by Carlton Mabee; poetry, *Western Star* by Stephen Vincent Benét; music, *Symphony No. 4 (Op. 34)* by Howard Hanson; special award, *Oklahoma!* by Rodgers and Hammerstein.

Most widely sung popular song of the year was "I'll Be Seeing You." Other hit tunes included "Mairzy Doats" and "I'll Walk Alone," "Don't Fence Me In," "Long Ago and Far Away," and "Besame Mucho."

In fiction, Lillian Smith's *Strange Fruit*, **John Hersey**'s *A Bell for Adano*, and **Irving Stone**'s *Immortal Wife* were popular successes, but at year's end the runaway best seller was **Kathleen Winsor**'s *Forever Amber*, a historical novel laced with sex. Nonfiction reading fare included **Ernie Pyle**'s *Brave Men*, **Van Wyck Brooks'** *The World of Washington Irving*, **Catherine Drinker Bowen**'s *Yankee from Olympus*, and heralding a revival of interest in Henry James, **F. O. Matthiessen**'s *Henry James: The Major Phase* and *The Great Short Novels of Henry James*, edited by **Philip Rahve.**

Encouraged by success of *Oklahoma!*, many writers and composers turned to the American past for romantic musicals: *Bloomer Girl* by **Harold Arlen** and **E. Y. Harburg** goes back to the hoopskirt days of 1860's; *Up in Central Park* (1945) by **Sigmund Romberg** is set in the days of Boss Tweed; *Annie Get Your Gun* (1946) by **Irving Berlin** recounts adventures of Annie Oakley of Ohio.

John Van Druten continued his success of *The Voice of the Turtle* (1943) with a play about a Norwegian-American family in San Francisco, *I Remember Mama.*

Postwar period saw a host of fantasy plays hit Broadway. Between 1944 and 1946 some of our best playwrights turned to this general theme: **Elmer Rice**'s *Dream*

SCIENCE; INDUSTRY; ECONOMICS: EDUCATION; RELIGION; PHILOSOPHY.

SPORTS; FASHIONS; POPULAR ENTERTAINMENT; FOLKLORE; SOCIETY.

Rabi's main contribution to nuclear physics in this prize-winning work was in the refinement of the experimental technique which enabled him, in the words of the president of the physics section of the Nobel Committee, "to establish radio relations with the most subtle particles of matter, with the world of the electron and of the atomic nucleus."

Nobel Prize in medicine and physiology awarded to **Joseph Erlanger** and **Herbert Spencer Gasser** "for their discoveries regarding the highly differentiated functions of single nerve fibers." Erlanger and Gasser collaborated on their prize-winning experiments at the medical school of Washington University in St. Louis. They discovered that nerve fibers conducted impulses at various speeds. The thickest fibers, called A-fibers, had the highest conduction velocity; the less thick fibers or B-fibers had a lower conduction velocity; and the thinnest or C-fibers had the lowest velocity of all. Through a study of the relatively simple structure of the nerve fibers (of frogs), Erlanger and Gasser hoped to gain clues to the more elaborate mechanisms of the nervous system.

Medical wonder of the year was **penicillin,** shown to be amazingly effective against a wide variety of infectious diseases and wounds. Further uses were also found for the sulfa drugs, and in one of the more important medical feats of the war, the armed forces used the insecticide DDT to control and wipe out typhus (transmitted by body lice) among troops and civilians.

In **salvage drives** this year, nearly 7 million tons of wastepaper, 84,807 tons of fats, 18.5 million tons of iron and steel scrap, 185,676 tons of tin cans, and 544,-739 tons of rags were collected.

Jan. 19 **Railways returned to owners** after final settlement of wage dispute.

Feb. 29 American **black marketeers** squeezed an estimated $1.2 billions from housewives during past year, according to OPA Director Chester A. Bowles.

Apr. 19 **Lend-lease** extended to June 30, 1945, by House of Representatives.

supporting actor. Ingrid Bergman was named best actress for her performance in *Gaslight* and Ethel Barrymore was named best supporting actress for her portrayal in *None But the Lonely Heart.* Margaret O'Brien received a special award as the "outstanding child actress of the year." A new award for "documentary productions" was shared by 2 combat films of World War II: *Fighting Lady,* an account of an aircraft carrier, and *With the Marines at Tarawa,* an on-the-spot record.

Top box-office attractions at motion-picture theaters, according to *Motion Picture Herald's* poll, were Bing Crosby, Gary Cooper, Bob Hope, Betty Grable, and Spencer Tracy.

Cartoonists **Bill Mauldin** and **George Baker** gave armed services newspapers their most popular features. In "Up Front with Mauldin" a pair of long-suffering GI's, Willie and Joe, endured stoically the rigors of combat ("Just gimme th' aspirin. I already got a Purple Heart"). Baker created the "Sad Sack," an unlucky, confused, ill-dressed, but well-meaning GI forever in trouble. In postwar years, Baker's "Sad Sack" became a regular feature of comic sections; Mauldin took naturally to political cartooning.

The **contribution of dogs to the war effort** was recognized by posthumous awards of certificates of outstanding achievment to 7 dogs killed in the South Pacific, and a German shepherd received the Distinguished Service Medal for charging a machine-gun nest in the invasion of Sicily.

This year's **National College Football Champion** was Army, coached by Earl Blaik.

The Heisman Memorial Trophy was awarded to Leslie Horvath, Ohio State quarterback named by sportswriters as the **outstanding collegiate football player of the year.**

Green Bay Packers defeated the New York Giants 14 to 7 for the **National Professional Football Championship.**

545

agement and loss at Saipan. His cabinet resigned.

July 19–21 **National Convention of the Democratic Party** met in Chicago and nominated Pres. Roosevelt for his 4th term and Harry S. Truman for the vice-presidency.

July 25 German defenses in **Normandy** crumbled under heavy attack by U.S. soldiers under Gen. Bradley.

Aug. 1 Americans pushed into **Brittany** driving forward relentlessly after taking Normandy.

Aug. 8 Americans swept through **Brittany** peninsula and launched a powerful drive eastward toward Paris.

Aug. 9 **Guam** fell to Americans after 20 days of bloody fighting. The conquest cost the Americans 1214 lives and nearly 6000 wounded, while 17,000 Japanese were killed and almost 500 prisoners were taken. Eisenhower, on this day, changed the location of his headquarters from England to France.

Aug. 15 **Southern France** invaded by the U.S. 7th Army under Lt. Gen. Patch.

Aug. 21 **Dumbarton Oaks Conference** opened at Washington, D.C.; attended by delegates of U.S., Great Britain, U.S.S.R. Conference agreed on "proposals for establishment of a general international organization."

Aug. 25 **Paris liberated** as German commander Von Choltitz surrendered to Gen. Leclerc.

Sept. 12 U.S. 1st Army pushed 5 mi. into **Germany.** For 1st time the Allies fought in territory where the inhabitants were not sympathetic to them.

Oct. 20 Americans landed at **Leyte,** Philippine Islands, fulfilling MacArthur's promise to return. It was during the Leyte campaign that the Kamikaze, or suicide plane, was 1st used.

Girl re-enacts daydreams of a young lady; *Harvey* by **Mary Chase** tells the story of an alcoholic and his imaginary rabbit; **Moss Hart's** *Christopher Blake* shifts between fantasy and realism in a dissection of the dreams of a boy whose parents are estranged; *Lute Song* by **Raymond Scott** is a fantasy based on a Chinese play concerning a true and faithful wife; **Tennessee Williams'** *The Glass Menagerie* recounts the touching story of a crippled girl who takes refuge in the unreality of glass animals.

Fancy Free, a ballet with music by the young composer **Leonard Bernstein,** presented at the Metropolitan Opera House by the Ballet Theater. The ballet drew large crowds, and Bernstein later incorporated part of the score in the music he wrote for the musical comedy, *On the Town.*

Late in the year, audiences and critics hailed the emergence of 2 great opera singers: **Dorothy Kirsten,** who sang several lyric and coloratura roles with the City Center Opera Co.; and **Regina Resnik,** who prepared in 24 hours to debut in *Il Trovatore* at the Metropolitan, replacing Zinka Milanov.

Mar. 5 Première performance of **Walter Piston's** 2d Symphony given in Washington, D.C. The symphony achieved an immediate and far-reaching success and brought Piston's name prominently before the music public.

Oct. 1 The **Declaration of Independence** and other historic documents, sent away from Washington for safekeeping in December 1941, were put on display again at the Library of Congress.

Oct. 30 *Appalachian Spring,* a ballet composed on commission from the Elizabeth Sprague Coolidge Foundation by **Aaron Copland,** performed by **Martha Graham** and her company at the Library of Congress, Washington, D.C.

SCIENCE; INDUSTRY; ECONOMICS: EDUCATION; RELIGION; PHILOSOPHY.

SPORTS; FASHIONS; POPULAR ENTERTAINMENT; FOLKLORE; SOCIETY.

Apr. 26 Montgomery Ward plant seized by army. Troops entered Chicago plant of company after Chairman Sewell Avery refused to extend firm's contract with CIO as ordered by WLB.

May 3 Development of **synthetic quinine** announced by 2 Harvard University chemists, Dr. Robert B. Woodward and Dr. William E. Doering.

May 3 Meat rationing ended, except for steak and choice cuts of beef, by order of the OPA.

May 8 New York Hospital, New York City, established 1st eye bank in plan which included 19 other New York hospitals. Eye bank was used to store human corneas which could be used to restore sight in certain kinds of blindness.

May 20 In convention at New York City the **Communist Party** of the U.S. voted to dissolve itself. Its leaders formed a non-party group, the Communist Political Association.

June 5 Insurance companies declared subject to Sherman antitrust laws because they engage in interstate commerce, according to U.S. Supreme Court decision.

June 22 Servicemen's Readjustment Act signed by Pres. Roosevelt. The measure provided broad benefits to returning veterans, including a generous educational program. Known as **"GI Bill of Rights."**

Aug. 14 Production of vacuum cleaners, electric ranges, cooking utensils, and other **consumer goods** resumed under order of WPB. Order was provisional and could be revoked depending upon war needs.

Sept. 14 A major **hurricane** with winds up to 134 mph raked the Atlantic coast from Cape Hatteras to Canada, killing 390 at sea (mostly on military vessels that sank) and about 50 civilians. Damage was estimated at $50 million.

In this year's **P.G.A. Championship,** held at Spokane, Wash., Byron Nelson lost, 1 down, to the relatively unknown Indiana pro Robert Hamilton.

U.S. lawn tennis men's singles champion, Sgt. Frank A. Parker; **women's singles champion,** Pauline M. Betz.

Pensive won the 68th annual **Preakness Stakes,** paying 33–20. Jockey was C. McCreary; time was 1:59⅕ on a fast track for winnings valued at $60,075.

Bounding Home won the 76th annual **Belmont Stakes,** paying 16–1. Jockey was G. L. Smith; time was 2:32⅕ on a fast track for winnings valued at $55,000.

Jan. 1 Southern California defeated Washington, 29 to 0, in the **Rose Bowl** at Pasadena, before a crowd of 68,000.

Mar. 3 Bob Montgomery outpointed Beau Jack in 15 rounds at Madison Square Garden to win the **lightweight championship.** His title, recognized by the N.Y. State Athletic Commission, came into dispute Mar. 8 when Juan Zurita defeated Sammy Angott in Hollywood and was named champion of the 135-lb. division by the N.B.A.

May 1 On the steps of the Capitol in Washington, 90-year-old Jacob S. Coxey delivered the speech he was prevented from making 50 years ago when he led **"Coxey's Army"** of unemployeds there to demand a program of federal works projects.

May 6 Winner of the 70th annual **Kentucky Derby** was the favorite, Calumet Farm's *Pensive,* ridden by C. McCreary. The time, 2:04⅕ on a good track; the prize, $64,675.

July 6 At an afternoon performance in Hartford, Conn., attended by nearly 7000, **fire destroyed the main tent of Ringling Brothers and Barnum & Bailey Circus.** Blazing canvas fell on fleeing spectators and in the scramble 167 were killed, more than 175 injured.

July 11 The National League won the 12th annual **All-Star baseball** game at Pittsburgh, 7–1.

POLITICS AND GOVERNMENT; WAR; DISASTERS; VITAL STATISTICS.

BOOKS; PAINTING; DRAMA; ARCHITECTURE; SCULPTURE.

Oct. 21   **Aachen** fell to the Allies after 7 days of house-to-house fighting.

Oct. 23–26   Japanese fleet failed to halt U.S. invasion of Philippines and in **Leyte Gulf** suffered heavy losses during largest naval battle of the war.

Nov. 7   Pres. Roosevelt defeated Thomas E. Dewey in the **presidential elections** by an electoral vote of 432–99. Popular vote: Roosevelt, 25,602,504; Dewey, 22,006,285.

Dec. 15   4 generals—Henry Arnold, Dwight Eisenhower, Douglas MacArthur, and George C. Marshall—elevated to new rank of **General of the Army** by special act of Congress. Called popularly "5-star generals," the new appointees wore insigne of rank consisting of 5 stars joined in a circle.

Dec. 16   Germans, under von Rundstedt, began their offensive into Belgium breaking through the center of the Allied line, to start the **battle of the bulge.**

Nov. 11   Ending a 2-year fight with American Federation of Musicians president **James C. Petrillo,** 2 major recording companies signed a contract agreeing to pay his union a fee on each record manufactured.

Dec. 23   Artist **Charles Dana Gibson,** whose illustrations of Victorian beauties and the famed "Gibson Girl" had wielded great influence on fashions in the U.S. and Europe, died at 77 in New York City.

1945

It was a monumental year—the end and the beginning of an era. Germany and Japan collapsed and were forced to accept unconditional surrender. The 1st atomic bomb was dropped—a fact that changed the entire complexion of future wars and of the world in general. A mighty new instrument of peace—the United Nations—was optimistically launched at San Francisco. The presidency of the United States changed hands as Franklin D. Roosevelt died in office.

Cordell Hull received this year's **Nobel Peace Prize.**

Jan. 9   American 6th Army landed on **Luzon** when 850 ships sailed into Lingayen Gulf, 100 miles above Manila.

Feb. 7   Gen. MacArthur entered **Manila** more than 3 years after he was forced out of the city by the Japanese.

Feb. 9   **Iwo Jima** invaded by U.S. Marines who established beachheads 2 hours after landing.

It seemed that the most profitable thing for a young man in 1945 was to become a writer. 2d and 3d printings were commonplace for novels as the paperback trade continued to create hundreds of thousands of new readers. Nor was this all. Hollywood, hungry for plots, was willing to pay $250,000 for the rights to a good story. Barely competent ones still commanded handsome figures. With such rich prizes before them, our writers tailored their techniques to fit the requirements of the screen. The result, by and large, was undistinguished. Books about the war continued to be widely written and widely read. In fact, on all artistic fronts, there was a frenzy of activity.

Pulitzer Prizes: novel, *A Bell for Adano* by John Hersey; drama, *Harvey* by Mary Chase; U.S. history, *Unfinished Business* by Stephen Bonsal; biography, *George Bancroft: Brahmin Rebel* by Russel Blaine Nye; poetry, *V-Letter and Other Poems* by

SCIENCE; INDUSTRY; ECONOMICS: EDUCATION; RELIGION; PHILOSOPHY.	SPORTS; FASHIONS; POPULAR ENTERTAINMENT; FOLKLORE; SOCIETY.

Sept. 27   Canadian-born evangelist **Aimee Semple McPherson,** 54, died in Oakland, Calif. Sister Aimee was a spellbinding fundamentalist preacher and faith healer whose followers remained faithful through her several marriages and divorces and a sensational "kidnapping" in 1926.

Oct. 4–9   St. Louis, NL, defeated St. Louis, AL, 4–2 in the 41st **World Series.**

Nov. 25   **Kenesaw Mountain Landis,** commissioner of organized baseball for nearly 24 years, died.

Nov. 18   Report on **living costs** showed rise of 29–30% over last year.

Dec. 2   **Army** defeated Navy, 23–7.

Dec. 24   Maj. **Glenn Miller,** trombonist and leader of the most popular "big name" dance bands of the prewar years, was reported missing on a flight from Paris to England. His hallmark was slow-paced, romantic music, in arrangements featuring the reed instruments. At his death he was director of the U.S. Air Force Band.

Nov. 22   At its convention in Chicago the CIO voted to make its **Political Action Committee** a permanent political instrument.

1945

Aside from victory, biggest news of the year was the development of atomic energy. Having seen what they had wrought, scientists took pause and questioned the moral and ethical value of their work. At first, the public refused to share the alarm of the physicists. They had created this new force and in all probability would next tell the world how to control it—so at least went the general thinking. The idolizing of science and the emergence of the laboratory worker into the status of a man of public affairs followed. Unfortunately, such blind trust was unfounded. No one could supply definite or even optimistic answers.

Roosevelt College established as Thomas Jefferson College in Chicago, Ill. 1st classes met same year. Present name adopted in 1954.

Vitamin research in America stimulated with discovery of folic acid, a component of the large vitamin B family and a necessary element in the growth of living cells. Folic acid was found effective in the treat-

By the end of the war, the Hollywood Victory Committee had arranged for 55,619 personal appearances of movie stars at bond rallies and for servicemen in camp. Celluloid personalities had taken 122 overseas junkets, 151 hospital and 254 camp tours, and had sparked 41 bond selling campaigns. At the same time, the industry kept up a high level of production, even though the major companies were under fire by government lawyers who charged them with conspiring to form illegal trusts. American fashion designers urged women to be more relaxed, stressed delicacy and "prettiness." Crime statistics recorded a startling upward swing. Experts interpreted it as symptomatic of the postwar uncertainty.

Academy Awards presented to *The Lost Weekend* as the outstanding motion picture of the year and to its star, Ray Milland, as the best actor. Joan Crawford was named best actress for her portrayal of *Mildred Pierce.* Anne Revere was chosen best sup-

549

| POLITICS AND GOVERNMENT; WAR; DISASTERS; VITAL STATISTICS. | BOOKS; PAINTING; DRAMA; ARCHITECTURE; SCULPTURE. |

Feb. 12 Declaration signed by Churchill, Roosevelt, and Stalin revealed they had met Feb. 4–11 at Yalta and agreed to aid liberated nations; exact stiff reparations from Germany and divide that country into 4 occupation zones; create a veto for UN Security Council votes; recognize the Lublin government of Poland. Full details of the **Yalta Conference** were not revealed until 1947. Secretly, Russia agreed to declare war upon Japan within 3 months of Germany's defeat, in return for concessions in Asia.

Feb. 23 American flag raised on Mt. Suribachi, **Iwo Jima,** by Lt. Harold C. Shrier.

Mar. 7 1st Army crossed over the **Rhine** at Remagen. Not since the days of Napoleon had an invading army crossed the Rhine.

Mar. 16 **Iwo Jima** fell to the U.S. Marines after 36 days of bitter and bloody fighting. More than 4000 Marines were killed and some 15,000 were wounded. The Japanese lost more than 20,000 men.

Apr. 1 Okinawa invasion begins.

Apr. 12 **Pres. Franklin D. Roosevelt** died in Warm Springs, Ga., on the 83d day of his 4th term; he was 63. He was succeeded by **Harry S. Truman.**

Apr. 24 **United Nations Conference** opened at San Francisco with delegates from 50 nations attending. UN charter signed June 26.

May 7 **Germany surrendered** unconditionally to the Allies after almost 6 years of war. The surrender was signed in Gen. Eisenhower's headquarters in Rheims.

June 21 Japanese surrendered at **Okinawa** after 2½ months of deadly struggle. More than 100,000 Japanese soldiers were killed; American deaths ran to almost 13,000, and nearly 40,000 were wounded.

July 5 Gen. MacArthur reported liberation of the **Philippine Islands.** In 10 months of fighting since the first American landings at Leyte, more than 400,000 Japanese soldiers were killed, while upwards of 12,000 Americans lost their lives.

Karl Shapiro; music, *Appalachian Spring* by Aaron Copland.

Outstanding novel of the year was **Richard Wright's** *Black Boy,* the story of a grim and frightening Negro childhood. Best nonfiction book was *The Age of Jackson* by newcomer **Arthur M. Schlesinger, Jr.,** a fascinating account of the life and times of Andrew Jackson. Most distinguished verse offering was **Robert Frost's** *A Masque of Reason,* a delightful debate between God, Job, and Job's wife.

Carousel, a musical comedy by **Richard Rodgers** and **Oscar Hammerstein II,** was hit of the season in New York.

Tennessee Williams' *Glass Menagerie* won the New York Drama Critics' Circle Award. The play starred Laurette Taylor and Eddie Dowling.

Use of sheet metal for sculpture furthered through work of **Jose de Creeft** and **Saul Raizerman.** De Creeft's head of *Rachmaninoff,* hammered in lead, received 1st Sculpture Prize at Pennsylvania Academy of Art.

New York Music Critics' Circle Award for the best symphonic composition went this year to **Walter Piston's** *2d Symphony.*

Ernst Krenek, 12-tone composer, wrote *The Santa Fe Time Table* for mixed chorus *a cappella.*

Charles Ives, pioneer American composer in the modern vein, elected to the National Institute of Arts and Letters. At the time Ives had never heard any of his works performed by a full orchestra.

Apr. 18 Newsman **Ernie Pyle** died in action on Ie Jima, an island near Okinawa. Probably the most widely read war correspondent, he had covered both European and Pacific campaigns, living with and writing sympathetically about ordinary GI's. His columns were collected into best-selling books, among them *Here Is Your War* (1943) and *Brave Men* (1944).

July 9 Frank Lloyd Wright displayed his model for the **Solomon R. Gug-**

ment of pernicious anemia but later analyses revealed adverse effects on the nervous system.

Gross product of U.S. goods and services valued at $215 billions for the year, two thirds more than in 1939.

Jan. 15   **Nationwide dimout** ordered to conserve diminishing fuel supplies.

Feb. 26   **Midnight curfew** on all places of amusement ordered.

Mar. 1   **10% royalty** on all coal mined asked by John L. Lewis of UMW.

Mar. 26   Power to cut **tariff rate** by 50% in reciprocal trade agreements asked by Pres. Roosevelt.

Apr. 30   **Sugar rations** cut 25% as reserves neared "rock bottom."

May 6   **12 million tons of food** needed to feed Europe during coming year, according to Agriculture Department.

May 8   **Nationwide dimout** lifted.

May 9   **Midnight entertainment curfew** lifted.

May 10   73 **consumer items** once more manufactured as WPB bans lifted.

May 25   30% reduction in production of **military aircraft** announced.

June 27   The FCC allocated 13 channels for **commercial television broadcasting.**

June 30   **OPA** granted 1 more year of life by House of Representatives vote.

July 1   **New York State Commission Against Discrimination** established; it was 1st state anti-discrimination agency. The commission was authorized to take the steps to prevent "discrimination in employment because of race, creed, color or national origin."

July 27   The Communist Political Association voted to disband itself and become again the militant **Communist Party.**

Aug. 14   All **manpower controls** lifted by War Manpower Commission.

Aug. 18   Full restoration of civilian **consumer production,** collective bargaining, and a return of free markets ordered by Pres. Truman.

porting actress for her work in *National Velvet* and James Dunn was picked best supporting actor for his characterization in *A Tree Grows in Brooklyn.*

Catchword **"Kilroy was here"** spread throughout the whole world, wherever the American GI had set his foot. Kilroy is a kind of abstract conglomerate of all the gagsters in the U.S. Army. The phrase was scribbled on streets, billboards, in latrines, etc., throughout the world.

This year's **national football champion** was again Army, coached by Earl Blaik. Their record: 9 wins, no losses, no ties.

U.S. lawn tennis men's singles champion, Sgt. Frank A. Parker; **women's singles champion,** Mrs. Sarah Palfrey Cooke.

Boxer of the year was newcomer Rocky Graziano, who in 5 fights at Madison Square Garden scored 5 knockouts, including 2 over welterweight champ Fred Cochrane.

Pavot won the 77th annual **Belmont Stakes,** paying 2–1. Jockey was E. Arcaro.

Polynesian won the 69th annual **Preakness Stakes,** paying 12–1. Jockey was W. D. Wright.

Jan. 1   Southern California defeated Tennessee 25 to 0 in the **Rose Bowl.**

Jan. 26   The **N.Y. Yankees baseball club was sold** by the heirs of the late Jacob Ruppert and Edward G. Barrow to a syndicate headed by Lawrence McPhail and including Daniel Topping and Del Webb. Estimated price was $2.8 million.

Apr. 24   Sen. **Albert B. "Happy" Chandler** named high commissioner of baseball to fill post caused by death of Judge Landis.

June 9   Jockey Eddie Arcaro rode his 3d **Kentucky Derby** winner, F. W. Hooper's *Hoop Jr.*

551

| POLITICS AND GOVERNMENT; WAR; DISASTERS; VITAL STATISTICS. | BOOKS; PAINTING; DRAMA; ARCHITECTURE; SCULPTURE. |

July 16   **1st atomic bomb** exploded near Alamogordo, N.M., at 5:30 A.M.

July 28   U.S. Senate ratified the **UN Charter** by a vote of 89 to 2.

Aug. 6   **U.S. atomic bomb** dropped on Hiroshima; Nagasaki bombed Aug. 9.

Aug. 14   Unconditional **surrender of Japan** announced by Pres. Truman.

Aug. 30   Gen. MacArthur landed in **Japan;** occupation hq were in Yokohama.

Sept. 2   **Surrender** document signed aboard the U.S.S. *Missouri* in Tokyo Bay.

genheim **Museum of Non-Objective Painting** in New York. The structure's main element is a round, blunt tower capped with a glass dome and tapered toward the base. Within it, exhibit areas are situated along a continuous spiral ramp.

Oct. 31   Booker T. Washington, Walter Reed, Thomas Paine, and Sidney Lanier were elected to the **Hall of Fame** on the New York University campus.

Nov. 21   Humorist **Robert Benchley** died in New York City.

1946

Formidable domestic problems—a spiraling inflation, acute shortage of housing, bitter labor disputes—were complicated by the first rumblings of the "cold war" with Russia and the appalling poverty of Europe which looked to us for aid. It quickly became apparent that the United States would not be allowed to lick its own wounds and mend its private fences. A menace, more frightening than Naziism, was seen by many as threatening our very way of life. There were those, of course, who disagreed that Communist Russia had ultimate territorial demands on the West, and there were some who felt that, if indeed it had, these demands were not our problems. The administration, however, took the view that complete isolation was a luxury we could not afford, primarily because of the existence of the atomic bomb. And so the U.S. assumed the role of stabilizer in a rocky world. It was a role that at times was not very confidently played.

John Raleigh Mott and Emily Greene Balch shared the **Nobel Peace Prize** for this year. Mott, Methodist layman and a leader in international church activities, headed the Y.M.C.A.'s relief activities for prisoners of war during World War I. Emily Greene Balch was a founder in 1915 of the Women's International League

Literary critics looked for a spate of fine books this year, calling up as their precedent the year immediately following World War I. Unfortunately they were disappointed, had to be content with noting a new development in fictional technique —a modified stream of consciousness in which a highly sensitive story was told by a perceptive observer. Chief practitioners of this style were 2 women: Elizabeth Bolton, who published *Do I Wake or Sleep?,* and Eudora Welty, who put out *Delta Wedding.* Architects were still being forced to be practical. With building costs per unit up, they designed houses with smaller rooms, compensated for it by enclosing them with more glass. U.S. painters were seen at an exhibition in London and succeeded in shocking (not boring) viewers. Theater-goers were treated to one of the most extensive revival seasons within memory. Broadway houses held Shakespeare, Shaw, Chekhov, Ibsen, Sophocles, Aristophanes, Wilde, Webster, Marlowe, others.

Pulitzer Prizes: novel, no prize; drama, *State of the Union* by Russel Crouse and Howard Lindsay; U.S. history, *The Age of Jackson* by Arthur M. Schlesinger, Jr.; biography, *Son of the Wilderness* by Linnie Marsh Wolfe; poetry, no prize; music, *The Canticle of the Sun* by Leo Sowerby.

552

SCIENCE; INDUSTRY; ECONOMICS: EDUCATION; RELIGION; PHILOSOPHY.	SPORTS; FASHIONS; POPULAR ENTERTAINMENT; FOLKLORE; SOCIETY.

Aug. 20   210 controls over **consumer production** lifted by WPB.

Oct. 30   **Shoe rationing** ended.

Nov. 21   **CIO United Auto Workers** struck all General Motors plants.

Nov. 23   **Meat, butter rationing** ended.

Dec. 20   **Tire rationing** ended.

Dec. 21   **Gen. George S. Patton,** died in Heidelberg of auto injuries.

Dec. 31   Office of **National War Labor Board** replaced by **National Wage Stabilization Board.**

July 28   This foggy Saturday morning the **Empire State Building was struck by a B-25 bomber** at the 78–79th floors.

Aug. 10   Controlling interest in the **Brooklyn Dodgers** baseball club was acquired by Branch Rickey, Walter O'Malley, and John L. Smith.

Sept. 6   N.Y.C. police commissioner **Lewis J. Valentine** resigned to preside over the radio show "Gang Busters."

Oct. 3–10   Detroit, AL, defeated Chicago, NL, 4–3 in the 42d **World Series.**

Dec. 2   Army defeated Navy, 32–13.

1946

A year of tremendous confusion and bitter warfare between management and labor. Held down by years of wage controls, practically all the large and powerful labor unions struck for higher pay. Industry insisted their demands were exorbitant, but could not afford walkouts at a time when the consumer market was at an unparalleled high. The country had a great deal of excess money, saved over from the days when nothing could be bought, and everyone had a new carefree desire to spend it. The agonizing changeover from war production to consumer goods took time, and tempers grew shorter when orders were not met immediately. The government, meanwhile, desperately tried to convince the people that the emergency was not yet over, that ruinous inflation still threatened, that the shift back to peacetime habits and living should be made slowly, cautiously.

Nobel Prize in physics awarded to **Percy Williams Bridgman** "for the invention of apparatus for obtaining very high pressures, and for the discoveries which he made by means of this apparatus in the field of high-pressure physics." Bridgman performed most of his prize-winning experiments at Harvard where he had been Hollis Professor of Mathematics and Natural Philosophy since 1926. Bridgman's

Repeal of the federal excess profit tax and generally increased admission prices upped box office receipts at movie houses to unprecedented highs. Quality of films produced was also up. But then it had to be as foreign producers made a strong bid for American markets by offering such colorful spectacles as Laurence Olivier's *Henry V.* Baseball stars, returning from service, improved the game, afforded fans a breathtaking pennant race, with a playoff necessary in the National League. In keeping with the sunny optimism of peace, and partly to retain their leadership in the fashion world now that styles were once more coming from Paris, our designers showed light-hearted feminine collections. Chief topics of conversation: rising prices, shortage of housing, menace of Russian communism, the atomic bomb.

Academy Awards presented to *The Best Years of Our Lives* as the outstanding motion picture of the year and to its star, Fredric March as the best actor. Olivia de Havilland was named best actress for her performance in *To Each His Own* and Anne Baxter was chosen best supporting actress for her work in *The Razor's Edge.* Harold Russell, an amputee who had never acted before, was named best supporting actor for his portrayal of an amputee-veteran in *The Best Years of Our Lives.*

| POLITICS AND GOVERNMENT; WAR; DISASTERS; VITAL STATISTICS. | BOOKS; PAINTING; DRAMA; ARCHITECTURE; SCULPTURE. |

for Peace and Freedom at The Hague, The Netherlands.

Apr. 11 Bill providing for Government monopoly over all U.S. **atomic energy** activities passed by Senate committee. It is known as the McMahon Bill.

May 14 **Selective Service Act** extended to Sept. 1.

July 1 **Atomic bomb tests** held at Bikini Atoll in Pacific. A Nagasaki-type bomb was dropped from 30,000 feet, destroying 5 ships, heavily damaging 9, and doing varying amounts of damage to 45 others.

July 4 "The independence of the **Philippines** as a separate and self-governing nation" proclaimed by Pres. Truman, thus keeping our promise made on acquiring the islands in 1898.

July 30 U.S. joined **UNESCO** (United Nations Educational, Scientific and Cultural Organization).

Aug. 1 Pres. Truman signed a bill creating the **Atomic Energy Commission,** composed of a 5-man control board without military representation but with military liaison. Bill allowed the army and navy to manufacture atomic weapons and prohibited the distribution of fissionable materials or atomic energy information.

Dec. 7 127 died and nearly 100 were injured in America's **worst hotel fire.** The Winecoff Hotel in Atlanta, Ga., having no outside fire escapes or sprinkler system, became a death trap when the 2 elevator shafts and the 2 narrow stairways caught fire. Many leaped to their deaths from the windows of the 15-story building to avoid the flames.

Dec. 14 Gift of $8½ million from John D. Rockefeller, Jr., accepted by UN to be used for purchase of property along New York city's East River for UN **permanent headquarters.**

Dec. 31 **State of hostilities** officially ended by Pres. Truman, who reminded the

Frenetic censorship issue raised over **Edmund Wilson's** *Memoirs of Hecate County* reminiscent of similar furor stirred up by **James Branch Cabell's** *Jurgen* in 1919. Cases against Wilson and publishers led to eventual withdrawal of book.

1st literary work affected by new Massachusetts statute relating to **obscene literature** was Kathleen Winsor's phenomenal best-seller *Forever Amber.* Book was exonerated in Suffolk County Superior Court and decision upheld in Massachusetts Supreme Court with observation of Judge Frank J. Donahue that the book was more of a "soporific . . . than an aphrodisiac."

High standard of New York theater reflected in the openings of many fine plays this season. **Eugene O'Neill** returned in *The Iceman Cometh;* **Lillian Hellman** offered an attack upon capitalism in *Another Part of the Forest;* **Maxwell Anderson** presented *Joan of Lorraine,* Ingrid Bergman starring in the lead; **George Kelly's** *The Fatal Weakness* continued his studies of marriage and divorce.

Most startling architectural innovation in years was the **Dymaxion House,** designed by Buckminster Fuller. A circular family dwelling, it could be mass produced by assembly line techniques, and was considered by many the answer to the critical housing shortage.

The **"ranch type" home** caught the architectural fancy of the public this year. Soon the countryside was mushrooming with low-slung, single-story (although sometimes split level) homes.

Biggest **popular song hit** was "The Gypsy." Others included: "They Say It's Wonderful," "Doin' What Comes Naturally," "I Got the Sun in the Morning," all 3 from Irving Berlin's score for *Annie Get Your Gun;* "To Each His Own";

SCIENCE; INDUSTRY; ECONOMICS; EDUCATION; RELIGION; PHILOSOPHY.

SPORTS; FASHIONS; POPULAR ENTERTAINMENT; FOLKLORE; SOCIETY.

experiments with high pressures have had immense value in determining the effects of these pressures on hitherto unexplained phenomena.

Nobel Prize in medicine and physiology awarded to **Hermann Joseph Muller** "for his discovery of the production of mutations by means of X-ray irradiations." Muller obtained his 1st evidence of mutations caused by X-rays in 1926. His discovery has been of invaluable assistance to the science of genetics. Muller's studies also instituted a spirit of caution among radiologists since most mutations are undesirable. Muller's work on the somatic effects of radiation have a continuing significance with the advent of atomic energy.

Nobel Prizes in chemistry presented to **Dr. James B. Sumner** for work in the crystallizing of enzymes, and to **John Northrop** and **Dr. Wendell M. Stanley** for preparation of enzymes and virus proteins in pure form. They are the 4th, 5th, and 6th American chemists to attain this distinction.

4,600,000 workers involved in **strikes** this year at a cost of 116 million man-hours.

Jan. 25 AFL voted to readmit **United Mine Workers** under John L. Lewis.

July 7 **Mother Frances Xavier Cabrini** canonized in ceremonies presided over by Pope Pius XII; she was 1st American to be canonized. Mother Cabrini was founder of the Missionary Sisters of the Sacred Heart of Jesus. Her principal shrine is at Mother Cabrini High School in New York city; her feast day is Dec. 22.

Oct. 15 **Price controls** on meat lifted.

Nov. 9 All **wage and price controls** ended except on rents, sugar, and rice.

Nov. 16 **Evangelical United Brethren Church** organized at Johnstown, Pa., in a

This year's **National Football Champion** was Notre Dame, coached by Frank Leahy. Their record: 8 wins, no losses, 1 tie.

U.S. lawn tennis men's singles champion, John A. Kramer; **women's singles champion,** Pauline M. Betz.

U.S.G.A. amateur championship won by Ted Bishop at Baltusrol G.C., Short Hills, N.J. He defeated Smiley Quick, 1 up. **Open championship** won by Lloyd Mangrum at Canterbury G.C., Cleveland, Ohio, with a score of 284.

Assault won the 70th annual **Preakness Stakes,** paying 7–5. Jockey was W. Mehrtens; time was 2:$1\frac{2}{5}$ on a fast track for winnings valued at $96,620.

Assault won the 78th annual **Belmont Stakes,** paying 7–5. Jockey was W. Mehrtens; time was 2:30$\frac{4}{5}$ on a fast track for winnings valued at $75,400.

U.S. defeated Australia 5 to 0 in the challenge round of the **Davis Cup** International Matches.

Jan. 1 Alabama defeated Southern California by a score of 34 to 14 in the **Rose Bowl** at Pasadena, Calif., before a crowd of 93,000.

May 4 King Ranch's *Assault* won the 72d annual **Kentucky Derby** at Churchill Downs, Louisville, Ky. He ran the 1¼ mi. in 2:06$\frac{3}{5}$ on a slow track, winning $96,400. The jockey was W. Mehrtens. He became the 7th Triple Crown winner.

July 9 American League shut out the National League, 12–0, in the 13th annual **All-Star game** held in Boston after a lapse of one year. Ted Williams hit 2 home runs for the winners and Charlie Keller hit one.

Oct. 1–3 National League pennant race ended in league's **1st tie:** Brooklyn and St. Louis had same season record of 96 wins, 58 losses. St. Louis won play-off on Oct. 3 by taking 2 games straight, 4–2 and 8–2.

Oct. 6–15 St. Louis, NL, defeated Boston, AL, 4–3 in the 43d annual **World Series.**

| POLITICS AND GOVERNMENT; WAR; DISASTERS; VITAL STATISTICS. | BOOKS; PAINTING; DRAMA; ARCHITECTURE; SCULPTURE. |

nation that a state of war still existed and that the states of emergency, proclaimed by Pres. Roosevelt, were not yet rescinded.

"Aren't You Glad You're You"; "Ole Buttermilk Sky"; and "Shoo-Fly Pie and Apple Pan Dowdy."

1947

Economic equilibrium was the administration's chief concern. A restless populace complained about constantly rising prices of food, clothing, rent, other necessities of life. Manufacturers blamed spiraling costs on industry-wide wage boosts. Housing conditions everywhere became so tight that Pres. Truman called the shortage "the foremost of the many problems facing the nation." Most dramatic successes of the year were scored in our foreign policy. The European Recovery program or "Marshall Plan," as it was more commonly called, earned us gratitude from Western European nations, abuse from Iron Curtain and satellite countries. The intensity of the "Cold War" was stepped up as an executive order banned all members or sympathizers of the Communist Party from holding office in the executive branch of the government.

Apr. 9 **Tornado** caused the death of 167 persons and the injury of more than 1300 in Texas and Oklahoma. ⅔ of Woodward, Okla., was destroyed by the storm.

Apr. 16–18 Upwards of 500 persons died as a result of a **ship explosion** in Texas City, Tex. The city itself was virtually annihilated by the blast.

May 22 Pres. Truman signed the **Greek-Turkish Aid Bill** which authorized some $400 million in aid to Greece and Turkey upon their request. This authorization was subject to withdrawal upon the disapproval of the interested countries, the U.N. Security Council or General Assembly, or of the president if he deemed the aid to have been either improperly used or entirely unnecessary. This legislation is known as the **"Truman Doctrine."** When Truman requested the legislation he had said: "I believe that it must be the policy of the United States to support free peoples

The 2 most noticeable trends in American publishing were a reawakening interest in our history and a striking turn toward philosophical introspection. The latter was, no doubt, prompted by an increased concern with the fate of the human race now that it had discovered the power to destroy itself. Symbols once more played an important part in the artistic life of the country. Exhibitions featured more nonobjective and expressionistic paintings, leaned less on realism and the once fashionable surrealism. Composers took heart as orchestral societies encouraged the programming of contemporary works. Despite a continued boom on Broadway, producers found it difficult to find backers for their plays; production costs were twice what they were 5 years ago. Reluctant to risk so much on new scripts, they resorted to revivals. Architects produced little individualistic work since ¾ of the building in the country was in the hands of the big operators who planned large-scale "developments."

Pulitzer Prizes: novel, *All the King's Men* by Robert Penn Warren; drama, no prize; U.S. history, *Scientists Against Time* by James Phinney Baxter III; biography, *The Autobiography of William Allen White;* poetry, *Lord Weary's Castle* by Robert Lowell; music, *Symphony No. 3* by Charles Ives, who had been composing since 1900. This was the 1st public recognition of his work.

2 delightful musical plays opened in New York this year and caught the hearts of the public. Both drew material from the British Isles: *Finian's Rainbow* by **E. Y. Harburg** is the fantasy tale of an old Irishman who has stolen a crock of gold from a leprechaun; *Brigadoon* by **Alan J. Lerner** tells the tale of two American

SCIENCE; INDUSTRY; ECONOMICS; EDUCATION; RELIGION; PHILOSOPHY.	SPORTS; FASHIONS; POPULAR ENTERTAINMENT; FOLKLORE; SOCIETY.

union of Evangelical Church and Church of the United Brethren in Christ. In 1953 Church membership was 727,549.

Nov. 30 Army defeated Navy, 21–18, to win the annual **Army-Navy football game** at Municipal Stadium, Philadelphia, Pa.

1947

Many of labor's hard-won gains guaranteed by the Wagner Act were erased this year by passage of the widely debated Taft-Hartley Bill. While many citizens applauded the law's effective curb on alleged union excesses, labor leaders pledged an all-out effort to eliminate the legislation, particularly the hateful (to them) provision outlawing all closed shop contracts. Despite this setback, organized labor grew more powerful as a continued business boom sent more and more workers into its ranks. American education was concerned with 5 major areas: (1) betterment of the economic lot of teachers; (2) finding ways to meet the challenge of increased enrollment; (3) trying to decide how to take advantage of federal aid for schools and still keep them free of government control; (4) how to settle the growing controversy over the role of religion in education; and, (5) how to implement a growing interest in international educational co-operation.

Nobel Prizes in medicine and physiology awarded to **Carl F. Cori** and his wife, **Gerty T. Cori** "for their discovery of how glycogen is catalytically converted." The significance of this discovery lies in its revelation of the chemical mechanism by which the hormones concerned in carbohydrate metabolism perform their task. The Coris' were born in Prague but entered the U.S. in 1922 to work on the staff of the State Institute for the Study of Malignant Diseases in Buffalo, N.Y.

Veteran enrollment in American colleges, spurred by the "G.I. Bill of Rights," reached its peak. Over 1 million ex-servicemen were included in the rolls of 2½ million college students.

38 **U.S. magazines** reached circulations of more than 1 million. In 1900 no Ameri-

Biggest news from Hollywood was the investigation of alleged Communism in movie studios. Senate committees claimed that 10 screen writers were either card-carrying members of the Party or had strong Red leanings. These men, it was argued, had no place in an industry strategically placed to transmit the propaganda of foreign ideologies. The studios, by and large, took the view that outside help was not needed to clean house. Meanwhile, large companies viewed with alarm the 20% federal amusement tax which encouraged people to stay home to watch ever-improving entertainment offered on television. Most general topic of conversation: the "New Look" in women's fashions inspired by Paris designer, Christian Dior, who screened milady's leg with a lower skirt, pinched in her waist, flattened her bosom.

Academy Awards presented to *Gentleman's Agreement* as the outstanding motion picture of the year, to Loretta Young as the best actress for her performance in *The Farmer's Daughter*, and to Ronald Colman as the best actor for his portrayal in *A Double Life*. Celeste Holm was chosen best supporting actress for her work in *Gentleman's Agreement* and Edmund Gwenn was named best supporting actor for his playing in *Miracle on 34th Street*.

1st Negro baseball player in National League when Jackie Robinson signed with Brooklyn Dodgers. Later in season Negro players played in American League for 1st time.

This year's **National College Football Champion** was again Notre Dame, coached by Frank Leahy. They were undefeated and untied in 9 games.

557

POLITICS AND GOVERNMENT; WAR; DISASTERS; VITAL STATISTICS.

BOOKS; PAINTING; DRAMA; ARCHITECTURE; SCULPTURE.

who are resisting attempted subjugation by armed minorities or by outside pressures."

June 5 **Marshall Plan** proposed at a Harvard commencement by Sec. of State George C. Marshall. He urged that a careful study of European needs (upon which U.S. aid could be based) was essential before any real progress could be made in the economic rehabilitation of Europe.

June 14 U.S. Senate ratified the **peace treaties** with Italy, Rumania, Bulgaria, and Hungary, and Pres. Truman formally signed them.

June 26–28 **National Convention of the Prohibition Party** met at Winona Lake, Ind., and nominated Claude A. Watson of California for the presidency.

July 18 Pres. Truman signed the **Presidential Succession Act** which designated the Speaker of the House and President of the Senate pro tempore next in succession after the vice-president.

July 25 Congress enacted bill to **unify armed services.** New Dept. of Defense united War, Navy, and Air Force departments under single secretary of cabinet rank. 1st Sec. of Defense was James V. Forrestal.

Sept. 17–19 Severe **hurricane** swept in from Gulf of Mexico, causing widespread damage in Florida, Mississippi, and Louisiana, killing at least 100 people. On Sept. 21, as aftermath of hurricane, flood waters near New Orleans destroyed many crops and killed about 60 people.

Dec. 27 **Greatest snowfall** in New York city's history, (25.8 in.) caused nearly 80 deaths in the North Atlantic states. Stalled trains stranded commuters. Marooned suburbanites crowded downtown hotels.

lads in a small Scotch town. Both plays abound in memorable tunes. From *Finian's Rainbow* came "How Are Things in Glocca Morra?" "If This Isn't Love," and "Old Devil Moon." From *Brigadoon,* "Almost Like Being in Love."

Powerfully moving play of the South, presenting the disintegration of a neurotic character, Blanche Dubois, in the face of the brutality of modern day life is **Tennessee Williams'** colorful *A Streetcar Named Desire.* The decay of Southern aristocracy is epitomized in the career of Blanche in sensual New Orleans.

1st performance of **Roger Sessions'** Symphony No. 2 in San Francisco provoked considerable hostile reaction. Dedicated "To the Memory of Franklin Delano Roosevelt," the symphony incorporates a dissonant contrapuntal texture, harmonic complexity, and a driving rhythm.

Jan. 28 **Bay Psalm Book** bought for $151,000 at an auction of the Parke-Bernet Galleries in New York. This was the highest price ever paid for a book.

Feb. 18 *The Medium,* a 2-act opera by **Gian-Carlo Menotti,** produced at the Heckscher Theater in New York by the Ballet Theater. On May 1, it opened on Broadway at the Ethel Barrymore Theater and achieved a resounding popular success.

Apr. 26 Première performance of the Symphony in A, by **John Powell,** given by the Detroit Symphony Orchestra. Commissioned by the National Federation of Music Clubs, the Symphony was one of the last major works in the avowedly nationalistic movement among American composers; it applied neo-romantic techniques to Anglo-American folk themes.

1948

Little love was lost between the administration and the lawmakers this year. Pres. Truman called the 80th Congress the

Our authors seemed preoccupied with 4 chief areas; World War II in fiction and fact, an evaluation of the meaning of the

SCIENCE; INDUSTRY; ECONOMICS; EDUCATION; RELIGION; PHILOSOPHY.

SPORTS; FASHIONS; POPULAR ENTERTAINMENT; FOLKLORE; SOCIETY.

can magazine had a circulation of more than half a million.

June 11 **Sugar rationing** ended.

June 17 Pan American Airways, Inc., inaugurated **1st globe-circling passenger line.** Fare was $1700.

June 23 Controversial **Taft-Hartley Act** passed over Pres. Truman's veto, reduced or eliminated many labor union advantages provided for in the Wagner Act, including the unconditional closed shop, the "check-off" system, unconditional right to strike at any time, immunity from employer lawsuits over breaches of contract and strike damage. New obligations for labor unions included publication of financial statements, and mandatory affidavit of all union leaders attesting nonmembership in the Communist Party.

Oct. 14 Capt. Charles E. Yeager, U.S. Air Force, piloted **1st plane to achieve supersonic speed** during test at Muroc Air Force Base, Calif. Plane was X-1 research model built by Bell Aircraft Corporation.

Oct. 29 General Electric Company "seeded" cumulous clouds with dry ice over a forest fire at Concord, N.H., and a rain fell drenching area. But since a natural rain followed soon after the experiment, it was impossible to determine exactly how effective the seeding had been. During 1947 press carried much comment about **"artificial weather,"** but the opinion of most meteorologists was that rain would result only from the seeding of clouds already at shower stage. Thus "making" rain over a drought area was considered nearly impossible.

U.S. lawn tennis men's singles champion, John A. Kramer; **women's singles champion,** A. Louise Brough.

U.S. defeated Australia 4 to 1 in the challenge round of the **Davis Cup** International Matches.

U.S.G.A. amateur championship won by Robert H. Riegel at Pebble Beach Course, Del Monte, Calif. He defeated Johnny Dawson, 2 and 1. **Open Championship** won by Lew Worsham at St. Louis, Mo., C.C., with a score of 282.

Faultless won the 71st annual **Preakness Stakes,** paying 21–5. Jockey was D. Dodson; time was 1:59 on a fast track for winnings valued at $98,005.

Phalanx won the 79th annual **Belmont Stakes,** paying 23–10. Jockey was R. Donoso; time was 2:29⅖ on a fast track for winnings valued at $78,900.

Jan. 1 Illinois defeated U.C.L.A. by a score of 45 to 14 in the **Rose Bowl** at Pasadena, Calif., before a crowd of 90,000.

May 3 The winner of the 73d **Kentucky Derby** at Churchill Downs, Louisville, Ky., was *Jet Pilot* ridden by Eric Guerin. He ran the 1¼ mi. in 2:06⅘ on a slow track, winning $92,160 for his owners, the Main Chance Farm.

July 8 The 14th annual **All-Star game** won by the American League, 2–1, at Chicago on July 8. Johnny Mize hit a homer to account for the losers' only run.

Sept. 30–Oct. 6 New York, AL, defeated Brooklyn, NL, 4–3 in the 44th annual **World Series.**

Nov. 29 **Army** defeated Navy, 21–0, in their annual contest at Municipal Stadium, Philadelphia.

1948

Bolstered by increased defense expenditures and a costly foreign aid program, American industry enjoyed a peak year.

The major leagues provided fans with the 1st postseason playoff in the history of the American League when Cleveland

"worst in our history." One of the chief areas of disagreement was the concern over the influx of Communists in responsible governmental positions. The House Committee on un-American activities (Thomas Committee) wrote alarming reports which the President largely ignored, calling one finding a "red herring." He maintained that the FBI together with the Justice Department was more than equal to the task of cleaning house. Some 2 million federal employees were investigated; as a direct result, 526 resigned and 98 were dismissed. The European Recovery Program continued with military aid sent to Greece, Turkey, and China. Most dramatic development of the year was the Berlin blockade which the U.S. breached by maintaining an airlift that kept the beleaguered city supplied.

Jan. 8   Minimum cost of **European relief** for 1st 15 mo. put at $16,800,000,000 by Sec. of State George C. Marshall.

Mar. 30   Pres. Truman signed the **Rent Control Bill** which extended controls until Mar. 31, 1949. Bill also designated an Emergency Court of Appeals to decide on decontrols or increases recommended by local boards but rejected by the Federal Housing Expediter.

Apr. 3   Pres. Truman signed the **Foreign Assistance Act** of 1948 which provided $5.3 billion for a 1-year European Recovery Program, known officially as ERP and popularly as the **"Marshall Plan."** Act also provided $275 million for military aid to Greece and Turkey, $463 million for economic and military aid for China, and $60 million for a U.N. Fund for Children.

May 2   **Socialist Labor party convention** at New York city nominated Edward A. Teichert for the presidency.

May 9   **Socialist party convention** at Reading, Pa., nominated Norman M. Thomas for the presidency for 6th consecutive time.

June 24   Gov. Thomas Dewey of New

atomic bomb, a search for peace of mind that evoked several best-selling homiletic tracts, and a concern for the sociobiological place of sex in society. The "big" or definitive novel of World War II was still awaited, and since, in a way, contemporary themes in fiction were meaningless until they had been given a foundation in the recent conflict, the next best thing was nonfiction. The newest communication medium, television, was cursed in many quarters as the eventual destroyer of American reading, theater, movies. Actually, it spurred audiences to experience these arts for themselves. Nowhere was this tendency more apparent than in music. TV broadcasts of concerts and operas created more music festivals, provided commissions for more new composers.

Pulitzer Prizes: novel, *Tales of the South Pacific* by James A. Michener; drama, *A Streetcar Named Desire* by Tennessee Williams; U.S. history, *Across the Wide Missouri* by Bernard DeVoto; biography, *Forgotten First Citizen: John Bigelow* by Margaret Clapp; poetry, *Age of Anxiety* by W. H. Auden; music, *Symphony No. 3* by Walter Piston.

This year's **Nobel Prize for Literature** won by Thomas Stearns Eliot, a naturalized Englishman born in the U.S. He is famous for *The Waste Land* (1922), *Ash Wednesday* (1930), *Murder in the Cathedral* (1935), *Four Quartets* (1944), *The Cocktail Party* (1949), and *The Confidential Clerk* (1954).

1st United States Supreme Court hearing on a state "obscenity" law as related to a specific book, deadlocked 4–4 on the question of **Edmund Wilson's** *Memoirs of Hecate County* and its suppression in New York state, thus upholding the lower court conviction of the publisher.

Tennessee Williams returned to Broadway with *Summer and Smoke,* a work reminiscent of his earlier successes. It was quietly received by both critics and audi-

SCIENCE; INDUSTRY; ECONOMICS; EDUCATION; RELIGION; PHILOSOPHY.

SPORTS; FASHIONS; POPULAR ENTERTAINMENT; FOLKLORE; SOCIETY.

Relations between labor and management were particularly mellow. General Motors granted an automatic cost-of-living increase to some 265,000 hourly workers. Strikes were fewer and less violent. Education had a number of new problems to consider: (1) sharply rising enrollments; (2) inadequacy of facilities; (3) failure of teaching personnel to gain better economic status, mainly because rising prices offset any salary increases; (4) the resultant shortage of teachers; (5) the beginning of decline of veteran enrollments at colleges and universities; (6) an ever-swelling tide of foreign students here on exchange scholarships.

Dr. Benjamin Minge Duggar, noted American botanist, produced **aureomycin** at Lederle Laboratories, Pearl River, N.Y.

Conquest of **pernicious anemia** complete with discovery of vitamin B-12, the substance in liver abstracts that was responsible for earlier cures. Vitamin B-12 was found to have a phenomenal efficiency with a daily dosage equivalent to $\frac{1}{100}$ of a grain of salt sufficient to cure victim of pernicious anemia and the same quantity taken twice a week sufficient to maintain victim in constant good health.

Mississippi became the last state in the Union to provide **workmen's compensation laws.**

Jan. 2 **Atomic research** for industrial development announced as major concern of a new partnership between the University of Chicago and 7 corporations.

Jan. 12 **Legal education facilities for Negroes** in Oklahoma ordered equal to those for whites by U.S. Supreme Court ruling.

Feb. 2 AFL executive council decided not to support **Henry A. Wallace's 3d party.** The CIO executive board previously passed a similar resolution.

ended the year with the same won-and-lost record as the Boston Red Sox. The nation's crime rate remained steady. Racketeers concentrated their talents on large scale gambling operations which had the tacit approval of local authorities. Dior's "New Look," so fashionable last year, was booed off the backs of mannequins. The inevitable reaction allowed the more natural lines of the body to show forth. The motion picture industry suffered a trying 12 months. Continued stiff competition from abroad lowered their income substantially. Major studios reported a 25% drop in employment.

Academy Awards presented to *Hamlet* as the outstanding motion picture of the year and to its title player, Sir Laurence Olivier as the best actor. Jane Wyman was named best actress for her portrayal in *Johnny Belinda*. Claire Trevor was chosen best supporting actress for her performance in *Key Largo* and Walter Huston was selected best supporting actor for his characterization in *The Treasure of the Sierra Madre*. In a rare display of family achievement, Walter Huston's son, John Huston, received an award for his direction of *The Treasure of the Sierra Madre*.

This year, the **National Football Champion** was Michigan, for their 1st title since 1933. The coach, Bernie Oosterbaan. The record: 9 wins, no losses, no ties.

U.S. lawn tennis men's singles champion, Richard A. Gonzales; **women's singles champion,** Mrs. Margaret Osborne du Pont.

U.S.G.A. amateur championship won by Willie Turnesa at Memphis, Tenn., C.C. He defeated Ray Billows, 2 and 1. **Open championship** won by Ben Hogan at Riviera C.C., Los Angeles, Calif., with a score of 276.

Citation won the 80th **Belmont Stakes,** paying 1–5. Jockey was E. Arcaro; time

561

POLITICS AND GOVERNMENT; WAR; DISASTERS; VITAL STATISTICS.

BOOKS; PAINTING; DRAMA; ARCHITECTURE; SCULPTURE.

York chosen by the **Republican National Convention** at Philadelphia as candidate for presidency. The following day, Gov. Earl Warren of California was chosen as the vice-presidential candidate.

June 24 Pres. Truman signed the **Selective Service Act** which provided for the registration of all men between 18 and 25 and the draft of enough men to constitute an Army of 837,000, a Navy and Marine Corps of 666,882, and Air Force of 502,-000.

June 25 Pres. Truman signed the **Displaced Persons Bill** which admitted 205,-000 European displaced persons, including 3,000 nonquota orphans.

July **States Rights Democrats** (a splinter party that walked out of the regular Democratic National Convention because they could not support party's civil rights platform) met at Birmingham, Ala., and nominated Gov. J. Strom Thurmond of South Carolina and Gov. Fielding L. Wright of Mississippi for the presidency and vice-presidency.

July 15 **Democratic National Convention** nominated Pres. Harry S. Truman and Sen. Alben W. Barkley of Kentucky for the presidency and vice-presidency.

July 20 12 **Communist party** leaders indicted by U.S. and charged with advocating the overthrow of the U.S. government.

July 23–25 **Progressive party convention** at Philadelphia, Pa., nominated Henry A. Wallace and Sen. Glen H. Taylor of Idaho for presidency and vice-presidency.

Aug. 2–6 **Communist party convention** at New York city supported Progressive party nomination of Henry A. Wallace for presidency.

Nov. 2 Harry S. Truman defeated Thomas E. Dewey for the **presidential election** by an electoral vote of 304–189. Popular vote: Truman, 24,104,836; Dewey, 21,969,500; Thurmond, 1,169,312; Wallace, 1,157,172; Thomas, 132,138; Watson, 103,343.

ences. Biggest hits of the year were musicals, 3 of them revues. They were *Lend an Ear, Make Mine Manhattan,* and *Inside U.S.A.,* the last named successful mainly because of the efforts of comedienne, **Bea Lillie.** Other musical hits were *Where's Charley?,* an adaptation of *Charley's Aunt,* and *Kiss Me, Kate,* **Cole Porter's** lighthearted, sophisticated treatment of Shakespeare's *Taming of the Shrew.*

Popular **song hits** of the year included: "Buttons and Bows," "Now Is the Hour," "Nature Boy," "You Call Everybody Darling," "On a Slow Boat to China," "All I Want for Christmas Is My Two Front Teeth."

Notable musical premières included **Howard Hanson's** *Piano Concerto No. 1;* **Bohuslav Martinu's** *String Quartet* for oboe, violin, cello, and piano, and his *Seventh String Quartet;* and **Arnold Schoenberg's** cantata, *Survivor from Warsaw.*

Painter with a social message is **Ben Shahn.** Son of an immigrant, he studied in Paris and returned to wage war against social injustice. Using modernistic techniques of distortion and coloring he tries to make an appeal to simple people. In his *Miners' Wives,* the news of the death of her husband is read in the eyes of a poor woman. Indignation as well as pity flows from the painting.

1st major postwar architectural competition, the design of the **Jefferson National Expansion** memorial in St. Louis, Mo., won by a team headed by Eero Saarinen. The group, which included, beside an architect, a sculptor, a painter, and a landscape architect, won the $40,000 prize with a huge parabolic arch made of stainless steel.

Red Cross Headquarters in San Francisco, Calif., built from designs by Gardner A. Dailey. Ribbed surface texture of poured concrete walls particularly notable.

SCIENCE; INDUSTRY; ECONOMICS; EDUCATION; RELIGION; PHILOSOPHY.

SPORTS; FASHIONS; POPULAR ENTERTAINMENT; FOLKLORE; SOCIETY.

Mar. 5 New record for **U.S. rocket missiles** set by Navy. Speed of 3000 mph. and altitude of 78 mi. were achieved during tests at White Sands, N.M.

Mar. 8 **Religious education** in public schools declared a violation of 1st amendment by U.S. Supreme Court.

Mar. 15 More than 200,000 **soft coal miners struck** for a more liberal old-age pension plan.

Apr. 12 **Striking soft coal miners** sent back to pits by John L. Lewis after compromise was reached on pension fund.

May 10 Nationwide **railroad strike** averted when government was granted injunction. Pres. Truman had threatened to order the army to seize the roads.

May 25 **1st sliding-scale wage contract,** in which wages depended on cost of living, signed by General Motors Corp. and auto workers union. It granted some 225,000 workers an immediate 11¢ per hour increase.

June 3 **World's largest reflector telescope** dedicated. It was the 200-in. Hale telescope at Palomar Mountain Observatory, maintained by the California Institute of Technology.

July 31 **Idlewild International Airport** in New York city, largest in the world, dedicated by Pres. Truman.

Aug. 16 **Anti-inflation Act** passed. On Aug. 17, Federal Reserve System instituted curbs on installment buying.

Sept. 25 The U.S. Air Force released news of a **jet plane** that could travel almost 900 mph.

Nov. 15 General Electric and American Locomotive Companies tested **1st U.S.-built electric locomotive** with gas turbine at Erie, Pa.

Nov. 20 **New balloon altitude record** claimed by U.S. Army Signal Corps. It was 140,000 ft. or 26½ mi.

was 2:28⅕ on a fast track for winnings valued at $77,700.

Citation won the 72d annual **Preakness Stakes,** paying 1–10. Jockey was E. Arcaro; time was 2:02⅗ on a heavy track for winnings valued at $91,870.

U.S. defeated Australia 5 to 0 in the challenge round of the **Davis Cup** International Matches.

Jan. 1 Michigan defeated Southern California by a score of 49 to 0 in the **Rose Bowl** at Pasadena, Calif., before a crowd of 93,000.

May 1 Eddie Arcaro rode his 4th **Kentucky Derby** winner, the horse who was to become the greatest money winner of all time, Calumet Farm's *Citation*, in the 74th running of the Churchill Downs, classic. *Citation's* time was 2:05⅖, winning $83,-400. He was the 8th horse to win the Triple Crown of American racing.

July 13 The American League defeated the National League, 5–2, to win the 15th annual **All-Star baseball** game at St. Louis, Mo.

July 29–Aug. 14 U.S. won the unofficial championship of the 14th **Olympic games** held at London, England, with a team score of 547.5. Sweden was 2nd with a score of 308.5.

Oct. 6–11 Cleveland, AL, defeated Boston, NL, 4–2 in the 45th annual **World Series.**

Oct. 24 Term **"Cold War"** to characterize Russo-American relationships after World War II is given national prominence after a speech by Bernard M. Baruch before the Senate War Investigating Committee. "Although the war is over," said Baruch, "we are in the midst of a cold war which is getting warmer."

Nov. 27 Army and Navy tied, 21–21, in the annual **Army-Navy football game** held at Municipal Stadium, Philadelphia, Pa.

563

1949

Pres. Truman's annual message to Congress presented a program of domestic legislation that he called the "Fair Deal." It included repeal of the Taft-Hartley law and a re-enactment of the Wagner Act, a minimum wage law of 75¢ an hour, generous farm price supports, expansion of social security, federal aid to local school systems, low rent public housing and slum clearance, and broad civil rights proposals. In foreign affairs, a bipartisan senate ratified the North Atlantic Treaty Alliance, pledged over $1¼ billion to finance a military assistance program. Worry over Communists at home continued as Russia disclosed that she too had atomic weapons. 11 Communist Party leaders in New York city were found guilty of teaching the overthrow of the government. Biggest headlines of the year: the Alger Hiss trial and the testimony of confessed former Communist Whittaker Chambers that linked the former state department official with Red activities.

Jan. 20 Pres. Harry S. Truman inaugurated at Washington, D.C. In his inaugural address Truman announced his Four Points of a major program to promote world peace. The most famous is the **"Point Four"** section, which formulated U.S. policy of making available to underdeveloped areas of the world American industrial knowledge and scientific advances. This "Point Four" program was sent to Congress June 24.

Feb. 7 1st section of the report of the **Hoover Commission on Organization of the Executive Branch of the Government,** recommending the reduction and streamlining of the executive branch. On Feb. 17 the Commission suggested that the Post Office Department should be placed beyond politics and run instead on a business basis. On Mar. 21 it further reported that a new cabinet post—director of a proposed department of national welfare and education

American book publishers noted an increasing popularity of nonfiction religious books, studies of world affairs, and books that discussed the plight of the American Negro. Architects rejoiced in slightly decreased building costs that allowed them to plan more luxury residences. The trend toward decentralization of cities afforded new opportunities to design factories, laboratories, offices in rural areas. The League of New York Theaters instituted an investigation into the ills of the theater. Findings recommended fairer policies toward the public in the matter of ticket distribution, pooling of production techniques, more careful advertising and promotion, training of theater staffs, and several others. The investigation neglected to mention, as a possible contributing cause, the dearth of good plays.

Pulitzer Prizes: novel, *Guard of Honor* by James Gould Cozzens; drama, *Death of a Salesman* by Arthur Miller; U.S. history, *The Disruption of American Democracy* by Roy Franklin Nichols; biography, *Roosevelt and Hopkins* by Robert E. Sherwood; poetry, *Terror and Decorum* by Peter Viereck; music, *Louisiana Story* music by Virgil Thomson.

This year's **Nobel Prize for Literature** won by William Faulkner (it was not announced until the awarding of the 1950 prizes). He is famous for his novels *The Sound and the Fury* (1929), *As I Lay Dying* (1930), *Sanctuary* (1931), *Intruder in the Dust* (1948), *Requiem for a Nun* (1951), and *A Fable* (1954).

Religious books enjoyed unprecedented popularity this year. Best **sellers** included *The Waters of Siloe*, a history of Trappist Order by **Thomas Merton,** *Peace of Soul,* by **Fulton J. Sheen,** *The Greatest Story Ever Told* by **Fulton Oursler,** and *A Guide to Confident Living* by **Norman Vincent Peale.** Other popular works were *Modern*

SCIENCE; INDUSTRY; ECONOMICS; EDUCATION; RELIGION; PHILOSOPHY.

SPORTS; FASHIONS; POPULAR ENTERTAINMENT; FOLKLORE; SOCIETY.

1949

A record national debt of $250 billion was offset by a rising national income—it was estimated at $222 billion. Agricultural productivity was at an all-time high. Economists noted a slight decline during the 1st half of the year, but pointed out that such a sag was inevitable after the inflation period of 1948. Total salaries and wages reached new highs; the automotive industry sent some 6 million cars and trucks off assembly lines—a new record. Unemployment increased by 1½ million. Labor pressed for a 4th round of wage increases since the end of the war. Most significant development in its ranks was a growing involvement in the national political scene. Candidates for elective office took great care to draw up platforms designed to attract the labor vote.

Nobel Prize in chemistry presented to **William Francis Giauque** "for his work in the field of chemical thermodynamics, particularly concerning the behavior of substances at extremely low temperatures." Giauque was born in Niagara Falls, Ont., but carried on most of his research at the University of California where he had been appointed professor of chemistry in 1934. Giauque's experiments were a major contribution to the continuing research on the effects of temperature on chemical and physical changes, particularly extremely low temperatures.

Jan. 3 The right of states to ban **closed shop** upheld by U.S. Supreme Court.

Jan. 8 Air Force XB-47 **jet bomber** crossed continent in 3 hr., 46 min. averaging 607.2 mph.

Jan. 14 **Antitrust** suit against American Telephone and Telegraph Company filed by Department of Justice. The action sought to separate the company from its manufacturing subsidiary, Western Electric, Inc.

Movie producers were cheered by the way their products were greeted everywhere in the world. An expanding market plus careful planning made for a healthier financial year than last, gave Hollywood new optimism. The 2 major league baseball leagues staged breath-taking shows for their fans as both pennants were clinched on the very last day of the season. For a change, American men cheered Parisian fashion designers as they decreed daring décolletage for evening wear, practically nonexistent bathing suits, called "Bikini" suits, for the beach. Whether this was a style or a fad was debatable, but while it lasted, both sexes made the most of it.

Academy Awards presented to *All the King's Men* as the outstanding motion picture of the year; to its star, Broderick Crawford as the best actor. Olivia de Havilland was named best actress for her portrayal of *The Heiress*. Mercedes MacCambridge was chosen best supporting actress for her performance in *All the King's Men* and Dean Jagger was selected best supporting actor for his performance in *Twelve O'Clock High*.

This year, the **national football champion** was Notre Dame—the 7th time they were honored and the 4th time under coach Frank Leahy, who was forced to retire at the end of the 1953 season because of ill health.

U.S. lawn tennis men's singles champion, Richard A. Gonzales; **women's singles champion,** Mrs. Margaret Osborne du Pont.

U.S.G.A. amateur championship won by Charles R. Coe at Oak Hill C.C., Rochester, N.Y. He defeated Rufus King, 11 and 10. **Open championship** won by Cary Middlecoff at Medinah, Ill., C.C., with a score of 286.

565

| POLITICS AND GOVERNMENT; WAR; DISASTERS; VITAL STATISTICS. | BOOKS; PAINTING; DRAMA; ARCHITECTURE; SCULPTURE. |

—should be created. In its final report on Apr. 1 Commission charged that corruption and inefficiency was involved in many of the government's business enterprises.

Apr. 4 **North Atlantic Treaty** signed in Washington, D.C., by Belgium, Canada, Denmark, France, Great Britain, Italy, Iceland, Luxembourg, The Netherlands, Norway, Portugal, and U.S.

May 18 **1st U.S. civilian high commissioner of Germany** appointed. He was John J. McCloy, president of the International Bank for Reconstruction and Development.

June 29 **Last U.S. troops evacuated from Korea.** Only a military mission remained in an advisory capacity.

July 21 U.S. Senate ratified the **North Atlantic Treaty** by a vote of 82 to 13.

Aug. 31 83d and last encampment of **Grand Army of the Republic,** Civil War veterans, attended by 6 of the 16 surviving veterans at Indianapolis, Ind.

Oct. 14 After a long, bitter trial marked by personal attacks on the presiding federal judge, Harold Medina, 11 top **U.S. Communists** found guilty of conspiring to advocate the violent overthrow of the government of the U.S. Each was sentenced on Oct. 21 by Judge Medina to $10,000 fine; 10 were sentenced to 5 years imprisonment, 1 to 3 years.

Oct. 24 Permanent **UN headquarters** in New York city dedicated.

Oct. 26 Pres. Truman signed a **minimum wage** bill which raised the minimum wage in certain industries engaged in interstate commerce from 40¢ to 75¢ an hour.

Arms and Free Men by **Vannevar Bush,** *Peace or Pestilence* by **Theodore Rosebury.** Top fiction entries of the year were *The Brave Bulls* by **Tom Lea,** *The Man with the Golden Arm* by **Nelson Algren,** *A Rage to Live* by **John O'Hara.**

Powerful tragedy of the common man is *Death of a Salesman* by **Arthur Miller.** Using a shifting sense of time, he tells the story of Willy Loman, all his life the go-getter with the great smile, who at the age of 63 is tossed on the rubbish heap, a wrecked man with nothing left but his loyal wife. Play was also 1st drama to become a Book-of-the-Month selection.

South Pacific, by **Richard Rodgers** and **Oscar Hammerstein II,** began a run on Broadway. It contained such songs as "Some Enchanted Evening" and "There Is Nothing Like a Dame."

New compositions by **U.S. composers** included the following: *Symphony No. 6* by **George Antheil,** *Viola Concerto* by **Béla Bártok,** *Symphony No. 2 for Piano and Orchestra* by **Leonard Bernstein,** *Concerto for Flute, Oboe, Clarinet, Bassoon, Harp, and Orchestra* by **Paul Hindemith,** and *Quartets No. 14 and No. 5* by **Darius Milhaud.**

Popular music this year was dominated by the songs of Rodgers and Hammerstein, Irving Berlin, and Cole Porter. Their hits included "Some Enchanted Evening," "A Wonderful Guy," "Bali Ha'i," "Younger than Springtime," "Were Thine That Special Face," "So in Love," "Just One Way to Say I Love You," "Let's Take an Old Fashioned Walk."

566

SCIENCE; INDUSTRY; ECONOMICS; EDUCATION; RELIGION; PHILOSOPHY.	SPORTS; FASHIONS; POPULAR ENTERTAINMENT; FOLKLORE; SOCIETY.

Feb. 13 **Voluntary medical care plan** supported by American Medical Association in opposition to compulsory health insurance plan purposed by Pres. Truman.

Feb. 25 American guided missile, the **WAC-Corporal,** launched at White Sands, N.M., and ascended to an altitude of 250 miles. Highest altitude ever achieved by a man-made projectile.

Feb. 25 **1st automobile price cuts** since end of war announced by General Motors Corp. It affected the company's entire line of passenger cars and trucks.

Mar. 2 *Lucky Lady II,* U.S. Air Force Superfortress, ended **1st circum-global nonstop flight** at Carswell Air Force Base, Tex. Plane refueled 4 times in air.

Mar. 11 **2-week soft coal walkout** ordered by John L. Lewis. UMW took the action in protest against appointment of Dr. James Boyd as director of Bureau of Mines.

Apr. 20 Discovery of **cortisone** announced. The hormone promised to bring relief to sufferers of rheumatoid arthritis, the most painful type of arthritis.

May 20 Reaffiliation bid by **United Mine Workers** refused by executive council of AFL.

Oct. 1–Nov. 11 Nation-wide **steel strike** of 500,000 workers. Dispute settled when companies agreed to pension demands.

Capot won the 73d annual **Preakness Stakes,** paying 5–2. Jockey was T. Atkinson; time was 1:56 on a fast track for winnings valued at $79,985.

Capot won the 81st annual **Belmont Stakes,** paying 11–2. Jockey was T. Atkinson; time was 2:30⅕ on a fast track for winnings valued at $60,900.

U.S. defeated Australia 4 to 1 in the **Davis Cup** International Matches.

Jan. 1 Northwestern defeated California by a score of 20 to 14 in the **Rose Bowl** at Pasadena, Calif., before a crowd of 93,000.

May 7 A 16–1 long shot, Calumet Farm's *Ponder,* won the 76th annual **Kentucky Derby** at Churchill Downs, Louisville, Ky., running the 1¼ mi. in 2:04⅕ on a fast track and winning $91,600. Jockey up was S. Brooks.

June 22 New **World's Heavyweight Champion,** Ezzard Charles, who outpointed "Jersey Joe" Walcott in 15 rounds in Chicago, after retirement of Champion Joe Louis. Louis came out of retirement in 1950 and was outpointed by Charles in 15 rounds.

July 12 The 16th annual **All-Star game** at Ebbets Field in Brooklyn, N.Y. was won by the American League, 11–7. Ralph Kiner and Stan Musial hit home runs for the losers.

Aug. 3 **Flag Day** designated by Congress to fall on June 14.

Oct. 5–9 New York, AL, defeated Brooklyn, NL, 4–1 in the 46th annual **World Series.**

Nov. 26 Army defeated Navy, 38–0, to win the annual **Army-Navy football game** at Municipal Stadium, Philadelphia, Pa.

567

POLITICS AND GOVERNMENT; WAR;   BOOKS; PAINTING; DRAMA;

DISASTERS;   VITAL   STATISTICS.   ARCHITECTURE; SCULPTURE.

1950

At mid-century, the nation was concerned with 3 major issues; inflation and the threat of internal communism, both domestic problems, and a foreign policy that never seemed to bring lasting or stable results. Profound pessimism gripped the country when North Korean troops crossed the 38th parallel and invaded South Korea. The action was given over to the United Nations to handle, who found the solution by sending an international "police force" to the Far East with orders to end the hostilities. Since no other nation could afford to enter the area in force, the U.S. embarked on a costly, unpopular war in miniature. Hatred of Communist influences within the country mounted as FBI director J. Edgar Hoover announced that there were 55,000 party members and 500,000 fellow travelers active within the U.S. The Senate appointed a special investigating committee to probe charges of alleged communistic activity within the State Department leveled by Sen. Joseph McCarthy of Wisconsin.

Population—150,697,361. Center of population: 8 miles north-northwest of Olney, Richland County, Ill.

Jan. 2 $24,802,000,000 in **grants and credits went to foreign nations** from July 1, 1945, to Sept. 30, 1949, according to report issued by U.S. Department of Commerce.

Jan. 21 **1st chairman of civilian mobilization office** appointed by Pres. Truman. He was Paul J. Larsen, whose responsibility was to streamline plans for wartime civilian defense.

Jan. 21 **Alger Hiss** found guilty of perjury on 2 counts, bringing to an end 2 long, very public trials highlighted by the dramatic confrontation of Hiss by the main witness against him, his onetime friend and alleged fellow party member, Whittaker Chambers. Hiss, protesting his in-

The confusion and uncertainty of the times fostered some curious literary panaceas. Best sellers were *Look Younger, Live Longer* by Gaylord Hauser which explored dietetic avenues to contentment and strength. *Dianetics* by L. Ron Hubbard promulgated a new science of mental health. Architects expended their talents on shopping centers, supermarkets, motels, outdoor movies, all in response to a general mass movement away from the city. That chronic invalid, the theater, reported bad times. Production costs were so exorbitant that only smash successes could afford to pay their backers. Yet, with characteristic perversity, the Broadway stage produced some of its most interesting work in recent years. Particularly noteworthy was a renaissance of poetic drama, as witnessed by plays of T. S. Eliot, Christopher Fry, and Robinson Jeffers, all of which met with public acclaim.

Pulitzer Prizes: novel, *The Way West* by A. B. Guthrie, Jr.; drama, *South Pacific* by Richard Rodgers, Oscar Hammerstein II, and Joshua Logan; U.S. history, *Art and Life in America* by Oliver W. Larkin; biography, *John Quincy Adams and the Foundations of American Foreign Policy* by Samuel Flagg Bemis; poetry, *Annie Allen* by Gwendolyn Brooks; music, *The Consul* by Gian-Carlo Menotti.

Best sellers included: *The Wall* by **John Hersey,** a story of the last days of the Warsaw ghetto under Nazi attack during World War II; *The Cardinal,* the story of the rise of a Catholic priest to the ermine, by **Henry Morton Robinson;** *The Disenchanted* by **Budd Schulberg,** a biting novel of a man's struggle for success in Hollywood; and *World Enough and Time* by **Robert Penn Warren,** a brawling historical romance of the Mississippi R. in the 19th century and the "Kentucky Tragedy."

The 2 best straight **plays** of the Broadway season were *The Country Girl* by

1950

A continued upward trend in prices led organized labor to press for higher wages and improved working conditions. The Korean war cut down the number of unemployed to 1,900,000. Average weekly earning in industry was up to $60.53, an all-time high. Having pledged the defeat of Sen. Robert A. Taft of Ohio, labor entered into the election campaign of that state with a determined strength. But this, their 1st real try to function as a political force, ended in a dismal failure as Taft was returned to office by an overwhelming majority. Educators had to face (1) the growing financial difficulties of colleges and universities, (2) the charge that Communists had filtered into the school systems of the country and were corrupting students, and (3) the issue of desegregation in classrooms. Religious leaders reported a rise in church membership. The Roman Catholic church announced a 2% gain, while the Protestant churches recorded a 2.9% upswing.

Nobel Prize in medicine and physiology presented to **Edward Calvin Kendall** and **Philip Showalter Hench** of the University of Minnesota, and to **Tadeus Reichstein** for "their discoveries concerning the suprarenal cortex hormones, their structure and biological effects." Kendall and Hench collaborated in America while Richstein, the Swiss organic chemist, pursued his research at the University of Basel. The main significance of their discoveries lay in the development of hormones like cortisone which removed many of the symptoms of diseases without removing the causes. All 3 prize winners insisted that their discoveries were only exploratory efforts on the threshold of a new aspect of medicine.

Phenomenal popularity of **antihistamines** for the treatment of the common cold reflected in sales amounting to $100 million despite warnings of responsible

The motion picture industry, faced with the challenge of television, produced some of its finest films this year. Many studios took advantage of frozen funds abroad by sending full-scale units on location all over the world. As a result, exotic backgrounds became commonplace on Main Street's local movie screen. Fashion designers acted with more becoming modesty as they again clothed American women. The "Bikini" bathing suit all but disappeared and dresses became more wearable and natural. Biggest single fashion note was the reappearance of stoles that proved popular during the day as well as at night. The younger set wore their hair short, dressed in dungarees and ballet shoes. This latter fad may have been prompted by an outburst of activity in the dance world. American companies won over European audiences, and dancers from abroad toured U.S., enjoying packed houses wherever they played.

Academy Awards presented to *All About Eve* as the outstanding motion picture of the year, to Judy Holliday as the best actress for her performance in *Born Yesterday,* and to José Ferrer for his portrayal of *Cyrano de Bergerac.* Josephine Hull was named best supporting actress for her playing in *Harvey* and George Sanders was chosen best supporting actor for his performance in *All About Eve.*

This year's **National College Football Champion** was Oklahoma, coached by Charles Wilkinson. Their record: 10 wins, no losses, no ties.

Man o' War named the greatest horse of the 1st half of the 20th Century by an Associated Press poll. Known as a super horse, that is, one excelling both as a sprinter and a distance runner, this great horse was run as a 2-year-old and a 3-year-old, winning 20 out of 21 starts and breaking 5 track records. He was never really

569

POLITICS AND GOVERNMENT; WAR; DISASTERS; VITAL STATISTICS.

BOOKS; PAINTING; DRAMA; ARCHITECTURE; SCULPTURE.

nocence, was sentenced to 5 years in prison.

Jan. 31 Pres. Truman ordered development of the **hydrogen bomb.**

June 25 **North Korean troops invaded Republic of South Korea** by crossing 38th parallel. UN ordered immediate cease fire, withdrawal of invading forces.

June 27 Pres. Truman ordered U.S. forces to the aid of South Korea when they were attacked by **North Korea.** The President received the approbation of Congress for his action, and the UN Security Council adopted a U.S. resolution for armed intervention.

June 30 Use of U.S. ground forces authorized by Pres. Truman. He also ordered a naval blockade of entire **Korean** coast.

July 1 1st U.S. ground forces landed in **Korea.**

Aug. 4 **62,000 enlisted reservists called up** for 21 months active duty by army.

Sept. 8 Pres. Truman granted **emergency powers** over entire national economy under Defense Production Act.

Sept. 23 **Internal Security Act** of 1950 became law as Congress overrode Pres. Truman's veto by a vote of 291 to 48 in the House of Representatives and a vote of 57 to 10 in the Senate.

Sept. 26 **Seoul,** capital of South Korea, recaptured by U.S. troops.

Sept. 29 **Counterattacking South Korean** troops reached 38th parallel.

Oct. 7 **U.S. forces invaded North Korea** by crossing 38th parallel.

Nov. 6 **Chinese Communist troops** reported in action along with North Korean forces by Gen. Douglas MacArthur.

Nov. 20 **U.S. troops reached Manchurian border** on Yalu R.

Nov. 29 **U.S. forces retreated** under heavy attack from Chinese Communist units.

Clifford Odets, the story of a man trying to make a comeback with the help of his wife, and *The Member of the Wedding* by **Carson McCullers.** This last was awarded the **Drama Critics' Circle award** as the best play of the season. It was marked by exceptional performances by **Julie Harris, Ethel Waters,** and a truly remarkable portrayal by child actor, **Brandon DeWilde.**

Popular music this year reached a new low of banality with such offerings as "Good Night, Irene," "Music! Music! Music!," "Tzena, Tzena, Tzena," a song based on Israeli folk music, "My Foolish Heart," and "Mona Lisa." Nearly every one of this list had a melody derived from some previous popular song.

Boiler plant at Illinois Institute of Technology, Chicago, built as part of over-all campus designed by **Ludwig Mies van der Rohe.** Campus style used exposed steel frames and buff-colored brick panels on major elevations.

United Nations Secretariat, designed by international board of architects under direction of Wallace K. Harrison, built in New York—a 39-story building with narrow end walls of white marble and wide elevations of green-tinted glass.

Construction begun on **Lever House,** one of New York's most impressive modern business buildings; completed 1952. Designed by Skidmore, Owings & Merrill, whole structure of glass seems to float on slim colonnade.

Mar. 1 Première performance of *The Consul,* an opera by **Gian-Carlo Menotti,** given at the Shubert Theater in Philadelphia. On Mar. 15, the Broadway run began at the Ethel Barrymore Theater.

Nov. New York Philharmonic-Symphony Orchestra, Dimitri Mitropoulos conducting, performed **Howard Swanson's** *Short Symphony,* which later was awarded the Music Critics' Circle award. The work

| SCIENCE; INDUSTRY; ECONOMICS; EDUCATION; RELIGION; PHILOSOPHY. | SPORTS; FASHIONS; POPULAR ENTERTAINMENT; FOLKLORE; SOCIETY. |

medical authorities and the dubious results of laboratory experiments.

Illiteracy in America reached a new low of 3.2% of the population, a decline of 1% from 1940 and a decline of 16.8% from 1870.

Jan. 24 **Minimum wage of 75¢** per hour went into effect under amendment to Fair Labor Standards Act.

Mar. 13 **Largest income ever reported by a corporation** was announced by General Motors Corp. Net earnings in 1949 were $656,434,232.

Mar. 17 **New element,** californium, announced by University of California, Berkeley. This, the heaviest yet known, was discovered in experiments with the cyclotron, which also yielded another element, berkelium. They are numbered 97 and 98 respectively.

Mar. 23 **Wages up 130%** since 1939 according to U.S. Labor Department report. However, **buying power** had only increased 35%.

May 11 **Grand Coulee Dam** in Washington dedicated by Pres. Truman.

May 25 **Longest vehicular tunnel in U.S.,** the Brooklyn-Battery, New York city, opened to traffic.

Aug. 25 Pres. Truman ordered **army to take control of all railroads** to prevent a strike of trainmen and yardmen on Aug. 28. He acted under a 1916 war emergency measure. Strike was called off as consequence of seizure.

Oct. 11 Federal Communications Commission licensed Columbia Broadcasting System to begin **color television broadcasting** on Nov. 20. Touched off tremendous industry controversy. Radio Corporation of America charged that CBS' device was

pressed and his only loss was incurred when he was left at the starting gate.

U.S. lawn tennis men's singles champion, Arthur Larsen; **women's singles champion,** Mrs. Margaret Osborne du Pont.

Australia defeated the U.S. in the challenge round of the **Davis Cup** International Matches, 4–1.

U.S.G.A. amateur championship won by Sam Urzetta at Minneapolis, Minn., G.C. He defeated Frank R. Stranahan, 1 up. **Open championship** won by Ben Hogan at Merion G.C. Ardmore, Pa., with a score of 287.

Middleground won the 82d annual **Belmont Stakes,** paying 27–10. Jockey was W. Boland; time was 2:28⅗ on a fast track for winnings valued at $61,350.

Hill Prince won the 74th annual **Preakness Stakes,** paying 7–10. Jockey was E. Arcaro; time was 1:59⅕ on a slow track for winnings valued at $56,115.

Jan. 1 Ohio State defeated California by a score of 17 to 14 in the **Rose Bowl** at Pasadena, Calif., before a crowd of 100,963.

May 6 The 77th annual **Kentucky Derby** at Churchill Downs, Louisville, Ky., was won by King Ranch's *Middleground,* who just missed tying Whirlaway's Derby record by ⅕ sec. With jockey W. Boland up he won $92,650, running the fast track in 2:01⅗.

July 11 The National League finally won an **All-Star game,** beating the American League, 4–3, at Chicago, after losing 4 straight mid-season classics. Ralph Kiner and Red Schoendienst hit homers for the winners.

Oct. 4–7 New York, AL, defeated

Dec. 16 **State of national emergency** declared by Pres. Truman. Charles E. Wilson appointed director of defense mobilization.

Dec. 19 **Gen. Dwight D. Eisenhower** appointed supreme commander of the Western Europe defense forces by the North Atlantic Council. Lt. Gen. Gruenther was named Chief of Staff.

established the reputation of Swanson, a young Negro composer from Atlanta, Ga.

Nov. 16 1st performance of **Aaron Copland**'s *Clarinet Concerto* given by Benny Goodman and the NBC Symphony Orchestra.

1951

An exasperated and irritated America hovered dangerously close to the brink of a 3d world war. The issue was this: Chinese Communist troops had unofficially entered the Korean campaign, operating from bases above the Yalu R. Our military men on the scene claimed that complete victory could never be won until United Nations forces could attack and destroy those strategic positions within Chinese territory. However, that would be tantamount to declaring war on China, who was linked by a military alliance to Russia. American casualties had reached 100,000 and tempers were getting short. With this crisis before them, government leaders framed a foreign policy whose main instrument was preparation for war. A huge increase in taxes was asked, universal military training was urged, a ring of bases around the U.S.S.R. suggested. General war was averted, however, as the administration stood firmly behind the UN on the decision not to attack Chinese bases.

Jan. 1 Chinese **Communist troops in Korea** broke through defense perimeter around Seoul, took Inchon and Kimpo airfield. Seoul was abandoned 3 days later.

Feb. 1 UN formally accused **Communist China of agression** in Korea.

Feb. 26 **22nd amendment** adopted stipulating that no person may be elected to the presidency for more than 2 terms. A vice president succeeding to the presidency and serving more than half the term of his predecessor would be eligible for only 1 more term.

Some 11,000 titles were published this year. 2 kinds of work proved especially popular; factual essays and volumes of opinion about the ever-increasing complexity of the world, political, social, scientific, psychological, etc., and a peculiarly introspective fiction that examined private emotions of adolescents. The phenomenal sale of paper back books led many publishers to launch a series of these editions. Architects were forced to concentrate on industrial and defense work, although considerable work of interest was accomplished in the design of school buildings whose chief feature was sunny congenial expansiveness, as opposed to a tightly regimented plan of corridor with classrooms on either side. Painters continued to work in abstractions. American regionalism all but vanished from contemporary exhibitions. After a brief season of experimentation, the theater returned to the tried-and-true musical.

Pulitzer Prizes: novel, *The Town* by Conrad Richter; drama, no prize; U.S. history, *The Old Northwest, Pioneer Period 1815–1840, vols. I–II* by R. Carlyle Buley; biography, *John C. Calhoun: American Portrait* by Margaret Louise Coit; poetry, *Complete Poems* by Carl Sandburg; music, music for opera *Giants in the Earth* by Douglas Stuart Moore.

More than 231,000,000 copies of **paperbound reprints** sold by the publishers of 25¢ books.

William Faulkner continued his "history" of mythical Jefferson, Miss., in a

not the best and workable only on its own systems. On Nov. 15 a temporary restraining order was issued by Chicago Federal District Court.

Philadelphia, NL, 4–0 in the 47th annual **World Series.**

Dec. 2 **Navy** defeated Army, 14–2, in their annual contest at Municipal Stadium, Philadelphia.

1951

Employment of women in American industry reached its highest point in history—even more than during the acute man shortage days of World War II. Wages were again up, but so were prices; employment figures were robust. Alarmed over the growing inflation, the administration tried to institute a program of production controls. 200,000 consumer items were placed under price ceilings, but attempts to freeze all prices and wages failed. Universities and colleges bemoaned a sharp drop in enrollment. These institutions, and particularly their intercollegiate athletic programs, made the headlines as star college basketball players confessed to accepting bribes and throwing games for gamblers.

Nobel Prize in Medicine and Physiology awarded to **Dr. Max Theiler** of Rockefeller Institute, an American who was born in South Africa, for his development of a vaccine to combat yellow fever.

Nobel Prize in chemistry awarded to **Dr. Edwin M. McMillan** and **Dr. Glenn T. Seaborg** of the University of California, the 8th and 9th American chemists to obtain this distinction, for their discovery of plutonium.

U.S. had over 12,000 **trade associations** —so many that in Chicago the managers gathered to form a trade association of managers of trade associations.

Jan. 15 30-day ban on all **commercial**

The baseball season afforded fans across the country what future historians of the sport may call the most dramatic home run of the game. The Brooklyn Dodgers and the New York Giants battled their way down to a tie for the National League Pennant. Each team had won 1 of the playoff games; Brooklyn led in 3d and deciding contest 4–1, going into the 9th inning. New York managed 1 run, then 2 men got on base. Finally, at the last moment, Bobby Thomson, Giants' 3d baseman, slammed a home run to decide the game and the season. Chief topic of conversation this year was the senate's special committee investigating organized crime in interstate commerce. Committee's chairman, Sen. Estes Kefauver of Tennessee, called for public televised hearings. For weeks, the nation stayed glued to its sets watching the infamous great and near-great of the underworld parade before the mercilessly objective eye of the camera. Ensuing revelations amused and shocked the entire country.

Academy Awards presented to *An American in Paris* as the outstanding film of the year, to Vivien Leigh as the best actress for her performance in *A Streetcar Named Desire*, and to Humphrey Bogart as best actor for his portrayal in *The African Queen*. Karl Malden and Kim Hunter, both in *A Streetcar Named Desire*, were named best supporting actor and best supporting actress, respectively.

This year's **National College Football Champion** was Tennessee, coached by Col.

POLITICS AND GOVERNMENT; WAR;
DISASTERS; VITAL STATISTICS.

BOOKS; PAINTING; DRAMA;
ARCHITECTURE; SCULPTURE.

Mar. 14 **Seoul** recaptured by U.S. forces.

Mar. 21 **U.S. armed forces** numbered 2,900,000 according to Defense Secretary George C. Marshall. This was double the strength of our armed forces at the outbreak of the Korean War.

Apr. 4 **SHAPE** (Supreme Headquarters, Allied Powers in Europe) established at Paris. Gen. Dwight D. Eisenhower assumed command, and he designated as his naval deputy Vice-Adm. André Lemonnier of France.

Apr. 11 **Gen. Douglas MacArthur** relieved of all commands by Pres. Truman. His posts as Supreme Commander, Allied Powers; Commander-in-Chief, UN command; Commander-in-Chief, Far East; Commanding General, U.S. Army, Far East were all filled by Lt. Gen. Matthew Ridgway.

June 19 **Selective service** extended to July 1, 1955. The bill also lowered draft age to 18½, lengthened time of service to 2 years, set universal military training.

June 23 Jacob Malik, U.S.S.R. delegate to UN, proposed a **cease-fire in Korea**, and withdrawal of troops from 38th parallel. On June 30 Gen. Matthew Ridgway sent to North Korea a proposal to negotiate a cease-fire agreement, and Kim Il Sung, North Korean commander, and Gen. Peng Teh-huai, Chinese communist commander, agreed the next day to meet UN representatives to discuss cease-fire proposals.

July 10 **1st Korean truce talks** held between UN and Communists at Kaesong.

July 11–25 **Costliest flood in U.S. history** when Missouri R. and tributaries flooded more than 1 million acres of farm land in Kansas, Oklahoma, Missouri, and Illinois. Kansas City suffered particularly severe damage July 14. Property damage estimated at more than $1 billion.

Sept. 8 **Japanese peace treaty** signed at San Francisco by delegates of 48 na-

novel written in play form, *Requiem for a Nun*. Action is centered around a character named Temple Drake, a young woman who had appeared in his *Sanctuary*.

Notable Broadway plays included *Darkness at Noon*, dramatized by **Sidney Kingsley** from the novel by **Arthur Koestler** (it won the Drama Critics' Circle Award); *The Rose Tattoo* by **Tennessee Williams;** *Billy Budd*, **Herman Melville**'s novelette adapted by **Louis O. Coxe** and **Robert Chapman;** *I Am a Camera*, **John van Druten**'s dramatization of **Christopher Isherwood**'s Berlin stories; and the musical smash hit, *The King and I* by **Richard Rodgers** and **Oscar Hammerstein II**, based on the book, *Anna and the King of Siam* by **Margaret Landon**. This last piece starred **Gertrude Lawrence** as Anna and **Yul Brynner** as the king.

Outstanding **popular song hit** of the year was "Too Young." Others included "Hello Young Lovers" and "Getting to Know You," from the Richard Rodgers-Oscar Hammerstein II score for *The King and I*.

Survey showed 659 **"symphonic groups"** in U.S., including 32 professional orchestras, 343 community, 231 college, and various amateur organizations. More than 1500 U.S. cities and towns supported concert series during year.

Rise of **record industry** in U.S. indicated by sale during the year of some 190 million records.

Friedman House, one of **Frank Lloyd Wright**'s best plans of his late period, built at Pleasantville, N.Y. Based on circular pattern of rough stone, it cuts away from stereotyped ideas of "modern" architecture.

One of best buildings by European-born **Marcel Breuer**, dormitory at Vassar College, built in Poughkeepsie, N.Y. Shows influence of Breuer's Bauhaus association.

Lake Shore Drive apartments, 2 26-story

574

construction ordered by National Production Authority.

Jan. 15 **Annual estimated budget:** revenues; $55,138,000,000; expenditures, $71,594,000,000 of which $41,421,000,000 was for military purposes.

Jan. 16 **Margin requirements** for stock purchasing upped from 50% to 75% by Federal Reserve System Board of Governors.

Feb. 28 **Organized labor** withdrew representatives from all government defense agencies in protest against administration mobilization policies. On Apr. 30 labor ended its boycott because administration's policies had changed as signalized by labor's new position on the National Advisory Board on Mobilization Policy and the creation of the new Wage Stabilization Board on Apr. 17. Board was to have power to settle all labor disputes threatening national defense effort.

Apr. 28 **Beef price ceilings** fixed by Office of Price Stabilization.

May 15 American Telephone and Telegraph Company reported that it was the **1st corporation to have in excess of 1 million stock holders.**

June 25 **1st U.S. commercial color telecast** presented by Columbia Broadcasting System, New York city.

July 11 New York state's decision to give school children "released time" for **religious studies** upheld by the New York state Court of Appeals. Upheld again by U.S. Supreme Court Apr. 28, 1952.

Sept. 4 **1st transcontinental television broadcast** reported Pres. Truman's opening address to the delegates of the Japanese Peace Treaty Conference in San Francisco,

Robert Neyland. The "Volunteers'" record: 10 wins, no losses, no ties.

U.S. lawn tennis men's singles champion, Frank Sedgman of Australia; **women's singles champion,** Maureen Connolly.

Australia defeated U.S. 3–2 in the challenge round of the **Davis Cup** International Matches.

U.S.G.A. amateur championship won by Billy Maxwell at Saucon Valley C.C., Bethlehem, Pa. He defeated Joseph F. Gagliardi, 4 and 3. **Open championship** won by Ben Hogan at Oakland Hills, C.C., Birmingham, Mich., with a score of 287.

Counterpoint won the 83d annual **Belmont Stakes,** paying 5–10. Jockey was D. Gorman; time was 2:29 on a fast track for winnings valued at $82,000.

Bold won the 75th annual **Preakness Stakes,** paying 4–1. Jockey was E. Arcaro; time was 1:56⅘ on a fast track for winnings valued at $83,110.

Jan. 1 Michigan defeated California by a score of 14 to 6 in the **Rose Bowl** at Pasadena, Calif., before a crowd of 98,939.

Feb. 3 **Largest amount of money earned by a horse in one race** was the $144,323 won by *Great Circle* in the Santa Anita Maturity at Santa Anita Park, Arcadia, Calif. The jockey was Willie Shoemaker.

May 5 Jockey Conn McCreary rode his 2d **Kentucky Derby** winner, J. J. Amiel's *Count Turf,* at Churchill Downs, Louisville, Ky. Time, 2:02⅗; prize, $98,050.

July 10 The 18th annual **All-Star game** was won by the National League, 8–3, at Detroit. 6 home runs were hit; Stan Musial, Bob Elliot, and Gil Hodges connecting for the National League and Vic Wertz and George Kell hitting for the losers.

July 14 **1st horse to win $1 million**

tions. U.S.S.R., Poland, and Czechoslovakia did not sign.

Oct. 10 Mutual Security Act of 1951 signed by Pres. Truman. It authorized $7,483,400,000 in U.S. foreign economic, military and technical aid; established new mutual security agencies. W. Averell Harriman was named head of the agency the following day.

Oct. 24 State of war with Germany officially declared at end by Pres. Truman.

Nov. 13–15 National Convention of the Prohibition Party met at Arcadia, Okla., and nominated Stuart Hamblen of California for the presidency and Enoch A. Holtwick of Illinois for the vice-presidency.

buildings, built in Chicago from plans by **Ludwig Mies van der Rohe.** Both buildings walled entirely in glass.

Mar. 28 Première of *Giants in the Earth,* Pulitzer Prize winning opera by **Douglas Moore.** It was given by the Columbia University Opera Workshop, New York city. Opera tells a story of Norwegian settlers in the Dakota Territory.

Dec. 24 *Amahl and the Night Visitors,* a television opera by **Gian-Carlo Menotti,** broadcast on Christmas Eve. Based on a theme suggested by Hieronymus Bosch's painting "The Adoration of the Magi," the opera had been commissioned by the National Broadcasting Co.

1952

Early in the year British Prime Minister Winston Churchill visited the U.S. in order to "re-establish the close and intimate relationship that he had with Pres. Roosevelt in wartime and to seek a common policy and approach on the grave problems facing the Western Alliance." These problems were, of course, the spreading danger of Communist domination. Our policy: to arm Western Europe and make it too costly for the U.S.S.R. to start a war. Opponents of this alliance included ex-president Herbert Hoover, who claimed we were carrying Europe at disastrous expense. A far better plan, he maintained, was to retire to the western hemisphere and build a "bastion of liberty." Although 1952 was an election year, this issue was never a serious part of the campaign since the 2 major candidates supported the NATO idea. While both Stevenson and Eisenhower enjoyed enormous popularity, the Democrats suffered from attacks on alleged corruption within the administration. Eisenhower's subsequent victory was interpreted by many as a personal rebuke to the Truman regime. In spite of truce negotiations in Korea, light ground and air action still continued, and intensified

The political events of 1952 were reflected in the literature of the year. Single most outstanding fiction trend was the regional novel dealing with the South. An unprecedented building boom spurred architects to design with distinction and to experiment with new methods of construction, notably prestressed concrete. The year was one of travel for musical organizations both here and abroad. The Boston Symphony essayed its 1st European tour; Gershwin's folk opera, *Porgy and Bess,* played to enthusiastic houses in Berlin, Vienna, London. Most noticeable trend was a growing acceptance of so-called modern works. Igor Stravinsky, for instance, was slowly achieving the stature of a classic composer. Cross pollination also occurred in painting with a flurry of international exhibitions. A movement away from abstractionism towards representationalism was noted. The theatrical year on Broadway so lackluster that George Jean Nathan refused to issue his annual volume on the season.

Pulitzer Prizes: novel, *The Caine Mutiny* by Herman Wouk; drama, *The Shrike* by Joseph Kramm; U.S. history, *The Uprooted* by Oscar Handlin; biography,

SCIENCE; INDUSTRY; ECONOMICS; EDUCATION; RELIGION; PHILOSOPHY.

SPORTS; FASHIONS; POPULAR ENTERTAINMENT; FOLKLORE; SOCIETY.

Calif. President was seen and heard over 94 stations all across the country.

Oct. 10 **Transcontinental dial telephone** service begun experimentally at Englewood, N.J.

Dec. 20 1st electricity generated from **atomic energy** at the U.S. Reactor Testing Station in Idaho.

was *Citation,* who brought his total earnings to $1,085,760 by winning the Hollywood Gold Cup, Inglewood, Calif. The great bay horse had run out of the money only once in 45 starts during a 4-year career.

July 18 **World Heavyweight Championship** won by "Jersey Joe" Walcott when he K.O.'d Ezzard Charles in 7th round at Pittsburgh. At 37 Walcott was oldest man to gain title.

Oct. 4–10 New York, AL, defeated New York, NL, 4–2 in the 48th annual **World Series.**

Dec. 1 **Navy** defeated Army, 42–7, in their annual contest at Municipal Stadium, Philadelphia.

1952

Inflation was no longer a threat, it was a reality. Employment had reached a record high of 62,500,000. Prices continued to zoom. The U.S. Treasury recorded a deficit of $4 billion. Major development along the labor front was the 3-way struggle among the steel industry, the U.S. Steel Workers of America (C.I.O.), and the president. When the union prepared to walk out for wage hikes, Pres. Truman seized the mills on the grounds that steel was vital to our defense effort. The management retaliated by bringing an injunction against the seizure; a Federal District court then pronounced the president's action unconstitutional, a ruling upheld by the Supreme Court. This sent the steel workers out on what developed into a 54-day strike. The president asked Congress for legislation permitting seizure of vital industries, but the Senate advised him to use the provisions of the Taft-Hartley Law. He refused to do this, called both sides to the White House, where they settled dispute in a conference.

Nobel Prizes in physics awarded to **Dr. Felix Bloch** and **Dr. Edward Mills Purcell,** both of Harvard, for work in measurement of magnetic fields in atomic nuclei. They

This was the year of flying saucers, panty raids, and prison riots. Unidentified aircraft, which appeared to be luminous disks or saucers, were reported flashing across the night skies all over the nation. The Air Force even published photographs of the phenomena. There was widespread conjecture that these objects were manned by emissaries from outer space, a theory unsupported by official spokesmen. Unfortunately, these spokesmen offered such a bewildering variety of answers that the confusion helped promote the "men-from-Mars" interpretation. Favorite outdoor sport of collegiates across the country seemed to be a harmless form of rioting whose ground rules called for male students to besiege sorority houses and girls' dormitories demanding, as token of submission, various articles of feminine underclothing, which were, as a rule, freely bestowed. Disturbances of a more serious nature plagued prison officials. Inmates, pressing for more liberal treatment, kidnaped guards and used them as hostages while they dickered with authorities. These riots led to a review of our prison system on both state and national level.

Academy Awards presented to *The*

577

POLITICS AND GOVERNMENT; WAR; DISASTERS; VITAL STATISTICS.

BOOKS; PAINTING; DRAMA; ARCHITECTURE; SCULPTURE.

in October when truce talks were temporarily postponed.

Jan. 24 Truce negotiations in Korea deadlocked according to statement issued by UN headquarters in Tokyo.

Mar. 8 Charges of **germ warfare** formally lodged against U.S. by Chinese Communist foreign minister Chou En-lai. Charges, reported by Peking radio, were supported by Soviet representative to UN Jacob A. Malik. Offer by International Red Cross to investigate was rejected by Malik, and on Mar. 28 UN ruled Malik's charges out-of-order.

Mar. 20 U.S. Senate ratified the **Japanese Peace Treaty** by a vote of 66 to 10.

May 30–June 1 National Convention of the Socialist Party met in Cleveland and nominated Darlington Hoopes of Pennsylvania for the presidency and Samuel H. Friedman of New York for the vice-presidency.

June 25 McCarran-Walter Bill, which sought to revise and limit immigration, vetoed by Pres. Truman as un-American and discriminatory. The following day the House of Representatives overrode veto by 278–113; Senate took similar action on June 27 by vote of 57–26. Act abolished racial restrictions on immigration and retained quota system derived from national origins count of 1920.

July 4–6 National Convention of the Progressive Party met in Chicago and nominated Vincent Hallinan of California for the presidency and Mrs. Charlotta A. Bass of New York for the vice-presidency.

July 11 Republican National Convention ..ominated General Dwight D. Eisenhower for the presidency. Sen. Richard M. Nixon of California was nominated for the vice-presidency.

July 16 President Truman signed the Korea **"G.I. Bill of Rights"** which offered

Charles Evans Hughes by Merlo J. Pusey; poetry, *Collected Poems* by Marianne Moore; music, *Symphony Concertante* by Gail Kubick.

National Book Award given to Negro novelist **Ralph Ellison** for his *Invisible Man,* the story of a Southern Negro's experiences in the modern world. Pictures of a small Southern town, a college campus and Harlem form the descriptive background.

Ernest Hemingway turns his masterful technique to a short account of man's struggle with nature, *The Old Man and the Sea.* With manifest symbolic overtones, the book tells the story of an old Caribbean fisherman and his unsuccessful contest with a giant marlin.

Major novel by **John Steinbeck** is *East of Eden,* a panoramic and symbolic story of a family from the Civil War to World War II. Details of a California valley are woven into the fabric of a Cain and Abel story.

The Collected Poems of **Archibald MacLeish** *1917–1952* published and presents many of his longer poems: "Pot of Earth," "Hamlet of A. MacLeish," "Einstein," and "Colloquy for the States."

Broadway successes included: *The Shrike,* a 1st effort by **Joseph Kramm** which won the Pulitzer Prize. The play dealt with life in the psychopathic ward of a large New York hospital. Also, *Point of No Return,* **Paul Osborn's** dramatization of **John P. Marquand's** successful novel; *The Fourposter,* by **Jan de Hartog,** a play that needed only 2 characters; *The Grass Harp,* a gentle comedy of life in a small Southern town by **Truman Capote,** his 1st play. Distinguished visitors from abroad were *Venus Observed,* a verse play by **Christopher Fry,** and the **Lawrence Olivier, Vivien Leigh** double productions of **Shaw's** *Caesar and Cleopatra* and **Shakespeare's** *Anthony and Cleopatra.*

Among the better received **musical compositions** heard for the 1st time this year were *Symphony Concertante* by **Gail Ku-**

were the 8th and 9th American physicists to attain this distinction.

Nobel Prize in Medicine and Physiology presented to **Dr. Selman A. Waksman** of Rutgers, an American who was born in the Ukraine, for his discovery (with others) of streptomycin.

Mar. 2 **Subversives barred from teaching** in public schools by U.S. Supreme Court decision.

Mar. 6 **Foreign military and economic aid** during fiscal year estimated at $7,900,-000,000 by Pres. Truman.

Apr. 8 **Striking steel mills seized** by Pres. Truman. The next day 3 major steel companies instituted legal action in federal court, Washington, D.C. to contest seizure. They were denied temporary restraint order.

Apr. 29 **Seizure of steel mills** declared unconstitutional by U.S. District Judge David A. Pine. Steelworkers immediately went on strike.

May 2 **Steel strike canceled** by union at presidential request.

May 8 **75-ton atomic cannon** announced by Army Secretary Frank C. Pace.

June 2 **Steel plant seizure** declared unconstitutional by U.S. Supreme Court. Pres. Truman ordered plants returned; steelworkers resumed strike.

June 14 Dedication of keel of **1st atomic submarine,** *Nautilus,* at Groton, Conn.

June 28 **Wage and rent controls,** priority and material allocations extended by Congress.

June 30 **American stock holders** numbered 6½ million, 76% of them earning less than $10,000 a year after taxes according to report made by Brookings Institute.

Greatest Show on Earth as the outstanding motion picture of the year, to Shirley Booth as the best actress for her performance in *Come Back, Little Sheba,* and to Gary Cooper for his portrayal in *High Noon.* Gloria Grahame was chosen best supporting actress for her work in *The Bad and the Beautiful* and Anthony Quinn was named best supporting actor for his characterization in *Viva Zapata!*

This year's **National College Football Champion** was Michigan State, coached by Clarence "Biggie" Munn. Their record: 9 wins, no losses, no ties. By the end of the season Michigan State had a winning streak of 24 games dating back to 1950.

U.S. lawn tennis men's singles champion, Frank Sedgman of Australia; **women's singles champion,** Maureen Connolly.

Australia defeated the U.S. 4 to 1 in the challenge round of the **Davis Cup** International Matches.

U.S.G.A. amateur championship won by Jack Westland at Seattle, Wash., G.C. He defeated Al Mengert, 3 and 2. **Open championship** won by Julius Boros at Northwood Club, Dallas, Tex., with a score of 281.

Blue Man won the 76th annual **Preakness Stakes,** paying 8–5. Jockey was Conn McCreary; time was 1:57⅗ on a fast track for winnings valued at $86,135.

One Count won the 84th annual **Belmont Stakes,** paying 13–1. Jockey was E. Arcaro; time was 2:30⅕ on a fast track for winnings valued at $82,400.

Jan. 1 Illinois defeated Stanford by a score of 40 to 7 in the **Rose Bowl** at Pasadena, Calif., before a crowd of 96,825.

May 3 Jockey Eddie Arcaro rode his 5th **Kentucky Derby** winner, Calumet Farm's *Hill Gail,* who fell ⅕ sec. short of Whirlaway's Derby record set in 1941, running the fast track in 2:01⅗. The winner's prize was $96,300.

579

POLITICS AND GOVERNMENT; WAR; DISASTERS; VITAL STATISTICS.

BOOKS; PAINTING; DRAMA; ARCHITECTURE; SCULPTURE.

Korean veterans with 90 days of service as of June 27, 1950, rights and benefits similar to those granted to veterans of World War II.

July 26 Democratic National Convention at Chicago, Ill., nominated Gov. Adlai E. Stevenson of Illinois for presidency. Sen. John J. Sparkman of Alabama was nominated for the vice-presidency.

Nov. 4 Gen. Dwight D. Eisenhower defeated Adlai E. Stevenson in the **presidential elections** by an electoral vote of 442 to 89. Popular vote: Eisenhower, 33,-938,285; Stevenson, 27,312,217; Hallinan, 140,138; Hamblen, 72,881; Hoopes, 20,189.

Nov. 29 Pres.-Elect **Eisenhower,** carrying out his campaign promise, flew to Korea to inspect UN situation. He made a 3-day tour, visiting front line positions. Trip was kept secret until after he had left dangerous zone.

bik, Pulitzer Prize winner for music; *Symphony No. 4* by **Paul Creston;** *Piano Concerto* by **Alexei Haieff;** *Symphony No. 7* by **Roy Harris;** *Temptation of St. Anthony,* a dance-symphony by **Gardner Read.**

Successful **popular music** this year included: "Cry," "Please," "Mr. Sun," "Kiss of Fire," "Wish You Were Here," "I Went to Your Wedding," "Domino," "Wheel of Fortune."

New operas that received their premières this year included *Trouble in Tahiti* by **Leonard Bernstein** (Brandeis University, Waltham, Mass.); *Acres of Sky* by **Arthur Kreutz** (New York city); and *The Farmer and the Fairy* by **Alexandre Tcherepnin** (Aspen, Colorado).

Alcoa Building, Pittsburgh, Pa., built from plans by Harrison & Abramovitz. Entire 30-story tower sheathed with 6 x 12 ft. prefabricated aluminum sheet panels.

1953

The nation watched with interest as a Republican administration took over the reins of government for the 1st time in 24 years. Pres. Eisenhower enjoyed an uncertain control of Congress; the Republicans ruled there by the grace of conservative Southern Democrats. The president made immediate attempts to secure the legislative by announcing he favored a close presidential-congressional "partnership." The new chief executive had 4 major areas of foreign policy to deal with. These were: (1) countering Russian expansion on all parts of the globe; (2) bolstering our European allies by economic and military aid; (3) fostering European unity; and (4) forcing an equitable armistice in Korea. Most explosive internal problem: Sen. McCarthy and his charges of Soviet espionage activities in America. Most outstanding success: signing of peace agreement in Korea. Pres. Eisenhower announced this fact to a relieved country, but warned, "We have won an armistice on a single battleground, not peace in the world."

American literature seemed to be taking inventory before going on to explore fresh areas. There was a bountiful supply of good books, but few really distinguished ones. Of particular interest was the unusual number of highly competent Negro writers who published their works, mostly novels. Architects looked forward to boom times with commercial construction up 43.2%. Most frequently designed buildings were schools. Important musical festivals here and abroad attracted many new manuscripts from composers. American painting had reverted to the abstract form, but had also discovered the so-called primitivism of Grandma Moses, who received world-wide recognition. Despite Broadway's usual complaints of rising production costs, shortages of houses and scripts, the season showed a marked improvement. Among playwrights, it was definitely a year for newcomers. 3 of the town's biggest hits were *Picnic* by William Inge (his 2d play), *The Seven Year Itch* by George Axelrod (his 1st), and *Tea and*

580

SCIENCE; INDUSTRY; ECONOMICS; EDUCATION; RELIGION; PHILOSOPHY.	SPORTS; FASHIONS; POPULAR ENTERTAINMENT; FOLKLORE; SOCIETY.

July 7 **Transatlantic speed record** set by S.S. *United States* on first round trip with eastward crossing of 3 da., 10 hr., 40 min. On July 14 she set westward crossing record of 3 da., 12 hr., 12 min.

July 14 **Price controls** removed from most fresh and processed meats and vegetables.

July 24 **Steel strike settled** as management and labor reached compromise agreement at special White House conference called by Pres. Truman.

Nov. 25 **George Meany** of New York appointed president of AFL to fill unexpired term of William Green, who had died Nov. 21.

Dec. 4 **Walter P. Reuther,** president of United Auto Workers, chosen head of CIO.

July 8 Baseball's 19th annual **All Star Game** at Shibe Park, Philadelphia won by the National League team, 3–2. Jackie Robinson and Hank Sauer hit home runs for the winners.

Sept. 23 World **Heavyweight Championship** won by Rocky Marciano, who knocked out Jersey Joe Walcott in 13th round at Philadelphia. It was Marciano's 43d straight win as professional boxer, no bouts lost.

Oct. 1–7 New York, AL, defeated Brooklyn, NL, 4–3 in the 49th annual **World Series.**

Nov. 29 **Navy** defeated Army, 7–0, in their annual contest at Municipal Stadium, Philadelphia.

1953

A population of nearly 161 million continued to enjoy unprecedented prosperity, even though it was estimated that the 1953 dollar was worth about 52¢ as compared with its 1935–39 equivalent. A greatly increased personal income more than made up the difference for much of the population. This year saw the end of all wage and salary controls; rent ceilings were also removed. Labor continued its fight for erasure of the Taft-Hartley Law. A broad economic program was announced by the administration. It included: (1) revision of tax laws—modification or elimination of excess profits tax—to benefit corporations—and double taxation of dividends; (2) shifting the national debt to long-term bonds; and (3) providing for a sliding scale interest rate that would go up or down depending upon the demand. This latter provision was designed as a check to inflationary borrowing.

Nobel Prizes in Medicine and Physiology presented to **Dr. Fritz A. Lipmann** and **Dr. Hans Adolph Krebs** for their research

Most frequently heard topics of conversation: the McCarthy investigations (this was far and away the most explosive subject of small talk in the nation); the trial and subsequent conviction and death sentence of Julius and Ethel Rosenberg for espionage; and the conquest of Mt. Everest, world's highest peak, by a British party whose guide, Tenzing Norkey, became an international hero. Biggest fashion news was a designers' invasion into the field of men's clothes. Bermuda shorts for the businessman were promoted and worn during the hot summer months. For the ladies, a mood of sleek elegance was decreed. Skirts were worn shorter, and so was the coiffure. The "Italian" haircut became the vogue. This style called for a carefully casual female crew cut that gave the wearer a gamin-like, wind-blown look that was still strikingly sophisticated. Various 3-dimensional wide-screen processes, plus stereophonic sound, helped boost movie attendance throughout the country. Most popular trend in films was the science fiction thriller.

581

| POLITICS AND GOVERNMENT; WAR; DISASTERS; VITAL STATISTICS. | BOOKS; PAINTING; DRAMA; ARCHITECTURE; SCULPTURE. |

U.S. armed forces **casualties in Korea** totaled 137,051; of this number, 25,604 were killed, 103,492 were wounded, and 7955 were reported missing.

Jan. 20 **Gen. Dwight D. Eisenhower** inaugurated 34th president at Washington, D.C.

Jan. 21 13 more top **Communists** convicted by federal jury in New York city of charges of conspiring to teach and advocate overthrow of U.S. government.

Mar. 9 **World peace** outlook brighter because of Stalin's recent death, according to Secretary of State, John Foster Dulles.

Apr. 1 **Department of Health, Education, and Welfare** formally created by joint congressional action.

Apr. 11 1st secretary of new **Department of Health, Education, and Welfare** sworn in. She was **Mrs. Oveta Culp Hobby** of Texas.

Apr. 20 **U.S. Communist Party** ordered to register with the Justice Department as an organization controlled and directed by Russia.

Apr. 24 **Record taxes** collected in 1952 according to U.S. Bureau of Internal Revenue. They totaled $68.5 billions.

Apr. 25 **Record speech in U.S. Senate** made by **Sen. Wayne Morse** (Ind.-Ore.) who spoke for 22 hr., 26 min. opposing a bill that would return offshore oil reserves to individual states. His marathon failed to .sway the Senate, which passed the measure May 5, by a vote of 56–35.

May 11 Vicious **tornadoes** hit Waco and San Angelo, Tex., killing 124 people.

June 8 **Tornado** sliced through Ohio and Flint, Mich., killing 139 persons.

June 9 **Tornado** hit western Massachusetts, killing 86 persons.

Sympathy by Robert Anderson (also a debut).

Pulitzer Prizes: novel, *The Old Man and the Sea* by Ernest Hemingway; drama, *Picnic* by William Inge; U.S. history, *The Era of Good Feeling* by George Dangerfield; biography, *Edmund Pendleton, 1721–1803* by David J. Mays; poetry, *Collected Poems, 1917–1952* by Archibald MacLeish; music, no prize.

A panoramic view of middle-class Chicago during the '20's and the depression is **Saul Bellow's** novel *The Adventures of Augie March.* A ubiquitous character, Augie touches upon countless aspects of society and thus in true picaresque fashion allows us a glimpse of a veritable cross section of life.

Novelist **John Steinbeck** published a series of sketches and stories *Sweet Thursday,* a sequel to his earlier *Cannery Row.* The comical and endearing antics of his Southern Californian *paisanos* are shown against the backdrop of World War II.

Camino Real by **Tennessee Williams** proved a disaster for its backers and a fretful puzzle for the critics, most of whom considered it an *avant garde,* symbolistic charade, too sprawling for a play, too suddenly serious to be a vaudeville. Its failure, despite violently partisan audiences, proved once more how unwise it is financially for Broadway producers to experiment. Both critics and audiences were much more at home with *Wonderful Town,* a musical version of *My Sister Eileen,* a successful farce of a few years back. It starred **Rosalind Russell** and boasted a score by **Leonard Bernstein.**

Popular **song hits** included: "I Believe," "Doggie in the Window," "Till I Waltz Again With You," and "I'm Walking Behind You."

Architectural Award of Merit for Distinguished Design went to Saarinen, Saarinen & Associates for the engineering staff building of the General Motors Technical Center, Warren, Mich., and also to William Henley Deitrick of Deitrick·Knight

| SCIENCE; INDUSTRY; ECONOMICS; EDUCATION; RELIGION; PHILOSOPHY. | SPORTS; FASHIONS; POPULAR ENTERTAINMENT; FOLKLORE; SOCIETY. |

on the mechanism of living cells. Both Dr. Lipmann, an American, and Dr. Krebs, an Englishman, were born in Germany.

The Ford Foundation established **The Fund for the Republic** and gave it $15 millions "to help fight restriction on freedom of thought, inquiry and expression."

Jan. 9   **Estimated budget** for fiscal year 1953–54 called for expenditures of $78,-587,000,000; revenues of $68,665,000,000.

Jan. 16   **Offshore oil deposits** set aside as national reserve by Pres. Truman.

Feb. 5   **U.S. steel production** up to 117,500,000 short tons per year, according to report issued by American Iron & Steel institute.

Feb. 6   All **controls** on wages and salaries lifted; order also affected many consumer goods.

Feb. 12   **Price ceilings** off many items, including tires, gasoline, poultry, eggs. All prices were decontrolled by Mar. 17.

Feb. 13   Allotment **controls on steel,** copper, aluminum renewed by Office of Defense Mobilization.

Feb. 20   Margin requirements for **stock purchases** reduced from 75% back to 50%, effective Feb. 24.

Feb. 22   Voluntary program of **health insurance** to be financed by federal, state, and municipal funds recommended by president's Commission on the Health Needs of the Nation.

Feb. 25   **Controls** lifted on cigarettes, dry groceries, copper, aluminum by Office of Price Stabilization.

Mar. 12   **Price controls** on all consumer goods lifted by Office of Price Stabilization.

Mar. 17   **Price controls officially ended** by Office of Price Stabilization.

Mar. 30   **Jet-propelled guided missiles** under production according to U.S. Navy.

May 25   **1st atomic artillery shell** fired at proving grounds in Nevada.

Academy Awards presented to *From Here to Eternity* as the outstanding motion picture of the year, to Audrey Hepburn as best actress for her performance in *Roman Holiday,* and to William Holden for his portrayal in *Stalag 17.* Donna Reed was named best supporting actress for her playing in *From Here to Eternity* and Frank Sinatra was chosen best supporting actor for his portrayal in *From Here to Eternity.*

U.S. lawn tennis men's singles champion, Tony Trabert; **women's singles champion,** Maureen Connolly.

U.S.G.A. amateur championship won by Gene Littler at Oklahoma City, Okla., G. and C.C. He defeated Dale Morey, 1 up. **Open championship** won by Ben Hogan for 4th time at Oakmont C.C., Pittsburgh, Pa., with a score of 283.

This year's **national college football champion** was Michigan State with a perfect season; team was coached by Clarence (Biggie) Munn who was named "coach of the year."

Native Dancer won the 77th annual **Preakness Stakes,** paying 1–5. Jockey was E. Guerin; time was 1:57⅖ on a fast track for winnings valued at $65,200.

Native Dancer won the 85th annual **Belmont Stakes,** paying 9–20. Jockey was E. Guerin; time was 2:28⅗ on a fast track for winnings valued at $82,500.

Australia defeated the U.S. 3 to 2 in the challenge round of the **Davis Cup** International Matches.

Jan. 1   Southern California defeated Wisconsin by a score of 7 to 0 in the **Rose Bowl** at Pasadena, Calif., before a crowd of 100,000.

Mar. 18   The shifting of the **Boston Braves'** baseball franchise to Milwaukee, Wisc., approved by the National League. This year Milwaukee became the most baseball-happy town in the U.S. leading

| POLITICS AND GOVERNMENT; WAR; DISASTERS; VITAL STATISTICS. | BOOKS; PAINTING; DRAMA; ARCHITECTURE; SCULPTURE. |

June 18 **Worst air accident** in history occurred near Tokyo, Japan, when a U.S. Air Force *Globemaster* crashed killing 129 men.

July 27 **Korean armistice** signed at Panmunjon by UN and Communist delegates.

Aug. 1 New **Foreign Operations Administration** given direction of all foreign aid programs.

Aug. 1 Broader **social security** act proposed by Pres. Eisenhower who recommended provisions be made to include another 10½ million persons under the law. Legislation subsequently passed, Sept. 1, 1954.

Aug. 7 **Refugee Relief Act** of 1953 signed. It admitted 214,000 refugees beyond the regular immigration quotas.

Associates for the North Carolina State Fair Building at Raleigh, N.C.

Jan. 1 *Suite Hebraïque* for viola and orchestra, by **Ernest Bloch,** introduced by the Chicago Symphony, Chicago, Ill.

Jan. 9 *Volpone,* an opera by **George Antheil,** produced in Los Angeles, Calif.

Feb. 7 **Bohuslav Martinu's** opera, *The Marriage,* premiered by the New York Opera Company at the New York City Center, New York city.

May 4 Première performance of *The Mighty Casey,* a 1-act opera by **William Schuman** based on the poem, "Casey at the Bat," given by the Julius Hartt Opera Guild in Hartford, Conn.

1954

The 83d Congress and the nation anxiously awaited Pres. Eisenhower's legislative program. The country's foreign policy, he declared, would be dedicated to an attempt to regain initiative in the world fight against communism and to a search for an equitable international program designed to win our allies' confidence. With regard to defense, the president advocated intensive research on atomic weapons, an integrated transcontinental transportation system that embraced the St. Lawrence Seaway proposal. He went on the record for greater discretion in loyalty investigations, but promised decisive action in all cases of actual espionage or sabotage. He revealed that some 2200 government employees had been dropped under the administration's new security system. Later on in the year, the president asked Congress to provide necessary legislation to allow the AEC to share certain atomic se-

Principal interest of American literature this year seemed to be journalistic. Books on the "cold war," U.S. foreign policy, government loyalty programs, subversion, and the A-bomb filled rental libraries and booksellers' racks. Novelists favored an exploration of the psychopathic mentality, but said little that was new or surprising. Major development for poets was an ever-increasing list of awards and prizes open to them; their response was to write more and better verse. The building boom of 1953 showed no signs of let-up; in fact, July set a monthly record of $3,135,000,-000 worth of new construction. All departments of musical endeavor reported a great demand. Established symphonic societies and widely popular musical festivals continued to give composers commissions.

Pulitzer Prizes: novel, no prize; drama, *The Teahouse of the August Moon* by John Patrick; U.S. history, *A Stillness at*

June 12 **Wage agreement** signed by U.S. Steelworkers of America (CIO) and U.S. Steel Corporation granting 8½¢ per hour wage boost plus ½¢ in benefits.

Sept. 10 Labor Secretary **Martin P. Durkin** resigned his cabinet post because of failure of administration to carry out alleged agreement to propose 19 amendments to the Taft-Hartley labor law.

Sept. 22 **International Longshoremen's Association** expelled from AFL for refusing to get rid of racketeering elements within its ranks.

Dec. 9 General Electric Co. announced that all **Communist employees** would be discharged.

Dec. 16 **Airplane speed record** achieved by U.S. Air Force Major Charles E. Yeager who flew a Bell X-1A rocket powered plane more than 1600 mph.

both leagues in attendance, 1,826,397, National League record.

May 2 A 25-1 long shot, *Dark Star,* won the 79th annual **Kentucky Derby** at Churchill Downs, Louisville, Ky., nosing out the favorite, *Native Dancer.* Dark Star's time was 2:02; his prize, $90,050. Jockey H. Moreno rode for the Cain Hoy Stable.

July 14 The National League won the 20th annual **All-Star game** at Cincinnati, Ohio, on July 14, beating the American League, 5–1.

Sept. 16 The shift of the **St. Louis Browns' baseball** franchise to Baltimore, Md., approved by the American League, the Browns to begin the following season as the **Baltimore Orioles.**

Sept. 30–Oct. 5 New York, AL, defeated Brooklyn, NL, 4–2 in the 50th annual **World Series.** This was the 1st time a team has won 5 consecutive World Series.

Nov. 28 Navy defeated Army, 7–0, at Philadelphia, Pa., to win the annual **Army-Navy football game.**

1954

A mild business recession coupled with slightly rising unemployment worried some Americans, but Administration spokesmen reminded the nation that a certain amount of rollback from previous unprecedented economic highs was not only natural, but desirable. However, the downward trend was reversed about the middle of the year, and by September personal income had exceeded the August figure by $2 billions. Unemployment, though, totaled 2,893,000, about twice the figure reported for 1953. The AFL and the CIO agreed to merge, and AFL president, George Meany, predicted that the marriage would take place some time in 1955. Huge crop surpluses resulted in the most stringent curbs ever imposed by the Agriculture Department. Secretary of Agriculture Ezra Benson was given legislation allowing him to barter U.S. crop surpluses on the world market for strategic goods. Schools were

The McCarthy investigations stirred most Americans to anger, to indignation, frequently to both. Another topic of concerned conversation was the rising rate of juvenile crime and delinquency. Families discussed discipline and examined outside influences. Lurid comic books and violence-spattered pulp magazines came under heavy attack from parents' groups and, in some cases, public legislation. Fashion designers introduced a new softer silhouette that de-emphasized the bust, showed a longer torso. Hollywood produced fewer, better films, concentrated on new techniques, most of which employed variants of the wide screen process. This resulted in a rash of spectacular historical epics and large-scale westerns which were shown in the 7448 movie houses throughout the country that had installed CinemaScope facilities.

Academy Awards presented to *On the*

585

POLITICS AND GOVERNMENT; WAR; DISASTERS; VITAL STATISTICS.

BOOKS; PAINTING; DRAMA; ARCHITECTURE; SCULPTURE.

crets with allies and to pave the way for peaceful industrial development of the atom.

Mar. 1 5 Congressmen shot on the floor of the House of Representatives by Puerto Rican nationalists. All recovered from their wounds.

Mar. 8 Nearly $8 billions in **foreign military aid** given by U.S. between Oct., 1949, and Dec. 31, 1954, according to report made by Pres. Eisenhower.

Mar. 8 Mutual defense agreement signed by Japan and U.S., providing for gradual rearming of Japan.

Mar. 10 1st atomic power plant planned for Duquesne Power Co., Pittsburgh, Pa., by U.S. Atomic Energy Commission. Pres. Eisenhower, using radioactive and electronic devices, broke ground for it from Denver Sept. 6.

Mar. 10 50% reduction in most **federal luxury taxes** and other excise taxes voted by House of Representatives.

Mar. 13 10th **Inter-American conference** adopted U.S. anti-Communist resolution.

Mar. 31 Hydrogen bomb capable of destroying any city on earth within possibility, declared Lewis L. Strauss, chairman of U.S. Atomic Energy Commission.

Apr. 1 U.S. Air Force Academy, similar to service schools at West Point and Annapolis, authorized.

Apr. 8 Construction of **early warning radar net** stretching 3000 miles across Canadian far north announced by U.S. and Canada.

May 21 Proposed constitutional amendment extending **vote to 18-year olds** defeated by U.S. Senate.

May 24 Membership in **Communist Party** declared sufficient grounds for deportation of aliens, according to U.S. Supreme Court decision which upheld constitutionality of Internal Security Act of 1950.

Appomattox by Bruce Catton; biography, *The Spirit of St. Louis* by Charles A. Lindbergh; poetry, *The Waking: Poems 1933–1953* by Theodore Roethke; music, *Concerto for Two Pianos and Orchestra* by Quincy Porter.

Ernest Hemingway won this year's **Nobel Prize for Literature.** He is best known for his novels and collections of short stories, including *The Sun Also Rises* (1926), *A Farewell to Arms* (1929), *Death in the Afternoon* (1932), *To Have and Have Not* (1937), *The Fifth Column and the First Forty-Nine* (1938), *For Whom the Bell Tolls* (1940), and *The Old Man and the Sea* (1952).

A retelling of the Crucifixion and Resurrection story against the background of World War I is **William Faulkner's** *A Fable.* The mature Faulkner employs all his previously perfected techniques: backtracking in time, rhetoric, stream of consciousness, etc.

The Teahouse of the August Moon, **John Patrick's** adaptation of **Vern Sneider's** novel about U.S. occupation of Okinawa, won both the Pulitzer Prize and the New York Drama Critics' Circle Prize. Other hits of the Broadway season included: *The Caine Mutiny Court Martial* by **Herman Wouk,** and *The Confidential Clerk,* a verse play by **T. S. Eliot** starring Ina Claire.

4 new works by **Igor Stravinsky** were heard this year. They were: *Septet* for violin, cello, viola, clarinet, horn, bassoon, and piano (Dumbarton Oaks, Jan. 24); *Three Songs from William Shakespeare* (Hollywood, Mar. 8); *In Memoriam: Dylan Thomas* (Hollywood, Sept. 20); and *Four Russian Peasant Songs* for female chorus and 4 horns (Los Angeles, Oct. 11).

Some **popular song hits** of the year were: "Stranger in Paradise," based on a melody of Alexander Borodin; "Hernando's Hideaway" and "Hey, There," both from the

SCIENCE; INDUSTRY; ECONOMICS; EDUCATION; RELIGION; PHILOSOPHY.

SPORTS; FASHIONS; POPULAR ENTERTAINMENT; FOLKLORE; SOCIETY.

still crowded to overcapacity, and, with the Supreme Court decision on May 14 outlawing segregation in all public schools, confusion reached alarming proportions.

Jan. 11 Widespread changes in the **Taft-Hartley labor law** urged by Pres. Eisenhower in a special message to Congress. He also advocated a return to flexible farm price supports.

Jan. 19 $1 billion expansion program announced by **General Motors Corporation.**

Jan. 20 **St. Lawrence Seaway** approved by Senate vote.

Feb. 2 1st thermonuclear **(hydrogen bomb)** explosion officially reported by Pres. Eisenhower. It took place at Eniwetok Atoll in the Pacific in 1952.

Feb. 23 **Antipolio inoculation** of school children begun by Dr. Jonas E. Salk, serum's developer, at Pittsburgh, Pa.

Mar. 24 **Hydrogen bomb** explosion in Marshall Islands on Mar. 1, 1954, exceeded all estimates of its power made by scientists, according to statement made by Pres. Eisenhower.

Apr. 2 **Longest and costliest strike** in history of New York city, a labor jurisdictional strike which began Mar. 3, terminated by International Longshoremen's Association.

May 13 **St. Lawrence Seaway** bill, authorizing construction of U.S.–Canadian artificial waterway connecting Great Lakes and Atlantic Ocean, signed by Pres. Eisenhower.

June 9 Defense Secretary Charles E. Wilson named director of **St. Lawrence Seaway** Development Corporation by Pres. Eisenhower.

June 29 2-year **labor agreement** signed between United Steelworkers of America (CIO) and U.S. Steel Corporation. The contract called for wage hikes, and increased pension and social insurance benefits.

Waterfront as the outstanding motion picture of the year, to its star, Marlon Brando, as best actor of the year, and to Grace Kelly as best actress for her performance in *The Country Girl*. Eva Marie Saint was named best supporting actress for her portrayal in *On the Waterfront* and Edmond O'Brien was selected best supporting actor for his playing in *The Barefoot Contessa*.

The average American's **favorite meal** was fruit cup, vegetable soup, steak and potatoes, peas, rolls and butter, pie à la mode.

90% of adult Americans drank 3 to 4 cups of coffee a day. 64% of American adults drank **beer, wine, or liquor:** 70% of the male adults and 58% of the female adults.

45 out of 100 adults in U.S. smoked 1 pack of **cigarettes** a day. 60% of the male population of U.S. and 30% of the female, smoke.

3 out of 5 households in the United States, about 29 million households, had **television** sets—on the market only 8 years, since 1947.

Only 17% of American adults were **reading** a book at the time of a recent survey as compared to 50% of the adults in England, and 33⅓% in Canada and Australia.

U.S. lawn tennis men's singles champion, E. Victor Seixas, Jr.; **women's singles champion,** Doris Hart.

U.S.G.A. amateur championship won by Arnold Palmer at Detroit C.C., Grosse Point Garms, Mich. He defeated Bob Sweeny, 1 up. **Open championship** won by Ed Furgol at Baltusrol G.C., N.J., with a score of 284.

High Gun won the 86th annual **Belmont**

587

| POLITICS AND GOVERNMENT; WAR; DISASTERS; VITAL STATISTICS. | BOOKS; PAINTING; DRAMA; ARCHITECTURE; SCULPTURE. |

June 24 Colorado Springs, Colo., announced as site of new **Air Force Academy** by Air Force Secretary Harold E. Talbott.

Sept. 1 **Hurricane "Carol"** struck Long Island, N.Y., and New England killing 68; property losses estimated at $500 million. On Sept. 10, **hurricane "Edna"** veered inland at Cape Hatteras, N.C., roared northward, killed 22, caused property damage of $50 million. **Most violent hurricane** of year was **"Hazel"** which hit U.S. on Oct. 15 causing 99 deaths in this country, 249 in Canada. Combined U.S.–Canadian property loss put at $100 million.

Sept. 3 **Espionage and sabotage** act of 1954 signed by Pres. Eisenhower. Death penalty was authorized for peacetime sabotage; statute of limitations done away with.

Sept. 30 **1st atomic powered submarine,** U.S.S. *Nautilus,* commissioned at Groton, Conn.

Oct. 25 **1st public and televised cabinet meeting** held. The President and his cabinet met in the White House to hear Secretary of State John Foster Dulles report on Paris agreements on Germany.

Dec. 11 **Largest warship** ever built, 59,650-ton aircraft carrier, U.S.S. *Forrestal,* launched at Newport News, Va.

Dec. 27 **Record land speed** of 632 mph announced by Air Force. Speed was achieved by experimental rocket sled.

Broadway musical hit, *Pajama Game;* "I Love Paris"; "Careless Love"; and "Young at Heart."

Highlight of a concert arranged by the Jewish Tercentenary Committee (honoring 300th anniversary of the 1st Jew to land in America) was **David Diamond's** symphonic eulogy, *Ahavah* (Brotherhood) The Concert was held at Constitution Hall, Washington, D.C.

The Tender Land, a new opera by **Aaron Copland,** premiered by the New York City Opera Co. at the City Center, New York city. It met with indifferent reviews and failed to excite popular interest.

Jan. 30 *Symphonic Fantasy* by **Roy Harris** introduced by the Pittsburgh Symphony at Pittsburgh, Pa.

Feb. 22 *Concerto No. 5* for piano and orchestra, by **Alan Hovhaness,** performed in New York by the National Orchestral Association.

Mar. 4 **Ernest Krenek's** *Violoncello Concerto* heard for 1st time at a performance of the Los Angeles Philharmonic in Los Angeles, Calif.

Dec. 27 **Gian-Carlo Menotti's** *The Saint of Bleecker Street* opened at the Broadway Theater in New York city to critical acclaim and subsequent popular success.

1955

The marked easing of the cold war brought about by the so-called Geneva spirit was engendered by Pres. Eisenhower's dramatic proposal for an exchange of military blueprints and aerial inspection with Russia. Nations which had previously been cool, indifferent, or even downright suspicious of U.S. foreign policy began to trust us a little more. At home, Americans enjoyed a fresh outburst of

American book publishers bombarded their readers with volumes of fact and opinion on current world affairs. A great deal of attention was paid to the vagaries of child behavior with a shower of handbooks finding a wide readership of bewildered parents. Novelists turned to a tired naturalism to tell their stories, produced little of note, although a considerable number of fiction entries achieved ex-

July 12 4-point program of **highway modernization** proposed by Pres. Eisenhower. The cost, estimated at several billions of dollars, would be shared by federal and state governments.

July 13 **Gross National Product** for 1953 put at $365,000,000,000 by Department of Commerce.

Aug. 15 2d assembly of **World Council of Churches** convened at Evanston, Ill.

Sept. 24 **Communists, Fascists,** members of the **Ku Klux Klan** banned by United Steelworkers of America (CIO).

Oct. 13 **1st supersonic bomber,** B-58, ordered into production by Air Force.

Oct. 21 **Nobel Prize** for medicine and physiology awarded to **John F. Enders** of Harvard School of Medicine, **Thomas H. Weller** of the Harvard School of Public Health, and **Frederick C. Robins** of Western Reserve Medical School, for work with cultivation of polio virus.

Nov. 3 **Nobel Prize** in chemistry went to **Linus Pauling** of the California Institute of Technology for study of forces holding together protein and other molecules.

Dec. 31 **New York Stock Exchange** prices were highest quoted since 1929; volume of shares traded during 1954 (573,-374,622) highest since 1933.

Stakes. Jockey was E. Guerin; time was 2:30⅘ for winnings valued at $89,000.

Hasty Road won the 78th annual **Preakness Stakes.** Jockey was J. Adams; time was 1:57⅗ for winnings valued at $91,600.

Jan. 1 Michigan State defeated U.C.L.A. by a score of 28 to 20 in the **Rose Bowl** at Pasadena, Calif., before a crowd of 100,000.

May The winner of the 80th **Kentucky Derby** at Churchill Downs, Louisville, Ky., was *Determine* ridden by R. York. His time was 2:03; the prize, $102,050.

July 13 The 21st annual **All-Star baseball game** at Municipal Stadium, Cleveland, Ohio, was a slugfest won by the American League 11–9, enlivened by 6 home runs, 4 by the winners.

Sept. 29–Oct. 2 New York, NL, defeated Cleveland, AL, 4–0 in the 51st annual **World Series.**

Nov. 8 The American League approved the transfer of the **Philadelphia Athletics** baseball franchise to Kansas City, Mo.

Nov. 27 Navy defeated Army, 27–20, in the annual **Army-Navy** football game.

Dec. 26 The Cleveland Browns defeated the Detroit Lions, 56–10, to win the **National Professional Football Championship.**

1955

The American economic scene enjoyed a healthy period of full employment and peak production. Net business income was up 33% over the previous year. Labor concentrated on consolidating its gains, stated new objectives, chief of which was a pledge to fight for a guaranteed annual wage. The organized labor force in America totalled 15 million after AFL and the CIO merged to become the American Federa-

1955 was the year of Davy Crockett and Rock 'n Roll. Originally Davy Crockett started as a Technicolor movie produced in Hollywood by Walt Disney. However, high pressure publicity agents snowballed the legend of the frontiersman who died at the Alamo until it became a major force in the social and economic activities of the nation—what with the millions of Davy Crockett coonskin hats being manufactured

prosperity, remodeled the faces of their cities with an unprecedented building boom, bought new, bigger, more expensive cars, planned dream homes of greater elegance, flocked in to buy home appliances, gadgets, color TV sets. More attention was paid to peaceful uses of atomic energy. A certain amount of relaxation in our defense policy was made possible by an easing situation in Europe. The Far East, however, was still a sorely troubled area; consequently our foreign policy emphasis shifted more toward winning the uncommitted nations of Asia.

Jan. 1 **Financial aid** to South Vietnam, Cambodia, and Laos begun by U.S. Foreign Operations Administration. $216 million was spent in 1955.

Jan. 3 3002 **security risks** discharged from federal employment between May 28, 1953, and Sept. 30, 1954.

Jan. 14 U.S. Senate voted 84–0 to continue its investigation of **communism.**

Jan. 17 **Estimated Budget** for 1955 fiscal year announced. Its expenditures totaled $62,408,000,000; revenues, $60 billions.

Jan. 19 **1st filmed presidential press conference** took place. Both TV and motion picture newsreel photographers covered the event.

Jan. 28 U.S. Senate pledged defense of **Formosa** and **Pescadores Islands** by a vote of 85–3. The following day Chinese Communists demanded that the U.N. order U.S. withdrawal from entire Formosan area.

Feb. 26 4000 **atomic bombs** stockpiled by U.S.; Russia's reserve, 1000, according to unofficial estimate of Prof. Cecil F. Powell, British Nobel physics prize winner.

Mar. 1 **Congressional salaries** and pay scale of federal judges increased by about 50% under bill passed by House of Representatives.

Mar. 16 **Atomic weapons** would be used in case of war according to statement made by Pres. Eisenhower.

tremely large sales. Architects hailed the continuing high level of construction. Church building reached its highest rate in history. Striking new materials such as aluminum and plastics were being used in construction. Once more musical organizations, both here and abroad, spent as much time traveling as playing. The New York Philharmonic and the Philadelphia Orchestras both embarked on extensive European tours. The Symphony of the Air headed east and played in Japanese concert halls. A showing of contemporary American and European painters revealed that for the 1st time our native artists seemed to surpass their European peers in imaginative styles and techniques. The showing at the Museum of Modern Art, New York city, featured Americans, William de Kooning, Jackson Pollock, Robert Motherwell, Adolph Gottlieb.

Pulitzer Prizes: novel, *A Fable* by William Faulkner; drama, *Cat on a Hot Tin Roof* by Tennessee Williams; U.S. history, *Great River, the Rio Grande in North American History* by Paul Horgan; biography, *The Taft Story* by William S. White; poetry, *Collected Poems* by Wallace Stevens; music, *The Saint of Bleecker Street* by Gian-Carlo Menotti.

Best Broadway plays were *Bus Stop*, **William Inge;** *Inherit the Wind*, dramatization of the famous Scopes trial, by **Jerome Lawrence and Robert E. Lee;** *The Bad Seed*, **Maxwell Anderson.** The only successful foreign play was **Christopher Fry's** adaptation of **Jean Giraudoux's** *La Guerre de Troie n'aura pas lieu*, which he entitled *Tiger at the Gates.* Top musicals were *Fanny*, **S. N. Behrman's** treatment of **Marcel Pagnol's** famous trilogy with music by **Harold Rome;** *Silk Stockings*, **Cole Porter's** version of *Ninotchka*; *Plain and Fancy*, an operetta whose scene was an Amish community in Pennsylvania; *Damn Yankees*, the saga of a baseball fan who sold his soul to devil; and *The Boy Friend*,

tion of Labor and the Congress of Industrial Organizations. Chief concern of labor leaders was an increasing use of automation in industrial plants. Walter P. Reuther, vice-president of the newly merged labor group, predicted a 2d industrial revolution due to the new science. Farm income was down 5½% from 1954. Educators reported a shortage of 250,000 classrooms; a need for 141,300 new teachers.

Nobel prize in chemistry went to **Vincent du Vigneaud** of Cornell Medical College for his work in developing 2 hormones that aided in childbirth. Physics prize shared by **Polykarp Kusch** of Columbia University and **Willis E. Lamb, Jr.,** of Stanford University for their work in atomic measurements.

Jan. 8 New York mental hygiene department announced a certain amount of success with 2 new **drugs for treatment of mental patients.** The drugs are **thorazine** and **reserpine.**

Jan. 9 Experimental **atomic power plants** to be operated by private industry according to Atomic Energy Commission announcement.

Feb. 9 Details of **AFL-CIO merger** agreement made public.

Apr. 12 Announcement was made of successful development of an **antipolio vaccine** by Dr. Jonas E. Salk. Tests, carried out in 44 states, indicated its effectiveness against paralytic polio.

May 19 Unprecedented number of **business mergers** reported—3 times the 1949 rate. Report was issued by Federal Trade Commission.

May 23 Ordination of **women ministers** approved by General Assembly of Presbyterian Church.

May 31 **Racial segregation** in U.S. public schools banned by U.S. Supreme Court.

and distributed, fur dealers in New York city enjoyed one of the most prosperous few months ever. Equally contagious was the mania for Rock 'n Roll music which was attacked from many quarters as "immoral," and contributing to juvenile delinquency, allegedly because of its monotonous, primitive beat. A gala year in Flatbush, the faithful rejoiced as the Brooklyn Dodgers won their 1st baseball championship from the mighty New York Yankees. Fashion designers combined a sophisticated sex appeal with fresh youthfulness, favored a semifitted sheath with Oriental design and color.

Academy Awards presented to *Marty* as the outstanding motion picture of the year, to Ernest Borgnine as the best actor for his performance in the same film, and to Anna Magnani for her work in *Rose Tattoo.* Jo Van Fleet was named best supporting actress for her portrayal in *East of Eden,* and Jack Lemmon was chosen best supporting actor for his performance in *Mr. Roberts.*

More than 1 billion **comic books** sold annually according to report issued by the University of California, at an estimated cost of $100 million, 4 times the total book budget of all U.S. public libraries combined. New York State passed a law banning sale of lurid crime and horror comic books to persons under 18 years of age. Violations punishable by 1 year imprisonment and/or $500 fine.

This year's **National College Football Champion** was Oklahoma, coached by Charles Wilkinson.

The Cleveland Browns defeated the Los Angeles Rams, 34–14 at Los Angeles, Calif., to win the **National Professional Football** Championship.

U.S.G.A. Amateur Golf Championship won by Harvie Ward at the Country Club of Virginia, Richmond, Va. He defeated William Hyndman, 9 and 8. **Open Cham-**

591

POLITICS AND GOVERNMENT; WAR; DISASTERS; VITAL STATISTICS.

BOOKS; PAINTING; DRAMA; ARCHITECTURE; SCULPTURE.

Apr. 9 Civil Defense Co-ordinating Board, to be headed by Civil Defense Administrator, Val Peterson, formed by presidential order. Duties of the new agency were to co-ordinate defense activities of all federal bureaus.

June 10 U.S. postal workers won 8% rise in salaries.

June 16 Selective Service extended to June 30, 1959, by House of Representatives.

June 21 Reciprocal Trade Agreements Act extended to June 30, 1958, by House of Representatives.

June 28 Over 1 million **federal employees** granted 7.5% pay boost.

July 7 $3,285,800,000 **foreign aid** bill passed by Congress.

July 11 U.S. **Air Force Academy** officially opened at temporary site, Lowry Air Force Base, Denver, Colo.

July 18 Geneva conference among heads of state of U.S., Great Britain, U.S.S.R., France, opened at Geneva, Switzerland.

July 26 U.S. **military reserve** to be increased from 800,000 to 2,900,000 by 1960 under bill passed by Congress.

Aug. 2 45,000 new **public housing** units approved by Congressional vote of 187–168. The units were to be built before July 31, 1956.

Aug. 20 Serious floods caused Pres. Eisenhower to declare following states major disaster areas; Connecticut, Massachusetts, Pennsylvania, South Carolina, parts of New Jersey and Rhode Island.

Nov. 25 Racial segregation on interstate trains and buses banned by Interstate Commerce Commission.

Dec. 27 U.S. **auto deaths** over Christmas weekend set a record of 609.

a gay spoof of the musical comedies of the '20's.

Among **operas** that received their premières this year were: *The Pot of Fat* by **Theodore Chanler** (Cambridge, Mass., May 8); *The Ruby* by **Norman Dello Joio,** (Bloomington, Ind.); *The Wish* by **George Antheil** (Louisville, Apr. 2); *Griffelkin* by **Lukas Foss,** an opera specially written for the NBC Opera Theater and produced Nov. 6.

Top **popular songs** were based on old melodies. "Melody of Love" was a 20th-century piano student's concert piece, "The Yellow Rose of Texas" was a Confederate Civil War song. Other song hits were "Let Me Go, Lover," "Learnin' the Blues," "Mr. Sandman," "Unchained Melody," "I Need You Now."

Premières of *Symphony No. 6* by **Darius Milhaud** held at Boston, Oct. 7, and *Symphony No. 5* by **Walter Piston,** also at Boston, Nov. 25.

5 buildings chosen for awards in the **American Institute of Architecture design competition** were: The American Embassy, Stockholm, Sweden, Ralph Rapson and John van der Meulen; Central restaurant, General Motors Technical Center, Warren, Mich., and Women's dormitories and dining hall, Drake University, Des Moines, Iowa, both by Eero Saarinen & Associates; The North Hillsborough (California) elementary school, Ernest J. Kump; and the General Telephone Company of the Southwest, San Angelo, Tex., by Pace Associates, Charles B. Benther, architect in charge.

592

July 5 91,960,366 shares of **General Motors common stock** to be split 3 for 1, according to decision of G.M. board of directors.

July 29 Plans for **1st earth-circling satellites** announced by U.S. They were scheduled to be launched some time in 1957.

Aug. 21 U.S. **private investments abroad** estimated at $26,600,000,000 by U.S. Department of Commerce.

Sept. 8 Large blue-green areas on planet **Mars** discovered by National Geographic Society. Announcement indicated that patches were living vegetation.

Sept. 12 American Foundations Information Service listed 7,300 charitable, welfare, research **foundations** in U.S., of which 4,162 had assets of over $4,700,000.

Sept. 26 Heaviest single day dollar loss in New York **Stock Exchange** history totaled $14 billion. 7,720,000 shares traded, highest since July 21, 1933. This sharp break in prices occurred 2 days after announcement that Pres. Eisenhower had suffered a heart attack at Denver, Colo.

Oct. 7 World's most powerful warship, U.S.S. **"Saratoga,"** 59,600 tons, launched at New York Naval Shipyard, Brooklyn, N.Y.

Oct. 18 **Antiproton,** a new atomic particle, discovered at University of California.

Nov. 3 Discovery of promising **"common cold" vaccine** announced by U.S. public health service.

Dec. 5 **AFL and CIO formally merged.** The new organization, to be called American Federation of Labor and Congress of Industrial Organizations, was headed by George Meany, ex-president of AFL.

Dec. 12 **Record educational grant** of $500 millions went to 4157 privately supported colleges, universities, and hospitals. Made by Ford Foundation.

pionship was won by Jack Fleck at Olympic C.C., San Francisco, Calif. He defeated Ben Hogan, 69 to 72 in a playoff match.

Nashua won the 87th annual **Belmont Stakes.** Jockey was E. Arcaro; time was 2:29. Winnings were valued at $83,700.

Nashua won the 79th annual **Preakness Stakes.** Jockey was E. Arcaro; record time was 1:54⅗.

U.S. lawn **Men's Tennis Singles Champion,** Tony Trabert; **Women's Singles Championship** won by Doris Hart.

Jan. 1 Ohio State defeated Southern California 20–7, before 89,191 in the annual **Rose Bowl** football game at Pasadena, Calif.

Jan. 27 Wealthy financier, **Serge Rubinstein,** convicted World War II draft dodger, strangled in his New York city home.

May 7 The 82d annual **Kentucky Derby** at Churchill Downs, Louisville, Ky., won by *Swaps.* Time was 2:01⅘. With jockey Willie Shoemaker up, he won $108,400.

July 12 The National League won the 22d **All-Star baseball game,** beating the American League, 6–5, in a 12-inning contest held at Milwaukee, Wis.

Sept. 28–Oct. 4 Brooklyn, NL, defeated N.Y. Yankees, AL, 4–3 in the 52d annual **World Series.**

Nov. 26 Army defeated Navy, 14–6 in the annual **Army-Navy game** at Philadelphia, Pa.

593

1956

Tension with Russia still dominated the American scene. John Foster Dulles summed up the Cold War in his "brink of war" statement: "The ability to get to the verge without getting into the war is the necessary art." At home, there was bitter rivalry between the armed services, heightened in May by army charges that the air force was not doing its job. Americans again found a conflict between the North and South. Southern states either ignored or rebelled against the Supreme Court ruling against segregation in the public schools. In Montgomery, Ala., Negroes boycotted buses, and on November 13 the Supreme Court ruled that segregation on buses and streetcars was unconstitutional. But 1956 was an election year, and Americans could relax from wars, internal and international, in the colorful national conventions.

Jan. 9 Virginia amended a state prohibition against the use of public funds for private schools. The amendment was interpreted as a vote for **segregation,** since it helped support private education in a state where public schools have been shut down because of the Supreme Court ruling against segregation in public schools.

Feb. 15 In New Orleans, La., a federal court banned all Louisiana laws contrary to the Supreme Court ruling against **segregation** in the schools.

Mar. 27 Internal Revenue agents **seized Communist newspaper** *Daily Worker* for nonpayment of income taxes. The New York, Chicago and Detroit offices were returned on Apr. 3 after *Daily Worker* officers posted $4500 against their tax bill.

Apr. 2–3 **Tornadoes** in Michigan, Wisconsin, Oklahoma, Kansas, Mississippi, Missouri, Arkansas and Tennessee killed at least 45 persons and damaged $15 million worth of property.

Americans' awareness of world problems started a new trend in book publishing. Formerly, American books had been exported and there had been few imports, but in 1956 there was a growing desire for cultural products from abroad. Fiction titles such as Edwin O'Connor's *The Last Hurrah* and John Hersey's *A Single Pebble* received extraordinary sales, but critics continued to complain that novels had become dull and sterile. In architecture, the volume of construction, particularly of industrial and commercial buildings, continued to increase. The outspoken elder statesman of architecture, Frank Lloyd Wright, was still extremely productive in 1956; he completed work on the Price Tower in Bartlesville, Oklahoma, and began construction of the Guggenheim Museum in New York. Contemporary American paintings by such men as Glarner and Pollock were characterized by a distinct abstractionism; indeed, abstractionism, once a rebel, had become the conventional mold into which new painters had to put their work.

An **important book** of literary history published this year was **The Letters of Thomas Wolfe,** edited by Elizabeth Nowell. In his letters, the stormy Wolfe reveals how close his novels were to his actual life.

Operas became more popular this year in the U.S. Among favorites were *La Boheme,* which was staged 162 times during the year, Mozart's comic opera *Cosi fan Tutte,* and *Boris Godunov,* the dramatic opera by Mussorgsky.

Pulitzer Prizes: novel, *Andersonville* by MacKinlay Kantor; drama, *The Diary of Anne Frank* by Frances Goodrich and Albert Hackett; U.S. history, *The Age of Reform* by Richard Hofstadter; biography, *Benjamin Henry Latrobe* by Talbot F. Hamlin; poetry, *Poems: North and South—*

SCIENCE; INDUSTRY; ECONOMICS; EDUCATION; RELIGION; PHILOSOPHY.	SPORTS; FASHIONS; POPULAR EN-TERTAINMENT; FOLKLORE; SOCIETY.

1956

About 2 million workers received pay increases during the first half of the year, while rising business investment and earnings were benefitting all of labor. The new federal hourly wage minimum of $1 an hour was expected to help approximately 2 million workers, and in September the AFL-CIO started a campaign for a shorter work week. Despite widespread drought and crop restrictions, American farmers produced a new all-time high in food and fiber output. Yields from crops were the highest in U.S. history. Although there were no great discoveries in physics or astronomy during 1956, scientists were active in plans for the approaching International Geophysical Year, to take place in 1957–58.

1956 was another good year for **automobile production.** Approximately 6 million cars and 1 million trucks came out of the assembly lines, ranking 1956 about the same as 1953, the industry's 3rd best production year. A slow **shift in body styling** took place; in 1956, about 1 out of 8 cars was a station wagon.

Nobel prize in physics went to Drs. **William Shockley, Walter H. Brattain** and **John Bardeen** of Bell Telephone Laboratories for their work in semiconductors and their discovery of the transistor effect.

Feb. 6 The **first Negro student** enrolled in the University of Alabama, Autherine Lucy, was suspended after 3 days of near riots. On Mar. 1 she was permanently expelled for her accusations against the school in a legal suit handled by the National Association for the Advancement of Colored People.

In 1956, movies were getting longer and more expensive than ever. *The King and I* cost $7 million, *The Ten Commandments,* $13½ million, and *War and Peace* $6½ million. Biographical films were popular with audiences; 1956 saw the production of the lives of celebrities from Rocky Graziano to Vincent Van Gogh. The year was notable also for the rise of a snake-hipped Tennessee "rock-and-roll" singer, Elvis Presley, who skyrocketed to fame despite objections from the parents of the nation. A cult grew up around a promising young actor who had been killed in an automobile accident—rebellious James Dean—and it was fostered enthusiastically by the nation's adolescents.

Academy Awards presented to *Around the World in 80 Days* as the outstanding motion picture of the year, to Yul Brynner as best actor for his performance in *The King and I,* and to Ingrid Bergman as best actress. Anthony Quinn won the best supporting actor award for his work in *Lust for Life,* and Dorothy Malone was named best supporting actress.

This year's **National College Football Champion** for the 2nd year in a row was Oklahoma, coached by Bud Wilkinson.

U.S.G.A. Amateur Golf Championship won by Harvie Ward, Jr., for the 2nd year in a row. **Open Championship** was won by Cary Middlecoff at Rochester, N.Y.

Fabius won the 80th annual **Preakness Stakes.** Time was 1:58 2/5. Jockey was Willie Hartack.

U.S. lawn **Men's Tennis Singles Champion,** Ken Rosewall; **Women's Singles Championship** won by Shirley Fry.

595

POLITICS AND GOVERNMENT; WAR; DISASTERS; VITAL STATISTICS.	BOOKS; PAINTING; DRAMA; ARCHITECTURE; SCULPTURE.

Apr. 8 On a disciplinary march at Parris Island, S.C., 6 **Marine recruits drowned.** Platoon Sgt. Matthew C. Mc-Keon was convicted on Aug. 3 of drinking on duty and negligent homicide. He was reduced to private and served a 3-months' sentence.

May 5–7 At the **Socialist Labor Party** convention in New York, Eric Haas, editor of the weekly Socialist Labor newspaper, was nominated for the presidency.

June 8–10 In its 30th national convention, held this year in Chicago, the **Socialist Party** nominated Pennsylvania lawyer Darlington Hoopes as candidate for President of the U.S.

June 30 In the **worst commercial air disaster** in history, 128 people were killed when 2 airliners crashed into Grand Canyon. The Trans-World Airline Super-Constellation and United Air Lines DC-7 probably collided in mid-air before the crash.

July 14–15 The famous old **Wanamaker Building destroyed** by fire. The building was located on Astor Place, New York.

Aug. 2 The **last Union Army veteran,** Albert Woolson, died at the age of 109.

Aug. 13–17 The colorful **Democratic National Convention** held in Chicago. Former Pres. Harry S. Truman backed Gov. Averell Harriman of New York, but Adlai E. Stevenson of Illinois won the nomination for the presidency on the first ballot. His running mate for vice-president was Senator Estes Kefauver of Tennessee, former chairman of the Senate Committee to Investigate Organized Crime in Interstate Commerce.

Aug. 20–24 The **Republican National Convention** in San Francisco, Calif., was more staid than the Democratic Convention, since everyone knew Pres. Dwight D. Eisenhower would be renominated with Vice-President Richard M. Nixon for his running mate.

A Cold Spring by Elizabeth Bishop; music, *Symphony No. 3* by Ernst Toch.

Best Broadway plays were *Middle of the Night,* **Paddy Chayefsky;** *My Fair Lady,* a musical adapted from George Bernard Shaw's *Pygmalion* by **Alan Jay Lerner** and **Frederick Loewe;** *The Happiest Millionaire,* **Kyle Crichton;** *Separate Tables,* an English import from the pen of **Terence Rattigan;** and *Auntie Mame,* a smash hit by **Patrick Dennis.** Orson Welles did Shakespeare's *King Lear;* Welles, after a series of accidents, played the aging king dynamically from a wheelchair.

Among **operas** that received their premières this year were: *The Unicorn, the Gorgon and the Manticore* by **Gian-Carlo Menotti** (Washington, D.C., Oct. 21); *The Ballad of Baby Doe* by **Douglas Moore** (Colorado, during the Central City Opera Festival, July 7); *Images of Youth* by **Felix Labunski** (Cincinnati, O., May 11); *The Trial at Rouen* by **Norman Dello Joio** (NBC Television, Apr. 8); *The Wife of Martin Guerre* by **William Bergsma** (New York, Feb. 15).

Top **popular hits** sung by Elvis Presley, a new young singer who had skyrocketed to stardom, included "Heartbreak Hotel," "Don't Be Cruel," "Hound Dog" and "Love Me Tender." Other hits were "True Love," "No, Not Much," "Poor People of Paris," "Standing on the Corner" and "Blue Suede Shoes."

Five buildings chosen for awards in the **American Institute of Architecture design competition** were: Hillsdale High School, San Mateo, Calif., John Lyon Reid and Partners; the Center for Advanced Study in the Behavioral Sciences, Palo Alto, Calif., Wurster, Bernardi and Emmons; the Lambert Municipal Airport Terminal, St. Louis, Mo., Hellmuth, Yamasaki and Leinweber; the Manufacturers Trust Company, Fifth Ave. Branch Bank, New York, N.Y., Skidmore, Owings and Merrill; and the

SCIENCE; INDUSTRY; ECONOMICS; EDUCATION; RELIGION; PHILOSOPHY.	SPORTS; FASHIONS; POPULAR ENTERTAINMENT; FOLKLORE; SOCIETY.

Mar. 20 The **longest major strike** at Westinghouse Electric Corp. in more than 20 years was settled after 156 days when the union accepted contract terms proposed by the company.

Apr. 5 A **hoodlum hurled acid** in the face of noted labor columnist Victor Riesel as the crusader against rackets left a New York restaurant. On May 4 it was announced that Riesel had lost the sight of both eyes.

Apr. 28 The New York Coliseum, the **world's largest exhibition building**, with 9 acres of floor space, opened in New York City. Total cost: $35,000,000.

May 2 The General Conference of the **Methodist Church** in Minneapolis, Minn., demanded abolishment of all racial segregation in Methodist churches.

May 4 **Private atomic energy plants authorized** by the Atomic Energy Commission. Consolidated Edison Company of New York constructed a $55 million plant at Indian Point, N.Y., and Commonwealth Edison Company put up a $45 million plant in Grundy Co., Ill.

June 11 In Chicago, the American Medical Assn. heard reports by Dr. Jonas A. Salk and Surgeon Gen. Leonard A. Scheele that **paralytic polio would be eliminated** as a threat within 3 years by use of the Salk vaccine.

Aug. 1 The **Salk anti-polio vaccine** was put on the open market by manufacturers

Jan. The Internal Revenue Bureau began **investigation of tipping.** On Jan. 20, Hans Paul, headwaiter of the Waldorf-Astoria Hotel in New York, was indicted on charges of not reporting tips averaging $500,000 to $1,000,000 a year. Paul was fined $7500 and jailed 4 months on April 25.

Jan. 1 Michigan State defeated U.C.L.A. by a score of 17 to 14 in the annual **Rose Bowl** football game at Pasadena, Calif.

Mar. 12 **Dr. Jesus de Galindez,** a vehement critic of the Trujillo régime in the Dominican Republic, disappeared on his way to his New York home. Police found a note in his apartment directing them to look for his enemies if anything happened to him, but Dominican officials denied any involvement in the disappearance.

Apr. 19 Actress **Grace Kelly, 26,** married in Monte Carlo to **Prince Rainier III** of Monaco, 32, in one of the most-publicized marriages of the century. Prince Rainier is a member of the Grimaldi dynasty founded in 1017.

May 5 *Needles* won the 83rd annual **Kentucky Derby** at Churchill Downs, Louisville, Ky. Time was 2:03 2/5. Ridden by jockey D. Erb, he won $123,450.

June 16 *Needles* won the 88th annual **Belmont States.** Time was 2:29 4/5. Jockey was D. Erb.

July 10 The National League won the 23rd **All-Star baseball game,** beating the American League 7–3 at Washington, D.C.

July 16 **Ringling Brothers and Barnum and Bailey Circus** performed its last show

POLITICS AND GOVERNMENT; WAR; DISASTERS; VITAL STATISTICS.

BOOKS; PAINTING; DRAMA; ARCHITECTURE; SCULPTURE.

Aug. 24 An army H21 helicopter completed the **first transcontinental helicopter flight** nonstop from San Diego, Calif., to Washington, D.C., in 37 hours. A crew of 5 flew 2610 miles.

Aug. 28 Johnny Dio, a notorious labor racketeer, was named by the F.B.I. **mastermind of the Victor Riesel blinding.** Dio and 6 other men were indicted by a Federal grand jury on conspiracy charges on Sept. 7.

Nov. 6 **Eisenhower won** the presidency by a landslide, the first Republican President to win re-election since William Mckinley in 1900. But although Eisenhower carried 41 states, the Democrats retained control of both houses of Congress. **Minor party candidates** pulled a few votes: Byrd, Independent and States Rights Party, received 134,128, the Prohibition Party netted 27,087 votes, Haas of the Socialist Labor group took 36,452, and Hoopes of the Socialist Party gained 1,763 votes. The **popular vote** of the two major candidates was 35,387,015 for Eisenhower and 25,875,408 for Stevenson. The **electoral vote** was 457 for Eisenhower and 74 for Stevenson.

Dec. 17 The **worst recorded single automobile accident** occurred near Phoenix, Ariz. Twelve out of 13 passengers were killed.

Richard Hodgson residence, New Canaan, Conn., Philip C. Johnson.

Phenomenal best-seller of the year was *Peyton Place,* a sensational story about sex in a small town.

New York's ordinarily conservative **Metropolitan Museum acquired an unconventional piece of sculpture,** Richard Lippold's *Variation Within a Sphere, No. 10: The Sun.* The sculpture contained almost two miles of gold wire and more than 14,000 hand-welded joints.

Aug. 11 One of the most controversial of the abstractionist painters, **Jackson Pollock, killed** in an automobile accident near East Hampton, N.Y. He had symbolized to young American painters the spirit of revolt.

Oct. 29 The new season of the Metropolitan Opera opened with the Metropolitan debut of fiery **Maria Callas** in the title role of Bellini's *Norma.* The opening made a box office **record for first-night receipts:** $75,510.50.

1957

On October 4, the Soviet Union launched the first earth satellite, popularly called Sputnik I; that launching brought to the fore the American need for faster development of intercontinental ballistic missiles. Thus 1957 was another year of world tension; the President developed his Eisenhower Doctrine to resist Communist aggression in the Middle East. Despite the race against Russia in outer space, the President continued to release uranium-235 for peaceful purposes; by the end of the year, a total of 100,000 kilograms of U-235 had

James Gould Cozzens' *By Love Possessed* was the major American novel of the year; critics praised it, and it stayed on top of the best-seller lists. It is the story of two days in the life of a middle-aged lawyer told with a sardonic humor and a keen insight into human nature. Another much publicized novel was Jack Kerouac's *On the Road,* an investigation of the themes of jazz, sex and dope; it was a major voice in a new group of American writers, the "beat" generation, who, in Kerouac's view, look to alcohol, dope and speed as a means

who sold it through normal distribution channels.

Sept. 24 The World's **first transatlantic telephone cable system** began operating. The twin cables, 2250 miles long, stretch from Clarenville, Newfoundland, to Oban, Scotland. The cable, which cost $42 million, has 3 times the capacity of radio telephone circuits between Europe and the U.S.

Nov. 25 **First successful parachute jump in Antarctica** was made by air force Sgt. Richard J. Patton. The 1500-foot test jump was made to determine the cause of parachute malfunctioning in below-zero weather.

Dec. 22 **First gorilla born in captivity, a female**, weighing 4½ lbs., was at the Columbus, Ohio, Zoo.

under canvas. Rising costs for a tented show forced the circus to fold.

Oct. 3–10 New York, AL, defeated Brooklyn, NL, 4–3 in the 53rd annual **World Series.** On Oct. 8, Don Larsen, New York Yankee right-hander, pitched the **first no-hit, no-run game in World Series history** to beat Brooklyn 2–0.

Nov. 30 Floyd Patterson knocked out Archie Moore in the 5th round of their **heavyweight championship fight** in Chicago to win the title vacated by retiring Rocky Marciano on April 27. Patterson, 21, was the youngest man ever to win the championship.

Dec. 1 The 57th annual **Army-Navy game** at Philadelphia, Pa., was tied 7–7.

Dec. 30 The New York Giants defeated the Chicago Cardinals 47–7 at New York to win the **National Professional Football** Championship.

1957

In September, wages for factory production workers averaged $2.08 per hour and $82.99 a week. Employment remained high during most of the year, but in autumn began to decline. Farmers exceeded the crop yield record set in 1956, and farm prices continued the advance begun in 1956. In religion, leaders of various faiths played important parts in the fight to implement the Supreme Court's decision to bar racial segregation in public schools. The official bodies of several Southern church groups requested peaceful compliance with the de-

The "sack" was the most-discussed fashion since the "New Look." The sack's silhouette was an unfitted drape, and men were heard to comment: "It looks like a *flour* sack." The most highly-praised man of the year in boxing was Carmen Basilio, who outpointed wily Sugar Ray Robinson in a savage fight for the middleweight championship. But by 1958 Robinson had defeated Basilio again. Baseball was marked by the departure of the New York Giants to San Francisco and the Brooklyn Dodgers to Los Angeles, leaving the pen-

| POLITICS AND GOVERNMENT; WAR; DISASTERS; VITAL STATISTICS. | BOOKS; PAINTING; DRAMA; ARCHITECTURE; SCULPTURE. |

been made available for research and for power fuel. The Air Force, which marked its golden anniversary in 1957, became the largest enterprise in the United States; its total assets for the year were over $70 billion.

Jan. 5 In a joint session of Congress, Pres. Eisenhower formally proposed a plan, soon known as the **Eisenhower doctrine,** to protect against Communist aggression any Middle Eastern nation requesting aid.

Feb. 4 **37 miners killed** when gas exploded in a coal mine near Bishop, Va.

Feb. 8 The U.S. pledged full **support to plans for the European Atomic Energy Community** for the establishment of an atomic energy industry in Europe in 10 years.

Feb. 9–12 The U.S. **Communist Party** held a convention in New York during which they adopted a new and more liberal party constitution. One of the new rules in the constitution: Party members can be expelled for subversion. F.B.I. chief **J. Edgar Hoover** stated the new rules were merely an attempt by the party to gain acceptance by U.S. citizens.

Feb. 17 A **fire** in a home for the aged in Warrenton, Mo., killed 72.

Mar. 30 The United States' **2nd atomic submarine,** the *Seawolf,* was commissioned. On May 16, *Skate,* the 3rd atomic submarine and the **first designed for assembly-line production,** was launched at Groton, Conn.

Apr. 30 A special committee of the U.S. Senate named 5 former members to the **Senate Hall of Fame:** Robert M. Taft, Robert M. La Follette, John C. Calhoun, Daniel Webster and Henry Clay.

June 27–28 **Hurricane Audrey** and a subsequent tidal wave hit the Louisiana

to the beatific. In 1957, extraordinary prices were being paid for painting and sculpture. The Edward G. Robinson collection was sold for well over $3 million, and one painting in the Georges Lurcy collection, Renoir's *La Serre,* brought $200,000.

Pulitzer Prizes: novel, no award, but a special citation to Kenneth Roberts for his historical novels; drama, *Long Day's Journey into Night* by Eugene O'Neill; history, *Russia Leaves the War* by George F. Kennan; biography, *Profiles in Courage* by John F. Kennedy; poetry, *Things of This World* by Richard Wilbur; music, *Meditations on Ecclesiastes* by Norman Dello Joio.

Best Broadway plays were **Leonard Bernstein's** musical, *West Side Story;* **John Osborne's** play from England, *Look Back in Anger;* **Ketti Frings'** adaption of the sprawling Thomas Wolfe novel, *Look Homeward, Angel; The Music Man,* a musical by **Meredith Willson; William Inge's** study of the Middle West, *The Dark at the Top of the Stairs;* **William Saroyan's** *The Cave Dwellers;* and *A Visit to a Small Planet,* a comedy by **Gore Vidal.**

Among **operas** that received their premières this year were: *Panfilo and Lauretto* by **Carlos Chavez** of Mexico (Columbia University, N.Y., May 9); *The Turn of the Screw* (adapted from the Henry James story) by **Benjamin Britten** (Straford, Ont., Aug. 20); and *The Portrait* by **Hilding Rosenberg** (Stockholm, Sweden).

Top **popular songs** included "Love Letters in the Sand," sung by Pat Boone, a young man who approached Elvis Presley in popularity, "Tammy," "Fascination," music from *My Fair Lady,* "Young Love" and "Round and Round."

New York's Museum of Modern Art gave a **comprehensive Picasso exhibition** in honor of the artist's 75th birthday. Attendance during the exhibit was 238,646.

A Death in the Family, **James Agee's** only full-length novel, published this year. It is an extremely moving and disturbing study of a boy's reaction to his father's

cision, and the Vatican approved the move by the archbishop of New Orleans to desegregate church schools. But at the end of the year, desegregation in the schools was still a major issue.

Nobel prizes in physics went to Dr. **Tsung Dao Lee** of Columbia University and Dr. **Chen Ning Yang** of the Institute for Advanced Study for their work leading to important discoveries about elementary particles.

In a survey of 60,000 **high school juniors and seniors,** Dr. Ernest V. Hollis of the U.S. Office of Education discovered that 51% with an IQ of 133 or higher do not attend college because of the expense or because of their not having any college goal.

Mar. 11 Admiral **Richard E. Byrd** died in Boston, Mass. Admiral Byrd, the leader of 5 expeditions to Antarctica, was the first person to fly over both the North and South Poles.

Apr. 4 The **National Education Association** celebrated 100th anniversary in Philadelphia. NEA, started in 1857 with a membership of 43, had grown to almost 1 million teachers and affiliates.

May 2 A federal grand jury in Seattle, Wash., **indicted Dave Beck,** president of the Teamsters Union, on charges that he had evaded payment of $56,000 in income taxes in 1950. Further investigation revealed that Beck had used union funds for himself and his family.

June 13 *Mayflower II* landed at Plymouth, Mass., 54 days after setting out from Plymouth, England, to **duplicate the voyage of the Pilgrims.**

July 1 The first major project in the **International Geophysical Year** was the firing of a rocket on San Nicolas Island, Calif., by the Naval Research Laboratory

nant-winning Yankees with sole dominion over the New York baseball scene.

Academy Awards presented to *The Bridge on the River Kwai* as outstanding motion picture of the year, to Alec Guinness as best actor for his performance in the same picture, and to Joanne Woodward as best actress of the year. Red Buttons and Miyoshi Umeki respectively received best supporting actor and actress awards for their work in *Sayonara*.

This year's **National College Football Champion** was Auburn (Alabama Polytechnic Institute), whose team finished the season undefeated.

The Detroit Lions defeated the Cleveland Browns 59–14 to win this year's **National Professional Football** Championship.

U.S.G.A. Amateur Golf Championship won by Air Force Lt. Hillman Robbins of Memphis, Tenn. **Open Championship** was won by Dick Mayer of La Jolla, Calif., who defeated defending champion Cary Middlecoff in an 18-hole playoff.

U.S. lawn **Men's Tennis Singles Champion,** Malcolm Anderson; **Women's Singles Championship** won by Althea Gibson.

The Milwaukee Braves set a **baseball attendance record** for the National League of 2,215,404 fans attending games during the year.

Jan. 1 At the annual **Rose Bowl** football game in Pasadena, Calif., Iowa beat Oregon State 35–19.

Feb. 23 The Yale Univ. freestyle relay **swimming team set a new record** of 3:18 3/10 in the 400-yard freestyle event at New Haven, Conn.

Apr. 27 Bob Gutowski, an Occidental College senior, set a new **pole-vault record** of 15 feet 8¼ inches at Palo Alto, Calif.

| POLITICS AND GOVERNMENT; WAR; DISASTERS; VITAL STATISTICS. | BOOKS; PAINTING; DRAMA; ARCHITECTURE; SCULPTURE. |

and Texas coasts, leaving 531 dead and missing.

July 16 A **transcontinental speed record** (Long Beach, Calif., to Brooklyn, N.Y.) was set by Maj. John H. Glenn, Jr., in a F8U-1P jet. The time was 3 hr., 23 min., 8.4 sec.

Aug. 30 After speaking 24 hours, 27 minutes against civil rights, Sen. Strom Thurmond, Dem., South Carolina, set a **new filibuster record.**

Sept. 19 **First underground atomic explosion** set off at the proving grounds near Las Vegas, Nev.

Sept. 24 Pres. Eisenhower sent about 1000 **U.S. Army paratroops to Central High School,** Little Rock, Ark. The President said that violence had caused the removal of 9 Negro students in the newly integrated school. The 9 Negroes entered the guarded school on Sept. 25.

Oct. 8 Confessed **Soviet spy** Jack Soble sentenced in New York to 7-year imprisonment for espionage.

Nov. 25 At the opening of **Senate Preparedness Subcommittee** hearings, noted scientist Dr. Edward H. Teller urged U.S. to strengthen heavy bomber bases as safeguard against Soviet missile attack.

death. Another book of interest was **William Faulkner's** *The Town,* a continuation of his Yoknapatawpha County saga; it deals with the cold-blooded cut-throat Snopes family.

Six buildings chosen for awards in the centennial **American Institute of Architecture design competition** were Chapel of Holy Cross, Sedona, Ariz., Ashen and Allen; St. Anselm's Priory for the Benedictine Fathers, Tokyo, Japan, Antonin Raymond and I.I. Rado; Edgemont Junior-Senior High School, Greenburgh, Scarsdale, N.Y., Warren H. Ashley; residence for Eliot Noyes, New Canaan, Conn., Eliot Noyes; Middlesex Mutual Bldg. Trust Office, Waltham, Mass., Anderson, Beckwith and Haible; and Brazos County (Texas) Courthouse and Jail, Caudill, Rowlett, Scott and Associates.

Feb. 25 In a **censorship decision** the Supreme Court ruled unanimously against the conviction of a Detroit, Mich., bookseller for selling John Howard Griffin's *The Devil Rides Outside.* The ruling slapped down the section of Michigan penal law declaring it a misdemeanor to sell books which might corrupt youth. Justice Felix Frankfurter said the Michigan law would reduce adults of the state to reading only what is fit for children.

June 17 **Igor Stravinsky's 75th birthday** was celebrated in Los Angeles with an all-Stravinsky program that included the world première of his ballet score *Agon: A Contest.*

Oct. 16 It was announced that **Leonard Bernstein** had been appointed to serve as one of the Philharmonic-Symphony Society of New York's two principal conductors. It was further announced on Nov. 19 that he would become the Philharmonic's sole musical director at the close of the season.

1958

The political scene was unusually heated for an off-election year. Republicans charged Democrats with "radicalism," and

With few exceptions, American literature was not noteworthy in 1958. Vladimir Nabokov's *Lolita* was a highly-touted book

SCIENCE; INDUSTRY; ECONOMICS; EDUCATION; RELIGION; PHILOSOPHY.	SPORTS; FASHIONS; POPULAR ENTERTAINMENT; FOLKLORE; SOCIETY.

in a study of effects of the sun's radiation on communications. Scientists of 67 nations participated in the International Geophysical Year.

Aug. 19–20 **A new balloon ascent record** was set when Maj. David G. Simons went up to 101,486 feet in a plastic balloon. The record also marked man's longest stay on the edge of space.

Sept. 1 **Billy Graham's** 16-week evangelist campaign for New York closed with a giant rally on Times Square. His meetings had drawn an attendance of almost 2 million, and 56,767 of his hearers in New York had made "decisions for Christ."

Sept. 18 The Ethical Practices Committee of the AFL-CIO charged James Hoffa fostered **criminals in the Teamsters Union** and told the union to expel Hoffa or leave the AFL-CIO. On Dec. 6 the Teamsters Union was expelled.

Oct. 16 The U.S. Air Force fired 2 **aluminum pellets into space** which escaped the earth's gravity.

Nov. 1 **World's longest suspension bridge,** the Mackinac Straits Bridge between Michigan's upper and lower peninsula, opened for traffic. Bridge cost an estimated $100 million.

Dec. 12 Maj. Adrian E. Drew set a **world speed record** in his F-101 Voodoo. Speed set over Mojave Desert, Calif., was 1,207.6 mph.

May 4 The 84th annual **Kentucky Derby** at Churchill Downs, Louisville, Ky., won by *Iron Liege*. Time was 2:02 1/5; jockey Willie Hartack rode for $107,950. Hartack's 341 winners made him riding champion for the 3rd straight year.

May 18 *Bold Ruler* won the 81st annual **Preakness Stakes** at Pimlico. Jockey was Willie Shoemaker; time was 1:56 1/5.

June 15 *Gallant Man* won the 89th annual **Belmont Stakes.** Jockey was Willie Shoemaker; time was 2:26 3/5.

July 9 The 24th **All-Star baseball game** in St. Louis, Mo., was won by the American League. Score was AL 6, NL 5.

July 19 Don Bowden was **first American to run mile in less than 4 minutes.** His time was 3 min., 58.7 seconds at Stockton, Calif.

Oct. 2–10 Milwaukee, NL, defeated New York, AL, 4–3 in the 54th annual **World Series.**

Oct. 25 **Umberto (Albert) Anastasia slain** by 2 gunmen as he sat in a barber shop. The gangster had been nicknamed "Lord High Executioner" of the crime syndicate Murder, Inc.

Nov. 30 Navy defeated Army 14–0 in the 58th **Army-Navy game** at Philadelphia, Pa.

1958

A serious recession affected the entire country. In February, the jobless represented 7.7% of the total labor force—the

At the fashionable America's Cup race at Newport, R.I., America retained the cup when the sleek yacht *Columbia* defeated

former Pres. Harry Truman countered with the claim that Pres. Eisenhower had "surrendered" in Korea. Informal polls showed that the Republicans were losing ground because of continued world tension, but they continued the fight until election day. The international picture was characterized by America's rush to beat Russia into space. Many highly publicized American rockets failed, but by October 11, America was the first nation to approach the moon.

Jan. 3 The U.S. Air Force announced the formation of the **first 2 squadrons armed with intermediate-range ballistic missiles.** The 2 squadrons fall under the Strategic Air Command.

Jan. 13 The *Daily Worker,* best known American **Communist newspaper, suspended daily publication,** becoming a weekly, because of declining revenue. The final edition headline: "We'll Be Back!"

Feb. 22 Former Pres. **Harry S. Truman** in a TV address charged the Eisenhower Administration with bringing on the recession and with inadvertently helping the Soviets.

Feb. 28 A school bus collided with a car and plunged into Big Sandy River near Prestonburg, Ky. The driver and **27 children drowned.**

Feb. 28 The Senate, approved an **increase in postal rates,** which went into effect Aug. 1. Regular mail rose from 3¢ to 4¢ an ounce, domestic air mail from 6¢ to 7¢.

Mar. 4 Secretary of the Air Force James H. Douglas reaffirmed the verdict of guilty of bringing discredit to the military service against **Brig. Gen William (Billy) Mitchell** almost 37 years ago, but added that Mitchell's faith in air power had been vindicated.

Mar. 5 The **President vetoed** an all-out effort to make the U.S. the first nation to put a nuclear-powered airplane in the air. He said that scarce talent would be wasted if the U.S. concentrated only on a prestige objective.

and a best-seller, but many critics complained that the author's potential talents were being wasted in just another sex story. Even T. S. Eliot received bad reviews; critics said his new play lacked the old Eliot power and importance. Music experienced a few changes. Under the direction of dynamic, young Leonard Bernstein, the New York Philharmonic Orchestra began to play many more works by contemporary American composers. Painters were still fighting the battle of abstractionism versus representation, but abstractionism was obviously the winner in most American exhibits.

Pulitzer Prizes: novel, *A Death in the Family* by James Agee (awarded posthumously); drama, *Look Homeward, Angel* adapted by Ketti Frings from Thomas Wolfe's novel of the same name; history, *Banks and Politics in America—from the Revolution to the Civil War* by Bray Hammond; biography, *George Washington* by Douglas Southall Freeman; poetry, *Promises: Poems 1954–56* by Robert Penn Warren; music, *Vanessa* by Samuel Barber.

Top **popular songs** during the year were predominately rock-and-roll: "Purple People-Eaters" and "Bird Dog" represented the rock-and-rollers, and among ballads were "A Certain Smile" and "Your Precious Love."

Archibald MacLeish's poetic drama *J.B.* published. It is a parable of our time based on the Bible story of Job.

World première of *Threni,* a sacred work by **Igor Stravinski,** at the International Festival of Contemporary Music in Venice.

Jan. 3 Publication of a notable **first novel by William Humphrey,** *Home from the Hill,* the story of a boy who tries to emulate a father obsessed by hunting and women.

SCIENCE; INDUSTRY; ECONOMICS; EDUCATION; RELIGION; PHILOSOPHY.

SPORTS; FASHIONS; POPULAR ENTERTAINMENT; FOLKLORE; SOCIETY.

lowest employment figures in 16 years; by March the number of unemployed jumped to 5,198,000. After anti-recession legislation, the lull began to improve by early fall. In education, desegregation was still a major issue. State authorities in Little Rock, Ark., closed the public schools and reopened them as private institutions which would not admit Negroes. A new cry was heard for better educational standards; critics of American education claimed that standards were lower then ever before.

Nobel Prize in physiology and medicine shared by **Joshua Lederberg** of the University of Wisconsin for his discovery of sex in bacteria and **George W. Beadle** of the California Institute of Technology and **Edward L. Tatum** of the Rockefeller Institute for their discovery that single chemical reactions in a living cell are related to single genes.

U.S. satellites detected the existence of **mysterious band of powerful radiation** about 600 miles in space. The radiation is 1000 times more intense than expected, but scientists report that we can protect space travelers with a lead shield.

At the conclusion of a nationwide study of the **American college student,** Dr. W. Max Wise announced that today's student is more serious than his predecessors; he is older, often married, and usually has a part-time job.

Jan. 20 Pres. Eisenhower stated in a letter to Congress that **unwarranted wage or price increases** could imperil the economic status of the U.S.

Jan. 23 Pres. Eisenhower urged Congress to legislate against **racketeers in labor unions.** He said most labor union officials are honest, but government action is needed.

Jan. 31 **First U.S. earth satellite,** Explorer, launched at 10:48 P.M. from Cape

Britain's untried sailing ship *Scepter.* Tennis was about to lose one of its amateur champions; Althea Gibson announced she would quit tennis for a year to launch a career as a popular singer. In boxing, middleweight champion Sugar Ray Robinson disproved the theory that former champions cannot make a comeback when he regained his crown for the fifth time; and young heavyweight champion Floyd Patterson showed in his title defenses that his incredibly fast hands were getting better than ever.

U.S.G.A. Amateur Golf Championship won by Charlie Coe when he defeated Tom Aaron 5 and 4. **Open Championship** was won by Tommy Bolt in Tulsa, Okla.

Jan. 1 Ohio State defeated Oregon State 10–7 in the annual **Rose Bowl** football game at Pasadena, Calif.

Jan. 15 According to Gallup Poll report, Mrs. Eleanor Roosevelt headed the annual list of **most-admired women** in the U.S.

Feb. 20 Nathan Leopold, Jr., in Statesville Prison, Joliet, Ill., since 1924 for the **thrill murder** of Bobby Franks, was granted a parole. He was released on Mar. 13.

Mar. 22 Flamboyant movie producer **Mike Todd** killed when his private plane exploded and burned near Grants, N.M. Todd was producer of academy-award winning *Around the World in 80 Days.*

Mar. 25 Sugar Ray Robinson won the middleweight boxing championship for the 5th time by outpointing Carmen Basilio in 15 rounds at Chicago. He became the **first champion to regain his crown 5 times.**

Apr. 4 Cheryl Crane, 14, daughter of actress Lana Turner, stabbed and **killed known hoodlum** Johnny Stompanato after she had heard Stompanato threaten her

605

POLITICS AND GOVERNMENT; WAR; DISASTERS; VITAL STATISTICS.

BOOKS; PAINTING; DRAMA; ARCHITECTURE; SCULPTURE.

Apr. 1 President signed the **first anti-recession legislation** of 1958, a bill to stimulate housing construction. On Apr. 4 the President eliminated the 2% down payment on GI home loans.

Apr. 16 In the midst of the **"clean" bomb controversy,** Dr. Edward Teller told a Senate subcommittee that if the U.S. ended nuclear tests it would sacrifice millions to a possible atomic war.

Apr. 23 During a practice jump at Fort Campbell, Ky., **strong ground winds caused death** to 5 members of the 101st Airborne Division; 137 were injured.

May 1 **4 pacifists seized** in their ship, the *Golden Rule,* by the Coast Guard when they attempted to leave Honolulu for Eniwetok, the atomic testing area, in protest to the tests.

May 16 Capt. Walter Irwin flew a single-jet F-104A Starfighter over Edwards Air Force Base, Calif., for an official **world speed record** of 1404.19 mph.

June 17 **Sherman Adams,** Assistant to the President, denied before a House investigating committee that he had interceded with federal agencies on behalf of industrialist Bernard Goldfine. The President backed Adams on June 18 by saying he was a likable man of integrity.

June 30 The Senate approved **Alaska's admission to the U.S.** as the 49th state with an overwhelming vote of 64–20. Only the President's signature remained. When Gov. Stepovitch of Alaska heard the news, he said: "I believe that we will show the United States of America that we will be one of the greatest states in the Union within the next 50 years."

July 7 Pres. Eisenhower signed the bill for **Alaskan statehood.** The President will issue a formal proclamation some time in 1959 announcing Alaska's official recognition as a state.

Aug. 5 The U.S. atomic-powered submarine *Nautilus* made the world's **first undersea crossing of the North Pole.** The ship

Jan. 5 Opening of an **off-Broadway** twin bill by **Tennessee Williams;** the two plays were put together under the title *Garden District.* This year saw a boom in off-Broadway productions.

Jan. 15 **Samuel Barber's** first opera, *Vanessa,* heard for first time in Metropolitan Opera House in New York. *Vanessa* won the Pulitzer Prize in music.

Jan. 16 Opening of **William Gibson's** *Two for the Seesaw,* a play about a divorced lawyer who falls in love with a New York girl. The comedy had a cast of 2.

Jan. 30 Opening of **Dore Schary's** play *Sunrise at Campobello.* The play pictures Franklin D. Roosevelt during his struggles with polio and his return to politics.

Apr. The Moiseyev Dance Company, **a ballet group from Russia,** played at the Metropolitan Opera House in New York. The troupe was received enthusiastically by U.S. theatre-goers, and some critics felt the U.S. might be able to get together with Russia on the cultural front.

Apr. 11 Texas pianist **Van Cliburn,** 23, won the Tchaikovsky International Piano and Violin Festival held in Moscow, Russia. His playing of the Rachmaninoff *3rd Piano Concerto* turned the auditorium of the Tchaikovsky Conservatory into a frenzy of applause.

Apr. 15 **Fire in the Museum of Modern Art** in New York killed one workman and caused an estimated $320,000 damage.

May 1 The U.S. entered **international cultural competitions** at the Brussels World's Fair with the European première of the motion picture *South Pacific.* Other American cultural events included the New York City Center Light Opera Company production of Rodgers and Hammerstein's *Carousel* (June 4–8 and June 17–22) and

Canaveral, Fla. It was bullet-shaped, 80 inches long and 6 inches in diameter with the last stage attached, and weighed 30.8 lbs.

Feb. 12 Pres. Eisenhower told the nation that **recession** is not permanent, that employment will pick up in March.

Mar. 8 Nobel Prize winning novelist William Faulkner said at Princeton University that parents and educators are **endangering U.S. education** by not facing up to important realities and that schools are turning into "baby-sitting organizations."

Mar. 17 After more than 3 months of highly publicized delays, a 3¼ lb. Vanguard **satellite went into orbit.** The 6.4 inch aluminum sphere, the smallest satellite launched so far, went into wider orbit than any other man-made satellite.

Apr. The **International Automobile Show** was held in New York. Most cars in the show were European models, but U.S. was represented by a few special cars: the Ford Thunderbird and a specially designed Buick.

Apr. 26 Samuel Cardinal Stritch given **highest Vatican post an American has ever received,** Pro-Prefect of the Vatican's Sacred Congregation for the Propagation of the Faith. On Apr. 28, a blood clot forced amputation of his right arm, and on May 27 he died after a stroke.

Apr. 28 Nobel Prize-winner Dr. Linus Pauling said that **radioactive carbon-14** already left in the air by detonated atomic bombs would cause 5 million genetically defective births and millions of cancer and leukemia cases in the next 300 generations.

May 2 Declines were recorded in the number of insured jobless in the U.S., with California showing the biggest **increase in employment.**

mother. A coroner's jury called it justifiable homicide on Apr. 11.

May 3 The 84th annual **Kentucky Derby** at Churchill Downs, Louisville, Ky., won by *Tim Tam.* Time was 2:05. With jockey Ismael Valenzuela up, he won $160,500.

May 17 *Tim Tam* won the 81st annual **Preakness Stakes.** Jockey was Ismael Valenzuela; winnings were $97,900.

June 3 Publication of *The Decline of the American Male,* a non-fiction work by Attwood, Leonard and Moskin. The book claims **American men** are totally dominated by women.

June 7 *Cavan* won the 90th annual **Belmont Stakes** for $73,440. Jockey was Pete Anderson.

June 28 Nancy Ramey of Seattle swam the women's 100-meter butterfly in a **world record** time of 1:9 3/5 during a meet in Los Angeles.

July 8 The American League won the 25th **All-Star baseball game,** beating the National League 4–3 before a crowd of 48,829 in Baltimore, Md.

Aug. 6 During a meet in Budapest, Hungary, Glenn Davis of Columbus. O., set a new **world record in the 400-meter hurdles** in 49.2 seconds.

Aug. 10 **Thieves broke 2 display windows** at Tiffany & Co. of New York and stole $163,300 worth of insured jewels.

Sept. 2 **Dr. and Mrs. Melvin Nimer** were slain in their home in Staten Island, N.Y., after they discovered a masked prowler in their sons' room. The older boy, Melvin, Jr., 8, later confessed to the crime, but after psychiatric examination, on Oct. 21 confession was declared invalid. At the

607

| POLITICS AND GOVERNMENT; WAR; DISASTERS; VITAL STATISTICS. | BOOKS; PAINTING; DRAMA; ARCHITECTURE; SCULPTURE. |

submerged near Point Barrow, Alaska, Aug. 1 and sailed under the 50-foot-thick ice cap for 96 hours before surfacing.

Aug. 25   Law granting pensions to ex-Presidents of the U.S. became effective. It was the **first law for pensions** for former heads of the country.

Sept. 5   A **commuters' train** of the Jersey Central R.R. went through an open drawbridge into Newark Bay, resulting in an estimated 40 killed. Autopsy on train's engineer revealed he had suffered heart attack and had been unable to respond to stop signals.

Sept. 22   The atomic-powered submarine U.S.S. *Skate* returned from a transpolar voyage during which she set a **world's record** by steaming for 31 days under polar ice without surfacing.

Sept. 22   **Sherman Adams,** Assistant to the President, resigned under pressure from fellow Republicans who felt he was endangering GOP chances in the Nov. elections. In nationwide radio-TV broadcast, Adams insisted he had done no wrong in accepting gifts and favors from Boston industrialist Bernard Goldfine.

Oct. 6   The atomic-powered submarine *Seawolf* set an **undersea endurance record** when it surfaced after 60 days.

Dec. 1   The **3rd most catastrophic school fire in the U.S.** occurred in Chicago. The fire spread rapidly through Our Lady of the Angels Roman Catholic Parochial School in Chicago and cost the lives of 87 children and 3 nuns. The two school fires more disastrous were: on Mar. 18, 1937, 294 died in New London, Tex., and on Mar. 4, 1908, 176 died in the Collinwood school fire in Cleveland.

a performance by the American Ballet Theatre (Aug. 5–10).

July   **Newport Jazz Festival** at Newport, R.I., featured work of jazz pioneer **Duke Ellington.** Ellington played several of his own works, including excerpts from his jazz suite *Black, Brown, and Beige.*

Aug. 18   American publication of **Vladimir Nabokov's** highly-publicized novel *Lolita.* The book is a satire based on a middle-aged European's love affair with a 12-year-old girl.

Aug. 20   World première of *Maria Golovin,* a new opera by **Gian-Carlo Menotti,** at the Brussels World's Fair.

Oct. 2   Opening of Eugene O'Neill's *A Touch of the Poet* in New York. The play, a historical piece, is expected to be the **last full-length posthumous play by O'Neill.**

Oct. 15   In a news conference, poet **Robert Frost** said of **Ezra Pound's** *The Cantos,* "I don't say I'm not up to them, I say they're not up to me. Nobody ought to like them, but some do, and I let them. That's my tolerance." Frost had helped to obtain Pound's release from a mental hospital in Washington, D.C.

Oct. 23   Opening of a comedy about television, *Make a Million,* by **Norman Barasch.** Experienced comedian **Sam Levene** made the show a sure hit.

Dec. 1   Opening of **Rodgers and Hammerstein's** new spectacular musical, *The Flower Drum Song.*

1959

Two world-famous figures, John Foster Dulles and George C. Marshall, died. Two others made official visits, Richard M. Nixon to the U.S.S.R. and Soviet Premier Khrushchev to the U.S.; the antics of both

American fiction underwent another dull year, with the exception of a few bright moments in John Updike's *Poorhouse Fair* and Allen Drury's *Advise and Consent* and some brilliant insights in Truman Capote's

June 27 An air force KC-135 piloted by Col. Harry Burrell, set a **new New York-to-London speed record** of 5 hours, 27 minutes, 42.8 seconds for an average of 630.2 mph.

Sept. 2–3 Harold J. Gibbons, chief aide to **Teamsters union** President James R. Hoffa, denied before a Senate investigating committee that he ran the union with the aid of hoodlums. He said he regretted violence in strikes but could not quarrel with a worker's right to protect his job.

Sept. 30 Gov. Orval E. Faubus of Arkansas defied Supreme Court ruling against **segregation** by closing 4 high schools in Little Rock. On Sept. 17 the Little Rock Private School Corp. was chartered in a move to reopen city's schools on a segregated basis as private but state-financed institutions.

Oct. 11 A Pioneer rocket was launched in attempt to circle the moon. Rocket failed on Oct. 12, but obtained a **record maximum altitude** of 79,193 miles—thirty times the altitude of any previous man-made object.

Oct. 12 **A bomb exploded in a Jewish synagogue** in Atlanta, Georgia. No one was in the building. On Oct. 14, a synagogue in Peoria, Ill., was bombed. Pres. Eisenhower said he was "outraged" at the action, and F.B.I. began investigations.

end of the year sensational crime was still a mystery.

Sept. 6 *Mark Antony,* a 4-year-old colt, set a **world record for the mile and 70 yards** when it won the Manchester Handicap at Rockingham Park, N.H., in 1:39.2.

Sept. 7 U.S. lawn **Men's Tennis Singles Championship** won by Ashley Cooper; **Women's Singles Champion** was Althea Gibson for the second year in a row.

Oct. 1 John Joseph Scanlon, 38, **notorious waterfront hoodlum,** was fatally shot. His murderers forced his automobile to crash into a telephone pole, apparently in attempt to make death appear accidental.

Oct. 1–9 New York, AL, defeated Milwaukee, NL, 4–3 in the 55th annual **World Series.**

Oct. 9 **Yogi Berra,** New York Yankee catcher, finished participating in his 10th World Series; he tied records for World Series participation set by **Babe Ruth** and **Joe DiMaggio.**

Dec 28 The Baltimore Colts defeated the New York Giants 23–17 at New York to win the **National Professional Football** Championship.

1959

After a 2-week delay at the request of Pres. Eisenhower, the United Steelworkers of America began a nationwide walk-out on July 15. Negotiations proceeded slowly and progress was infinitesimal. On the or-

The U.S. suffered a major sports defeat when Floyd Patterson lost the world's heavyweight boxing title to Ingemar Johansson in the 3rd round of a Yankee Stadium bout. Archie Moore retained the

men were widely publicized. The 1960 Presidential election was beginning to cause great activity among Republicans and Democrats alike. Contention for the Republican nomination seemed limited to Gov. Nelson A. Rockefeller and Vice-Pres. Richard M. Nixon, while the Democrats numbered John F. Kennedy, Adlai E. Stevenson, Lyndon B. Johnson, Hubert Humphrey, Stuart Symington, Edmund G. Brown, Robert B. Meyner, and G. Mennen Williams as possible nominees.

Jan. 3 **Alaska was proclaimed 49th state** by Pres. Eisenhower at 12:02 P.M. EST. An executive order was then signed adding a 49th star to the U.S. flag in a new design of 7 rows of 7 stars with alternate rows indented, this flag to become official July 4.

Jan. 6 Rep. Charles A. Halleck (R-Ind). became **House Republican leader** by a 74–70 vote in a GOP caucus, thus ending Rep. Joseph W. Martin's (R-Mass.) 20-year career in that post.

Feb. 3 An American Airlines **plane crashed** into New York City's East River, killing 65 of 73 persons aboard. Survivors were 3 of 5 crew members and 5 of 67 passengers.

Feb. 10 **St. Louis** was declared a **disaster area** by Pres. Eisenhower after a tornado struck, killing 22 persons, injuring 350, leaving 5,000 homeless, and causing damages estimated at $12 million.

Mar. 18 Pres. Eisenhower signed the **Hawaii statehood bill,** and, on receiving certification that Hawaii's voters have signified their approval of statehood, will proclaim Hawaii the 50th state.

Mar. 30 **Double jeopardy was upheld** in two U.S. Supreme Court decisions stating that a person could be tried for the same offense in both federal and state courts.

Apr. 7 The New York City Council adopted a resolution which provided for a committee to study New York City's **possible emergence as the 51st state.**

Breakfast at Tiffany's. The drama was well represented by Lorraine Hansberry's *A Raisin in the Sun;* but poetry underwent a particularly bleak season, unaided by the multitudinous Beatnik efforts. One of the most spectacular musical undertakings of the season was the extensive foreign tour of Leonard Bernstein and the New York Philharmonic Orchestra. Commencing in Athens (Aug. 5) and concluding in London (Oct. 10), the tour included a notable series of 18 concerts in the U.S.S.R. The U.S.S.R. was the scene of another notable artistic event when "Welcome Home," a painting by Jack Levine which had been sharply criticized by Pres. Eisenhower, proved to be very popular with the Russian people.

Among the **musical shows** popular during the year were Rodgers and Hammerstein's *Flower Drum Song,* and Jule Styne's *Gypsy.* Other flourishing musicals were *Once upon a Mattress* and *La Plume de Ma Tante.*

Popular music of the year was made slightly more interesting by the welcome intrusion of occasional folk tunes into the ranks of best sellers. Among these were "Tom Dooley," "Stagger Lee," "The Battle of New Orleans," and "He's Got the Whole World in His Hands."

Jazz made itself felt as an ever-expanding influence on the cultural scene. The number of jazz festivals was increasing, as was the incidence of jazz performances in European music festivals. TV also felt the beat as jazz found its way into the

SCIENCE; INDUSTRY; ECONOMICS; EDUCATION; RELIGION; PHILOSOPHY.

SPORTS; FASHIONS; POPULAR ENTERTAINMENT; FOLKLORE; SOCIETY.

der of Pres. Eisenhower, an 80-day Taft-Hartley injunction was issued Oct. 21 and, after a court fight ending in the Supreme Court, was executed Nov. 7, halting the 116-day steel strike, the longest in U.S. history. The United States scored a spectacular success when it launched an entire Atlas missile designed to function as a satellite. This was the 5th and largest earth satellite successfully launched by the U.S. Besides much information-collecting instrumentation, the missile contained a recording of Pres. Eisenhower's voice which was automatically broadcast. The message was subsequently received and recorded by U.S. radio stations and distributed throughout the world.

Jan. 19 Virginia State Supreme Court ruled invalid state laws designed to prevent **school integration** by automatically closing schools receiving final federal court orders to integrate.

Feb. 2 Following the Virginia State Supreme Court ruling, **schools were desegregated** in both Arlington and Norfolk, with no serious disorders.

Feb. 17 A Vanguard satellite designed to function as the **1st weather station in space** achieved orbit after being launched from Cape Canaveral, Fla., by the U.S. Navy.

Mar. 31 Pres. Eisenhower signed a compromise bill granting a limited 3-month extension of the emergency federal **employment compensation** program.

Apr. 5 An increase in **atmospheric radioactivity** of 300% in the eastern United States after the U.S.S.R. nuclear tests of Sept.–Oct., 1958, was reported by the U.S. naval research laboratory.

Apr. 7 The Commerce and Labor Departments announced an **unemployment drop** from 4,749,000 in mid-Feb. to 4,362,-000 in mid-Mar., a drop about two thirds larger than usual for the season and the largest drop since Feb.–Mar., 1950.

Apr. 9 Seven **astronauts** were picked from the ranks of military test pilots by the NASA. After a vigorous training pro-

light heavyweight title by knocking out challenger Yvon Durelle of Canada, also in the third round. Los Angeles replaced New York as U.S. boxing center as boxing, in general, tended to move from the East to the West Coast following the trend set by similar moves in major league baseball. The Los Angeles Dodgers, in their second season on the West Coast, gave California its first baseball championship by defeating the Chicago White Sox to win the 1959 World's Series.

Jan. 5 Marie Torre of the New York *Herald Tribune* began a **10-day jail sentence for contempt of court.** In refusing to reveal her source of information for one of her columns, Miss Torre invoked the Fifth Amendment.

Feb. 1 Zachariah Davis was designated for the **Baseball Hall of Fame.** Ceremonies for the former outfielder of the Brooklyn Dodgers were held July 20.

Feb. 14–15 In a 2-day raid throughout New York City, narcotics agents and police smashed a major U.S. **heroin** ring. Recovering an estimated 28½ lbs. of heroin valued at $3,600,000 and $50,000 in cash, agents arrested 27 wholesale importers and distributors.

Apr. 7 Oklahoma **repealed 51 years of prohibition** by a decisive margin of 80,000 votes, thus legalizing the sale of liquor and leaving Mississippi the only dry state.

May 20 4,978 **Japanese-Americans** who had renounced U.S. citizenship during World War II and later applied for restitution were restored to citizenship by the U.S. Justice Department.

May 25 A Louisiana ban on bouts between **Negro and white boxers** was declared unconstitutional by the United States Supreme Court.

June 15 The U.S. Federal Communications Commission ruling requiring TV

| POLITICS AND GOVERNMENT; WAR; DISASTERS; VITAL STATISTICS. | BOOKS; PAINTING; DRAMA; ARCHITECTURE; SCULPTURE. |

Apr. 15 Due to incapacitating illness **John Foster Dulles** resigned as Sec. of State. Pres. Eisenhower requested that he remain as consultant and accept some office that would make him useful to the State Dept.

Apr. 18 **Christian Archibald Herter** was named Sec. of State by Pres. Eisenhower. The Senate waived the 7-day interval between introduction and confirmation of a presidential appointment, confirming Sec. Herter in 4½ hours by a 93–0 vote.

May 20 Highest U.S. civilian award, the **Medal of Freedom,** was presented to John Foster Dulles by Pres. Eisenhower.

May 22 Brig. Gen. Benjamin O. Davis, Jr., USAF, was appointed to the rank of **Major General.** He was the **first Negro** to achieve such rank in the U.S. armed forces.

May 24 **John Foster Dulles,** 71, former U.S. Sec. of State, died in Washington, D.C. An official funeral with full military honors was ordered by Pres. Eisenhower, who described Dulles as "one of the truly great men of our time."

June 8 The right of Congress and of individual states to **investigate Communism** was upheld by the U.S. Supreme Court in two 5–4 decisions.

June 19 **Gov. Earl Long** being committed to a state mental institution, Lt. Gov. Lether Frazar became Acting Governor of Louisiana.

June 21 On his return to Washington from the Geneva conference, Christian Herter, U.S. Sec. of State, announced that the West was convinced that the **U.S.S.R.'s goal** was to absorb both West Berlin and eventually all Germany into the Communist camp.

June 23 Gen. **Maxwell Taylor resigned** as U.S. Army chief. He stated that his decision had been influenced by rejection of his efforts to modernize the Army.

July 4 At 12:10 A.M. the U.S. **49-star flag** was raised for the first time at the

scores for such programs as *Richard Diamond, Peter Gunn,* and *M Squad.*

Mar. 3 The *Symphony No. 13* (Madras) by American composer **Henry Cowell** was given its world premier in Madras, India. The work was performed by the Little Orchestra of New York (Thomas Scherman, director) during its tour of Asian countries.

Mar. 5 *Wozzeck,* a modern operatic masterpiece by Alban Berg, received its **first Metropolitan Opera production.** The opera was first heard 34 years previously in Berlin.

Apr. 7 Negro playwright Lorraine H. Hansberry was the first Negro to receive the N.Y. **Drama Critics Circle Award** for her first play, *A Raisin in the Sun.*

Apr. 26 **Hugo Weisgall's** musical play *Six Characters in Search of an Author,* based on Pirandello's play of the same name, was produced by the New York City Opera.

May 2 **George Grosz** announced plans to move to West Berlin but to retain his U.S. citizenship. The satirical and impressionist painter fled Nazi Germany in 1933 to become a U.S. citizen.

May 4 **Pulitzer Prizes:** novel, *The Travels of Jamie McPheeters* by Robert Lewis Taylor; drama, *J. B.* by Archibald MacLeish; history, *The Republican Era: 1869–1901* by Leonard D. White with Jean Schneider, who shared the prize with

SCIENCE; INDUSTRY; ECONOMICS; EDUCATION; RELIGION; PHILOSOPHY.

SPORTS; FASHIONS; POPULAR ENTERTAINMENT; FOLKLORE; SOCIETY.

gram, 1 of the 7 was picked to ride a Project Mercury space capsule into earth-circling orbit in 1961.

May 3 By vote of the **Unitarian and Universalist churches** and fellowships, the American Unitarian Association and the Universalist Church of America merged.

May 28 Two **monkeys in the nose cone** of an IRBM launched by the U.S. Army from Cape Canaveral, Fla., were recovered unhurt from the Caribbean area after a 300-mile-high space flight.

June 3 Using the **moon as a reflector,** a message recorded by Pres. Eisenhower was transmitted from Westford, Mass., to Canadian Prime Minister Diefenbaker in Prince Albert, Sask.

June 15 It was announced by the New York Stock Exchange that early in 1959 12,490,000 persons owned U.S. **public-held corporations' stock.**

June 18 A 3-judge U.S. federal court declared unconstitutional the Arkansas law under which Gov. Orval Faubus closed the **public schools in Little Rock.**

June 22 A technical conference on means of **detecting nuclear tests** above 50 km. was opened by scientists from U.S., Britain, and the U.S.S.R.

June 30 A bill raising the temporary **debt limit** to $295,000,000,000 and the permanent limit to $285,000,000,000 was signed by Pres. Eisenhower.

July 7 The Evangelical Lutherans and United Evangelical Lutherans merged to form the **American Lutheran Church.**

July 7 In Oberlin, Ohio, the General Synod of the **United Church of Christ** issued its first major pronouncement stressing the church's role in social, international, and political problems, and urging an end to segregation.

July 14 The Labor Department reported a rise in **employment** from 66,016,000 in mid-May to 67,342,000 in mid-June. As 2 million students graduated or left school to seek summer jobs, unemployment rose simultaneously; however, the

and radio stations to give **equal time to all political candidates** in both debate and news broadcasts was affirmed (4–3).

June 22 A 1957 congressional statute restricting defendants' access to pretrial statements made by witnesses was upheld by the U.S. Supreme Court.

June 26 Ingemar Johansson of Sweden won the **world's professional heavyweight boxing title** by knocking out Floyd Patterson in a bout in New York City.

July 13 Cliff Lumsden won the Atlantic City (N.J.) professional swim marathon. Finishing in 10 hr. 54 min. 5 sec., he won $5,000.

July 20 **Tennis national clay court championships** were won by Bernard Bartzen, men's singles; Sally Moore, women's singles; Bernard Bartzen and Grand Golden, men's doubles; Sandra Reynolds and Renée Schuurman, women's doubles.

Aug. 16 The **American Soap Box Derby** was won by Barney Townsend, an Indiana 13-year-old.

Aug. 26 Alfredo Camerero, from Argentina, won a $4,400 **English Channel race.** He swam from Cap Gris Nez, France, to Dover, England (a distance of 22 miles), in 11 hr. 48 min. 26 sec.

Aug. 28–31 Australia retained the **Davis Cup** as its team (Neale A. Fraser, Roy Emerson, Rod Laver) defeated the U.S. challangers (Alex Olmedo, Barry MacKay, and Earl Buchholtz, Jr.) at Forest Hills, N.Y.

Sept. 7 **Pan American Games** concluded with the U.S. first and Argentina second. The games were held Aug. 27–Sept. 7 in Soldier Field and Portage Park, Chicago, Ill.

Sept. 13 **U.S. tennis amateur championship winners** included: Neale Fraser,

Capitol in Washington, D.C., and at Ft. McHenry, Md.

July 7 Pres. Eisenhower vetoed an **omnibus housing bill,** terming it excessive, defective, inflationary, and an obstacle to constructive progress toward better housing for Americans.

July 24 After his "debate" with Soviet Premier Khrushchev in the kitchen exhibit, Vice-Pres. Nixon, on an official U.S.S.R. visit, **opened the American exhibition** in Moscow.

July 29 National Safety Council announced the lowest **accident death rate** since 1954 for 1958, 52.5 persons in 100,-000, giving total deaths at 91,000, 37,000 of which were auto accident deaths, raising the all-time U.S. death toll in auto accidents to 1,265,000.

Aug. 1 In a **radio-TV address from Moscow,** Vice-Pres. Nixon told the Russian people that they would live in tension and fear if Premier Khrushchev attempted to propagate Communism in countries outside the U.S.S.R.

Aug. 7 A warehouse fire caused the **explosion** of a truck loaded with 6½ tons of dynamite and ammonium nitrate, which killed at least 11 persons, injured 100, and leveled 8 blocks in Roseburg, Ore.

Aug. 21 Pres. Eisenhower officially proclaimed **Hawaii the fiftieth state** of the Union. The President also issued the order for a new flag of 50 stars arranged in staggered rows: 5 6-star rows and 4 5-star rows, this flag to become official July 4, 1960.

Aug. 24 The seating of Senators Hiram L. Fong (R) and Oren E. Long (D), and Rep. D. K. Inouye (D) of Hawaii increased U.S. **Senate membership** to 100, and **House membership** to 437.

Aug. 26. Extension of the U.S. **nuclear test ban** from Oct. 31 to Dec. 31, 1959, was announced by the U.S. State Dept. The U.S. government hoped that Britain and the U.S.S.R. would make similar extensions.

White's estate; biography, *Woodrow Wilson* by Arthur Walworth; poetry, *Selected Poems, 1928–1958* by Stanley Kunitz; music, *Concerto for Piano and Orchestra* by John La-Montaine.

May 18 President Eisenhower presented Spanish painter, Joan Miro, with the $10,000 **Guggenheim international art award** for his mural *Night and Day.*

June 11 **Lady Chatterley's Lover** was banned from the mails by Postmaster General Arthur E. Summerfield, who said, "Any literary merit the book may have is far outweighed by the pornographic and smutty passages and words, so that the book, taken as a whole, is an obscene and filthy work."

Aug. 5–Oct. 10 The New York Philharmonic under the direction of **Leonard Bernstein** toured 17 countries giving a total of 50 concerts. Among the American music programed was Bernstein's *The Age of Anxiety* and Charles Ives's *The Unanswered Question.*

Aug. 11 Publication date of Allen Drury's popular **Advise and Consent,** which revealed much of the inner conflicts and workings of the Senate centering on the appointment of a highly controversial figure as Sec. of State.

Sept. 14 "Modern works" were among the **art objects made duty free** in a bill signed into law by President Eisenhower.

Oct. 19 **The Miracle Worker** opened at the Playhouse with Anne Bancroft playing the leading role of Helen Keller's first

| SCIENCE; INDUSTRY; ECONOMICS; EDUCATION; RELIGION; PHILOSOPHY. | SPORTS; FASHIONS; POPULAR ENTERTAINMENT; FOLKLORE; SOCIETY. |

number of unemployed family heads dropped 180,000 below May.

July 15 After a breakdown of negotiations, the **United Steelworkers** began a nationwide **strike** against the 28 steel companies normally producing 85–95% of the U.S.'s steel. It was the 6th such strike since World War II.

July 21 At its launching in Camden, N.J., the **1st U.S. nuclear merchant ship** was christened the *Savannah* by Mrs. Dwight D. Eisenhower.

Aug. 4 Teamsters' president James Hoffa and two of his chief aides were denounced for **union abuses** in a special U.S. Senate committee report.

Aug. 6 In a radio-TV address Pres. Eisenhower called for a strong **labor reform law** to purge corruption from the labor-management field.

Aug. 7 U.S. Explorer VI, **"Paddlewheel,"** a 142-lb. satellite, was orbited from Cape Canaveral, Fla.; this was the first satellite to be handled from initiation to orbit by the NASA.

Aug. 12 **High schools in Little Rock,** Ark., reopened, integrating two previously all-white schools. About 200–250 segregationists demonstrated near Central High School but policemen held them back with fire hoses and clubs.

Sept. 7 The National Council of Churches announced that in 1958 **church membership** increased to 109,557, 741. This showed a gain of 5% since 1957 and indicated that 64% of the population were church members.

Sept. 11 Congress voted affirmation of a bill designed to **relieve depressed areas.** This legislation grants the Secretary of Agriculture the power to distribute, by means of food stamps, large quantities of surplus food to impoverished Americans.

Sept. 18 The **12th successful U.S. satellite,** "Vanguard III," was launched at Cape Canaveral, Fla. Two other satellites, Discoverers V and VI, were launched Aug. 13 and 19.

men's singles; Maria Bueno, women's singles; Neale Fraser and Roy Emerson, men's doubles (played Aug. 23).

Sept. 14 A bill exempting radio-TV news of U.S. political candidates from **FCC equal-time requirements** was signed by Pres. Eisenhower; the bill had been passed by Congress Sept. 2–3.

Oct. 8 National League Los Angeles **Dodgers won the World Series** by defeating the American League's Chicago White Sox, 13–6 in the 6th game.

Oct. 10 The PGA announced that Art Wall, golf pro of Pocono Manor, was the **leading golf prize winner** for 1959. Wall had won $53,142 on the PGA tournament circuit.

Oct. 29 The **Cy Young award** was given to Chicago White Sox' Early Wynn as the best major league pitcher of 1959.

Nov. 4 The Baseball Writers' Association named **Ernie Banks,** shortstop for the Chicago Cubs, the most valuable National League player of 1959.

Nov. 5 The **American Football League** announced that eight professional teams will begin play in 1965. The newly formed American League will rival the National Football League.

Nov. 7 **Martyn Green,** famous for his comic baritone roles in the English D'Oyly Carte productions of Gilbert & Sullivan, suffered amputation of his left leg, which had been crushed in an elevator accident.

Nov. 9 Housewives were warned against buying **cranberries** grown in Washington and Oregon. A. S. Fleming, U.S. Health, Education, and Welfare Secretary, announced that a weed killer causing cancer in rats had contaminated cranberries

Sept. 7 Pres. Eisenhower was asked by the U.S. Civil Rights Commission to **appoint federal registrars** to supervise in areas where local officials had prevented Negroes from voting.

Sept. 15. **Premier Khrushchev arrived at Andrews Air Force Base** to the official welcome of Pres. Eisenhower. The Soviet Premier stated that he was visiting the U.S. with "open heart and good intentions."

Sept. 19 Pres. Eisenhower called the 1st session of the **86th U.S. congress one of many "disappointing failures."** He particularly criticized the "extravagant proposals" and the "shortsighted cuts in military outlay."

Sept. 27 Upon Premier **Khrushchev's departure from Washington, D.C.** for Moscow, it was revealed that he and Pres. Eisenhower had reached understandings designed to relieve world tensions, including the withdrawal of the U.S.S.R. Berlin ultimatum.

Oct. 12 New Jersey authorities reported that **deaths from equine encephalitis** in that state had claimed 20 lives. It is believed that the disease, commonly known as sleeping sickness, is carried by mosquitos from birds to horses and humans.

Nov. 15 In the process of **reshaping state government,** 18 departments were established and 80 discontinued by Hawaiian state legislature.

Nov. 16 Pres. Eisenhower asked $41 billion for the 1961 **defense budget.** It was also decided that there would be no immediate reduction in U.S. troops overseas.

Dec. 3 Leaving Washington, Pres. Eisenhower began a **three-week visit to 11 nations** in Asia, Africa, and Europe.

Dec. 7 The Supreme Court, by refusing to consider lower court decisions banning **Red China travel** to Americans, upheld the right of the President to make such prohibitions.

Dec. 10 In a speech before the Indian parliament in New Delhi, Pres. Eisenhower

childhood teacher. The play was an immediate success.

Oct. 21 **Dmitri Shostakovich** arrived in New York City to begin a one-month tour with various U.S. symphony orchestras. With him were several other Russian composers including Dmitri Kabalevsky, Fikret Amirov, and Konstantin Dankevich.

Oct. 21 The Solomon R. **Guggenheim Museum of art** was opened. The only building in New York City designed by Frank Lloyd Wright, the museum has become one of the most controversial structures in the U.S.

Nov. 4 The $5000 **Academy of American Poets Award** fellowship was won by **Leonie Adams** while the Lamont Poetry Selection for an unpublished first manuscript was awarded to **Donald B. Justice.**

Nov. 13 **William Faulkner** published *The Mansion,* the final work of several dealing with the Snopes family.

Nov. 19 **Discovery of paintings** said to be the work of Michelangelo da Caravaggio, Il Tintoretto (Jacopo Robusti), Titian, Lorenzo Lotto, Claude Gile, Luca Giordano, Bernardo Cavallino, Artemisia Gentileschi, and Raffaello Santi (Raphael) in the home of Pasadena, Calif., TV repairman Alfonso Follo, was announced by an associate of the family. The announcement was later declared premature as the owners sought expert opinion.

616

SCIENCE; INDUSTRY; ECONOMICS; EDUCATION; RELIGION; PHILOSOPHY.

SPORTS; FASHIONS; POPULAR ENTERTAINMENT; FOLKLORE; SOCIETY.

Sept. 22 The **International Longshoremen** were readmitted on 2-year probation to the AFL–CIO. The ILA had been expelled from the labor organization because of corruption and criminal elements, conditions which AFL–CIO Pres. Meany said were much improved.

Sept. 23 The **AFL–CIO 3rd biennial convention** ended. At the close of the convention, which was held Sept. 17–23 in San Francisco, the issue of racial bias in the locals was hotly debated by George Meany, president, and A. Philip Randolph, vice-president, of the labor organization.

Oct. 1 70,000 members of the **International Longshoremen's Union walked off the job** in Atlantic and Gulf Coast ports. Pres. Eisenhower invoked the Taft-Hartley Act Oct. 6 by appointing a board of inquiry. An injunction Oct. 8 halted the strike.

Oct. 1 **$2,000,000,000 in U.S. notes** was offered by the U.S. treasury at a 5% interest rate, the highest for U.S. securities since 1929.

Oct. 10 Initiation of the **first passenger service circling the globe** was announced by Pan American World Airways.

Oct. 13 A missile fired into space by a U.S. B-47 bomber crew came very near **Explorer VI,** U.S. earth satellite.

Oct. 15 Severo Ochoa and Arthur Kornberg received the 1959 **Nobel prize in medicine** for their joint work on the chemistry of heredity.

Oct. 26 Emilio Segre and Owen Chamberlain (U.S.) received the **Nobel prize for physics.**

Nov. 7 A Taft-Hartley injunction against the **steel strike** was upheld by the U.S. Supreme Court (8–10). Strikers were immediately ordered to comply with the decision.

Nov. 13 Allen W. Dulles, director of Central Intelligence Agency, branded as "a gross exaggeration" Khrushchev's statement that the U.S.S.R.'s **standard of living** would exceed that of the U.S. by 1970.

grown in Washington and Oregon during the 1958–1959 season.

Nov. 12 The Baseball Writers' Assn. named Nellie Fox, 2nd baseman for the Chicago White Sox, the **most valuable American League Player** of 1959.

Nov. 17 Willie McCovey, first baseman of the San Francisco Giants, was named **rookie of the year** in the National League, 1959.

Nov. 18 Bob Allison, center fielder for the Washington Senators, was named **rookie of the year** in the American League, 1959.

Nov. 21 *Progressing,* ridden by Hedley Woodhouse, won the **Pimlico Futurity** in Baltimore for $71,635.

Nov. 30 Martha Graham was announced the recipient of the 9th annual **Capezio Award** of $1,000.

Dec. 1 The **Heisman Trophy** for outstanding 1957 college football player was awarded to Billy Cannon, halfback for Louisiana State University.

Dec. 2 Joe Brown retained the **world lightweight title** by scoring a TKO over Dave Charnley.

Dec. 4 Gene Fullmer successfully defended his **world middleweight championship** by a 15-round decision over Ellsworth "Spider" Webb.

Dec. 6 The New York Giants won the **Eastern Championship of the National Football League** by defeating the Cleveland Browns 48–7.

Dec. 8 Boxing Writers Association selected **Ingemar Johansson** "fighter of the year."

617

POLITICS AND GOVERNMENT; WAR; DISASTERS; VITAL STATISTICS.	BOOKS; PAINTING; DRAMA; ARCHITECTURE; SCULPTURE.

stated that the U.S. **would defend its friends and allies** against aggression.

Dec. 10–14 Gus Hall was named general secretary of the **American Communist Party.** Hall, 48, had formerly been the party's Midwest secretary.

Dec. 16 At the NATO Council in Paris, U.S. Sec. of Defense Gates said that, at present, the **U.S. had "nuclear superiority"** over the U.S.S.R. in weapons and their delivery.

Dec. 23 In a radio-TV speech, Pres. Eisenhower stated that he had perceived a profound **wish for peace** everywhere he went during his 11-nation goodwill tour.

Dec. 1 *The Self,* a cast-iron figure, won for sculptor **Isami Noguchi** the Logan Art Institute Medal for painting or sculpture.

1960

For the United States, 1960 was marked by explosions and shocks. Relations with the U.S.S.R., which were somewhat improved after Nixon's trip to Moscow, and Khrushchev's tour of the United States and amicable Camp David talks with Pres. Eisenhower, perilously deteriorated when a U.S. U-2 reconnaissance plane was shot down well inside the U.S.S.R. on May 1. The event gave Premier Khrushchev a tremendous propaganda advantage, of which he made maximum use, culminating in the disintegration of the Paris Summit Meeting. The U-2 incident and later U.S. plane–U.S.S.R. incident involving an RB-47, together with events, pressures, and contentions involving the U.S. in Laos, Congo, Germany, Cuba, and Japan, caused a sharp increase in the American public's concern with and interest in the apparent deterioration of U.S. world position and

One of Beatnikism's brighter spokesmen, Jack Kerouac, published a new novel, *Tristessa,* which exhibits a somewhat frantic fascination with and magnetic attraction to the misery of the world of a kind-hearted prostitute-addict in Mexico City. A certain aura of sweetness and near insipidity deprived the book of the saving flavor of some of Kerouac's other work. Both John O'Hara (*Ourselves to Know*) and Harper Lee (*To Kill a Mockingbird*) attained considerable commercial success, while Ezra Pound, literary god-devil of half a century, published the latest installment, *Thrones,* of his distinctly uncommercial poem, *Cantos,* an epic obscurity. Musical obscurity was not without its airing as Richard Strauss' *Die Frau ohne Schatten,* a gigantic operatic-symbolic music-drama replete with strange people, flying fish, and splitting beds, was performed

SCIENCE; INDUSTRY; ECONOMICS; EDUCATION; RELIGION; PHILOSOPHY.	SPORTS; FASHIONS; POPULAR ENTERTAINMENT; FOLKLORE; SOCIETY.

Nov. 18 The development of a 220-lb. nuclear reactor designed to provide **electrical power for space vehicles** was made public by the U.S. Atomic Energy Commission.

Nov. 19 It was announced that U.S.S.R. and U.S. scientists had held preliminary talks on a plan to cooperate in **space exploration.**

Nov. 22 The U.S. Chamber of Commerce predicted a steady rise of **prosperity** in 1960. An annual productivity rate of $525 billion was predicted.

Dec. 15 **John L. Lewis** announced that he would resign as president of the United Mine Workers early in 1960, the year of his 80th birthday.

Dec. 28 Stimulation of the **U.S. rate of growth** by considerable alterations in federal economic policies was recommended by the U.S. joint congressional economic committee.

Dec. 30 The **1st U.S. nuclear submarine** capable of carrying and launching missiles was commissioned at Groton, Conn.

Dec. 12 The Sebring (Fla.) Grand Prix, auto racing classic, was won by Bruce McLaren of New Zealand. Driving a Cooper-Climax, he drove 218.4 miles in 2 hr. 12 min. 36.6 sec.

Dec. 16 **Roger Touhy,** 61, was shot and killed on the steps of his sister's home in Chicago. Touhy, a former underworld figure, had only recently been released from Stateville (Mich.) prison.

Dec. 18 The **Bert Bell award** for the outstanding National Football League player of 1959 was given to John Unitas, quarterback for the Baltimore Colts.

Dec. 19 The **last veteran** of the American Civil War, Walter Williams, died in Houston, Tex., at the age of 117.

Dec. 27 The **Baltimore Colts** retained the National Football League Championship by defeating the New York Giants 31–16.

1960

The United States achieved considerable space progress by launching 17 space satellites and probes. Of the more spectacular of the objects hurled into space by the U.S. were: Tiros I, which took 22,952 pictures of the earth cloud cover; Discoverer XIII, whose capsule was the first orbited object ever returned to earth; and Discoverer XIV, whose capsule was caught in mid-air at an altitude of 8,500 feet. In some other areas the United States was not so fortunate. The national economy was showing some symptoms of instability both in the dangerous outflow of gold that prompted the government to curtail foreign spending by military personnel, and also in the maintenance of a high rate of unemployment. The government continued its fight for Southern school integration; but progress was token, some public schools remaining closed, and marred by

Floyd Patterson, using a conglomerate boxing style, became the first man in history to regain the heavyweight championship of the world. In an exciting and evenly matched bout in the New York Polo Grounds, Patterson knocked out Ingemar Johansson in the fifth round of a scheduled 15-round fight. Another famous fighter, 40-year-old Sugar Ray Robinson, failed to regain the middleweight title as he fought to a draw with middleweight champion Gene Fullmer, and lost twice to Paul Pender. Boxing, in general, was under fire and under congressional investigation to determine the nature and extent of underworld influence on the sport. Congress also investigated the practice of "payola" in the recording and broadcasting industries. The investigation, which included questioning of Dick Clark, teen idol, culminated in the arrest of Alan Freed

POLITICS AND GOVERNMENT; WAR;
DISASTERS; VITAL STATISTICS.

BOOKS; PAINTING; DRAMA;
ARCHITECTURE; SCULPTURE.

stature. These events played a definite and perhaps decisive role in the Nov. elections, which changed the political rule of the White House by electing John F. Kennedy President. The election, which involved one of the most colorful campaigns and closest votes in U.S. political history, reflected the heightening of concern and divergencies of opinion in the U.S. public which historically characterize such turbulent and hectically dynamic times.

Jan. 2 **U.S. manned space flight projects** were, according to the *New York Times*, Jan. 2 and 5, being hampered and curtailed by increased cost and budget restrictions.

Jan. 3 Sen. John F. Kennedy announced that he would be a **candidate for the Democratic presidential nomination.** Sen. Kennedy also stated that he would not be interested in the vice-presidency.

Jan. 6 **A trip to various Latin American countries by Pres. Eisenhower** was announced by the White House. Among the countries to be visited were Brazil, Argentina, Chile, and Uruguay. The President's departure was scheduled for Feb. 23.

Jan. 7 In his State of the Union message, Pres. Eisenhower said that **prospects of improvement in East-West relations** were somewhat greater in view of "recent Soviet deportment."

Jan. 9 Vice-President Richard M. Nixon announced his **candidacy for the Republican presidential nomination.** He stated that he would begin his campaign Jan. 15 in Florida.

Jan. 11 The United States issued a **stiff protest to Cuba** regarding Cuban appropriation and confiscation of U.S. property. The note was delivered by U.S. Ambassador Philip W. Bonsal in Havana and was rejected by the Cuban government the same day.

Jan. 18 The Japanese and U.S. governments signed the explosively controversial **mutual security treaty.** Among other pledges, the treaty stated that both

in San Diego. The music season was, however, more significantly and tragically marked by the deaths of renowned musicians, Ernst von Dohnanyi, Dimitri Mitropoulos, Jussi Bjoerling, and Leonard Warren.

Jan. 4 **U.S. military prowess and competency was described as dangerously diminishing** by Gen. Maxwell D. Taylor in his book, *The Uncertain Trumpet.* Gen. Taylor, former U.S. Army Chief of Staff, resigned in 1959, stating as his reason the Defense Department's failure to follow his recommendations for the reappraisal and modernization of the Army.

Jan. 4 **Errol Flynn's autobiography,** *My Wicked, Wicked Ways,* was published posthumously. The book proved to be one of the most popular of several such works in recent years.

Jan. 6 The donation of **Billy Rose's modern sculpture collection** to the newly completed National Museum in Jerusalem, Israel, was made public. Among the sculptors represented in the collection were Rodin, Maillol, Epstein, and Zorach.

Feb. 4 **Grant Moves South,** by Bruce Catton, was published. Reflecting the tremendous interest of the author and, indeed, of the literary world, in the Amer-

SCIENCE; INDUSTRY; ECONOMICS; EDUCATION; RELIGION; PHILOSOPHY.

SPORTS; FASHIONS; POPULAR ENTERTAINMENT; FOLKLORE; SOCIETY.

mob violence and vandalism such as that which errupted in the November integration attempts in New Orleans.

Jan. 2 Dr. John H. Reynolds of the University of California (Berkeley) has placed the **age of the solar system** at 4,950,000,000 yrs. His estimate was based on study and analysis of a meteorite that fell 41 yrs. previously near Richardton, N.D.

Jan. 4 The **longest steel strike** in the nation's history was settled when the steel companies and United Steel Workers agreed on a package wage increase.

Jan. 7 A new **world ocean diving record** was established when Lt. Donald Walsh and Jacques Piccard descended 24,000 ft. in the bathyscaph *Trieste*. The record dive was made in the Pacific Marianas trench, 60 miles from Guam, and was later surpassed when the *Trieste* made a dive of 37,800 ft.

Jan. 7 A **$200 million budget surplus** was predicted for 1960 by Pres. Eisenhower in his annual State of the Union message to Congress. The President stated that "1960 promises to be the most prosperous year in our history."

Jan. 9 Bishops and other leaders of the Protestant Episcopal Church approved some methods and instances of **birth control**. The approbation was limited to countries in which the population increase posed a definite threat to the general welfare.

Jan. 23 Dependence on **local governmental financing for education** was described as "unbusinesslike" by the National Education Association. Local governments provide 56%, state governments 40%, and federal government 4% of school funds.

Feb. 8–16 The AFL–CIO Executive Council blamed the Eisenhower Administration's **"19th-century budget policy"** for a recession they predicted would hit the United States in 1961.

and other disc jockeys on charges of "commercial bribery." And in California, a 12-year battle for life ended when Caryl Chessman, author and convicted sex attacker, was executed in the gas chamber at San Quentin.

Jan. 1 **Rose Bowl game,** Pasadena, Calif.: Washington defeated Wisconsin, 44–8.

Jan. 2 Brooklyn's 16-year-old chess wonder, Bobby Fischer, successfully defended the **U.S. chess championship** in a tournament in New York City.

Jan. 12 Dolph Schayes, of the Syracuse professional basketball team, reached a **15,013 point total** for his career. Schayes, famed for his rebounding ability, was the first player in NBA history to score more than 15,000 points.

Jan. 22 **The National Basketball Association all-star game** was won by the Eastern Division in a 125–115 victory over the West.

Jan. 22 Paul Pender defeated Sugar Ray Robinson in a 15-round split decision to gain world recognition as **middleweight boxing champion.**

Jan. 24 Richard Morrison, ex-convict awaiting trial for burglary, named 8 Chicago policemen as confederates. In the ensuing scandal and investigation, **17 policemen were suspended** for robbery, bribery, and burglary.

Jan. 25 **"Payola,"** offered or accepted, would bring a $500 fine and 1-year prison term in a law proposed by Pres. Donald H. McGannon of the Westinghouse Broadcasting Co., chairman of the Natl. Assn. of Broadcasters' TV code review board. The proposal followed extensive investigations

621

POLITICS AND GOVERNMENT; WAR; DISASTERS; VITAL STATISTICS.	BOOKS; PAINTING; DRAMA; ARCHITECTURE; SCULPTURE.

the U.S. and Japan would "maintain and develop . . . their capacities to resist armed attacks."

Feb. 22 Pres. Eisenhower in Puerto Rico began an extended **Latin American tour** which was scheduled to include Brazil, Argentina, Chile, and Uruguay.

Feb. 23 Senator Symington charged in the Senate that the "American people are being misled" concerning the **missile gap** between the U.S. and the U.S.S.R. Pres. Eisenhower vehemently denied the charge.

Feb. 25 A **plane collision** over Rio de Janeiro took the lives of 35 U.S. Navy men and 26 Brazilians.

Feb. 29 A filibuster designed to impede **civil rights legislation** was begun by 18 Southern Senators. Such civil rights filibusters had never been lost by the Southern minority in the past.

Mar. 7 Pres. Eisenhower, just returned from a **Latin American goodwill tour,** stated that U.S.–Latin American relations were better than ever before. He also mentioned that during the tour, Sec. of State Herter had held useful conferences with various Latin American leaders.

Mar. 16 Pres. **Eisenhower endorsed Vice-Pres. Nixon as his successor.** The President said that he would do whatever he could to further Nixon's chances for the presidency.

Mar. 17 The **explosion of an airborne Lockheed Electra** plane bound from Chicago to Miami killed 63 persons. The explosion occurred over Tell City, Ind.

Apr. 8 A **civil rights bill** was passed by the Senate, 71–18. Though the bill was the first civil rights legislation to survive a Southern filibuster, Sen. Joseph S. Clark (D-Pa.), an advocate of civil rights, said that his side had "suffered a crushing defeat" calling the bill "only a pale ghost of our hopes."

May 2 Pres. Eisenhower appealed to the U.S. public to exert their influence in persuading Congress not to cut his **foreign aid proposals.**

ican Civil War, the book deals with the 1861–63 campaign of U. S. Grant.

Feb. 11 A congressional hearing on **"payola"** and other deceptive practices in the broadcasting industry ended. Legislation was recommended for the legal curtailment of broadcasting activities not in the public interest.

Feb. 25 A new play by **Lillian Hellman,** *Toys in the Attic,* opened in New York at the Hudson Theater. The play received excellent reviews.

Feb. 26 A **Thurber Carnival:** *Sketches with Music* opened at the ANTA theater in New York City. The musical is based on the works of humorist James Thurber.

Mar. 4 **Leonard Warren,** renowned Metropolitan Opera baritone, died of a stroke while on stage. The 49-year-old singer had been with the Metropolitan since 1938.

Mar. 11 Publication of **Apologies to the Iroquois** by **Edmund Wilson.** This book, by the author of *Memoirs of Hecate*

SCIENCE; INDUSTRY; ECONOMICS; EDUCATION; RELIGION; PHILOSOPHY.

SPORTS; FASHIONS; POPULAR ENTERTAINMENT; FOLKLORE; SOCIETY.

Feb. 17 It was announced that a Defense Dept. study had been ordered of the possibility of using **unmanned seismic stations** for the detection of underground nuclear tests.

Feb. 25 Communist infiltration of the U.S. clergy in general and the National Council of Churches in particular was affirmed by Dudley C. Sharp, Air Force Sec., in his statement before the House Un-American Activities Committee.

Feb. 26 James R. Hoffa, pres. of the Teamsters Union, was **accused of "complete dishonesty"** with respect to his promise to eliminate gangster elements from the Teamsters Union. The charge was made by the Senate Select Committee on Improper Activities in the Labor or Management Field.

Mar. 11 The **third man-made object to be hurled into orbit around the sun,** Pioneer V, was launched by the United States from Cape Canaveral. The other two planetoids were the U.S. Pioneer IV and the U.S.S.R. Lunik I (Mechta).

Mar. 22 Incidence of **stomach cancer** was reported to be declining and that of **lung cancer** to be increasing by Dr. J. R. Heller, director of the National Cancer Institute.

Mar. 30 The Special Senate Committee on Unemployment cautioned that if more jobs were not created, **unemployment would be steadily increased** by the constant growth of the population.

Apr. 1 The first **weather satellite** was orbited by the U.S.; pictures of cloud cover were sent back to earth.

Apr. 2 The Cabinet Committee on Price Stability for Economic Growth predicted considerable **expansion of the U.S. economy** in the 1960's. The report was released by Pres. Eisenhower Apr. 16.

Apr. 9 *Southern School News* reported that in spite of the fact that the Supreme Court decision against segregation was in

into "payola" practices in the broadcasting industries.

Jan. 30 The $166,490 **Santa Anita Maturity** was won by C. T. Chenery's *First Landing* for $80,490. Eddie Arcaro was up in the racing classic run at Arcadia, Calif.

Jan. 30 U.S. figure skating championships were won in Seattle by: Carol Heiss, women's singles; David Jenkins, men's singles; Margie Ackles and Charles Phillips, Jr., dance pairs.

Feb. 7 Arnold Palmer, 30-year-old professional golfer, won the $100,000 **Palm Springs Desert Classic** for $12,000. In the same tournament, Joe Campbell won a special $50,000 prize for shooting a hole in one.

Feb. 11 Jack Paar, popular comedian, walked out of his late-night show in **protest of the NBC censoring** of one of his jokes of the night before. Later, at a meeting with network officials in Florida, Paar agreed to return to the program Mar. 7.

Feb. 14 The **Daytona International** 500-mile stock car race was won for $19,600 by Robert Johnson, driving a 1959 Chevrolet. The $88,245 race was run at Daytona Beach, Fla.

Feb. 18–28 Unofficial team championship of the 1960 Winter Olympics was won by the U.S.S.R. at Squaw Valley, Calif. Sweden was 2nd and the U.S. 3rd.

Feb. 23 Demolition of Ebbets Field, one-time home park of the Brooklyn Dodgers (now the Los Angeles Dodgers), was begun. An apartment project will replace the time-worn structure.

623

POLITICS AND GOVERNMENT; WAR;	BOOKS; PAINTING; DRAMA;
DISASTERS; VITAL STATISTICS.	ARCHITECTURE; SCULPTURE.

May 5 The **downing of an unarmed U.S. plane over Russian territory** on May 1 was announced by Soviet Premier Khrushchev. Khrushchev called the captured pilot of the plane, Francis Gary Powers, a spy and vowed that he would be put on trial. On May 7 the U.S. government admitted that the plane was on a spy mission.

May 9 It was announced that U.S. **U-2 flights similar to that one intercepted would be discontinued.** One of the reasons given was that the flights, if continued, would cause difficulty for some of our allies.

May 16 The U-2 spy plane incident was used by Soviet Premier Khrushchev to kill the **Paris Summit Conference.** An invitation for Pres. Eisenhower to visit the U.S.S.R. was canceled by Khrushchev.

June 4 The U.S. State Dept. accused the Cuban government of undertaking a **"campaign of slander" against the U.S.** The accusation was made in a note delivered to the Cuban Foreign Ministry in Havana.

June 16 Pres. **Eisenhower's trip to Japan was canceled** in view of the security risk created by Japanese riots.

June 26 At the completion of his **Far East goodwill tour,** Pres. Eisenhower supported his foreign policies and proclaimed his tour a success in spite of elimination of Japan from the schedule.

July 4 The **50-star U.S. flag,** made necessary by the admission of Hawaii to the Union, became official.

July 11 A U.S. RB-47 reconnaissance bomber was **shot down by a Soviet fighter.** The U.S.S.R. alleged that the U.S. plane was in Soviet air space at the time and accused the U.S. of a continuance of the espionage program revealed by the downing of a U-2 earlier in the year.

July 13 The **Democratic National Convention nominated Sen. John F. Kennedy for the presidency.** Kennedy was the second Roman Catholic in the party's history to be nominated for that office.

County, is concerned with the history and social spirit of the Iroquois.

Mar. 25 **Lady Chatterley's Lover** by D. H. Lawrence was ruled not obscene and therefore mailable by the U.S. Circuit Court of Appeals in New York. Chief Judge Charles E. Clark, alluding to Postmaster General Arthur E. Summerfield, asked, "Should a mature and sophisticated reading public be kept in blinders because a government official thinks reading certain works of power and literary value are not good for him?"

Mar. 31 Rave revues were accorded Gore Vidal's play, **The Best Man,** when it opened at the Morosco Theater in New York City. The play concerns a fight for the presidential nomination.

Apr. 11 It was announced by the **National Institute of Arts and Letters** that the Brunner Award ($1000 to an outstanding architect) would be given to **Louis Kahn** of Philadelphia.

Apr. 18 The annual $1000 **Rosenthal Award** for Painting (to a young, distinguished, and unknown artist) was given to Ann Steinbrocker.

June 5 **No High Ground** by Fletcher Knebel and Charles W. Bailey was published. This timely book concerns the advancement of the A-bomb to its use at Hiroshima and the residue of that use.

June 14 **Out of the Burning;** the story of Frenchy, a boy gang leader, by Ira Henry Freeman, was published. The book is a factual account of the activities of a New York gang and of its leader and his eventual reformation.

1954, only **6% of the schools in the South** had been integrated.

Apr. 13. A Thor-Able-Star rocket launched an experimental satellite, **Transit I-B.** The satellite, achieving an elliptical orbit 500 miles high, is expected to be of great use for navigational purposes.

Apr. 14 A **Polaris missile** was fired from under water in California for the first time.

Apr. 27 The National Council of the Protestant Episcopal Church reiterated a previous stand endorsing the **Negro "sit-ins"** in the South.

Apr. 28 **Marital sex relations** without procreative intentions were declared unsinful by leaders of the 100th General Assembly of the Southern Presbyterian Church.

May 10 The *U.S.S. Triton,* nuclear submarine, completed the **first undersea voyage around the world.** The *Triton* was the largest submarine in the world.

May 15 A Tax Foundation report stated that most Americans paid approximately 25% of their earnings in federal, state, and local **taxes.**

May 20 The U.S. set a **world record** by firing an Atlas missile 9,000 miles to beyond the tip of Africa.

May 20 "When a public official is inescapably bound by the dogma and demands of his church, he cannot consistently separate himself from these," stated the Southern Baptist Convention in Miami Beach in a resolution decrying the **election of Roman Catholics** to public office.

May 21 **Human sperm** was reported to exist in two varieties: one with round heads, producing male babies, and the other with oval heads, producing female babies. The disclosure was made by Dr. Landrum B. Shettles, assistant clinical professor of obstetrics and gynecology, Columbia University.

Feb. 24 According to a Census Bureau estimate, the **population of the United States** had reached 179,245,000 by Jan. 1, 1960.

Mar. 7 **KKK carved on his chest,** beaten with tire chains, Felton Turner, a 27-year-old Houston, Tex., Negro was hung upside down in an oak tree. Turner had been abducted by 4 masked youths who explained that their actions were related to the sit-down strikes of Texas Southern University Negro students.

Mar. 25 **Wilt Chamberlain, Negro pro basketball star, retired** from professional basketball. Though he decried the rough opposition tactics, he admitted that racial difficulties had influenced his decision. Chamberlain relented later in the year and signed another pro basketball contract.

Apr. 29 Dick Clark, one of the nation's best paid and most powerful disc jockeys, denied any implication in **"payola"** payments. Clark stated before the Special House Subcommittee on Legislative Oversight, "I believe in my heart that I have never taken 'payola.' "

May 2 After 12 years of avoiding the death penalty, **Caryl Chessman was executed** in San Quentin Prison, Calif.

May 12 The Lockheed Aircraft Corp. announced that a structural deficiency had caused the **Electra crashes** in Sept., 1959 and Mar., 1960. Cost of correcting the deficiency was estimated at $25 million.

May 19 Alan Freed, originator of the term "rock 'n roll" and the person who popularized the teen craze, was arrested on charges of commercial bribery. 7 other persons involved in **"payola"** scandals were also arrested.

May 30 The 44th **500-mile race at the Indianapolis Speedway** was won by Jim

| POLITICS AND GOVERNMENT; WAR; DISASTERS; VITAL STATISTICS. | BOOKS; PAINTING; DRAMA; ARCHITECTURE; SCULPTURE. |

July 25 The **Republican National Convention nominated Vice-Pres. Richard M. Nixon for the presidency.** Nixon was virtually unchallanged for the nomination, although Sen. Barry Goldwater did receive 10 votes when his name was put into nomination against his wishes.

Aug. 19 Francis Gary Powers, pilot of the U-2 spy plane shot down in Russia, was sentenced by the Russians to 10 years' "deprivation of freedom."

Aug. 26 The **AFL–CIO endorsed Sen. John F. Kennedy** and his Democratic ticket for President. Kennedy was described by the labor leaders as "intelligent, articulate, and forceful."

Sept. 9–12 30 persons were killed and heavy damage done as **Hurricane "Donna,"** most destructive in U.S. Weather Bureau history, ravaged the U.S. Atlantic Coast from Florida to New England.

Sept. 12 In a speech in Houston, Tex., Sen. John F. Kennedy stated that his **actions as President would be solely dictated by the public welfare** rather than by the Roman Catholic hierarchy. Kennedy stated that he would resign "if the time should ever come . . . when my office would require me to either violate my conscience or violate the national interest."

Sept. 26 The first of a series of **television debates** between Vice-Pres. Nixon and Sen. John F. Kennedy took place in Chicago, Ill.

Oct. 10–12 Ex-Pres. **Harry S. Truman** was reported to be **campaigning vigorously for Sen. John F. Kennedy** in the 1960 presidential campaign. Various reports stated that Truman had said that Vice-Pres. Nixon "never told the truth in his life," told a San Antonio audience that if they voted for Nixon "you ought to go to hell," and responded to an apology demand for his San Antonio remark by saying, "Tell 'em to go to hell."

Oct. 20 The U.S. State Dept. placed an **embargo on exports to Cuba.** Some medicines and foods were excluded from this embargo.

July 11 **To Kill a Mockingbird** by Harper Lee was published. The novel concerns the story of two Southern children, whose father, a lawyer, defends a Negro.

Aug. 2 **The Liberal House,** a volume of essays by John Kenneth Galbraith was published. It details the author's views on the advancement and improvement of the U.S. economic situation.

Aug. 8 **All Fall Down,** a novel of adolescence by James Leo Herlihy, was published.

Sept. 19 **Countdown for Decision** by Maj. Gen. John B. Medaris was published. The book criticized the U.S. missile and space programs and accused Pres. Eisenhower of being somewhat behind the times in his military knowledge and thinking.

Sept. 20 *The Hostage* by **Brendan Behan** opened at the Cort Theater in New York City to good reviews and a delighted audience, ever aware of the author's presence in New York and of his famed interruptions of his own plays.

Sept. 26 Publication of **John Hersey's** *The Child Buyer,* a brilliant novel con-

SCIENCE; INDUSTRY; ECONOMICS; EDUCATION; RELIGION; PHILOSOPHY.

SPORTS; FASHIONS; POPULAR ENTERTAINMENT; FOLKLORE; SOCIETY.

May 24 Midas II, a 5,000-lb. satellite designed to act as an **early warning system** against surprise missile attacks, was launched from Cape Canaveral, Fla.

May 31 The Joint Commission on Mental Illness and Health stated that 25% of all Americans have at one time or another been sufficiently **mentally disturbed** to require professional advice.

June 2–13 After an Actors' Equity strike against one theater, all 22 Broadway legitimate **theaters closed.** The strike, the first since 1919, ended on June 13.

June 6 According to the American Heart Association, **coronary death rates in middle-aged men** "were found to be from 50% to 150% higher among heavy cigarette smokers" than among nonsmokers.

July 3 Cuban Premier Castro's anti-U.S. policies resulted in a severe cut in the quota of **Cuban sugar exports** to the United States.

July 7 The Modern Language Association criticized the **low requirements for language teaching** in the U.S. public schools. In a report to the U.S. Office of Education, the Association pointed out that Kansas was the only state that offered special certification to instructors proficient in the languages they taught.

July 20 An atomic submarine, the *U.S.S. George Washington,* accomplished the first successful launching of **Polaris missiles** from a submerged craft. The missiles were fired 1,150 miles.

Aug. 3 The first 2-way phone conversation in which **voices were bounced off the moon** was held by U.S. scientists.

Aug. 4 The X-15 experimental U.S. rocket plane set a **world air speed record** of 2,196 mph. The plane was piloted by Joseph A. Walker, civilian test pilot.

Aug. 11 The **first payload recovered from orbit** was lifted from the Pacific ocean by a U.S. helicopter. The capsule was orbited by Discoverer XIII Aug. 10.

Rathmann of Miami. Completing the course in 3 hr. 36 min. 11.36 sec., with an average speed of 138.757 mph, Rathmann won $110,000.

June 18 **The U.S. Open golf championship** was won by Arnold Palmer. The tournament was played in Denver, Col.

June 20 By a knockout of **world heavyweight boxing champion,** Ingemar Johansson, Floyd Patterson became the first fighter in boxing history to lose and then regain the heavyweight championship.

July 13 The **baseball all-star series** was won by the National League. Walter Alston managed the National League team; Al Lopez managed the American League team.

July 13 The **Powder Puff Derby** (women's transcontinental air race) was won by Mrs. Aileen Saunders. She flew 2,709 miles in 18 hr. 27 min.

Aug. 12 A Troy, Mich., cemetery **rejected the body of Winnebago Indian** George V. Nash because he was not white. Nash, a World War I veteran, was buried in Pontiac, Mich., after his family refused to permit burial in Arlington National Cemetery.

Aug. 28 The U.S. tennis men's **doubles championship** was won by Roy Emerson and Neale A. Fraser of Australia. The women's championship was won by Darlene R. Hard of Calif. and Maria Esther Bueno of Brazil.

Sept. 10 Nancy Anne Fleming, 18, from Michigan, was crowned **"Miss America"** at the annual pageant in Atlantic City, N.J.

Oct. 3 U.S. narcotics agents confiscated **$3½ million worth of heroin** (110

627

| POLITICS AND GOVERNMENT; WAR; DISASTERS; VITAL STATISTICS. | BOOKS; PAINTING; DRAMA; ARCHITECTURE; SCULPTURE. |

Oct. 29 16 members of the California State Polytechnic College football team were killed when their plane crashed shortly after take-off. A total of 22 were killed in the Arctic Pacific Line crash.

Nov. 8 John Fitzgerald Kennedy, Sen. (D. Mass.), **was elected President** of the United States. Kennedy was the 2nd-youngest man ever to win the nation's highest office. Lyndon Baines Johnson, Sen. (D. Tex.), was elected Vice-President.

Nov. 15 The 1960 census indicated the population of the U.S. had undergone a sufficient shift to necessitate an **alteration in the number of House seats** for each of 25 states.

Dec. 12 President-Elect Kennedy announced the appointment of David Dean Rusk as **Secretary of State.**

Dec. 16 The worst **air disaster** in the history of aviation occurred when a United Air Lines DC-8 jet and a Trans-World Airlines Lockheed Super-Constellation collided in a fog over New York Harbor; 132 died as a result of the crash.

Dec. 28 Completion of the **presidential popular vote** count showed that Kennedy won 49.7% and Nixon 49.6% of the popular votes counted, making the election one of the closest in history.

concerning the attempts of a corporation to purchase a male child.

Sept. 30. The Waste Makers by Vance Packard was published. The book is a penetrating study of U.S. market economics.

Oct. 8 Rave reviews greeted the opening of **An Evening with Mike Nichols and Elaine May** at the St. James Theater. The entire show was written and played by the two performers.

Oct. 26 Publication of Maurice Zolotow's **Marilyn Monroe,** a biographical anatomy of the irrepressible actress.

Oct. 31 It was announced in New York that Karel Appel had been selected to receive the 1960 **Guggenheim international art award** ($10,000) for his abstract painting *Woman with Ostrich.*

1961

John F. Kennedy was inaugurated President of the U.S. in a year that provided many explosive and dangerous situations to try the intellect and administrative ability of the nation's youthful President. In the field of foreign policy and entanglements, Kennedy was met with a civil war in Laos, one in the Congo, and continued Russian threats and ultimatums in Berlin. In domestic areas the President's was by no means an easy task. Unemployment continued to be a major problem as Congress discarded the President's notion of job re-education. Congress also proved disappointing to the President when it ren-

Tropic of Cancer by Henry Miller became available in the U.S. after many years of prohibition on grounds of obscenity. Imported and reprinted by the same company that was responsible for the U.S. publication of *Lady Chatterley's Lover, Tropic of Cancer* encountered considerably less legal difficulty than did the D. H. Lawrence novel. If the U.S. literary scene was somewhat enhanced by the admission of Henry Miller to the union, it was sadly marred by the death of Ernest Hemingway, one of the country's greatest literary personalities. There was, perhaps, an element of mystery in a man ex-

SCIENCE; INDUSTRY; ECONOMICS; EDUCATION; RELIGION; PHILOSOPHY.	SPORTS; FASHIONS; POPULAR ENTERTAINMENT; FOLKLORE; SOCIETY.

Aug. 19 A 300-lb. space capsule ejected from Discoverer XIV was **snagged at an altitude of 10,000 ft.** by the U.S. Air Force.

Oct. 15 2,000 members of the AFL–CIO Oil, Chemical, and Atomic Workers International Union struck the Union Carbide Nuclear Co. The strike was ended Oct. 31 when a wage settlement was reached.

Oct. 18 **Heredity not dependent on genes** was reported observed by Dr. Tracy Sonneborn of Indiana University.

Nov. 3 Prof. Willard Frank Libby, of the University of California, received the $43,627 **Nobel prize in chemistry.**

Nov. 3 Prof. Donald A. Glaser, of the University of California, received the $43,627 **Nobel prize in physics.**

Nov. 16 In an effort to stop the **outflow of gold** from the U.S. and reduce U.S. balance-of-payments deficits, Pres. Eisenhower ordered curtailment of overseas spending wherever possible.

Nov. 18 The Chrysler Corp. made public its intention to **discontinue the manufacture of the De Soto** line. The De Soto had been manufactured by the company since 1928.

lbs.) and arrested 4 in one of the biggest raids in history. Among those arrested was the Guatemalan ambassador to Belgium, Mauricio Rosal.

Oct. 5–13 The **World Series** was won by the Pittsburgh Pirates, defeating the New York Yankees 4 games to 3.

Oct. 8 The P.G.A. designated Arnold Palmer the **professional golfer of the year.**

Oct. 17 **Charles Van Doren,** former star contestant on TV's quiz show "21," and 13 others connected with the quiz show scandal were arrested on charges of perjury based on original statements that the quiz shows involved had not provided questions and answers.

Oct. 18 Manager of the New York Yankee baseball team, **Casey Stengel, was fired.** Although the official announcement was that Stengel had reached retirement age, the manager of the N.Y. Yankees since 1949 attributed his dismissal to a controversy with the owners of the club.

Nov. 17 New Orleans was the scene of the worst **anti-integration riots** since the initiation of school integration there. 194 people were arrested.

1961

This was the year for space, as two Americans and two Russians invaded the frontier of the future. Although the U.S. was unable to equal the impressive Soviet feat of putting men into orbit, it did manage to propel two men to the threshold of space and then recover them safely. The U.S. also launched a highly impressive series of earth satellites and space probes, mostly designed to transmit space data to earth. Progress of a different and much slower sort was being made in the much-discussed area of civil rights in educational facilities. Court after court voided and upheld various state laws designed to

In Miami Beach the frantic fists of Floyd Patterson proved their efficiency again in a close but quick battle with Ingemar Johansson. Patterson withstood the power of the Swedish ex-champion's savage right hand to score a knockout, the second in a row for the Rockville Centre heavyweight. In New York, Jack Paar, popular clown-conversationalist for night-owls, fought a lengthy public battle with Ed Sullivan, columnist and MC, when Sullivan threatened to pay Paar show entertainers the minimum that Paar paid. The feud contributed to the momentum of Paar vs. the press, a battle of months and intensity.

dered no substantial aid to U.S. education and only an impotent civil rights bill. Congress did, however, manage to sustain the longest filibuster on record and enact elaborate "payola" legislation. The year was, in short, as many recent years have been: full of dangerous situations for the whole world and tempests in teapots for various segments of it, both met by customary and frequently misplaced moments of hysteria, disinterest, and amusement.

Jan. 3 **U.S. broke diplomatic relations with Cuba.** The break came as the climax to a long series of mutual antagonisms, the last of these being Cuba's demand that the U.S. reduce its Havana embassy staff to 11 members.

Jan. 6 20 persons died as the result of a **fire in the Thomas Hotel** in San Francisco.

Jan. 20 John F. Kennedy was **inaugurated the 35th President** of the U.S. Earl Warren administered the oath that made Kennedy the first Roman Catholic and the youngest President of the U.S.

Mar. 3 **Legalized prostitution,** lotteries, and off-track betting were urged by a grand jury of 13 women and 8 men in Philadelphia.

Mar. 8 Concern was voiced in the Senate over the spread of the **John Birch Society,** an ultraconservative, secret society dedicated to fighting Communism with Communism's own means. The society has named Harry S. Truman, Franklin D. Roosevelt, John Foster Dulles, Dwight D. Eisenhower, and other key political figures as members of the Communist movement.

Mar. 13 Mrs. Elizabeth Gurley Flynn, 70, was named to succeed Eugene Dennis as **national chairman of the U.S. Communist Party.** She was the first woman to fill the office.

Apr. 3 Calling the **Castro regime a "Soviet satellite,"** the U.S. government

pert in the use of firearms accidentally killing himself while cleaning a shotgun, but the loss was no less great. A notable literary year was further colored by two new productions from established novelists of high repute: *The Winter of Our Discontent* by John Steinbeck and *Franny and Zooey* by J. D. Salinger. Both works served to bolster the standing of their authors. The musical events of the season were as colorful and spectacular as the literary events. Joan Sutherland made an impressive U.S. debut at the Metropolitan Opera, in which she displayed the tremendous capacity for combining agility, color, and volume of sound with subtle musicianship. Equally impressive but far from a debut was a tremendous New York recital series by pianist Artur Rubinstein. Playing 10 Carnegie Hall recitals within 40 days, Rubinstein, at 72, announced joyfully that he had decided *not* to make the series his "final touch."

Webster's Third New International Dictionary (Unabridged) was published. The new dictionary was greeted with a mixed response. Many linguists objected to its refusal to set standards of English and felt that too much valuable old material had been omitted to make way for new.

"Lost" recordings of **Dinu Lipatti** were released. Both performances—Mozart's *Concerto No. 21* and Enesco's *Sonata No. 2*—were amateur tapes of broadcast concerts. Discovery and issuance of the recordings was warmly received by the music world, which had long lamented the lack of recordings by the famous pianist who died at the age of 33.

630

SCIENCE; INDUSTRY; ECONOMICS; EDUCATION; RELIGION; PHILOSOPHY.

SPORTS; FASHIONS; POPULAR ENTERTAINMENT; FOLKLORE; SOCIETY.

prevent school integration. Even though individual civil rights battles were being won, actual integration was sluggish and colored by sporadic violence such as that occurring during the "Freedom Rides." Education as a whole became more and more a cause for concern as it became increasingly evident not only that present educational facilities were inadequate and growing more so but also that the quality of instruction in many areas left much to be desired.

Jan. 28 The U.S. State Department made public plans for the initiation of the **"Peace Corps"** project of Pres. Kennedy.

Jan. 30 Pres. Kennedy, in his first State of the Union message, decried the **crisis in U.S. education,** mentioning that there was an excess of 2 million children being instructed by 90,000 teachers "not properly qualified."

Jan. 31 The U.S. shot a 37½-lb. **chimpanzee into space** and recovered him successfully. The Project Mercury rocket containing the animal traveled 5,000 mph to a height of 155 miles.

Feb. 6–7 29 top manufacturers of electrical equipment were found guilty of **price fixing** and bid rigging by U.S. District Judge J. Cullen Ganey. The penalties exacted included 30 jail sentences, 23 of which were suspended, and $1,924,500 in fines.

Feb. 9 Dr. Luis W. Alvarez of the University of California received the $5,000 **Albert Einstein Award** for contributions to physical theory.

Feb. 9. It was revealed that Vanguard I and II had provided photographic grounds for calculations revealing that the **earth is a "slightly irregular ellipsoid."**

Feb. 18 **Discoverer XXI** was launched into orbit by a Thor-Agena-B rocket. An unusual feature of the shot was a control mechanism which permitted the rocket's engine to be restarted while in orbit.

Feb. 22–23 **Birth control** as a means of family limitation was endorsed by the

Another battle of some interest was that of Sugar Ray Robinson for the middleweight boxing championship of the world. Ex-champion Robinson fought frequently and diligently to regain his lost crown, but was unable to muster the fire and KO's responsible for his past greatness. And there was also Newton Minow, FCC head, who, asserting that TV was a "wasteland" and that the nation's needs were more important than the nation's tastes, began a violent assault on TV violence.

Jan. 1 Washington defeated Minnesota 17–7 in the annual **Rose Bowl** football game in Pasadena, Calif.

Jan. 2 Bobby Fischer, 17-year-old **chess champion,** defeated Paul Benko, Hungarian Grand Master, to assure himself the U.S Chess Championship, his fourth.

Jan. 23 The U.S. Supreme Court ruled constitutional a controversial Chicago, Ill., **ordinance forbidding the showing of any motion picture** without permission of the city censors.

Feb. 1 Edward L. Bernays announced that a poll of 276 newspapers had voted the *New York Times* the **best daily newspaper** in the U.S.

Feb. 25 Northrup R. Knox defended the **U.S. Amateur Tennis Championship** by defeating Jimmy Bostwick. Earlier in the year he retained the U.S. Open Championship with his defeat of Jimmy Dunn.

Feb. 25 The $145,000 **Santa Anita Handicap** was won by *Prove It* for $100,000. Willie Shoemaker was up.

Mar. 13 Floyd Patterson retained the **heavyweight championship of the world** when he knocked out Ingemar Johansson in the 6th round of a bout in Miami Beach, Fla.

| POLITICS AND GOVERNMENT; WAR; DISASTERS; VITAL STATISTICS. | BOOKS; PAINTING; DRAMA; ARCHITECTURE; SCULPTURE. |

urged Cuba to separate itself from the Communist movement.

Apr. 24 Pres. Kennedy stated that he accepted full responsibility for the abortive **Cuban invasion.** In his statement of Kennedy's position, Pierre Salinger, White House Press Sec., said that the President opposed anyone's "attempting to shift the responsibility."

Apr. 27 In a message sent to Congress, Pres. Kennedy said the "ultimate answer to **ethical problems in government** is honest people in a good ethical environment."

May 16–17 Pres. and Mrs. Kennedy paid a **2-day visit to Canada.** The President urged Canada to augment its "hemispheric role" in aid to underdeveloped countries and in the strengthening of NATO.

May 25 Pres. Kennedy read his **second State of the Union message.** The President urged the U.S. to "take a clearly leading role in space achievements," and asked for $1.8 billion for space and other programs.

June 3–4 **Pres. Kennedy and Soviet Premier Khrushchev met** in Vienna for discussions of major world problems. The major topics discussed were Laos, Germany, and disarmament.

June 22 Returning to Washington after an 18-day **goodwill tour to 10 South American countries,** U.S. Amb. to UN Adlai Stevenson stated that "popular discontent" had grown and governmental "stability" had diminished since his 1960 South American tour.

July 8 Pres. Kennedy ordered a **reappraisal and review of U.S. military prowess.** The action was generally attributed to the pressures of the Berlin crisis and of increased U.S.S.R. military expenditures.

July 14 The 3rd week in July was designated by Pres. Kennedy **"Captive Nations Week."** The captive nations week resolution had been adopted by Congress in 1959.

July 19 Pres. Kennedy urged the bolstering and improvement of "all programs

The New York City Opera opened its fall season with Pucinni's **Il Trittico.** This operatic trilogy comprises three one-act operas: *Il Tabarro, Suor Angelica,* and *Gianni Schicchi.* Although *Gianni Schicchi* has attained considerable popularity as an individual production, *Il Trittico,* as a whole, is rarely performed.

Pulitzer Prizes: novel, *To Kill a Mockingbird* by Harper Lee; drama, *All the Way Home* by George Ault Mosel, Jr.; history, *Between War and Peace: The Potsdam Conference* by Herbert Feis; biography, *Charles Sumner and the Coming of the Civil War* by David Donald; poetry, *Times Three: Selected Verse from Three Decades* by Phyllis McGinley; music, *Symphony No. 7* by Walter Piston.

Mar. *Mary, Mary,* a play by writer-wit **Jean Kerr** opened at the Helen Hayes Theater in New York to good reviews.

Mar. 17 *The Agony and the Ecstasy,* a novel by **Irving Stone** based on the life of Michelangelo, was published.

Mar. 19 A 4-year grant of $244,000 was announced by the **Ford Foundation** to "stimulate communication among the various branches of the American theater."

Apr. 16 **The Antoinette Perry (Tony) Awards** for "achievement" in New York theater were announced. Winners included Jean Anouilh, for his play *Becket,* Zero Mostel, for his performance in *Rhinoceros,* and Joan Plowright for her performance in *A Taste of Honey.*

Apr. 30 The award of $1,350,000 in fellowships to 265 scholars, scientists and artists was announced by the **John Simon Guggenheim Memorial Foundation.**

July 2 **Ernest Hemingway,** 61, died of a gunshot wound in the head. His wife claimed that he had shot himself accidentally while cleaning a shotgun. Among Hemingway's more famous novels are *The Old Man and the Sea, The Sun Also Rises,* and *A Farewell to Arms.*

Aug. 19 **Aaron Copland** received the Edward MacDowell Medal for major con-

SCIENCE; INDUSTRY; ECONOMICS; EDUCATION; RELIGION; PHILOSOPHY.

SPORTS; FASHIONS; POPULAR ENTERTAINMENT; FOLKLORE; SOCIETY.

National Council of Churches at a meeting in Syracuse, N.Y.

Feb. 23 The **most costly airline strike in aviation history** ended. The strike had completely shut down Trans-World, Eastern, Flying Tiger, American, and National airlines and had hampered operations of several others.

Mar. 2 It was announced that the **projected U.S. space exploration** efforts will in a 10-year period include 12 space probes to the moon and 5 to Mars and Venus.

Apr. 27 A Juno II rocket orbited the 95-lb. **Explorer XI** satellite. Carrying a "lensless telescope," the satellite's function was to determine the nature of interstellar matter.

Apr. 30 72% of elementary and high school teachers approve the "judicious use of **corporal punishment** as a disciplinary measure."

May 4 2 Navy scientists **ascended a record 113,500 ft.** in a 411-ft. balloon called "Stratolab High No. 5." A mishap occurred when one of the balloonists was drowned as he fell from the sling of the helicopter that had picked him up.

May 5 Pres. Kennedy signed into law a bill raising the **minimum wage** from $1 to $1.25 and expanding coverage to include 3,624,000 workers not covered previously.

May 5 **Sub-orbital space flight** was achieved by U.S. Navy Cmndr. Alan Bartlett Shepard, Jr. The flight was accomplished by means of a 2,300-lb. Project Mercury capsule called "Freedom 7."

June 6 A plan for the mass and general **detection of heart defects in children** was announced perfected by the Chicago Heart Assoc. The plan involves recording the heart sounds of children on hi-fidelity tapes which are later read by cardiologists.

June 16 **Discoverer XXV** was launched, its capsule being ejected and recovered June 18. The satellite carried samples of

Mar. 25 The **world championship endurance auto race** in Sebring, Fla., was won by Phil Hill of Santa Monica, Calif., and Olivier Gendebien of Belgium, who shared the $1,500 prize.

May 6 The 87th annual **Kentucky Derby** was won by *Carry Back* for $120,000. Johnny Sellers was up in the $163,000 racing classic.

May 9 Newton N. Minow, Chrmn. of FCC, called TV **"a vast wasteland."** In a vehement criticism of TV programing, Minow said, "It is not enough to cater to the nation's whims—you must also serve the nation's needs. . . ."

May 14 White citizens of Anniston and Birmingham attacked 2 racially mixed groups of **"Freedom Riders"** on a bus tour from Washington to New Orleans.

May 30 The $383,000, 45th **Indianapolis Speedway Memorial Day 500-mile race** was won by A. J. Foyt, Jr., for $111,400.

June 5 The $148,650 **Belmont Stakes** was won by *Sherluck* for $104,900. Braulio Baeza was the jockey.

June 9 4 ex-college basketball players and 17 current players were accused of bribery in connection with a college basketball **"point shaving"** plot. Gamblers Aaron Wagman and Joseph Hacken were accused as co-conspirators.

June 10 Archie Moore retained the **world light-heavyweight championship** by defeating Giulio Rinaldi in a 15-round decision. The title is recognized in New York, Massachusetts, California, the British Commonwealth, and Europe.

June 16–17 The 40th annual **National Collegiate Athletic track and field cham-**

633

POLITICS AND GOVERNMENT; WAR; DISASTERS; VITAL STATISTICS.

BOOKS; PAINTING; DRAMA; ARCHITECTURE; SCULPTURE.

which contribute to the **physical fitness of our youth."**

July 24 An **Eastern Air Lines Electra was hijacked** while flying from Miami to Tampa. The pilot of the plane was forced at gunpoint to Cuba. The plane was later entrusted to the UN Security Council, according to the Cuban government, to discourage the "imminent military aggression" of the U.S. against Cuba.

July 24 In a report of his recent **Latin American tour,** Adlai Stevenson, U.S. Amb. to UN, stated that the real danger of Soviet control of Cuba was to the Latin American democracies rather than to the U.S.

July 31–Aug. 1. Pres. Kennedy held talks with Gen. Chen Cheng, during which he promised that the **U.S. would uphold the rights of Nationalist China** to UN membership and oppose the admission of Communist China to UN membership.

Sept. 1 78 died in what was described as **U.S. commercial aviation's worst single plane crash** when a TWA Constellation crashed in Hinsdale, Ill., 4 minutes after take-off from Chicago's Midway Airport.

Sept. 4 Pres. Kennedy signed the 1961 **Foreign Assistance Act,** which authorized $4,253,500,000 for use in foreign military and economic programs.

Sept. 5 Pres. Kennedy signed into law a bill making punishable by death or imprisonment the crime of **airplane hijacking.** The law followed several such mid-air crimes.

Sept. 27 In announcing his **candidacy for the governorship of California,** Ex-Vice Pres. Nixon stated: "I shall not be a candidate for President in 1964."

Oct. 6 Pres. Kennedy stated that any "prudent family" should build or obtain a **shelter against fall-out** resulting from thermonuclear attack. He said that U.S.

tributions to American music. Pres. Kennedy called Copland "a significant force in the cultural life of this nation and the the world community."

Oct. Esquire Inc. announced that the October issue of **Coronet magazine** would be the last. The 25-year-old magazine had 2,310,000 subscribers but had steadily lost money for two years.

Oct. 2 – **Sinclair Lewis:** *An American Life* by Mark Schorer was published. This "official" biography of Sinclair Lewis, 814 pages in length, received good reviews, although it was criticized as being somewhat "excessive."

Oct. 12 **World, a national weekly newspaper** went on sale. Published in Washington, D.C., by Willard W. Garvey of Wichita, Kansas, had an initial circulation in about 100 U.S. cities.

Oct. 17 Grants of $1,470,000 for five new visual arts programs were announced by the **Ford Foundation.**

Oct. 23 **Spirit Lake** by MacKinlay Kantor was published. This massive novel (951 pp.), by the author of *Andersonville,* concerns frontier life in the 1850's, with emphasis on the relationships of the Indian and white populations.

Oct. 26 **The International Exhibition of Contemporary Painting and Sculpture** awarded $13,250 in prizes at the Carnegie Institute in Pittsburgh.

Oct. 31 The first $2,500 **Bollingen Translation Prize** was awarded to Robert Fitzgerald, Geneva, N.Y., poet, for his translation of Homer's Odyssey.

Nov. 15 The **Academy of American Poets** awarded its 1961 $5,000 fellowship to Horace V. Gregory for his "distinguished" achievements.

Nov. 15 A record price of $2,300,000 was paid by the N.Y. Metropolitan Museum of Art for **Rembrandt's masterpiece,** "Aristotle Contemplating the Bust of Homer." The painting was formerly in the

| SCIENCE; INDUSTRY; ECONOMICS; EDUCATION; RELIGION; PHILOSOPHY. | SPORTS; FASHIONS; POPULAR ENTERTAINMENT; FOLKLORE; SOCIETY. |

various minerals to determine how they would be affected by space conditions.

June 29   A 79-ft. Thor-Able-Star rocket accomplished the **launching of 3 satellites.** These satellites, Transit IV-A, Greb III, and Injun, comprised the first such triple launching in history.

June 30   Pres. Kennedy signed a bill **increasing the national debt limit** by $5 billion to a $289 limit for the fiscal year ending 1962.

July 3   A Taft-Hartley injunction was issued at the request of the U.S. Dept. of Justice, halting the 18-day **maritime strike.** According to the Justice Dept., the strike was "cutting the lifelines to Puerto Rico and Hawaii."

July 7   **James R. Hoffa** was re-elected president of the International Brotherhood of Teamsters by a tremendous vote of confidence. The election was held at the Teamsters' convention in Miami Beach, Fla.

July 21   Capt. Virgil Grissom, U.S. Air Force, became the **third known human in space** when he ascended to an altitude of 118 miles in a Mercury capsule.

July 28   Henry F. Garrett, psychologist and past president of the American Psychological Assoc., called the notion that all races are equal in ability potential, the **"scientific hoax of the century."** He stated that evidence tends to indicate that racial differences in mental ability are "innate and genetic."

Aug. 11   Pres. Kennedy signed into law a bill reducing the **value of duty-free goods** which travelers may bring into the country from $500 to $100.

Sept. 8   In a report in the *Journal* of the American Medical Association it was held that there was "statistical evidence" indicating a connection between **smoking and heart disease.**

Sept. 13   An **"artificial astronaut"** was orbited in a Project Mercury space capsule launched from Cape Canaveral.

pionships in Philadelphia were won by Southern California.

June 17   Gene Littler won the U.S. Open golf championship.

July 11   The National League defeated the American League, 5–4, in the first game of the annual **all-star baseball series.** The second game of the two-game series ended in a tie, 1–1, as the game was called because of rain at the end of the ninth inning.

July 29   *Ridan,* with Bill Hartack up, won the $211,750 **Arlington Futurity** in Chicago for $127,050.

July 30   Jerry Barber defeated Don January to win the **P.G.A. national golf championship** for $11,000.

Aug. 27   A Cuban campaign to seek sympathy and support among American Negroes had failed, according to **"Cuba and the American Negro,"** a U.S. Senate Internal Security Subcommittee report.

Sept. 22 $30,000,000 was authorized in a bill signed by Pres. Kennedy to fight **juvenile delinquency** in the U.S. The 3-year bill was passed by the House Aug. 30, and the Senate Sept. 11.

Nov. 6–9   447 homes, including some owned by famous Hollywood figures, were destroyed by **fire in the Bel Air–Brentwood suburbs** of Los Angeles. The fire was another of a series that has caused extensive damage in the 4-year California drought.

Nov. 15   Roger Maris of the N.Y. Yankees was designated **the most valuable player** of the year in the American League. Frank Robinson received the award for the National League on Nov. 22.

| POLITICS AND GOVERNMENT; WAR; DISASTERS; VITAL STATISTICS. | BOOKS; PAINTING; DRAMA; ARCHITECTURE; SCULPTURE. |

Civil Defense should provide such protection for every American.

Nov. 8 74 U.S. Army recruits were killed when a chartered Imperial Airlines Constellation crashed and burned near Richmond, Va. It was later revealed that the airline had previously been twice penalized for rules infractions.

Dec. 5 President Kennedy called for **"broad participation in exercise"** by the people of the United States. The President noted that 5 of 7 men called for the Army were rejected and complained that the U.S. was becoming a nation of "spectators" rather than a nation of "athletes."

private collection of the late Alfred W. Erickson and his wife.

Dec. 17 The gold medal and $5,000 first prize of the **Dimitri Mitropoulos International Music Competition** was won by Agustin Anievas of New York City.

Dec. 28 *West Side Story* was named the best film of the year by the **New York Film Critics.** *La Dolce Vita* was designated the best foreign film of the year while **Sophia Loren** (*Two Women*) and **Maximilian Schell** (*Judgment at Nuremberg*) received honors as best actress and actor.

1962

The Cuban crisis, created by the presence of Russian-built missiles and missile sites within the shadow of the U.S. mainland, constituted the nation's most serious potential military conflict. Pres. Kennedy's quarantine of the island and the display at the UN of photographic proof of the presence of weapons resulted in their withdrawal by Premier Khrushchev. The year also saw U.S. troops in Thailand, and military aid to India in its struggle against Communist China. There was an abatement in the tension over Berlin, although the Berlin wall remained. An interruption of nuclear-test-ban talks was followed by U.S. resumption of testing in the atmosphere. Pres. Kennedy made 298 specific legislative requests to Congress of which he was given only 44.3%. Granted the Trade Expansion Act, a tax-reform law, and new control of drugs, the President was awarded only $3.9 billion of the $4.8 billion requested for foreign aid and was defeated in his proposals for medical care for the aged under social security (medicare) and the establishment of a Cabinet-level Dept. of Urban Affairs and Housing. Pres. Kennedy met British Prime Minister

1962 was a year of disappointments in literature. Katherine Anne Porter's *Ship of Fools,* while treated politely by the critics, was not the masterpiece many had hoped for. *Letting Go,* Philip Roth's 1st novel after winning the National Book Award, was a distinct falling off in both style and content. James Baldwin, however, solidified his position as a leading force among young writers with *Another Country.* One of the year's most popular books was Joseph Heller's hilarious *Catch-22.* Action painting began to lose ground in the New York galleries as the interest of both the general public and collectors focused incredulously on "pop art," the depiction and sometimes the actual display of the most banal objects of American life: canned foods, electric appliances, comic strips, and the like. The "Century 21 Exposition" in Seattle, Wash., did not produce any buildings of real architectural merit, but the 600-foot "Space Needle" with a revolving restaurant on top was a popular attraction of the fair. An international art scandal broke when Canadian authorities questioned the genuineness of many of the paintings from Walter P. Chrysler's famous collection

636

SCIENCE; INDUSTRY; ECONOMICS; EDUCATION; RELIGION; PHILOSOPHY.	SPORTS; FASHIONS; POPULAR ENTERTAINMENT; FOLKLORE; SOCIETY.

NASA officials described the flight as "very successful."

Oct. 30 In a report published by 7 specialists, the "whole-word" method of reading instruction was decried as vastly inferior to the "phonic method." The report stated that the "whole-word" method had caused **reading retardation in 35% of American youths.**

Dec. 14 Secretary of Labor Arthur J. Goldberg made public the conclusion of a contract settlement between the Metropolitan Opera Association and Local 802 of the American Federation of Musicians. With the announcement of the settlement, Goldberg urged federal **aid to the performing arts.**

Nov. 19 It was reported that Michael Rockefeller, 23, son of Nelson Rockefeller, Gov. of N.Y., was **missing at sea** off the coast of New Guinea. Governor Rockefeller and his daughter, Mrs. Mary Rockefeller Strawbridge, flew to New Guinea to aid the unsuccessful search.

Dec. 4 **Floyd Patterson** remained **world heavyweight champion** by knocking out Tom McNeeley in the 4th round of a bout in Toronto, Canada.

Dec. 31 **The pro-championship of the National Football League** was won by The Green Bay Packers of the West defeating the New York Giants of the East.

1962

The U.S.'s "space year" included the launching of Telstar, a communications satellite, and the orbiting of 3 astronauts in perfect missions. Experimentation with nuclear submarines and with thermonuclear detonations in the atmosphere and below ground added to U.S. technological development. In the South, segregation in education at the university level was broken following mob violence and death. A Roman Catholic archbishop excommunicated 3 persons who protested against the desegregation of parochial schools in New Orleans. Official nondenominational prayers in public schools were held a constitutional infringement by the Supreme Court. Congress took no steps to assist financially the improvement of educational facilities for the nation's youth. In industry, an effort by steel-industry management to raise prices was successfully stopped by Pres. Kennedy. The AFL-CIO announced a drive to establish a 35-hour work week for the country. In the headlines were the merger of the nation's two largest railroads, and the creation by merger of the world's largest airline system. The value of shares on the New York Stock Exchange suffered the

Hollywood produced 1 large scale epic in *Lawrence of Arabia* that was also an artistic success. However, of the 200 movies released in the U.S. during the year, the 2 that caused the greatest sensation and provoked the most comment were French: Resnais' *Last Year at Marienbad* and Truffaut's *Jules et Jim.* TV watchers had a chance to compare symptoms with patients on "Dr. Kildare," "Ben Casey," "The Nurses," and "The Eleventh Hour." Situation comedies, however, dominated the evening hours on TV, the comical situations being in some cases World War II! In boxing Floyd Patterson lost his heavyweight crown to Sonny Listòn in less than 3 minutes. The New York Yankees turned an old trick by winning the World Series, their 20th. Arnold Palmer, who was voted P.G.A. "golfer of the year," bettered his own record by winning $81,000 in prize money. A national dance craze was the twist, which had its origin in a small New York night club known as The Peppermint Lounge. In women's fashions wigs became not only acceptable but popular. Boots, too, became a fashion accessory rather than a sometime necessity. The romance

Macmillan in Bermuda. With Mrs. Kennedy he received a warm reception on an official visit to Mexico. Among international figures who met with the President at the White House were Premier Ahmed Ben Bella of Algeria, Congolese Prime Minister Cyrille Adoula, Russian cosmonaut Gherman S. Titov, and Archbishop Makarios, president of Cyprus.

Jan. 12   State Dept. announced new regulations **denying passports to Communist Party members.**

Jan. 15   **U.S. removed its tank force from the Berlin wall** in an effort to improve relations in that city. 2 days later 12 Soviet tanks stationed near the wall since October 1961 were removed.

Jan. 29   **Nuclear-test-ban conference** of U.S., U.S.S.R., and Great Britain at Geneva adjourned after 353 sessions over 3-year period. Talks were deadlocked over monitoring system for international control.

Feb. 3   **A ban on almost all trade with Cuba,** effective Feb. 7, was ordered by Pres. Kennedy.

Feb. 8   Defense Dept. announced the creation of new U.S. military command in South Vietnam, to be known as **Military Assistance Command (MAC).**

Feb. 10   U-2 pilot **Francis Gary Powers was released** in Berlin by Russian authorities in exchange for Soviet spy **Rudolf Abel.** Another American, student Frederic L. Pryor, was released at the same time.

Feb. 14   Pres. Kennedy said that U.S. **troops in Vietnam** on training missions had been instructed to **fire to protect themselves** if fired upon, but were "not combat troops in the generally understood sense of the word."

Feb. 26   Supreme Court ordered a federal court in Mississippi to act on state segregation laws in travel terminals, holding that **no state could require racial segregation of interstate or intrastate transportation facilities.**

then on tour in Canada. The formation of the Citizens for Decent Literature kept the question of censorship in the news; 2 particular targets of this watchdog group were Harold Robbins' *The Carpetbaggers* and Henry Miller's *The Tropic of Capricorn.*

2 of the fastest-selling albums in the history of the recording industry were issued this year. In "The First Family," Vaughn Meader and others mimicked members of the Kennedy clan. "My Son, the Folk Singer" had Allan Sherman singing absurd parodies of folk songs ("Sarah Jackman, Sarah Jackman, how's by you?" to the tune of "Frère Jacques"; "The Catskill ladies sing this song," to "The Camptown Races").

In the controversial best seller *Silent Spring,* author-scientist Rachel Carson raised the possibility of a world made uninhabitable by the indiscriminate use of pesticides and other harmful chemicals. Her angry, well-documented book cited dozens of cases in which insecticides and chemical pollutants had seriously upset the balance of nature. It made an impassioned plea for strict curbs on the use of such poisons while their side effects were studied, and for research into alternate methods of controlling insects.

Jan. 20   Poet **Robinson Jeffers, 75,** died at Carmel, Calif. A tragic poet, basically at odds with "progress" and modern civilization, Jefferson dealt mainly with themes of timeless significance from the Bible and classical mythology. His greatest popular success was the poetic drama *Medea* (1947), a free adaptation of the Euripides play.

Jan. 29   **Fritz Kreisler,** a resident of the U.S. since 1940 and a citizen since 1943, died at age 86. Kreisler was 1 of the greatest violinists of his day; he had retired in 1950 after a career that spanned 62 years.

Feb. 19   The **boyhood home of Abraham Lincoln** in Lincoln City, Ind., was established as a national monument.

Feb. 26   Arthur Kopit's ingenious but

biggest drop since 1929 but rallied over-night.

Jan. 12   Directors of the 2 largest U.S. railroads—**Pennsylvania and New York Central**—approved their merger.

Jan. 16   U.S. and Common Market nations initialed an agreement for mutual **reduction of tariffs.**

Jan. 18   A **25-hour work week,** plus 5 hours overtime, was established when electrical workers concluded a contract with employers in New York after an 8-day strike.

Jan. 23   The **merger of American Airlines and Eastern Air Lines** was approved by their directors. Stockholders approved the creation of the world's biggest airline system in assets and revenue on Apr. 17.

Jan. 26   Ranger III, a rocket designed to transmit close-up **TV pictures of the moon** to earth before landing scientific instruments on its surface, was launched from Cape Canaveral. 2 days later it passed by the moon because of excessive velocity and went into orbit around the sun.

Feb. 14   The American Telephone & Telegraph Co. announced plans for an $84 million **underwater telephone cable** between Hawaii and Japan, via Midway, Wake, and Guam islands.

Feb. 20   Lt. Col. John Glenn **orbited the earth 3 times** in his space capsule *Friendship 7,* launched from Cape Canaveral. He was the 1st U.S. astronaut to achieve orbit.

Mar. 1   In the **biggest antitrust case** in history E.I. du Pont de Nemours & Co. was ordered by a federal district court to divest itself of 63 million shares of General Motors stock.

Mar. 4   U.S. Atomic Energy Commission announced that the 1st **atomic power plant in Antarctica** was in operation at McMurdo Sound.

Mar. 7   Pres. Kennedy told Congress

between Elizabeth Taylor and Richard Burton on the *Cleopatra* set in Rome was in and out of the headlines all year.

The country's **1st municipally-owned television station,** WNYC-TV, began operations in New York, which also received its 1st educational TV station, WNDT, which offers completely noncommercial programs, supported entirely by private donations. FCC chairman Newton Minow received a Peabody award for his efforts to "rescue the (television) wasteland from the cowboys and private eyes."

Maury Wills of the Dodgers was named **most valuable player in the National League.** Wills stole 104 bases in 165 games, breaking the major-league record set by Ty Cobb in 1915.

Academy Award winners for 1962: best film, *Lawrence of Arabia;* best actor, Gregory Peck (*To Kill a Mockingbird*); best actress, Anne Bancroft (*The Miracle Worker*); best director, David Lean (*Lawrence of Arabia*); best foreign-language film, *Sundays and Cybèle;* best supporting actor, Ed Begley (*Sweet Bird of Youth*); best supporting actress, Patty Duke (*The Miracle Worker*).

A survey by UPI showed that in the 24 states with legalized on-course betting, 33,-881,860 **horse racing fans** bet a total of $2,679,461,505. Attendance was up 1.28% over 1961, betting was up 5.57%. Mrs. Richard C. du Pont's *Kelso* was named "horse of the year" for the 3rd straight year. His earnings of $254,585 boosted his lifetime earnings to $1,011,940, and made him the 5th horse in racing history to top the $1 million mark.

Jan.   Christina Paolozzi, a 22-year-old model, **appeared in the nude in a full-page color ad** in *Harper's Bazaar.* The photograph, taken by high-fashion photographer Richard Avedon, caused a furor all over the U.S.

Jan. 1   In the **Rose Bowl,** Minnesota defeated U.C.L.A. 21–3; Alabama won 10–3 over Arkansas in the Sugar Bowl; Texas beat Mississippi 12–7 in the Cotton

Mar. 1 All **95 persons aboard a jetliner were killed** when the plane crashed into Jamaica Bay seconds after take-off from Idlewild International airport for flight to Los Angeles.

Mar. 19 The Justice Dept. filed a **civil suit in New York against the Communist Party** and 4 of its officials—Elizabeth Gurley Flynn, Gus Hall, Benjamin J. Davis, and Philip Bart—to collect $500,-000 in income taxes and interest for 1951.

Mar. 26 By a vote of 6 to 2 the Supreme Court held that the constitutionality of **distribution of seats in state legislatures was subject to the scrutiny of the federal courts.**

Apr. 3 Defense Dept. ordered full **racial integration in military reserve units** exclusive of National Guard.

Apr. 5 U.S. and Soviet army commanders in Berlin agreed on **resumption of normal relations** between their military missions.

Apr. 8 Cuba announced that 1,179 prisoners seized in the 1961 invasion were convicted of treason and sentenced to 30 years in prison. Officials offered to free all prisoners upon payment of **$62 million ransom.** 6 days later, 60 sick and wounded prisoners were returned to U.S. upon a promise to pay $2.5 million ransom.

Apr. 13 Under an agreement signed by U.S. and Brazil in Washington, $276 million in **Alliance for Progress** funds were allocated to be used for development of northeastern Brazil.

Apr. 25 U.S. **resumed nuclear testing** in the atmosphere after 3 years with the explosion of a device of intermediate yield in the Pacific testing area near Christmas Island. Pres. Kennedy announced that testing would be resumed on Mar. 2, saying that the U.S.S.R. had broken the U.S.-U.S.S.R. moratorium the preceding September.

May 12 Naval, air, and land forces, including a battle group of 1,800 U.S. Marines, were ordered to Thailand for de-

sometimes baffling *Oh Dad, Poor Dad, Mamma's Hung You in the Closet and I'm Feeling So Sad* opened off-Broadway in New York. It was a financial success.

Mar. 20 **Henry Moore** exhibited 29 bronzes at the Knoedler Gallery. This was the great English sculptor's first 1-man show in New York in 8 years.

Mar. 26 At the White House Pres. Kennedy presented to **Robert Frost on his 88th birthday** a special medal voted to him by Congress. Frost's 1st book of poetry in 15 years, *In the Clearing*, was published later. At the time he claimed it would be his final work.

Apr. 2 **Katherine Anne Porter's** *Ship of Fools*, long-awaited and 20 years in preparation, was published. Called by its author a novel "of character rather than of action," it records a 27-day sea voyage from Mexico to Germany aboard a German ship in 1931. Miss Porter's primary concern was with the German ethos immediately before Hitler came to power. The book received mixed reviews.

Apr. 27 The home of **Alexander Hamilton** on Convent Ave. in New York City, known as "The Grange," was established as a national monument.

May 7 **Pulitzer Prizes** were awarded: novel, *The Edge of Sadness* by Edwin O'Connor; drama, *How to Succeed in Business Without Really Trying* by Frank Loesser and Abe Burrows; history, *The Triumphant Empire: Thunder-Clouds Gather in the West* by Lawrence Gipson; poetry, *Poems* by Alan Dugan; nonfiction, *The Making of the President, 1960* by Theodore H. White; music, *The Crucible*, an opera by Robert Ward.

May 8 *A Funny Thing Happened on the Way to the Forum*, a musical comedy based on Plautus, opened starring Zero Mostel. In an especially weak theater season this was the **outstanding new stage work.** Even so, a great deal of its success could be attributed only to Mostel's brilliant performance.

SCIENCE; INDUSTRY; ECONOMICS; EDUCATION; RELIGION; PHILOSOPHY.	SPORTS; FASHIONS; POPULAR ENTERTAINMENT; FOLKLORE; SOCIETY.

he had drastically reduced a wide range of U.S. **import duties** to save American overseas markets and to avoid the collapse of trade negotiations with other nations.

Mar. 8 The U.S. signed a new two-year **agreement with the U.S.S.R.** to expand cultural, scientific, technical, and educational exchanges.

Mar. 13 House passed a compromise bill establishing a 3-year **manpower retraining program** for unemployed workers with obsolete or insufficient skills.

Mar. 16 Titan II, the **most powerful U.S. I.C.B.M.**, on its maiden flight covered more than 5,000 miles from Cape Canaveral to a spot near Ascension Island in the South Atlantic.

Mar. 27 Archbishop Joseph Francis Rummel ordered all **Roman Catholic schools in the New Orleans, La., diocese to end segregation.**

Apr. 10 United States Steel announced a **steel price increase** averaging 3.5% or $6 a ton after signing new union contract on Apr. 1. The following day Pres. Kennedy accused union steel companies of "irresponsible defiance" of the public interest in raising steel prices.

Apr. 11 A **27-day shipping strike** on the west coast was halted by an injunction issued under the Taft-Hartley Act.

Apr. 13 Major steel companies rescinded their previously announced price increases after **Inland Steel refused to raise prices.**

Apr. 16 Catholic Archbishop Rummel of New Orleans, La., **excommunicated 3 persons** for their attempts to provoke opposition to desegregation of parochial schools.

Apr. 19 Skybolt, the **1st U.S. airborne ballistic missile**, was launched from a B-52 bomber at Cape Canaveral; its 2nd stage failed to fire and the missile fell short of its target.

Apr. 21 **"Century 21 Exposition,"** Seattle, Wash., world's fair, was opened by

Bowl; Penn State downed Georgia Tech 30–15 in the Orange Bowl.

Feb. 2 Marine corporal John Uelses became the **1st man to pole-vault 16 ft.**, at the Milrose games in Madison Square Garden. Using a springy fiberglass pole, he cleared 16 ft. ¼ in. The following night at Boston he raised the mark to 16 ft. ¾ in.

Feb. 10 Jim Beatty, the **1st American to run an indoor mile in less than 4 minutes**, was clocked at 3:58.9 in Los Angeles, a new indoor mile record. On June 8, also at Los Angeles, he set a new world record of 8:29.8 for 2 miles. He won the James E. Sullivan Memorial Trophy as the outstanding amateur athlete of 1962.

Feb. 13 Ch. Elfinbrook Simon, a West Highland White Terrier, won the "best in show" award at the **Westminster Kennel Club Dog Show.** He was the first of this breed to win "best in show."

Feb. 14 Mrs. John F. Kennedy, accompanied by Charles Collingwood of CBS, led TV viewers on a **tour of the White House.** The program was broadcast simultaneously by CBS and NBC and was seen by an estimated 46.5 million persons.

Mar. 2 **Wilt (the Stilt) Chamberlain**, star of the Philadelphia Warriors, dropped in 36 goals and 28 foul shots against the N.Y. Knicks, to become the 1st basketball player to score 100 points in a game. Despite his box-office appeal, an economic pinch forced the Warriors to move their franchise to San Francisco at the end of the season.

Mar. 9 **Jacqueline Kennedy**, wife of Pres. Kennedy, left on a goodwill mission to Italy and India. After an audience with Pope John XXIII, she flew to India and Pakistan. Mrs. Kennedy was greeted everywhere she went by large and friendly crowds, and her trip was considered both a personal and political success.

Mar. 24 TV fight fans watched **welterweight contender Emile Griffith** hammer champion Benny (Kid) Paret sense-

fense against a possible attack by Communist forces from Laos. By May 29, more than **5,000 U.S. military personnel were in Thailand.**

May 20   **Cyrus R. Vance** was named Secretary of the Army.

May 21   **Supreme Court** set aside on technical grounds the contempt convictions of 6 men who refused to answer questions of Congressional committees relating to Communism.

June 3   122 Americans were killed when a **French jet crashed** and burned in Paris. All but 2 of the 132 passengers died in the worst single-plane disaster in aviation history.

June 16   **2 U.S. Army officers were killed** in a convoy ambush by Communist guerrillas north of Saigon, South Vietnam.

July 19   Diplomatic relations were suspended and economic and military aid to Peru were stopped following a **military coup in Peru** on July 18.

July 19   Treasury Dept. announced that federal government **expenditures for fiscal year ended June 30, 1962,** were **$87,667,980,000** as against revenue of $81,360,367,000.

July 27   **Withdrawal** of last U.S. Marines from Thailand.

Aug. 1   Senate passed and sent to the White House a bill appropriating **$48,136,-247,000 for the armed forces** during fiscal year ending June 30, 1963.

Aug. 14   A record cash haul of $1,-551,277 was taken during the **robbery of a mail truck** at Plymouth, Mass.

Aug. 15   The **national debt** exceeded $300 billion for the 1st time in history.

Aug. 17   U.S. **resumed diplomatic relations with Peru** and restored economic aid to that country.

Aug. 23   U.S., Great Britain, and France declared they would **maintain their position in Berlin** against Communist encroachment.

May 13   Artist **Franz Josef Kline,** 1 of the foremost exponents of abstract expressionism, died at 51 in New York City.

May 28   The poured-concrete **Trans World Airlines passenger terminal** opened at New York International Airport (Idlewild). Designed by Eero Saarinen before his death in 1961, it resembled a graceful bird in flight. The TWA building was the most eye-catching at the airport which was on its way to becoming something of an architectural showpiece.

May 31–June 3   The **1st International Jazz Festival,** presented in Washington by the President's Committee of the People-to-People Program, proved to be a disappointment. There was unanimous praise for the Duke Ellington orchestra and the old-style jazz of the Eureka Brass Band of New Orleans, but the classical-jazz hybrid compositions (called "Third Stream") of Ellington, Gunther Schuller, and André Hodeir were received coolly.

June 4   **William Beebe,** famed naturalist, explorer, and author, died at 84 in Trinidad. He became a world celebrity in 1934 when he descended 3,028 ft. into the ocean near Bermuda in a bathysphere. Beebe also led expeditions to the Himalayas, to the Galápagos Islands, to the Sargasso Sea, and to tropic jungles, and wrote of them in popular books. A collection of his writings, *Adventuring With Beebe,* was published in 1955.

June 14   **Igor Stravinsky celebrated his 80th birthday** when his new ballet, *Noah and the Flood,* was performed on network television. It was the first work that the composer had written expressly for TV. The choreography was by Stravinsky's old friend and collaborator George Balanchine, the director of the New York City Ballet, which danced the work.

July 6   **William Faulkner,** Nobel laureate (1949) and 1 of America's greatest novelists, died at age 64 in Oxford, Miss. His last novel, *The Reivers,* had been published earlier in the year. A comic novel, *The Reivers* disappointed many re-

SCIENCE; INDUSTRY; ECONOMICS; EDUCATION; RELIGION; PHILOSOPHY.	SPORTS; FASHIONS; POPULAR ENTERTAINMENT; FOLKLORE; SOCIETY.

Pres. Kennedy from Palm Beach, Fla. He activated the carillon in the 600-ft. Space Needle by remote control.

Apr. 23   U.S. and Soviet scientists were revealed to have agreed to establish a **"world weather watch"** network linked by meteorological satellites.

Apr. 26   **1st international satellite,** Ariel, bearing 6 British experiments and propelled aloft by a U.S. Delta rocket, was launched from Cape Canaveral. Its purpose was to study the ionosphere.

Apr. 26   U.S. spacecraft Ranger IV crashed onto the **dark side of the moon** 64 hours after being launched from Cape Canaveral. After 55 hours' flight, its radio system had gone dead.

May 6   Polaris missile armed with a nuclear warhead and launched from the nuclear submarine *Ethan Allen* was successfully exploded near Christmas Island, the 1st U.S. test of a **nuclear warhead carried by a long-range missile,** and the 1st nuclear warhead launched from a submarine.

May 24   Astronaut M. Scott Carpenter was launched by an Atlas rocket from Cape Canaveral, **orbited the earth 3 times** in *Aurora 7,* and landed near Puerto Rico.

May 25   George Meany, president of AFL-CIO, stated his union would institute a nationwide campaign to **cut the standard U.S. work week from 40 to 35 hours.**

May 28   **Shares on the New York Stock Exchange lost $20.8 billion** in value in the biggest 1-day drop since Oct. 29, 1929.

June 8   Pres. Kennedy named Jerome Wiesner to head the newly created **Office of Science and Technology.**

June 18   Supreme Court ruled 5 to 3 that an **injunction against a strike is not included in employers' recourse** when a strike is called in violation of a collective-bargaining agreement.

June 25   Supreme Court held 6 to 1 that reciting a 22-word official **prayer in**

less in Madison Square Garden. Paret died 10 days later without regaining consciousness.

Mar. 24   In the final of the **NCAA basketball tournament** at Louisville, Cincinnati for the 2nd year beat Ohio State, 71–59. Nevertheless, Ohio State was voted best collegiate team by the news service polls; Ohio State star Jerry Lucas was named outstanding college player of the year.

Apr. 3   **Eddie Arcaro,** the greatest American jockey in modern turf history, retired from racing. During his 31-year career he had ridden 4,779 winners and had brought home purses totaling $30,039,543.

Apr. 9   In a 3-way playoff of the **Masters tournament** at Augusta, Ga., Arnold Palmer scored a 68 to win by 3 strokes over Gary Player. Dow Finsterwald finished 3rd. Palmer, who was voted P.G.A. "player of the year," won a total of $81,000 this year.

Apr. 22   The National Hockey League's **Stanley Cup** was won by the Toronto Maple Leafs for the 1st time since 1951, as they defeated the Chicago Black Hawks 4 games to 2.

May 5   *Decidedly* won the **Kentucky Derby** with Hartack up. The time was 2:00⅖; the purse was $119,650.

May 19   *Greek Money* won the **Preakness Stakes** with Rotz up. The time was 1:56⅕; the purse was $135,800.

May 30   Roger Ward, driving a Leader Card, set a new race record of 140.292 mph, to win the Memorial Day classic at the **Indianapolis Speedway.**

June 4   Sports announcer **Clem McCarthy,** 79, died in New York City. Since 1928, his rapid-fire, precise descriptions of major sporting events, especially prizefights and horse races, had made his voice 1 of the most familiar voices of radio.

June 9   *Jaipur* won the **Belmont Stakes** with Shoemaker up. The time was 2:28⅘; the purse was $109,550.

643

| POLITICS AND GOVERNMENT; WAR; DISASTERS; VITAL STATISTICS. | BOOKS; PAINTING; DRAMA; ARCHITECTURE; SCULPTURE. |

Aug. 27   U.S. and Great Britain proposed at **Geneva disarmament conference** either an internationally inspected total **ban on nuclear weapons tests** or an uninspected limited ban. U.S.S.R. rejected the proposals.

Aug. 27   A constitutional amendment (the 24th) barring **poll tax** as a requirement for voting in federal elections was approved by Congress.

Aug. 29   Associate Justice **Felix Frankfurter retired** after 23 years on the Supreme Court. Secretary of Labor Arthur J. Goldberg succeeded him. Undersecretary of Labor W. Willard Wirtz was named new Secretary of Labor Aug. 30.

Sept. 11   The appointment of Negro **Thurgood Marshall** as a judge of the 2nd Circuit Court of Appeals was confirmed by the Senate after 8 months of consideration.

Sept. 24   Pres. Kennedy was authorized by the House to call up to **150,000 reservists** for 1 year and to **extend active duty** of servicemen without declaring a state of emergency.

Oct. 2   Bill authorizing a U.S. **loan of $100 million to the UN** to help meet its financial crisis was signed by Pres. Kennedy.

Oct. 4   Congress approved the **foreign trade bill** giving Pres. Kennedy authority to negotiate tariff reductions and to assist firms and individuals injured by the lowering of tariffs.

Oct. 22   U.S. naval and air "quarantine" effective Oct. 24 on shipment of offensive military supplies to Cuba was announced by Pres. Kennedy. In a TV address he said that the U.S.S.R., contrary to

viewers who remembered the great, somber masterpieces of Faulkner's past: *As I Lay Dying, The Sound and the Fury, Absalom, Absalom!,* and *Light in August.*

July 25   Congress authorized the establishment of the **Sagamore Hill National Historic Site** to preserve the home of Theodore Roosevelt at Oyster Bay, N.Y., and the preservation of his birthplace on East 20th St. in New York City.

Sept. 23   Philharmonic Hall, the 1st building to be completed in New York's **Lincoln Center for the Performing Arts,** opened with a gala concert. Live television coverage was supplied as Leonard Bernstein conducted the New York Philharmonic before a glittering audience of dignitaries, musicians, and patrons of the arts. The hall's acoustics proved disappointing, and for months after the opening engineers made adjustments of the ceiling baffles and other sound-control devices.

Sept. 29   The musical **My Fair Lady** closed. It was the longest-running musical in Broadway history, with 2,717 performances since its opening on Mar. 15, 1956.

Oct. 3   *Stop the World—I Want to Get Off,* starring Anthony Newley and Anna Quayle, was 1 of 2 British imports that brightened the **Broadway** scene. It had a book, music, and lyrics by Leslie Bricusse and Mr. Newley, and 1 of its songs, "What Kind of Fool Am I?" became a popular hit. On Oct. 27, a quartet of young Englishmen opened in *Beyond the Fringe,* a comedy review with delightfully satiric sketches.

Oct. 4   Expatriate author and publisher **Sylvia Woodbridge Beach** died in Paris. In 1922 she published the first com-

644

New York State public schools violates the 1st Amendment to the U.S. Constitution.

July 6   The 2nd explosion of a **thermonuclear device for non-weapons purposes** by the U.S. was set off underground at the Nevada proving grounds.

July 9   The U.S. set off a **thermonuclear explosion equal to about 1.4 million tons of TNT** at an altitude of 250 miles over Johnston Island.

July 10   Telstar, the **experimental communications satellite** developed and owned by American Telephone & Telegraph Co. and Bell Telephone Laboratories, was orbited from Cape Canaveral and later relayed live TV pictures from Andover, Me., to France and Great Britain.

July 27   The Justice Dept. announced that General Electric had agreed to pay the U.S. $7,470,000 in damages for **excess profits received through price fixing.**

Aug. 14   Senate invoked **cloture for the 1st time since 1927** when it voted to limit debate on a bill to create a communications satellite corporation.

Aug. 17   Dr. Frances O. Kelsey of the Food and Drug Administration was awarded the gold medal for distinguished public service by Pres. Kennedy for her resistance to "rigorous" demands to clear the drug thalidomide for the U.S. market. Tranquilizing drug was found to cause **severe fetal deformities.**

Aug. 22   Pres. Kennedy announced that 2 U.S. nuclear submarines had effected an under-ice rendezvous at the North Pole. On the same day the *Savannah,* the world's **1st nuclear-powered cargo ship,** completed her maiden voyage from Yorktown, Va., to Savannah, Ga.

Aug. 27   A compromise bill creating **a satellite communications corporation** was passed by the House 372 to 10.

Aug. 27   Spacecraft Mariner II was launched successfully from Cape Canaveral on a projected 15-week trajectory toward the **planet Venus.**

June 17   Jack Nicklaus, amateur golf champion of 1961, capped his smashing 1st year as a pro by winning the **U.S. Open championship** at Oakmont, Pa. He and Arnold Palmer had finished regulation play in a tie at 283; Nicklaus won the playoff 71 to 74.

July 21–22   In the 4th annual meeting between **track and field teams of the U.S. and Russia,** the American men's team won by a score of 128–107, at Palo Alto, Calif. As usual, the U.S.S.R.'s strong women's team bested the U.S. ladies, 66–41.

July 22   Gary Player of South Africa became the 1st non-resident of the U.S. to win the **P.G.A. championship,** carding a 278 to defeat Bob Goalby by 1 stroke at Newton Square, Pa.

Aug. 5   **Marilyn Monroe** died in her Los Angeles home, an apparent suicide from an overdose of sleeping pills. Famous first for her beauty and subsequently exploited as Hollywood's reigning sexgoddess, at the end of her career she was recognized as a competent actress and a fine comedienne. Her 23 films, which included *Gentlemen Prefer Blondes, The Seven-Year Itch, Bus Stop,* and *Some Like It Hot,* grossed millions and earned her countless fans. Her 3 marriages, the 2nd to Joe Dimaggio and the 3rd to Arthur Miller, all ended in divorce.

Sept. 8   The **richest purse in thoroughbred racing history,** $357,250, was offered in the Arlington-Washington Futurity, a race for 2-year-olds. The winner's share, $142,250, went to *Candy Spots.* Manuel Ycaza, who finished 2nd on *Never Bend,* drew a suspension for making a flimsy claim of foul.

Sept. 15–25   The U.S. successfully defended the **America's Cup,** yachting's most important international trophy, for the 18th time. The challenging Australian 12-meter sloop *Gretel* was defeated in 4 races out of 5 by *Weatherly,* the U.S. defender. It was the closest competition in years and the 1st time since 1934 that the U.S. boat had not swept the 1st 4 races.

| POLITICS AND GOVERNMENT; WAR; DISASTERS; VITAL STATISTICS. | BOOKS; PAINTING; DRAMA; ARCHITECTURE; SCULPTURE. |

its assurances, had been building missile and bomber bases in Cuba. The next day the Council of the Organization of American States voted unanimously to authorize the **use of armed force to prevent shipment of offensive weapons to Cuba.**

Oct. 24   Premier **Khrushchev** in a letter to British philosopher Bertrand Russell **denounced the U.S.** quarantine of shipment of aggressive weapons to Cuba as "piratical" and suggested a summit meeting to discuss the situation in order to avert nuclear war.

Oct. 25   Amb. Adlai Stevenson displayed to the UN **aerial photographs of offensive missile bases in Cuba.** The next day the U.S. Navy boarded and searched a Soviet-chartered freighter en route to Havana.

Oct. 27   Premier Khrushchev offered to **remove missile bases in Cuba** under UN supervision, demanding that the U.S. take corresponding action in Turkey. A U-2 reconnaissance plane was shot down over Cuba.

Oct. 28   Premier Khrushchev agreed to **halt construction of bases in Cuba** and remove rockets under UN inspection. Pres. Kennedy agreed to lift quarantine when the UN had acted, and pledged the U.S. would not invade Cuba.

Oct. 29   The U.S. suspended its naval quarantine of Cuba for the duration of a trip by Acting UN Secretary-Gen. U Thant for a conference with Prime Minister Castro. **No agreement was reached on UN inspection.**

Nov. 2   Pres. Kennedy reported to the nation that missile bases in Cuba were being dismantled and "progress is now being made toward **restoration of peace in the Caribbean.**"

plete text of James Joyce's *Ulysses* under the imprint of Shakespeare & Co. (the name of the Paris bookstore she ran from 1919 to 1941), and shared with Joyce the literary and legal assaults the book provoked. Her autobiography, *Shakespeare and Company* (1959), contains many details of her friendships with Gide, Valéry, Hemingway, and other writers of the post-World War I era.

Oct. 13   Edward Albee's first full-length play, *Who's Afraid of Virginia Woolf?* opened on Broadway. A solid cast headed by George Grizzard and Uta Hagen helped make this fierce and exhausting drama into a box-office success and **the most talked about play of the season.**

Oct. 14   **E. E. Cummings**, poet, novelist, and painter, died at North Conway, N.H. Cummings was influenced by the great artistic innovators he met in Paris during the 1920's, and in much of his work (except in his frankly sentimental paintings) he makes use of novel forms and eccentric typography, spelling, and punctuation, visual devices which in combination with sound and meaning, helped him convey the immediacy of the artistic experience. He was a gifted satirist, and is considered to be 1 of the great erotic poets in the English language.

Oct. 23   Several eagle-eyed collectors spotted an error of inversion in **commemorative stamps** issued today in honor of the late U.N. Secretary-General Dag Hammarskjöld. Postmaster General J. Edward Day created a sensation when he ordered 10 million of the errors printed to prevent speculation in the rarities. A suit against Day by a New Jersey collector was halted when the Post Office Dept. authenticated his 50-stamp pane as a "discovery" item.

SCIENCE; INDUSTRY; ECONOMICS; EDUCATION; RELIGION; PHILOSOPHY.	SPORTS; FASHIONS; POPULAR ENTERTAINMENT; FOLKLORE; SOCIETY.

Sept. 15 A bill authorizing $900 million for **public works in economically depressed areas** of U.S. was signed by Pres. Kennedy.

Sept. 20 The application by **James H. Meredith,** a Negro, for admission to the University of Mississippi was denied by Mississippi Gov. Ross R. Barnett in defiance of a federal court order.

Sept. 21 Agreements between the U.S. and West Germany, France, and Italy for the purchase of U.S. military equipment to offset **U.S. gold losses** was announced by the Dept. of Defense.

Sept. 27 Pres. Kennedy signed the Food and Agricultural Act of 1962, a compromise bill providing for some of the **increased crop controls** he had requested.

Sept. 28 Gov. Ross R. Barnett of Mississippi was found guilty of civil contempt by a U.S. court of appeals and ordered to cease interference with **desegregation at the University of Mississippi** or face arrest and a fine of $10,000 for each day of continued interference.

Sept. 30 Negro student James H. Meredith was escorted onto the University of Mississippi campus by U.S. marshals. **2 men were killed** in the ensuing mob violence which was quelled with the aid of 3,000 federal soldiers.

Oct. 1 Negro student **James H. Meredith was enrolled** and began classes at the University of Mississippi as federal law officers and troops held back rioters.

Oct. 3 Astronaut Walter M. Schirra, Jr., orbited the earth 5¾ times in his capsule *Sigma 7.* He landed near Midway Island in the Pacific within 4 miles of the recovery carrier *Kearsarge.*

Oct. 18 **Nobel prize for medicine** was awarded jointly to Dr. James D. Watson of Harvard, Dr. Maurice H. F. Wilkins of King's College in London, and Dr. Francis H. C. Crick of Cambridge for their discovery of the molecular structure of deoxyribonucleic acid (DNA), the physical basis of heredity.

Sept. 25 After 2 minutes 6 seconds of the 1st round in their **heavyweight boxing title match** Sonny Liston knocked out Floyd Patterson to gain the crown. This was 1 of the shortest title bouts in history and an understandable disappointment to fans who had paid $100 for ringside seats. Total revenue from the fight reached a record $5 million.

Sept. 27 **The New York Mets,** a new National League baseball team, finished their 1st season under ex-Yankee manager Casey Stengel. During the season the Mets had lost 3 out of every 4 games they played. The fans loved it; nearly 1 million of them came to the Polo Grounds to witness the heroic ineptitude of the players and the antics of their manager.

Oct. 8 The U.S. Supreme Court rejected an appeal by theater owners who sought to prevent the large-scale tryout of **pay TV** which began in June in Connecticut.

Oct. 16 The New York Yankees won the 7th game of the **World Series** 1–0 against the San Francisco Giants, to become world baseball champions for the 20th time. The regular season ended with a tie in the National League between the Giants and the Dodgers, a duplicate of the close of the 1951 season. The Giants won the 3-game playoff, as they had done in 1951, and entered the Series as tired underdogs.

Nov. 5 The **U.S. Supreme Court** ruled unanimously that a film distributor cannot require a TV station to buy a "package" of motion pictures to get films it wants.

Nov. 15 The long career of heavyweight **Archie Moore,** now close to 50, seemed ended after he was stopped in the 4th round by 20-year-old Cassius Clay. It was Clay's 16th victory, and his 13th knockout.

Dec. 23 The Dallas Texans defeated the Houston Oilers 20–17, to win the AFL championship. The game went to 2 extra

Nov. 4   Pres. Kennedy announced that the current series of U.S. **nuclear tests** in the atmosphere had been concluded, although underground testing was continuing.

Nov. 7   **Billie Sol Estes,** Texas financier whose business manipulations involving the Dept. of Agriculture created a political scandal, was sentenced to 8 years in prison on a charge of swindling a Texas farmer. Other state and federal indictments remaining against him were for theft, swindling, mail fraud, false statements, and criminal antitrust violations.

Nov. 10   The State Dept. said that U.S. emergency **military aid to India** in its border war with China had been completed with the delivery of $5 million worth of infantry weapons, ammunition, and equipment.

Nov. 20   Pres. Kennedy announced the **lifting of the naval blockade of Cuba** following assurances by Premier Khrushchev that all U.S.S.R. jet bombers in Cuba would be removed within 30 days.

Nov. 20   Pres. Kennedy signed an **executive order prohibiting racial discrimination in housing** built or purchased with federal funds.

Dec. 17   U.S. **Communist Party was convicted** by a federal jury in Washington, D.C., of committing a criminal act by failing to register as an agent of the U.S.S.R. and fined $10,000 on each of 12 counts.

Dec. 23   **Cuban government began releasing prisoners** captured in the April 1961 invasion under an agreement with a U.S. private committee by which Cuba would get more than $50 million in food and medical supplies.

Oct. 25   John Steinbeck received the **Nobel prize for literature** in Stockholm. Among his best-known works are *Tortilla Flat* (1935), *Of Mice and Men* (1937), and *The Grapes of Wrath* (1939). The award cited his "realistic and imaginative writing . . . distinguished by a . . . social perception." Earlier in 1962 his latest book, *Travels With Charley: In Search of America,* had been published. He was the 6th American to win a Nobel prize for literature.

SCIENCE; INDUSTRY; ECONOMICS; EDUCATION; RELIGION; PHILOSOPHY.	SPORTS; FASHIONS; POPULAR ENTERTAINMENT; FOLKLORE; SOCIETY.

Nov. 1 New York Newspaper Guild members struck the *Daily News*. Although that union signed a new contract, other unions' demands resulted in the **suspension of publication by Dec. 8 of all 9 New York daily newspapers.**

Nov. 4 The current series of U.S. atmospheric nuclear tests was concluded with a **high-altitude explosion** over the Johnston Island testing area in the Pacific.

Dec. 2 Deposits of thorium in the White Mountains, N.H., were found to be 10 times as great as earlier estimates, constituting a **reserve for nuclear fuel** equal to the nation's uranium deposits.

Dec. 8 Rt. Rev. John Melville Burgess was consecrated as suffragan bishop of Massachusetts, the 1st U.S. **Negro bishop** of the Protestant Episcopal Church to serve a predominantly white diocese.

Dec. 13 Relay I, the **intercontinental communications satellite,** was sent into orbit. 2 days later transmission was turned off for an indefinite period because of a power failure.

Dec. 14 U.S. space probe Mariner II, on its 109th day of flight, **transmitted information about Venus** for 42 minutes.

Dec. 18 The Navy launched a Scout rocket at Point Arguello, Calif., carrying a satellite that was sent into orbit to act as an **electronic star,** visible in all weather.

Dec. 21 Mississippi Gov. Ross R. Barnett and Lt. Gov. Paul B. Johnson were charged with **criminal contempt of court** in the U.S. 5th Circuit Court of Appeals at New Orleans for actions in September violating court orders for admission of James H. Meredith to the University of Mississippi.

Dec. 23 A strike by the 90,000-member **International Longshoremen's Association** went into effect along the eastern seaboard.

quarters, and was decided by a field goal by Tommy Brooker.

Dec. 30 For the 2nd year, the NFL championship was won by the Green Bay Packers, who defeated the N.Y. Giants 16–7 in the playoff at New York.

POLITICS AND GOVERNMENT; WAR;	BOOKS; PAINTING; DRAMA;
DISASTERS; VITAL STATISTICS.	ARCHITECTURE; SCULPTURE.

1963

The death of Pres. John F. Kennedy on Nov. 22 shocked the nation and the world. The 34th person to have been elected President of the U.S., Kennedy was the 4th President to die by an assassin's bullet. His youthfulness, vigor, and idealism, and the personal images which he and his family conveyed to the nation made his sudden death seem a personal loss to many citizens. The respect which he evoked throughout the world was attested by the presence at his funeral of representatives of 92 nations, among them Pres. Charles de Gaulle of France, Premier Anastas I. Mikoyan of the U.S.S.R., and Prince Philip of Great Britain. Although Kennedy did not live to see the passage of his civil rights bill, his program of medical care for the aged, or the tax-reduction bill, Congress did approve his proposal for aid to the mentally retarded. $3.6 billion for foreign aid was appropriated, a saving of $300 million over the previous year. In spite of continued conflict with Cuba, the U.S.S.R. in Berlin, and in Vietnam, the international situation improved generally when the U.S., the U.S.S.R., and Great Britain signed a treaty banning nuclear testing in the atmosphere, in space, and under water. Traffic deaths reached an all-time high of 40,804.

Jan. 17   Pres. Kennedy sent to Congress a **federal budget** of $98.8 billion, the biggest in history, with a deficit of $11.9 billion forecast.

Jan. 31   U.S.S.R. broke off informal **nuclear-test-ban talks** with the U.S. which had opened in New York on Jan. 14 and were joined by Great Britain on Jan. 23.

Feb. 5   Program of federal aid to **combat mental illness and mental retardation** was proposed to Congress by Pres. Kennedy.

Feb. 8   U.S. **resumed underground tests of nuclear weapons** in Nevada. Suspension of tests had been ordered on Jan. 20 during U.S.–U.S.S.R. test-ban talks.

The year in literature was dominated by familiar, established names. Mary McCarthy's *The Group* was an immediate best seller. Two J.D. Salinger stories were published in 1 volume: *Raise High the Roofbeam, Carpenters* and *Seymour, An Introduction.* The book most appreciated by the critics was Bernard Malamud's *Idiots First*, a collection of short stories. The theater season was the most vapid in years—there was not a single new American work of any substance. The best plays to be seen on Broadway were revivals (O'Neill's *Strange Interlude*), British imports (Sheridan's *School for Scandal* and Osborne's *Luther*), and translations (Brecht's *Mother Courage and Her Children*). New buildings at Harvard and Yale made most of the architectural news. Le Corbusier, the great Swiss-French master, designed the Visual Arts Center at Harvard, his 1st building in this country. At Yale 2 new colleges, the 1st built since the '30's, were completed. The work of Eero Saarinen and Associates, the adjoining college complexes were inspired by small Italian hill towns. Also new at Yale were the Beinecke Rare Book and Manuscript Library and Paul Rudolph's Art and Architecture building, a 6-story structure that incorporated 36 different floor and ceiling levels. The Ford Foundation made the largest grant ever given to one art form when it allocated $7.7 million for the development of ballet in the U.S. The pervasive music news of the year concerned the very poor acoustics of the new Philharmonic Hall in New York. In mid-April Lincoln Center president William Schuman announced that $300,000 would be spent on adjustments to the hall that summer, and more later if it were needed.

Managed news became a hot subject of debate between newsmen and government officials as an aftermath of the Cuban crisis. Journalists had decried official suppression of information during the crisis, and the administration's answer to the crit-

1963

Continued efforts to achieve full Negro civil rights resulted in violence in Alabama, Mississippi, North Carolina, Virginia, and Maryland. New York City and Chicago were also centers of racial demonstrations. Progress toward civil rights was made when the last Southern state to maintain segregation, South Carolina, opened its colleges to Negroes. The University of Alabama admitted 2 Negroes, and restaurants and hotels in Nashville, Tenn., were peacefully desegregated. The building and construction trades union of the AFL-CIO adopted a program to eliminate racial discrimination. During the year, the nation's unemployment rate rose. George Meany, president of the AFL-CIO, condemned automation as a "curse to society." A threatened national railroad strike resulted in a Congressional act requiring arbitration, the 1st time arbitration was imposed in a peacetime labor dispute. Federal legislation required that women receive pay equal to that of men for similar work. The nation's farmers overwhelmingly voted down a government program to decrease wheat production and to support the price of wheat. A move toward the improvement of education was made with a federal appropriation of nearly $2 billion for the construction and improvement of college facilities and for student loans.

Jan. 3   Relay I, a **communications satellite** launched Dec. 13, 1962, but silent since Dec. 15 due to malfunction, was reactivated by radio signal from the ground and began transmissions between North and South America and Europe.

Jan. 26   East coast and Gulf coast **longshoremen returned to work**, ending a strike that had tied up shipping since Dec. 23, 1962, and cost more than $800 million.

Jan. 28   Harvey B. Gantt, a Negro student, enrolled in Clemson College, Clemson, S.C., **breaking segregation in the last state to hold** out against integration.

Tragedy struck in the boxing ring again when featherweight champion Davey Moore died shortly after losing his title to Sugar Ramos. The sports world lost 2 of its most popular competitors in the retirements of baseball slugger Stan Musial and basketball's back-court artist Bob Cousy. The strike zone in major-league baseball was enlarged at the beginning of the season, and to compensate for the bigger target, perhaps, National League umpires began applying the rule that a pitcher must wait 1 second between windup and delivery. Their rigorous enforcement evoked so many outraged howls from fans and players that the Rules Committee dropped the 1-second rule within a month.

Thoroughbred racing's "horse of the year," for a record 4th time, was *Kelso*, a great-grandson of the famed *Man o' War*. His earnings this year came to $569,762, which boosted his career total to $1,581,702, 2nd only to that of the retired *Round Table*. The year's biggest money-maker was *Candy Spots*, who earned $604,481.

Without taking any of the 4 major tournaments, **Arnold Palmer** became the 1st golfer to win over $100,000 in a year. His official P.G.A. prize money came to $128,230. In his 2nd year as a pro, 23-year-old **Jack Nicklaus** became the youngest man ever to win the Augusta Masters tournament; he went on to take the P.G.A. title, too. **Mickey Wright** took the Ladies P.G.A. championship and in 13 victories amassed earnings of $31,269, the record for women pros.

The vogue of **folk-singing** entered a new phase, with group concert programs, often with audience participation, called "Hootenannies." NBC's "Hootenanny" became 1 of the more popular TV programs. Singer Joan Baez and singer-composer Bob Dylan remained the most popular concert and recording folk artists.

"Tom Swifties," witticisms based on the overuse of adverbs in the popular juvenile

Feb. 12   17-nation UN Disarmament Committee reconvened in Geneva with U.S.S.R. calling for **elimination of foreign missile and nuclear submarine bases.**

Feb. 14   Pres. Kennedy proposed a program for youth including a Youth Conservation Corps and a **domestic Peace Corps.**

Feb. 21   2 Cuban-based Russian jets **fired rockets at** a disabled U.S. shrimp boat the *Ala,* adrift in international waters about 60 nautical miles north of Cuba.

Feb. 21   **Medicare,** a medical-hospital insurance plan financed through social security, was submitted to Congress by Pres. Kennedy.

Feb. 25   Cuba formally denied the attack on U.S. shrimp boat *Ala* in response to **strong U.S. protests.**

Feb. 27   U.S.–British plan for a sea-based **multilateral NATO force** armed with Polaris missiles was presented in Paris.

Mar. 16   The U.S. formally protested to the U.S.S.R. the flights of 2 **Soviet reconnaissance planes over Alaska** on Mar. 13, the "first clearly established incident of a Soviet overflight of the U.S."

Mar. 18   Supreme Court held that states must supply **free counsel for all indigents** facing serious criminal charges.

Mar. 19   Pres. Kennedy signed the Declaration of San José following conference in Costa Rica with presidents of 6 Central American countries. The Declaration called for perfection of a **Central American common market,** economic development, and political strengthening.

Mar. 21   Presidential 10-member study commission headed by Gen. Lucius D. Clay submitted report suggesting tightening and **reduction of U.S. foreign aid,** saving U.S. about $500 million over 3 years.

Apr. 9   Sir Winston Churchill was proclaimed an **honorary U.S. citizen** in a

icism was that its news dissemination policies were guided solely by the "national interest." One far-reaching result of the controversy was a decided falling-off of public confidence in the truth of official versions of developments in Cuba, Vietnam, and other trouble spots.

The William A. Farnsworth Library and Art Museum, Rockland, Me., bought **Andrew Wyeth's** *Her Room* for $65,000, the highest price ever paid by a museum for the work of a living American artist.

Pulitzer Prizes: novel, *The Reivers* by William Faulkner; history, *Washington, Village and Capital, 1800–1878* by Constance McL. Green; biography, *Henry James: the Middle Years* and *Henry James: the Conquest of London* by Leon Edel; poetry, *Pictures from Brueghel* by William Carlos Williams; nonfiction, *The Guns of August* by Barbara Tuchman; music, *Piano Concert No. 1* by Samuel Barber. A furor was caused when it was announced that there would be no drama award made: the Advisory Board had recommended Edward Albee's *Who's Afraid of Virginia Woolf?* and when their recommendation was not accepted both John Mason Brown and John Gassner resigned.

The most controversial book of the year was Jessica Mitford's *The American Way of Death,* an exposé of and attack on **American funeral and burial customs.** The book brought on storms of denial and rebuttal from undertakers and cemetery owners, considerable praise from clergymen and other interested parties, and created a great deal of interest in burial societies that offered low-cost, dignified burials.

Eichmann in Jerusalem: A Report on the Banality of Evil by **Hannah Arendt** was one of the most widely discussed books of the year. An unemotional account of the trial of the Nazi officer and the preceding events during and after the war, the book was praised by some, attacked by others, and misunderstood by many.

SCIENCE; INDUSTRY; ECONOMICS; EDUCATION; RELIGION; PHILOSOPHY.

SPORTS; FASHIONS; POPULAR ENTERTAINMENT; FOLKLORE; SOCIETY.

Feb. 14 Syncom I, an experimental forerunner of a series of 3 satellites which would hover at different points over the earth in synchronous orbits and conduct **communications between most points on earth,** was launched from Cape Canaveral. Although a near-synchronous orbit was achieved, radio contact with earth was lost the same day.

Mar. 11 **Unemployment** was termed the nation's "No. 1 economic problem" and the achievement of full employment the nation's "most pressing internal challenge" by Pres. Kennedy in a message to Congress. He said unemployment had averaged 5.6% in 1962 and had risen to 6.1% in February 1963.

Mar. 17 Elizabeth Ann Bayley Seton was **beatified by Pope John XXIII,** the 1st U.S. native to be so honored. Since beatification is generally a prelude to canonization, Mother Seton could become the 1st U.S.-born saint.

Apr. 1 New York City **newspapers resumed publication** following settlement of strike that began Dec. 8, 1962. Loss during the period was estimated at $190 million. The longest newspaper shutdown in history was of Cleveland papers, struck between Nov. 29, 1962, and Apr. 8, 1963, with an estimated loss of $25 million.

Apr. 1 U.S. Steel Corp. and 6 other steel manufacturers were indicted by a federal grand jury on charges of **price fixing.**

Apr. 5 J. Robert Oppenheimer, U.S. physicist declared a security risk in 1954, was named winner of the **Atomic Energy Commission's 1963 Fermi award.**

Apr. 9 Wheeling Steel Corp. announced a price increase averaging $6 a ton. Within the next few days, other major **steel companies announced price increases.**

Apr. 12 The Rev. Martin Luther King, Jr., was arrested as racial disturbances, marking **antisegregation drive** begun Apr. 2, continued in Birmingham, Ala.

series of 30 years ago, amused the public for some time in the spring and summer. Example: "Take the prisoner to the deepest dungeon," he said condescendingly.

Motion-picture **Academy Award** winners for 1963: best picture, *Tom Jones;* best actor, Sidney Poitier (*Lilies of the Field*); best actress, Patricia Neal (*Hud*); best director, Tony Richardson (*Tom Jones*); best foreign-language film, *8½;* best supporting actor, Melvyn Douglas (*Hud*); best supporting actress, Margaret Rutherford (*The V.I.P.'s*).

Jan. 1 In the **Rose Bowl** U.S.C. defeated Wisconsin 42–37; Mississippi won 17–13 over Arkansas in the Sugar Bowl; Louisiana State beat Texas 13–0 in the Cotton Bowl; and Alabama defeated Oklahoma 17–0 in the Orange Bowl.

Jan. 5 **Rogers Hornsby,** 1 of the great sluggers of major-league baseball, died in Winters, Tex. His 1924 season batting average of .424 has never been equaled, and his lifetime average of .358 is topped only by that of Ty Cobb. Hornsby was made a member of baseball's Hall of Fame in 1942.

Mar. 20 **Hope Cooke,** recent graduate of Sarah Lawrence College, married Crown Prince Palden Thondup Namgyal of Sikkim in a Buddhist ceremony at Gangtok. On Dec. 2 the prince succeeded to the throne as maharajah at the death of his father, Sir Tashi Namgyal.

Mar. 21 1 hour after he had lost his featherweight title to Sugar Ramos in the 10th round at Los Angeles, **Davey Moore collapsed and died** without regaining consciousness.

Mar. 23 In the finals of the **NCAA basketball tournament** at Louisville, Loyola of Chicago defeated the University of Cincinnati, 60–58.

Apr. 7 At the Augusta Masters golf tournament, **Jack Nicklaus** edged Tony Lema by 1 stroke, to win with a score of 286. At Las Vegas on May 5, Nicklaus won the Tournament of Champions with a score of 273, and on Sept. 8 he carded a

POLITICS AND GOVERNMENT; WAR; DISASTERS; VITAL STATISTICS.	BOOKS; PAINTING; DRAMA; ARCHITECTURE; SCULPTURE.

ceremony internationally televised from the White House.

Apr. 10   U.S. nuclear-powered submarine *Thresher* was lost in the Atlantic with 129 men on board during a test dive. A Navy board of inquiry concluded that probably a system failure created progressive flooding; the interference with electrical circuits caused loss of power and the ship had sunk.

Apr. 22   Units of the U.S. 7th Fleet were sent to the Gulf of Siam as a "precautionary" measure during fighting in Laos.

May 11   Acceptance by Canada of U.S. nuclear warheads for missiles installed on Canadian soil toward fulfillment of defense commitments in North America was announced.

June 3   U.S. resumed normal diplomatic relations with Haiti and withdrew a naval task force from Haitian waters. The task force was sent in April during the Haitian-Dominican crisis. The crisis was an outgrowth of Haitian Pres. François Duvalier's determination to continue in office in spite of popular opposition and violence.

June 25   Pres. Kennedy in a major speech of his 10-day tour of Europe said that the U.S. "will risk its cities to defend yours."

July 8   U.S. banned virtually all financial transactions with Cuba in another move toward economic isolation of that country.

July 15   Conference opened in Moscow between the U.S., Great Britain, and the U.S.S.R. on a treaty to ban nuclear testing.

July 23   Pres. Kennedy in a special message to Congress requested abolition of

"Happenings," an ultra avant-garde theatrical form, were performed in various places (except in theaters) all over the country. A series of abstract events generally of an absurd or comic nature, "Happenings" combined mime, painting, music, modern dance, etc.

Folk singers Peter, Paul and Mary, Joan Baez, and the Kingston Trio dominated the recording world for most of the year, but in November a Belgian nun, Sister Luc-Gabrielle, became an overnight sensation with a single record, "Dominique," a song she wrote and sang under the pseudonym Soeur Sourire. Her album "The Singing Nun," released in December, also became an immediate best seller. Shortly after President Kennedy's assassination, recording companies began issuing excerpts from his speeches and other documentaries, and by the end of the year sales of these records had passed the 5 million mark.

Richard Lippold's "space-sculpture" was completed at Philharmonic Hall in New York. Called *Orpheus and Apollo* by the artist, it was a collection of gold metal planks suspended from the ceiling.

Jan. 8–Mar. 4   New Yorkers and Washingtonians had a chance to view Leonardo da Vinci's Mona Lisa on a short-term loan from the Louvre to this country. Nearly a million people, both art lovers and the simply curious, lined up to see the painting. Another Louvre masterpiece, Whistler's *Portrait of my Mother*, was shown at Atlanta in February as a memorial tribute to a group of Georgia art lovers killed in a plane crash near Paris in 1962.

Jan. 29   **Robert Frost,** 4-time Pulitzer Prize winner and 1 of America's best-loved poets, died at 88 in Boston. Born in California, his poetry celebrated the traditional rugged, individual, and patriotic virtues of New England where he lived most of his life. His last book, *In the Clearing* (1962), was a best seller, and it won the Bollingen prize for the best book of poems.

Mar.–June   The 1st large-scale exhibition of the phenomenon known as **"pop**

Apr. 18   Successful **transplants of human nerves** were reported by Dr. James B. Campbell of the New York University Medical Center.

May 7   Telstar II, the **2nd communications satellite,** was launched from Cape Canaveral, Fla., and began relaying color and black-and-white TV between U.S. and Europe.

May 9   A secret satellite which dispensed 400 million tiny copper hairs in the earth's polar orbit was launched by the Air Force from Point Arguello, Calif. The cloud of "needles" bounced signals back to earth, providing **coast-to-coast radio transmissions.**

May 12   Federal troops were dispatched to bases near Birmingham, Ala., after bombings touched off a 3-hour **race riot.**

May 15   Maj. L. Gordon Cooper, Jr., was launched on a 22-orbit, 2-day trip around the earth in *Faith 7,* the final flight of **Project Mercury.**

May 15   Presidential science advisory committee issued a cautionary report on the **use of pesticides,** an outgrowth of the book *Silent Spring* by Rachel Carson which had called attention to toxicity of pesticides used on food crops.

June 3   The Supreme Court held unanimously that an **agency shop labor contract,** in which an employee is not required to join a union but must pay it the equivalent of dues and fees, is constitutional where it is permitted by states. The Court ruled that a state could bar the agency shop.

June 4   Bill changing the **backing for U.S. $1 and $2 bills from silver to gold** was signed by Pres. Kennedy.

June 8   American Heart Association became the 1st voluntary public agency to open a **drive against cigarette smoking.**

June 10   Pres. Kennedy signed bill requiring **equal pay for equal work,** regardless of sex.

140 to win the World Series of Golf at Akron.

Apr. 18   The Toronto Maple Leafs won the National Hockey League's **Stanley Cup,** defeating the Detroit Redwings 4 games to 1. Gordie Howe of the Wings was voted most valuable player of the 1962–63 season. The following Nov. 10, in a game against Montreal, Howe scored the 545th goal of his career, 1 more than the record held by Maurice Richard of the Canadiens.

Apr. 24   Boston Celtics' brilliant guard **Bob Cousy,** 34, retired from competition after leading his team to their 5th straight NBA championship. The Celtics downed Los Angeles 4 games to 2 in the title playoffs.

May 4   John Galbreath's *Chateaugay,* the year's top 3-year-old colt, won the **Kentucky Derby,** with Baeza up. *Chateaugay* also took the Belmont Stakes, but missed racing's "triple crown" by finishing 2nd to *Candy Spots* in the Preakness.

May 4   Gov. **Nelson Rockefeller** of N.Y. married Mrs. Margaretta Fitler Murphy shortly after both had been divorced. The governor was an announced candidate for the Republican nomination for President in 1964, and newsmen began calculating how much his chances had been hurt.

May 6   **Monty Woolley,** white-bearded, mustachioed actor, died at 74 in Albany, N.Y. He achieved fame as Sheridan Whiteside in the comedy *The Man Who Came to Dinner* (stage, 1939; movie, 1941).

May 18   *Candy Spots,* with Shoemaker in the saddle, won the **Preakness Stakes** and a purse of $127,500.

May 30   In the 47th annual 500-mile race at **Indianapolis Speedway,** Parnelli Jones drove an Agajanian-Willard Battery Special an average speed of 143.137 mph to take top prize of $148,513.

June 7   Actress **ZaSu Pitts,** 63, died in Hollywood. She began her career as a

655

the quota system of immigration within 5 years.

July 25   A treaty prohibiting nuclear testing in the atmosphere, in space, and under water was initialed in Moscow by the U.S., Great Britain, and the U.S.S.R.

Aug. 21   Pres. Kennedy reported to Congress that during the fiscal year ended June 30, 1963, $1.5 billion in U.S. farm commodities had been shipped abroad under the Food for Peace program.

Aug. 30   The "hot line," an emergency communications link between Washington and Moscow proposed by the U.S. to reduce the risk of accidental war, went into operation.

Oct. 2   White House issued a statement indicating that aid to South Vietnam would be continued and that the war there might be won by the end of 1965 if the political crisis did not significantly affect the military effort.

Oct. 7   Robert G. Baker resigned as secretary to the Senate majority after being charged with using his position for personal financial gain.

Oct. 7   U.S. formally ratified the treaty to limit nuclear testing when Pres. Kennedy affixed his signature. The treaty went into effect Oct. 10.

Oct. 9   Pres. Kennedy approved the sale of 4 million metric tons of wheat worth about $250 million to the U.S.S.R. through private commercial channels at the world price for cash or on short-term credit.

Oct. 11   U.S. protested strongly to U.S.S.R. against the blocking of a U.S.

art" was held at the Solomon R. Guggenheim Museum, New York. The show moved on to other major American cities later in the year, bemusing critics and public alike with its representational paintings of such prosaic subjects as soup cans and re-created comic strips. Prominent in the 3-year-old movement were artists Andy Warhol, Jasper Johns, Robert Rauschenberg, and Roy Lichtenstein.

Mar. 4.   **William Carlos Williams,** poet and physician, died at 79 in Rutherford, N.J. The National Institute of Arts and Letters awarded him its 1963 gold medal for poetry.

Mar. 7   The new **Pan Am Building,** designed by Emery Roth and Sons, was dedicated. It is an octagonal 59-story structure built over a portion of Grand Central Station. Most critics found it an architectural blight, decried its contribution toward congestion in an area already crowded with traffic and buildings, and lamented the destruction of the grand design of Grand Central. The prospect of future noisy flights from its rooftop heliport made other tenants in the area uneasy. Meanwhile, efforts to save N.Y.'s Pennsylvania Station failed, and that classic edifice began to fall to the wrecker's ball to make way for a new Madison Square Garden.

Mar. 11   An all-star cast from the Actors Studio revived **Eugene O'Neill's** *Strange Interlude* on Broadway. Directed by José Quintero, who was making a name for himself as an interpreter of O'Neill, it was staged in the original 9-act version and ran from 6 P.M. to midnight. There was a 1-hour intermission for supper.

Apr.   The famous **Armory Show** was re-created in its original setting, the 69th Regiment Armory in New York. First presented in 1913, the Armory Show gave Americans their first look at the works of Braque, Picasso, and other European modernists and is considered a decisive factor in the development of modern American art. Of the 1,300 works on exhibit in 1913, 370 were assembled for the anniversary show. After 50 years Marcel Duchamps'

SCIENCE; INDUSTRY; ECONOMICS; EDUCATION; RELIGION; PHILOSOPHY.

SPORTS; FASHIONS; POPULAR ENTERTAINMENT; FOLKLORE; SOCIETY.

June 11 **2 Negro students were enrolled** at the University of Alabama after Gov. George C. Wallace stepped aside when confronted by federalized National Guard troops.

June 12 The **murder by a sniper** of Medgar W. Evers, Mississippi field secretary for the NAACP, was followed by mass demonstrations in Jackson, Miss.

June 19 Pres. Kennedy requested Congress to enact **civil rights legislation** which would provide equal access of all citizens to public businesses in interstate commerce, and would enable the Attorney General to initiate school integration suits.

July 1 United Brotherhood of Carpenters, largest U.S. building trade union, ordered its locals to **end racial discrimination.**

July 7 Railroad operating unions rejected a plan by Labor Secretary Wirtz to resolve dispute with U.S. railroads over work rules. The plan was one of several efforts by the government to resolve the **labor-management deadlock.**

July 11 Demonstrations continued at New York City construction sites in an effort to win **more jobs for Negroes and Puerto Ricans.** During the month more than 700 persons were arrested.

July 12 Modified form of **martial law was imposed in Cambridge, Md.,** after National Guard troops were sent into city for 2nd time in a month to control racial violence.

July 26 Syncom II was successfully launched and on Aug. 15 placed over Brazil in a **synchronous orbit with the earth.** It transmitted telephone and Teletype between U.S. and Nigeria.

July 30 **Atoms for Peace prize** was awarded to Edwin M. McMillan of the U.S. and Vladimir I. Veksler of the U.S.S.R.

tragedienne in silent films, but her high-pitched, dry voice was a natural for comedy roles when talkies arrived. She played opposite Charles Laughton in *Ruggles of Red Gap* (1935).

June 8 The **Belmont Stakes** purse of $101,700 was won by *Chateaugay*, Baeza up.

June 12 The **most expensive motion picture** in movie history, *Cleopatra* opened in New York and at 69 theaters in the U.S. and Canada. The film cost $37 million, but by the end of the year it was obvious that 20th Century-Fox was well on its way to the $63 million set as its break-even point. The picture received mixed reviews, with most praise going to Rex Harrison's performance as Julius Caesar; Richard Burton's Antony and Elizabeth Taylor's Cleopatra were judged so-so. The couple's torrid romance during the filming probably played no little part in the picture's record advance sales. After the première, the 4-hour running time was cut by editing.

June 23 In a playoff match at Brookline, Mass., Julius Boros won the **U.S. Open** golf title, defeating Arnold Palmer and Jacky Cupit.

July 7 U.S. tennis amateur Chuck McKinley downed Fred Stolle of Australia 9–7, 6–1, 6–4 in the finals, to win the **Wimbledon singles title.**

July 9 Baseball's **All-Star** game in Cleveland was won 5–3 by the National League team.

July 22 In a return **heavyweight title bout** at Las Vegas, Sonny Liston knocked out Floyd Patterson in 2 minutes 10 seconds of the 1st round.

Aug. 5 Craig Breedlove set an unofficial **world auto speed record** of 407.45 mph on the Bonneville Salt Flats, Utah, driving a sleek 3-ton, 3-wheeled, jet-powered auto. The U.S. Auto Club established a new class for its records: "Jet-Powered Vehicles."

Aug. 24 Swimming star **Don Schollander** of Santa Clara became the 1st man

POLITICS AND GOVERNMENT; WAR; DISASTERS; VITAL STATISTICS.

BOOKS; PAINTING; DRAMA; ARCHITECTURE; SCULPTURE.

military convoy by Soviet troops outside West Berlin.

Oct. 16   2 U.S. **nuclear satellites** were secretly launched from Cape Canaveral for detection of any violation of the treaty ban on nuclear tests in space.

Oct. 24   Operation "Big Lift," the airlift of the 2nd Armored Div. from Texas to West Germany to demonstrate **U.S. ability to increase its ground forces in Europe quickly,** was completed in 63 hours, about 9 hours ahead of schedule.

Oct. 31   A **gas explosion** in the Indiana State Fair Grounds during an ice show caused the deaths of 68 spectators and injured 340.

Nov. 4   Soviet guards **halted a U.S. troop convoy** at the western border of Berlin. It was released after 41 hours following U.S. protests.

Nov. 7   U.S. recognized the provisional government of South Vietnam headed by a Buddhist premier, following **overthrow of Ngo Dinh Diem's government** by a military coup d'état in November.

Nov. 12   State Dept. **barred diplomats of Bulgaria, Czechoslovakia, Hungary, Poland, and Rumania** from 355 counties, about 11% of the continental U.S., for "reasons of national security."

Nov. 16   Prof. Frederick C. Barghoorn of Yale, a specialist on Soviet affairs, was released from the U.S.S.R. following **arrest and imprisonment on charges of espionage.**

Nov. 22   John F. Kennedy, 35th President of the U.S., was **assassinated** and pronounced dead at 1 P.M. in Dallas, Tex.

Nude Descending a Staircase was still the main attraction.

Apr. 30   Gov. John W. King of New Hampshire signed into a law a sweepstakes bill which authorized the institution of a government-operated lottery, to help finance the state's educational programs. Former F.B.I. man Edward J. Powers was named director of the lottery, which was to become operative in March 1964.

May 2   **Van Wyck Brooks,** critic and biographer, died at 77. In his early writings, Brooks was highly critical of the Puritan influence on 19th-century American literature. In the 5 volumes of his "Makers and Finders" series (the best-known, *The Flowering of New England,* won a Pulitzer Prize in 1936), he created the 1st composite picture of cultural and literary developments in the U.S.

May 3   *Labyrinth,* a new opera by Italian-born composer **Gian Carlo Menotti,** was performed on TV. On May 18 another new work, *Death of the Bishop of Brindisi,* "a dramatic cantata of the Children's Crusade," was 1st performed in Cincinnati.

Aug.   **Larry Rivers,** a painter and graphic artist, created an original billboard poster to advertise the 1st New York Film Festival. The 10 ft. by 16 ft. painting was placed at Broadway and 65th St. in New York during the month of August. A private collector had bought the work before it was even finished.

Aug. 1   **Theodore Roethke,** 55, poet and teacher, died at Bainbridge Island, Wash. His collection *The Waking: Poems, 1933–53,* won a Pulitzer Prize for 1954.

Aug. 2   **Oliver La Farge,** author and anthropologist, died at 83. He was a tireless fighter for the welfare of the American Indian, and his 1st novel, *Laughing Boy* (1929), is noted for its sensitive and accurate depiction of Navaho culture and psychology.

Aug. 14   Clifford Odets, 57, the outstanding proletarian dramatist of the 1930's, died in Los Angeles. His first 2 plays, *Waiting for Lefty* and *Awake and*

658

| SCIENCE; INDUSTRY; ECONOMICS; EDUCATION; RELIGION; PHILOSOPHY. | SPORTS; FASHIONS; POPULAR ENTERTAINMENT; FOLKLORE; SOCIETY. |

Aug. 28   An estimated 200,000 Negroes and whites participated in a "Freedom March" on Washington, supporting demands for full Negro civil rights immediately. National civil rights leaders met with Pres. Kennedy in the White House.

Aug. 28   Congressional legislation requiring **compulsory arbitration** of 2 key issues in the work-rules dispute and barring a strike for 18 days, averted a nationwide railroad strike scheduled for midnight.

Sept. 7   Food and Drug Administration announced that the controversial "miracle" drug **Krebiozen** was creatine, a common amino acid, and was ineffective against tumors.

Sept. 10   **Alabama National Guard was federalized** by Pres. Kennedy to prevent Gov. George C. Wallace's using guardsmen to stop public-school desegregation.

Sept. 14   **Quintuplets**—4 girls and a boy—were born to Mrs. Andrew Fischer in Aberdeen, S.D.

Sept. 27   Joseph M. Valachi, hoodlum turned informer, publicly identified the men who he said were the **chiefs of organized crime** in the U.S. in televised testimony before the Senate Permanent Investigations Subcommittee.

Oct. 10   The deferred **1962 Nobel Peace Prize** was awarded to Dr. Linus C. Pauling of the California Institute of Technology. Pauling had won the 1954 Nobel prize in chemistry.

Oct. 22   About 225,000 pupils were absent from Chicago public schools in a 1-day **boycott protesting de facto school segregation.**

Nov. 5   1963 **Nobel prize in physics** was awarded to Eugene P. Wigner of Princeton, Maria G. Mayer of the University of California, and Hans Jensen, a German scientist.

to break the 2-minute mark for the 200-meter freestyle swim. At Osaka, Japan, he won the event with the time of 1:58.4.

Aug. 24   At Miami, John Pennel became the **1st man to pole-vault 17 ft.** Using a fiber glass pole, he cleared 17 ft. ¾ in., a feat which won him the James E. Sullivan Memorial Award as the outstanding amateur athlete of the year.

Sept. 7   At Atlantic City, Donna Axum of El Dorado, Ark., was crowned **Miss America 1964.**

Sept. 29   **Stan (The Man) Musial** played his last game today for the St. Louis Cardinals, retiring at 42 to take an executive position with the club. In his 22 years in baseball, all with the Cards, the great batsman had set or tied 17 major-league records and 30 National League records.

Oct. 2–6   Sparked by the pitching of Sandy Koufax, the Los Angeles Dodgers won the **World Series** in 4 straight games from the New York Yankees. Dodger pitching held the Yanks to 4 runs in the Series. In the opener, Koufax set a Series record by striking out 15 men; he came back in the 4th game to win 2–1 over Whitey Ford. His Series performance capped a brilliant season for Koufax: he had fanned 306 men, hurled a no-hitter, and won 25 of his 30 games. He was named the National League's most valuable player, and won the Cy Young award as the outstanding player in the majors.

Oct. 29   **Adolphe Menjou,** 73, died in Beverly Hills. The actor was seen in more than 200 films from 1923 to 1960. He was noted for his suavity and the elegance of his attire. His autobiography is *It Took Nine Tailors* (1948).

Nov. 1   **Elsa Maxwell,** world-famed as a professional party giver since the 1920's, died in N.Y.C. Earlier in her life Miss Maxwell had been a vaudeville trouper and piano accompanist. In 1957 she wrote *How to Do It, or, The Lively Art of Entertaining.*

| POLITICS AND GOVERNMENT; WAR; DISASTERS; VITAL STATISTICS. | BOOKS; PAINTING; DRAMA; ARCHITECTURE; SCULPTURE. |

Texas Gov. John B. Connally was severely wounded. Vice-Pres. Lyndon B. Johnson took the presidential oath at 2:39 P.M. at Love Air Field, Dallas.

Nov. 24   Lee Harvey Oswald, **accused assassin of Pres. Kennedy,** was shot and killed by Jack Ruby while in the custody of Dallas police as millions watched on TV.

Nov. 25   John F. Kennedy was **buried at Arlington National Cemetery** with full military and state honors. His funeral was attended by world leaders.

Nov. 27   Pres. Johnson signed a bill increasing temporarily the **national debt limit** to $315 billion for the remainder of the fiscal year.

Nov. 29   A special commission, headed by Chief Justice Earl Warren, was named by Pres. Johnson to **investigate the assassination of Pres. Kennedy** and the murder of his accused assassin.

Sing!, which deal with social conflicts, are considered his best. Both were produced in 1935 by The Group Theater, an association he helped to found in 1931.

Sept. 11   A retrospective show of the work of **Hans Hofmann** opened at the Museum of Modern Art in New York. Hofmann, who emigrated from Germany in the '30's, was the greatest influence on the abstract-expressionism movement in America during the '40's and '50's.

Oct. 16   The *New York Mirror,* a Hearst paper, ceased publication. Although its circulation was 2nd largest among U.S. dailies, the paper fell victim to an economic squeeze, partly the result of the 114-day strike which closed 8 papers, partly because of decreasing advertising income. The *Mirror's* name, goodwill, and other assets were sold to the rival morning tabloid, the *Daily News.*

Nov. 22   While conducting the regular Friday afternoon concert of the Boston Symphony, Eric Leinsdorf learned of the **death of Pres. Kennedy.** He stopped the performance to announce the news and then played portions of Beethoven's 3rd Symphony, the *Eroica.*

Dec. 12   Contralto **Marian Anderson** announced that after her 1964–65 tour was completed she would retire from the concert stage.

Dec. 28   Paul Hindemith, German-born composer who became a U.S. citizen in 1946, died in Frankfurt, Germany. His most widely performed works are the symphony *Mathis der Mahler* (1934), adapted from his 7-scene opera with the same title, and the ballet *Nobilissima visione* (1938), based on the life of St. Francis of Assisi.

1964

Campaigning on the promise of achieving the "Great Society," Lyndon B. Johnson and Hubert H. Humphrey were elected President and Vice-President on Nov. 3 with a record-breaking landslide vote. For

The publishing event of the year was the posthumous appearance of Ernest Hemingway's *A Moveable Feast,* a collection of impressionistic sketches of Paris and its artistic colony of the years 1921–1926. The

SCIENCE; INDUSTRY; ECONOMICS; EDUCATION; RELIGION; PHILOSOPHY.	SPORTS; FASHIONS; POPULAR ENTERTAINMENT; FOLKLORE; SOCIETY.

Nov. 20 U.S. losses in the "chicken war" with Common Market over its **levies on U.S. poultry imports** were placed at $26 million by a special panel of experts. The U.S. in retaliation increased its tariffs on imports from market members.

Nov. 26 Congressionally created arbitration board for the railroad work-rules dispute ruled that 90% of diesel **locomotive firemen's jobs in freight and yard service were unnecessary** and should be eliminated gradually. Railroads had sought to eliminate all of the 40,000 firemen's jobs.

Dec. 4 Roman Catholic Ecumenical Council authorized the use of **vernacular languages**—English in the U.S.—in place of Latin for parts of the Mass and for the sacraments.

Nov. 8 6 of 8 trotters in the 6th race at **Roosevelt Raceway, N.Y.,** were involved in a pile-up. Fans who had laid bets on the daily double were outraged when the race was declared official, rioted all over the track and started a $20,000 fire. In the melee, 20 persons were injured.

Nov. 10 **"That Was the Week That Was,"** a U.S. version of the popular British program of the same name, had its TV première. The new series, known also as TW3, aimed its barbs at persons and subjects currently in the news and recognized no sacred cows, but on the whole, its sketches contained more cynicism than wit, more sarcasm than satire.

Dec. 8 **Frank Sinatra, Jr.,** son of the singer-actor, and himself an aspiring popular singer, was kidnapped at Lake Tahoe. He was released unhurt in Los Angeles Dec. 11 after his father paid ransom of $240,000. Most of the money was recovered 2 days later when the F.B.I. arrested 3 suspects.

Dec. 26–29 In Adelaide, Australia, the U.S. tennis team won the **Davis Cup** for the 1st time since 1958, defeating an Australian team 3–2.

1964

The first close-up pictures of the moon's surface, of assistance in achieving a lunar landing, were obtained by the U.S. At the same time, the U.S. successfully launched a ship to fly by and photograph the surface

At the New York World's Fair the General Motors Futurama proved to be the most popular attraction in terms of the number of people who queued up to "see the future." Ranking just behind GM in at-

661

POLITICS AND GOVERNMENT; WAR;
DISASTERS; VITAL STATISTICS.

BOOKS; PAINTING; DRAMA;
ARCHITECTURE; SCULPTURE.

the 1st time since 1920, the conservative wing of the Republican Party dominated its campaign, alienating its moderate and liberal voters. At the same time, the Democratic Party lost 5 Southern states because of civil rights legislation. Pres. Johnson succeeded in putting through the long-debated civil rights bill in July. He was equally successful with the other primary legislative aim of his Administration, the anti-poverty bill. His economy-in-government drive was reflected in his 1st budget which contained a $1.1 billion cut in defense spending, and he asked for $3.4 billion for foreign aid, the smallest amount requested in 16 years. Congress granted income and corporate tax reductions of more than $11 billion over a 2-year period, and appropriated $5.2 billion for NASA's space program, $1.1 billion for federal housing and urban renewal, and $375 million for a 3-year program of transportation development in congested urban areas. The Administration's $228 million program to aid the impoverished 10-state Appalachia area was refused as was the renewed plea for Medicare. Foreign relations were marked by continued tension with Cuba and in Berlin. Steady deterioration of the situation in Southeast Asia resulted in greater U.S. military and economic assistance to South Vietnam. In the Congo, Americans died in spite of U.S. efforts to help solve the internecine conflict. The U.S. and U.S.S.R. made efforts to reduce fear of nuclear war by reducing their stockpiles of materials for nuclear weapons. Steps were taken for international cooperation in developing peaceful uses of atomic energy and for sharing technological advances.

Jan. 9   Diplomatic relations with U.S. were severed by Panama following riots over flying of U.S. and Panamanian flags within the **Panama Canal Zone.**

Jan. 22   U.S. and Canada signed agreements for a multimillion dollar hydroelectric and **flood-control project in the Columbia River Basin.**

Jan. 23   The 24th Amendment abol-

book received mixed critical reactions. To many, the sketches were vintage Hemingway, a fitting memorial to a great writer, and valuable for the light they shed on his mode of writing. Others were offended by their malicious gossip about dead literary associates, by the author's purported anti-intellectualism, and by his preoccupation, at 60, with boasts of his capacity for liquor and his sexual prowess. Saul Bellow's 6th novel, *Herzog,* was the year's outstanding work of fiction, sharing best-seller status with Louis Auchincloss' *The Rector of Justin,* Gore Vidal's *Julian,* and the sex-farce *Candy,* written by Terry Southern and Mason Hoffenberg. Great interest was aroused by the purchase of the G. & C. Merriam Co., publishers of *Webster's Third New International Dictionary,* by Encyclopaedia Britannica, Inc. The Warren Commission's report on the assassination of President Kennedy was published by the U.S. Printing Office and, in paper and cloth editions, by 5 private publishers. Bantam Books, with the help of the *New York Times* national staff, prepared a paperback edition that was available to the public 80 hours after the report was released.

In the year that followed the death of Pres. Kennedy more than 50 books were published on aspects of his life. While many were rushed into print with the hope of catching part of this popular market, others were moving and thoughtful tributes to the dead President. Among the latter was *Of Poetry and Power,* a collection of verse eulogies.

The Repertory Theater of Lincoln Center had its 1st season in a temporary theater off Broadway while its permanent home, the Vivian Beaumont Theater, was still under construction at Lincoln Center. The company offered 2 new plays by Arthur Miller, *After the Fall* and *Incident at Vichy.* Both Miller plays stirred controversy, but in the end must be considered inferior to his early works. Another new play was S. N. Behrman's *But for Whom Charlie,* which was also one of that au-

| SCIENCE; INDUSTRY; ECONOMICS; EDUCATION; RELIGION; PHILOSOPHY. | SPORTS; FASHIONS; POPULAR ENTERTAINMENT; FOLKLORE; SOCIETY. |

of Mars. The 1st cooperative U.S.-U.S.S.R. space program—Echo II, a communications satellite—was established. Racial violence in both the North and South marked the nation's continuing efforts to assure civil rights to Negro citizens. Harlem, Brooklyn, Rochester, northern New Jersey, Jacksonville, Fla., Chicago, and Philadelphia, Pa., were scenes of violent rioting. Schools were boycotted in New York City, Cleveland, Cincinnati, Cambridge, Md., Boston, and Chicago to protest de facto segregation. Federal aid to university-level education was increased and extended. The 1964 New York World's Fair was opened. The Surgeon General's report on cigarette smoking found that the habit definitely contributed to an increased mortality rate.

Jan. 11 U.S. Surgeon Gen. Luther Terry's committee reported that the **use of cigarettes "contributes substantially to mortality** from certain specific diseases and to the over-all death rate."

Jan. 25 Echo II, the **1st U.S.-U.S.S.R. cooperative space program,** was launched from Vandenberg Air Force Base, Calif., and sent messages around the world by reflecting radio signals from one point on earth to another.

Jan. 29 The 5th Saturn rocket test, in preparation for the manned Apollo program, was launched from Cape Kennedy with a **20,000-lb. payload,** surpassing the U.S.S.R. weight-in-orbit record of 14,292 lbs.

Feb. 25 9-day **boycott on loading wheat** for the U.S.S.R. ended after U.S. assured International Longshoremen's Association that 50% of wheat under future contracts would be shipped in U.S. vessels.

Mar. 4 James R. Hoffa, president of the International Brotherhood of Teamsters, was found **guilty of tampering with a federal jury** in 1962 by a Chattanooga, Tenn., federal jury. He was sentenced to 8 years in prison and fined $10,000.

Mar. 25 2-day **race riot** in Jacksonville, Fla., triggered by student attempt to

tendance was the Vatican Pavilion, its chief attraction being Michelangelo's *Pietà.* Among the most admired pavilions were those of New York State and Spain. The Spanish Pavilion was also judged to have the fair's best restaurants. One of the most ubiquitous personages at the fair was Walt Disney whose firm had designed and constructed exhibits for the Ford Motor Company, the State of Illinois, and the Pepsi-Cola Company. While this was the largest, most lavish, and in many ways the best fair of all time, attendance lagged behind fair president Robert Moses' predictions and many exhibitors began to feel an economic pinch. Worst hit were the extravagant shows in the Lake Amusement Area that had been so popular at the 1939-1940 fair. Most of these shows had closed before the end of the fair's 1st season.

It was a year of upheavals in baseball. Just before the start of the season, American League owners refused a request of Kansas City to move its franchise to Louisville. In August, the Columbia Broadcasting System secured majority stockholder control of the Yankees, a move widely decried by baseball officials because it might result in baseball's being reclassified as a business, and as such, subject to antitrust legislation. The day after he led his team to victory in the World Series, Johnny Keane of the St. Louis Cardinals resigned as manager. Yogi Berra, manager of the losing Yankees, was fired and given another job in the club. A week later, Keane was hired as Yankee manager and Berra, after 19 years with the Yankees, was named player-coach of the N.Y. Mets. In the fall, the courts blocked a proposed move of the Milwaukee Braves to Atlanta for the 1965 season, but National League officials thought the move could be accomplished in 1966.

In boxing there was a great deal more noise than fighting. The racket came mostly from Cassius Clay, who touted his own beauty and prowess in doggerel verses on the theme "I am the greatest." He was good enough to wrest the heavyweight

ishing the poll tax was ratified by the 38th state, South Dakota, and was declared part of the U.S. Constitution on Feb. 4. It had been submitted to the state legislatures on Sept. 14, 1962.

Jan. 27   Sen. Margaret Chase Smith of Maine announced she would seek the **Republican nomination for President.**

Feb. 6   Cuba cut off the **water supply of the U.S. naval station** at Guantánamo in retaliation for the seizure of 4 Cuban fishing vessels within U.S. territorial waters near Florida on Feb. 2.

Feb. 13   Treasury Dept. announced the **1st U.S. drawing from the International Monetary Fund.**

Feb. 17   Supreme Court held by a 6 to 3 vote the controversial decision that **Congressional districts within each state must be substantially equal in population.**

Feb. 29   Pres. Johnson disclosed U.S. development of an advanced **experimental jet plane** the A-11, capable of flying at more than 2,000 mph and at an altitude of over 70,000 ft.

Mar. 4   Pres. Johnson announced the **appointment of 10 women** to major governmental posts.

Mar. 10   Soviet air defense forces **shot down a U.S. reconnaissance plane** which accidentally crossed into East German airspace, the 2nd such incident in 6 weeks. Following U.S. protests, the plane's 3 crewmen were released.

Mar. 10   **Henry Cabot Lodge** won the Republican presidential primary in New Hampshire with a write-in vote.

Mar. 14   Jack Ruby was **found guilty** by a Dallas, Tex., jury of the murder of Lee Harvey Oswald, accused assassin of Pres. Kennedy, and was sentenced to death.

thor's minor efforts. Things went better with the 2 revivals that completed the season: O'Neill's *Marco Millions* and Thomas Middleton and William Rowley's 17th-century tragedy *The Changeling*. Both artistic directors, Elia Kazan and Robert Whitehead, quit at the end of the season when they learned that efforts had been made to replace them. The over-all critical reaction to the company and its productions was that it takes more than 1 year to make a repertory group.

Much bitter feeling was generated over the Ford Foundation's announcement last December that most of the $7.7 million it had granted to dance groups was to go to the New York City Ballet, and none at all to such noted companies as the American Ballet Theatre and the Robert Joffrey Ballet, nor to any modern dance group. Friction between Robert Joffrey and the Harkness Foundation resulted first in withdrawal of the Foundation's subsidy of the Robert Joffrey Ballet, and then in June in the formation of the new Harkness Ballet, which was given all the sets, scores, and ballets created for the Joffrey company. In November, the Ford Foundation made a grant of $155,000 to keep the Robert Joffrey Ballet company together.

The Pulitzer Prizes again made more news this year for the awards not made than for the ones that were. The 2 most important categories, fiction and drama, along with music, were ignored by the trustees of Columbia University who make the awards. Prizes were given in history, *Puritan Village: The Formation of a New England Town* by Sumner Chilton Powell; biography, *John Keats* by Walter Jackson Bate; poetry, *At the End of the Open Road* by Louis Simpson; and general nonfiction, *Anti-Intellectualism in American Life* by Richard Hofstadter.

Jan. 16   The biggest **musical comedy hit of the season** opened on Broadway:

organize a school boycott and demonstration, subsided following appointment of a biracial committee in that city.

Apr. 2 Mrs. Malcolm Peabody, the 72-year-old mother of Gov. Endicott Peabody of Massachusetts, was released after 2 days in a St. Augustine, Fla., jail. Her arrest with 282 other persons, including several clergymen, had followed **4 days of civil rights demonstrations** in that city.

Apr. 8 Gemini spacecraft without occupants was **successfully launched into orbit** from Cape Kennedy.

Apr. 11 Pres. Johnson signed a farm bill providing for major **changes in federal wheat and cotton price subsidies.**

Apr. 16 Texas Gulf Sulphur Co. confirmed a **major find of zinc, copper, and silver ore,** estimated at more than 25 million tons, near Timmins, Ont., Canada.

Apr. 22 **New York World's Fair** opened on schedule in spite of civil rights demonstrations on the fairground and threat of a "stall-in" on roads to the fair by militant civil rights groups.

Apr. 27 Supreme Court refused to hear a suit brought by the railroad union challenging the arbitration award of the previous year under which thousands of firemen's jobs were eliminated. The Court left standing a lower court decision **upholding the constitutionality of the** Congressional act under which the **arbitration panel** was created.

May 19 The AFL-CIO Executive Council issued a statement opposing the Johnson Administration's **non-inflationary wage guidelines.**

May 21 World's 1st **nuclear-powered lighthouse** went into operation in Chesapeake Bay.

crown from Sonny Liston, but the World Boxing Association, which has a rule against return bouts, withdrew recognition of Clay's title when he announced plans for a rematch with Liston. Along the way, Clay became known as Muhammad Ali, his name in the Black Muslim movement.

Although musicals and comedies predominated in movie fare (*Mary Poppins, My Fair Lady, The Unsinkable Molly Brown, The Americanization of Emily, A Hard Day's Night*), there was a significant trend toward films which attempted to assess contemporary realities. The horrors of nuclear warfare were explored in *Fail Safe* and *Dr. Strangelove or: How I Learned to Stop Worrying and Love the Bomb.* In the 1st, an electronic malfunction triggers the holocaust; in the latter, the villain is a fanatical Air Force general. *Dr. Strangelove* was viewed variously as a brilliant satire, a piece of subversion, or a sick joke. *Seven Days in May* depicted an attempted coup d'état by a jingoistic Air Force general out of step with U.S. nuclear policy. In a presidential election year, Gore Vidal's *The Best Man* pitted an egghead against a ruthless old-line politician in a struggle for the nomination. The best documentary of the year, *Point of Order,* recapitulated the 1954 Senate hearings which aired countercharges of the Army and Sen. Joseph McCarthy. The year's more serious dramas, with the exception of *Beckett* and *Night of the Iguana,* came from abroad. Notable among them were Ingmar Bergman's *The Silence,* the British film *The Servant,* and *The Organizer,* an Italian picture in which Marcello Mastroianni portrayed a labor leader at the turn of the century.

Popular rock 'n' roll dances of the younger set had animal names: the Dog, the Monkey, the Chicken; but the favorites were the Watusi and the Frug. They were dances in which the partners gyrated, squirmed, jerked, and waved the arms—at a distance, of course. The swinging set crowded into "discothèques," where the music was supplied by records. The "in" places were Shepheard's and Trude Hel-

| POLITICS AND GOVERNMENT; WAR; DISASTERS; VITAL STATISTICS. | BOOKS; PAINTING; DRAMA; ARCHITECTURE; SCULPTURE. |

Mar. 28 Alaska was declared a major disaster area by Pres. Johnson following a tremendous **earthquake centered on Anchorage,** the state's largest city, the preceding day in which 117 persons died.

Apr. 3 U.S. and Panama agreed to the immediate **resumption of diplomatic relations** and to take steps to eliminate the "causes of conflict" between the 2 countries.

Apr. 14 The Defense Dept. published an inventory of U.S. and Soviet nuclear power to demonstrate the **increasing military superiority of the U.S.**

May 11 Pres. Johnson and Latin American leaders signed loan agreements and commitments bringing total U.S. funds for **Alliance for Progress** since Dec. 1963 to $430 million.

May 18 Supreme Court by a vote of 5 to 3 held **unconstitutional** a federal statute depriving naturalized citizens of their citizenship if they return to the land of their birth for 3 years.

May 19 U.S. State Dept. revealed that a network of more than 40 **microphones had been found embedded in the walls of the U.S. Embassy in Moscow.**

June 9 George Gessner, a 28-year-old Army deserter and defector, was convicted of **having passed U.S. nuclear secrets to the U.S.S.R.** and sentenced to life imprisonment, the 1st conviction under the 1946 Atomic Energy Act.

June 10 Senate by a vote of 71 to 29 invoked **cloture on the civil rights bill,** ending a 75-day filibuster.

June 15 Supreme Court held by a vote of 6 to 3 that both houses of **state legislatures must be apportioned on basis of population.** Previously, upper houses had geographical bases. Both houses of Congress made efforts to block the Court's decision.

Hello, Dolly! The show was based on Thornton Wilder's *The Matchmaker* and starred Carol Channing who was at the top of her form. The title song from the show became a hit record with jazz-man Louis Armstrong's version selling over 1 million copies.

Jan. 18 **Dylan,** a drama based on incidents in the life of the late Welsh poet Dylan Thomas, opened. The title role was taken by Sir Alec Guinness who won the Antoinette Perry Award for best actor for his performance. The play was written by Sidney Michaels.

Jan. 22 Composer **Marc Blitzstein,** 58, was murdered in Fort-de-France, Martinique. He is best known for his adaptation of Kurt Weill's *Threepenny Opera* (1952).

Jan. 23. The newly formed **Repertory Theater of Lincoln Center,** playing in a temporary shed near Washington Square Park, gave its 1st performance with Arthur Miller's new play *After the Fall.* Strongly autobiographical in character, it was not well received by most critics. Many people felt that Miller's view of himself was somewhat biased in his own favor.

Feb. 26 **The Deputy,** a play by Rolf Hochhuth, opened. A sensation even before its 1st performance, it charged Pope Pius XII with partial responsibility for the death of millions of Jews during World War II, by reason of his refusal to take a stand against the Nazis. Needless to say the play was bitterly attacked by some and righteously defended by others. The play itself was not an artistic triumph.

Mar. 9 The U.S. Supreme Court unanimously reversed a $500,000 **libel**

SCIENCE; INDUSTRY; ECONOMICS; EDUCATION; RELIGION; PHILOSOPHY.

SPORTS; FASHIONS; POPULAR ENTERTAINMENT; FOLKLORE; SOCIETY.

May 25 Supreme Court held unanimously that the **closing of public schools in Prince Edward Co., Va., in 1959 to avoid desegregation was unconstitutional.** The Court ordered the schools to reopen by a 7–2 vote.

June 11 The Rev. Martin Luther King, Jr., was 1 of 18 arrested as **civil rights demonstrations,** accompanied by violence, continued in St. Augustine, Fla., the oldest city in the nation.

June 14 United Steelworkers of America and 11 steel companies announced an agreement **not to practice racial discrimination in the steel industry.**

June 24 Federal Trade Commission announced that beginning in 1965 it would require cigarette packages to carry a warning that **cigarette smoking is dangerous to health.**

July 9 The **New Orleans Cotton Exchange,** 2nd largest in the U.S., **stopped "futures" trading** after 93 years of operation, announcing its action was due to government control exercised by the Agricultural Act of 1964.

July 18 **A race riot broke out in Harlem** after the shooting by an off-duty policeman of a Negro boy who allegedly attacked him with a knife. Serious riots in Brooklyn and Rochester, N.Y., followed. Property damage during the riots was several million dollars.

July 22 Federal court in Atlanta, Ga., **upheld the key section of the Civil Rights Act** of 1964 barring discrimination in public accommodations and ordered a restaurant and a motel in Atlanta to admit Negroes.

ler's in New York, and the Whiskey à Go-Go in Los Angeles. Dancers on the floor were often abetted by scantily clad "go-go girls" who performed in relays on raised platforms.

Oscar awards of the Academy of Motion Picture Arts and Sciences: best film, *My Fair Lady;* best actor, Rex Harrison (*My Fair Lady*); best actress, Julie Andrews (*Mary Poppins*); best supporting actor, Peter Ustinov (*Topkapi*); best supporting actress, Lila Kedrova (*Zorba, the Greek*); best director, George Cukor (*My Fair Lady*); best foreign-language film, *Yesterday, Today, and Tomorrow.*

Feb. 11 Best-in-show at the **Westminster Kennel Club** show in New York City was a whippet, Ch. Courtenay Fleetwood of Pennyworth.

Feb. 25 At Miami Beach, heavyweight boxing champ Sonny Liston could not answer the bell for the 7th round because of an injury to his left arm, and surrendered his title to **Cassius Clay** on a TKO. Clay announced he would give Liston a rematch, but the World Boxing Association claimed it had a rule forbidding return bouts, announced the heavyweight title vacant, and made plans for an elimination tournament. When their contender Cleveland Williams was shot by Texas highway police, the W.B.A. postponed its plans until 1965. The Clay-Liston bout, scheduled for Nov. 16 in Boston, was called off 70 hours before the bell when Clay went to the hospital for a hernia operation.

Mar. 15 After a tempestuous courtship that began during the filming of their co-starring extravaganza *Cleopatra,* film stars **Elizabeth Taylor and Richard Burton were married** in Montreal. Miss Taylor had been divorced 10 days earlier from singer Eddie Fisher; it was her 5th marriage, Mr. Burton's 2nd.

Mar. 21 At Aintree, England, the **Grand National Steeplechase** was won by *Team Spirit,* the 1st American horse to win the event in 26 years.

667

June 22   Supreme Court, by vote of 6 to 3, **held unconstitutional the provisions of the Internal Security Act** of 1950 denying U.S. passports to Communists.

July 2   **Civil Rights Act of 1964** was signed by Pres. Johnson in a televised ceremony a few hours after the House approved Senate amendments by vote of 289 to 126.

July 8   Senate Rules Committee reported that it had found Robert G. Baker, former secretary to the Democratic Senate majority, guilty of **"many gross improprieties"** while employed by the Senate, but did not accuse him of any specific violation of law.

July 15   Sen. Barry Goldwater of Arizona was nominated for President on the 1st ballot by the **28th Republican National Convention** in San Francisco. The next day Rep. William E. Miller of New York was nominated for Vice-President.

July 19   Gov. George C. Wallace of Alabama withdrew his **segregationist candidacy for President.** He had been committed to run in at least 16 states.

July 24   18 nations initialed agreements in Washington, D.C., on **international management and ownership of the global communications satellite** system being developed by the U.S.

Aug. 2   3 North Vietnamese PT boats **attacked U.S. destroyer** *Maddox* in Gulf of Tonkin in international waters, but were fought off by fighter planes from U.S. carrier *Ticonderoga.* 3 days later U.S. planes bombed North Vietnamese installations and naval craft.

Aug. 7   Senate and House passed a joint resolution approving U.S. action in

judgment against the **N.Y. Times** by the Alabama Supreme Court. The case arose out of factual misstatements in a paid political ad which criticized the conduct of state officials. The Supreme Court ruled ·that the Constitution prohibits a public official from recovering damages for defamatory statements about his official conduct unless he can prove they were made with actual malice—that is, knowing they were false, or with reckless disregard of whether they were false or not.

Mar. 16   The **Gallery of Modern Art,** New York's newest museum, opened in its brand-new building on Columbus Circle. Sponsored by A & P heir Huntington Hartford, the museum's name was faintly ironic since its permanent collection and special exhibitions did not include anything even remotely avant-garde. (The 1st big show, which opened the next month, was a retrospective of the Pre-Raphaelites.) While New Yorkers generally were puzzled over why they had the new museum, some critics were hostile to Hartford's intentions. The museum building, however, designed by Edward D. Stone, was praised for its beauty and functional efficiency.

Apr. 14   **Rachel Carson,** biologist and author, died at 56 in Silver Spring, Md. Miss Carson's *The Sea Around Us* (1951) and *The Edge of the Sea* (1956) were popular scientific works acclaimed also as fine literary achievements. In *The Silent Spring* (1962), she focused attention on the hazards to wild life and to people of the indiscriminate use of weed killers and insecticides.

Apr. 18   **Ben Hecht,** playwright, novelist, journalist, died at 70 in New York City. Hecht will be best remembered for the 2 plays he wrote in collaboration with Charles MacArthur, *The Front Page*

SCIENCE; INDUSTRY; ECONOMICS; EDUCATION; RELIGION; PHILOSOPHY.

SPORTS; FASHIONS; POPULAR ENTERTAINMENT; FOLKLORE; SOCIETY.

July 26   **James R. Hoffa,** president of the International Brotherhood of Teamsters, was **convicted of fraud and conspiracy** in the handling of his union's pension fund by a federal jury in Chicago. He was sentenced to 5 years in prison and fined $10,000.

July 31   U.S. lunar probe Ranger 7 crashed into the moon after sending to earth **4,316 photographs of the lunar surface** taken within a 1,300-mile range.

Aug 4   The **bodies of 3 civil rights workers** who had been missing since June 22 were found by the F.B.I. in a dam near Philadelphia, Miss.

Aug. 5   House passed and sent to the White House for signature a bill authorizing the creation of a National Commission on Technology, Automation and Economic Progress to **study the effect of automation on unemployment.**

Aug. 14   **Negro students registered without incident** at previously white elementary schools in Biloxi, Miss., the 1st desegregation of schools below the college level in that state.

Aug. 19   **Communications satellite** Syncom III was sent into space. In October it transmitted live the Olympic Games from Tokyo to California.

Aug. 28   Nimbus I, an **advanced meteorological satellite,** was fired from Vandenberg Air Force Base, Calif. Although it missed its intended circular orbit, it sent back exceptionally clear close-up pictures of the earth's nighttime cloud cover.

Aug. 29   In Philadelphia, Pa., 125 blocks were quarantined by Mayor James H. J. Tate following outbreak of **racial rioting.** Over 500 persons were injured and

Mar. 21   In the final game of the **NCAA basketball tournament** at Kansas City, U.C.L.A. defeated Duke University 98–83. The victory climaxed a perfect season for U.C.L.A., which won all 30 of its games, the 1st major team to have an undefeated season since 1957.

Mar. 23   **Peter Lorre,** famed for his screen portrayals of soft-spoken villains, died at 59 in Hollywood.

Apr. 22   Opening-day ceremonies of **N.Y. World's Fair** of 1964–65 were marred by threats of a massive traffic tie-up by members of the Congress of Racial Equality, whose members planned to have their cars "run out of gas" on all major arteries leading to the fairgrounds. The "stall-in," intended to dramatize CORE's demand for city action against racial discrimination, did not materialize, but it was probably a major factor (along with bad weather) in cutting attendance from an expected 250,000 to 92,646. Pres. Johnson's dedication speech was interrupted by the demonstrators' chants. When the fair closed its 1st season on Oct. 18, it was apparent that it was in dire financial straits. Low attendance was blamed on fear of racial violence, high prices, and criticism of the fair as a cultural desert.

Apr. 25   In the **Stanley Cup** playoffs, the Toronto Maple Leafs won the cup for the 3rd year in a row, defeating the Detroit Red Wings 4 games to 3.

May 2   *Northern Dancer,* Bill Hartack up, won the 90th **Kentucky Derby,** beating *Hill Rise* by a neck.

May 16   The **Preakness Stakes** was won by *Northern Dancer,* Hartack up.

May 30   A. J. Foyt of Texas, driving a Sheraton-Thompson Special, won the annual Memorial Day race at **Indianapolis Speedway.** He averaged 147.350 mph on the 500-mile course, a new record. During the race, a spectacular pile-up and fire claimed the lives of Eddie Sachs and Dave MacDonald.

May 31   In the **longest game in baseball history,** the Giants finally defeated the

669

POLITICS AND GOVERNMENT; WAR; DISASTERS; VITAL STATISTICS.

BOOKS; PAINTING; DRAMA; ARCHITECTURE; SCULPTURE.

Southeast Asia. A resolution passed on Aug. 1 had granted authority to the President to use all necessary measures to **repel armed attack and to provide help to any SEATO nation** asking assistance in defense of its freedom.

Aug. 26   Pres. Johnson and Sen. Hubert H. Humphrey of Minnesota were named by acclamation their party's choice of presidential and vice-presidential candidates by the **34th Democratic National Convention** in Atlantic City, N.J.

Aug. 30   Pres. Johnson signed the **anti-poverty bill,** Economic Opportunity Act of 1964, authorizing $947.5 million for youth programs, community action anti-poverty measures in rural areas, small-business loans, and job training, including Job Corps for youth.

Aug. 31   Census Bureau reported that as of July 1, 1964, California had passed New York as the nation's **most populous state.**

Sept. 3   A permanent **national wilderness** system comprising 9.2 million acres was established by Congressional act and signed by Pres. Johnson.

Sept. 17   Pres. Johnson disclosed that the U.S. had perfected 2 weapons systems —the Nike-Zeus rocket and the Thor rocket—that could **intercept and destroy armed satellites** circling the earth in space.

Sept. 27   The **Warren Commission** report on the assassination of John F. Kennedy was released with the finding that there was no conspiracy, either domestic or international, in the assassination, and that Lee Harvey Oswald alone was responsible for it. The report found that Jack Ruby, convicted murderer of Oswald, had had no prior contact with Oswald.

(1928) and *Twentieth Century* (1933). Both were made into successful films.

Apr. 19   **Michelangelo's Pietà,** on loan from St. Peter's in Rome, was unveiled at the Vatican Pavilion at the New York World's Fair. The famous marble statue had arrived by ship from Italy 6 days before. For its transportation, a special waterproof, floatable crate, designed to free itself from a sinking ship, had been constructed. Placed in a dramatic setting by stage designer Jo Mielziner, the *Pietà* was 1 of the most popular attractions at the fair.

Apr. 23   The 400th anniversary of the **birth of William Shakespeare** was celebrated all over the U.S. During the entire year there was unprecedented attention given to the poet and his works. Dozens of books were published that related to Shakespearean scholarship and a number of national magazines, including *Life* and the *Saturday Review,* devoted entire issues to the anniversary. In festivals and single performances from coast-to-coast, 30 of Shakespeare's 37 plays were performed. Among the finest productions of the year were Richard Burton's *Hamlet* (with Hume Cronyn and Alfred Drake) in New York and the Royal Shakespeare Company's *King Lear* (starring Paul Scofield), which played in Boston, Philadelphia, Washington, and New York.

Apr. 24   The **New York City Ballet,** under the direction of George Balanchine, opened its 1st season in its new house, the New York State Theater at Lincoln Center for the Performing Arts. A new ballet, *A Midsummer Night's Dream,* was performed in celebration of the 400th anni-

more than 350 persons were arrested during 3 days of rioting (Aug. 28–30).

Sept. 9   Chrysler Corp. and the **AFL-CIO United Automobile Workers** agreed to a new 3-year national contract 55 minutes before 74,000 workers were scheduled to strike.

Sept. 12   6 persons won $100,000 each in the **1st legalized sweepstakes** in U.S. horse-racing history at Rockingham Park, N.H.

Sept. 18   Another national strike of auto workers was averted when **Ford Motor Co.** and the UAW reached agreement on a new union contract less than an hour before deadline. However, plants went out on strike over local grievances on Nov. 6, tying up production until Nov. 23.

Sept. 25   AFL-CIO United Automobile Workers began a nationwide strike against **General Motors Corp.**, the world's largest industrial corporation, after failure to reach a new labor agreement. A new 3-year national contract was agreed to on Oct. 5 but local strikes tied up production until Nov. 7.

Oct. 2   4 Philadelphia, Miss., law-enforcement officers and a former sheriff were indicted by a federal grand jury on charges of **depriving 7 Negroes of their civil rights** by unlawfully detaining and beating them.

Oct. 14   1964 Nobel Peace Prize was awarded to the Rev. Martin Luther King, Jr., Negro civil rights leader of Atlanta, Ga. He donated the award, valued at $54,600, to the civil rights movement.

Oct. 15   The 1964 Nobel prize for physiology or medicine was awarded jointly to Dr. Conrad E. Block of Harvard and

Mets 8–6 after 7 hours and 23 minutes of the 2nd game of a doubleheader. The end came in the 23rd inning, matching the 4th longest game in innings played.

June 6   A total of $5,834,896 was bet on a 9-race program at Aqueduct, setting the world record for a single day's wagers at a horse-racing track. Highlight of the day was the **Belmont Stakes,** on which a crowd of 61,215 bet $903,948. Winner of the event was *Quadrangle,* whose share of the purse was $110,850.

June 20   Golfer Ken Venturi, making a comeback from illness, scored a personal and popular triumph in the **National Open,** winning by 2 strokes over Tommy Jacobs at the Congressional Club in Washington, D.C. Venturi was voted pro golfer of the year.

June 21   At Shea Stadium pitcher Jim Bunning of the Phillies pitched a **perfect game** against the Mets, the 1st regular season perfect game since 1922.

Aug. 27   Comedienne Gracie Allen, for 35 years the zany half of a comedy team with her husband George Burns, died at 58 in Hollywood.

Sept. 15–21   Defending the America's Cup, yachting's oldest trophy, the U.S. boat *Constellation* easily outdistanced a British challenger in 4 races off Newport, R.I. 1st won by the *America* in 1851, this was the cup's 19th successful defense by the U.S., and the 16th failure by an English contender. The loser was the *Sovereign,* built by Tony Boyden and skippered by Peter Scott. The *Constellation* was the product of a U.S. syndicate of yachtsmen; its nominal skipper, Eric Ridder, took over on the final legs from helmsman Robert Bavier. In a total of 97.2 miles and about 17 hours of sailing, the *Constellation* racked up a victory margin of 48 minutes and 11 seconds. At times she was practically out of sight of her rival.

Sept. 25–28   For the 1st time in the history of **Davis Cup** tennis competition, the challenge round was played on clay courts. The scene was a school playground

671

POLITICS AND GOVERNMENT; WAR; DISASTERS; VITAL STATISTICS.

BOOKS; PAINTING; DRAMA; ARCHITECTURE; SCULPTURE.

Oct. 1 FCC held, by vote of 4 to 3, that any radio or TV station carrying a presidential press conference in full must grant **equal air time** to other presidential candidates.

Oct. 14 Presidential aide Walter W. Jenkins resigned following his **arrest in Washington, D.C.,** on a morals charge. An F.B.I. investigation later revealed that Jenkins had not compromised the security or interests of the U.S.

Oct. 20 **Herbert Hoover,** President of the U.S. from 1929 to 1933 and a noted humanitarian, **died in New York at the age of 90.** A 30-day mourning period was proclaimed.

Nov. 3 **Lyndon B. Johnson and Hubert H. Humphrey were elected President and Vice-President** with more than 42,676,-000 votes to the Republicans' 26,860,000. The Democrats carried 44 states and the District of Columbia, the first time the District voted in a presidential election, and increased their majorities in both houses of Congress.

Nov. 25 U.S. Air Force planes **dropped 600 Belgian paratroopers into Stanleyville to rescue white hostages** held captive by Congolese rebels. Minutes before they landed, 29 hostages were executed, including Dr. Paul E. Carlson, U.S. medical missionary. A total of 80 whites were discovered to have been slain in rebel territory.

Dec. 5 U.S. determination to fight Communism in Vietnam was reaffirmed as Pres. Johnson presented the **Medal of Honor** to U.S. Army Capt. Roger H. C. Donlon, the 1st serviceman to receive that honor for heroism since the Korean War.

versary of Shakespeare's birth. This was also the opening night of the new theater that had been designed by Philip Johnson. Attempting a modern interpretation of traditional theater elegance, the interior was red and gold, studded with giant, faceted lamps that resembled jewels.

May 25 In New York the **Museum of Modern Art** opened its 2 new wings and expanded sculpture garden. The new construction provided enough space for 2 major special shows to be given at the same time and allowed room for a changing display of new acquisitions. Above the special exhibition galleries, the museum's 1st permanent photographic gallery was installed.

Aug. 20 Mrs. Lyndon Johnson, representing the U.S., and Mrs. Lester Pearson, wife of the Canadian Prime Minister, attended a ceremony dedicating **Campobello Island** as a memorial to President Franklin D. Roosevelt. It was at his vacation estate here that the President was stricken with polio, and where he began his recovery. By terms of an agreement signed in January, the New Brunswick island was designated Roosevelt Campobello International Park, and is to be administered by a commission made up of 3 members from each country.

Sept. 22 Destined for a long run, the musical **Fiddler on the Roof** opened on Broadway. It was based on the stories of Shalom Aleichem and starred Zero Mostel.

Oct. 13 German pianist **Wilhelm Kempff,** now 69 and long familiar to American music lovers through his recordings, made his U.S. debut at Carnegie Hall.

SCIENCE; INDUSTRY; ECONOMICS; EDUCATION; RELIGION; PHILOSOPHY.	SPORTS; FASHIONS; POPULAR ENTERTAINMENT; FOLKLORE; SOCIETY.

Feodor Lynen, a German professor, for their work in the relationship between heart disease and cholesterol.

Oct. 16   Pres. Johnson signed a bill **increasing appropriations of the National Defense Education Act** and extending it to June 30, 1968.

Oct. 29   1964 **Nobel prize** in physics was awarded to Charles H. Townes of M.I.T. and 2 Russian scientists, Nikolai Basov and Aleksandr Prokhorov.

Nov. 21   The **longest strike-induced shutdown by major newspapers** in U.S. history—132 days—was ended when pressmen for the *Detroit News* and *Detroit Free Press* accepted a new settlement.

Nov. 21   Verrazano-Narrows Bridge between Brooklyn and Staten Island, N.Y. —at 6,690 ft. the **world's longest suspension bridge**—was formally opened.

Nov. 28   Mariner IV was launched from Cape Kennedy **to transmit close-up TV pictures of Mars** on its projected fly-by within 8,600 miles of that planet in July 1965.

Dec. 4   **21 white men in Mississippi were arrested** by F.B.I. on charges of conspiring to violate the victims' civil rights in connection with the murder of 3 civil rights workers near Philadelphia, Miss., in June.

Dec. 10   **Conspiracy charges against 19 of the 21** men arrested in Mississippi in connection with the murder of 3 civil rights workers were dismissed in Meridian, Miss. Charges against the other 2 were dismissed at the federal government's request.

in Cleveland, where champions Roy Emerson and Fred Stolle led a strong Australian team that took the trophy from the U.S. Emerson had won the U.S. title 2 weeks earlier at Forest Hills.

Oct. 7–15   Pitcher Bob Gibson of the St. Louis Cardinals struck out 31 batters in 3 games, a Series record, as his team took the **World Series** 4 games to 3 from the N.Y. Yankees. Gibson lost the 2nd game but came back to win 2 games in 4 days, including the 7th game at St. Louis, a 7–5 victory. In the 3rd game, the Yanks' Mickey Mantle hit his 16th Series homer, breaking the record held by Babe Ruth. The regular season had ended with the most exciting pennant races in years: the Yankees won 30 of their last 40 games but did not clinch the AL flag until the next-to-last day of the season; the Cards won the NL pennant in the fading sunlight of the last day of season play, a victory that spared the league a 3-way tie involving also the Phillies and Cincinnati.

Oct. 10   **Eddie Cantor,** banjo-eyed comedian of vaudeville, movies, radio, and TV, died at 72 in Hollywood.

Oct. 10–24   At the 18th **Olympic Games** in Tokyo, strong swimming and track and field teams wor. the U.S. 36 gold medals for 1st place. The Russians took 30 1st-place medals, the Japanese 16.

Oct. 29   Thieves made off with some of the most magnificent jewels in the collection of rare stones in the Museum of Natural History in New York City. The value of the stolen jewels was estimated at $410,000; actually, being irreplaceable, they were priceless. Among them were the world's largest sapphire, the 565-carat Star of India, and the 100-carat DeLong ruby. A tip-off led to the arrest of professional swimmers Allan Kuhn and Jack (Murph the Surf) Murphy, and beach boy Roger Clark. Most of the gems were recovered as part of an agreement by which the trio received a lenient sentence (Apr. 6, 1965). The DeLong ruby was finally ransomed on Sept. 2, 1965.

673

Dec. 18   Plans for a **new, deeper sea-level canal between the Atlantic and Pacific oceans** to be built in either Central America or Colombia were announced by Pres. Johnson. At the same time he said a new treaty with Panama will be negotiated to replace the 1903 treaty under which the Panama Canal is administered.

Dec. 22   Oregon and 4 northern California counties were declared **major disaster areas** because of heavy snow, rain, and floods. Deaths in Oregon, California, Idaho, Washington, and Nevada totaled at least 40.

Oct. 15   **Cole Porter,** 1 of the most successful song writers of all time, died at age 71. He wrote the music and lyrics for nearly a dozen hit shows, among them *Kiss Me Kate* and *Panama Hattie*. Some of his best-known songs are: "Begin the Beguine," "Night and Day," "Don't Fence Me In," "You're the Top," and the Yale "Bulldog Song."

Oct. 21   The U.S. Supreme court declined to review a lower court's decision that there had been no **copyright infringement** on the songs of Irving Berlin which were parodied in *Mad* magazine.

1965

Greatly increased U.S. participation in the war in Vietnam was protested by thousands of citizens in demonstrations across the nation. Before year's end, the U.S. losses in Vietnam since January 1961 exceeded 1,300 dead and 6,100 wounded. The 1st large-scale use of helicopters in war helped to keep the fatality rate less than 2% of wounded, where it had been 2.7% in the Korean War, 3.3% in World War II, and 5.5% in World War I. The Johnson Administration obtained passage of most of its programs by one of the nation's most productive Congresses in terms of bulk and scope of legislation enacted. Total appropriations were a record high for peacetime: $119.3 billion, of which $46.9 billion were for defense. At the same time, Pres. Johnson's request for foreign aid was the smallest in the history of this program—$3.38 billion, of which $3.2 billion was granted. The Medicare program was passed, as were anti-poverty and voting-rights bills and increased aid to education. Although turned down on his requests for repeal of Section 14-b of the Taft-Hartley Act, which permits state "right-to-work" laws, and for self-government of the District of Columbia, Pres. Johnson was given a $1.1 billion appropriation for development in Appalachia, ex-

The most sensational theatrical offering of the year was Peter Weiss's *The Persecution and Assassination of Marat as Performed by the Inmates of the Asylum of Charenton Under the Direction of the Marquis de Sade,* a production of the Royal Shakespeare Company directed by Peter Brook, which opened Dec. 27. The playwright's cynical view of the French Revolution, and all revolutions, was conveyed by actors manifesting a wide variety of psychoses; audiences, and especially the players, found the experience harrowing. Edward Albee's new play, *Tiny Alice,* which opened Dec. 29, 1964, was a religious allegory that defied interpretation. Revivals of the Kaufman-Hart success of the 1930's, *You Can't Take It With You,* and Tennessee Williams' *The Glass Menagerie,* were well received. Backers poured $650,000 into the hapless musical *Kelly,* which opened and closed Feb. 6.

The Repertory Theater of Lincoln Center occupied its new home, the Vivian Beaumont Theater, but the company continued to draw adverse criticism with its substandard productions.

The most significant development in art this year was a rather abrupt shift in emphasis from "pop" to "op" (optical) art,

| SCIENCE; INDUSTRY; ECONOMICS: EDUCATION; RELIGION; PHILOSOPHY. | SPORTS; FASHIONS; POPULAR ENTERTAINMENT; FOLKLORE; SOCIETY. |

Dec. 16 AFL-CIO **International Longshoremen's Association and the New York Shipping Association reached agreement on a 4-year contract,** the union's first long-term settlement in its 92-year history. Before ratification of the agreement, a series of wildcat strikes broke out in New York and elsewhere.

Oct. 31 At Aqueduct race track in New York, the 7-year-old gelding **Kelso** won the Jockey Club Gold Cup for the 5th straight time. His time, 3:19.2, broke his own American record for 2 miles. For the 5th time in a row, *Kelso* was voted Horse of the Year. His 1964 earnings of $311,660 boosted his lifetime total to $1,893,362, and made him the biggest money winner of all time.

Dec. 27 In Baltimore, fullback Jimmy Brown led the Cleveland Browns in a massive ground offensive that swamped the Baltimore Colts 27–0, and brought the Browns the **National Football League championship.**

1965

The 1st U.S. "walk" in space and the successful rendezvous of 2 Gemini capsules 185 miles above the earth assisted the nation in its preparations for a manned trip to the moon. Photographs of the surface of Mars showed no trace of the famous "canals" and provided evidence that the planet has little earth-like atmosphere. Commercial communication by an earth satellite was realized with the aid of Early Bird. The most spectacular comet since Halley's in 1910 was spotted by 2 amateur Japanese astronomers, and was named the Comet Ikeya-Seki. Demonstrations for civil rights continued in the South with Alabama the site of a struggle for voting rights. The nation's most violent and destructive race riot erupted in Watts, a Negro section of Los Angeles, highlighting the disadvantageous conditions under which many Northern residents live. The nation's gross national product rose from $628 billion to $672 billion, exceeding by $14 billion the predictions of the President's economic advisors.

Feb. 1 **Dr. Martin Luther King, Jr., was arrested** and spent 4 days in jail before posting the $200 bond set in Selma, Ala., during demonstrations protesting discrimination against Negro applicants for voter

In both clothes and hair styles, the trend was toward sexual ambivalence. Young men sprouted shoulder-length hair and girls wore bangs and shingles, a style designed by London hairdresser Vidal Sassoon. The "Mod" look, also emanating from London, put the young of both sexes into tight, bell-bottom trousers; but for dress-up the girls wore skirts 2 inches above the knees and ruffles at the throat and wrists. The Courrèges look was the high-fashion sensation. It featured a solid color "A-line" dress trimmed with contrasting bands, high white boots, and often a helmet-type hat. Art-inspired fashions included the "Mondrian" dresses of Yves St. Laurent and "op" art fabrics favored by Capucci.

Two of the more popular TV series capitalized on the vogue for James Bond-type spy thrillers: "The Man From U.N.C.L.E." featured the tongue-in-cheek adventures of special agent Napoleon Solo (Robert Vaughn) and his sidekick Ilya Kuryakin (David McCallum); the comedy "Get Smart" had befuddled agent Maxwell Smart (Don Adams), whose retraction of exaggerated claims gave currency to the puckish query "Would you believe . . . ?"

675

cise taxes were cut, a new immigration law abolished the 41-year-old national-origins quota system, and a new Cabinet Dept. of Housing and Urban Development was established. The nation's rate of population growth was the slowest since 1945, 1.21%, as a result of a declining birth rate.

Jan. 4   In his **State of the Union** message, Pres. Johnson listed among his goals improved public education, medical research, national beautification, development of poverty-stricken regions, crime prevention, and the elimination of all voting obstacles.

Jan. 20   **Lyndon B. Johnson and Hubert H. Humphrey were inaugurated as** President and Vice-President.

Jan. 28   Pres. Johnson requested Congress to propose **constitutional amendments** which would cover presidential disability, provide for filling vice-presidential vacancy, and reform the Electoral College system so that voters could not be overridden by electors.

Feb. 5   **Water in New York City's storage reservoirs reached an all-time low** of 24.5% of capacity in the drought which began in September 1961 and covered an area from Maine to northern Delaware.

Feb. 10   Pres. Johnson, in a special message to Congress, requested redoubled efforts to promote exports and asked that U.S. businessmen and bankers reduce investing and lending abroad to help **eliminate deficits in the nation's balance of payments.** He urged U.S. and other tourists to "See the U.S.A."

Mar. 4   The **U.S. Information Agency closed its facilities in Indonesia** due to "intolerable" harassment, the first time it had withdrawn its facilities from any of the 100 nations in which it operates. The Peace Corps was withdrawn the following month.

Mar. 8   The Supreme Court held unanimously that a **conscientious objector** who has a sincere belief in a Supreme Being, even though differing from that held

abstract painting which arrests the attention by the dazzling interaction of colors, and/or optical illusion. Most critics welcomed the resurgent mode as a delightful change from the commonplace treatments of "pop" art. The most important "op" show, "The Responsive Eye," opened at N.Y.'s Museum of Modern Art, and was seen subsequently in St. Louis, Seattle, Pasadena, and Baltimore. Predominating in the show were works by Josef Albers and Victor de Vasarely, the best-known masters of perceptual abstraction.

Two biographies of the late President Kennedy were the nonfiction standouts of the year. Theodore Sorensen's *Kennedy* was a fast-paced, intimate account of Kennedy's career since 1953, criticized only because it was deemed too discreet. In *A Thousand Days,* on the other hand, Arthur M. Schlesinger, Jr., provoked much hostility by his assertion that Kennedy planned to depose Dean Rusk as Secretary of State after the 1964 elections; it was felt the disclosure would seriously handicap Mr. Rusk, who still held the position under Pres. Johnson. Richard Whalen's *The Founding Father: The Story of Joseph P. Kennedy* was a frank portrait of the late President's father. Samuel Eliot Morison's *The Oxford History of the American People* was acclaimed as a robust and expert, albeit highly personal, survey of the U.S. from the aboriginal Indians to the accession of Pres. Johnson. With *Never Call Retreat,* Bruce Catton concluded his massive 3-volume *Centennial History of the Civil War.* The American Library Association's Newbery Medal for the most distinguished children's book was awarded to Maia Wojciechowska for *Shadow of a Bull.*

Jan. 4   **T. S. Eliot,** U.S.-born British poet, critic, and playwright, died at 76 in London. With the publication of his earliest books of poetry, *Prufrock and Other Observations* (1917) and *The Wasteland* (1922), Eliot established himself as a ma-

| SCIENCE; INDUSTRY; ECONOMICS; EDUCATION; RELIGION; PHILOSOPHY. | SPORTS; FASHIONS; POPULAR ENTERTAINMENT; FOLKLORE; SOCIETY. |

registration. More than 3,000 persons were arrested during the voter registration drive begun Jan. 2.

Feb. 3   Following an Academy investigation, 105 of 2,560 cadets resigned from the Air Force Academy for **cheating on examinations.** Later 4 more resigned when the cadet wing honor board found they had had knowledge of the cheating but had not reported it.

Feb. 7   A contract based on attrition to **reduce the labor force** was signed by 5 AFL-CIO non-operating railroad unions and railroad management, solving the last remaining collective-bargaining dispute for the 1st time in over 5 years.

Feb. 16   Pegasus 1, a **micrometeoroid detection station** with 96-ft. wings as sensors, was launched into orbit.

Feb. 20   Ranger 8, launched Feb. 17, sent back to earth **7,137 photos of the moon's surface** before crashing into the Sea of Tranquillity.

Feb. 21   **Malcom X,** founder of the extremist Black Nationalist movement and a former leader of the Black Muslims, was shot to death as he addressed a rally in Harlem. Members of the Black Muslim movement were later convicted of the murder. On Feb. 23 Black Muslim headquarters in San Francisco and New York were burned.

Mar. 11   The **Rev. James J. Reeb** of Boston, a Unitarian minister who had gone to Selma, Ala., to assist in the Negro-rights drive, **died following a beating** he received Mar. 9. 3 white men were indicted for the murder.

Mar. 21   About 3,200 marchers from all over the country, led by Dr. Martin Luther King, Jr., began a 5-day, 54-mile **march from Selma to Montgomery, Ala.,** demonstrating for equal civil rights for Negroes. Demonstrators numbered 25,000 when the march ended in front of Montgomery's state capitol.

Mar. 23   The 1st **U.S. manned Gemini flight** was launched from Cape Ken-

Oscar awards of the Academy of Motion Picture Arts and Sciences: best film, *The Sound of Music;* best actor, Lee Marvin (*Cat Ballou*); best actress, Julie Christie (*Darling*); best supporting actor, Martin Balsam (*A Thousand Clowns*); best supporting actress, Shelley Winters (*A Patch of Blue*); best foreign-language film, *The Shop on Main Street;* best director, Robert Wise (*The Sound of Music*).

In **popular music,** the rock 'n' roll beat lost ground to the "folk-rock," a kind of blues-message-protest music whose high priest was singer-composer Bob Dylan. Often, current events provided the themes, as evidenced by some typical titles: "Selma, Alabama," "Hello, Vietnam," "Eve of Destruction." Nevertheless, British singers and groups continued to produce many of the best-selling single records: "Satisfaction" (Rolling Stones), "Downtown" (Petula Clark), "Help!" (The Beatles), and "Can't You Hear My Heartbeat?" (Herman's Hermits). In midyear, Herb Alpert's Tijuana Brass introduced a new sound that caught on immediately; it was a combination of Dixieland and Mexican Mariachi.

A **truth-in-packaging bill** was introduced in Congress by Sen. Philip Hart (D., Mich.). It would require establishment of standard weights for food packages, so consumers could readily compare prices of similar products. The food industry set up the Food Council of America as its propaganda and lobbying agent.

Jan. 1   Michigan beat Oregon State 34–7 in the **Rose Bowl;** Louisiana State won 13–10 over Syracuse in the Sugar Bowl; Texas beat Alabama 21–17 in the Orange Bowl; and Arkansas defeated Nebraska 10–7 in the Cotton Bowl.

Feb. 13   16-year-old Peggy Fleming of Pasadena won the U.S. ladies **senior figure-skating** title at Lake Placid; Gary Visconti of Detroit took the men's title.

Feb. 15–16   A Scottish terrier, Ch. Carmichael's Fanfare, was chosen best in show at the **Westminster Kennel Club** show in New York.

677

POLITICS AND GOVERNMENT; WAR;
DISASTERS; VITAL STATISTICS.

BOOKS; PAINTING; DRAMA;
ARCHITECTURE; SCULPTURE.

by accepted religions, may be **exempted from combatant training and service.**

Mar. 8–9 More than **3,500 U.S. Marines landed in South Vietnam** to guard the U.S. Air Force base at Danang, the first combat troops sent to that country. They joined 23,500 other Americans serving as advisors to the Vietnamese armed forces.

Mar. 15 Pres. Johnson, in an address to a joint night session of Congress which was televised nationally, asked for speedy passage of **legislation to remove every barrier of discrimination against citizens trying to register and vote.** Later he submitted a voting-rights bill to Congress, 1 provision of which would empower the Attorney General to assign federal registration examiners in the 6 states in which literacy tests or other voter-qualification tests are used.

Mar. 22 U.S. spokesmen in Saigon confirmed the use by Vietnamese fighting forces of a U.S.-supplied nonlethal type of tear gas. Many members of Congress joined in **worldwide denunciations of the use of gas.**

Apr. 11 A series of 37 tornadoes swept through Indiana, Iowa, Illinois, Wisconsin, Michigan, and Ohio, killing 271 persons and injuring 5,000. It was the nation's **worst tornado disaster in 40 years.**

Apr. 26 Secretary of Defense Robert McNamara estimated the **cost to the U.S. of the Vietnamese war at $1.5 billion annually,** with economic aid at $300 million, food and agricultural supplies at $70 million, military assistance at $330 million, and the cost of U.S. forces at $800 million.

Apr. 28 Over 400 **Marines were sent to the Dominican Republic** to protect U.S. citizens there and to return them to the U.S. during the struggle for control of that country. By May 5, the U.S. had 12,439 Army men and 6,924 Marines in the Dominican Republic.

May 7 4,000 men of the 3rd Marine Div. arrived in Vietnam, bringing the **total U.S. forces in Vietnam to 42,200.**

jor 20th-century poet, and his reputation grew to almost mythic proportions during his own lifetime. Other major poems are *Gerontian* (1919), *Ash Wednesday* (1930), and *Four Quartets* (1943). He wrote 5 verse-dramas, the 1st of which, *Murder in the Cathedral* (1935), is generally regarded as the best. His early critical essays were published in *The Sacred Wood* (1920). In the collection *For Lancelot Andrews* (1929) Eliot declared himself "an Anglo-Catholic in religion, a classicist in literature, and a royalist in politics," and the labels stuck, despite frequent modifications and reversals of his opinions. He was awarded the Nobel Prize in 1948.

Feb. 16 A **plot to dynamite the Statue of Liberty,** the Liberty Bell, and the Washington Monument was foiled through the combined efforts of New York City police, the F.B.I., and the Royal Canadian Police. A rookie N.Y. cop infiltrated the 4-member conspiracy group, which included the self-styled leader of the Black Liberation Front and a woman member of the Separatist Party advocating the secession of Quebec from Canada. On June 14 3 men were convicted of conspiracy; the woman pleaded guilty of smuggling dynamite and testified for the government.

Mar. 1 The U.S. Supreme Court struck down a Maryland **movie censorship law** as a violation of the 1st Amendment. The Court ruled that pictures may be censored before showing only if provision is made for swift court relief; that the burden of proving a film should not be shown must rest on the censor. Citing this decision, the Court on Mar. 15 declared unconstitutional New York's censorship procedures. That case involved the Danish film *A Stranger Knocks* in which the plot crisis occurs during an act of sexual intercourse.

Mar. 19 At Christie's, the London auction house, U.S. industrialist Norton Simon created an uproar by claiming an irregularity after bidding had closed on

nedy. The craft, nicknamed "Molly Brown," was put through a series of delicate maneuvers by its pilots, Maj. Virgil Grissom and Lt. Cmdr. John Young, during its 3-orbit flight and was retrieved by the carrier *Intrepid* in the Atlantic Ocean.

Mar. 24   Ranger 9 transmitted back to earth **5,814 pictures of the moon's surface** before crashing in the Alphonsus Crater following a 3-day journey from earth.

Apr. 6   The world's 1st **commercial communications satellite,** Early Bird, was launched and placed in orbit 22,300 miles above the earth. Owned by ComSat, Early Bird transmitted phone calls, TV, Teletype, and other communications.

Apr. 16   Saturn S-1C, to be the 1st stage for the Apollo lunar flight and the **largest U.S. booster ever produced,** was successfully fired at Cape Kennedy.

Apr. 26   An interim agreement between steel workers and major steel companies providing for **wage increases for 400,000 steel workers** averted a nationwide strike scheduled for May 1. Negotiations for a new contract continued.

Apr. 29   Commissioner of Education announced that all of the nation's 27,000 public-school districts would be required to **desegregate all public schools** completely by the beginning of the autumn 1967 term.

May 9   **A record arbitration award** was made when more than 800 retired employees of the Fifth Ave. Coach Lines in New York received over $9 million. The city had taken over the bus line in 1962; in 1964 the courts ruled that the company must continue its obligations to its retired employees.

June 3   Maj. Edward White, co-pilot of Gemini 4, took the 1st **U.S. "space walk"** of 20 minutes while 135 miles above North America and attached to the craft by a lifeline. The 4-day, 62-orbit flight, piloted by Maj. James McDivitt, set the endurance record to date for 2-man space flight.

Feb. 19   In Washington, **Henry Ford 2nd** married Italian-born Mrs. Maria Cristina Vettore Austin. It was the 2nd marriage for both.

Feb. 23   **Stan Laurel,** sad-faced, skinny half of the film comedy team of Laurel and Hardy, died at 74 in Santa Monica.

Mar. 17   "Grand old man of football" **Amos Alonzo Stagg,** a coach for more than 60 years, died at 102 in Stockton, Calif.

Mar. 21   The Boston Celtics won their 7th consecutive pro **basketball championship,** defeating Los Angeles 4 games to 1. Their big guard Bill Russell won the Sam Davis Award as the most valuable pro player of the year. The Celtics gave him a new 3-year contract that called for an annual salary of about $100,000.

Apr. 3–4   At the **International Kennel Club** Show in Chicago, best-in-show honors were awarded to a Doberman pinscher, Ch. Ru-Mar's Tsuchima C.D.

Apr. 11   Jack Nicklaus won the **Masters Golf Tournament** at Augusta, Ga., with a score of 271.

May 1   At Montreal, the Montreal Canadiens won the **Stanley Cup,** defeating the Chicago Black Hawks 4 games to 3. Bobby Hull, Hawks' left wing, was named most valuable player in the National Hockey League.

May 1   *Lucky Debonair,* ridden by Shoemaker, won the **Kentucky Derby** purse of $112,000.

May 2   Arnold Palmer won golf's **Tournament of Champions** at Las Vegas.

May 15   *Tom Rolfe,* Turcotte up, won the **Preakness Stakes** and a purse of $128,100.

May 25   Defying a new rule of the World Boxing Association that prohibited their return bout, Cassius Clay and Sonny Liston fought a 1-minute skirmish at Lew-

POLITICS AND GOVERNMENT; WAR; DISASTERS; VITAL STATISTICS.

BOOKS; PAINTING; DRAMA; ARCHITECTURE; SCULPTURE.

June 7 The Supreme Court held unconstitutional an 1879 Connecticut law forbidding the use of contraceptives by anyone, including married couples. The law was considered a **violation of the "right of privacy"** guaranteed by various constitutional amendments.

June 7 The Supreme Court by a 5–4 vote upset the 1962 swindling conviction of Billie Sol Estes by a Texas state court on the ground that televising "notorious" criminal trials is a violation of the due process clause of the 14th Amendment, and that the **presence of TV cameras might affect jurors, witnesses, and judges.**

June 17 Guam-based B-52's bombed a Vietcong concentration 30 miles north of Saigon, the 1st combat use of the heavy jet bombers since they were placed in use in 1952. It was the **1st mass bombing raid in Vietnam.**

June 30 The Senate Rules Committee, in its **final report on the investigation of Robert G. Baker,** former secretary to the Senate Democratic majority, recommended the Senate consider indicting Baker for violation of conflict-of-interest laws, and recommended Senate rules for control of outside business activities of Senate employees. Republican members of the committee termed the majority report "a whitewash" and filed a minority report criticizing the conduct of the investigation.

July 27 The 18-nation UN **Disarmament Committee** resumed talks in Geneva after a recess since September 1964. France continued to boycott the negotiations.

July 28 Pres. Johnson announced that the **U.S. armed forces in Vietnam would be increased from 75,000 to 125,000 men,** and the **draft would be doubled** from 17,000 to 35,000 a month to support the war in the Far East.

Aug. 16 Total **U.S. casualties in Vietnam** from Jan. 1, 1961, were announced as 561 killed, 3,024 wounded, 44 missing

Rembrandt's portrait of his son Titus. Bidding was reopened and Simon got the picture for $2,234,000. It was reported that Prince Franz Josef II of Liechtenstein had refused Simon's offer of $6 million for Leonardo da Vinci's *Portrait of a Young Woman.*

Mar. 30 The **Los Angeles County Art Museum** was dedicated. It is the largest art museum west of the Mississippi, and the largest built since the National Gallery was opened in 1941.

Apr. 9 Pres. Johnson was among the honored guests at an exhibition game between the Houston Astros and the N.Y. Yankees which marked the inauguration of a new architectural wonder, the **Houston Astrodome.** The players were troubled by glaring light transmitted by the stadium's plastic dome, which was later painted over.

Apr. 26 Leopold Stokowski and his American Symphony Orchestra presented the world première of the late **Charles Ives'** 4th Symphony. The 50-year-old work was laboriously reconstructed from a badly organized manuscript, and 2 assistant conductors were required for its performance.

May 9 Pianist **Vladimir Horowitz,** 60, returned to the concert stage after an absence of 12 years. A wildly enthusiastic audience in Carnegie Hall gave him standing ovations before and after his recital; critics found the virtuoso pianist at the peak of his musical powers.

May 14 At Runnymede, where in 1215 King John had signed the Magna Carta, Queen Elizabeth dedicated a monument to the late **President Kennedy.** Its inscription reads: "This acre of English ground was given to the United States of America by the people of Great Britain in memory of John Fitzgerald Kennedy."

SCIENCE; INDUSTRY; ECONOMICS; EDUCATION; RELIGION; PHILOSOPHY.

SPORTS; FASHIONS; POPULAR ENTERTAINMENT; FOLKLORE; SOCIETY.

June 10   Mass demonstrations, including street sit-downs, began in Chicago as protest against **slow pace of desegregation in public schools.** By June 15, 530 marchers had been arrested.

June 12   The discovery of new celestial objects known as blue galaxies lent support to the **"big bang" theory of the creation of the universe**—that it began in one place set off by an explosion and has been expanding ever since and is not static and infinite as some theories propose.

June 18   Titan 3C was launched into orbit with a **total thrust of 2.4 million lbs.,** the greatest of any rocket ever to leave the earth's surface. The launching was the first to use large solid-fuel rockets to lift a large spacecraft.

July 15   Mariner 4 began transmission of **21 pictures of the surface of Mars,** taken at a range of between 10,500 and 7,000 miles. Transmitting data to earth since its launch Nov. 28, 1964, the craft flew within 5,700 miles of Mars.

July 24–26   Dr. Martin Luther King, Jr., conducted a **civil rights campaign in Chicago's Negro neighborhoods** and the white suburb of Winnetka against that city's "symbol of de facto segregation."

Aug. 11–16   35 were killed and hundreds injured during **riots in Watts,** a Negro section of Los Angeles, set off when a white policeman stopped a Negro driver suspected of being drunk. About $200 million in property was burned, looted, and detroyed.

Aug. 21   Gemini 5 was launched on an **8-day, 120-orbit space flight,** piloted by Lt. Col. Gordon Cooper and Lt. Cmdr. Charles Conrad. The flight took as long as a round trip to the moon. There was some difficulty with the new fuel-cell system.

Aug. 29   A **75-day shipping strike,** by 3 unions against 8 shipping lines with losses to lines and employees estimated at $1.8 million daily, **was settled.** One of the issues was procedures by which to solve

iston, Me. Few fans saw the alleged punch that floored Liston. Clay retained the **N.B.A. heavyweight crown,** but on Mar. 5 Ernie Terrell had won the W.B.A. title by outpointing Eddie Machen in New York. In the aftermath of this debacle, Congress held some inconclusive hearings on the need for a boxing commission, and Connecticut banned the sport entirely.

May 31   At **Indianapolis Speedway,** Jim Clark of Scotland won a record $166,-621 and hit the all-time high average speed of 150.680 mph in the Memorial Day classic. He drove a Ford-powered Lotus.

June 5   The **Belmont Stakes** purse of $125,000 was won by *Hail to All,* ridden by Sellers.

June 21   **U.S. Open** golf championship was won by Gary Player of South Africa. He became the 3rd man to win golf's 4 top pro titles; only Gene Sarazen and Ben Hogan had taken the U.S. and British Opens, the Masters, and the P.G.A. during their careers. Elated, Player gave his $26,000 winnings to charity and his caddy.

Aug. 15   Dave Marr won the **P.G.A. championship** with a record score of 280, at Ligonier, Pa. He was named P.G.A. player of the year.

Aug. 30   N.Y. Mets manager **Casey Stengel** announced his retirement, after 55 years in baseball. On July 25, just a few days before his 75th birthday, he had broken his hip in a fall. Coach Wes Westrum became interim manager, and at the season's end was given the job permanently.

Sept. 2   The DeLong ruby, stolen last Oct. 29 from the American Museum of Natural History, was ransomed in Florida for $25,000 by millionaire John D. MacArthur.

Sept. 9   Sandy Koufax of the L.A. Dodgers pitched a **perfect game** (no man got to 1st base) against the Chicago Cubs. Koufax fanned 14 batters in the 1–0 victory. It was the 4th no-hit game of his ca-

| POLITICS AND GOVERNMENT; WAR; DISASTERS; VITAL STATISTICS. | BOOKS; PAINTING; DRAMA; ARCHITECTURE; SCULPTURE. |

in action, and 269 Americans dead of non-combat causes.

Aug. 17   A **treaty to prevent the spread of nuclear weapons** proposed by the U.S. to the UN Disarmament Committee in Geneva was dismissed by the U.S.S.R. delegate as a "joke." The committee adjourned 2 days later.

Aug. 20   Pres. Johnson said **crime prevention was one of the nation's most difficult problems** and would receive priority attention.

Sept. 4   The U.S. **recognized the new provisional government of the Dominican Republic,** established on Organization of American States proposals, and pledged to give it $20 million in economic aid.

Sept. 24   Pres. Johnson announced the agreement in principle to terms of a treaty between the U.S. and Panama to supersede the 1903 pact under which the U.S. had sole control of the Canal. The new treaty would provide for **shared administration and operation of the Panama Canal.**

Oct. 4   **Pope Paul VI visited New York to address the UN General Assembly** in an appeal for peace. During the visit he celebrated a low papal mass in Yankee Stadium and went to the World's Fair.

Oct. 15–16   **Demonstrations against U.S. participation in the war in Vietnam** were held in cities from New York to Berkeley, Calif. They were followed by a series of rallies and petitions supporting U.S. policy. Several persons burned their draft cards publicly, and 1 person was arrested 3 days later under a law effective on Aug. 31 which made destruction of a draft card a crime.

Oct. 17   **New York World's Fair closed** after 2 years. It had the largest total attendance of any international exposition in history, 51,607,037 persons, but not the 70 million predicted.

Oct. 19   The House Committee on Un-American Activities opened public hearings in its **investigation of the Ku Klux**

May 24   The U.S. Supreme Court declared unconstitutional a federal law which empowered the Postmaster General to hold **foreign mail deemed to be Communist propaganda** and make the addressee submit a written request for it. The law, the Court said, violated rights protected by the 1st Amendment.

May 27   In a rare stage appearance, choreographer **George Balanchine** danced the title role at the New York City Ballet's première performance of his new work, *Don Quixote.*

June 5   **Thorton Burgess,** 91, author of "Peter Rabbit" stories for children, died in Hampden, Mass.

June 14   Pres. Johnson played host to some 400 artists at a 13-hour **Festival of the Arts and Humanities** at the White House. It included exhibitions of paintings, sculpture, and photography, prose and poetry readings, recitals of music, and a ballet performance. Poet Robert Lowell set off a controversy when he refused an invitation because of his distrust of current U.S. foreign policy.

July 16   Simon Rodilla (Sam Rodia), immigrant Italian builder of the controversial **Watts Towers** in Los Angeles, died at 90 in Martinez, Calif. The sometime sculptor spent years constructing his fantastic towers; pronounced them finished in 1954. In 1963 they were named a historical cultural monument by the Los Angeles Cultural Heritage Board.

Aug. 8   Author **Shirley Jackson,** best known for her macabre novels and short stories, died at 45 in North Bennington, Vt. Her short story "The Lottery," published 1948 in *The New Yorker,* is regarded as a classic horror tale.

| SCIENCE; INDUSTRY; ECONOMICS; EDUCATION; RELIGION; PHILOSOPHY. | SPORTS; FASHIONS; POPULAR ENTERTAINMENT; FOLKLORE; SOCIETY. |

disputes over manpower and automation of new ships.

Sept. 3   A new 3-year **pact between major steel companies and steel workers,** including wage increases and other employee benefits, **was agreed to** immediately before a nationwide strike was scheduled to begin.

Sept. 16   A New York Newspaper Guild strike against the *New York Times* set off a **suspension in publication of most New York City dailies** for more than 3 weeks, at a loss to the industry of between $10 million and $15 million.

Oct. 12   The U.S. Navy completed its Sealab 2 research program, a series of 15-day periods **205 feet below the surface of the Pacific Ocean.** The purpose was to study the effects on men of living under water and to conduct experiments with equipment.

Oct. 21   1965 **Nobel prize in physics** was awarded to Richard P. Feynman of Caltech, Julian S. Schwinger of Harvard, and Shinichero Tomonaga, a Japanese scientist, for their work in quantum electrodynamics. The **chemistry prize** was awarded to Robert Burns Woodward of Harvard for his work in synthesizing complicated organic compounds.

Nov. 10   **Aluminum price rises of 2%** planned by Alcoa, the U.S.'s largest aluminum producer, and 3 other companies to take effect on Nov. 5 were rescinded after the government announced it would sell some of its aluminum stockpile.

Dec. 3   **Collie LeRoy Wilkins and 2 other Ku Klux Klansmen were found guilty of conspiracy** charges in the death of Mrs. Viola Liuzzo on Mar. 25 in Selma, Ala. They were convicted by a federal court in Montgomery, Ala., under an 1870 federal statute making it a crime to conspire to deprive a citizen of his constitutional rights, and were given the maximum sentence of 10 years in prison. They had

reer, a major-league record, and only the 8th perfect game in baseball history. The left-hander also set a major-league record this season with a total of 382 strikeouts, breaking the 1946 record of 348 by Bob Feller.

Sept. 10   **Father Divine,** religious cult leader, died in Philadelphia. He was thought to be George Baker, born about 1882 near Savannah, but to members of his Peace Mission (or Kingdom of Peace) cult, he was God incarnate. The group enjoyed its greatest period of growth in the '30's and '40's. Most of its members are American Negroes and many live a communal life in which peace, asceticism, and celibacy are emphasized.

Sept. 11   Deborah Bryant (Miss Kansas) was chosen **Miss America** at Atlantic City.

Sept. 12   In the quarter-finals of the U.S. singles and doubles tournament at Forest Hills, tennis fans thrilled as U.C.L.A. students Arthur Ashe and Charles Pasarell knocked off the Australians who had been rated 1–2. Ashe defeated Roy Emerson, holder of the Australian and Wimbledon titles; Pasarell beat Fred Stolle, holder of the French championship. Neither student made it to the finals on Sept. 12, however, when Manuel Santana of Spain won the U.S. singles title. Ashe was the 1st Negro chosen for the U.S. Davis Cup team.

Oct. 14   At Metropolitan Stadium, Bloomington, Minn., the L.A. Dodgers won their 4th game of the **World Series,** defeating the Minnesota Twins 2–0. The players' shares were $10,297 to the Dodgers, $6,634 to the Twins.

Oct. 17   The closing day of the **N.Y. World's Fair** drew 446,953 people, the biggest crowd of its 2-year run. The final days were marred by pandemic vandalism and looting, and souvenir hunters made off with anything portable. Robert Moses,

683

POLITICS AND GOVERNMENT; WAR; DISASTERS; VITAL STATISTICS.

BOOKS; PAINTING; DRAMA; ARCHITECTURE; SCULPTURE.

Klan. Several Klansmen called as witnesses refused to answer questions, pleading several constitutional amendments.

Nov. 2 **John V. Lindsay was elected mayor of New York** in the closest race in that city in 25 years. A liberal Republican and former New York representative to the national Congress, he was the first non-Democratic mayor since Fiorello La Guardia ended his 3rd term in 1945.

Nov. 9–10 A **massive electric-power failure** blacked out more than 30 million persons in an 80,000-square-mile area comprising New York, most of New England, parts of New Jersey, Pennsylvania, and Ontario and Quebec, Canada. The blackout, lasting as long as 13 hours in some areas, was caused by the malfunction of an automatic relay device at a generating plant near Niagara Falls.

Nov. 15 The Supreme Court ruled unanimously that **individuals may refuse to register with the government as members of the Communist Party,** as had been required by the Subversive Activities Control Act of 1950, on grounds that such registration could be self-incriminating under the 1940 Smith Act and other criminal statutes.

Nov. 20 **U.S. loses at the end of the week-long battle in the Iadrang Valley in Vietnam** were 240 dead, 470 wounded, and 6 missing, exceeding the Korean War weekly average of 209 Americans killed. Communist dead were estimated from 2,262 by body count to as high as 4,000.

Nov. 27 Between 15,000 and 25,000 protesters from 140 groups **demonstrated in Washington, D.C., against the war in Vietnam.** Organized by SANE (National Committee for a Sane Nuclear Policy), they marched around the White House and to the Washington Monument.

Dec. 2 A 13,200-square-mile area with about 1 million persons and containing 50 cities and 4 military bases in southwest Texas, southern New Mexico and Ciudad Juárez, Mexico, was **blacked out**

Sept. 24 Russian-born conductor **Nikolai Sokoloff,** 79, died at La Jolla, Calif. Sokoloff entered the Yale School of Music at 13; at 17 he was a violinist with the Boston Symphony; in 1918 he organized and conducted the Cleveland Orchestra; from 1935 to 1939 he was director of the WPA music project.

Sept. 30 Pres. Johnson signed the Federal Aid to the Arts Act, which established a **National Foundation on the Arts and the Humanities,** and appropriated $63 million to finance the 1st 3 years of the program.

Oct. 21 The **Ford Foundation** announced grants totaling $85 million to 50 symphony orchestras throughout the U.S., to enable them to lengthen their seasons and improve the salary scales of musicians.

Oct. 21 The **Vivian Beaumont Theater,** permanent home of the Lincoln Center Repertory Theater, was opened with an adaptation of Georg Büchner's *Danton's Death.* The playhouse, the 3rd unit to be completed of the Lincoln Center for the Performing Arts, was designed by Eero Saarinen and Jo Mielziner. In January it was announced that Elia Kazan and Robert Whitehead were to be replaced as directors of the company by Herbert Blau and Jules Irving of the famed San Francisco Actors' Workshop. The new directors' offerings fared no better at the hands of critics than did those of their predecessors. *Danton's Death* and the company's 2nd production, Wycherley's *The Country Wife,* were harshly criticized as badly acted and ineptly staged.

Oct. 28 The year's most awesome architectural project, Eero Saarinen's steel **Gateway Arch in St. Louis,** was topped out. The 630-ft. parabolic arch commemorates the Louisiana Purchase and the city's role in westward expansion. It is part of

SCIENCE; INDUSTRY; ECONOMICS; EDUCATION; RELIGION; PHILOSOPHY.

SPORTS; FASHIONS; POPULAR ENTERTAINMENT; FOLKLORE; SOCIETY.

earlier been tried twice by state courts on murder charges but not convicted.

Dec. 4   Gemini 7, piloted by Lt. Col. Frank Borman and Cmdr. James A. Lovell, Jr., was launched by a Titan 2 rocket from Cape Kennedy on a **14-day, 206-orbit mission** and rendezvous in space with Gemini 6.

Dec. 5   The FAA announced that medical tests on travelers showed that **jet travel through a number of time zones "causes measurable disruptions in both physiological and psychological functions in humans,"** and that body functions are disturbed for 3 to 5 days.

Dec. 5   The **Federal Reserve Board raised the discount rate**—the amount charged its 6,235 commercial bank members for borrowing funds—from 4% to 4½%, the highest in 35 years, in an effort to stabilize prices and counter inflation. Other banks then increased their interest rates.

Dec. 6   California Gov. Edmund G. Brown's commission, headed by John A. McCone, to investigate the Watts riots released its report that **worse riots might occur** unless the educational gap is closed, unemployment is reduced through job training, mass transit facilities are greatly increased, and a new procedure for dealing with charges of police brutality is established.

Dec. 7   International Telephone and Telegraph announced it would acquire the American Broadcasting Co., contingent on the approval of stockholders and federal agencies. The new company would have more than **$1.8 billion in assets** and would outrank the Radio Corp. of America and its NBC subsidiary.

Dec. 10   3 white men in Selma, Ala., were found **not guilty of the murder of the Rev. James J. Reeb** of Boston. Reeb died of a beating on Mar. 11 during demonstrations in Selma for Negro civil rights.

president of the fair corporation, called it an "artistic, cultural, and educational success," but financial backers faced the prospect of a return of 39¢ on the dollar of the $30 million they had invested. The most popular attractions of the fair were General Motors' Futurama and the Vatican Pavilion, to which the Pope had lent Michelangelo's *Pietà*. Most of the fairgrounds were to be restored as a public park, but among the structures to be retained are the Unisphere, the Port of N.Y. Authority heliport, the New York City building, and the United States Pavilion, 1 of the few architectural adornments of the event. The Spanish Pavilion, another of the more handsome attractions, was to be reconstructed near the Gateway Arch in St. Louis.

Nov. 16   William D. Eckert, retired U.S.A.F. lieutenant general, was elected **baseball commissioner.** He succeeded Ford Frick, who retired after having held the post since 1952.

Nov. 22   At Las Vegas, Cassius Clay stopped ex-champ Floyd Patterson in the 12th round of what had been billed as a fight for the **heavyweight championship.** Although the bout had been set up by Jim Deskin, new head of the World Boxing Association, that organization afterward classified Clay as merely No. 1 contender for the crown the WBA had given to Ernie Terrell on Mar. 5.

Dec. 24   Engagement of President Johnson's daughter **Luci Baines** to Airman Patrick Nugent was announced.

Dec. 26   The Buffalo Bills defeated the San Diego Chargers 23–0 to win the **American Football League championship,** their 2nd straight, at San Diego. The same day, in a "sudden-death" extra period at Green Bay, Wisc., the Green Bay Packers took the Western Conference title in the National Football League with a 13–10 win over the Baltimore Colts; a field goal by Don Chandler did the trick. On Jan. 2,

685

POLITICS AND GOVERNMENT; WAR;
DISASTERS; VITAL STATISTICS.

BOOKS; PAINTING; DRAMA;
ARCHITECTURE; SCULPTURE.

for 2 hours when the El Paso Electric Co. experienced a failure.

Dec. 2   The U.S. Labor Dept. announced that **over-all unemployment fell** to 4.2% in November, an 8-year low. A shortage of skilled labor was also reported.

Dec. 4   **2 airliners** carrying a total of 112 persons **collided in midair** over Danbury, Conn. Only 4 persons were killed.

Dec. 6   The Defense Dept. announced that **149 military installations would be closed, consolidated, or reduced in size,** bringing to 852 the number of installations affected by cutbacks since 1961, with a saving of about $1.5 billion a year.

the 40-block Jefferson National Expansion Memorial along the city's riverfront. The Spanish Pavilion from the N.Y. World's Fair is to be reconstructed near the arch.

Nov. 6   **Edgar Varèse,** Paris-born U.S. composer regarded as "the father of electronic music," died at 90 in New York City.

Nov. 17   The Ford Foundation announced a grant of $3.2 million to the **New York City Ballet and the New York City Opera** to help them finance productions at the New York State Theater in Lincoln Center.

1966

A steadily escalating U.S. participation in the Vietnamese war resulted in 5,008 U.S. troop deaths and 30,093 wounded in 1966, bringing the total casualties since Jan. 1, 1961, to 6,664 killed and 37,738 wounded. By the end of the year, the U.S. had almost 400,000 troops in Southeast Asia. Among the series of sometimes violent antiwar demonstrations was the International Days of Protest (Mar. 25–27), during which parades and rallies were held in 7 U.S. and 7 foreign cities. High school students beat 7 antiwar demonstrators in Boston, and in Berkeley, Calif., the headquarters of the antiwar Vietnam Day Committee was bombed. The proposed Administration budget for fiscal 1967 was the largest ever: expenditures were set at $112.8 billion, up $6.4 billion from 1966; estimated receipts at $111 billion, up $11 billion from 1966; and a predicted deficit of $1.8 billion, smallest in 7 years. U.S. aid to foreign countries for the year was set at $2,940,-000,000 and for foreign economic and military aid at $3,501,735,000. Among legislation requested by the Administration were antipollution programs, forest and historic sites preservation, consumer protection, anticrime appropriations, and

The few new works offered this year by U.S. playwrights added no luster to the theater. Edward Albee's *Malcolm* was set down as a pretentious fable. Tennessee Williams' *Slapstick Tragedy,* a pair of 1-acters, was panned by the critics and dismissed by the public in 5 days; William Inge's *Where's Daddy?* lasted but 2 weeks. Albee's *A Delicate Balance,* despite puzzling rhetoric, enjoyed a moderate success that was partially credited to fine performances by Hume Cronyn and Jessica Tandy. The only new critical successes on the legitimate stage were imports: Brian Friel's *Philadelphia, Here I Come!;* Frank Marcus' *The Killing of Sister George;* and James Goldman's *The Lion in Winter*— and the last-named was a commercial failure. Tickets for the late-1965 offerings, *Marat/Sade* and *Man of La Mancha,* remained at a premium, but principally it was the new musical comedies that kept the Broadway box offices busy. Most of these were adaptations: *Mame,* the 4th incarnation of Auntie Mame of the novel, play, and film, had Angela Lansbury in a sensational musical-comedy debut; Lotte Lenya and Joel Grey starred in *Cabaret,* a musical version of John Van Druten's *I Am a Camera* (out of Christopher Isher-

| SCIENCE; INDUSTRY; ECONOMICS: EDUCATION; RELIGION; PHILOSOPHY. | SPORTS; FASHIONS; POPULAR ENTERTAINMENT; FOLKLORE; SOCIETY. |

Dec. 15   Gemini 6, piloted by Capt. Walter Schirra and Maj. Thomas Stafford, was launched and rendezvoused with Gemini 7 185 miles above the earth. During its 14-orbit flight, it came within 6 ft. of Gemini 7 and traveled in close formation with the sister ship, achieving man's first **rendezvous in space.** Gemini 6 came down the next day.

1966, the Packers defeated the Cleveland Browns 23–12, to win the league championship.

Dec. 27   **N.Y. Film Critics** gave top acting awards to Oskar Werner (*Ship of Fools*) and Julie Christie (*Darling*). They named *Darling* the best film, and *Juliet of the Spirits* the best foreign film of the year.

1966

The introduction of the slogan "Black Power" into the civil rights struggle signaled a serious split in Negro ranks between pacifist followers of the Southern Christian Leadership Conference of Martin Luther King, Jr., and militants such as Stokeley Carmichael of the Student Nonviolent Coordinating Committee and Floyd McKissick of the Congress of Racial Equality. Conflicting explanations of the new concept helped create widespread uneasiness. In fiery moods Carmichael proclaimed that "Black Power" meant the destruction of the western civilization; in calmer moments he explained that the phrase was intended to rally blacks and encourage them to make their own way in self-respect by acting in concert politically and economically. A corollary catchphrase, "white backlash," came into use to describe the vocal and sometimes violent reaction to this emerging militancy and to continuing efforts by local and federal governments to end both de jure and de facto discrimination in education, housing, and jobs. Enforced desegregation of schools in the South generated resentment and riots and prompted establishment of privately financed schools. In urban areas elsewhere, proposals to end

Southpaw Sandy Koufax made the Los Angeles Dodgers pay $130,000 for the use of his pitching arm for the season and demonstrated its worth by winning 27 games and the National League pennant for his club, even though he had to take cortisone shots before each game for his arthritic arm. But the Baltimore Orioles, sparked by nearly flawless pitching and the hitting of the American League's MVP Frank Robinson, swept the World Series in 4 straight games. After the season Koufax retired from baseball lest he damage permanently his ailing arm. The Giants' Willie Mays hit 37 home runs for a career high of 542, 2nd only to Babe Ruth's 714.

Girl-watchers rejoiced as young ladies adopted the miniskirt. The new fashion rage put hemlines 4 or 5—and occasionally a daring 7—inches above the knee. The lower thigh and the knee became the new erogenous zone as bust, waist, and hips were deemphasized. This year also saw a short-lived fad for paper throwaway clothes, especially inexpensive, 1-wearing dresses.

British performers continued to domi-

appropriations to expand facilities for medical care and education. Congress turned down the Administration's proposed civil rights bill largely because of its open housing provisions, but did pass measures giving the government a major role in determining automobile and highway safety standards, in attacking urban decay, and in controlling air and water pollution. Income tax payments were speeded up and excise taxes increased to help finance the Vietnamese war and to counter inflationary pressures in the national economy. Pres. Johnson received Indian Prime Minister Indira Gandhi, West German Chancellor Erhard, Burma's chief of state Gen. Ne Win, and Philippine President Marcos. He also made an informal 24-hr. visit to Mexico City.

Jan. 17   The Senate unanimously confirmed Robert C. Weaver as Secretary of the newly created Dept. of Housing and Urban Development. He was the **1st Negro Cabinet member in the U.S.**

Jan. 17   A U.S. Air Force B-52 jet bomber and a KC-135 jet tanker collided over Spain's Mediterranean coast during refueling, killing 7 of the 11 men aboard the planes. 4 **hydrogen bombs** fell from the B-52, 3 on land. 2 of these split apart; the other was recovered intact. The 4th bomb fell in the Mediterranean, where it was recovered Apr. 7.

Jan. 29–31   The **worst blizzard in 70 years** in an area stretching from North Carolina to New England caused 165 deaths.

Jan. 31   Pres. Johnson announced that the U.S. had resumed **bombing raids on North Vietnam,** which had been suspended Dec. 24, 1965. He said that the halt and a major U.S. peace offensive had brought only negative responses from North Vietnam and Communist China. Johnson also said that the UN Security Council would be asked to take up the Vietnam question.

wood's *Berlin Stories*); Mary Martin and Robert Preston sang *I Do! I Do!,* an adaptation of Jan de Hartog's *The Fourposter;* and Gwen Verdon romped in *Sweet Charity,* a reworking of the Fellini film *Nights of Cabiria.* In March, Hal Holbrook returned to the stage to electrify New York audiences once again with his impersonation of Mark Twain as a lecturer (*Mark Twain Tonight!*). The New York Drama Critics Circle gave Holbrook a special citation for his 1-man show, and named *Marat/Sade* the best play of the 1965–66 season and *Man of La Mancha* the best musical. Off-Broadway, the most interesting plays carried strong social and political charges: Megan Terry's *Viet-Rock* was antiwar; Jean-Claude Van Itallie's *America, Hurrah!* was 3 short plays that made strident comments on television and its viewers, sex in motels, and job interviews; Arnold Wesker's *The Kitchen* was a naturalistic allegory about life in a restaurant kitchen; John Arden's *Serjeant Musgrave's Dance* dealt with violence and pacifism in a Victorian mining town; and Henry Livings' *Eh?* was a machine-age farce. The Repertory Theater of Lincoln Center, after 3 harshly criticized productions earlier in the season, finally had a success in Brecht's *The Caucasian Chalk Circle.* Poor attendance imperiled the future of the Ypsilanti Greek Theatre, a summer festival that was inaugurated with Dame Judith Anderson starring in the *Oresteia* of Aeschylus and with Bert Lahr in Aristophanes' *The Birds.*

In the book world it was a year of controversy, sex, and violence. The Supreme Court found the sexually explicit novel *Fanny Hill* not without "redeeming social value" and reversed a Massachusetts obscenity decision, and startled publishers and legal scholars by making "titillating advertising" a major factor in upholding the conviction of Ralph Ginzburg, a publisher of erotic material. Mrs. Ernest Hemingway vainly sought to suppress A. E. Hotchmer's biography of her late husband, *Papa Hemingway.* A multi-

SCIENCE; INDUSTRY; ECONOMICS; EDUCATION; RELIGION; PHILOSOPHY.

SPORTS; FASHIONS; POPULAR ENTERTAINMENT; FOLKLORE; SOCIETY.

de facto school segregation by redrawing district lines and busing children to and from Negro areas provoked bitter controversies.

Drugs and narcotics became a national preoccupation, with the spotlight on the hallucinogenic or "psychedelic" drugs, especially LSD (lysergic acid). Since about 1962 LSD had been bootlegged and concocted by amateurs and its traffic had created a rapidly growing cult of users. Their high priest was Timothy Leary, a psychologist fired from Harvard in 1963 for letting undergraduates experiment with drugs. Because a "bad trip" on LSD can induce psychoses, panic, and suicidal behavior, it and other hallucinogens were added to the federal list of "dangerous drugs," making their criminal misuse a felony.

The U.S. program to land a man on the moon before the end of the decade was significantly advanced by the successful completion of the manned Gemini series of space probes and the moon-mapping of the Lunar Orbiters. NASA officials were especially delighted with the "soft" moon landing by Surveyor I, and its photographs demonstrating that the moon's surface was firm enough to support the weight of astronauts and their vehicles.

Jan. 1 On his first day as mayor of New York, John Lindsay was faced with the **1st "official" transit strike** in the city's history. Monumental traffic jams developed as people used autos to get to work, and morning and evening crowds trudging along the streets gave New York the air of a city of refugees. The strike ended Jan. 13.

Feb. 9 Topping off a 3½-year bull market, the Dow-Jones industrial averages hit an all-time high of 995. A downslide in **stock prices** for most of the rest of the year set market analysts worrying

nate the pop music field. During an American tour the Beatles' John Lennon said that his group was more popular than Jesus Christ, and his subsequent explanation that he had not meant to imply that this was a desirable situation did not quell criticism. Frank Sinatra's rendition of "Strangers in the Night" was the smash song hit of the year.

By the time the fall TV season began, practically all major network shows, and many local programs, were being televised in color. Nearly half of the 11 million TV sets sold this year were equipped for color reception.

Jan. 1 Michigan State, unbeaten in regular-season play, bowed to UCLA, 14–12, in the **Rose Bowl.**

Jan. 13 Entertainer **Sophie Tucker,** "Last of the Red Hot Mamas," died at about 79.

Feb. 10 Showman **Billy Rose** died at 66. He wrote the lyrics for more than 400 popular songs and was famed as a nightclub owner, producer, philanthropist, financial wizard, art collector, and ladies' man.

Mar. 5 At Albuquerque, Bob Seagren set a new indoor record of 17 ft. ¼ in. for the **pole vault.**

Mar. 11 The grand old man of horse racing, **James (Sunny Jim) Fitzsimmons,** died in Miami at 91. Sunny Jim was active in racing for 78 years, first as a jockey and then as the sport's most famous trainer. At his retirement in 1963, he had saddled nearly 2300 winners and had earned his stables more than $13 million.

Mar. 12 In **hockey,** Bobby Hull of the Chicago Black Hawks scored his 51st goal, in a game with the New York Rangers at Chicago. Hull thus became the 1st player to score more than 50 in a season, and later ran the total to 54.

689

POLITICS AND GOVERNMENT; WAR; DISASTERS; VITAL STATISTICS.

BOOKS; PAINTING; DRAMA; ARCHITECTURE; SCULPTURE.

Feb. 2 The House of Representatives voted 344 to 28 to cite 7 **Ku Klux Klan leaders** for contempt for refusing to co-operate with a HUAC committee investigation into the KKK. Robert Shelton, Jr., imperial wizard of the United Klans of America, was found guilty and on Oct. 14 sentenced to a year in prison and a $1000 fine.

Feb. 8 Pres. Johnson and South Vietnamese Premier Ky ended a 3-day conference and issued the **Declaration of Honolulu,** which outlined major U.S. and South Vietnamese political and military policy in South Vietnam and stressed economic and social reform.

Feb. 21 The 1st **air strike against North Vietnam** since the Jan. 31 resumption of bombing was made against a training center at the old French fort of Dienbienphu.

Feb. 22 **Operation White Wing,** a month-long search and destroy mission by more than 20,000 U.S., South Vietnamese, and South Korean troops in Quang Ngai Province was wound up after resistance by 2 Vietcong and 2 North Vietnamese regiments collapsed. Communist troop deaths were reported at 1130.

Feb. 28 **Astronauts Elliot See, Jr., and Charles Bassett II,** scheduled to fly the Gemini IX mission, were killed in the crash of a jet trainer.

Mar. 1 Congress passed a bill authorizing an additional $4.8 billion for the **Vietnamese war.** The Senate rejected an amendment repealing the Gulf of Tonkin resolution of Aug. 1964.

Mar. 2 Defense Secretary Robert McNamara announced that **U.S. forces in Vietnam** numbered 215,000 and another 20,000 troops were on the way.

Mar. 7 The Supreme Court unanimously upheld the **Voting Rights Act of 1965.**

faceted dispute involved the Kennedy family, William Manchester (the "authorized" chronicler of the presidential assassination), Manchester's publisher, and *Look* magazine, which was about to serialize parts of Manchester's forthcoming *The Death of a President.* The Kennedys claimed they had not, as per an agreement with the author, approved the manuscript, and they won the right to delete from it some particularly sensitive material. The Warren Commission's investigation of the assassination was harshly criticized in Mark Lane's *Rush to Judgment,* Harold Weisberg's *Whitewash: The Report on the Warren Report,* and Jay Epstein's *Inquest: The Warren Commission and the Establishment of Truth.* The growing demand for more stringent gun controls was eloquently promoted in Carl Bakal's *The Right to Bear Arms.* Critics scoffed at Truman Capote's claim to have invented a new literary form, the "nonfiction novel," but were unstinting in their praise of his exhaustive study of a multiple murder in Kansas, *In Cold Blood,* which was the result of years of research and interviews with the convicted murderers and all others associated with the case. Gerold Frank's *The Boston Strangler* was a chilling depiction of a mad killer and the city he terrorized. Bernard Malamud's novel *The Fixer* told a harrowing tale of the torture and persecution of a Czarist Russian Jew on a trumped-up charge of ritual murder. The power and passion of the Afro-American struggle were expressed in *The Autobiography of Malcolm X, Malcolm X Speaks* (a collection of speeches by the Black Muslim leader), and LeRoi Jones' *Home: Social Essays.* In pop fiction, Jacqueline Susann's *Valley of the Dolls* was consigned to most critics' trash cans but became a runaway commercial success. A major American lexicographical effort, *The Random House Dictionary of the English Language,* received guarded approval.

Jan. 18 **Kathleen Norris,** popular author of romantic novels, died at 85.

about a recession. A low of 744 was reached Oct. 7.

Mar. 15 2 were killed and 20 injured in **rioting in Watts,** a Negro area of Los Angeles.

Mar. 16 Astronauts Neil Armstrong and David Scott guided Gemini VIII to the **1st successful space docking,** closing on the target vehicle after a 6½-hour chase. A yaw thruster rocket on the Gemini malfunctioned, throwing the connected crafts into a frightening tumble and bringing the projected 71-hr. flight to an end in less than 11 hr.

Mar. 22 General Motors president James Roche apologized before the Senate Subcommittee on Traffic Safety for the company's **spying into the private life of Ralph Nader.** Nader's late-1965 book *Unsafe at Any Speed* had singled out models of GM's Corvair as dangerous.

Apr. 6 Cesar Chavez' National Farm Workers Union, which started a **strike against California grape growers** Sept. 8, 1965, scored its 1st victory when it was recognized as bargaining agent for farm workers of Schenley Industries, a major grower.

Apr. 13 Pan American Airways announced that it was ordering 25 new **Boeing 747 jet transports** for delivery in 1969. The huge craft can carry up to 500 passengers. As other lines put in orders during the year, concern mounted about airport congestion, safety factors, and fare wars when the planes came into common use.

Apr. 24 The **longest newspaper strike** in a major city of the nation began. Fearing loss of jobs as a result of a merger of 3 ailing New York City papers —the *World-Telegram and Sun,* the *Journal-American,* and the *Herald Tribune*— the Newspaper Guild struck the new World-Journal-Tribune Inc. The strike lasted until Sept. 11.

Mar. 12 Jockey **Johnny Longden,** 59, retired after 40 years of racing and after riding his 6032nd 1st-place horse—the most ever for a jockey—in the San Juan Capistrano Handicap at Santa Anita. Longden had also ridden 4914 2nds and 4272 3rds in a total of 32,397 races. His mounts earned $24,665,800.

Mar. 27 Ken Miles and Lloyd Ruby won the **Sebring 12-hr. endurance race** in a Ford Roadster XL with an average speed of 98.631 mph.

Mar. 29 In Toronto, **heavyweight boxing champ** Cassius Clay won a 15-round decision over George Chuvalo, Canadian title-holder.

Apr. 11 At Augusta, golfer Jack Nicklaus won the **Masters** tournament for the 3rd time and became the 1st man to do it 2 years running.

Apr. 25 Jack Valenti, former special assistant to Pres. Johnson, was elected **president of the Motion Picture Association,** an office vacant since the death of Eric Johnston in 1963.

Apr. 25 In Madison Square Garden, New Yorker Emile Griffith won the **middleweight boxing title** from Dick Tiger of Nigeria in a 15-round decision.

Apr. 28 The Boston Celtics won the **National Basketball Association** playoffs, beating the Los Angeles Lakers, 4 games to 3, and allowing coach Red Auerbach to retire with his 8th successive championship. Auerbach was replaced by Bill Russell, Celtic center, the 1st Negro to coach a major U.S. sports team.

May 5 At Detroit, the Montreal Canadiens beat the Red Wings 3–2, winning the finals of the **Stanley Cup playoffs,** 4 games to 2, and the team's 2nd consecutive National Hockey League championship.

POLITICS AND GOVERNMENT; WAR;

DISASTERS; VITAL STATISTICS.

BOOKS; PAINTING; DRAMA;

ARCHITECTURE; SCULPTURE.

Mar. 10 A U.S. Special Forces (Green Beret) camp at **Ashau Valley** fell to about 2000 North Vietnamese troops after a 72-hr. siege. About 200 U.S. and South Vietnamese troops were killed or captured.

Mar. 25 The Supreme Court by a 6 to 3 decision outlawed **poll taxes** on the ground that an economic barrier to voting is unconstitutional.

Apr. 12 8-engined **B-52 strategic bombers,** used for the 1st time on targets in North Vietnam, dropped more than a million tons of bombs and blocked the main infiltration route into the south.

Apr. 23 U.S. aircraft flying over North Vietnam were attacked in strength by **Communist planes** for the 1st time.

May 1 U.S. artillery shelled targets in Cambodia after U.S. troops operating along the Caibac R. came under fire from the Cambodian shore. It was **the 1st time the U.S. intentionally fired on Cambodian soil.**

May 10 The **UN Disarmament Committee** recessed, having made no progress on a treaty to prevent the spread of nuclear weapons.

May 15 More than 10,000 persons picketed the White House to protest the **Vietnamese war** and to express support of Congressional candidates who were pledged to seek peace. At a rally at Washington Monument 63,000 "voters' pledges" to vote only for antiwar candidates were displayed.

May 30–31 In the **heaviest air raids of the war on North Vietnam,** more than 300 U.S. planes bombed North Vietnamese targets on May 30; on May 31 an important North Vietnamese arsenal was virtually destroyed by U.S. bombers.

June 1–2 The **White House Conference on Civil Rights,** attended by 2400

Jan. 18 An emergency grant of $100,000 from the National Council on the Arts, the 1st federal grant to a performing arts group, enabled the American Ballet Theatre to open its season at the New York State Theater in Lincoln Center. The **National Foundation on the Arts and the Humanities,** created Sept. 30, 1965, made other grants this year through its 2 agencies, the National Councils on the Arts and for the Humanities. The principal beneficiaries were Jerome Robbins' American Lyric Theatre Workshop ($300,000); the Laboratory Theatre for Education ($500,000); Playwrights' Experimental Theatre Project ($250,000); and Martha Graham's dance company ($141,000 for a nationwide tour and $40,000 to aid in the production of 2 new works). An endowment of $25,000 was made to the Association of American Dance Companies, a new service group for professional and nonprofessional performing companies.

Feb. 17 German-born U.S. painter **Hans Hofmann,** 85, died. He was one of the leading exponents of abstract expressionism.

Feb. 22 For the 1st performance in its new home, the New York State Theater in Lincoln Center, the **New York City Opera** gave Alberto Ginastera's *Don Rodrigo* its North American premiere.

Mar. 10 **Mari Sandoz,** novelist and historian of the Old West, died in New York City.

Mar. 21 The Supreme Court upheld the obscenity conviction of **Ralph Ginzburg,** publisher of *Eros* and other erotica, principally because the materials were advertised with the "leer of the sensualist." In past obscenity cases the Court had considered the material itself, rather than the circumstances of its production and promotion. At the same time, the Court reversed a Massachusetts ruling that the 18th-century novel *Fanny Hill* was ob-

Apr. 27 The ICC authorized **merger of the Pennsylvania and New York Central railroads,** greatest corporate merger in U.S. history.

May 13 12 school districts in the deep South were denied federal funds, the 1st such action against violators of the **desegregation guidelines** of the 1964 Civil Rights Act.

May 14 The Student Nonviolent Co-ordinating Committee elected black militant Stokeley Carmichael its chairman and embraced the concepts of **"Black Power"** and retaliatory violence.

June 2 Surveyor I, launched May 30, made the **1st U.S. soft landing on the moon** after a flight of 231,483 mi. in 63 hr. 36 min. It immediately began televising pictures of the moon's surface, and by July 14, when its batteries went dead, it had sent more than 11,000 of them. Shots of indentations made by the craft's legs showed that the surface was strong enough to support an astronaut.

June 3 The Gemini IX space-docking mission having been scratched May 17 because of failure of the Agena Target vehicle, **Gemini IXA** was launched in pursuit of an unpowered substitute target. As astronauts Thomas Stafford and Eugene Cernan closed on the target they found its nose shroud only partially detached, gaping open like the "jaws of an angry alligator" and making docking impossible. In the 2nd day of flight Cernan spent a record 2 hr. 5 min. in a space "walk," but found his equipment so troublesome that he terminated his extravehicular activity a bit early. Gemini IXA splashed down on June 6 after 70 hr. 20 min. aloft.

June 6 James Meredith, on a lone march from Memphis, Tenn., to Jackson, Miss., to encourage voter registration by blacks, was shot and slightly wounded. Groups came from all over to complete

May 7 *Kauai King,* a son of the great *Native Dancer,* led all the way to win the 92nd **Kentucky Derby** and $120,500 prize money.

May 21 Derby winner *Kauai King,* ridden by D. Brumfield, came from behind to win the **Preakness** at Pimlico. The purse was $129,000.

May 21 World **heavyweight boxing champion** Cassius Clay defeated England's Henry Cooper in 6 rounds in London.

May 30 At the **Indianapolis Speedway** nearly half of the 33 starters were involved in a 1st-lap crash, but only 1 driver was hurt. Graham Hill won the classic 500 as only 6 cars finished.

June 4 *Amberoid,* ridden by W. Boland, won the $117,700 purse of the **Belmont Stakes.** Derby and Preakness winner *Kauai King* ran 4th, lost his bid to become the 9th holder of racing's triple crown.

June 8 The **National and American football leagues** announced that they would merge for the 1970 season. The move provided for a common draft of college players in 1967, putting an end to costly competition between the leagues, and set up a Super Bowl game between the league champions of the 1966–67 season.

June 19 Comedian **Ed Wynn,** billed as "The Perfect Fool," died at 79. Late in life he won acclaim as a dramatic actor.

June 20 Billy Casper, PGA Golfer of the Year, won his 2nd **U.S. Open** in a playoff with Arnold Palmer.

June 25 **Buckpasser** set a new world record of 1:32⅗ for the mile in winning the Arlington Classic. The horse, named the champion 3-year-old and racing's horse of the year, earned more than

POLITICS AND GOVERNMENT; WAR; DISASTERS; VITAL STATISTICS.

BOOKS; PAINTING; DRAMA; ARCHITECTURE; SCULPTURE.

persons, adopted resolutions urging Congress to pass the Administration's proposed civil rights bill and asking for more effective enforcement of existing civil rights laws, more federal support for establishing civilian review boards to hear charges of police brutality, and more protection by the FBI in racially troubled areas. Floyd McKissick, national director of CORE, termed the conference a "hoax." Stokeley Carmichael, chairman of SNCC, refused to attend.

June 3   At Amherst College, 20 of the 270 graduating seniors walked out of their commencement ceremony when **Secretary of Defense Robert S. McNamara** was presented with an honorary degree. At New York University and Brandeis University, graduating seniors and faculty also protested the war in Vietnam.

June 3–13   One of the biggest battles of the **Vietnamese war** was fought in the Central Highlands province of Kontum. No figures on U.S. casualties were made available.

June 11   Secretary of Defense Robert S. McNamara announced that **U.S. troops in Vietnam** would be increased by 18,000 men within 45 days, bringing the total number to 285,000. He also said that since Jan. 1 a total of 2100 Americans, 4000 South Vietnamese, and 250 Australian, New Zealander, and South Korean soldiers had been killed. During the same period 21,000 Vietcong had been killed.

June 13   The Supreme Court ruled 5 to 4 in **Miranda v. Arizona** that the provision in the 5th Amendment to the Constitution against self-incrimination applies to police interrogation of a criminal suspect. Among other guidelines, the Court specified that a suspect must be told he has the right to have a lawyer present while being questioned, and that, if a suspect chooses to make a confession without a lawyer and is subsequently put on trial, the prosecution must prove that

scene, by granting that it was not without "redeeming social value."

Mar. 31   Sculptor **Paul Manship** died at age 80. His most famous work is the statue of Prometheus in Rockefeller Center, New York City.

Apr. 3   **Russel Crouse,** playwright, died at 73. His *Life with Father* (1939) was one of the longest running Broadway hits of all time. It was written in collaboration with Howard Lindsay, with whom Crouse also wrote the Pulitzer Prize winning *State of the Union* (1945). Crouse and Lindsay first teamed together to stage Cole Porter's *Anything Goes* (1934). Their other productions included *Arsenic and Old Lace* (1941) and *Detective Story* (1945).

Apr. 16   Performers and audience joined hands to sing *Auld Lang Syne* at the end of a 5-hr. gala, the last performance of the **Metropolitan Opera** in its venerable house at Broadway and 39th Street in New York. The fabulous gold curtain later was cut up into small patches and packaged with souvenir recordings of the occasion. A committee formed to preserve the old house failed to prevent its demolition.

Apr. 29   Douglas Moore's new opera **Carry Nation,** commissioned for the occasion, was given its premiere performance during the centennial of the University of Kansas. The work was later also performed by the Spring Opera of San Francisco.

May 2   The **Pulitzer Prize** in history went to the late Perry Miller for *The Life of the Mind in America: From the Revolution to the Civil War;* biography, Arthur M. Schlesinger, Jr., for *A Thousand Days: John F. Kennedy in the White House;* fiction, Katharine Anne Porter's *Collected Stories;* nonfiction, Edwin Way Teale's *Wandering Through Winter;* poetry, Richard Eberhart's *Selected Poems.* The 1st music award in 3 years went to Leslie

the march with Meredith on June 26. This **most important civil rights demonstration** of the year had a traveling debate between pacifist Martin Luther King, Jr., and militants Stokeley Carmichael and Floyd McKissick over their respective approaches to Negro problems.

July 1 The **Medicare program for the aged** was inaugurated. The new insurance plan, damned by some as the 1st step toward "socialized medicine," covers costs of care in hospitals and, after Jan. 1, 1967, in nursing homes.

July 8 The International Association of Machinists called an **airline strike** that grounded the planes of all major airlines until Aug. 19.

July 10 **Martin Luther King, Jr.,** at a huge rally in Soldiers Field, Chicago, demanded that the city end discrimination in housing, schools, and jobs, and stop police brutalities. The city had a riot-torn summer.

July 15 National guardsmen restored order after **3 nights of rioting** in Chicago's predominantly Negro West Side. The trouble started when police shut off fire hydrants opened to cool off children during a hot spell.

July 18 Astronauts John Young and Michael Collins, aboard **Gemini X,** successfully docked in space with an Agena target vehicle. Both suffered eye irritation when lithium hydroxide leaked from their life-support system. The Gemini splashed down on July 21 in full view of TV cameras after a 71-hr. flight.

Aug. 8 At Methodist Hospital in Houston, a team headed by heart surgeon Michael DeBakey installed the **1st successful artificial heart pump** (a left ventrical bypass) in a patient.

Aug. 10 **Lunar Orbiter I,** designed to photograph possible landing sites on the moon, was launched from Cape Ken-

$600,000 this year. With the $568,096 he had earned as a 2-year-old, he became the 1st 3-year-old to have won more than $1 million. **Kauai King,** Derby and Preakness winner, went lame in the Arlington Classic and his retirement from racing was announced 3 days later. He was syndicated for breeding purposes at a record $2.6 million.

July 2–3 The world **decathlon** record of 8089 points, held by C. K. Yang, was bested twice at Salina, Kans., by Russ Hodge (8130) and Bill Toomey (8234).

July 9 Jack Nicklaus won the British Open, joining Gene Sarazen, Ben Hogan, and Gary Player as the only men to have won the 4 major **golf championships** of the world (the others being the PGA, the Masters, and the U.S. Open).

July 12 In St. Louis, baseball's **all-star game** was won by the National League 2–1 in 10 innings.

July 13–14 During the night **8 student nurses were slain** in an apartment-dormitory in Chicago. As the killer took the girls one by one from a bedroom and coldly stabbed or strangled them, one girl escaped by rolling under a bed in his absence. On July 17 a sometime seaman and ex-convict, Richard Speck, was arrested for the crime. His left arm bore the tattoo "Born to Raise Hell."

July 16–17 All other countries lost out in a **5-nation swimming meet** in Moscow that saw the long-awaited match of the U.S. and Soviet teams of both sexes. The U.S. won 11 of the 17 events, the Soviets the remaining 6.

July 17 Jim Ryun, 19-year-old college freshman, ran **the mile** in 3:51.3, trimming 2.3 sec. from the world record.

July 18–21 In the U.S. Amateur Athletic Union's **national outdoor swimming championships** at Lincoln, Neb., Don Schollander won 5 gold medals and

the defendant understood his rights when he confessed.

June 22–26 At the 18th national convention of the U.S. **Communist Party** in New York City, Gus Hall was elected party general secretary and Henry Winston national chairman. Hall reported that membership was 12,000, up 2000 since 1965.

June 29 For the 1st time in the **Vietnamese war,** the North Vietnamese capital of Hanoi and the principal port of Haiphong were bombed by U.S. jet fighter-bombers. Oil storage and loading installations, highways, railroads, bridges, and ships were attacked. Approximately ⅔ of North Vietnam's oil supply was destroyed within a week. Between Feb. 7, 1965, and July 19, 1966, 299 U.S. planes were lost over North Vietnam.

July 30 The **demilitarized zone (DMZ)** separating North and South Vietnam was bombed by U.S. planes for the 1st time.

Aug. 4 The Defense Dept. announced the **highest monthly draft call** since the Korean war: 46,200 for Oct.

Aug. 6 **Demonstrations against the Vietnamese war** were held across the country on the anniversary of the atomic bombing of Hiroshima. In Washington pickets demonstrated in front of the White House and the church where Pres. Johnson's daughter Luci was being married. In New York 5000 marched to Times Square. On Aug. 9, the anniversary of the atomic bombing of Nagasaki, 200 demonstrators tried to stage a sit-in at the New York office of the Dow Chemical Co., a manufacturer of napalm.

Sept. 18–24 The U.S. had a record 970 casualties in the **Vietnamese war** for the week, 142 killed, 825 wounded, 3 missing. During the same period South Vietnamese losses were 98 killed, 280 wounded, 71 missing.

Bassett for his *Variations for Orchestra.* For the 3rd time in 4 years there was no award in drama.

July 3 **Deems Taylor,** composer and music critic, died at 80 in New York City. He wrote more than 50 orchestral, choral, and operatic works. He collaborated with Edna St. Vincent Millay on the opera *The King's Henchman,* considered the 1st successful American opera, which was given its premiere by the Metropolitan Opera in 1927.

July 10 Sculptor **Malvina Hoffman** died in New York City.

July 11 **Delmore Schwartz,** poet and critic, died in New York City.

Aug. 6 The **Actor's Workshop of San Francisco,** a resident company that had generated excitement and controversy for 14 years, was disbanded.

Sept. 15 **Anne Nichols,** author of one of Broadway's longest running hits, *Abie's Irish Rose* (1922), died at 75. Her most successful play, it ran for 5 years in New York and 20 on the road. There were Broadway revivals in 1937 and 1954, and 2 film versions.

Sept. 16 The **Metropolitan Opera** inaugurated its 84th season and its new house in Lincoln Center for the Performing Arts with Samuel Barber's *Antony and Cleopatra,* commissioned for the occasion. The backstage facilities and acoustics were rated excellent; the new opera and the nondescript architecture and decor of the house were faintly praised or damned. Practically everyone, however, loved the murals by Marc Chagall and the elegant crystal chandeliers that grace the foyer.

Sept. 28 The new home of the **Whitney Museum of American Art** was inaugurated in New York City. The building, designed by Marcel Breuer and Associates, is a

nedy. It went into lunar orbit on Aug. 14 and televised 215 "fair" pictures. On Oct. 29 it was crashed into the dark side of the moon, lest its radio signals interfere with Orbiter II, launched Nov. 6.

Aug. 15   The **New York Herald Tribune,** strike-bound since Apr. 24, closed forever. The paper had been formed in 1924 by a merger of the *New York Herald* (founded 1835 by James Gordon Bennett) and the *New York Tribune* (founded 1841 by Horace Greeley).

Aug. 22   The Labor Dept. announced that the July **Consumer Price Index** had hit a record high, making 1966 the most inflationary year since 1957.

Aug. 26   After the Chicago Real Estate Board agreed to support open occupancy in housing, Martin Luther King, Jr., called off a planned **civil rights march** into suburban Cicero. Robert Lucas of the Congress of Racial Equality charged that King had "sold out" to whites and, on Sept. 4, led a group into Cicero. Violence erupted as angry whites attacked the marchers; 15 were wounded, 39 arrested.

Sept. 9   Pres. Johnson signed the **Traffic Safety Act,** which established safety standards for autos sold to the public.

Sept. 12   **Gemini XI** lifted off with astronauts Charles Conrad and Richard Gordon and docked with an Agena target vehicle 94 min. after launch. On Sept. 14 the joined crafts achieved a record height of 851 mi. Gemini XI landed Sept. 15, its descent controlled entirely by on-board instruments—a space 1st.

Sept. 12   The new **World-Journal-Tribune,** formed by a merger of 3 defunct dailies, published its 1st edition in New York City after the longest **newspaper strike** in U.S. history had come to an end the previous day.

set world records in the 200- and 400-meter freestyle events. In all, 5 world records were broken at the meet, and 15 American records fell and 3 were tied.

July 23   John Pennel set an outdoor record of 17 ft. 6¼ in. in the **pole vault.**

July 24   Golfer **Tony Lema** was killed in the crash of a private plane near Munster, Ind.

July 24   Al Geiberger, with an even par score of 280, won the **PGA championship** at Akron, Ohio.

Aug. 1   From a tower of the University of Texas at Austin, Charles J. Whitman, who had already slain his mother and wife, shot and wounded 31, killed 13, in one of the worst 1-man **murder rampages** in U.S. history. Whitman was himself shot and killed.

Aug. 6   **Luci Baines Johnson,** daughter of the President, married Patrick Nugent in the Shrine of the Immaculate Conception, Washington.

Aug. 6   In London, Brian London failed to land a single solid punch against **heavyweight champion Cassius Clay** and was knocked out in the 3rd round.

Sept. 10   At Frankfurt, **heavyweight king Cassius Clay** defeated the German champion Karl Mildenberger in 12 rounds.

Sept. 14   Gertrude Berg, actress known to millions as **Molly Goldberg** of radio and TV situation comedy, died at 66. The radio show *The Rise of the Goldbergs* made its debut in 1929. The Goldbergs were last seen on TV in 1954.

Sept. 18   **Valerie Jeanne Percy,** 21 daughter of Republican Senate candidate Charles Percy, was killed by an intruder in the family home in Kenilworth, Ill.

697

Sept. 23 U.S. military command announced that U.S. planes were **defoliating dense jungle areas** immediately south of the DMZ between North and South Vietnam to destroy cover to North Vietnamese military units.

Oct. 13 Record U.S. air attacks were made against **North Vietnamese targets** with 173 planes. The next day 175 bombers renewed the raid. On Oct. 15 it was announced that 403 U.S. planes and 3 helicopters had been lost over North Vietnam since Feb. 7, 1965.

Oct. 14 Pres. Johnson signed into law a bill extending the **exclusive U.S. fishing zone** to 12 mi. off the coast.

Oct. 15 A bill creating a **new federal Dept. of Transportation** was signed by Pres. Johnson. It is the 12th Cabinet department.

Oct. 18 **12 firemen died** and 9 were injured when fire destroyed an old commercial building in New York City. It was the worst disaster in the 100-year history of the department.

Oct. 26 A fire on the U.S. carrier **Oriskany** in the Gulf of Tonkin killed 43 men and injured 16.

Nov. 2 Pres. Johnson returned to Washington after attending a **7-nation conference on Vietnam in Manila** and a 17-day, 26,000-mi. trip which took him to the U.S. base at Camranh Bay in South Vietnam, Thailand, Malaysia, and South Korea.

Nov. 8 Massachusetts, with a 2.2% black population, elected Republican Edward W. Brooke U.S. Senator, the **1st Negro in the Senate** since Reconstruction and the 1st ever elected by popular vote.

Nov. 25 J. Edgar Hoover, chief of the Federal Bureau of Investigation, said that no evidence had been found which would indicate that Lee Harvey Oswald, alleged

5-story granite structure with the shape of an inverted ziggurat. It has a sunken sculpture garden, and its walls are pierced at random with 7 trapezoidal windows.

Sept. 28 Author **Lillian Smith**, 68, died. Her controversial novel *Strange Fruit,* a literary sensation of 1944, dealt with the tragic love of a Negro girl and a white man.

Oct. 2 In Houston, the handsome **Jesse H. Jones Hall for the Performing Arts** was inaugurated with a week of concerts. The new theater–concert hall can accommodate audiences of from 1800 to 3000, and its foyer is graced with a pair of sculptures by Richard Lippold entitled *Gemini II.* It is part of a projected $40 million arts and entertainment complex in the Civic Center. The newly formed **Chamber Symphony of Philadelphia** gave its 1st concert in that city.

Oct. 12 *The Visitation,* 1st opera of U.S. composer **Gunther Schuller**, received the extraordinary tribute of 50 curtain calls at its world premiere in Germany by the Hamburg State Opera. The work, a blend of jazz and atonal music, deals with the persecution of a Negro in the South.

Oct. 13 Actor **Clifton Webb** died at 72.

Oct. 30 A phone call led police to Chicago's Grant Park and to a trash can containing an Italian Renaissance painting just stolen from the **Chicago Art Institute.** It was Correggio's *Madonna, Child, and St. John,* worth $500,000, one of the most valuable art works ever stolen in the U.S.

Nov. 2 The management of the **New York Philharmonic** announced that Leonard Bernstein, its music director for a decade, would retire from that post in 1969 and would then become laureate conductor.

Nov. 5 The off-Broadway production

SCIENCE; INDUSTRY; ECONOMICS;
EDUCATION; RELIGION; PHILOSOPHY.

SPORTS; FASHIONS; POPULAR
ENTERTAINMENT; FOLKLORE; SOCIETY.

Sept. 12 At 2 newly integrated public schools in **Grenada, Miss.,** police stood idly by as white mobs assaulted Negro children and their parents with ax handles, pipes, and chains, injuring 40.

Sept. 22 **Surveyor II,** launched 2 days earlier, crashed into the moon as attempts to correct its tumbling flight failed.

Oct. 7 **Stock prices** hit the year's low, with the Dow-Jones industrial averages down to 744 from a Feb. high of 995. It was the worst decline since the 1-day crash of 1962.

Nov. 6 **Lunar Orbiter II launched.** On Nov. 17 it went into orbit about the moon, photographing possible landing sites along the equator. NASA scientists said that photographs of domelike formations indicated that the moon once had volcanic activity.

Nov. 11 Bringing the Gemini series of manned space flights to a successful close, astronauts James Lovell and Edwin Aldrin rode **Gemini XII** to a successful docking in space. On Nov. 12 they took pictures of a solar eclipse. Aldrin spent a total of 5½ hr. in extravehicular activity, without the fatigue and equipment difficulties that had marked earlier Gemini flights. The pair landed safely Nov. 15.

Nov. 11 The **Methodist Church** (10 million members) and the **Evangelical United Brethren Church** (750,000) voted to merge in 1968 as the United Methodist Church, which would be the largest U.S. Protestant church. The move was subject to ratification by members of both sects.

Nov. 18 Roman Catholic bishops announced that, effective Dec. 2, U.S. Catholics would no longer have to **abstain from meat on Fridays,** except during Lent.

Dec. 10 The **Nobel Prize in chemistry**

Sept. 20 Hollywood's **Motion Picture Association** replaced its 1930 production code with new, and brief, guidelines for classifying films as to their suitability for audiences. The new rules were advisory only; they urged producers to use caution and restraint in dealing with sex, nudity, sin, crime, evil, and the like, and provided that some films be designated SMA (Suggested for Mature Audiences).

Oct. 5 The Texas Court of Appeals **reversed the conviction of Jack Ruby** for the murder of Lee Harvey Oswald, alleged assassin of Pres. Kennedy.

Oct. 9 In Baltimore the Orioles shut out the Dodgers for the 3rd straight game —and 33 consecutive innings—to sweep the **World Series** in 4 games, 5–2, 6–0, 1–0, 1–0.

Oct. 22 In Mexico City the crowd began fighting after referee Billy Conn stopped the **lightweight title bout** between Carlos Ortiz and challenger Sugar Ramos in the 5th round because of a cut over Ramos' eye. An official overruled the referee and gave the title to Ramos when Ortiz refused to continue the fight. The next day the World Boxing Association declared the title vacant and it was agreed that the 2 fighters would meet again in 1967.

Nov. 1 The Kennedy family released to the National Archives **autopsy photos and X-rays** of the murdered President.

Nov. 8 Despite criticism that he was a far-right conservative without any experience in government, movie star **Ronald Reagan,** a Republican, won himself a new career, being elected governor of California by nearly a million votes over 8-year incumbent Edmund G. "Pat" Brown, a Democrat. Reagan himself had been a Democrat most of his life, and during his earlier screen career had espoused liberal causes.

Nov. 12 In a Mesa, Ariz., beauty

assassin of Pres. John F. Kennedy, had accomplices. Hoover's statement was evoked by criticism of the **Warren Commission's report** on the assassination.

Nov. 29 Pres. Johnson announced that **federal programs totaling $5.3 billion were being canceled or postponed** to save $3 billion in the current fiscal year. Some cuts were in the areas where Congress had authorized higher expenditures than the President had requested; other cuts were made in the President's budget.

Dec. 3 Pres. Johnson inspected the $78-million **Amistad Dam** on the U.S.–Mexican border and had a 4-hr. visit with Mexican President Gustavo Díaz Ordaz. The cost of the dam is being shared equally by the 2 countries.

The Fantasticks became the **longest-running musical in New York theater history,** exceeding the record run of 2717 performances of *My Fair Lady.*

Dec. 14 The **Metropolitan Opera** announced that its 2-year-old touring company, the Metropolitan Opera National Company, had cost over $3 million more than anticipated and would be disbanded in 1967.

1967

Greatly intensified U.S. involvement in the Vietnamese war meant concomitant casualties: by mid-November more than 17,000 Americans had died in Vietnam since 1961; 2,000 more in the 1st 10 months of the year than in the period 1961–66. U.S. bombing of the demilitarized zone, through which North Vietnamese were infiltrating into the South, and of North Vietnam marked air activity. On the ground, the capture of Quang Tri was considered the most important Communist victory of the war. U.S. and UN efforts to achieve peace were entirely unsuccessful, with UN Secretary-Gen. U Thant asserting that the impasse was caused by U.S. bombing of North Vietnam. At home, Pres. Johnson got a $69.9 billion defense appropriation for the 1967–68 fiscal year, the largest single

The most important art news in the U.S., as in the rest of the world this year, was the international effort to save the priceless cultural treasures damaged by a disastrous flood which struck Florence on Nov. 4, 1966. U.S. art conservationists and concerned nonprofessionals volunteered their personal services, and the Red Cross, the Boy Scouts, the Lions, and extemporaneous committees raised money for the work of salvage and restoration. Mrs. John F. Kennedy was honorary president of the Committee to Rescue Italian Art, which collected several million dollars through subcommittees in 25 cities. Sen. Claiborne Pell of Rhode Island helped form an Anglo-American committee, the Florentine Relief Fund, Inc.

The theatrical season beginning this fall

700

was awarded to Robert S. Mulliken for his work on the chemical bond of atoms in a molecule. The prize in **medicine** went to Charles B. Huggins and F. Peyton Rous, for cancer research.

Dec. 31 After government officials studied Boeing and Lockheed designs for the **1st U.S. supersonic transport airliner (SST),** Pres. Johnson announced a decision in favor of Boeing, and of an engine by General Electric (over Pratt & Whitney) to power the craft. The Boeing 2707 has a movable wing and can carry 300 passengers at a top speed of 1800 mph. Controversy already raged about the effects of the plane's sonic boom, about the congestion it might create at airports, and about the cost of development, which was estimated at $6.4 billion.

parlor Robert Smith, 18, forced 5 women and 2 children to lie on the floor, then shot them; 5 died. Smith said he got the idea from recent **mass killings** in Chicago (July 13) and Austin (Aug. 1).

Nov. 14 In the Houston Astrodome, the **largest indoor crowd in boxing history** (34,420) saw heavyweight champion Cassius Clay defeat Cleveland Williams by a TKO in the 3rd round.

Nov. 19 In the **collegiate football game of the year,** the undefeated teams of Michigan State and Notre Dame battled to a 10–10 tie at East Lansing.

Nov. 28 **Truman Capote,** celebrating the smashing success of his nonfiction novel *In Cold Blood,* threw a party at New York's Plaza Hotel that was the year's social sensation.

Dec. 15 Motion picture cartoonist **Walt Disney,** winner of 29 academy awards, died in Los Angeles at 65.

Dec. 16 Boxer José Torres lost the **light heavyweight title** to Dick Tiger of Nigeria.

1967

The "long hot summer" saw the worst race riots in the nation's history. Riots occurred in more than 100 cities, the worst in Detroit where 43 persons were killed during 5 days of violence. 26 persons were killed and more than 1300 injured in the 5-day riot in Newark, N.J. In off-year elections, 2 Negroes won mayoralty races in Northern cities and a Negro was elected to the Mississippi legislature, signaling progress in the fight for civil rights. At the same time, segregationist restaurateur Lester G. Maddox was elected governor of Georgia by the state's General Assembly.

The worst disaster yet in the space program occurred when 3 astronauts, taking their Apollo I vehicle through tests at Cape Kennedy, were killed when a fire

Baseball had one of its most exciting pennant races in years as the season neared its end with 3 teams in the American League only 1½ games apart. Boston, up from 9th place the previous year with the help of the big bat of left fielder Carl Yastrzemski, took 2 in a row from Minnesota to clinch the title. The Red Sox then faltered in the World Series and lost to St. Louis, 4 games to 3. Yastrzemski joined baseball's small circle of triple-crown batters, with a year's average of .326, 44 home runs, and 121 runs batted in. After the Series the Kansas City franchise was moved to Oakland for the 1968 season; later the American League decided to expand to a complement of 12 teams in 1969, by replacing the Kansas City club and in addition awarding a franchise in Seattle.

appropriation ever passed by Congress, although he was unsuccessful in his request for an income tax surcharge which he said was needed to fight the war, to conduct the Great Society programs, and to fight inflation. Congress passed bills providing for increased Social Security benefits, aid to education, and antipoverty funds. Administration legislation requests included the smallest appropriation for foreign aid in 20 years, a Civil Rights Act that would end discrimination in housing by 1969 and prevent discrimination in selecting juries, funds to stimulate state and local crime-control efforts, revision of the Selective Service system through substitution of a lottery to select draftees, pay rises for civilian and military employees of the government, and an increase in 1st, 2nd, and 3rd class mail rates. Pres. Johnson attended former West German Chancellor Konrad Adenauer's state funeral in Bonn and Prime Minister Henry Holt's funeral in Australia, visited U.S. troops in South Vietnam and Thailand, conferred with Pope Paul VI in Rome, and attended a conference with South Vietnamese and U.S. military and diplomatic advisors in Guam. West German Chancellor Kurt Kiesinger and Foreign Minister Willy Brandt, Japanese Prime Minister Eisaku Sato, and Emperor Haile Selassie of Ethiopia made official visits to the U.S.

Jan. 3 **Jack Ruby died** in a prison in Dallas. He was the killer of Lee Harvey Oswald, alleged assassin of Pres. Kennedy.

Jan. 27 The U.S. signed a 63-nation **treaty concerning the use of outer space.** The treaty, signed also by the Soviet Union, prohibited the orbiting of nuclear weapons and forbade territorial claims on celestial bodies. It took force on Oct. 10.

Jan. 29 **Robert G. Baker,** former secretary to the Senate Democratic majority, was convicted of income tax evasion, theft, and conspiracy to defraud

was one of the leanest ever, with fewer openings than any this century and no significant new plays by U.S. dramatists. Eugene O'Neill's *More Stately Mansions,* an unfinished play from a projected autobiographical cycle, was judged a failure. Equally disappointing was *Everything in the Garden,* Edward Albee's adaptation of a play by Giles Cooper. The only provocative dramas for the legitimate stage were provided by British playwrights Harold Pinter (*The Homecoming* and *The Birthday Party*), Tom Stoppard (*Rosencrantz and Guildenstern Are Dead*), and John Bowen (*After the Rain*). Herbert Blau resigned from the Lincoln Center Repertory Company in January and Jules Irving, now sole artistic director, had an unqualified triumph with a revival of Brecht's *Galileo.* The APA-Phoenix under Ellis Rabb scored successes early in the year with Ibsen's *The Wild Duck,* Hart and Kaufman's *You Can't Take It with You,* and Piscator's *War and Peace.* In the fall it offered equally splendid revivals of Ghelderode's *Pantagleize* and George Kelly's *The Show-Off.* Welcome visitors from abroad were the Jewish State Theater of Poland and its star Ida Kaminska, and the Bristol Old Vic company. The smash musical *Hello Dolly!* was restaged to general acclaim with an all-Negro cast led by Pearl Bailey and Cab Calloway. Joseph Papp's New York Shakespeare Festival produced *Hair,* a "love-rock" musical with scenes of total nudity and a score that soon had everyone singing about the dawning of "the Age of Aquarius." Charles Schultz's comic strip *Peanuts* provided the basis for an amusing off-Broadway musical revue, *You're a Good Man, Charlie Brown.* The Tyrone Guthrie Theatre in Minneapolis offered John Lewin's *The House of Atreus,* a striking adaptation of Aeschylus' *Oresteia* with an all-male cast looming larger than life in costumes, masks, stilts, and platformed boots designed by Tanya Moiseiwitsch. Robert Lowell's adaptation of Aeschylus' *Prometheus Bound* was less successful in its premiere production by the Yale Drama School.

broke out in their capsule. The U.S. made 3 "soft landings" on the moon in order to get data about the lunar surface and possible landing sites for manned flights. Mariner V gave us information about the atmosphere of Venus, and the new Saturn V rocket, the world's largest launch vehicle, orbited the earth in a test to determine its use for eventual manned flights to the moon.

Jan. 9 **Julian Bond,** the Negro Democrat from Atlanta who had twice been barred from taking his seat in the Georgia legislature, was seated in the House of Representatives after the U.S. Supreme Court ruled that his statements against the Vietnamese war and in defense of draft-card burning did not disqualify him as a member of the legislature.

Jan. 10 **Lester G. Maddox,** the restaurateur who received national attention in 1964 when he sold ax handles to roughneck whites and stood in the door of his fried-chicken diner with a pistol in order to prevent desegregation of his eatery, was elected governor of Georgia by the state's General Assembly with a vote of 182 to 66. None of the 3 candidates in the state's Nov. 1966 election had received a majority vote, and Maddox, a Democrat, had run second to Republican Howard H. Callaway, who had received 453,665 votes to Maddox' 450,626.

Jan. 15 The Commerce Dept. announced that the **gross national product** of the U.S. had risen by 5.4% during 1966.

Jan. 16 The **1st Negro sheriff in the South** in this century, former paratrooper Lucius Amerson, took his oath in Tuskegee, Ala.

Jan. 27 **Astronauts Virgil I. (Gus) Grissom, Edward H. White, 2d, and Roger B. Chaffee** were killed when a fire broke out in their Apollo I capsule during tests on the ground at Cape Kennedy, Fla. An investigation concluded that a faulty electrical wire was the probable cause.

For the 1st time in pro football history the National and American leagues played preseason games, with the NFL winning 13 and losing 3. The NFL granted a franchise to the New Orleans Saints, and split itself into 2 conferences and 4 divisions: Eastern (Century and Capitol) and Western (Central and Coastal).

Sitarist Ravi Shankar played to sell-out crowds of both classical and pop music fans interested in the instrument and the subtle Indian harmonies used increasingly by pop groups. The Beatles, always innovating, maintained their popularity in the U.S., although there was some protest that their latest album, *Sgt. Pepper's Lonely Hearts Club Band,* had lyrics that tended to glamorize the drug scene.

The biggest motion picture attractions at the box office were the 1965 releases *The Sound of Music* and *Dr. Zhivago.* Among the new Hollywood productions, critics gave greatest praise to the adaptation of Edward Albee's play *Who's Afraid of Virginia Woolf?* and to its director Mike Nichols.

Clothing styles remained relatively unchanged this year, except that a few daring young ladies began wearing "maxis" (ankle-length coats) over their miniskirts. Britain's fashion rage, a thin, boyishly styled model aptly named Twiggy, received much attention from fashion editors and humorists as she toured the U.S.

Some 62.6 million bettors laid out an all-time high of $4.8 billion at thoroughbred and harness tracks this year. Among other records, $365,000 was paid for *Quill,* an 11-year-old brood mare in foal to *Native Dancer; Damascus* won more than $800,000; and Braulio Baeza set a 1-year high for a jockey's earnings when his mounts won $3,088,888.

Jan. 18 Albert DeSalvo, self-confessed **"Boston Strangler"** of 13 women, was given a life sentence after conviction for armed robbery, assault, and sex offenses. DeSalvo, who has been compared

POLITICS AND GOVERNMENT; WAR; DISASTERS; VITAL STATISTICS.

BOOKS; PAINTING; DRAMA; ARCHITECTURE; SCULPTURE.

the government. He was sentenced Apr. 7 to from 1 to 3 years in prison.

Feb. 10 The **25th Amendment** to the U.S. Constitution, providing a contingency plan for presidential succession, took effect when Nevada became the 38th state to ratify it.

Feb. 13 The **National Student Association** admitted that it had secretly received more than $3 million from the Central Intelligence Agency between 1952 and 1966 for use in its overseas programs. The Soviet newspaper *Pravda* charged that the CIA had financed student organizations for the purpose of subverting Communist groups.

Feb. 21 The 18-nation **UN Disarmament Committee** reconvened in Geneva after a 6-month recess. France continued its boycott of the negotiations.

Mar. 1 **Adam Clayton Powell** was denied his seat in the 90th Congress by a vote of 307 to 116. This was the 3rd time the House had taken such action against a duly elected member. A committee investigating Powell's activities found that he had "wrongfully and willfully" misused approximately $46,000 of government money for private purposes and had "improperly maintained" his wife on his office payroll.

Mar. 28 UN Secretary-Gen. U Thant revealed that he had proposed **a general truce in Vietnam** and talks preparatory to a reopening of the Geneva conference, and had been rebuffed by the North Vietnamese. The U.S. and the South Vietnamese had accepted his plan with qualifications.

Mar. 31 Pres. Johnson signed the 1st **U.S.-U.S.S.R. consular treaty** since the Russian Revolution.

Apr. 4 Military authorities announced that the U.S. had lost its **500th plane**

The book sensation of the year was William Manchester's *The Death of a President,* published after author, publisher, and the Kennedy family reached an out-of-court agreement to delete certain material. Critics found the book a somewhat turgid but nonetheless fascinating account of the assassination, and complained that history had not been served well by the cuts. The Rev. James Cavanaugh generated much controversy with *A Modern Priest Looks at His Outdated Church,* and at its height he left the Roman Catholic priesthood and married. Among other nonfiction best sellers were Stephen Birmingham's *Our Crowd: The Great Jewish Families of New York;* Robert K. Massie's study of the last Czarist regime, *Nicholas and Alexandra;* Studs Terkel's *Division Street,* edited tape interviews with Chicagoans of all walks of life; and Cornelia Otis Skinner's biography of the great actress Bernhardt, *Madame Sarah.* Marshall McLuhan and designer Quentin Fiore collaborated on *The Medium Is the Massage* (a pun on McLuhan's pronouncement that "the medium is the message"), which sought to show through words and correlated pictures how electronic technology in the mass media is reshaping social and private life. G. E. Stearn collected comments and criticisms from the growing mass of writing on McLuhan in *McLuhan: Hot & Cool.* William Styron's *The Confessions of Nat Turner,* a fictionalized account of the 19th-century slave rebel, got rave reviews as fiction and some harsh criticism as distorted history. *Rosemary's Baby,* by Ira Levin, was a chillingly convincing novel of witchcraft in Manhattan.

Jan. 10 Artist **Charles Burchfield,** known especially for his watercolors of scenes from nature, died at 73 in Gardenville, N.Y.

Jan. 31 In Seattle, famed Metropolitan Opera tenor **Giovanni Martinelli,** 81, agreed to pinch-hit for a performer with laryngitis and sang the role of the aged emperor Altoum in Puccini's *Turandot.*

704

SCIENCE; INDUSTRY; ECONOMICS; EDUCATION; RELIGION; PHILOSOPHY.

SPORTS; FASHIONS; POPULAR ENTERTAINMENT; FOLKLORE; SOCIETY.

Feb. 3 **Walter P. Reuther,** head of the United Auto Workers, resigned from the executive council of the AFL-CIO in a widening split between Reuther and AFL-CIO president George Meany.

Feb. 4 **Lunar Orbiter III** was launched from Cape Kennedy on its 92-hr. mission to the moon. The spacecraft relayed back to earth pictures of possible landing sites for manned space vehicles.

Mar. 7 **James R. Hoffa,** president of the International Brotherhood of Teamsters, began serving an 8-year prison sentence for jury tampering, when the Supreme Court refused to review his 1964 conviction.

Mar. 10 The **New York Stock Exchange** had the 2nd greatest trading day in its history, exceeded only by Oct. 29, 1929.

Mar. 29 **Complete school desegregation** no later than the fall term was ordered for 6 Southern states by the U.S. Court of Appeals for the 5th Circuit. The states affected were Alabama, Florida, Georgia, Louisiana, Mississippi, and Texas.

Apr. 2 16% of the Negro students in 11 Southern states were attending **desegregated schools** in 1967, an increase of 10% over 1966, the Southern Education Reporting Service announced.

Apr. 10 A 13-day **strike against major TV and radio networks** ended.

Apr. 19 The 2nd U.S. spacecraft to make a soft landing on the moon, **Surveyor III,** completed its 65-hr. flight from Cape Kennedy and began transmitting pictures of the lunar surface.

May 5 The New York City afternoon daily, the **World-Journal-Tribune,** born the past Sept. 12, ceased publication after piling up deficits at the rate of $700,000 a month.

to "Jack the Ripper" and called "possibly the most famous sex offender of the twentieth century," was not tried for the "Strangler" murders because of lack of evidence.

Feb. 2 Formation was announced of a 2nd pro basketball league, the **American Basketball Association,** with former NBA star George Mikan as commissioner. The new league, with 11 teams, failed to lure stars from the NBA. San Francisco's Rick Barry tried to jump to the new Oakland team but had to sit out the season when his old team sued.

Mar. 4 At the **women's world figure-skating championships** in Vienna, Peggy Fleming of the U.S. fell during her free-style event but went on to win the world title the 2nd year in a row.

Mar. 12 The Chicago Black Hawks clinched the **National Hockey League** championship, the team's 1st title in its 41 years of existence, but then lost the Stanley Cup semifinals to Toronto, 4 games to 2. Toronto won the finals May 2, defeating Montreal, 4 games to 2.

Mar. 22 A Louisiana grand jury indicted Clay Shaw, New Orleans businessman, for his role in an **alleged conspiracy that led to the assassination of Pres. Kennedy.** Shaw claimed that he was being persecuted by District Attorney James Garrison.

Mar. 25 UCLA, undefeated in 30 games this season, beat Dayton, 79–64, to win the **NCAA basketball championship** for the 3rd time in 4 years. UCLA's center, sophomore Lew Alcindor, had an all-time high season field-goal percentage of .667 in this, his 1st varsity year, and was everyone's collegiate player of the year.

Apr. 9 Gay Brewer edged out playing partner Bobby Nichols to win the **Masters golf championship.**

POLITICS AND GOVERNMENT; WAR; DISASTERS; VITAL STATISTICS.

BOOKS; PAINTING; DRAMA; ARCHITECTURE; SCULPTURE.

since the air raids on North Vietnam began in 1964.

Apr. 12–14 Pres. Johnson and Secretary of State Dean Rusk attended a conference of 18 chiefs of Western Hemisphere nations at **Punta del Este, Uruguay.** The conference issued a declaration calling for a start toward creating a Latin American common market by 1970, for improved transportation and communications facilities, for increased efforts to boost trade earnings, and for the elimination of unnecessary military spending.

Apr. 15 From 100,000 to 400,000 **protesters against the Vietnamese war** marched from New York's Central Park to UN Headquarters. A similar protest in San Francisco drew about 50,000.

Apr. 20 **U.S. bombers** raided the major port city of **Haiphong** in North Vietnam, hitting 2 power plants. North Vietnamese **MIG airfields** were struck for the 1st time.

Apr. 21 **Svetlana Aliluyeva,** daughter of the late Russian dictator Joseph Stalin, **arrived in New York** after requesting political asylum at the U.S. embassy in New Delhi, India.

Apr. 21 **Tornadoes in northeastern Illinois** killed 55, injured 1000.

Apr. 30 **Southern Minnesota tornadoes** killed 12, injured more than 100.

May 13 About 70,000 persons staged an 8-hr. parade in New York to show **support of U.S. troops in Vietnam.**

May 19 U.S. planes bombed a power plant in Hanoi in the **1st air strike at the heart of North Vietnam's capital.** U.S. and South Vietnamese forces also made an offensive attack in the DMZ.

June 1 U.S. officials reported 313 Americans killed, 2616 wounded during the week of May 21–27. It was the **great-**

Feb. 14 A retrospective show of more than 200 works by **Andrew Wyeth** opened at the Whitney Museum of American Art in New York. There, and at museums in other cities where it was shown, the exhibit attracted record crowds. A few critics found Wyeth's objective style too "photographic" but most praised the evocative studies created by the most popular living U.S. painter.

Feb. 15 The formation of a new opera touring group, the **American National Opera Company,** was announced. The company was organized, with the help of a grant from the National Council on the Arts, to fill the gap left by the foundering of the Metropolitan Opera's touring group. In the fall, the new company began its 1st tour with productions of Verdi's *Falstaff,* Puccini's *Tosca,* and Berg's *Lulu.*

Feb. 20 The **National Gallery of Art** announced that it had bought Leonardo da Vinci's *Ginevra dei Benci* from the Prince of Liechtenstein. The price was said to be between $5 and $6 million.

Feb. 28 **Henry Luce,** of the *Time* and *Life* publishing empire, died at 68 in Phoenix.

Mar. 7 **Alice B. Toklas,** long-time associate of poet Gertrude Stein, died in Paris at 89.

Mar. 10 **Geraldine Farrar,** 85, one of the Metropolitan Opera's great lyric sopranos, died in Ridgefield, Conn. She had retired in 1922.

Mar. 17 Marvin David Levy's **Mourning Becomes Electra,** adapted from the O'Neill play, was given its world premiere by the Metropolitan Opera. Critics found its music uninteresting.

Apr. 5 **Mischa Elman,** violin virtuoso, died at 76 in New York City. Born in the Ukraine, he studied with Leopold Auer in St. Petersburg and made his profes-

SCIENCE; INDUSTRY; ECONOMICS; EDUCATION; RELIGION; PHILOSOPHY.

SPORTS; FASHIONS; POPULAR ENTERTAINMENT; FOLKLORE; SOCIETY.

May 10–11 1 man was killed and 2 others wounded on the campus of all-Negro **Jackson State College** in Jackson, Miss., during riots which reportedly started when 2 Negro policemen arrested a speeder on the campus. About 1400 national guardsmen were called up to quell the disorders.

May 11 Pres. Johnson and representatives of the Bell System and the U.S. Independent Telephone Association took part in ceremonies marking installation of the **100 millionth telephone in the U.S.** This number is approximately half of all telephones in the world.

May 22 The Confession of 1967 was adopted by the General Assembly of the **Presbyterian Church** in the U.S., the 1st major new confession by the Presbyterians since the Westminster Confession of 1647.

May 29 The Supreme Court ruled that a California law permitting property owners "absolute discretion" over the **renting and selling of housing** was unconstitutional because it was discriminatory and thus violated the 14th Amendment.

June 3 During a riot in the **Roxbury district of Boston,** over 1000 Negroes threw bottles, looted stores, and battled with 1700 policemen.

June 14 An 8-day **strike by merchant marine deck officers** began, tying up shipping in Atlantic and Gulf Coast ports.

June 14 The U.S. launched **Mariner V** on its probe of Venus.

June 19 U.S. district judge J. Skelly Wright ordered an end to **de facto segregation in the public schools of Washington, D.C.,** by the autumn. His ruling was considered a historic extension of the Supreme Court's ruling against segregation imposed by state laws.

July 5 The **American Telephone and**

Apr. 10 **Academy Awards** for 1966 films: best movie, *A Man for All Seasons,* and best actor, Paul Scofield, for his role in that film; best actress, Elizabeth Taylor in *Who's Afraid of Virginia Woolf?;* best supporting actor and actress, Walter Matthau in *The Fortune Cookie* and Sandy Dennis in *Who's Afraid of Virginia Woolf?;* best foreign-language film, *A Man and a Woman.*

Apr. 15 Richard Speck was found guilty of the **murder of 8 Chicago nurses in 1966;** the jury recommended the death penalty.

Apr. 24 The Philadelphia 76ers, led by center Wilt Chamberlain, defeated the San Francisco Warriors, 4 games to 2, to win the **National Basketball Association championship.**

May 6 *Proud Clarion,* a 30–1 shot, won the **Kentucky Derby.** *Damascus* ran 3rd, lost his chance at racing's triple crown.

May 14 On his home field, Yankee outfielder **Mickey Mantle** hit his 500th home run, the 6th man in baseball to reach that lifetime mark.

May 20 *Damascus* won the **Preakness Stakes.**

May 31 A. J. Foyt drove his Coyote-Ford an average of 151.205 mph to win the **Indianapolis 500,** which was started May 30 and postponed by rain after 18 laps. Andy Granatelli's turbine-engine car, allowed in the race over protests by owners of piston cars, led with 3 laps to go, but then a transmission part failed.

June 3 *Damascus* won the **Belmont Stakes.** The 3-year-old colt was the first to win 3 divisional titles: Horse of the Year, best 3-year-old, and best handicap racer. He won 12 of 16 races and earned $817,-941, the most ever in a year.

June 18 Jack Nicklaus won golfing's

POLITICS AND GOVERNMENT; WAR; DISASTERS; VITAL STATISTICS.

BOOKS; PAINTING; DRAMA; ARCHITECTURE; SCULPTURE.

est weekly casualty toll of the Vietnamese war.

June 5 A band of Mexican-Americans seized the county courthouse at **Tierra Amarilla, N.M.,** wounded 2 policemen, took 2 hostages, and freed 11 prisoners held for unlawful assembly. The rebels were members of the Political Confederation of Free City States, which sought to reclaim some 2500 sq. mi. of northern New Mexico that they said the Spanish crown had granted to their forebears. Most of the rebels were later captured.

June 5 A **10-hr. power failure** in New Jersey, eastern Pennsylvania, northern Delaware, and eastern Maryland affected about 40 million people.

June 8 Israeli torpedo boats and planes attacked the **U.S. communications ship Liberty** in international waters 15 mi. north of the Sinai Peninsula, killing 34 seamen and wounding 75. Israel apologized for what it said was an accidental attack.

June 12 The Supreme Court ruled unanimously that state laws against **interracial marriages** are unconstitutional.

June 23 The Senate voted 92 to 5 to **censure Sen. Thomas J. Dodd** (D–Conn.) for personal use of political funds.

June 23 and 25 Pres. Johnson and Soviet Premier Kosygin met for a total of 10 hours of "useful" **talks at Glassboro, N.J.** Kosygin had headed his nation's delegation to the UN during its attempt to have Israel branded the aggressor during the 6-day war with the Arab league.

June 30 In Geneva, the U.S. and 45 nations signed the **General Agreement on Tariffs and Trade** (GATT), the result of 4 years of Kennedy Round talks.

July 6 The Joint Economic Committee predicted the **Vietnamese war** would cost $4 to $6 billion more in 1967 than the $20.3 billion requested by Pres. Johnson.

sional debut in Berlin in 1904. He was famed as the creator of a distinctively warm and vibrant tone. He became a U.S. citizen in 1923.

Apr. 15 Thomas Hoving, former parks commissioner for New York City, became **director of the Metropolitan Museum of Art** at age 36. Hoving had also been curator of the museum's medieval collection at the Cloisters.

Apr. 26 At an auction at Sotheby's in London, New York art dealer David Mann bought a **Picasso Blue Period painting,** *Mother and Child,* for $532,000, the most ever paid for a work of a living artist.

May 1 **Pulitzer Prizes** awarded this year for 1966 works: fiction, Bernard Malamud (*The Fixer*); nonfiction, David Brion Davis (*The Problem of Slavery in Western Culture*); poetry, Anne Sexton (*Live or Die*); history, William H. Goetzmann (*Exploration and Empire*); biography, Justin Kaplan (*Mr. Clemens and Mark Twain*); drama, Edward Albee (*A Delicate Balance*); music, Leon Kirchner (*Quartet No. 3*).

May 8 Playwright **Elmer Rice,** 74, died in Southampton, England. His *Street Scene* (1929) was given in 1947 in an operatic version by Kurt Weill, with lyrics by Langston Hughes.

May 15 Realist painter **Edward Hopper,** 84, died at Nyack, N.Y.

May 19 The Washington Opera Company presented the world premiere of **Bomarzo,** 2nd opera of the Argentinian composer Alberto Ginastera. The work was banned in Buenos Aires, the composer's home town, because the mayor found it "obsessed with sex and violence."

| SCIENCE; INDUSTRY; ECONOMICS; EDUCATION; RELIGION; PHILOSOPHY. | SPORTS; FASHIONS; POPULAR ENTERTAINMENT; FOLKLORE; SOCIETY. |

Telegraph Co. was ordered by the FCC to decrease its costs for long distance and overseas telephone service by $120 million per year.

July 12 In Newark, N.J., Negroes in the city's ghetto began looting stores, setting fires, and sniping from rooftops and windows at police and firemen. There were 26 deaths and more than 1300 injuries before the **race riot** was brought to an end on July 17 with the help of the national guard and state police.

July 17 **Surveyor IV,** programmed to land in the center of the near side of the moon, lost radio contact with earth seconds before it landed.

July 23 The **worst race riot in the nation's history** erupted in Detroit, resulting in 43 dead and 5000 homeless during 5 days and nights of violence. The national guard was called in when the riot first began; the next day 4700 Army paratroopers were ordered in to assist. Property damage was estimated at over $200 million.

July 24 A riot broke out in **New York City's Spanish Harlem** lasting 3 nights and resulting in 2 deaths. In Rochester, N.Y., a riot resulted in 2 deaths and widespread property damage.

July 25 Blacks rioted and set fires in the Negro business district of **Cambridge, Md.,** after a speech by H. (Rap) Brown, chairman of the Student Nonviolent Coordinating Committee. Brown was seized next day by FBI agents in Alexandria, Va., and on Aug. 14 he was indicted in Cambridge for arson, inciting to riot, and disturbing the public peace.

July 26 A 3-month **strike by the United Rubber Workers** ended when the union signed 3-year contracts with the nation's largest tire manufacturers. One of the companies, Firestone, announced price increases on July 31.

July 31 **A riot in Milwaukee's Negro**

U.S. Open championship with a score of 275, 1 stroke better than the record set by Ben Hogan in 1948. Nicklaus, named the PGA Golfer of the Year, won more than $200,000 in prize money this year.

June 20 Heavyweight boxer **Muhammad Ali** (Cassius Clay) was given a 5-year sentence and fined $10,000 for refusing to be drafted. Ring authorities had earlier stripped him of his world title, rejecting, as did the jury, his claim to exemption as a minister of the pacifist sect the Nation of Islam.

June 23 Jim Ryun cut 0.2 sec. from his own **world record for the mile** with a run of 3:51.1 in the AAU Championships at Bakersfield, Calif. At the same meet, Paul Wilson cleared 17 ft. 7¾ in., adding ¾ in. to the **world record for the outdoor pole vault** just set June 10 by Bob Seagren.

June 25 *Our World,* the **1st global TV hookup** in history, originated live from 19 countries on 5 continents, and was seen in 39 nations via 3 U.S. and 1 Soviet satellites.

July 8 At Wimbledon, England, **Mrs. Billie Jean King** of the U.S. swept the women's singles, the doubles (with Rosemary Casals), and the mixed doubles (with Owen Davidson).

July 11 At Anaheim, the National League won baseball's **all-star game,** 2–1.

July 14 Eddie Mathews of the Houston Astros became the 7th man in baseball to hit **500 home runs.**

July 21 **Jimmy Foxx,** member of the Baseball Hall of Fame and one of the great hitters of all time, died at 59. His lifetime batting average was .325, and at his death his record of 534 home runs had been surpassed by only Babe Ruth and Willie Mays.

POLITICS AND GOVERNMENT; WAR; DISASTERS; VITAL STATISTICS.

BOOKS; PAINTING; DRAMA; ARCHITECTURE; SCULPTURE.

July 7   U.S. and North Vietnamese troops suffered heavy casualties in 5 days of fierce fighting near the **U.S. Marine base at Con Thien,** just south of the DMZ.

July 19   Near Hendersonville, N.C., 82 died after a **midair collision** of a private plane and a Boeing 727.

July 22   The number of **U.S. troops in Vietnam** was to be increased to 525,000 by the end of 1968, the Administration announced.

July 23   By 60.5% of votes cast in a plebiscite, **Puerto Rico chose to remain a commonwealth** of the U.S., rejecting statehood and full independence.

July 29   Fire from a punctured fuel tank swept the **aircraft carrier Forrestal** in the Gulf of Tonkin, killing 134 U.S. seamen and injuring 62.

Aug. 14–15   Flooding of the Chena R. killed 3 and caused about $176 million damage in **Fairbanks, Alas.**

Aug. 21   The Defense Dept. announced that **2 U.S. Navy jets had been shot down** over Communist China after straying off course from a bombing mission over North Vietnam.

Aug. 24   The House of Representatives cut $247 million from the **foreign aid bill** in protest against Administration policies.

Aug. 24   The draft of a **treaty to stop the spread of nuclear weapons,** sponsored by the U.S. and U.S.S.R., was presented to the 18-member UN Disarmament Committee meeting in Geneva.

Aug. 25   U.S. Nazi Party chief **George Lincoln Rockwell** was shot to death in Arlington, Va. John C. Patler, his former aide, was arrested for the shooting.

Sept. 7   Secretary of Defense Robert McNamara announced that the U.S. would

May 22   Writer **Langston Hughes,** 65, died. His poems, novels, stories, plays, and essays dealt, often humorously, with the tribulations of Negro life in the U.S.

June 7   Writer **Dorothy Parker,** 73, died in New York City. Her trenchant and caustic wit was dispensed in poems, short stories, critical essays, and plays.

June 10   Actor **Spencer Tracy,** 67, died in Beverly Hills.

June 16   Art dealer **Sidney Janis** gave his $2 million collection of modern art (100 works by 54 artists) to New York's Museum of Modern Art.

July 22   **Carl Sandburg,** 89, poet, biographer, and folklorist, died at Flat Rock, N.C. He was a vigorous critic of political, religious, and commercial hypocrisy and chicanery, an authority on Lincoln, and a major contributor to U.S. folklore as a collector and singer of local ballads.

July 27   The **Santa Fe Opera House** was destroyed by fire just after the opening of the summer season. Enough sets, costumes, and scores were saved to enable the company to continue the season in a high school gym.

Aug. 15   A steel sculpture designed as a gift to the city by Pablo Picasso was unveiled in the plaza of Chicago's Civic Center. The untitled work (usually referred to as **"Chicago's Picasso"**) stands 50 ft. high, weighs 163 tons, and looks disconcertingly like a winged baboon.

Aug. 25   Actor **Paul Muni,** 71, died in Santa Barbara. He began his career in Yiddish drama, gained world fame for his motion picture roles, especially his

SCIENCE; INDUSTRY; ECONOMICS; EDUCATION; RELIGION; PHILOSOPHY.	SPORTS; FASHIONS; POPULAR ENTERTAINMENT; FOLKLORE; SOCIETY.

inner city resulted in 3 persons dead and 100 injured.

Aug. 15 Martin Luther King, Jr., called for a **civil disobedience campaign in Northern cities** to force the federal government to act on Negro demands.

Aug. 17 In a broadcast from Havana, Cuba, where he was attending the Latin-American Solidarity Organization conference, **Stokeley Carmichael,** militant black leader, told U.S. Negroes to arm for "total revolution."

Aug. 23 5 days of **rioting ended in New Haven, Conn.** Arson, looting, and vandalism occurred in various parts of the city.

Aug. 30 **Republic Steel Corp.** announced a price increase of 1.8% on its steel bars. By Sept. 1, 6 other steel producers announced price rises.

Sept. 6 159,816 employees of the **Ford Motor Co.** were idled when the AFL-CIO United Automobile Workers went out on strike as their contract expired. Contracts with General Motors and Chrysler expired at the same time but the UAW members reported for work. The union sought a 6% wage hike and extensive fringe benefits.

Sept. 8 **Surveyor V** was launched from Cape Kennedy and soft-landed on the moon 65 hr. later. By Sept. 24 it had transmitted a total of 18,006 pictures to earth along with important technical data.

Sept. 28 Walter E. Washington was sworn in as commissioner of the District of Columbia, a post equivalent to mayor of the city of Washington. He was the **1st Negro to head a major city government** in the nation's history.

Sept. 29 **New York City public school teachers** returned to their classrooms after an 18-day strike which began on the day schools opened. The teachers won a new

July 23–Aug. 6 A U.S. team of 401 athletes overwhelmed all opponents at the 5th **Pan-American Games** in Winnipeg. The U.S. squad won 120 of 171 gold medals, 63 silver medals, and 42 bronze; its wrestlers won all 23 of their bouts and its swim team broke 13 world records.

July 24 Golfer Don January won the **PGA championship** in Denver, in a play-off with Don Massengale.

Aug. 20 In the Women's National AAU Outdoor Championships at Philadelphia, swimmer **Debbie Meyer,** 15, cut an incredible 22.9 sec. from the world record to win the 1500-meter freestyle event in 17:50.2. **Catie Ball** set a new world record of 2:39.5 for the 200-meter breaststroke. On Aug. 19 she had set a new record of 1:14.6 for the 100-meter breaststroke, and she set 2 more world records on Sept. 30. Miss Meyer this year also set new world freestyle record times of 4:29 for 400 meters, 9:22.9 for 800 meters, and 9:44.1 for 880 yd.

Aug. 21–29 In the U.S. doubles championships at Brookline, Mass., **Mrs. Billie Jean King and Rosemary Casals** won the women's title. Mrs. King, with Owen Davidson, also won the mixed doubles.

Sept. 10 At Forest Hills, N.Y., **Mrs. Billie Jean King** won the U.S. women's singles tennis championship, completing her sweep of both the U.S. and British singles, doubles, and mixed doubles championships. She was the 1st to achieve this feat since Alice Marble's victories in 1939. John Newcombe of Australia won the men's singles.

Sept. 12–18 The U.S. yacht *Intrepid* bested Australia's *Dame Pattie* in 4 straight races to win for the U.S. the **America's Cup** for the 20th consecutive time.

Sept. 24 Jim Bakken of the St. Louis Cardinals broke all **pro football kicking records** with 7 field goals in 1 game.

build a barrier of land mines, barbed wire, and electronic devices just below the **demilitarized zone in Vietnam.**

Sept. 18 Washington announced plans to build the **Sentinel system,** a "thin-line" antiballistic missile (ABM) system capable of hitting ICBM's launched from Communist China.

Oct. 3 The House Ways and Means Committee voted 20 to 5 to shelve the **10% tax surcharge** requested by Pres. Johnson until the national budget had been cut by $5 billion.

Oct. 4 The month-long siege of the **Marine base at Con Thien** by North Vietnamese guns located in the DMZ was stopped by U.S. air and artillery attacks.

Oct. 14 The U.S. charged the North Vietnamese with **mistreatment of prisoners of war** in violation of the 1949 Geneva Convention.

Oct. 18 The House of Representatives by a vote of 238 to 164 ordered Pres. Johnson to **cut nonmilitary spending** in the current fiscal year by $5 to $7 billion.

Oct. 21–22 Over 50,000 **antiwar protesters** marched in Washington. At least 647 were arrested, most after a clash with police and troops at the Pentagon.

Oct. 26 Selective Service chief Lewis Hershey ordered **cancellation of draft deferments** of college students who violated draft laws or interfered with recruiting.

Oct. 28 Pres. Johnson and Mexican President Díaz Ordaz met for ceremonies at El Paso to transfer to Mexico the 437-acre border area of **El Chamizal,** separated from Mexico in the 1850's when the Rio Grande changed its course.

Nov. 3 The 5-day Vietcong and North Vietnamese assault on **Loc Ninh** near the Cambodian border, marked by unusual

portrayals of Louis Pasteur and Emile Zola.

Aug. 30 Painter **Ad Reinhardt,** a developer of "minimal art," died at 53 in New York City.

Sept. 29 **Carson McCullers,** novelist, short-story writer, and playwright, died at 50 in Nyack, N.Y. Her work dealt with love, loneliness, and society's misfits, as in her 1st novel, *The Heart Is a Lonely Hunter.*

Oct. 11 An exhibit of 275 **Picasso sculptures,** assembled and shown in Paris in honor of the artist's 85th birthday (1966), opened at New York's Museum of Modern Art.

Oct. 18 The **La Scala Opera Company,** in its 1st appearance in the U.S., sang Verdi's *Requiem* at New York's Carnegie Hall.

Dec. 1 In an auction at Christie's, London, Monet's *La Terrasse à Sainte-Adresse* was bought for New York's Metropolitan Museum of Art for $1.4 million, the **highest auction price ever for an impressionist work.**

Dec. 4 Actor-comedian **Bert Lahr,** 72, died. He was best known as the Cowardly Lion in the movie *The Wizard of Oz* and for the role of Estragon in Beckett's *Waiting for Godot.*

Dec. 6 At an art forgery seminar at New York's **Metropolitan Museum of Art,** the museum revealed that one of its most prized pieces was a 50-yr.-old forgery. It was an elegant statue of a horse, estimated to be 2400 years old when it was

SCIENCE; INDUSTRY; ECONOMICS; EDUCATION; RELIGION; PHILOSOPHY.

SPORTS; FASHIONS; POPULAR ENTERTAINMENT; FOLKLORE; SOCIETY.

contract calling for $135,400,000 in pay hikes over a 26-month period. A 2-week strike by teachers in Detroit ended Sept. 18 when they won a 2-year contract increasing salaries by $850 each year.

Oct. 2 Thurgood Marshall, the **1st Negro to be appointed to the nation's highest court,** took his oath as a Supreme Court justice.

Oct. 19 **Mariner V** passed within 2480 mi. of the planet Venus and sent back to earth scientific data indicating that the planet is unfit for human habitation.

Oct. 20 7 men who took part in a 1964 **Ku Klux Klan** conspiracy to murder 3 civil rights workers were found guilty by an all-white Mississippi federal jury. The jury acquitted 8 others and could not reach a verdict on 3 defendants. Those found guilty were sentenced to prison terms ranging from 3 to 10 years.

Oct. 25 United Automobile Workers union members voted to end a 49-day **strike against the Ford Motor Co.** Their new 3-year contract raised pay and fringe benefits from 5% to 7% a year.

Oct. 30 **Dr. Martin Luther King, Jr.,** began serving a 5-day jail sentence in Birmingham, Ala., growing out of a 1963 civil rights demonstration.

Nov. 7 In off-year elections, Negro Democrat **Carl B. Stokes** was elected mayor of Cleveland, the 8th largest city in the nation, and Gary, Ind., chose Negro Richard G. Hatcher, also a Democrat, for mayor. Robert G. Clark was elected representative to the Mississippi legislature, the first Negro to sit in that house since Reconstruction.

Nov. 9 The unmanned **Apollo IV** completed an 8-hr. 37-min. test orbit of the earth. The capsule was recovered in the Pacific Ocean just 10 mi. from its target area. It was lifted off from Cape Kennedy

Sept. 30 In London, U.S. swimmer **Catie Ball** set 2 new world records, winning the 110-yd. breaststroke in 1:17 and the 220-yd. breaststroke in 2:46.9.

Oct. 3 Folk singer and composer **Woody Guthrie,** 55, died in New York City. He was credited with more than 1000 songs, including "This Land Is Your Land" and "So Long, It's Been Good to Know You."

Oct. 12 St. Louis Cardinals' pitcher Bob Gibson won his 3rd game of the **World Series,** defeating the Boston Red Sox, 7–2, in the 7th and deciding game.

Oct. 23 Leo Held of Loganton, Pa., went on a **murder rampage,** shooting 12 neighbors and coworkers; 6 died. Held, shot by police, died Oct. 25 without regaining consciousness.

Oct. 24 Robert Smith was convicted of the **1966 murders of 5 persons** in a Mesa, Ariz., beauty parlor.

Nov. 7 Pres. Johnson signed a law creating the **Corporation for Public Broadcasting,** a nonprofit public corporation charged with raising the quality of noncommercial television.

Nov. 14 **Shirley Temple Black,** former child movie star, failed in a bid to win the Republican nomination for a California seat in the U.S. Congress.

Nov. 18 In the **collegiate football game of the year,** Southern California and its star runner O. J. Simpson defeated UCLA and its great quarterback Gary Beban, 21–20. Beban won the Heisman Trophy as the best player of the year; Simpson, a junior, led major-college players in rushing, with 1415 yd.

Dec. 9 **Lynda Byrd Johnson,** the President's older daughter, was married to Marine Capt. Charles Robb in the White House.

713

desperation and fanaticism, was finally broken by U.S. and South Vietnamese troops.

Nov. 16   The Administration announced the names of 63 U.S. cities which would participate in a $300 million **slum-clearance program.**

Nov. 20   Despite the lowest yearly birthrate in history, 17.8 per 1000, the **U.S. population reached 200 million.**

Nov. 22 U.S. Army forces captured **Hill 875** near **Dak To** after a 19-day battle, one of the bloodiest of the Vietnamese war.

Dec. 5 More than 1000 **antiwar protesters** attempted to close down a New York induction center. Among the 264 arrested were Dr. Benjamin Spock and poet Allen Ginsberg.

Dec. 15 The **collapse of a suspension bridge** on the Ohio R. between Point Pleasant, W.Va., and Kanauga, Ohio, killed 46 persons.

Dec. 20 The number of **U.S. troops in South Vietnam** reached 474,300.

acquired in 1923 and since then widely reproduced in casts and used as an illustration in many books on Greek art. A gamma-ray shadowgraph confirmed that it was cast by a technique developed in the 14th century.

Dec. 7 The **New York Philharmonic** celebrated the 125th year of its founding with Leonard Bernstein conducting a repeat of the orchestra's first program on the same date in 1842.

1968

Popular concern about national policies and social change reached unusual heights even for an election year. Dissent and doubt regarding the war in Vietnam and the economy at home affected the traditional party system, attracting contenders to Pres. Johnson from within his own party and stimulating the reactionary, 3rd-party candidacy of George C. Wallace. In Mar., Pres. Johnson announced that he would not seek another term. Later, the country was shocked by the assassination of 2 national leaders, Martin Luther King, Jr., and Sen. Robert F. Kennedy, and by violence surrounding the party conventions in Miami and Chicago. The Republican candidate, Richard M. Nixon,

Concern with political events dominated the literary scene this year. Norman Mailer, writing better than ever, made a strong comeback with 2 powerful books on recent political events: *Armies of the Night,* a personal account of the march on the Pentagon (Oct. 1967), and *Miami and the Siege of Chicago,* an equally personal and vivid view of the political conventions of 1968. The controversial *The Confessions of Nat Turner* (published in 1967) continued to provoke acrimonious discussion, and copies of the real confession of Nat Turner were advertised in numerous literary journals. 2 other books concerned with the difficulties of Negroes in America were Black

by the Saturn V rocket, world's largest launch vehicle, designed for eventual manned flights to the moon—the 1st time the Saturn V was used. On the same day, **Surveyor VI** landed on the moon and began sending back pictures of possible landing sites for manned flights.

Nov. 24 **Surveyor VI,** which had landed on the moon and sent more than 20,000 photographs of the lunar surface back to earth, made a unique maneuver when it moved itself 8 ft. to photograph its original landing site.

Dec. 8 Maj. Robert H. Lawrence, Jr., the **1st Negro astronaut** in the nation's space program, was killed in the crash of his F-104 jet at Edwards Air Force Base, Calif.

Dec. 14 Biochemists at Stanford University announced that they had produced **synthetic DNA,** the substance that controls heredity.

Dec. 29 Bandleader **Paul Whiteman,** famed in the 1920's and early 1930's as the "King of Jazz," died at 77.

Dec. 31 At Green Bay, with the temperature at −13° and 13 sec. left to play, Packers' quarterback Bart Starr sneaked the ball from the 1-yd. line for a touchdown that beat the Dallas Cowboys, 21–17, for the **National Football League championship.** The Oakland Raiders routed the Houston Oilers, 40–7, to win the **American Football League title.**

1968

The economy was seriously threatened by inflation, while unemployment remained low, averaging 3.6% of the labor force for the year, and there was a record 9% increase in the GNP, bringing it to $860.6 billion. In Apr. and June, William McChesney Martin, chairman of the Federal Reserve Board, warned that unless something were done to correct weaknesses in the economy, in particular inflation and the balance-of-payments deficit, the nation faced a serious crisis. Following the passage of the income-tax surcharge bill in June, along with other fiscal restraints, interest rates dropped. By Dec., however, the prime rate had risen again, to a record 6.75%. Labor made strong

In fashion, hemlines remained high, and efforts to introduce the "midi" length (hemline at midcalf) were unsuccessful. Pantsuits for evening wear, with full, flowing lines, gained wide acceptance. More and more men began to favor bold, extravagant fashions, and both men and women were wearing leather garments.

The major television networks provided comprehensive and distinguished coverage of the many shocking news events of the year. Some critics, however, maintained that the reporting was unfairly biased toward the liberal end of the political spectrum. The year's most

POLITICS AND GOVERNMENT; WAR;

DISASTERS; VITAL STATISTICS.

BOOKS; PAINTING; DRAMA;

ARCHITECTURE; SCULPTURE.

running on pledges to end the war and restore calm, narrowly won the presidency in November. Although inflation had become critical, Pres. Johnson's budget was a record $186 billion, with the year's expenditure on Vietnam approximating $25 billion. The foreign-aid request of $3.04 billion was the lowest in 20 years. The most heartening events of the year were the flights of Apollo VII and Apollo VIII, in Oct. and Dec.

Jan. 1 To combat the U.S. **balance-of-payments deficit,** Pres. Johnson called for restraint in travel abroad and placed limits on overseas private investment and government spending.

Jan. 5 **Dr. Benjamin Spock,** eminent pediatrician, and the Rev. William Sloane Coffin of Yale were **indicted** with 2 other antiwar critics **for conspiracy** to aid and abet draft evasion.

Jan. 17 In his **State of the Union message,** Pres. Johnson called for a **10% income-tax surcharge to** reduce the budget deficit (estimated at $20 billion for fiscal 1968) and to curb inflation.

Jan. 19 Pres. Johnson appointed **Clark M. Clifford** to succeed Robert McNamara, who had resigned 2 months earlier, as secretary of defense.

Jan. 21 A U.S. **B-52 plane carrying 4 hydrogen bombs crashed** near Greenland, causing radioactivity in the area.

Jan. 23 The **Pueblo,** a U.S. Navy intelligence ship, **was captured by North Korean patrol boats** and taken to Wonson.

Jan. 25 **John W. Gardner resigned** as secretary of health, education, and welfare, reportedly because of dissatisfaction with the U.S. war policy.

Jan. 30 A massive attack, the **Tet (New Year) offensive,** was launched by Communist troops against 35 Allied cen-

Panther leader Eldridge Cleaver's *Soul on Ice,* a book of essays, and John Hersey's *The Algiers Motel Incident,* which dealt with police brutality toward blacks in an incident in Detroit. Both were best sellers. In fiction, 2 of the most talked-about books of the year were John Updike's *Couples* and Gore Vidal's *Myra Breckinridge.* Both emphasized flagrant sexuality but were otherwise regarded as disappointing, given the talents of the authors. 3 books of poetry by Rod McKuen made various best-seller lists although virtually condemned universally as sentimental and callow. *The Money Game* by Adam Smith, a disarmingly gossipy but also shrewd analysis of the psychology of playing the stock market, became an immediate best seller. Smith's cautionary note, however, was generally ignored as the market continued to rise and younger brokers, inclined toward speculation, continued to operate successfully. James D. Watson's book *The Double Helix,* describing the discovery of the structure of DNA, a Nobel Prize winning achievement, became a best seller, and was praised for its frank account of the intramural maneuvers of the scientists involved. The trend toward mergers in the publishing industry continued.

Once again there was no Pulitzer Prize given for drama in 1968, and Broadway productions seemed unable to create theater of serious contemporary interest. Neil Simon's skilled and amusing *Plaza Suite* was successful in attracting audiences, mostly of older people, but was criticized as slick and superficial. 2 serious plays that did well were *The Great White Hope* by Howard Sackler and *The Man in the Glass Booth* by Robert Shaw, both of which dealt with political and social problems. The most interesting musical of the season was *Hair* by Gerome Ragni and James Rado, described as "tribal love rock," but this was originally an off-Broadway production. Off-Broadway, political and social concerns affected not only content but

716

SCIENCE; INDUSTRY; ECONOMICS; EDUCATION; RELIGION; PHILOSOPHY.

SPORTS; FASHIONS; POPULAR ENTERTAINMENT; FOLKLORE; SOCIETY.

gains, but some of these were offset by inflation and taxes.

In education, administrators were plagued by increased militancy on the part of both students and teachers. Major strikes by teachers hit New York City and Florida. Across the nation students demanded numerous reforms, including the complete separation of universities from government defense or military projects, a greater participation by students in the administration of schools, more university involvement in the neighborhoods, an increase in the enrollment of Negro and poor students, and the addition of more black-studies programs to the curricula. The students pressed their demands with calls for strikes. In cases where student sit-ins and agitation were answered by calling in the police (as at Columbia and San Francisco State), moderate students became further radicalized.

The space program, designed to prepare for a manned flight to the moon, proceeded successfully in the series of Apollo flights. In medicine, numerous organ transplants were attempted, many successfully. Dr. Denton Cooley of Texas was the most active heart-transplant surgeon, performing 17 such operations.

Drug abuse at all levels of society became more severe, and for the 1st time some public concern began to rise over the spreading use of heroin by middle class youths.

Jan. 9 **Surveyor VII** made a soft landing on the moon and began sending back data, including photographs. This was the last flight of the Surveyor series.

Jan. 22 An unmanned spacecraft, **Apollo V,** was launched on an earth orbital flight, during which the LM (lunar module) was tested.

Feb. 2 In New York City, **sanitationmen went out on strike.** The action lasted 9 days.

popular show was *Laugh-In,* a goofy, bright comedy hour that relied heavily on sight gags and 1-liners, and somehow usually escaped censorship.

For the 1st time the Gallup Poll recorded that crime ranked number 1 among matters that concerned the public.

The movie industry still seemed unable to adjust to changing audience tastes. Stanley Kubrick's science fiction extravaganza *2001: A Space Odyssey* was visually exciting and extremely popular with youthful moviegoers. 3 of the best movies of the year were documentaries: *Warrendale,* which was filmed in a home for emotionally disturbed children; *The Queen,* which dealt with a beauty contest for transvestites; and *The Legendary Champions,* on early heavyweight boxing heroes, from Sullivan to Tunney. On Nov. 1, a new voluntary rating system, designed to counteract the criticism that children were being exposed to excessive sex and violence in the movies, went into effect. A rating of "G" was adopted for movies suitable for persons of all ages; "M" for movies recommended for adults and mature young persons only; "R" for movies that might not be seen by children under 16 unless accompanied by an adult; and "X" for movies that might not be viewed by children under 16.

The baseball season of 1968 was known as "the year of the pitcher," with righthander Denny McClain of the Detroit Tigers leading the field. Only 6 regular players managed to hit over .300 for the season. The sports world was further distressed by organized demands and protests on the part of the players, the most notable being the demand for better pensions, set forth by the new National Football League Players Association, and protests against South Africa's apartheid policies that led to that country's being excluded from the Olympic Games in Mexico. The American Basketball Asso-

POLITICS AND GOVERNMENT; WAR; DISASTERS; VITAL STATISTICS.

BOOKS; PAINTING; DRAMA; ARCHITECTURE; SCULPTURE.

ters in Vietnam, including Saigon, Hue, and the marine base at Khe Sanh.

Feb. 1 Former Vice-President **Richard M. Nixon** declared himself a candidate for the Republican nomination for the presidency.

Feb. 8 Former Gov. of Alabama **George C. Wallace** announced that he would run for president as a 3rd-party candidate on a law-and-order platform.

Feb. 13 Pres. Johnson ordered **10,500 new combat troops into Vietnam.**

Feb. 14 Talks began at Panmunjom between the U.S. and North Korea on the fate of the **Pueblo's crew.**

Feb. 16 Occupational and graduate-student **draft deferments were sharply cut back.**

Feb. 24 **Hue was recaptured** from Vietcong and North Vietnamese forces.

Feb. 28 Gov. **George Romney unexpectedly withdrew from the New Hampshire Republican primary** following Gov. Nelson Rockefeller's statement 4 days earlier that he might be available in a draft for the presidency.

Feb. 29 The President's National Advisory Committee on Civil Disorders (the "Kerner Commission") released a report condemning **white racism** in the U.S. and calling for aid to Negro communities to avert further racial polarization and violence.

Mar. 4 The U.S. received **a letter from the crew of the Pueblo** asking the Administration to concede that the ship had entered North Korean waters, and stating that the U.S. should apologize and promise that no such future violations would occur. The release of the crew depended upon these conditions being met.

Mar. 6 **Joseph Martin, Jr.,** Republican

form. 2 of the most widely discussed productions were *Dionysus 69,* produced by the Performance Group, and the Living Theater's *Paradise Now;* both relied heavily on improvisation and audience participation via more or less spontaneous expressions of emotion. Foreign imports, including *The Prime of Miss Jean Brodie* by Muriel Spark, *Joe Egg* by Peter Nichols, and *Loot* by Joe Orton, competed more than successfully with American productions. Among the new companies that opened, 2 were regarded as particularly interesting: The Negro Ensemble Company and Theatre Atlanta, which opened its season with the very sharp and funny *Red, White and Maddox,* a satirical attack on Georgia's eccentric governor.

In both music and art, technology continued to play a major role, with the emphasis on mixed media. New facilities for the production and performance of electronic music were established all over the country. The Museum of Modern Art opened on Nov. 27 a major exhibition, *The Machine,* which featured machine designs created for both industry and art. Exhibits based on the aesthetic use of light were displayed in both museums and private galleries. The John Hancock Building in Chicago, having 100 stories, was completed. The outside of the building is crisscrossed with diagonal braces, and it is tapered toward the top for greater stability.

Jan. 17 The respected Boston publishing company of **Little, Brown and Co.** was acquired by Time, Inc., at a price of $17 million.

Feb. 11 **Howard Lindsay,** coauthor, with Russel Crouse, and star of *Life with Father* (1939), which broke box office records, died at age 78. As an author, director, and actor, Lindsay had been active in the theater for almost 60 years. Among his other works written with Crouse are *Life with Mother* (1948) and *State of the Union* (1945), which won a Pulitzer Prize.

718

SCIENCE; INDUSTRY; ECONOMICS; EDUCATION; RELIGION; PHILOSOPHY.

SPORTS; FASHIONS; POPULAR ENTERTAINMENT; FOLKLORE; SOCIETY.

Feb. 14 The New York Local of the International Longshoremen's Union voted to accept a settlement and go back to work. This marked the beginning of the **end of the longshoremen's strike** that began on Dec. 20, 1967.

Feb. 19 Florida public school teachers began a strike that lasted until Mar. 8. This was the **1st statewide teachers' strike.**

Mar. 1 Carl G. Hartmann, whose studies of the relationship between hormone changes and fertility led to the development of **birth control pills,** died at age 88.

Mar. 8 Pope Paul VI appointed the Rev. **Terence J. Cooke archbishop of New York,** succeeding the late Cardinal Spellman.

Mar. 8 In Orangeburg, S.C., a clash between Negro students and police resulted in the **deaths of 3 Negroes.** The national guard was called in to restore order.

Mar. 17 Representatives of the U.S. and the 6 European members of the London Gold Pool met in Washington and worked out a **2-price system for gold,** whereby all gold transactions between governments would be at the official price of $35 an ounce and the private market would be allowed to fluctuate. This resolved a critical rush on gold that had threatened to disrupt the international economy.

Mar. 28 Violence erupted in Memphis, Tenn., during a march supporting a sanitationmen's strike. 1 Negro was killed and the national guard was called in. The march was led by Dr. Martin Luther King, Jr., who tried unsuccessfully to preserve calm. Despite the danger, he promised to attend another rally in Apr. He was assassinated while preparing for this event, and shortly thereafter the 65-day strike was ended.

ciation concluded its 1st season of play with a loss of $2.5 million. In boxing, there were 2 official heavyweight champions, Jimmy Ellis and Joe Frazier, in addition to the unrecognized but undefeated Muhammad Ali (Cassius Clay), who was still barred from competition. In golf, there was a split between the established Professional Golfers' Association and the new American Professional Golfers, with both groups struggling for control of the tours while purses reached a record $4 million. A satisfactory compromise agreement was worked out on Dec. 13. In tennis, for the 1st time, tournaments were opened to professionals as well as amateurs. Jogging became a popular activity, enabling the enthusiast to get away from it all and improve his health simultaneously.

In popular music, hard rock became more complex and difficult to listen to, as in the case of the successful Jimi Hendrix. Many fans turned for relief to the sound of "soul"—especially the recordings of Aretha Franklin, and even to older and fine blues singers such as B. B. King.

Jan. 1 In the **Rose Bowl,** Southern California, with powerful running back O. J. Simpson, defeated Indiana 14–3.

Jan. 14 In the **Super Bowl,** the Green Bay Packers of the National Football League defeated the Oakland Raiders of the American Football League 33–14. The Packers thus gained the world championship for the 2nd year in a row. Shortly thereafter, their formidable coach, **Vince Lombardi,** retired, taking an executive position with the organization.

Jan. 18 A luncheon at the White House, given by Mrs. Lyndon B. Johnson for a group of nationally influential women, was disrupted when Negro actress Eartha Kitt stated with great emotion that it was pointless to discuss remedies for the troubles at home as long as the war in Vietnam continued.

719

congressman from Massachusetts for 42 years, died at age 83. He twice served as speaker of the House (1946–48, 1952–54).

Mar. 12 In the New Hampshire Democratic presidential primary, **Sen. Eugene McCarthy,** campaigning on an antiwar platform and aided by student volunteers, won an astonishing 42% of the vote.

Mar. 13 It was reported that more than **6400 sheep had been killed by nerve gas** being tested by the Army at Dugway Proving Grounds in Utah.

Mar. 16 **Sen. Robert F. Kennedy** announced that he was a candidate for the Democratic nomination for president.

Mar. 31 In a dramatic television appearance **Pres. Johnson announced that he would not seek the presidency again,** and also called for a partial halt to the bombing of North Vietnam and the opening of peace negotiations.

Apr. 4 Civil rights leader and Nobel Prize winner **Dr. Martin Luther King, Jr., was assassinated** at age 39 by a sniper in Memphis, Tenn. The event was followed by **a week of rioting** in urban ghettos. New York remained calm but Washington was seriously disrupted. **King's funeral** on Apr. 9 was attended by approximately 75,000 marchers.

Apr. 5 **The siege of** the U.S. Marine base at **Khe Sanh was lifted.**

Apr. 8 **Operation Complete Victory,** involving 100,000 Allied troops, was begun. It aimed to drive Communist forces from the provinces around Saigon.

Apr. 11 **24,000 military reservists** were called to active duty.

Apr. 11 The **1968 Civil Rights Act** was signed by Pres. Johnson. Discrimination in housing was made illegal for almost all types of dwelling.

Feb. 15 **Henry Lewis** was appointed director of the New Jersey Symphony, thus becoming the 1st Negro in the U.S. to head a major orchestra.

Feb. 23 Popular novelist **Fannie Hurst** died at the age of 78. Although criticized for sentimentality, her works, including *Back Street* (1930), sold exceptionally well, especially to women readers.

Mar. 6 **National Book Awards** were given for the following works: Thornton Wilder's *Eighth Day* (fiction); Jonathan Kozol's *Death at an Early Age* (science, philosophy, and religion); Robert Bly's *The Light Around the Body* (poetry); George F. Kennan's *Memoirs 1925–1950* (history and biography); and William Troy's *Selected Essays* (arts and letters). Prize winner Bly at the awards ceremony gave his check to a draft protestor to dramatize his dissent from U.S. war policies.

Mar. 14 The eminent German-born art historian **Erwin Panofsky** died at age 75.

Apr. 6 San Antonio, Tex., celebrated its 200th anniversary with **the opening of HemisFair 68,** an attractive world's fair that featured many permanent buildings, including the 622-ft.-high Tower of the Americas, the largest such construction since the Eiffel Tower. One of the permanent buildings, the **Theater for Performing Arts,** opened with a performance of Verdi's *Don Carlo.* The fair was widely praised but suffered financial difficulties, partly as a result of bad weather. On Sept. 15, a monorail accident killed 1 person and injured 48.

Apr. 10 **George M! a musical** by Michael Stewart and John and Fran Pascal based on the life of George M. Cohan, was welcomed as pleasant and nostalgic entertainment.

Apr. 16 Best-selling novelist **Edna Ferber** died at age 82. Her works in-

720

Apr. 4 **Apollo VI** was launched on an unmanned mission designed to test, for the 2nd and last time, the Saturn 5 vehicle preparatory to a manned flight.

Apr. 18 The **Bell System was struck, for the 1st time in its history,** by 178,000 members of the Communications Workers union. The strike scarcely affected telephone service but the record-breaking settlement on May 5, amounting to increases of 19.58% over 3 years, set a high standard for other unions.

Apr. 23 Students at **Columbia University,** protesting in particular the university's plan to build a gymnasium (primarily for students) that encroached on land needed by the neighboring community, began a sit-in that led to the closing of the university on Apr. 26.

Apr. 30 The **police ended the sit-in at Columbia University** in a nighttime clearing action that resulted in at least 150 injuries and was widely criticized as unnecessarily brutal.

May 2 **Donald Hall,** designer of the airplane *Spirit of St. Louis,* which was flown by Charles Lindbergh in the 1st transatlantic flight, died at age 69.

May 4 The Curtis Publishing Co. announced that it would cut the subscription list of its debt-ridden **Saturday Evening Post** from 6.8 to about 3 million, lopping off those from poor sections of the nation. Restricting the *Post*'s markets to areas of high-income consumers, it was hoped, would increase revenues by attracting more expensive advertising. The move evoked much humorous publicity as names of unwanted subscribers became known, for among them were Martin Ackerman, new president of Curtis, and Winthrop Rockefeller, governor of Arkansas. The device did not save the magazine, which failed early in 1969.

May 16 The **United Auto Workers union was suspended by the AFL-CIO**

Feb. 1 **Lawson Little,** famed golfer, died at age 57. In 1934 and 1936, he won both the British and U.S. amateur open championships.

Feb. 6–18 In the **Winter Olympic Games,** held in Grenoble, France, the U.S. won only 1 gold medal, taken by figure skater Peggy Fleming.

Feb. 13 In the **Westminster Kennel Club Show** a Lakeland terrier, Ch. Stingray of Derrybah, won the best-of-show.

Feb. 13 Silent-screen star **Mae Marsh** died at age 72. Her most famous role was that of Little Sister in D. W. Griffith's classic *Birth of a Nation.*

Feb. 22 **Peter Arno,** popular *New Yorker* cartoonist, died at age 64. He was noted for his worldly treatment of the erotic foibles of the well-to-do.

Mar. 22 The UCLA basketball team, sparked by **Lew Alcindor** (7 ft. 1½ in. tall), defeated their arch-rivals of the University of Houston in the **NCAA** semifinals, and went on the next day to win the championship easily.

Apr. 10 The **Oscar awards** of the Academy of Motion Picture Arts and Sciences, given for films released in 1967, went to *In the Heat of the Night* (best film); Katharine Hepburn (best actress), for her role in *Guess Who's Coming to Dinner?;* Rod Steiger (best actor), for his performance in *In the Heat of the Night;* and Mike Nichols (best director) for his work on *The Graduate.*

Apr. 14 Bob Goalby won the **Masters golf tournament** when leader Roberto DeVincenzo was disqualified for having signed an incorrect scorecard.

Apr. 16 Movie actress **Fay Bainter** died at age 74. In the course of her long and distinguished career, she won an Oscar award (1938) as best supporting actress for her performance in *Jezebel.*

Apr. 15   Mayor Richard Daley of Chicago told police to "shoot to kill" in cases of arson, looting, or rioting—an order that was credited with provoking police violence in Aug.

Apr. 25   UN Amb. **Arthur Goldberg resigned.**

Apr. 27   Vice-Pres. **Hubert H. Humphrey** declared himself a candidate for the Democratic nomination for president.

Apr. 30   After weeks of vacillation, New York's Gov. Rockefeller announced that he would run for the **Republican presidential nomination.**

May 2   The **Poor People's March on Washington,** planned by the late Dr. Martin Luther King, Jr., got under way headed by the Rev. Ralph Abernathy. Later in the month some 3000 marchers camped on a muddy site, dubbed "**Resurrection City,**" near the Washington Monument.

May 3   The U.S. and North Vietnam agreed to hold **peace talks in Paris.**

May 5   Communist forces in South Vietnam began another major offensive against Allied strongholds. Although Saigon was under attack from mortar and sniper fire, the offensive was judged to be not as severe as the January assault.

May 10   Peace talks opened in Paris with W. Averell Harriman representing the U.S. and Xan Thuy representing North Vietnam.

May 29   The U.S. **nuclear submarine Scorpion was reported missing** off the Azores with 99 men aboard.

June 4   Sen. Robert F. Kennedy, following a loss to Sen. McCarthy in the Oregon primary, **came back to win the California primary.**

June 6   Sen. Robert F. Kennedy, age

cluded **Giant** and **So Big,** which won a Pulitzer Prize in 1924.

Apr. 16   The Boys in the Band by Mart Crowley opened off-Broadway. It was acclaimed as a witty, mature, and frank treatment of homosexuality.

Apr. 21   The **Antoinette Perry (Tony) Awards** were nationally televised for the first time. Zoe Caldwell won the best-actress award for her role in *The Prime of Miss Jean Brodie,* and Martin Balsam the best-actor award for his performance in *You Know I Can't Hear You When the Water's Running.* Tom Stoppard's *Rosencrantz and Guildenstern Are Dead* was voted the best play, and *Hallelujah, Baby!* the best musical.

Apr. 25   The **New York Drama Critics Circle** for the 1st time gave one of its awards to an off-Broadway production, **Your Own Thing** by Don Driver, which was voted the best musical. **Rosencrantz and Guildenstern Are Dead** by Tom Stoppard won the best-play award.

Apr. 29   Anthony Boucher (real name William White), noted mystery-story critic and writer, died at age 56.

May 8   Pulitzer Prizes awarded to the following: Bernard Bailyn's *The Ideological Origins of the American Revolution* (history); George F. Kennan's *Memoirs 1925–1950* (biography); Anthony Hecht's *The Hard Hours* (poetry); William and Ariel Durant's *Rousseau and Revolution* (general nonfiction); and William Styron's *The Confessions of Nat Turner* (fiction). George C. Crumb received the music award for his orchestral suite *Echoes of Time and the River.* No award was given for drama.

May 15   Merce Cunningham's exciting and respected modern-dance company began its 1st major season in New York City.

May 20   Concert pianist **Ray Lev** died at age 56.

SCIENCE; INDUSTRY; ECONOMICS; EDUCATION; RELIGION; PHILOSOPHY.	SPORTS; FASHIONS; POPULAR ENTERTAINMENT; FOLKLORE; SOCIETY.

for nonpayment of dues. The longstanding split between the two groups culminated in a formal separation in July.

May 18 **Sanford L. Cluett,** inventor of Sanforizing, died at age 93.

June 1 **Helen A. Keller** died at age 87. Deaf, dumb, and blind since infancy, she had with the aid of her teacher, Anne M. Sullivan, learned to communicate with the outside world. She was internationally admired for her courage, intelligence, and sensitivity.

June 13 **Trading on the New York Stock Exchange reached a record high,** with 2,350,000 shares traded. The marked upsurge in business had begun in Apr., and was attributed to general optimism that the war in Vietnam was coming to an end. The volume of paperwork became so great in this period that, starting on June 12, **the Stock Exchange closed down trading on Wednesdays.**

June 17–July 1 **Yehuda Leib Levin, the chief rabbi of Moscow, visited the U.S.,** apparently with the purpose of persuading U.S. Jews that there was no anti-Semitism in the U.S.S.R. Although he spoke to large groups and was respectfully heard, most Jews remained unconvinced concerning the good will of Moscow.

July 1 The **Kennedy Round tariff reductions,** affecting 18 nations, went into effect.

July 1 A formal **separation of the United Auto Workers from the AFL-CIO** was announced. The split followed years of conflict during which UAW head Walter Reuther had accused AFL-CIO head George Meany of blocking labor reforms and allowing the movement to stagnate. 3 weeks later, the UAW joined with the Teamsters to form the Alliance for Labor Action.

July 2 **Francis Cardinal Brennan of Philadelphia died** at age 74. Having

Apr. 19 **Tommy Bridges,** who had pitched for the Detroit Tigers in 4 winning World Series efforts, died at age 61.

Apr. 20 **Rudolph Dirks,** creator of the perenially popular comic strip *The Katzenjammer Kids,* died at age 91.

May 2 The supposedly aging Boston Celtics won the **National Basketball Association Championship** by defeating the Los Angeles Lakers, 4 games to 2.

May 4 *Dancer's Image* won the **Kentucky Derby,** but was disqualified 3 days later on the grounds that he had been given a pain-killing drug. *Forward Pass* was then declared the winner. Peter Fuller, the owner of *Dancer's Image,* denied any wrongdoing and initiated legal action to have his horse reinstated.

May 8 Jim (Catfish) Hunter, Pitching for the Oakland Athletics, turned in a **perfect game,** the 1st in the American League since 1922.

May 9 **Harold Gray,** creator of the comic strip *Little Orphan Annie,* died at age 74.

May 11 The **Stanley Cup** was won by the Montreal Canadiens, who swept the series from the St. Louis Blues, taking the 4th game by a score of 3–2.

May 18 The **Preakness Stakes** were won by *Forward Pass,* who was also the official winner of the Kentucky Derby, *Dancer's Image* having been disqualified.

May 27 **George Halas,** a leading figure in the National Football League since the 1920's and owner of the Chicago Bears, retired as coach of the Bears.

May 30 Bobby Unser, driving an Eagle-Offenhauser, won the **Indianapolis 500** when a turbine car holding the lead broke down on the 191st lap. Unser set a track record of 152.882 mph for the 200 laps.

723

42, died of gunshot wounds inflicted at 12:15 A.M. on June 5, immediately following his victory speech in Los Angeles.

June 7 **Sirhan B. Sirhan was indicted** as the assassin of Sen. Kennedy. **150,000 mourners lined up to view Sen. Kennedy's coffin** at St. Patrick's Cathedral in New York on June 7 and 8.

June 8 Ex-convict **James Earl Ray was arrested** in London for the murder of Martin Luther King, Jr.

June 10 Gen. **William C. Westmoreland turned over command of the troops in Vietnam to Gen. Creighton W. Abrams.** On Mar. 22, Gen. Westmoreland had been appointed chief of staff by Pres. Johnson. This promotion was considered in fact a reflection of disappointment with the progress of the war.

June 13 Supreme Court Chief Justice **Earl Warren submitted his resignation** to Pres. Johnson, effective upon the approval of a successor.

June 14 A **verdict of guilty** was reached **in the Spock conspiracy case.**

June 17 The **Supreme Court ruled against discrimination** in the purchase or lease of property.

June 23 The war in Vietnam became the **longest war in U.S. history.**

June 24 The police cleared **Resurrection City,** arresting 124 persons, after the expiration of the campers' permit.

June 26 **Pres. Johnson nominated** Associate Justice **Abe Fortas as chief justice** of the U.S.

June 28 Pres. Johnson signed the **income-tax surcharge bill,** which Congress had tied to a $6 billion decrease in government spending.

July 1 The U.S., U.S.S.R., and 59

May 21 Miss **Helen Hayes,** "first lady" of the U.S. theater, was given a special Drama Desk Award for her performance in *The Show-Off,* a revival of George Kelly's 1924 comedy, produced by the APA-Phoenix Repertory Company.

May 25 The **Gateway Arch in St. Louis,** designed by the late Eero Saarinen, was formally dedicated.

June 3 **Andy Warhol,** controversial pop artist and film maker, **was shot** and seriously wounded by Valerie Solanis, an advocate of female chauvinism, who had appeared briefly in one of Warhol's films. Later she was adjudged not mentally competent to stand trial.

June 5 Distinguished actress **Dorothy Gish** died at age 70. She and her sister, Lillian, starred together since childhood in theater and films, working notably with the pioneer director D. W. Griffith.

June 12 The newly built **Garden State Arts Center in New Jersey** opened with a performance by the Philadelphia Orchestra, with Van Cliburn as a soloist and Eugene Ormandy conducting.

June 20 A **4-day strike by the members of Actors Equity** against the League of New York Theaters was concluded.

July 21 Pioneer choreographer of modern dance **Ruth St. Denis** died at age 90(?). With her husband Ted Shawn, she headed the influential Denishawn Company 1915–1931.

July 23 The **Whitney Museum** opened the show *Light: Object and Image,* dedicated entirely to works of art created with light.

Aug. 13 **René d'Harnoncourt,** a leading figure in the art world and former director of the Museum of Modern Art in New York, died at age 67.

Aug. 22 16 **art works worth approxi-**

served on the powerful Roman Curia for 28 years, he was one of the most influential of U.S. Roman Catholic clergymen.

July 4 A giant **radio astronomy satellite** was launched into an earth orbit. With its antennas extended, the satellite was 1500 ft. in diameter.

July 15 **A U.S.S.R. commercial jet landed at Kennedy Airport in New York.** On the same day, a U.S. commercial jet took off for Moscow. Thus began the 1st direct flights between the 2 countries.

July 28 **Charles W. Mayo,** surgeon and member of the Board of Governors of the Mayo Clinic, died at age 70.

July 30 **11 steel companies reached a settlement with the United Steel Workers** that averaged a 6% increase in a 3-year contract. The next day Bethlehem Steel announced **a 5% rise in steel prices.**

July 31 The National Council of Catholic Bishops issued a statement supporting Pope Paul VI's encyclical of July 25 that had reiterated the **Church's condemnation of artificial methods of birth control.** Nevertheless, many Roman Catholic priests and laymen in the U.S. and overseas openly expressed dissent from the Pope's position.

Aug. 7 U.S. Steel, reacting partly to government pressure directed against inflationary steel prices, announced price increases averaging 2½%. This was approximately 2% below other steel prices, and following this action **steel prices were adjusted downward** by other companies.

Aug. 8 Wealthy financier **Louis E. Wolfson and 3 associates were found guilty** of violating SEC regulations by manipulating stock in connection with the liquidation of Merritt-Chapman & Scott Corp.

Aug. 9 A **264-day strike against** Detroit's **major newspapers** was finally ended.

June 2 The **Belmont Stakes** were won by *Stage Door Johnny,* thus destroying *Forward Pass'* chance to win the triple crown.

June 7 Veteran actor **Dan Duryea** died at age 61. He appeared in more than 60 films, including *Johnny Stool Pigeon* (1949), *Underworld Story* (1950), and *Battle Hymn* (1957).

June 14 In a surprise victory, Lee Trevino won the **U.S. Open golf championship,** beating Jack Nicklaus by 4 strokes.

June 15 **Sam Crawford,** member of baseball's Hall of Fame, died at age 88. He was a home run hitting outfielder for the Detroit Tigers and the Cincinnati Reds.

June 26 **Ziggy Elman,** former trumpeter with the Benny Goodman and Tommy Dorsey bands, died at age 54.

July 6 Billie Jean King won the women's singles championship at Wimbledon for the 3rd straight year.

July 9 In **baseball's all-star game,** played at the Astrodome, the National League beat the American League, 1–0, in a low-hitting game typical of the season.

July 21 Julius Boros won the PGA golf championship by 1 stroke, beating Arnold Palmer and Bob Charles.

Aug. 20 **Earl Sande,** highly successful jockey, died at age 69. He won the Kentucky Derby 3 times and took almost $3 million in purses.

Aug. 24 *Dr. Fager,* the **Horse of the Year, set a world record** for the mile, running it in 1:32⅕ at Arlington.

Sept. 9 Arthur Ashe won the **U.S. Open tennis** championship for men's singles by beating Tom Okker of the Netherlands.

POLITICS AND GOVERNMENT; WAR; DISASTERS; VITAL STATISTICS.

BOOKS; PAINTING; DRAMA; ARCHITECTURE; SCULPTURE.

other countries signed **a nuclear nonproliferation treaty,** concluding 4 years of negotiations. U.S. ratification by the Senate was pending at the year's end.

July 23 **A sniper attack on police in Cleveland, Ohio, initiated 4 days of rioting** in the Negro ghetto. The national guard was called in. 7 persons, including 3 policemen, were killed.

Aug. 8 In Miami, **Richard M. Nixon won the Republican nomination for the presidency,** easily defeating the more conservative Gov. Ronald Reagan and the more liberal Gov. Rockefeller. Maryland's Gov. Spiro T. Agnew won the vice-presidential nomination on Aug. 9. **Riots in the Negro district of Miami,** beginning on Aug. 7, left 3 Negroes dead and hundreds injured. The national guard was called in.

Aug. 10 **Sen. George McGovern** of South Dakota, backed by many supporters of the late Sen. Kennedy, announced that he was a candidate for the presidency.

Aug. 21 The U.S. was shocked by the news that **Soviet troops had entered Czechoslovakia** to end the movement toward autonomy and liberalism that had begun there in Jan.

Aug. 28 **John Gordon Mein,** U.S. amb. to Guatemala, was killed by terrorists.

Aug. 29 In Chicago, **Hubert H. Humphrey** won the Democratic nomination for president. Sen. Edmund S. Muskie of Maine was named the vice-presidential candidate. **The convention,** which began Aug. 26, **was the most violent in U.S. history.** Young antiwar protestors, embittered by the faint impact of the campaigns of Sens. McCarthy and McGovern, clashed with police and national guardsmen. Hundreds of persons, including bystanders and newsmen, were beaten by

mately **$1.4 million were stolen** from the Edward Hanley Collection in Pennsylvania. Among the missing items was a $500,000 Picasso. The FBI recovered the works on Aug. 29, but would not discuss the case. No arrests were made.

Sept. 26 **The Man in the Glass Booth** by Robert Shaw and starring Donald Pleasance opened. A serious drama treating the problem of guilt in relation to the Nazi regime, the play was received with respect if not enthusiasm.

Sept. 28 The **Metropolitan Museum** opened an exhibit, *The Great Age of Fresco,* displaying 70 Italian Renaissance frescoes, which had for the 1st time been removed from their settings. The show was beautiful, widely acclaimed, and extremely crowded.

Oct. 3 **The Great White Hope,** a play by Howard Sackler based on the career of Negro heavyweight champion Jack Johnson, opened on Broadway. The performance of James Earl Jones in the lead conveyed brilliantly the frustration of a black man in a white society who has the misfortune to be the best in his field.

Oct. 5 The **report of the Cox Commission** on the disturbances at Columbia University was released. Later, published by Random House, it became a nationwide best seller.

Oct. 9 At a Parke-Bernet auction in New York, Norton Simon, the California industrialist, paid **$1,550,000 for Renoir's Le Pont des Arts.** This set a record for an impressionist painting, as art prices continued to escalate.

Oct. 29 The **Atlanta Memorial Arts Center officially opened.** This 13-million complex incorporated the High Museum, and also includes facilities for the Atlanta Symphony; ballet, opera, and theater companies; a children's theater; and an

SCIENCE; INDUSTRY; ECONOMICS; EDUCATION; RELIGION; PHILOSOPHY.

SPORTS; FASHIONS; POPULAR ENTERTAINMENT; FOLKLORE; SOCIETY.

Sept. 7 Well-known Harvard historian **Crane Brinton** died at age 70.

Sept. 9 **New York City public-school teachers went out on strike,** protesting policies associated with the program of school decentralization. The conflict centered on the actions of the board of the experimental Ocean Hill–Brownsville school district in Brooklyn, which refused to assign classes to teachers that it claimed were undermining its authority. The teachers' union and the board members accused each other of racism.

Sept. 19 **Chester F. Carlson,** the inventor of xerography, died at age 62.

Oct. 11 **Apollo VII,** manned by Commander Walter M. Schirra, Jr., Donn F. Eisele, and Walter Cunningham, began an 11-day earth orbital flight during which the crew transmitted live television broadcasts from the spaceship. The men successfully performed a docking maneuver with the lunar module.

Oct. 25 **Cardinal Cushing of Boston announced his retirement,** stating that he was partly motivated by hate mail relating to his defense of Mrs. John F. Kennedy's marriage to Aristotle Onassis.

Nov. 6 Dissident students demanding reforms, especially in the area of black-studies programs, called **a strike at San Francisco State College.** This initiated almost 4 months of turmoil, during which the president of the school, S. I. Hayakawa, called upon the police to help end the strike.

Nov. 15 **U.S. Roman Catholic bishops** in a pastoral letter **defended Pope Paul's** condemnation of artificial methods of birth control.

Nov. 18 The **New York City school-teachers' strike,** which had been in effect for 36 of the 48 days of school this term, was finally settled. One of the terms of

Sept. 14 New Zealand bred **Cardigan Bay,** the 1st harness racer to earn more than $1 million, was retired at age 12 by his trainer, Stanley Dancer.

Sept. 18 **Franchot Tone,** star of stage and film for more than 30 years, died at age 63.

Oct. 10 The Detroit Tigers won the **World Series** for the 1st time since 1945, beating St. Louis, 4–1, in the 7th game.

Oct. 12–27 In the **Olympic Games** at Mexico City, the U.S. took 45 gold medals, the U.S.S.R. took 29, and Hungary finished 3rd with 10. Despite the altitude many records were broken, and spectacular performances were turned in by U.S. athletes Bob Beamon, who broke the world broad-jump record by 21 in. with a jump of 29 ft. 2½ in., and Dick Fosbury, who won the high jump at 7 ft. 4½ in., going over the bar backwards.

Oct. 18 U.S. track stars Tommie Smith and John Carlos were suspended from Olympic competition for giving **a black-power salute** during the ceremony in which they were awarded victory medals.

Oct. 19 **Mrs. John F. Kennedy married** Greek multimillionaire shipping magnate Aristotle Onassis in a private ceremony on his island of Skorpios. This was both the most fabulous and most controversial social event in many seasons. Cardinal Cushing of Boston publicly defended Mrs. Kennedy's decision.

Oct. 25 Pres. Johnson's older daughter, **Mrs. Charles S. Robb, gave birth** to a baby girl, Lucinda Desha Robb.

Nov. 17 In a critical game between the New York Jets and the Oakland Raiders televised on NBC, the network cut away the last minute of the game to broadcast a production of *Heidi.* In what became known immediately as the **"Heidi game,"** Oakland scored twice in 9 seconds to win, 43–32.

police, even in full view of television cameras.

Oct. 2 Justice **Abe Fortas** asked to be withdrawn from consideration for the chief justiceship. The Senate had objected to his advisory services to the President while on the Court.

Oct. 3 George Wallace named former Air Force Chief of Staff **Gen. Curtis E. LeMay** as his vice-presidential running mate. LeMay was widely regarded as a hawk on the issue of nuclear war.

Oct. 31 Pres. Johnson announced a **stop to the bombing of North Vietnam.**

Nov. 5 In the **presidential election** Republicans **Richard M. Nixon and Spiro T. Agnew beat Hubert H. Humphrey and Edmund S. Muskie** with 43.4% of the popular vote, the slimmest margin since 1912, and 302 of the 538 electoral votes. The Wallace-LeMay ticket won 13.5% of the popular vote, carrying 5 Southern states. The Democrats kept control of both houses of Congress but lost 5 governorships to the Republicans.

Nov. 20 **78 coal miners died** in Farmington, W.Va., as a result of explosions and fires in a mine.

Dec. 1 The National Commission on the Causes and Prevention of Violence termed the police action in Chicago during the Democratic Convention a **"police riot,"** and warned against a **national tendency toward violence.**

Dec. 19 **Norman Thomas,** U.S. Socialist leader, died at age 84.

art school. It was built in memory of 122 Atlanta citizens killed in an airplane accident in Europe in 1962.

Oct. 30 Novelist **Conrad Richter,** author of the Pulitzer Prize winning *The Town* (1931), died at age 78. His last book, *The Aristocrat,* concerning an old woman struggling to survive, was published this year.

Nov. 2 The publishing company of **Funk & Wagnalls** was acquired by Reader's Digest Association.

Nov. 6 **Charles Münch,** Austrian-born conductor who led the Boston Symphony 1949–1962, died at age 77.

Nov. 25 **Upton Sinclair,** prolific and influential author of muckraking novels, died at age 90. His works include *Oil!* (1927) and *The Jungle* (1906).

Dec. 12 **Tallulah Bankhead,** star of stage and film since the 1920's, died at the age of 65. Daughter of William B. Bankhead, a former congressman and speaker of the House, she was internationally known for her beauty, striking performances, reckless and often outrageous behavior, honesty, and wit. She created the roles of Regina in Lillian Hellman's *The Little Foxes* (1939) and of Sabina in Thornton Wilder's *The Skin of Our Teeth* (1942).

Dec. 20 Novelist **John Steinbeck,** who received the Nobel Prize for literature in 1962, died at age 66. His best-known work, *The Grapes of Wrath* (1939), awakened the nation to the plight of impoverished rural families who fled the Dust Bowl in the 1930's. His other works include *Tortilla Flat* (1935), *Of Mice and Men* (1937), *The Long Valley* (1938), a book of short stories containing the classic *Red Pony,* and *East of Eden* (1952).

| SCIENCE; INDUSTRY; ECONOMICS; EDUCATION; RELIGION; PHILOSOPHY. | SPORTS; FASHIONS; POPULAR ENTERTAINMENT; FOLKLORE; SOCIETY. |

the agreement provided for the continued suspension of the board of the Ocean Hill–Brownsville school district.

Dec. 2 In New York City, **high school students began 4 days of disorderly protests** against the additional time added to the school schedule to make up for the days lost during the teachers' strike. Most of the outbreaks involved Negro students, especially from the troubled Ocean Hill–Brownsville district.

Dec. 4 **A new standard of death** was formulated by the American Medical Association in an effort to resolve controversy surrounding organ-transplant operations. The AMA declared that a person could be considered dead when death was irreversible. This criterion was termed **"brain death"** by Dr. Henry K. Beecher of Harvard on Dec. 12.

Dec. 9 **Thomas Merton,** Trappist monk and famed author on religion and mysticism, died at age 53.

Dec. 10 5 Americans were presented **Nobel Prizes.** Luis W. Alvarez was honored for his work in physics, particularly for the development of the bubble chamber used to investigate subatomic particles. Lars Onsager received the award in chemistry for his work in thermodynamic theory. Robert W. Holley, H. Gobind Khorana, and Marshall W. Nirenberg received the award in physiology or medicine for their work in genetics.

Dec. 12 It was announced that the spread of **Hong Kong flu** had attained epidemic proportions.

Dec. 27 **Apollo VIII,** manned by Commander Frank Borman, James Lovell, Jr., and William Anders, completed a pioneering 5-day mission that included 10 orbits of the moon and yielded spectacular photographs of the earth and moon.

Nov. 18 Movie producer **Walter Wanger,** one of the giants of Hollywood, died at age 74. His films included *Stagecoach* and *Cleopatra.* His "discoveries" included Claudette Colbert and Hedy Lamarr.

Dec. 6 **Baseball Commissioner William D. Eckert** was relieved of his post at a meeting of team owners.

Dec. 15 Former world heavyweight champion (1915–1919) **Jess Willard** died at age 86. He won his title from Jack Johnson on a 26th-round knockout, and lost it to Jack Dempsey in a controversial fight in which Dempsey was not disqualified for hitting Willard before he could get to his feet. The story surrounding the Johnson fight was dramatized in the play *The Great White Hope* (1968).

Dec. 22 Pres.-elect **Richard Nixon's younger daughter, Julie, was married** in New York to Dwight David Eisenhower, grandson of former Pres. Eisenhower.

Dec. 28 The U.S. tennis team, led by Arthur Ashe and Clark Graebner, won the **Davis Cup** from the Australians by a score of 4–1.

Dec. 30 *Motion Picture Herald* magazine announced that **Sidney Poitier** was the top box office star in the U.S. In 1967, he had become the 1st Negro to make the top-10 list.

POLITICS AND GOVERNMENT; WAR;

DISASTERS; VITAL STATISTICS.

BOOKS; PAINTING; DRAMA;

ARCHITECTURE; SCULPTURE.

1969

Richard Milhous Nixon assumed the presidency carrying the burden of the most unpopular war in our history, and Congressional "doves" allowed him nearly 8 months to make good on his campaign promise to end the conflict in Vietnam. While peace talks in Paris dragged on futilely, but after the new President had ordered a start on withdrawal of U.S. troops, antiwar sentiment in Congress was again unleashed by a Republican, Sen. Charles Goodell of New York, who demanded a complete pullout by the end of 1970. In mid-Oct. and mid-Nov., mammoth peace demonstrations were held in the nation's capital and other major cities, and these rallies sparked prowar marches and meetings by what the President called "the great silent majority." As the year wore on, the new Administration came under increasingly vocal criticism for allegedly pursuing a "Southern strategy," a plan purportedly concocted by Attorney Gen. John Mitchell to frame federal policies and make appointments that would mollify the South and encourage Republican victories there in coming years. Pentagon spending and lax military procurement policies came under strong Congressional scrutiny; the $70 million armed services budget was cut by $5 billion, and Congress failed by but 1 vote to defeat an appropriation to begin construction of the Safeguard antiballistic missile system. Pres. Nixon asked $2.6 billion in foreign aid, but Congress slashed that even though it was the lowest request since the program was started. Political observers speculated that Sen. Edward Kennedy's lame explanation of the accident in which a young lady died in his car had probably ruined his chances for a try at the presidency in 1972, if not forever. Hijackers made off with 65 planes (most of them to Cuba), a number that exceeded the total for all years since the 1st such seizure in 1952.

Jan.–Mar. Heaviest rains in 100 years caused **vast mudslides in southern Cali-**

Most of the theatrical excitement this year was generated on off-Broadway stages. Jerzy Grotowski's Polish Laboratory Theatre, a strong influence on avant-garde companies for several years, demonstrated its innovative techniques in 3 productions. Elaine May directed a successful twin bill consisting of her own 1st play, *Adaptation,* and Terrence McNally's *Next.* There were an unusual number of interesting works by black playwrights: the Negro Ensemble Company made a truly moving experience of *Ceremonies in Dark Old Men* by Lonne Elder III; the New York Shakespeare Festival offered Charles Gordone's *No Place to Be Somebody; A Black Quartet* was a set of 1-acters by LeRoi Jones, Ronald Milner, Ed Bullins, and Ben Caldwell; and the late Lorraine Hansberry was represented with a compilation from her works entitled *To Be Young, Gifted, and Black.* The off-Broadway sensations, however, were productions that regressed from the previous season's nudity to simulated copulation and assorted perversions. Police arrested practically everyone connected with *Che!* a lewd diatribe about U.S. relations with Latin American nations. Kenneth Tynan put together *Oh! Calcutta!* a pastiche of pornographic songs, dances, and sketches by such writers as Samuel Beckett, John Lennon, and Jules Feiffer. Critics panned the entertainment, but it quickly became a sellout, with best seats going for $25. 2 wretched plays suggested by the works of the Marquis de Sade did not fare as well. Broadway itself had another season devoid of a significant new work by a U.S. playwright, and only 2 new musicals that caught the public fancy: *1776,* based on events surrounding the signing of the Declaration of Independence, and *Coco,* a rather feeble story about couturier Gabrielle Chanel that was made a hit only by Katharine Hepburn's performance in the title role. Arthur Kopit's *Indians* dealt with exploitation of the American Indian, and Heinar Kipphardt's *In the Matter of*

SCIENCE; INDUSTRY; ECONOMICS; EDUCATION; RELIGION; PHILOSOPHY.	SPORTS; FASHIONS; POPULAR ENTERTAINMENT; FOLKLORE; SOCIETY.

1969

The U.S. economy continued to display critical danger signs throughout the year as inflation was not adequately checked and a recession threatened. The GNP rose to $932.3 billion, approximately a 7.7% increase. This gain was smaller than the 1968 increase, and moreover did not reflect a corresponding increase in output, since by the end of the year GNP gains were based on price increases only. Averaged over the year, the Consumer Price Index rose a sharp 7.2%. In an effort to fight inflation, the Federal Reserve Board acted to impose monetary restraint, and by June 9 the prime bank rate had reached a record high of 8.5%.

In science, the flights of Apollo XI and Apollo XII to the moon dwarfed all other achievements. These manned missions, exploring for the first time a heavenly body other than earth, caused 1969 to be popularly called "the year of the moon."

In education, the year was marked by continuing student unrest, provoked primarily by the lack of change in the Vietnam situation. Police and even the national guard were called in on college and university campuses across the country. Among the schools most affected were Cornell, Harvard, Hampton Institute (Virginia), San Francisco State College, Dartmouth, and City College (New York).

Jan. 16 It was announced by Merck Laboratories and Rockefeller University that 2 teams of scientists, working independently, had for the 1st time **synthesized an enzyme** (ribonuclease).

Jan. 20 Astronomers at the University of Arizona announced that they had made the **1st optical identification of a pulsar** (a dense neutron star), in the Crab Nebula.

Jan. 21 A government study stated that **chronic hunger and malnutrition**

Big league baseball's 100th anniversary year was one of change and excitement. The National League expanded to San Diego and Montreal, the American League to Kansas City and Seattle. Each league was split into Eastern and Western divisions, and playoffs for league pennants were inaugurated. Players refused to report for spring training until owners increased their pension benefits. The outfields of 6 ball parks were shortened to make it easier to hit home runs, and, in a further attempt to spark offensive play, the strike zone was narrowed and the pitcher's mound lowered. The moves had the desired effect: average runs per game jumped to 8.16 from the 1968 mark of 6.84, and the combined team batting average in the majors rose from .237 to .248. Ted Williams came out of retirement to manage the Washington Senators; Mickey Mantle and Don Drysdale retired. The New York Mets, long the laughingstock of the majors, astounded everyone with their 1st season of championship ball. Mets' pitcher Tom Seaver won the Cy Young Award as the best pitcher in the National League; Mike Cuellar (Baltimore) and Denny McLain (Detroit) shared that honor in the American League. Harmon Killebrew, 3rd baseman with Minnesota, and Willie McCovey, San Francisco's 1st baseman, were voted Most Valuable Player in the American and National leagues, respectively.

Fashion designers let up on their effort to dictate a lower hemline this year, and offered women a choice of mini, midi, and maxi lengths. Bellbottom pants were in vogue for both sexes, as was the heavy look in shoes: blunt toes and buckles. "Unisex," matching outfits for couples, was much talked about but not much worn.

Jan. 1 In the **Rose Bowl,** Ohio State defeated favored Southern California and its powerful running back O. J. Simpson by a score of 27–16.

POLITICS AND GOVERNMENT; WAR;
DISASTERS; VITAL STATISTICS.

BOOKS; PAINTING; DRAMA;
ARCHITECTURE; SCULPTURE.

fornia, killed more than 100, destroyed nearly 10,000 homes. Damage exceeded $60 million. The worst storms hit Jan. 18–26, Feb. 23–26.

Jan. 3 The House voted to seat **Adam Clayton Powell** in the 91st Congress, but fined him $25,000 for improper use of government funds and stripped him of seniority.

Jan. 14 Fires and explosions on the aircraft carrier **Enterprise** killed 27 men, injured 82 at Pearl Harbor.

Jan. 16 After weeks of debate, to worldwide derisive criticism, U.S. and North Vietnamese delegates finally agreed on the shape of the table to be used when the South Vietnamese and the National Liberation Front joined the **peace talks in Paris.** 4-party talks began Jan. 18.

Jan. 20 Protesters against the Vietnamese war, a few hurling objects and obscenities, marred **inaugural ceremonies for Pres.-elect Richard Nixon.**

Jan. 20 Henry Cabot Lodge replaced W. Averell Harriman as chief U.S. negotiator at the **Vietnam peace talks in Paris.**

Feb. 8 A well that leaked oil for 12 days off **Santa Barbara** was capped. 40 miles of beaches were despoiled.

Mar. 1 A New Orleans jury found **Clay Shaw** not guilty of conspiring to assassinate Pres. Kennedy.

Mar. 4 The Defense Dept. admitted that it had regularly shipped lethal **nerve gas** by rail and was spending $350 million a year on **chemical and biological weapons.**

Mar. 10 **James Earl Ray,** assassin of Dr. Martin Luther King, Jr., was sentenced to 99 years in prison.

Mar. 14 Pres. Nixon asked Congress for funds to start construction of an **anti-**

J. Robert Oppenheimer painfully evoked an era of political repression. In a British import, Peter Luke's *Hadrian VII,* Alec McCowen won acclaim as a would-be pope. Otherwise, the New York stage had the air of summer stock, with an extraordinary number of revivals. Among these were 2 productions of *Hamlet,* and *Our Town, Private Lives, The Front Page, The Three Sisters, Henry V, The Miser, The Time of Your Life, Three Men on a Horse, Tiny Alice,* and *Oklahoma!*

Capitalizing on the demand for ever more salacious fiction, 24 writers for the Long Island (N.Y.) paper *Newsday* collaborated as "Penelope Ashe" on a randy novel they called *Naked Came the Stranger.* Any section that might have rated a "B" in a creative-writing course was rewritten to the level of trash. This obscene gumbo made the best-seller lists and brought a tidy sum as movie material, but it was not the publishing sensation of the year. That distinction belonged to Philip Roth's *Portnoy's Complaint,* the protagonist of which is an urban Jew with an assortment of sexual and social hangups. The public went wild for this, Roth's 3rd novel, but the critics gave it a mixed reception. Many of them preferred the more elegant prurience of Vladimir Nabokov's *Ada.* Jacqueline Susann ground out another commercially successful chunk of subpornography, *The Love Machine.* Kurt Vonnegut's novel *Slaughterhouse-Five* depicted the awesome World War II destruction of Dresden by Allied bombs and a fantastic firestorm that killed 100,-000 people. Mario Puzo's *The Godfather* and Peter Maas's *The Valachi Papers* offered purportedly fictional and nonfictional accounts, respectively, of the inner workings of Mafia-type criminal groups. Among other notable nonfiction works this year were the late Robert Kennedy's recollections of the Cuban missile crisis, *Thirteen Days;* Dean Acheson's *Present at the Creation,* about the years during which he served as Pres. Truman's secretary of state; Carlos Baker's *Ernest Hemingway:*

732

SCIENCE; INDUSTRY; ECONOMICS; EDUCATION; RELIGION; PHILOSOPHY.	SPORTS; FASHIONS; POPULAR ENTERTAINMENT; FOLKLORE; SOCIETY.

were **widespread in the U.S.,** accompanied by diseases related to malnutrition and unhealthy living conditions.

Jan. 29   5 Southern school districts were allowed 60 additional days to comply with **desegregation orders** before federal funds would be cut off. This reprieve was widely interpreted as a sign that the Nixon Administration was not committed to enforcing integration.

Feb. 14   The 57-day strike of Port of New York dock workers ended with agreement on a new 3-year contract. But 43,000 other members of the International Longshoremen's Association continued to strike, closing ports along the Atlantic and Gulf coasts until Apr. 2. This strike, which began on Dec. 20, 1968, was **the longest U.S. dock strike in history.**

Feb. 26   4.9 million possibly **defective cars and trucks** were recalled by General Motors, the largest recall ever.

Mar. 13   In **Apollo IX,** astronauts James A. McDivitt, Russell L. Schweickart, and David R. Scott completed a 10-day earth orbit flight, during which they tested the lunar excursion module (LEM).

Apr. 4   The world's **1st totally artificial heart**—made of Dacron and plastic—was implanted in a human by Dr. Denton A. Cooley in Houston, Tex. The patient died Apr. 8.

Apr. 9   A group of 300 protesting **Harvard University** students took over the main administration building and evicted 8 deans. The next day 400 state and local police cleared the building.

Apr. 14   Dr. Gerald Edelman announced that he and other scientists at Rockefeller University had discovered the **chemical structure of an antibody.**

Apr. 20   Following a 36-hr. sit-in at the student union building of **Cornell University,** Negro students emerged armed with shotguns and other weapons.

Jan. 12   Fulfilling the confident prediction of its colorful quarterback Joe Namath, the New York Jets scored a stunning 16–7 upset over the Baltimore Colts, giving the American Football League its 1st major triumph over the National League and its 1st **Super Bowl** victory.

Feb. 7   At Hialeah, Diana Crump became the **1st woman jockey** to race at a U.S. parimutuel track. Her mount finished 10th in a field of 12.

Feb. 22   Barbara Jo Rubin became the **1st winning woman jockey** at a U.S. thoroughbred track, with a victory at Charles Town in West Virginia.

Feb. 25   A 3-year pact was signed ending a **baseball players' boycott of spring training** in a pension dispute. Club owners agreed to increase their pension contributions and to reduce eligibility for a pension to 4 years.

Mar. 2   Tim Wood of Detroit won the **men's world figure-skating championship** at Colorado Springs. Gabriele Seyfert of East Germany won the women's title.

Mar. 2   During a **drag race at Covington, Ga.,** a car going 180 mph smashed into spectators, killing 11 and injuring scores.

Mar. 22   UCLA, sparked by 7-ft. 1½-in. center Lew Alcindor, won the **NCAA basketball tournament** for the 3rd straight year, beating Purdue 97–92. Alcindor became the 1st to win the tourney's MVP award 3 years in a row. Later, the Milwaukee Bucks allegedly paid $1.2 million for Alcindor's services during the next 5 years.

Apr. 4   The **Smothers Brothers Comedy Hour,** one of TV's most popular shows, was canceled by the CBS network because the brothers failed to submit a show for prescreening. The brothers said

POLITICS AND GOVERNMENT; WAR; DISASTERS; VITAL STATISTICS.

BOOKS; PAINTING; DRAMA; ARCHITECTURE; SCULPTURE.

ballistic missile (ABM) system as a "safeguard" for the U.S. nuclear-missile deterrent. Heretofore the ABM had been promoted as protection for cities.

Mar. 28   Former Pres. **Dwight D. Eisenhower,** 78, died of heart disease.

Apr. 3   **U.S. combat deaths in Vietnam** since Jan. 1, 1961, reached 33,641, topping the 33,629 killed in the Korean war.

Apr. 15   North Korean MIG's **shot down a U.S. reconnaissance plane** over the Sea of Japan; 31 crewmen were lost.

Apr. 23   **Sirhan Sirhan** was sentenced to die in the gas chamber for the murder of Sen. Robert Kennedy.

Apr. 24   U.S. B-52's dropped nearly 3000 tons of bombs on enemy positions near the Cambodian border northwest of Saigon, thus far **the most intense bombing raid of the Vietnamese war.**

May 6   Navy Secretary John Chaffee overruled a court of inquiry, said that no action would be taken against the captain or crew of the **USS Pueblo.**

May 14   Pres. Nixon proposed an **8-point peace plan for South Vietnam,** including a pullout of most foreign troops within a year and elections supervised by an international body.

May 15   **Justice Abe Fortas** announced his resignation from the Supreme Court. He had been criticized for accepting a fee from the family foundation of Louis E. Wolfson, who was jailed for stock manipulation.

May 16   The $50 million **nuclear submarine Guitarro sank at dockside** in San Francisco while undergoing final fitting. A House report later charged the Navy with "inexcusable carelessness."

May 20   U.S. and South Vietnamese troops captured **Hamburger Hill** after 10

A Life Story; Lillian Hellman's autobiographical *An Unfinished Woman;* and Gay Talese' *The Kingdom and the Power,* a history of *The New York Times.* Theodore White's *The Making of the President 1968* was a straightforward study of the campaigns of the major presidential candidates. Joe McGinniss, who had traveled with the Nixon entourage, penned an unflattering depiction of that group and its activities which he called *The Selling of the President 1968.*

Jan. 2   Theatrical producer **Gilbert Miller** died at age 84. Among his successful plays were *Victoria Regina, Journey's End,* and *Under Milk Wood.*

Jan. 8   On the Mall near the Smithsonian Institution, Pres. Johnson broke ground for the **Joseph H. Hirshhorn Museum and Sculpture Garden.** The building, expected to cost $15 million, was to house the extensive art collection Hirshhorn donated to the federal government in 1966.

Jan. 9   The UCLA Committee on Fine Arts Production sponsored the world premiere of Harry Partch's **Delusion of the Fury,** a mixed-media musical drama.

Jan. 10   New York's Museum of Modern Art announced that it had bought the **art collection of poet Gertrude Stein.** The purchase price was reported to be more than $6 million. The collection includes 38 Picasso works painted before 1915.

Feb. 8   The date borne by the last issue of **The Saturday Evening Post,** once the nation's most popular magazine, which failed after losing $5 million in 1968. The *Post* for many years carried the boast, "Founded in 1728 by B. Franklin"; but this was a myth, adopted in 1898 after the magazine was acquired by Cyrus H. K. Curtis. Vol. 1, No. 1, was dated Aug. 4, 1821.

Feb. 22   **Giovanni Martinelli,** star dramatic tenor of the Metropolitan Opera for 33 years, died at age 83.

SCIENCE; INDUSTRY; ECONOMICS; EDUCATION; RELIGION; PHILOSOPHY.

SPORTS; FASHIONS; POPULAR ENTERTAINMENT; FOLKLORE; SOCIETY.

Apr. 26 The National Black Economic Development Conference, led by James Forman, issued a **Black Manifesto,** demanding $500 million in "reparations" from white churches and synagogues for complicity in racism.

May 13 In Fayette, Miss., Negro civil rights activist **Charles Evers** won the Democratic nomination for mayor. His election was guaranteed, since no other party put forward a candidate.

May 15 In Berkeley, students and members of the neighboring community who had made a **People's Park** on property owned by the University of California were attacked by police and national guardsmen. Shotguns and tear gas were used. 5 days later a national guard helicopter dropped a stinging chemical powder on demonstrators, including faculty members.

May 26 Astronauts Thomas P. Stafford, Eugene A. Cernan, and John W. Young returned to earth safely in their Apollo X craft after making the **1st manned orbital flight around the moon** and descending in the lunar excursion module to within 9 miles of its surface. The mission had begun May 18.

July 1 The **Truth-in-Lending Law,** requiring that the charges for credit and loans be made clear to the creditor, went into effect.

July 3 The Administration announced that it would require compliance with the Sept. 1969 **desegregation deadline** by all Southern school districts except those with "bona fide educational and administrative problems." The next day, the million-member National Education Association voted overwhelmingly to demand restoration of the deadline without modification.

July 16 Apollo XI was launched, and man's **1st attempt to land on the moon** was under way. The spaceship was manned by Commander Neil A. Arm-

that CBS had been mindlessly censoring their topical jokes in an effort to enforce a bland inoffensiveness; they later instituted 3 suits asking more than $31 million in damages from the network.

Apr. 13 George Archer won the **Masters golf championship** at Augusta, Ga.

Apr. 14 **Academy Awards** for the "bests" in 1968 motion pictures were made to the following: *Oliver!* (film); *War and Peace* (U.S.S.R.—foreign film); Cliff Robertson (actor, *Charly*); Barbra Streisand and Katharine Hepburn (tie for best actress, *Funny Girl* and *The Lion in Winter,* respectively); Jack Robertson (supporting actor, *The Subject Was Roses*); Ruth Gordon (supporting actress, *Rosemary's Baby*).

Apr. 29 Pres. Nixon presented the Presidential Medal of Freedom to **Duke Ellington** at a White House dinner honoring the composer-bandleader on his 70th birthday. A stellar group of jazz musicians played Ellington compositions.

May 3 *Majestic Prince,* Bill Hartack up, won the **Kentucky Derby** by a neck over *Arts and Letters.* The winner's prize was $113,200.

May 5 Once again the aging Boston Celtics took the **National Basketball Association championship,** beating the Lakers, 108–106, in the 7th game. Following this 10th victory in 11 years, the brilliant player-coach Bill **Russell** announced his retirement.

May 10 Plans were completed for the 1970 **merger of the 2 pro football leagues** into a new National Football League with 2 conferences of 13 teams each. The old NFL was renamed the National Conference and 3 of its teams (Baltimore, Cleveland, and Pittsburgh) were shifted to the American Conference (the old AFL).

May 10 National guardsmen dispersed

735

POLITICS AND GOVERNMENT; WAR;

DISASTERS; VITAL STATISTICS.

BOOKS; PAINTING; DRAMA;

ARCHITECTURE; SCULPTURE.

days of bloody battle. Sen. Edward Kennedy criticized such "senseless" assaults. The hill was abandoned May 27 and later was reoccupied by North Vietnamese troops.

May 22 A Canadian official said that his country, which had been admitting **U.S. draft evaders,** would also admit Army deserters who qualified as immigrants.

June 2 The U.S. destroyer **Frank E. Evans** was sliced in two by the Australian carrier *Melbourne* in the South China Sea. 74 U.S. seamen were lost.

June 6 Testimony in a federal court in Houston revealed that the **FBI had tapped the phones of Martin Luther King, Jr.,** even after a 1965 order by Pres. Johnson to tap only for "national security."

June 8 After meeting with Pres. Thieu of South Vietnam on Midway I., Pres. Nixon announced that **25,000 U.S. troops would leave Vietnam** by Aug. 31.

June 19 It was learned that the Pentagon, without public announcement, had let contracts worth $87 million for **68 MIRV's** (Multiple Independently-Targetable Reentry Vehicles). The President had been talking of a halt on tests for such a weapon.

June 23 Earl Warren retired as Chief Justice of the U.S., swore in **Warren Earl Burger** as his successor.

July 8 The 1st step of Pres. Nixon's plan to **reduce U.S. troop strength in South Vietnam** was taken, as 814 men of the 9th Infantry Division left that country.

July 11 A U.S. court of appeals overturned the convictions of **Dr. Benjamin Spock** and 3 codefendants for conspiring to counsel draft evasion.

July 18 It was disclosed that the U.S. had for years deployed lethal **nerve gases** at bases around the world.

Mar. 10 Leopold Stokowski led the American Symphony in the world premiere of **Gian-Carlo Menotti's** *Triple Concerto.*

Mar. 14 Lithuanian-born painter **Ben Shahn** died at age 70. Despite changing fashions, he had maintained a distinctive style combining realism, fantasy, and concern with social issues, exemplified in his famous series *The Passion of Sacco and Vanzetti.*

Mar. 16 Noted lecturer, critic, and author **John Mason Brown** died at age 68. Throughout his professional life Brown was involved in a unique effort to convey high critical standards to a wide audience.

Mar. 25 **Max Eastman,** author, poet, and political commentator, died at age 86. A leading leftist in the early part of his career, Eastman became increasingly disillusioned with Communism during the 1920's and '30's. In 1941 he became a roving editor for *Reader's Digest.*

Mar. 27 The date of the formal establishment of the **Black Academy of Arts and Letters,** an organization to honor and encourage writers, artists, and scholars who make notable contributions to black culture.

Apr. 7 The Supreme Court ruled unanimously that **laws against the private possession of obscene materials** are unconstitutional. Justice Thurgood Marshall wrote: "Our whole constitutional heritage rebels at the thought of giving government the power to control men's minds."

Apr. 20 **Antoinette Perry (Tony) Awards** for the 1968–69 season were given to *The Great White Hope* (best play); James Earl Jones (best actor), for his performance in *The Great White Hope;* Julie Harris (best actress), for her role in *Forty Carats;* Peter Hunt (best director), for *1776,* which also won the best-musical award.

May 2 Peter Mennin's secular cantata

strong, Edwin E. Aldrin, Jr., and Michael Collins.

July 20 **Astronauts Armstrong and Aldrin landed their lunar excursion module Eagle on the moon, near the Sea of Tranquillity,** at 4:17 P.M. EDT. Approximately 6½ hr. later Armstrong set foot on the lunar surface. The event was seen on television by hundreds of millions of people. His first words were, "That's one small step for [a] man, one giant leap for mankind." He was followed by Aldrin, and both men talked with Pres. Nixon via telephone, set out equipment for gathering scientific data, and collected samples of moon rock and soil during their more than 2-hr. walk. Astronaut Collins, alone in the command-service module *Columbia,* piloted it in its lunar orbit.

July 21 The **lunar excursion module** *Eagle* successfully lifted off from the surface of the moon, and later docked with the *Columbia.*

July 23 **Consumer prices** up 6.4% since Jan. 1, the biggest jump since the war year 1951.

July 24 At 12:50 P.M. EDT, **Apollo XI splashed down,** landing in the Pacific Ocean about 250 miles south of Johnston I. Pres. Nixon was on hand to greet the astronauts aboard the carrier *Hornet.*

July 29 The **stock market** hit its year's low of 88.04, according to Standard & Poor's 500-stock index.

July 30 **Mariner VI,** an unmanned spaceship launched toward Mars on Feb. 25, passed over the surface of that planet at an altitude of 2120 miles, sending back 74 photographs.

Aug. 5 **Mariner VII,** an unmanned spaceship launched toward Mars on Mar. 27, passed across the south pole of Mars and sent back 91 photographs.

college students who turned a **beer bust in Zap, N.D.,** into a huge donnybrook.

May 17 *Majestic Prince,* Bill Hartack up, won the **Preakness Stakes** by a head over *Arts and Letters,* ridden by Braulio Baeza. Baeza got nowhere with his complaint that the winner had bumped his mount early in the race.

May 30 In the **Indianapolis 500,** Mario Andretti won driving a turbo-powered Ford-Brawner Hawk designed by Andy Granatelli, and set a track record of 156.867 mph. The win was popular with the fans, marking a long-sought 1st for both Granatelli and Andretti, who had never won the 500.

June 6 **Joe Namath,** quarterback of the New York Jets, announced that he would retire from football rather than give up his interest in a restaurant that Commissioner Pete Rozelle said had become a hangout for gamblers. On July 18, Namath reversed his decision.

June 7 *Majestic Prince,* having edged out *Arts and Letters* in the 1st 2 events of racing's triple crown, finished 5 lengths behind the chestnut colt in the **Belmont Stakes.** *Arts and Letters,* who won 5 other major races and $555,064 during 1969, easily took Horse of the Year honors.

June 8 Movie actor **Robert Taylor** died at age 57. During his 30-year career, Taylor appeared in 75 films, his most famous role being that of Armand in *Camille* (1936), in which he played opposite Greta Garbo.

June 8 In ceremonies at Yankee Stadium, star outfielder **Mickey Mantle** formally retired after 18 years with the Yankees.

June 15 Orville Moody won the **U.S. Open golf championship** at Houston by a single stroke over Deane Beman, Al

POLITICS AND GOVERNMENT; WAR;

DISASTERS; VITAL STATISTICS.

BOOKS; PAINTING; DRAMA;

ARCHITECTURE; SCULPTURE.

July 19 **Sen. Edward Kennedy** (D–Mass.) told Edgartown police this morning that 10 hr. earlier his car had plunged into the water from a bridge on Chappaquiddick I. and he had been unable to rescue his passenger, Mary Jo Kopechne.

July 25 **Sen. Edward Kennedy** pleaded guilty to leaving the scene of the July 18 accident in which Mary Jo Kopechne drowned. On TV this evening Kennedy called his late report of the accident "indefensible," asked his constituents to help him decide on continuing his career. The response was reported as favorable; Kennedy resumed his Senate duties July 31.

July 26–Aug. 3 **Pres. Nixon visited 5 Asian capitals and Romania.** He indicated that the U.S. expected its Asian allies to assume chief responsibility for that area's security and economic development. On Aug. 2, crowds gave him an enthusiastic welcome to Bucharest.

July 31 Col. Robert Rheault, Green Beret commander in Vietnam, and 7 of his men were charged by the Army with the **murder of a Vietnamese said to be a double agent.** The charges were dropped Sept. 29 after the CIA, which was involved in the affair, refused to cooperate in the prosecution.

Aug. 4 Congress extended the **10% income-tax surcharge** through Dec. 31.

Aug. 17 **Hurricane Camille** killed more than 300 and left 70,000 homeless in Mississippi, Louisiana, and Alabama. On Aug. 23, floods caused by the storm killed 100 in Virginia.

Aug. 24 Exhausted after 5 days of battle in Vietnam, a decimated U.S. infantry company for hours **refused direct orders to fight,** finally was coaxed into battle again by a seasoned veteran.

Sept. 7 **Everett McKinley Dirksen,** 73, U.S. Senator from Illinois, died in Wash-

The Pied Piper of Hamelin was given its world premiere by the Cincinnati Symphony during the Cincinnati May Festival. Max Rudolf conducted and New York's mayor, John Lindsay, narrated.

May 5 **Pulitzer Prizes** were announced for the following persons: Leonard W. Levy, for *Origins of the Fifth Amendment* (history); B. L. Reid, for *The Man from New York* (biography); George Oppen, for *Of Being Numerous* (poetry); Howard Sackler, for *The Great White Hope* (drama); N. Scott Momaday, for *House Made of Dawn* (fiction); Norman Mailer, for *Armies of the Night* (nonfiction); Dr. René Jules Dubos, for *So Human an Animal* (nonfiction); and, in music, Karel Husa, for *String Quartet No. 3.*

May 8 **Nelson Rockefeller,** governor of New York, announced that he had donated his extensive collection of primitive art to the Metropolitan Museum of Art in New York City. The collection was to be housed in a new wing, the Michael C. Rockefeller Memorial Collection of Primitive Art, named for the governor's son who disappeared in 1961 while on an expedition in New Guinea.

May 15 The **New York Drama Critics Circle** voted *The Great White Hope* the best drama of 1968–69, and *1776* the best musical.

May 17 **Leonard Bernstein** conducted Mahler's 3rd Symphony in his last concert as music director of the New York Philharmonic. His successor was named in June.

May 17 A copy of the 1st printing of the **Declaration of Independence,** 1 of 16 known to exist, was bought by Ira G. Corn of Dallas for $404,000. Corn outbid Hans P. Kraus of New York, who on Apr. 15 had bought a copy of the 1st printing of the **U.S. Constitution** for $155,000. The copy of the Declaration was found in late

Aug. 8 Pres. Nixon called for comprehensive reform of the welfare system and an unprecedented **minimum income for families with children.**

Aug. 27 About half of the lawyers in the Justice Dept.'s Civil Rights Division openly **protested the Administration's desegregation policies,** following a government request that 33 Mississippi school districts be allowed to delay integration.

Sept. 7 The body of **Dr. James Pike,** 56, controversial former Episcopal bishop of California, was found in Israel near the Dead Sea. It was estimated that he had died about Sept. 3 after he and his wife became lost and then separated during an auto trip through the Judean desert. In 1966 Pike had been accused, but never tried, of heresy for the liberalism of his doctrinal opinions. He left the Episcopal Church in 1968.

Sept. 14 The SS *Manhattan,* an icebreaking tanker, sailed through the Prince of Wales Strait, thus becoming the 1st commercial ship and the **1st large vessel to voyage through the Northwest Passage.** She left Chester, Pa., Aug. 24 and arrived at Point Barrow, Alas., Sept. 21. The project, a test of the feasibility of transporting crude oil by sea from northern Alaska, cost 3 oil companies $40 million.

Sept. 23 Secretary of Labor George Shultz ordered into effect the **Philadelphia Plan,** which set guidelines for the hiring of minority-group members by 6 skilled-craft unions working in Philadelphia on projects receiving federal funds.

Sept. 24 The trial of the **Chicago 8** —radical leaders accused of conspiring to incite riots during the Democratic Convention in Chicago in 1968—began, with Judge Julius J. Hoffman presiding. The defendants claimed that they were being unfairly tried for their ideas, and were disruptive. On Oct. 29 the judge ordered Black Panther Chairman Bobby G. Seale bound and gagged. On Nov. 5, 2

Geiberger, and Bob Rosburg. The PGA named Moody Golfer of the Year.

June 21 John Pennel added 1½ in. to the **world pole vault record,** clearing the bar at 17 ft. 10½ in. in a night meet at Sacramento.

June 23 **Joe Frazier** defeated leading heavyweight contender Jerry Quarry with a KO in the 7th round. Frazier was the recognized champ in 7 states; Jimmy Ellis, recognized by the World Boxing Association as champion, did not defend his title this year. Muhammad Ali (Cassius Clay) remained absent from the ring as he fought his draft case in the courts.

July 23 In Washington, D.C., the National League won baseball's **all-star game** for the 7th year in a row, beating the American League 9–3.

Aug. 9 The bodies of actress **Sharon Tate** and 4 others were discovered in and about her Los Angeles home. In Dec., Charles Manson and several members of his nomadic hippie cult were indicted for the bizarre murders.

Aug. 13 Bowie Kuhn, temporary **commissioner of baseball** since Feb., was formally appointed to that post with a 7-year contract.

Aug. 15–18 Poor planning and bad weather threatened for a time to make a disaster area of a farm near Bethel, N.Y., as a massive throng of young people gathered there for a weekend folk-rock festival, the **Woodstock Music and Art Fair.** The crowd was estimated at 300,000 to 400,000, and many more failed to reach the fair as monumental traffic jams clogged all roads leading to the Catskill area. Helicopters were pressed into service to replenish local supplies of food, water, and medicine. Rains made a quagmire of the festival grounds; all forms of drugs circulated freely, with many treated for bad narcotic reactions; and there were 3 deaths. But the police adopted a hands-

739

ington, D.C. Republican leader in the Senate since 1959, Dirksen was noted for his honey-bass voice and old-fashioned oratorical style.

Sept. 9 Near Indianapolis, 83 died when a **light plane crashed into a jet.**

Sept. 21 Auto traffic from Mexico slowed to a snail's pace when federal law officers began an intensive drive against **drug smugglers.** "Operation Intercept" eased considerably Oct. 10 after strenuous complaints by the Mexican government.

Oct. 1 An AWOL U.S. Marine **hijacked at gunpoint a TWA Boeing 707** flying out of San Francisco and ordered it flown to Rome. He was captured a few hours after he left the plane.

Oct. 5 In an apparent **breach of U.S. air defenses,** a Cuban defector landed a MIG-17 at Homestead AFB near Miami, where Pres. Nixon's plane was waiting to return him to Washington.

Oct. 15 Millions observed the 1st **Vietnam Moratorium Day** with prayer vigils, candlelight processions, mass meetings, and black armbands. Pres. Nixon ignored it; Vice-Pres. Agnew on Oct. 19 called protest leaders "an effete corps of impudent snobs."

Oct. 28 J. William Fulbright, chairman of the Senate Foreign Relations Committee, charged that the U.S. had been conducting a **war in Laos** without the knowledge or consent of Congress.

Nov. 3 In a TV speech, Pres. Nixon said that the North Vietnamese had rejected **secret U.S. peace proposals** and asked the nation to support his plans to "Vietnamize" the war and withdraw U.S. troops.

Nov. 6 Congress approved a weapons procurement bill that included funds to make a start on the **Safeguard ABM system.**

1968 in a defunct bookstore in Philadelphia.

June 10 Composer-conductor Pierre Boulez was appointed music director of the **New York Philharmonic** for 3 years beginning in 1971. George Szell, director of the Cleveland Orchestra, was named to fill the post in a part-time capacity until then.

July 5 German-born architect **Walter Gropius,** founder in 1919 of the Bauhaus School of Design, died at age 86. His severe use of concrete, steel, and glass established him as the father of the modern international style. After the Nazis closed his "degenerate" school in 1933, Gropius first went to England and then came to the U.S., where in 1938 he became head of the architecture division of Harvard's Graduate School of Design. He advocated the team approach in architecture. Among his later designs were the Pan Am Building in New York City (with Pietro Belluschi) and the U.S. Embassy in Athens.

July 7 **Gladys Swarthout,** leading mezzosoprano with the Metropolitan Opera from 1929 to 1945, died at age 64.

July 15 A & P heir Huntington Hartford announced that he had relinquished ownership of his **Gallery of Modern Art** in New York City to Fairleigh Dickenson University.

Aug. 1 The Santa Fe Opera Company presented the world premiere of Gian-Carlo Menotti's **Help! Help! The Globolinks!** a light, satirical attack on electronic music.

Aug. 17 Innovative and influential architect **Ludwig Mies van der Rohe** died at age 83. Born in Germany, he was one of the leaders of the pioneering Bauhaus School of Design; he fled to the U.S. in 1938, where he became the head of the Armour Institute in Chicago. His creative use of steel and glass is exemplified in one

SCIENCE; INDUSTRY; ECONOMICS; EDUCATION; RELIGION; PHILOSOPHY.

SPORTS; FASHIONS; POPULAR ENTERTAINMENT; FOLKLORE; SOCIETY.

days after his restraints were removed, Seale was sentenced to 4 years for contempt and his case was declared a mistrial. The trial of the others was still in progress at the end of the year. It attracted numerous protesters, and the national guard was called into Chicago Oct. 9–11 to keep order.

Oct. 8 The Dept. of Health, Education, and Welfare, it was reported, had **blacklisted hundreds of renowned scientists** from its advisory panels for offenses such as antiwar statements.

Oct. 16 It was announced that the **Nobel Prize for physiology or medicine** was awarded to U.S. scientists Max Delbruck of the California Institute of Technology, Alfred D. Hershey of the Carnegie Institute (Cold Spring Harbor, N.Y.), and Salvador E. Luria of the Massachusetts Institute of Technology, for their work on the genetic structure of viruses.

Oct. 18 The Dept. of Health, Education, and Welfare **banned the use of cyclamates**—a type of artificial sweetener —in diet foods. The ban was modified Dec. 20 to permit the use of specified amounts, except in soft drinks.

Oct. 27 150,000 workers went out on strike against the **General Electric Co.** The strike was still in effect when the year ended.

Oct. 29 Nixon appointee Chief Justice Warren Burger, in his 1st decision, joined in an indirect rebuke of the Administration as the Supreme Court unanimously ordered **integration "at once"** in the 33 Mississippi school districts for which the government had asked a delay.

Oct. 30 It was announced that the **Nobel Prize in physics** was awarded to Murray Gell-Mann of the California Institute of Technology for his contributions to the theory of elementary particles.

off posture, and the youths enjoyed themselves in a general spirit of peace, cooperation, and enthusiasm. Many commentaries on the social significance of the affair treated it as an idyll; some expressed alarm at the incontrovertible evidence of a mass drug culture.

Aug. 30 At Oakmont, Pa., Steve Melnyk won the **USGA men's amateur golf championship** with a record 5-stroke margin.

Aug. 31 Former world heavyweight boxing champion **Rocky Marciano** was killed in a plane crash near Newton, Iowa. He had retired undefeated in 1956.

Aug. 31 In a time trial at Indianapolis, **Nevele Pride** trotted a 1-mile track in 1:54⅘, breaking the record of 1:55¼ set by *Greyhound* in 1938. The 4-year-old stallion, named Harness Horse of the Year for the 3rd straight time, was syndicated for $3 million in Oct. and retired to stud. His career earnings were $871,738.

Sept. 9 Australian Rod Laver, who had already won the Australian, French, and Wimbledon singles titles, completed the **grand slam of tennis** by winning the U.S. men's singles championship at Forest Hills. It was only the 3rd such sweep in history: Laver had done it in 1962, Don Budge in 1938.

Sept. 19–21 The U.S. retained the **Davis Cup,** defeating the Romanian tennis team, 5 matches to 0, at Cleveland Heights. Arthur Ashe and Stan Smith played the U.S. singles, Smith and Bob Lutz the doubles.

Sept. 22 San Francisco Giants outfielder **Willie Mays hit his 600th home run,** becoming the only player other than Babe Ruth to reach that mark.

Oct. 5 **Walter Hagen,** one of the all-time golfing greats, died. At his retirement

Nov. 11 **Veterans' Day** marked by demonstrations, supporting U.S. policy in Vietnam, by those Pres. Nixon had called "the great silent majority."

Nov. 13 Speaking in Des Moines, **Vice-Pres. Agnew** said that a dozen newsmen of the 3 major television networks constituted a biased "unelected elite" that dictated what news the U.S. would learn about each day. In Montgomery, Ala., Nov. 20, he charged that newspapers were often unfair and had monopolistic powers over public opinion.

Nov. 14 The **2nd Vietnam Moratorium** began with a long, single-file "March Against Death" in Washington, D.C. The next day 250,000 marched there against the war. A San Francisco protest drew 100,000.

Nov. 16 News reports charged a U.S. infantry unit with a **massacre at Songmy,** South Vietnam, on Mar. 16, 1968. More than 450 villagers, including many women and babies, were said to have been slain.

Nov. 17 Preliminary discussions in the **strategic arms limitation talks** (SALT) between the U.S. and the Soviet Union opened in Helsinki.

Nov. 20 **Henry Cabot Lodge** resigned as chief U.S. negotiator at the Paris talks on the Vietnamese war.

Nov. 21 It was announced that the U.S. would return control of **Okinawa and other Ryukyu islands** to Japan by 1972.

Nov. 21 After a 3-month debate, the Senate rejected the nomination of **Clement Haynsworth** to the Supreme Court.

Nov. 24 The U.S. and the U.S.S.R. became the 23rd and 24th signatories to the **nuclear nonproliferation treaty.**

Nov. 25 Pres. Nixon said that the U.S. would not engage in **biological war-**

of his best-known works, the Seagram Building in New York City.

Sept. 11 A concert by the new Chamber Music Society of Lincoln Center inaugurated **Alice Tully Hall** in the new home of the Juilliard School in New York City. The school building itself was dedicated late in Oct.

Sept. 17 The **Milwaukee County Performing Arts Center** was formally opened. This $12-million complex had been in planning for 25 years.

Sept. 25 New York's **Metropolitan Museum of Art** announced that the recently deceased (Aug. 9) chairman of its board of trustees, investment banker Robert Lehman, had bequeathed to the museum the nearly 3000 works in his art collection, worth more than $100 million. Included in the gift, considered one of the world's most important private collections, were works by Rembrandt, Goya, El Greco, Dürer, Picasso, Renoir, Van Gogh, and many other old masters and moderns.

Oct. 21 **Jack Kerouac,** novelist and leading figure of the "beat generation," died at age 47. The publication of his novel *On the Road* in 1957 is credited with popularizing the rejection of middle class values and the interest in Oriental mysticism and drug-induced experiences that were taken up by the "hippies" of the '60's.

Oct. 26 The new $29.5-million home of the **Juilliard School** at New York's Lincoln Center was dedicated with a nationally televised concert.

Nov. 25 The **American Symphony Orchestra League,** sponsor of a meeting in New York of 77 presidents of major U.S. symphonies, announced that it would seek increased appropriations from the federal government. It was reported that the 5 most important orchestras

Nov. 14 **Apollo XII,** manned by Commander Charles Conrad, Jr., Richard F. Gordon, Jr., and Alan L. Bean, was launched on a lunar flight in rainy weather. 36.5 sec. after liftoff, it was hit by an electric charge, which briefly knocked out power in the spaceship but not in the rocket.

Nov. 19 Astronauts Conrad and Bean became the **2nd team of men to land on the moon** when they brought down the *Intrepid,* their lunar excursion module, on the plain of the Ocean of Storms. They made 2 moon walks, and the next day successfully blasted off to rejoin Gordon in the command ship, the *Yankee Clipper.*

Nov. 20 In the 1st step toward a **total ban on the use of DDT** by 1971, the U.S. Dept. of Agriculture ordered a halt to its use in residential areas.

Nov. 22 Harvard scientists announced that they had **isolated a single gene,** the basic unit of heredity. Their feat promised to facilitate the study of the mechanism of gene control.

Nov. 24 **Apollo XII** splashed down only 3 miles from the recovery ship USS *Hornet.*

Dec. 2 The **Boeing 747 giant jet,** which cost $21.4 million to develop, made its 1st public flight, from Seattle, Wash., to New York City.

Dec. 4 Fred Hampton, Illinois chairman of the **Black Panther** Party, was killed along with another party leader during a predawn raid by police on an apartment in Chicago. The next day the Illinois ACLU and other groups demanded an investigation of the Panthers' charge that Hampton had been "murdered in his bed."

Dec. 8 Los Angeles police attempting an early-morning raid on a local **Black Panther** headquarters were met with gun-

in 1929, Hagen had won 17 major titles and more than $1 million.

Oct. 6 On their home field the New York Mets won the **National League playoffs,** having defeated the Atlanta Braves in 3 straight games, 9–5, 11–6, 7–4. In Minnesota the Baltimore Orioles routed the Minnesota Twins in 3 consecutive games also, 4–3, 1–0, and 11–2, to win the **American League playoffs.**

Oct. 7 **14 blacks were dropped from the University of Wyoming football team** after they defied the coach's ban against protests and wore black armbands in support of a stand by the Black Students' Alliance. The BSA wanted the university to sever sports ties to Brigham Young University, a school run by Mormons, who have barred Negroes from their church's ministry.

Oct. 16 The New York Mets won the **World Series,** taking 4 of 5 games from the favored Baltimore Orioles: 1–4, 2–1, 5–0, 2–1, 5–3. The "Amazin'" Mets had finished either in the cellar or next to last in every season since their 1st in 1962.

Oct. 18 Chester Marcol of Hillsdale (Michigan) College kicked a **62-yd. field goal,** the longest on record for either amateur or pro football.

Oct. 24 Actor **Richard Burton** bought for his wife, Elizabeth Taylor, a 69.42-carat diamond from Cartier, New York jeweler. The price was not revealed, but Cartier had paid $1,050,000 for the gem the previous day and said it had made a profit on the sale to Burton.

Nov. 22 Ohio State, acclaimed by all polls as a superteam, lost, 24–12, to longtime rival Michigan before a massive crowd of more than 103,000 at Ann Arbor. The game tied the 2 clubs for the **Big 10 football championship** and qualified Michigan for the Rose Bowl.

743

POLITICS AND GOVERNMENT; WAR;
DISASTERS; VITAL STATISTICS.

BOOKS; PAINTING; DRAMA;
ARCHITECTURE; SCULPTURE.

fare nor make "first use" of lethal or incapacitating chemicals. The White House later said that tear gas and defoliants were not included in the ban.

Nov. 26 Pres. Nixon signed into law a bill providing for a **lottery for Selective Service draftees.** The first drawing was held Dec. 1.

Dec. 15 Pres. Nixon said that **U.S. forces in Vietnam would be cut to 434,000** by Apr. 15—a total reduction of about 110,000 since he took office.

Dec. 22 Congress sent to the President **the most far-reaching tax reform bill in history.** Although it removed 9 million of the very poor from federal tax rolls, it was criticized as a hodgepodge measure that aided the rich. The bill, signed by Pres. Nixon Dec. 30, reduced the tax surcharge to 5% and extended it for 6 months, reduced the oil depletion allowance from 27.5% to 22%, closed numerous tax loopholes, and increased Social Security benefits by 15%.

(Cleveland, Philadelphia, Boston, Chicago, and New York) had deficits totaling $5.7 million for the 1967–68 season, up from an aggregate loss of $2.9 million in 1963–64.

Dec. 29 The **Metropolitan Opera** in New York opened late in the season. A strike by performers and musicians had been in effect throughout the fall.

(Text for the years from 1970 begins on page 891.)

fire. 11 Panthers surrendered after a 4-hr. battle.

Dec. 17 In a controversial decision, Congress appropriated $80 million for the construction of 2 prototype **supersonic transport planes** (SST's).

Dec. 18 Congress sent to the President a law that established **stricter safety standards in the coal mining industry** and provided for compensation of "black lung" victims.

Dec. 28 The ACLU charged, after a survey of 9 large cities, that law enforcement officials were subjecting the **Black Panther Party** to provocative and punitive harassment.

Dec. 31 The **stock market** closed near the low for the year (reached on July 29) —at 92.06 on Standard & Poor's 500-stock index.

Dec. 6 A protest by the governor of Pennsylvania (where Penn State was undefeated in 30 games in 3 years) failed to deter Pres. Nixon from presenting a plaque to Texas as the **best football team in the nation** after it defeated Arkansas, 15–14.

Dec. 10–11 **Bill Toomey** set a new world record of 8417 points for the decathlon. He won the Sullivan Award as the best amateur athlete of the year.

Dec. 17 Singer **Tiny Tim** (Herbert Buckingham Khaury) and Miss Vicki (Victoria May Budinger)—he in his mid-40's and she 17—were wed in a nondenominational ceremony on Johnny Carson's TV show, *Tonight*.

Dec. 29 The **New York Film Critics' Circle** chose *Z* as the best picture of 1969; Jon Voight (*Midnight Cowboy*) the best actor; and Jane Fonda (*They Shoot Horses, Don't They?*) the best actress.

(Text for the years from 1970 begins on page 891.)

INDEX

(See also Index to the Supplement, beginning on p. 916.)

NOTE: References are to year and column, columns I and II being on the left-hand page and III and IV on the right. The dates in the index indicate the place at which an item is entered and should not necessarily be taken for the date of the event.

747

Amateur Athletic Union of the U.S., 1888, IV
Amateur sports, 1st track and field meet, 1868, IV
Ambassador, creation of rank, 1893, I
Ambassadors, The, Henry James, 1903, II
Ambers, Lou, 1938, IV
Ambler, Richard, 1706, I
Ambrister, Robert, 1818, I
Amelia Goes to the Ball, Gian-Carlo Menotti, 1938, II
Amendments to Constitution, *see* Constitution
America:
　1st reports, 986, I
　1st use of word, 1507, II
"America," Samuel Francis Smith, 1831, II
America Hurrah!, Jean-Claude van Itallie, 1966, II
American Academy of Arts, N.Y., 1802, II
American Academy of Arts and Letters, 1904, II
American Academy of Arts and Sciences, 1780, II
American Academy of Political and Social Science, 1889,
　III
American Airlines, 1962, III
American Angler, 1881, IV
American Antiquarian Society, 1812, III
American Antislavery Society, 1833, I
American Anti-Vivisection Society, 1883, IV
American Art Union, 1839, II
　membership of, 1848, II
American Association for the Advancement of Science,
　founded, 1848, III
American Ballet Theatre, 1964, II; 1966, II
American Bar Association, 1878, III
American Bible Society, 1816, II
American Board of Commissioners for Foreign Missions,
　1810, III; 1812, III
American Bowling Congress, 1895, IV
American Broadcasting Co., sold, 1965, III
American Civil Liberties Union, 1969, III
American Coast Pilot, The, Capt. Lawrence Furlong,
　1796, III
American Commonwealth, The, James Bryce, 1888, III
American Company of Booksellers, 1801, III
American culture, defense of, 1823, III
American Dante Society, 1890, III
American Democrat, The, James Fenimore Cooper, 1838,
　II
American Derby winner, *Modesty,* 1884, IV
American Dialect Society, 1889, III
American Dictionary of the English Language, Noah
　Webster, 1828, II
American Economic Association, 1885, III
American Farmer, 1819, III
American Federation of Labor, 1886, III
　boycotts German-made products, 1933, III
　merger with CIO, 1955, III
　no-strike policy in war industries, 1941, III
　opposes Johnson administration, 1964, III
　organized, 1886, III
　repudiates socialism, 1894, III
　separation of United Auto Workers, 1968, III
　stand for shorter work week, 1933, III
American Federation of Musicians, 1942, II; 1944, II
American Fine Arts Society, 1892, II
American Fire Insurance Co., Philadelphia, 1810, III
American Fistiana, The, 1849, IV

American Folklore Society, 1888, III
American Forestry Association, 1882, III
American Gazetteer, The, . . . , 1793, III
American girl, glorified in art, 1880, II
American Gothic, Grant Wood, 1930, II; 1942, II
American Heart Association, 1963, III
American Historical Association, 1884, III
American Horologue Company, 1849, III
American Humane Association, 1877, III
American in Paris, An, George Gershwin, 1928, II
　motion picture, 1951, IV
American Institute of Architecture awards, 1955, II;
　1956, II; 1958, II
American Institute of Christian Philosophy, 1881, III
American Institute of Electrical Engineers, 1884, III
American Institute of Instruction, 1830, III
Americanization of Edward Bok, The, 1921, II
Americanization of Emily, The, 1964, IV
American Journal of Education, 1855, III
American Journal of Obstetrics, 1862, III
American Journal of Science, 1818, III
American language, 1st formal study, 1816, II
American Laryngological Association, 1861, III
American Law Journal, 1808, III
American Legion:
　Forty and Eight Society, 1918, IV; 1919, I
American Library Association, 1876, III
American Lyric Theatre Workshop, 1966, II
American Magazine, Andrew Bradford's, 1741, II
American Magazine, The, 1757, II
American Magazine and Historical Chronicle, Boston,
　1743, II
American manufactures, growth of, 1787, III
American Mathematical Society, 1888, III
American Medical Association:
　criticism of medical-care study, 1932, III
　formulates new standard of death, 1968, III
　guilty of violating antitrust laws, 1943, III
　organized, 1847, III
American Mercury, and subsequent mergers, 1793, II
American-Mexican Joint Commission, 1916, I
American Moral Reform Society, 1837, IV
American Museum, N.Y.C., 1811, III
American Museum, publication, 1787, II
American Museum of Natural History, 1964, III
American National Opera Company, 1967, II
American Orchestra and Theodore Thomas, The, Charles
　Edward Russell, 1928, II
American Ornithology, Alexander Wilson, 1808, III
American Party (*see also* Know-Nothing Party):
　control of, 1855, I
　national convention, 1888, I
American Peace Society, 1828, IV; 1837, I; 1860, III
American Philosophical Society, 1743, III
American Physical Association, 1889, III
American Poems, Selected and Original, early anthology,
　1793, II
American Pottery Manufacturing Co., 1828, III
American Protective Association, 1887, I
American Psychological Association, 1892, III
American Quarterly Review, founded, 1827, II
American Railroad Express Co., 1918, III
American Red Cross, The, 1881, III

opened, 1883, II
Brooks, Gwendolyn, *Annie Allen*, 1950, II
Brooks, Rev. John A., 1888, I
Brooks, Joseph, 1874, I
Brooks, Preston S., 1856, I
Brooks, Van Wyck, 1937, II; 1944, II; 1963, II
Brotherly Love, George Grey Barnard, 1887, II
Brough, A. Louise, 1947, IV
Brougham, James, 1854, II
Broun, Heywood, 1933, III
Browder, Earl, 1936, I; 1940, I
Brower, Frank, 1843, II
Brown, Al, 1934, IV
Brown, B. Gratz, 1872, I
Brown, Charles Brockden, 1800, II
   novels of, 1798, II
Brown, Rev. Daniel, 1722, III
Brown, David Paul, *The Prophet of St. Paul's*, 1837, II
Brown, Edmund G. (Pat), 1959, I; 1966, IV
Brown, George, 1843, I
Brown, Henry Kirke, equestrian statue of Washington,
   Union Square, N.Y.C., 1856, II
Brown, H. Rap, 1967, III
Brown, Jackie, 1934, IV
Brown, Jimmy, 1964, IV
Brown, Joe, 1959, IV
Brown, John:
   death of, 1859, I
   joins Free State Forces, Kan., 1855, I
   massacres 5 pro-slavery men, 1856, I
Brown, John Mason, 1963, II; 1969, II
Brown, Olympia, 1860, III
Brown, Saul:
   1st rabbi, 1655, III
Brown, Dr. William, *Pharmacopoeia . . .* , 1778, III
Brown, William Hill, *The Power of Sympathy*, 1789, II
Browne, Charles Farrar, 1852, II; 1862, II
Browne, Mary K., 1912, IV; 1913, IV; 1914, IV
Browning, Elizabeth Barrett, *Aurora Leigh*, 1857, II
Brownlow, William G., *Parson Brownlow's Book*, 1862, II
"Brown October Ale," Reginald De Koven, 1890, II
Bruce, Sen. Blanche Kelso, 1880, I
Bruce, Philip Alexander, 1665, II
Brugière, Madame, 1829, IV
Brumfield, D., 1966, IV
Brunner Award for arts and letters, 1960, II
Brush, Charles F., 1879, III
Brush, rival of Ford car, 1910, III
Brushaber v. *Union Pacific Railroad Company*, 1916, III
Brussels Peace Conference, 1848, III
Brutus, or the Fall of Tarquin, John Howard Payne, 1818,
   II
Bry, de, *Voyages*, 1591, II
Bryan, Charles W., 1924, I
Bryan, Thomas Jefferson, 1853, II
Bryan, William Jennings, 1900, I; 1908, I
   addresses on evolution, 1923, III
   appeal for free silver, 1895, I
   "Cross of Gold" speech, 1896, I, IV
   editor of *World-Herald*, Omaha, Neb., 1894, I
   elected to Congress, 1890, I
   1st recorded political speech, 1871, I
   leads Democratic Silver Convention, 1894, I

proposes gov't ownership of railroads, 1906, III
Bryan Gallery of Christian Art opened, 1853, II
Bryant, William Cullen:
   Poems, 1832, II; 1876, II
   "Thanatopsis" printed, 1817, II
   Thirty Poems, 1863, II
   24 poems published, 1826, II
Bryant's Minstrels, 1859, II
Bryce, James, 1888, III
Bryn Mawr College for Women, 1880, III; 1885, III
Brynner, Yul, 1951, II
   wins Academy Award, 1956, IV
Buchanan, James, 1854, I; 1856, I
   birth of, 1791, I
   death of, 1868, I
   elected president, 1856, I
   inaugurated 15th president, 1857, I
Buchholtz, Earl, Jr., 1959, IV
Büchner, Georg, *Danton's Death*, 1965, II
Buck, Dudley, 1889, II
Buck, Paul Herman, *The Road to Reunion*, 1938, II
Buck, Pearl S., *The Good Earth*, 1931, II
Buckingham, James, 1841, IV
Bucknell University, Lewisburg, Pa., chartered as the Uni-
   versity at Lewisburg, 1846, III
Buckner, Simon P., 1896, I
Budge, J. Donald, 1937, IV; 1969, IV
Budgets, *see* National budgets
Buena Vista, battle of, 1847, I
Bueno, Maria Esther, 1959, IV; 1960, IV
Buffalo Bill (William F. Cody), 1883, IV
"Buffalo Gals," 1844, II
Buffalo hunting:
   1st account of, 1693, IV
Building, nonessential, ban on, 1942, III
Building materials:
   hollow tile, 1st design, 1871, II
Buley, R. Carlyle, 1951, II
Bulfinch, Charles, 1742, II; 1794, IV; 1795, II; 1804, II
Bulfinch, Thomas, *Age of Fable; or the Beauties of
   Mythology*, 1855, II
Bulge, battle of the, 1944, I
Bull, Dixy, 1632, IV
Bull baiting, 1774, IV
Bullins, Ed, and others, *A Black Quartet*, 1969, II
Bull Moose Party, *see* Progressive Party
Bullock, James, 1673, IV
Bullock, William, 1863, III
Bull Run, battle of, 1861, I
Bull-Us, Hector (James K. Paulding), 1812, II
Bulwer-Lytton, Edward, *The Last Days of Pompeii*, 1834,
   II
Bundling, 1785, IV
Bungalow Book, The, . . . , Henry L. Wilson, 1910, II
Bunker Hill, battle of, 1775, I
Bunker Hill, play, 1797, II
Bunner, H. C., 1886, II
Bunning, Jim, 1964, IV
Bunyan, John, 1681, II
Burbank, Luther, 1875, III; 1909, IV
Burchard, Dr. Samuel D., 1884, IV
Burchfield, Charles, 1932, II; 1967, II
Burden, Henry, 1835, III

767

785

1st recorded, 1859, III
incandescent lamp, 1879, III
light bulb frosted inside, 1928, III
in railroad train, 1905, III
Electric-power failure, 1965, I; 1967, I
Electric trains:
  electric lights in, 1905, III
  1st streamlined engine, 1935, III
  miniature train, 1847, III
  passenger train, 1930, III
  third rail invented, 1874, III
Electric trolley, 1888, III
Electron microscope, 1940, III
Elegy on the Reverend Thomas Shepard, Oakes, 1677, II
Elements:
  californium, 1950, III
  mendelevium, 1955, III
Elevated railroads, 1st U.S., 1867, III
Elevators:
  1st office building to contain, 1868, III
  1st passenger elevator, 1859, III
  hydraulic, 1st safety device, 1852, III
Eleventh Hour, The, 1962, IV
Elinot, Rev. Jared, 1739, III; 1748, II
Eliot, Charles W., 1909, III
Eliot, Rev. John, 1631, III; 1646, III; 1660, III; 1670, III
  Catechism in the Indian Language, 1653, II
  Christian Commonwealth, The, 1659, II
Eliot, Thomas Stearns, 1948, II; 1965, II
  new play attacked, 1958, II
Eliot Seminary, St. Louis, Mo., chartered, 1853, III
Elizabeth, Queen, and King George visit Washington, D.C., 1939, I
Elizabeth the Queen, Maxwell Anderson, 1930, II
Elks, Benevolent and Protective Order of, 1868, IV
Ellington, Duke, 1962, II; 1969, IV
Elliott, B. B., 1872, I
Elliott, Lt. Jesse D., 1812, I
Ellis, E. S., *Seth Jones,* 1853, II
Ellis, Jimmy, 1968, IV; 1969, IV
Ellis Island, receiving station for immigrants, 1892, I
Ellison, Ralph, 1952, II
Ellsworth, James Sanford, 1840, II
Elman, Mischa, 1908, II; 1967, II
Elman, Ziggy, 1968, IV
Elsberg, Prof. Louis, 1862, III
Elsie Venner, Holmes, 1861, II
Ely, Eugene, 1910, III
Ely, Prof. Richard T., 1889, III
Emancipation Day celebrated, 1863, IV
Emancipation Proclamation, 1862, I
Emancipator, 1820, III
Embargo Act:
  passed, 1807, I
  repealed, 1809, I
Embury, Rev. Philip, 1766, III
Emergency Relief Appropriation Act, 1935, I; 1938, III
Emerson, Ralph Waldo, 1841, III
  American Scholar address, 1837, II
  bust of, by French, 1879, II
  Conduct of Life, The, 1860, II
  English Traits, 1856, II
  Essays, 1841, II; 1844, II

Nature, 1836, II
  Representative Men, 1850, II
Emerson, Roy, 1959, IV; 1960, IV; 1964, IV; 1965, IV
Emery, Walter, 1935, IV
Emery Roth and Sons, 1963, II
Emigrant, weekly newspaper, 1832, III
Emigrant Aid Society, New England, 1854, I
Emlyn, Thomas, *The Humble Inquiry into the Scripture Account of Jesus Christ,* 1756, III
Emmett, Daniel Decatur, 1842, II; 1843, II; 1859, II
Emmons, Alexander H., 1840, II
Emory University, Oxford, Ga., chartered as Emory College, 1836, III
Emperor Jones, The, Eugene O'Neill, 1920, II
Empire State Building, 1929, II; 1931, III
  struck by plane, 1945, IV
Employer's Liability Act:
  Congress approves, 1906, I
Emporia Gazette, 1896, II
  purchased by William A. White, 1895, II
Emree, Elihu, 1820, III
Encyclopaedia Britannica, American edition, 1790, II; 1964, II
Encyclopaedia Americana, 1827, III; 1829, III
Enders, John F., Nobel Prize, 1954, III
"End of a Perfect Day, The," Carrie Jacobs Bond, 1910, II
Engineering:
  American Society of Civil Engineers, N.Y.C., 1852, III
  American Society of Mechanical Engineers, 1880, III
  school of, Rensselaer Polytechnic Institute, 1824, III
  world's largest cantilever bridge, 1876, III
Engines (*see also* Locomotives):
  caloric, 1856, III
  1st internal combustion, 1826, III
  gas, invented, 1844, III
England (*see also* Great Britain; War of 1812):
  emigration from, to America, 1834, I
  1st U.S. minister to, 1792, I
English, William H., 1858, I; 1880, I
English Classical School, opened, 1821, III
English sparrows imported, 1850, III
English Traits, Ralph Waldo Emerson, 1856, II
Engravings:
  1st caricature, 1762, II
  Peter Pelham, 1751, II
  portrait, of Richard Mather, 1670, II
Enjoyment of Poetry, The, Max Eastman, 1913, II
Enormous Room, The, E. E. Cummings, 1923, II
"Entangling alliances," expression coined, 1801, IV
Enterprise, U.S.S., 1813, I
Enterprise (aircraft carrier), 1969, I
Enthusiasms Described and Cautioned Against, Chauncey, 1742, III
Entomology:
  Association of Economic Entomologists, 1890, III
Episcopal Church, Jamestown, Va., burned, 1676, III
Epstein, Jacob, 1960, II
Epstein, Jay, *Inquest: The Warren Commission and the Establishment of Truth,* 1966, II
Equal Rights Party, 1884, I
  national convention, 1888, I
Equitable Life Assurance Society:
  1st building to contain elevator, 1868, III

791

frozen, in essential industries, 1942, III
Georgia Contract Labor Act, 1942, I
major setback, in Kan., 1915, III
minimum 48-hr. work week in war plants, 1943, III
minimum wage, 1949, I; 1950, III
National Labor Congress, 1866, III
no-strike truce, AFL and CIO, 1942, III
Preparedness Day bombing, 1916, I
railroads, 1963, III; 1964, III
right-to-work laws, 1965, I
state laws limiting working hours unconstitutional, 1905, III
Taft-Hartley Bill, 1947, I
Section 14-b, 1965, I
10-hr. day established for federal employees, 1840, III
trial of "Wild Bill" Haywood, 1907, III
12-month wage contracts guaranteed for immigrants, 1864, III
unrest, 1886, III; 1892, III
U.S. Board of Mediation and Conciliation, 1913, III
wage formula, Truman's, 1946, III
women, equal pay for equal work, 1963, III
Laboratory Theatre for Education, 1966, II
Labor Day:
legal holiday in N.Y., 1887, IV
made legal holiday, 1894, IV
Labor paper, *Fincher's Trades' Review,* 1863, II
Labor Party, national convention, 1884, I
Labor unions and organizations (*see also* Strikes):
actors', 1900, II
AFL-CIO convention, 1959, III
antitrust laws and, 1908, III
Colored National Labor Convention, 1869, III
decline in influence, 1877, III
declining membership, 1931, III
8-hour-day goal, 1867, III
Federal Society of Journeymen Cordwainers, 1794, III
Federation of Organized Trades and Labor Unions, 1881, I
1st appeal to courts by struck employer, 1805, III
1st general strike, 1934, III
1st national Negro group, Colored National Labor Convention, 1869, III
1st organization, Mass., 1648, I
gains of, 1933, III; 1937, III; 1948, III
I.L.G.W.U., 1900, III
Industrial Congress of the U.S., 1845, III
Journeymen Cordwainers, trial, 1810, III
Longshoremen's union, 1959, III
Mass. Supreme Court decisions, significance of, 1842, III
membership, 1870, III
Molly Maguires, 1862, III
Noble Order of the Knights of Labor, 1869, III
Order of the Knights of St. Crispin (shoe industry), 1867, III
political organization of, 1868, III
railway brotherhoods, 1863, III; 1873, III
rising living costs and, 1864, III
Southern Tenant Farmers' Union, 1934, I
Supreme Court pronouncement re, 1921, III
Teamsters union, 1959, III; 1960, III; 1961, III
Labunsky, Felix, *Images of Youth,* 1956, II

Labyrinth, Gian-Carlo Menotti, 1963, II
Lachaise, Gaston, *Standing Woman,* 1912, II
Lacoste, René, 1926, IV; 1927, IV
Lacrosse, 1763, I
Cherokee Indians, Fla., 1775, IV
deadly game of, 1763, I
Indians playing, 1585, IV
Intercollegiate Lacrosse Association, 1882, IV
Ladd, William, 1860, III
Ladenburg, Mrs. Adolph, 1902, IV
Ladies' Home Journal, 1883, II; 1889, II
Ladies' Magazine, 1827, IV
La Dolce Vita, 1961, II
Lady Chatterley's Lover, D. H. Lawrence, 1959, II; 1960, II; 1961, II
"Lady or the Tiger, The," Frank R. Stockton, 1884, II
Lae, New Guinea, battle of, 1943, I
LaFarge, John, 1876, II; 1888, II
La Farge, Oliver, 1930, II; 1963, II
Lafayette, Morse's portrait of, 1826, II
Lafayette College, chartered, 1826, III
"Lafayette, we are here," 1917, IV
La Follette, Senator Robert M. (Bob), 1884, I; 1911, I; 1924, I
named to Senate Hall of Fame, 1957, I
LaGuardia, Fiorello, 1933, III
Lahr, Bert, 1966, II; 1967, II
Laidlie, Rev. Dr., 1764, IV
Laine, Jack (Papa), Ragtime Band, 1892, II
Lake Denmark, N.J., explosion, 1926, I
Lake Mead Reservoir, 1936, III
Lake Ontario, 1st English-made vessel on, 1755, III
Lake Washington Floating Bridge, 1940, III
Lallement, Pierre, 1866, III
Lamarr, Hedy, 1968, IV
Lamb, Willis E., Jr., Nobel Prize, 1955, III
Lambeth Walk, 1938, IV
Lamb in His Bosom, Caroline Miller, 1934, II
Lame Duck Amendment, 1932, I
LaMontaine, John, *Concerto for Piano and Orchestra,* 1959, II
Lamplighter, The, Maria Susanna Cummins, 1854, II
Lampoon, Harvard U., 1876, III
Lancaster, Joseph, 1806, III
Lancaster, Mass., destroyed by Indians, 1676, I
Lancaster turnpike, 1794, III
Lancastrian school, Adm. Sir Isaac Coffin's nautical school, 1827, III
Lancastrian system of education, introduced, 1806, III
Land, Edwin H., 1932, III
Land, Frank S., 1919, IV
Land fraud, Yazoo, 1795, I
Land grants:
1st land grant act, 1862, III
1st federal, for education, 1785, I
1st large, for railroads, 1850, III
Land holdings, Charles Carroll's, 1832, IV
Landis, Judge Kennesaw Mountain, 1910, III; 1920, IV; 1944, III
Land mine, invented, 1840, I
Lando, Sebastiano, 1929, III
Land office, opened in Kansas, 1854, I
Land of the Free, MacLeish, 1938, II

Landon, Alfred M., 1936, I
Landon, Margaret, 1951, II
Landreth, David, 1784, III
Landscape gardening, Andrew Jackson Downing's book on, 1841, II
Landslides, southern California, 1938, I
Landsteiner, Dr. Karl, Nobel Prize, 1930, III
Lane, Joseph, 1860, I
Lane, Mark, *Rush to Judgment,* 1966, II
Lang, Margaret Ruthven, 1889, II
Langley, Samuel P., airplanes of, 1896, III; 1903, III
Langmuir, Irving, 1917, III
  Nobel Prize in chemistry, 1932, III
Langtry, Lily, 1882, II
Language, American:
  "Americanisms," "wigwam words," 1806, IV
  "doughface," 1820, IV
  first formal study, 1816, II
  "half horse and half alligator," 1820, IV
  Modern Language Association, 1883, III
  Southern planters, and change, 1817, II
  Webster's *Dictionary,* 1806, II
Languages:
  1st French course, 1733, II
  1st instruction in German, 1754, III
Lanier, James F. D., 1844, II
Lanier, Sidney:
  Boy's Froissart, The, 1878, II
  compositions for flute, 1873, II
  Hall of Fame, 1945, II
  Psalms of the West, 1876, II
  Revenge of Hamish, The, 1878, II
  Tiger Lilies, 1867, II
Lansbury, Angela, 1966, II
Lansky, J. G., 1931, III
Lantern, N.Y., 1st Uncle Sam cartoon, 1852, I
Laos, 1969, I
  financial aid to, 1955, I
  U.S. troops in, 1963, I
Lapowinsa, portrait of, 1735, II
Lark, The, 1895, II
Larkin, Oliver W., *Art and Life in America,* 1950, II
Larkin, Thomas Oliver, 1843, I
Larkin Administration Building, Buffalo, N.Y., 1903, II
Larned, William A., 1901, IV; 1902, IV; 1907, IV; 1908, IV; 1909, IV; 1910, IV; 1911, IV
Larsen, Arthur, 1950, IV
Larsen, Don, 1956, IV
Larsen, Paul J., 1950, I
Laryngologist, 1st, 1862, III
La Salle, Sieur de, 1678, III; 1685, III
La Scala Opera Company, 1967, II
Lassen Peak, Calif., erupts, 1914, III
Last Mile, The, John Wexley, 1930, II
Last of the Mohicans, The, James Fenimore Cooper, 1826, II
Last Puritan, The, George Santayana, 1935, II
Last Year at Marienbad, 1962, IV
Late Christopher Bean, The, Sidney Howard, 1932, II
Late George Apley, The, John P. Marquand, 1937, II; 1938, II
Lathrop, Rose Hawthorne, 1896, III
Latimer, Rear Adm. Julian L., 1926, I

Latin America, 1967, I
  cultural ties with, 1811, II
  and Eisenhower, 1960, I
  U.S. recognition of republics, 1822, I
Latin-American Conference:
  re Mexico, 1915, I
Latin schools, 1765, III
Latrobe, Benjamin H., 1799, II; 1803, III; 1805, II; 1819, II
Latta, Alexander Bonner, 1852, III
Laudonnière, René de, 1564, I, IV
Laughing Boy, Oliver La Farge, 1930, II
Laughton, Charles, 1933, IV; 1935, IV
Laurel, Stan, 1965, IV
Laver, Rod, 1959, IV; 1969, IV
Law, Andrew, *Plain Tunes,* 1767, II
Law, John, 1732, I
Lawes, John Bennet, 1842, III
Lawler, Charles, "The Sidewalks of New York," 1894, II
Lawn tennis, *see* Tennis
Law of Nations, The, Briggs, 1939, III
Lawrence, Amos, 1837, IV; 1854, I
Lawrence, D. H., *Lady Chatterley's Lover,* 1959, II; 1960, II; 1961, II
Lawrence, Ernest Orlando, Nobel Prize in physics, 1939, III
Lawrence, Florence, 1907, IV
Lawrence, Gertrude, 1937, II; 1951, II
Lawrence, Capt. James, 1813, I
Lawrence, Kan.:
  sacked by Border Ruffians, 1856, I
  settled, 1854, I
Lawrence, Richard, 1835, I
Lawrence, Robert H., Jr., 1967, III
Lawrence, U.S. flagship, 1813, I
Lawrence College, Appleton, Wis., chartered as Lawrence Institute, 1847, III
Lawrence of Arabia, 1962, IV
Laws:
  against blasphemers and atheists, Mass., 1697, III
  against drinking toasts, 1639, IV
  baking of bread, 1656, IV
  banning of priests, Mass., 1647, IV
  "Body of Liberties," Mass., 1641, I
  conviction for adultery, Plymouth, 1639, IV
  dueling prohibited in D.C., 1839, I
  education of poor, Va., 1646, II
  1st breach of promise suit, 1623, IV
  1st convict labor law, Va., 1642, I
  1st gambling legislation, Boston, 1630, I
  1st highway, 1634, I
  1st immigration law, 1819, I
  1st law book, 1687, II
  1st law digest published, 1803, III
  1st law magazine, 1808, III
  1st lawyers' association, 1747, III
  1st volume of commentaries, 1826, III
  heresy law, 1646, III
  law governing smoking, Mass., 1646, IV
  Missouri Compromise, 1820, I
  Molasses Act, 1733, I
  New Amsterdam, 1659, IV
  proclamation by Pres. Jackson, 1832, I

819

829

Oklahoma, Rodgers and Hammerstein, 1943, II; 1944, II; 1969, II

Oklahoma Territory, Removal Bill, Indian resettlement, 1830, I

Old age benefits, 1935, I

Old age pensions laws, enacted by Mont. and Nev., 1923, I

Old Art Museum, Boston, 1872, II

"Old Black Joe," Stephen Foster, 1860, II

"Old Dan Tucker," popular song, 1843, II

Oldfield, Barney, speed record, 1910, III

"Old Folks at Home," 1851, II

Old Friends and New, Sarah Orne Jewett, 1879, II

Oldham, John, 1628, I

"Old Ironsides," Oliver Wendell Holmes, 1830, II

Old Maid, The, Zoe Akins, 1935, II

Old Man and the Sea, The, Ernest Hemingway, 1952, II; 1953, II; 1961, II

Old North Church, Boston, 1723, II
  carillon in, 1745, II

Old Northwest, Pioneer Period, R. Carlyle Buley, 1951, II

"Old Oaken Bucket, The," Samuel Woodworth, 1826, II

Old Régime in Canada, The, Parkman, 1874, II

Old Road to Paradise, Margaret Widdemar, 1919, II

Olds Company, Detroit, 1900, III

Old Ship Meeting House, Hingham, Mass., 1681, II

Old South Church, Boston, mass meeting in, 1768, I

Old South Meeting House, Boston, 1729, II

Old Swimmin' Hole, The, James Whitcomb Riley, 1883, II

Oldtown Folks, Harriet Beecher Stowe, 1869, II

Olin, Bob, 1934, IV

Oliver! (motion picture), 1969, IV

Olivet College, Mich., gives up traditional system, 1934, III

Olivier, Sir Laurence, 1946, IV; 1948, IV; 1952, II

Olmedo, Alex, 1959, IV

Olmsted, Frederick Law, 1857, IV

Olney, Richard, 1895, I

Olustee, Fla., battle of, 1864, I

Olympic Ball Club, Phila., 1833, IV

Olympic Games:
  American team, 1908, IV
  Amsterdam, 1928, IV
  Athens, 1906, IV
  Belgium, 1920, IV
  1st held in America, 1904, IV
  1st modern, Athens, 1896, IV
  Grenoble, France, 1968, IV
  London, 1948, IV
  Mexico City, 1968, IV
  Paris, 1924, IV
  Stockholm, 1912, IV
  Tokyo, 1964, IV
  U.S., 1932, IV; 1960, IV

Omoo, Herman Melville, 1847, II

Onassis, Aristotle, 1968, IV

Once upon a Mattress, 1959, II

Oneida Community, founded, 1848, IV

O'Neill, Eugene, 1915, II
  Ah, Wilderness!, 1933, II
  All God's Chillun Got Wings, 1924, II
  Anna Christie, 1921, II; 1922, II
  Beyond the Horizon, 1920, II
  Days Without End, 1934, II

  Desire Under the Elms, 1924, II; 1925, II
  Emperor Jones, The, 1920, II
  Great God Brown, The, 1926, II
  Hairy Ape, The, 1922, II
  Iceman Cometh, The, 1946, II
  Lazarus Laughed, 1928, II
  Long Day's Journey into Night, 1957, II
  Marco Millions, 1928, II; 1964, II
  More Stately Mansions, 1967, II
  Mourning Becomes Electra, 1931, II
  Nobel Prize, 1936, II
  one-act dramas, 1924, II
  Strange Interlude, 1963, II
  Touch of the Poet, A, 1958, II

O'Neill, Oona, 1943, IV

One of Ours, Willa Cather, 1923, II

One World, Wendell L. Willkie, 1943, II

Only a Tramp, Bronson Howard, 1878, II

Ontario, Lake, 1st vessel on, 1678, III

On the Nature, Extent, and Perfection of the Divine Goodness, Mayhew, 1763, III

On the Road, Jack Kerouac, 1957, II

On the Town, Leonard Bernstein, 1944, II

On the Waterfront, 1954, IV

On Trial, Elmer Rice, 1914, II

On Your Toes, Rodgers and Hart, 1936, II

OPA, *see* Office of Price Administration

Opechancanough uprising, 1644, I

Open Boat and Other Stories, The, Stephen Crane, 1898, II

Opera:
  Astor Place Opera House, 1847, III
  1st based on American theme, 1905, II
  1st broadcast, *Hansel and Gretel,* 1931, II
  1st by American, performed, 1796, II
  1st by American produced at Met., 1910, II
  1st produced, Charleston, S.C., 1734, II
  Four Saints in Three Acts, 1934, II
  Italian, introduced in N.Y., 1825, II
  Italian Opera House opened, 1833, II
  Lenora, William H. Fry, 1845, II
  New Orleans as center, 1808, II
  Puccini, *The Girl of the Golden West,* 1910, II
  Rip Van Winkle, 1855, II
  Warrior, The, 1947, II

O Pioneers!, Willa Cather, 1913, II

Oppen, George, *Of Being Numerous,* 1969, II

Oppenheim, E. Phillips, *The Great Impersonation,* 1920, II

Oppenheimer, J. Robert, 1963, III

Orange, Aaron M., 1940, I

"Orange Blossom," implausible stories by, 1880, IV

Orangeburg, S.C., racial violence in, 1968, III

Orator (Edward Everett), 1826, II

Orchestral score, 1st printed, 1791, II

Ordaz, *see* Díaz Ordaz

Oregon:
  admitted as 33rd state, 1859, I
  American Society for Encouraging Settlement of, 1829, I
  Anglo-American friction over boundary, 1844, I
  Astoria, William Hunt arrives at, 1812, I
  boundary settlement, 1844, III

847

Puerto Rico (*cont.*)
requests statehood, 1934, I
Pulaski, Count, 1779, I
Pulitzer, Albert, 1882, II
Pulitzer, Joseph, 1878, II; 1895, I; 1917, II
Pulitzer Prizes:
1917, II; 1918, II; 1919, II; 1920, II; 1921, II; 1922, II;
1923, II; 1924, II; 1925, II; 1927, II; 1928, II;
1929, II; 1934, II; 1935, II; 1937, II; 1938, II;
1939, II; 1940, II; 1941, II; 1942, II; 1943, II;
1945, II; 1946, II; 1947, II; 1948, II; 1949, II;
1950, II; 1951, II; 1952, II; 1954, II; 1955, II;
1956, II; 1957, II; 1959, II; 1961, II; 1962, II;
1963, II; 1964, II; 1966, II; 1967, II; 1968, II
1st for play, 1917, II
Pullman, George M., 1859, III
Pullman Palace Car Co., 1867, III
Pullman sleeper, 1st, 1859, III
Pullman strike, Chicago, 1894, III
Punishment:
ducking stool, 1691, IV
exclusion from church, Boston, 1638, IV
New Amsterdam, 1638, IV
Pupin, Michael Idvorski, *From Immigrant to Inventor,*
1924, II
Purcell, Dr. Edward Mills, Nobel Prize, 1952, III
Purchas, Samuel, 1613, II
Purdue University, 1865, III
Pure food and drug laws (*see also* Foods and food indus-
try):
advocacy of, 1898, III
national law, 1848, I
Pure Food and Drug Act, 1906, I
Puritans:
and Catholics, in Md., 1655, I
and singing, 1720, II
Puritan Village: The Formation of a New England Town,
Sumner Chilton Powell, 1964, II
"Purple Cow, The," Gelett Burgess, 1895, II
Purple Heart, decoration, 1782, I
Pusey, Merlo J., 1952, II
Putnam, Gideon, 1802, IV
Puzo, Mario, *The Godfather,* 1969, II
Pygmalion, George Bernard Shaw, 1938, IV
Pyle, Ernie, 1943, II – 1945, II
Pyramiding, banking phenomenon, 1825, III

Quadrant, navigating, invented, 1730, III
Quaker City, The, George Lippard, 1840, II
Quakers:
executed, Boston, 1659, III; 1661, III
1st in America, 1656, III
1st emancipation petition submitted to Congress, 1790,
I
1st large group, 1677, I
1st legislation against, 1656, III
1st in Manhattan, 1657, III
1st private home for mental illness, 1709, III
1st treatment on stage, 1795, II
1st yearly meeting, 1661, III
found public almshouse, Phila., 1732, III
Haverford College, 1856, III
oppose use of umbrellas, 1738, IV

persecution halted, 1661, III
slavery and, 1696, III
and Underground Railroad, 1838, I
West Jersey, 1677, III
women, Sewall's account of, 1677, III
Woolman, John, 1743, III
Quarry, Jerry, 1969, IV
Quartering Act, 1774, I
Quayle, Anna, 1962, II
Quebec, battle of, 1759, I
Quebec Act, 1774, I
Quebec Conference, 1943, I
Queen, The, 1968, IV
Queen Anne style furniture, 1725, II
Queen Anne's War, 1713, I
Queen Mary, maiden voyage, 1936, III
Queensboro Bridge, N.Y.C., 1909, III
Queen's College (Rutgers University), 1766, III
Quick, Smiley, 1946, IV
Quilting Party, The, painting, 1830, II
Quimby, Fred, *The Milky Way,* 1940, IV
Quincy, Mass., First Church (Unitarian), 1828, II
Quincy Market, Boston, 1826, II
Quinine, synthetic, 1944, III
Quinn, Anthony, 1952, IV
Quintero, José, 1963, II

Rabaul, Japanese defeat at, 1943, I
Rabb, Ellis, 1967, II
Rabble in Arms, Kenneth Roberts, 1933, II
Rabi, Isidor Isaac, Nobel Prize, 1944, III
Race horses, *see* Horses
Racetracks, *see* Horse racing
Rachmaninoff, Sergei, 1943, II
Racial prejudice:
doctrines, 1928, III
plays dealing with, 1945, II
white racism condemned, 1968, I
Racial segregation, *see* Integration
Racing (*see also* Automobile racing; Foot racers; Horse
racing; Rowing):
bicycle, 1898, IV
greyhound, 1884, IV
horse and locomotive, 1830, IV
relay, 1893, IV
sculling, 1851, IV
sprint, Childs Cup, 1879, IV
Racquets, sport introduced, 1863, IV
Radar, 1943, III
early warning net, N. Canada, 1954, I
1st tests of, by Coast Guard, 1938, III
1st U.S. research, 1922, III
Radburn, N.J., 1st garden community, 1929, III
Radcliffe College, 1879, III; 1882, III
Radio:
between U.S. and Japan, 1915, III
1st coast-to-coast broadcast, 1937, II
1st FM transmitter, 1941, III
1st important patent, to Edison, 1891, III
1st message, N.Y.-Chicago, 1909, III
1st national beacon for air transportation, 1927, III
1st program broadcast, 1906, III
1st regular broadcasting service, 1920, III

861

Selective Service Acts, 1940, I; 1941, I; 1946, I; 1948, I;
   1951, I; 1955, I; 1962, I; 1965, I
Self, The, Isami Noguchi, 1959, II
Selfridge, Lt. Thomas W., 1908, III
Sellers, Johnny, 1961, IV; 1965, IV
Selling of Joseph, Sewall, 1700, II
Selling of the President 1968, The, Joe McGinniss, 1969,
   II
Seminole Indians:
   ordered to evacuate Florida, 1834, II
   treaty with, 1821, I
Seminole War, 1817, I
   1st, end of, 1818, I
   2nd, begun, 1835, I
Senate:
   bomb destroys reception room, 1915, I
Senators:
   1st woman, 1922, I
   popular election of, 1913, I
Seneca Falls convention, women's rights, 1848, III
"Seneca oil," 1841, III
Seneca Oil Company, Titusville, Pa., 1859, III
Senf, Christian, 1800, III
Sennett, Mack, 1914, IV; 1932, IV
Sentinel (ABM) system, 1967, I
Seoul, Korea, 1950, I; 1951, I
Separate Tables, Terence Rattigan, 1956, II
Sequoia National Park, 1890, III
Sequoyah, invented Cherokee alphabet, 1828, II
Sergeant, John, 1826, I
Serjeant Musgrave's Dance, John Arden, 1966, II
Serra, Fr. Junipero, 1769, II
Servant, The, 1964, IV
Servant's staircase, 1720, IV
Servicemen's Readjustment Act, 1944, III
Sesquicentennial Exposition, Phila., 1926, IV
Sessions, Roger:
   Symphony No. 2, 1947, II
Seth Jones, E. S. Ellis, 1853, II
Seton, Elizabeth Ann Bayley, 1963, III
Settlement houses:
   Hull House, 1889, III
   Neighborhood Guild, N.Y.C., 1886, III
Settle table, 1650, II
Seven Days in May, 1964, IV
Seven Pines, battle of, 1862, I
Seventeen, Booth Tarkington, 1914, II
1776, Edwards and Stone, 1969, II
Seventh Day Baptist Church:
   1st, 1671, III
Seventh Heaven, Austin Strong, 1922, II
*Several Poems Compiled with Great Variety of Wit and
   Learning,* Bradstreet, 1678, II
Severance, Carolina, 1868, III
Sewage systems:
   Chicago, Ill., 1856, III
Sewall, Arthur, 1896, I
Sewall, Judge Samuel, 1699, IV; 1714, III
   Diary, 1674, II; 1677, III
   Selling of Joseph, 1700, II
   and witch trials, 1697, III
Seward, William Henry, 1867, IV
   nominated gov. of N.Y., 1834, I

   phrase "an irrepressible conflict," 1858, IV
Seward Day, Alaska, 1867, IV
Sewell, Anna, *Black Beauty,* 1890, II
Sewer construction:
   1st underground sewer, 1704, IV
Sewing machine:
   electric, 1889, III
   improvements, 1857, IV
   invented, 1846, III
   loop-stitch single thread, 1857, III
   Singer, 1st successful manufacturer, 1851, III
Sexton, Anne, *Live or Die,* 1967, II
Sexual conduct, Puritan enforcement of, 1649 – 1660, IV
Seyfert, Gabriele, 1969, IV
Seymour, Harry, *Capture of Fort Donelson,* 1861, II
Seymour, Horatio, 1868, I
Shackleford Good Roads Bill, 1916, III
Shadow of a Bull, Maia Wojciechowska, 1965, II
Shadows on the Rock, Willa Cather, 1931, II
Shadrach, mob rescue of, 1851, I
Shaftesbury, Lord, *Characteristics,* 1711, III
Shahn, Ben, 1948, II; 1969, II
Shakers, 1774, III
   slat-back chair, 1700, II
Shakespeare, 1610, II; 1916, II; 1964, II
Shaler, Dean, 1869, III
Shame of the Cities, The, Lincoln Steffens, 1904, II
Shankar, Ravi, 1967, IV
Shannon, Wilson, 1855, I
SHAPE:
   established at Paris, 1951, I
Shapiro, Karl, *V-Letter and Other Poems,* 1945, II
Sharkey, Jack, 1932, IV; 1933, IV
Sharp, Dudley C., 1960, III
Sharpe, Col., murder of, 1825, II
Shaver:
   electric dry, 1931, III
   invention, 1833, IV
Shaw, Clay, 1967, IV; 1969, I
Shaw, George Bernard, 1905, II; 1906, II; 1956, II
Shaw, Henry W. (Josh Billings), *Sayings,* 1865, II
Shaw, Irwin, 1936, II; 1939, II
Shaw, Louis Agassiz, 1927, III
Shaw, Robert, *The Man in the Glass Booth,* 1968, II
Shaw, Maj. Samuel, 1786, I
Shawn, Ted, 1916, II; 1968, II
Shays' (Daniel) Rebellion, 1787, I
She, Sir Henry Rider Haggard, 1887, II
Shearer, Norma, 1930, IV
Sheeler, Charles, 1932, II
Sheen, Fulton J., 1949, II
Sheep, Merino, 1st in country, 1802, IV
Sheik, The, Edith M. Hull, 1921, II
Sheldon, Charles M., *In His Steps,* 1897, II
Sheldon, Edward, 1908, II; 1913, II
Shelton, Robert, Jr., 1966, I
Shenandoah, Bronson Howard, 1889, II
Shenandoah (dirigible) wrecked, 1925, III
Shepard, Alan Bartlett, Jr., 1961, III
Shepard, Mrs. Finley J., 1900, III
Shepard, Odell, *Pedlar's Progress,* 1938, II
Shepard, Thomas, 1641, II
Shepardson College, 1832, III

863

871

877

886

Supplement of the 70s

1970

Pres. Nixon was confronted throughout the year with large-scale problems both at home and abroad. Perhaps his most pressing problem was the disappointing performance of the U.S. economy, which was considered the main cause of the Republicans' poor showing in the congressional and gubernatorial elections. Although the Republicans gained 4 seats in the Senate, they lost 10 seats in the House of Representatives and 11 state governorships. The President also suffered a setback in his desire to put a strict constructionist and a Southerner on the Supreme Court. After his 2nd nominee was rejected by the Senate, he proposed Judge Harry A. Blackmun, of Minnesota, who was confirmed. Part of the President's response to the growing inflationary trend in the economy was to offer a reduced federal budget and to curtail the space program severely. The latter move added to the unemployment problem, as aeronautical and space-oriented companies laid off many workers, including scientists and engineers. With public concern over the environment on the increase, the President proposed a $10 billion program to build municipal waste-treatment plants and called for a coordinated policy to improve the nation's environment. As Pres. Nixon continued to stress the reduction of U.S. military activity in Vietnam, the U.S. participated in a surprise sweep into Cambodia in May; all American troops were withdrawn from the country in June. Although the number of American troops in Vietnam had been reduced to 340,000 by late Dec., many factions in the U.S. continued to clamor for withdrawal of all American forces from Indochina. By the end of the year the total death toll of U.S. personnel had passed 44,000.

Jan. 2 A Defense Department survey reported **1,403 servicemen had deserted** into foreign countries since July 1, 1966.

The perennial invalid, the Broadway theater squeaked through another season, with less interest being shown in serious plays and more in comedies and musicals. Several hits did emerge to keep the theater lights burning. One of the best received was Robert Marasco's *Child's Play,* a psychological thriller set in a boys' school. Producer David Merrick chose the play as his first motion-picture production, because, as he said, "I cannot find enough good plays to do on Broadway." The musical stage rose to the challenge with *Applause,* based on the now-classic motion picture *All About Eve.* The musical starred Lauren Bacall in the famed Bette Davis role of a stage actress supplanted by her understudy. *Company,* a caustic and sophisticated musical by librettist George Furth and composer Stephen Sondheim, examined the institution of marriage as seen through the eyes of a bachelor and 5 of his married friends. The season was augmented by several imports, including the huge success *Sleuth,* a clever thriller by Anthony Shaffer given spectacular performances by Keith Baxter and Anthony Quayle, and *Conduct Unbecoming,* by Barry England, a melodramatic portrayal of 19th-century military life in British-controlled India. At the end of the season Danny Kaye returned to Broadway in Richard Rodgers' musical *Two by Two,* a story of Noah and the Ark adapted from Clifford Odets' play *The Flowering Peach.* Off-Broadway, the prize winner was *The Effect of Gamma Rays on Man-in-the-Moon Marigolds,* a perceptive and moving drama by Paul Zindel about a neurotic mother and her teen-age daughters, featuring a striking performance by Sada Thompson.

By far the best-selling books of the year concerned the age-old subject of sex. *Everything You Always Wanted to Know About Sex,* by Dr. David Reuben, and *The Sensuous Woman,* by "J," headed the

1970

The declining pace of the U.S. economy that became evident in 1969 continued, making 1970 a disappointing year. The word recession, not heard for almost a decade, crept back into the public vocabulary. Of primary concern were the high level of unemployment and the reduction in industrial output. The economic policies of Pres. Nixon called for a concerted contraction in the economy to break the inflationary spiral that had begun some 3 years earlier. At the end of the year, it was apparent that more contraction had taken place than was desired. Estimates placed the Gross National Product, or GNP, at $982 billion, about 5.4% above the level at 1969. The slower growth rate compared to the 7.7% of the previous year was further diminished by increased inflation. The most disturbing factor, however, was unemployment, which rose to 5.8% in Nov. While consumer income rose, the rate of savings also increased, an indication of the caution sweeping through the economy. By the end of the year, the government and particularly the monetary authorities were moving toward expansionary policies by reducing interest rates as a means of stimulating the economy.

In science the cliff-hanger of the year was the aborted Apollo XIII moon mission. The explosion of a tank of liquid oxygen crippled the spacecraft so that it could not make a lunar landing, but it still had to travel around the moon before it returned to earth.

In education, campus unrest was expressed by continued student demonstrations, some involving bombings, arson, riots, strikes, seizures of public buildings, boycotts, and other disorders. The climax was reached at Kent State University, in Ohio, in May, when 4 students were killed by National Guardsmen firing into a crowd of demonstrators. A few days later at Jackson State College, Miss., 2 students

Professional sports were plagued by the same symptoms of rebellion and unrest that affected society at large. Curt Flood, outfielder with the St. Louis Cardinals baseball team, objected to being traded to the Philadelphia Phillies and brought an anti-trust suit against organized baseball over the reserve clause. The case was headed to the Supreme Court. Dave Meggyesy of the St. Louis Cardinals quit football and leveled charges of hypocrisy at college and professional football in his book *Out of Their League*. Jim Bouton, former New York Yankees pitcher, criticized the baseball establishment in his successful book *Ball Four*. Big money epitomized professional sports in general. Pro golfers shared prize money of nearly $7 million; the Indianapolis 500 automobile race provided a purse of more than $1 million; and pro basketball teams signed unprecedented contracts in excess of $1 million with collegiate stars Pete Maravich, Dan Issel, and Bob Lanier. On the comeback trail after 3½ years of inactivity, Muhammad Ali (Cassius Clay) returned to the ring in 2 bouts, defeating Jerry Quarry and Oscar Bonavena. Joe Frazier, a knockout winner over Jimmy Ellis and Bob Foster, was recognized as the heavyweight champion, opening the way to a showdown fight with Muhammad Ali, who had been stripped of his world heavyweight title in 1967 after a conviction for refusing induction into the Army.

In fashion, controversy raged over dress length, with many in the industry pushing the midi look which accentuated a longer line with skirts at mid-calf length. Reaction against the look was typified by a woman's group, POOFF, for Preservation of Our Femininity and Finances. Design turned to a naked, braless, girdleless look. Among the young, costumes played a big role, with granny dresses, old military uniforms, and tie-dyed materials very popular. The more conservative retreated

| POLITICS AND GOVERNMENT; WAR; DISASTERS; VITAL STATISTICS. | BOOKS; PAINTING; DRAMA; ARCHITECTURE; SCULPTURE. |

Jan. 6 Nixon Administration officials announced a diplomatic agreement with France to cooperate in halting **illegal production of heroin** in France, as part of an increased effort to curb the flow of the drug into the U.S.

Jan. 19 The Supreme Court ruled that the **Selective Service System** lacked authority to speed up induction of young men who violated draft regulations.

Jan. 22 Pres. Nixon delivered his first **State of the Union** message to Congress, in which he stressed the pressing need for environmental control.

Feb. 4. As part of his goal to improve the environment, Pres. Nixon proposed a $10 billion program to construct **waste-treatment plants.**

Feb. 14 Reaffirming that the U.S. would not be the first to use lethal and incapacitating chemicals, and having previously renounced the use of biological weapons, Pres. Nixon extended the renunciation of **chemical warfare** to include toxins.

Feb. 18 Pres. Nixon sent to Congress the 1st of what may become an annual **State of the World message.** The foreign policy statement emphasized the need for continuing U.S. global commitments, but with U.S. allies sharing more of the costs.

Feb. 26 After much protesting by civil liberty organizations, the Army announced that it would discontinue **surveillance of peaceful civilian demonstrations** and the maintenance of records of civilians who might be involved in riots.

Feb. 28 Leaked to the press was a private memorandum from Daniel P. Moynihan, domestic adviser to Pres. Nixon, in which Moynihan proposed "the time may have come when the issue of race could benefit from a period of **'benign neglect.' "** Later he explained that blacks could fare better if extremists on both sides of the political spectrum were less vocal.

Mar. 4 Defense Secretary Melvin R.

list. *Human Sexual Response,* by Dr. William H. Masters and Mrs. Virginia Johnson, a highly technical work based on extended research, spawned half a dozen explanatory paperbacks. The battle between the sexes was continued in Kate Millett's *Sexual Politics.* This explanation of the unequal relationship between man and woman soon became the manifesto of the women's liberation movement. Biographies abounded, particularly about unusual women, including John Keats's *You Might as Well Live: The Life and Times of Dorothy Parker,* and Nancy Milford's *Zelda.* Known primarily for her wit, Dorothy Parker emerged as a tragic figure, as unhappy as Zelda Fitzgerald, wife of the famous chronicler of the 1920's, F. Scott Fitzgerald. *Roosevelt: The Soldier of Freedom 1940–45* was a 2nd volume on Pres. Franklin D. Roosevelt by the historian James MacGregor Burns. Notable works of fiction included a posthumous novel by Ernest Hemingway, *Islands in the Stream,* which concerned the adventures of an American painter living in the Caribbean area. A modest, old-fashioned romantic novella, *Love Story,* by Yale professor Erich Segal, long led the best-seller lists, followed by John Fowles' *The French Lieutenant's Woman.* Two works that explored the "alternate culture" of American society, or the generation gap, were Margaret Mead's *Culture and Commitment* and Charles A. Reich's *The Greening of America.*

Jan. 22 The young and enterprising Seattle Opera presented the world premiere of composer **Carlisle Floyd's** opera *Of Mice and Men,* based on the novel by John Steinbeck.

Jan. 29 Leonard Bernstein led the New York Philharmonic in the world premiere of William Schuman's *In Praise of Shahn.* The canticle for orchestra was a **tribute to the late artist Ben Shahn.**

Feb. 5 New York City Ballet director George Balanchine was awarded the

were killed as demonstrators were fired on by city and state police. A Commission on Campus Unrest was established by Pres. Nixon to determine the causes of campus violence and to suggest solutions. The commission report warned of the alarming discontent among students over U.S. military involvements, lack of racial justice, and the current state of American culture. The commission urged Pres. Nixon to exercise his reconciling moral leadership to prevent further violence and create understanding.

Jan. 2 Secretary of Health, Education, and Welfare Robert H. Finch said his department had dropped its **blacklist of prominent scientists.** The scientists were blacklisted from HEW's advisory panels for alleged anti-administration statements, including antiwar statements.

Jan. 5 **Joseph Yablonski,** unsuccessful candidate for president of the United Mine Workers, was found murdered in his home along with his wife and daughter.

Jan. 14 The Supreme Court set a Feb. 1, 1970, **deadline for desegregation** of public schools in Alabama, Florida, Georgia, Louisiana, Mississippi, and Texas, overturning the Sept. 1970 deadline set by a lower court.

Jan. 18 David O. McKay, president of the Church of Jesus Christ of Latter-Day Saints since 1951, died at age 96. He was succeeded Jan. 23 by Joseph Fielding Smith, 93, great-nephew of the founder of the **Morman Church.**

Jan. 30 An agreement was reached between **General Electric Co.** and its electrical unions settling a strike that began Oct. 27, 1969.

Feb. 4 A Space Electric Rocket Test (SERT-2) **ion-propulsion engine** was launched into earth orbit to test ion-propulsion, long recognized as the most efficient form of reaction power for space flight.

Feb. 18 In the **Chicago 7 trial,** 5 of the defendants were found guilty of cross-

to pants suits until a well-defined style should emerge.

The motion-picture industry, in the economic doldrums and making 25% fewer pictures, was sparked by remembrances of things past when MGM held an auction of more than 50 years' accumulation of sets, props, and costumes. Items steeped in nostalgia fetched handsome prices, such as $1250 for Clark Gable's raincoat from *It Happened One Night* and $3000 for Debbie Reynolds' brass bed from *The Unsinkable Molly Brown.* In television, the show that attracted the most attention was the educational television series *Sesame Street,* aimed at educating disadvantaged preschoolers but appreciated by older generations as well. Kenneth Clark's television series *Civilisation,* which traced the development of the arts through history, was also widely acclaimed.

Rock music lived on the screen with two film documentaries that attracted large audiences. *Woodstock* was based on the 1969 rock festival that attracted 400,000 young people to a historic gathering; and *Gimme Shelter* was a devastating revelation of behind-the-scenes activities during the American tour of the popular rock group The Rolling Stones.

Jan. 1 The University of Southern California, playing its 4th consecutive **Rose Bowl** game, upset Michigan 10–3.

Jan. 11 In professional football's **Super Bowl** game, played in Tulane Stadium, New Orleans, the Kansas City Chiefs defeated the Minnesota Vikings 23–7.

Feb. 7 At Tulsa, Okla., the U.S. **men's figure-skating championship** was won for the 3rd straight year by Tim Wood of Colorado Springs, Colo.

Feb. 15 Billy Kidd of Stowe, Vt., won the men's combined title in the **Alpine World Ski Championships** at Val Gardena, Italy. Kidd's was the 1st U.S. world title in Alpine combination.

Feb. 16 **Joe Frazier** became recog-

Laird announced that **371 military bases in the U.S. and abroad would be closed** or cut back in an economy move expected to save $914 million in defense spending.

Mar. 5 The treaty on the **nonproliferation of nuclear weapons** came into force after ratification by more than 40 countries, including the Soviet Union and the U.S.

Apr. 1 Enumeration date of the 19th Decennial **Census of Population and Housing.** In taking the census, the Bureau of the Census made greater use of the mails and more sophisticated census techniques. The preliminary population count approached 205 million.

Apr. 1 Pres. Nixon signed a bill **banning cigarette advertising** on radio and television after Jan. 1, 1971.

Apr. 8 After a prolonged debate, the Senate rejected the nomination of **Judge G. Harrold Carswell** to the Supreme Court. It was the 2nd rejection of a nominee for the seat vacated by the resignation of Abe Fortas.

Apr. 18 In Texas, **tornadoes battered 11 Panhandle towns** and killed 25 persons.

Apr. 20 Pres. Nixon announced he would **withdraw an additional 150,000 troops from Vietnam** by early 1971.

Apr. 29 Some 20,000 U.S. and South Vietnamese troops launched a **major drive into Cambodia,** aimed at destroying North Vietnamese sanctuaries and capturing the command post of the Vietcong.

May 8 Dozens of demonstrators were bloodied by **construction workers who broke up an anti-war rally** in New York's Wall Street. At a White House meeting on May 26, leaders of N.Y. longshoremen's and building trades' unions gave Pres. Nixon a safety helmet, a symbol of continuing "hard hat" support for his policies.

May 9 Huge crowds gathered in Washington, D.C., to protest **expansion of the Southeast Asian war into Cambodia** and the student deaths at Kent State University on May 4.

Handel Medallion, New York City's highest award for cultural achievement. Balanchine celebrated his 50th year as a working choreographer.

Feb. 12 The centennial of the **Metropolitan Museum of Art** opened with the exhibition *The Year 1200,* which featured all art forms that flourished from 1180 to 1220.

Feb. 19 Artist **Andrew Wyeth** was honored at the opening of an exhibition of his works at the White House. The one-man show at the presidential mansion was thought to be the 1st such recognition of a living artist.

Feb. 25 At the Parke-Bernet Galleries in New York, a **record price was paid** for a Vincent van Gogh painting. The picture of cyprus trees in a cornfield, *Le Cypres et l'Arbe en Fleur,* sold for $1.3 million.

Feb. 25 **Mark Rothko,** Russian-born American painter, was found dead in New York City at age 66. He changed from a realist painting style in the 1940's to a highly individual abstract style on which his reputation was based.

Mar. 3 The **Metropolitan Opera** in New York premiered a landmark revival of Vincenzo Bellini's *Norma,* with Joan Sutherland in the title role and Marilyn Horne in her Met debut singing Adalgisa.

Mar. 11 The creator of the Perry Mason tales, **Erle Stanley Gardner,** died in Temecula, Calif., at age 80. His detective stories were among the most successful of the genre.

Apr. 11 **John O'Hara,** the popular author known for his novels and stories chronicling the social history of America in the 1st half of the 20th century, died in Princeton, N.J., at age 65. *Appointment in Samarra* was one of his most popular works.

Apr. 16 One of the influential architects of the 20th century, **Richard Neutra,** died in Wuppertal, West Germany, at age 78. His functional residential designs used

ing a state line with intent to incite a riot and sentenced to 5-year prison terms. The charges and conviction resulted from disturbances caused by demonstrators during the Democratic National Convention in Chicago in Aug. 1968. Previously there were 8 defendants, but 1 was convicted of contempt of court and his case was declared a mistrial.

Mar. 7   As part of the new U.S. space goals, Pres. Nixon announced that during the 1970's 2 **"grand tour" probes of the outer planets** by unmanned spacecraft would be undertaken.

Mar. 16   1st publication of the complete text of the **New English Bible.** Like the New American Bible, published in Sept. of this year, the NEB was translated directly from ancient texts. It was the work of British scholars of the major Protestant churches, assisted by a panel of literary experts, and was the subject of debate because its language departed radically from the rich sonorities of the King James version.

Mar. 23   The National Guard was called out by Pres. Nixon to alleviate the delays caused by the first widespread **strike of postal employees.** The strike began Mar. 18 and ended Mar. 25.

Apr. 11   Apollo XIII was launched, manned by astronauts James A. Lovell, Jr., John L. Swigert, Jr., and Fred W. Haise, Jr. The **lunar mission was aborted** after a tank of liquid oxygen exploded on April 13, damaging the spacecraft. The crew was able to bring the crippled spacecraft safely back to earth on Apr. 17.

Apr. 22   **Earth Day** was celebrated to dramatize the dangers of environmental pollution.

Apr. 28   The **Dow Jones industrial stock average** plummeted to 724.33, the lowest level since that recorded on the day of Pres. John F. Kennedy's assassination, Nov. 22, 1963.

nized as the heavyweight champion of the world by winning over Jimmy Ellis in a 5th-round knockout in New York City. The title was taken from Muhammad Ali (Cassius Clay) in 1967 because of his conviction for draft evasion.

Mar. 7   At Ljubljana, Yugoslavia, Tim Wood won the **men's world figure-skating championship** for the 2nd consecutive year.

Mar. 21   UCLA won the **NCAA basketball tournament** for the 4th straight year, defeating Jacksonville University, 80–69.

Apr. 7   The annual **Academy Awards** for 1969 presented by the motion-picture industry were given to: *Midnight Cowboy* (best film); *Z* (best foreign film, Algeria); John Wayne (best actor, *True Grit*); Maggie Smith (best actress, *The Prime of Miss Jean Brodie*); Gig Young (best supporting actor, *They Shoot Horses, Don't They?*); Goldie Hawn (best supporting actress, *Cactus Flower*).

Apr. 13   Billy Casper won the **Masters golf championship** at Augusta, Ga.

Apr. 26   Famed striptease artist, actress, and writer, **Gypsy Rose Lee** (real name Rose Louise Hovick) died in Los Angeles at age 56.

May 2   The **Kentucky Derby** was won by *Dust Commander,* an outsider ridden by Mike Manganello. The purse was $170,300.

May 3   The 1st of a series of **auctions to sell MGM memorabilia** was held in Culver City, Calif. Included in the sale was a 50-year accumulation of set decorations, costumes, and props.

May 8   The **New York Knickerbockers** won the NBA title for the 1st time in 24 years, beating the Los Angeles Lakers 113–99 in the 7th and deciding game of the playoffs.

May 10   The Boston Bruins won the National Hockey League's **Stanley Cup**

| POLITICS AND GOVERNMENT; WAR; DISASTERS; VITAL STATISTICS. | BOOKS; PAINTING; DRAMA; ARCHITECTURE; SCULPTURE. |

May 12 After rejecting 2 nominees, the Senate confirmed the appointment of **Judge Harry Andrew Blackmun** to the Supreme Court. Controversy over the 2 earlier nominees had centered on their alleged white-supremacist views.

June 15 The Supreme Court ruled that a person was entitled to **conscientious objector status** for moral reasons. Previously such status was usually given only on grounds of long-standing affiliation with a religion that opposed war.

June 22 The Supreme Court ruled that the Constitution permitted **juries of fewer than 12 persons.** Some states required only a 6-man jury, whereas tradition stipulated 12.

July 4 **Honor America Day** was observed in Washington, D.C., as thousands gathered to display their confidence in the nation's policies.

Aug. 3–5 **Hurricane Celia** swept across the Gulf Coast, killing 26 persons in Texas and Florida.

Aug. 12 The **Postal Reorganization Act** was signed by Pres. Nixon, establishing the U.S. Postal Service as an independent agency within the Executive branch of the government.

Sept. 12 Drug advocate and philosopher **Dr. Timothy Leary** escaped from prison near San Luis Obispo, Calif., and fled to Algeria.

Sept. 22 A bill authorizing the **District of Columbia** to send a nonvoting delegate to the House of Representatives was signed by Pres. Nixon. The District had not been represented in Congress since 1875.

Sept. 22–28 In southern California, **brush and forest fires,** worst in the state's history, destroyed thousands of acres of forest and hundreds of homes.

Sept. 26 Pres. Nixon signed a bill authorizing $20 million to purchase remaining privately held land within the glass extensively, and he specialized in architecture for the California environment.

Apr. 19 **Antoinette Perry (Tony) Awards** for the 1969–70 season were given to *Borstal Boy* (best play) and *Applause* (best musical). *Child's Play* won five awards, including Fritz Weaver (best actor) and Joseph Hardy (best director). Tammy Grimes received best-actress award for her performance in *Private Lives.*

Apr. 30 The **New York Drama Critics Circle** selected *The Effect of Gamma Rays on Man-in-the-Moon Marigolds* as the best American play and *Company* as the best musical. *Borstal Boy* was chosen as the best foreign play.

May 4 **Pulitzer Prizes** were announced for the following persons: T. Harry Williams, for *Huey Long* (biography); Ada Louise Huxtable, the first award in criticism, for her articles on architecture for *The New York Times;* Charles Gordone, for *No Place to Be Somebody* (drama); Jean Stafford for *Collected Stories* (fiction); Dean Gooderham Acheson, for *Present at the Creation: My Years in The State Department* (history); Eric H. Erikson for *Gandhi's Truth: On the Origins of Militant Non-violence* (general nonfiction); Charles W. Wuorinen, for *Time's Encomium* (music); and Richard Howard for *Untitled Subjects* (poetry).

May 29 **John Gunther,** author of the popular "Inside" series, such as *Inside Russia Today* (1958), died in New York City at age 68. By 1969 more than 3.9 million of his books had been sold.

June 24 At the opening of the **Venice Biennale art festival,** 20 American artists withdrew in opposition to U.S. actions in Vietnam and Cambodia.

July 3 A leader of the color-field school of painting, **Barnett Newman** died in New York City at age 65. He was a pioneer in his field and a precursor of the shaped canvas and Minimal Art of the 1960's.

May 4 At a campus antiwar demonstration, 4 students were killed and 9 wounded at **Kent State University,** Ohio, by National Guardsmen firing into a crowd.

May 9 Jet-setter and financial entrepreneur **Bernard Cornfeld** was forced to resign as chief executive of the vast conglomerate Investors Overseas Services. Cornfeld's $2 billion empire, staggering under falling security prices, had been started with a firm selling U.S. securities abroad on the installment plan.

May 10 **Walter Reuther,** 62, president of the United Automobile Workers, was killed with his wife and 4 others in a plane crash in Michigan.

May 15 At Jackson State College, Miss., **2 students were killed** when city and state police opened fire on demonstrators.

June 4 The FDA approved the use of the **drug L-dopa for treatment** of Parkinson's disease.

June 5 **Henry Cabot Lodge,** former chief U.S. negotiator at the Paris peace talks, was named as Pres. Nixon's personal envoy to the Vatican.

June 13 Pres. Nixon named a 9-member **Commission on Campus Unrest** to report on the principal causes of campus violence and to suggest solutions. The commission was headed by William W. Scranton, former Republican governor of Pennsylvania.

June 21 The **Penn Central Railroad Co.,** operator of the nation's largest railroad system, was granted a petition for reorganization under U.S. bankruptcy laws.

June 30 In Pittsburgh, Bell Telephone inaugurated the nation's first commercial **Picturephone** service. Basic cost of the "face-to-face" service was $165 a month.

July 3 The National Communicable Disease Center reported that **no known deaths from polio** were recorded in 1969, the 1st year without fatalities since the keeping of records began in 1955.

for the 1st time in 29 years, defeating the St. Louis Blues 4–3 to complete a 4-game sweep. The Bruins' Bobby Orr was named the league's most valuable player.

May 16 *Personality,* with Eddie Belmonte up, won the **Preakness Stakes** at Baltimore. The colt, best of the 3-year-olds, won $444,049 in purses during the year.

May 30 The **Indianapolis 500** was won by Al Unser, driving a Colt-Ford.

June 6 The **Belmont Stakes,** the 3rd of the triple-crown horse races, was won by *High Echelon,* with John Rotz up, earning $115,000.

June 18–20 At the NCAA outdoor championships at Des Moines, Iowa, Ralph Mann of Brigham Young University broke the **world record 440-yd. hurdles** with 48.8 seconds.

June 21 The **U.S. Open golf championship,** held at Chaska, Minn., was won by Tony Jacklin, of Great Britain, by 7 strokes over Dave Hill. He was the first Englishman in 50 years to win it.

July 14 In Cincinnati the National League won baseball's **all-star game** for the 8th consecutive year, defeating the American League in the 12th inning 5–4.

Aug. 16 In Tulsa, Okla., golfer Dave Stockton won the **PGA championship** by 2 strokes.

Aug. 23 At the **AAU national outdoor swimming meet,** at Los Angeles, Gary Hall of Indiana University broke 3 world records.

Aug. 29–31 Led by Arthur Ashe and Cliff Richie, the U.S. retained the **Davis Cup** by defeating West Germany, 5–0, in Cleveland.

Sept. 3 **Vince Lombardi,** one of the great coaches of football, died in Washington, D.C., at age 57. In 9 seasons he led the professional Green Bay Packers to 6 Division titles and 5 National Football League championships.

Everglades National Park in Fla. The government thus assured preservation of the parklands.

Sept. 27 Pres. Nixon began a 9-day **tour of Europe.** In an effort to improve relations he met with the leaders of Italy, Yugoslavia, Spain, Great Britain, and Ireland.

Oct. 7 Pres. Nixon proposed a **5-point peace plan** for Indochina, which included an immediate cease-fire and release of all prisoners of war. The plan was rejected by the North Vietnamese.

Oct. 13 **Angela Davis,** the object of a 2-month nationwide hunt, was seized in New York City. She was wanted on kidnapping, murder, and conspiracy charges for her alleged role in the Aug. 7 courtroom shoot-out in San Raphael, Calif.; a judge and 3 others were killed. A black militant and Communist, she was not re-hired to the UCLA faculty in June because of her "extreme" speeches outside the classroom.

Oct. 15 The **Organized Crime Control Act** was signed by Pres. Nixon as he pledged a "total war against organized crime."

Oct. 26 The **Legislative Reform Act,** 1st attempt since 1946 to improve the legislative process, was signed by Pres. Nixon. The seniority system, long considered outmoded, was retained.

Nov. 2 The **Strategic Arms Limitation talks** between the U.S. and the Soviet Union were resumed in Helsinki, Finland.

Nov. 12 The **court-martial of Lt. William L. Calley, Jr.,** a principal figure in the alleged massacre of 102 South Vietnamese civilians at Mylai, also known as Songmy, began at Ft. Benning, Ga.

Nov. 21 A task force of U.S. military men raided a camp in Sontay, North Vietnam, in an attempt to free **American prisoners of war.** The camp was deserted.

Nov. 23 The U.S. signed a **treaty with Mexico** settling long-standing border disputes. On Aug. 20 Pres. Nixon had reached

July 30 **George Szell,** conductor of the Cleveland Orchestra since 1946, died in Cleveland at age 73.

Aug. 13 The **Santa Fe Opera** Company presented the world premiere of Luciano Berio's multimedia work *Opera.*

Sept. 9 The **New York City Opera** opened its season with a revival of Boito's *Mefistofele,* the 1st New York performance of the work in more than 40 years.

Sept. 28 Author **John Dos Passos** died in Baltimore at age 74. He was best known for his trilogy *U.S.A.,* completed 1938, which explored a panorama of life in the U.S. from pre-World War I up to the first years of the Depression in the 1930's.

Sept. 29 The **National Gallery of Art** in Washington, D.C., received Paul Cézanne's early work *The Artist's Father* from patron Paul Mellon, who reportedly paid more than $1.5 million for the painting.

Oct. 11 **Natalia Makarova,** prima ballerina with the Leningrad Kirov Ballet who defected from the Soviet Union in September, joined the American Ballet Theatre.

Oct. 24 **Richard Hofstadter,** American historian, died at age 54. He was a leading interpreter of American politics in cultural and noneconomic terms and had received Pulitzer Prizes for his books *The Age of Reform* and *Anti-Intellectualism in American Life.*

Oct. 25 The eighth annual international **Chopin Festival** competition in Warsaw, Poland, was won by 22-year-old Garrick Ohlsson of White Plains, N.Y.

Nov. 3 The New York City Opera gave the 1st New York performance of Leoš Janáček's *The Makropoulos Affair* with soprano **Maralin Niska** being widely acclaimed for her performance in the leading role.

Nov. 16 A strike by members of Actors Equity Association over pay and

SCIENCE; INDUSTRY; ECONOMICS; EDUCATION; RELIGION; PHILOSOPHY.

SPORTS; FASHIONS; POPULAR ENTERTAINMENT; FOLKLORE; SOCIETY.

Aug. 11   FBI agents seized the **Rev. Daniel J. Berrigan,** a Jesuit priest who had been a fugitive for 4 months. Berrigan, together with his brother, the Rev. Philip F. Berrigan, and 7 other Roman Catholics had been convicted of burning draft records in 1968 at Catonsville, Md. They were known as the "Catonsville 9."

Sept. 12   A **Trans World Airline** Boeing 707 was 1 of 3 Western-owned airplanes blown up in Jordan by Palestinian guerrillas. The aircraft had been hijacked on Sept. 6.

Sept. 15   The United Auto Workers struck against the **General Motors Corporation,** idling nearly 400,000 workers. The strike was finally settled on Nov. 11.

Sept. 21   The Nixon Administration announced a series of **steps to deal with aircraft hijacking.** The government offered an insurance plan and proposed a 2500 federal armed-guard force to accompany international flights.

Sept. 30   1st publication of the **New American Bible** in its entirety. This was the 1st Roman Catholic translation in English done directly from original sources. A new translation for Protestants, the New English Bible, was published Mar. 16.

Oct. 14   The Department of Commerce announced that, for the 1st time, **personal income surpassed $800 billion,** on a seasonally adjusted annual basis.

Oct. 15   The **Nobel Prize in medicine and physiology** was awarded to an international trio of scientists for their research on the nature of substances found on the ends of bodily nerves that keep blood vessels from distending and man from losing consciousness. Dr. Julius Axelrod, a professor of pharmacology at the National Institute of Mental Health in Bethesda, Md., shared the award with British and Swedish scientists.

Oct. 16   The 2nd **Alfred Nobel Memorial Prize in economic science** was

Sept. 7   At the Del Mar horse racing track in California, **Willie Shoemaker** rode his 6033rd winner, breaking Johnny Longden's record. In his career, Shoemaker had earned more than $4 million.

Sept. 13   Veteran Australian tennis player Ken Rosewall won the **U.S. men's singles championship** at Forest Hills, N.Y.

Sept. 18   Rock superstar **Jimi Hendrix** died from an overdose of drugs in London at age 27.

Sept. 28   Off Newport, R.I., the **America's Cup** was won by the U.S. yacht *Intrepid* which took 4 of 7 heats from the Australian contender *Gretel II.*

Oct. 2   14 members of the **Wichita State University football team** were killed when their chartered plane crashed in the Rocky Mts.

Oct. 4   A leading rock singer in the country-blues tradition in American popular music, **Janis Joplin** died at age 27. She was known for her shrieking and wailing of the blues, as in "Little Girl Blue."

Oct. 5   In the **National League playoffs,** the Cincinnati Reds beat the Pittsburgh Pirates in 3 straight games: 3–0, 3–1, 3–2. The Baltimore Orioles routed the Minnesota Twins in 3 straight games, 10–6, 11–3, 6–1, to win the **American League playoffs.**

Oct. 15   The Baltimore Orioles won the **World Series,** taking 4 of 5 games from the Cincinnati Reds: 4–3, 6–5, 9–3, 5–9, 9–3. Brooks Robinson, the Baltimore 3rd baseman, was named the outstanding player of the series.

Oct. 23   A **land speed record** of 622.407 mph was set by Gary Gabelich of Long Beach, Calif., driving a rocket-powered car.

Oct. 26   **Muhammad Ali** (Cassius Clay) fought his first regulation bout in 3½ years in Atlanta, Ga. The fight with Jerry Quarry was stopped after 3 rounds

POLITICS AND GOVERNMENT; WAR;
DISASTERS; VITAL STATISTICS.

BOOKS; PAINTING; DRAMA;
ARCHITECTURE; SCULPTURE.

an agreement on the treaty during talks with Mexican Pres. Gustavo Díaz Ordaz.

Nov. 23 A Lithuanian sailor sought **political asylum on a U.S. Coast Guard cutter** off Martha's Vineyard, Mass. Public outcry followed later disclosure that his shipmates had been allowed to board the cutter and drag the sailor back to a Soviet trawler.

Nov. 27 FBI director J. Edgar Hoover testified before a Senate subcommittee that a group known as the **East Coast Conspiracy to Save Lives** was conspiring to kidnap a high-level government official and to blow up underground heating equipment of federal buildings in Washington, D.C., to disrupt government operations. The purpose of the conspiracy was to seek an end to the U.S. involvement in the war in Vietnam. Named as leaders of the plot were Philip and Daniel Berrigan, brothers and both priests; the official was later identified as presidential adviser Henry Kissinger.

Dec. 2 **William D. Ruckelshaus** was confirmed as director of the Environmental Protection Agency on the day the agency was activated. Most federal pollution control functions were channeled through the new independent agency.

Dec. 21 The Supreme Court upheld the constitutionality of **18-year-olds voting in national elections,** but did not rule on voting rights in state and local elections where a higher age was required by law.

Dec. 26 The White House announced plans for an orderly and quick **phase-out of herbicide operations** in Vietnam.

Dec. 28 U.S. Representative **L. Mendel Rivers** died in Birmingham, Ala., at age 65. As chairman of the House Armed Services Committee, he was one of the most powerful members of Congress.

Dec. 30 Near Wooton, Ky., an **explosion killed 38 miners** in a coal mine.

benefits closed 17 **off-Broadway productions.** The disagreement was submitted to binding arbitration on Dec. 16.

Nov. 18 The **National Gallery of Art** in Washington, D.C., awarded a medal for distinguished service to Kenneth Clark, who created the widely acclaimed television series *Civilisation.*

Nov. 27 At Christie's, London, a **world-record auction price for a single painting** was paid by Wildenstein Gallery of New York, which bought Velázquez's portrait of his assistant, Juan de Pareja, for $5,544,000. The work was bought by the Metropolitan Museum in 1971.

Nov. 30 **Leopold Stokowski** conducted the first concert ever given in St. Patrick's Cathedral, New York, a charity benefit honoring the late Francis Cardinal Spellman.

Dec. 9 The head of the Stockholm Opera, **Goeran Gentele,** was named to succeed Rudolph Bing as general manager of the Metropolitan Opera in New York City. Gentele, who was to assume command after July 1972, expressed an interest in directing opera, as well as serving as general manager.

Dec. 10 A **record auction price for an American painting** was set at Parke-Bernet Galleries when Thomas Eakins' *Cowboys in the Badlands* sold for $210,000.

Dec. 16 The **200th birthday of Ludwig van Beethoven** was celebrated by the Metropolitan Opera with a performance of his only opera, *Fidelio.*

Dec. 23 The North tower of the World Trade Center in New York City was topped out, making it the **tallest building in the world.** At 1350 ft., the twin structures are 100 ft. taller than the Empire State Building.

Dec. 27 **Hello, Dolly!** the longest running Broadway musical, closed after 2844 performances. The previous record was held by *My Fair Lady,* with 2717 performances.

SCIENCE; INDUSTRY; ECONOMICS; EDUCATION; RELIGION; PHILOSOPHY.

SPORTS; FASHIONS; POPULAR ENTERTAINMENT; FOLKLORE; SOCIETY.

awarded to Paul A. Samuelson of the Massachusetts Institute of Technology.

Oct. 21   Agronomist Norman E. Borlaug was awarded the **Nobel Peace Prize** for his role as prime mover in the "green revolution," the development of strains of wheat and rice with prodigious yields.

Oct. 30   Pres. Nixon signed a bill establishing the **National Railroad Passenger Corporation,** as a quasi-governmental corporation to run passenger service between big cities.

Nov. 2   **Richard Cardinal Cushing** of Boston died at age 75. The Roman Catholic prelate was noted for his modernizing of the Boston archdiocese and as a confidant of the Kennedy family.

Nov. 7   A Princeton University biochemist announced discovery of a **plant protein that arrested the multiplication of cancer cells.**

Nov. 18   Linus Pauling, Nobel Prize-winning scientist, asserted that **high doses of vitamin C can ward off the common cold and flu.** Other scientists argued that high doses of vitamin C on a long-term basis may be harmful.

Dec. 1   The Atomic Energy Commission announced that during the year 24 **underground nuclear-weapon-related tests** were made at the Nevada test site.

Dec. 4   The Department of Labor announced that the **unemployment level was 5.8%,** the highest rate in 7½ years.

Dec. 18   The appropriation of $3.2 billion approved for NASA for fiscal 1971 was the lowest since 1962, causing a **reduction in current and future space programs** and a stretch-out of the Apollo lunar program.

Dec. 31   A **National Air Quality Control Act** was signed by Pres. Nixon to tighten air-pollution standards and penalties; the measure required a 90% reduction in pollution from automobile exhaust by 1975.

because of cuts over Quarry's left eye, and Ali was declared the winner.

Nov. 8   Tom Dempsey of the New Orleans Saints pro football team kicked a **record 63-yard field goal** to give the Saints a 2-point victory over the Detroit Lions.

Nov. 14   In Kenova, W.Va., 43 members and coaches of the **Marshall University football team** were killed when their chartered plane crashed.

Nov. 18   **Heavyweight title defended** by Joe Frazier in Detroit, Mich. Frazier won with a 2nd-round knockout of Bob Foster of Washington, D.C., the light-heavyweight champion.

Nov. 24   **Jim Plunkett,** Stanford University quarterback, was named winner of the Heisman trophy as the nation's outstanding collegiate player.

Dec. 7   Before a sold-out Madison Square Garden crowd, **Muhammad Ali** (Cassius Clay) fought his 2nd big return bout, knocking out Oscar Bonavena of Argentina in the 15th round.

Dec. 7   Cartoonist **Rube Goldberg** died at age 87 in New York City. He was best known for drawings of outlandish contraptions that did work of no consequence.

Dec. 23   **Mimi Benzell,** the Metropolitan Opera singer who turned to a career in nightclubs and on Broadway, died at age 47. She had starred in the Broadway musical *Milk and Honey.*

Dec. 28   The **New York Film Critics Circle** voted *Five Easy Pieces* the best film of 1970; George C. Scott (*Patton*) was voted best actor and Glenda Jackson (*Women in Love*), best actress.

1971

The announcement in July by Pres. Nixon that he proposed to visit China and the Soviet Union in 1972 aroused international excitement. Earlier in the year in a series of steps to improve relations with China, Pres. Nixon relaxed a more than 20-yr. embargo on trade and announced a willingness to undertake a dialogue to normalize relations. At home, the Administration was confronted with economic problems that threatened to undermine Pres. Nixon's chances for re-election in 1972. The economic pressures resulted in the startling announcement in Aug. of a "New Economic Policy," which had worldwide repercussions as the U.S. dollar was untied from its traditional convertibility into gold and a 10% surcharge was placed on imports. The domestic aspect of the new policy included a 90-day price and wage freeze followed by a Phase II system of controls and guidelines. The acrimony surrounding the President's previous nominations for an Associate Justice of the Supreme Court was avoided when he nominated 2 candidates who received Senate confirmation without serious opposition. Associate Justices Lewis F. Powell, Jr., and William H. Rehnquist joined the Court, adding to the so-called strict constructionist membership and giving the Court a more conservative majority. Active American participation in the war in Vietnam continued to wind down as more U.S. troops were withdrawn, leaving a 184,000-man contingent in Dec. The scars of the 1968 Mylai massacre, first revealed in 1969 and earlier referred to as the Songmy massacre, remained as the trial of Lt. William L. Calley, Jr., ended with his conviction; a sentence of life imprisonment was later reduced to 20 yrs. In addition, Pres. Nixon announced that he would personally review the case after it had gone through all appeal channels. Two other trials related to the massacre, those of Capt. Ernest L. Medina and Col. Oran K. Henderson, resulted in exonera-

The lackluster state of the economy was evident in the theatrical and art worlds, with the Broadway season offering fewer shows and many museums being forced to economize and reduce their hours of operation. Much anticipation on Broadway preceded the arrival of *Jesus Christ Superstar,* a rock opera based on the Passion of Christ. The work had aroused nationwide interest; 3 million records of the music were sold, and 2 touring companies gave concert versions of the opera across the country. The Broadway production, starring a newcomer, Jeff Fenholt, as Jesus of Nazareth, turned out to be a gaudy superspectacle. A popular and charming small musical, *Godspell,* drew on the parables and life of Christ, but revealed them in a lively circus-like setting. Nostalgia played a major role in the season. *Follies* was an extravagant musical that explored the recollections of 2 ex-Follies dancers 30 years after they left Broadway. The show brought Alexis Smith to the musical stage for the 1st time and also starred Dorothy Collins. *No, No, Nanette,* the 1925 Vincent Youmans musical, was successfully revived, featuring Ruby Keeler, Bobby Van, Helen Gallagher, and Jack Gilford. An unsuccessful revival was Leonard Bernstein's musical *On the Town.* Shakespeare was represented in 2 adaptations that caught the public fancy. Peter Brooks brought from England his psychedelic and sensual version of *A Midsummer Night's Dream,* and Joseph Papp had *Two Gentlemen of Verona* transformed into a contemporary musical for his free Shakespeare festival in Central Park. The adaptation, with music by Galt McDermot, of *Hair* fame, and lyrics by John Guare, author of the award-winning *The House of Blue Leaves,* was directed by Mel Shapiro; it was later transferred to Broadway. *Lenny,* a powerful drama based on the life of the comedian Lenny Bruce, gained much admiration for Cliff Gorman's performance in the title role. Two of the

904

1971

The U.S. economy continued to show such a slow rate of growth that in Aug. Pres. Nixon announced a "New Economic Policy." The Gross National Product, or GNP, failed to meet the expected $1065 billion by some $18 billion. Unemployment rose to a high of 6%, and inflation continued to increase in excess of 4%, as did the cost of living. For the first time in the 20th century, U.S. imports exceeded exports, by $2 billion. The President's policy sought to reduce inflationary tendencies and unemployment by a wage and price freeze, followed by control and review boards to keep price and wage increases within acceptable limits. To improve the U.S. balance of trade, the Administration agreed to a devaluation of the U.S. dollar by 8.57%, accompanied by the realignment of other international currencies.

The year's advances into space were highlighted by 2 manned lunar landing missions and man's closest view of the planet Mars. Both Apollo XIV and XV crew members explored the lunar surface. Men of the latter crew stayed on the moon for 76 hours and traveled some 17 miles on the lunar surface in a 4-wheeled, battery-powered vehicle. One of the rock samples they collected was later found to be 4 billion years old and was dubbed "Genesis rock." The Mariner IX orbital mission to Mars began taking pictures in Nov. and sent back many spectacular photographs of the surface of the planet. Research at various institutions in the country also revealed new information about outer space. At the NASA Ames Research Center scientists found amino acids in a meteorite, strengthening the possibility of chemical evolution of life elsewhere in the universe. Astronomers at the California Institute of Technology reported they had successfully tested Einstein's General Theory of Relativity. Underwater research produced a successful

Even in sports, China was on everyone's mind when a team of U.S. table-tennis players was invited to China in April for an impromptu tournament. They were consistently beaten by the Chinese, but their visit opened the door for future contests. Lee Trevino sparked the golf tournament circuit with his ready quips and winning play as he won the U.S., the Canadian, and the British Open contests within a 4-week period. Trevino, Jack Nicklaus, and Arnold Palmer won more than $200,000 in prize money during the year, as did stock-car drivers Richard Petty and Bob Allen and tennis star Rod Laver. One of the richest sports events of all time was the long-awaited Muhammad Ali-Joe Frazier world heavyweight championship fight, which grossed nearly $20 million, primarily through closed-circuit television. Frazier retained his title. Ali, having gained a Supreme Court decision overturning his 1967 conviction for refusing induction into the Army, scheduled other matches looking toward another crack at the title. A fresh crop of sports stars sprang up during the year; among them, in baseball, Vida Blue, a 21-year-old left-handed pitcher for the Oakland Athletics. The surprise track star of the season was Dr. Delano Meriwether, a 27-year-old hematologist, who won the 100-yd. dash in the national championships: Chris Everett, a 16-year-old schoolgirl, attracted huge crowds at the U.S. tennis championships as she won 4 matches. She lost in the finals to Mrs. Billie Jean King, who was the 1st woman athlete to win more than $100,000 in a single year. Professional football emerged as the most popular sport. Superstar Joe Namath of the New York Jets was out for most of the season with an injured knee. The Dallas Cowboys, after a slow start, became the outstanding team of the season when quarterback Roger Staubach led the team to 7 straight victories to win the National Football Conference championship. The Cowboys had a

tion of the defendants. Another scar of Vietnam, drug addiction among servicemen, caused Pres. Nixon to seek funds for treatment and rehabilitation of addicted military personnel. As the 1972 Presidential election year approached, a wide array of Democratic Party aspirants declared their candidacy for the nomination, with 11 candidates scheduled to enter various primaries. Leading contenders appeared to be Senators Edmund S. Muskie of Maine, Hubert H. Humphrey of Minnesota, Henry M. Jackson of Washington, and George S. McGovern of South Dakota. Others included former Senator Eugene J. McCarthy of Minnesota, New York City Mayor and former Republican Representative John V. Lindsay, and the 1st black woman candidate, U.S. Representative Shirley Chisholm of New York. Senator Edward M. Kennedy continued to disavow ambitions for the Presidency. Expected to enter the race was Gov. George C. Wallace of Alabama who ran as a 3rd party candidate in 1968. Two members of his own party challenged Pres. Nixon for the Republican nomination. Representative Paul N. McCloskey, Jr., of California, a liberal Republican, called for a faster withdrawal of U.S. forces from Indochina. Representative John M. Ashbrook of Ohio, a conservative, wanted to end deficit spending and wage and price controls and prevent a guaranteed income from becoming law.

Jan. 2   Pres. Nixon signed the **Omnibus Crime Control Act,** authorizing $3.6 billion for federal aid to state and local law-enforcement agencies.

Jan. 12   The Rev. **Philip F. Berrigan** and 5 others were indicted on charges of conspiring to kidnap Henry A. Kissinger, assistant to Pres. Nixon for national security affairs, and for plotting to blow up the heating systems of federal buildings in Washington, D.C. At the time of the indictment Berrigan was serving a prison sentence for burning draft cards in 1968.

Jan. 19   **Carl B. Albert,** Democrat of Oklahoma, was selected as Speaker of the

greatest English actors, Sir John Gielgud and Sir Ralph Richardson, dazzled audiences with their performances in David Storey's *Home,* an English import concerning 2 men in a mental home. Also imported was Harold Pinter's *Old Times,* another of his puzzling dramas, about a man and his wife and a visiting woman friend discussing their past after being apart for 20 years. The perennial Neil Simon returned with another smash hit, *The Prisoner of Second Avenue,* a serio-comic play about urban paranoia. Simon's previous play, *The Gingerbread Lady,* provided Maureen Stapleton with a Tony award-winning role, although the play was not entirely successful. Edward Albee's *All Over,* about a dying man as seen through the eyes of his family and friends, was considered a dismal play. Two works by Ibsen were revived, with Claire Bloom gaining much acclaim in *A Doll's House* and *Hedda Gabler.* The most active playhouse was the Public Theater operated under the auspices of the New York Shakespeare Festival, directed by Joseph Papp. The playhouse had 4 plays running simultaneously. *The Basic Training of Pavlo Hummel* and *Sticks and Bones,* both by David Rabe, concerned aspects of the war in Vietnam and its effects on individuals. *Black Terror,* by Richard Wesley, presented a militant black viewpoint toward society, and a musical, *The Wedding of Iphigenia plus Iphigenia in Concert,* was loosely adapted from the classic by Euripides by Doug Dyer, Peter Link, and Gretchen Cryer.

The revelation of the Pentagon Papers resulted in a Supreme Court test, which upheld the right of newspapers to print classified material without prior government approval. The decision left undecided whether or not the publication of the papers could be prosecuted criminally after the fact. The Pentagon Papers, which were allegedly stolen by Dr. Daniel Ellsberg, who was later indicted on federal charges, concerned the historical development of the decision-making process on Vietnam policy. In his memoirs *The Vantage Point,*

and economically feasible mining system and chemical separation process for the harvesting of manganese nodules from the deep ocean bottom, indicating once again that the frontiers of science still offered great opportunities.

In education the unrest that had disturbed colleges throughout the country in 1970 was largely dissipated and there were no occurrences of the violence that had so shocked the nation, such as at Kent State University in Ohio. Many major problems still confronted educational institutions. The National Science Foundation reported that federal aid to colleges and universities was the lowest since 1966, with education also being caught in government budgetary considerations. The foundation also forecast an oversupply of scientists and engineers with Ph.D. degrees by 1980. This forecast, added to the high unemployment rate among certain types of engineers and scientists, presented a dark picture for persons in those professions for the next few years. The National Education Association also revealed that current teacher demand was the lowest in 20 years, indicating another profession with problems. Concern over the use of drugs in American society was increased by a sampling of 10,000 students at 50 colleges which revealed that 31% had tried marijuana at least once and that 14% were using it every week or so.

Jan. 11   Derek Curtis Bok was named 25th president of **Harvard University,** succeeding Nathan Pusey.

Jan. 12   Ralph Nader, the consumer advocate, announced the formation of the **Earth Act Group,** designed to organize high-school and college students to raise funds for support of court actions and scientific efforts to fight rural and urban environmental problems.

Jan. 25   The Supreme Court, in its **1st sex discrimination ruling** on equal hiring provisions of the 1964 Civil Rights Act, ruled that companies could not deny

problem star in Duane Thomas, their outstanding running back, who froze out all communication with public and press alike because of a disagreement with the management over his contract.

Fashion took a series of definite turns, ending some of the uncertainty of previous seasons. Skirt length was settled at just below the knee for daytime and above the ankle for night. An outrageous look persisted, particularly in footwear, which featured the ugly, the bizarre, and the absurd. Blue denim was big, and tie-dye gave way to leather. Fads brought back the 40's look, following the swing toward nostalgia, with short-shorts being redubbed "hot pants."

The motion-picture industry continued to be depressed, with fewer pictures being made by the major studios in California and more independent productions being filmed on location throughout the country. Some states provided special subsidies to attract motion-picture production, for example, New Mexico, Arizona, and Texas. Typical of this type was the Peter Bogdanovich film, *The Last Picture Show,* shot in Texas, which became one of the biggest hits of the year. Musicals and spectaculars, though fewer, were still being made with *The Boy Friend, Fiddler on the Roof,* and *Nicholas and Alexandra* sustaining interest in these special genres.

Jan. 1   In the **Rose Bowl,** Ohio State, unbeaten all season, was upset by Stanford University, 27–17.

Jan. 5   World heavyweight boxing champion (1962–1964) **Sonny Liston** was found dead at age 38. He lost the title to Muhammad Ali (Cassius Clay) in 1964.

Jan. 17   With 5 seconds left to play, Jim O'Brien kicked a field goal to break a tie and give the Baltimore Colts a 16–13 **Super Bowl** victory in Miami over the Dallas Cowboys.

Jan. 25   **Charles M. Manson** and 3 female codefendants were convicted in

POLITICS AND GOVERNMENT; WAR; DISASTERS; VITAL STATISTICS.

BOOKS; PAINTING; DRAMA; ARCHITECTURE; SCULPTURE.

House of Representatives, replacing John W. McCormack, who retired in 1970.

Jan. 21   The senior Democratic member of the U.S. Senate, **Richard B. Russell,** of Georgia, died in Washington, D.C., at age 73.

Jan. 22   In his State of the Union Message, Pres. Nixon proposed a **revenue-sharing plan** with state and local governments, worth $16 billion annually.

Feb. 3   A **fire and explosion** at the Thiokol Chemical Corp. in Woodbine, Ga., killed 25 persons and injured many more.

Feb. 9   An **earthquake in southern California** caused extensive damage and took more than 60 lives, with over 40 lost at a Veterans Administration hospital in Sylmar, near San Fernando.

Feb. 11   A treaty prohibiting installation of **nuclear weapons on the seabed** was signed by 63 nations; it would become effective when ratified by 22 nations.

Feb. 21   90 persons were killed and more than 500 injured by **tornadoes** in Louisiana, Mississippi, and Texas.

Feb. 24   In a 5–4 decision, the Supreme Court ruled that **illegally obtained evidence** generally inadmissible in a criminal trial could be used by the prosecution to contradict a suspect's testimony if he chose to take the stand in his own defense. This ruling limited the protection to the defendant that resulted from the 1966 Miranda decision.

Mar. 1   In Washington, **a bomb exploded in a rest room of the Senate wing of the Capitol,** causing damage of about $300,000. "Weather Underground" claimed credit for the bombing.

Mar. 8   The Supreme Court ruled that draft exemption for **conscientious objectors** must be based on opposition to all wars, not just the war in Indochina.

Mar. 25   **Files stolen from an FBI office** in Media, Pa., Mar. 8 and mailed to newspapers revealed the agency was in-

former Pres. Lyndon B. Johnson reviewed his years in office and covered many of the sensitive details that so concerned the government about the Pentagon Papers. Other biographies concerning political figures were less controversial. *Eleanor and Franklin: The Story of Their Relationship Based on Eleanor Roosevelt's Private Papers,* by Joseph P. Lash, brought to light many facets of Pres. Roosevelt's private and public life and revealed the moral fiber that made Eleanor Roosevelt into the public figure she became. A return of interest in the occult and the unexplainable was evident in the popularity of William P. Blatty's *The Exorcist* and Thomas Tryon's *The Other,* which had a feeling of Henry James's *The Turn of the Screw.* Sigmund Freud was given a sympathetic biography by Irving Stone in *The Passions of the Mind.* Another kind of biography appeared in Gay Talese's *Honor Thy Father,* an inside-organized crime report on the life style of a member of a syndicate family. Novels that attracted wide attention were Vladimir Nabokov's *Glory,* Joyce Carol Oates' *Wonderland,* and Bernard Malamud's *The Tenants.* One of the best nonfiction works, *Bury My Heart at Wounded Knee,* by Dee Brown, was a history of the American Indians' loss of their tribal lands.

Mar. 13   **Rockwell Kent,** artist and illustrator of international reputation, died at age 88. He specialized in stark, rugged landscape painting.

Mar. 18   The Whitney Museum of Art in New York announced it had been bequeathed about 1500 works from the estate of painter **Edward Hopper.**

Mar. 28   The 25th annual **Antoinette Perry (Tony) Awards** for the 1970–71 Broadway season were presented to *Sleuth* (drama); *Company* (musical); Brian Bedford (dramatic actor) in *The School for Wives;* Maureen Stapleton (dramatic actress) in *The Gingerbread Lady;* Peter Brook (dramatic director) for *A Mid-*

employment to women with preschool children unless the same criteria applied to men.

Jan. 31–Feb. 9 **Apollo XIV,** manned by astronauts Alan B. Shepard, Jr., Edgar D. Mitchell, and Stuart A. Roosa, made the 3rd lunar landing.

Feb. 12 **J. C. Penney,** founder of the department-store chain, died in New York City at age 95. He expanded his stores into the 5th-largest merchandising enterprise in the U.S.

Mar. 1 Commerce Secretary Maurice Stans issued an **order ending the licensing of commercial whale hunters.** Many species of whales were being placed on the list of endangered species.

Mar. 29 The New York University Research Center reported that it had apparently succeeded in **immunizing children against serum hepatitis,** a highly infectious and sometimes fatal liver disease.

Apr. 5 The New York Stock Exchange instituted a controversial system of **negotiated commission rates** on the portion of large stock transactions that exceeded $500,000.

Apr. 14 Pres. Nixon announced the relaxing of the more than 20-year **embargo on trade with Communist China.**

Apr. 20 The Supreme Court, in a series of decisions, held that **busing children** as a means of dismantling dual school systems was constitutional.

May 1 The quasi-governmental National Railroad Passenger Corporation, known as **Amtrak,** went into operation. It was to provide the service of 182 trains to more than 300 cities.

May 8 **Mariner VIII,** intended to orbit Mars, had a malfunction of the 2nd stage booster rocket and fell into the Atlantic Ocean.

May 25 Pres. Nixon signed a bill authorizing funds to terminate a project to develop a commercial **supersonic transport (SST).** In March the Senate refused addi-

California of the murders of Sharon Tate and 6 other persons in 1969. They were sentenced to death Apr. 19. Another defendant, Charles Watson, was sentenced to death on Oct. 21 for his participation in the murders.

Feb. 20 Radio and television stations across the country were thrown into confusion by a **false nuclear alert** when an operator at the National Emergency Warning Center in Colorado mistakenly wired them into an emergency alert tape instead of a mere test. Some stations went off the air after telling listeners of the "emergency." It took officials 40 minutes to cancel the alert.

Feb. 28 The **PGA championship** tournament at Palm Beach Gardens, Fla., was won by golfer Jack Nicklaus by 3 strokes over Billy Casper.

Mar. 8 The much publicized confrontation between Joe Frazier and Muhammad Ali (Cassius Clay) for the **heavyweight championship of the world** resulted in a unanimous decision in favor of Frazier in the 15-round bout.

Mar. 8 **Harold Lloyd,** famed in both silent and talking motion pictures, died at age 77. He appeared in more than 500 films.

Mar. 25 For the 5th straight year UCLA won the **NCAA basketball championship** in a 4-game sweep over Villanova.

Apr. 7 Horseplayers flocked to betting windows in New York when the city began operation of the country's 1st legal **off-track betting system (OTB).**

Apr. 10–14 A U.S. **table-tennis team visited Communist China** and played several exhibition matches in Peking. The unprecedented invitation by the Chinese also included visas for 7 Western newsmen, reversing a policy that had been maintained since 1949.

Apr. 11 The **Masters golf championship** was won by Charles Coody by 2 strokes over Jack Nicklaus and John Miller

volved in large-scale surveillance of black and pacifist militants and intended to create a climate of fear to discourage their activities.

Mar. 27   Tanker *Texaco Oklahoma* split in two off Cape Hatteras, N.C., causing the **drowning of 31 crew members.**

Mar. 29   **Lt. William L. Calley, Jr.,** was convicted of the premeditated murder of at least 22 South Vietnamese civilians at Mylai, a hamlet of Songmy, on March 16, 1968. His life-imprisonment sentence was reduced to 20 years on Aug. 20 and was still under appeal at the end of the year.

May 3–5   After several weeks of **antiwar protests in Washington, D.C.,** highlighted by young veterans' deposit of decorations and military paraphernalia on the steps of the Capitol Apr. 23 and a huge parade Apr. 24, police made more than 12,000 arrests, sweeping up curious bystanders along with militants bent on disrupting all government affairs. Most charges were subsequently dropped; the police action drew a mixed chorus of praise and condemnation.

June 11   U.S. **marshals removed 15 Indians** from Alcatraz Island in San Francisco Bay and ended a 19-month occupation of the former prison island. The Indians had claimed the land under a treaty privilege they said gave them unused federal lands.

June 30   The **26th Amendment to the U.S. Constitution became law** when Ohio became the 38th state to ratify it. The amendment lowered the voting age to 18 for all elections.

July 10–11   More than 200 women attended the National Women's Political Caucus to mobilize for **equal representation of women** with men at all levels of the nation's political system.

July 15   Pres. Nixon announced that he would **visit China before May 1972,** as the 1st American president to be received by a Chinese government.

summer *Night's Dream;* and Harold Prince (musical director) for *Company.*

Apr. 6   One of the most influential 20th-century composers, **Igor Stravinsky** died at age 88. His ballet scores that became classics included: *The Firebird, Petrouchka, The Rite of Spring, Les Noces,* and *Pulcinella.*

Apr. 30   **Elmo Roper,** one of the 1st public-opinion analysts and political polltakers to use the sampling techniques of market research, died at age 70.

May 3   **Pulitzer Prizes** were announced for the following persons: Lawrance R. Thompson, for *Robert Frost: The Years of Triumph, 1915–1938* (biography); James MacGregor Burns, for *Roosevelt: The Soldier of Freedom* (history); John Toland, for *The Rising Sun* (general nonfiction); William S. Merwin, for *The Carrier of Ladders* (poetry); Mario Davidowsky, for *Synchronisms No. 6 for Piano and Electronic Sound* (music); and Paul Zindel for *The Effect of Gamma Rays on Man-in-the-Moon Marigolds* (drama).

May 7   The **New York Drama Critics Circle** voted *Home,* a British import, the best play of the 1970–71 season. *Follies* was chosen best musical, and *The House of Blue Leaves* the best American play.

May 12   The Metropolitan Museum of Art in New York City announced the **acquisition of the Velázquez painting** *Portrait of Juan de Pareja.* One of its most important single acquisitions, the museum paid $5.5 million for the painting.

May 19   **Ogden Nash,** poet and humorist, died at age 68. He was a master of light satirical verse, including the classic "Candy is dandy/but liquor is quicker."

May 22   Dedication of the **Lyndon Baines Johnson Library,** an $18.6 million complex at the University of Texas that houses documents of the former President's administration.

tional government funds to continue the project, but the House tried to revive government support. The compromise appropriation provided phase-out funds to the prime contractors.

June 1   Protestant theologian **Reinhold Niebuhr** died at age 78. His religious philosophy stressed neo-orthodoxy, which recognized the importance of original sin and rejected utopianism.

June 10   The Federal Trade Commission announced that it would require big manufacturers to **substantiate claims made in advertising,** and that the auto industry would come under scrutiny first.

June 25   The New York Stock Exchange voted into membership, for the 1st time in its history, a **black-operated securities firm,** Daniels & Bell of New York City.

June 28   The Supreme Court declared **unconstitutional state programs to underwrite nonreligious instruction** in parochial schools.

July 1   Inauguration ceremonies were held at the White House for the semi-independent **U.S. Postal Service,** which replaced the Post Office Department, founded in 1789.

July 2   A research team in Texas announced that it had **isolated a cancer virus** from cells taken from a cancer patient. The discovery was considered a significant new lead in the search for human cancer viruses.

July 26–Aug. 7   Apollo XV made the **4th lunar-landing mission,** manned by astronauts David R. Scott, James B. Irwin, and Alfred M. Worden who remained in the command module. Using a 4-wheeled, battery-powered lunar roving vehicle, the 2 astronauts traveled 17.3 miles on the lunar surface.

Aug. 2   Legislation providing a $250 million loan guarantee to **Lockheed Aircraft Corp.** was narrowly passed by Congress, after much controversy over such precedent-setting aid to private industry.

Apr. 14   At the **Academy Awards** presentation *Patton* won 7 awards, including best film, best director (Franklin J. Schaffner), and best actor (George C. Scott). Other major awards went to Glenda Jackson (best actress) for her performance in *Women in Love,* John Mills (best supporting actor) in *Ryan's Daughter;* and Helen Hayes (best supporting actress) in *Airport.* Orson Welles received a special award for contributions to the film industry.

Apr. 30   In a 4-game sweep, the **Milwaukee Bucks won the National Basketball Assn. title,** defeating the Baltimore Bullets.

May 1   *Canonero II,* Gustavo Avila up, won the **Kentucky Derby** over a field of 20. The win was worth $145,500.

May 15   The **Preakness Stakes** was won by 1½ lengths by *Canonero II,* Gustavo Avila up. The winner's purse was worth $137,400.

May 28   **Audie Murphy,** the most decorated hero of World War II, having received 28 medals, died at age 46. Murphy became a motion-picture actor after the war.

May 29   For the 2nd straight year Al Unser won the **Indianapolis 500** in a P.J. Colt chassis with a Ford rear-mounted engine.

June 5   *Canonero II* failed to win the triple crown of horse racing, finishing 4th in the **Belmont Stakes.** *Pass Catcher* was the winner.

June 12   The eldest daughter of Pres. Nixon, **Patricia Nixon,** married Edward Finch Cox at a ceremony in the rose garden of the White House.

June 15   **Frank Sinatra** announced his decision to retire at 53, after a much publicized career as a singer and an Academy Award-winning actor for his role in *From Here to Eternity.*

June 21   Lee Trevino won the **U.S. Open golf championship** in Ardmore, Pa.

911

POLITICS AND GOVERNMENT; WAR; DISASTERS; VITAL STATISTICS.

BOOKS; PAINTING; DRAMA; ARCHITECTURE; SCULPTURE.

July 28 The U.S. Army Vietnam command announced that it was expanding its drive against narcotics and virtually all U.S. servicemen in South Vietnam are to be **tested for heroin use.**

Aug. 2 After more than 20 years of opposition, the U.S. announced it would not oppose the **entry of Communist China into the United Nations.** At the same time the U.S. stated that it would not agree to the expulsion of Nationalist China from the U.N. or deprive it of U.N. representation. In the U.N., voting on the question on Oct. 25, the General Assembly voted to admit Communist China and to expel the National Chinese government based on Taiwan.

Aug. 15 Pres. Nixon announced his **"New Economic Policy"** which included a 90-day freeze on prices and wages and a 10% surcharge on imports.

Aug. 21 **George Jackson,** 1 of 3 black convicts who became known as the Soledad Brothers after being charged with killing a prison guard at Soledad state prison in Calif., was killed while attempting to escape from San Quentin. He was a militant who became known through his prison memoir *Soledad Brother.*

Sept. 4 **Crash of a jetliner** west of Juneau, Alaska, killed 111 people. It was the worst air accident involving a single airplane in U.S. history.

Sept. 9–13 **A prison riot** at Attica State Correctional Facility, Attica, N.Y., resulted in the loss of 43 lives after 1500 state troopers and other officers staged an air and ground assault to quell the uprising.

Sept. 17 Supreme Court Justice **Hugo L. Black** resigned because of ill health; he died Sept. 25 at 85. On Sept. 23 Justice **John Harlan,** 72, also retired for reasons of health; he died on Dec. 29.

Sept. 22 **Capt. Ernest L. Medina** was cleared of all charges in connection with the killing of South Vietnamese civilians at Mylai, also known as Songmy; for

May 28 The New York City Ballet premiered the ballet *The Goldberg Variations,* by **Jerome Robbins,** set to the piano music of Johann Sebastian Bach.

June 10 **Raphael Kubelik** was named to the newly created position of musical director of the Metropolitan Opera in New York.

June 13 *The New York Times* began publishing excerpts from the **Pentagon Papers,** popular name for *History of the U.S. Decision-making Process on Vietnam Policy,* a top-secret study begun during the Johnson Administration. Federal courts stopped publication, but were reversed by the Supreme Court June 30. On June 28 a former Defense Dept. official, Dr. Daniel Ellsberg, admitted he had given the papers to *The Times;* he was later indicted for theft and possession of secret documents.

June 16 An **El Greco painting,** a sketch for *The Immaculate Conception* stolen in Spain in 1936 during the Civil War, was recovered in New York City by the FBI.

June 19 The **Brandywine River Museum** opened in Chadds Ford, Pa., as a permanent repository of the works of Brandywine valley artists, the most famous being the realist painter Andrew Wyeth and his son Jamie.

June 28 The J. Paul Getty Museum in Malibu, Calif., brought Titian's *Death of Actaeon* from art dealer J. H. Weitzner who had paid $4.032 million for it June 25 at Christie's in London. The **auction price was the 2nd highest** ever paid for a painting.

June 30 In a historic decision, the Supreme Court held that the government cannot impose prior restraint on published material. The ruling allowed 2 newspapers to continue publication of the controversial **Pentagon Papers.**

July 21 Harold Prince's production of *Fiddler on the Roof* became the **longest-running Broadway musical,** its 2845 performances surpassing *Hello, Dolly!*

SCIENCE; INDUSTRY; ECONOMICS; EDUCATION; RELIGION; PHILOSOPHY.

SPORTS; FASHIONS; POPULAR ENTERTAINMENT; FOLKLORE; SOCIETY.

Aug. 5   William McChesney Martin, Jr., former head of the Federal Reserve Board, released a report calling for a full-scale **reorganization of the New York Stock Exchange** and creation of a national stock-exchange system.

Aug. 15   Pres. Nixon outlined an economic program including a **90-day wage and price freeze,** reductions in federal spending, and a temporary 10% surcharge on imports. The U.S. dollar was also allowed to float from its formerly fixed exchange rate of $35 per ounce of gold.

Aug. 20   In Washington, D.C., 50 countries signed the permanent **INTELSAT agreements** for the international control of communications satellites in the 1970's.

Aug. 30   A significant court ruling was handed down in California declaring that the state **school-financing system based on property taxes** favored affluent districts and discriminated against children in poorer neighborhoods.

Sept. 29   The **Orbiting Solar Observatory VII** was launched to study for the 1st time, in X-ray observations, the beginning of a solar flare.

Oct. 14   The **Nobel Prize in physiology and medicine** was awarded to Dr. Earl W. Sutherland of Vanderbilt University for his work with hormones.

Oct. 15   The 3rd **Alfred Nobel Memorial Prize in economic science** was awarded to retired Harvard professor Simon Kuznets, a major developer of the use of Gross National Product as a means of measuring economic output.

Oct. 29   University of Pennsylvania surgeons reported the 1st success in use of direct **electric current to knit a bone fracture.**

Nov. 6   The **most powerful underground nuclear test** was exploded on the remote Alaskan island of Amchitka, after much protest from environmental-protection and antiwar groups, who took their case to the Supreme Court.

On July 10 he won the British Open championship, to become the 4th U.S. player to win both titles in the same year.

June 27   Two of the largest and best-known showplaces of rock music, **Fillmore East in New York and Fillmore West in San Francisco,** were closed, being no longer financially feasible according to the owner.

June 28   Boxer **Muhammad Ali** (Cassius Clay) won a 4-year legal battle for vindication when the Supreme Court reversed his 1967 draft-evasion conviction.

July 6   Master showman and world-renowned jazz trumpeter **Louis Armstrong** died in New York City at age 71.

July 25   Golf's richest tournament, the **Westchester Classic** played in Harrison, N.Y., was won by Arnold Palmer who received a top purse of $50,000.

July 26   Heavyweight fighter **Muhammad Ali** (Cassius Clay), defeated by Joe Frazier in March, fought Jimmy Ellis in Houston and stopped him in 12 rounds. In Nov. Ali outpointed Buster Mathis in 12 rounds in Grand Rapids, Mich.

Aug. 8   The **U.S. professional tennis championship** was won by Australian Ken Rosewall, one of the top contenders on the international pro circuit.

Aug. 25   Song-and-dance man **Ted Lewis** died at age 80. With a cane and battered top hat he began his act shouting "Is ev'rybody happy?"

Aug. 26   Wellington Mara, owner of the club, announced that the **New York Giants football team** would move to New Jersey when a new 75,000-seat stadium was completed in 1975.

Aug. 27   **Bennett Cerf,** head of the Random House publishing firm and a well-known television personality, died in Mount Kisco, N.Y., at age 73. He appeared for 16 years on *What's My Line,* a TV panel show.

Aug. 28   **Nathan Leopold,** sentenced to life imprisonment in 1924 for the "thrill" murder of Bobby Franks, died in Puerto Rico at age 66. He was paroled in 1958.

which Lt. William L. Calley, Jr., was convicted on Mar. 29.

Sept. 26 Pres. Nixon greeted Emperor Hirohito of Japan in Anchorage, Alaska, marking the 1st foreign trip of a Japanese emperor and the **1st meeting of an American president and a Japanese monarch.**

Sept. 30 The U.S. and the Soviet Union signed agreements to **reduce the risk of accidental nuclear war.**

Oct. 12 It was announced that **Pres. Nixon will visit Moscow in May 1972,** the 1st trip of a U.S. president to the Soviet Union since Pres. Roosevelt attended the Yalta Conference in 1945.

Oct. 12 **Dean G. Acheson,** former secretary of state and a major architect of U.S. post-World War II policy, died in Sandy Spring, Md., at age 78.

Nov. 12 Pres. Nixon announced an additional **U.S. troop withdrawal** of 45,000 men from South Vietnam by Feb. 1972, leaving a force of 139,000.

Nov. 13 Aubran W. Martin, 1st of 5 defendants brought to trial for the 1970 murders of United Mine Workers' leader **Joseph Yablonski** and his wife and daughter, was sentenced to death.

Nov. 25 An **airliner hijacker** parachuted with $200,000 ransom into a wilderness in Washington state.

Dec. 6 **Lewis F. Powell, Jr.,** was confirmed as associate justice of the Supreme Court by the Senate. Powell, a former president of the American Bar Association, was to take the seat vacated by the late Hugo L. Black.

Dec. 10 The Senate confirmed the nomination of **William H. Rehnquist** to fill the Supreme Court seat vacated by Justice John Marshall Harlan, after heated debate on Rehnquist's view on civil rights.

Dec. 26–30 U.S. Air Force and Navy planes carried out massive **sustained air attacks** on military installations in North Vietnam, the heaviest attack since the Nov. 1968 bombing halt.

Aug. 6 **Fausto Cleva,** Italian-born orchestra conductor, died in Athens, Greece, at age 69. He had conducted at the Metropolitan Opera in New York City for more than 50 years.

Aug. 10 Pres. Nixon signed a bill providing $61.2 million for **National Arts and Humanities Endowments** administered by the National Foundation on the Arts and the Humanities.

Aug. 27 **Margaret Bourke-White,** acknowledged as one of the world's great photographers and one of the early photojournalists, died at age 67.

Sept. 8–9 The **Kennedy Center for the Performing Arts** in Washington, D.C., held a gala 2-day opening highlighted by the premiere of Leonard Bernstein's *Mass,* a theater piece for singers, dancers, and players, requiring more than 200 performers.

Sept. 11 *Beatrix Cenci,* an opera by **Alberto Ginastera,** was given its world premiere at the Kennedy Center for the Performing Arts, in Washington, D.C.

Oct. 2 **Lorin Maazel** was named musical director of the Cleveland Orchestra, succeeding the late George Szell.

Oct. 19 **Look magazine** ceased publication, citing mounting revenue losses, the depressed economy, and rising postal rates.

Oct. 25 **Pablo Casals** conducted the premiere of *Hymn to the United Nations,* composed by him with words by W. H. Auden. Casals received the U.N. Peace Medal from Secretary-General U Thant. On Dec. 29 Casals celebrated his 95th birthday at his home in Puerto Rico.

Nov. 10 The author of the Western classic *The Ox-Bow Incident,* **Walter Van Tilburg Clark,** died in Reno, Nev., at age 62.

Nov. 16 After 31 years as editor of the *Saturday Review,* **Norman Cousins** resigned over a disagreement on the editorial policy the new owners of the magazine intended to effectuate.

SCIENCE; INDUSTRY; ECONOMICS; EDUCATION; RELIGION; PHILOSOPHY.	SPORTS; FASHIONS; POPULAR ENTERTAINMENT; FOLKLORE; SOCIETY.

Nov. 8 The House of Representatives rejected a **proposed constitutional amendment** permitting voluntary prayers in public schools.

Nov. 13 **Mariner IX,** launched on May 30 for orbiting Mars, began to take pictures and was expected to transmit to earth 5000 pictures over a 3-month period.

Nov. 14 **Phase II** restraints of Pres. Nixon's "New Economic Policy" began after expiration of the 90-day freeze on prices and wages begun on Aug. 15. A Pay Board, responsible for setting wage-increase standards, adopted a 5.5% guideline for pay increases. The Price Commission, set up to oversee prices, announced a guideline to limit price increases to 2.5% a year.

Nov. 18 The **hunting of birds, fish, or other animals** from airplanes was made a federal crime in a bill signed by Pres. Nixon.

Nov. 19 The Consumer Price Index for October, after seasonal adjustment, was reported to have risen by only .1%, the **smallest monthly increase in consumer prices** since April 1967.

Dec. 4 General Motors Corp. announced the **largest voluntary safety recall** in the auto industry, as 6.7 million vehicles were recalled to secure engines against mount breakage.

Dec. 9 **Dr. Ralph J. Bunche,** United Nations undersecretary-general for special political affairs, died at age 67. He won the 1950 Nobel Peace Prize for negotiating the 1949 armistice between Israel and the Arab states.

Dec. 12 **David Sarnoff,** broadcasting pioneer who helped found the electronics and communications industry, died at age 80.

Dec. 20 The 10% **surcharge on imports was removed.** It had been imposed Aug. 15 as part of the "New Economic Policy."

Sept. 9 **Gordie Howe,** one of the all-time greats of the National Hockey League, announced his retirement at age 43 to take a position in the front office of the Detroit Red Wings, his team for 25 seasons.

Sept. 15 Winners of the singles titles at the **U.S. Open tennis championship** at Forest Hills, N.Y., were Stan Smith and Mrs. Billie Jean King. It was the 1st time in 16 years that the U.S. won both titles.

Sept. 21 It was announced that the **Washington Senators** would move to Texas for the 1972 season of the American League in baseball.

Oct. 3 Tennis star **Mrs. Billie Jean King** became the 1st female athlete in history to earn more than $100,000 in a single year.

Oct. 17 In a surprise finish, the underdog Pittsburgh Pirates defeated the favored Baltimore Orioles in baseball's **World Series.** The Pirates won 2–1 in the deciding 7th game.

Oct. 26 In Buenos Aires, Bobby Fischer defeated the Soviet Union's Tigran Petrosian and became the 1st American to clear elimination matches for the **world chess championship.** He was scheduled to meet world champion Boris Spassky of the Soviet Union in 1972.

Oct. 30 Ed Marinaro of Cornell set a new **collegiate rushing record** with a 3-year career total of 4132 yards.

Nov. 19 The loquacious and colorful sports broadcaster **Bill Stern** died in Rye, N.Y., at age 64.

Dec. 18 **Bobby Jones,** one of the world's great sports figures, died at age 69. He was the only golfer to win the golfing grand slam in 1 year—the British Amateur, the U.S. Open, the British Open, and the U.S. Amateur—a feat he accomplished in 1930.

Dec. 25 Survivors of the **National Football League playoffs** were the Dallas Cowboys and the Miami Dolphins. They were to meet each other in the Super Bowl in New Orleans.

915

INDEX TO THE SUPPLEMENT

(The index to pre-1970 material begins on p. 747)

NOTE: References are to year and column, columns I and II being on the left-hand page and III and IV on the right. The dates in the index indicate the place at which an item is entered and should not necessarily be taken for the date of the event.

916

922

Reference
E
174.5
.C3
1972

6078

REFERENCE DO NOT
TAKE FROM THIS ROOM

REFERENCE DO NOT
TAKE FROM THIS ROOM